THE OXFORD ENCYCLOPEDIA OF

BRITISH LITERATURE

EDITORIAL BOARD

THE OXFORD ENCYCLOPEDIA OF

BRITISH

LITERATURE

David Scott Kastan

Editor in Chief

Volume 3

TONY HARRISON–*A MIRROR FOR MAGISTRATES*

OXFORD

UNIVERSITY PRESS

2006

OXFORD

UNIVERSITY PRESS

Oxford University Press, Inc., publishes works that further
Oxford University's objective of excellence
in research, scholarship, and education.

Oxford   New York
Auckland   Cape Town   Dar es Salaam   Hong Kong   Karachi
Kuala Lumpur   Madrid   Melbourne   Mexico City   Nairobi
New Delhi   Shanghai   Taipei   Toronto

With offices in
Argentina   Austria   Brazil   Chile   Czech Republic   France   Greece
Guatemala   Hungary   Italy   Japan   Poland   Portugal   Singapore
South Korea   Switzerland   Thailand   Turkey   Ukraine   Vietnam

Copyright © 2006 by Oxford University Press, Inc.

Published by Oxford University Press, Inc.
198 Madison Avenue, New York, New York, 10016
http://www.oup.com/us

Library of Congress Cataloging-in-Publication Data
The Oxford encyclopedia of British literature / David Scott Kastan, editor in chief.
p. cm.
Includes bibliographical references and index.
ISBN-13: 978-0-19-516921-8 (alk. paper)
ISBN-10: 0-19-516921-2 (alk. paper)
1. English literature—Encyclopedias.
2. Great Britain—Literatures—Encyclopedias.
3. Great Britain—In literature—Encyclopedias.
4. Great Britain—Intellectual life—Encyclopedias.
I. Title: The Oxford encyclopedia of British literature.
II. Kastan, David Scott.
PR19.095 2006
820′.3—dc22
2005025187

Printing number: 9   8   7   6   5   4   3   2   1

Printed in the United States of America
on acid-free paper

THE OXFORD ENCYCLOPEDIA OF

BRITISH LITERATURE

TONY HARRISON

Sandie Byrne

Tony Harrison (born 1937) was born in a working-class district of Leeds, in the North of England, to the baker Harry Harrison and his wife Florence (Florrie). He was educated at a local primary school where he won one of the very few state scholarships to the prestigious Leeds Grammar School. After studying classics at Leeds University, he embarked on postgraduate research into translations of the *Aeneid*, but abandoned academic life in order to devote himself to poetry. He has lived and worked in Africa, Prague, Cuba, the United States, and Greece, but has made Newcastle upon Tyne in the North of England his base for many years. He has been married twice and has two children.

Harrison's early poems appeared in student magazines such as *Poetry and Audience*, and were later taken by periodicals such as *London Magazine* and *Stand*. His first collection was a pamphlet-length publication, *Earthworks*, printed in 1964, and his first book proper was *The Loiners* (a dialect word for residents of Leeds), which was published in 1970. Since then he has published numerous volumes of poetry, verse plays, and verse film scripts, including two editions of his *Selected Poems*, and he is still publishing poetry in periodicals such as *The Guardian*, the *Times Literary Supplement*, and the *London Review of Books*. Harrison has been awarded a number of prizes, including the Geoffrey Faber Memorial Prize, the Whitbread Poetry Prize, the Prix Italia, the Royal Society's Best Original Programme Award, the William Heinemann Prize, and the Northern Rock Award, but he remains a determinedly antiestablishment figure, and made it known that he would not accept the poet laureateship if it were to be offered to him after the death of Ted Hughes. (It was given to Andrew Motion.)

A number of Harrison's verse plays and adaptations have been performed at the London National Theatre as well as in northern locations such as Salt's Mill, in Saltaire, Yorkshire, and in other European locations such as the ancient stadium at Delphi, in Greece. Although he has written some entirely original dramatic work, he is better known for his verse adaptations of classical and other

plays such as *The Oresteia*, *The Mysteries*, *The Common Chorus*, *The Trackers of Oxyrhynchus*, *Medea: A Sex-War Opera*, *The Kaisers of Carnuntum*, and *The Labourers of Herakles*. His television and cinema work has led to collaborations with a number of leading producers and directors, including George Cukor, Peter Hall (whom Harrison later pilloried for accepting a knighthood), Richard Eyre, and Peter Symes, on projects such as *The Gaze of the Gorgon*, *v.*, and *Black Daisies for the Bride*; but on more recent work, such as the film *Prometheus*, Harrison himself has taken on the director's role.

Harrison lists among his poetic influences his "household gods," John Milton and John Keats, but also the music-hall artists Max Miller and "Professor" Leon Cortez. Embracing both "high" and "low" culture, and insisting that neither should be the exclusive province of any sector of society, Harrison combines in his work elements from classical literature and myth, canonical poetry of many cultures, popular song, and jokes. The language he employs to convey this eclectic mix is highly flexible, incorporating dialectal and Standard English, non-English languages, profanity, and specialized registers. A master of form, he uses strict metrical and rhyme schemes, but often when depicting subjects and using language not usually associated with the conventions of canonical poetry.

THEMES

The main theme of Tony Harrison's work is introduced in his linked sonnets "Them & [uz]" I and II, which articulate the anger of a bright working-class schoolboy despised and disparaged for his dialect and accent ("[uz]" is a phonetic representation of the word "us" pronounced in a northern English accent, while "[ʌs]" represents the same word spoken by a someone whose accent is R.P., the more prestigious Received Pronunciation).

> 4 words only of *mi 'art aches* and . . . "Mine's broken,
> you barbarian, T.W.!" He was nicely spoken
> "Can't have our glorious heritage done to death!"

Harrison's Leeds Grammar School scholarship amounted to cultural kidnap. It gave him a classical education and introduced him to the arts, but also divorced him from working-class culture and the family background he portrays as, at least for his earliest years, warm and loving. Another sonnet, "Illuminations," depicts this background as a circuit through which flowed a kind of current, uniting the family. Education broke the circuit, and experience, travel, and his profession widened the break. The scholarship boy cannot have his wish to be the poet that his father reads. In "A Good Read" he writes:

> I've come round to your position on the Arts
> but put it down in poems, that's the bind

Nonetheless, Harrison cites his family as the source of his poetic power. "Heredity" answers a question about where he got "his talent" from:

> I say: I had two uncles, Joe and Harry—
> one was a stammerer, the other dumb.

The uncles' painful strained articulacy remains Harrison's gold standard, and in "Self-Justification," writing of both his ancestors and his contemporaries, he states:

> Their aggro towards me, my need of them 's
> what keeps my would-be mobile tongue still tied—
>
> aggression, struggle, loss, blank printer's ems
> by which all   eloquence   gets justified.

The last line is "justified"—that is, made to fit across the whole line width by the insertion of spaces. (An "em," or two "ens," was a width measurement of a piece of type, and a blank em would insert that much space in a line typeset in the old way, by hand, using actual metal pieces for each symbol.)

These are all Meredithian sonnets, named for the Victorian poet George Meredith, who employed a sixteen- rather than a fourteen-line form in his sonnet sequence *Modern Love* (1862). The extra two lines enable Harrison to develop his argument and—a favorite device—to spring a surprise at the end, fit in a punch line, or turn his argument around, pulling the rug out from under our feet. Many of his Meredithian sonnets are part of the "School of Eloquence" sequence that has been growing since the late 1960s. Among these are some of Harrison's most moving lines, in elegies for his parents, and some of his most powerful political statements, in his attempts to give a voice to the voiceless and dispossessed.

Harrison often breaks up his forms on the page and includes typographical devices (italic and bold type, Gothic script, small caps) to represent political, social, and personal division and fragmentation. Harrison's remedy for this fragmentation and dispossession is not the restoration of the continuum; not a return to a family, class, and peer-centered life, but instead the embracing of *self*-centeredness. Poems such as "The Heartless Art," representing the poet seizing on a personal tragedy as good poetic copy, show an achieved ruthlessness and self-interest presented as essential for the pursuit of poetry. Other poems depict characters finding refuge in sex, which in Harrison's work is an affirmation of life set against the void of personal and possible global extinction.

Sexual union is important to the poems and verse plays because the dramatis personae of Harrison's work are divided from one another and within. Their sense of self, however divided, is strong, but they are dispossessed from the very things that, for most people, constitute the sense of self: family, language, culture, rights. The place of origin and original belonging establishes identity, and accent (pronunciation) is its marker, particularly for Harrison's "Loiners," or natives of Leeds, but Harrison does not romanticize the poorer areas of Leeds. The streets of uniform, cramped, back-to-back houses are shown as having nothing going for them other than this status as common origin, but his Loiners feel their disconnection from these places and from one another, moving from connection to disconnection and from separation to contact.

Classics may have interrupted the continuum of Harrison's family life, but it also gave him a model of a society with a dynamic culture in which religion, entertainment, philosophy, art, and community were integrated. The prefaces to his verse plays suggest that classical Greek drama incorporated high and low culture into an indivisible whole by staging tragedy, comedy, and satyr play together, and it acknowledged the necessity for both poet and hooligan in the human makeup. Silenus, the loutish, drunken leader of the satyrs in Harrison's *Trackers of Oxyrhynchus* (1990), sets out the case:

> Satyrs in theatre are on hand to reassess
> doom and destiny and dire distress.
> Six hours of tragedy and half an hour of fun.
> But they were an entity conceived as one.

Silenus argues that later teachers and critics have "elbowed the satyrs with embarrassing erections" out of high art. But can classical high art—art from a highly hierarchical society and the catalyst for the division in Harrison's life—really be the cement that rebinds society? Later in the same play, Silenus's satyrs employ the same kind of aggressive language as the narrator of "Them & [uz]," but literalize the narrator's attack on the canon, tearing up and burning the papyrus fragment of *The Ichneutae*, the play they came from; they then metamorphose into football hooligans. The message seems to be that you can take a half-man-half-goat to culture but you cannot make him respect it. The acts of destruction are offered as tragic yet acceptable. One remembers that Harrison, claiming his kinship with the "skinhead" football hooligan in his earlier long poem *v.*, lays claim to his own act of hooliganism, triggered by anger at the idealist rhetoric of politics and "high" art. Harrison's satyrs, soldiers, and vandals are associated with Dionysus, the god of outdoors, celebration, loss of inhibition, libido, community; while the scholar who discovered the fragments of Sophocles' play becomes Apollo: god of music and other aspects of high culture, control, balance, the autonomous self. The play makes an association, characteristic of Harrison's work, between working-class culture and male bonding, between "masculinity" and energy, and between ruling-class culture and cold ruthlessness. In *Trackers*, Harrison uses Marsyas, who was flayed by Apollo for daring to aspire to the high art form of music, to represent the culmination of a number of acts of exclusion from high culture visited by the ruling classes on upstart working-class artists. In another play, *The Big H*, a chain of hyperbolic logic is made to lead from the same mockery and silencing of language seen in "Them & [uz]" to gagging, censorship, imprisonment, murder, and war.

Classical literature is not Harrison's only source of reference material, quotation, and adaptation. Many of his longer poems engage with other texts, borrowing their method or form, or addressing their themes and assumptions. One of his justly most famous poems, "A Kumquat for John Keats," takes as intertext Keats's Odes, and wonders what the Romantic poet would have made of the ambivalently bitter and sweet kumquat, had it been available to him instead of the grape. "The Fire-Gap" and "The Lords of Life" build on Lawrentian ideas about the wild and the Christian demonization of our animal and primitive instincts. "Newcastle is Peru" is an energetic and witty innovative rediscovery of a metaphysical mode. "The Blasphemers' Banquet" was an intervention in the Salman Rushdie controversy.

Although in "Them & [uz]" Harrison affirms "[uz] [uz] [uz]" and expresses a longing to restore the "continuous" of "our Tony" and the family, geographical, or social group, it is "my name" and my "own voice" that are loudest in his work; not "we," but "I." The starting point of many of the "School of Eloquence" poems is, crucially, the loss of membership in a group (for example, "Me Tarzan," "Confessional Poetry") or the loss of a "sense of place," or is a pairing (for example, "Isolation," "Cremation"). Harrison has refused to join "us," but dropping "T.W.," the initials by which he was known at school, did not restore "our Tony" to assimilation with "uz." Harrison represents his textual persona, the narrative "I," as an artist, observer, outsider; a man alone and between, divided and dualistic, sometimes dueling.

Although the narrators of the poems are often exiled and alienated, their alienation is mitigated. They resist the tags of "sellout" and "softy" by performing physical exertion: digging, sawing, fire making, sex (for example, in "Cypress and Cedar" and "The Lords of Life"). They seek and find solace in interpersonal and erotic, rather than social and familial, relations. Libidinous release sometimes brings oblivion and sometimes brings a sense of connection; to the woman, to the life force, in a way that Harrison associates with the pulse of life and the beat of meter. Arguing that sex obliterates class, nation, and other differences, Harrison comes close to arguing "make love not war" (for example, in "Chopin Express"). "Durham," however, comes around to the view that neither sex nor love nor any other human transaction is exempt from politics.

While relationships with working-class men are strained in Harrison's work, in "The Lords of Life" the "Cracker" neighbors in Florida are said to assume that the narrator is a "fairy" or "cissy," and he competes in pointless displays of machismo; sexual relationships with women seem to represent a literally plugging in to a stream that is a composite of life-energy, poetic rhythm, and language, perhaps because, for him, his mother was the conduit of literacy, as he shows in "Blocks." "Uz" in Harrison's work remains eternally lost, and "ʌs" (or "them") a club he is desperate not to join; but women, at least women available for heterosexual relations, represent a way of reinserting himself into a continuum.

Any short introduction to Harrison's work could lead the reader to expect stereotypical working-class "chip on the shoulder" aggression or the guilt of the social climber, but there is more to Harrison's work than that. He is a wonderful formalist; a master of meter and a master manipulator of the ambivalent image, of the contradiction, of the qualification. The worldview of his poetry is an equilibrium permanently compromised and permanently in tension.

CRITICAL EVALUATION AND SELF-EVALUATION

Harrison is a former editor of literary magazines, former president of the Classical Association, and a polyglot. The cover of his *Selected Poems* acclaims him as "one of the most prodigiously gifted and accessible poets alive today . . . our best English poet," and quotes Stephen Spender referring to "poems written in a style which I feel I have all my life been waiting for." Conversely, Harrison has been accused of being a "Bolshy," of writing "a torrent of four-letter filth" (*Daily Mail*, 12 October 1987), of contributing to the decline of broadcasting standards (Early Day Motion, House of Commons, 27 October 1987), and it has often been implied that he brings poetry into disrepute by inappropriately using the "high" cultural forms of poetry to represent the "low" life of popular culture. If one aspect of Harrison does acknowledge that the critics' praise is justified, another seems instantly compelled to turn his work against the "poetry lovers," and thus himself, by giving a voice to those who have no value for poetry or the poet. In the last scene of his *Labourers of Herakles*, the published text has the portentous direction, "*Enter* **Tony Harrison** *to speak as* **The Spirit of Phrynichos**." At the first (and thus far unique) performance of the play, at Delphi, the respectful silence following the playwright's highly referential as well as moving speech on war, genocide, and Greek drama was broken by the querulous and irritated voice of one of the laborers: "Who the fuck was that?"

Although he is both a highly literate and a technically accomplished poet, Harrison is never in danger of becoming complacent or pretentious while aspects of himself detach themselves to shout, "*A book, yer stupid cunt, 's not worth a fuck!*" (the offensive sexism there is the character's, not Harrison's, of course), as happens in his long poem *v.*, which contemplates, with some sympathy, the unemployed youths who turn to vandalism and defile the graves in the Leeds cemetery where Harrison's parents are buried. Nor is he in danger of overrating his intellect at the expense of his roots or his feelings. His writing can be a roller-coaster ride through one of the most exciting minds we are ever likely to encounter, but it is as visceral as it is cerebral, and as emotional as it is sensual. It is also, sadly, as removed from its contemporary audience as it is linked to its poetic ancestors, or so Harrison suggests. He could be accused of peddling stereotypes in his insistence that working-class men do not read poetry, but it also has to be admitted that his representations of oppressed workers are mostly politely applauded by middle-class "poetry supporters." A poem to a long-dead child mine laborer, Patience Kershaw, tells her, "You're lost in this sonnet for the bourgeoisie."

The poetry evinces a pained awareness of the price paid for the products of high culture. First in his first "proper book," and later in *Selected Poems*, Harrison included "Thomas Campey and the Copernican System," a poem for a secondhand book dealer whose diseased spine is bowed by the weight of the old, crack-spined volumes he pushes in his handcart through the Leeds streets. The frontispiece in Harrison's own books is a woodcut of Thomas Campey, bent almost double in flat cap and mackintosh, with a quotation from the poem:

And every pound of this dead weight is pain
to Thomas Campey (Books)

Just as Thomas Campey is before Harrison when he opens his books, and Patience Kershaw is before him when he looks into a coal fire, so, perhaps, the trace of the burden of volumes bound in heavy boards, the metaphorical weight of the capital-intensive publishing industry on its workers, and the moral responsibility of the writer for his or her words, are present in each "sonnet for the bourgeoisie."

[*See also* Ted Hughes.]

SELECTED WORKS

Earthworks (1964)
Aikin Mata, with James Simmons (1966)
Newcastle Is Peru (1969)
The Loiners (1970)
Palladas: Poems (1975)
Phaedra Britannica (1975)
Bow Down (1977)
From "The School of Eloquence" and Other Poems (1978)
Looking Up, with Philip Sharpe (1979)
Continuous: Fifty Sonnets from "The School of Eloquence" (1981)
A Kumquat for John Keats (1981)
The Oresteia (1981)
U.S. Martial (1981)
Selected Poems (1984; 2nd ed. with additional poems, 1987)
Dramatic Verse 1973–1985 (1985)
The Fire-Gap (1985)
The Mysteries (1985)
v. (1985)
Theatre Works 1973–1985 (1986)

Anno 42 (1987)

Ten Sonnets from "The School of Eloquence" (1987)

The Trackers of Oxyrhynchus (1990)

A Cold Coming (1991)

*The Common Chorus: A Version of Aristophanes'
    "Lysistrata"* (1992)

The Gaze of the Gorgon (1992)

Square Rounds (1992)

Black Daisies for the Bride (1993)

Poetry or Bust (1993)

The Shadow of Hiroshima and Other Film/Poems (1995)

*Plays 3: Poetry or Bust, The Kaisers of Carnuntum, The
    Labourers of Herakles* (1996)

The Prince's Play, Le Roi S'Amuse (1996)

Prometheus (1998)

Laureate's Block and Other Occasional Poems (2000)

Plays 4 (2002)

Plays 5 (2004)

Under the Clock and Other Poems (2005)

FURTHER READING

Astley, Neil, ed. *Bloodaxe Critical Anthologies I: Tony Harrison.* Newcastle upon Tyne, U.K., 1991. An indispensable collection of articles from newspapers and periodicals as well as some of the poet's own prose introductions.

Byrne, Sandie. *H, v. & O: The Poetry of Tony Harrison.* Manchester, U.K., 1998. A full-length study based on three central images in Harrison's work.

Byrne, Sandie, ed. *Tony Harrison: Loiner.* Oxford, 1997. A collection of essays by critics and collaborators in celebration of Harrison's sixtieth birthday.

Kelleher, Joe. *Tony Harrison.* Writers and Their Work Series. Plymouth, U.K., 1996. A short introduction to the poet and his poetry.

Rowland, Antony. *Holocaust Poetry: Awkward Poetics in the Work of Sylvia Plath, Geoffrey Hill, Tony Harrison, and Ted Hughes.* Edinburgh, 2005. An interesting comparison of the representation of the Holocaust and the use of holocaust imagery in the work of these poets.

Rowland, Antony. *Tony Harrison and the Holocaust.* Liverpool, U.K., 2001. A scholarly, theoretically engaged study of Harrison's representations of mass destruction.

Spenser, Luke. *The Poetry of Tony Harrison.* London, 1994. An accessible and readable work that includes summaries of and introductions to the poems.

STEPHEN HAWES

Antony J. Hasler

Once a victim of the condescension and neglect usually afforded early sixteenth-century literature, the Tudor courtman and poet Stephen Hawes (1485?–1529?) is now a partaker in its revaluation. His fascination lies partly in his work's strange protomodernity and the prospect it opens on his place in cultural history. Hawes is heir to a fifteenth-century tradition of public and advisory poetry, and to the more intimate love narratives, allegories, and lyrics of late-medieval England and Europe. He regularly lauds the authority of Chaucer, John Gower, and in particular John Lydgate, the poet-monk whose gargantuan endeavors had ushered in the Lancastrian dynasty a century before Hawes was writing. Yet such well-buttressed vernacular lineages had in Hawes's lifetime to contend both with an enduring sense of English's endemic backwardness and with the Latin lives, odes, and panegyrics, written by such career humanists as Bernard André, which after Henry VII's accession in 1485 became the literary prestige models of the new Tudor regime. Hawes's poetry is also responsive, in vivid yet unsettlingly indefinable ways, to the more direct pressures of courtly power. Against this background Hawes practices a curious eclecticism, almost as if to suggest that the competing modes and genres available to him offer no single and secure vantage point. The enticements and frustrations his poems offer the modern reader both measure a struggle to narrate self-formation in a desperately heterogeneous cultural and political world—hence both their allurements and their frustrations.

Next to nothing is known about Hawes's life. He may have been from East Anglia, where the name is common enough to have foiled a number of would-be identifications; he may have been the Stephen Hawes who attended Magdalen College, Oxford, in 1493. In 1503, he received four yards of black cloth for the funeral of Henry VII's queen Elizabeth of York. Royal accounts from 10 January 1506 show a payment to Hawes of ten shillings "for a ballett [balladeo] that he gave to the king's grace." All his poems were printed by William Caxton's disciple and follower Wynkyn de Worde. The first to appear, *The Example*

of Virtue, refers to him as "one of the gromes [grooms] of the most honorable chambre of our souerayne lorde King Henry VII"; its followers take up this designation, but a change occurs, as we shall see, after Henry VIII's accession in 1509.

PROMOTING POETRY

The Example of Virtue (composed 1503/04, published 1509), on all the evidence Hawes's earliest published poem, is typical of his longer works. After professing, in good fifteenth-century style, its author's modesty and indebtedness to his precursors, the poem settles into a personification allegory in which the narrator–protagonist Youth undertakes a quest to seek the lady Cleanness (purity or chastity). In a dream the narrator finds himself in a "medowe amerous," the familiar landscape of love literature, but is quickly taken under the tutelage of Sapience and Discretion, spiritual virtues both, who bombard him with strings of maxims from advisory texts. These figures guide him onward to a strangely anomalous island, an earthly paradise strewn with exotic coral and pebbles but also an English nation where yet more personifications debate the relative importance of wisdom, nature, hardihood, and fortune, and consider the perils of a boldness that improperly harnessed is as likely to foster treasonous rebellion as it is defense of the commonweal. What is at issue on this wondrous terrain, it soon turns out, is the proper condition not just of the religious self but also of political subjecthood under monarchy. Later Youth passes the portals of a peculiarly syncretic King of Love, an indecipherable blend of classical and Christian iconography, and meets Cleanness herself, whose cloistered virtue relates her to lay devotional writings about the "mixed life," an idealized union of action and contemplation.

The long expository speeches that gloss the allegory are offset by much more abrupt and bewildering interminglings of sacred and secular, one of which carries an autobiographical signature. Youth becomes groom to the chamber of Dame Sapience, who tells him that perseverance in her commandments will ultimately bring him to "a much better room." The royal chamber of Henry VII's reign was, as David Starkey's researches have shown, the center of far-reaching changes in governmental style, as a monarch wary of household conspiracy selected his closest attendants from outside the ranks of traditional privilege. There is no evidence that Hawes belonged to the intimate circle of the king's privy-chamber grooms, as some have claimed. The passage nevertheless negotiates hopes of court preferment most skillfully, asserting the courtier's emulous wishes even as they vanish into a command to win heaven through the pursuit of wisdom, self-advancement authorizing itself through self-annihilation. This mixture of political ambition, doctrine, and otherworldly, hypnotic scenery was to reach a long way; not for nothing has Hawes been seen as a forerunner to Edmund Spenser.

FATAL FICTIONS

The conclusion of *The Example* has a decidedly clerical bent; Youth and Cleanness marry in a feast sponsored by every figure of doctrine Hawes can lay hands on (moral personifications, Church fathers), then go on a tour of heaven and hell. The much longer *Pastime of Pleasure* (composed 1505/06, published 1509), Hawes's most famous poem, is structurally more subtle. Once more it is an allegorical quest, but here the love fiction dominates; the narrator is called Graunde Amour, his love La Belle Pucelle (the fair maiden). Pucelle, however, is also the object of desire in a more general way. Long before she appears as a character, her desirability is announced by Dame Fame—not the skeptical Chaucer's fickle goddess but, rather, stable and everlasting renown decked out in the "brennyrge tongues" of an admiring future, a figure borrowed from the poetry and court festivities of contemporary Burgundy. What follows, once again, is an exercise in generic instability, as the poem wanders between love narrative, the poet's quest for fame, and a marked—if more subdued—religious strand. There is low-style comedy, too, in the shape of Godfrey Gobelive, a ribald dwarf who scorns Amour's refined love. Also of note is the particular path that Amour must follow; in accordance with the period's increasing insistence that the gentleman be educated in letters as well as arms, Amour spends much of the poem in the Tower of Doctrine with the Seven Liberal Arts, before fighting giants and monsters who take on the roles of traditional obstacles—slander, "disdain"—to the medieval literary lover's success.

A. S. G. Edwards has shown close correspondences between Hawes's first two poems and the woodcuts that accompany them, implying that Hawes and his printer de Worde are especially aware of the potential of print. This perhaps accounts for the poem's fluid treatment of narrative voice. The poems move sectionally among genres, sometimes marked by affiliations with other texts printed by de Worde (the woodcuts in *The Pastime's* Tower of Doctrine scenes, for instance, also appear in instructional works). In *The Pastime*, accordingly, the fiction of a speaking lover, Graunde Amour, takes second place to Hawes's sense of what genre the poem is in at any given point. Such apparent discontinuity, however, goes with statements about the general nature of poetry that are consistent, serious, and self-conscious. The Tower of Doctrine episodes assign overwhelming importance to rhetoric, which gives Hawes the chance to praise past poets who, Lydgate-like, used their talents in the service of the realm. Hawes's vocabulary, too, derives from Lydgate; true poets "enlumyne" and "encense," their words, as though viewed through some strange sensorium, pouring out light and fragrance. The narrator's voice is highly Latinate, and Gobelive, its opponent within the poem, speaks in the unreconstructed "rude" English (here a Kentish dialect) that Hawes openly rejects. Coupled with this, however, is a persistent stress on secrecy. Poets write "fatal fictions," which conceal truth beneath "cloudy figures"; rhetoric in the Tudor state, as Rita Copeland notes, is seen as the preserve of an initiate elite wielding a veiled power. *The Pastime's* own fatal secret, however, is a structural one. After its long expanses, the poem suddenly collapses, concertina-style. Amour marries his Pucelle, but the poem hurries him, in a very few lines, into avaricious old age, a death that he himself narrates ("Out of my body my soule than it went"), and purgatory. As C. S. Lewis observed, the blurred narratorial articulation of the entire poem turns out in retrospect to have been death-haunted. A final sequence of triumphal entries—of time, fame, and eternity—gradually move away from Amour himself, to suggest that time and narrative are fictions, subplots built on an eternity into which the poem must at last disappear. Hawes, much concerned with poetic "authority," once again enacts an authority attested by its own dissolution.

THE DISCOMFORTS OF HISTORY

The records that note Hawes's presence at the 1503 obsequies for Henry VII's queen do not include him among the mourners for her royal husband in 1509. After this, he is identified in his poems as "somtyme grome" of the "late" king's chamber, suggesting that after the accession of Henry VIII he may have lost or left office. Most of his work in the new reign tells us little of what, if anything, changed in the poet's circumstances. *The Conversion of Swearers* (1509) remarkably anticipates the pattern poems of later poets such as George Herbert. His surviving panegyric of the new ruler, *A Joyful Meditation* (1509), is more revealing, though of what we cannot know. The poem's praise of the young Henry VIII is partly swamped by a timid defense of the late king's "avarice" (shown in the bonds and recognizances imposed on the nobility in Henry VII's latter years) and edgily equivocal claims that it was geared to the preparation for a new crusade. As Hawes's editors suggest, building also on fragments of political fable that hang sinisterly in the air in *The Example of Virtue*, Hawes may have been overclosely associated with Sir Richard Empson and Edmund Dudley, the unpopular lawyer-councillors who implemented Henry VII's fiscal policies and were executed once the new reign began.

Whatever the truth, Hawes's remarkable *Comfort of Lovers* (composed 1510/11, published c. 1515) reads like nothing so much as a powerful record of the experience of exclusion. Again we meet a lover in a garden, here remembering a "lady excellent" of higher station whom he has loved and longs to recover. This time, however, Hawes's customary eclecticism has become a traumatic fragmentation. This lover is compassed about by terrifying necromantic plotters; a venerable lady interrogates him as in earlier works, but here the usual sententious utterances are combined with questions of riddling obliquity, to which he responds in kind. Love complaint mingles here with late-medieval political prophecy, in which hopes and fears of political change found expression in cryptic figurative speech. The poem offers other keys. It features a total absorption in books—the lover even claims that the poems of Chaucer, Gower, and Lydgate, the forefathers of English poetry, prophesy his own sufferings. Such matter is intercut with episodes of romance recognition; the lover sees magical mirrors and gems; a sword that, Excalibur-style, marks its discoverer as a hero-elect; and an image of the Holy Ghost suggesting divine inspiration. The poem seems to be reaching toward some dramatic gesture of closure that will heal the split identities of this narrator-protagonist, who is at once lover, ambitious courtier, romance hero, poet and prophet—and who, like *The Pastime of Pleasure's* central figure, is named Amour. Yet such fantasies of completion are undermined by the appearance of the lady herself—La Belle Pucelle *rediviva*, who calmly rejects the promises held out by the genres previously evoked and preserves a chilly distance, even claiming that the sword he took was not ordained for him. This most secretive of Hawes's poems—does it refer to some concealed history? is it an allegory of his poetic career?—is also the most reflexive, as Amour, again resting his desires on the slender thread of a literary signature, tries to write *The Pastime* into the story of his love. This achieves nothing, however; the lover-poet, locked in his own obscure words ("I speke vnknowen") is left wishing that his lady would recognize the "preuyte" [privity] of his heart and "remembre" him.

AFTERLIFE

We hear no more of Hawes until a later reference by the poet Thomas Feylde to "Yonge Steuen Hawse whose soule god pardon," in a poem published in 1529, provides a *terminus ante quem* for his death and poignantly hints that he may have died young. Feylde was also published by De Worde, who evidently strove to keep Hawes's reputation alive, and in the 1530s some of the more self-contained lyrics from his poems appear in manuscript. Hawes received little attention in the eighteenth and nineteenth centuries, although the exceptions to this rule include such notable names as Thomas Wharton and Elizabeth Barrett Browning. The twentieth century, if we discount Lewis's superb and sympathetic account, also gave him short shrift. Even its final decades, with their fresh exploration of fifteenth- and early-sixteenth-century poetry (which did much to rehabilitate Hawes's adored Lydgate), tended to repeat the standard accusations of clunking prosody, weak rhyme, and narrative longueurs, without heeding Hawes's real if sometimes uncertainly handled experimentalism of form and genre. Lately, however, a sharper scholarly attentiveness to the ways in which late medieval poets read one another, and their own historical involvement, has brought Hawes's work, once interesting merely as a symptom of a supposed "transition from medieval to Renaissance," into fresh focus. The critical results suggest that despite his unpromising reputation, reading Hawes can still be a pastime of pleasure.

[*See also* John Lydgate.]

SELECTED WORKS

The Example of Virtue (1503/04)
The Pastime of Pleasure (1505/06)

The Conversion of Swearers (1509)
A Joyful Meditation (1509)
The Comfort of Lovers (1510/11)

FURTHER READING

Copeland, Rita. "Lydgate, Hawes, and the Science of Rhetoric in the Late Middle Ages." *Modern Language Quarterly* 53 (1992): 57–82. Highly suggestive on the politics of Hawes's rhetorical practice.

Edwards, A. S. G. *Stephen Hawes.* Boston, 1983. Useful overview, full bibliography.

Lewis, C. S. *The Allegory of Love.* Oxford, 1936. Classic, often wrongheaded, still perceptive on Hawes.

Starkey, David. "Intimacy and Innovation: The Rise of the Privy Chamber, 1485–1547." In *The English Court: From the Wars of the Roses to the Civil War,* edited by David Starkey et al., 71–118. London, 1987. Invaluable for the historical context of the early Tudor court.

ELIZA HAYWOOD

Ellen Pollak

Eliza Fowler Haywood (c. 1693–1756) was one of the most popular and prolific writers of the first half of the eighteenth century, celebrated in her own day as one of the three most influential women writers of the age by the poet-critic James Sterling, who included her, along with Aphra Behn (c. 1640–1689) and Delarivier Manley, in the "fair Triumvirate of Wit" ("To Mrs. Eliza Haywood, on Her Writing," dedicatory verse to Haywood's *Secret Histories, Novels, and Poems*, 1725). An extraordinarily versatile writer, Haywood experimented with a remarkable range of genres (including drama, poetry, the political essay, the scandal chronicle, periodical writing, theater history, and translation, in addition to the prose fiction for which she is best known), publishing more than seventy works over almost forty years.

Her first novel, *Love in Excess; or, The Fatal Enquiry*, a story of amorous intrigue published in three parts between 1719 and 1720, was a best seller, going through two editions and multiple reissues before 1724 and appearing in two collected editions of Haywood's works in 1724 and 1725, respectively. It has been argued that only two other works appearing prior to the 1740 publication of Samuel Richardson's acclaimed novel *Pamela*—Daniel Defoe's *Robinson Crusoe* (1719) and Jonathan Swift's *Gulliver's Travels* (1726), now both classics—enjoyed comparable popularity.

Haywood's best-known works are *The Female Spectator*, the first English periodical for women written by a woman, which appeared monthly between April 1744 and May 1746; and *The History of Miss Betsy Thoughtless* (1751), a narrative of female development that has earned her distinction as a pioneer in the early history of the English novel. Although the dominant character of her writing changed conspicuously over the course of her career, from the explicitly erotic fiction of the 1720s to the more morally decorous didactic prose and domestic fiction of the 1740s and 1750s, Haywood demonstrated a sustained commitment throughout her life to analyzing and critiquing eighteenth-century gender politics and their influence on the dynamics and representation of heterosexual love.

Despite her importance and visibility in eighteenth-century literary and theatrical circles, until very recently Haywood has cut a rather poor figure in the annals of literary history. Certainly she has not enjoyed the kind of critical reception that kept controversial male writers like Defoe and Swift in print and at the forefront of public consciousness throughout the nineteenth and twentieth centuries. For over two hundred years after her death she was known primarily as a licentious hack writer, best remembered for Alexander Pope's disparaging portrait of her in his mock-epic poem *The Dunciad* (1728), where she appears as the prize in a urinating contest between two rival booksellers whom Pope considered among the most unprincipled of his contemporaries. Figuring his "Eliza" as an offering to the farthest pisser, Pope insinuates that as a professional writer Haywood habitually sold herself (her body as well as her work) to the highest bidder. As has often been the case in treatments of women writers of the past, Haywood's sexuality has been a focus of attention while her work itself has been neglected and undervalued.

Since the early 1990s, however, Haywood's critical fortunes have begun to change. An increasing number of her works are now available in modern editions and are receiving the serious critical and scholarly attention they deserve; works not formerly attributed to her are still in the process of being identified. No longer regarded merely as a minor precursor to the great canonical novelists of the mid to late eighteenth century, she is now emerging in her own right as a leading figure in the early development of the British novel—one whose innovations in the genre had a shaping influence on many better-known writers, including Richardson, Henry Fielding, Frances Burney, and Jane Austen.

LIFE AND EARLY CAREER

Little information about Haywood's life survives. Born Eliza Fowler, probably in London in 1693, her first known appearance as Eliza Haywood occurred in 1715, when she made her acting debut at Dublin's prestigious Smock Alley Theater. Until recently, the theory of the early-twentieth-century biographer George Frisbie Whicher that Haywood was the runaway wife of the cleric Valentine Haywood dominated the scholarly field (Whicher's is still the only full-length biography of Haywood); but the work of Christine Blouch has since demonstrated that this conjecture is based on tenuous evidence. Although we know from Haywood's own later testimony that "an unfortunate marriage . . . reduc'd [her] to the melancholly necessity of depending on [her] Pen for the support of [her]self and two children" (letter from Haywood to an unidentified potential patron, quoted in Blouch, p. 537), nothing is known about the identity of her husband or the circumstances under which their relationship ended. Be that as it may, Haywood was almost certainly on her own by the time she returned to London in 1717, where she performed at Lincoln's Inn Fields, one of the city's two royal theaters, and became a member of the vibrant literary circle of the playwright and essayist Aaron Hill. During this period (1717–1724) she developed a personal and professional relationship with the writer Richard Savage, who may have been the father of one of her two children. The father of her other child was probably the playwright and actor William Hatchett, with whom she lived for twenty years and collaborated on a number of theatrical projects.

After the triumphant success of *Love in Excess* (1719), Haywood continued to act and write plays, and she collaborated with Daniel Defoe on a series of pamphlets about the deaf-mute prophet Duncan Campbell; but her energies during the decade of the 1720s were primarily focused on the production of prose fiction. Her own words suggest that this shift in emphasis was market-driven: "The Stage not answering my Expectations, . . . made me turn my Genius another Way" (quoted in Ingrassia, Introduction, p. 30). Her literary output between 1719 and 1729 was prodigious; in all, she wrote more than fifty texts, averaging a new novel every three months. Her preferred genre was the amatory novel, in the tradition of Behn and Manley, a form distinguished by the frank sexuality and rhetorical extravagance of passages like this one from *Love in Excess*, in which Amena, despite misgivings, is overcome by the seductions of Count D'Elmont:

> she had only a thin Silk Night-Gown on, which flying open as he caught her in his Arms, he found her panting Heart beat Measures of Consent, her heaving Breast swell to be

> press'd by his, and every Pulse confess a Wish to yield; . . . in fine, there was but a Moment betwixt her and Ruin. (*Secret Histories* [1725], vol. 1, p. 26)

Haywood followed the example of Behn and Manley in exploring the relationships between power and seduction, at once exploiting the erotic potential of the seduction plot and deriding her society's sexual double standard, but she also initiated an important transformation in the amatory genre. Where Behn's and Manley's stories of power and sexual intrigue had been inextricably embedded in party political rivalries and ideologies (the two rival political parties of the time were the Whigs and the Tories), Haywood's work, though it does not altogether abandon Tory political concerns, harks back to earlier traditions of romantic fiction in addressing a more general and less directly party-political reader, thus expanding its appeal and ultimately paving the way for the later development of the domestic novel. Although there is some debate over whether Haywood's fictions were directed primarily at a female readership, scholars tend to agree that the formidable productivity and popularity that inspired Henry Fielding to portray her as "Mrs. Novel" in his 1730 play *The Author's Farce* and James Sterling to praise her as the "Great Arbitress of Passion" derived in large part from her sustained focus on the universal force of desire and on sexual seduction as an instrument of power.

Although Haywood produced at least eight new works between 1729 and 1739, her voluminous output and public visibility during this period underwent a relative decline. Consequently, some scholars have speculated that Pope's 1728 attack on her as a "Juno of majestic size, / With cow-like udders, and with ox-like eyes" (*Dunciad*, book 2, lines 155–156) had effectively shamed her into silence and eventual moral reform, supporting their conjecture by pointing to the uncharacteristically didactic character of most of the work she produced in the 1740s and 1750s. In fact, far from being silenced during the decade of the 1730s, Haywood had merely shifted direction professionally in an attempt to capitalize on growing markets for theatrical and political writing, particularly writing critical of the Whig government of Robert Walpole, England's controversial first prime minister (1721–1742). During these years she resumed her acting career; she collaborated with Hatchett on *The Opera of Operas; or, Tom Thumb the Great* (1733), a musical adaptation of Fielding's anti-Walpole play *The Tragedy of Tragedies*; she produced a critical history of the British theater (*The Dra-*

matic Historiographer; or, The British Theatre Delineated, 1735; later retitled The *Companion to the Theatre*) that went into seven editions by 1756; and she anonymously published *The Adventures of Eovaai, Princess of Ijaveo* (1736, 1741), a sophisticated satiric fantasy mocking Walpole and his government. In 1737 she joined Fielding's Great Mogul's Company at the Little Theatre in Haymarket, which she later referred to as "F——g's scandal-shop," alluding to the radical political nature of the plays performed there (*The History of Miss Betsy Thoughtless,* 1751). A benefit performance of Fielding's wildly popular *Historical Register,* in which Haywood appeared as Mrs. Screen, was held for her on the night before Parliament passed the Stage Licensing Act—a statute designed to prevent the performance of plays (especially those by Fielding) satirizing Walpole's administration. This legislation brought about the closing of Fielding's theater and ended both of his and Haywood's theatrical careers.

HAYWOOD AND THE NOVEL AT MIDCENTURY

In 1741, in an extraordinary move for a woman, Haywood set up shop as a bookseller in Covent Garden, calling her business The Sign of Fame. In the same year, she wrote and anonymously issued (from her own shop) *Anti-Pamela; or, Feign'd Innocence Detected.* With this work she joined the groundswell of public response to Samuel Richardson's supreme best seller, his first novel, *Pamela*—a wave of reaction that generated not only numerous imitations, rewritings, continuations, and commentaries but also a new market for such fashionable commodities and entertainments as Pamela fans and Pamela waxworks. Like Fielding, who also participated in this "Pamela-craze" with his two parodies, *Shamela* (1741) and *Joseph Andrews* (1742), Haywood—ever attuned to new commercial opportunities—capitalized on her competitor's popularity while entering into a larger cultural conversation about the nature of the novel genre and its readers. Through the adventures of its heroine, Syrena Tricksy, a servant girl who uses her wit and seductive wiles to turn her position of sexual and economic dependence to profit, Haywood's *Anti-Pamela* at once exposes the vulnerable position of female servants in the eighteenth century and impugns the jealously guarded purity of Richardson's heroine, whose virtuous resistance to the sexual advances of her young, aristocratic master ultimately pays off in the form of a marriage proposal and a dramatic class ascent.

Richardson captured the market for fiction in the 1740s by producing titillating novels of seduction with an expressly moral aim, thus capitalizing on popular taste for amatory intrigue while at the same time distancing his work from the "scandalous" romances of Haywood and her predecessors Behn and Manley, whose narrative techniques he nevertheless freely incorporated. With her finely attuned commercial and cultural sensibilities, Haywood understood the gendered stakes of Richardson's commercial success and the shift in literary tastes it represented. Recognizing the new cultural authority of the figure of the virtuous domestic woman, and being "something of a discursive contortionist who could manipulate her skills to fit the appropriate niche markets" (Ingrassia, Introduction, p. 35), Haywood responded cannily by reinventing her public persona. In the first issue of *The Female Spectator* of April 1744, she pays direct lip service to the doctrine that readers should be edified as well as entertained:

> It is very much, by the Choice we make of Subjects for our Entertainment, that the refine'd Taste distinguishes itself from the vulgar and more gross: Reading is universally allowed to be one of the most improving, as well as agreeable Amusements; but then to render it so, one should, among the Number of Books which are perpetually issuing from the Press, endeavour to single out such as promise to be most conducive to those Ends.

At once confronting and forestalling readerly concern about authorial reputation, Haywood issued her periodical anonymously while introducing herself to her readers as a reformed coquette:

> I . . . acknowledge, that I have run through as many Scenes of Vanity and Folly as the greatest Coquet of them all . . . . My Life, for some Years, was a continued Round of what I then called Pleasure, and my whole Time engross'd by a Hurry of promiscuous Diversions.—But whatever Inconveniences such a manner of Conduct has brought upon myself, I have this Consolation, to think that the Publick may reap some Benefit from it.

Her experience, she archly hopes, will prove "in some measure both useful and entertaining to the Publick."

Haywood cultivated this new, more respectable and high-minded persona throughout the remainder of her career, publishing three "moral" novels—*The Fortunate Foundlings* (1744), *The History of Miss Betsy Thoughtless* (1751), and *The History of Jemmy and Jenny Jessamy* (1753), as well several works on conduct: *Epistles for the*

Ladies (1748–1750), *The Wife* (1756), and *The Husband: In Answer to the Wife* (1756). She did not, however, abandon political controversy altogether, bringing out several issues of a Tory periodical, *The Parrot*, in 1746, and writing, anonymously publishing, and possibly distributing an allegedly seditious pamphlet for which she was arrested and jailed for some weeks (but not prosecuted) in 1750. In 1756 she became ill while working on a new weekly publication, *The Young Lady*. She died on 25 February and was buried on 3 March at St. Margaret's Church, in an unmarked grave in sight of Westminster Abbey, where many British literary figures are memorialized by burial in the Poet's Corner, and where Aphra Behn lies in the cloister.

WOMEN WRITERS IN THE LITERARY MARKETPLACE

Women occupied a prominent but vexed position in the new literary marketplace within which the novel flourished. Because the new profession of writing was open to authors of diverse socioeconomic backgrounds and did not require a formal education, women were able to compete within it on the same footing as men. On the other hand, as Paula McDowell observes, "Augustan political and cultural élites recognized . . . women's . . . access to their culture's most important mode of mass communication as a significant new threat to the established order, and expended considerable energy working to shut down their voices in print" (p. 6). Such viciously sexualized attacks on Haywood as Pope's make it clear that women writers in the early modern print market faced unique and difficult challenges. Since authorship was traditionally considered a male activity, the very act of entering the public sphere as a writer—not to mention publishing racy and sometimes libelous narratives—called a woman's sexual character into question. Jonathan Swift was content to refer to Haywood as "a stupid, infamous, scribbling woman," even as he confessed never having "seen any of her productions" (*Correspondence of Jonathan Swift*, ed. Harold Williams, vol. 3 [Oxford 1963], 501). Pope's "Eliza,"—with her "cow-like udders" and "Two babes of love close clinging to her waste" (*Dunciad Variorum*, 2.150)—represents the "profligate licentiousness of . . . shameless [s]cribblers" generally, but mainly those of "That sex, which ought least to be capable of such malice or impudence" (149 n.). In the context of *The Dunciad*'s sustained attack on literary hacks, her grotesquely breeding reproductive body (whose "babes of

love" just as readily suggest her amorous literary progeny as her illegitimate children) comes to stand for the monstrous fecundity of print culture itself, with its proliferating glut of inferior authors and bad writing. In much the same satiric vein, Haywood's one-time lover Savage referred to her as a former "Strolling Actress" who should have turned washerwoman rather than scandal writer, so that she might have usefully cleaned others' "sullied linen" instead of simply displaying it in public (Richard Savage, *An Author To Be Lett*, [London, 1729], Publisher's Preface).

Haywood lamented the impossible cultural condition of the woman writer on more than one occasion, alluding to "that Tide of Raillery, which all of my Sex . . . must expect once they exchange the Needle for the Quill" (dedication to *The Fair Captive*) and inveighing against "the numerous Difficulties a Woman has to struggle through in her Approach to Fame" (preface to *The Memoirs of the Baron de Brosse*). Her first biographer, David E. Baker, nonetheless praised her posthumously for her unsurpassed "virtue" and "purity":

> whatever Liberty she might at first give to her Pen, to the Offence either of Morality or Delicacy, she seem'd to be soon convinced of her Error, and determined not only to reform, but even attone for it; since, in the numerous Volumes which she gave to the World towards the latter Part of her Life, no Author has appear'd more the Votary of Virtue, nor are there any Novels in which a stricter Purity, or greater Delicacy of Sentiment, has been preserved. (*Companion to the Play House* [London, 1764])

Clara Reeve followed suit in her famous essay *The Progress of Romance* (1785), but without the hint of doubt implicit in Baker's use of the terms "seem'd" and "appear'd." Here, in a dialogue concerning the romance genre, the voice of Euphrasia is resolute in her defense of Haywood's ultimate respectability: "I would be the last to vindicate her faults, but the first to celebrate her return to virtue, and her atonement for them."

Whether or not Haywood's midcareer "conversion" has been accepted at face value, the wonder is that it has taken so much longer in her case than in, say, Swift's, for critics to begin to explore her manipulation of literary masks. Haywood's heroines are often victims of male power and duplicity, but they are just as often plotters themselves who use masquerade to outwit men. The heroine of *Fantomina; or, Love in a Maze* (1725) brilliantly secures the interest and desire of her straying lover by impersonating an array of different women with whom he, quite unsuspecting, has a series of what he believes are secret liaisons. In *The Female Spectator* Haywood included several stories about the dangers of public masquerades for young women, in part perhaps to deflect attention from her own private masquerade as a reformed coquette. She would revisit the theme of the reformed coquette in Betsy Thoughtless, a high-spirited young woman with a good heart but a lack of prudence who, like Fielding's Tom Jones, must learn not just to *be* virtuous but also to *appear* so. The strategies whereby Haywood distanced herself from her characters and even sometimes from her own narrative voice can make it difficult for readers to locate her in her writing. Like the narrator in her semifictional journalistic treatise *The Invisible Spy* (1754) who wears a magic belt of invisibility, she seems to disappear into the fictional spaces she occupies. She seems to have understood that character is a fiction in life as well as in art. Haywood's conflicting self-representations work to expose this fictionality and to make it impossible to pin her down. In a world all too ready to collapse her into her characters, or to confuse her romances with her life, this elusiveness may have been her most powerful strategy of survival, both during her lifetime and beyond.

[*See also* Delarivier Manley; The Novel; Popular Romance; *and* Samuel Richardson.]

SELECTED WORKS

Love in Excess; or, the Fatal Inquiry (1719–1720)

The Fair Captive (1721)

The British Recluse; or, The Secret History of Cleomira, Suppos'd Dead (1722)

The Injur'd Husband; or, The Mistaken Resentment (1722)

Idalia; or, The Unfortunate Mistress (1723)

Lasselia; or, The Self-Abandon'd (1723)

The Rash Resolve; or, The Untimely Discovery (1723)

A Wife to Be Lett (1723)

The Works of Mrs. Eliza Haywood, Consisting of Novels, Letters, Poems, and Plays (3 vols. 1723; vol. 4, 1724)

The Arragonian Queen: A Secret History (1724)

Bath Intrigues; In Four Letters to a Friend in London (1724)

Fantomina; or, Love in a Maze (1724)

The Fatal Secret; or, Constancy in Distress (1724)

The Force of Nature; or, The Lucky Disappointment (?1724)

The Masqueraders; or, Fatal Curiosity (1724; part two, 1725)

Memoirs of the Baron de Brosse (1724)

Memoirs of a Certain Island Adjacent to the Kingdom of Utopia (1724; vol. 2, 1725)

Poems on Several Occasions (1724)

Secret Histories, Novels, and Poems (4 vols. 1725)

A Spy upon the Conjuror; or, A Collection of Surprising Stories, with Names, Places, and Particular Circumstances Relating to Mr. Duncan Campbell . . . (1724)

The Surprise; or, Constancy Rewarded (1724)

The Tea-Table (1724; periodical)

The Dumb Projector; Being a Surprizing Account of a Trip to Holland made by Mr. Duncan Campbell (1725)

The Fatal Fondness; or, Love Its Own Opposer (1725)

Mary Stuart, Queen of Scots (1725)

The Tea-Table; or, A Conversation between Some Polite Persons of Both Sexes, at a Lady's Visiting Day (1725)

The Unequal Conflict; or, Nature Triumphant (1725)

The City Jilt; or, The Alderman Turn'd Beau (1726)

Cleomelia; or, The Generous Mistress. To which is added The Lucky Rape; or, Fate the Best Disposer and The Capricious Lover; or, No Trifling with a Woman (1726)

The Distress'd Orphan; or, Love in a Mad-house (1726)

The Double Marriage; or, The Fatal Release (1726)

Letters from the Palace of Fame (1726)

The Mercenary Lover; or, The Unfortunate Heiress (1726)

Reflections on the Various Effects of Love, According to the Contrary Dispositions of the Persons on Whom It Operates (1726)

The Secret History of the Present Intrigues of the Court of Caramania (1726)

The Fruitless Inquiry; Being a Collection of Several Entertaining Histories (1727)

The Life of Madam de Villesache (1727)

The Perplex'd Dutchess; or, Treachery Rewarded (1727)

Philidore and Placentia; or, L'Amour Trop Delicat (1727)

Secret Histories, Novels, &c. (2 vols. 1727)

The Agreeable Caledonian; or, Memoirs of Signiora di Morella (1728; part two, 1729) Reprint as *Clementina; or, The History of an Italian Lady* (1768)

Irish Artifice; or, The History of Clarina. In The Female Dunciad [Edmund Curll] (1728)

The Padlock; or, No Guard without Virtue. Appended to *The Mercenary Lover*, 3rd ed. (1728)

The Parrot (1728) By Mrs. Prattle. Attributed to Haywood.

Persecuted Virtue; or, The Cruel Lover (1728)

The City Widow; or, Love in a Butt (1729)

The Fair Hebrew; or, A True, but Secret History of Two Jewish Ladies (1729)

Frederick, Duke of Brunswick-Lunenburgh (1729)

Love-Letters on All Occasions Lately Passed between Persons of Distinction (1730)

Secret Memoirs of the Late Mr. Duncan Campbell, the Famous Deaf and Dumb Gentleman. (1732)

The Opera of Operas; or, Tom Thumb the Great (1733; with William Hatchett.)

The Dramatic Historiographer; or, The British Theatre Delineated (1735; repr. as *A Companion to the Theatre; or, A View of our Most Celebrated Dramatic Pieces,* 2 vols., 1747)

The Adventures of Eovaai, Princess of Ijaveo (1736; repr. as *The Unfortunate Princess; or, The Ambitious Statesman,*1741)

Anti-Pamela; or, Feign'd Innocence Detected (1741)

A Present for a Servant-Maid; or, The Sure Means of Gaining Love and Esteem (1743)

The Fortunate Foundlings (1744)

The Female Spectator (4 vols. 1744–1746)

The Parrot:With a Compendium of the times, by the Author of the Female Spectator (1746)

Epistles for the Ladies (monthly, Nov. 1748–May 1749; vol. 2, 1750)

Life's Progress through the Passions; or, The Adventures of Natura (1748)

Dalinda, or, The Double Marriage (1749)

A Letter from H----- G-----, Esq (1750)

The History of Miss Betsy Thoughtless (4 vols. 1751)

The History of Jemmy and Jenny Jessamy (3 vols. 1753)

Modern Characters; Illustrated by Histories in Real Life, and Address'd to the Polite World (1753)

The Invisible Spy. By Explorabilis (4 vols. 1755)

The Wife. By Mira, one of the Authors of *The Female Spectator,* and *Epistles for Ladies* (1756)

The Husband: In Answer to the Wife (1756)

The Young Lady. By Euphrosine (1756)

The History of Leonora Meadowson (1788)

FURTHER READING

Ballaster, Ros. *Seductive Forms: Women's Amatory Fiction from 1684 to 1740.* Oxford, 1992. A seminal study of the amatory fiction of Behn, Manley, and Haywood.

Blouch, Christine. "Eliza Haywood and the Romance of Obscurity." *Studies in English Literature* 31 (1991): 535–552. An important recent corrective to Whicher's 1915 biography.

Craft-Fairchild, Catherine. *Masquerade and Gender: Disguise and Female Identity in Eighteenth-Century Fictions by Women.* University Park, PA, 1993. Includes a chapter on masquerade in several of Haywood's fictions.

Gonda, Caroline. *Reading Daughters' Fictions: 1709–1834: Novels and Society from Manley to Edgeworth.* Cambridge, U.K., 1996. Includes a brief but interesting discussion of some of Haywood's fictions, especially those involving incest.

Hollis, Karen. "Eliza Haywood and the Gender of Print." *The Eighteenth Century: Theory and Interpretation* 38 (1997): 43–62. An analysis of Haywood's concern with women's ability to control the public circulation of their private writing.

Ingrassia, Catherine. *Authorship, Commerce, and Gender in Early Eighteenth-Century England: A Culture of Paper Credit.* Cambridge, U.K., 1998. Two chapters on Haywood contextualize her in relation to the professionalization of authorship and the development of new literary and financial practices; also reassesses her importance in relation to Pope and Richardson.

Ingrassia, Catherine. Introduction. In *Anti-Pamela by Eliza Haywood and Shamela by Henry Fielding,* 7–43. Peterborough, Ont., 2004.

McDowell, Paula. *The Women of Grub Street: Press, Politics, and Gender in the London Literary Marketplace, 1678–1730.* Oxford and New York, 1998.

Richetti, John. *Popular Fiction before Richardson: Narrative Patterns 1700–1739.* Oxford, 1969, repr. 1992. An important early contribution to the study of eighteenth-century popular writing, with discussion of the plots of Haywood among others; reprinted with a new introduction in the wake of feminist criticism.

Saxton, Kristen T., and Rebecca P. Bocchicchio, eds. *The Passionate Fictions of Eliza Haywood: Essays on Her Life and Work.* Lexington, KY, 2000. This edited collection of essays on Haywood's fiction is the first book-length critical study of Haywood.

Spedding, Patrick. *A Bibliography of Eliza Haywood.* London, 2004. The first descriptive bibliography of the works of Haywood (and William Hatchett), covering more than twice as many imprints as the last available (1915) bibliography.

Spencer, Jane. *The Rise of the Woman Novelist: From Aphra Behn to Jane Austen.* Oxford and New York, 1986. An important thematic treatment of women writers' contributions to the early history of the English novel; notes Haywood's effect on the development of the plot of the reformed coquette.

Straub, Kristina. "Women, Gender, and Criticism." In

Literary Criticism and Theory: The Greeks to the Present, edited by Robert Con Davis and Laurie Finke, 855–876. New York and London, 1989. Includes a fine extended discussion of Haywood's *Invisible Spy.*

Todd, Janet. *The Sign of Angellica: Women, Writing, and Fiction, 1660–1800.* New York, 1989. One of the first important literary histories of women writers in the eighteenth century, this book includes a brief but valuable reading of *Betsy Thoughtless.*

Turner, Cheryl. *Living by the Pen: Women Writers in the Eighteenth Century.* London and New York, 1992. An important book on the rise of women's prose fiction and the emergence of female literary professionalism in England.

Warner, William B. *Licensing Entertainment: The Elevation of Novel Reading in Britain, 1684–1750.* Berkeley, 1998. A revisionary account of the emergence of the British novel as an "overwriting" of novels of amorous intrigue; includes a sustained reading of Haywood's *Love in Excess.*

Whicher, George Frisbee. *The Life and Romances of Mrs. Eliza Haywood.* New York, 1915. The first full-length biography of Haywood, now partially superseded by the work of Blouch.

WILLIAM HAZLITT

Jon Klancher

William Hazlitt (1778–1830) was a Romantic-age critic and essayist of remarkable gifts—a strikingly original thinker on theater, painting, and poetry; a combative political journalist in an age of intense public controversy; and a brilliantly unpredictable, incisive prose stylist. His aesthetic and political reach has been compared to that of his contemporary Samuel Taylor Coleridge. Yet to a far greater extent than Coleridge, Hazlitt was a prolific and rapid producer for the weekly journals, monthly magazines, lecture halls, quarterly reviews, and on one occasion the *Encyclopaedia Britannica*, registering some of the most dynamic tendencies of his times. He could stimulate equal pleasures in the popular art of boxing and the high-spoken sport of poetics. He proclaimed the virtues of "plain speaking," yet in his prose he delighted in paradox, antithesis, and the display of wide cultural reference. He misquoted many of the writers he cited, but the rich allusiveness of his essays wove cultural memory into the pungent immediacy of his topics and arguments. He was, by his own phrase, a "good hater" in intellectual combat; he could also be a painfully inept lover and left a public trail of amorous embarrassments. His Victorian admirer Leslie Stephen called Hazlitt the "pure literary critic," yet many later readers have instead concurred with David Bromwich's assessment that Hazlitt was a critic "distinctly placed in history, conscious that literature and politics belong to one world."

EARLY LIFE

Hazlitt was born 10 April 1778, in Maidstone, England, to a family of Dissenters who stocked the house with books written by iconoclastic Enlightenment writers such as Joseph Priestley, William Godwin, Jean-Jacques Rousseau, and Benjamin Franklin. His father, the Reverend

William Hazlitt
Engraving by J. Hyatt, after John Hazlitt,
c. 1813
NATIONAL PORTRAIT GALLERY, LONDON

William Hazlitt Sr., leavened his Unitarian teaching with studies of Scottish Enlightenment philosophes, and imparted to the younger Hazlitt a lifelong taste for responding vigorously to the key controversies of the age. In the 1780s Hazlitt's father took him to America in the flush of colonist victories against the British, then brought him back to England to enroll, at the age of fifteen, at the Unitarian New College at Hackney. But this was 1793, when English public opinion turned decisively against the French Revolution and its Enlightenment roots. Stimulated by contemporary debates, the younger Hazlitt grew impatient with the secluded ministry training offered at Hackney and left the New College without a degree in 1795. "I started in life with the French Revolution" he later wrote of this period, and would remain a defender of its principles to his death in 1830. In that spirit he penned one of the period's most powerful replies to the socially pessimistic theories of Thomas Malthus in 1807. But it was characteristic of Hazlitt's complex sensibility that he could also develop keen admiration for the writings of such conservatives as Jonathan Swift and Edmund Burke, learning to distinguish his antipathy for their politics from a certain thrill at the complexity of their rhetorical powers.

After quitting the New College, Hazlitt set out on two very different career paths—painting and moral philosophy—that proved disappointing in the short run but unexpectedly productive in the long run. In his early twenties he learned to paint, prompted by his brother John, who had been painting portraits in London under the guidance of the British master of visual art, Sir Joshua Reynolds. From the start Hazlitt emulated ambitious models (Titian, Raphael, Rembrandt) and roamed the London art galleries to find British painters of comparable strength. But it may have been during his visit to the Louvre in 1802, during a brief truce in England's war against France, that Hazlitt began thinking about how the arts speak to the wider urgencies of historical change. The masterpieces on the Louvre's walls, he would write breathlessly many years later, were infused with the spirit of revolutionary change: "Art, no longer a bondswoman, was seated on a throne, and her sons were kings!" Few writers in Romantic-age Britain were so vividly to articulate that republican aesthetic, which, long after the French Revolution had become infamous to England, echoed in the pages of its aesthetic criticism.

Still, Hazlitt's unsystematic tutelage in painting—later echoed in his professed hostility to the British art academies—cost him self-confidence. Feeling he would never be more than a derivative portrait painter, he pinned new hopes on a long manuscript of moral philosophy he published in 1805 as *An Essay on the Principles of Human Action*. Here Hazlitt drew on his father's beloved Scottish Enlightenment to argue the case against egotism and self-interest, especially as it had been articulated in the seventeenth century by Thomas Hobbes. Against selfishness he argued for the human propensity to sympathetic identification with others, drawing in equal parts on David Hume's skepticism toward a fixed personal identity and Godwin's philosophy of social benevolence. Hazlitt's work on the project was long and painstaking, and the *Essay*'s poor reception by critics struck again at his confidence in the capacity to forge a sustained philosophic argument. By 1812 he was turning to the short prose forms of essay, review, and polemical article and finding them far more effective ways to engage readers and editors in the fray of public controversy.

THE CRITIC:
ART, THEATER, POETRY, POLITICS

We might identify a key term in the title of his earlier *Essay* as a leitmotif in his now-burgeoning volume of literary, theatrical, and art criticism: "action." When Hazlitt began writing art and theater criticism for London's *Morning Chronicle* in late 1813, his characteristic vocabulary would speak to the "force," "power," "impact," or (to use the term he made famous in his time) the "gusto" of the arts. "Gusto in art is power or passion defining any object," he wrote; it appeared in the way Titian colored his canvases ("sensitive and alive all over"), the arching power in Michelangelo's human forms, and the vibrancy of Rubens's sensual human shapes. By contrast, painters

such as Claude Lorraine gave spectators little gusto insofar as their works revealed only "the visible language of nature." Nothing as intellectualized as the aesthetic of "transport" or the sublime seems to have been intended by Hazlitt's prizing of gusto. The term seems rather almost onomatopoeic, a word that in its physical sound seems to grasp a conception of "nature" as something like what Aristotle had understood as the crystallizing of human action in tragedy and other genres. Hazlitt located gusto in Greek statues, Shakespeare's histories and tragedies, Milton's odes and epics, and Dryden's satires. The curious word took him across visual, theatrical, and poetic genres in his most productive years of writing criticism on the arts (1814–1819).

Hazlitt was forging this aesthetics of action in tandem with a growing effectiveness in writing political essays and polemics. Leigh Hunt's radical weekly newspaper on politics and the arts, *The Examiner* (begun in 1808), offered Hazlitt an ideal opportunity to punch out essays defending Napoleon, attacking the English politicians who prosecuted the war on France, and rethinking the meaning of "patriotism" in those deeply reactionary times. The culmination of this period for Hazlitt came in a burst of lectures and books from 1817 to 1819: *The Round Table* (1817), a collection of essays on the arts and public topics; *Lectures on the English Poets* (1818), which traced an English poetic lineage from Chaucer to Wordsworth, Coleridge, Byron, and other contemporaries; *A View of the English Stage* (1818), which focused on performances in theater; and *Lectures on the English Comic Writers* (1819). His *Political Essays* (1819), published in the volatile aftermath of the Peterloo massacre in August of that year, offered what remains the most wide-ranging perspective on the public context of second-generation Romantic writing.

Although he often wavered on whether to celebrate or distrust the twists and turns of public opinion, Hazlitt sustained a lifelong conviction about the power of books and the force of writing—even when it meant finding strength and brilliance in an ideological adversary such as Edmund Burke. "He unites every extreme and every variety of composition," Hazlitt wrote admiringly. "He exults in the display of power, in shewing the extent, the force, and intensity of his ideas." Burke's texts became Hazlitt's own rhetorical mentor despite the political gulf between them. To Burke's agile rhetoric Hazlitt opposed Samuel Johnson's "*set* or formal style," which excludes "the low and vulgar" and "destroys all force, expression, truth, and character" by abstracting away the particularity and "confounding the differences of things." And it was Johnson's writing model, Hazlitt believed, that increasingly dominated the monthly magazines and quarterly reviews, producing a "uniformity" of public discourse that dulled the combat of ideas and prevented the grounding of thought that Hazlitt often called "the sphere of practice."

Even in his most topical essays, Hazlitt linked contemporary affairs to the wider historical impact of the printed book and the genres of writing. He construed the French Revolution, when it was still being regarded in England as a regrettable upsurge of popular violence, as "a remote but inevitable result of the art of printing." True, cosmopolitan "liberality" lay in grasping the role of the printed word and the visual arts in the larger trajectory of the growth of equality and liberty. Often this meant distinguishing between the arts themselves (whether print or visual) and the more rational or argumentative modes of printed discourses. The arts are not "progressive" in the same sense that modern political thought or scientific work is progressive; the imagination that gives so keen a feeling and grasp of "action" in the arts is a crude instrument when it comes to the finer distinctions and reasoning processes required by the complexity of modern politics. This was why Hazlitt could interrupt his lecture on Shakespeare's *Coriolanus* to offer a somewhat startling explanation for Shakespeare's seeming sympathy for kings rather than crowds. "Poetry is right-royal," he declares here; "the language of poetry *naturally* falls in with the language of power." Although modern readers may interpret this passage as asserting simply that "poetry is political," Hazlitt seems to have been suggesting instead that when it comes to the kind of complexity required by modern political thinking, poetry cannot really be political enough. The arts may not be "progressive" in the usual sense, but criticism about poetry, drama, and theater could and had to be. In Hazlitt the moral philosopher and the practical painter were still meeting in a form unparalleled elsewhere in British criticism of the Romantic age.

Hazlitt waged prolonged battles with the Tory critics and reviewers who had been trying to discredit him, along with Keats, Hunt, and others, as cultural pretenders without the social status or classical learning to justify their poetic and critical ambitions. The question for contemporary literary culture, he argued, was whether the imagination could be "free and sympathetic" or would have to "curdle into service to illegitimate power." The first-generation Romantic poets gave him the ideal test case

for such possibilities of imagination. The young Hazlitt's legendary meeting with Coleridge and Wordsworth, at the time of their writing and publishing *Lyrical Ballads* in 1798, furnished the occasion for Hazlitt's most appreciative—and since then his most widely anthologized—essay, "My First Acquaintance with Poets" (1823). He credits Coleridge with an effervescent, hypertalkative "genius" and with making him begin to think more seriously about the arts. In *Lectures on the English Poets* (1818) he lined up their achievements in poetry with those of the strongest precursors in the tradition and ranked them (in some of his most influential formulations) high above the neoclassical poets Dryden and Pope. Yet the admiration he communicated for *Lyrical Ballads* and other Lake poetry was qualified by sharp criticism of their critical postures. "The Spirit of Jacobin poetry," he wrote of Wordsworth's claim to democratize poetry in the preface to *Lyrical Ballads* (1800), "is rank egotism." Like Keats he drew attention to Wordsworth's effort to impose a philosophy on his materials while calling it "nature" or "humanity." Often Hazlitt linked the earlier Romantic writers' egotistical or metaphysical claims to their now frankly nationalist politics, and he held up Shakespeare as an alternative cosmopolitan and poetic ideal. Shakespeare's capacity to be disinterested—the quality that Keats, following Hazlitt's lead, called "negative capability"—was an important foil for the characteristic egotism of contemporary poets such Byron and Wordsworth.

The rich diversity of Shakespearean characters had social implications that Hazlitt extended to the theater more generally when he called it "a test and school of humanity." His lectures and articles on theater tend to focus not on the philosophical design of the printed play (as Coleridge was doing in rival London lectures on Shakespeare) but on dramatic character in relation to both performers and audience. "Play-going people," he noted, become "the most sociable, gossiping, good-natured and humane members of society." What focused the sociable interchange of playgoers was, Hazlitt thought, the key role of the performer onstage who establishes empathy between performers and audience, and of spectators with one another. Hazlitt's theater criticism burnished the reputations of leading London actors—especially Edmund Kean, Sarah Siddons, and John Kemble—in weekly lecture series and in books, including *A View of the English Stage* (1818) and *Characters of Shakespeare's Plays* (1817). Unlike Coleridge, who interpreted Shakespeare's characters as integral to the aesthetic design of the plays on the printed page, Hazlitt constantly refers the texts' characters to performances, trying to show how the players' physical and emotive presence on stage links the literary work to the sociable awareness of spectators.

Hazlitt often idealized sociability, but his frequently acidic treatment of rivals also earned a reputation, in Thomas De Quincey's words, for "inveterate misanthropy." Today's readers may note instead a lifelong strain of misogyny in his writings. Hazlitt was married twice, to Sarah Stoddart in 1808 and to Isabella Bridgewater in 1824, but seemed unable to sustain lasting relationships with women his own age and became notorious for trying to seduce servant or country girls—"humble beauties," as he called them—especially in the failed but well-publicized romance he attempted with Sarah Walker, the daughter of his landlord, which ended his marriage to Stoddart in 1823. Hazlitt's Rousseauesque account of this affair in *Liber Amoris; or, The New Pygmalion* (1823) made for one of the oddest books of the nineteenth century. Elsewhere he habitually denigrated the sorts of books known to be widely read by women and often the books women wrote (Frances Burney was a recurring critical target). A republican notion of literary masculinity runs through almost everything Hazlitt wrote about contemporary letters, especially when, as in the 1820s, it began to seem as if the older republic of letters was rapidly disintegrating and that various kinds of female taste or authorship were part of the decline.

LATE WRITINGS: CULTURAL CRITICISM

When the political battles of Regency England faded into the uneasy calm of the 1820s, Hazlitt, long an admirer of Montaigne's essays, turned to a more personal mode of writing that he best defined in the 1821 essay "On Familiar Style." This decade saw the rapid emergence of what literary historians commonly call "Romantic prose," the flamboyantly personal yet culturally and critically ambitious mode of nonfiction writing stimulated by such newer literary periodicals as the *London Magazine* and the *New Monthly Magazine*. Hazlitt's essays now appeared in these sophisticated magazines geared to an urbane London audience, alongside those of Thomas De Quincey, Charles Lamb, and P. G. Patmore. Even so, Hazlitt's preoccupation with the world of "things" sets apart his 1820s writing from that of more pronouncedly introspective magazine writers such as De Quincey (*Confessions of an English Opium Eater*, 1821) or Lamb (*Essays of Elia*, 1820–1823). As in his art criticism, "gusto" and the exceptionally mobile figure of the observing writer made a good

number of his "familiar" essays a means of interpreting how Londoners thought, acted, and worked. "The Fight," "On Londoners and Country People," and similar essays took middle-class readers to decidedly unfamiliar locations in the metropolis where they met boxers, fishmongers, or prostitutes as often as the fashionable or "the fancy." Often these essays jarred with upper-class characterizations of the "low and vulgar" and, alternating between literary phrasings and the slang of the streets, became vivid essays in cultural criticism and a kind of investigative journalism.

Often ebullient, his later essays could also be dark, pessimistic, or cynical about what was changing in British literary culture. In "On the Aristocracy of Letters" Hazlitt writes entertainingly but bitterly of how the older republic of letters has degenerated into a kind of star system, in which the most highly valued writers are those who have published the least but have been able to flash their academic or other credentials to win "credit" in the market of literary goods. In this picture, workaday, prolific authors such as Hazlitt himself were increasingly marginalized as the "dandies," or fashionable class, were exchanging their family escutcheons for pens and publishing contracts. The new passion for expensive rare books (the "bibliomania" of this period) seemed further to isolate the "poor author," about whom Hazlitt indulged in some uncharacteristically sentimental prose. The beleaguered tone of loss and isolation dominates Hazlitt's writing in his last years (1826–1830) and may have contributed to the deeply nostalgic tenor of his four-volume *Life of Napoleon Buonaparte*. That book celebrates, among other legacies of the French Revolution, the liberating vocation of the arts that had first struck him at the Louvre. It was now feeling like a very remote world; the Napoleon biography found few readers on publication.

But a masterpiece also emerged in Hazlitt's last decade. *The Spirit of the Age* (1825), the culmination of his career, is a brilliant gallery of intellectual portraits ranging from the poets (Wordsworth, Coleridge, Byron) and moral philosophers (Jeremy Bentham, Godwin) to novelists (Walter Scott), critics (William Gifford, Francis Jeffrey), and political figures. Hazlitt's finest prose and widest range of critical powers animate a book that, as James Chandler has argued, gives an extraordinarily full and complex articulation to the Romantic period's feeling that its own time was historically unique and dense with contradictions in literature, politics, and cultural change.

[*See also* Samuel Taylor Coleridge; Thomas De Quincey; Eighteenth-Century Journalism; William Godwin; Thomas

Hobbes; Leigh Hunt; Samuel Johnson; John Keats; John Locke; Romanticism; *and* William Shakespeare.]

SELECTED WORKS

An Essay on the Principles of Human Action (1805)

A Reply to the Essay on Population by the Rev. T. R. Malthus (1807)

The Round Table (1817)

Characters of Shakespeare's Plays (1817)

A View of the English Stage; or, A Series of Dramatic Criticisms (1818)

Lectures on the English Poets (1818)

Lectures on the English Comic Writers (1819)

Political Essays, with Sketches of Public Characters (1819)

Lectures on the Dramatic Literature of the Age of Elizabeth (1820)

Table-Talk; or, Original Essays (1821)

Liber Amoris; or, The New Pygmalion (1823)

The Spirit of the Age, or, Contemporary Portraits (1825)

The Plain Speaker: Opinions on Books, Men, and Things (1826)

The Life of Napoleon Buonaparte, 4 vols. (1828–1830)

EDITIONS

Cook, Jon, ed. *William Hazlitt: Selected Writings.* Oxford, 1991. A good, easily available paperback selection representing the range of Hazlitt's writing in politics, the arts, poetry, theater, and British urban culture.

Howe, P. P., ed. *The Complete Works of William Hazlitt.* London, 1930–1934. The largest and most widely cited collection of Hazlitt's essays and books. Contains an invaluable index for finding individual essays and topics in the twenty-one-volume collection.

Wu, Duncan, ed. *The Selected Writings of William Hazlitt.* London, 1998. This nine-volume collection omits lesser works by Hazlitt but features newly edited versions of the major writings.

FURTHER READING

Bromwich, David. *Hazlitt: The Mind of a Critic.* New York, 1983. Influential study of Hazlitt's work as literary critic that compares him with Coleridge and other leading Romantic literary writers.

Chandler, James. *England in 1819: The Politics of Literary Culture and the Case of Romantic Historicism.* Chicago, 1998. Important study of the Romantic period's self-consciousness about its place in history and Hazlitt's key role in formulating "the spirit of the age."

Gilmartin, Kevin. *Print Politics: The Press and Radical Opposition in Early Nineteenth-Century England.* New York, 1996. Valuable account of Hazlitt's contribution to English radical writing in relation to the popular radical press.

Howe, P. P. *Life of William Hazlitt.* London, 1922. Although outdated by more recent and historically detailed biographies, such as Jones's, Howe's intimate portrait is filled with passages from Hazlitt's writing, and views of him by others, that are not easily found elsewhere.

Jacobus, Mary. "The Art of Managing Books." In *Romanticism and Language,* edited by Arden Reed. Ithaca, NY, 1984. An astute study of Hazlitt's generally overlooked writings on print culture and the cultural dimensions of the book.

Jones, Stanley. *Hazlitt: A Life.* Oxford, 1989. The most recent and thorough biography detailing Hazlitt's career.

Kinnaird, John. *William Hazlitt: Critic of Power.* New York, 1978. A wide-ranging critical study that puts Hazlitt's literary and art criticism into the context of his philosophical and political outlook.

Whale, John. "Hazlitt: the Limits of Imagination." In his *Imagination under Pressure, 1789–1832: Aesthetics, Politics, and Utility.* Cambridge, U.K., 2000. An insightful chapter that puts into perspective Hazlitt's lifelong defense of the French Revolution in terms of his late-career hostility to the new framework of democratic reform, Utilitarianism.

SEAMUS HEANEY

John Goodby

Seamus Heaney
Painting by Tai-Shan Schierenberg
© TAI-SHAN SCHIERENBERG/NATIONAL
PORTRAIT GALLERY, LONDON

Seamus Heaney grew up in rural County Derry, Northern Ireland, where he was born in 1939. He came from a moderately prosperous farming family with no history of higher education. Heaney, however, won a scholarship to Saint Columb's College in Derry and went on to read English at Queen's University, Belfast, after which he qualified as a teacher and took an MA, writing his dissertation on the Belfast literary scene of the 1940s. He taught at Saint Joseph's College of Education before taking up a lectureship in English at Queen's University from 1966 to 1972. He had begun writing poems in the early 1960s, and he soon became a central figure in the so-called Belfast Group, a regular gathering of poets, fiction writers, dramatists, and critics presided over by Philip Hobsbaum, a lecturer at Queen's University. The group met from 1963 until 1966.

Hobsbawm used his London contacts to draw attention to the Belfast poets, and Heaney's first collection, *Death of a Naturalist,* was published by Faber and Faber in 1966. The work established him as the leading figure in the Northern Irish poetry renaissance, which would, by the 1970s, be immensely influential within mainstream British and Irish poetry. His early poems were written in an energetic, mimetic style influenced by John Keats, Gerard Manley Hopkins, and Thomas Hughes, and he was concerned with rendering Irish rural life in a way that owed much to William Wordsworth and—above all—Patrick Kavanagh. Heaney charted vanishing customs and trades (e.g., mumming, thatching, butter churning, eel fishing), as well as his growing up within, and then out of, a life of instinct. The "naturalist" of the title is the young Heaney "dying" out of his early rural life, out of his inheritance and childhood, and into a literary education, intimations of sexuality, and wider intellectual horizons.

The concern with roots and the sense of enlargement are symbolized in the volume's opening poem, "Digging," a talismanic lyric with which Heaney always begins readings of his work, and which stands at the head of all his subsequent volumes of selected and collected poems. The poem compares the potato-digging and turf-cutting labor of his father and grandfather to his own work with a pen; though he admits to not having "a spade to follow men like them," he concludes: "Between my finger and my thumb / The squat pen rests. / I'll dig with it." In "Digging," however, the pen is not merely phallic but "snug as a gun," a reminder that in this collection Heaney was also sublimating the aggrieved Catholic and nationalist side of his inheritance. The mid-1960s were a time of struggle by Northern Irish Catholics to reverse decades of discrimination by the Unionist Stormont government; and, largely historical though it is at this stage, Heaney's sympathy with the civil rights movement can be seen in poems such as "For the Captain of the *Eliza*," set at the time of the Irish Famine; "Docker," whose "fist would drop a hammer on a Catholic"; and a sonnet he wrote in 1966 (but which he did not include in his readings because of its potential for sectarian identification), "Requiem for the Croppies," in memory of those who rose against British rule in 1798.

Unlike most other contemporary poets, Heaney was, simply by virtue of his origins, viewed as a community spokesman from the start of his career, and so he was keenly aware of the dangers of lapsing into propaganda or sentimentality. When the "Troubles" erupted in 1968–1969, he realized that "the problems of poetry moved from being simply a matter of achieving the satisfactory verbal icon to being a search for images and symbols adequate to our predicament"—as he put it in the essay "Feeling into Words"—thus making the task of representation still more demanding. However, Heaney was able to use events as an opportunity and a goad, exploring the link between memory and digging in order to produce new and startling images of the past that had produced the violent present. His second collection, *Door into the Dark* (1969), was written before the outbreak of hostilities and largely pursued conflicts and anxieties familiar from the first book. But if some pieces, such as the title poem, are frankly nostalgic, in the concluding "Bogland" he also shows a keen sense of his developing strengths in envisioning the vertical cross-section through a bog as the Irish equivalent of the horizontal expansionism of American and British history:

> Our pioneers keep striking
> Inwards and downwards,
>
> Every layer they strip
> Seems camped on before.
> The bogholes might be Atlantic seepage.
> The wet centre is bottomless.

Gesturing towards the Irish writer and scholar Daniel Corkery's characterization of Irish identity under British tutelage as "a quaking sod," this lyric points to the rich instabilities of Heaney's best poetry. Accordingly, the major innovation of *Wintering Out* (1972) is a turn "inwards and downwards" into history and the history of language (or philology), as these emerge from Ireland's complex, layered, and inevitably strife-torn cultural residue. The title poem maps the survival of the Catholic population's sense of dignity, culture, and integrity in Penal Law times into the present; though "impenitent," like the cow-herd of the poem, Catholic Ireland "nurses the eggs" of a better future as it "winters out" in the cold and darkness. Elsewhere, Heaney explores the apparent paradox of the cultivated Elizabethan scholar-poets whose brutal actions as soldiers and planters in Ireland helped destroy Gaelic culture and the Irish language. In linguistic mode, however, he seeks connections and exploits the resources of Northern Irish English dialects and the Irish words within them. In the 1972 essay "Belfast," he had written of the "bawn" part of the name of his family's farm, Mossbawn, coming to be pronounced "bánn"—the English for "fortified farmstead" changing into the Irish for "white." A similar process of peaceful linguistic assimilation and blending is at work in "Broagh," "Anahorish," and "Toome," which draw on ancient Irish tradition of place-name lore known as *dinnseanchas*, as well as on Anglophone Ulster dialects. "Broagh" exemplifies the tactic of proposing tentative linguistic amities in the face of enormous political hostilities:

> Riverbank, the long rigs
> pending in broad docken
> and a canopied pad
> down to the ford.
>
> The garden mould
> bruised easily, the shower
> gathering in your heelmark
> was the black O
>
> in *Broagh*,
> its low tattoo
> among the windy boortrees
> and rhubarb-blades
>
> ended almost
> suddenly, like that last
> *gh* the strangers found
> difficult to manage

Here, vocabulary drawn from English, Ulster-Scots, and Hiberno-Irish ("rigs," "docken," "pad," "boortree"), not to mention the hovering syntax of the opening sentence, prepares us for a conclusion in which the Catholic and Protestant members of the community are united in their ability to pronounce the "*gh*" so difficult for "the strangers." Such names, for Heaney, are "vocables" in which, according to his own gendered model of linguistic interaction, the "masculine" consonants of English were ploughed into the "feminine" vowels of Irish.

Yet if these poems remain tentatively hopeful, some details suggest darker forces. The "black O" is both the "heelprint" of Heaney's wife and of an *aisling* (an Irish visionary maiden figure), but it is also a figure of negation, absence, and death, while "tattoo" is a term associated with the beating of Lambeg drums on Orange parades held on 12 July and often intended to intimidate the Catholic population. After a year at the University of California, Berkeley, in 1969–1970, the shock of returning to the spiraling violence in Belfast, combined with personal threat, led to Heaney's departure for the Republic of Ireland with his family in 1972. He worked at Carysfort College in Dublin, and, after 1980, as a freelance writer and part-time professor at Harvard University.

It was in considering the significance of that move that *North* (1975) was incubated. As before, a germ for a collection lay in its predecessor, in this case *Wintering Out*'s "The Tollund Man." The poem is a meditation on a two-thousand-year-old body, the victim of ritual murder, discovered preserved in a Danish bog and reputed to have been sacrificed to the earth goddess Nerthus. Heaney likens it to the bodies of men murdered by the Black and Tans (British conscripts to the Royal Irish Constabulary) in the 1920s, and in speaking of visiting the body at Aarhus Museum, he anticipates feeling "lost / Unhappy and at home." In this way "Tollund Man" anticipates *North*, which elaborates a myth based on northern Europe's history of violent invasions. The major elements of this myth appear in the essay "Feeling into Words," which attempts to place the Troubles within a long continuum, arguing that imperial, masculine power (in the form of Vikings, Elizabethans, and, later, the British in Northern Ireland) intermittently usurps the sovereignty of a indigenous female territorial goddess, from Iron Age cults to the present-day IRA's bombing campaign. Within *North*, a sequence of "Bog Poems" develops from the point reached in "The Tollund Man," using other bodies discovered in Danish and Irish bogs, and exploring their meaning in the light of the myth. In "The Grauballe Man," for example, the "perfected memory" of the ancient body is weighed against "the actual weight / of each hooded victim, / slashed and dumped."

As a result of such concerns, *North* is Heaney's most controversial collection. Despite the fact that he was trying to explore how his community perceived the violence, a deep abjection and resignation to division and violence does hold sway. At the time, he was both praised for speaking the truth about the "awful intensity" of the conflict by the historian Conor Cruise O'Brien and lambasted by the writer Ciaran Carson and the literary critic Edna Longley as a "laureate of violence" guilty of ritualizing bloodshed. The ambiguities of Heaney's situation are particularly contentious in "Punishment," in which the speaker arraigns himself as one who "would connive in civilized outrage" at the tarring and feathering of women by the IRA, "yet understand the exact / and tribal, intimate revenge." Yet for all the mystification Heaney risked in depicting a modern conflict as tribal and racial, the outrage he provoked now seems somewhat excessive. "Strange Fruit," like other poems, questions the tendency of the lyrical impulse to aestheticize violence. The poem deals with the Windeby Girl, an Iron Age body found in the 1950s in Ireland, and as the head returns his gaze, it is described as "outstaring / What

had begun to feel like reverence." Arguably more damaging in the long term, in several of these poems, is the unthinking use of traditional gender stereotypes, already visible in the notion of the "vocable": Ireland is female, and the female is passive, yet castrating and devouring. In addition, there is the dubious trope of imperialism as rape.

Whatever its successes—and the collection gave Heaney an international reputation—*North* left Heaney with the problem of dismantling his elaborate myth of northernness. A series of prose poems, published in a limited edition as *Stations* in 1975, show a more relaxed side of the poet; however, it was in *Field Work* (1979) and *Station Island* (1984), his midcareer collections, that Heaney began to break out of being "mired in attachment" to his place and community obligations. These books show a more elegiac and wary mood, respectively, in accordance with a new tendency to take stock. A collection of his critical prose, *Preoccupations*, was published in 1980, and Heaney was also beginning to look for new exemplars and figures against whom to measure himself. Robert Lowell, Dante, and Osip Mandelstam are presiding spirits in *Field Work*, in which Heaney looks outward from the matter of Ireland to international sources of inspiration. For all that, the book is a sorrowful one, commemorating several victims of the Troubles. It is also a celebration of domestic and family life, particularly in the central "Glanmore Sonnets" section.

In *Station Island*, the model is the Irish one of Sweeney, the legendary king of Ulster who was driven mad after committing an act of impiety. (The Middle Irish tale *Buile Suibhne* recounts the story of Sweeney as an outcast from society, restless and unable to settle, fleeing human contact, and living in trees like a bird; and Heaney published a translation of it as *Sweeney Astray* in 1983.) *Station Island*'s eponymous title poem, in twelve sections, sees Heaney follow in the footsteps of Kavanagh and the nineteenth-century Irish poet William Carleton to a site of pilgrimage at Saint Patrick's Purgatory in Lough Derg, in order to look back over his life and formative influences. As in the "Glanmore Sonnets" and *Sweeny Astray*, what are being sought, in retreat, recuperation, and meditation, are role models for skeptical engagement, proper sympathy, and an ideal poetry. In a final encounter with James Joyce, the older writer's ghost tells Heaney that "That subject people stuff is a cod's game, / infantile . . . You lose more of yourself than you redeem / doing the decent thing." If this fails to convince (Heaney avoids the radical formal implications of Joyce's art), Heaney is far more persuasive in his self-searching in the final "Sweeney Redivivus" section of *Station Island,* which maps his own struggle to escape into "a kingdom / of such scope and neuter allegiance / my emptiness reigns at its whim" ("The Cleric"). That this "emptiness" is a form of negative theology, or at least a secular approximation of it, is clear from section XI of "Station Island," in which Heaney fulfilled a penance by translating Saint John of the Cross.

In *The Haw Lantern* (1987), *Seeing Things* (1991) and *The Spirit Level* (1996), Heaney opens up fruitful absences (as in the "Clearances" sonnet sequence in memory of his mother), credits miracles and wonders, and writes in a "weightless" style of short, unfinished sentences or phrases, using an almost Neoplatonic imagery of light and buoyancy. In these books Heaney also returns to his use of the image of the circle, though it is now changed from the sense of constriction which had attended it in the wedding poems of *Wintering Out* or the swaddling bands of *Field Work*'s "Casualty" to a near-mystic wholeness and completion, as in "Wheels within Wheels" in *Seeing Things*, and to circular self-awareness, as in "A Brigid's Girdle" in *The Spirit Level*: "As strange and lightsome and traditional / As the motions you go through going through a thing." This collection ends with "Postscript," a poem that, with typical indirection (and punningly ambiguous phrasing), celebrates the IRA ceasefire of 1994, the beginning of the peace process in Northern Ireland:

> You are neither here nor there,
> A hurry through which known and strange things pass
> As big soft buffetings come at the car sideways
> And catch the heart off-guard and blow it open.

Successful though it can be, as here, the later poetry does not always escape the blandness that results from having it too many ways, a tendency that also informs some of the more sweeping statements made in Heaney's second and third collections of criticism, *The Government of the Tongue* (1988) and *The Redress of Poetry* (1995): "In that liberated moment when the lyric discovers its buoyant completion . . . of self-justification and self-obliteration, the poet . . . is at once intensified in his being and detached from his predicaments."

Even so, it was no coincidence that Heaney, who had worked so hard to rethink and rewrite the bitter and entrenched polarities of the Northern Irish violence, was awarded the Nobel Prize for Literature the year after the ceasefire, in 1995, crowning a career in which he had won almost all of the major honors the literary world can bestow on a poet. He has continued to write prolifically since then, publishing a popular and critically acclaimed translation of *Beowulf* in 2000, as well as a 2001 collection of poetry, *Electric Light* (2001), which resembles its immediate predecessors in style and theme, but with a new consciousness of mortality. By some distance the most prominent of living Irish writers, Heaney's importance ultimately lies in the persistence, tact, and power with which he has consistently charted and given memorable artistic form to "the scared, irrevocable steps" by which he and his generation in Northern Ireland advanced—against the political odds, and despite bloodshed and bitterness—toward a historic measure of social justice and self-discovery.

[*See also* Patrick Kavanagh.]

SELECTED WORKS

Death of a Naturalist (1966)
Door into the Dark (1969)
Wintering Out (1972)
North (1975)
Field Work (1979)
An Open Letter (1983)
Sweeney Astray (1982)
Station Island (1984)
The Haw Lantern (1987)
The Cure at Troy (1990)
Seeing Things (1991)
The Spirit Level (1996)
Opened Ground: Poems 1966–1996 (1998)
Beowulf (2000)
Electric Light (2001)
Finders Keepers: Selected Prose 1971–2001 (2002)
The Burial at Thebes (2004).

FURTHER READING

Andrews, Elmer, ed. *The Poetry of Seamus Heaney.* Cambridge, 1998.

Corcoran, Neil. *Seamus Heaney: A Critical Guide.* London, 1998.

Coughlan, Patricia. " 'Bog Queens': The Representation of Women in the Poetry of John Montague and Seamus Heaney." In *Theorizing Ireland.* Edited by Claire Connolly. Basingstoke, U.K., 2003.

Curtis, Tony, ed. *The Art of Seamus Heaney.* 4th ed. Bridgend, South Wales, 2001.

Deane, Seamus. "Seamus Heaney: The Timorous and the Bold." In his *Celtic Revivals: Essays in Modern Irish literature, 1880–1980.* London, 1985.

Hart, Henry. *Seamus Heaney: Poet of Contrary Progressions.* Syracuse, NY, 1992.

Lloyd, David, " 'Pap for the dispossessed': Seamus Heaney and the Poetics of Identity." In his *Anomalous States: Irish Writing and the Post-Colonial Moment.* Durham, NC, 1993.

Malloy, Catharine, and Phyllis Carey, eds. *Seamus Heaney: The Shaping Spirit.* Newark, DE, 1996.

O'Donoghue, Bernard. *Seamus Heaney and the Language of Poetry.* New York, 1994.

Vendler, Helen. *Seamus Heaney.* London, 1998.

FELICIA HEMANS

Susan J. Wolfson

By the late 1820s, beset by budding poets seeking advice and support, and fans seeking autographs, album-inscriptions, or just a glimpse of the famous "poetess," Felicia Hemans (1793–1835) was waxing wry and rueful about what she called "the dust of celebrity" and sighing of "the nothingness of Fame, at least to woman." The career that brought this sigh was far from nothing. An international best seller, Hemans was one of the first women to make a decent living as a poet. Nineteen volumes appeared between 1808 and 1835, some in multiple editions. Versatile and literate, imaginative and intellectually appetitive, talented and disciplined, industrious and ambitious, working with business acumen and with alertness to the marketplace, Hemans found fame by shaping popular themes along a transhistorical, international range of subjects, drawing on sources past and present, English and Continental. "Mrs. Hemans" was England's premier "poetess," its boast of "feminine" excellence. Well into the century, her poetry was widely admired. *Casabianca* ("The boy stood on the burning deck") became a standard for recitation; Americans took *The Landing of the Pilgrim Fathers* ("The breaking waves dashed high") to heart, while *The Homes of England* and *England's Dead* became virtual British anthems.

Yet by the century's end these favorites had lost their luster, and Hemans's more varied corpus was nearly forgotten. Then, as new interests at the end of the twentieth century began to reshape the critical study of Romanticism, her poetry compelled fresh interest, especially for its dissonance about "feminine" ideals, about the glory of war, and even (occasionally) about the adequacy of religious consolation. Hemans is now a key reference in the story of women's poetry in the age of Romanticism, in the measurings of aesthetic value in gendered culture, and

Felicia Hemans
Plaster bust by Angus Fletcher, 1829
NATIONAL PORTRAIT GALLERY, LONDON

not least, in the terms by which "feminine" icons get established, cherished, or dismissed.

THE FEMININE POETESS

From her own day and long after, Felicia Hemans figured as the epitome of "feminine" sensibility, her poetry a primer of domestic affections, of religious and patriotic piety, and of the female responsibility to bind all this together. When the *Edinburgh Monthly Review* said in 1820, on the cusp of her popularity, that she "never ceases to be strictly *feminine* in the whole current of her thought and feeling," it meant that "delicacy which belongs to the sex, and the tenderness and enthusiasm which form its finest characteristic." "Critics and casual readers have united in pronouncing her poetry to be essentially feminine," the poet Lydia Sigourney (the "American Hemans") summed up the praises in 1840; "the whole sweet circle of the domestic affections—the hallowed ministries of woman, at the cradle, the hearthstone, and the death-bed, were its chosen themes," all sites of "the disinterested, self-sacrificing virtues of her sex." Yet these praises could entail limitations, as even a friend, Henry Chorley, managed to suggest in his *Memorials of Mrs. Hemans* (1836): her sensibility is "essentially womanly—fervent, trustful, unquestioning, 'hoping on, hoping ever'—in spite of a painfully acute consciousness of the peculiar trials of her sex." The critic Francis Jeffrey, writing in 1829 at the height of Hemans's fame, put it more directly in the *Edinburgh Review*: this "fine exemplification of Female Poetry" has nothing to do with "the fierce and sullen passions of men . . . scenes of actual business or contention—and the mixed motives, and strong and faulty characters, by which affairs of moment are usually conducted on the great theatre of the world"—all this due to the "disabling delicacy" that pervades female "conceptions and feelings." Female poets, Jeffrey blandly stated, are no better at "long moral or political investigations, where many complex and indeterminate elements are to be taken into account, and a variety of opposite probabilities to be weighed. . . . They rarely succeed in long works, . . . their natural training rendering them equally averse to long doubt and long labour."

Strangely and strikingly, Jeffrey ignores the poetry by Hemans, including such long works as *The Forest Sanctuary* (one of the occasions of his essay, even), fraught with long doubt, long labor, and many complex and indeterminate elements. He cast Hemans into the preferred image of the "poetess," reflecting and freshening the pattern. If Chorley meant only to be descriptive when he wrote at the conclusion of his *Memorials* that "the woman and the poetess were in [Hemans] too inseparably united to admit of their being considered apart," the compound was another way of saying she was no poet. Writing in *Tait's Edinburgh Magazine* in the next decade, another admirer, George Gilfillan, decided that "in its highest sense, the name of poet" had to be denied Hemans: "A *maker* she is not" (alluding to the etymology of *poet* as *maker*); "Mrs. Hemans's poems are strictly effusions. And not a little of their charm springs from their unstudied and extempore character . . . in fine keeping with the sex." A woman mustn't seem to be working at it. In 1820 the *Quarterly Review* was willing to recognize a poetry of "reflection and study," but only because Hemans's "talent and learning have not produced the ill effects so often attributed to them; her faculties seem to sit meekly on her." "You are saved the ludicrous image of a double-dyed Blue, in papers and morning wrapper, sweating at some stupendous treatise or tragedy," Gilfillan would put it, wielding that male-club contempt for learned ("bluestocking") women.

This bias in favor of female meekness implied esteem for the "not un-feminine"—Mrs. Hemans was not one of those politically vocal female poets of the 1790s, lambasted in 1798 by Reverend Richard Polwhele in *The Unsex'd Females* (Lady Macbeth their patent godmother). In 1820 the *Edinburgh Monthly Review* praised "the modesty of Mrs. Hemans, for whose gentle hands the auxiliary club of political warfare, and the sharp lash of personal satire are equally unsuited," admiring her for "scrupulously abstaining from all that may betray unfeminine temerity." A late-Victorian edition of her poetry blamed the waning popularity of her "essentially feminine" genius on a "lamentable change in the tone of modern society,"

especially its "cry of '*Women's Rights*,' . . . the unfeminine imitators of masculine habits [are] not likely to appreciate the voice of the *true* woman that spoke in Felicia Hemans."

THE PROFESSIONAL POET, THE COMPLEX POETRY

Yet Felicia Hemans herself did not always speak in one tone. Even the sentimental favorites are fraught with contradictory awarenesses. *England's Dead* produces the British Empire not just as a realm on which the sun never sets, but also as a global graveyard, where everywhere, "*There* slumber England's dead!" *Casabianca* gushes over the purity of filial martyrdom (and thus the parodies), but it is also a dead-serious reflection of the fatal grip of patriotism and patriarchy. A French boy's call to his dead father ("unconscious of his son") for release from his post aboard a burning ship in the Battle of the Nile, Admiral Nelson's signal triumph over Napoleonic ambition, is far from simple sentiment; with French deflection, *Casabianca* is a grim anecdote of son-sacrificing warfare. Hemans's fictional displacements (this French boy, women in Carthage, medieval Valencia, Renaissance Italy, Tudor England, the American West) are not distancing and derealizing; there is a universalizing import. Living in an era of prolonged conflict with Revolutionary and then Napoleonic France—warfare that involved her brothers and her husband—Hemans can channel patriotic romance, but her poetry can also alternate into the anguished conflict, spectacularly in her drama about a son-sacrificing siege in medieval Spain (a palimpsest for Napoleonic warfare): *The Siege of Valencia*, published the same year, 1823, as Lord Byron's mordant critique of military glory in *Don Juan Canto 7* (about the siege of Ismail).

Hemans could tap into conflicting currents because she was so adept in the mainstream—a rippling also coursing through those famed "feminine" devotions. Reworking history and iconic figures and events from the perspective of women's lives, desires, and dissatisfactions, her signature genre was "Records of Woman" (titling her best-selling volume of 1828). Under the categorical sign of *Woman*—featuring women as historical figures, as repositories of cultural values (heroines of "domestic affection"), as interpreters (Hemans included) of history and social structure, and as perpetual victims of men's rivalries, political contentions, and wars—Hemans created a macrotext of female social fate in a man's world. In scenes of suffering and love-longing, of destitution, of desperate suicides and infanticides, of salvation only through death, Hemans does not stint to record the oppressions and devastations of domestic life, along with its cherished affections. A related genre is given by the title (again, categorical) of her iconic poem, "Woman and Fame." The *and* is deceptive, for the link spells a culturally determinate conflict between artist and woman, female affection and female ambition, family and fame. One symptom, which Hemans's contemporaries noted, was a characteristic "melancholy." The nineteenth-century tendency was to diagnose a hyper-susceptible femininity (the dark side of the ideal) that could be transvalued into heroic forbearance and patience, faith, and martyrdom, all warding off a cultural unconscious of the connection of the political to the personal, of public to private—what readers today discern as critique of the ideology of "feminine" virtue or "universal" female fate.

When poet-laureate-to-be William Wordsworth added Hemans (unnamed, but legible) to his elegy for the poets he had known, *Extempore Effusion* (1836), he could not forbear lamenting in his headnote her ignorance of household skills. Byron, who did not know her personally, wrote letters in 1820 to their common publisher John Murray, gibing at "your feminine *He-Man*" and "Mrs. Hewoman's"—the punning and pointed misspelling aimed at her learning and commercial force. Like many he-poets, Byron preferred women in their place, not his. "I do not despise Mrs. Heman—but if [she] knit blue stockings instead of wearing them it would be better," he snarked. Yet Byron and Wordsworth were at least alert to the contradiction that Victorian representations of and affections for "Mrs. Hemans" tended to elide: her considerable education, her rather casual domestic skills, her failed marriage, and, not least, her canny professionalism.

HEMANS'S LIFE

Born in Liverpool in 1793 (the year of the onset of nearly a quarter of a century of war against France), Felicia Browne lived in this bustling city until 1800, when her merchant father suffered reversals, closing up shop and moving the family to a coastal village in North Wales. The serene beauty nurtured the girl's imagination, and so did her mother, who undertook her education. Felicia read everything, memorized poetry, studied music and art, and learned French, Portuguese, Spanish, and Italian from her mother, then Latin from the local vicar, and later, German. She wrote poetry (her first subjects were her mother and Shakespeare), and by age fourteen, with her mother's

management, published a handsome illustrated quarto, *Poems* (1808), meant to help pay for her education. One of its purchasers was a comrade of her brother in the war against Napoleon, Captain Alfred Hemans.

Poems was not well reviewed, and although Felicia was stung, she was persistent. *England and Spain; or, Valour and Patriotism* appeared in 1809 (to no sales and no notice), and she was soon working at *War and Peace*, a long pacifist oration. The same year she met and fell in love with Captain Hemans, who returned from war in 1811, scarred by wounds and in ill health. They married in 1812, the year *The Domestic Affections, and Other Poems* (including *War and Peace*) was published, again to little notice. When the Captain's postwar appointment was terminated, they and a baby son joined her mother's household (her father had left in 1810 for a fresh start in Canada, where he died two years later). Hemans's first success came with a poem keyed to Britain's triumphant emergence as a world power after the fall of Napoleon, *The Restoration of the Works of Art to Italy* (1816); Byron admired it, and it was purchased by his publisher Murray for a second edition. Soon after, Murray published Hemans's *Modern Greece* (1817) and then a volume of translations and original poetry (1818).

There was a fifth son on the way in 1818 when Captain Hemans left for Italy, never to return. The "story" was his health, but insiders sensed his unease with a professional wife; a posthumous memoir would report his complaint (echoing Byron) that "it was the curse of having a literary wife that he could never get a pair of stockings mended." The marriage never mended either. While the ideal of hearth and home for which "Mrs. Hemans" became famous was haunted by two broken marriages, her parents' and her own, there were material benefits. Now the sole supporter of five boys (ages 3 to 10), Hemans determined to make a living as a poet. Situated in her mother's home with adult siblings, and no husband to require care and to be obedient to, she found time to read, study, and write. Even so, the home front was a challenge. So beset was she by "the household troops" that she thought of retreating to the cellar to work. All that "talk of tranquillity and a quiet home" (she sighed to a friend) made her "stare about in wonder, having almost lost the recollection of such things, and the hope that they may probably be regained." Yet she soon produced *Tales, and Historic Scenes* (1819), a compendium of crises that was well reviewed and commercially successful. By 1820 she was winning prize competitions, getting warm reviews in major presses, and enjoying good sales, fanned by the increasing influence of women as purchasers and readers. In rapid succession she published *Wallace's Invocation to Bruce, The Sceptic, Stanzas to the Memory of the Late King* (George III), *Dartmoor*, and *Welsh Melodies*. New venues for poetry opened with the founding of *Blackwood's Edinburgh Magazine* in 1817 and the gift-book annuals of the 1820s. Hemans capitalized on both, often getting double value by collecting the publications for her volumes. Her fame was clinched with *The Forest Sanctuary, and Other Poems* (1825 and 1829), *Records of Woman, with Other Poems* (1828, with several further editions), and *Songs of the Affections, with Other Poems* (1830).

Amidst this success, her domestic situation helped her image: "Mrs. Hemans" was a poet not only *of* home but *at* home, under "the maternal wing" (a common phrase in the nineteenth-century biographies). The "literary lady" who would dismay Wordsworth by seeming "totally ignorant of housewifery" could thus deflect the stigma of "unfeminine" independence. Even as the Victorian editor W. M. Rossetti groused at a feminine "monotone" in the poetry, he warmed to the "admired and popular poetess" as a "loving daughter" and a "deeply affectionate, tender, and vigilant mother." The death of Hemans's mother in 1827 was a devastating loss, deepened by the breakup of the household as older sons left for school and siblings married or moved away. To escape the emptiness, Hemans moved with her younger sons to a village near Liverpool, where she found schooling for them and literary and musical society for herself: Chorley, the poets Rose Lawrence and Mary Howitt, the vivacious writer Maria Jane Jewsbury, and a charming young musician, John Lodge, with whom she flirted and who arranged musical settings for her poems. She met Wordsworth and Walter Scott, enjoying summer sojourns with each. But her health was weakening from emotional and physical stress, and in 1831 she moved to Dublin, to be near the care of her brother and his wife. Although she again found good society and continued to write and publish, the climate was a disaster. She grew very ill and then bedridden in 1834, and died a few months shy of her forty-second birthday, in 1835, only eight years after her mother—and with regrets about poetry never realized: "My wish ever was to concentrate all my mental energy in the production of some more noble and complete work."

[*See also* Bluestockings; George Gordon Byron; *and* William Wordsworth.]

SELECTED WORKS

Poems by Felicia Dorothea Browne (1808)
England and Spain; or, Valour and Patriotism (1808)
The Domestic Affections and Other Poems (1812)
The Restoration of the Works of Art to Italy: A Poem (1816)
Modern Greece: A Poem (1817)
Translations from Camoens and Other Poets, with Original Poetry (1818)
Tales and Historic Scenes in Verse (1819)
Wallace's Invocation to Bruce: A Poem (1819)
The Sceptic: A Poem (1820)
Dartmoor: A Poem (1820)
A Selection of Welsh Melodies, with Symphonies and Accompaniments by John Parry and Characteristic Words by Mrs. Hemans (1822)
The Siege of Valencia, a Dramatic Poem, and The Last Constantine, with Other Poems (1823)
Vespers of Palermo: A Tragedy in Five Acts (1823)
Hymns for Childhood (1824)
The Forest Sanctuary and Other Poems (1825)
The League of the Alps, The Siege of Valencia, The Vespers of Palermo, and Other Poems (1826)
Hymns on the Works of Nature, for the Use of Children (1827)
Records of Woman, with Other Poems (1828)
Songs of the Affections, with Other Poems (1830)
Hymns for Childhood (1834)
National Lyrics, and Songs for Music (1834)
Scenes and Hymns of Life, with Other Religious Poems (1834)

EDITIONS

Wolfson, Susan J., ed. *Felicia Hemans: Selected Poems, Letters, and Reception Materials*. Princeton, NJ, 2000. Ample authoritative collection with introduction, chronology, generous annotation, and comprehensive bibliography.
Wolfson, Susan J. and Elizabeth Fay, eds. *The Siege of Valencia: A Parallel Text*. Peterborough, Ont., 2002. The 1823 publication with a newly discovered manuscript showing significant variants; introduction, bibliography, reviews, and supplementary materials.

FURTHER READING

Chorley, Henry Fothergill. *Memorials of Mrs. Hemans*. 1836. The first posthumous memoir; controversial for including private correspondence.
Clarke, Norma. *Ambitious Heights: Writing, Friendship, Love*. London, 1990. Hemans's celebration of and oppression by the "feminine" ideal.

Curran, Stuart. "Women Readers, Women Writers." In *Cambridge Companion to British Romanticism.* Edited by Stuart Curran, 177–195. Cambridge, U.K., 1993.

Feldman, Paula R. "The Poet and the Profits: Felicia Hemans and the Literary Marketplace." *Keats-Shelley Journal* 46(1997): 148–176. Important account of Hemans the businesswoman.

Hughes, H. "Memoir of the Life and Writings of Felicia Hemans, by Her Sister." In *The Works of Mrs. Hemans.* 7 vols. 1839. An attempt to remedy the image cast by Chorley.

Leighton, Angela. *Victorian Women Poets: Writing against the Heart*, 8–44. Charlottesville, VA. 1992. Conflicts of affection and vocation.

Lootens, Tricia. "Hemans and Home: Victorianism, Feminine 'Internal Enemies,' and the Domestication of National Identity." *PMLA* 109 (1994): 238–253. A pioneering essay, probing fractures, contradictions, and dissonances of the "feminine" sensibility.

Mellor, Anne K. *Romanticism and Gender*, 123–143. New York, 1992. Hemans's pressure against the ideals of "feminine" sensibility.

Melnyk, Julie, and Nanora Sweet, eds. *Felicia Hemans: Reimagining Poetry in the Nineteenth Century.* London, 2001. The first, and still only, collection of critical assessments.

Ross, Marlon B. *The Contours of Masculine Desire: Romanticism and the Rise of Women's Poetry.* New York, 1989. See pp. 232–310; one of the first modern assessments of Hemans's "feminine" difference from canonical male Romanticism.

Wolfson, Susan J. "The Domestic Affections and Spear of Minerva: Felicia Hemans and the Dilemma of Gender." In *Women Writers in the Age of English Romanticism.* Edited by Carol Shiner Wilson and Joel Haefner, 128–167. Philadelphia, 1994. Conflicting images of women in relation to "feminine" ideals.

Wolfson, Susan J. "Felicia Hemans and the Revolving Doors of Reception." In *Romanticism and Women Poets: Opening the Doors of Reception.* Edited by Stephen C. Behrendt and Harriet Kramer Linkin, 14–41. Lexington, KY, 1999. The reception of Hemans as "feminine" poet, and the pressure of *The Siege of Valencia* against the ideal.

ROBERT HENRYSON

R. James Goldstein

Although Robert Henryson (c. 1425–c. 1490) was not a prolific writer, the outstanding quality of his work has ensured his reputation not only as one of the most accomplished poets of late-medieval England and Scotland but also as arguably the greatest Scottish poet of all time. To many modern readers, Henryson's work invites comparison with the poetry of Geoffrey Chaucer, whose example and influence have led to the label, "Scottish Chaucerian." Yet very little is known about Robert Henryson, the man himself. Born c. 1425, Henryson must have died by 1505, when the Scots poet William Dunbar mentioned him in his elegy for English and Scottish poets known as "The Lament for the Makaris." The considerable learning demonstrated in his poetry helps confirm the likely identification of the writer as the same Robert Henryson who was incorporated into Glasgow University in 1462, which means that he was already a graduate of another university, either in Britain or on the Continent. We know that he was active as a notary public in Dunfermline in 1477–1488, which indicates that he possessed a working knowledge of legal documents and may well have studied law. Later sixteenth-century evidence also claims that Henryson was schoolmaster of the grammar school at Dunfermline, an important royal burgh. The impression of the poet gained from his work meshes nicely with these bits of external evidence, since he is well versed not only in the law but in the various branches of the medieval arts curriculum, comprising the trivium (grammar, logic, and rhetoric) and the mathematical arts of the quadrivium (including music and astronomy). He evidently flourished during the troubled reign of James III (r. 1460–1488), an early Stewart monarch whose tyrannical rule, based on his highly inflated view of kingship, led to serious clashes with the nobility and his eventual death in 1488 during a rebellion whose participants included his young son, James IV. None of Henryson's poetry may be firmly dated; thus, it remains uncertain whether he continued to write into the next reign. Able to deploy his considerable learning with a light touch, Henryson strikes most readers as humane, witty, and wise, able to laugh at human frailties but ultimately possessed of a strong religious faith. In short, though he has his own distinctive qualities, he reminds us of no other medieval writer more than Chaucer.

ORPHEUS AND EURYDICE

Of his three major works, Henryson's account of the mythical couple Orpheus and Eurydice is the one most undervalued by modern readers, not because it is less skillful but because shifts in aesthetic and philosophical tastes separate us from late-medieval literary culture. Indeed, the poem is a virtuoso piece of work, packing into 633 lines much of the received philosophical wisdom of the ancients as reconceived by generations of Christian moralizers—mythographers who interpreted classical myths as integuments, or poetic fictions that allegorically concealed moral or cosmological truth. Henryson's main source for the well-known story of Orpheus's failed attempt to retrieve his wife Eurydice from hell is the short poem at the end of book three of Boethius's *Consolation of Philosophy;* for his allegorical interpretation Henryson relies on the most widely known Latin commentary on Boethius from the later Middle Ages, by the early fourteenth-century Dominican scholar Nicholas Trivet. In keeping with the traditional doctrine of the correspondences between the cosmos and the human soul, the poet introduces the notion of celestial harmony while identifying Orpheus as the offspring of the muse Calliope and the god Apollo. With this noble lineage, Orpheus is both king and master musician; more than a gifted harpist, he is a musical theorist who understands the ordered harmonies of *musica mundana*, the music of the spheres.

The central metaphor of the narrative is the marriage between Orpheus and Eurydice, which represents, as the *moralitas* or allegorical interpretation explains, the concord between the two principal aspects of the human soul, the intellectual and the appetitive. When the herdsman Aristeus (whose name the early Christian mythographer Fabius Planciades Fulgentius links etymologically with the

Greek word for virtue) attempts to rape Eurydice, she accidentally treads on a venomous serpent and is called to the underworld by Proserpine. The stylistic contrast between the Latinate diction in passages that display the poet's encyclopedic learning and the plain style he uses to voice the hero's fraught emotion upon discovering the loss of his wife demonstrates Henryson's mastery of the full resources of the Scottish vernacular. The poem traces Orpheus's ascent through the celestial spheres in search of his wife in a Neoplatonic soul-journey in which he learns the mathematical proportions of heavenly harmony. The poet does not wait until the poem's conclusion to signal the allegorical significance of Orpheus's troubles: when he looks back as he leads his wife out of the underworld, we are told he lost her forever because he was blinded by great affection. The *moralitas* soon follows, explicitly identifying the hero with the intellectual faculty of the soul, and his wife with the appetitive, which drags the rational part of the mind downward toward false worldly goods. The philosophical tenor of the poem, in a way typical of Henryson's other work, both celebrates the inherent dignity and worth of human beings (with the proviso that the masculine should dominate the feminine) and laments the tragic inevitability, at least in the absence of grace, of a downward drift toward sensuality. By choosing a semidivine singer as his hero, moreover, Henryson implies that the poem is also about the nature of true poetry itself: eloquence capable of moving an audience to embrace philosophical wisdom.

MORALL FABILLIS

Henryson's most ambitious work is his collection of thirteen animal fables with a prologue, mostly derived from the twelfth-century Aesopic collection in Latin by Walter the Englishman, which along with its commentary was a standard grammar-school text well into the early modern period. Henryson also draws on the medieval French beast epic of Renard the Fox, and for his tale of the Cock and Fox, on Chaucer's *Nun's Priest's Tale*. Henryson enjoys creating ironic contrasts between the literal sense of the fables and the allegorical interpretations offered in the moralities, a technique that parallels his using Eurydice's would-be rapist to represent virtue. Much of the pleasure of the collection derives from the skillful use of dialogue and descriptive detail as the talkative animals deftly hover between their all-too-human and beastly identities, often shifting rapidly from one to the other in surprising ways. We smile at the foolish cock of the first fable, who in

scratching out a living on a dunghill discovers a gemstone, which he tosses away because it is of no use to him. In the subsistence economy of medieval Scottish society, the earnestness with which the cock describes his hunger for corn would have resonated powerfully, even as the *moralitas* chastises the human lack of prudence in rejecting true wisdom. Similarly, the tender country mouse and her burgh-dwelling sister feast on human delicacies until we are reminded of their rodent nature when they season their food with candles instead of spices; Chantecleir's wife Pertok in the tale of "The Cock and the Fox" delicately straddles the division between poultry and human when she describes her husband as a loving provider who used to break bread with his sweet bill.

Henryson manages to include a variety of social and political concerns in the collection, often using these to provide links between tales. For example, corrupt churchmen are satirized in "The Fox and the Wolf," when the wolf assigns an easy penance despite the fox's lack of true contrition (lamb's flesh is so honey sweet that he cannot bring himself to renounce it). The next tale, "The Trial of the Fox," follows the career of the previous fox's son, who, when he helps himself to a fat lamb, violates the lion king's decree that no beast shall molest another within a twenty-mile radius of his parliament. The tale is replete with powerful images of a well-governed society with the ideal king sitting in majesty, though the fraudulent fox nearly gets away with murder until the lamb's mother appears in court and points to his bloody snout and the wool and flesh of her son still stuck on the fox's teeth. After the culprit is summarily judged and executed, the *moralitas* calls for good government and the rule of law in a society where these often were lacking.

The two central tales show Henryson's complex artistry at its best. In "The Lion and the Mouse," the poet creates a frame tale in which the persona wanders outdoors and encounters his master Aesop, who complains that poetic fables can do little good when even the preaching of God's word falls on deaf ears. The revered master reluctantly consents to tell his protégé the tale about the mouse who repays her debt to the merciful lion. Henryson's conservative social vision is evident in the *moralitas*, which allegorizes the mice as the common folk in need of correction by the sovereign, who must mitigate the ferocity of his justice with true mercy. Aesop's voice returns in the final stanza of the *moralitas*, calling on churchmen to pray for treason to be exiled and for justice to reign. Notwithstanding attempts to read this and similar moments as topical references to events from the reign of James III, the political sentiments in the *Fabillis* are expressed in the general and universalized terms of traditional advisory literature.

"The Preaching of the Swallow" is perhaps the high point of the entire collection. Following a majestic opening that depicts the providential natural order visible in the changing seasons, the narrator encounters a flock of swallows who foolishly ignore his warnings to beware the peasant farmer who eventually ensnares them in his net. Overheard by the narrator, the swallow's preaching to deaf ears offers another example of Henryson's embedding figures for the moral function of his art within his poetry even while registering doubts about its efficacy. Indeed, the vision sustained in the second half of the collection grows increasingly dark and pessimistic when innocence is destroyed in both "The Wolf and the Wether" and "The Wolf and the Lamb." "The Paddock and the Mouse" brings the collection to a startling and disturbing conclusion. The frantic struggle between the frog who ferries a mouse across a river with the malicious intent of drowning her ends abruptly when a kite swoops down and disembowels them both. The morality concludes by allegorizing the mouse as the soul struggling against evil in the water that represents the world, and the poet turns to God with a final prayer, though with no assurance that justice will prevail in the present world.

THE TESTAMENT OF CRESSEID

Henryson's best-known work radically rewrites the ending of Chaucer's *Troilus and Criseyde* to reopen questions raised by his predecessor about the value of sexual love and the moral obligations of loyalty. Henryson frames his abbreviated, intensely imagined narrative of 616 lines by creating the fictive persona of a sexually frustrated old man, a servant of Venus, whose vital bodily heat during a frosty evening utterly fails him. After rereading Chaucer's book, he wonders whether it is entirely true, then turns to another book, clearly invented by the poet, which tells a different story. Drawing on this fictitious source, Henryson traces the career of the abject figure of Cresseid, who after settling her love on the Greek Diomede is soon abandoned. The poem's complex mixture of misogyny and compassion for her suffering is most striking in the harsh description of how she changed her femininity into filth by going among the Greeks "sa giglotlike takand thy foull plesance" (like such a strumpet taking your foul pleasure [line 83]), which is followed by the narrator's expression of pity for her misfortune. Taking a cue from Chaucer, the narrator goes out of his way to make excuses for her behavior by attributing it to feminine frailty. With no one else to protect her she returns to her father's house, where a terrifying scene unfolds immediately after she expresses resentment against the god and goddess of love. Ravished in an ecstasy, she is subjected to the wrath of the planetary deities in all their malignant force as they convene an assembly to put her on trial for blasphemy. Saturn, the most destructive god, sentences her to a life of disease and penury for her insolence and wantonness. Diana confirms the sentence, specifying that Cresseid must suffer leprosy and beg for the rest of her days; it is important to recall that leprosy was associated with venereal disease in earlier periods. After her nightmare vision, Cresseid beholds her deformed image in a mirror and is soon discovered by her father. Like the lepers of medieval and early modern Scotland who were forbidden to mix with the healthy population, Cresseid assumes her new position in a lazar house on the outskirts of town. She voices a formal complaint over her unjust fate: surely nothing she has done, the poem invites us to conclude, deserves such cruel punishment. In the most powerful scene of the poem, Troilus (who in this version has not yet died in battle) encounters his former lover as he passes on his way home from battle. They fail to recognize each other, but her image somehow rekindles the spark of love within him, and he tosses a purse of gold into her lap. When a beggar companion informs her that the knight was in fact Troilus, Cresseid is overcome by a sense of guilt and self-recrimination for betraying her faithful lover. Able to connect her fate with her own moral responsibility at last, she makes her last will and testament, dies, and is buried at Troilus's expense. Yet the strong formal devices of closure leave the poem's moral complexities unresolved; the narrator merely observes laconically that since she is dead he will say no more. Unlike Henryson's other major works, the *Testament* offers no concluding morality outside the narrative proper, leaving the reader a greater interpretive freedom that parallels the author's artistic license to rewrite his predecessor's work. Careful never to break the fictional pagan framework of the tale, Henryson leaves the poem tottering on the brink between the consolation of offering his heroine final spiritual redemption and abandoning her diseased body to a tragic and unredeemable fate.

THE CRITICAL RECEPTION

Henryson was greatly valued by fifteenth- and early-sixteenth-century Scottish and English readers and fellow poets. At least one of his works was issued c. 1508 by the first Scottish printers, Chepman and Myllar, and we have already seen that Dunbar lamented his passing c. 1505. Both Gawin Douglas and Sir David Lindsay borrow from Henryson, and the Asloan and Bannatyne MSS, the two most important manuscript compilations of Middle Scots poetry, devote considerable space to his work. The *Fables* and the *Testament* were printed several times well into the seventeenth century. Shakespeare alludes to Henryson's *Testament* more than once. Yet Henryson's reputation in England took a strange turn when William Thynne (d. 1546) appended a somewhat anglicized version of the *Testament* to his 1532 edition of Chaucer's *Troilus*, leading generations of English readers to attribute Henryson's work to Chaucer. By the eighteenth century his work was little known in either Scotland or England, but scholars of the next century resuscitated his reputation and devoted serious attention to establishing a modern critical text of all his works. It was not until the flourishing of scholarly and critical attention to Middle Scots poetry in the second half of the twentieth century, however, that Henryson finally began to receive the attention he deserves.

[*See also* Geoffrey Chaucer; William Dunbar; *and* David Lindsay.]

EDITION

Fox, Denton. *The Poems of Robert Henryson.* Oxford English Texts. Oxford, 1981. Magisterial edition of his works, with detailed introduction, commentary, and review of biographical material.

FURTHER READING

Gray, Douglas. *Robert Henryson.* Leiden, 1979. Learned and humane, most valuable general study.

Kratzmann, Gregory. *Anglo-Scottish Literary Relations, 1430–1550.* Cambridge, U.K., 1980. Best study of literary relations with Chaucer.

MacQueen, John. *Robert Henryson: A Study of the Major Narrative Poems.* Oxford, 1967. Still valuable, though overstates the case for the poet's debt to Italian humanism.

Stearns, Marshall W. *Robert Henryson.* New York, 1949. Still valuable on life and times, but exaggerates claims for poet's democratic sympathies.

Wheatley, Edward. *Mastering Aesop: Medieval Education, Chaucer, and His Followers.* Gainesville, FL, 2000. Includes chapter on the relation of the *Fables* to Latin commentary tradition.

GEORGE HERBERT

Michael Schoenfeldt

The fifth son of an important English family, George Herbert (1593–1633) combines in his poetry an elegant sense of aristocratic decorum with a Christian eye for the gritty spiritual truths that challenge the claims of class, wealth, and privilege. His single volume of posthumously published poetry, *The Temple* (1633), begins with a long poem on proper behavior in and out of church, "The Church-porch," and concludes with a long prophetic poem following the historical trajectory of the true church to the new world, *The Church-Militant*. In between are the poems for which Herbert is best known—177 of the most emotionally intense and formally accomplished devotional lyrics since the Davidic Psalms. Herbert's poems exhibit a remarkable capacity for self-directed irony; they also display an equally impressive stanzaic variety. Herbert's poetry, though, is most marked by its remarkable ambience of spiritual authenticity, an ambience won through a clear-eyed engagement with the uncomfortable material demands and gracious spiritual comforts of Christianity.

George Herbert's background exposed him to the centers of political and spiritual power in early modern England. His elder brother Edward, Lord Herbert of Cherbury, served as ambassador to France. His younger brother Henry became Master of the Revels, in charge of court entertainment before the civil war and after the Restoration. His mother, Magdalene Herbert, was famous for her piety, her intelligence, and her beauty; her funeral sermon was preached by John Donne. George Herbert was educated at Westminster School and later at Trinity College, Cambridge. He climbed quickly through the academic hierarchies at Cambridge, and was appointed university orator, a position that normally led to a career at court. But Herbert never made the transition to court,

George Herbert
Engraving by Robert White, 1674
NATIONAL PORTRAIT GALLERY, LONDON

for reasons we will never fully understand. It may have been a progressive disenchantment with the possibilities of uniting spiritual and political work. Or it may simply have been an unexpected shift in the vagaries of courtly favor. Between his last public oration in 1623, and his acceptance of the parsonage at Bemerton in 1630, Herbert is nearly absent from the historical record.

EARTHLY AND HEAVENLY AUTHORITY

Herbert spent most of his creative life writing to one form of authority or another. This proved to be a remarkable preparation for a career as a sacred poet. Indeed, in his hands, prayers to God and supplications to earthly power share an artful language of courtship. There is in Herbert's verse a profound sense that his relationship with God pervades all meaningful relationships; thus God can be to him a lord, a master, a father, a king, a friend, and a beloved, sometimes in different poems, sometimes in the same poem. Whether writing to an earthly lord or the Lord, to King James or heaven's king, Herbert allows the strategies of courtly utterance to mingle with the spiritual aspirations of prayer. In "The Thanksgiving," Herbert's God is addressed as the "King of grief," while in "Affliction (I)," he is a "King . . . of pleasures." The speaker of "The Odour, 2 Cor. 2. 15" addresses God as "My Master," and longs to be accepted as "my servant." "Redemption" brilliantly tells the story of human relations with God in terms of terrestrial landlord-tenant relations. The poem "Unkindnesse" compares the speaker's relationship with human companionship: "I would not use a friend as I use thee," the speaker declares to his infinitely accommodating Lord. In the final lyric of *The Temple*, "Love (III)," the sublimely gracious and nourishing deity is addressed at once with the deference of "Lord" and the intimacy of "My dear"; the deity in turn responds with the epitome of coercive hospitality: "You must sit down, sayes Love, and taste my meat."

THE RESOURCES OF FORM

Compared with John Donne's obvious pyrotechnics, Herbert's verse seems quiet, even simplistic on a first acquaintance. But this is deceptive. Herbert is engaged in a deeper exploration of the emotional and spiritual resources of lyric form than any previous English poet. *The Temple* includes poems that are carefully shaped to represent the spiritual truth they describe—"The Altar" and "Easter Wings"—as well as a poem about spiritual rebellion—"The Collar"—that approaches free verse in its unflinching portrait of spiritual disorder. Even this literally amazing poem manages to resolve itself into a kind of formal order that represents the speaker's emergent submission:

But as I rav'd and grew more fierce and wild
At every word,
Me thoughts I heard one calling, *Child!*
And I reply'd, *My Lord.*

A poem entitled "Deniall" similarly uses the failure of the final lines of various stanzas to rhyme to represent spiritual sterility, and signals a progressive spiritual acceptance with the achievement of rhyme in the poem's last line.

Herbert aggressively explores in his poetry the paradox that God deserves his best efforts, but that the aesthetic display that seems appropriate to such an elevated subject may just be needless bustling. Part of this paradox derives from the two audiences of devotional lyrics: there is a human reader, whom Herbert hopes to "Ryme . . . to good, and make a bait of pleasure" ("The Churchporch"); but there is also the divine audience, by definition omnipotent and omniscient, who would not be susceptible to such blandishments. The reader of one of Herbert's lyrics often feels like she or he is eavesdropping on a deeply artful conversation between the speaker and God.

Herbert in fact writes wonderfully about the difficulty of writing religious poetry. He considers the project of composing religious poetry in two poems entitled "Jordan," taking their name enigmatically from the river one must cross to enter the Promised Land. In the first "Jordan" poem, Herbert's speaker wants to identify himself not with those who value the artifice of "fictions only

and false hair" but with those "Who plainly say, *My God, My King.*" But the plea for a simple poetry collapses on its own complex scaffolding, particularly under an absolutist monarch. In "Jordan (II)," Herbert even parodies a poem by his kinsman Sir Philip Sidney (*Astrophel and Stella*, 1) in his sincere effort to depict his misguided aspirations to give God the best of his poetic efforts. The poem concludes:

But while I bustled, I might heare a friend
Whisper, *How wide is all this long pretence!*
There is in love a sweetnesse readie penn'd:
Copie out onely that, and save expense.

But just what labor this entails is never explained. In "Praise (II)" Herbert promises his God that "with my utmost art / I will sing thee," while in "The Forerunners" the speaker declares that "my God must have my best, ev'n all I had." Yet in "A true Hymne," the speaker argues that the phrase "My joy, my life, my crown" can "If truly said, . . . take part / Among the best in art." Here it is the sincerity of the speaker rather than the formal ingenuity of the utterance that determines its aesthetic success. The poem "Sion" suggests that God prefers inarticulate cries to elaborate edifices: "All Solomons sea of brasse and world of stone / Is not so deare to thee as one good grone." Herbert continues to ponder but never resolves the respective claims of sincerity and artifice, of aspirant heartfelt sighs and aspiring aesthetic edifices, in his poetry; rather he allows this tension to energize his spiritual quest, asking highly wrought lyrics to gesture toward an aesthetic of simple sincerity.

EARTHLY AND HEAVENLY LOVE

Herbert's first lyric impulse, expressed in a letter to his pious mother when he was sixteen, was to castigate "those many Love-poems, that are daily writ and consecrated to Venus," and to add to those embarrassingly few love poems that "are writ, that look towards God and Heaven." Along with this letter Herbert sent to his mother two sonnets comparing love for God with love for human beauty; the final line of the second encapsulates the ascetic mood of both poems:

Open the bones, and you shall nothing find
In the best face but filth, when Lord, in thee
the beauty lies in the discovery.

The first lesson of "The Church-porch," the long poem of advice prefacing the lyrics of *The Temple*, continues this sense of disgust with corporeal desire: "Beware of lust; it doth pollute and foul." The poetry of *The Temple*, though, is far more equivocal when dealing with the relations between terrestrial and heavenly love. A poem entitled "The Size" seems to sanction pleasure —"Thy Saviour sentenc'd joy"—before relocating it from earth to heaven—"And in the flesh condemn'd it as unfit." Two sonnets entitled "Love" imagine contiguity rather than competition between earthly and heavenly desire; the second begins: "Immortall Heat, O let thy greater flame / Attract the lesser to it." In the poem "The Invitation," Herbert even imagines that the Eucharistic banquet epitomizes the kinds of sinful pleasure that it should repudiate. "Come ye hither all," Herbert's speaker shouts, "whose taste / Is your waste, / . . . whom wine / Doth define, / . . . whom pain / Doth arraigne, / . . . whom joy / Doth destroy, / . . . whose love / Is your dove." In this profoundly capacious vision of Christianity, Herbert sees the feast of love as a special invitation to those sinners—the glutton, the drunk, and the lecher—that Christianity would normally shun.

The poetry of *The Temple*, then, is marked by a careful attention to the corollary experiences of corporeal suffering and of corporeal pleasure. In "The Forerunners" Herbert advertises the fact that the medium of his religious devotions is an erotic language of "sweet phrases, lovely metaphors" that "before / Of stews and brothels only knew the doores." He has "washed" them, "brought [them] to church well drest and clad." But still they desire to "leave the Church, and love a stie"—which the speaker treats as a moment of erotic abandonment: "But will ye leave me thus?" The poem "Longing" addresses God as "My love, my sweetness," while the poem "Even-song" remarks, "My god, thou art all love." Herbert would argue not that divine love is a sublimation of earthly love, but rather that earthly love is a diminished and misguided version of divine love, the source and ultimate object of all desire.

DEATH AND POSTHUMOUS PUBLICATION

Herbert spent the last three years of his short life as a country parson at Bemerton, a village close to Salisbury, geographically and socially distant from the court whose favors he had originally sought. He was terribly ill much of this time, but nonetheless served his divine monarch, and his earthly congregation, with industrious devotion. He continued as well to work on the poems of *The Temple*, and composed a conduct manual for rural clergy, *A Priest to the Temple; or, The Country Parson His Character,*

and Rule of Holy Life. Both *The Temple* and *A Priest to the Temple* were published posthumously. Izaak Walton, author of the first extensive biography of Herbert, relates a moving story thirty-seven years after Herbert's death, about how Herbert on his deathbed asked that his friend Nicholas Ferrar read the poems of *The Temple*, "and then, if he can think it may turn to the advantage of any dejected poor Soul, let it be made publick: if not let him burn it: for *I and it, are less than the least of God's mercies.*" The story deserves to be true. Ferrar did indeed ensure that the poems were published, and they were published in a small but beautiful edition by Cambridge University Press, the university where Herbert had begun his academic and political career. The collection proved so popular that a second edition came out in the first year, and the tenth edition by 1674, when it was published with Walton's *Life,* and with Christopher Harvey's *The Synagogue,* one of the many works imitating Herbert's accomplishment published in the period. Herbert's lyrics were read with appreciation by believers of all creeds—Puritans and Catholics, Parliamentarians and Royalists—over the course of that volatile century. There is perhaps no greater testimony to the rigor and capaciousness of his poetry.

[*See also* John Donne; Metaphysical Poets; *and* Henry Vaughan.]

SELECTED WORKS

The Temple (1633)
A Priest to the Temple (1652)

FURTHER READING

Bloch, Chana. *Spelling the Word: George Herbert and the Bible.* Berkeley, CA, 1985.

Fish, Stanley. *The Living Temple: George Herbert and Catechizing.* Berkeley, CA, 1978.

Fish, Stanley. *Self-Consuming Artifacts: The Experience of Seventeenth-Century Literature.* Berkeley, CA, 1972.

Hodgkins, Christopher. *Authority, Church, and Society in George Herbert: Return to the Middle Way.* Columbia, MO, 1993.

Lewalski, Barbara Kiefer. *Protestant Poetics and the Seventeenth-Century Religious Lyric.* Princeton, NJ, 1979.

Malcolmson, Cristina. *Heart-Work: George Herbert and the Protestant Ethic.* Stanford, CA, 1999.

Martz, Louis L. *The Poetry of Meditation: A Study in En-*

glish Religious Literature of the Seventeenth Century. New Haven, CT, 1954; revised 1962.

Schoenfeldt, Michael. *Bodies and Selves in Early Modern England: Physiology and Inwardness in Spenser, Shakespeare, Herbert, and Milton.* Cambridge, U.K., 1999.

Schoenfeldt, Michael. *Prayer and Power: George Herbert and Renaissance Courtship.* Chicago, 1991.

Stein, Arnold. *George Herbert's Lyrics.* Baltimore, 1968.

Strier, Richard. *Love Known: Theology and Experience in George Herbert's Poetry.* Chicago, 1983.

Summers, Joseph. *George Herbert: His Religion and Art.* Cambridge, MA, 1954.

Targoff, Ramie. *Common Prayer: The Language of Public Devotion in Early Modern England.* Chicago, 2001.

Tuve, Rosemond. *A Reading of George Herbert.* Chicago, 1952.

Vendler, Helen. *The Poetry of George Herbert.* Cambridge, MA, 1975.

Walton, Izaak. *Lives.* Edited by George Saintsbury. London, 1927.

ROBERT HERRICK

Elizabeth Clarke

Robert Herrick (1591–1674) was born in Goldsmith's Row in the south of Cheapside. Before he was two years old, his father Nicholas seems to have committed suicide, a terrible act that his family tried to cover up; perhaps this personal history explains the recurrence in his poetry of an obsession with proper burial rites. He was brought up, with his two elder brothers, by his uncle William Herrick, who does not seem to have treated his nephews as well as his own sons. He probably went to Merchant Taylor's school, like his cousins, before being apprenticed to his uncle as a goldsmith in 1607. However, he had served only five years of his ten-year apprenticeship when he entered St. John's College, Cambridge, in 1613; while there he began writing poetry. He met many friends and patrons in Cambridge, most importantly Mildmay Fane, later the second earl of Westmoreland. The Devonian John Weekes, who remained a close friend for much of his life, was a fellow at St. John's (see H43, H336). Herrick's poems are conventionally referred to in scholarly literature by their sequential numbers in his published volume, with "H" denoting the first part of the book, "Hesperides," and "N" for "His Noble Numbers," the second section.

There is evidence that Herrick became known in London in the 1620s: the poet Mildmay Fane addressed two poems to him there, and in 1625 Richard James in *The Muses Dirge* deplored the fact that the death of James I had not been lamented by "Some *Jonson, Drayton,* or some *Herrick.*" In 1627 Herrick and Weekes were chaplains to George Villiers, the duke of Buckingham, on the doomed expedition to La Rochelle to relieve French Protestants. Herrick probably continued in the duke's service until the latter's assassination in 1628. The Church was probably not the first choice of Herrick or Weekes, but they both eventually found livings in Devon, in southwestern England. Herrick was presented to the vicarage of Dean Prior, which was in the king's gift, in September 1629. It was on the edge of Dartmoor, and not a rich living: Herrick seems to have enjoyed saying good-bye to his parishioners, "rude (almost) as rudest savages" rather

more than living among them (H86). Paradoxically, he admits that he wrote his best poetry there, "where I loathed so much" (H51). He wrote some poems to local patrons such as Thomas Shapcot (H443, H444). Less favored locals, such as Scobble, Mudge, Dundridge, and Coone, are memorialized in sharp, satirical epigrams. He had a curate, William Greene, who made possible Herrick's visits to London. His brother's widow, Elizabeth, kept house for him until her death in 1643 (H376).

Herrick was probably in Whitehall in May 1630 for "A Pastoral upon the Birth of Prince Charles, Presented to the King, and Set by Master Nicholas Lanier" (H213). He clearly valued participation in London literary culture, even at a distance, as his poems to Ben Jonson and John Denham reveal. "An Ode for Him" (H911) suggests that he participated in the lively coterie of poets around Ben Jonson, and he certainly would have been among those who considered themselves "sons of Ben." Like much poetry of the period, his poems can be considered as "occasional verse," responding to individual events or the observations of a specific moment. His work is deeply permeated with the classicism that characterizes Jonson's poetry; Jonson had perfected the art of the epigram, and Herrick both mastered the classical precedents and went beyond them. *Hesperides* draws heavily on Martial, Anacreon, and Horace.

PUBLICATION OF *HESPERIDES*

From 1635 to 1640 only four of Herrick's poems were published, although many had appeared in manuscript miscellanies, but in 1640 his poems were entered for publication in the Stationers' Register by Andrew Crooke. However, this edition never appeared. In 1648 his poems were published as *Hesperides; or, The Works Both Humane & Divine of Robert Herrick Esq.* It was a unique attempt by an English poet to publish all his work in one volume, amounting to nearly 1,400 poems. The volume was divided into two parts, "Hesperides" and the shorter "His Noble Numbers," which was entirely on religious subjects. The poetry was well known in its time: more than seventy-five of Herrick's poems appeared in the various editions of *Witts Recreations*, a Royalist miscellany, in the 1650s. Some critics have attributed the problems many modern readers have in making sense of such a large and disparate volume to the fact that conventions for the organization of "complete works" were not established at this date. Others have suggested that the volume only makes sense as an epigram book, a genre followed in the early modern period by Sir Thomas More and Sir John Harrington. Gordon Braden argues that the overwhelming sense of a debt to classical models gives a degree of substance to a work that might otherwise suffer from the slightness of some individual lyrics. But he points out that many of the borrowings from the classics are decontextualized and equate to a general preoccupation with classical paraphernalia for which he coins the word "décor." Even astonishing words that sound like Latinisms turn out to have no source, and to have been thought up by Herrick himself, such as the word "liquefaction" in "Upon Julia's Clothes" (H779):

> Whenas in silks my Julia goes
> Then, then, methinks, how swiftly flows
> The liquefaction of her clothes.

The *Hesperides* offer up a cornucopia of small poems, often concerned with small objects—what one critic christened "microphilia," illustrated in the poem that opens the volume:

> I sing of brooks, of blossoms, birds and bowers:
> Of April, May, of June and July-flowers.
> I sing of maypoles, hock-carts, wassails, wakes,
> Of bridegrooms, brides, and of their bridal-cakes.

In effect Herrick offers literary critics of all persuasions ample evidence with which to pursue their particular theories. The psychoanalyst in particular has plenty of material to work from: many of the poems are sexualized, including several dreams, and many of the epigrams involve bodily functions and bodily fluids. Theories have been formed about the nature of Herrick's sexuality, suggesting that it was not fully adult, and that Herrick always pulls back from describing full intercourse, although there is plenty of foreplay in his poetry. Some critics observe that Herrick idealizes his "mistresses"—Anthea, Electra, Corinna, Perilla, but above all Julia—and is actually put off by the bodily functions of real women; however, Herrick's conscious stance is that no physical unpleasantness will deter the true lover. Herrick never

married, and his claim in the last line of "Hesperides" is a line from Ovid: "Jocund his Muse was, but his life was chaste." Critics and biographers have speculated on what exactly is the nature of the "cleanly-wantonness" aspired to in the first poem of the book. An intriguing informer's note in the State Papers accuses Herrick of nonresidence at Dean Prior, since he had been living for some time in Westminster in the same house as Thomasin Parsons, about whose childhood beauty Herrick had written. The implication is that Herrick is responsible for the birth of Thomasin's bastard child.

CRITICAL RESPONSES TO HERRICK'S POETRY

This puzzle illustrates an aspect of Herrick's work that critics have returned to again and again—its heterogeneity. Although the Hesperides of myth contained an enclosed garden, what went on within it was without too many rules, perhaps like the sacred Garden of Love that many poets of Herrick's period used as the site for erotic encounters. In its very superficiality the volume is profoundly anti-Puritan. It is fascinated by surfaces, by glitter, by light falling on silk, by clothes in general. As Achsah Guibbory has pointed out, "Hesperides" is as concerned with aspects of religion as "His Noble Numbers": it celebrates different kinds of ritual, particularly funeral rites, including "Julia's Churching, or Purification," the church service for cleansing after childbirth that Puritans particularly abhorred. The words "rites" and "ceremonies" appear in the titles of many poems, including "Ceremonies for Candlemas Eve," a feast-day that Puritans wanted removed from the church calendar long before they abolished all such feasts in 1648. Altars and sacrifices abound in various contexts; pagan and Christian: candles, which had been banned from church altars in 1643, flicker brightly along with the "the shine of snails," and dew, "disparkling" in some of the dim corners of "Hesperides." However, the whole enterprise is deeply unserious. Describing the time of day "When He Would Have His Verses Read" (H8), Herrick rejects "sober mornings" and plumps for boozy evenings when he would wish "rigid Cato" to read his poems, which are described as "holy incantations." Despite the apparent separation of the volumes into "sacred" and "profane," and the repudiation of his "unbaptised rhymes" at the start of "His Noble Numbers," the imaginative vision expressed in the entire volume is inclusive and eclectic. In the same severe poem at the start of "His Noble Numbers," Herrick asks God to "blot each line / Out of my book that is not thine." If this prayer has been answered, it means that a variety of sexually explicit and scatological poems are in fact included in the category "divine." He calls his Hesperides a "sacred Grove," and in mythology this garden is considered as a kind of Paradise, but one where all kinds of pleasures are gratified. The poem called "The Temple," which must have reminded the 1640s reader of George Herbert's famous and very serious volume, is actually about the fairies' temple, and the religion practiced there is extremely heterodox, "Part Pagan, part Papisticall." It is impossible to take the fairy religion seriously—it is on such a miniature, and bizarre scale—but Herrick is surely being mischievous here in expressing his delight in a spirituality and ritual that runs so counter to the dominant temper of the 1640s. The introduction to "Hesperides" finishes in extremely non-Puritan fashion: "I write of hell; I sing (and ever shall) / Of heaven, and hope to have it after all." His is a "mixt religion" indeed, reluctant to exclude or condemn. The epigram on "The Number Two" (N249) expresses Herrick's hatred of the polarities characteristic of Puritanism:

> God hates the dual number, being known
> The luckless number of division.

Perhaps it is this deep opposition to the politics of the 1640s that has made Robert Herrick a source of fascination for New Historicist critics, who have studied his royalism, aligning him with other "Cavalier Poets." His title, "Hesperides," has a Royalist significance: the birth of Prince Charles had been marked by a bright midday manifestation of Hesperus, the evening star. Several of his poems celebrate Royalist victories in the English Civil War; Devon was one of its fiercest arenas, and in 1646 Herrick was replaced with a Presbyterian minister. His royalism has been detected in his consistent celebration of the traditional social order, and his liking for traditional festivals has been seen as in line with the Book of Sports—reissued by Charles I (r. 1625–1649) and enforced by his archbishop, William Laud—which encouraged traditional sports and pastimes, even on a Sunday. Several of Herrick's longer poems are enlisted in the canon of Royalist poetry: "Corinna's Going a-Maying" (H178) celebrates the May Day festival when the young went into the woods at dawn for sexual fun and to gather hawthorn branches, "the proclamation made for May" in the Book of Sports. Corinna's name would seem to suggest she was up for such sport—it is that of Ovid's mistress—but the poem is apparently occasioned by her refusal to get out of bed on May morning. Characteristically, Herrick reverses Puritan morality in order to persuade her to join in this rather suspect activity: "tis sin—nay profanation" to stay in bed while the birds are singing matins in the woods. It is typical of Herrick that he urges her not to take time over dressing; elsewhere, as here, he celebrates a carelessness in clothing. The third stanza is also characteristic in that it depicts a natural scene as if it were a religious site where a solemn religious festival is in train. A picture of a country May Day observance is given that acknowledges the sexual implications of the event—the eating of cakes and cream to the accompaniment of jokes about "locks picked," and even actual betrothals. However, by the end of the poem the speaker seems to have accepted that he and Corinna have missed all the fun, and his thoughts turn to another preoccupation of Herrick's. The last stanza is a beautiful *carpe diem* exercise:

> Come, let us go while we are in our prime
> And take the harmless folly of the time.
>   We shall grow old apace, and die
>   Before we know our liberty,
>   Our life is short, and our days run
>   As fast away as doth the sun.
> And, as a vapour or a drop of rain,
> Once lost can ne'er be found again:
>   So when you and I are made
>   A fable song, or fleeting shade,
>   All love, all liking, all delight
> Lies drowned with us in endless night.

A festival for the other end of the year is commemorated in another frequently anthologized poem, "The Hock-Cart, or *Harvest Home*," addressed to Herrick's patron, Mildmay Fane (H250). The festive cart that brings home the last of the harvest is described in loving detail, "Dressed up with all the country art." As elsewhere, this art is seen as a kind of devotion:

> Some bless the cart; some kiss the sheaves;
> Some prank them up with oaken leaves;
> Some cross the fill-horse: some with great
> Devotion stroke the home-borne wheat.

The menu of the feast at the lord's house is given in specifics typical of Herrick: beef, mutton, veal, bacon, custard, and frumenty. The happy scene seems significant of a cozily feudal relationship between lord and peasant, until the final lines, which give away a pragmatic reason for the lord's benevolence:

> And, you must know, your lord's word's true—
> Feed him ye must, whose food fills you;

And that his pleasure is like rain,
Not sent ye for to drown your pain
But for to make it spring again.

In some ways Herrick's poems, deeply "occasional" in nature, reflect the vicissitudes and acquaintances of his own life. Reading "Hesperides" in particular, there is a sense of a very particular personality infusing the poems, but this is a deliberate self-construction, like the harmless persona created in classical epigram books. Like many Royalist male poets, Herrick creates a social sense of masculine solidarity, which has been seen as itself political, contributing to the survival of Royalist culture throughout the dark days of the Interregnum. The controlled lack of seriousness throughout his volume is part of the strategy of resistance to Puritan domination. Very little verse survives from the later part of his life, although it is unlikely that he ceased to write. Perhaps surprisingly, he petitioned the House of Lords to return him to Dean Prior in 1660, and he died there in 1674. The printed volume *Hesperides*, which contains many premonitions of the poet's own death, is prefaced by an engraving. On a carved monument stands a living bust, thought to be modeled on Herrick's actual features: a symbol of Herrick's fascination with his own death, and his belief that he would be memorialized as a famous poet.

[*See also* Cavalier Poetry *and* Ben Jonson.]

SELECTED WORKS AND EDITION

Hesperides; or, The Works Both Humane & Divine of Robert Herrick Esq. (1648)

Martin, L. C. ed. *The Poetical Works of Robert Herrick.* Oxford, 1956.

FURTHER READING

Braden, Gordon. *The Classics and English Renaissance Poetry: Three Case Studies.* New Haven, CT, 1978. One of these case studies, beautifully written and extremely influential, is on Herrick's use of the classical epigrammatists.

Coiro, Ann Baynes. *Robert Herrick's "Hesperides" and the Epigram Tradition.* Baltimore, 1988. Usefully revises Braden and places Herrick's volume in the tradition of the early modern epigram book.

Guibbory, Achsah. *Ceremony and Community from Herbert to Milton: Literature, Religion, and Cultural Conflict in Seventeenth-Century England.* Cambridge, U.K., 1998. See pp. 79–118. This chapter places Herrick's "generally ceremonialist, and probably specifically Laudian, mentality" within the religious and cultural conflicts of the 1640s and suggests that "Hesperides" as well as "His Noble Numbers" is concerned with the question of what constitutes "the religious."

Marcus, Leah S. *The Politics of Mirth: Jonson, Herrick, Milton, Marvell, and the Defense of Old Holiday Pastimes.* Chicago, 1986. See pp. 140–168. This substantial chapter in an influential book is the classic New Historicist treatment of Herrick.

Schoenfeldt, Michael C. "The Art of Social Disgust: Civility and the Social Body in *Hesperides.*" In *George Herbert Journal* 4 (1990–1991). This article in a special issue of the *George Herbert Journal* devoted to Herrick considers some of his more unpleasant and scatological verse.

JOHN HEYWOOD

Kent Cartwright

The singer, virginals player, dancer, musical composer, dramatist, actor, wit, poet, and epigrammatist John Heywood (c. 1497–c. 1578) is best known to later generations for his high-spirited farces and debate plays. Those plays offer the most sophisticated theatricality of any Henrician interludes and represent a new phase in the development of English drama. With John Bale, Heywood is one of the two most important playwrights during the time of the two Tudor Henrys—Henry VII (r. 1485–1509) and Henry VIII (r. 1509–1547). Born in the reign of Henry VII and a steadfast Catholic during an era of religious turmoil, Heywood nonetheless prospered as an entertainer and intimate at the courts of four English monarchs of strongly differing Protestant and Catholic view—Henry VIII, Edward VI (r. 1547–1553), Mary I (r. 1553–1558), and Elizabeth I (r. 1558–1603)—before his self-exile to the Continent in 1564. Tall, playful, intelligent, convivial, and charming, Heywood forged a distinctive artistic career at court with his wit. His raucous and multifaceted writings blend old-world values and new humanist realism; they celebrate proverbial wisdom yet reveal the enigma of human experience; they parody political and religious figures but yield finally to an optimistic vision of social harmony.

LIFE

Heywood achieved unusual success and prosperity as an entertainer at court, such that he was rewarded with close association with the monarch and enough gifts and annuities—some of it from Henry's dissolution of the monasteries—to allow him to rise to the level of landed gentry. He was also an important figure in the More circle, the group of family and friends around Sir Thomas More, chancellor of England and Catholic martyr (executed in 1535). By his marriage, Heywood became the nephew of More and the son-in-law of the famous printer, dramatist, and entrepreneur John Rastell. He was himself the father of the Jesuit Jasper Heywood, the first translator of Seneca's plays into English, and the grand-

father of one of England's greatest poets, John Donne (who finally abandoned the family's Catholicism).

Born around 1497, Heywood possessed musical abilities that took him to court by at least 1519. First a singer, then a player of the virginals (a keyboard instrument), Heywood by the end of the 1520s had been appointed to the longtime position of Steward of the Royal Chamber, as an official in the king's household. About 1529 Heywood married Rastell's daughter Eliza. His surviving plays probably date from this period, the late 1520s and the early 1530s, undoubtedly fostered by his association with his playwriting and play-producing father-in-law and his play-loving uncle-in-law. And it was Heywood's brother-in-law, the printer William Rastell, who published most of those works. In 1533 Henry VIII married Anne Boleyn, having divorced Catherine of Aragon and begun his break with the Catholic Church. In that same year appeared at least two of Heywood's dramatic farces, *Johan Johan* and *The Pardoner and the Friar*, plays that acknowledge Catholic abuses but also call for reason and toleration toward the traditional Church—a difficult negotiation in a time of turmoil. During the same period, Heywood became associated as a musician with the future queen, the Catholic Mary (daughter of Henry and the divorced Catherine of Aragon), now estranged from her father. In 1544 Heywood was almost executed for conspiring to overthrow the Protestant archbishop Thomas Cranmer; after making a public recantation he was forgiven and restored to the good graces of Henry. In the later view of the Elizabethan Sir John Harrington, Heywood had "scaped hanging with his mirth" (*The Metamorphosis of Ajax*, 1596, p. 40). Heywood continued as a musician and producer of court entertainments during Edward's Protestant reign but reached the height of his worldly success during the reign of Mary.

In 1546 Heywood published his *Dialogue conteinyng the number in effect of all the prouerbes in the englishe tongue, compacte in a matter concernyng two maner of mariages*, a verse narrative putting traditional folk sayings (already echoed through his plays) into humanistic literary form. The *Dialogue* was followed by a collection of a hundred epigrams (1550), which he subsequently expanded and republished until it reached six hundred in his nondramatic *Works* of 1562. With such publications, Heywood advanced the new humanist interest in literary and philosophical epigrams launched by William Caxton and developed by Desiderius Erasmus (c. 1467–1536), More, Nicholas Udall, and Robert Crowley. Heywood also wrote short, sometimes occasional poems, and in 1556 he published his long, gnomic, pro-Mary allegorical poem, *The Spider and the Fly*. Heywood produced entertainments for Elizabeth, but he left England for the Continent in 1564, along with his Jesuit son Ellis, because of actions to enforce Protestant worship. There followed years of transient exile and poverty until his death at Louvain, probably in 1578.

DRAMATIC WORKS

Although Heywood wrote and produced various entertainments—such as his 1539 *Masque of King Arthur's Knights*, or his "parts of man," written for Cranmer sometime after the events of 1544, and his "play of children" for Elizabeth—only six early plays have survived, ones likely published for political purposes. Criticizing venal Church officials, corrupt religious practices, and even prominent figures at court, Heywood's plays undertake an impressively immediate political satire. Heywood stands out not only as a satirist but also as an innovator. He was England's first adapter of French drama, first truly literary playwright, first important writer of stage comedy, and first secular dramatist to emphasize acting and theatricality. In *Johan Johan*, Heywood made the original translation of a French farce. Adapting the French spirit in his other plays, Heywood rejected the allegorical and didactic morality-play model then followed in English theater. Instead, he based his dramas on incidents and disputes, filled them with common (sometimes disreputable) contemporary characters, added realistic details from homely life, and reveled in broad humor and highjinks. Such drama was new in England. Heywood was surely influenced, too, by the witty dialogues of the ancient Roman writer Lucian, some of whose works had been translated by More. Although Heywood was not an academic playwright, his comedies demonstrate an undervalued literariness, arising at a time when the printers William Caxton and Wynken de Worde had begun to make an English (and Continental) literary heritage available. Heywood drew freely on other writers, not only Eu-

ropeans such as Erasmus and Giovanni Pico della Mirandola (1463–1494) but also English such as Geoffrey Chaucer (preeminently), John Skelton, Henry Medwall (1462–after 1501), John Rastell, and of course, More.

Heywood's dramatic vision is comic. Structured as debates—Is it better to love or not to love? Is the intelligent man or the witless man happier? Who should be in charge of the weather?—his plays nonetheless involve farcical narratives, puns, absurd logic, sexual jokes, and parodies. They also end in the spirit of expansive insight and social reconciliation that is a hallmark of comedy. Heywood's comedic tendencies are repeated in his sense of theatricality. Characters sing, dance, gesticulate, and posture; the Potycary hops about in *The Four PP*, as does the "Vice," in *The Play of Love*, who also comes on stage wearing a hat with exploding fireworks. Heywood loved physical action and eruptions of spectacle, and it is likely that he himself played some of the most comedic roles (perhaps the Potycary, No Lover Nor Loved, or Merry Report). Heywood's theater showcases the virtuosity of the performer—far more than does the drama of his predecessors—and, thus, his characters sometimes emerge in unexpected lights as a play progresses: the initially sympathetic Friar is exposed as a rapscallion in *The Pardoner and the Friar*, the seemingly transparent Palmer becomes an enigmatic liar—or truth-teller?—in *The Four PP*. Although Heywood's characters begin as representative types, they take on an individuality and complexity expressive of the nature of their performances. They acquire, that is, a specifically theatrical mode of existence, a theatrical ontology.

Such dynamism is enhanced by Heywood's positioning of characters rhetorically against each other, as with the two dramatis personae Lover Not Loved and Loved Not Loving. Implications arise from contrasts and parallels, in a manner not unlike that of Thomas Elyot's humanistic *The Governor*. As the action proceeds, moreover, characters surprise, become complicated, so that clear winners and unambiguous meanings disappear. Perhaps more intellectual than emotional, such a drama employs speech characterized by language jokes and comic logic rather than by poetic devices (although Heywood's verse lines and rhyme patterns provide sensual pleasure). Yet the debates often involve surprisingly subtle distinctions among mental and emotional states, such as the relative suffering of a short but intense pain as compared to a longer but duller one. Heywood's intellectual dramas are further softened by their intimacy. Casts are small, typically three or four characters (except for the ten roles, many for children, in *The Play of the Weather*, 1533), and actors perform in banquet rooms or great halls, often addressing, gesturing inclusively toward, or entering through the audience.

Heywood's first play (following the order presented by Richard Axton and Peter Happé) is *Witty and Witless* (the standard modern title for an untitled play preserved in manuscript as British Library MS Harley 367, fols. 110r–119r; first published in 1846 under the title *A Dialogue on Wit and Folly*). Here John and James argue whether the intelligent or the foolish person experiences the greater physical and mental pleasures and pains. The interlude is striking for its richness of psychological discrimination, as when the two discuss "inward delyght" or the kinds and degrees of joy and disappointment—early evidence of the sense of subjectivity often noted as emerging in the Renaissance. Heywood's lone narrative play is *Johan Johan*, translated from the French *Farce du Pasté*. The henpecked village husband, John, must chaff wax to mend a leaky pail while watching his presumably unfaithful wife share a pie with her apparent seducer, the priest Sir John. Heywood adds considerable English color and local detail to this translation; Tyb emerges as an aggressive version of Chaucer's Wife of Bath; while the exaggerated sexual symbolism of pail, wax, and pie, along with the husband's fleetingly felt triumph, give the narrative a disturbing poignancy beyond its French original.

In *The Pardoner and the Friar* the two main characters defend the relative merits of their professions and progressively reveal their venality. The Pardoner derives from Chaucer, while the argument reflects More's attack on heresy. When the Curate and Neighbor attempt to apprehend the now-brawling Pardoner and Friar, the two increasingly demonic villains, surprisingly, beat the good villagers and stroll off threatening return. With its shocking outcome, the play offers a parable of the real dangers of Church corruption and division (the Friar seems to voice Lutheranism) on the eve of the Reformation. In *The Four PP* another duplicitous Pardoner appears, joined by a shrine-obsessed Palmer, an apothecary with life-threatening medications, and a peddler. The first three proceed to debate which among them represents the best means to salvation and agree to determine supremacy with, ironically, a lying contest, in which the Palmer defeats the previous two tellers of misogynistic tales by claiming never to have seen a woman "out of patience." One of the theatrical pleasures of this play is the possibility that the enigmatic Palmer may mean to tell the truth, a possibility that underscores Heywood's message of tolerance.

In *The Play of Love* Heywood parodies the vicissitudes of romantic love, perhaps as preoccupations of aristocratic culture (in which figures such as Sir Thomas Wyatt were writing Petrarchan poetry). The play's most interesting character is the madcap, somewhat cruel, self-determining "Vice," No Lover Nor Loved. In *The Play of the Weather*, another antic Vice-figure, Merry Report, undertakes, on behalf of the god Jupiter, to gather disputants over the question of who should determine the weather. Merry Report interviews representatives of different occupations and classes, but Jupiter decides to leave the weather unchanged. The play's satire embraces court rivalries, officials who control royal access, and the management of factional and class conflicts. It also may contain some veiled allusions to the sexual activities of Anne Boleyn.

NONDRAMATIC WORKS

Heywood was best known to contemporaries as a wit, epigrammatist, and nondramatic poet. His *Dialogue of Proverbs* (1546) is a verse conversation between the narrator and a young man, the latter considering whether to marry a young, lovely, but poor maiden or an old, wizened, but rich widow. The speakers proceed by trying out proverbs—that is, short, pithy, colloquial statements, often metaphoric, of popular wisdom—applicable to the situation. Infused with humor and realistic detail, the *Dialogue* manages to give color to its speakers and the figures in its inset tales. It also contributes to the growing list of proverbs collections in the late fifteenth and sixteenth centuries. An interest in proverbs saturates Renaissance literature, and Heywood's collection is cited as exemplary in Thomas Wilson's *Art of Rhetoric* (1560). Not scholarly like the compilations of Erasmus or Udall, Heywood's proverb collection marks the telling intersection of a folk sensibility with a humanist drive to amass and organize knowledge. Heywood's success with proverbs likely inspired his subsequent collections of epigrams. He first published *An Hundred Epigrams* in 1550, expanding the number progressively through the remainder of his career. Heywood's epigrams are short (sometimes two lines), anecdotal, often earthy verses on a particular subject culminating in a witty turn of phrase, for example the epigram *Of a man's head*: "Thy head is great, and yet seemth that head but thin: / Without hair without, and without wit within." Sometimes familiar, sometimes invented, they reflect Heywood's blending of the popular with the learned, as well as his connection to More and to Continental humanist epigrammatists.

Heywood's poetic oeuvre includes miscellaneous ballads, songs, and topical poems, and, notably, his long (over four hundred pages) political allegory *The Spider and the Fly*, published in 1556 but begun twenty years earlier. *The Spider and the Fly* seemingly alludes to a variety of events, figures, and conflicts: the Catholic peasant uprising of 1536 (the Pilgrimage of Grace); Robert Kett's peasant rebellion of 1549; the arbitrary legal practices of Cardinal Thomas Wolsey (1470/71–1530); the fall of Sir Thomas More; the anti-Catholic persecutions by Archbishop Cranmer; the class conflicts between nobility and peasantry over rents and enclosures of public grazing land; the 1553 execution of John Dudley, the Protestant duke of Northumberland; and the religious turmoil between Catholics and Protestants. Although significations are shifting and illusive, the spiders often stand for nobility and Protestants, the flies for peasants and Catholics, while the victorious maid clearly represents Queen Mary. Heywood intended the poem as his *magnum opus*, but the Elizabethan William Harrison delivered a more typical verdict: "neither he himself that made it, neither anyone that readeth it, can reach unto the meaning thereof." The poem may testify to an era when transparency of meaning could be dangerous and likewise to the difficulty of describing the fraught Tudor years allegorically.

EVALUATION

Although Heywood's reputation now rests on his drama, critics have sometimes argued that his plays had no successors. As Altman demonstrates, however, sixteenth-century humanist drama structures its action into a presentation of multiple sides of an issue, as do Heywood's plays. Heywood, moreover, introduced homely characters into English drama; he made original use of literary tradition; he introduced dramatic farce; and he created characters who bespeak a new theatrical mode of existence. Heywood may not have directly influenced later Elizabethan playwrights, but he richly expanded for those figures the possibilities of dramatic form and theatrical representation.

[*See also* John Bale.]

SELECTED WORKS

A mery play betwene the pardoner and the frere, the curate and neybour Pratte (1533)

The play of the wether A new and very mery enterlude of all maner wethers made by Iohn[n] Heywood (1533) The first work with Heywood's name on the title page.

A play of loue, A newe and a mery enterlude concernyng pleasure and payne in loue, made by Ihon[n] Heywood (1534)

The playe called the foure PP. A new and a very mery enterlude of A palmer. A pardoner. A potycary. A pedler. Made by Iohn Heewood (c. 1544)

A dialogue conteinyng the number in effect of all the prouerbes in the englishe tongue, compacte in a matter concernyng two maner of mariages, made and set foorth by Iohn[n] Heywood (1546)

An hundred epigrammes. Inuented and made by Iohn Heywood (1550)

A balad specifienge partly the maner, partly the matter, in the most excellent meetyng and lyke mariage betwene our Soueraigne Lord, and our Soueraigne Lady, the Kynges and Queenes highness. Pende by Iohn Heywod (c. 1554)

Two hundred epigrammes, vpon two hundred prouerbes, with a thyrde hundred newely added and made by Iohn Heywood (1555)

The spider and the flie. A parable . . ., *made by Iohn Heywood* (1556)

A breefe balet touching the traytorous takynge of Scarborow castell (1557)

A fourth hundred of epygrams, newly inuented and made by Iohn Heywood (1560)

A ballad against slander and detraction (1562)

Iohn Heywoodes woorkes (1562)

EDITIONS

Axton, Richard, and Peter Happé, eds. *The Plays of John Heywood.* Cambridge, U.K., 1991. The definitive scholarly edition of Heywood's dramatic works; rich in explanatory notes and source information, with something of a political and religious orientation.

Habenicht, Rudolph E., ed. *John Heywood's A Dialogue of Proverbs.* Berkeley, CA, 1963. The best scholarly edition of Heywood's *Dialogue*, with an introduction that locates Heywood's work with the traditions of proverb collections and dialogue debates.

Milligan, Burton A., ed. *John Heywood's Works and Miscellaneous Short Poems.* Urbana, IL, 1956. A critical edition of Heywood's 1562 *Works*, containing his *Dialogue of Proverbs*; his collections of epigrams; and his short poems, including ballads, songs, occasional poems.

Ward, A. W., ed. *The Spider and the Flie by John Heywood.* New York, 1967 [1894]. A reprint of Heywood's 1556 edition, with a critical introduction explaining its political context.

FURTHER READING

Altman, Joel B. *The Tudor Play of Mind: Rhetorical Inquiry and the Development of Elizabethan Drama.* Berkeley, CA, 1978. Sees Heywood's debate structure as representative of the interest by humanist dramatists in exploring multiple sides of an issue.

Bevington, David. *Tudor Drama and Politics: A Critical Approach to Topical Meaning.* Cambridge, MA, 1968, 64–74 and *passim*. An early and important analysis of the treatment of political issues in Heywood's farces.

Cartwright, Kent. *Theatre and Humanism: English Drama in the Sixteenth Century.* Cambridge, U.K., 1999. See pp. 25–48. Chapter on Heywood argues that his theatricality, as represented in *The Four PP*, illustrates a playful humanist interest in the enigmatic.

Holstun, James. "The Spider, the Fly, and the Commonwealth: Merrie John Heywood and Agrarian Class Struggle." *ELH* 71 (2004): 53–83. Argues that *The Spider and the Fly* shows sympathy for Kett's rebellion, criticizes monarchical absolutism, and reveals incipient sympathies for the idea of a commonwealth.

Johnson, Robert Carl. *John Heywood.* New York, 1970. The most recent comprehensive treatment in English of Heywood's times, life, and literary oeuvre, emphasizing Heywood as an important Tudor playwright (particularly for his use of farce) but also as a writer with limited influence on sixteenth-century drama.

Reed, Arthur William. *Early Tudor Drama: Medwall, the Rastells, Heywood, and the More Circle.* London, 1926. An early critical biography of the dramatists around Sir Thomas More, rich in information, and helpful in locating Heywood in his literary and political context.

Walker, Greg. *The Politics of Performance in Early Renaissance Drama.* Cambridge, U.K., 1998. See pp. 76–116. Argues that Heywood's writings express strongly felt dissent toward royal policy instituting the Reformation.

THOMAS HEYWOOD

Benedict S. Robinson

In 1633, in a letter to the readers of his play *The English Traveler*, Thomas Heywood (c. 1574–1641) paused to explain why no collected edition of his plays was available. "Many of them by shifting and change of Companies, have been negligently lost," he wrote, while "others of them are still retained in the hands of some Actors." To these plausible reasons he then added one that sounds a little disingenuous: "It never was any great ambition in me, to be in this kind Voluminously read." In fact, Heywood had tried to publish a volume of his plays the previous year; another letter to his readers promised to bring together a set of plays—the so-called Age plays—in "an handsome Volume," also to include an "Explanation of all the difficulties, and an Historical Comment of every hard name, which may appear obscure or intricate to such as are not frequent in Poetry."

Both the project and its failure reveal quite a bit about Heywood, his place in Tudor and Stuart theater, and his subsequent critical reputation. He was very much a professional of the stage, and he worked for theater companies that largely performed in outdoor amphitheaters, such as the Red Bull, which had the reputation of drawing a "citizen" crowd from London's middle classes. Heywood's letter of 1633 describes the fate of his scripts, circulating among various actors and theater companies, who may have tried, as he alleges, to resist their publication. Late in his life, Heywood claimed to have been an author of or collaborator on as many as 220 plays. Whether or not we take this claim at face value—if it is anywhere near true, we have lost the bulk of his work—it is indicative of a pattern of writing. Heywood was a professional actor, a playwright, and a shareholder in a theater company; this was his primary means of support and the primary forum for his writing, and for most of his career he showed little interest in publishing his plays. This choice of the stage over the page itself reveals a populist impulse: according to the theater historian Andrew Gurr, it is estimated that in 1620 nearly twenty-five thousand Londoners attended the theater each week. By comparison, a published book usually was legally limited to twelve hundred copies, and most publishers did not print that many, fearing they would not find buyers.

During Heywood's lifetime, however, English dramatists were increasingly trying to get their plays accepted as works of literature in the more elite forum of the printed book. In 1616 Ben Jonson issued a collection of works of which nearly half were plays performed on the London stage, and in 1623 Shakespeare's fellow actors put together a huge posthumous volume containing exclusively his plays. Heywood seems to have ignored this trend or to have attended to it only too late. Even when he did consider producing something like a collected works, albeit on a smaller scale, the book he imagined had a distinctly populist edge: it would have been a book for those "not frequent in Poetry," not one whose margins were peppered with references to classical literature, like Jonson's. During Heywood's lifetime, London's population was exploding and a new urban, civic culture was emerging, centered in large measure on London's artisans, shopkeepers, merchants, and apprentices. This was an urban middle-class culture of which the commercial theater was one of the most visible institutions. Heywood devoted himself to writing for this London, for people with time and money enough to attend the theater and to buy a few books, but not for leisured sophisticates or the country gentry, for whom London was increasingly a place to come for tasteful and elegant recreation in the social "season," but not a permanent home. Heywood self-consciously set out to write for what the period called the "middling sorts."

LIFE AND CAREER

Outside of Heywood's professional life, we know little about him. He was probably born around 1574 in Lincolnshire, but the relevant parish registers have been lost. His parents may have been the Robert and Elizabeth Heywood resident at either Rothwell or Ashby-cum-Fenby; Robert was rector of both village churches until his death. If this was his family, there were ten children younger than he, but Robert and Elizabeth seem to have been able to send Thomas to Emmanuel College, Cambridge, in 1591, although his academic career was probably cut short by his father's death two years later. By 1594 Heywood was in London seeking to earn a living as a writer. By the early seventeenth century he had settled in the suburb of Clerkenwell, where he stayed until his death on 16 August 1641. He may have married twice, to Anne Butler in June 1603 and to Jane Span in January 1633.

On arriving in London, Heywood clearly become involved with the theater almost immediately, and he remained so through most of his life, except for its last decade, when he may have retired from acting, and a mysterious period between about 1612 and 1622, when he seems to have done no work for the theater, perhaps as a result of the legal and financial troubles of his acting company at the time, the Queen's Men. We know something about his early professional life because by 1596 he was working with the theatrical entrepreneur Philip Henslowe, from whose detailed expense accounts we get a great deal of our information about the workings of the Elizabethan theater. Heywood started by revamping older plays for new runs and by collaborating on plays, perhaps including *Sir Thomas More* (c. 1592–1594), on which Shakespeare was another collaborator. He was clearly prolific: between September 1602 and March 1603, Henslowe's disbursements show that Heywood had a share in at least nine plays, for which he earned over £28. He seems to have parlayed a career in the theater into a fairly steady income, although he was probably never as successful as Shakespeare; Shakespeare retired from the theater to his "New House" in Stratford, but Heywood seems to have spent his last years working as a kind of journalist in London. Whatever we may think about their plays, Shakespeare was clearly the better entrepreneur.

Comparisons with Shakespeare have dogged Heywood. Charles Lamb called him a "prose Shakespeare," praising his generosity and his ability to render ordinary life vividly but claiming that he never produced real poetry; T. S. Eliot similarly wrote of him that his "sensibility is merely that of ordinary people in ordinary life," inadvertently singling out the very quality that would produce a critical revaluation of Heywood in the mid-twentieth century. Heywood was probably about ten years younger than Shakespeare, but their careers overlapped and they were always writing for rival companies. Heywood may be responsible for inaugurating the comparisons when he borrowed heavily from Shakespeare's brief erotic poem *Venus and Adonis* (1593) for his own poem *Oenone and Paris* (1594). In 1612, the two were again linked when William Jaggard published several hundred lines of poetry by Heywood under Shakespeare's name. Heywood pointed out the theft, self-deprecatingly writing that Shakespeare would resent having such work passed off as his. The modesty is typical of him, yet he had made a name for himself: as early as 1598, he appeared listed alongside Shakespeare among "the best for Comedy" in the English theater.

Heywood did not write exclusively for the theater. His *Troia Britannica* (1609) is a verse redaction of classical mythology and history, parts of which became the basis for his plays *The Golden Age*, *The Silver Age*, *The Brazen Age*, and *The Iron Age* (all c. 1609–1612). He also wrote *The Hierarchy of the Blessed Angels* (1635), which compiles popular stories about angels and witchcraft, and *Gunaikeion* (1624), a collection of stories about women intended as an entry into a controversy sparked in 1615 by a violently misogynist pamphlet by Joseph Swetnam. In the 1630s, Heywood increasingly wrote for the press, producing pamphlets on topics from piracy to drunkenness to the story of a recluse who went forty-four years without stepping outside. It was at this time that he tried to get his "Age" plays published, and he may also have worked as an agent for his longtime publishers, John and Nicholas Okes, procuring scripts like Christopher Marlowe's *The Jew of Malta*, which he edited in 1633, perhaps even writing new material for it. But his most famous nondramatic publication was still about the theater: *An Apology for Actors* (1612), a tract defending the theater from the charge of immorality leveled against it by Puritans and other staunch Protestants. For Heywood, the theater was an institution with a long and glorious history, capable of shaping the ethical consciousness of its audience: "so bewitching a thing is lively and well-spirited action," he wrote, "that it hath power to new-mold the hearts of the spectators."

THE PLAYS

As a playwright, Heywood tended toward pathos and sentimentality, often focusing on difficult reconciliations between couples after one has betrayed or abandoned the other. He generally avoided satire, bitter social commentary, and other kinds of invective, even though that kind of sharper comedy was at times in fashion during his lifetime, particularly among playwrights like Ben Jonson and Thomas Middleton, who in the new dramatic genre of "city comedy" mocked the culture and behavior of

London's citizen or middling classes. Heywood probably began by writing plays based on English history, such as *Edward IV, Parts 1 and 2* (c. 1599) and *If You Know Not Me You Know Nobody, Parts 1 and 2* (c. 1604–1605), the latter loosely dramatizing the life of Elizabeth I. He also had a penchant for adventure: in one of his earliest plays, *The Four Prentices of London* (c. 1599), the sons of a French aristocrat living in exile become apprentices in four London guilds and then travel to Jerusalem to become heroes of the First Crusade. In *The Fair Maid of the West, Parts 1 and 2* (c. 1600–1610 and 1631), a tavern girl named Bess captains a ship that sails from Plymouth to Morocco and Italy, searching for her fiancé Spenser, plundering Spanish ships, and narrowly escaping from the advances of a sultan and an Italian duke. In one plot of *Fortune by Land and Sea* (c. 1608–1609), a younger brother fights pirates after he is forced to flee England because he has killed the man who killed his older brother; for his victory over the pirates, he is pardoned and even earns his fortune, thereby also helping his sister, who has been forced into servitude by a father-in-law who disapproves of her family's poverty. Many of these plays engage issues of class or social status; the dramas of piracy and foreign travel also address questions of national identity and cross-cultural contact, vital issues at a moment when English cities were increasingly functioning as centers of an expanding global economy.

But it is for domestic drama that Heywood is most famous. Even *Edward IV* is largely a domestic story. Its major plot line concerns Edward's love for Jane Shore, the wife of a goldsmith who helps defend London from a rebel army at the start of the first play. Persuaded by Edward, Jane goes to the court as his mistress, and her husband leaves England for self-imposed exile. The second play takes up with Michael Shore's return to England, to end with the reconciliation and the deaths of both husband and wife. Problems of marriage, infidelity, and forgiveness absorbed Heywood's attention in some of his best plays, including undoubtedly the most famous one, *A Woman Killed with Kindness* (c. 1603). That play begins with the marriage of Anne Acton and John Frankford, and with the arrival at their house of Wendoll, a poor but handsome gentleman who becomes Frankford's close friend. But Wendoll falls in love with Anne and persuades her to love him, and the two are caught together by Frankford. The remainder of the play details the difficult process leading up to the reconciliation of Anne and John on her deathbed, a scene whose pathos is complicated by the knowledge of John's complicity in her death: he banished her from his sight, refused to acknowledge her as his wife or the mother of their children, and allowed her to starve herself out of grief and guilt. In Heywood's best work, our sympathies in the story of betrayal are never uncomplicated; what we witness is a push and pull between revenge and forgiveness in which reconciliation often comes too late.

A number of Heywood's plays offer detailed scenes of middle-class London life or celebrations of London culture; fittingly, between 1631 and 1639 he was seven times invited to write pageants for the inauguration of the Lord Mayor. City life is often as much a subject as a scene in his plays. The second part of *If You Know Not Me* shows the merchant Thomas Gresham founding the Royal Exchange, for which he is knighted by Elizabeth; a little less realistically, it also shows him drinking Elizabeth's health from a glass into which he has powdered a pearl worth £1,500, clearly a fantasy about merchant wealth easily won from London's new trades with Asia and Africa. The first scene of *The Wise-Woman of Hogsdon* (c. 1603) shows us four dissolute "young Gentlemen" from the country gambling in a London tavern, and the play takes its name from a suburb notorious for drinking and prostitution. London doubled in size between 1550 and 1650, growing into a complex cultural site inhabited by artisans, merchants, courtiers, and gentlemen, a place where migrants from the provinces—like Heywood—came to seek a living, and where anxieties about social mobility, overpopulation, disease, and crime found expression in new genres like the underworld pamphlets of the late sixteenth century or the dramas of city life popular in the early seventeenth. Much of Heywood's work clearly responds to London life, from its staging of London locations to the forms of social conflict it explores.

Heywood's reputation has been uneven, even in his own lifetime. *Four Prentices* was mercilessly parodied onstage as fit only for the tastes of ignorant citizens, in Francis Beaumont's *Knight of the Burning Pestle* (1607). In the mid-seventeenth century, the bookseller Francis Kirkman disparagingly remarked, "Many of his Plays being composed and written loosely in Taverns, occasions them to be so mean." Heywood's theatrical professionalism, his commitment to the always collaborative work of the theater, prevented him from easily entering the first rank of Tudor and Stuart dramatists, when the plays first produced for the commercial stage began instead to be published, collected, and canonized for a reading audience. Since the mid-twentieth century, however, with rising scholarly interest in popular culture, Heywood has earned increasing critical attention. Recent concern with nationalism, gender, and the city have also contributed to a revitalized study of his work, divested now of the patronizing tone of Eliot's appraisal of him as a writer of "ordinary life." Heywood has emerged as a distinctive and important voice in a conception of early modern theater and culture more diverse than that valued by Eliot's generation.

[See also William Shakespeare.]

SELECTED WORKS

Oenone and Paris (1594)

The Four Prentices of London (c. 1599)

Edward IV, Parts I and II (c. 1599)

The Fair Maid of the West, Part I (c. 1600–1610)

How a Man May Choose a Good Wife from a Bad (c. 1601–1602)

The Fair Maid of the Exchange (c. 1602–1605; authorship uncertain)

A Woman Killed with Kindness (c. 1603)

If You Know Not Me You Know Nobody, Part I (c. 1604)

The Wise Woman of Hogsdon (c. 1604)

If You Know Not Me You Know Nobody, Part II (c. 1605)

The Rape of Lucrece (c. 1607)

Troia Britannica (1609)

Fortune by Land and Sea (c. 1608–1609)

The Golden Age (c. 1609–1611)

The Silver Age (c. 1609–1611)

The Brazen Age (c. 1609–1611)

The Iron Age, Parts I and II (c. 1612)

The Captives (1624)

Gunaikeion (1624)

Dick of Devonshire (authorship uncertain) (1626)

The English Traveler (1627)

The Fair Maid of the West, Part II (1631)

A Maidenhead Well Lost (1632)

The Late Lancashire Witches (1634)

Love's Mistress, or The Queen's Masque (1634)

The Challenge for Beauty (1634)

The Hierarchy of the Blessed Angels (1635)

FURTHER READING

Brooks, Douglas A. *From Playhouse to Printing House: Drama and Authorship in Early Modern England.* Cambridge, U.K., 2000.

Christensen, Ann. "Business, Pleasure, and the Domestic Economy in Heywood's *A Woman Killed with Kindness.*" *Exemplaria* 9 (1997): 315–340.

Clark, Arthur M. *Thomas Heywood: Playwright and Miscellanist.* New York, 1958.

Eliot, T. S. *Selected Essays.* New York, 1932.

Gurr, Andrew. *The Shakespearean Stage, 1574–1642.* 3d ed. Cambridge, U.K., 1992.

Hammill, Graham. "Instituting Modern Time: Citizen Comedy and Heywood's *Wise Woman of Hogsdon.*" *Renaissance Drama* 29 (1998): 73–105.

Howard, Jean E. "An English Lass amid the Moors: Gender, Race, Sexuality, and National Identity in Heywood's *The Fair Maid of the West.*" In *Women, 'Race,' and Writing in the Early Modern Period*, edited by Margo Hendricks and Patricia Parker. New York, 1994.

Howard, Jean E. "Competing Ideologies of Commerce in Thomas Heywood's *If You Know Not Me You Know Nobody Part II.*" In *The Culture of Capital: Property, Cities, and Knowledge in Early Modern England*, edited by Henry S. Turner. New York, 2002.

Howard, Jean E. "Scripts and/versus Playhouses: Ideological Production and the Renaissance Public Stage." *Renaissance Drama* 20 (1989): 31–49.

Kamps, Ivo. *Historiography and Ideology in Stuart Drama.* Cambridge, U.K., 1996.

Lamb, Charles. *Specimens of English Dramatic Poets, Who Lived about the Time of Shakespeare.* 2 vols. London, 1808; repr. New York, 1970.

Leggatt, Alexander. *Citizen Comedy in the Age of Shakespeare.* Toronto, 1973.

Leinwand, Theodore B. *The City Staged: Jacobean Comedy, 1603–1613.* Madison, WI, 1986.

McLuskie, Kathleen E. *Dekker and Heywood: Professional Dramatists.* New York, 1993.

Robinson, Benedict S. "Thomas Heywood and the Cultural Politics of Play Collections." *Studies in English Literature* 42 (2002): 361–380.

Wall, Wendy. "Forgetting and Keeping: Jane Shore and the English Domestication of History." *Renaissance Drama* 27 (1996): 123–156.

Wright, Louis, B. *Middle-Class Culture in Elizabethan England.* Chapel Hill, NC, 1935; repr. New York, 1980.

GEOFFREY HILL

Vincent Sherry

Among British poets moving into prominence in the years after World War II, probably none has prompted claims of importance more exalted than has Geoffrey Hill (born 1932). "The finest British poet of our time," writes John Hollander; "the strongest British poet now alive," asserts Harold Bloom; "the best poet we have," goes *The Evening Standard*, while William Logan labels Hill's work as a whole "the major achievement of late-twentieth-century verse." These assertions occur, however, on the back covers of volumes that may not even appear on the shelves offering contemporary poetry in otherwise respectable bookstores. At once established and overlooked, invoked as the major voice and unheard as the recondite talent, Hill occupies an emblematic site, providing perhaps the most vivid instance of the conditions dividing critical acclaim from popular readership in current literary culture. Such tensions are hardly remarkable in the circumstances of postwar poetry, when literary modernism, or one strain of literary modernism, has established difficulty as the hallmark quality of the most significant work. Yet Hill lives this contradiction forward in ways especially relevant to the struggles of poetry in his own time.

Born in 1932, opening into sentience (by his own account) at the same moment that exposed the existence of the death camps in Europe, he seems to have been born to stand as witness, and challenge, to Theodor Adorno's claim that there could be no poetry after Auschwitz. Where modern atrocity seems to have given the final lie to the romantic notion that poetry can save us—reducing Percy Bysshe Shelley's claim that "poets are the unacknowledged legislators of the world" to the irony and pathos of its own impossibility—it is the special distinction of Hill's work to submit those ambitions of poetry to the worst that history has to offer and to maintain the high ground of Parnassus as vantage and advantage of his poetic calling. The result is a verse at once urgent and opaque, one that assumes the task of speaking truths that are equally necessary and difficult, essential yet secret, since what is already open to public view appears to have been compromised beforehand. This conceit leaves a body of writing that features a high degree of obvious posture in its accomplishment. If this quality leads at its worst to a sort of contorted, almost costive hermeticism, at its best it reclaims the loftiest responsibilities of poetry, and it does so in a language that bears the accent and validation of absolute modernity.

POETRY AFTER AUSCHWITZ

As an undergraduate at Oxford in the early 1950s, Hill was already striking a note recognizably his own. A vatic exaltation consorts and contrasts with an idiomatic concision, a sometimes deliberately roughed-up vernacular, which gives the tone of prophetic privilege the pressure, the handprint, of contemporary necessity. The title of Hill's first book, *For the Unfallen* (1959), locates its poems in the immediate postwar moment, and its initial sequence (written in 1952), fittingly titled "Genesis," introduces the character-in-voice that will carry this first collection. This speaker fits the fiction of biblical creation to his task of making poetry; he assumes the role of the deity, turning the word of God to the language of his own verse:

> And first I brought the sea to bear
> Upon the dead weight of the land;
> And the waves flourished at my prayer,
> The rivers spawned their sand.

The sequence concludes by setting out a mythos as well as a poetics for the speech of contemporary verse:

> By blood we live, the hot, the cold,
> To ravage and redeem the world;
> There is no bloodless myth will hold.
>
> And by Christ's blood are men made free,
> Though in close shrouds their bodies lie
> Under the rough pelt of the sea;
>
> Though Earth has rolled beneath her weight
> The bones that cannot bear the light.

Highly verbal, mythic, and ritualistic, Hill's invocation of the legends of blood and suffering draws its authority on one side from the ceremonies of moral warning in the prophetic books of the Old Testament but on the other, obliquely yet unmistakably, from the dire circumstance of current history—the aftermath of global cataclysm, the unearthed sepulchres of Auschwitz and Bergen-Belsen.

"For all that must be gone through, their long death / Documented and safe, we have enough / Witnesses (our world being witness-proof)," opens the second of his "Two Formal Elegies," where the dedicatory subtitle, *For the Jews in Europe*, identifies the difficult motive and problematic aim of these sonnets. How can poetry, in the role of the conventional elegy, provide explanation and consolation for the massive, staggering fact of genocide on the Continent? The poem gives the issue depth and specificity. While there is no shortage of official "witnesses" in the verbal culture of historical record, its sordid story is actually "witness-proof"—a "witness" usually offers "proof," but here the idiomatic sense of "witness-resistant" is obviously germane. Beyond the unspeakable horror of the event, the pun highlights the essential unreliability of language, the inadequacy of single word to integral fact. And adequacy itself is the problem: there is the indecency of the sufficient ritual, which "documents" the horrific "death" and so makes it "safe." This acknowledgment of the basic limitations and slipperiness of language and the devious appeasements of words locates the complex provocation for Hill's idiosyncratic prosody. His twisting syntax, go-and-stop rhythms, and often impacted vocabulary resist the ready translation of awful events into soothing formulas, formulaic solutions—as in the octave of this first sonnet:

> Knowing the dead, and how some are disposed:
> Subdued under rubble, water, in sand graves,
> In clenched cinders not yielding their abused
> Bodies and bonds to those whom war's chance saves
> Without the law: we grasp, roughly, the song.
> Arrogant acceptance from which song derives
> Is bedded with their blood, makes flourish young
> Roots in ashes.

The oddly angled cadences, the grammatical suspensions and puzzling ellipses respect the unspeakability of recent history. This "song," made "rough" in ways characteristic of the prosody of this first volume, provides an apology for contemporary poetry at its own ethical and aesthetic pitch.

Throughout this book and the next (*King Log*, 1968), Hill deepens his engagement with the problem of art's duty to represent modern atrocity. Two of his most justly famous pieces, "Ovid in the Third Reich" and "September Song," depict the role of the poet in the midst of history at its worst, in the belly of modern Leviathan. In the first, the speaker compounds his identity as Ovid, the poet banished from Rome for the offense he gave to a member of the family of Augustus, with the task of speaking out against the programs of Nazi Germany. This new Ovid sells out with the usual apologies, however, taking the spirit of W. H. Auden's claim that "poetry makes nothing happen" to excuse himself: "I love my work and my children. God / Is distant, difficult. Things happen." The condensed, bitter eloquence in this obviously ironic disclaimer speaks with the force of the author's own moral conviction, which, if overridden in the rhetorical fiction of this piece, underlies the extraordinary subtlety and complexity in the representation of "September Song."

Here the speaker's attempt to write an elegy for a Jewish child, who has been "deported" from Germany in 1942, uses the brutal euphemism in that word (in the subtitle) as a kind of ethical and aesthetic tuning fork. Hill is alerting us to the wrong note, to words' capacity to delude and appease, and he turns this caution through the poem. He transforms the conventional lyric moment (which the title promises) into a dramatic occasion, presenting a process in which the speaker struggles both with and against the conventional susceptibilities of language. "Undesirable you may have been, untouchable / you were not. Not forgotten / or passed over at the proper time." How inappropriate to recall the first Passover without capitalizing the reference, with just a casual loquacity (especially when the child has not been spared), and how "*im*proper," after all, to attach the correctness of a bureaucratic timetable to ethnic murder. Thus Hill displays the inertial drag of habitual idiom, which serves to standardize and normalize even this atrocity. The effort to particularize this death and to represent its exceptional outrage is an impetus Hill needs to speak against poetic convention itself, as evidenced in the poem's startling finale:

> September fattens on vines. Roses
> flake from the wall. The smoke
> of harmless fires drifts to my eyes.
>
> This is plenty. This is more than enough.

Deploying the imagery and motifs of the pastoral elegy, the speaker envisions death within the scheme of the annual seasonal cycle and so invokes an order in which life may be reborn. This promissory consolation is taken to the extremity of the final line, however, which exposes the poetic genre as a rudely self-serving, self-satisfying enterprise. And so in the end the poem emerges as a kind of inverted triumph, revealing the devious facility of routine speech and the inadequacy of any conventional measures to the unconventional event of this child's death.

POST-POSTWAR POETRY

More distant history frames the work of poetic imagination in Hill's next book, *Mercian Hymns* (1971), where the eighth-century Anglo-Saxon kingdom of Mercia, encompassing the West Midlands region of Hill's own childhood, is recovered as a site of poetic archaeology. This book-length sequence consists of thirty "versets," prose hymns or canticles, which recast the genre of the Anglo-Saxon psalter. Hill's sequence proceeds as a seriocomic ritual, a playful ceremony of identification between the poet, variously as child and adult, and the royal personage, the semilegendary King Offa.

> So much for the elves' wergild, the true governance
> of England, the gaunt warrior-gospel armoured in
> engraved stone. I wormed my way heavenward for
> ages amid barbaric ivy, scrollwork of fern.
>
> Exile or pilgrim set me once more upon that ground:
> my rich and desolate childhood. Dreamy, smug-faced,
> sick on outings—I who was taken to be a king of
> some kind, a prodigy, a maimed one.

The kingliness of childhood, the majesty of poetic imagination, and the childishness of king and poet alike are the conceits the sequence plays out in engaging combinations of humor, learning, and fantasy. A newly personal note, fictionalized as it may be through the legendary histories of Offa, adds a fresh dimension of interest to the sequence, which gained Hill a considerable increase in readership through the 1970s.

The publication in 1975 of *Somewhere Is Such a Kingdom: Poems 1952–1971* gathered Hill's first two decades of work, while Harold Bloom's introduction offered a strong and influential characterization of this poet, who was still in his early forties. For many readers the poems of this (long) early phase record Hill's signature achievement and contribution. Any major talent must reinvent itself in a process of renewal and transformation—as evidenced, say, in William Butler Yeats's attempts to contemporize his voice in the 1910s, or T. S. Eliot's turn to the more sustained, single voice of discursive and contemplative lyric after *The Waste Land*. In the work of subsequent years, Hill centers his energy and invention in his ongoing, deepening preoccupations with questions of religion and politics, not just as areas of human activity or subjects of impartial representation but as ideas to believe in or critique. From the tortured spirituality of the devotional sonnets in *Tenebrae* (1978) he moves to the brink of the spirit's garden in *The Orchards of Syon* (2002). From his homage to the cultural politics of *l'ancienne* France in *The Mystery of the Charity of Charles Péguy* (1983) he goes back to contemporary England in *Canaan* (1994), where the biblical topos of the fallen city provides reference and resonance for his chronicle of current political folly. This is an attitude and a character-in-voice that he elaborates through the classical rhetorical genre of *laus et vituperatio* (roughly, "praise and blame") in *The Triumph of Love* (1998) and *Speech! Speech!* (2000).

In the work of these subsequent decades, Hill has moved to a dominant and obvious position the set of concerns that had remained latent or recessive in his earlier work. Despite these continuities, the more recent poetry has generated a new intensity of both enmity and defense. The tremendous claims made for his achievement, overstated or not, seem to have been spurred by the hecklers. Granted, the inward life of Christian orthodoxy is not among the more popular topics in the contemporary literary world. And Hill's political perspective is informed by his deep and abiding sympathy with Tory radicalism, which represents an idealization of the rural economies in which he was raised. But this vision of agrarian hierarchy, a sort of medieval or vertical socialism, is hardly gaining strength among current partisans, even among (urban) Conservatives, who, in Hill's view, have nothing to conserve. The recent work is also characterized by a surprising (by Hill's standards) speed and volume in production, and in a now famous interview in the *Paris Review* he attributes his new fluency to the influence of spirituality, marital love, and antidepressants. Earlier, Hill might well have testified that there was a good deal in history to be depressed about, and depression, clinical or not, could be understood as the condition that provided those early poems their imaginative traction, their extraordinary gravitas. Extending but altering this condition, Hill's new work is most often satirical. If anger (to turn the Freudian adage around) is depression turned outward, this underlying emotional strain remains in place as the powerful coadjutor of his most characteristic poetic speech.

Hill is, perhaps, fundamentally an elegist. He is a poet of lost possibilities; his rhetorical occasions have developed from the story of the biblical Fall in Genesis to the plaints of the recent books, which record this falling away equally in spiritual and political spheres. "A heretic's dream of salvation, expressed in the images of an orthodoxy from which he is excommunicate," goes the formula that positions Hill's poetry of religion outside the temple. And Tory radicalism, committed to an order that is sensed as having passed always and already into history, is tinged with a similar aura of glories forgone. This sense of loss is not contrived for poetic effect, however; it is not merely topical, politically or religiously. It begins in the verbal fabric of his craft and art, in the memory of words themselves. "In handling the English language," he avers elsewhere, "the poet makes an act of recognition that etymology is history. The history of the creation and the debasement of words is a paradigm of the loss of the kingdom of innocence and original justice." A sensibility steeped so deeply in the presentiment of loss leans inevitably perhaps to the lost cause, or to the cause of loss itself. Given the immense validity of such feelings in an adult consciousness of modern history, Hill's elegies are as densely and richly expressive as any contemporary verse can be. As in "Dark-Land," from *Canaan*:

> Wherein Wesley stood
> up from his father's grave,
> summoned familiar dust
> for strange salvation:
>
> whereto England rous'd
> ignorant, her inane
> Midas-like hunger: smoke
> engrossed, cloud-cumbered,
>
> a spectral people
> raking among the ash;
> its freedom a lost haul
> of entailed riches.

[*See also* W. H. Auden; T. S. Eliot; Paul Muldoon; *and* William Butler Yeats.]

SELECTED WORKS

For the Unfallen: Poems 1952–1958 (1959)
King Log (1968)
Mercian Hymns (1971)
Somewhere Is Such a Kingdom: Poems 1952–1971 (1975)
Tenebrae (1978)
The Mystery of the Charity of Charles Peguy (1983)
The Lords of Limit: Essays on Literature and Ideas (1984)
The Enemy's Country: Words, Contexture, and Other Circumstances of Language (1991)
Canaan (1994)
New and Collected Poems: 1952–1992 (1994)
The Triumph of Love (1998)
Speech! Speech! (2000)
The Orchards of Syon (2002)
Style and Faith (2003)

FURTHER READING

Bloom, Harold, ed. *Geoffrey Hill*. New York, 1986. Essays by various hands on individual volumes and specific critical topics in Hill's poetry.

Hart, Henry. *The Poetry of Geoffrey Hill*. Carbondale, IL, 1986. A close reading of the first five books of Hill's poetry, developing the major themes.

Knottenbelt, E. M. *Passionate Intelligence: The Poetry of Geoffrey Hill*. Amsterdam, 1990. A close reading of the first five books of Hill's poetry, mainly in thematic paraphrase.

Robinson, Peter, ed. *Geoffrey Hill: Essays on His Work*. Milton Keynes, U.K., 1985. Essays by various hands on individual volumes and specific critical topics in Hill's poetry.

Sherry, Vincent. *The Uncommon Tongue: The Poetry and Criticism of Geoffrey Hill*. Ann Arbor, MI, 1987. A reading of Hill's critical prose and the first five books of poetry in the framework of British literary history after World War II.

THOMAS HOBBES

Stephen A. State

Thomas Hobbes (1588–1679) was born in Westport near Malmesbury, Wiltshire, the second son of a minor clergyman who died when Hobbes was a schoolboy. A relative supported his education at Magdalen Hall, Oxford, where he graduated in 1608. For most of his life he was employed as a tutor and secretary and supported by several generations of the Cavendish family. Hobbes would likely not have troubled himself about his place in British literature, but he would have been very concerned for his influences on three principal issues of his time: science, religion, and politics. He successfully achieved fame, or notoriety, in each.

Thomas Hobbes
Portrait by John Michael Wright,
c. 1669–1670
NATIONAL PORTRAIT GALLERY, LONDON

SCIENCE

In the domain of science and method, the period of Hobbes's lifespan witnessed a widespread assault on the Aristotelian world view. That scientific perspective, most commonly associated with a Ptolemaic, earth-centered universe of perfect spheres, was challenged by many Renaissance thinkers, including Copernicus and Galileo. The latter had been forced by the Catholic Church to recant his cosmological theories. Hobbes had met Galileo while escorting one of the young Cavendish sons on a grand European tour. Although he did not follow Galileo's empirical bent, he was greatly alarmed by the way in which the Church had sought to intervene in what he thought were properly matters of science and not of faith. A lifelong concern of Hobbes was to clarify the appropriate domain of each to the benefit of both.

The prevailing Aristotelian scientific perspective (Hobbes labeled it with the equally imprecise term "Scholastic") more generally involved teleological explanations of events in the world—that is, explanation in terms of ends or purposes. Thus, birds have wings for the purpose of flight; humans have speech and reason for the purpose of political life and moral discourse. For Hobbes this was patent nonsense, and the only thing that counted as an explanation was one framed in terms of matter in motion. He took the universe to be a corporeal "plenum," entirely filled with contiguous particles or "corpuscles." Even if we cannot experience them, we should assume that they are present and that they account for everything that happens.

Science for Hobbes did not involve experimentation and testing of hypotheses in a laboratory or in nature, in contrast to the direction taken by Francis Bacon and the scientists who founded the Royal Society. Interestingly, Hobbes was for a time the secretary of Bacon—although not much is known about their relationship. In any case, Hobbes was not impressed by this empiricism. There would always be too many variables, he thought, to make the testing of hypotheses anything more than prudential guesswork. The proper scientist would undertake only thought experiments and speculate as to how causes could, mechanistically, generate possible effects, or how effects might be generated by possible causes. The genuine scientist needed only to think and reflect.

A further signature element of Hobbes's method was the incorporation of arguments of deductive entailment, which he consciously imported from geometry. He proposed that we start our moral and political arguments from settled, proper definitions, in the way that geometers begin, say, with the proper definition of a circle. Since, for example, a circle can be constructed by rotating a straight line about a point, it necessarily follows that each radius is equal in length to every other. Only a very dull student, he said, would assert otherwise. If in politics—and, importantly, he took political communities to be artificial constructs that we make ourselves—we were to begin from the proper definitions of law and right and contract and justice and so forth, we should be able to reach conclusions that are self-evident and as certain as those of geometry.

RELIGION

One of the domains where Hobbes's thinking on science and method played out with enormous controversy was that of religion and theology. Most of his contemporaries, and many later critics as well, were reluctant to see his position here as an acceptable expression of the Reformation spirit of personal interpretation of revealed texts. The problem began with Hobbes's suspicious zeal for the new science of matter in motion. Christianity had developed a long and cozy relationship with the old Aristotelian world view, and a universe of corporeal mechanics was decidedly awkward for theologians.

Hobbes had no problem in believing in a God who is omnipotent, omnipresent, and ubiquitous, and who is revealed in the holy texts of the Judeo-Christian tradition. We cannot know God, Hobbes would happily affirm, along with every other theologian. But what should we say about this God in whom we believe but whom we cannot know? Does the word "spirit" that we read in the Bible necessarily require that this God operates in a non-corporeal manner? Well, we cannot know that, so why talk about something as manifestly absurd as incorporeal matter? Why not believe in a scientifically progressive material God, albeit an invisible one?

Christians had come to understand their rituals through the lenses of the old science. Transubstantiation, though much contested in its particular details, was most often understood as a nonmaterial, spiritual presence, a separated essence in the wafer and wine of consecration. For Hobbes, this bluster about separated essences was, again, nonsense. Why evoke absurdities in religious practice when we can construe these rituals in metaphorical ways and preserve our common sense and scientific understanding? Hobbes made few friends with these positions. Although most of his attacks were directed at the Catholic Church, he made it clear that he included the Church of England in his criticism.

Hobbes had debated these matters in the 1630s in a private exchange of letters with a noted Anglican theologian, John Bramhall, the onetime bishop of Derry. Bramhall put forward the Anglican position influenced by the Dutch theologian Arminius. One particular feature of that perspective concerns the issue of free will. The Arminians—the orthodox Anglicans—supported it;

Hobbes did not. In his view, if everything has a corporeal mechanical cause, then how can we exempt human behavior? Although this position was not unprecedented in Reformation thought—Martin Luther had defended it in a debate a century earlier with Erasmus—it was not popular in England. Bramhall complained that such a position would make humans "the tennis balls of destiny," and most of his British contemporaries agreed. Hobbes may not have been a real atheist, some said; even worse, he was an atheist-by-consequence. His heterodox theology was deemed more offensive than the complete denial of God.

Hobbes raised that most difficult of problems posed by an omnipotent deity believed to cause all things that happen: How can people justifiably be punished by a God who causes their immoral behavior in the first place? Either they are not responsible and should not be punished; or, if they are responsible and punishable, should we then deny that God actually does cause all things to happen, or should we wonder why he causes bad things to happen to good people? Hobbes found his answer in the book of Job, which was also the source of the title for his greatest work, *Leviathan*: we were not around when the universe was created, and we simply do not understand everything that God does.

POLITICS

In the political and military struggles that came to be called the English Civil Wars, Hobbes was firmly on the side of monarchy, but not for reasons that most monarchists would likely accept. The arguments laying out his position took their finished form in *Leviathan* (1651), although versions can be found in earlier works, including *De Corpore Politico* (On the Body Politic, 1640) and *De Cive* (On the Citizen, 1642). The date of publication of his masterpiece is significant; the book appeared during the politically and religiously ambiguous days after the execution of Charles I and before the consolidation of the Protectorate, when there was no settled political authority and no orthodox church. Hobbes could expound at length on both politics and religion without worrying about the contradiction involved in arguing that both were matters of authoritative stipulation by the sovereign.

The conflicts that led to civil war and regicide were very much conflicts over the nature and scope of political authority. Contemporary arguments in this matter were varied. Some held that political authority was a matter of constitutional precedent and the courts should decide;

others, like Robert Filmer, held that political authority was a matter of divine grant and that religious faith should prevail; still others claimed that it rested on principles of natural law and that reason should decide. Hobbes would undercut and annoy all of these factions.

His argument begins with some key assumptions. First of all, humans will always act so as to advance what they desire (their personal sense of felicity) and to avoid what they fear, which is principally their own death and destruction. He explicitly denies that people are naturally evil, but in a situation where there is no formal polity with the rule of law and effective policing, things will not go well.

In such a hypothetical situation the natural condition of humankind would be, as he famously remarked, "solitary, poor, nasty, brutish, and short." Although most people are content to get by with what they need, there are those who will take in excess and still others who simply enjoy the fighting that a state of war occasions. For that reason, sensible people will, in order to preserve their own lives and the lives of their families, undertake the sort of actions that in other situations would be deemed immoral: preemptive attacks, disregarding some categories of contracts entered into with others, or hoarding.

Hobbes contended that the properly understood right of nature which people have in these circumstances allows extraordinary measures in the interest of self-preservation or conservation. It is not a right to anything, but it is a right to anything which is in good faith (*in foro interno*, "in the court of conscience") deemed required for preservation. I would have no right to kill my neighbor in order to enjoy gratuitous violence; I would be justified in killing him if I believed him to constitute a threat.

The situation is a case of both freedom and its opposite. It is free because we all have the right to choose what instruments will advance our felicity; it is not free in the sense that the condition produced by this apparent freedom universally pursued in fact limits everyone. The chaos and uncertainty—much like the civil war, which turned son against father and brother against brother—does not permit successful living. The state of nature is a state of war. Moral principles are present, but too often overridden by legitimate concern for staying alive. Promises of mutual trust, where we rely on others and they on us for something to be done in the future, are never obligatory in the state of nature. The situation is too unpredictable for people to foresee their needs down the road. Other kinds of contracts, however, are obligatory.

In general, the understanding of moral principle that Hobbes advanced is one in which a moral good is an instrumental good, a good which advances the preservation of human life from the individual perspective. Without reflection from a moral point of view, good and evil are simply the labels attached to things we like or fear. Hobbes's point is that reason suggests some very general principles which, if followed, will advance almost everyone's version of felicity. The effect of this is to turn moral obligation into prudential obligation, and to understand the Laws of Nature as if they were rational theorems conducive to survival. (More than one commentator has pointed out that they become like doctors' orders of a particularly compelling kind.) Hobbes said as much in *Leviathan* but adds that the prudential rationality involved, when believed to be commanded by God in revelation, makes these prudential theorems into divinely obligatory laws. Subsequent liberal moralists have largely dropped the theological dimensions of this mode of argument, but the implication that we ought to be free to live our own lives as long as we leave others to do the same thing has had a long run. Morality for Hobbes was less about the detailed picture of the good life—the *summum bonum*—and more about the rules and procedures that allow people to paint their own pictures of the good life.

These moral, rational, religious obligations—which Hobbes called "the Laws of Nature"—suggest a set of principles which will advance human life; they turn out to be the unsurprising principles of justice, equity, mercy, and sociability. In political terms, what is needed is a permanent solution to the uncertainty and violence that characterize the state of nature. The solution is the creation through contract of a sovereign and, by virtue of that office, the creation as well of a political community. It is preferable but not essential that the sovereign be a single person; it is essential that the office contain all the powers needed to sustain it from forces that might compromise the freedoms that sovereignty makes possible.

It is here that Hobbes's very liberal concern for human freedom has faced most of its criticism. *Leviathan* is by no means a democratic tract. Hobbes contended that popular criticism of the late Stuart regime had been a significant driver of the violence and bloodshed of the civil wars: too much pride, and too little deference. People did not realize, he argued in *Behemoth* (1679), that the creation of civil society must entail that authority over all matters sacred and secular becomes the sole right of the sovereign. Authority is not to be divided or shared if there is to be a successful polity; human freedom can, paradoxically, have political success only in authoritarian regimes. Leviathan will be the king of the proud and so prevent human presumption from undermining civil life.

The argument in effect reverses all of the limitations on sovereignty that had been added incrementally in England since the Magna Carta, and which many hoped to extend in making a recalcitrant king accountable to reason, law, and legislature. Even most supporters of monarchy did not reject the existing constitutional limitations on executive power; rather, they denied that the limits had been breached. *Leviathan*'s sovereign would give no independent standing to a legislature to question what the sovereign proposed as law. As well, no court would have the right to interpret, against the sovereign, what the law meant. Law would be the command of the sovereign. Nor would there be any independent religious authority to question the sovereign in matters of doctrine or ritual. In the interests of peace and on the basis of his reading of scripture, the sovereign would be deemed God's lieutenant.

If Hobbes had moved to disengage religion from science, with regard to politics and religion his goal was to merge the two. He thought it acceptable to honor private beliefs and wrote with disdain about the fires of Smithfield, where people were burned at the stake after being tortured into admitting they believed the wrong things. In the interests of civil peace, however, he thought we should always limit public speech to what was officially allowed. His strategy lost out to the practice of religious toleration championed by John Locke. The close merging of church and state was not unprecedented in that early period of English Reformation, but it was decidedly unpopular both among clerics in the Church of England if the sovereign dominated clerical authority, and among minority religious sects, who put no trust in political power and preferred to say what they believed without hypocrisy. As time went on, Hobbes's position became overshadowed in the West by the principle of the separation of church and state.

The concentration of powers in the authority of the sovereign, Hobbes argues, comes about in the way that the office is created. Right holders in the natural state come to mutual agreement to set up such a sovereign and to obey him. They do not make a contract with the sovereign directly; the sovereign is rather the third-party beneficiary of contracts made by others. Hobbes made much of this imagined detail, which turns importantly on his understanding of justice.

Justice, Hobbes would say, is properly understood as the result of a valid contract. Whatever terms the contractors happen to agree to are what constitutes justice. There is not some other natural notion of justice to compare to what contractors decide. Whereas medieval jurists would invoke, for example, a notion of a just remuneration for a fair day's work, Hobbes would say that whatever employer and employee agreed to was just. Even where contracts are entered into because of fear or where the distribution of power among contractors is lopsided, Hobbes would say justice has been done and all contracting parties are obliged to comply with the terms of their agreement. Thus, he felt vindicated in claiming that the sovereign can commit no injustice because he did not enter into a contract. How can he be called unjust if there was no agreement to break? And his subjects are bound by their mutual agreement to accept his word, his power, and his law without complaint.

Both natural law discourse and social contract discourse—as well as the constitutional principles invoked against the Stuarts—had hitherto produced a check on the exercise of government and more than a dash of revolutionary potential. If a ruler disobeyed the laws of nature, should he perhaps be removed? If a ruler broke the contract under which he came to power, then should he perhaps be replaced with one more respectful of the agreements on which the exercise of power rest? A generation later, the Glorious Revolution would demonstrate the popularity of political accountability. Hobbes undercut both of these arguments and transformed revolutionary potential into a conservative defense of the status quo.

Why this stunningly unaccountable understanding of sovereignty? Hobbes's only rejoinder was to say that the state of war likely to result without such concentration of powers is more to be feared than a bad ruler. Now, of course, if the sovereign were rational and concerned about his own survival, he too would do a good job, make good laws, look to the welfare of the population, and so forth. The rashness of delinquent princes, after all, was apt to cause rebellion even if rebellion was never justified. Nevertheless, *Leviathan*—and to some extent its author as well—has always attracted more criticism than conviction.

[*See also* Francis Bacon.]

SELECTED WORKS

Dates follow, for the most part, J. C. A. Gaskin's notes and introduction to the Oxford World Classics edition of *Leviathan* (1996).

Translation of Thucydides, *History of the Peloponnesian War* (1629)

Elements of Law, Natural and Politic (1640; containing *Human Nature* and *De Corpore Politico*, each published separately in 1650)

De Cive (1642; English translation published in 1651)

Leviathan (1651)

Of Liberty and Necessity (1654; unauthorized publication of private correspondence with Bishop John Bramhall by the latter)

De Corpore (1655; English translation, *Of Body*, published 1656)

Questions Concerning Liberty, Necessity and Chance (1656; further, authorized debate with Bramhall)

De Homine (1658)

A Dialogue between a Philosopher and a Student of the Common Laws of England (written 1666; not published until 1681)

Behemoth (written 1668; not published until 1679; authorized version published 1682)

An Answer to Bishop Bramhall (written 1668; published 1682)

A True Ecclesiastical History, from Moses to the Time of Martin Luther, in Verse (written 1670; published 1688 in Latin and 1722 in English)

Translation of Homer, *Odyssey* (1673)

Translation of Homer, *Iliad* (1676)

FURTHER READING

Brandt, Frithiof. *Thomas Hobbes' Mechanical Conception of Nature.* Translated by Vaughan Maxwell and Anne Fausbøll. London, 1928. Still the best account of Hobbes's scientific arguments.

Gauthier, David. *The Logic of Leviathan.* Oxford, 1969. A lucidly analytical treatment, especially of Hobbes's notion of right.

King, Preston, ed. *Thomas Hobbes: Critical Assessments.* 4 vols. London, 1993. An excellent collection of essays.

Macdonald, Hugh, and Mary Hargreaves. *Thomas Hobbes: A Bibliography.* New York, 1952. Itemizes the publishing history of Hobbes's works during his lifetime.

Martinich, A. P. *The Two Gods of Leviathan: Thomas Hobbes on Religion and Politics.* Cambridge, U.K., 1992. Excellent account of Hobbes's religious views.

McNeilly, F. S. *The Anatomy of Leviathan.* London, 1968. A useful overview.

Mintz, Samuel I. *The Hunting of Leviathan.* Cambridge, U.K., 1962. Examines some contemporary reactions to Hobbes.

Peters, R. S. *Hobbes.* Harmondsworth, U.K., 1967; reprinted Westport, CT, 1979. Good overview.

Spragens, Thomas A., Jr. *The Politics of Motion: The World of Thomas Hobbes.* Lexington, KY, 1973. Engaging comparison with Aristotle on the linkage of science and theorizing generally.

Strauss, Leo. *The Political Philosophy of Hobbes.* Chicago, 1952.

Warrender, Howard. *The Political Philosophy of Hobbes: His Theory of Obligation.* Oxford, 1957. Places Hobbes in the tradition of natural law theorizing.

Watkins, John W. N. *Hobbes's System of Ideas: A Study in the Political Significance of Philosophical Theories.* London, 1965; repr. Aldershot, U.K., 1989. A brief and elegant treatment of science and ethics in Hobbes's work.

THOMAS HOCCLEVE

John M. Bowers

When Geoffrey Chaucer died in 1400, Thomas Hoccleve (c. 1367–c. 1426) was middle-aged but had not yet written any of his major poems. Hoccleve (sometimes spelled Occleve) became in 1387 a clerk of the Privy Seal, the Westminster writing office responsible for royal warrants and instructions to government officials, and thus began moving in the same literate circles of courtiers and civil servants who formed Chaucer's first audience. Hoccleve's later writings implied a personal connection with the great author, even a teacher–student relationship:

> My deer maistir, God his soule qwyte,
> And fadir, Chaucer, fayn wolde han me taght,
> But I was dul and lerned lyte or naght.
>
> (ll. 2077–2079)

After Chaucer's death, Hoccleve quickly moved to fill the opening in the literary scene. In furtherance of this ambition, he became the first to celebrate Chaucer as the father of English poetry, he claimed his position as the poet's rightful heir, and in general he originated the entire notion of the English literary tradition as a genealogy descending from Chaucer as the founding father.

We know more about Hoccleve than about any other English writer of the period. First, more than sixty documents trace his career as a clerk at an official government writing office. Second, he wrote extensively about his London life and provided far more autobiographical detail than had any of his predecessors, even Chaucer himself. Hoccleve also left three autograph manuscripts of his poetry, written entirely in his own hand, as concrete evidence of his language, his exact metrical practices, and his connections with aristocratic patrons as well as fellow professionals in the growing London book trade.

Dated 1402, Hoccleve's first major poem, *The Letter of Cupid*, is a free adaptation of a work by the French poet Christine de Pisan, who had recently turned down an invitation from Henry IV to join the English court. Clearly Hoccleve was making his move, catering to the literary tastes of the new Lancastrian monarch. Although notoriety as a poet won attention in the right quarters, Hoccleve never operated as a "court poet" steadily supported by patronage from king, prince, or duke.

The poet's own annotations in his autograph manuscripts help to date other poems. Around 1405, his *Male Regle* (Bad Lifestyle) described an ill-regulated period of drinking and dicing, flirting with tavern wenches, and squandering money on boat-taxis. The more he fretted about his financial situation, the sicker he felt. Government bureaucrats had trouble collecting their pay during this period, and Hoccleve was never shy about sending petitionary poems to various officials at the Exchequer.

Other poems were tied to royal occasions. The poet's handwritten notes state (in French) that one lyric was written "to King Henry V when the lords of the realm did their homage to him" (1413), another "when the bones of Richard II were transported to Westminster" (1414). His fiercely orthodox poem *To Sir John Oldcastle* followed in the wake of the Lollard uprising of 1414. Supporting the Lancastrians meant opposing anyone who stood in the way of their grand nationalist ambitions.

In the midst of these social upheavals, the year 1414 was terrible for Hoccleve personally. He suffered some severe medical crisis, which he described in his later *Complaint* as a form of mental illness; he took nearly a year to recover, and even longer to convince colleagues and friends that he was no longer insane. The shadow of this psychological catastrophe darkened the rest of his career, coming as it did after his greatest literary success with *The Regiment of Princes*.

THE REGIMENT OF PRINCES

Hoccleve completed the *Regiment* in 1411. It survives in forty-three copies, six of them high-quality manuscripts with expensive illuminations. Composed in the rhyme-royal stanzas perfected by Chaucer in *Troilus and Criseyde*, the 5,463-line masterpiece forms a peculiar literary diptych. The lengthy Prologue is autobiographical, describing how Hoccleve, upset as usual about his financial problems, encounters an Old Man who preaches the virtues of poverty and the fickleness of Fortune. The narrator proceeds to confess the disarray of his personal and professional life, also lodging sharp comments on the abuses of the age—simony, heresy, child marriage, and the government's neglect of old soldiers. Toward the end of this moralizing dialogue, covering subjects as diverse as the quality of one's wardrobe and the advisability of marriage, the Old Man recommends that the poet appeal for financial assistance directly to Prince Henry. This suggestion leads to the second and longer part of the *Regiment*.

The "mirror of princes" was a piecemeal genre that gathered a large number of worthy topics for the convenience of the royal reader, who could select whatever he liked in the encyclopedic contents, passing over whatever he found useless or annoying. The general drift was that princes should avoid vice and follow virtue. Gower had used the *Secretum secretorum*, an apocryphal letter from Aristotle to his pupil Alexander the Great, extensively in his voluminous English story collection *Confessio amantis* (*The Lover's Confession*), first dedicated to Richard II and then rededicated to the earl of Derby, the future Henry IV. Hoccleve may have been encouraged by the success of Gower's work as well as that of his acknowledged source, Giles of Rome's popular *De regimine principum*. Working out of these well-established practices, Hoccleve offered a wide range of pious and practical suggestions, peppered throughout with exemplary stories, for achieving well-regulated royal governance.

Toward the end of the *Regiment*, Hoccleve included several stanzas commending Chaucer as his artistic father-figure and the originator of the English literary style:

> The firste fyndere of our fair langage
> Hath seid, in cas semblable, and othir mo,
> So hyly wel that it is my dotage
> For to expresse or touche any of tho.
> Allas, my fadir from the world is go,
> My worthy maistir Chaucer—him I meene;
> Be thow advocat for him, hevenes queene.

(ll. 4978–4984)

Addressed as a prayer to the Virgin, this almost hagiographic passage provided the occasion for inserting, in the British Library's manuscript Harley 4866, the famous portrait of Chaucer that closely resembles the poet's likeness in the Ellesmere Manuscript of the *Canterbury Tales*. Thus Hoccleve helped to create a visual representation of the founding author as a counterpart to the name recognition fostered throughout his writings. The *Regiment* also suggests two parallel dynasties originating in the late fourteenth century: the Lancastrian dynasty descending from John of Gaunt to his grandson Prince Henry, and the literary dynasty descending from Chaucer to Hoccleve himself.

Although the work has proved most fascinating for its autobiographical contents, several passages allude to national events to make larger political points. For example, the account of the 1410 burning of the heretic John Badby, attended by the Prince of Wales, seems calculated to banish suspicion that Henry of Monmouth, the future Henry V, neglected the threat of the Lollards. Scholars now suspect that Hoccleve's enterprise was a put-up job encouraged by Henry of Monmouth's followers in order to flatter the prince as the promoter of good governance. Or perhaps Henry himself commissioned the work, on the quiet, in order to bolster his image as a prince willing to heed sage counsel—playing the English Alexander to Hoccleve's touchy, moralizing Aristotle.

THE *SERIES* AND HOCCLEVE'S FINAL YEARS

Critical opinion has split on the work dubbed the *Series*. Derek Pearsall dismissed it as an attempt to make a longish poem out of nothing, while John Burrow has praised the linked collection as Hoccleve's *Canterbury Tales* in miniature. The sequence begins with his *Complaint*, in which the poet describes regaining his sanity and literary competence after a period of mental illness. These personal disclosures owe less to Chaucer's ironic self-deprecations and more to the brutal, unnerving honesty of the Pardoner and the Wife of Bath.

Next comes the *Dialogue with a Friend*, in which the invalid gets a visit from a concerned acquaintance. The conversation has a jolly verve as the Friend cajoles the poet back into a more optimistic mood, and Hoccleve rises to the occasion, joking back with his visitor about his next writing projects. He thinks that he might translate a military treatise for Humphrey, duke of Gloucester, while the Friend recommends cultivating female readers who, like Chaucer's Wife of Bath, want to hear no slanders about themselves. There follow two moralistic translations favorable to women—the *Tale of Jerelaus's Wife* and the *Tale of Jonathas*—and then the verse treatise *Lerne to Dye*, in the sobering medieval tradition of the *ars moriendi* or "art of dying."

Hoccleve is often reckoned to be one of the professional textwriters who were recruited to sort through Chaucer's literary papers in order to produce the first circulated copies of the *Canterbury Tales*. As a trained scribe, he was also able to produce "definitive editions" of his own works during the last years of his life. Already he was worrying about posterity. The poet's own handwritten copy of the *Series* closes with a stanza dedicating the work to the countess of Westmoreland, who was both Chaucer's niece and Henry V's aunt. Such a patroness attests to the intersection of literary and political worlds in Lancastrian England. Two other autograph manuscripts, now at the Huntington Library in California, gather shorter poems such as Hoccleve's *Marian Hymns*, many of which are reckoned early works inspired by Chaucer's *ABC to the Virgin*. The author's headnotes indicate the original occasions and well-placed recipients, who included the Prince of Wales, the dukes of York, Bedford, and Gloucester, and the earl of Arundel.

Hoccleve was right to worry about his literary fortunes. By the time he died in 1426, his reputation as a poet was already in decline. Perhaps his confessions of mental instability disqualified him as a respectable author, or perhaps he had tied his career too closely to Henry V, whose early death in 1422 disrupted the literary as well as the political scene in England. Or perhaps, despite his claims as Chaucer's student, Hoccleve's writings were not really "Chaucerian" enough. He failed in exactly the areas where Chaucer succeeded most brilliantly. He was not a good storyteller, and he was not funny. His *Regiment* is a sprawling medley of autobiography, complaint, social satire, and moral reflection, stamped by a quirky poetic personality, that aligns itself more readily with Langland's *Piers Plowman*, another London work that steadily lost favor among elite readers. The rate of scribal productions of the *Regiment* fell off during the course of the fifteenth century. William Caxton, the first English printer, did not select the work for commercial printing. The Renaissance took no notice. There was no complete edition of the *Regiment* until 1860. The Early English Text Society brought all of Hoccleve's poetry into print at the end of the nineteenth century, but largely as a service to the *Oxford English Dictionary*.

Modern readers were first drawn to the highly personal content of his poetry, which made Hoccleve a prime witness to English life in the first decades of the fifteenth century. He was a confirmed Londoner, living mostly at Chester Inn in the western suburb and spending his entire professional life in neighboring Westminster. He provided a more lively, nitty-gritty view of the capital than did any other medieval poet, including his fellow Londoner Chaucer. The unnerving directness of his autobiographical disclosures earned him both respect and sympathy. He told how he was embarrassed about the need for reading glasses later in life, for example, and after his mental breakdown, he would stand in front of the mirror arranging his facial expression so that nobody in the street would suspect he was insane. Always a quill-pushing bureaucrat, Hoccleve never enjoyed the windfall of ecclesiastical preferment, eventually stooping to a marriage that he viewed as a sign of professional failure. C. S. Lewis paid tribute to Hoccleve as the first poet to explore "worry" as his predominant state of mind.

As a final reversal of fortune, Hoccleve has now become one of the most written-about poets of the medieval period. His explorations of unsettled states of mind and emotion are as self-referential as any postmodernist might wish. Moreover, his involvement in the meteoric career of his royal patron, Henry V, has made him a darling of the New Historicists. But perhaps his most enduring contribution to the English literary tradition was his innovative campaign to create this tradition itself, as a family tree that descended from Chaucer as the "father of English poetry."

[*See also* Geoffrey Chaucer *and* Middle English.]

EDITIONS

Blyth Charles R., ed. *The Regiment of Princes*. Kalamazoo, MI, 1999.

Burrow J. A., ed. *Thomas Hoccleve's Complaint and Dialogue*. Early English Text Society, original series 313. London, 1999.

Furnivall, Frederick J. and I. Gollancz, eds., revised by Jerome Mitchell and A. I. Doyle. *Hoccleve's Works: The Minor Poems*. Early English Text Society, extra series 61 and 73. London, 1892 and 1925; rev. ed., 1970.

Furnivall, Frederick J., ed. *Hoccleve's Works: The Regement of Princes*. Early English Text Society, extra series 72. London, 1897.

FURTHER READING

Bowers, John M. "*Thomas Hoccleve and the Politics of Tradition.*" *Chaucer Review* 36 (2002): 352–369.

Burrow, J. A. *Thomas Hoccleve*. Authors of the Middle Ages, vol. 1, no. 4. Aldershot, U.K., 1994.

Knapp, Ethan. *The Bureaucratic Muse: Thomas Hoccleve and the Literature of Late Medieval England.* University Park, PA, 2001.

Mitchell, Jerome. *Thomas Hoccleve: A Study in Early Fifteenth-Century English Poetic.* Urbana, IL, 1968.

Patterson, Lee. " 'What Is Me?': Self and Society in the Poetry of Thomas Hoccleve." *Studies in the Age of Chaucer* 23 (2001): 437–470.

Pearsall, Derek. "Hoccleve's *Regiment of Princes: The Poetics of Royal Self-Representation.*" *Speculum* 69 (1994): 386–410.

Perkins, Nicholas. *Hoccleve's "Regiment of Princes": Counsel and Constraint.* Cambridge, U.K., 2001.

Scanlon, Larry. "The King's Two Voices: Narrative and Power in Hoccleve's *Regement of Princes.*" In *Literary Practice and Social Change in Britain, 1380–1530,* edited by Lee Patterson, 216–247. Berkeley, CA, 1990.

Strohm, Paul. "Hoccleve, Lydgate and the Lancastrian Court." In *The Cambridge History of Medieval Literature,* edited by David Wallace, 649–661. Cambridge, U.K., 1999.

JAMES HOGG

Penny Fielding

James Hogg (1770–1835) was the son of a small-scale sheep farmer in Ettrick, a valley in the southeastern Scottish Border country. Although born into a laboring class, Hogg would normally have expected to attend a parish school, receiving a basic education in literacy. Because of the failure of his father's farm, however, he had only a few months of formal schooling and spent his early years herding sheep and cattle. Yet despite a popular image of him as an unlettered peasant poet, Hogg was very much in touch with intellectual currents of his day. As an adult, he educated himself through independent reading—from newspapers to works of theology—and by attending meetings of literary societies organized among

James Hogg
Watercolor by Charles Fox, 1830
NATIONAL PORTRAIT GALLERY, LONDON

shepherd communities. In 1810 Hogg moved to Edinburgh, and the following year he joined a public debating society, the Forum, which met to address philosophical propositions relating to current affairs and which introduced Hogg to men in the professional worlds of the law, the church, and medicine.

Hogg was known throughout his publishing life as the "Ettrick Shepherd," and his career reveals the various resonances of the term. He was associated with an eighteenth-century tradition of laboring-class poets (such as Robert Burns, "the Ayrshire Ploughman") and seen by an increasingly urban readership as part curiosity, part primitive genius. In some ways Hogg collaborated in this picture of himself and saw the fashion for popular and vernacular forms as a way of advancing his literary career. He describes his earliest ventures into writing as the composition of songs with which the local girls might amuse themselves. He assisted and learned from Walter Scott in the compilation of Scott's collection of Scottish ballads, *Minstrelsy of the Scottish Border*—many of them transcribed from recitals by Hogg's own neighbors and

family—which brought Scott fame and profit in 1802. With Scott's encouragement and assistance, Hogg's own volume of ballad imitations, *The Mountain Bard*, followed in 1807, and his collection of traditional songs suitable for drawing-room performance, *The Forest Minstrel*, in 1810. "The Ettrick Shepherd," a useful brand name for him, appeared on the title page of many of his works, sometimes without the additional "James Hogg." But Hogg was also a professional shepherd who published (more profitably than his farming ventures) *The Shepherd's Guide: Being a Practical Treatise on the Diseases of Sheep* (1807) on husbandry and veterinary practices. Even while they use an ironic pastoral idiom, his tales insist that they are about real shepherds and other country workers, and that they are generated from within the local communities they describe. They resist the popular sentimentalizing of the rural poor that was common elsewhere in the literature of the period. These forms of social realism were not always appreciated by Hogg's fellow authors, reviewers, and journal editors who ran the Edinburgh cultural scene. Frequently punning on Hogg's surname (which can mean either "pig" or "young sheep"), they portrayed him as uncouth and lacking in good taste. Even the hugely influential figure of Scott, who remained on affectionate terms with Hogg throughout their careers, blended his genuine admiration for Hogg's powerful writing with a sense of his friend's humble origins.

Hogg's career was inextricably entwined with the media of the early nineteenth century, both as an editor and contributor of poems and stories to magazines and newspapers, and as a literary figure represented in them. In his own short-lived periodical *The Spy* (1810–1811), Hogg assumes the editorial role of "Mr. Spy," a deceptively self-deprecating fellow who satirically observes the foibles of literary Edinburgh. "The Shepherd" was a frequent character in the "Noctes Ambrosianae," a series of fictional conversations between many of the luminaries of literary Edinburgh and the wider cultural world (versions of Lord Byron and Thomas De Quincey put in appearances), which were published in the monthly *Blackwood's Edinburgh Magazine* between 1822 and 1835. Combative and garrulous, "the Shepherd" combines deference to the gentlemen around him with a refusal to be intimidated by their superior education. Hogg was very conscious of literary celebrity and allegorized his own perceived status in his most financially successful work, *The Queen's Wake* (1813). This long poem describes a poetic contest performed before Mary, Queen of Scots. The winner is the most showy of the competitors, but the second-placed bard, who produces simpler and more heartfelt songs, is awarded the more musical harp. Hogg makes clear his feelings that his own poetry, based on the songs and ballads from the Scottish Borders, did not receive the acclaim of more ostentatious authors, but his apparent celebration of artlessness is more than it seems. Hogg was an extremely crafty and complex performer whose grasp of different poetic idioms was put to good effect in his collection of parodies of big-name poets such as William Wordsworth, Scott, and Byron, *The Poetic Mirror* (1816). Nor did he have any problem mastering complicated poetic forms for nonparodic purposes: *Mador of the Moor* (1816) is written in the difficult Spenserian stanza form.

NOVELS AND TALES

Although Hogg was writing while the novel was taking a consolidating overview of history and the nation, he rarely tried to emulate Scott's success with the genre. Only *The Brownie of Bodsbeck* (1818), covering ground similar to that in Scott's *Old Mortality* (1816), approaches what was becoming the recognized form of the historical novel. Instead of a symmetrical novel tracing the protagonist's journey through demarcated historical events and ending with a clearer prospective on the contours of that history, Hogg's work rebels against the possibility of taking any kind of measured or unified perspective. Characters frequently disappear out of a story, never to be seen again, or reappear without its being at all clear where they have been in the meantime. The beginnings and endings of Hogg's texts merge into each other; sections of them move from one location to another; texts that initially appeared as magazine stories, apparently demonstrating

some authentic ethnographic illustration of Scottish rural life, might find their way into longer novels as tales told by a fictional character. Hogg also fictionalized himself as author. In 1823, *Blackwood's* published a letter from Hogg to John Wilson, the editor of the magazine, describing a strange local-interest tale of the discovery of the corpse of a suicide. This letter, still signed by "James Hogg," then reappeared the following year in the novel *The Private Memoirs and Confessions of a Justified Sinner*, with the suicide incident now inserted into the fictional plot. Hogg refuses to let us decide between the positions of the antiquarian unearthing the evidence of authentic history, and the novel reader entertained by implausible fictions.

Hogg's own "tales" are vernacular and local, in contrast to the increasingly popular "national tale," a form of the novel in which an educated but often inexperienced stranger visits the rustic inhabitants of peripheral parts of the kingdom (usually Scotland or Ireland) and learns of their value to the nation as a whole. In Hogg's tales the peasants are allowed to speak for themselves, and they often emphasize their own specificity and the way particular localities function, rather than becoming absorbed into the larger flow of national history. This is true of both Hogg's short stories and his novel-length fiction. *The Three Perils of Man* (1822), which Hogg himself styled "A Border Romance," is structured not according to novelistic traditions with their established narrative structures but by the more anarchic, unpredictable logic of storytelling. This exuberant and sprawling tale intercuts a narrative of medieval warfare with a storytelling competition among a bizarre group of characters only loosely related to the supposedly central, important historical event: the siege of Roxburgh Castle in the fifteenth century. Hogg parodies the style of chivalric romance associated with Scott, deflecting his readers' attention from the linear, reported narrative of official history and onto the local tale. In this mode stories may be local, functional, or told for specific and conditional reasons; in the case of this competition, the storytellers are trapped in a tower and the loser stands to be cannibalized by the others.

The Three Perils of Woman (1823) is an equally bold experiment with form, juxtaposing a modern-day romance between a young Borders woman and a medical student from the Highlands with a tragic story of the savage aftermath of the failed 1745 Jacobite rebellion and the resultant Highland clearances that depopulated northern Scotland. The novel is an unsettling mixture of genres and styles, combining the domestic fiction of polite society, raunchy comedy, and elegiac lament. Its bleak outcome finally suggests that no form of conventional novel writing—or perhaps of writing altogether—can encompass the complex history and regional differences of Scotland.

MODERNITY AND TRADITION

Hogg's short autobiographical "Memoir of the Author's Life" (1821) recounts his early experience of reading books without fully understanding their social or literary contexts, and this acute awareness of the process of reading influenced all his fiction. Hogg's texts challenge their readers to recognize themselves *as* readers, and reading as a socially identifying process. Hogg understands that the traditional tales he grew up with can be thought of as specifically traditional (rather than normative or customary) only when they become claimed by a antiquarian or literary culture interested in reviving or imagining a shared past. His stories continually return to the border between his own sense of the rural, laboring-class communities that inspired them and the modern, sophisticated context in which they might be read, and he rarely makes it easy to draw a precise line between the two.

Despite his success with local tales and legends, Hogg had an exceptionally wide-ranging and absorptive imagination that also drew him to science, philosophy, and current events. "The Pongos," set in southern Africa, tells of a child abducted and brought up by apes, tapping Scottish Enlightenment interest in anthropology and the possibility, expressed by Lord Monboddo, that the orangutan occupied a point midway between human and animal. The hero of "The Surpassing Adventures of Allan Gordon" visits the North Pole in the spirit of adventure generated by the upsurge of Arctic exploration in the 1820s. The frequent appearance of ghosts, wraiths, and corpses that return to life in his stories points not only to his interest in supernatural tradition but also to the medical experimentation that gave rise to grave-robbing scandals in the 1820s. Hogg's readers are often left in a position where it is difficult to chose between materialist and magical explanations for phenomena: in *The Three Perils of Man*, the Eildon Hills are split into three both by the scientifically minded friar (who does it with a trick of perspective) and the wizard Michael Scott (who uses a spell).

Hogg undercuts the possibility of a grand sweep of historical time by showing how time is relative and subjective. History to him is more complicated than a distinction between a modern, enlightened present and an earlier traditional past. "Time" is something that is dependent on memory and experience and on shared pointers. "Some Terrible Letters from Scotland" takes place "that summer that Burke was hanged." "Storms" reminds the reader that a shepherd's calendar (the story is the first of the 1829 collection of that title) is mapped by the meteorological events that "constitute the various areas of the pastoral life." Hogg uses supernatural traditions to challenge notions that we can order the world through the shaping structures of space and time: the hero of "The Mysterious Bride" manages, though an unaccountable agency, to be simultaneously in Scotland and Ireland; in the poem "Kilmeny" and the short story "Mary Burnet," other possible worlds seem to exist alongside the familiar one, as Hogg exploits tales of a fairyland that overlaps with the space inhabited by mortals. Nor is time always linear—Hogg's stories are full of prophecies, curses, and events experienced in dreams before they take place in waking life.

Hogg's greatest account of the difficulty of reading the past through an enlightened modernity is now his most celebrated novel, although it was considered virtually unreadable at its first appearance. *The Private Memoirs and Confessions of a Justified Sinner* was published anonymously in 1824. The novel consists of two narratives, each telling the story of the murder in the early eighteenth century of George Colwan, supposedly by his brother Robert Wringhim. The first is a reconstruction of events by an early nineteenth-century "Editor," and the second is a version recorded by the accused murderer. The Editor's narrative relies on the "powerful monitors" of history and local tradition, but Robert's is a deeply personal, increasingly paranoid tale of his relationship with Gil-Martin, a persuasive figure who may be the Devil or a product of Robert's disintegrating psyche. As is typical with Hogg, no single explanation is forthcoming; after we have read Robert's own first-person account we are returned to the Editor, who tries to disinter Robert's body but finds that the corpse crumbles away into dust. Even the most empirical and physical act of investigation fails to produce a truth in fact. Although the novel is strikingly modern in its use of fractured narrative and divided psyches, *Confessions of a Justified Sinner* also returns to an earlier world of extreme Protestant theology to enter dark psychological territory. As Robert himself confesses, "My life has been a life of trouble and turmoil of change and vicissitude; of anger and exultation; of sorrow and of vengeance." Hogg explores the theological idea that some people are preordained to be spiritually saved, coupled with the imperative for the Calvinist to police continually his or her own actions for signs of that salvation. Robert is sure that he is one of "the elect" and cannot be damned; he abandons his conscience and does everything Gil-Martin tells him, including committing murder. Gil-Martin, who can transform himself into Robert's physical double, acts both as Robert's internal psychological drives and as an external voice of godlike authority. But this act of extreme Calvinist logic results in the dislocation of Robert's mind between the scrutinizing authority of Gil-Martin and his own failure to remember the crimes of which he is accused, driving him finally to madness and suicide.

Hogg's later books brought him little money, and he resorted to publishing shorter pieces in Edinburgh and London magazines while he tried to negotiate for a collected edition of his works. He died on 21 November 1835 and was buried in Ettrick churchyard. Although respect for his work later declined—his stories appeared in a chopped-up and bowdlerized edition in the 1860s—more than two thousand people attended a ceremony in 1860 to erect a statue of him overlooking St. Mary's Loch in the Ettrick valley; even as his works fell out of literary fashion they remained important to the local, rural readership for which they were in part written. Hogg's work remained neglected during much of the twentieth century, with only *Confessions of a Justified Sinner* becoming established in the canon of gothic fiction. In 1995, however, the first volume of a modern, authoritative collection of his works appeared, allowing the full scope of this complex and experimental author to reappear.

[*See also* The Gothic; Romanticism; *and* Walter Scott.]

SELECTED WORKS

The Queen's Wake (1813)
The Brownie of Bodsbeck and Other Tales (1818)
Winter Evening Tales (1820)
The Three Perils of Man (1822)
The Three Perils of Woman (1823)
The Private Memoirs and Confessions of a Justified Sinner (1824)
The Shepherd's Calendar (1829)
Altrive Tales (1832)
Familiar Anecdotes of Sir Walter Scott (1834)

EDITION

Mack, Douglas S., ed. *The Stirling/South Carolina Research Edition of the Works of James Hogg*. Edinburgh, 1995–. The introductions to the individual volumes of this fine edition provide the best available way of approaching Hogg's works and the literary contexts in which he wrote.

FURTHER READING

Duncan, Ian. "The Upright Corpse: Hogg, National Literature, and the Uncanny." *Studies in Hogg and His World* 5 (1990): 29–54. An essential article that explains Hogg's double relation to Scottish culture.

Fielding, Penny. *Writing and Orality: Nationality, Culture, and Nineteenth-Century Scottish Fiction*. Oxford, 1996. Sets Hogg in the context of early nineteenth-century ideas about oral storytelling.

Miller, Karl. *Electric Shepherd: A Likeness of James Hogg*. London, 2003. A modern and lively biography.

GERARD MANLEY HOPKINS

Julia F. Saville

In a fragmentary text entitled "Poetry and Verse," believed to belong to lecture notes written in 1873–1874, Gerard Manley Hopkins (1844–1889) described poetry as "speech framed to be heard for its own sake" (*Journals*, p. 289). Later, he declared that his own verse was "less to be read than heard" (*Letters . . . to Robert Bridges*, p. 46). It was this characteristic that years later struck the American poet Hart Crane as a revelation when he wrote of Hopkins's work, "I did not know that words could come so near a transfiguration into pure musical notation—at the same [time] retaining every minute literal signification!" Today Hopkins's poetry remains renowned for the playfulness of its sound patterns, the emotional power of its rhythms, and the idiosyncrasy of the word choices that make both of these possible.

Very little of Hopkins's work was published during his lifetime; the first anthology of his poetry appeared posthumously in 1918 under the editorship of his friend, long-standing correspondent, and literary executor, Robert Bridges. This delayed appearance, combined with his experiments in poetic form, led to his initial association with the modernist poetics exemplified in the work of T. S. Eliot and Ezra Pound. Since the 1970s, however, the Victorian character of his work has been more widely explored and recognized. With the 1989 publication in facsimile of his early poetic manuscripts and confessional notebooks, followed in 1991 by his later poetic manuscripts, Hopkins's lifelong attraction to young men has become openly acknowledged and has stimulated lively scholarly debate about the degree to which his sexual orientation contributed to the passionate intensity of his devotional poetry.

Gerard Manley Hopkins
Photograph by
Forshaw & Coles, 1880
NATIONAL PORTRAIT GALLERY,
LONDON

HOPKINS'S POETIC THEORY AND TERMINOLOGY

Hopkins was unusually self-conscious in his approach to poetry writing, as is clear both from the numerous discussions of his craft in his correspondence with other poets such as Bridges, Richard Watson Dixon, and Coventry Patmore, as well as from his early lecture notes and the preface he wrote in 1883–1884 for a collection of his poems that Bridges had assembled. Among the most useful terms for understanding Hopkins's poetic theory are four neologisms—inscape, instress, pitch, and stalling—which begin to appear in his journals and notebooks shortly after his graduation from Oxford in 1868. "Inscape" could be described as the species-specific pattern that becomes distinguishable to the viewer's eye when the features of a figure or object (for instance, the arrangement of the branches of an oak tree) become defined against the figure's unnoticed ground (perhaps the sky behind the tree's branches). The energy that sustains the pattern of inscape and the viewer's experience of it is termed "instress." The inscape of an object arrests the movement of a wandering, scanning eye and directs it to focus on the hidden singularity of the object, which it might otherwise miss. Hopkins called this singularity the object's "pitch" or "self." The following journal entry of spring 1871 provides a useful illustration of his own usage: "End of March and beginning of April—This is the time to study inscape in the spraying of trees, for the swelling buds carry them to a pitch which the eye could not else gather" (*Journals*, p. 205).

Inscape can be seen as a means to an end rather than an end in itself. It is a device developed in response to the peculiarly mid-Victorian cultural experience of instability and flux exacerbated by the spread of industrial capitalism. Its effect is to encourage a contemplative frame of mind as an antidote to the "getting and spending" of urban life. To this end Hopkins recommended the use of delaying strategies, or "stalling," that intensify the experience of inscape and so encourage finer discriminations of pitch enabled by the synthesizing energy of instress. This is reminiscent of Walter Pater's exhortations in the "Conclusion" of his *Studies in the History of the Renaissance* (1873), where he urges his readers to resist Heraclitean flux and maximize the interval of life between birth and death by refining their perceptions through art and song. However, where Pater's aesthetic theory is neo-Hellenic and draws on a skeptical tradition that does not accept the possibility of an afterlife, Hopkins's finer discriminations are directed toward a heightened awareness of Christ's redemptive presence in the world. In contrast with Pater's Hellenism, Hopkins corroborated his theory of inscape with the writings of the medieval Franciscan scholastic Johannes Duns Scotus (1266?–1308), whose commentary on the *Sententiae* (1148–1151) of Peter Lombard (c. 1095–1160) he had found in the Badeley Collection in the library of the Jesuit complex, Stonyhurst, during the summer of 1872.

Duns Scotus encouraged a fine appreciation of the temporal world and was preoccupied with revealing the kinds of fine distinctions and shades of meaning that made his thirteenth-century philosophy unexpectedly compatible with Hopkins's Victorian project of celebrating Christ through his poetry. In the view of Duns Scotus, the human intellect has a gift for generalization and is easily able to grasp the common nature of objects. It is, however, less able to recognize what is uniquely individual to each object, its *haecceitas* or "thisness." What is obvious to the eye is recognized with ease, but more effort is needed to see finer distinctions. In these terms, access to the Supreme Being does not require special genius, but effort, so that one who exercises greater efforts of inquiry may recognize truths that another who does not expend effort will not come to know. The terms Scotus uses in his philosophy correspond closely to the neologisms in Hopkins's poetic theory: Scotus's "common nature" is equivalent to Hopkins's "inscape"; "effort" is like "stalling"; and *haecceitas* corresponds to "pitch."

In his spiritual writings of 1881, Hopkins was at pains to distinguish inscape or the common nature (for instance, those patterns of an oak tree that make it distin-

guishable from a willow) from the self or pitch or *haecceitas* that must be drawn out, or instressed, by dwelling on that inscape. It is pitch, therefore, not inscape, that Hopkins saw as the equivalent to Duns Scotus's *haecceitas*. By inducing individuation, the effort of stalling on inscape permits the viewer to infer Christ in his infinite difference from the pitch or selfhood of objects. These principles apply as readily to language as to any other material objects. From this it follows that when the crafted language of poetry—and in particular, the sounds of spoken poetry—is the focus of intense attention, its own inscape emerges in structural patterning. In Hopkins's own words, "Poetry is in fact speech only employed to carry the inscape of speech for the inscape's sake—and therefore the inscape must be dwelt on" (*Journals*, p. 289). His "sprung rhythm" is one of various techniques Hopkins developed to heighten the patterns and thus the inscape of his poetic language. This in turn describes the patterns of creatures and objects (the kingfishers, dragonflies, windhovers, clouds, and landscapes) that populate Hopkins's verse and are all in their own way manifestations of Christ's presence and beauty. In other words, the inscape or patterning of poetic language mediates the freshness of vision and therefore of spiritual experience produced by observing inscape in the surrounding world.

SPRUNG RHYTHM

Although frequently praised for its originality, sprung rhythm was in fact less an invention, or a break with tradition, than an unusually shrewd version of the new prosody that developed in Victorian poetic circles between 1850 and 1900. The accomplishment of Victorian prosodists such as Patmore was to recognize that the rhythmic effects of poetry are produced by negotiating between the regularity of abstract metrical form and the variations possible in the actual execution of verse. Experimenting with this negotiation, Hopkins saw scope for unprecedented variation in sense stressing—that is, the placing of emphasis where intense feeling called for it, rather than where formal metrical pattern required it.

In retrospect, scholars have recognized that sprung rhythm is both isochronal and dipodic. First, this means that each metrical foot is a single unit in a series of units, each of which is of the same duration. Second, while conventional running rhythm has only one stressed syllable in any single foot, dipodic rhythm permits two feet to count as one, and two stressed syllables of varying stress to occur in one metrical foot. Consider, for example, the rhythm of the simile that describes Hopkins's famous falcon, turning in flight and gathering itself: "As a skate's heel sweeps smooth on a bow-bend" ("The Windhover"). Depending on how the reader scans the whole line, the succession of monosyllables in these first three feet can add up to as many as six stressed syllables interspersed with an unlimited number of unstressed beats contributing to a five-foot line of fifteen syllables, an extraordinary length for a pentameter line in English. This in turn allows the surging pattern (or inscape) of the rhythm to be repeated often enough to be viscerally experienced (or instressed) by the listener.

The exaggerated patterns of Hopkins's sprung rhythm became audible only in his mature work beginning with his great thirty-five-stanza ode, "The Wreck of the *Deutschland*" (1875), and continuing in his numerous sonnets, the latter being a verse form he favored to the end of his life. For convenience's sake, one might divide his most significant work into three phases: the Welsh period (1875–1877), the nomadic period—when he was moved from one professional assignment to the next, mainly in the industrial Midlands, but never remaining in one place longer than nineteen months (1878–1883)—and the Irish period (1884–1889).

THE WELSH PERIOD

Hopkins began writing poetry in the early 1860s but burned his early work in 1868 (presumably as a gesture of renunciation), a few months before he joined the Society of Jesus (the Roman Catholic Jesuit order). Many of the early poems survived in the form of copies sent to friends, but for the next seven years he wrote almost nothing further. In December 1875, the German ship *Deutschland*, bound for New York, was wrecked off the coast of Kent. Among the passengers drowned were five Franciscan nuns exiled from the new German empire after the passage of the May Laws by Adalbert Falk, Chancellor Otto von Bismarck's minister of public worship and education. Hopkins, then in his second year of the Jesuit theologate or seminary at Saint Beuno's College in Wales, read of the wreck in the newspapers. Written in two parts, the first describing Hopkins's own revelatory experience, and the second the epiphany of a drowning nun, this ode interprets the shipwreck typologically. Hopkins presents it as both a fulfillment of Christ's promise and power to redeem humanity through suffering, and as a prefiguration of Britain's rebirth into a new age of faith.

From a literary perspective, "The Wreck of the *Deutschland*" in fact marks the renaissance of Hopkins's own poetic career, for it was followed by some of his most highly acclaimed and anthologized Petrarchan sonnets, among them "God's Grandeur," "The Starlight Night," "As Kingfishers Catch Fire," "Spring," "The Windhover," "Pied Beauty," "The Sea and the Skylark," and "Hurrahing in Harvest." Just as "The Wreck" presents Christ as lover and bridegroom of the soul to whom he is united in death, almost all the Welsh poems celebrate Christ as the beloved, "Lovely in limbs, and lovely in eyes not his" who offers "a / Rapturous love's greeting" to those who recognize him in the inscapes of nature.

THE NOMADIC YEARS

In the years that followed his ordination in September 1877, Hopkins produced a small but constant stream of poems as he shuttled from one pastoral or teaching assignment to the next, often in or near large industrial towns such as Sheffield, Liverpool, and Glasgow. Many of these poems, such as "Binsey Poplars," "Inversnaid," and "Ribblesdale," express the poet's deep concern about the effects of industrialization and urban development on the quality of the air and water in the surrounding countryside. Such lyrics have lent themselves recently to consideration as proto-ecological works. Alongside these poems is a corpus of verses that eulogize manly beauty: for instance, a second shipwreck poem, "The Loss of the *Eurydice*," "The Bugler's First Communion," and "Felix Randal." Like the rural inscapes threatened by indiscriminate industrial development, manpower is represented as an invaluable but limited national resource under threat from natural disaster, urban pollution, and continual wars abroad.

THE "TERRIBLE" SONNETS AND OTHER POEMS OF THE IRISH PERIOD

Early in 1884 Hopkins moved to Ireland, where he had been appointed professor of Greek at University College, Dublin, and fellow in classics of the Royal University of Ireland. The sense of personal isolation, alienation, and oppression from onerous pedagogical duties made him subject to severe bouts of depression. He articulated his distress both in his letters and in a cluster of sonnets that have been variously named the "Sonnets of Desolation," the "Dark Sonnets," and the "Terrible Sonnets"—the latter phrase referring to their harrowing misery. A prevailing motif in these poems is the speaker's dread that he is no longer loved by Christ, who is represented repeatedly as an exacting master and the source of the speaker's anguish rather than a resource for relieving it. Christ is, for instance, variously described as "The hero whose heaven-handling flung me, foot trod / Me," or "my peace / my parting, sword and strife," or "dearest him that lives alas! away."

Alongside the Terrible Sonnets and in some cases drafted on the same manuscript sheets are further eulogies to the beauty of the young male body, of a kind with those composed during the years in the Midlands. For instance, on the recto side of the manuscript on which the agonized "Carrion Comfort" is drafted appears the aesthetic contemplation "To what serves mortal beauty," where beauty is illustrated by the image of young slave lads. On the verso of this manuscript sheet are more drafts of "Carrion Comfort" together with "The Soldier," a eulogy to soldiers and sailors ("Our redcoats, our tars") whose work is represented as specially valued and blessed by Christ. Such juxtapositions suggest a complex connection between Hopkins's admiration for male beauty and the intense self-loathing expressed in the Terrible Sonnets.

LASTING INFLUENCE

Although he engaged in lively epistolary debates with his poetic contemporaries, Hopkins received little public recognition during his lifetime. "The Wreck of the *Deutschland*" was rejected by the Jesuit journal *The Month*, and a sample of his sonnets, submitted for an anthology, was returned to him as unacceptable. In the twentieth century, however, he came into his own, particularly in North America. "What a man—and what daring!" enthused Crane. "It will be long before I shall be quiet about him." The poet Elizabeth Bishop's letters of the mid-1930s are peppered with enthusiastic allusions to Hopkins and his work, and the composer Aaron Copland borrowed the term *Inscape* in 1967 for the title of his last major work. But perhaps the most touching recognition comes in John Berryman's elegiac *Dream Song*, #377, announcing at last that "Hopkins's credits, while the Holy Ghost / rooted for Hopkins, hit the Milky Way."

[*See also* Robert Bridges.]

EDITIONS

Abbott, Claude Colleer, ed. *The Correspondence of Gerard Manley Hopkins and Richard Watson Dixon*. London, 1955.

Abbott, Claude Colleer, ed. *Further Letters of Gerard Manley Hopkins Including His Correspondence with Coventry Patmore*. London, 1956.

Abbott, Claude Colleer, ed. *The Letters of Gerard Manley Hopkins to Robert Bridges*. London, 1955.

Devlin, Christopher, ed. *Sermons and Devotional Writings of Gerard Manley Hopkins*. (1959) London, 1967.

House, Humphry, ed. *Journals and Papers of Gerard Manley Hopkins*. Completed by Graham Storey. (1959) London, 1966.

MacKenzie, Norman H., ed. *The Early Poetic Manuscripts and Note-Books of Gerard Manley Hopkins in Facsimile*. New York, 1989.

MacKenzie, Norman H., ed. *The Later Poetic Manuscripts of Gerard Manley Hopkins in Facsimile*. New York, 1991.

MacKenzie, Norman H., ed. *The Poetical Works of Gerard Manley Hopkins*. Oxford, 1990.

FURTHER READING

Bristow, Joseph. "'Churlsgrace': Gerard Manley Hopkins and the Working-Class Male Body." *ELH* 59 (1992): 693–711. This essay provides an informative aesthetic context for understanding Hopkins's later poems on manly beauty.

Culler, Jonathan. "Lace, Lance, and Pair." In *Profession* 94 [Modern Language Association] (1994): 5–10. Culler provides concise study of the pleasures invited by the playfulness of Hopkins's linguistic patterns.

Gardner, W. H. *Gerard Manley Hopkins, 1844–1889: A Study of Poetic Idiosyncrasy in Relation to Poetic Tradition*. 2 vols. London, 1949. One of the first exhaustive studies of Hopkins's poetry, this documents how he was understood in the mid-twentieth century.

Mariani, Paul. *A Commentary on the Complete Poems of Gerard Manley Hopkins*. Ithaca, NY, 1970. This remains one of the most reassuring companions for the reader approaching Hopkins for the first time.

Ong, Walter. "Hopkins' Sprung Rhythm and the Life of English Poetry." In *Immortal Diamond: Studies in Gerard Manley Hopkins*, edited by Norman Weyand, 93–174. New York, 1969. This long essay provides a thorough but accessible account of how sprung rhythm heightens the emotional intensity of poetry.

Parham, John. "Green Man Hopkins: Gerard Manley Hopkins and Victorian Ecological Criticism." *Nineteenth-Century Contexts* 25 (2003): 257–276. A helpful, readable introduction to Victorian eco-consciousness with an intriguing account of Hopkins's sprung rhythm within it.

Saville, Julia F. *A Queer Chivalry: The Homoerotic Asceticism of Gerard Manley Hopkins*. Charlottesville, VA,

2000. A study of the psychic economy that allowed moral scrupulosity, spiritual intensity, sensuality, and eroticism to coexist in Hopkins's verse.

Sulloway, Alison. *Gerard Manley Hopkins and the Victorian Temper*. London, 1972. A perennially absorbing, suggestive discussion of Hopkins in relation to his Victorian intellectual and cultural context.

Taylor, Dennis. *Hardy's Metres and Victorian Prosody*. Oxford, 1988. The opening chapters of this study provide an invaluable overview of Victorian debates on prosody.

White, Norman. *Hopkins: A Literary Biography*. Oxford, 1992. A meticulously researched, highly detailed, and informative account of Hopkins's life.

A. E. HOUSMAN

Benjamin F. Fisher

Alfred Edward Housman (26 March 1859–30 April 1936) has been known far better as a poet than as a classical scholar who specialized in Latin and textual analysis. His poetical output in no way matches the extensive quantity of Alfred, Lord Tennyson, Robert Browning, or George Gordon Byron, or, for that matter, of his own publications in classical studies. His first book of poetry, *A Shropshire Lad*, originally published in 1896, contained sixty-three poems. It initially attracted little notice, but when reissued by a different publisher two years later, the slender volume became popular, and it has been reprinted for more than a century. *A Shropshire Lad* thus bears witness that what is compact is not consequently negligible. The book, along with *Last Poems* (1922), includes some of the most memorable poems in English. After Housman's death his brother Laurence published two more collections, *More Poems* (1936) and *Additional Poems* (1937), from manuscripts that had been written much earlier.

Born in Worcestershire, the eldest of seven children, Housman was drawn early to the works of many poets in several languages. He and his siblings often wrote verse, much of it humorous, as was then a widespread custom. Housman's more mature poetry often displays touches of grim comedy, perhaps a carryover from the juvenilia. Then, and into his adult life, despite the rise in importance of the novel as a literary (but bourgeois) form, poetry continued to have a reputation as possibly the greatest type of creative writing. Given also Housman's interest in classics, especially in classical verse, that he should have become a poet is not surprising. An additional youthful fascination—astronomy—came to figure into both his verse and his major scholarly effort, an edition of the five books of the *Astronomicon*, a long verse work on astronomy by Manilius, a minor Latin poet.

Housman's early years were saddened by his mother's illness and early death, which left a lasting impact, although he came to bear great affection for his stepmother. His father's irresponsibility as a husband and parent often caused financial and other problems for the family. These circumstances instilled in Housman a sense that life's injustices and failures were inescapable and had to be endured. While at Bromsgrove School he excelled scholastically and had a prize poem published. He then attended Oxford, where he pursued classical studies, continued to write humorous verse, and met A. W. Pollard and Moses Jackson. The latter became the consuming passion in Housman's personal life, but his feelings were not reciprocated, and the rejected lover's turbulent emotions may have loomed large in his failure in "Greats" (classical literature, philosophy, and history), although his disdain for the curriculum in classical studies predisposed him to ill preparation for his examinations. A failure in his own eyes and, as he would have presumed, in the eyes of others whose high expectations for him were dashed, he left Oxford (from which, however, he ultimately earned a BA) and found employment in the Patent Office in London, where he worked for eleven years. He spent his spare time in the library of the British Museum, developing his classical interests and bringing out significant publications based on his research.

When a teaching post in Latin opened at University College, London, Housman submitted such compelling recommendations that he easily won the position, and he remained a faculty member there for nineteen years. Feelings of failure, self-loathing, and loneliness continued to afflict him, so he may have resorted to composing poetry for therapy. His reputation as an authority in classical studies grew, and in 1911 he was offered a professorship in Latin at Cambridge and subsequently became Kennedy Professor of Latin, a position he held until his death in 1936.

Readers' responses to meaning in Housman's poems are divergent, and his own reticence on such topics has prompted continuing interest. That he often forestalled those who might be too curious may be attested by his calling attention, in the annual Leslie Stephen Lecture at Cambridge in 1933 (published as *The Name and Nature of Poetry*), to his method of composition of "I hoed and trenched and weeded," the final poem in *A Shropshire*

Lad. After his death it was discovered that he had cut the draft of the poem from his notebook, as if to ensure no scrutiny of that manuscript.

Throughout Housman's writings, brevity is paramount; it suits the bleak themes of human existence typical in his verse, and suggests an awareness that intense emotion would disperse were the expression allowed more space. He claimed as chief inspirations the old ballads and the poetry of Shakespeare and Heinrich Heine, although sources in writings of Matthew Arnold, Thomas Hardy, Robert Bridges, and others are also evident. To a casual reader the majority of Housman's poems, as they appear on the printed page, look like ballads, but thoughtful examination reveals that they are more sophisticated and polished than many of the old popular ballads. In form, some of the poems also resemble hymns—for example, "Reveille" (IV, *A Shropshire Lad*), "As I gird on for fighting" (II, *Last Poems*), and the poem Housman wrote to be used during his funeral, "Oh thou that from thy mansion" (XLVII, *More Poems*)—although his ironies impart vastly different implications to the content within these verse structures than we find in hymns of joy and uplift.

A question also arises, principally in regard to *A Shropshire Lad*, although the same might be said of *Last Poems*: should we regard the book as one extended poem or as an anthology of separate lyrics? Housman repeatedly opted for compactness, but he emerged as a poet when respect for the long, often book-length, poem was still great, and when such sonnet sequences as Dante Gabriel Rossetti's *The House of Life* and George Meredith's *Modern Love* might have served as models. Another work that appeared first serially then as a unified poem, Tennyson's *Idylls of the King* may be seen as analogous to *A Shropshire Lad* with its cyclical structure. However, just about any individual poem within the overarching structure of these sequential works may be read as an independent, self-contained entity. *A Shropshire Lad* may be read as one extended poem loosely unified by the perspective of Terence, in much the same way that such short-story cycles or sequences as Sherwood Anderson's *Winesburg, Ohio* and Ernest Hemingway's Nick Adams stories function. Housman had called his manuscript "Poems by Terence Hearsay," but Pollard recommended changing that pedestrian title to the far more felicitous *A Shropshire Lad*.

In the course of the book Terence relocates to urban environs from his native "Shropshire" (an invented fantasy world rather than the actual English county) and its agricultural life: farm work, courtship, sex, family rela-tionships, rural pleasures such as drinking, dancing, fairs—pursuits and pastimes often tinged with violence and death. Terence's life journey takes him from the festive aura of Queen Victoria's Golden Jubilee, in 1887, to diminished buoyancy as the book concludes. The poignancy of these episodes is pointedly conveyed. The poems featuring soldiery emphasize loss and bewilderment, appealing though military life may seem, because soldiers' lives are bound up with rootlessness, that is, dislocation from domesticity, along with all the other uncertainties inherent in their careers. A soldier's life may seem enviable in its adventurousness—on the field or in amours—but it may terminate without warning. The disjointed nature of the military world mirrors Terence's own unsureness as he leaves behind his long-familiar life. Themes of early deaths—literal deaths, emotional deaths, and the swift passage (the "death") of youth—recur throughout *A Shropshire Lad*, reaching an emotional climax in the concluding four poems. Thus, the book depicts a journey from youthful spirits, both cheerful and dour, to age with its diminished vigor and increased contemplations of death, metaphorically if not actually for Terence, who justifies his grim poems on grounds that life is in the main troubling.

Another constant in Housman's poems—motion, or travel—leads characters through life's fleeting pleasures inexorably toward death. An excellent example is "White in the moon the long road lies" (XXXVI, *A Shropshire Lad*), which recounts a disconsolate traveler's treading a seemingly endless road to reach his lover, the speaker's journey neatly counterpointed by that of the moon across the sky. A more ironic rendering of like circumstances appears in "The half-moon westers low, my love" (XXVI, *Last Poems*), in which the sea's separation of the two lovers seems to be permanent. One may not be sure whether the speaker refers to the distant lover's sleep as pleasant, if the sleep is death, or if the faraway person is so satisfied with life that sleep comes easily while the torment of separation makes the speaker wakeful. Such ambiguities occur frequently in Housman's poetry, perhaps to keep unwary readers from discerning that many of the poems center on homosexual love. Those ambiguities have done good service because these poems also permit readings from a heterosexual viewpoint. Often the emotional plight of a character is intensified by positioning human disturbances against a backdrop of lovely natural scenery, where cyclicalness hints at a timelessness that contrasts sharply with the comparatively short spans of human life, as in "Loveliest of trees" (II, *A Shropshire Lad*), in which the measure of human life appears minuscule when contemplated alongside the apparent infinity of natural seasonalness.

If a creative writer's personal experiences provide signal origins for artistic work, Housman's tumultuous emotions related to sexuality and to frustrations and sorrows in other areas of life are transfused by means of his creative imagination into exquisite poems, wherein love—not explicitly same-sex love—is unpleasant and unrewarding. Misunderstandings, strife, disappointments, and bitter disillusionments await those who seek enjoyment and contentment in love. The deceptions that befall idealistic lovers are couched in biting, if understated, ironies, for example, those in "Is my team ploughing" (XXVII, *A Shropshire Lad*). As the dialogue involving a dead man's queries to and answers from his living friend proceeds subtly, we begin to detect where the conversation will lead, to the revelation that the living man has with ease become the sexually satisfied and satisfying lover of the dead man's sweetheart. The gradual shift from work to male group sports to sex is expressed in unmistakable sexual wordplay. "Ploughing" is a colloquialism for sexual intercourse, and the phallic suggestions in the "stands" in repetitions concerning games are evident, culminating in the "hearty" man's conscious—and probably taunting—repetition of "lie," another term for sexual intercourse, as he reveals the relationship that he and his interlocutor's former sweetheart enjoy, and that apparently required no long delay. Contrasts are strongly wrought in depicting differences between inactivity and debilitation in the dead speaker, whom the living friend urges to remain "still" (with no doubt several implications of the word in his mind), and the motion, sounds, and other sensory dynamics among the living. One is left with an impression that the living man achieves extra vitality because of the absence of a rival; he seems to work with the dead man's horses (animals often symbolic of rampant sexuality), to play games in which both men had been participants, and to enjoy sexual play with the girl he's bedding. The shift from "sleep" and "weep" to the more aggressively sexual bedtime scenario sharpens contexts of the active nature of their relationship. This poem concludes a cluster in which the survivor of a dead lover soon finds satisfaction with another. "Fancy's Knell" (XLI, *Last Poems*) is a companion piece to these poems. The title appropriately forecasts what follows; that is, the lilting measure within the text mimes a dance through life and the dancers sport until a cloud, or sunset, or autumn with its warning of winter darkens their world and the speaker's flute is silenced by this symbolic death knell. The terse concluding line adds significantly to the sense of the shutting down of youthful vitality.

Love relationships in Housman's verse are not, however, the sole causes of tragedies. In general, all but the nonsense poems recognize little other than bleakness in human existence, although no wailing or gnashing of teeth ensues from that realization. Instead, the poems advocate resistance to surrender and forging onward, albeit resignation is a concomitant of life's journey. Death will bring release and, presumably, oblivion. Admiration for the soldier and the athlete is tempered by contemplation of those who seem to be brimful of vital life but die before their promise is realized. "To An Athlete Dying Young" (XIX, *A Shropshire Lad*) is in part a lament for the early loss of a champion, but the elegiac nature of this poem offers a reconciling conclusion: the dead hero will never suffer the sorrows and physical ravages that accompany aging. The movement of the funeral procession and the later observation of the setting of the runner's foot on the doorsill of death are fitting tropes for travel through life. This poem addresses situations similar to those in the military poems in that both athletes and soldiers are considered excellent physical specimens yet are not guaranteed longevity or happiness.

Brevity in the typical Housman poem reinforces themes of short-lived pleasures and satisfactions. The lyrical effects produce music—specifically, choral music—that is perforce fleeting. Those effects blend well with thematic contexts of very temporary enjoyment. Shifts from formal to colloquial diction indicate that no social level or occupation escapes life's tragedies. Such features place these poems firmly within the ranks of literary modernism, in which indecisiveness and disorientation surface at crucial moments. The fragmentary nature of the two books of Housman's poetry that he oversaw, from which the posthumously published poems show no departure, bolsters these hallmarks of modernist writing. In *A Shropshire Lad* and *Last Poems*, we find clusters of poems that focus on a single theme, but the books are so well knit that transitions from one poem to another are inconspicuous. These two books provide the essentials for understanding Housman as poet, although most of the posthumously published poems are also worthy of attention.

SELECTED WORKS

Introductory Lecture Delivered before the Faculties of Arts and Laws and of Science in University College, London (1892, reprinted 1933)

A Shropshire Lad (1896, reissued 1898)
M. Manilii Astronomicon (1903–1930)
Last Poems (1922)
"The Application of Thought to Textual Criticism" (1922)
The Name and Nature of Poetry (1933)
More Poems (1936)
Additional Poems (1937)

EDITIONS

Burnett, Archie, ed. *The Poems of A. E. Housman.* New York and Oxford, 1997.

Maas, Henry, ed. *The Letters of A. E. Housman.* London, 1971.

Ricks, Christopher, ed. *A. E. Housman: Collected Poems and Selected Prose.* London, 1988.

FURTHER READING

Bayley, John. *Housman's Poems.* Oxford, 1992. A sensible reading of Housman's poetical canon.

Bourne, Jeremy. *The Westerly Wanderer: A Brief Portrait of A. E. Housman.* Bromsgrove, U.K., 1996. Written for the centenary of publication of *A Shropshire Lad.* Although brief, it takes account of critical materials published after Page's book and offers more critical thought than older biographies and sketches tend to.

Efrati, Carol. *The Road of Danger, Guilt, and Shame: The Lonely Way of A. E. Housman.* Madison, NJ, and London, 2002. Although Efrati's readings of Housman's poems as emanating chiefly from his homosexuality have provoked dissension, she argues convincingly for what has previously been a much avoided or guarded topic, and she likewise neatly compares his poems with those of other British poets.

Holden, Alan W., and J. Roy Birch, eds. *A. E. Housman: A Reassessment.* Basingstoke, U.K., and New York, 2000. Essays by various critics that range over biographical, analytical, and bibliographical topics.

Housman, Laurence. *My Brother, A. E. Housman: Personal Recollections Together with Thirty Hitherto Unpublished Poems.* London, 1937; New York, 1938. A biography by one whose knowledge of Housman's life carries immediacy.

The Housman Society Journal. An annual published since 1974 in which analytical criticism and bibliographical and biographical information appear along with appreciations of the writings of Housman and other members of his family.

Jebb, Keith. *A. E. Housman.* Bridgend, U.K., 1992. Judiciously threads the way through controversies regarding Housman's sexuality and his achievements as classical scholar and poet. Within a narrow scope, offers all the essentials relating to Housman's life and career.

Leggett, B. J. *Housman's Land of Lost Content: A Critical Study of "A Shropshire Lad."* Knoxville, TN, 1970. Along with Efrati and Leggett's *Poetic Art,* the best extended critiques of Housman's art and poetic theories.

Leggett, B. J. *The Poetic Art of A. E. Housman: Theory and Practice.* Lincoln, NE, and London. 1978. Leggett's sensitive readings of the poems and criticism make this book indispensable for those who wish to know Housman's poetry. His linking of Housman's ideas about poetry with those of T. S. Eliot—particularly as Eliot expressed his ideas in the Harvard Norton Lectures in 1932–1933—demonstrate that, contrary to his detractors' contentions, Housman's principles, set forth in *The Name and Nature of Poetry,* were closely aligned with those of critics who were considered more mainstream.

Naiditch, P. G. *Problems in the Life and Writings of A. E. Housman.* Beverly Hills, CA, 1995. Meticulous investigations and scholarship illuminate many shadowy corners of Housman's life and work.

Page, Norman. *A. E. Housman: A Critical Biography.* London and New York, 1983. A biographical-critical account based on discoveries made after the death of Laurence Housman.

Pugh, John. *Bromsgrove and the Housmans.* Bromsgrove, U.K., 1974. A Housman Society publication that chronicles the early lives of Housman and his family; a valuable source of biographical information.

Ricks, Christopher, ed. *A. E. Housman: A Collection of Critical Essays.* Englewood Cliffs, NJ, 1968. Some of the foremost critiques of Housman's overall ideas and techniques, as well as discussions of textual issues, many of the selections being the work of major poet-critics themselves (e.g., W. H. Auden, Richard Wilbur, and Randall Jarrell). Serves as complementary reading to Leggett's books.

TED HUGHES

Ryan Hibbett

Edward James Hughes (1930–1998; known as Ted Hughes) emerged onto the English poetic landscape as an alternative to the war-chastened, allegedly insular vernacular of Philip Larkin and his fellow "Movement" poets. In an essay titled "Beyond the Gentility Principle" (1962), the influential critic A. Alvarez contrasted Larkin's "At Grass," which he found representative of an emotionally depleted, overly cautious brand of contemporary English poetry, with Hughes's "A Dream of Horses"—a poem Alvarez found more daring in its approach to the same subject matter, and more attuned to the powers and mysteries of prerational existence.

Hughes, who absorbed the effects of war indirectly through his shell-shocked father, likewise found the prevalent poetry of his day anesthetized by "death camps and atom bombs," and set out instead to meet the collective "wound" head-on. For Hughes, this meant using poetry to access those deeper levels of being that he considered dangerously repressed, and reconciling them with conscious expression. Influenced no doubt by early anthropological studies such as James Frazer's *The Golden Bough* (1922; Hughes dropped English literature to study anthropology at Cambridge) and by the psychologist Carl Jung's archetypal theories, Hughes came to envision the poet's role as akin to that of the shaman—a member of tribal societies who could mediate between the spiritual and material worlds, and heal the sick through magic and ritual. This notion lent the laureateship a special appeal for Hughes when it was offered to him in 1984.

NATURE AND VIOLENCE

As in shamanism, animals figure centrally throughout Hughes's work, often as concentrated symbols of uninhibited being. Growing up on the moors of west Yorkshire, Hughes would eagerly chase down the game hunted by his older brother Gerald, and began what would become his lifelong adventurous pursuit of fishing. He soon pursued poetry with equal fervor, penning his first lines at fifteen, and would go on to forge an enduring connection between the worlds of animals and of poetry: "I think of poems as a sort of animal. They have their own life. . . . And they have a certain wisdom . . . something perhaps which we are very curious to learn" (*Winter Pollen*). Many of Hughes's poems focus on a particular animal, and display the author's talent for scrupulous observation and mimesis—an ability to seem to climb into the creature's skin and, as in these lines from "Second Glance at a Jaguar," capture its energy and essence: "Skinful of bowls he bowls them, / The hip going in and out of joint, / dropping the spine / With the urgency of his hurry / Like a cat going along under thrown stones." Hughes's poems express an affinity with the sheer will to survive observed in the animal kingdom, and seem to lament the advent of consciousness—and, ultimately, the Western bias toward purely rational and scientific discourse—that severs humanity from nature.

Hughes's creatures grow more strange and mythical as his writing strains to escape the formal conventions of the English poetic line; the title poem from *Wodwo* (1967), for example, presents a creature just on the brink of self-awareness, curiously exploring the boundaries between himself and his environment: "I seem / separate from the ground and not rooted but dropped / out of nothing casually I've no threads / fastening me to anything I can go anywhere." Stripped of any clear identity ("wodwo" is borrowed from *Sir Gawain and the Green Knight*, where it refers to a wandering wood spirit) and lent a kind of rudimentary speech, the creature becomes less an animal-object of human observation than a "naturalized" embodiment of human consciousness in an embryonic state—baffled, yet full of potential. Hughes made a similar creature the subject of an entire volume in 1970, when, in his quest for a "super-ugly" language, he stunned the literary world with *Crow*. Inspired by the drawings of Hughes's friend and collaborator Leonard Baskin, *Crow* draws on sources as richly diverse as Native American mythology, journalistic phrasing, biblical narrative, and comic books in constructing a dark and turbulent universe where contemporary atrocities become entangled with sacred texts. The sequence features a series of trials, mishaps, and encounters—often disastrous in consequence—in the life of its protagonist, Crow. Like the trickster character of Native American folktales, Crow makes a habit of thwarting God's plans for creation, becoming responsible in some instances ("A Childish Prank," "A Horrible Religious Error") for the fundamental struggles confronted by humanity. But Crow appears as a victim in his own right, as he struggles, much like Wodwo, to make sense of his own divided existence; in "Crow Tyrannosaurus," his bid for enlightenment is painfully undermined by his insatiable appetite: "'ought I / To stop eating / And try to become the light?' // But his eye saw a grub. And his head, trapsprung, stabbed."

Celebrated by many as a bold inquiry into the horrors of modern existence, Crow for others exacerbates a problem of violence intrinsic to Hughes's work; Crow's many instances of dismemberment, bloodshed, and battle seem a pronounced enactment of a terror that elsewhere in Hughes's poetry is more ominous and abstract. The brooding subject of the early poem "Hawk Roosting," for example, arguably contains in his tightly controlled monologue something of the dictator's logic: "For the one path of my flight is direct / Through the bones of the living. / No arguments assert my right." Hughes's inclination toward nature in its fiercest, most predatory manifestations leaves his audience divided: what some readers find an essential component of the healer's vision strikes others as a troublesome fascination with power and violence, or as a nihilistic response to tragic events of both historical and personal dimensions. Far from leaving the industrial, war-plagued world of humanity behind, one might argue, Hughes's nature presents a vast canvas onto which that world is projected, producing a markedly mechanical and vicious array of birds and beasts.

Such violent content—combined with the powerful, mantralike cadences of Hughes's language and the highly publicized events of his marriage to Sylvia Plath—has made Hughes an obvious subject for feminist critique. The power invoked by Hughes, however, does not appear as an overtly masculine power; rather, it assumes the form of a primitive, maternal energy, attempting to reintegrate itself to a restrictively masculine consciousness. Adopting Robert Graves's theory of the "White Goddess," Hughes inverts the hierarchy of life established in Genesis—where an abstracted, male creator gives humanity complete dominion over "every living thing"—by representing nature instead as the supreme divinity, or Goddess, who has since been usurped by the masculine God that is projected from

human consciousness. In her current repressed state, the Goddess, believed to be the source of all genuine poetry, appears vengeful and terrifying. This alternative theology informs the bulk of Hughes's poetry, including the blood-stained pages of Crow; attempting, in "Crow and Mama," to escape his "mother" by any means necessary, a self-deceived Crow finally blasts his way to the moon in a rocket, only to crawl out from "under his mother's buttocks."

From Crow until the end of his career, Hughes wrote predominantly in sequences. Moortown Diary (1979), a record of life at his father-in-law's farm in Devon, maintains Hughes's focus on animals and his attention to violence, though in a more plainly descriptive style. Hughes collaborated with Leonard Baskin for the vastly illustrated Season Songs (1976) and Cave Birds (1978), and also collaborated with Fay Godwin, whose black-and-white photographs of the Calder Valley accompany Hughes's poems throughout Remains of Elmet (1979). In the later stages of his career, Hughes revisited works of classical mythology, producing, among others, translations of Ovid (1997) and Aeschylus (1999). The publication of Hughes's Collected Poems in 2003 makes clear just how prolific he was: over a thousand pages in length, the collection not only presents Hughes's many well-known Faber and Faber volumes but reveals a number of small, privately published volumes printed originally by family-run presses, often in a highly ornate, visually embellished form. Well received by critics, Collected Poems makes a powerful argument for Hughes's centrality to postwar British poetry.

In addition to his major poetic works, Hughes produced a long list of children's books, including The Iron Man (1968)—later transformed into Warner Brothers' animated film The Iron Giant (1999); a collection of short stories, Difficulties of a Bridegroom (1995); introductions to the poetry of Keith Douglas (1964), Emily Dickinson (1968), and Sylvia Plath (1985); and a large critical study, Shakespeare and the Goddess of Complete Being (1992). Hughes worked diligently to promote the work of Eastern European poets, publishing such poetry with coeditor Daniel Weissbort in the journal Modern Poetry in Translation, and introducing collections by Vasko Popa (1969) and János Pilinszky (1976). Hughes also played a major role in establishing the Arvon Foundation, which continues to offer valuable educational opportunities for young creative writers.

TED HUGHES AND SYLVIA PLATH

Hughes's marriage to and poetic partnership with American author Sylvia Plath has become a major part of his cultural legacy, as well as the subject of much controversy and popular interest. After meeting at Cambridge, Hughes and Plath married in 1956. With an unwavering intensity, they devoted the ensuing years of their marriage to writing poetry, and had two children. Their relationship, however, grew increasingly strained, and in 1963, months after their separation, Plath committed suicide. Since then, Hughes has faced fierce accusations of his own culpability (by way of infidelity and abandonment) in Plath's death, as well as criticisms of his decisions as her literary executor and editor. After many years of silence on the subject, Hughes published *Birthday Letters* in 1998—shortly, as it turned out, before his own death. The collection, which brings together poems written over the decades after Plath's death, gazes retrospectively on their relationship, addressing Plath directly in a reflective and plain-speaking idiom: "Spain frightened you. Spain / Where I felt at home" ("You Hated Spain"). The poems are mostly narrative in style, and sweep chronologically and geographically across the couple's holiday on the Continent, their brief tenure in America, and their return to England. Over the course of eighty-eight poems, Plath's inner demons spiral out of control, producing her greatest literary achievements while diminishing her ability to cope.

Birthday Letters met with tremendous popular success—quickly topping the best-seller list and spawning the major motion picture *Sylvia* (2003)—as well as critical acclaim; it won the Forward Prize for Poetry, the T. S. Eliot Prize for Poetry, the South Bank Prize for Poetry, and, finally, the Book of the Year Prize. It did not, however, put an end to the Hughes–Plath controversy. Hughes's dissenters regret the volume's preoccupation with fate—Hughes's frequent characterization of his younger self as a hapless and naive victim of an externally scripted narrative—which they feel works to absolve the author of any moral responsibility. Others find in its pages an honest and thoughtful account of a deeply painful subject, and celebrate a close-up portrait of Plath that only Hughes could provide. Also at issue is a matter of textual appropriation versus collaboration. Hughes and Plath worked in close tandem during their marriage, providing mutual inspiration and encouragement. Hughes was greatly dismayed, however, to find their personal lives so thinly disguised in such poems of Plath's as the now-famous "Daddy." In *Birthday Letters*, Hughes revisits, engages with, and provides companion pieces to many of Plath's poems, occasionally duplicating their titles ("Apprehensions"; "The Rabbit Catcher"), or imitating them

stylistically. Ultimately, the collection advances the Freudian narrative explored by Plath herself, which locates her illness in her father's premature death, and binds the young couple's tragic relationship to their unflinching devotion to poetry itself: "Poetry listened, maybe, but we heard nothing / And poetry did not tell us. And we / Only did what poetry told us to do" ("Flounders").

The biographical nature of *Birthday Letters* marks in some ways a radical departure from Hughes's previous work, which, true to the modernist vein, strains to distance itself from personal, author-centered experience in both its use of myth and its fixed concentration on the external image. The speaker in Hughes's work prior to *Birthday Letters* seems to disappear altogether within the subject matter, while a densely musical language, reminiscent of Gerard Manley Hopkins and Dylan Thomas, predominates over that of ordinary speech: "Pike, three inches long, perfect / Pike in all parts, green tigering the gold" ("Pike," 1959). *Birthday Letters* delivers a less autonomous form of poetry, greatly reducing the distance between speaker and author, and in some sense entering a dialogue with the popular imagination. While prompting scholars to reconsider Hughes's relationship to other poets and traditions—Does Hughes remain distant from the Confessional school of Robert Lowell and Anne Sexton, to which Plath is sometimes relegated? Is he a difficult, experimental poet, or an accessible and popular one?—*Birthday Letters* complicates traditional distinctions between "high art" and popular culture, and revives unresolved questions about the role of an author's personal life in determining the meaning and merit of his or her work. The question of whether *Birthday Letters* ranks among Hughes's finest work, or merely appeals to a voyeuristic audience, is likewise subject to debate.

Despite its disorienting style and subject matter, *Birthday Letters* maintains much of what characterizes Hughes's earlier poetry: the fundamental role of animals, the profuse literary allusions, the overarching mythic formulas, and the haunting presence of "the Goddess" are all categorically present, rounding out what appears to be, at least in these respects, an intensively unified body of work.

[*See also* Robert Graves *and* Philip Larkin.]

SELECTED WORKS

The Hawk in the Rain (1957)

Lupercal (1960)

Wodwo (1967)

Crow (1970)
Moortown Diary (1979)
Winter Pollen: Occasional Prose (1994)
Tales from Ovid (1997)
Birthday Letters (1998)
Collected Poems (2003)

FURTHER READING

Alvarez, A. "Beyond the Gentility Principle." In *The New Poetry*, edited by A. Alvarez, 21–32. London, 1962.

Feinstein, Elaine. *Ted Hughes: The Life of a Poet.* New York, 2001. To date the only biographical work focusing specifically on Ted Hughes.

Sagar, Keith. *The Laughter of Foxes: A Study of Ted Hughes.* Liverpool, U.K., 2000. Includes an extensive timeline of Hughes's life and work, and a select bibliography of primary and secondary sources.

Sagar, Keith, ed. *The Challenge of Ted Hughes.* New York, 1994. A wide-ranging collection of essays on Ted Hughes.

Wagner, Erica. *Ariel's Gift: Ted Hughes, Sylvia Plath, and the Story of "Birthday Letters."* New York, 2001. A helpful synopsis of the poems in relation to the biographical material that informs them.

Walder, Dennis. *Ted Hughes.* Philadelphia, 1987. An excellent introduction to Hughes's poetry.

T. E. HULME

Scott Cohen

Thomas Ernest Hulme (1883–1917) stands as one of the most important intellectuals of British modernism, an essential conduit and interpreter of contemporary European thought on art, politics, philosophy, literature, and history. One of the more accessible and coherent voices on modern art, Hulme endeavored to explain what radical breaks from tradition might signal; he helped popularize Henri Bergson's epistemology, Wilhelm Worringer's art theory, and Georges Sorel's political philosophy. His writing on how individuals experience art as well as his own philosophy of human nature helped shape the direction of twentieth-century literature, especially the modern poetry of Ezra Pound and his Imagist movement, and the work of T. S. Eliot.

Yet for all Hulme's influence, the bibliography of works published during his lifetime—which includes several dozen short articles and reviews and six poems, all printed between 1909 and 1916—is deceptively modest. The case of Hulme reveals much about how ideas circulated during the most formative years of modernism and avant-gardism in Britain. It was largely through short published articles and letters, a handful of poems, lectures, translations, and personal contact with members of the flourishing London art scene that Hulme's ideas were initially disseminated throughout prewar Britain.

EARLY LIFE AND WRITING

Hulme was born 16 September 1883 in Endon, Staffordshire, England. The oldest of three children of Thomas and Mary Hulme, he attended Newcastle High School for Boys, where he excelled in mathematics and the sciences. After Newcastle he studied at St. John's College, Cambridge, until he was expelled in 1904. He moved to London and took courses in biology and physics at University College. After brief stays in Canada, where he worked on farms and in timber mills, and in Brussels, by 1908 Hulme was back in London. Over the next five years he became a prominent figure in the city's vibrant intellectual community. He never married. As a poet-philosopher, Hulme synthesized his own thinking about poetry as the highest form of human expression with contemporary philosophical and scientific thought.

In 1906 Hulme began working on "Cinders," a collection of observations that Herbert Read would later characterize as "a personal philosophy . . . having as its final object the destruction of the idea that the world has unity." Hulme's emerging nominalist, or antiabstractionist, thinking is clear in this fragmentary collection of notes, which was not published until 1922, as "The Note-Books of T. E. Hulme" in the *New Age*; it was then collected in *Speculations*, edited by Read in 1924. In "Cinders" Hulme set out to undermine the explanatory credibility of all universalizing theories. At the same time, he recognized the attraction of such thinking, positing that abstractions offer humans a sense of power over the world's chaos, allowing them to hope for a semblance of order and to find sanctuary in the possibility of originality. Hulme responded with a strong dose of skepticism, insisting that the objective world is merely "cinders," the residual yet infinite gritty stuff that composes the world. Accordingly, the universe accrues meaning, value, organization, and even substance only through human thought or will.

Hulme's "Notes on Language and Style" extends this perspective to the discussion of language and literature. Written around 1907, before his return to London, these notes read like a manifesto for modern poetry. In a tone both prescriptive and ponderous, he offers a formula, dense in mathematical and geometric metaphors, for a poetry that would take its proper place as "the advance guard in language." Since form is central to poetry's ability to create an "intensity of meaning," poems should be concise attempts to express emotions at a given moment. Attacking prose as clumsy, Hulme welcomes poetry that creates new images in an antiromantic and nonheroic manner.

Hulme's early writing gestured to future projects and navigated the intellectual currents of the day. Uniting the concerns of a new poetics with the dynamics of the modern world, he drew on contemporary thinking in psychology and philosophy, especially the work of Henri Bergson and Edmund Husserl as well as late-nineteenth-century discussions of language, including the writings of Friedrich Nietzsche and Rémy de Gourmont.

MAJOR WORKS

In 1908 Hulme was instrumental in forming the Poets' Club, a group of poets and critics who gathered once a month. During this time Hulme was also writing his own poetry. His "Autumn" and "A City Sunset" are often considered the earliest Imagist poems. Putting his poetics into practice, his short (three- to fourteen-line) poems demonstrate the economy, precision, and concentration that would define the poetry of the Imagist movement. At the Poets' Club Hulme presented "A Lecture on Modern Poetry" which reflects many of the principles found in his earlier notes. The lyric of Alfred Tennyson, Percy Bysshe Shelley, and John Keats has run its course. Meter in modern poetry is "cramping, jangling, meaningless." Poetry is not "akin to religion" but rather an intense form of thought and expression. Criticism should discuss poetry in the plainest terms. A new "impressionist" poetry and creative procedure is necessary in light of the decay and obsolescence of old verse.

In March 1909 Hulme started his own poetry collective, which met to consider the state of English poetry. Around the same time he began publishing in A. R. Orage's recently reinvented *New Age*. For Hulme the magazine offered a venue for communicating his opinions about modern art, culture, politics, and philosophy. His articles reflect his growing interest in the philosophy of Bergson, whose thinking Hulme cast into a poetics that could exist in the midst of the cindery flux that constitutes reality. Such poetry, Hulme writes, "always endeavours to arrest you, and to make you continuously see a physical thing, to prevent you gliding through an abstract process." Over the next few years Hulme's interest in poetry showed signs of declining as his interest in philosophy increased. His translation of Bergson's *Revue de Métaphysique et de Morale*, introducing English readers to the epistemology underpinning the new poetics, was published in 1913, and his translation of Sorel's *Réflexions sur la Violence* appeared the following year.

In his frequently anthologized "Romanticism and Classicism" Hulme trumpeted the revival of a "classical spirit" and railed against romanticism's enduring belief in human progress. If romanticism views the individual

as "an infinite reservoir of possibilities," the classical view, he argues, recognizes the fact the "man is an extraordinarily fixed and limited animal whose nature is absolutely constant." Consequently, progress—or "anything decent," in Hulme's words—can be achieved only through discipline, tradition, and organization. By this time he had come under the influence of Pierre Lasserre and Charles Maurras and others associated with the right-wing group L'Action Française. By arguing that Bergson was "but the last disguise of romanticism" Lasserre encouraged Hulme to question whether romanticism lurked in the shadows of his favorite French philosopher's works.

During these years Hulme hosted a weekly salon in Soho Square. Attended by a large cast of intellectuals and artists, the salon drew its vibrancy from its inclusiveness and figured as a crossroads where traditionalists and avant-gardists mingled to discuss literature, art, and politics. Having immersed himself in London's intellectual scene, Hulme found particularly accurate and useful the work of Wilhelm Worringer, who proposed a wide-ranging theory and history of art that suggested intimate connections among art, religion, and philosophy, particularly in non-Western and ancient cultures, in order to counter the assumption that mimesis was the highest aesthetic achievement. Such thinking dovetailed with Hulme's arguments about a new age of classicism in arts and politics and informed his eloquent defense of Jacob Epstein's sculptures in "Mr. Epstein and the Critics" (1913). Hulme's 1914 lecture "The New Art and Its Philosophy"—later published as "Modern Art and Its Philosophy"—offers a compelling rationale for and vivid introduction to modern and avant-gardist art, insisting that in its geometrical and angular character modern art corresponds to the contemporary state of mind. Art, Hulme suggests, "cannot be understood by itself, but must be taken as one element in a general process of adjustment between man and the outside world." In a chaotic and alienating world, the artist endeavors to shape, order, and ultimately "create a certain abstract geometrical shape, which, being durable and permanent shall be a refuge."

In 1915–1916 Hulme's seven-part essay "A Notebook" appeared in the *New Age*. Later published and anthologized as "Humanism and the Religious Attitude," these notes encapsulate many of his core beliefs: that the world was witnessing the imminent decline of Romantic humanism, that original sin is the connective tissue between religious and classical attitudes, and that false categories present serious dangers for thought and life. At this final stage in his philosophy, he was largely preoccupied with the negation and falsification of commonly held beliefs, taking aim at humanism and romanticism in particular. Even classicism, his longstanding antidote to humanism, does not avoid criticism as Hulme curiously dismisses a classical revival as a "partial" and ultimately "inadequate reaction against humanism."

At the start of World War I, Hulme enlisted in the army. He served at the Western Front, first as a private and later, after recovering from wounds, as an officer in the Royal Marine Artillery. In September 1917, Hulme was killed in action near Nieuport in Flanders. He was thirty-four.

Since his death Hulme's significance has been hotly debated. From suggestions that he was merely an amateur philosopher to exasperation at apparent inconsistencies in his work, his reputation has suffered. Pound both dismissed and acknowledged his importance; T. S. Eliot celebrated him as "the forerunner of a new attitude of mind, which should be the twentieth-century mind, if the twentieth century is to have a mind of its own"; F. S. Flint insisted on his importance as the founder of Imagism; Laura Riding suggested that his preoccupation with the past only ensured that he failed the present. But for decades it was Pound's dismissal of Hulme—who he insisted was not as influential as many of his friends had suggested—that stood. Attempting to reconcile positions concerning Hulme's influence, Michael Levenson has commented, " 'T. E. Hulme' might be seen merely as the name of an intellectual site, a place where intellectual currents converged. If that does not make him a 'serious thinker,' it at least makes him worth treating seriously." As recent scholarship returns its gaze to modernism, many of these misconceptions have been resolved, and Hulme is widely recognized as an important if not crucial figure for understanding cultural production in the first half of the twentieth century.

[*See also* Modernism.]

SELECTED WORKS

"The Complete Poetical Works of T. E. Hulme," in Ezra Pound's *Ripostes* (1912)

An Introduction to Metaphysics (translation) (1913)

Reflections on Violence (translation) (New York, 1914; London, 1916)

EDITIONS

Csengeri, Karen, ed. *The Collected Writings of T. E. Hulme* (1994)

Hynes, Sam, ed. *Further Speculations* (1955)

McGuinness, Patrick, ed. *Selected Writings* (1998)

Read, Herbert, ed. *Notes on Language and Style* (1929)

Read, Herbert, ed. *Speculations: Essays on Humanism and the Philosophy of Art* (1924)

FURTHER READING

Coffman, Stanley K. *Imagism: A Chapter for the History of Modern Poetry*. Norman, OK, 1951.

Eliot, T. S. "A Commentary." *Criterion* 2 (1924): 231. An early and influential assessment of Hulme inspired by the publication of *Speculations*.

Ferguson, Robert. *The Short Sharp Life of T. E. Hulme*. London, 2002. A recent biography that sheds light on Hulme's personal life and relationships.

Jones, Alun R. *The Life and Opinions of T. E. Hulme*. London, 1960. An essential biography and early republication of Hulme's writing.

Krieger, Murray. "The Ambiguous Anti-Romanticism of T. E. Hulme." *ELH* 20 (1953): 300–314. An early attempt to resolve many of the apparent contradictions in Hulme's philosophy and aesthetics.

Levenson, Michael H. *A Genealogy of Modernism: A Study of English Literary Doctrine, 1908–1922*. Cambridge, U.K., 1984. Contextualizes and situates Hulme within early literary modernism.

Martin, Wallace. "The Sources of the Imagist Aesthetic." *PMLA* 85 (1970): 196–204. A study of the philosophical foundations of imagism's break with Romantic traditions, finding common influences between Hulme and Pound.

The New Age (1907–1922). http://www.modjourn.brown.edu. A groundbreaking digital archive of the magazine that printed more than three dozen letters and articles by Hulme.

Roberts, Michael. *T. E. Hulme*. London, 1938. Important early introduction to the life and works.

Shusterman, Richard. "Remembering Hulme: A Neglected Philosopher-Critic-Poet." *Journal of the History of Ideas* 46 (1985): 559–576. Prefigures modernist studies' revival of Hulme, stressing the ingenuity of his thought.

LEIGH HUNT

Robert Morrison

Leigh Hunt (1784–1859) is often remembered as the victim of malicious assaults and the cheery friend of more substantial talents. Beginning in 1817, the Tory critics of *Blackwood's Edinburgh Magazine* tarred him as ringleader of the so-called Cockney School of Poetry, an informal group of London writers that included John Keats and whose members *Blackwood's* maligned as vulgar, suburban mediocrities with ideas well above their social station. Hunt suffered again when his friend Charles Dickens pilloried him in *Bleak House* (1852–1853) as the insolvent and unscrupulous Harold Skimpole, an unfair portrait that has nevertheless endured because it successfully if callously exploited two central aspects of Hunt's character: his dedication to beauty and his irresponsible attitude toward money. Hunt has been further diminished by invidious comparisons that set him beside contemporaries and almost inevitably find him wanting: he is important as a radical journalist, but he is not William Cobbett; he is a good literary critic, but he cannot match William Hazlitt or Samuel Taylor Coleridge; he is a fine familiar essayist, but he is no Charles Lamb; he had gifts as a poet, but they paled beside those of Keats and Percy Shelley.

Hunt has a good deal more decency, range, and grit than such assessments allow. At the heart of his writings is a double bind: how to reconcile a dedication to the world of action and unfairness with an equally strong devotion to art, beauty, and aesthetics. Hunt was fervently committed to radical politics and lashed out at contemporary abuses and injustices for over three decades, on one occasion with a recklessness that landed him in prison for two years for libeling the prince regent. Yet he also found great pleasure in books and beauty and in scores of instances produced that conversational familiarity and genial optimism that delighted many of his contemporaries and that continues to attract admirers. His political diatribes are occasionally misdirected, and sometimes his amiable conversation dwindles into a kind of sentimental pap, but much of his finest writing combines his two central preoccupations. In his eyes a love of beauty was deeply consonant with a love of freedom, and highly various literary and aesthetic concerns were sharpened and enriched when directed to political ends. As editor, critic, poet, essayist, and autobiographer, he was repeatedly bold and insightful, and throughout his long career he remained remarkably receptive to new ideas, voices, mediums, and friendships. His writings played a crucial role in pushing Britain toward social and political change, and they challenged and galvanized many of his leading contemporaries, including close friends like Keats and Shelley.

THE EARLY YEARS

Hunt began as a poet when at only seventeen he published his *Juvenalia* (1801), a series of imitations that revealed his early fascination with the work of Edmund Spenser and his extensive knowledge of eighteenth-century poets such as Alexander Pope, Mark Akenside, Thomas Gray, and especially William Collins. The volume was remarkably successful and went through four editions within two years, but it was another decade before Hunt began to publish poetry on a regular and extensive basis. *The Feast of the Poets* (1811) is his truculently satirical survey of contemporary poetry that awards the laurel to Thomas Campbell, Thomas Moore, Walter Scott, and Robert Southey but is most notable for its rough handling of William Wordsworth and Coleridge, both of whom are banished from the feast, the former for puerility and the latter for bombast. Hunt later issued revised and enlarged versions of the poem, adding a series of wide-ranging notes to the second edition of 1814 and modifying his reaction to Wordsworth to the point of admitting him to the feast in the version of 1815. *The Descent of Liberty: A Mask* (1815), a political drama written while Hunt was in prison, responds to the French emperor Napoleon Buonaparte's abdication in April 1814 and characterizes him as an apostate from liberty who has been defeated by a military alliance that must now keep its promises to spread freedom among the citizenry of Europe (though Hunt had soon to accept that such promises were empty). Hunt's most famous long poem, *The Story of Rimini* (1816), was written over a five-year period and took for its central action Dante's story in the *Inferno* of Francesca da Rimini's adulterous love affair with her brother-in-law, Paolo Malatesta. The poem is characterized by bold and innovative linguistic experimentation as Hunt abuts an impassioned historical narrative against neologisms, the vernacular, idiosyncratic expressions, and a less rigid use of the rhyming couplet. Tory publications like *Blackwood's* and the *Quarterly Review* flailed him as ignorant, vulgar, coarse, and depraved, but the depth of their outrage is perhaps the best indication of how thoroughly unnerved they were by his freer spirit of versification and his broadening and subversion of established literary models.

Hunt was also active throughout these early years as an editor, essayist, and critic. On 3 January 1808 he and his brother John Hunt founded the *Examiner*, a sixteen-page, double-columned Sunday newspaper, with Leigh as editor and chief writer and John as publisher. Within a year the paper had established itself as a significant political and cultural voice, and by 1812, at the height of its success, it had a circulation of seven thousand. The *Examiner* attracted a series of key writers, including Hazlitt, Keats, and Lamb, and it printed poems by Lord Byron, Keats, Shelley, and Wordsworth. But there is little question that it owed its success primarily to Hunt's diversity and fearlessness. He was a political critic, a literary critic, and a superb theater critic whose prose style was by turns erudite, familiar, ruminative, satirical, and hotly indignant. He took on issues ranging from military atrocities, Catholic emancipation, poverty, and government corruption to monarchical abuse, industrial advance, imperialism, slavery, and the periodical press. He filled the paper with his own shorter poetry, including squibs, satires, verse epistles, songs, and sonnets. He reviewed contemporary books and magazines, referred repeatedly to his favorite older writers, commemorated holidays, celebrated friendships, attended Parliament and the opera, enjoyed country walks, and recounted life in the streets and parlors of London. Yet at the core of this immense variety stands Hunt's unifying and ceaseless push for reform and a broadly arrayed series of styles, topics, preoccupations, and ideas marshaled into a campaign for renovation, sympathy, tolerance, and fairness.

During these years Hunt also founded and edited two other periodicals, the *Reflector* (1811–1812) and the *Indicator* (1819–1821), both of which were ostensibly dedicated to more literary matters but in which a political

subtext often lurked just below the casual surface. Characteristically, Keats's ballad "La Belle Dame sans Mercy" was first published in the *Indicator* in May 1820, and Hunt in his introduction established a liberal if not radicalized context for the poem by invoking his own recent *Examiner* defenses of sexual liberty in Shelley's work. Hunt has often been condemned for retreating from his political commitments after serving his two-year jail term, but his release in 1815 marked no decline in his criticism of public authority or his intense dissatisfaction with privilege and complacency. Hunt blazed throughout the *Examiner* years, remaining productive even while in prison, fostering hope in a repressive age, and challenging the boundaries between the literary and the journalistic in penetrating critiques that often got well under the skin of Tory reviewers and government officials. By 1821, however, his financial fortunes were at a low ebb, and he decided to give up the editorship of the *Examiner* in order to join Shelley and Byron in Italy, where the three planned to embark on a bold new venture to produce a quarterly journal aptly named the *Liberal*.

THE MIDDLE YEARS

It was of course not to be. Tragedy struck shortly after Hunt and his large family arrived in Italy when Shelley drowned at sea in July 1822. Hunt was devastated by the loss of his closest friend, and while plans for the *Liberal* went ahead, there was little realistic chance of success without the tempering influence of Shelley. The first issue appeared on 15 October 1822 and was highlighted by Hunt's prefatory essay on the goals and allegiances of the *Liberal* and by Byron's brilliantly satiric "Vision of Judgement." But the relationship between Hunt and Byron had already begun to deteriorate, and though subsequent issues featured work by Hazlitt and Mary Shelley, as well as continuing contributions from Byron and especially Hunt, the *Liberal* lasted only four numbers and collapsed within a year, its enormous potential unable to overcome tragedy, hostility, and indifference. Hunt's badly strained finances prevented him from returning to England until 1825, when the publisher Henry Colburn advanced him £200 and engaged him as a regular contributor to his highly popular *New Monthly Magazine*, where Hunt published more than fifty articles over the next twenty-five years. Colburn got his money back in 1828 when he published Hunt's *Lord Byron and Some of His Contemporaries*, a thoroughly uncharitable account of Byron and his involvement with the *Liberal* that brought the full vindictiveness of the Tory press down upon Hunt and turned a tidy profit for Colburn.

Hunt returned to founding and writing his own journals. The *Companion* (1828) featured his pleasure in the progress of liberal opinion and his delight at the repeal of the notorious Test and Corporation Acts. This journal carried apparently desultory essays, such as "On the Graces and Anxieties of Pig-Driving," that were nevertheless politically charged by Cockney place names and working-class subject matter. The *Companion* was discontinued after only seven months. Hunt's next venture, the *Chat of the Week* (1830), lasted only thirteen issues, for his enthusiasm at the outbreak of the second French Revolution of late July brought him again to the attention of government censors, who quickly had the paper shut down. Hunt, however, was not to be quenched. He reemerged only a week later with the *Tatler* (1830–1832), a daily that featured an enormous range of material, including an examination of Hazlitt's political thought, book reviews of reissues of Thomas Paine's *The Rights of Man* and William Godwin's *Adventures of Caleb Williams*, theater reviews of Richard Brinsley Sheridan's comedy *The Rivals* and Byron's tragedy *Werner*, great praise for the young Alfred Tennyson's *Poems, Chiefly Lyrical*, a lashing of Walter Scott for his benighted attitude toward political reform, and a celebration of Christmas Day in which Hunt tellingly observes that the rich have too much Christmas all year round.

In 1833 Hunt went to work for a series of radical publications buoyed by the recent passage of the Reform Bill, including *Tait's Edinburgh Magazine*, the *True Sun*, and the *Weekly True Sun*, where he produced a nine-part series called "The Townsman," in which he extolled the walks, stones, and trees of London and revealed it as a place richly endowed by unespied beauty and the memory of past events. *Leigh Hunt's London Journal* (1834–1835) featured Hunt's sadness at the death of his close friend Charles Lamb, his keen appreciation of Robert Browning's poem *Paracelsus*, and his account of Twelfth Night as an evening of games in which rigid class barriers are dismantled and all are kings and queens. In 1837 Hunt briefly became editor of the *Monthly Repository*, where he campaigned vigorously for household suffrage and national education, and a year later his career seemed to come full circle when he returned to the *Examiner* and reviewed the work of new friends, such as Thomas Carlyle and Charles Dickens, whose *Oliver Twist* he praised for its combination of wit, tenderness, and social utility.

Throughout these middle years Hunt also stayed active as a poet. He denounced the Tory editor William Gifford in *Ultra-Crepidarius* (1823) and war in *Captain Sword and Captain Pen* (1835). He collected his *Poetical Works* (1832) and prefaced them with one of his most important explorations of poetry and the poetic imagination. He surveyed contemporary women's writing in "Blue-Stocking Revels" (1837); and produced a series of oft-anthologized set pieces, such as "Rondeau" (1838) and "Abou Ben Adhem and the Angel" (1838). Hunt's personal fortunes during the 1820s and 1830s were in a state of perpetual crisis that no amount of hard work seemed to restore, and while he grew more conscious of producing lighter works that would sell, he remained highly productive and determinedly political, encouraged no doubt in great part by the reforms of these decades that he had done so much to inspire and assist.

THE FINAL YEARS

Hunt had long harbored ambitions as a dramatist. Although he wrote several plays, he met with his only success in February 1840, when his *Legend of Florence* was staged to great acclaim at Covent Garden and was even praised by his old nemesis, *Blackwood's Magazine*. Queen Victoria attended twice and in 1852 ordered a command performance at Windsor Castle. Hunt, his antimonarchical sentiments displaced by his admiration for the young queen, responded by dedicating to her one of his most impressive later poems, *The Palfrey* (1842), and by unsuccessfully jockeying for the position of poet laureate, which went to Wordsworth in 1843 and Tennyson in 1850.

Hunt continued to publish in periodicals ranging from *Fraser's Magazine* and the *Edinburgh Review* to *Ainsworth's Magazine* and Dickens's *Household Words*. In 1850 he founded *Leigh Hunt's Journal*, though like many of his previous attempts in a similar line, it soon failed. Hunt produced books on a wide variety of subjects, from the amusements and anecdotes of *Readings for Railways* (1849) and the meditations of *The Religion of the Heart* (1853) to a series of works on London, including *The Town* (1848) and *The Old Court Suburb* (1855). As anthologist, literary critic, and cultural guru, he issued volumes such as *Imagination and Fancy* (1844), *Wit and Humour* (1846), and *A Jar of Honey from Mount Hybla* (1847), in which he quoted long sections of his favorite English and Italian poets and, with italics, footnotes, and introductions, highlighted what he found most impressive and important in their work. His essay "An Answer to the Question, 'What Is Poetry?' " appeared as the preface to *Imagination and Fancy*, and both recalibrated these two central terms and offered the finest account of his poetic theory.

Hunt's most significant publication during these years, however, was his *Autobiography* (1850; revised 1860), which is widely regarded as the first example of its type in English literature. In it he surveyed the whole of his career but highlighted the political cut and thrust of the *Examiner* years and his seminal friendship with Shelley. It is an engaging and revealing account of a writer who spent much of his life in the thick of the political fray, whose highly varied output is bent repeatedly to the cause of cultural and social reform, and whose many irresponsible decisions were outweighed by his courage, his insight, his ability to command affection, and his lifelong commitment to the ideals of tolerance and equality.

[*See also* George Gordon, Lord Byron; William Hazlitt; John Keats; Charles Lamb; Mary Wollstonecraft Shelley; *and* Percy Bysshe Shelley.]

SELECTED WORKS

The *Examiner* (1808–1821)
The Story of Rimini (1816)
The *Indicator* (1819–1821)
The *Liberal* (1822–1823)
Lord Byron and Some of His Contemporaries (1828)
The *Tatler* (1830–1832)
Poetical Works (1832)
Captain Sword and Captain Pen (1835)
Imagination and Fancy (1844)
The Autobiography (1850)

EDITION

Cox, Jeffrey N., Greg Kucich, Charles Mahoney, Robert Morrison, and John Strachan. *The Selected Writings of Leigh Hunt*. 6 vols. London, 2003. A wide-ranging selection of Hunt's journalism, literary criticism, and poetry, with a general introduction and individual volume introductions.

FURTHER READING

Blunden, Edmund. *Leigh Hunt: A Biography*. London, 1930. Highly readable account of Hunt, his writings, and his many friendships and disappointments.

Cox, Jeffrey N. *Poetry and Politics in the Cockney School*. Cambridge, U.K., 1998. Places Hunt at the center of a group of writers that included Shelley, Keats, Hazlitt, and Byron, and that sought to put literature into the service of cultural and political reform.

Edgecombe, Rodney Stenning. *Leigh Hunt and the Poetry of Fancy*. Madison, NJ, 1994. A detailed consideration of Hunt as poet.

Gates, Eleanor M., ed. *Leigh Hunt: A Life in Letters*. Essex, CT, 1998. An extensive selection of Hunt letters, chronologically arranged, introduced, and annotated.

Holden, Anthony. *The Wit in the Dungeon: A Life of Leigh Hunt*. London, 2005. Comprehensive biography of Hunt, with attention to his many friendships and his versatility as nineteenth-century England's most productive man of letters.

Marshall, William Harvey. *Byron, Shelley, Hunt, and the "Liberal."* Philadelphia, 1960. An engaging account of the brilliant but ill-fated journal.

McCown, Robert A., ed. *The Life and Times of Leigh Hunt*. Iowa City, IA, 1985. A bicentenary commemoration of six essays that features work on Hunt as Skimpole and as dramatist, essayist, and poet.

Roe, Nicholas. *Fiery Heart: The First Life of Leigh Hunt*. London, 2005. Focuses on Hunt's life until 1822.

Roe, Nicholas, ed. *Leigh Hunt: Life, Poetics, Politics*. London, 2003. A collection of twelve essays covering various aspects of Hunt's career, including his cockneyism, aesthetics, misjudgments, and influence.

Thompson, James R. *Leigh Hunt*. Boston, 1977. An introductory overview of Hunt's many-faceted career.

ALDOUS HUXLEY

Gavin Keulks

Aldous Leonard Huxley (1894–1963) was without question one of the most productive and versatile writers in history, publishing a breathtaking number of books over a five-decade period. Writing at a pace that rivaled Anthony Trollope's legendary output, Huxley regularly published two or more books per year, even when his contract with Chatto & Windus did not require it. The expansive scope of Huxley's career makes summary difficult. His literary output ranges across poetry, short stories, novels, essays, and a smattering of plays for stage and screen. In addition, Huxley traveled extensively; was a husband, father, lecturer, and scholar; and socialized with some of the world's finest minds.

His earliest introduction to intellectual society actually occurred on 26 July 1894, when he was born to Leonard and Judith Arnold Huxley. The Huxleys formed one of the greatest intellectual dynasties in history, one that easily rivaled similar coteries among the Rossettis and the Woolfs. Huxley's father was the son of Thomas Henry Huxley, the celebrated writer, biologist, and champion of Darwinian theory; his mother was the niece of Matthew Arnold and the sister of Mrs. Humphrey Ward, a successful novelist. Huxley's brother, Julian, eventually followed in their grandfather's path, becoming a noted biologist, and in 1963 Huxley's half-brother, Andrew, won the Nobel Prize for his physiology research. Some children would no doubt be silenced by such precedent family fame; one of the world's most encompassing, inquisitive thinkers, Aldous Huxley found it inspiring.

EARLY NOVELS, EMERGENT FORMS

Huxley's continued fame will likely rest on the reputation of his novels rather than his nonfiction, poetry, or

Aldous Huxley
Photograph by Howard Coster, 1934
NATIONAL PORTRAIT GALLERY, LONDON

drama—especially *Point Counter Point* (1928) and *Brave New World* (1932), two sophisticated satires of intellectual complacency and institutionalized oppression. His detractors might argue that these works, especially the latter, have disproportionately skewed his historical significance, and they would be partly correct. But they would also fail to note Huxley's lifelong engagement with these novels' social themes, which Huxley strived to develop in earlier books and continued to refine even at the end of his career.

Like most writers, Huxley struggled with direction, form, and voice at the beginning of his career. After publishing a few volumes of poetry, he switched to short stories and drama with *Limbo* (1920). Huxley's first novel, *Crome Yellow*, appeared in 1921, to be followed by *Antic Hay* (1923) and *Those Barren Leaves* (1925). These early novels are united not only in theme but also in inspiration: their biographical genesis lay in Huxley's visits to Garsington, a country estate owned by Philip Morrell and his wife, Lady Ottoline. At Garsington Huxley met such artistic luminaries as T. S. Eliot, Virginia Woolf, and especially D. H. Lawrence, who became a lifelong friend. He also made the acquaintance of Maria Nys, a war refugee he would marry in 1919. Garsington was the site of numerous lively discussions, and the themes and rhythms of such debates migrated effortlessly to Huxley's novels.

Many of Huxley's books feature elements of the country-house novel and the novel of ideas; *Crome Yellow* and *Those Barren Leaves* feature elements of Menippean satire as well. In comparison with Horatian and Juvenalian satire, Menippean works are far more grotesque and discursive, modeled on the work of François Rabelais and Thomas Love Peacock rather than Henry Fielding or Jonathan Swift. Characters function as symbolic mouthpieces for the ideologies they espouse; often they meet in isolated locations, such as ancestral estates, and their compressed universes yield metaphorical depth. Huxley's first novel, for instance, satirizes the solipsistic delusions of the guests at Crome Yellow, the country estate owned by Henry Wimbush. Their conversations meander through various subjects that held Huxley's interest—notably Freud, poetry, and art—but the characters' imprisoning self-concern prohibits synthesis. They fail to perceive that underneath such subjects lies the unifying need to communicate—to connect. Barring such epiphanies, they endorse no meaningful ethical or moral imperatives. They represent action (and opinion) lacking cause or consequence. In the end, only Denis Stone, a poet, perceives the waste of time that Crome Yellow signifies. Fittingly, Huxley does not bestow any existential gravity on his character's recognition, refusing to redeem his insular, claustrophobic world.

If Huxley had intended the novel to be a satiric re-imagining of the time he had spent at Garsington, then he was successful: Lady Ottoline took great offense. Huxley, however, was a far more serious writer than her offense would imply. Although biographical connections loom throughout his work—notably his connection with D. H. Lawrence—Huxley's horizons were vast. Traversing issues both timeless and contemporary, his work supports satire's primary historical mandate: to expose moral blindness and ethical failing.

Huxley's next two novels, *Antic Hay* and *Those Barren Leaves*, deepen his critique of monomaniacal modernism. The first book exposes the narrow, limited world of post-war London, where the novel's lead character, Theodore Gumbril Jr., pursues his dream of becoming the "Complete Man." Having abandoned altruism for egotism, he leaves teaching to sell inflatable pants. Among the other characters, Myra Viveash and Gumbril's father are the most interesting. A sensualist and socialite, Viveash epitomizes the narcissism of a generation pursuing effervescent goals. A recluse, Gumbril senior symbolizes exile and retreat; arguably, however, he is the novel's only moral center, working quietly without hope of recognition, willing to sacrifice for others.

Huxley returned to the thematic structures of *Crome Yellow* for his third novel, which fails to match the depth of his earlier books. Completed in five months—a startling pace, though common for Huxley—*Those Barren Leaves* portrays life at an Italian villa called Cybo Malaspina. As in *Crome Yellow*, the characters in this microcosmic world pursue selfish, stillborn goals. Among the most important, Mary Thriplow, a young novelist, struggles to balance the competing demands of art and life; Mr. Calamy, a traveler, romantically pursues her. When their fleeting relationship dissolves, Calamy rejects the sensual world and journeys toward enlightenment on a mountaintop. His departure from the facetious gathering at Cybo Malaspina recalls Gumbril senior's seclusion in *Antic Hay* and foreshadows later Huxley journeymen and exiles, including Uncle Eustace in *Time Must Have a Stop* (1944), Poole and Loola in *Ape and Essence* (1948), and Will Farnaby in *Island* (1962).

POINT COUNTER POINT AND BRAVE NEW WORLD

Although Huxley's three earliest novels certainly established their author as one of the most incisive satirists of his day, they could not, even in the aggregate, portend the mature masterpieces that would follow. Dissimilar in form and direction, *Point Counter Point* and *Brave New World* ensured Huxley's international fame. Decidedly complex, ambitiously innovative, these books achieve a fineness of execution that is absent from his lesser work.

Point Counter Point ranges across diverse attitudes and literary styles without succumbing to any tempting, reductive simplification. Such multiplicity of perspective renders the novel complex, too demanding for some readers, yet its content is more substantive than its tour de force techniques. Alternating portraits of modern morality appear as contrasting fragments, and meaning arises from dual sources: juxtaposition and the reader's synthesizing mind.

Three characters chiefly animate the narrative. Philip Quarles acts as an authorial surrogate and is arguably the most important. A writer, Quarles seeks new narrative forms that could mirror the polyphony of music rather than the linearity of prose. Huxley's experiments, through Quarles, with self-referentiality as well as musical structure are historically important, too: the novel anticipates later works such as Lawrence Durrell's *The Alexandria Quartet* as well as better-publicized movements such as postmodernism. The other significant characters in *Point Counter Point*, Mark Rampion and Maurice Spandrell, are set in binary opposition, a common practice for Huxley, especially with female characters. Rampion—modeled on D. H. Lawrence—repudiates stigmatized belief, preferring a more dynamic moral outlook. Admired by Quarles, Rampion's ideas fail to sway the other characters or, for that matter, the reader. Far less malleable, Maurice Spandrell seeks uniformity of belief. His nihilism is the counterpoint to Rampion's faith in integrated living. Convinced that life has been unjustly preordained, Spandrell gleefully provokes disorder, reveling in disruptive actions that bracket two deaths: the murder of a Fascist leader and Spandrell's suicide. In the end, the novel rejects all vested ideologies. Like musical instruments or compositions, the characters' voices vie for legitimacy; their discourse, however, terminates only in the reader's mind. The novel ranks among the finest showcases for Huxley's narrative and structural innovations, his perspectival complexity, and his contrapuntal technique. Four years later Huxley's most famous novel, *Brave New World*, would appear, portraying one of the most celebrated examples of modern technocratic dystopias.

For many Huxley scholars, *Brave New World* signals a shift in Huxley's work, marking the onset of the social prophecy that would characterize the second half of his career. That is not to say that Huxley foreswore such a theme in his earlier work; rather, the scope and the tenor of analysis expanded, so that instead of scrutinizing characters' individual failings, Huxley concentrated on leveling society's institutional forces. With its regimented classes and pharmaceutically controlled emotions, its scientific incubation and somnambulant education, *Brave New World* conjures a world that is perfectly ordered yet palpably sterile. When a catalytic agent in the form of an outsider, John the Savage, is introduced to this world, coexistence proves impossible.

The offspring of two cultures—son of the Chief Controller but also of a mother who raised him on an Indian reservation—John remains ostracized from both of his symbolic worlds. Transplanted by Bernard Marx and Lenina Crowne, the novel's other main characters, his passionate, "savage" humanity cannot withstand the dehumanization that lies at the core of his new life. His feelings of love—for literature as well as for Lenina—cannot insulate him from conformity, and in the end he commits suicide, having failed to balance his humanity with his homogenizing new world, which proves anything but brave. More than seventy years after its publication, the novel continues to inspire new generations of readers who have witnessed with creeping trepidation such developments as cloning, the proliferation of psychotherapeutic drugs, and the advent of genetic engineering.

LATER WORK: PROPHETIC CELEBRITY

Huxley's novels after 1932 remain a vital source for literary scholarship but lack a general readership. *Eyeless in Gaza*, published in 1936, inspires debate about its loose narrative structure, which is composed of dated scenic fragments. Some critics contend that the novel reveals another level of Huxley's structural innovations. Others feel that *Eyeless in Gaza* fails to satisfy the substance of its themes; closure arises too conventionally, arguably through cliché.

The novel that followed, *After Many a Summer Dies the Swan* (1939), was the first to emerge from Huxley's residence in the United States. An inveterate traveler and therefore never confined to any nationality, Huxley emigrated to America in 1937. It remained his home until his death. During this period he continued to publish an astonishing number of books, and, like William Faulkner, F. Scott Fitzgerald, Graham Greene, and others, even tried his hand at Hollywood screenwriting. In addition, this period of Huxley's career seems devoted to three interrelated subjects: peace, perception, and science.

The characters in *After Many a Summer* (the abbreviated English title) perfectly reflect Huxley's modified life: one character is a scientist; another is a rich, art-collecting Californian; another is a transplanted Englishman trying to make sense out of his strange new world. In brief, despite moments of comic brilliance, the novel's morality seems diffuse. Its narcissistic, superficial characters rank among the most memorable in Huxley's gallery of grotesque talking heads, but for many readers, the resolution seems problematic, too quickly achieved. The novel ends without reckoning, as two characters observe the animalistic mating of a half-human English nobleman who has sacrificed his humanity for longevity. It is as though Huxley spared his misguided egotists the comeuppance they deserved—and which similar characters in earlier books had received.

Five years would pass before Huxley's next novel appeared. Such an intermission—absent from the early stages of his career—became more and more common in the second half. *Time Must Have a Stop* and *Island* are arguably his finest novels to emerge from their decades. They are intersected by two overly didactic works, *Ape and Essence* (1948) and *The Genius and the Goddess* (1955). Concerned to varying degrees with the creation and consequences of the atomic bomb, these didactic books accelerate the rhetoric of *Brave New World*, presenting archetypal characters who flail helplessly against the boundaries of their prophetic worlds. Willful allegories of inverted progress and humanist defeat, the novels are historically significant, especially in the contexts of postwar politics and apocalyptic fear. With the exception of Huxley scholars, however, their audience is dwindling.

By contrast, *Time Must Have a Stop* presents a less stentorian, more refined treatment of the themes of experience, diminishment, and death. Sebastian Barnack, a young Englishman, leaves London for Italy to seek happiness under the protection (and financial auspices) of his uncle Eustace. The novel improves upon the narrative inventiveness of *Eyeless in Gaza* by offering a more linear and controlled structure that nonetheless facilitates multiple perspectives. When Eustace dies, his spirit simply migrates to a different temporal realm, for instance. Continuing to speak from the afterlife, his voice mediates the novel's more serious, philosophical matter through light comic wistfulness.

As would be expected, not all readers welcome such experimentation. Some find the nonlinear sections of the novel tendentious; others find them distracting. Regardless, such artistic decisions confirm Huxley's lifelong interest, from *Those Barren Leaves* onward, in probing the limits of literary realism. Later writers, especially those grouped under the labels "nouveau roman" and "magical realism," would attempt far more extreme manipulations yet receive far greater credit. Furthermore, such choices directly reflect, and stylistically facilitate, Huxley's increasing fascination with themes of perception and altered states of consciousness. Famously, Huxley would experiment with altered states outside of his fiction, culminating in his controlled use of mescaline and LSD, the effects of which he described in *The Doors of Perception* (1954).

The other significant novel of this period, *Island* (1962), stands alone in Huxley's canon for its attempt to envision a utopia. Will Farnaby, the novel's protagonist, journeys to the island of Pala and discovers an enlightened society that apparently has balanced the competing demands of spirituality and subsistence, transcendence and mundanity. As with all such paradisiacal constructions, their isolation proves unstable: external forces loom, and a cloud of international commerce threatens the island's future. Attesting to Huxley's late swerve from didacticism, some of the novel's most serious words come from a comically playful source—the Mynah birds, whose chants remind the Palanese to pay "attention" and stay in the "here and now."

Although it may be argued that Huxley wrote too much and that much of what he published may one day be forgotten, startlingly few writers can rival his productivity or the quality of his satiric masterpieces, especially *Brave New World* and *Point Counter Point*. His persistent critique of society's superficiality, fragmentation, and decay positioned him at the heart of modern socio-literary debates, and his stylistic and structural experimentations remain undercredited by nonspecialists, overshadowed by his modernist contemporaries. As Huxley scholars have rightfully concluded, he is the last of the great Victorian types—the intellectual polymath, the archetypal man of letters. Although Huxley wrote much that fell below his highest level of achievement, in our contemporary era of isolationist, often exclusionary, specialization, it seems increasingly tempting to say of Huxley what Hamlet said of the ghost of his father—that "he was a man, take him for all in all"; the literary world may never look upon his like again.

[*See also* D. H. Lawrence; George Orwell; *and* Utopianism.]

SELECTED WORKS

The Burning Wheel (1916)

Crome Yellow (1921)

Antic Hay (1923)

Those Barren Leaves (1925)

Point Counter Point (1928)

Brave New World (1932)

Beyond the Mexique Bay (1934)

Eyeless in Gaza (1936)

Stories, Essays, and Poems (1937)

The Gioconda Smile (1938)

After Many a Summer (1939; republished as *After Many a Summer Dies the Swan*)

Grey Eminence: A Study in Religion and Politics (1941)

Time Must Have a Stop (1944)

Science, Liberty, and Peace (1946)

The World of Aldous Huxley: An Omnibus of His Fiction and Non-Fiction over Three Decades (1947)

Ape and Essence (1948)

The Devils of Loudun (1952)

The Doors of Perception (1954)

The Genius and the Goddess (1955)

Adonis and the Alphabet, and Other Essays (1956; republished as *Tomorrow and Tomorrow and Tomorrow, and Other Essays*)

Collected Short Stories (1957)

Brave New World Revisited (1958)

Collected Essays (1959)

Island (1962)

Literature and Science (1963)

The Crows of Pearlblossom (1967)

EDITIONS

Ferrucci, Piero, ed. *The Human Situation: Lectures at Santa Barbara, 1959*. New York, 1972.

Smith, Grover, ed. *Letters of Aldous Huxley*. London, 1969.

Watt, Donald, ed. *The Collected Poetry of Aldous Huxley*. London, 1971.

FURTHER READING

Baker, Robert S. *The Dark Historic Page: Social Satire and Historicism in the Novels of Aldous Huxley 1921–1939*. Madison, WI, 1982.

Bass, Eben E. *Aldous Huxley: An Annotated Bibliography of Criticism*. New York, 1981.

Bedford, Sybille. *Aldous Huxley: A Biography*. 2 vols. London, 1973–1974.

Bradshaw, David, ed. *The Hidden Huxley: Contempt and Compassion for the Masses, 1920–1936*. New York, 1994.

Dunaway, David King. *Aldous Huxley Recollected: An Oral History*. Chapel Hill, NC, 1995.

Firchow, Peter E., et al. *Reluctant Modernists: Aldous Huxley and Some Contemporaries*. Münster, Germany, 2002.

Huxley, Julian, ed. *Aldous Huxley, 1894–1963: A Memorial Volume*. London, 1965.

Huxley, Laura Archera. *This Timeless Moment: A Personal View of Aldous Huxley*. New York, 1968.

Kuehn, Robert E., ed. *Aldous Huxley: A Collection of Critical Essays*. Englewood Cliffs, NJ, 1974.

Mechier, Jerome. *Aldous Huxley: Satire and Structure*. London, 1969.

Mechier, Jerome, ed. *Critical Essays on Aldous Huxley*. New York, 1996.

Nugel, Bernfried, ed. *Now More Than Ever: Proceedings of the Aldous Huxley Centenary Symposium, Münster, 1994*. Münster, Germany, 1995.

ELIZABETH INCHBALD

Amanda Gilroy

A successful playwright, theater critic, and novelist as well as a celebrated beauty, Elizabeth Inchbald (1753–1821) was at the center of literary life in late-eighteenth-century London. She was born Elizabeth Simpson on 15 October 1753, the daughter of a middle-class Catholic farming family that lived near Bury St. Edmunds, Suffolk. Determined to see the world, she ran away to London at the age of eighteen to become an actress. She married the much older actor Joseph Inchbald in June 1772 (she was eighteen and he was thirty-seven). Soon afterward they both joined a Bristol theater company, and Elizabeth Inchbald made her debut on stage as Cordelia in *King Lear* despite a stammer that she never completely overcame. Inchbald was already writing during these early years with provincial theater companies. She kept pocketbooks in which she recorded her daily activities with a wealth of detail about plays, politics, her fears, her friends, and her financial accounts, and in 1777 she was at work on drafts of the novel that was to become *A Simple Story*. After her husband's sudden death in 1779, Inchbald continued to act until 1789 but supplemented her income by writing for the stage.

Inchbald appeared on stage with some of the era's most famous actors, including John Kemble and Sarah Siddons, and among her friends were other women writers, such as Amelia Anderson Opie and Anna Laetitia Barbauld. She had a long-standing but discreet relationship with the divorced Sir Charles Bunbury and flirtatious friendships with the radical writers William Godwin and Thomas Holcroft, whose works she read in manuscript, as they did hers. Samuel Taylor Coleridge could not understand Godwin's professional and personal intimacy with Inchbald—which included a proposal of marriage in 1793—and he anxiously noted her "heart-picking look." Across

Elizabeth Inchbald
Pencil drawing by George Dance, 1794
NATIONAL PORTRAIT GALLERY, LONDON

her oeuvre, which includes two novels, more than twenty plays, and biographical and critical prefaces to popular drama, Inchbald picks away with cool precision at repressed emotions and desires. She managed to charm her audiences and readers while offering an unsentimental probing of social norms of gender, race, and class subordination.

PLAYS

Inchbald's first success as a writer was her farcical afterpiece *The Mogul Tale; or, The Descent of the Balloon*, which was accepted by George Colman and opened at the Haymarket in July 1784. From then until her final play in 1805, she was the unofficial writer in residence at the Haymarket in the summer and Covent Garden in the winter. *The Mogul Tale* features a party of London ballooners—a "quack" doctor and a cobbler and his wife—who accidentally land in the middle of the seraglio of a great Mogul. Inchbald played one of the Mogul's many wives. The Mogul decides to test the effect of his visitors' fears, and on the advice of his eunuch, the three English characters pretend to be an ambassador from the British king, the pope, and a nun doing penance for the sin of bearing the pope's children. The play satirizes George III's prolific family and British imperial ambitions—France appears in the list of the British king's dominions. Inchbald's technique of parodic inversion defines the play's politics. The English characters display stereotypical signs of Oriental excess, while the Mogul's despotism is a dramatic pretense that exposes the stereotype assigned to him by Europeans. Many jokes about deflated balloons indicate the impotence of the Englishmen and suggest the enervation of British subjects involved in colonialism. Characteristically for Inchbald's plays, *The Mogul Tale* is full of topical interest. It exploits the pervasive balloon mania of 1784 in the wake of the

Mongolfier brothers' successful flight. Inchbald also cleverly dramatized contemporary political cartoons linking the instabilities of balloon travel to Indian affairs. Her mild Mogul effectively endorses reformers' support for Indian self-government and aligns her play with Charles Fox's East India Bill, defeated in December 1783, which aimed to restructure the East India Company. At the same time Inchbald plays to her audience and celebrates English patriotism, allowing the English couple to insist sentimentally that "there's no place like home."

The following year Inchbald consolidated her reputation as a dramatist with the comedy *I'll Tell You What* (1785), in which two elderly gentlemen return from a long stay in the West Indies and encounter a complicated plot of intrigue, divorces, and remarriages, concluding with the divorced Lady Harriet's recognition that women "of the world" are condemned to unhappiness. Of Inchbald's other original plays, perhaps the most interesting is *Such Things Are*, a combination of farce, pathos, and satirical social commentary first performed in 1787. The play revolves around the visit of Mr. Haswell, a character modeled on the British prison reformer John Howard, to the dungeons of a Sumatran despot, and it alternates between a sad story of love and imprisonment (the sultan, another closet Christian like Inchbald's earlier Mogul, has mistakenly imprisoned his own European wife, Arabella) and a satire on the social climbing and fashionable pretensions of the British subjects in the colony. Through the intervention of Haswell, the sultan's wife is freed, and the Eastern couple offer a model of conjugal happiness that contrasts with the bickering of Sir Luke and Lady Tremor. That Arabella exchanges imprisonment for a life of "sweet captivity" suggests something of Inchbald's satirical take on the way the institution of marriage oppresses women. In the context of the impending trial of Warren Hastings, the former governor general of the East India Company, the play links an Oriental career with familial, sexual, and economic exploitation and thus exposes the fiction of benevolent colonialism onstage at the heart of the empire.

In an 1807 essay in *The Artist*, Inchbald claimed that "a dramatist must not speak of national concerns, except in one dull round of panegyrick," but she broke this rule many times, especially in the five plays that ridicule Anglo-Indian relations as well as in *Every One Has His Fault* (1793), which concerns domestic and social problems to do with paternal authority and financial and moral obligations. Conservative writers claimed that the play promoted radical social "disorganisation," but the theatergoing public and press loved it. As well as writing original dramas, Inchbald also sensitively adapted the plays of French and German dramatists for the English stage. The sophistication of the French comedies on which she worked helped her achieve greater levels of refinement in her own work. *Animal Magnetism*, adapted from Antoine-Jean-Bourlin Dumaniant (1752–1828) in 1788, became one of her most popular and frequently performed plays. This three-act farce features a quack doctor who wants to marry his ward, Constance, but is outwitted by her, the young marquis she loves, their two servants, and a magic wand. Topical interest in the play focuses on the theories of the Swiss physician Anton Mesmer regarding the hypnotic effects of animal magnetism and on the quack treatments of contemporary London "doctors" (such as James Graham, whose Temple of Health offered milk baths, electrical treatments, and a giant "Celestial Bed" that apparently guaranteed procreation). Inchbald's wildly successful adaptation of August von Kotzebue's *Das Kind der Liebe* as *Lovers' Vows* opened at Covent Garden in October 1798 and had forty-five performances in its first run. GG and J. Robinson reprinted it thirteen times in the next five years, and it played all over England and Ireland for many years, including fifteen performances in Bath during the period 1801–1806, while Jane Austen was living there. It is best remembered in the early twenty-first century as the play that throws the Bertram household into chaos in *Mansfield Park* (1814).

NOVELS

Inchbald's first novel, *A Simple Story*, was published in 1791 and quickly went through several editions. Although not part of the traditional canon of eighteenth-century novels, it has always had its admirers. The tale combines two plots separated by a time span of seventeen years. The first two volumes recount the on-off courtship and eventual marriage of the beautiful and willful heiress Miss Milner and Dorriforth or Lord Elmwood. Dorriforth is a taboo object of desire for Miss Milner not only because he is her guardian but also because he is a Catholic priest, who, however, is released from his vows to assume the title Lord Elmwood. Volume three opens with the death of the heroine in self-imposed exile, following her adultery many years earlier while her husband was absent at his West Indian plantation (another sly dig at the consequences of colonialism). Lord Elmwood agrees that their daughter, Matilda, can live on one of his estates following her mother's death, but she is forbidden to see or speak to her father. The second half of the novel details the perverse estrangement of father and daughter and their final reconciliation after Lord Elmwood rescues Matilda from abduction by a villainous rake.

In contemporary reviews as well as in modern criticism, Inchbald's skillful characterization has been praised for its "dramatic" quality. It is generally supposed that Miss Milner is in part a self-portrait and that Dorriforth is modeled on the charismatic Kemble, who had also trained for the priesthood and with whom Inchbald had an intense relationship. Generic modification is evident as Inchbald imports aspects of the newly naturalistic style of late-eighteenth-century acting into her fiction. She demonstrates a theatrical control of the action and allows characters to reveal themselves in dialogue and through significant physical attitudes, often using a standardized language of theatrical gesture. Throughout the novel, bodies express inexpressible desire. Thus Miss Milner faints dramatically upon hearing that Dorriforth is to fight a duel and turns "pale as death" at news of his engagement to another, rendering her prohibited passion for him visible for the reader; in turn, when Lord Elmwood catches his swooning daughter in his arms, he presses her once to his bosom, unconsciously acting out the feelings he refuses to acknowledge. The novel brilliantly reveals emotional distress and repressed feelings by little signs and partially hidden expressions and confirms the reputation Inchbald had among her contemporaries of being able to expose "the labyrinth of the passions."

However, critics have often been bothered by the novel's apparent lack of unity. The two halves of the novel are self-sufficient, and some readers find them mechanically rather than organically joined. Indeed the second part was written some ten years later than the first. Even characters seem to metamorphose between volumes two and three. One solution to this aesthetic problem is to focus on psychological continuities and thus to see the fraught Oedipal attachment of the second part replaying the transgressive erotic pattern of the first. It is notable that in the famous scene on the stairs, when Lord Elmwood saves his fainting daughter from falling, he calls her "Miss Milner." Another is to think historically rather than aesthetically and thus to see Inchbald as deliberately resisting harmonious novelistic closure and instead showing two of the dominant versions of power available to eighteenth-century women. Miss Milner has some of the features of a conduct-book heroine (kindness, stoicism, obedience), but she is also a compulsive shopper who seems to embody the reckless female consumerism against which conduct books inveighed. Impetuous and passionate, she provokes a crisis when, determined to test her power over Dorriforth, she attends a masquerade in defiance of his prohibition. The feisty Miss Milner is replaced in the second half of the novel by her daughter Matilda, who is less a psychologically rounded character than a pattern of femininity. Passive, silent, submissive, tenderhearted as a sentimental heroine, Matilda is always a victim—of her father's tyranny and of Margrave's plot to kidnap and rape her. Inchbald's novel supports both female resistance to male authority and passive submission to it. Both heroines get Lord Elmwood as their reward, but the split narrative suggests that these two modes of female power cannot be reconciled and exposes the limited options available to late-eighteenth-century women. The novel's conventional concluding moral message that Miss Milner lacked "A PROPER EDUCATION" seems tacked on, more a gesture to literary respectability than an adequate summation of this not-so-simple novel.

Inchbald's second and final novel, *Nature and Art* (1796), returns to the issues of education, familial disjunction, and clerical fallibility, telling the story of the contrasting sensibilities of two brothers, William and Henry Norwynne, and their equally dissimilar sons of the same names. The elder William, university-educated through his brother's generosity, is snobbish and upwardly mobile. Ecclesiastical corruption is exposed in his career as a sycophantic dean. His miseducated son seduces and abandons the lower-class Hannah Primrose; as a magistrate, this William later sentences Hannah to death. Thus the legal system, like the church, is foregrounded as part of the apparatus of class and gender oppression. The novel offers a fascinating scrutiny of masculinity, suggesting that men are made, not born, in that the character deformations of the two Williams occur within a burgeoning capitalist society that offers new opportunities for middle-class men. The elder Henry raises his son as a Rousseauvian child of nature on an African island. On his return to England, the younger Henry's sincerity is the medium of Inchbald's cutting social critique. As a noble savage, he calls a spade a spade, or "*compliments, lies,*" and thereby unmasks the conventions of polite society. His naïveté in valuing objects as equal to the people who own them (he pays as much respect to expensive earrings as to the woman they adorn) ironically shows the shallowness of consumer culture. He is rewarded finally with a happy marriage and reunion with his long-lost father in a utopian rural retreat. The novel was generally well received by critics but was never as popular as *A Simple Story*. Its overt didacticism and generic ambiguity as a "sociopolitical fable" (Maurer) have helped keep it on the margins of Inchbald's oeuvre.

DRAMATIC CRITICISM

In addition to her success as a playwright and novelist, Inchbald was also a distinguished theatrical critic. Chosen by the series' publisher, Thomas Longman, to pen the prefaces to 125 popular plays, she produced a monumental record of the early-nineteenth-century British repertory, including 25 Shakespeare plays, work by John Dryden and Nicholas Rowe as well as her contemporaries Holcroft and Joanna Baillie, and of course some of her own plays. *The British Theatre* was published one play at a time beginning in 1806, followed in 1808 by the bound set of twenty-five volumes. Inchbald's collection helped rescue the theater from widespread moral censure, especially by emphasizing its didactic function. Her lively, anecdotal style avoided the abstruse scholarship of famous Shakespeare scholars like Samuel Johnson and was popular with readers and critics. Like her other work, Inchbald's theatrical criticism interrogates the social constraints of gender. She is not fond of the female passivity that colludes with male oppression (Rowe's heroine Lady Jane Grey is too virtuous to inspire imitation), and she is less interested in whether Calista is insufficiently penitent (in Rowe's *The Fair Penitent*) than in the heroine's lack of taste in choosing the "skipping, dancing" Lothario over his worthy rival. She is drawn to those heroines who violate social norms, especially the legendary adulteress Jane Shore, a role she herself played many times.

Inchbald's status as the leading authority on drama in the early nineteenth century was confirmed by two further dramatic collections for which she selected the plays, *A Collection of Farces and Afterpieces* (1809) and *The Modern Theatre* (1811). After these projects, Inchbald suffered from increasing ill health, and she died on 1 August 1821 in Kensington House, a Roman Catholic residence. She had an unusually successful career as a professional woman writer. Her celebrity status and the sophisticated politics of her works fully justify the renewed critical interest in them and in her.

[*See also* Anna Laetitia Barbauld *and* Romantic Drama.]

SELECTED WORKS

The Mogul Tale (performed as *A Mogul Tale* 1784; published 1788)

I'll Tell You What (performed 1785; published 1786)

Appearance Is against Them (performed and published 1785)

The Widow's Vow, adapted from Joseph Patrat's *L'hereuse erreur* (performed and published 1786)

Such Things Are (performed 1787; published 1788)

The Midnight Hour, adapted from Antoine-Jean-Bourlin Dumaniant's *Guerre Ouverte* (performed and published 1787)

All on a Summer's Day (performed 1787; published 1980)

Animal Magnetism, adapted from Dumaniant's *Le medecin malgre tout le monde* (performed and published 1788)

The Child of Nature, adapted from Mme. de Genlis's *Zelie; ou, L'ingenue* (performed and published 1788)

False Appearances, adapted from M. de Boissy's *Les dehors trompeurs* (performed 1789; previously attributed to Henry Seymour Conway)

The Married Man, adapted from Philippe Destouches's *Le philosophe marié* (performed and published 1789)

A Simple Story (1791)

Hue and Cry, adapted from Dumaniant's *La nuit aux aventures* (performed 1791; published 1980)

Next-Door Neighbours, adapted from Louis-Sébastien Mercier's *L'indigent* and Destouches's *Le dissipateur* (performed and published 1791)

Young Men and Old Women, adapted from Gresset's *Le mechant* (performed 1792)

Every One Has His Fault (performed and published 1793)

The Wedding Day (performed and published 1794)

Nature and Art (1796)

Wives as They Were, and Maids as They Are (performed and published 1797)

Lovers' Vows, adapted from August von Kotzebue's *Das Kind der Liebe* (performed and published 1798)

The Wise Man of the East, adapted from Kotzebue's *Das Schreiberpult, oder Die Gefahren der Jugend* (performed and published 1799)

To Marry or Not to Marry (published 1805)

Untitled essay in *The Artist* (1807)

The British Theatre; or, A Collection of Plays, . . . with Biographical and Critical Remarks by Mrs. Inchbald, 25 vols. (1808)

Collection of Farces and Other Afterpieces, 7 vols. (1809)

Modern Theatre, 10 vols. (1811)

The Massacre (written 1792; published 1833)

A Case of Conscience (written 1800; published 1833)

FURTHER READING

Bolton, Betsy. "Farce, Romance, Empire: Elizabeth Inchbald and Colonial Discourse." *Eighteenth Century* 39, no. 1 (1998): 3–24. Argues that *A Mogul Tale* and *Such Things Are* criticize early British imperialism, especially by mocking dominant assumptions of gender and racial subordination.

Carlson, Marvin. "Elizabeth Inchbald: A Woman Critic in Her Theatrical Culture." In *Women in British Romantic Theatre: Drama, Performance, and Society, 1790–1840*, edited by Catherine Burroughs, 207–222. Cambridge, U.K., 2000. Notes Inchbald's distinction as the first British critic of either sex to undertake such a prominent project as *The British Theatre*.

Castle, Terry. "Masquerade and Utopia II: Inchbald's 'A Simple Story.'" In *Masquerade and Civilization: The Carnivalesque in Eighteenth-Century English Culture and Fiction*, 290–330. Stanford, CA, 1986. Argues that the masquerade episode condenses the transgressive concerns of Inchbald's fiction. Also places Inchbald in company with Austen, James, and Sade.

Jenkins, Annibel. *I'll Tell You What: The Life of Elizabeth Inchbald*. Lexington, KY, 2003. A biography of Inchbald; useful plot summaries of each of her plays and novels and much detail from the pocketbooks, or miniature diaries, Inchbald kept throughout her life.

Lott, Anna. "Sexual Politics in Elizabeth Inchbald." *Studies in English Literature* 34 (1994): 635–648. Examines the feminist message of Inchbald's collection of prefaces assembled under the title *The British Theatre* and the critical disdain for these essays despite their contemporary popular success.

Maurer, Shawn L. "Introduction." In *Nature and Art*, by Elizabeth Inchbald, xi–xlv. London, 1997. Examines the novel's social critique, its scrutiny of masculinity, and the evasions of its conclusions.

Nachumi, Nora. "'Those Simple Signs': The Performance of Emotion in Elizabeth Inchbald's *A Simple Story*." *Eighteenth-Century Fiction* 11, no. 3 (1999): 317–336. Argues that Inchbald drew on a widely recognized repertoire of theatrical gesture to dramatize her characters' emotions through their bodies.

Osland, Dianne. "Heart-picking in *A Simple Story*." *Eighteenth-Century Fiction* 16, no. 1 (2003): 79–101. Analyzes the unconscious motivations of the novel's characters.

Parker, Jo Alyson. "Complicating *A Simple Story*: Inchbald's Two Versions of Female Power." *Eighteenth-Century Studies* 30, no. 3 (1997): 255–270. Reads the novel through the contradictory theories of female power offered by Mary Wollstonecraft and Hannah More.

THE INDUSTRIAL NOVEL

Catherine Gallagher

All nineteenth-century British novels are "industrial" in the sense that they were written during the Industrial Revolution, which made Britain the largest exporter of mass-produced goods in the world and helped consolidate its international economic dominance. But surprisingly few of the ten thousand novels published in Britain between 1800 and 1900 attempt to depict that great transformation or to grapple with its significant social dislocations. Only about twenty-five full-fledged novels belong to this subgenre, and most of them are quite obscure. The major instances of this small group, however, were disproportionately influential in shaping the development of the nineteenth-century novel.

Their influence derived partly from the fact that they were written by some of the period's most important and accomplished novelists: Benjamin Disraeli (*Sybil*, 1845), Elizabeth Gaskell (*Mary Barton*, 1848, and *North and South*, 1855), Charlotte Brontë (*Shirley*, 1849), Charles Kingsley (*Alton Locke: Taylor and Poet*, 1949), Charles Dickens (*Hard Times*, 1854), and George Eliot (*Felix Holt, The Radical*, 1866). The weight of this handful of books can also be attributed to an amalgamation of the topic of industrialism with the most profound philosophical issues of the day. "Industrialism" may sound mundane to us, but the nineteenth-century "sages" whose writings set the intellectual tone of the period (for example, Samuel Taylor Coleridge, Thomas Carlyle, John Stuart Mill, and John Ruskin) loaded the topic with weighty significance, making it a battleground for disputes over the nature of free will, the sources of social cohesion, and the relation between ethical facts and values. From the 1810s until the 1870s, a vast amount of British intellectual energy was expended on what came to be called the "Condition of England debate," a combined philosophical, social, economic, political, and literary discourse with the topic of industrialism at its center.

THE CONDITION OF ENGLAND

The novelists were attracted by both the breadth of this discourse and its depth, and when they entered it, they took on as well its deep philosophical considerations. For example, Kingsley wrote *Alton Locke: Tailor and Poet* under the strong influence of Carlyle's writings; even the title of the novel recalls Carlyle's *Sartor Resartus* (The Tailor Retailored). The eponymous hero and first-person narrator (a worker in the "sweated" London trade of clothes manufacturing) engages in numerous Carlylean reflections on the nature of human life, the relation between the immanent and the transcendent, and the definition of causality. *Alton Locke*'s plot structure, too, carries philosophical themes, as the severe Carlylean view of cosmic "consequences" tears the protagonist apart into an incoherent "multiplicity" and renders him temporarily mad. A long dream sequence, in which Alton Locke evolves through various stages of animal life, takes the novel altogether out of the realm of realist fiction and into the mode of evolutionary fantasy—a kind of early science fiction. Like Carlyle, Kingsley turns a social exposé (in this case, of the London clothing trade) into an interrogation of the meaning of human life. In taking his working-class hero to the extremes of recognizable human "character" and making him into a figure for the development of life itself, Kingsley finds a narrative equivalent for Carlyle's insistence that the most common forms signify the largest and loftiest verities.

Alton Locke's lurid surrealism is only an extreme version of the departures from novelistic realism that occur frequently in industrial novels, prompting a high degree of narrative self-reflection. For example, both Gaskell's *North and South* and Dickens's *Hard Times* stress the rupture between familial and socioeconomic life in the industrial city and seem to promise illustrations of renewed social cohesion. However, the novels actually deliver extended and structurally inconclusive meditations on how to connect private and public spheres without altogether collapsing them, and consequently they bring one of the novel's key generic presuppositions (that private and social life are complexly intertwined) to the level of explicit—and unresolved—thematic treatment. To take another example, the problem of working-class political representation central to Disraeli's *Sybil* and Eliot's *Felix Holt* becomes in both novels an instance of the unreliability of representation generally, including literary representation. Although the novels try to exempt themselves from the general skepticism they create about the substitution of signs for referents, offering their own procedures as superior to most novelistic and all political representation, they can do so only by concentrating attention on their forms. And thus, in writing industrial novels, Victorian novelists frequently examined the bases and the limits of their genre.

But the industrial novels were not composed without philosophical and formal reflection; indeed, one of their hallmarks is the mixture of such elements with documentary description and reformist exhortation. They often incorporate large amounts of material from government reports and investigative journalism describing the lives and occupations of working-class people in industrial cities—their "living and working conditions"—in the 1830s, 1840s, and 1850s. As the Condition of England debate developed, it focused on a succession of different issues, collecting and processing information that was relevant to specific pieces of legislation. These different issues seemed to call for novels with different plot types, different generic treatments, and different narrative strategies. The history of the industrial novel is not long— almost all of them were produced in the 1840s and 1850s—but we can trace a development in the subgenre from the earliest instances at the end of the 1830s and beginning of the 1840s, to the late 1840s and into the 1850s, paralleling the shift of public attention from the Ten Hours Movement (factory reform), to Chartism (working-class political representation), and then to trade unionism.

FOCUS ON THE TEN HOURS MOVEMENT

Two of the earliest industrial novels—Charlotte Elizabeth Tonna's *Helen Fleetwood* (1841) and Frances Trollope's *The Life and Adventures of Michael Armstrong, Factory Boy* (1839–1840)—are primarily concerned with child labor, for children were the first people to be considered victims of the "factory system," which was at that time almost entirely confined to the production of cloth in Lancashire and Yorkshire. Throughout the 1830s and into the 1840s, the Ten Hours Movement, which sought a legislative limit to the number of hours during the day when a factory could operate, used the overworking of factory children as their primary rationale. When, in response to the criti-

cism, many factory owners began working children in shorter shifts, the movement insisted that women, too, were physically unable to work a twelve-hour day. In the course of this campaign, which resulted in the Ten Hours Act of 1847, the "women and young people" who formed the great bulk of the factory workers became the objects of numerous medical and social investigations. Similar legislative attempts to protect chimney sweeps (1840) and women and children in mines and collieries (1842) further swelled and disseminated the literature about working-class women and children. The tiniest details of their lives (how many miles they walked a day, what they ate for breakfast, how many people slept in their beds, the average year of the onset of their menses, the state of their underclothes) were brought into public discourse and imbued with significance. Sanitary reports detailed the dangers that lurked in their water supply, in the dust they breathed, and the temperature of the rooms where they worked. These became the indicators of the true (but usually hidden) Condition of England. And in the course of these campaigns, reformers discovered women and children to be not only unfit for strenuous labor but also incapable of the autonomy required for protecting themselves or pursuing their interests.

The fragmented images of miserable, undernourished, ignorant, and injured children that appeared in "blue books" and other official reports, as well as in the propaganda of the Ten Hours Movement, were expanded by Trollope and Tonna into full-length narratives in which helpless, famished children are beaten by sadistic overseers, and fresh, saintly young women from the countryside are menaced and harassed by depraved fellow workers whose minds and bodies have been twisted by lives of unremitting labor in a literally overheated environment. The "documentary" purposes of these novels often sit uneasily inside their narrative conventions—Trollope's novel is gothic, whereas Tonna's is a sentimental Protestant hagiography—but the forms were obviously chosen for their tendencies toward the schematic contrast of good and evil. As later novelists detached their industrial novels from immediate propagandistic purposes, topical material, although still present, tended to be better integrated. In Gaskell's *Mary Barton*, for example, the labor of young women is still depicted as perilous, but it is neither a sensational nor a sentimental focus. It is merely a normal part of working-class life, to be explored fictionally like any other social condition so that middle-class readers might find an imaginative opening into working-class experience.

FOCUS ON CHARTISM

Moreover, by the time *Mary Barton* was written, Chartism had displaced factory abuses as the main indicator of the Condition of England. The Ten Hours Movement had brought together Tory reformers and working-class activists, creating a coalition in which novelists such as Tonna and Trollope could legitimately claim to share the goals of the workers themselves. But Chartism was an almost exclusively working-class movement, dominated by northern trade unionists who insistently pressed their demand for the franchise. Their egalitarian program as well as their method (petitions to Parliament accompanied by large public demonstrations) were unpalatable to many of the paternalistic supporters of the Ten Hours Movement. Whether paternalists or not, middle-class novelists seldom identified their narrative point of view with that of the Chartists. They undertook the literary representation of the industrial working class as an alternative to its political representation and claimed thereby to be overcoming the division between what Disraeli called "the Two Nations" without having to alter the franchise. The proposed charter, with its five points for parliamentary reform, often seems irrelevant to this fiction, which concentrates instead on the underlying social pathology the charter indicated: the mutual estrangement between classes that had resulted in this mass movement for separate political representation.

The habit of treating Chartism and other working-class movements not as purposeful programs but as a paroxysm of anger was initiated by Carlyle in his influential *Chartism*, which interpreted the movement as an expression of an unconscious desire for stronger leadership from above. Although the novelists do not seem quite as certain as Carlyle does that working men and women cannot know or articulate their own political desires, they adopted his method of reading working-class activism as symptomatic rather than substantial. The movement's messages were not evaluated in their own terms, but were instead decoded as pleas for sympathy, charity, or firmer direction. In both *Sybil* and *Mary Barton*, for example, the eponymous heroines are the daughters of intelligent and politically active working-class men who are the novels' real centers of gravity, and whose feelings of disaffection from the established order (rather than their proposed reforms) are the phenomena under scrutiny. We are to sympathize not with their ideas but with the pathos of the fact that their ideas are bound to be mistaken because "we" have abandoned them to ignorance and mis-

ery. Thus, Gaskell's narrator develops the metaphor of Frankenstein and his monster to describe class relations:

> The people rise up to life; they irritate us, they terrify us, and we become their enemies. Then, in the sorrowful moment of our triumphant power, their eyes gaze on us with a mute reproach. Why have we made them what they are; a powerful monster, yet without the inner means for peace and happiness? (pp. 219–220)

The point is not that the narrator dehumanizes working-class men by this analogy, but that she makes them into permanent dependents, incapable of arriving at a legitimate but separate view of the world, and entirely reliant on "us" for the "means for peace and happiness." Even when the trope is expanded and revised—"John Barton became a Chartist, a Communist, all that is commonly called wild and visionary. Ay! But being visionary is something. It shows a soul, a being not altogether sensual; a creature who looks forward for others, if not for himself"—Barton's "visionary" ideas are just a series of labels, not to be examined for their possible validity but only to be noticed as minimal indicators of a soul in distress.

In this example we can see the negative side of inflating every social problem into a metaphysical issue. That habit may have encouraged readers to take industrial issues seriously, but it also made some potential solutions impossible to consider. Since the industrial novelists were intent on exploring whether or not working men and women are fully developed free agents, they were diverted from the more practical task of evaluating the merits of the Chartists' program. Thus, the novels written at the height of Chartist organizing, *Mary Barton* and *Alton Locke*, take the proposal for franchise reform almost as a declaration of civil insurrection: the protagonists, in their bitterness and frustration, are driven to desperate lawlessness, murder, and riot. In these novels of the late 1840s Gaskell and Kingsley envision a British society so deeply riven by class antagonism that the possibility of a desirable future is precluded; in the end, death and immigration seem the only "solutions."

FOCUS ON TRADE UNIONISM

By the mid-1850s, when Gaskell wrote *North and South* and Dickens contributed *Hard Times* to the subgenre, the Chartist crisis was over; the campaign for manhood suffrage had been lost for the time being, and the North of England was experiencing another mode of working-class activism in renewed trade union activity. Compared to

Chartism with its mass demonstrations, trade unionism seemed like small-scale, endurable tension, merely class conflict as usual. The novels from this period prophesy no extreme disasters; they are more focused on the soul of the middle-class family than on that of the working-class rebel; and they are more optimistic than their predecessors about improving the Condition of England. Both novels use the family as a metaphor for the nation and ostensibly propose that sympathetic ties should bind parent to child, husband to wife, and master to workman. Although Gaskell and Dickens use the analogy differently, they both imagine affective relations spreading outward from the family circle to embrace the social whole. Hence, Dickens presents class alienation as one sign of the larger dearth of fellow-feeling, created by utilitarianism and afflicting both the home and the factory, and Gaskell also attributes it to the underdevelopment of sensibility in the masters' private lives. Setting the middle-class family right thus becomes the first step in a meliorist program of individual moral and social reform. The usual episodes of industrial novels—for example, strikes and factory accidents—become primarily elements of middle-class domestic dramas that focus on the struggles of misunderstood heroines. Different as they are in tone (Dickens's is a biting satire and Gaskell's an earnest domestic tale), they seem to share a matter-of-fact acceptance of class antagonism as a normal part of Britain's social dynamics. Sometimes the enmity heats up, sometimes it cools down, and yet it is generally amenable to local relief by private individuals whose home lives have trained their capacity for sympathy and their ability to manage the tension, anger, and frustrations of industrial life. Thus, these novels of the 1850s attempted to normalize class conflict by bonding it to the standard concerns of the novel—middle-class courtship and family life—but the very strenuousness of the effort called attention to the novelistic quality of that particular resolution.

Each phase of the Condition of England debate, in short, exaggerated some common aspects of novelistic representation, bringing the generic assumptions into the light of thematic prominence. The novel's usual job was to create the sense that freedom and causality, private and public life, facts and values exist in a productive state of tension, which is relaxed by the operations of the novel. Since it was feared that the new arrangements of industrial society would increase those very tensions to the breaking point, it is not surprising that novelists thought they might be able to invent models of resolution. There was, that is, a strong attraction between the discourses of industrialism and the function of the novel; instead of being inimical to the form, industrial subject matter was all too appropriate. But it turned out that novelists could not compose normally while simultaneously asking the questions prompted by the discourses of industrialism, for those were also questions about the genre's own presuppositions: What is the nature of freedom? Are members of all classes equally free? Can we apply the same standards of morality to public and private action? Will any representation of reality ever lead to a better state of things? Industrial novels thus tended to spin metanarrative inquiries rather than to resolve the issues at hand, and yet it was this very tendency that made them an important stage in the development of the self-conscious realism of the later nineteenth century.

[*See also* The Brontës; Thomas Carlyle; Chartist Literature; Charles Dickens; Benjamin Disraeli; George Eliot; *and* Elizabeth Gaskell.]

FURTHER READING

Bodenheimer, Rosemarie. *The Politics of Story in Victorian Social Fiction.* Ithaca, NY, 1988.

Brantlinger, Patrick. *The Spirit of Reform: British Literature and Politics, 1832–1867.* Cambridge, MA, 1977.

Cazamian, Louis. *The Social Novel in England, 1830–1850: Dickens, Disraeli, Mrs. Gaskell, Kingsley.* Translated by Martin Fido. London, 1973.

Childers, Joseph. *Novel Possibilities; Fiction and the Formation of Early Victorian Culture.* Philadelphia, 1995.

Colby, Robert. *Fiction with a Purpose: Major and Minor Nineteenth-Century Novels.* Bloomington, IN, 1967.

Gallagher, Catherine. *The Industrial Reformation of English Fiction; Social Discourse and Narrative Form, 1832–1867.* Chicago, 1985

Keating, Peter. *The Working Classes in Victorian Fiction.* London, 1971.

Plotz, John. *The Crowd: British Literature and Public Politics.* Berkeley, CA, 2000.

Williams, Raymond. *Culture and Society, 1780–1950.* London, 1958.

THE INKLINGS

Bruce L. Edwards

The writers' group known as the Inklings met weekly between 1933 and 1949, and its members produced some of the twentieth century's most popular and enduring works of fantasy, science fiction, and "supernatural thrillers." Led by the Oxford University literary scholars C. S. Lewis, creator of the *Chronicles of Narnia*, and J. R. R. Tolkien, creator of *The Hobbit* and *The Lord of the Rings*, this now legendary troupe read aloud from their works in progress over pints of stout and equal parts of uproarious laughter and earnest criticism, producing an astonishing number of works over a period of sixteen years and creating a legacy that continues to influence the world of genre fiction.

Tolkien bestowed the group's nickname, referring to the label as "a pleasantly ingenious pun in its way, suggesting people with vague or half-formed intimations and ideas plus those who dabble in ink." The "group" began in fact as a duo, a mutual admiration society between Lewis and Tolkien, who met at Oxford in the 1920s and discovered their common interest in all things ancient and medieval, as well as a shared romantic temperament that leaned toward the "mythopoeic"—toward the creation of fictional alternative worlds, entire landscapes populated by creatures and driven by story lines reflective of great myth, dark legend, and innocent fairy tale. Both were World War I veterans, both were refugees from the modern world and from the rising trend of modernism in literature and criticism, and both wished to rally to themselves others who were like-minded and equally disaffected. These two formidable talents invested a great deal of time in forging their metaphysical credo before sharing it with others.

THE INKLINGS IN ACTION

Before the Inklings' roll call grew beyond Lewis's and Tolkien's ardent private conversations and animated excursions into the never-never lands of fantasy and science fiction, Tolkien published *The Hobbit* (1937) and Lewis published *Out of the Silent Planet* (1938). Once they had begun to meet in earnest and with the regularity that characterized them during most of the 1940s, Lewis and Tolkien became even more prolific—though Tolkien's masterpiece, *The Lord of the Rings*, remained unpublished until the early 1950s. The Inklings eventually included professional friends (Lewis's family physician, Humphrey Havard, attended), admired writers and stimulating thinkers (Charles Williams, who gained some fame as a writer of supernatural fiction, earned Lewis's special acclaim for his Arthurian poetry cycle; Owen Barfield, a longtime friendly philosophical combatant of Lewis, who first met Lewis in 1919, commuted to Oxford from London where he practiced law), family members (both Lewis's brother Warren and Tolkien's son Christopher participated), and enterprising students (most prominent among them the poet John Wain), who were judged by Lewis or Tolkien to possess the right stuff to engage in the rough-and-tumble of a typical Inklings meeting.

Lewis's Magdalen College rooms were a usual Tuesday morning setting, while the more jovial Thursday evening gatherings were at a famous Oxford pub, The Eagle and Child. And what were the meetings like? They usually began with Lewis as host inviting someone to share a chapter from a manuscript, read aloud, and then submit to the assembled crew's commentary. It was a veritable writer's studio, with no holds barred, but all commentary focused on improving and not denigrating the works; it was an exhilarating experience for all. Lewis's brother Warnie, himself a surprisingly productive nonprofessional historian, expressed it this way: "We were no mutual admiration society: praise for good work was unstinted, but censure for bad work—or even not-so-good work—was often brutally frank. To read to the Inklings was a formidable ordeal."

Within their rich, layered, often boisterous and bawdy discussions, Lewis read from some or all of his most important works of the era, including *The Problem of Pain* (with a chapter supplied by Dr. Havard), *The Screwtape Letters*, *Perelandra*, *The Great Divorce*, and at least some portion of *The Lion, the Witch, and the Wardrobe*; while

Tolkien read frequently from his burgeoning "new Hobbit," *The Lord of the Rings.* (Tolkien acknowledged long after Lewis's death that *The Lord of the Rings* would never have seen the light of day without Lewis's helpful criticism and constant exhortation to complete it and send it to his publisher.) Barfield shared his prose explorations and expositions of metaphor, and what, as an advocate of Rudolph Steiner's occult anthroposophism, he termed "the evolution of consciousness"; Charles Williams submitted for Inklings review his most famous Stephen King–like thriller, *All Hallows' Eve,* which was admired by T. S. Eliot.

In retrospect, perhaps the most remarkable aspect of their association and productivity was that the Inklings were successful amateurs at the very things they loved— each of them became accomplished as a writer outside the profession that brought him his livelihood. They wrote and they met for the sheer joy of it, as well as for the reinforcement of their unabashed countercultural convictions about the world at large and the world to come. In one form or another, each embraced Christianity (Barfield's "faith" being the least articulated or pronounced), and this worldview was decidedly present in nearly every aspect of their published work, either on the surface (in Lewis and Williams) or somewhat latent (in Tolkien).

Though in many ways the genius behind the Inklings was Tolkien's—the Inklings was a surrogate for an earlier "writer's club" which he had helped found but which was decimated by World War I—Lewis was its center of gravity, its draw, and its ongoing source of energy. His ebullient personality was in great contrast to Tolkien's retiring demeanor. Lewis's group criticism could be pointed and personal, but always rendered for the sake of making a work more "seaworthy"; Tolkien's was more muted and focused on encouragement. What brought them together week after week, besides the pleasure of their company (which was enormous), was a shared conviction that the twentieth century had started abysmally and that one of the best ways to maintain or restore the glories of the "true West" was to create and promote grand works of mythopoeia—myth, fantasy, and speculative fiction that would "steal past the watchful dragons" of conventional wisdom and decadent culture and instill what Lewis called "a taste of the other"—a vision of a transcendent realm.

LEWIS AND TOLKIEN: THE HEART OF THE INKLINGS

If one were to codify Lewis's and Tolkien's shared aesthetic, it would be something like this: The world as we know it is not the world as it once was. The world as we see it and experience it is not the world as it was designed and ordained at its origin. The world as it is now is a world of spoiled goodness, a world of decay, withstood and understood only by those with an unfathomably wild sense of the anticipation of certain redemption. The world of shadows, of almosts, and neither/nors, close calls, what-ifs will give way to the bright sunshine of a world free of evil, pain, and death. There are the secret facts that inform our every attempt to explain, or explain away, the universe and of our place in its "Shadowlands." These are the stubborn rumors of a lost Eden, an elusive Nirvana, a passage to eternity that no civilization has been able entirely to dismiss or disavow in all the millennia that we have traversed the earth, and they are, in the end, the truest estimation of our predicament and of our destiny.

These in particular are the theological and aesthetic premises of the works both Lewis and Tolkien produced during their sojourn within the Inklings meetings, and they are evident in Lewis's space trilogy, *Screwtape, The Great Divorce,* and *The Chronicles of Narnia,* and in every aspect of Tolkien's *Hobbit/Lord of the Rings/Silmarillion* epics. Myth for them was not defined as a legendary tale told with dubious authority; but instead as the overarching narrative that created the reason to be, and to become, for members of the village, polis, and nation touched by its encompassing themes, images, characters, and plot lines.

Neither antihistorical, nor ahistorical, the Inklings' view of myth was that it evokes awe, wonder, passion, and, what is more, pursuit—a culture's myth is the story that has the power to explain the origin and destiny of a people, the text that orients them in history, guides them in the present, and points them to a future in which they and their offspring will exist—hence *The Lord of the Rings* and *The Chronicles of Narnia.* Myth places its believers in the presence of their creator and benefactor, judge and advocate, and answers the questions when, how, who, and why. A "true myth" has the power to explain where we came from, to shape our identity and purpose, to instill hope, to promote justice, and to sustain order. That is why Lewis can describe the Christian Gospel in these terms: "As myth transcends thought, Incarnation transcends myth. The heart of Christianity is a myth which is also a fact. . . . Christians also need to be reminded . . . that what became Fact was a Myth, that it carries with it into the world of Fact all the properties of a myth."

The Inklings' modus operandi was to create fantasies and new myths that could serve as an "alternate history," a winsome, redemptive, inclusive worldview that would restore personal dignity and a promised destiny to those with ears to hear and eyes to see. A history alternate to what, though? Simply put, it is alternate to what they regarded as the distorted false history written in the rise of a dehumanizing and disenchanting naturalism, which reduces men, women, children, and even whole civilizations to instincts, impulses, genetics, and environment: a cosmic accident. Neither Lewis nor Tolkien was a tame writer, and both believed that we long to know there is a homeland where we truly belong, an enchanted world, a neverland that calls to us in the midst of confusion and doubt, a world that we can see "if the eyes of our hearts are enlightened."

From Middle-Earth to Narnia, from Perelandra to Cair Paravel, and on to Mordor and Malacandra, Lewis and Tolkien and the rest of the Inklings called on readers to reenchant the cosmos, keeping alive the promise and animating the search for the world beyond the world. This is what Lewis was getting at in an early review of Tolkien's *The Hobbit*: "To define the world of *The Hobbit* is, of course, impossible because it is new. You cannot anticipate it before you go there, as you cannot forget it once you have gone." In a later review of the completed *Lord of the Rings*, Lewis encapsulated its achievement: "it rediscovers reality" by making of this world a myth; "the value of myth is that it takes all the things we know and restores to them the rich significance which had been hidden by the veil of familiarity." "The veil of familiarity" is a telling phrase; in the realm of the fantastic, within mythic landscapes, vistas, perspectives, anything might happen, anything might be discovered. One is not restricted by what he or she knows of the real world, its colors, shapes, creatures, languages, predicaments. The author of fantasy can use these but also invent others, intermixing them with the familiar and the real to create a "secondary" world that envelops and surpasses both. These alternate histories rescue readers from the "veil of familiarity," ushering them into a transcendent realm un-reachable by mere reason or coldhearted induction. This is certainly the ongoing legacy of the Inklings, whose work has inspired the rehabilitation and expansion of the genres of fantasy and science fiction well beyond their own century.

[*See also* C. S. Lewis *and* J. R. R. Tolkien.]

SELECTED WORKS

For works of C. S. Lewis and J. R. R. Tolkien, see their separate entries.

BY OWEN BARFIELD

Poetic Diction (1928)
Saving the Appearances (1957)
Speakers Meaning (1967)
Worlds Apart (1963)

BY CHARLES WILLIAMS

War in Heaven (1930)
Many Dimensions (1930)
The Place of the Lion (1931)
The Greater Trumps (1932)
Shadows of Ecstasy (1933)
Descent into Hell (1937)
All Hallows' Eve (1945)

FURTHER READING

Duriez, Colin, and David Porter. *The Inklings Handbook*. St. Louis, MO, 2001. A one-volume encyclopedia that covers all key questions regarding the Inklings.

Glyer, Diana. *The Company They Keep: C. S. Lewis and J. R. R. Tolkien as Writers in Community*. Kent, OH, 2005. The most up-to-date and accurate treatment of the relationships among Lewis, Tolkien, and the other Inklings.

Humphrey Carpenter. *The Inklings: C. S. Lewis, J. R. R. Tolkien, Charles Williams, and Their Friends*. Boston, 1978. The original biographical treatment of the Inklings, somewhat dated but still useful for overall perspective.

CHRISTOPHER ISHERWOOD

Stuart Christie

Christopher William Bradshaw-Isherwood (1904–1986) was born a Briton in Cheshire, England, and died an American in Santa Monica, California. His residence in two cities, Berlin and Los Angeles, marks distinctive phases of his long career, and each served as the locale for one of his two best works: Berlin for the collected stories making up *The Berlin Stories* (*The Last of Mr. Norris*, 1935; *Good bye to Berlin*, 1939), and Los Angeles for *A Single Man* (1964). Isherwood's love of these two cities, and of international travel more generally, suggest his fascination with life experiences beyond Britain. He wrote or cowrote two travel books: *Journey to a War* (with W. H. Auden, 1939) about the ongoing Sino-Japanese war, and *The Condor and the Cows* (photography by William Caskey, 1949), based on his travels in South America.

BEYOND BRITAIN

An iconoclast by nature, Isherwood as a young writer was greatly influenced by the early poetry of T. S. Eliot and the idealism of his classmate at Cambridge, Edward Upward, with whom he collaborated on a series of acerbic sketches (*The Mortmere Stories*, 1924–1927). Bred for, as well as bound by, the norms and conventions of the British ruling classes, Isherwood felt stifled by them, including the milieu embodied in his mother, Kathleen: "I was an upper-middle class Puritan, cautious, a bit stingy, with a stake in the land" (*Lions and Shadows*, 1938). Increasingly resentful, Isherwood engineered his own dismissal from university in 1925, making it all the more remarkable that his fiction was widely perceived as heralding a better future for the English novel.

Too young for Edwardian literature as well as its earliest modernist critics, Isherwood nevertheless cherished strong bonds with many of the period's most distinguished writers. His relationship with E. M. Forster grew from protégé to peer and became a friendship that lasted a lifetime. The prominent critic Cyril Connolly declared Isherwood "a hope of English fiction." While at dinner with Lady Sibyl Colefax in November 1938, W. Somerset Maugham praised Isherwood as "hold[ing] the future of the English novel in his hands." A guest at the same dinner, Virginia Woolf, wrote in her diary: "Isherwood and I met on the doorstep. He is a slip of a wild boy: with quicksilver eyes: nipped; jockeylike." Recalling Woolf's diary entry decades later in his own autobiographical work, *Christopher and His Kind* (1976), Isherwood approved of the description.

A theme common to Isherwood's 1930s writing was what he called "the Test" of British masculinity, imposed by society on young men succeeding the World War I generation. (Isherwood's father, Frank, was killed in combat at Ypres in May 1915.) For Isherwood's characters to fail this test of manhood, in the form of a defiant anti-heroism rejecting society's mandates, was, paradoxically, to pass it.

Along with his lifelong friend and collaborator W. H. Auden, Isherwood felt constrained by the British tradition even as it had defined, for better and worse, his most basic and self-identified characteristics. Isherwood cowrote three short plays with Auden for the London-based Group Theatre (directed by Rupert Doone, with musical scores by Benjamin Britten), including *The Dog Beneath the Skin* (1935), *The Ascent of F6* (1936), and *On the Frontier* (1938). Isherwood's enduring love of collaboration dates from this period and spoke of even greater work to come.

Yet for many of Isherwood's critics, his was a literary promise unfulfilled, at least when defined as exclusively British. It was after 1939 that the historical events in Germany fictionalized by Isherwood so capably, and to some extent disinterestedly, caught up with him. Perceived as fleeing Britain prior to the September 1939 outbreak of World War II, Isherwood and Auden (who had emigrated to the United States in January 1939) received rebuke in the House of Commons and faced eroding support, on grounds of lack of patriotism, from erstwhile supporters such as Connolly and Harold Nicolson. Such criticism was not universal—Forster defended him—but it smarted. It also bolstered Isherwood's resolve to remain in the United States as a pacifist (as recounted in *Christopher and His Kind*) and to continue with his spiritual explorations, recently begun in California, of mystical Hinduism under the teaching of the Vedantist monk Prabhavananda. Isherwood's remarkable relationship with Swami Prabhavananda lasted from 1939 until 1976 and is recounted in *My Guru and His Disciple* (1980). Isherwood collaborated with Prabhavananda on three translations of Vedantic scriptures and teachings, notably *The Song of God: Bhagavad-gita* (1944).

AUTOBIOGRAPHICAL FICTION

Through the use of a bold cross-genre technique, Isherwood's fiction links autobiographical prerogative and veracity (using the first-person "I") to the power of fictionalized characterization (using the third-person "she" or "he"). His narrators usually bear his name (Christopher or Christophe), or some approximate version of it (William Bradshaw or Herr Issyvoo). In his more expressly autobiographical (or quasi-autobiographical) writings, ranging from *Lions and Shadows* to *Christopher and His Kind*, Isherwood occasionally refers to himself in the third person, striving for greater fidelity toward actual happenings unclouded by sentiment.

Isherwood's experiments predated by decades other attempts to combine fictional modes with documentary-style accuracy (such as Truman Capote's *In Cold Blood*,

Christopher Isherwood
Isherwood (center) with W. H. Auden and Stephen Spender.
Photograph by Howard Coster, 1937
NATIONAL PORTRAIT GALLERY, LONDON

1966, or Norman Mailer's *The Armies of the Night*, 1968). While still marketed as fiction today, Isherwood's various Berlin writings, combined by New Directions editor James Laughlin into the one-volume *The Berlin Stories* (1954), remain unflinching social texts, at once compelling and authoritative, recording the last months and years of the Weimar Republic prior to the rise of Adolf Hitler.

Overall, Isherwood's style is marked by a hungry restlessness and striving for accuracy that Gore Vidal called his "objective narcissism," a merciless eye for detail and great appreciation for the complexity of human character when viewed from all possible (and probable) angles. A description of Arthur Norris in *The Last of Mr. Norris* (1935; titled *Mr. Norris Changes Trains* in England) is characteristic of Isherwood's taut and evocative realism, which subordinates pat generalizations to a pleasurable aggregate of perceptions:

> As a final test, I tried to look Arthur in the eyes. But no, this time-honored process didn't work. Here were no windows to the soul. They were merely part of his face, light-blue jellies, like naked shell-fish in the crevices of a rock. There was nothing to hold the attention; no sparkle, no inward gleam. Try as I would, my glance wandered away to more interesting features; the soft, snout-like nose, the concertina chin.

As specific entries among his voluminous *Diaries* (1997) indicate, Isherwood could be ruthless when depicting others, but he never exempted himself. He undertook all writing in the name of an ultimate sincerity toward the most honest and complete rendering of subjectivity possible. It is in this respect that the style of Isherwood's autobiographical fiction is both absolute and unique.

An excerpt from *Down There on a Visit* (1962) expresses clearly Isherwood's often-stated aims for writing autobiographical fiction:

> We [author and persona] have in common the label of our name, and a continuity of consciousness; there has been no break in the sequence of daily statements that I am I. But *what* I am has refashioned itself throughout the days and years, until now almost all that remains constant is the mere awareness of being conscious. And that awareness belongs to everybody.

Isherwood described such a continuous and collaborative consciousness elsewhere as "interplay," the tension between individual expression and more objective commentary on how all people fashion differently meaningful myths from living. This interplay can be most readily observed in his last novel, *A Meeting by the River* (1967), the story of two brothers searching for emotional honesty and going in opposite directions in attempts to achieve it. Patrick, a repressive figure, attempts to convince his younger brother, Oliver, not to take monastic Hinduism's final vows. The form of the novel is distinctive. A series of interlinked letters, journal entries, and telephone conversations conveys a documentary unity even as it fragments any totalizing perspective concerning religious conversion or the emotional dependence that would counter it.

LOS ANGELES

After emigrating to the United States, Isherwood found steady work as a screenwriter in Hollywood, writing or contributing to numerous screenplays, several of which (notably *The Great Sinner*, 1949) established his reputation. His American network and income developed on other fronts as well. Isherwood's friend John van Druten adapted *The Berlin Stories* to the stage under the title *I Am a Camera*, and the run of the play at the Empire Theatre on Broadway (from November 1951 through July 1952) was a commercial success. Its subsequent film adaptation under the same title (1955) brought Isherwood some measure of financial independence and public acclaim.

Isherwood used proceeds earned from the stage and film adaptations of *The Berlin Stories* to purchase a home in Santa Monica, where with his life partner, Don Bachardy, he lived the remainder of his life. Approaching a very active retirement, Isherwood witnessed the further and highly successful adaptation of his Berlin stories to music and film, with Bob Fosse's *Cabaret* (1972) starring Liza Minnelli and having been based on Kander and Ebb's earlier musical of the same name (1966). Collaborating with Bachardy, Isherwood subsequently adapted Mary Shelley's novel *Frankenstein* to television (*Frankenstein: The True Story*, 1973); the adaptation focuses on the theme of creation as an ultimate power for good as well as evil. The delicate and delightful symbol of a butterfly, signaling rebirth and positive change, flutters throughout the occasionally dark tale.

After 1959, Isherwood began teaching creative writing regularly to students at Los Angeles–area universities and as a guest lecturer nationally. His experiences in the classroom directly informed the writing of *A Single Man*, which is generally considered the best among his later works. Sloughing off earlier suspicions of institutional containment, Isherwood relished teaching both inside and beyond the classroom. Like E. M. Forster's, Isherwood's legacy may be most meaningfully observed in this role as educator and mentor to younger writers. As Berg and Freeman have shown, Isherwood was a remarkable teacher, exacting and generous in equal measure, who profoundly influenced numerous writers and artists including Don Bachardy (*Stars in My Eyes*, 2000; *Christopher Isherwood: Last Drawings*, 1990), Michael S. Harper (*Dear John, Dear Coltrane*, 1970), Armistead Maupin (*Tales of the City*, 1978–), Edmund White (*Fanny: A Fiction*, 2003; *A Boy's Own Story*, 1982), James P. White (*Birdsong*, 1978), and Carter Wilson (*A Green Tree and A Dry Tree*, 1972; *Hidden in the Blood*, 1995).

ISHERWOOD'S TRIBE

If Isherwood's realism does not always take sides, his private life was another matter. As the American Isherwood matured, "the Test" of his earlier realist fiction became at once more spiritually abstract and more emotionally honest. It was his homosexuality that was, as he put it, "never satisfactorily expressed" in his earlier work and, with *A Single Man* and *Christopher and His Kind*, became the test of his fiction and his entire career as he saw it: "not so much from the point of view of the question of sexual preference but as . . . belonging to a rather small minority, a tribe, which is sometimes overtly persecuted but always . . . subtly slighted." Writing from the position of a strong and comfortable sexual identity, Isherwood was visibly active in the gay rights movement once its public dimension emerged after 1968. But he was also careful, as in his fiction, not to limit gay subjectivity—or that of other "minorities," in his own words—to specific caricatures that might upset the effective equivalence of all experiences within an eternal, indeed transcendental, frame of being.

Acknowledging Isherwood's mastery of fiction as belonging to an eminent author who enjoyed the love of men unabashedly neither defines his corpus expressly nor liberates it from what he termed the "Other" (heterosexual) tradition in any superficial sense. Both defining and liberating, homosexuality in his work presents different aspects of what, for Isherwood, was a broader truth in life. Yet to deflect the important fact that Isherwood's fiction was written by a gay or homosexual man—he appreciated neither term—would be also to be what he called "fakey," to strike a false pose. A consummate play-actor, affable and comfortable with almost everyone who knew him, Isherwood did not want to play at, or to flatter, whatever version of identity majority society had, however imperfectly, imagined for him. He simply claimed the right to love men in peace and to write about it openly.

On this point of principle, Isherwood refused after 1939 either to pose or to hide, and this refusal motivated his emigration to, he hoped, more tolerant climes. America, even California, was not always to be so, but at least there he found measurable room for his defiance of homophobia, using "a test by which every political party and government must be judged. . . . 'Does that include us or doesn't it?' " (*Christopher and His Kind*). Later Isherwood enjoyed the esteem of communities, gay as well as literary, he had done so much to establish and nurture within English letters, in Berlin and Britain and beyond, in Los Angeles and the United States and beyond.

[*See also* W. H. Auden.]

SELECTED WORKS

The Berlin Stories (1954)
Down There on a Visit (1962)
A Single Man (1964)
A Meeting by the River (1967)
Frankenstein: The True Story (screenplay, with Don Bachardy, 1973)
Christopher and His Kind, 1929–1939 (1976)
My Guru and His Disciple (1980)
Diaries: Volume One, 1939–1960 (1997)

FURTHER READING

Berg, James, and Chris Freeman, eds. *The Isherwood Century: Essays on the Life and Work of Christopher Isherwood*. Madison, WI, 2000. A significant, if scattered, collection of essays, memoirs, and recollections by scholars and thinkers, including many of Isherwood's closest friends and contemporaries.

Heilbrun, Carolyn G. *Christopher Isherwood*. New York, 1970. This groundbreaking, first critical monograph on Isherwood established still useful critical parameters for his work.

Parker, Peter. *Isherwood: A Life Revealed*. New York, 2004. An exhaustively researched biography focusing on Isherwood's connection to British letters.

Summers, Claude J. *Christopher Isherwood*. New York, 1980. A thoughtful and carefully balanced review of Isherwood's fiction-making in its biographical context.

KAZUO ISHIGURO

Gavin Keulks

Born on 8 November 1954 in Nagasaki, Japan, Kazuo Ishiguro has matured into one of the most respected contemporary British writers. After accompanying his family to England at the age of six, he took a BA with honors at the University of Kent and an MA in creative writing at the University of East Anglia. Ishiguro then published three novels over seven years that earned him some of England's most coveted awards and freed him to pursue writing full-time. *A Pale View of Hills* (1982) secured the Royal Society of Literature's Winifred Holt by Award for best first novel of the year; *An Artist of the Floating World* (1986) was honored with the Whitbread Book of the Year Award, one of England's most lucrative; and *The Remains of the Day* (1989) garnered the Booker Prize, England's highest literary commendation. These novels solidified Ishiguro's reputation as a highly intelligent, artistically controlled novelist whose stylistic finesse was wildly celebrated. As the later stage of his career now confirms, Ishiguro has never been comfortable with such early affiliations, prompting the increasing experimentation of his more recent work.

Kazuo Ishiguro
Portrait by Peter Edwards, 1995
NATIONAL PORTRAIT GALLERY, LONDON

EARLY NOVELS:
REALISM AND ITS DISCONTENTS

The trademark techniques and themes of Ishiguro's early period are easy to define: narrative unreliability, cultural dislocation, memorial conflict, and revelatory self-examination. Ishiguro's narrators routinely challenge traditional concepts of realist credulity to inspire questions about the ways that memory, nationality, and missed opportunity undermine presumptively stable constructs of identity.

A Pale View of Hills unfolds as a contrapuntal tale of disillusionment and displacement, both cultural and personal. The dual foci of the novel—the narrator Etsuko and her double Sachiko, a war widow—offer dueling glimpses of cross-cultural romance during war. In the process of mourning her daughter Keiko's suicide, Etsuko recounts her friendship with Sachiko, a neglectful mother whose relationship with an American soldier became fodder for neighborhood gossip. Questions about maternal competence predominate in Etsuko's recollections until, at the novel's end, she quietly, almost inadvertently, reveals her subjects to be psychological projections. The lives of Sachiko and her daughter wither as the interpolated tale implodes, subsumed by Etsuko's guilt. Through its powerful psychological contraction, the novel illumines the sacrifices of self, love, and relationship that are invariably enlisted in spiritual and spatial relocation.

Published four years later, *An Artist of the Floating World* extends Ishiguro's investigation of identity, memory, and disillusion, both Japanese and English. As in the earlier novel, issues of reliability assume central importance. The novel centers upon Masuji Ono, who is attempting to arrange the marriage of his youngest daughter, Noriko. Over the course of his preparations he finds he must make peace with his past, negotiating a record of increasingly disconcerting revelations. As the novel deepens, however, the reader begins to question Ono's confessions. Ishiguro patiently undercuts his narrator's recollections, contrasting Ono's responsibility toward his daughter with his guilt over past betrayals, a litany that includes his own father as well as his mentors and prize pupils. This bifocal vision of modernized Japan suggests that the "floating world" of the novel's title should be read equally as Japan and as memory. Mourning the increasing westernization of his country in 1949–1950, Ono recalls a prewar Japan in which patriotic and nationalist codes predominated. Like *A Pale View of Hills*, *The Artist of the Floating World* concludes by enacting a variation upon a theme: realist stability (and exteriority) again succumbs to psychology. What persists is not the pathos of Ono's guilt but instead a vision of unmediated suffering, the emotional residue of Ono's self-lacerations. Neither time nor honesty triumphs over pain, and Ono remains a failed artist, unable to structure his confession.

Ishiguro's career had already flourished, therefore, by the time he commenced work on *The Remains of the Day*, the novel for which he is best known. Upon its release, Ishiguro's third novel rose quickly in significance, assuming its position as one of the central texts of late-twentieth-century historiography, reimagining a world as vividly and inventively as such other masterpieces as Salman Rushdie's *Midnight's Children*, Jeanette Winterson's *The Passion*, and Graham Swift's *Waterland*. All these novels were published during the 1980s, at the height of the postmodernist period; Ishiguro's novel is decidedly unpostmodernist, however, and instead carefully, methodically, and thoroughly realistically creates one of the most sympathetic failures in all of British literature: Stevens, the self-abnegating butler of Darlington Hall.

The Remains of the Day clarified that Ishiguro's primary theme was national transition, especially during the postwar period. His characters, while quietly vivid, are entirely emblematic. Whereas his first two novels analyze Japan from the vantage point of the late 1940s and mid-1950s, his third novel scrutinizes England at the same period. Set in 1956, the novel is predominantly introspective: Stevens recollects his life while driving to visit Miss Kenton (now Mrs. Benn), who was the housekeeper at Darlington Hall from 1922 to 1936. Disappointingly married, she represents Stevens's last hope for an emotionally sustaining life. Stultified by his sense of decorum, Stevens sadly cannot respond and is unresponsive to the limited opportunities life affords.

Love is not the only thing that Stevens has repressed, either; ordered on vacation by his current employer—Mr. Farraday, an American—Stevens must come to grips with the fact that his earlier master, Lord Darlington, was a Nazi sympathizer, thereby violating his noble title as well as Stevens's respect. In typical Ishiguro fashion, Stevens's epiphanies occur slowly, powerfully, with metronomic precision. When Stevens recounts the night of his father's death—when he remarkably kept working—the reader recoils from his exacting rationalizations; when Stevens recalls Miss Kenton's final day of service, in 1936, however, the reader comprehends the wrenching depth of his

self-deprivation: he has sacrificed his entire life embracing empty ideals—the delusional dignity he attributes to his position. There is something crushingly conclusive in Stevens's resolution, upon returning to Darlington Hall—alone—that "in bantering lies the key to human warmth."

The Remains of the Day bids somber farewell to Stevens and his diminishing world without the fanfare of raging storms, blinded advisers, or dead bodies. Yet like Shakespeare's Lear, Stevens too is "more sinned against than sinning"; of course, he is also symbolically blind and dead—like the past he revisits, like his retreating opportunities, like his perfidious ideals. "You see, I *trusted*," he says in one of the novel's more poignant lines; "I trusted in his lordship's wisdom. All those years I served him, I trusted I was doing something worthwhile. I can't even say I made my own mistakes."

Besides winning the Booker Prize, *The Remains of the Day* was made into a successful feature-length film by the celebrated English duo of Ismail Merchant and James Ivory. Featuring a screenplay by the Indian writer Ruth Prawer Jhabvala and a theatrically distinguished cast (with Anthony Hopkins as the lead and Emma Thompson as Miss Kenton), it received eight Academy Award nominations in 1993.

LATE NOVELS: POSTMODERN EXPERIMENTATION

To his credit, Ishiguro has never rested upon the heated acclaim his early novels have generated. He certainly could have. Instead, he lamented the rote contextualization of his work as realist, retrograde countermeasures to more contemporary postcolonial and postmodern trends. His stylistic control, he explained to interviewers, was not simply a tribute to Japanese literary traditions, a form of Buddhist self-denial. Critics, he felt, continually underestimated the depths to which he manipulated realist protocol, overlooking the significance of his delayed subversion of such conventions, which often occurred in the novel's final pages. In short, by the early 1990s, Ishiguro felt artistically constrained.

That feeling, many critics contend, is the probable reason why Ishiguro's fourth novel, *The Unconsoled* (1995), bears so little resemblance to his earlier work. Other answers could of course be offered: six years had passed since *The Remains of the Day* and during that time, new governments had succeeded those of Margaret Thatcher in England and Ronald Reagan in the United States; the Internet had flourished, promising new revolutions in language and identity, and imaginative theories in quantum physics made the nightly news; finally, the nuclear desperation of the 1980s evaporated as the Soviet Union fragmented into disparate states. Whatever the reasons, many readers were surprised at, and some bewailed, Ishiguro's artistic redirection.

Among other things, *The Unconsoled* is decidedly postmodern, counterbalancing the realism of his earlier period. Stylistically effusive, structurally unstable, the novel uses language far more excessively than in any of Ishiguro's earlier narrative experiments, offering the reader surrealism instead of reticence. The narrator, Mr. Ryder, a famous pianist, wanders through an unnamed European city, lacking knowledge of the purpose, reason, or schedule for his visit. As with similar urban wanderers, or postmodern flâneurs, Ryder's idealized amnesia comes to symbolize the disjointed, disconnected frenzy of life at the cusp of the new millennium. His narrative authority devolves as he strives to read (and interpret) the text of his life, deprived of either background or context.

Whereas Ishiguro's earlier novels had achieved closure through contraction, *The Unconsoled* proceeds with relentless expansion. Information proliferates, breeding interpretive pluralities out of supposition and confusion. Throughout the book Ryder encounters numerous people who play significant roles in his life. One is a lover, one is his son, one is a musician who squandered his career for drink. In the end, and despite these various quests, Ryder remains ontologically and existentially lost, deprived of a sense of self or of place. Lacking motivation and character—the foundations of classical realism—he remains disconcerted, unconsoled.

Many reviewers shared such disconsolate feelings, pondering Ishiguro's new directions. With its fondness for conjecture and teleological contingency, *The Unconsoled* seemed to borrow from detective fiction; in its rampant indeterminacy, the book seemed indebted to chaos theory and quantum physics; with its surreal temporal logic and paranoiac revelations, the book confirmed postmodern influences. The first-person narration remained quasi-confessional, epiphanic, yet Ryder's revelations seemed to lack the emotional depth of previous work, as though saturated by signification. These hypotheses would be tested again when Ishiguro released *When We Were Orphans* in 2001.

Ishiguro's fifth novel, after another six-year quiet period, is, at first glance, a detective story. It is also a work of historical fiction, a moralistic novel of ideas, and a tragedy of manners. Its narrator, the prominent English detective Christopher Banks, attempts to reconcile his past by using the deductive skills of his profession. Commencing in 1930, the novel probes the most powerful incident of Banks's youth: the mystery of his parents' disappearance. Eventually his investigation takes him back to Shanghai, his boyhood home, where he encounters not only a Japanese siege but, like Ryder in *The Unconsoled*, multiple versions of himself—redefinitions, reconfigurations, previously repressed. Both novels suggest the need to mediate one's past and present, the quintessential will-to-power underlying all formations of identity. Yet in typical Ishiguro fashion, such sustaining answers remain untenable. At the end of their respective journeys, Ryder and Banks face similarly bleak decisions: either accept the present with its lacunae and ghosts, or sacrifice one's life chasing the shadows of the past.

More moderate—or moderated—in style, *When We Were Orphans* also attempts to broker an accord between the minimalism of *The Remains of the Day*, where every emotion is checked and guarded, and the unbridled expressionism of *The Unconsoled*. Although Ishiguro's new novel received mixed reviews—some found its suspense unconvincing, its ratiocinations monotonous—it was clear that the author had reclaimed his authorial freedom, reinvigorated to embrace risk without fear of classification.

Never Let Me Go, Ishiguro's subsequent novel, appeared in 2005. Arguably the most experimental book in the author's oeuvre, it combines science fiction and humanism in the voice of Kathy H, the thirty-one-year-old narrator. Glimmers of this combination had previously appeared in *The Unconsoled*, yet Kathy's deficit of autonomy and selfhood far outstrip similar quandaries faced by Ryder, her thematic forbearer. As the novel progresses, the reader discovers that Kathy is a genetically engineered clone whose sole purpose is to furnish vital organs for the "normal" people of the world. The clones are monitored by "guardians" who teach them to appreciate the refinements of life, including music and art. Yet despite all this, Ishiguro strives to avoid sentimentality, paradoxically reaffirming that, even among clones, Heraclitus was right: "Character is fate."

As in *When We Were Orphans*, the prose in *Never Let Me Go* is controlled, poignant in understatement. Caring for the "donors" at Hailsham—a quasi-boarding-school for clones, where she is an alumna—Kathy reflects on her adolescence, resurrecting feelings of alienation, regret, and even love. An important part of her cautionary tale involves the description of the romantic triangle between herself and two other clones, one generous, the other manipulative. Conscious that she is speaking to a "normal" person in the form of the reader, she offers her story as a confession, a means of rapprochement. Reflecting upon the stares of people who "dread the idea of your hand brushing against theirs," she mourns that "the first time you glimpse yourself through the eyes of a person like that, it's a cold moment." Echoing the title's plea for connection, such meditations interject a tone of wounded emotionalism into the novel, one that rises in volume when juxtaposed against Kathy's absence of family ties.

Beyond the claims of culture or class, Ishiguro's greatest strength as a novelist may lie in his depictions of familial strife, the beloved horror of kinship. His solipsistic, self-abnegating narrators navigate the alleyways of their fading hopes, but human relationships reside at the center of such labyrinths. It is therefore unsurprising that the clones in *Never Let Me Go* suffer as palpably as do any of Ishiguro's damaged, disconnected characters. Their feelings of duty—and fears of erasure—seem sadly disembodied, already withdrawn. These inner divisions partly derive from the depthlessness of their identities, which they evolve by watching television and movies—the avatars of consumerist popular culture. Yet as in many of Ishiguro's other novels, art and music ultimately fail to redeem the crises of self from which his characters suffer. That does not mean, however, that no hope awaits his patiently observant souls. Even at the end of *Never Let Me Go* Ishiguro hints about the potential for redemption, which, although unrealized, nonetheless tempers the somber fatalism of Kathy's tale.

Poised at the midpoint of his career, nearing the completion of what may one day be termed his middle period, Kazuo Ishiguro seems to be a writer in transition. Throughout the 1980s he sculpted a style of unassuming power and grace. Disillusioned by the pigeonholing success of his first three novels, he then courageously veered, risking his reputation on audacious experiments with setting and voice. Over the past ten years he has reclaimed his artistic autonomy, reaffirming his independence from the movements to which he is generally enlisted: neorealism, postmodernism, postcolonialism. Until his subsequent novels appear, it will prove difficult to assess the fullness of his career; but it seems likely that for decades to come Ishiguro will continue to be followed with spirited anticipation. Few contemporary writers can match the stylistic sophistication with which he scrutinizes war-torn cultures and classes, national identities, individual isolation, and the indelible presence of the past.

[*See also* The Novel.]

SELECTED WORKS

A Pale View of Hills (1982)
An Artist of the Floating World (1986)
The Remains of the Day (1989)
The Unconsoled (1995)
When We Were Orphans (2001)
Never Let Me Go (2005)

FURTHER READING

Lewis, Barry. *Kazuo Ishiguro*. Manchester, U.K., 2000. One of the better introductions to Ishiguro's work.

Parkes, Adam. *Kazuo Ishiguro's* The Remains of the Day: *A Reader's Guide*. New York, 2001. A brief guide.

Schaffer, Brian W. *Understanding Kazuo Ishiguro*. Columbia, SC, 1997. The first full-length study of Ishiguro's work; designed for both general and academic audiences.

Wong, Cynthia F. *Kazuo Ishiguro*. Tavistock, U.K., 2000. A short introduction for students.

JACOBIN AND ANTI-JACOBIN FICTION

Nancy E. Johnson

The rubric "Jacobin" was applied to fiction, primarily of the 1790s, that engaged the political discourse of the period and advocated widespread reform in Britain. This fiction, dominated by the novel, was labeled "Jacobin" by the self-proclaimed "Anti-Jacobin" movement, in a provocative gesture to associate British radicals with the notoriously violent Jacobin Party during the French Revolution. The title "Jacobin" is therefore misleading. Although radical authors in Britain supported the French Revolution in its earliest days, they did not promote revolution within Britain. They embraced gradual change and an evolutionary process toward improvement. Thus, as Gary Kelly has suggested, they were more closely aligned with the Girondins, a moderate and more judicious political party in France.

Jacobin fiction was informed by the philosophy of sentimentalism (see Butler) and the theories of contractarianism, which merged in the campaign for rights of the 1790s. From the philosophers Anthony Ashley Cooper, third earl of Shaftesbury, and Francis Hutcheson, Jacobin authors gleaned the concept of innate goodness. They believed that, if properly educated and raised in an environment of enlightened thought, all members of a society would be capable of behaving well and acting with compassion and benevolence. The philosopher and novelist William Godwin and the novelist and playwright Thomas Holcroft, in particular, saw the power of the human mind as an unexplored resource of unlimited potential. They entertained notions of human perfectibility and, based on philosophical sentimentalism, suggested that vice is mere error resulting from ignorance. Correct these errors, they believed, and one might rid the world of evil. Sentimentalism, when combined with Godwin's assertion that circumstances determine the character of an individual, became an important political expedient. Such views made widespread social change seem possible, and they rendered the populace worthy of the social, legal, political, and economic authority they would receive as citizens in a nation governed by contract.

Contractarianism was another important theoretical source for Jacobin fiction. John Locke's identification of the origin of political power in law and of proprietorship located in self-ownership were concepts put forth in *Two Treatises of Government* (1690), and rigorously investigated by Jacobin authors in their novels. Locke's debate with political theorist Sir Robert Filmer, whose *Patriarcha* (1680) was a justification for the divine right of kings and an articulation of formal patriarchalism, elucidated the shift taking place from monarchy to government by contract, from subjecthood to citizenship. Locke's arguments empowered the individual who was regarded as a proprietor in society, endowing this "citizen" with certain privileges that could not be violated by civil actions. Locke's recasting of the relationship between the individual and the state as one of consent was supported by the contractarian thought of the seventeenth century. The political theorist James Harrington envisaged a citizenry of "proprietors" who would be protected by their rights of property (*The Commonwealth of Oceana*, 1656), and the English politician Algernon Sidney described the civil body as "a collation of every man's private right into a publick stock," driven by the assumption that one will gain from the investment (*Discourses Concerning Government*, 1698).

The principles of contractarianism were revisited in the political debate on rights in the 1790s, and it is to this debate that Jacobin fiction made its contribution: its critique of the social contract. Richard Price's sermon *A Discourse on the Love of Our Country*, delivered on 4 November 1789, an anniversary of the Glorious Revolution, is often acknowledged to have been the spark that ignited the fiery exchanges on Britain's political structure. Price used the occasion to propose three resolutions to expand British liberty; he concluded the sermon, however, with congratulations to France on her rebellion against tyranny, thereby initiating an impassioned controversy. Price's comments invited numerous responses, including the statesman Edmund Burke's *Reflections on the Revolution in France* (1790), which in turn precipitated its own rejoinders. The debate that ensued focused on definitions of natural and civil rights and the constitution of the legal subject. While Burke argued for "inherited rights"—civil liberty that is an "entailed inheritance" bequeathed to heirs by their forefathers—his opponents advocated for "individual inalienable rights" given by God as a birthright. Burke's adversaries, who included, most prominently, Thomas Paine, Mary Wollstonecraft, and James Mackintosh, saw in Burke's fashioning of rights an attempt to limit the franchise and deny "proprietorship" to the newly conceived citizenry.

Jacobin authors enlisted fiction to pursue their political goals and to conduct an inquiry into the issues and concepts under debate in the 1790s. Godwin explained that essayists turned to the novel to veer the dialogue on rights away from "refined and abstract speculation" and toward "a study and delineation of things passing in the moral world" (*Caleb Williams*, 1794). In early Jacobin fiction, Robert Bage and Thomas Holcroft offered sanguine, optimistic representations of social change. Their protagonists were often worthy figures of enfranchisement who flourished when endowed with Paine's "rights of man." These early novels were imbued with philosophical sentimentalism. As the genre of Jacobin fiction developed, however, the authors' endorsement of the rights of man began to give way to a critique of contractarianism. When Mary Wollstonecraft and Mary Hays began to investigate the impact of political advancements on women, they discovered the persistence of patriarchalism in the social contract. The rights of man were indeed the rights of men, not women. Additionally, nearly all of the Jacobin authors began to grapple with the role of property in determining one's relationship to civil society. If "proprietorship" was to be the mechanism for one's participation in a social contract, then what was to become of those members of society who could not make claims to self-ownership, such as women, servants, and beggars? This problem resonates through Jacobin fiction as characters find themselves the property of others, thereby negating opportunities to become full legal subjects in a social contract.

JACOBIN AUTHORS

The most prominent Jacobin authors were Robert Bage, William Godwin, Mary Hays, Thomas Holcroft, Elizabeth Inchbald, Charlotte Smith, and Mary Wollstonecraft. Others who expressed Jacobin sympathies in their fiction were Maria Edgeworth, Mary Robinson, and Helen Maria Williams.

Robert Bage (1728–1801) was a paper manufacturer in Elford, Staffordshire, who published two Jacobin novels:

Man As He Is (1792) and *Hermsprong; or, Man As He Is Not* (1796). In his novels Bage incorporated the socially progressive theories of Voltaire, Wollstonecraft, and Paine. William Godwin, perhaps the best-known of the Jacobin novelists, was first and foremost a political philosopher, author of the influential and controversial *Enquiry Concerning Political Justice* (1793). Godwin's most important Jacobin novel is *Things As They Are: or, The Adventures of Caleb Williams* (1794), in which Godwin fictionalized many of the ideas he examined in his *Enquiry*. Mary Hays (1760–1843) was a Dissenter who met in London the leading political authors, Godwin and Wollstonecraft. Her two Jacobin novels are *Memoirs of Emma Courtney* (1796) and *The Victim of Prejudice* (1799), in which she explored radical philosophy and the socio-political lives of women. Thomas Holcroft (1745–1809), friend and confidant of William Godwin, was a central figure in Jacobin fiction. His literary productions are predominantly in drama, but he wrote two Jacobin novels, *Anna St. Ives* (1792) and *Hugh Trevor* (1794–1797), that build a case for reform and celebrate the potential for social transformation. Elizabeth Inchbald was an actress, dramatist, and novelist. Her novel *Nature and Art* (1796) investigates the power of education and enlightenment. The poet and novelist Charlotte Smith was active in radical circles in the 1790s and wrote two of the most significant Jacobin novels: *Desmond* (1792) and *The Young Philosopher* (1798). Her novels record the movement from optimism to skepticism that characterizes Jacobin fiction. Mary Wollstonecraft, one of the first respondents to Burke, emerged initially as a political theorist at the forefront of republican thought. She wrote only one Jacobin novel, *The Wrongs of Woman; or, Maria* (1798). Though it was published unfinished, it provides a comprehensive and cogent review of laws of the time that oppressed the lives of women.

ANTI-JACOBIN FICTION

Anti-Jacobin fiction entered into a dialogue with Jacobin fiction, defining itself against "the new philosophy" of Jacobinism. The goal of Anti-Jacobin thought was clarified in the prospectus to *The Anti-Jacobin* magazine, founded by George Canning, William Gifford, and John Hookham Frere in 1797: "of JACOBINISM in all its shapes . . . We are avowed, determined, and irreconcilable enemies" (1.7). Thus, Anti-Jacobin fiction, also dominated by the novel, concentrated its efforts on revealing the dark intentions of progressive narratives and dismantling their underlying philosophical assumptions, rather than providing a positive conservative ideology to counter Jacobinism. Anti-Jacobin novels appeared in the later 1790s and early 1800s, and they were far more numerous than Jacobin novels; M. O. Grenby estimates the number to be near 200. By the mid-1790s, the political landscape had changed. Revolutionary France had turned into Napoleon's France, and, beginning in 1793, Britain was again at war with its longtime enemy. Rebellion was brewing in Ireland, and British radicals were being arrested, jailed, and charged with sedition and treason. Many Jacobin authors were distancing themselves from France, given the violent turn of the revolution and its spawning of Napoleon Buonaparte, but Anti-Jacobin fiction was relentless in staying focused on France as an example of the potential fate of Britain, should the nation abandon its illustrious traditions and welcome a new age based on individual talent and personal merit.

Embracing the traditional literary forms of satire and allegory, Anti-Jacobin writers frequently ridiculed central Jacobin figures such as Godwin, Wollstonecraft, and Hays, and they worked to discredit the ideas presented in Jacobin political theory. Anti-Jacobin fiction took an antisentimental stance. In these novels, characters who deem themselves to be innately good and full of unlimited potential undergo a process of disillusionment and experience a deflation of their expanded egos. Sentimental philosophers are weak and deluded (if men) and "manly" and aggressive (if women). Utopian societies founded on individual entitlements are shown to be corrupt, violent communities, driven by personal greed. To counter philosophical sentimentalism, Anti-Jacobins posed traditional Christian values. Rather than encourage a universal benevolence supported by the state, Anti-Jacobin fiction embraced private charity, positing that it is better to help one's neighbor than to try to reform society at large. Social obligation, therefore, is not about citizenship but about acknowledging one's limitations and taking one's rightful place in society.

Anti-Jacobin fiction also attacked the emphasis on individualism and self-governance in contractarianism. Seeking political authority and legal subjecthood through inalienable rights was represented in Anti-Jacobin fiction as a selfish pursuit, driven by hubris and resulting in social decay. The "new philosophy" is most often spread by French or French-trained philosophes: Isaac D'Israeli's Vaurien, Henry James Pye's Jean Le Noir, and Jane West's Fitzosborne. The proselytizing philosophe is at best misleading, and at worst a malicious villain interested only in personal gain. His victim is either a guileless young man, coming of age intellectually and socially, or an attractive young woman (sometimes married) who becomes the object of sexual desire. The latter case provides an opportunity to illustrate one of the most alarming dangers of Jacobinism, the destruction of the British family, which would mean the ruin of the British nation. The infiltration of a British family by a French or French-trained philosophe, as occurs in Jane West's *A Tale of the Times* (1799), is akin to a French invasion of Britain's shores. The family was the site of Burke's "inherited rights," and it was the cornerstone of British society. The "new philosophy" that glorified the individual distinct from his or her place in a family—and was imported from France—threatened the foundation of Britain itself.

Despite their vast ideological differences, Jacobin and Anti-Jacobin fiction shared some common ground: an advocacy of reason and, at times, support of female education. Quite consistently, Anti-Jacobin fiction encouraged the containment of passion and the liberal use of one's rational faculties. Jacobin fiction also argued for the dominance of reason. However, reason in Anti-Jacobin fiction was most often presented as "common sense," not the liberating human faculty of Godwin's political theory. The emphasis on reason also surfaces in the Anti-Jacobin novels of women, when they insist on the importance of female education. Jane West and Elizabeth Hamilton, like Mary Wollstonecraft and Mary Hays, promoted formal instruction for women. Yet, again, they did so for differing motives. For West and Hamilton, the goal was to nurture good wives and mothers who would be charged with moral authority in the home, whereas for Wollstonecraft and Hays the aim was to prepare women for citizenship.

Jacobin and Anti-Jacobin fiction made important contributions to political debates at the turn of the century, identifying the critical points of controversy for Britain as a nation in transformation. Hence, this literature maintains a significant place in political history. Jacobin and Anti-Jacobin fiction were also important to the development of the novel, producing a new genre of the sociopolitical novel, reexamining sentimentalism and sensibility in social thought, and ushering fiction into the age of Romanticism.

ANTI-JACOBIN AUTHORS

The most notable of the Anti-Jacobin authors were Robert Bisset, Isaac D'Israeli, Elizabeth Hamilton, Charles Lloyd, Charles Lucas, Henry James Pye, George Walker, and Jane West. Robert Bisset (1759–1805) was a lawyer, historian and reviewer for *The Anti-Jacobin* magazine. His Anti-Jacobin novel, *Douglas; Or, the Highlander,* (1800) ferrets out those intellectuals, including Godwin, Wollstonecraft, and Hume, responsible for putting Britain in danger. Charles Lucas (1769–1854) fashioned an evil protagonist, Marauder, in his novel *Infernal Quixote* (1801) to convey and catalogue the satanic strategies of radical thinkers. Although best known for his critical and historical writings, Isaac D'Israeli (1766–1848) wrote six novels, at least one of which, *Vaurien: or, Sketches of the Times* (1797), espouses Anti-Jacobin views. In this novel, the French philosophe, in the figure of Vaurien, is also examined and found to be not just duplicitous but villainous. The essayist and novelist Elizabeth Hamilton (1756–1816) began an attack on "the new philosophy" in her first novel, *Translations of the Letters of a Hindoo Rajah* (1796), but she confronted Jacobin thought with full force in her second novel, *Memoirs of Modern Philosophers* (1800). The poet Charles Lloyd (1775–1839) does not easily fit the mold of Anti-Jacobin author. His novel *Edmund Oliver* (1798) depicts the seductive but ultimately destructive qualities of Jacobinism; however, it also considers a humane redistribution of wealth. Henry James Pye (1745–1813), an English poet laureate, published two Anti-Jacobin novels, *The Democrat* (1795) and *The Aristocrat* (1799). In both, the very espousal of French ideas demonstrates their futility, and democracy is revealed to be impractical at best. The bookseller and novelist George Walker (1772–1847) published *The Vagabond* (1799), a novel that depicts the potential violence resulting from reform and naive assumptions about social transformation. Jane West (1758–1852), a novelist, dramatist, and poet, wrote two novels—*Advantages of Education* (1793) and *A Gossip's Story* (1796)—that are not overtly political, though they promote a conservative approach to marriage choices. Her most important Anti-Jacobin novel is *A Tale of the Times* (1799), in which domestic decisions are infused with political ideology.

[*See also* Maria Edgeworth; William Godwin; Elizabeth Inchbald; John Locke; Mary Robinson; Charlotte Smith; Helen Maria Williams; *and* Mary Wollstonecraft.]

FURTHER READING

JACOBIN FICTION

Butler, Marilyn. *Jane Austen and the War of Ideas.* Oxford, 1975. The first book to categorize Jacobin fiction and compare it to Anti-Jacobin fiction.

Clemit, Pamela. *The Godwinian Novel.* Oxford, 1993. Studies Godwin's novels in relation to his radical political philosophy and as paradigms for other novelists.

Johnson, Nancy E. *The English Jacobin Novel on Rights, Property, and the Law.* Basingstoke, U.K., 2004. Considers Jacobin fiction as a critique of contractarianism.

Keane, Angela. *Women Writers and the English Nation in the 1790s.* Cambridge, U.K., 2000. Includes chapters on nationalism in the works of Williams, Smith, and Wollstonecraft.

Kelly, Gary. *The English Jacobin Novel.* Oxford, 1976. Examines the structure of the English Jacobin novel and provides a helpful historical context for Jacobin fiction.

McCann, Andrew. *Cultural Politics in the 1790s: Literature, Radicalism and the Public Sphere.* New York, 1999. Addresses the conflation of aesthetics and politics in literature; chapters on Burke, Paine, and Wollstonecraft.

Paulson, Ronald. *Representations of Revolutions, 1789–1820.* New Haven, CT, 1983. An important discussion of the aesthetics of representing revolution and utopian visions.

Taylor, Barbara. *Mary Wollstonecraft and the Feminist Imagination.* Cambridge, U.K., 2003. A comprehensive study of Wollstonecraft's theoretical and fictional work.

Ty, Eleanor. *Unsex'd Revolutionaries: Five Women Novelists of the 1790s.* Toronto, 1993. Uses feminist theory to analyze novels by Wollstonecraft, Hays, Smith, Inchbald, and Williams.

Watson, Nicola. *Revolution and the Form of the British Novel, 1790–1825: Intercepted Letters, Interrupted Seductions.* Oxford, 1994. Examines the narrative form of novels in relation to national identity; includes discussions of Edgeworth, Smith, and Wollstonecraft.

ANTI-JACOBIN FICTION

Butler, Marilyn. *Jane Austen and the War of Ideas.* Oxford, 1975. Identifies Anti-Jacobin fiction and discusses its dominant ideologies in relation to Austen.

De Montluzin, Emily L. *The Anti-Jacobins, 1798–1800: The Early Contributors to the "Anti-Jacobin Review."* Basingstoke, U.K., 1988. Historical study of conservative thought and language gleaned from Anti-Jacobin poetry, fiction, and essay writing.

Dinwiddy, John. "Interpretations of Anti-Jacobinism." In *The French Revolution and British Popular Politics,* edited by Mark Philp. Cambridge, U.K., 1991. Explores political motivations of Anti-Jacobin authors.

Dyer, Gary. *British Satire and the Politics of Style, 1789–1832*. Cambridge, U.K., 1997. Includes some discussion of Anti-Jacobin satire.

Grenby, M. O.. *The Anti-Jacobin Novel: British Conservatism and the French Revolution*. Cambridge, U.K., 2001. The most thorough study of Anti-Jacobin fiction; provides important historical and theoretical contexts.

Johnson, Nancy E. "The 'French Threat' in Anti-Jacobin Novels of the 1790s." In *Illicit Sex: Identity Politics in Early Modern Culture*, edited by Thomas DiPiero and Pat Gill. Athens, GA, 1997. Examines the use of "fears of France" to distract from issues of British reform.

Kelly, Gary. *Women, Writing, and Revolution, 1790–1827*. Oxford, 1993. Includes a chapter on Elizabeth Hamilton.

Ty, Eleanor. *Empowering the Feminine: The Narratives of Mary Robinson, Jane West, and Amelia Opie, 1796–1812*. Toronto, 1998. Analyzes works by Jane West.

KING JAMES I OF SCOTLAND

John M. Bowers

King James I of Scotland (1394–1437) secured his place in British history as the Stewart ancestor of Mary Queen of Scots and James I of England. His claim on literary history, however, rests on a single 1,379-line poem that survives in only one manuscript, Oxford Bodleian MS Arch. Selden B.24, copied half a century after his death. *The Kingis Quair* (*The King's Booklet*) is one of the most charming and accomplished Chaucerian imitations written in the fifteenth century. The royal poet's use of the elegant seven-line stanza of iambic pentameter rhyming *ababbcc*, perfected by Chaucer in *Troilus and Criseyde* during the 1380s, actually gave this verse form the name still used today: "rhyme royal." Even Shakespeare admired this stanza enough to employ it in *The Rape of Lucrece.*

The Kingis Quair was written about 1423 or 1424, and James himself signaled his indebtedness to Chaucer as well as to John Gower in its final stanza:

> Unto th'inpnis of my maisteris dere,
> Gowere and Chaucere, that on the steppis satt
> Of rethorike quhill [while] thai were lyvand [living] here,
> Superlative as poetis laureate
> In moralitee and eloquence ornate,
> I recommend my buk in lynis sevin—
> And eke thair saulis unto the blisse of hevin.
>
> (Norton-Smith, ed., p. 50, ll. 1373–1379)

It was extraordinary that the heir to the Scottish crown had read Chaucer's poetry at such an early date, and more so that he knew the *Knight's Tale* as well as *The Parliament of Fowls* so thoroughly that he seemed compelled to write only in echoes. Biographical background is required to account for James's unlikely emergence as the first major Scottish Chaucerian in a line that would include Robert Henryson and William Dunbar.

When the eleven-year-old James was intercepted en route to the French court in 1406, Henry IV exclaimed jokingly that the Scots should have sent the boy to him for his education in the first place, "for I too know the French language!" But this teaching process, perhaps begun by Chaucer's old friend Henry Scogan, was different from the education given to other hostages. Specifically, James's education included Chaucer's poetry at a time when the English author's works were not easy to obtain except in deluxe aristocratic copies, such as the Ellesmere *Canterbury Tales* and the Pierpont Morgan manuscript of *Troilus* owned by Henry V while Prince of Wales. During his eighteen years in England, James had become a member of what might be called Chaucer's "captive audience." This small group of noble hostages, including Charles of Orléans, was maintained in custodial imprisonment and systematically schooled in Chaucer's poetry. James's reading and later writing of courtly poetry were exercises intended to fashion him as a courtier, a specifically *English* courtier. But rather than remain a passive imitator, he composed his poetic autobiography as a cunning fabric of linguistic and narrative borrowings that can be read as a textual counterassault on the English. Even his poem's dialect represents a willful attempt to "Scotticize" vocabulary and poetic rhetoric that remain essentially Chaucerian.

Henry IV kept the heir to the Scottish throne in the shadows, but when he succeeded his father in 1413, Henry V started using James as a royal figurehead. In 1420, for example, the Scotsman contributed his regal prestige at the wedding of Henry V and Catherine of Valois. Henry then moved to create a larger role for James as a military figure, knighting him as a member of the Order of the Garter at Windsor in 1421. *The Kingis Quair* belongs to this later phase of high visibility on the international stage, leading up to his release from English captivity in 1424.

King James wrote a courtly dream-vision whose allegory conceals not only moral truths but also autobiographical facts. At the beginning of *The Kingis Quair*, the narrator muses on Boethius's *Consolation of Philosophy* in order to make better sense of his own experience, since he too was a prisoner, held in strongholds such as the Tower of London. Buoyed by Good Hope, he is passed along by Venus to the goddess Minerva to learn about the superior form of love grounded in Christian wisdom. Further reflection leads the poet to conclude that Fortune, once his enemy, has now become a friendly supporter of his love life. Her turning wheel would elevate him to new heights. Thus his dream counters Chaucer's *de casibus* tragedies with a jubilant Boethian comedy.

Self-regulating discipline characterized advisory writings such as Thomas Hoccleve's *Regiment of Princes*, a privileged text at the Lancastrian court in the years following its completion around 1411. James incorporated the most admirable traits of this "mirror of princes" genre into his own account of princely self-fashioning. James was writing about love while rehearsing his own long-deferred reign as the Scottish monarch. The challenge became how much Englishness would remain in him.

As a deliberate reminiscence of the *Knight's Tale*, for example, James described how his prison tower abuts on a flower garden. Like Chaucer's Palamon, he looks into the garden and sees a beautiful woman walking among the trees and flowers:

> And therwith kest I doun myn eye ageyne,
> Quhare [where] as I sawe, walking under the tour,
> Full secretly new cummyn hir to pleyne,
> The fairest or the freschest yonge floure
> That ever I sawe, me thought, before that houre.
> For quhich [which] sodayn abate anon astert
> The blude of all my body to my hert.

(p. 10, ll. 274–280)

Like Palamon, he immediately falls in love and begins wondering if she is a goddess. But there are important differences. He is a Palamon without an Arcite, a young lover without a rival. This is a poetic fiction, since we know that he actually shared his captivity with other Scotsmen. His pursuit of the lady also proceeded without the visible dominance of any penal authority. He is a Theban without a Theseus, a prisoner without a jailer. The poem completely banishes the presence of the Lancastrian captors. Far from being depressing, his whole love experience becomes joyous and liberating.

By using Boethius to translate his captivity into a philosophical issue, James eliminated the power and even the presence of his Lancastrian hostage-takers, just as the *Consolation* displaced the *Knight's Tale* as the acknowledged textual inspiration. He also changed the Boethian conclusion imposed in Theseus's "Fair Chain of Love" speech in the *Knight's Tale*, with its insistence on the crude mechanics of succession, for the grander providential vision "Of him that hiest in the hevin sitt." Challenging the English court in its own poetic medium, James discovered in the official Chaucerian tradition the resources for constructing the kind of savvy, self-determining identity—a true discourse of subjectivity—that modern readers have so consistently valued in Chaucer himself. James's over-optimistic ambition as a lover intent upon writing his own happy ending, however, foreshadowed the heavy-handed political tactics that later cost him his throne and his life.

The Kingis Quair moves from an autobiographical narrative into a poetic performance, then back into an autobiography that opens out onto a real-life royal triumph. By making access to the lady contingent on his freedom from prison, the narrator establishes marriage as the symbol of that liberation. James's whole account moves toward his union with the lady, who is unnamed by the narrative but fully known to history: Joan Beaufort, daughter of the earl of Somerset and granddaughter of John of Gaunt through his third wife, Katherine Swynford. This means that Joan's genealogy included Geoffrey Chaucer, husband of Katherine's sister Philippa. This convergence of dynastic history and literary tradition would have deep implications for James's national project after his return to Scotland.

The death of Henry V in 1422 accelerated the pace of negotiations for James's release, completed in December 1423 with promise of a £40,000 ransom. In February 1424, he married Joan Beaufort in Southwark, not far from the site of Harry Bailey's Tabard Inn whence the Canterbury pilgrims depart. It is significant that the wedding feast was hosted by the bride's uncle, Henry Beaufort, bishop of Winchester, because the marriage clearly worked to his political advantage. The union linked the Stewart monarch with the Beaufort half-bloods of the royal house of Lancaster. The Beaufort-Stewart marriage promised an alliance that ideally neutralized the long-standing threat on the northern border so that England could concentrate on Continental expansion, specifically the colonization of Normandy.

James I had spent his formative years in a kingdom with the most centralized governance in western Europe, and he had personally observed the most dazzling and aggressive monarch of the age, Henry V. Once back in Scotland and securely on the throne, he used what he had learned to fullest advantage. He sprang upon the scene as an impressive prince skilled at jousting, wrestling, and archery, as well as music-making with the flute, harp, and organ. The new king moved quickly to impose on Scotland a centralized form of government based on the Lancastrian practices of strong crown authority, well-enacted laws, heavy taxation, efficient bureaucracy, an enfranchised commons, a bicameral parliament, a reformed system of monasteries, and obedient, politically weakened barons. The Scottish historian Michael Brown has dubbed him "an angry man in a hurry."

Instead of paying his ransom raised by special taxation, James went on a spending spree to supply his court with the luxuries that he had witnessed in England and France. Palaces such as Linlithgow were constructed, and Flemish agents were charged with purchasing jewels, silks, furs, and satins. These extravagant acquisitions reflected James's desire to lift his kingship out of the reach of his magnates. His sole surviving poetic composition can be situated within this larger cultural enterprise. *The Kingis Quair* offered itself as a foundational text, exquisitely crafted, for a national literary tradition that discovered its origins in an English court already working hard at installing Chaucer as the "father of English poetry."

In England, there had been a division of labor. The Lancastrian kings claimed a viable dynasty, while Chaucerian writers such as John Lydgate constructed a parallel literary lineage that would prove more durable. In Scotland, King James ambitiously set himself the assignment of creating both a strong centralized monarchy and a poetic masterpiece as the starting point for a Scottish literary tradition. He was poised to become father of the Scottish nation *and* the father of Scottish poetry, with a work documenting his self-formation, his discovery of an ideal queen, and his liberation to pursue these long-range goals.

Although James's ruthless tactics for reducing the power of the magnates led to his assassination in 1437, his initiatives for creating a stronger sense of national identity deserve full recognition. He had established himself as a prince of international stature and a potential adversary on England's northern border. But just as James's governmental innovations came too much too soon, his literary efforts also fell short. *The Kingis Quair* attracted no widespread readership and no school of name-dropping imitators. The poem survived in a single anthology of Chaucerian poems produced around 1488 for James's longtime followers, the Sinclairs.

Despite the tragic conclusion to their marriage, King James and Queen Joan had twin sons in 1430, and one of them succeeded his father as James II. Throughout the next two centuries, Scotland enjoyed a degree of political stability based on an orderly succession of Stewart kings,

in marked contrast to England, thrown into disorder by the Wars of the Roses. James I's farsighted project had succeeded in lifting the status of the Stewart dynasty in the eyes of neighboring rulers, and this status was eventually accepted by the Scottish people themselves. So solid was the Stewart line that his descendant James VI of Scotland was available to succeed Elizabeth I on the English throne after the extinction of the Tudor line. In a sense, Scotland turned the tables on Lancastrian ambitions by reversing the direction of cross-border expansion and dynastic encroachment. Perhaps the ultimate tribute to the cultural project of James I of Scotland emerges in the fact that Scottish kings were so thoroughly "Englished" that King James VI arrived as a wholly acceptable successor to Queen Elizabeth.

[*See also* Geoffrey Chaucer; John Gower; *and* Thomas Hoccleve.]

EDITIONS

Norton-Smith, John, ed. *The Kingis Quair*. Oxford, 1971.

Skeat, Walter W., ed. *The Kingis Quair*. Scottish Text Society, vol. 1. Edinburgh and London, 1884.

The Works of Geoffrey Chaucer and "The Kingis Quair": A Facsimile of Bodleian Library, Oxford, MS Arch. Selden B.24. Introduction by Julia Boffey and A. S. G. Edwards. Cambridge, U.K., 1997.

FURTHER READING

Balfour-Melville, E. W. M. *James I, King of Scots, 1406–1437*. London, 1936.

Bowers, John M. "Three Readings of *The Knight's Tale*: Sir John Clanvowe, Geoffrey Chaucer, and James I of Scotland." *Journal of Medieval and Early Modern Studies* 34 (2004): 279–307.

Brown, Michael. *James I*. Edinburgh, 1994.

Fradenburg, Louise O. *City, Marriage, Tournament: Arts of Rule in Late Medieval Scotland*. Madison, WI, 1991. See the chapter "Speaking of Love: *The Parliament of Fowls, The Kingis Quair,* and *The Thrissill and the Rois,*" pp. 123–149.

Goldstein, R. James. "Writing in Scotland, 1058–1560." In *The Cambridge History of Medieval English Literature*, edited by David Wallace, 229–254. Cambridge, U.K., 1999.

Mapstone, Sally. "Kingship and the *Kingis Quair*." In *The Long Fifteenth Century: Essays for Douglas Gray*, edited by Helen Cooper and Sally Mapstone, 51–69. Oxford, 1997.

KING JAMES VI AND I

Neil Rhodes

James VI of Scotland and I of England (1566–1625) has been the only monarch of either nation to pursue authorship as well as authority in any systematic way. His ancestor James I of Scotland, an accomplished poet, and his immediate predecessor in England, Queen Elizabeth, also have claims to literary distinction, but no other British sovereign has been so dedicated a writer or so keen to publish the results of his or her literary labors. The *Short Title Catalogue* lists nearly seventy separate items, at the center of which is the 1616 folio *Workes* (actually published in 1617). Why James chose to publish so much is something of a mystery. Although he claimed that he wrote merely for intellectual pleasure ("for exercise of mine owne ingyne"), his works are far from being aristocratic jottings. In another life he would probably have been an academic. In the royal role that he was required to assume (from the age of two), he used the printing press for public relations purposes—as a projection of his personality and an extension of his rule.

POETRY

The desire to see his writings in print began early for James. He was eighteen when *Essayes of a Prentise in the Divine Art of Poesy* (1584) was published at Edinburgh. This was a collection of poetry that included a treatise on versemaking, "The Reulis and Cautelis to be Observit and Eschewit in Scottis Poesie," as well as "The Phoenix," an elegiac love poem (the homoerotic elements are somewhat coded) written for his friend and relation, Esmé Stuart, Seigneur d'Aubigny. James imagines his beloved phoenix fleeing from his enemies to his protection:

> she fled at last
> To me (as if she wolde wishe me to judge
> The wrong they did her) yet they followed fast
> Till she betwixt my leggs her selfe did cast.

Essayes was followed by a second volume, *His Majesties Poeticall Exercises at Vacant Houres* (1591), which contains his translation from the French poet Guillaume de Sallust Du Bartas, titled "The Furies," which discourses on the

tribulations of the Fall, and an epic in fourteeners (verse lines of fourteen syllables) called "Lepanto," celebrating the naval victory over the Turks by the Christian forces of Don John of Austria in 1574. This early literary work was the product of James's association with a group of court poets that included Alexander Montgomerie and William Fowler, known (perhaps misleadingly) as the Castalian band. The association was probably quite loose, but there is no doubt that James himself drew inspiration from the example of the Pléiade (a group of sixteenth-century French poets), and in particular from Pierre de Ronsard and Joachim du Bellay, who provided a model for the "Reulis." The French connection is evident, too, in his admiration for Du Bartas, whom he was later to meet, as well as (rather more personally) for Esmé Stuart.

James wrote less poetry as he grew older, partly because he had fewer vacant hours. "Amatoria," a collection of love poems written for Anne of Denmark whom he married in 1589 (honeymooning in Elsinore), remained unpublished, but this was not on account of its being overly personal. James says in the "Reulis and Cautelis" that love is the most hackneyed subject for poetry, and in the "Amatoria" he admits that he has told a "willfull lye" since he has "sung of sorrows never felt by me." Some later poems did find their way into print, but as part of other texts. The best known of these is "God gives not Kings the stile of *Gods* in vaine," a more heartfelt sonnet on the subject of divine right, which prefaces his treatise on the art of kingship, *Basilicon Doron* (1599). Of the few poems that we have from his later years, perhaps the most interesting is "The wiper of the peoples teares," his response to a verse lampoon on him that had been widely circulated but is now lost. Here he describes himself as "a Cradle King" whose life has been one of unending responsibility. He will call Parliament, he explains, "When I see things more out of joint: / Then will I sett all wry things straight."

PROSE: THE SCOTTISH YEARS

James's marriage to Anne of Denmark was also the occasion for his first major prose work, *Daemonologie*, published at Edinburgh in 1597. James's voyage to Denmark to claim his bride had been marked by terrible storms. In 1590, Agnes Sampson, one of a number of people from North Berwick who were being investigated for witchcraft, confessed that she had raised the storms herself in order to kill the king. This appalling discovery was the cue for James to write a polemic against those such as Reginald Scot, the author of *The Discovery of Witchcraft* (1584), who were sceptical about the existence of witches. It takes the form of a dialogue between the "learned" Epistemon, who represents James himself, and Philomathes, "the lover of knowledge." It is divided into three short "books": the first deals with "Magie," the second with "Sorcerie and Witchcraft," and the third offers "a description of all these kindes of Spirites that troubles men or women." There are some Faustian touches to the work, such as his account of how academic curiosity leads to "the horrors of Hell," but its most obvious relationship with the English drama of the period is the contribution it made to the witchcraft elements in *Macbeth*.

At the end of the 1590s, before ascending the English throne, James wrote the two works that constitute his statement on governance, *Basilicon Doron* and *The Trew Law of Free Monarchies*. The first is a practical manual of kingship dealing, in turn, with a king's Christian duties, the duties of his office, and, lastly, "of a King's Behaviour in Indifferent Things." It was written for his elder son, Prince Henry, who was to die at the age of eighteen, and its title means "the royal gift," so it falls into the "advice to princes" tradition. Since on Henry's death this "royal gift" passed to Prince Charles, who was eventually executed for high treason, *Basilicon Doron* must be regarded as one of the least successful handbooks of practical advice ever written. It does, however, tell us a good deal about James's interests and obsessions, one of which is secrecy. This is the book where he famously describes the king "as one set on a stage, whose smallest actions and gestures, all the people gazingly doe behold," yet it is also full of references to "the secretest of my drifts," "their secretest actions," "the more secret and close keeping of them," and so on. He even forbids the wearing of defensive armor called "secrets" (worn underneath the clothes), despite relying for his own security on heavily padded clothing.

Another theme that might also be regarded as a security issue is the subject of the Union between England and Scotland. At the time of writing *Basilicon Doron*, this was only a gleam in James's eye, but he took the opportunity to advise his own son against "dividing your king-

domes . . . as befell to this Ile" at the time of Brutus, the mythical founder of Britain. This glimpse ahead to *King Lear* is presented here in a specifically Scottish context. His own kingdom was divided between Highlanders and Lowlanders, and it was frayed at the edges by "alluterly barbarous" Islanders and Borderers. Internal colonization was the answer: a project that was to have far-reaching consequences when repeated beyond the shores of Britain in Ulster, Virginia, and elsewhere.

The private/public, Scottish/British aspects of *Basilicon Doron* are reflected in its publishing history. Originally written in Middle Scots in 1598, it was Anglicized and published the following year in a clandestine manner in an edition of only seven copies. When Elizabeth died in 1603, a second Edinburgh edition and a London edition were rushed from the presses. All told, about 14,000 copies were printed, enabling people south of the border to get a preview of their new monarch. The book was then translated into the major European languages, into Latin, and also (to penetrate the deepest parts of James's new kingdom) into Welsh. *Basilicon Doron* traveled from being virtually a private talk from father to son in a strange tongue to its eventual status as a printed book with a pan-European audience.

The Trew Law of Free Monarchies was also written in 1598 and published at Edinburgh in the same year. It is a companion text to *Basilicon Doron* in that it provides a theoretical framework for the more practical account of kingship set out in that book. It could also be described as a statement of James's views on divine right, the theory that kings are divinely appointed and therefore answerable only to God for their actions. But it is also directed specifically at people (like his former tutor, the Scottish humanist George Buchanan) who argued for a contractual theory of kingship. The "free" monarchy advertised in the title of the work is one in which the king is free of any contractual obligations toward his subjects. The main purpose of the work is indeed to support a concept of "divine right," but it does so by arguing against both contract theory and resistance theory, the latter being the belief that, in certain circumstances, subjects may have the right to depose their king. James bases his arguments on "two similitudes": one, which appears elsewhere in his writing, is that the king is the "head of a body composed of divers members"; the other is that at his coronation the king is placed by the law of nature in the role of a father toward his subjects, who are required to show the obedience expected of children. The words "free" and "freedom," then (as well as "true" and "truth"), provide a specious rationale for oppression. This is a point that may have occurred to Ben Jonson when, in *Sejanus*—a play dedicated, incidentally, to Esmé Stewart's son—he made Tiberius reiterate the view that, under his rule, Rome is a "free state."

PROSE: THE ENGLISH YEARS

James's first publication after ascending the English throne was the *Counterblaste to Tobacco*, which might be regarded as the first H. M. Government Health Warning against the noxious weed. Here James adopts the persona of the good physician, listing in his typically methodical way the objections to a series of arguments in favor of smoking: that it is medicinal, working on the principle of the cure by contraries (and is also used as a prophylactic against syphilis by the native Americans); that it has a purgative effect; that it is popular, so it must have some benefit; and that it never did anyone any harm. What most concerns James, however, is that it is a symptom of the "sluggishness" brought on by the peace with Spain, and therefore the first seed of disobedience and rebellion.

This brief polemic coincided with the issuing of his first speech to Parliament, and it is these political speeches that constitute the major part of his published work after 1603. The speech to Parliament of 1604 is concerned particularly with the Union, a project dear to James's heart but to very few others in either England or Scotland. He begins by evoking the bloody memory of the civil wars between York and Lancaster, recently staged by the Lord Chamberlain's Men, who had now been granted his royal patronage. The union that exists in his person is, firstly, he argues, a union between those two houses, and it is this that underlies the greater union between the two nations. He continues with the well-known metaphor of marital embrace, a variation on the family metaphor of father and children: "I am the Husband, and all the whole Isle is my lawfull Wife: I am the Head, and it is my Body; I am the Shepherd, and it is my flocke." The speech ends with a promise that he intends in these orations "to use no other Eloquence than plainnesse and sinceritie," an allusion, presumably, to the notoriously Delphic and evasive utterances of his predecessor, Elizabeth. He returned to the subject of the Union in the speech of 31 March 1607, and to the subject of transparency in the speech of 12 March 1610, where he compared his words to a mirror, laying open the heart of the king for all his subjects to see. There are three ways of "wronging" a mirror, he claimed: by looking upon it "with a false light"; by soiling it "with a false breath"; and by letting it "fall or breake." These warnings against misinterpretation might themselves be regarded as somewhat opaque, and James's mirror certainly reflects his ambiguous feelings about secrecy and publicity that are so much in evidence elsewhere.

James's name will always be associated with the Authorized Version of the Bible of 1611, otherwise known as the King James Bible, but he also wrote religious works of his own in the form of biblical commentary and reflection. The earliest of these was the *Paraphrase upon Revelation* (1588), a popular exercise at the time that enabled the writer to elaborate on apocalyptic themes, as Edmund Spenser does in the first book of *The Faerie Queene*. Toward the end of his life he also wrote the *Meditation upon the Lord's Prayer* and the *Meditation upon Matthew 26*. The second of these harks back to the apocalyptic strains of the work on Revelation, as James meditates on the Crucifixion of Jesus as a prototype of the suffering of kings. "As a croune of thornes then represents the stinging cares of Kings, so a croune of platted thornes doth more vively represent the anxious and intricate cares of Kings," he muses, before returning to the persona of the king as a good physician. By a strange coincidence, it was this very passage from Matthew that was the appointed reading on the day that his son, King Charles, the royal martyr indeed, was led out to execution on 30 January 1649.

When James decided to publish his writings in folio in 1616, he engaged James Montague, bishop of Winchester, to supervise the work and write the preface. "Yet hath it been ever esteemed a matter commendable to collect [works] together, and incorporate them into one body, that we may behold at once, what divers Off-springs have proceeded from one braine," wrote Montagu, uniting James's favorite metaphors of the body and the family. 1616 was also the year that James's court poet, Ben Jonson, published his plays as his *Workes*. James may well have felt that if a playmaker, however learned, could publish his plays as "works," then why not the king, whose own writings were much more serious. James did not, however, include his poetry in the 1616 folio, and it was not until 2003 that James's poetry and prose works were published together in a single volume.

[*See also* The English Bible; Queen Elizabeth I; *and* Ben Jonson.]

EDITIONS

Rhodes, Neil, Jennifer Richards, and Joseph Marshall, eds. *Selected Writings*. Aldershot, U.K., 2003. Freshly edited and annotated complete texts of all the major prose works and most of the poetry. Glossary and bibliography.

Sommerville, Johann P., ed. *Political Writings.* Cambridge, U.K., 1994. Good introduction and notes, with glossary.

FURTHER READING

Fischlin, Daniel, and Mark Fortier, eds. *Royal Subjects: Essays on the Writings of James VI and I.* Detroit, MI, 2002. The first critical collection to survey the full range of James's writing.

Goldberg, Jonathan. *James I and the Politics of Literature: Jonson, Shakespeare, Donne, and Their Contemporaries.* Baltimore, 1983. Pioneering New Historicist account of James's writing within the political and cultural contexts of the literature of his reign.

Jack, R. D. S. "Poetry under King James VI." In *The History of Scottish Literature: The Origins to 1660,* edited by R. D. S. Jack, 125–139. Aberdeen, Scotland, 1988. Places James's poetry within the context of his court circle.

Rhodes Neil. "Wrapped in the Strong Arms of the Union: Shakespeare and King James." In *Shakespeare and Scotland,* edited by Willy Maley and Andrew Murphy. Manchester, U.K., 2005. Discusses Unionist ideas in the work of both writers.

Sharpe, Kevin. "The King's Writ: Royal Authors and Royal Authority in Early Modern England." In *Culture and Politics in Early Stuart England,* edited by Kevin Sharpe and Peter Lake, 117–138. Stanford, CA, 1993. Excellent overview of James as a writer and his conjunction of royal and poetic authority.

Sharpe, Kevin. "Private Conscience and Public Duty in the Writings of James VI and I." In *Public Duty and Private Conscience in Seventeenth-Century England: Essays Presented to G. E. Aylmer,* edited by John Morrill, Paul Slack, and Daniel Woolf, 77–100. Oxford, 1993. Argues that these two terms were not regarded as opposites by James and explores the consequences of that view in his poetry and religious writings.

Wormald, Jenny. "James VI and I, *Basilikon Doron* and *The Trew Law of Free Monarchies*: The Scottish Context and the English Translation." In *The Mental World of the Jacobean Court,* edited by Linda Levy Peck. Cambridge, U.K., 1991. Authoritative account of the circumstances of publication and the reception of James's two principal political works.

HENRY JAMES

Eric Haralson

As Virginia Woolf summed up his achievement and the powerful imprint he left upon the writers of modernism—"to some an oppression, to others an obsession"—Henry James's exemplary genius made him "undeniably present to all." Henry James (1843–1916) was born in New York City into a gifted, quirky, well-to-do family. His father, Henry senior, was a prominent author of Swedenborgian tracts, his older brother William would become the premier psychologist-philosopher of the era, and his sister Alice was a shrewd social commentator and diarist. James passed what he later called his "rootless & accidental childhood" with sporadic bouts of schooling in venues as varied as Albany, Newport, Boston, Paris, Geneva, and London, as his father sought in Europe the kind of "sensuous education" denied to children in puritanical America. The James family's means and standing were substantial, as were young Henry's charm and intelligence, so that by his mid-twenties he had encountered a veritable "who's who" of the British and American cultural elite, including Ralph Waldo Emerson, Washington Irving, William Makepeace Thackeray, William Morris, Dante Gabriel Rossetti, Charles Darwin, John Ruskin, and George Eliot. An emerging writer with better connections is scarcely imaginable, as his next decade of circulating in Europe brought him in contact with Alfred Tennyson, Robert Browning, George Meredith, Ivan Turgenev, Gustave Flaubert, Émile Zola, and Guy de Maupassant. James's first international success came with the long story "Daisy Miller: A Study" (1878), about an American ingenue abused by snobbish compatriots abroad. Over the course of five decades, this quintessential bachelor-artist "dedicated himself to literature, with growing self-denial, lucidity, and happiness" (in Jorge Luis Borges's formula), writing or dictating up to the moment of his

Henry James
Portrait by John Singer Sargent, 1913
NATIONAL PORTRAIT GALLERY, LONDON

death in early 1916: "the pen drops from my hand," his last letter declares.

Even aside from James's reputation and influence, the bare facts of his literary production are staggering. Beginning in earnest with *Roderick Hudson* (1875)—which follows a talented New England sculptor going to the dogs amid Old World decadence—and extending to the autobiographical *Notes of a Son and Brother* (1914), James's oeuvre ultimately comprised twenty-two novels, more than a hundred tales or novellas, fifteen plays, and roughly three hundred pieces of criticism. His novels include the indisputable masterpieces *The Portrait of a Lady* (1881) and *The Golden Bowl* (1904), and his tales the chilling gothic riddle "The Turn of the Screw" (1898) and the melodramatic parable of missed life "The Beast in the Jungle" (1903). James's criticism addresses a breathtaking array of American, British, and other world authors; favorite subjects are Nathaniel Hawthorne, Anthony Trollope, George Eliot, Honoré de Balzac, George Sand, and his close friend Turgenev. In addition to these many works, James produced extensive travel writings—notably those collected in *English Hours* (1905), *The American Scene* (1907), and *Italian Hours* (1909)—and the essential, retrospective prefaces to the New York Edition of his major fiction (1907–1909). This would-be monument to his career suffered disappointing sales, yet the prefaces have proven invaluable for illuminating the life circumstances and narrative "germ" of his key works, the challenges posed by his groundbreaking techniques—the so-called scenic method and the use of "reflectors" or "centers of consciousness"—and the process of revising, or "re-dreaming," the earlier writings. James's paean to the novel as "the most independent, most elastic, most prodigious of literary forms" made clear that his own practice demanded keen "attention of perusal" from readers; in exchange he promised the "divinely great" pleasure derived from art that can "bear without cracking the strongest pressure we throw on it." Shouldering aside predecessors like Charles Dickens and tasking contemporaries like Zola, James did not master fiction so much as he "overmastered" it, as the poet Robert Lowell said, becoming "the first American to be unassailably at home" in the English novel.

THE INTERNATIONAL THEME

James's biography of Hawthorne (1879) conveniently supplies his motives for having settled in England, where he lived with only occasional returns to the United States for the forty years of his maturity. The creation of meaningful artworks, he contended, required a substantial accumulation of cultural history, whereas the American landscape could boast only a "thin and impalpable . . . deposit." James's well-known inventory of "the items of high civilization . . . absent from the texture of American life"—pronounced social classes, picturesque antiquities, storied institutions of learning, repositories of art—explains his preference for the "denser, richer, warmer European spectacle," with its "infinitely more various" customs and types for fictional appropriation. Yet in his formative years James also believed that being raised an American made "an excellent preparation" for immersion in other cultures, conferring a "spiritual lightness and vigour" of temperament unknown in older civilizations and equipping American-born writers for the "intellectual fusion and synthesis of the various National tendencies of the world." James's transplantation, that is, did not mean that he ever truly relinquished his native land or forgot its inhabitants, with both their strengths and liabilities of character. T. S. Eliot went so far as to doubt whether "anyone who is not an American can *properly* appreciate James" or the "fullness of existence" embodied in his protagonists, for James's grasping imagination (unlike that of British authors) "preyed not upon ideas, but upon living beings." Indeed James's most memorable heroines, from the cruelly exploited Isabel Archer (*The Portrait of a Lady*) to the passionate, doomed Milly Theale (*The Wings of the Dove*, 1902), as well as his sympathetic heroes from Christopher Newman (*The American*, 1877) to Lambert Strether (*The Ambassadors*, 1903), constitute studies in the confrontation between American idealism—well-meaning but naive—and European worldliness, in which avarice, duplicity, and intrigue are the order of the day. It must be added that some of the more distinguished villains in the Jamesian plot, such as Gilbert Osmond and Serena Merle of *The Portrait of a Lady*, are themselves deracinated Americans.

In point of fact, no nationality corners the market on dubious, even pernicious moral behavior in James. His social critique is evenhanded, and taken together his fictional writings, whether satiric or tragic, render an Anglo-American world in which the most basic institutions of society have become profoundly unstable. Marriage and sexual mores waver, and the bonds of friendship strain under temptations of self-interest; in the creaky class system "the working and the worked [are] the parties to every relation" (as is matter-of-factly observed in *The Wings of the Dove*), and the bourgeois family falters as a socializing unit and seat of honor. Even protocols for the transmission of family name and property are sorely tested or utterly break down. As for nationalities, if the unscrupulous schemers in *The Portrait of a Lady* are American expatriates, then the calculating lovers in *The Wings of the Dove*—"handsome" Kate Croy and her hapless conspirator Merton Densher—are products of the English middle classes. If the vicious, neglectful parents and adulterous stepparents of *What Maisie Knew* (1897) and the lax, chatty fast set of *The Awkward Age* (1899) typify modern London, then the weakened, destructive ethics of Americans must also come under scrutiny, as in "Daisy Miller" and "The Pupil" (1891). In *Washington Square* (1880), an American father, the harsh Dr. Austin Sloper, wields the threat of disinheritance against his daughter Catherine's romantic aspirations, if not her very selfhood, while in *The Spoils of Poynton* (1897), an English widow and her affianced son wrestle over the ownership of an estate and its furniture until the contested "spoils" go up in proverbial smoke. And although a cash-strapped European aristocracy often factors into the social and sexual machinations at the core of James's plots, the quietly but mercilessly acquisitive American capitalist Adam Verver of *The Golden Bowl* may stand as the prime manipulator in the author's corpus. Not coincidentally, one of the few women in James to dominate her marital and economic fate is Verver's daughter and protégée, the "much-thinking little" Maggie, as the novel pursues a critique of an ascendant American imperialism and its ramifications for family and social structure.

ORDEALS OF CONSCIOUSNESS AND EXPERIENCE

Whether one interprets the Ververs as "nice monsters," in Stephen Spender's terms, or as a considerably naughtier "superbly monstrous couple" (à la Gore Vidal), James's broad postulate about the human predicament still holds: everybody pays some price for living in societies in which conduct is governed by material greed or emotional self-seeking. Occasionally the cage may be gilded or the leash silken, such as the one Charlotte Stant is imagined to wear after her affair with Prince Amerigo (a double adultery) is exposed in *The Golden Bowl*, but ultimately both individual freedom and the chances of love are compromised. No social station is spared: trapped in a "frail structure of wood and wire," the young telegraphist of "In the Cage" (1898) jeopardizes her own prospects when she dallies in the seamy liaisons of the British upper crust. The captive condition of humanity, dramatized in the spirit of what James called his "imagination of disaster," is seldom in question. As Graham Greene forcefully put it, however much James came to pity his fallen creatures, they could expect "no victory" while on this mortal coil; instead, "you were punished in your own way, whether you were of God's or the Devil's party." Or as Borges concluded, despite James's immense energy and stylistic buoyancy, he is best understood as "a resigned and ironic inhabitant of Hell" masquerading as a psychological novelist of manners.

The most common victims of earthly punishment in James—or rather, of the transatlantic degeneracy and skullduggery that inform his plots—are women. Those already mentioned include Catherine Sloper, Isabel Archer, and Milly Theale, heiresses whose "thumping bank-accounts" combine with their romantic desires to make them targets of deception or subjects of sinister leverage. Or take the strenuous suffragist Olive Chancellor of *The Bostonians* (1886), who loses a precious ally and the love of her life when the mesmerizing Verena Tarrant runs off with an unreconstructed Southern male chauvinist. James handles the Parisian enchantress Madame de Vionnet of *The Ambassadors* more tenderly, but she is still left sundered by her amorous plunge—not the "virtuous attachment" it is advertised to be—with the suave, feckless scion of a New England manufacturing family. No less ravaged, May Bartram of "The Beast in the Jungle" epitomizes a recurrent Jamesian type, the woman who waits in vain for "overwhelming" ardor—the only true kind—while devotedly serving a man who will never fully reciprocate, either because he obeys a selfish propriety or because his amatory drift is decidedly not heterosexual.

Although James was no feminist in the political sense, his women often emerge as fiercer and stronger than his men, more willing to be "hit" by love, incur its risks, and absorb its abjection; intensely committed to life, they also manage their dying better, according to James, as men suffer "more grossly than women, and resist with . . . an inferior strategy." Notably, even his female perpetrators—like Kate Croy, Charlotte Stant, the rampaging governess in "The Turn of the Screw," and the child-murderer Rose Armiger of *The Other House* (1896)—elicit a degree of sympathy from readers for being in themselves disenfranchised, haunted, and self-defeating figures. The culpable but nonetheless poignant Madame Merle tries to instruct a dangerously "theorizing" Isabel Archer that all persons, especially women, are constrained by a "whole envelope of circumstances" and are never unitary or invulnerable subjects: "What shall we call our 'self'? Where does it begin? where does it end? It overflows into everything that belongs to us—and then it flows back again." Or as a choric female voice in *The Ambassadors* succinctly puts it: "What woman was ever safe?" The signal exception that proves the rule might be Miriam Rooth, the Anglo-Jewish actress of *The Tragic Muse* (1890), although her triumphs of self-assertion as a woman artist are imperiled by modern mass culture.

Not only James's women pay for experience so exquisitely and pathetically. His fond fascination with the young, part of his curiosity about the way that complex adult knowledge accrues, finds expression in a retinue of child or adolescent characters who also must undergo experiential ordeals. In "The Pupil," precocious Morgan Moreen's fatal defect in "the region of the heart" emblematizes the failure of both his hypocritical parents and his hard-pressed tutor to nurture his growth. Little Maisie Farange, reduced to a pawn in the bed-hopping, social-climbing games of devious adults, endures trials of affiliation and "knowing." In the coming-of-age narrative of Nanda Brookenham in *The Awkward Age*, James cannot allow her a more satisfying escape from the debasing London marriage market than a retreat into rustic quietude with avuncular Mr. Longdon. The (apparently) innocent young Miles and Flora in "The Turn of the Screw," (seemingly) harrowed by ghosts and governess alike, are abandoned by the tottering institutions of British society. And although Hyacinth Robinson, the delicate "prostitute's bastard" of *The Princess Casamassima* (1886), survives his adoptive childhood, he also belongs on this roster of souls damned or damaged early on, since his ruinous flirtation with European anarchism is rooted in his nativity.

Even though James's women and children bear many burdens—burdens of suffering and thus of meaning—his men do not fare much better, for all the privileges of patriarchy. To speak in rough categories, James's male gallery consists of ambivalent suitors, callow fellows on the make, wooden manly men, elusive aesthetes, family-ridden sons, and a host of "poor, sensitive gentlemen" who do not quite fit the conventional mode of Anglo-American manhood, or necessarily conform to norms of sexuality. Nationality inflects this catalog to an extent, in the guise of an anxious British bureaucrat, for example, or a dull but effusive American businessman, or English lords and captains by turns too earnest, stuffy, or slippery; but the sum total suggests a pervasive cross-cultural crisis in masculinity. Those who settle most comfortably into the established order are perhaps the tradesmen, like patient Butcher Mudge of "In the Cage," or their ambitious descendants, like the nouveau-riche shoemaker's son "Mitchy" Mitchett of *The Awkward Age*. James also specialized in the late-blooming bachelor type who comes through life's experiences only relatively intact, as exemplified by Strether of *The Ambassadors* or Spencer Brydon of "The Jolly Corner" (1908). Yet these men must face their own rites of passage, and their revelations—or spiritual "revolutions," to use James's term—come at the cost of painful episodes of self-recognition and appreciable self-abnegation. Indeed, Strether may best capture James's ethos for right living when he summarizes the "only logic" of his conduct as being a concerted bid "not, out of the whole affair, to have got anything for myself."

THE MODERN ARTIST AND JAMES'S LATE STYLE

James's works also show concern for the plight of serious artists, especially creative writers, striving to maintain excellence in an overcommercialized, journalistically ravenous, "cheap" modernity. Anglo-American mass culture gravitated toward the "huge and ornamentally vulgar," to quote a critical voice in *The Tragic Muse*, and its "most distinctive sign" was a "colossal, deafening newspaperism" that promoted ephemeral talents while threatening the livelihood of the genuinely gifted. As melodramatically portrayed in "The Author of 'Beltraffio'" (1883) and then expounded with ironic verve in "The Aspern Papers" (1888), "The Middle Years" (1893), and "The Death of the Lion" (1894), writers both living and dead had much to fear from incursions of the press, facile critics, zealous admirers, and would-be disciples conspiring to ferret out the artist's secret and pursuing nothing less than the "immediate exposure of everything." Little wonder that

James burned heaps of his personal correspondence, or that he ultimately left London for what he called his "little old celibatoirean oak-parlour" of Lamb House in Rye, Sussex. The fading author Dencombe of "The Middle Years" is not a stand-in for James, but his last breath utters the Jamesian conviction that literature harbors a mystery not for the fingering of profane hands: "We work in the dark. . . . Our doubt is our passion and our passion is our task. The rest is the madness of art." Despite James's skepticism about "the newnesses, the queernesses, above all the bignesses" that made up modern society, as in the urban spaces revisited in *The American Scene*, he never deviated from the credo of artistic receptivity first announced in "The Art of Fiction" (1884). Writers of genius opened themselves to an endlessly evolving social life and therefore had to be observers "upon whom nothing is lost": "Experience . . . is an immense sensibility, a kind of huge spiderweb of the finest silken threads suspended in the chamber of consciousness, and catching every airborne particle in its tissue." Only an unflinching alertness to a shifting, sometimes shocking reality could secure what he later heralded as the radical "plasticity and liberality" of the novel as preeminent literary genre.

No account of James would be complete without addressing his late manner, which contemporary reviews routinely taxed for displaying "too much brilliancy" or presenting a "verbal hedge" resisting the reader's penetration. His elaborate style, rich in apposition and circumlocution as if testing the limits of English prose, has had its famous detractors and has invited clever parodies, such as H. G. Wells's "The Spoils of Mr. Blandish" in *Boon* (1915). Some readers, like James's own brother William, simply asked for more straightforward expression to save them from reading "innumerable sentences twice over to see what the dickens they could possibly mean." Others complained that James burnished his surface at the expense of depth; Mark Twain, for instance, held that James "analyzed the guts out of emotion" with excessive discourse. This charge was repeated in slightly different terms both by Oscar Wilde, who thought James was masking an inaptitude for deep feeling, and by E. M. Forster, who claimed that James's textual fiddling (as he saw it) resulted in cerebral fables about enervated, "castrated" characters. The most stinging attack, however, came from the combative Wells: James's "adverbial stuffing" only made his "vast paragraphs sweat and struggle" like a hippopotamus trying to pick up a pea. Even later admirers like Spender noted that in James the most quotidian events might be "drowned by waves, or smothered in flowers" of verbiage owing to the author's "inescapable individualism": "The privilege the reader is offered is to become Henry James, a highly sensitive, cultured man, with extremely isolated spiritual experiences."

James's poetics and substance have attracted staunch defenders as well, however. Joseph Conrad's praise of James as "the historian of fine consciences" implies that his valorized characters, with their discriminating ethics and "energetic acts of renunciation," could not be dramatized without rhetorical finesse and narrative intricacy. To Ford Madox Ford, who considered this "un-Americanised American" uniquely suited to depict transatlantic cultures in transition, James's fictional voice was "simply colloquial" even with all the embroidery, his sentences perfectly clear when read aloud. The point is well taken: Henry James, like all powerful innovators, trains the responsive reader in how to read Henry James. Unwilling to relinquish her countryman to the British tradition, Gertrude Stein nominated James as "the only nineteenth-century writer who being an American felt the method of the twentieth century," and as her own most influential precursor. As Stein's testimony suggests, along with accolades from Eliot and Ezra Pound, James's stylistics and subjects have found special favor among poets. Marianne Moore, for example, esteemed the ornate finish of his works as a token of "diffidence, reserve, and strong feeling," of his "respectful humility" toward the range of human emotions in general. Borrowing James's diction, Moore also celebrated the way that things in his created universe "glow, flush, glimmer, vibrate, shine, hum, bristle, reverberate," reminding us that literary language carries its own sensual intensity and meaningful pleasures. W. H. Auden eulogized James as "poet of the difficult, dear addicted artist," one whose "nuance and scruple" in matters both formal and ethical made him the ideal mentor for those confronting a troubled century. To fortify the case, writers as diverse as Evelyn Waugh, James Baldwin, A. S. Byatt, and Philip Roth have continued to attest to the importance of James's example in Anglo-American letters.

But James himself was the most ardent proponent and steadfast explicator of his own brand of literary art, graciously answering even his toughest critics until the end of an epoch-spanning career. As his own health declined with age and as world war thrust his familiar Victorian world into the abyss, he resolutely reissued his dictum that the writer must engage experience, take in all that expands consciousness, and remain true to a private vision and "measure of fullness." In keeping with values

subtly advanced in his works, especially a commitment to freedom and self-accountability under conditions of trial and constraint, James threw his "moral weight and personal allegiance" into the English war effort, visiting wounded soldiers, rallying Americans to the cause, and finally assuming British citizenship. By living passionately on his own terms and striving ceaselessly to realize what he saw as literature's "best gift" of beguiling readers with a vivid "extension of life," James affirmed his faith that art "*makes* life" through the very "force and beauty of its process." Moreover, his ideal of authorship, which aspired to a calculated "ambiguity" of national identity and a "melting together" of cultures across boundaries, anticipated the transnational mobility of mind now associated with global cosmopolitanism. It seems fitting that his ashes lie buried in the James family plot in Cambridge, Massachusetts, while a commemorative plaque honors his accomplishments in the Poets' Corner of Westminster Abbey.

HENRY JAMES IN CONTEMPORARY CULTURE

Wells's image of James as the finicky mandarin of "copious emptiness" has been refuted by the continuing interest in his work long after his death. The many successful film adaptations of his novels and novellas, the enduring vitality of his fiction in the classroom and the academy, and the ongoing commercial appeal of his writings would have astounded even the author himself. The gothic psychodrama of "The Turn of the Screw" has proven particularly irresistible to filmmakers, resulting in no fewer than ten movie renditions, the most haunting and compelling being *The Innocents* (1961). The merits of other film treatments of James have provoked lively debate, but noteworthy adaptations include *The Heiress* (1949), featuring Olivia de Havilland's Oscar-winning portrayal of Catherine Sloper; feminist embellishments of both *The Portrait of a Lady* (1996) and *Washington Square* (1997), directed by Jane Campion and Agnieszka Holland, respectively; and a steamy, opulent take on *The Wings of the Dove* (1997). Director James Ivory and screenwriter Ruth Prawer Jhabvala, after warming up with versions of *The Europeans* (1979) and *The Bostonians* (1984), teamed with producer Ismail Merchant to offer a darkly captivating film version of *The Golden Bowl* (2000). Cumulatively, these movies uncover the insistent subtext of power, desire, and pathos in James's fiction—the often perverse dynamics of "freedom and domination, glamour and stigma," that animated late-Victorian Anglo-American culture (Moon, p. 25).

A more curious tribute to James's popular relevance is paid by a steady stream of novels based on aspects of his biography—not only his creative life, but also his affective experience as a closeted gay man. These include Emma Tennant's *Felony* (2002), Colm Tóibín's *The Master* (2004), and David Lodge's *Author, Author* (2004). Within the university curriculum and the ever-burgeoning body of literary scholarship, James's work has enjoyed vibrant readings and shown a remarkable hospitality to new interpretations under such rubrics as women's studies, gay and lesbian studies, and postmodern theory—his intricate novel *The Sacred Fount* (1901) amounts to a primer in avant-garde narrative. All these various testimonials to Henry James's legacy confirm that he embodied what he once called "that queer monster the artist, an obstinate finality, an inexhaustible sensibility."

[*See also* Aestheticism; Narrative; The Novel; *and* H. G. Wells.]

SELECTED WORKS

Roderick Hudson (1875)

The American (1877)

"Daisy Miller: A Study" (1878)

Washington Square (1880)

The Portrait of a Lady (1881)

The Bostonians (1886)

The Princess Casamassima (1886)

The Spoils of Poynton (1897)

What Maisie Knew (1897)

"The Turn of the Screw" (1898)

"In the Cage" (1898)

The Awkward Age (1899)

The Wings of the Dove (1902)

"The Beast in the Jungle" (1903)

The Ambassadors (1903)

The Golden Bowl (1904)

The American Scene (1907)

"The Jolly Corner" (1908)

A Small Boy and Others (1913)

Notes of a Son and Brother (1914)

EDITIONS

Blackmur, Richard P., ed. *The Art of the Novel: Critical Prefaces by Henry James.* New York, 1962.

Horne, Philip, ed. *Henry James: A Life in Letters.* London, 1999.

FURTHER READING

Blair, Sara. *Henry James and the Writing of Race and Nation.* Cambridge, U.K, 1996. An ambitious social-historical study that corrects the elitist image of James by showing how his writings engaged popular culture as part of a larger project in rethinking dominant ideologies of nation, race, and gender.

Cameron, Sharon. *Thinking in Henry James.* Chicago, 1989. An important reconsideration of James's most challenging works, arguing that consciousness is represented not as internalized psychology but as an intersubjective mode of relationship and power.

Edel, Leon. *Henry James: A Life.* New York, 1987. A condensed, revised edition of the first major biography of James, dated and reductive in its psychoanalytic premises.

Freedman, Jonathan. *Professions of Taste: Henry James, British Aestheticism, and Commodity Culture.* Stanford, CA, 1990. An incisive account of James's unique position within Anglo-American aestheticism, as concepts of authorship and literature grew increasingly commodified.

Freedman, Jonathan. *The Temple of Culture: Assimilation and Anti-Semitism in Literary Anglo-America.* Oxford, 2000. A trenchant survey of the topic that features two crucial chapters on James in the context of contemporary representations of Jewishness and historical discourses of anti-Semitism.

Hadley, Tessa. *Henry James and the Imagination of Pleasure.* Cambridge, U.K., 2002. A strong treatment of ten major works, showing James's departure from traditional novelistic moralizing about sexuality and female character, and movement toward a continental European emphasis on pleasure and play in modern relationships.

Haralson, Eric. *Henry James and Queer Modernity.* Cambridge, U.K., 2003. An expansive inquiry into far-reaching changes in the gender system and the emergent politics of male homosexuality as depicted by James and the American modernists whom he influenced.

Kaplan, Fred. *Henry James: The Imagination of Genius, A Biography.* London, 1992. A competent biography that draws James's homosexuality within its compass; occasionally formulaic readings of the fiction.

Moon, Michael. *A Small Boy and Others: Imitation and Initiation in American Culture from Henry James to Andy Warhol.* Durham, NC, 1998. A far-ranging study of the dynamics of sexual identity in twentieth-century

America that innovatively incorporates James's memoirs, fiction, and social observation.

Pippin, Robert B. *Henry James and Modern Moral Life.* Cambridge, U.K., 2000. A perceptive, accessible explication of the subtle theory of moral comprehension and behavior informing James's fictions about a newly complex social life.

Posnock, Ross. *The Trial of Curiosity: Henry James, William James, and the Challenge of Modernity.* Oxford, 1991. A powerful case for James as a relentless, avant-garde cultural analyst, based on careful readings of the fiction and *The American Scene* juxtaposed with writings by seminal American and European theorists of modernity.

Rowe, John Carlos. *The Other Henry James.* Durham, NC, 1998. A groundbreaking interpretation of the Jamesian canon applying recent theoretical models (feminist, queer, postcolonial) that fundamentally revises the iconic figure of James as aloof, high-formalist master.

Stevens, Hugh. *Henry James and Sexuality.* Cambridge, U.K., 1998. A theoretically and historically rich study revealing James's representations of transgressive desires, including same-sex passion, and of various sexual identities on the margins.

Taylor, Andrew. *Henry James and the Father Question.* Cambridge, U.K., 2002. An insightful consideration of intellectual affinities and conflicts between James and his idiosyncratic philosopher-father, and their implications for his theories of fiction and autobiography, gender politics, and psycho-ethical concepts of the self.

RICHARD JOHNSON

Richard Proudfoot

Richard Johnson (fl. 1592–1621) poses a peculiar problem for the compiler of a literary encyclopedia. Although the name is attached to a number of popular publications of the late sixteenth and early seventeenth centuries, it remains quite uncertain to what London tradesman of those decades it belonged. Of the author's career it is known, on the basis of information included in several of his books, that he was not a Londoner by birth, but he pursued his career there and was reasonably successful. In dedicating one of his two most popular works, the prose romance *Tom o' Lincoln* (the presumed first edition of 1599 has not survived, the earliest extant being the 1631 reprint), to Simon Wortedge of "Okenberrie" (Alconbury), Huntingdonshire, he signs himself "Your worships deuoted, and Poore Country-man, R. I.," and speaks of the "great friendship" shown by Wortedge's "renowned" father to his own parents. Local records yield no information about a Wortedge family in Alconbury (though the name Worledge is recorded).

The stages of Johnson's career in London are recorded in other publications. In 1592 he was "a poore prentice" and nine years later "a poore freeman" of the city of London. In 1608, 1616, and 1621 he dated reprints of his most successful book, *The Seven Champions of Christendom*, "from my house at London." He never specified his trade, and though a train of allusion could associate him with the Merchant Taylors, whose company included a Richard Johnson of appropriate age, the name was so common at the time as to make this identification no more than a possibility, and no direct link has yet been established. Here if anywhere is a clear instance of the author as "author function." The assumption that the books published in the name of Richard Johnson, or sometimes "R. I.," had a single author is based on the evident selling power of that name and the consistent address and appeal of his miscellaneous publications to a wide citizen readership, with some emphasis on young male readers. It may reasonably be assumed that his prose romances were read by London prentices as avidly as the prentices in Francis

Beaumont's *The Knight of the Burning Pestle* (act 1, lines 207–219) read the English translation of *Palmerin of England.*

PLACING JOHNSON

Three of Johnson's publications are dedicated to lord mayors of London. The first of these, indeed Johnson's earliest certain publication, is *The Nine Worthies of London* (1592), a Chaucerian dream poem, "proceeding from the barren braine of a poore apprentice, that dare not promise moul-hils, much less mountaines," which adopts the form of *The Mirror for Magistrates* to celebrate nine famous mayors of London. Johnson dedicated it to the current lord mayor, Sir William Webbe (Salter). Johnson's allegiance to the City and its governors continued with *Anglorum Lacrimae* (Tears of the English, 1603), his elegy on Queen Elizabeth, dedicated to Robert Lee, lord mayor (Merchant Taylor), and the knights and aldermen of the City. His last pamphlet, *Look on Me London* (1613), in which he denounces the vices of the London suburbs, is addressed to all "the yong Men of London, as well *Gentlemen as others*," and is dedicated to Sir Thomas Middleton, lord mayor (Grocer) and zealous inquisitor into London crime and vice. The formula was varied for *The Pleasant Walks of Moorefields* (1607), which celebrates local improvements and City history and is dedicated to the knights and aldermen of London. The same year Johnson chose Sir Robert Stone, mercer to the queen, as dedicatee of *The Pleasant Conceits of Old Hobson the Merry Londoner* (1607), a collection of thirty-five humorous anecdotes mostly well known from earlier jest books but here loosely attached to the figure of William Hobson, haberdasher, who died in 1581.

Johnson aimed higher with his most ambitious book, *The Seven Champions*, dedicating its first part (1596) to Lord Thomas Howard, a hero of the victory over the Spanish Armada and of the 1596 raid on Cádiz, and its second part (1597) to Howard's brother, Lord William, later an eminent antiquary. Though the dedication of part 1 to Thomas Howard was never reprinted, that of part 2 to William Howard appears in most seventeenth-century reprints. A second dedication to Thomas Howard had a more immediate bearing on the subject of the pamphlet in question, *A Lantern-Light for Loyal Subjects*, occasioned by the treason trial of Sir Walter Ralegh in November 1603 before a commission headed by Robert Cecil and Howard himself. In a later pamphlet, *A Remembrance of the Honours due . . . to Robert, Earl of Salisbury*, Johnson claims that on 9 June 1612 he was present on the occasion of the funeral of Robert Cecil, earl of Salisbury, at Hatfield. The Howard brothers had as children been wards of Cecil's father, William Cecil, Lord Burghley, after the execution of their father, Thomas, fourth duke of Norfolk, in 1572.

Mention of their dedicatees indicates something of the aspirations of these publications. Johnson's noble dedicatees belonged to the court faction in the ascendant, and City dignitaries generally received dedications while in office. The absence of any such dedication makes it clear that Johnson's other popular publications, collections of songs and ballads, were more simply commercial ventures on the part of his publishers. Two such anthologies, *A Crown Garland of Golden Roses* (1612, revised in 1631, perhaps still by Johnson himself) and *The Golden Garland of Princely Pleasures* (1620), "The third time imprinted, enlarged and corrected by Rich. Iohnson," testify by their history of reprinting to his success as ballad writer and collector. A third, "Johnson*s hearb-John*. by Richard Johnson," was entered for publication in the Stationers' Register on 31 January 1622. This is the latest clear reference to Johnson as a writer. No copy of the book is now known. Whether he died about then or merely gave up working for the press, no later work can be attributed to him. His last extant book, a prose version of the story of Tom Thumb, survives in a single copy of its first part, dated 1621, while the "*first and 2. parte of Tom Thombe*" are named in the Stationers' Register on 13 December 1620.

AUTHOR OR PLAGIARY?

If Johnson's identity is in doubt, so too is the extent of his original composition. Modern scholarship has demonstrated to what extent his more ambitious publications simply recycle earlier works by other writers. Thus, of the 180 lines of his elegy on Queen Elizabeth, 130 are lifted from the *Celestial Elegies of the Goddesses and the Muses* (1598) by Thomas Rogers of Bryanston. *A Lantern-Light for Loyal Subjects* is a mosaic of quotations from George Whetstone's *Censure of a Loyal Subject* (1587), on the trial of the Babington plotters, and contains no more than three or four paragraphs of Johnson's own. Whetstone was also Johnson's quarry for his last pamphlet, *Look on Me London*, though this time the adaptation (combining two associated pamphlets, *A Mirror for Magistrates of Cities* and *A Touchstone of the Time* [1584] into one) was effected by heavy cutting, especially of specific details but also of Whetstone's frequent classical allusions—a pointer to Johnson's intended down-market readership of "the yong Men of London, as well *Gentlemen as others*," where Whetstone had targeted the "yong Gentlemen, of the Innes of Court." Even in *The Pleasant Walks of Moorfields*, which celebrates local improvements and City history, substantial sections are lifted verbatim from John Stow's *Survey of London* (1598). Though such recycling is a familiar phenomenon of pamphlet publication in the period, the extent and pervasiveness of Johnson's borrowing may still come as a surprise. Whether one chooses to characterize his flagrant and extensive borrowings as plagiarism or to dignify them with the modish sixteenth-century designation "imitation" is in the end a matter of personal opinion and historical perspective.

That Johnson earns a place among the notable popular writers of late Elizabethan and Jacobean London is not due to his more socially ambitious and heavily plagiaristic literary projects. In his own time and for many years later, he was valued as a writer of prose fiction and a compiler of jest books and ballad collections.

Johnson may or may not have written all those ballads and songs in his popular compilations that have not been traced to other writers, among them Thomas Deloney, George Wither, Richard Alison, Nicholas Breton, John Dowland, Thomas Ford, and Robert Jones. The subjects of the ballads include English royalty (especially from the fourteenth century to his own time), City history and mythology, and love and marriage. *The Golden Garland* is the earliest known source for ballads on *Titus Andronicus* and *King Lear* that appear to derive from knowledge of Shakespeare's plays (perhaps in performance, though both were in print before 1620, the date of the third edition and earliest surviving copy of Johnson's collection). That Johnson might be the author of these would be congruous with apparent allusions to *Titus* and to *Hamlet* in the second part of *Tom o' Lincoln* (1607, by which time both plays were in print). Lighthearted dramatizations of *Tom o' Lincoln* and *The Seven Champions*, the former for private performance at Gray's Inn, and the latter, printed in 1638 and attributed to John Kirke, for the public theater, seem to have been written in the second decade of the seventeenth century. Thomas Heywood has been mooted as a possible contributor to both, and they reveal the ease with which such romances could become butts of good-natured ridicule. Certainly Heywood's own *If You Know Not Me You Know Nobody*, part 2 (1605), had been plundered by Johnson both for the character of Old Hobson and for three of the best anecdotes in his jest book *The Pleasant Conceits of Old Hobson the Merry Londoner*, which largely comprises jests already well known from earlier such collections but here loosely attached to the figure of the memorable London worthy William Hobson (who appears in Heywood's play).

JOHNSON'S CLAIM TO FAME

Johnson's prose romances had a long history of adaptation, abridgment, and ubiquitous reprinting. Indeed, it was only as late as the 1930s that that hardy perennial *The Seven Champions*, in its latest children's version, finally went out of print (to reemerge in 2003 in its first scholarly edition by Jennifer Fellows). Allusions to it persist at late dates. For instance, in chapter 12 of Thomas Hardy's 1873 *A Pair of Blue Eyes*, Elfride Swancourt comforts herself that "if ill report should come . . . why, the orange-tree must save me, as it saved virgins in St George's time from the poisonous breath of the dragon" (*A Pair of Blue Eyes*, p. 171), associating the bridal bouquet with one of the more memorably outlandish motifs of Johnson's tale.

The structure of the romance is revealing. Despite its title, the first part centers on Saint George, patron saint of England, and devotes only a single chapter each to the independent narratives of the remaining six saintly champions, Andrew of Scotland, David of Wales, Patrick of Ireland, Denis of France, James of Spain, and Anthony of Italy, whose roles are elsewhere related and subordinated to the narrative of George's adventures. The romance narrative is derivative. The principal events in George's story, for instance, all occur in the medieval romance of *Bevis of Hampton*. Part 1 ends with a triumphant crusade led by the champions; part 2 takes up the stories of George's twin sons, related in similarly episodic manner. The offer of a third part never materialized beyond provision of the narrative closure of seven chapters, added at the end of part 2 in 1616, which relate the deaths of the seven champions in turn.

The motifs of the romance are common to the genre, from Edmund Spenser's *Faerie Queene* downward. The typical activities of the champions include killing mon-

sters, wild beasts, and giants; overcoming magicians; converting (or butchering) pagans; enduring hardships; winning the love of princesses; adopting disguises (frequently as hermits); and honoring and burying their dead parents. The tone is set at the start of part 1, with its promise to relate

> how troublesome warres ouerspread the whole earth. . . . Likewise of the bloody tragedies of many vnchristian Princes: whereat the heauens will mourne to see the effusion of blood trickle from the breasts of murthered Infants, the heapes of slaughtered damsels trampled to peeces by souldiers horses, and the streetes of many a Cittie sprinckled with the blood of reuerent age: Therefore gentle Reader accept of this my labour with a smoothe brow & a kinde countenance, and my wearie Muse shall neuer rest, till I haue finished the true Historie of these Heroicall Champions.

The emphasis on cities is not coincidental, and Johnson's intended readership is sharply evoked by a revealing simile in part 1, chapter 16, when George and his wife Sabra, lost in a forest, are likened to "solitarie Pilgrims, spending the daie with wearie steps, and the night with vaine imaginations, euen as a childe when hee hath lost himselfe in a populous Cittie, runneth vp and downe not knowing how to returne to his natiue dwelling."

Whether or not, as has been suggested, Thomas Heywood's popular play *The Four Prentices of London* (1615) was directly indebted to the writings of Johnson, it certainly implements the military and romantic fantasies of City prentices that fill the pages of Johnson's prose romances and are exemplified in ballads on such popular heroes of London mythology as Dick Whittington or Thomas Stukeley (both of whom figure in Johnson's collections).

[*See also* Thomas Heywood *and* Walter Ralegh.]

SELECTED WORKS

The Most Pleasant History of Tom a Lincolne/ R. I. (1599?; 1631), edited by Richard S. M. Hirsch (1978). Old-spelling text with informative introduction.

The Seven Champions of Christendom, 1596–7 (1596–1597), edited by Jennifer Fellows (2004). Makes Johnson's most popular work once more accessible in a lightly annotated old-spelling text.

The History of Tom Thumbe/ R. I., edited by Curt F. Bühler (1965). Scholarly reprint of all that survives of *Tom Thumb* (1621).

The Nine Worthies of London (1592)

Anglorum Lacrimae (1603)

A Remembrance of the Honours due . . . to Robert, Earl of Salisbury (1612)

A Crown Garland of Golden Roses (1612)

Look on Me London (1613)

The Golden Garland of Princely Pleasures (1620), "Third Impression"

The Pleasant Walkes of Moore-fieldes (1607), in *Illustrations of Early English Popular Literature*, vol. 2, edited by John Payne Collier (1966). Only modern reprint.

The Pleasant Conceites of Old Hobson the Merry Londoner (1607), in *Old English Jest-Books*, edited by W. C. Hazlitt, vol. 3 (1864). Only modern reprint.

FURTHER READING

Clark, Sandra. *The Elizabethan Pamphleteers*. Rutherford, NJ, 1983. Readable and informative survey of a wide and various field of Elizabethan publication.

Hardy, Thomas. *A Pair of Blue Eyes.* Edited by Roger Ebbatson. Harmondsworth, U.K., 1986.

Liebler, N. C. "Elizabethan Pulp Fiction: The Example of Richard Johnson." *Critical Survey* 12, no. 2 (2000): 71–87. *Seven Champions* meet literary theory.

Plett, H. F. "An Elizabethan Best Seller: Richard Johnson's *The Seven Champions of Christendom* (1596)." In *Modes of Narrative*, edited by Reingard M. Nischik and Barbara Korte, 234–251. Würzburg, Germany, 1990. Contextualizing Johnson.

Proudfoot, Richard. "Richard Johnson." In *Oxford Dictionary of National Biography*, edited by H. C. G. Matthew and Brian Harrison, 30:295–296. Oxford, 2004. Brief statement of current facts about Johnson and his works.

Willkomm, H. W. *Über Richard Johnson's "Seven Champions of Christendom."* Berlin, 1911. A book-length scholarly study of Johnson.

SAMUEL JOHNSON

Robert Folkenflik

The later eighteenth century in England is often regarded as the "Age of Johnson" because the range and quality of Samuel Johnson's writings and his role as the subject of the best-known biography in English impressed him upon his own time and the centuries following. Today Johnson (1709–1784) seems the embodiment of the professional writer and for many the foremost representative of English literary culture. The compiler of *A Dictionary of the English Language* (1755), the editor of Shakespeare (1765), and the author of *The Lives of the English Poets* (1779–1781), he was more responsible than anyone else for the growth of English literary nationalism ("the chief glory of every people arises from its authors," as he claimed in his preface to the *Dictionary*), although in many ways he was far from being a nationalist.

Samuel Johnson
Portrait by James Barry, c. 1778–1780
NATIONAL PORTRAIT GALLERY, LONDON

EARLY LIFE AND THE *GENTLEMAN'S MAGAZINE*

The son of Michael Johnson, a Lichfield bookseller, Samuel Johnson was born "almost dead," as he put it, in 1709. From his early years his prodigious intelligence was recognized, although his many ailments—scrofula, near blindness in one eye, and, as is now thought, Tourette's syndrome—led some to mistake him for an idiot before he began talking. He spent only thirteen months at Pembroke College, entering in 1728, but Oxford remained a highly formative influence and a place of fond associations. After writing some now lost essays for the *Birmingham Journal* (1733), translating Father Jerome Lobo's *A Voyage to Abyssinia* (1735), and teaching unhappily at Market Bosworth grammar school and in his own school at Edial, he joined Edward Cave's *Gentleman's Magazine* in 1738 and published the first of his Juvenalian "imitations" and first major poem, *London*.

London, an imitation—a form looser than a translation (in this case of Juvenal's third satire)—adapts modern instances to Juvenal's original examples of Roman decadence. An attack on the government of Sir Robert Walpole and the Hanoverian rule of George II, the poem pours scorn on English politics and culture broadly. Thales, the narrator's friend (who may or may not be based on Johnson's own friend, the poet Richard Savage), leaving London for Wales, excoriates the corruption of the city that extends from thieves and avaricious lawyers to unfair taxes, poorly built houses, and especially "publick Crimes." He contrasts this state of affairs with "Britannia's Glories," England under Elizabeth, which was able to quash its Spanish enemy, as opposed to Walpole's inaction in the face of Spanish provocations. This forceful poem was especially admired by opposition Whigs (the "patriots" praised in it), Tories, Jacobites (supporters of the dethroned James II and his successors), and opponents of Walpole generally. Alexander Pope accurately predicted that the anonymous poet would be "*déterré*" ("unearthed").

The following year Johnson published two prose satires, *Marmor Norfolciense* and *A Compleat Vindication of the Licensers of the Stage*, both indebted to Jonathan Swift. Again his targets are Walpole's government and the German king. *Marmor Norfolciense* is the account by an obtuse progovernment scholar of an "ancient prophetical inscription" on a marble found in Norfolk (hence the title) that predicts in runic form the current plight of England, although the scholar is too dense to understand it in his zeal for the government. The *Compleat Vindication* ironically defends the government's prohibition of Henry Brooke's antigovernment play *Gustavus Vasa* (1739) through its use of the Stage Licensing Act of 1737 effectively to censor and circumscribe English theater.

During these years and the early 1740s as a writer and editor for Cave, Johnson wrote poetry, reviews, and biographies of scholars, physicians, and naval heroes (these last, of Admiral Robert Blake and Sir Francis Drake, were clearly salvos in antigovernment attacks), but the largest of his undertakings for the *Gentleman's Magazine*—at first with William Guthrie and then on his own—was a series of "Debates in the Senate of Magna Lilliputia," a thinly disguised and largely imagined re-creation of the actual debates in the House of Commons, which were illegal to publish.

MATURITY AND RECOGNITION

Johnson's major publication of this period, *An Account of the Life of Mr. Richard Savage, Son of the Earl Rivers* (1744)—the sensational biography of his friend, the poet who claimed to be the son of an earl and murdered a man in a tavern brawl—was the first of his great biographies. The title indicates Johnson's unskeptical acceptance of the claim, but the biography itself is very clear-eyed about Savage's shortcomings and self-deceptions: "He proceeded throughout his Life to tread the same Steps on the same Circle; always applauding his past Conduct, or at least forgetting it, to amuse himself with Phantoms of Happiness, which were dancing before him; and willingly turned his Eyes from the Light of Reason, when it would have discovered the Illusion, and shewn him, what he never wished to see, his real State."

Johnson begins with pathos. At the outset he announces that his biography of the author of *The Bastard* and *The Wanderer* will be an addition to "the mournful Narratives" of the "Miseries of the Learned." But his biography mixes satire with sentiment (often with the balance carefully calibrated to tip in the direction of the former), and after warning that "those are no proper Judges of his Conduct who have slumber'd away their Time on the Down of Plenty" he concludes by pronouncing, in a series of oxymoronic phrases, harsh judgment on a man whose abilities he greatly admired and whom he frequently defends in the biography: "Negligence and Irregularity, long continued, will make Knowledge useless, Wit ridiculous, and Genius contemptible." Johnson would later quote his own *Life of Savage* in his *Dictionary*, appropriately under "dissipate."

Johnson's first significant work published under his name, and his second imitation of Juvenal, *The Vanity of Human Wishes* (1749), is the greatest of his numerous poems. "Vanity" is a rich concept in a poem that draws on religion for its ultimate values. "All is vanity," according to Ecclesiastes, and the combination of emptiness and arrogance that follows from human pride is central to the poem. One can feel the presence of Pope's *Essay on Man* at times, but the voice is all Johnson's own. His famous opening provides a global perspective: "Let observation with extensive view, / Survey mankind, from China to Peru." In an alternating series of concise historical portraits (of, among others, Thomas Cardinal Wolsey, archbishop of York, Charles XII of Sweden, and the Persian king Xerxes I) and accounts of generalized human types (the traveler, the rich man, the beauty, the scholar), the poem exempts no one. The account of the scholar, who suffers from "the fever of renown," concludes with a litany of woes: "There mark what ills the scholar's life assail, / Toil, envy, want, the patron, and the jail." The shift in 1755 from "garret" to "patron" made a good line great, not because it registers Johnson's own experience with the earl of Chesterfield, his putative patron for the *Dictionary*, but because—as with Pope's litter on Belinda's table in the *Rape of the Lock* ("Puffs, Powder, Patches, Bibles, Billet-doux")—it brilliantly complicates our response by slipping a seemingly out-of-place item into an otherwise congruous series, only to jolt us into recognizing the justice of the placement.

Among the portraits of the historical characters Johnson singles out to embody the tragic fates of leaders, both religious and secular, the one of Charles XII is arguably the best: "On what foundation stands the warrior's pride, / How just his hopes let Swedish Charles decide." Nearly thirty lines later Johnson dispatches this combination of stoic self-denial and military impetuousness with withering scorn in couplets singled out by T. S. Eliot for great admiration:

> His fall was destin'd to a barren strand,
> A petty fortress, and a dubious hand;
> He left the name, at which the world grew pale,
> To point a moral, or adorn a tale.

Recently, the portrait of Charles has been taken (unconvincingly) as a sympathetic depiction of a tragic hero and a coded allusion to Johnson's putative Jacobite sympathies. In *Adventurer* 99, Johnson wishes Charles, along with Peter the Great, "huddled together in obscurity or detestation." Johnson's treatment of the great displays few images less heroic or sympathetic than this one. The point, however, is not that the bad overreach, but that all human desires will fail: "Fate wings with every wish th' afflictive dart." In their stead he recommends—in place of Juvenal's famous *mens sana in corpore sano* ("a sound mind in a sound body")—"patience," which although religious bears an analogy to stoicism, and together with "Faith" and "love" stands in for the New Testament's faith, hope, and charity.

Johnson's only drama was performed in 1749. Set in Greece, the tragedy *Irene* is based on Richard Knolles's *History of the Turks*, a favorite of Johnson's. David Garrick, who had been one of his few students at Edial and was now England's foremost actor and the manager of the Drury Lane Theatre, staged the play with a strong cast. Johnson had written an excellent prologue for the opening of the theater and another for Garrick's farce *Lethe* (1740). Garrick kept *Irene* running for nine days, although his own additions—including the onstage strangling of Irene by Sultan Mahomet (played by Garrick)—led the audience to protest. Johnson was unable to devise speaking styles suitably differentiated for his characters, and the play has proved unmemorable, his least successful major work.

Johnson's next work of first importance was *The Rambler* (1750–1752), a series of 208 essays that he considered "pure wine," that is, not watered down. In addition to writing twice a week essays on morality (his dominant concern) and ethics, he wrote criticism (of biography, the novel, poetry, and drama, as well as of the literary life), Oriental tales, and allegorical fictions. He also described the daily activities of life in essays very different in tone and weight from those of his influential predecessor, Joseph Addison, in *The Spectator*. He wrote infrequently on politics, but he argued against capital punishment in *Rambler* 114. A number of the essays adapt the standard contrivance of letters ostensibly from readers. Friends—including Samuel Richardson, David Garrick, Elizabeth Carter, Hester Mulso, Joseph Simpson, and Catherine Talbot—in fact wrote a handful of the essays for him. (He encouraged women writers in a variety of ways.) *The Rambler* did not originally sell strongly (about five hundred copies an issue), but the essays were frequently reprinted in newspapers and in book form. Johnson purposely did not attach his name so that the morality of the works would not be linked to his own traits or behavior. His wife, Tetty—the widow Elizabeth Porter, whom he had married in 1735—died 17 March 1752, three days after his last *Rambler* essay was published. The following year he contributed twenty-nine essays to *The Adventurer*, edited by his friend and fellow contributor to the *Gentleman's Magazine*, John Hawkesworth. Much of this work of the late 1740s and early 1750s appeared while Johnson's greatest undertaking, his *Dictionary of the English Language*, proceeded invisibly as far as the public was concerned, except for the *Plan of the English Dictionary*, published in 1747.

More than any other publication, the *Dictionary* (contracted in 1746, published in 1755) gave Johnson his greatest fame during the eighteenth century, as well as a typifying nickname, "Dictionary" Johnson. With 42,773 entries it did not contain the most words, but its definitions and its illustrations of usage through what the full title called "Examples from the Best Writers" quickly made it the standard English dictionary. That decision turned the book to some extent into an ideological document—a conduct book—because the "best writers," chosen from the time of Queen Elizabeth forward, omitted those whose words in Johnson's view might inculcate bad moral lessons, not merely bad English usage. Hence, philosophers such as Thomas Hobbes, considered an atheist, are not quoted. Henry St. John, lord Bolingbroke, is quoted very infrequently and usually negatively. Johnson's definition of "irony" makes his animus clear: "A mode of speech in which the meaning is contrary to the words; as, *Bolingbroke was a holy man*." Johnson thought only two English books were "wished longer" by their readers. Yet Bunyan's *Pilgrim's Progress* does not appear in the *Dictionary*, and Defoe makes only a few appearances, for *Robinson Crusoe*. This is not simply a matter of animus against the novel (a suspect form), for Johnson includes a number of examples from *The Female Quixote* by Charlotte Lennox, one of a handful of living people whom friendship or necessity led him to quote. Among the others were Samuel Richardson, Joshua Reynolds, and Hester Thrale.

The *Dictionary*'s definitions have been controversial from his time to ours. Not many—in fact, a minuscule percentage—of the definitions appeared to embody Johnson's politics, but those few have become very well known, for example, the entry for "pension": "An allowance made to any one without an equivalent. In England it is generally understood to mean pay given to a state hireling for treason to his country." (This one was quoted back at Johnson when he accepted his own pension from the government in 1762.) "Excise," one of his satiric targets in *London*, is "a hateful tax levied upon commodities, and adjudged not by the common judges of property, but wretches hired by those to whom excise is paid." The earl of Chesterfield, to whom Johnson sent a letter (made famous forty-six years later by James Boswell's biography) full of the defensive pride of the author ignored by his professed patron, could read that a patron is "one who countenances, supports, or protects. Commonly a wretch who supports with insolence, and is paid with flattery." "Whig" is defined as "the name of a faction," although "Tory," equally a party or "faction," is "one who adheres to the antient constitution of the state, and the apostolical hierarchy of the church of England, opposed to a whig." Earlier dictionary makers had not always been more objective than this. Nathan Bailey's *An Universal Etymological English Dictionary* (1721) defines "Tory" as "a Nick-name to such as call themselves *High Church Men*, or to the Partisans of the Chevalier *de St. George*." That is, the Tory, according to Bailey, is a Jacobite—a position taken by many, but a partisan view. Johnson's definition of "lexicographer," however, is one of his self-deflating moments: "A writer of dictionaries; a harmless drudge, that busies himself in tracing the original, and detailing the signification of words." The *Dictionary* contains some other famous self-referential moments, such as his salute to his native Lichfield in a phrase from Virgil's *Georgics*, under "lich": "Salve magna parens" ("Hail great mother [of the crops]").

There are limits to such considerations. Johnson was firmly against the idea of a national academy to fix usage, as existed in France. His definitions were overwhelmingly descriptive, not prescriptive, prejudiced, or autobiographical. He did not control all aspects of the *Dictionary* completely. We now know that some books marked for use in the *Dictionary* were not marked by him. And he warns us ruefully in his preface, after recognizing that he would need to scale back the length of his illustrative quotations, "by hasty detruncation . . . the general tendency of the sentence may be changed: the divine may desert his tenets, or the philosopher his system." He prided himself on doing two things "very well": "One is an introduction to any literary work, stating what it is to contain, and how it should be executed in the most perfect manner; the other is a conclusion, shewing from various causes why the execution has not been equal to what the authour promised to himself and the publick." This is a personal recognition of the vanity of human wishes, and in the preface he characterizes the difference between what he intended and what he accomplished as "the dreams of a poet doomed at last to wake a lexicographer." Posterity has been greatly impressed with what the awakened lexicographer accomplished.

The History of Rasselas, Prince of Abissinia (1759), Johnson's one long fiction, was written in a week to defray the expenses of his mother's funeral. It is an Oriental tale

and more gently satirical than the *Vanity of Human Wishes*. The very opening of this exemplary tale warns the credulous (all of us) of the disappointments to come in the pursuit of "the phantoms of hope." Rasselas must escape the ironically named Happy Valley, where everyone is jaded with pleasures, in order to seek happiness and "the choice of life." But this quest of Rasselas, his sister Nekayah, her servant Pekuah, and the poet Imlac (generally taken to be the mouthpiece of Johnson, although he has no exclusive purchase on wisdom) turns out to be wide-ranging but circular. Going through Egypt but ending up on the outskirts of the Happy Valley, which cannot be reentered by any who leave, the group returns to Abyssinia. In desiring to know how to live, the little group encounters a range of people, often with antithetical ideas, whose example or advice is generally undercut by events that prove their inadequacy for their own lives. The implication is that they consider a mutually exclusive and exhaustive series of possibilities: wealth (including high station) and poverty, youth and age, marriage and singleness ("Marriage has many pains, but celibacy has no pleasures"), city dwelling and country dwelling. The stoic sage, unable to contain his grief when a member of his own family unexpectedly dies, is hardly the "wise and happy man" promised by the chapter's title. The pastoral life of shepherds proves to be filled with ignorance, "discontent," and "malevolence" rather than the simplicity promised in poetry. The hermit's solitary life leads him to return to society. The astronomer, who convinces himself that he controls the weather, provides an example of "the dangerous prevalence of imagination," but the wish-fulfilling daydreams of all the characters lie behind Imlac's claim that "if we speak with rigorous exactness, no human mind is in its right state." Perhaps the most famous episode is Imlac's hyperbolic "Dissertation upon Poetry" (chapter 10), with its famous claim that the poet "does not number the streaks of the tulip" (an activity that sounds straight out of *Alice in Wonderland*). Although it has often been ripped from its context and taken as Johnson's own view of the poet, Imlac's account, which has some things in common with what Johnson believed, is better seen as a last Renaissance statement about the poet and a critique of that position at the same time. The next chapter, after all, continues, "Imlac now felt the enthusiastic fit and was proceeding to aggrandize his own profession, when the prince cried out, " 'Enough! Thou hast convinced me, that no human being can ever be a poet.' "

Like Voltaire's *Candide*, which had appeared earlier the same year, *Rasselas* is a philosophical tale, and the undifferentiated speaking styles of the characters, which would be a weakness in a novel, are not a drawback in a fiction in which characters represent intellectual positions. In effect a satire on the "pursuit of happiness" before the Lockean idea was enshrined in the Declaration of Independence of the United States, *Rasselas* is a fiction that stresses through its Middle Eastern characters a universalism that goes beyond nations and religions and promotes the necessity of choosing over the "choice of life": " 'It seems to me,' said Imlac, 'that while you are making the choice of life, you neglect to live.' " The aphoristic wisdom of *Rasselas* often shuts down possibilities: "Human life is every where a state in which much is to be endured, and little to be enjoyed." The final chapter, a "Conclusion, in Which Nothing Is Concluded," leaves the little group still full of wishes that cannot be satisfied, despite the wisdom they have gained.

The Idler (1758–1760), another essay series, was begun before *Rasselas* but completed after. It is Johnson's last major work in what proved to be an extraordinary decade, starting with the *Vanity of Human Wishes*. The work is mainly lighter in tone than *The Rambler* and contains half as many essays; the self-described idler of the title appears as the autobiographical "Mr. Sober" in essay 31. *Idler* 84 prefers autobiography to biography, the subject of an important earlier essay, *Rambler* 60. One much-admired pair of essays satirizes the stockbroker turned critic Dick Minim (*Idler* 60–61), who spouts a combination of clichés and wrongheaded opinions. If this is a lighter series, Johnson's most mordantly satirical essay, number 22, presents an old vulture lecturing her young on the killing propensities of man that make him "a friend to vultures." Written during the Seven Years' War, when Johnson unpopularly opposed English nationalism, it was not reprinted in book form.

Johnson's eight-volume edition of Shakespeare, contracted the year after the publication of the *Dictionary*, which prepared him uniquely for the task, appeared only a decade later (1765). With a fresh honorary doctorate from Trinity College, Dublin (Oxford would follow suit in 1775)—which led Boswell and others to call him Dr. Johnson, although he did not use the title himself—he edited Shakespeare's plays but not *Pericles* or the poems. He prefaced the edition with his single greatest critical essay. Johnson had been preparing for this work since his *Miscellaneous Observations on the Tragedy of Macbeth* (1745) skewered the edition by Sir Thomas Hanmer and put forward proposals for an edition of his own. The Tonsons, whose threatened suit as the putative owners of the

copyright to Shakespeare's works had scared off Cave then, published Johnson's edition twenty years later. As editor, Johnson attempted to establish the best text (purged of later corruptions) and to conclude each play with a general comment. Johnson's annotations, at once substantial and succinct, are one of the glories of his edition. They often forgo the self-aggrandizement of emendation for the humbler task of explication. His close study of Shakespeare's diction and that of his contemporaries, whose books he read widely, informs this work.

Johnson begins his preface with a rejection of the notion that "praises are without reason lavished on the dead, and that the honours due only to excellence are paid to antiquity" (only after letting us think, typically, that he believes the statement) and an inquiry into how and when a great author is received into the canon. Upholding Shakespeare's claims, he insists they are based on "just representations of general nature." Hence, he praises Shakespeare's tragic heroes not for their individuality but for the common humanity that they share with the audience: "Shakespeare has no heroes; his scenes are occupied only by men." This conception runs against the grain of Romantic and modern criticism, but it enables Johnson to overcome the narrow decorum of Thomas Rymer, John Dennis, and Voltaire that insisted that men of great station should be consistently represented as great: "He knew that Rome, like every other city, had men of all dispositions; and wanting a buffoon, he went into the senate-house for that which the senate-house would certainly have afforded him." As he says elsewhere in the preface, "That this is a practice contrary to the rules of criticism will be readily allowed; but there is always an appeal open from criticism to nature." It is easy to miss the fact that when Johnson claims Shakespeare is "the poet that holds up to his readers a faithful mirrour of manners and of life" he is drawing not on neoclassical critics but on Hamlet's advice to the players. When he later asserts that "it is time therefore to tell [the critics] by the authority of Shakespeare" that the unities of time and place are unnecessary for effective dramas and that the audience does not believe in the reality of representation, he has already implicitly drawn on Shakespeare's authority. Others had previously attacked the unities, but Johnson's powerful rejection was decisive.

THE LATER YEARS

Johnson began to spend a great deal of time with the wealthy and sociable Thrales, Henry and Hester, most often at their house at Streatham but also on trips to Wales and France. The unlikeliest of his journeys was to the Hebrides, in 1773. He had always been interested in such a venture but undertook it only after having been lured by James Boswell. Although the product of his trip, *A Journey to the Western Islands of Scotland* (1775), was attacked by many Scots, the book is the eighteenth century's best account of its subject and an excellent addition to travel literature, a genre of great importance at the time. His account is historically informed, sociological and anthropological in its interests, and attentive to the lives of the common people. He apologizes for attention to "Scotch windows" by adding:

> These diminutive observations seem to take away something from the dignity of writing, and therefore are never communicated but with hesitation . . . But it must be remembered, that life consists not of a series of illustrious actions, or elegant enjoyments; the greater part of our time passes in compliance with necessities, in the performance of daily duties, in the removal of small inconveniencies, in the procurement of petty pleasures; and we are well or ill at ease, as the main stream of life glides on smoothly, or is ruffled by small obstacles and frequent interruption. The true state of every nation is the state of common life.

The year after Johnson's death Boswell published his very different account, *The Journal of a Tour to the Hebrides*. The men had met in 1763, when the twenty-two-year-old Boswell visited London, and Boswell's remarkably detailed journals, arguably his greatest work, provided the basis for both *The Journal of a Tour to the Hebrides* (1785) and *The Life of Samuel Johnson, LL.D.* (1791).

In the early 1770s Johnson also wrote four controversial political pamphlets in support of the government. *The False Alarm* (1770) supported the decision of the House of Commons to deny readmission to the louche John Wilkes and made light of the constitutional claims (and a petition campaign on Wilkes's behalf) connected to the case. *Thoughts on the Late Transactions Respecting Falkland's Islands* (1771) opposed a war with Spain over "tempest-beaten barrenness." This essay gained new admiration in the late twentieth century, when Argentina threatened another conflict with Great Britain over the ownership of these largely ignored islands.

Johnson famously snorted, "Patriotism is the last refuge of a scoundrel," and in the 1773 revision of the *Dictionary* he defined "patriot" as "a factious disturber of the government." He had in mind his allies of the late 1730s and early 1740s, who, after driving Walpole from office,

shifted to the views they had attacked. *The Patriot* (1774) tries to define true and false patriotism in an election year. One can hear in his dicta a reprehension of some of his own earlier political behavior: "A man may hate his King, yet not love his country" and "A true Patriot is no lavish promiser: he undertakes not to shorten parliaments; to repeal laws; or to change the mode of representation, transmitted by our ancestors." Finally, *Taxation No Tyranny* (1775), notorious in the American colonies and in later years for its opposition to American independence, argued with some justification that the colonists who would have had the vote in England (and only a small percentage of men and no women in England were enfranchised to vote) were voluntarily absent, and it famously asked, "How is it that we hear the loudest yelps for liberty from the drivers of Negroes?" This was more than a rhetorical stick with which to beat the colonists. Johnson had consistently opposed slavery and colonialism for many years in print and conversation. In "An Introduction to the Political State of Great Britain" (1756) he calls Jamaica "a place of great wealth and dreadful wickedness, a den of tyrants and a dungeon of slaves." Revealingly, the proslavery Boswell complains: "His violent prejudice against our West Indian and American settlers appeared whenever there was an opportunity." Johnson, who wished Columbus had never been born and recommended in *Idler* 81 that the Indians slaughter the Europeans who did not slaughter each other (that is, the French and the English) until they left America, considered the European colonists tyrants and robbers.

After Boswell and the Romantics, it is difficult to recognize properly the achievement of Johnson as literary biographer. Boswell claimed that "to write the Life of him who excelled all mankind in writing the lives of others . . . may be reckoned in me a presumptuous task," but he knew that their biographies were not alike. Boswell wrote a huge life-and-times biography of Johnson. Most of Johnson's fifty-two biographies in *The Lives of the Poets* (1779–1781), all but a handful chosen by the booksellers (in our terms, publishers), are short, and were written to serve as prefaces to volumes of poetry (the original title was *Prefaces, Biographical and Critical, to the Works of the English Poets*). The anecdotes that interested him were characteristic, not idiosyncratic. The more developed biographies' tripartite form (life–character–works) appears old-fashioned, and some twentieth-century scholars have objected that Johnson lagged in integrating life and work. But Johnson, who regarded writing as in some sense a performance, thought, as he says in the "Life of Addison," that "to write and to live are very different." Believing in a disparity between the morality put forward in his works and the way he himself lived, he thought one could obtain apt lessons of morality from those whose practice was flawed: "The vicious moralist may be considered as a taper, by which we are lighted through the labyrinth of complicated passions; . . . he guides all that are within view, but burns only those who make too near approaches" (*Rambler* 77). *The Lives of the Poets* is full of such recognitions, as well as moral aphorisms, witty anecdotes, and fresh information about his subjects. However, it has long been superseded as a source of factual accuracy for most of the poets. The style of these biographies is easier than in the *Rambler*—not because, as Thomas Babington Macaulay put it, late in life "he had written little and had talked much," nor because biographical details restrained his characteristically more ornate and polysyllabic rhetoric, but because he thought historical writing required a middle style. "Pope" is the longest and best. Others among the longer and most important include "Dryden," "Milton," and "Addison" (the included reprint of the 1744 *Savage* is a special case). But mini-masterpieces can be found among the shorter biographies, for example, "Collins" and "Shenstone."

Johnson's critical achievement is less difficult to recognize, although his criteria tend to be different from ours. Johnson impresses by the sheer range of genres in which he wrote, but he is best known as a critic of literature. He is often praised for common sense and attacked for dogmatism, yet his criticism is characterized by sinewy coherence and a flexibility that belies familiar notions of his dogmatism. To give a mere list of the critical terms Johnson employs would be to distort their use. Typically, he coordinates his terms and looks not for just one criterion but a combination: "If . . . that be considered as Wit which is at once natural and new, that which though not obvious is, upon its first production, acknowledged to be just; if it be that, which he that never found it, wonders how he missed; to wit of this kind the metaphysical poets have seldom risen." This definition appears as part of the "disertation," as Boswell called it, on the metaphysical poets in the "Life of Cowley," the first of the biographies (which are ordered by date of death rather than birth of the poets).

Johnson once claimed that "no man but a blockhead ever wrote except for money," but he was such a blockhead: he frequently wrote prefaces for friends gratis and was far from a hard bargainer with publishers. Following *The Lives of the Poets* until his death on 13 December

1784, he mostly contributed to the writings of friends and wrote death notices and epitaphs. Volumes of his letters, prayers and meditations, and sermons, as well as a fragment of autobiography, all appeared posthumously. A phrase from the epitaph Johnson wrote for his friend Oliver Goldsmith in 1776 could appropriately appear on his own monument: *Qui nullum feré scribendi genus / non tetegit* ("who almost none of the kinds of writing did not touch"). Johnson's writing is remarkable in a wide range of genres. The modern standard edition of the works, still in progress, of this self-confessed idler is expected to fill nineteen volumes. Until he was nearly forty only one of the works he published—proposals for an edition of the neo-Latin author Politian—bore his signature. When he died he was the most famous English writer of his time.

[*See also* Joseph Addison; James Boswell; Eighteenth-Century Journalism; David Garrick; John Gay and Ned Ward; Hannah More; Neoclassicism; Alexander Pope; Satire; William Shakespeare; Jonathan Swift; *and* Hester Thrale.]

SELECTED WORKS

London: A Poem in Imitation of the Third Satire of Juvenal (1738)

Marmor Norfolciense (1739)

A Compleat Vindication of the Licensers of the Stage (1739)

An Account of the Life of Mr. Richard Savage, Son of the Earl Rivers (1744)

The Vanity of Human Wishes (1749)

Irene: A Tragedy (1749).

The Rambler (1750–1752)

A Dictionary of the English Language, 2 vols. (1755)

The Idler (1758–1760)

The History of Rasselas, Prince of Abissinia, 2 vols. (1759)

The Plays of William Shakespeare, 8 vols. (1765)

The False Alarm (1770)

Thoughts on the Late Transactions Respecting Falkland's Islands (1771)

The Patriot (1774)

Taxation No Tyranny (1775)

A Journey to the Western Islands of Scotland (1775)

Prefaces, Biographical and Critical, to the Works of the English Poets, 10 vols., best known as *The Lives of the Most Eminent English Poets with Critical Observations on their Works* (1779–1781)

EDITIONS

Chalmers, Alexander, ed. *The Works of Samuel Johnson.* 11 vols. Oxford, 1825. Standard for some writings not in the Yale edition or other modern editions.

Fleeman, J. D., ed. *The Complete English Poems.* New Haven, CT. 1982. A useful collection.

Greene, Donald, ed. *Samuel Johnson.* Oxford, 1984. The best one-volume anthology.

Hazen, Allen T., and John H. Middendorf, eds. *The Yale Edition of the Works of Samuel Johnson.* New Haven, CT, 1958–. The best edition, still in progress.

Hill, George Birkbeck, ed. *The Lives of the English Poets.* 3 vols. Oxford, 1905. The standard edition until the Yale Edition of the *Lives* appears, although *Johnson's Lives of the Poets: A Selection*, edited by J. P. Hardy (Oxford, 1971), is preferable for the lives he chooses.

Lynch, Jack, ed. *Samuel Johnson's Dictionary.* Delray Beach, FL, 2002. The best modern abridgement.

Redford, Bruce, ed. *The Letters of Samuel Johnson.* 5 vols. Princeton, NJ, 1992–1994. Known as the Hyde Edition, this is the standard edition.

Tracy, Clarence, ed. *Life of Savage.* Oxford, 1971. The best modern edition of *An Account of the Life of Mr. Richard Savage.*

FURTHER READING

BIBLIOGRAPHIES

Clifford, James L., and Donald J. Greene. *Samuel Johnson: A Survey and Bibliography of Critical Studies.* Minneapolis, MN, 1970. Contains around four thousand items. Supplemented by Donald Greene and John A. Vance, *A Bibliography of Johnsonian Studies, 1970–1985* (Victoria, BC, 1987) and Jack Lynch, *A Bibliography of Johnsonian Studies, 1986–1998* (New York, 2000). Recent work can be found in *The Age of Johnson: A Scholarly Annual* and the quarterly *Johnsonian News Letter.*

Fleeman, J. D., ed. (with James McLaverty). *A Bibliography of the Works of Samuel Johnson.* 2 vols. Oxford, 2000. The standard bibliography, remarkably full.

BIOGRAPHIES

Bate, W. Jackson. *Samuel Johnson.* New York, 1977. A critically distinguished, psychoanalytically inflected biography.

Boswell, James. *The Journal of a Tour to the Hebrides with Samuel Johnson, LL.D.* London, 1785. Boswell's first published account of Johnson on their trip in 1773.

Boswell, James. *The Life of Samuel Johnson, LL.D.* 2 vols. London, 1791. The best modern edition of this most famous of biographies is edited by George Birkbeck Hill, revised and enlarged by L. F. Powell, 6 vols. Oxford, 1934–1950.

Clifford, James L. *Dictionary Johnson: Samuel Johnson's Middle Years.* New York, 1979. Takes the narrative up to the meeting with Boswell.

Clifford, James L. *Young Sam Johnson.* New York, 1955 (also published as *Young Samuel Johnson*, London, 1955). A scholarly account, full of fresh discoveries.

DeMaria, Robert, Jr. *The Life of Samuel Johnson: A Critical Biography* Oxford, 1993. The most recent of major biographies; emphasizes Johnson the European scholar.

Wain, John. *Samuel Johnson.* London, 1974, revised 1988. A vigorous biography, full of fellow-feeling for a writer from the midlands.

CRITICAL AND GENERAL STUDIES

Bate, W. Jackson. *The Achievement of Samuel Johnson.* New York, 1955. A powerful general reading of Johnson's life and works.

Cannon, John. *Samuel Johnson and the Politics of Hanoverian England.* Oxford, 1994. Johnson as middle-of-the-road Tory.

Clark, J. C. D. *Samuel Johnson: Literature, Religion, and English Cultural Politics from the Restoration to Romanticism.* Cambridge, U.K., 1994. A provocative case for Johnson as Jacobite and Nonjuror.

Clingham, Greg, ed. *The Cambridge Companion to Samuel Johnson.* Cambridge, U.K., 1997.

Folkenflik, Robert. *Samuel Johnson, Biographer.* Ithaca, NY, 1978. Considers Johnson's biographies as different in principles and practice from those of Boswell.

Fussell, Paul. *Samuel Johnson and the Life of Writing.* New York, 1971. Strongly attuned to the genres in which Johnson wrote.

Greene, Donald J. *The Politics of Samuel Johnson.* New Haven, CT, 1960. 2d ed., Athens, GA., 1990. Opposes notions of Johnson as reactionary Tory.

Greene, Donald. *Samuel Johnson.* New York, 1970, revised 1989. The widest-ranging informed account of Johnson's writings.

Hagstrum, Jean H. *Samuel Johnson's Literary Criticism.* Minneapolis, MN, 1952. Good introduction to Johnson as critic.

Lipking, Lawrence. *Samuel Johnson: The Life of an Author.* Cambridge, MA, 1998. Fresh account of the writing life of Johnson.

McIntosh, Carey. *The Choice of Life: Samuel Johnson and the World of Fiction.* New Haven, CT, 1973. The fullest account of *Rasselas* and the shorter fictions.

Rogers, Pat. *The Samuel Johnson Encyclopedia.* Westport, CT, 1996. Topical consideration of all things Johnsonian.

DAVID JONES

Gareth Joseph Downes

In *Goodbye to All That* (1929), the memoir of his experiences as a young officer with the Royal Welch Fusiliers during World War I, Robert Graves (1895–1985) recalls that "hardly one soldier in a hundred was inspired by religious feeling of even the crudest kind. It would have been difficult to remain religious in the trenches even if one survived the irreligion of the training battalion at home." However, for the poet and painter David Michael Jones (1895–1974), a similarly young infantryman in the London Welsh Battalion of the same regiment, it was in the midst of the inimical and irreligious wasteland of the trenches that he had an epiphanic encounter that would lead to his becoming a Roman Catholic on 7 September 1921. While foraging for firewood in the Ypres sector in 1917, Jones stumbled on a ruined outbuilding. Peering through a chink in the building, he witnessed not the darkness he had expected but a Catholic chaplain celebrating Mass. He marveled at the sight of the golden-colored vestments of the priest and the few khaki-clad soldiers kneeling in the straw beneath the improvised altar table, and he "felt immediately the oneness between the Offerent and those toughs." Jones came to perceive World War I in apocalyptic terms, viewing it as a monstrous symbol of the disintegration of Western Christian culture and the encroachment of an alienating and dehumanizing technological phase of civilization. However, amid the destruction and waste of the Western Front he was able to countenance a holistic and sacramental mode of vision that would have a profound influence on his poetry and painting.

Jones was born in Brockley, Kent, on 1 November 1895. His father, James Jones, a native of Holywell in North Wales, was a printer's overseer who had moved to London in 1885 and married Alice Ann Bradshaw, the daughter of a mast- and block-maker. While he received little formal education, his love of drawing was encouraged and from 1909 to 1914 he attended the Camberwell School of Art, an institution that prepared students for a career in trade. At the outbreak of World War I, he attempted to volunteer for service with the Artist's Rifles

but was rejected due to his insufficient chest expansion. On 2 January 1915 he enlisted as a private soldier with the London Welsh Battalion of the Royal Welch Fusiliers. He was posted to France and remained in or near the trenches from December 1915 to July 1916, when he was wounded in the attack on Mametz Wood as part of the Somme offensive. He returned to the Western Front in October 1916 and remained there until February 1918, when he was returned to England with trench fever. Unlike Graves, Wilfred Owen (1893–1918), Siegfried Sassoon (1886–1967), or Isaac Rosenberg (1890–1918), Jones never wrote about the war while he was in the trenches. Indeed, his only artistic output during this period was a series of life sketches. It was not until 1928, when he began to write *In Parenthesis*, that he started to experiment with literary form and attempted to find a "shape in words" to represent his experiences as a foot soldier in the war.

After demobilization, and with the aid of an ex-serviceman's grant, Jones enrolled at the Westminster School of Art, where he worked under the influence of the painter Walter Sickert (1860–1942). Here he was exposed to contemporary modernist practices in the arts, particularly impressionism and postimpressionism. Jones was struck by the postimpressionist theory of significant form, in which artistic form was held to have an actuality in its own right and was not merely a secondary impression of reality. During this period he became a confessed Catholic. As his involvement with Catholicism deepened and he came under the tutelage of the Catholic sculptor and typographer Eric Gill (1882–1940), he began to contemplate analogies between Roman Catholic sacramental theology and postimpressionism. Jones's belief that a made "thing" was "a signum of reality" was a synthesis of the postimpressionist theory of significant form and his belief that the human subject, as a maker of gratuitous, nonutile forms, was fundamentally a sacramental creature. This making or representation of forms or "signs" is analogous to the mystical role of the Catholic priest in celebrating the Eucharist (the sacrament in which the Last Supper, Crucifixion, and Resurrection of Jesus Christ are commemorated by the consecration of bread and wine). *Epoch and Artist,* a volume of essays on his sacramental understanding of art, was published in 1973.

Through his association with Gill—and his sojourn with the religious and artistic communities over which Gill presided during the 1920s at Ditchling Common, Sussex, and Capel-y-ffin in the Welsh borders—Jones became increasingly involved with Catholic intellectuals and artists. During the 1930s he was closely associated with a coterie of avant-garde and rightist intellectuals called the Chelsea Group. The late 1920s and early 1930s were also an intensely creative period in which he established himself as a watercolor painter and wood engraver, and in 1928 he was invited to join the 7 & 5 Society by the abstract painter Ben Nicholson (1894–1982).

THE ARTIST AS WRITER

In 1932 Jones suffered his first major breakdown, which was in part the result of overwork, and in part a delayed reaction to the trauma of World War I. *In Parenthesis* was composed between 1928 and 1932. It was published in 1937 by T. S. Eliot (1888–1962) at Faber and Faber and received the Hawthornden Prize in 1938. Written in prose and free verse, *In Parenthesis* possesses a dramatic narrative structure that is based on Jones's own experiences as an infantryman on the Western Front between December 1915 and July 1916. There is specificity of time, place, and action. The narrative is in seven parts and describes the movement of a company of Royal Welch Fusiliers from the parade ground before embarkation to France and deep into the trenches; the text culminates with the attack on Mametz, where most of the protagonists are either killed or wounded. While the narrative voice is impersonal, in its intimate representation of the consciousnesses of Private John Ball and his Cockney and Welsh comrades, it is relentlessly attentive to the deprivations and vulnerability of the ordinary foot soldiers. The dominant voice of the text is that of the private soldier, and it is a voice that speaks of being cold, overburdened, and weary. The empathy that Jones expresses for these men is also extended to the German infantry, and the book is dedicated to the men of both sides. The conflict is ultimately represented as a fratricidal and tragic encounter in which the individual human subject is exposed to the "relentless, mechanical" nature of modern civilization.

In Parenthesis was certainly influenced by Eliot's *The Waste Land* (1922). It employs a complex and textured network of allusion to order the confusion of the present in the context of the past—a modernist technique that Eliot identified as the "mythical" method. Jones had a strong and enduring affinity with his Welsh heritage, and although he was unable to read classical Welsh literature in the original, it was a tradition that he knew intimately and employed strategically in *In Parenthesis* (a collection of Jones's essays on the Welsh and Arthurian traditions was published posthumously in 1978 in a volume entitled *The Dying Gaul*). The two key texts that Jones appropriates to lend order and significance to the narrative are the *Goddodin* and the *Mabinogion*. The *Goddodin* is a long elegiac poem attributed to the poet Aneirin. It commemorates the individual heroic deeds of a war-band of Britons who died in a battle against the Saxons around the year 600. Each of the seven sections of *In Parenthesis* begins with an epigraph from the *Goddodin*, and the force of this textual trace serves to honor the fallen comrades of Ball. The *Mabinogion* is an anonymous collection of twelve medieval Welsh tales. The epigraph that prefaces *In Parenthesis* is taken from the tale of "Branwen Daughter of Llŷr" and concerns a pandoran door that, once opened, will reveal the horrors of a previous wasteful conflict. Jones was a supporter of appeasement during the 1930s, and the epigraph thus serves as both a warning to avoid further conflict and an admission that such a destructive expeditionary war might again be inevitable.

As the political circumstances of the 1930s worsened and World War II broke out, Jones's cultural pessimism increased. Influenced by the thought of the German philosopher Oswald Spengler (1880–1936), he perceived the war as symptomatic of the collapse of Western Christian culture rather than its cause. He remained in London during the war, where he was a witness to the destruction of the Blitz. During this period he worked on an epic poem that he had begun in 1938. A revised version of this work was published in 1952 as *The Anathemata*. As a "Londoner of Welsh and English parentage, of Protestant upbringing, of Catholic subscription," Jones felt himself to be an inheritor of the mythic, historic, and literary deposits of Wales and England, and of the spiritual and cultural traditions of the Christian West. Subtitled "Fragments of an Attempted Writing," *The Anathemata* is a complex, discontinuous, and highly allusive poem. The disembodied and impersonal voice of the poem, as the custodian and rememberer of the "data" of this cultural inheritance, attempts to gather together the shards and fragments of these traditions. The mode of vision is avowedly sacramental, as well as a response to the wider political and cultural disintegration Jones saw around him. Divided into eight titled sections with illustrations and a lengthy preface, *The Anathemata* is both devotional and commemorative. It is a celebration of the central mystery of the Catholic faith and an evocation of the geological and cultural development of Britain. Together with Eliot's *Four Quartets* (1944) it is the most significant civilian poetic response to World War II to emerge from Britain, and it was regarded by W. H. Auden as "probably the finest long poem in English this century."

In 1934 Jones had traveled to Palestine, then under British mandate, as part of his treatment and recuperation for his first severe breakdown. The sight of British troops there evoked not only his wartime experience but also the Roman soldiers who had occupied Palestine at the time of the death of Christ. Conceiving of the Roman soldiers as both the agents and the victims of imperialism, he attempted to write a narrative poem concerning a group of legionaries on duty on the night of the Last Supper. As he revised the poem, he inserted meditative evocations of Celtic Britain, but he found that he could not make the poem cohere. He had wished to publish the sequence as a "continuation, or Part II of *The Anathemata*" and he made repeated but unsuccessful attempts to complete the project during the remainder of his life. Fragments from this sequence were published as *The Sleeping Lord* in 1974 and posthumously as *The Roman Quarry* in 1981.

Jones was betrothed to Eric Gill's daughter, Petra, in 1924. However, the relationship broke down in 1927 and he never married. After another breakdown in 1946 he moved into Bowden House, Harrow-on-the-Hill, London, where he lived under medical supervision. His depression manifested itself in his increasing agoraphobia, and he became a reclusive figure, refusing to leave the clutter of books, manuscripts, and paintings in his "dugout." He remained in private lodging houses in the vicinity until a fall in 1970 necessitated his going into Calvary Nursing Home, Sudbury Hill, where he died on 28 October 1974. While *In Parenthesis* and *The Anathemata* were regarded highly by W. B. Yeats, Eliot, Auden and Seamus Heaney, Jones sadly remains a peripheral figure in the history of English literary modernism.

[*See also* T. S. Eliot; Mabinogian; Modernism; *and* World War I Poetry.]

SELECTED WORKS

In Parenthesis (1937)

The Anathemata: Fragments of an Attempted Writing (1952)

Epoch and Artist: Selected Writings (1973)

The Sleeping Lord and Other Fragments (1974)

The Dying Gaul and Other Writings (1978)

The Roman Quarry and Other Sequences (1981)

Wedding Poems (2002)

FURTHER READING

Alldritt, Keith. *David Jones: Writer and Artist.* London, 2003. In the absence of Thomas Dilworth's long-awaited scholarly biography of Jones, this is a useful if limited account of Jones's life and works.

Corcoran, Neil. *The Song of Deeds: A Study of "The Anathemata" of David Jones.* Cardiff, Wales, 1982. An astute and careful exegesis of Jones's postwar modernist epic that also explores its affinities with the work of T. S. Eliot and James Joyce.

Dilworth, Thomas. *The Shape of Meaning in the Poetry of David Jones.* Toronto, 1988. A substantial and sympathetic critical reading that is particularly attentive to the influence of Roman Catholic sacramental theology and liturgy on Jones's aesthetics.

Hague, René. *A Commentary on "The Anathemata" of David Jones.* Wellingborough, U.K., 1977. An important reference guide and critical companion to *The Anathemata.*

Hague, René, ed. *Dai Greatcoat: A Self-Portrait of David Jones in His Letters.* London, 1980. An idiosyncratic and selective life of Jones made up of excerpts from his letters to a coterie of close friends with background commentary from Hague.

Mathias, John, ed. *David Jones: Man and Poet.* Orono, ME, 1989. An important collection of essays on Jones's biography, writings, and art by leading scholars.

Miles, Jonathan. *Backgrounds to David Jones: A Study in Sources and Drafts.* Cardiff, Wales, 1990. A detailed and thorough analysis of the philosophical backgrounds and intellectual sources of Jones's work.

Miles, Jonathan, and Derek Shiel. *David Jones: The Mythmaker Unmade.* Bridgend, Wales, 1995. An in-depth critical analysis of Jones's art and writing that draws on extensive archival and biographical research.

Ward, Elizabeth. *David Jones: Mythmaker.* Manchester, U.K., 1983. A controversial and groundbreaking study that analyzes the ideological status of Jones's mythopoesis.

INIGO JONES

Stephen Orgel

Inigo Jones (1573–1652), architect and stage designer, was born in London, the eldest surviving child of a clothworker originally from Wales. The unusual Christian name is the vernacular form of Ignatius, also his father's name, and may suggest that in his grandfather's time the family was Roman Catholic. Inigo himself, however, was baptized an Anglican in the Church of St. Bartholomew the Less, in Smithfield. His early years are largely undocumented, but he was referred to in 1605 as "a great traveller," and his knowledge of Italy and proficiency in Italian recommended him to Thomas and Alathea Howard, the earl and countess of Arundel as a companion on their Italian travels in 1613. His traveling must have been undertaken, and his expertise acquired, before 1603, when he is recorded as being in England. The first artistic reference to him, in that year, is as a "picture-maker" to Roger Manners, the earl of Rutland. In 1604 Jones accompanied Rutland to Denmark to bestow the Order of the Garter on Queen Anne's brother King Christian IV, and by the end of 1604 he was employed with Ben Jonson on a Christmas masque for the queen, *The Masque of Blackness*, performed on Twelfth Night 1605. For this, Jones designed a revolutionary stage, with perspective settings and complex machinery, recognizably Italianate, but unlike anything that had been seen in England. Six months later, for a royal visit to Oxford, Jones created scenes and machines for three Latin academic plays. As with the masques at court, the settings required a new kind of theater, in which the king sat at the apex of the optical perspective, and this time there were complaints from the university officials that the royal visitor was not visible enough—James at these events was both the central spectator and the center of the spectacle, and the design of the hall was

Inigo Jones
After an engraving by Robert Van Voerst,
after a portrait by Anthony Van Dyck
NATIONAL PORTRAIT GALLERY, LONDON

determined, for the first time in England, not by the rules of protocol but by the science of optics.

Jones's first work as an architect was for the stage; his earliest designs for buildings date only from 1608, two unexecuted projects for Britain's Burse (Robert Cecil's new exchange in the Strand), and a central tower for St. Paul's Cathedral. In 1610 he became surveyor to Henry, Prince of Wales; his tenure in this post seems to have lasted little more than a year. His stage architecture in this period, however, grew increasingly grand and complex. In 1606, for Jonson's *Hymenaei*, Jones created a gigantic globe of gold and silver seemingly floating in midair, which turned to reveal eight masquers seated in "a mine of several metals; to which the lights were so placed as no one was seen" (Orgel, *Complete Masks*, lines 584–585). In 1609, in *The Masque of Queens*, a hell scene with fire and smoke was made to vanish in an instant, replaced with "a glorious and magnificent building figuring the House of Fame . . . filled with several-coloured lights" (ibid., lines 338–339, 461). The two masques related to Prince Henry's creation as Prince of Wales, *Prince Henry's Barriers* in 1610 and *Oberon* in 1611, both included a subtle progression of architectural sequences, from the classical ruins of ancient heroism to the English gothic House of Chivalry restored, and from a mountainous wilderness to a splendid palace combining Palladian balustrades, a dome, and Michelangelesque figures, with the crenellated towers of an English castle, all designed to reflect the national hopes invested in the young prince with his military ambitions and idealistic Protestantism.

Throughout these years Jones was also employed by the great collectors—Arundel, Cecil, Prince Henry, and, after his death in 1612, Prince Charles—as a connoisseur and adviser on acquisitions. It was not until 1615 that his career as an architect really began. In that year he replaced Simon Basil as surveyor to the works—becoming, in effect, the royal architect—and began work on one of his masterpieces, the Queen's House at Greenwich. The work on the building was abruptly halted by Queen Anne's illness and death in 1619, and the magnificent version that now stands was only completed in the 1630s for Queen Henrietta Maria. But at the age of forty-three Jones had finally emerged as a major architect. At first he did mainly alterations and additions to great estates—a massive gate at the queen's palace at Oatlands; renovations to Cecil's house at Greenwich, and also to Arundel House there; a two-story classical portico at Byfleet Lodge. At last, from 1619, he was building houses in the English Palladian style he perfected—Prince Charles's lodging at Newmarket, a town house for Sir Fulke Greville in Holborn; and, in 1619–1622, the great Banqueting House that still stands in Whitehall.

From this period on Jones was constantly employed as both an architect and artistic adviser, a universal authority on the arts, so that when King James became interested in Stonehenge, it was Jones, rather than any of the antiquarian experts, who was commissioned to explain and re-create it. *The Most Notable Antiquity of Great Britain Vulgarly Called Stonehenge*, posthumously published in 1655, declared Stonehenge to be the ruins of a Roman temple, and restored it, in a series of striking woodcuts, as a severe and elegant monument. The urge to see the most notable British antiquity as classical is characteristic of his imagination. When Charles I came to the throne in 1625, Jones became a key figure in the creation of the royal style. For the masques of the Caroline years, Jones created ideal civic fantasies, celestial visions, miraculous transformations—theatrical realizations of the royal program of purification and reform. The mechanics of his theater grew increasingly sophisticated, allowing many changes of setting both on the stage and in the heavens; he devised elaborate and ingenious flying machines—much of the action in these works by Aurelian Townshend, Thomas Carew, and especially William Davenant took place in midair. In the 1630s, too, plays began for the first time to be performed in the perspective settings Jones had introduced. These included William Strode's *Floating Island*, William Habington's *Queen of Aragon*, Lodowick Carlell's *Passionate Lovers*, Walter Montagu's *Shepherd's Paradise*—the plays are utterly forgotten, but

the stage they pioneered became, with the reopening of the public theaters after the Restoration, the standard one for the next three centuries. The architecture of this period included major renovations to the several royal palaces, a new theater for Whitehall (the Cockpit-in-Court), the chapel and major renovations at Somerset House, a lodge in Hyde Park, an anatomy theater for the Barber Surgeons, a new masquing hall for Whitehall (when the Banqueting House became unusable in 1637, after the installation of the Rubens ceiling, which was damaged by the smoke of the torches and candles required for performances), restorations to the ancient, crumbling cathedral of St. Paul's, including a splendid baroque façade for the west front and a classical portico for the east; and the redesign of the Covent Garden piazza for Francis Russell, the earl of Bedford, a restrained and elegant piece of city planning.

In 1638 the king proposed that Jones design a splendid royal palace to rival the Escorial and the Louvre, completing the architectural scheme implied in the Whitehall Banqueting House. For a monarch chronically in debt, the project was clearly a fantasy, but the several surviving drawings indicate how fully Jones was the architect of his master's imagination. The civil war put an end to all such schemes, which were scarcely less fantastic than the court masques, which also came to an end. After 1640 Jones's fortunes were closely linked with the king's. He deputized his work as surveyor to his assistant John Webb, and followed Charles to war, even lending him £500, a debt that was never repaid. He was captured at the siege of Basing House in 1645, brought back to London and deprived of his estate, though a year later he was pardoned, and the sequestration of his property converted to a fine. In his last years he was working with Webb on the rebuilding of Wilton House for Philip Herbert, the earl of Pembroke, though it is not clear that Jones served as anything more than an adviser for this project. He died in 1652, at Somerset House in the Strand, having transformed both the character of English architecture and the nature of the English stage.

[*See also* Masque.]

FURTHER READING

Gotch, J. Alfred. *Inigo Jones*. London, 1928.
Harris, John, and Gordon Higgott. *Inigo Jones: Complete Architectural Drawings*. London, 1989.
Harris, John, Stephen Orgel, and Roy Strong. *The King's*

Arcadia: Inigo Jones and the Stuart Court. London, 1973.

Jones, Inigo. *The Most Notable Antiquity of Great Britain Vulgarly Called Stonehenge.* Edited by John Webb. Menston, U.K., 1972.

Orgel, Stephen, ed. *Complete Masques.* New Haven, CT, 1969.

Orgel, Stephen, and Roy Strong. *Inigo Jones: The Theatre of the Stuart Court.* London and Berkeley, CA, 1973.

Parry, Graham. *The Golden Age Restor'd: The Culture of the Stuart Court, 1603–42.* Manchester, U.K., 1981.

Peacock, John. *The Stage Designs of Inigo Jones: The European Context.* Cambridge, U.K., 1995.

Summerson, John. *Architecture in Britain, 1530–1830.* Harmondsworth, U.K., 1953. See part two: "Inigo Jones and His Times, 1610–1660."

Summerson, John. *Inigo Jones.* Harmondsworth, U.K., 1966.

BEN JONSON

Martin Butler

Ben Jonson (1572–1637) is arguably the most important English Renaissance writer after Shakespeare. Unlike his great rival, who pursued his career single-mindedly in the theater, Jonson achieved eminence in several different spheres. As a dramatist, his reputation rests on seventeen completed plays, and particularly on his five great comedies, which have never been surpassed for their combination of brilliant plotting, breadth of social panorama, and exuberantly inventive language. But his poetry, too, was valued highly and widely imitated by contemporaries; a long-standing servant of the court, he produced dozens of masques that were staged annually at Whitehall's Christmas festivals; and as friend of scholars, historians, and intellectuals, he was one of England's first professional writers to live the semi-independent life of a man of letters. In effect, he had three or four overlapping careers, and his work made a correspondingly profound impact on the culture of his time.

Ben Jonson
Portrait by Abraham van Blyenberch, c. 1617
NATIONAL PORTRAIT GALLERY, LONDON

sensitive to accusations of social inferiority, and his insistence, in prologues and prefaces, on the superiority of his art to that of fellow playwrights bred resentment among his peers. Much of his life was passed in quarrels, mostly intellectual but occasionally physical. These were part and parcel of the congested world of London's professional theater, but they were also symptomatic of Jonson's intensely competitive mindset. A self-made writer, he was determined to prove that his achievement was valuable, and that it was entirely his own hard-won accomplishment. Perhaps the most striking instance of this reinvention of himself was his decision, in 1603, to drop the *h* from his surname, so that Ben Johnson thereafter became known, distinctively, as "Jonson."

Jonson was fortunate in being educated at Westminster School, where his master was the historian William Camden, one of the great intellectuals of the age, who bred in his pupil a critical mentality and profound respect for learning. But Jonson did not go to university, and the formidable scholarship that he later acquired came through independent study. Instead, he passed some of his youth laboring at his stepfather's uncongenial trade, then spent a short time as a common soldier, fighting with English troops stationed in the Netherlands. Subsequently he may have been a strolling player in the provinces before emerging as a commercial playwright in London.

In 1597, payments to Jonson appear in the account book of the theatrical entrepreneur Philip Henslowe for the first of several plays which have not survived. His earliest surviving play, *The Case Is Altered* (1597), is an idiosyncratic comedy modeled on classical sources. The same year, with Thomas Nashe, he cowrote a satire, *The Isle of Dogs*, which caused such offense that the Privy Council imprisoned him and temporarily closed all

THE ELIZABETHAN PLAYWRIGHT

Jonson's social origins were complex. His father was a clergyman, and through him the poet claimed a connection to an ancient Anglo-Scottish clan, the Johnstouns of Annandale, enabling him to regard himself as descended from gentlemen. But the senior Johnson (as the family name was originally spelled) died in 1572, shortly before his son was born, and his widow took as her second husband a prosperous Westminster bricklayer named Robert Brett, who eventually rose to become master of his guild. This background invested Jonson with profoundly divided attitudes. He was always proud of his writing as a craft and keenly displayed the intellectual labor and self-conscious artistry that it cost him, but he was also acutely

London's theaters. This was the first of several brushes with authority. Another came the following year, when he killed an actor in a duel, and two more in 1605, when he was questioned by the Privy Council for seditious remarks in his tragedy *Sejanus*, and imprisoned for offensive jokes about the Scots in his comedy *Eastward Ho!* (cowritten with George Chapman and John Marston). During the 1598 imprisonment Jonson converted to Catholicism, a dangerous choice at this time; in 1605 some of his Catholic acquaintances would be implicated in the Gunpowder Plot, and he was employed by the government as intermediary in part of the investigation. He did not return to the Protestant faith until 1610.

In 1598 Jonson produced his first masterpiece, *Every Man in His Humour*. This satirical comedy was set in Florence, though when Jonson printed a revised version in 1616, he relocated it in London. It is a landmark play, the first wholly urban comedy in English. It depicts a day in the life of a great Renaissance city, focusing on the interactions of a tight-knit group of citizens and gentlemen who are followed through almost in real time, from breakfast to supper. There is some romantic intrigue, but the primary concern is the exposure of follies, the "humours" of the title. These are the character traits of a gallery of fools, the antitypes against whom the play's norms are established: the bragging but cowardly captain Bobadilla, the ambitious but incompetent poet Matheo, the country bumpkin Stephano, the city clown Cob, and the pathologically jealous merchant Thorello. Each has a "humour"—an ingrained foible or tic of behavior—which the satire "purges" by exposing its irrationality. Such purgative comedy has its basis in contemporary medical theory, which held that defects of character were produced by imbalances in the bodily fluids, but at root Jonson's satire is social: all the fools are social aspirers, and their eccentricities arise mostly from the disparity between their real worth and their fantasies of social distinction. So the comedy seems conservative, for it satirizes the inanities of upstarts and would-bes, though its social vision is actually more ambivalent than this suggests. Implicitly, anyone can lead Jonson's community of wits, so long as he has sufficient merit. Although his heroes are gentlemen, their birth counts less than their intelligence, urbanity, and culture.

Every Man in His Humour helped to create a vogue for "humours" comedy, and Jonson followed it up with *Every Man Out of His Humour* (1599), which presents a broader panorama of eccentrics; *Cynthia's Revels* (1600), which transfers the humors to Whitehall, faintly disguised as the court of Cynthia; and *Poetaster* (1601), which puts them in ancient Rome, a faintly disguised version of contemporary London. But the possibilities of humors comedy were limited. Each play repeats the same stereotypical contrast between good wits and incompetent fools, and typically the theatrical energies belong with the fools. The success of the satire depends on one's willingness to believe in the authority of the wits who are the playwright's standards of value, but often Jonson found it hard to make these good characters convincing. All too frequently their victories seem contrived, the moral lessons imposed rather than achieved. Moreover, with *Poetaster*—which includes lampoons of Jonson's literary competitors John Marston and Thomas Dekker—he became embroiled in the so-called War of the Theaters, a highly personalized series of rivalries among companies and playwrights. Jonson found himself the victim of a devastating dramatic satire by Dekker, and he wrote an "Apologetical Dialogue" to be played after *Poetaster* which expresses a growing discomfort with the stage: he had a sense that audiences did not understand him, that tastes were against what he wanted to do, and that his satirical ideals were failing. When he returned to comedy, it would be of an entirely different stamp.

THE JACOBEAN COURT SERVANT

The death of Elizabeth and the arrival of James I changed the horizons of Jonson's world. This enabled him to find a foothold in the territory of the court from which he could begin to realize his self-image as man of letters working—in a respectful but nonetheless detached way—in the service of the state. He had already begun to make a name for himself as a nondramatic poet, and he attracted the interest of some well-placed patrons. His big break came in 1603, when he cowrote the civic pageant to welcome King James on his formal entry into his new capital.

Jonson helped to design and provided speeches for two triumphal arches and a pyramid past which the king rode, and he used the event to show the tremendous range of his learning and his ambitious vision of the Stuart monarchy. In the speeches he welcomed James as a new Augustus, a reborn Roman emperor taking possession of a renewed state. He alluded tactfully but noticeably to the shortcomings of Elizabeth's reign, the darkness of her last years, and the warfare in which she had embroiled the nation. By contrast, he hailed James as a monarch who would bring peace, stability, and justice, whose arrival changed old England to new Britain and marked a turning point in national history. He also complimented James in dense and often arcane reference to learned sources, framing him as the knowing inheritor of a great classical past. Unsurprisingly, when Queen Anne needed a poet to write *The Masque of Blackness*, her entertainment for the court's next Christmas festival, she turned to Jonson.

For the next twenty years Jonson was the favored writer of court masques and regularly supplied the texts for Whitehall's winter festivities, a prestigious and rewarding occupation. Masques were high-profile events, attended by only a tiny proportion of the population but still with high public visibility. They represented the monarchy at play and staged little dramatic fictions that expressed its culture and power. For example, in *The Masque of Blackness*, Queen Anne and her ladies disguised themselves as Negroes and pretended to arrive at Whitehall in quest of a new magic name that would wash their skins white. "Britannia," it turned out, was that name, so the solution to their quest was a testimony to the Stuart state's authority. Typically, such elegant fictions prefaced an evening of formal dancing by the masquers, followed by social dancing, and were mounted with stupendous spectacle. There was perspective scenery that moved and changed in marvelous manner (seen nowhere else on the English stage), provided by the court architect Inigo Jones; the performers wore bejeweled costumes; and there was music from the court's best composers. Each masque was performed only once and was expected to be expensive, for it proclaimed Whitehall's wealth and prestige. The poet was just one artist among many working on the event, but his part was crucial. He supplied the graceful mythological device that linked together all these components while complimenting the king and his state.

Jonson's three dozen masques are the single most sustained achievement in English court festival, and they made London's court seem as glorious as those of Paris, Florence, and Madrid. His fictions were endlessly inventive. In *The Masque of Queens* (1609), Queen Anne performed as *Bel-Anna, queen of the ocean*, and defeated a band of witches that threatened Whitehall. In *Oberon* (1611), Prince Henry danced as king of the fairies, leading in his glorious knights. In *The Golden Age Restored* (1616), the goddess of justice descended from the heavens and proclaimed that the golden age had begun again. In *Pleasure Reconciled to Virtue* (1618), Prince Charles was brought in by Hercules, the ancient prototype of heroic endeavor. And in *The Gypsies Metamorphosed* (1621),

James's favorite, the marquis of Buckingham, pretended to be a fortune-teller who did not know James personally but realized from his hand that he must be a great hero. Such fables—simultaneously glorious and witty, flattering yet lightly ironic—established Jonson as the one of the most influential figures in court culture who defined the imagery and values of Jacobean kingship. Little wonder that in 1616 James granted him a pension, making him poet laureate in all but name.

Today Jonson's masques seem rather fanciful, especially given what we know about the Jacobean court. James was not a heroic monarch, nor was his court orderly, and there must always have been a gap between Jonson's idealizations and the reality that audiences knew. Yet masques gave Jonson an opportunity to use his art in the service of power and to find a role for himself as a kind of poetic counselor to the king. In his commonplace book, *Discoveries*, he wrote, "Learning needs rest: sovereignty gives it; sovereignty needs counsel: learning affords it." This symbiosis between the intellectual and the state was exemplified in his masques, with their combination of flattering compliment and ethical advice, their conviction that the court might be simultaneously entertained and educated. Moreover, James was a monarch of a stamp that Jonson could admire, proud of his intellectual interests, respectful of culture, scornful of fanaticism, and committed to peace. It was no compromise to Jonson's values to write in his praise. At the same time, though, service to a prince necessitated some tact. Jonson was proud of the moral independence that he brought to court panegyric: as he described himself in the preface to the 1616 printing of *Cynthia's Revels*, he was the court's "servant, but not slave." Nonetheless, his ideas were expressed more robustly and in a less veiled way in the plays that he was simultaneously writing for the public stage.

THE JACOBEAN PLAYWRIGHT

Jonson's association with the court and acquisition of patronage brought him some financial independence, and during the decade after James's accession he ceased to do hackwork or to work full-time for the playhouses. Unlike Shakespeare, who was tied to one theater and generally wrote two plays a year, Jonson produced a play every other year and gave them to companies of his own choosing. This slow productivity allowed him to put more energy into each play, and his Jacobean dramas are intensely artful and well labored. But he could write fast when he wanted to—he claimed to have created *Volpone* in just five weeks—so the masterpieces he produced in this decade were not simply the result of leisure. Rather, the new reign inaugurated a changed attitude in his work: his drama became more ironical, searching, and caustic. The five great Jacobean plays—*Sejanus His Fall* (1603), *Volpone* (1606), *Epicene, or the Silent Woman* (1609), *The Alchemist* (1610), and *Bartholomew Fair* (1614)—are products of a new realism. They all share an underlying pessimism about the world that they represent.

Of these five, only *Sejanus* is not a comedy, but it marked a crucial departure. Depicting a tragic and violent period in the reign of the Roman emperor Tiberius, it is a humors comedy turned inside out. There is the same cast of good, virtuous, and rational men who deplore the follies and crimes of the world where they find themselves, but in this play the vicious characters are in control. Tiberius and his henchman, Sejanus, are amoral machiavels who run their state through fraud, violence, and fear, ruling with a show of law but ruthlessly cutting down anyone who opposes their will. Rome is a slaughterhouse, and although the good characters win the ethical arguments, they stand helplessly on the sidelines, waiting for their own destruction. Probably Jonson had the later years of Elizabeth in mind: this society of informers and flatterers, political violence and lost freedom of speech suggests a Catholic's memory of the Elizabethan state. But theatrically, the darkness of the tragedy is liberating. By putting power in the hands of the villains, Jonson acknowledged that the world is not ethically ordered, and that virtue, if it is to survive, has to be pragmatic. The play accepts the Machiavellian dicta that men are driven by self-interest and that victory goes to the strongest or cleverest. Indeed, the way that Tiberius and Sejanus seek to outmaneuver one another is grimly fascinating: each protects his position through the arts of power and exercises control through his knowledge of men's weaknesses. In the end, the vicious are kept in check only because they threaten one another, and Sejanus's ambitions become so monstrous that Tiberius has to destroy him. But there is no guarantee that Tiberius can be restrained in future. The world being what it is, the mob will inevitably give its allegiance to the next tyrant who comes along.

Translated into comedy, this ethically conflicted story, in which the bad men prevail, enabled Jonson to invent a radical new form. In the Machiavellian comedies that follow, the audience's subversive sympathy with the crooks became the mainspring through which a brilliant but perplexing theatrical dynamic was created. In *Volpone*, the Venetian confidence trickster Volpone and his servant Mosca have devised a scheme that draws victims into their clutches. Volpone is a childless aristocrat who pretends to be dying, attracting dupes who offer him valuable gifts in the hope of being written into his will. However much one may deplore Volpone's criminality—his worst act is an attempted rape of the wife of one of his victims—one cannot ignore the fact that the dupes deserve to be rooked, for their avarice and folly lay them open to exploitation by the clever rogues. *The Alchemist* takes this idea a step further by applying it to contemporary London. Here the crooks Subtle, Face, and Doll have set up a shop in the city from which they sell all kinds of illusions and fantasies, and it draws them idiotic customers, from the gluttonous knight Sir Epicure Mammon, through the country gentleman Kastril and the lawyer's clerk Dapper, to the small citizen Drugger, and a brace of Puritans. What they pretend to sell is the philosopher's stone, which can turn base metal into gold, as well as horoscopes, rules for quarreling, familiar spirits to help gamblers win, and cabbalistic charms for good luck. These are all paraphernalia for the gullible, but they are also devices with which to exploit men's aspirations: the victims are seduced by their intense desire to advance themselves and become something more than they are. But the teasing irony of the alchemy is that, while it holds out hope of transformation, the dupes will remain stubbornly base metal. Their greed is punished, but so is their folly. The worst pain they encounter is to realize their intellectual blindness, the fact that they had been too stupid to recognize the reality in front of them.

Jonson's great comedies thus brilliantly exploit the tension between the audience's enjoyment of the clever villain and the desire for enforcing some kind of ethical standard. As in *Sejanus*, there is no external authority to constrain bad men, and the crooks' plans collapse only when they start to compete among themselves. In each play, the justice that eventually prevails is entirely compromised: we are left with no expectation that, out of its own resources, good will win through. Moreover, Jonson's tricksters are all improvisers and performers who weave theatrical illusions around their victims and thus exploit the dangerous power of the stage. To that extent, Jonson implied that his theater audience could not be trusted either. They had paid the actors to deceive them, and so were no less prone than those they laughed at to be taken in by lies.

The other achievement of these comedies is the standard they set for dense and particular depiction of the

London space, and their exhibition of the developing habits and modes of speech of city life. *The Alchemist* succeeds in part because of its inhabitants' linguistic virtuosity, the dazzling blizzard of dialects, and the impression that it creates of real material life. Jonson takes this effect to its limits in *Epicene* and *Bartholomew Fair*. *Epicene* presents the casual games and good manners of a group of gentlemen living in and around the Strand. Effectively the very first West End comedy, it single-handedly established the genre of comedy of manners as well as the association of that form with the emergence of a metropolitan leisured class. The main butt of *Epicene*'s humor is Morose, a gentleman who lives in London even though he is morbidly allergic to noise. Morose's alienation from city life and the noisy torments that the play's gallants contrive to draw into his house from the city streets cement the connection between English comedy and the establishment of modern modes of urban living. The baffling of Morose is a victory for wit and urbanity over unsociability—though Jonson complicates the picture in that the wits are highly competitive, as keen to get an edge over each other as they are to defeat their external enemies. The play celebrates the emerging London *beau monde*, the fashionable elite, but it also registers the fragmentation and paradoxically enhanced sense of the isolation of the self that comes with the city space.

Even more impressive in its exploration of urban life is *Bartholomew Fair*, which provides the most vigorous cityscape of any Renaissance comedy. The play follows the fortunes of a congeries of city dwellers who visit the annual Saint Bartholomew's Day fair in Smithfield, a London suburb, to see the sights. They are headed by a group of gentlemen who look forward complacently to the display of credulousness that it will provide, but no one is immune to the fair's commercial appeal. Everyone is rooked by the stallholders, entertainers, and cutpurses; no one can avoid being seduced by the sounds, sights, and smells; and under the pressure of hard sell, pretensions of class and status start to evaporate. The most spectacular victims are the would-be social leaders—the magistrate, the Puritan, and the tutor, who all forfeit their claims to moral superiority when they fall prey to the fair's temptations—but by the end, the fair has leveled all differences and subordinated all visitors to its arbitrary, haphazard logic. As in Jonson's other comedies, the cleverest and most opportunist character comes out best, but in this comic version of *King Lear* everyone has been stripped bare (some quite literally) and no principle of authority is left—save King James, who is appealed to in the Epilogue, and the poet, who in the Induction emphasizes that the play belongs to him, not to his customers. The play suggests how unpredictable and ungovernable are men's desires, and it questions the ability of any member of this society effectively to govern it.

THE MAN OF LETTERS

In 1616 Jonson collected his plays, poems, and masques in an expensively printed volume which he titled *The Works of Benjamin Jonson*. This gesture met with skepticism from contemporaries, as some were amused by the idea that mere "plays" could be taken for "works." However, not only did the *Works* demonstrate the scale of Jonson's achievement, but it also projected his claim to being a man of letters, his status in the slowly crystallizing world of professional literature. Jonson presented his texts in monumental typography, as if they were already classics; he included addresses to future readers; and, by his editorship of his own writings, he laid an implicitly revolutionary claim to ownership of them, since at this time copyrights were not normally held by authors but by theater companies or publishers. The book proclaimed Jonson's ability to live off his own writing: he was neither a hack writer for the market, a slave to playhouse managers, nor a toady of the court. He was the first writer to present an image of himself as essentially working for his own artistic satisfaction.

Jonson's artistic individualism emerges most strongly in the poetry, for here he created a fully rounded voice that gave full expression to his private personality. Even more than Chaucer, Skelton, or Wyatt, Jonson emerges from his poetry as a many-sided individual, involved in complex interactions with a dense social world. He eschewed the popular modes of erotic and mythological verse with their stereotypical situations, tinkling rhymes, and fanciful language. Instead he wrote epigrams, odes, and epistles which focus on the poet's everyday life in sober, clear, thoughtful language. This is a poetry of friendship and acquaintance, directed to named individuals and dealing with shared experiences and common situations. The topics include marriages and birthdays, illnesses, and the deaths of friends and children—such as the moving epigram "On my first son" (*Epigram* 45) and the highly wrought commemorative ode for Sir Henry Morison (*Underwood* 70). There are reflections on journeys, fashions, and manners, expressions of congratulation and thanks, discussions of books and literary taste, and satires on the vicious, immodest, and stupid. But many of the poems have no "occasion" as such and simply praise in general terms the individual to whom they are addressed, celebrating the feelings of affinity between the poet and his circle. What counts is the intensely personalized voice with which Jonson speaks. Almost every poem includes the word "I," so that the world is re-created as if through the poet's eyes and in terms of values with which he identifies.

Jonson's poetry is ethical without being moralistic. It celebrates the good life, understood as a constant struggle to preserve one's sanity and self-control in face of wickedness, folly, and banality. There are, in Jonson's verse, a few good men and women, but most of the world is populated by fools. The people Jonson admires are notable for their stoicism and difference from the herd, above which they rise like monuments. As Jonson says of his friend the earl of Pembroke, his "noblesse keeps one stature still, / And one true posture, though besieged with ill" (*Epigram* 102). Yet there is nothing puritanical about this virtue: fastidiousness and austerity are as much enemies of the good life as is vice. The typical Jonson situation is the convivial feast, when some of the few come together to enjoy themselves decently but liberally, taking pleasure from wine, conversation, and good company. In later life Jonson himself kept court in the Apollo room at the Devil and St Dunstan's tavern near Temple Bar, and in "Inviting a friend to supper" (*Epigram* 101) he set out this attractively sociable ideal in the form of a bill of fare. No less convivial are his great "country house" poems, "To Penshurst" and "To Sir Robert Worth" (*The Forest* 2 and 3), which celebrate the lives of two of his wealthy friends on their country estates. These men are depicted as old-fashioned landlords who feast their tenants and friends and keep up now-declining traditions of hospitality. In Jonson's verse, city and country are held together by values of amity which are threatened by the commercialism or puritanism of the modern world.

Jonson's poetry was influential among his successors in defining a new verse aesthetic. "To Penshurst" is an important precursor of "country house" poems written by Robert Herrick, Thomas Carew, Andrew Marvell, and Alexander Pope, but his poetry also had a wider general currency as a stylistic model for social verse. His poems are saturated with allusions to Latin writers such as Horace, Catullus, Seneca, and Martial. He did more than any other poet to domesticate the classical tradition, and to show how English verse could be learned while remaining graceful. He also helped to create the ground for "cavalier" poetry by writing lyrics that managed to remain casual in effect while being highly poised and artful; and in poetic language, he promoted a diction that was polished and current, and which (unlike, say, John Donne's "metaphysical" poetry) did not depend on far-fetched metaphorical effects. Even in his own lifetime, a number of poets regarded themselves as "Sons of Ben," looking up to the elder poet as patron and example of rationalistic, critical writing. The history of later seventeenth-century English verse is unthinkable without his contribution.

LATER CAREER AND REPUTATION

After 1616 Jonson ceased to write for the playhouses, producing only poems and the annual court masque while busying himself with a life of scholarship. He compiled an English grammar and various historical works, and he cemented his friendships with intellectuals such as the jurist John Selden, the historian Robert Cotton, and the patron and politician Viscount Falkland. But his later years were not entirely happy. He lost several unpublished writings in a fire; he suffered a stroke and was possibly afflicted by Parkinson's disease; his royal pension fell into arrears, resulting in real impoverishment; he was questioned on suspicion of authoring a poem celebrating the assassination of the royal favorite Buckingham; and his working relationship with the court architect Inigo Jones fell into acrimony, following which he ceased to receive commissions for masques. After ten years' absence he returned to writing for the stage, but his late plays did not please: *The New Inn* (1629) was so badly received that he wrote an "Ode to Himself" excoriating the spectators as "swine" and vowing—once again—to abandon the "prostitute" stage. Yet although his contemporaries were baffled by these plays, they include some of his most attractive and inventive work, from the lyrical *New Inn*, through the pastiche Elizabethan farce *A Tale of a Tub* (1633), to the beautiful but unfinished pastoral *The Sad Shepherd* (1637). Even in his declining years, his work continued to move creatively in surprising directions.

Jonson was buried in Westminster Abbey in August 1637; a friend paid for the inscription "O rare Ben Jonson" to be carved above his grave. Despite the mixed success of his later years, his reputation at his death was that of a literary colossus. Throughout the seventeenth century, he, Shakespeare, and Beaumont and Fletcher were remembered as the giants of English theater: in *An Essay of Dramatic Poesy* (1668), John Dryden called him "the most learned and judicious writer which any theatre ever had." However, his reputation suffered by his proximity to Shakespeare. His plays kept the stage well into the eighteenth century, but as Shakespeare was increasingly admired for "naturalness," so Jonson became linked, pejoratively, with "art"—meaning that in comparison with Shakespeare's his plays seemed difficult, cold, and excessively labored. A myth also arose of his supposed envy of Shakespeare, which further damaged him in readers' minds: in the nineteenth and early twentieth centuries he was respected, but hardly ever performed. In recent years, however, there has been growing recognition of the stature and complexity of his writings, fostered particularly by the monumental Oxford edition of his works (1925–1952), on which a burgeoning academic industry has arisen. His complex, intelligent drama, too, appeals to modern tastes. All his major plays have had successful revivals, to which (ironically) the Royal Shakespeare Company at Stratford-upon-Avon has contributed the most. Jonson will perhaps never entirely escape the shadow of Shakespeare, but his achievement is now seen on its own terms more than at any time since 1700.

[*See also* Queen Elizabeth I; King James VI and I; Masque; *and* William Shakespeare.]

SELECTED WORKS

The Case Is Altered (1597)

Every Man in His Humour (1598)

Every Man out of His Humour (1599)

Cynthia's Revels (1600)

Poetaster, or The Arraignment (1601)

Sejanus His Fall (1603)

Ben Jonson His Part of King James His Magnificent Entertainment (1604)

The Masque of Blackness (1605)

Eastward Ho! (with George Chapman and John Marston; 1605)

Hymenaei (1606)

Volpone, or The Fox (1606)

The Masque of Beauty (1608)

The Haddington Masque (1608)

The Masque of Queens (1609)

Epicene, or The Silent Woman (1609)

The Speeches at Prince Henry's Barriers (1610)

The Alchemist (1610)

Oberon, or The Fairy Prince (1611)

Love Freed from Ignorance and Folly (1611)

Catiline His Conspiracy (1611)

Love Restored (1612)

The Irish Masque (1613)

Bartholomew Fair (1614)

Mercury Vindicated from the Alchemists at Court (1614)

The Golden Age Restored (1616)

Every Man in His Humour (revised version; 1616)

Epigrams (1616)

The Forest (1616)

The Devil Is an Ass (1616)

Christmas His Masque (1616)

The Vision of Delight (1617)

Pleasure Reconciled to Virtue (1618)

Informations to William Drummond (1619)

News from the New World Discovered in the Moon (1620)

Pan's Anniversary (1621)

The Gypsies Metamorphosed (1621)

The Masque of Augurs (1622)

Time Vindicated (1623)

Neptune's Triumph for the Return of Albion (1624)

The Fortunate Isles and Their Union (1625)

The Staple of News (1626)

The New Inn (1629)

Love's Triumph through Callipolis (1631)

Chloridia (1632)

The Magnetic Lady (1632)

A Tale of a Tub (1633)

The King's Entertainment at Welbeck (1633)

Love's Welcome at Bolsover (1634)

The Sad Shepherd (printed 1641)

The Underwood (printed 1641)

The English Grammar (printed 1641)

Timber, or Discoveries (printed 1641)

EDITIONS

Herford, Charles H., Percy Simpson, and Evelyn Simpson, eds. *Works*. 11 vols. Oxford, 1925–1952. The standard old-spelling edition of all Jonson's works.

Bevington, David, Martin Butler, and Ian Donaldson, eds. *The Cambridge Edition of the Works of Ben Jonson*. 25 vols. Cambridge, U.K., forthcoming. A complete modern-spelling edition, with old-spelling texts in electronic format.

FURTHER READING

Barish, Jonas A. *Ben Jonson and the Language of Prose Comedy*. Cambridge, MA, 1960. An unsurpassed critique of Jonson as a prose stylist.

Barton, Anne. *Ben Jonson, Dramatist*. Cambridge, U.K., 1984. A critical study with an important reassessment of Jonson's late plays.

Boehrer, Bruce Thomas. *The Fury of Men's Gullets: Ben Jonson and the Digestive Canal*. Philadelphia, 1997. The body as it is represented by Jonson.

Burt, Richard. *Licensed by Authority: Ben Jonson and the Discourses of Censorship*. Ithaca, NY, 1993. A study of Jonson in relation to political control of the literary text.

Butler, Martin, ed. *Re-Presenting Ben Jonson: Text, History, Performance*. Basingstoke, U.K., 1999. Essays focusing on the history of Jonson's texts in print.

Cave, Richard, Elizabeth Shafer, and Brian Woolland, eds. *Ben Jonson and Theatre: Performance, Practice, and Theory*. London, 1999. A collection of essays studying Jonson in relation to the modern theater.

Donaldson, Ian. *Jonson's Magic Houses: Essays in Interpretation*. Oxford, 1997. Classic and subtle essays on Jonson's major plays and on approaches to his life.

Duncan, Douglas. *Ben Jonson and the Lucianic Tradition*. Cambridge, U.K., 1979. Views Jonson's plays in relation to the classical and humanist traditions of satire.

Dutton, Richard. *Ben Jonson, Authority, Criticism*. Basingstoke, U.K., 1996. The most useful study of Jonson as a writer of criticism.

Goldberg, Jonathan. *James I and the Politics of Literature*. Baltimore, 1983. Jonson's work in relation to the language and iconography of Jacobean court life.

Harp, Richard, and Stanley Stewart, eds. *The Cambridge Companion to Ben Jonson*. Cambridge, U.K., 2000. A collection of essays surveying the major areas of Jonson's work.

Haynes, Jonathan. *The Social Relations of Jonson's Theatre*. Cambridge, U.K., 1992. A study of Jonson's earlier plays in the context of economic and social change.

Helgerson, Richard. *Self-Crowned Laureates: Spenser, Jonson, Milton, and the Literary System*. Berkeley, CA, 1983. Studies the shape of Jonson's career in relation to ideas of laureateship.

Kay, W. David. *Ben Jonson: A Literary Life*. New York, 1995. A thorough and informative biography.

Loewenstein, Joseph. *Ben Jonson and Possessive Authorship*. Cambridge, U.K., 2002. Explores Jonson as editor and shaper of his own printed texts.

Marcus, Leah. *The Politics of Mirth*. Chicago, 1986. Studies the works of Jonson's middle period in relation to the cultural changes of the time.

Norbrook, David. *Poetry and Politics in the English Renaissance*. London, 1984. Jonson's poetic career seen in relation to the political history of the period.

Orgel, Stephen. *The Jonsonian Masque*. New York, 1965. The classic analysis of Jonson's masques, and the first book to approach them as valuable literary texts.

Orgel, Stephen, and Roy Strong, eds. *Inigo Jones: The Theatre of the Stuart Court*. 2 vols. Berkeley, CA, 1973. A complete catalogue and edition of the costume and stage designs for Jonson's masques.

Partridge, E. B. *The Broken Compass: A Study of the Major Comedies of Ben Jonson*. London, 1964. An influential account of the imagery of Jonson's plays.

Peterson, Richard S. *Imitation and Praise in the Poems of Ben Jonson*. New Haven, CT, 1981. An intelligent study of the intellectual and iconographical meaning of Jonson's poems.

Riggs, David. *Ben Jonson, A Life*. Cambridge, MA, 1989. The best and most colorful biography.

Sanders, Julie, Kate Chedzgoy, and Susan Wiseman, eds. *Refashioning Ben Jonson: Gender, Politics, and the Jonsonian Canon*. New York, 1998. Groundbreaking essays developing some new critical approaches to Jonson.

Wayne, Don E. *Penshurst: The Semiotics of Place and the Poetics of History*. Madison, WI, 1984. An intensive study of Jonson's most important single poem.

Womack, Peter. *Ben Jonson*. Oxford, 1986. A reappraisal of Jonson's significance in relation to modern theoretical and political perspectives.

JAMES JOYCE

Derek Attridge

Any roll-call of the three or four most important writers of the twentieth century, irrespective of language or nationality, would be certain to include James Augustine Aloysius Joyce (1882–1941), and his name would probably head a large proportion of such lists. Importance can be measured in many ways, but Joyce's preeminence may be registered in at least four: the amount of commentary, learned and popular, that his writing has generated; the frequency with which his books appear on school and college syllabi; the global dimensions of his readership; and—perhaps the most meaningful in the long run—the impact of his work on the course of literature in the twentieth and twenty-first centuries.

James Joyce
Portrait by Jacques-Émile Blanche, 1935
NATIONAL PORTRAIT GALLERY, LONDON

A striking fact is that this enormous reputation is due largely to one work, a book that occupied some eight years of a creative life of about forty years. *Ulysses*, published in 1922, was the work that catapulted a relatively little-known author into the category of "great writer," and it remains the work that any ambitious novelist in any language has to take account of. This is not to say that Joyce's other works are of minor significance; *Dubliners* (1914), *A Portrait of the Artist as a Young Man* (1916), and *Finnegans Wake* (1939) all made highly original contributions to twentieth-century literature, and each in its own way has had a continuing influence on writers of fiction. One cannot be sure, however, that they would be as widely known today were it not for the phenomenal success of *Ulysses*, and this is even more the case with Joyce's other, shorter works.

Joyce's importance is a fact of literary and cultural history; of more immediate interest is what readers value in his work today. The adjective that is probably most often associated with Joyce is "difficult," but the qualities that give rise to this view of his work are inseparable from the rewards it offers. Many readers have testified to the apparent inexhaustibility of the major works: no matter how many times they are reread, they continue to offer new pleasures and new insights. This richness would not be possible without complexity, a complexity that (even in the apparently simple stories of *Dubliners*) requires of the reader an energetic involvement in the text. One does not, however, need to be particularly learned; knowledge of music-hall songs or brands of soap is likely to be just as useful in reading *Ulysses* as knowledge of Wagnerian opera or Greek idioms.

One of the most far-reaching effects of Joyce's writing is to make us aware that there can be far more in a page of literary writing than can be absorbed on first reading, and, just as important, that this is not a cause for regret. On the contrary, it is what makes rereading so fulfilling, as new knowledge and experience illuminates new aspects of the writing. It is also what makes reading Joyce in a group so pleasurable, as the fruits of varied personal histories contribute in different ways to comprehension and enjoyment. This principle—that any reading, no matter how well informed, is partial—became more and more central to Joyce's writing, culminating in *Finnegans Wake*, many of whose pages remain largely unexplained even after decades of prodigious scholarship. The complementary principle—that no kind of information, however apparently trivial, can be ruled irrelevant in advance—also became increasingly operative.

The density of allusion and the intricacy with which Joyce's works are constructed have given commentators and annotators immense scope, although their indefatigable labors may run the risk of diminishing the adventure, and therefore some of the pleasures, of reading

Joyce's books for the first time. (Fortunately, most readers will come to such commentaries at a late stage of their engagement with Joyce.) Too much emphasis on density and complexity, however, can deflect attention away from the many other qualities of Joyce's writing. These include a superb ear for the modulations of the English language, a wonderful sense of humor, acute observation of human behavior and feeling, a powerful descriptive ability, and a breathtaking inventiveness in handling the inherited resources of the short story and the novel. The most important aspect of Joyce's importance, one might say, can be seen in the smiles on the faces of readers around the world as they encounter for the first time the adolescent intensities of Stephen Dedalus, the engaging curiosity of Leopold Bloom, and the generous reflections of Anna Livia Plurabelle.

THE BEGINNINGS

A version of Joyce's early life is familiar from *A Portrait of the Artist as a Young Man*, whose title signals its autobiographical mode—if, that is, we take "the artist" to refer, as with paintings with similar titles, to the author of the work. It is important to note that we can also understand "the artist" generically; the book is, after all, narrated in the third person and the central character is called Stephen Dedalus, not James Joyce. The broad lines of the portrait are, however, accurate. Joyce was born on 2 February 1882 into a fairly well-off Catholic family living in Rathgar, Dublin, and his boyhood was marked by the gradual decline in his father's fortunes and in the Joyces' mode of life. It was also marked by frequent changes of abode, a pattern that Joyce kept to all his life, partly out of necessity—major incentives included poverty, hopes of employment, and world wars—and partly, it seems, out of some inner need. John Joyce was not the best of fathers or husbands, but his stories and witticisms provided a fund on which Joyce was to draw throughout his career as a writer. Joyce's mother was pregnant for much of the time he was at home; he was the first of fifteen children, five of whom died in infancy. As the family grew larger, the Dublin houses they lived in grew smaller, and the glimpses provided in *Portrait* and *Ulysses* of the circumstances in which Stephen's siblings are growing up carry a note of anguish unusual in Joyce's writing.

In spite of the increasingly straitened circumstances of the family, Joyce was given an excellent education at Jesuit institutions, first at Clongowes Wood College, then, after a spell of home study and a short time at a Christian Brothers school, at Belvedere College in north Dublin. There he was tempted for a while by the prospect of the priesthood, but in rejecting it rejected religion altogether, a painful but finally exhilarating process that Stephen Dedalus, too, goes through in *Portrait*. In 1898 he entered a third Jesuit institution, University College, from which he graduated in 1902. Although he left Belvedere as a star pupil, his interests at University College began to diverge from the academic path, and his greatest successes as a college student were as a writer and a speaker. However, some way of earning a living had to be found, and he went to Paris in 1902 with the aim of studying medicine—and, no doubt more importantly in his own mind, to experience at first hand the cultural ferment of the Continent.

It is at this point that the diary of his alter ego Stephen Dedalus ends, with the famous words that form the conclusion of *Portrait*: "I go to encounter for the millionth time the reality of experience and to forge in the smithy of my soul the uncreated conscience of my race. . . . Old father, old artificer, stand me now and ever in good stead." If James Joyce left for Paris feeling that the world of creative literary work was all before him, he was to return two years later in a much less buoyant mood, drawn back by the illness of his mother and still no more than a would-be author. His medical career had come to nothing, the family situation was worse than ever (his mother died in 1903), and he felt excluded from the Dublin literary scene. Later he was to give powerful verbal realization of these experiences in continuing the story of Stephen Dedalus in the pages of *Ulysses*.

Yet it was one of the figures of the Dublin literary world who gave him his breakthrough. In 1904 George Russell (whose penname was A.E.) invited Joyce to contribute a story to the *Irish Homestead*, a weekly agricultural newspaper. Thus "The Sisters" was published, over the name "Stephen Daedalus" (the spelling was changed for the character in *Ulysses*); later Joyce was to rewrite the story as the opening of the collection he entitled *Dubliners*. Two more stories for the *Irish Homestead* followed, and Joyce undertook a number of other writing projects: poetry, reviews, an autobiographical essay, short sketches he called "epiphanies," and a lengthy semiautobiographical novel entitled *Stephen Hero* and featuring a Dubliner called Stephen Daedalus. (The surviving part of *Stephen Hero* was eventually published in 1944; the other works are available in *Poems and Shorter Writings*.)

Joyce still felt that to stay in Ireland would be to stifle his potential, and he began to plan another departure.

Only in a Continental city, he believed, could he fulfill his vocation as an artist. Whether he decided that this time he should not go alone, or the possibility arose only when he found himself in love, when he sailed on 8 October 1904 it was with a twenty-year-old woman he had met four months earlier on a Dublin street. Nora Barnacle was to remain his constant companion until his death.

EARLY ACHIEVEMENTS

After failing to find employment in Zurich and Trieste, Joyce began teaching English at a Berlitz school in Pola (now Pula, in Croatia). In 1905 he moved to Trieste to take up a similar post, remaining there—with a short break in Rome as a bank clerk—until the outbreak of World War I in 1914, when he faced internment in Trieste (then part of Austro-Hungary) and decided to leave. By this time he and Nora had a son and a daughter.

As these bare facts indicate, Joyce's life in this period was far from easy. His spendthrift habits and frequent drinking bouts did not help. He continued to give English lessons, building up a loyal group of private students, and engaged in unsuccessful business ventures, including the establishment of the first cinema in Dublin, which necessitated a trip to Ireland in 1909. He contributed some journalistic pieces to the local newspaper and gave a few public lectures, in which his simultaneous support for Irish independence and mistrust of the nationalist movement were given expression (see *Occasional, Critical, and Political Writing*). In spite of his dedication to writing, for which he and his family were continually making sacrifices, by the middle of 1914 he had very little—in terms of either publication or monetary gain—to show for it.

Yet he went on writing. *Dubliners* continued to grow during his first year abroad, until by 1905 he felt able to submit the collection to a publisher. It was accepted, then turned down on the grounds that the printer objected to some passages; thus began what was to be a long struggle to find someone who would put into print the words that Joyce had written—including swearwords, references to sexual matters, and names of real Dublin establishments. By 1907 he had written three more stories but still had no publisher. In 1909 he visited Dublin (before his visit to establish a cinema) to negotiate with an Irish publisher; in 1912 he returned—on his last visit to Ireland—to continue the battle, without success. He had not lost his faith in himself as a writer, however, and, exhibiting an extraordinary capacity for self-criticism, had started rewriting his unwieldy autobiographical novel *Stephen Hero* in a radi-

cally different style. Although less than half of *Stephen Hero* survives (pages 519–902, and some thirty additional pages, of Joyce's handwritten manuscript), the magnitude of the change in Joyce's approach is evident. In place of the somewhat distanced, occasionally ponderous narrative it has a radiant, honed style, inviting the reader to participate with the hero as he grows in experience and maturity. The only concrete affirmation of his talent he received in these years was the publication of a collection of poems, *Chamber Music*, in 1907—poems that, had they not been written by James Joyce, would by now have been largely forgotten.

The tide, which had run against him for so long, turned in 1914. *Dubliners* finally appeared, the publisher to whom he had first sent the volume nine years earlier suddenly having decided that the world was ready for Joyce's uncompromising stories. In this year, too, the influential American poet Ezra Pound, to whom Joyce had sent the first chapter of his revised autobiographical novel and who had responded with huge enthusiasm, arranged for the work to appear in serial form in the London journal *The Egoist*. This was probably also the year in which he wrote an account of a flirtation with one of his language pupils in Trieste, *Giacomo Joyce* (published in 1968). And in this same year, with only a hint of the possibility of a successful artistic career gleaming on the horizon, he started a new novel, a work on a much more ambitious scale than *Dubliners* or *Portrait*, in which a Greek epic would be reincarnated in the streets of the city that Joyce had, imaginatively, never left.

DUBLINERS

The most striking feature of the stories of *Dubliners* is how little happens in them. A boy hears of the death of a priest who had befriended him and visits the old man's sisters to view the corpse and take refreshments ("The Sisters"); another boy (the same one?) plans to buy a gift for the girl across the street at a bazaar but gets there too late ("Araby"); a clerk has a bad day at the office followed by a miserable evening drinking and takes it out on his son ("Counterparts"); a group of election canvassers converse idly as they wait to be paid ("Ivy Day in the Committee Room"). The readerly pleasure offered by these stories is not one of dramatic eventfulness or breathtaking action. Their minimal plots might seem to owe something to Anton Chekhov, although Joyce told Herbert Gorman, his first biographer, that he had not read Chekhov when he wrote them. Perhaps the most important model was

Gustave Flaubert's exquisitely crafted story "Un Coeur Simple" in *Trois Contes*.

Once the reader's lens has been adjusted to the small-scale, close-up nature of the stories, however, a great deal can be seen to be happening, and this sharpness of attention also has the effect—as some of the best criticism of *Dubliners* has shown—of multiplying the mysteries that haunt each story. The eponymous heroine of "Eveline" is facing a decision that will determine the rest of her life, and yet the reader knows no more than the character about the true motives of the man who has offered to take her away to a new home in South America. "Clay" gives us, in vivid detail, the events and experiences of a day in the life of a Dublin spinster, a day that is special only in the context of her humdrum existence; in this story, too, the closeness of the narration to the character's own perspective leaves us in uncertainty: does her avoidance of humiliation extend beyond her own mind, or is she a figure of fun, or worse, to those she encounters?

A great deal—too much, perhaps—has been made of Joyce's comment that he wished to depict the "paralysis" of his native city, and of the occurrence of this word at the beginning of the first story. Although there is a pervading sense of entrapment—by economic constraints, social conventions, corrupted institutions, and endemic alcoholism and sexism—Joyce's Dubliners are extremely active as they develop and carry out their strategies for keeping afloat for one more day. They play truant, they gamble, they manipulate impressionable young men or recalcitrant committees, they hook up with flamboyant characters, they encourage then break off relationships, they recite poetry, they devise ways of achieving spiritual renewal, they orchestrate celebrations and come to terms with imperfect marriages. It is true that in almost every case the strategies fail to achieve their highest aims—or the aims themselves are such that the reader has little sympathy with them—but the characters survive to live another day and devise another plan. If they are often unpleasant and unethical as individuals, they never entirely forfeit our sympathy, because of the skill with which Joyce has conveyed the conditions that have made them what they are.

A PORTRAIT OF THE ARTIST AS A YOUNG MAN

Joyce's second published work of fiction is painted on a very different canvas. Dublin is still the background, but in place of what Joyce called his style of "scrupulous meanness" is a style that changes as its subject develops, capturing the young child's innocent apprehension of the mysteries of the adult world (and, perhaps even more baffling to him, that of boys older than himself), the adolescent's earnest grapplings with religion and sex, and the university student's ironies and self-scrutinies. And through it all runs a fluctuating engagement with language, from the first confused responses to the linguistic universe into which the child is born to the sophisticated experiments with poetic style in the young man's diary. *Portrait* achieves its economy not by utilizing spare language but by zooming in on key passages in its subject's life. As the book begins, hardly more than a page—but one of the most revolutionary pages in the history of fiction—gives us Stephen's initiation into language ("the geen wothe botheth"), art (story, poetry, song and dance), politics (Dante's brushes for Michael Davitt and Charles Parnell), religion (the Protestant Vances at number seven), family loyalties and tensions, and prepubescent stirrings of sexuality (wetting the bed; planning to marry Eileen Vance).

The rest of the first chapter consists of three scenes, two of which take place in Clongowes Wood College. In the first Stephen falls ill and is moved to the infirmary; in the second he is unjustly punished and makes a heroic complaint to the rector. Between them is a scene devoted to a Christmas dinner in the Dedalus home. In all, Joyce gives us perhaps thirty hours out of Stephen's years (probably around three) at Clongowes, yet we gain a strong sense of the boy's intense engagement with the environments in which he finds himself and of his resulting inner growth. All the themes announced on the opening page are developed and their interconnections made evident; for Stephen there is no separation among art, politics, religion, family relationships, and sex. The Christmas dinner scene, for example, involves a family argument hinging on politics, religion and sex—on, that is, the Catholic Church's response to the downfall of Parnell after the exposure of his adulterous affair. The energetic language of the quarrel—especially the colorful outbursts from Stephen's father—provides a hint of one of the resources on which the budding artist would draw later in life.

Each of the following four chapters works similarly, plunging the reader into particular moments in Stephen's life without providing any connecting summary, thus avoiding the distancing effect that the biographical mode, with its sense of a life looked back on, encourages. Part of the originality of the work lies in Joyce's incorporation of material that earlier writers would have summarized or massaged into a more conventional fictional form: he gives in full the sermons preached by Father Arnall at the retreat Stephen attends, repeats the stanzas of a bad poem Stephen composes, recounts in detail Stephen's long conversations with his university acquaintances on art, religion, politics, and other topics and ends the book with a series of diary entries as Stephen prepares to leave Ireland. He also incorporates, in chapter 2, some of his early epiphanies, as examples of the kind of writing young Stephen is doing—although he introduces them, characteristically, without any explicit announcement: "He chronicled with patience what he saw, detaching himself from it and tasting its mortifying flavour in secret. He was sitting on the backless chair . . . "

The external events of Stephen's life in *Portrait* follow those of Joyce's life; the inner story—of sexual temptation and torment, of religious fervor and loss of faith, of literary ambitions and artistic dedication—has its own unfolding logic and narrative power, whether or not it is faithful to Joyce's own experience. At no point, however, do we receive guidance in our judgment of Stephen from an authorial voice or an adult perspective. How seriously are we to take Stephen's self-assessments? (At times he takes himself very seriously indeed, but there is no requirement that we follow him in this.) How real is his promise as a writer? How much irony plays around the bravura conclusion quoted above? How much should we be influenced by the knowledge that the Stephen Dedalus of *Ulysses* is back in Dublin, his dreams unfulfilled? Is the hidden title *A Portrait of the Would-Be Artist*? Joyce provides no answers to these questions—and therein lies part of the book's continuing fascination.

THE MASTERPIECE

Joyce obtained permission to leave Trieste for Switzerland in 1915, and the family established themselves in Zurich, where they were to remain for four years, living their customary nomadic existence. These were important years for Joyce's reputation: they saw the publication of his play *Exiles* (1915), the book publication, to much acclaim, of *Portrait* (1916), and the start of the serialization of *Ulysses* in the *Little Review*, an American magazine edited by Margaret Anderson and Jane Heap. They were years in which his financial situation began to improve, thanks largely to the support of Harriet Shaw Weaver, the wealthy editor of *The Egoist*. They were also highly creative years during which Joyce wrote twelve of the eighteen episodes of *Ulysses* and moved from the style of the opening chapters—already hugely innovative—to the unprecedented inventiveness of the chapters set in the Ormond Hotel ("Sirens") and Barney Kiernan's pub ("Cyclops"). (The episode titles do not appear in the book, but Joyce circulated them to friends and they have become standard in critical commentaries.) The one blot on the horizon was the beginning of severe eye problems, necessitating the first of several operations in 1917.

The ending of the war made it possible for Joyce and his family to return to Trieste in 1919, but life in what was now an Italian city in decline was very different, and he took up Pound's suggestion to move to Paris in 1920. There followed the usual constant changing of abode and long spells in crowded conditions. Joyce often had to work in the bedroom that he, Nora, and Lucia, now a teenager, shared. Miraculously, under these adverse conditions, Joyce completed the final, hugely ambitious chapters of *Ulysses*, and revised the whole book extensively (he added about a third of the work by expanding successive proofs). For much of the time he did not even know if he would find a publisher—the editors of the *Little Review* had been convicted of publishing obscene material after the appearance of the thirteenth episode—but Sylvia Beach, the American owner of a Paris bookstore, came to the rescue. Just in time for Joyce's fortieth birthday on 2 February 1922, Shakespeare and Co. published *Ulysses*, and before very long Joyce was known across the literary world, by those who had read the work and by very many more who had not.

The richness and complexity of *Ulysses* are of a kind unprecedented in literary history. One means of appreciating its extraordinary qualities is by considering the number of ways in which the novel can be read (while acknowledging that any actual reading is likely to deploy several of these in combination). Here are five possible ways of approaching the novel.

It is the story of a day and a night in the lives of three Dubliners. Stephen Dedalus is a young writer, back from Paris and mourning the death of his mother, and attempting to gain a foothold in the Dublin literary world. Leopold Bloom is a middle-aged, part-Jewish advertising agent who takes a fatherly interest in Stephen while postponing his return home. Molly Bloom is his wife of nearly sixteen years who is visited by Blazes Boylan, the manager of her forthcoming singing tour, during the afternoon—for more than professional reasons. These characters are among the most fully realized in all fiction, and we follow the course of their hopes and fears, longings and frustrations, triumphs and defeats with all the involvement that accomplished fictional writing can produce. We also find ourselves privy to actions, thoughts, and feelings that earlier novelists, and their readers, would have considered too intimate for the printed page; here, as in so many other ways, Joyce effected a shift in the possibilities of the novel.

As this frankness suggests, the novel is also a minute investigation of the way our minds and emotions work. Joyce made brilliant use of the technique of interior monologue, which he transformed into a subtle and flexible instrument. By moving easily between a narrator's words and the thoughts of the character, often represented in broken sentences or single words, Joyce is able to present with remarkable immediacy both inner and outer worlds, and the interchange between them. Here is Bloom in the "Lestrygonians" episode, after noticing pincushions in a silk mercer's window:

> He bared slightly his left forearm. Scrape: nearly gone. Not today anyhow. Must go back for that lotion. For her birthday perhaps. Junejulyaugseptember eighth. Nearly three months off. Then she mightn't like it. Women won't pick up pins. Say it cuts lo.
>
> Gleaming silks, petticoats on slim brass rails, rays of flat silk stockings.
>
> Useless to go back. Had to be. Tell me all.

The sight of the pincushions prompts an inspection by Bloom of his own scraped arm, a reminder to himself to go back to the pharmacist he had visited earlier, a calculation about Molly's birthday (in Bloom's thoughts "her" usually refers to Molly), and a recollection of a female superstition. But the last word going through his mind—"love"—is sharply cut off as the underwear in the display triggers another association: Molly's coming assignation with Boylan. Bloom's insistence on the inevitability of Molly's adultery is an attempt to deal psychologically with the pain by which he is threatened, and is followed by an echo of earlier thoughts about the confessional that bespeak a desire for honesty. The trivial is thus seamlessly woven with the psychologically momentous.

Ulysses is also, as the title tells us, a rewriting of Homer's *Odyssey*, an epic for the modern world in which the hero is no battle-scarred adventurer encountering gods and monsters but an ordinary man dealing with the tribulations of early-twentieth-century urban life. Odysseus's tricking of the one-eyed Cyclops becomes Bloom's verbal offensive against a bigoted nationalist in a pub; the seaside meeting between the Phaeacian princess Nausicaa and the Greek hero becomes a young woman's exposure of her

underwear to a silently masturbating Bloom; and the slaying of the suitors becomes Bloom's acceptance of Molly's infidelity. The larger divisions of the novel are also Homeric: the Telemachiad (episodes 1–3: Stephen's need for paternal care mirroring the search by Telemachus for his father, Odysseus), the Odyssey (episodes 4–15: Odysseus's and Bloom's wanderings), and the Nostos, or Return (episodes 16–18: the hero's reunion with his faithful, or faithless, wife). The "schema" that Joyce drew up to assist commentators on the novel alerts us to the repeated references to each episode's specified "organ": in "Hades," for instance, the word "heart" appears in numerous apparently casual phrases such as "Wear the heart out of a stone, that," "Vain in her heart of hearts," "That touches a man's inmost heart," and "Warms the cockles of his heart."

Another way of approaching *Ulysses* is as a portrait of a city: Dublin on 16 June 1904. Joyce expended a great deal of effort on getting the details right, from street numbers to world events recorded in that day's newspapers, and the outcome of his meticulous research and astonishing memory allied to his verbal skill is that the Dublin of that day is a lively presence in the minds of millions of readers. This is perhaps the best way to understand Joyce's boast to Frank Budgen: "I want to give a picture of Dublin so complete that if the city one day suddenly disappeared from the earth it could be reconstructed out of my book." In fact, the picture is far from complete; for one thing, Joyce concentrates his attention on the experience of the kind of people he knew best—those whose economic security as members of the middle class was never completely assured. He does, however, convey with unparalleled vividness the opportunities and pitfalls, the struggles and compromises, that make up the lives of these inhabitants of a city entering the modern age and uneasily incorporated in the British Empire.

These four approaches to *Ulysses*, comprehensive though they may seem, fall far short of exhausting what the work has to offer. The story could be related in a few pages; the Odyssean allusions constitute only a small portion of the book; the minute exploration of thoughts and feelings becomes less and less central in the later episodes (except for the very last); and the portrait of Dublin emerges only sporadically. Tying them all together, and going beyond them, is a fifth way of reading: taking pleasure in the book's comic exploitation of the traditions of the novel and all the devices and varieties of language associated with it. It has often been observed that *Ulysses* teaches us how to read it. We start with the first six episodes' interior monologue, a style to which we quickly become accustomed; in the seventh episode, "Aeolus," we encounter newspaper headlines that are clearly not part of the scene depicted or thoughts of the characters; and in the ninth episode, "Scylla and Charybdis," the language of the narrator begins to be infected by what is being narrated ("—It is clear that there were two beds, a best and a secondbest, Mr Secondbest Best said finely"). From then on each episode adopts a distinctive style, and although arguments can be made for a relation between the style and the particular Homeric theme, the procedure is hardly organic: it is as if Joyce wished to offer a compendium of modes of comic fictional writing, and to explore each one to the fullest extent of which he was capable. The tenth episode, "Wandering Rocks," breaks with narrative continuity altogether; the eleventh, "Sirens," uses the sounds and patterns of language to mimic music and the emotions it arouses; the twelfth, "Cyclops," combines a monologue in Dublin vernacular with interpolated parodies; and the thirteenth, "Nausicaa," divides into a pastiche of romantic magazine literature and a stretch of continuous interior monologue.

From here on the sequence of styles plays a large part in conditioning the reader's response. A fairly simple narrative—Bloom follows Stephen into the red-light district of Dublin, gets him out of a tricky situation, and takes him home for cocoa and conversation before they part—is the occasion for a hugely elaborate stylistic extravaganza accounting for nearly half the book's length. We are released from the thickets of "Oxen of the Sun," in which Joyce recapitulates the history of English prose, to find ourselves in the phantasmagoria of "Circe," the climax of the novel's central section. The Nostos begins with comic long-windedness of "Eumaeus," which is followed by another hugely inventive and varied episode, the question-and-answer chapter, "Ithaca." "Penelope," the final episode, comes as something of a postscript, returning us, via yet another stylistic invention, to a character's inner world and, in tracing Molly's thoughts as she lies awake, offering us a new perspective on the day's events.

THE FINAL WORK

Soon after the publication of *Ulysses*, Joyce began work on an even more ambitious book. Unlike *Ulysses*, which was written sequentially (albeit with frequent reversions and expansions), *Finnegans Wake* was created in a non-linear fashion. Out of a few sparse narrative vignettes and a large accumulation of notes, and by means of a tech-

nique of word fusion that he had employed in a limited fashion in some of the *Ulysses* episodes, Joyce constructed a massive work that has still not been integrated into the literary tradition. This project was to occupy most of the remainder of his life, his only other creative production during the period being a scattering of poems, a collection of which was published in 1927 under the title *Pomes Penyeach*. He kept secret the title of what he regarded as his magnum opus, with the result that during the years of his increasing fame after the publication of *Ulysses*— the years of its banning in much of the world, the historic 1933 verdict of Judge John Woolsey allowing publication in the United States, and publication in the United Kingdom in 1936—one of the most famous authors in the English-speaking world was known only to be writing something called *Work in Progress*.

Work in Progress was not a completely unknown quantity during the sixteen years of its writing, however. Beginning in 1927 sections appeared in the Paris avant-garde magazine *transition* and were published as slim volumes by a number of presses. As Joyce's fame grew, so did the number of visitors who arrived at his door, and he was able to call on the aid of a large team of helpers (including the young Samuel Beckett). The family continued to live in Paris, moving, as always, from address to address, and in spite of increasing income from Joyce's publications and the continuing generosity of his patrons, seemed always on the brink of financial disaster. Joyce's eye troubles continued, and a new source of anxiety (and financial expenditure) arose as his daughter Lucia developed signs of mental illness, culminating in a breakdown in 1932. For the remainder of Joyce's life, Lucia's suffering was to remain a constant concern.

Joyce managed to repeat the birthday celebrations that had greeted *Ulysses* when, on 2 February 1939, he was presented by his publisher, Faber and Faber, with the page proofs of his new book, now bearing its real title, *Finnegans Wake*. But the world was preoccupied with other matters, and again war forced the Joyces (we can now call them this, as James and Nora were married in 1931) to seek refuge in neutral Switzerland. Joyce had been back in Zurich for less than a month when he suffered a perforated ulcer and died, on 13 January 1941. Nora Joyce remained in Zurich, where she died in 1951.

If *Ulysses* repays attentive reading, rereading, and reading in groups because so much is going on at so many levels on every page, *Finnegans Wake* does so to an even greater extent. Joyce was not one to repeat a previous achievement; as *Portrait* had marked a new start after

Dubliners, and *Ulysses* had struck out in a fresh direction after that, so *Finnegans Wake* involved Joyce in yet another reinvention of the tradition of the novel. If we revisit the five ways of reading sketched above in connection with *Ulysses*, it is easy to see how much farther Joyce traveled.

The story of *Finnegans Wake* is even less significant in the reading process than that of the earlier novel; in fact it is not even clear what the "story" is. Although heroic efforts have been made to translate the strange language of the book's seventeen chapters—divided into four sections—into a linear narrative with fully realized characters, perhaps the best way to think of this aspect of the work is as an endlessly repeated and multiply interpreted structure or template. The key event is a fall that is in some way redeemed, and the closest the book comes to instantiating this in a novelistic plot is in the many versions of an event in Dublin's Phoenix Park involving, it seems, a married man who takes pleasure in observing two girls urinating and who is in turn observed by three soldiers. The soldiers spread the story about, but the man is defended by his tolerant wife. As in *Ulysses*, a sexual misdemeanor and its acceptance by the one most offended is at the heart of the book, although now the genders are reversed. The "sin in the park" is not, however, a narrative event in the usual sense; it is retold over and over again, in shorter and longer forms, and with a huge number of variations. Its biblical form is, of course, the story of the Fall; its major political manifestation is the fall of Parnell (so significant in *Portrait*). It is sometimes transmuted into a story of a homosexual encounter, which itself sometimes becomes a version of a favorite story of Joyce's father involving an Irish soldier and a bare-bottomed Russian general; it takes on overtones of incest when the two girls are the daughters of the voyeur; and it is reflected in the ballad from which the book takes its title, as the fallen Tim Finnegan is revived by a splash of whiskey. The members of the cast of this kernel story are all, in fact, versions of the family group that provides the main characters in the book: the father, known by his initials, HCE, which sometimes stand for Humphrey Chimpden Earwicker; the mother, Anna Livia Plurabelle or ALP; the twin sons, Shem and Shaun (who are sometimes transformed into a threesome), and the daughter, Issy (who is often accompanied by a kind of mirror sister).

Finnegans Wake continues *Ulysses*' exploration of the inner realms of human experience, but this time goes on a longer journey: into the unconscious motivations, fantasies, and fears that underlie human conscious behavior.

Although publicly Joyce was wary of Sigmund Freud's theories, he was familiar with some key psychoanalytical writings, and when he came to explain his strange new book he found a useful parallel in the processes of dreaming. Although attempts to treat the whole work as a single dream leave unexplained many of the book's teeming details, the fissions and fusions, the manipulations of identity, and the linguistic transformations that characterize dreams are everywhere in the *Wake*. Other illuminating comparisons are to Freud's accounts of jokes and slips of the tongue.

The next two ways of reading proposed earlier are less fruitful for Joyce's last work. The nearest parallel to the Homeric scaffolding is the use of a simplified version of the sequence of ages suggested by the Italian philosopher Giambattista Vico in *The New Science* (1725): the ages of gods, heroes, and humans, followed by the *ricorso*, or return. The idea of history as cyclic structures the book, both in its repetition of motifs and in the running on of the last word (syntactically at least) to the first. But Vico does not provide Joyce with manifold opportunities for inventiveness in the way that Homer does, and is only one of many authors to whom the *Wake* makes repeated reference. Nor is there anything like *Ulysses*'s portrait of Dublin: the Irish capital is certainly important in *Wake*, but it is often merged with other cities. The city, or its more primitive form, the castle, is identified with the male principal, HCE, while the river—the Liffey, but also rivers around the globe—is identified with ALP, the female in her motherly and wifely aspect.

It is the fifth mode of reading, however, that responds most fully to what is new in the *Wake*. Joyce's exploitation of cultural materials and linguistic possibilities (now ranging far outside English) enriches, and sometimes undermines, all the other approaches, and offers its own substantial rewards. The "portmanteau word," in particular, makes it possible for Joyce to combine disparate meanings into a single moment of illumination, open his writing to future interpretations that he could not foresee, and achieve an unparalleled comic richness. Thus the exclamation "O foenix culprit!" (coming after a story of kidnapping and reconciliation involving male and female adults, twin boys, and a baby girl—versions, of course, of the primal family) combines "felix culpa" (the happy fall that is central to the book), Phoenix Park (the scene of HCE's disgrace and an allusion to Eden), the phoenix as the symbol of death and resurrection (exemplified by the story of Tim Finnegan as well as that of Jesus), and "culprit," a reminder of HCE's guilt.

Finnegans Wake cannot be read in the sense that most other literary works can, and there will perhaps always be only a relatively small number who, undisturbed by its refusal to observe the norms of the literary tradition, take delight in its exorbitant games with language, and languages, and its comic conflation of high and low cultures. Whereas *Ulysses* established a marker that later writers of fiction could not but acknowledge, *Finnegans Wake* has had few imitators, and fewer who have been able to be genuinely creative in further developing Joyce's innovations. It remains, still, at the limit of literary possibilities.

THE CRITICAL RECEPTION

Although Joyce's fame, or, perhaps more accurately, his notoriety, spread rapidly after the publication of *Ulysses*, his acceptance into the canon of great English literature—the literature studied in the classroom and featured in learned journals—was a slower process, in spite of praise by a number of other writers, notably Pound and T. S. Eliot, and his own encouragement of scholarly criticism, most importantly by Stuart Gilbert. Disowned by the cultural establishment in Ireland and rejected by the leading British critic F. R. Leavis, he found his strongest support in the United States; studies in the 1930s and 1940s by Edmund Wilson, Harry Levin, Richard M. Kain, and Joseph Campbell and Henry Morton created a strong foundation for later critics and scholars. By 1960 American criticism of Joyce, buoyed by the growth of New Criticism, with its emphasis on complexity and irony in literary works, included many impressive achievements; among the names one might list are Hugh Kenner, William York Tindall, Adaline Glasheen, and Richard Ellmann, whose magisterial 1959 biography did as much as any critical work to establish Joyce's reputation as an artist to be matched against, say, Alexander Pope and Charles Dickens, if not (yet) against Shakespeare and Milton. The 1960s saw further work in a New Critical vein, and an increasing flow of reference works and scholarly studies of manuscripts and sources.

Most of Joyce's creative life had been spent on the Continent, and it was there that he found some of his strongest supporters. His writing played an important part in the theoretical revolution of the late 1960s and 1970s: among those who acknowledged his influence, and commented on his work, were Jacques Derrida, Julia Kristeva, Jacques Lacan, and Hélène Cixous. Joyce was therefore an important presence when this theoretical work transformed the study of literature in the English-speaking world, and the renewal of Joyce studies at this time was profound. Later waves of literary and cultural theory have discovered equally fertile ground in Joyce. Postcolonial studies have explored the importance of Ireland's "semicolonial" condition; studies of popular culture have found much of relevance in Joyce; gay and lesbian studies have opened up areas of his work that had been passed over. Feminism has had a complicated impact on Joyce criticism; earlier work tended to fault Joyce for his use of gender stereotypes, but more recent commentary has found in his treatment of gender a sophisticated awareness of the operation of cultural norms. There is no reason to think that future developments in literary criticism will find Joyce's work any less responsive. Once an outsider, too difficult to be widely read, too experimental to be mainstream, too jokey to be taken seriously, too coarse to be put on a syllabus, Joyce is now the most canonical of writers. The comparison to Shakespeare and Milton is no longer an unusual or a surprising one.

SELECTED WORKS

Chamber Music (1907)

Dubliners (1914)

Exiles (1918)

A Portrait of the Artist as a Young Man (1916)

Ulysses (1922)

Pomes Penyeach (1927)

Finnegans Wake (1939)

Stephen Hero, edited by John J. Slocum and Herbert Cahoon (1944)

Giacomo Joyce, edited by Richard Ellmann (1968)

Poems and Shorter Writings, edited by Richard Ellmann, A. Walton Litz, and John Whittier-Ferguson (1991)

Occasional, Critical, and Political Writing, edited by Kevin Barry (2000)

FURTHER READING

GENERAL STUDIES

Attridge, Derek. *Joyce Effects: On Language, Theory, and History*. Cambridge, U.K., 2000. On the pleasures of reading, and being challenged by, Joyce.

Attridge, Derek, ed. *The Cambridge Companion to James Joyce*. 2nd ed. Cambridge, U.K., 2004. Studies of Joyce's major works, and of a range of related topics.

Attridge, Derek, and Marjorie Howes, eds. *Semicolonial Joyce*. Cambridge, U.K., 2000. Essays on Joyce in the context of Ireland's relationship to the British Empire.

Beja, Morris. *James Joyce: A Literary Life.* Columbus, OH, 1992. A short account of Joyce's life and major works.

Ellmann, Richard. *James Joyce.* Rev. ed. New York, 1982. The standard biography, full of illuminating and entertaining detail.

Kenner, Hugh. *Dublin's Joyce* (1955). Repr. New York, 1987. A scintillating commentary by one of Joyce's most influential critics.

Leonard, Garry. *Advertising and Commodity Culture in Joyce.* Gainesville, FL, 1998. Joyce's work in the light of early-twentieth-century consumer capitalism.

Levin, Harry. *James Joyce: A Critical Introduction.* Norfolk, CT, 1941; rev. ed, New York, 1960. One of the first introductions to Joyce, still well worth reading.

Seidel, Michael. *James Joyce: A Short Introduction.* Oxford, 2002. A brief, up-to-date introduction.

Senn, Fritz. *Joyce's Dislocutions: Essays on Reading as Translation.* Edited by John Paul Riquelme. Baltimore, 1984. Examples of the criticism of one of Joyce's best close readers.

Valente, Joseph, ed. *Quare Joyce.* Ann Arbor, MI, 1998. A collection of essays on the gay and lesbian dimensions of Joyce's work.

STUDIES OF INDIVIDUAL WORKS

Attridge, Derek, ed. *James Joyce's "Ulysses": A Casebook.* New York, 2004. A selection of essays, some classic, some less well known.

Devlin, Kimberly J., and Marilyn Reizbaum, eds. *"Ulysses"—En-Gendered Perspectives: Eighteen New Essays on the Episodes.* Columbia, SC, 1999. Each chapter of *Ulysses* discussed by a different critic, with particular attention to gender issues.

Gifford, Don, with Robert J. Seidman. *"Ulysses" Annotated: Notes for James Joyce's "Ulysses."* 2d ed. Berkeley, CA, 1988. A useful reference source.

Glasheen, Adaline. *Third Census of "Finnegans Wake": An Index of the Characters and Their Roles."* Berkeley, CA, 1977. Although out of print, still one of the most illuminating and enjoyable reference books on *Finnegans Wake.*

Kenner, Hugh. *"Ulysses."* Rev. ed. Baltimore, 1987. A reading of *Ulysses* of value to both beginners and experts.

McCarthy, Patrick A., ed. *Critical Essays on James Joyce's "Finnegans Wake."* New York, 1992. A useful collection of essays from various perspectives.

McHugh, Roland. *Annotations to "Finnegans Wake."* Rev. ed. Baltimore, 1991. The indispensable tool in reading *Finnegans Wake.*

Norris, Margot. *Suspicious Readings of Joyce's "Dubliners."* Philadelphia, 2003. Suggestive, sometimes controversial, interpretations of Joyce's short stories.

Norris, Margot, ed. *A Companion to James Joyce's "Ulysses."* Boston, 1998. A helpful introductory volume.

Sherry, Vincent B. *James Joyce: "Ulysses."* 2nd ed. Cambridge, U.K., 2004. An introduction to *Ulysses* that is particularly good on the historical context.

Thornton, Weldon. *Allusions in "Ulysses": An Annotated List.* Chapel Hill, NC, 1968. A valuable reference book.

Wollaeger, Mark A. *James Joyce's "A Portrait of the Artist as a Young Man": A Casebook.* New York, 2003. A selection of the best essays on *Portrait.*

JUDITH

Karma Lochrie

Beowulf, warrior and king, has become the central figure of Old English literature for his embodiment of male heroism in the warrior culture of early Germanic society. In the same manuscript that uniquely preserved the poem for modern readers, cataloged as British Library Cotton Vitellius A.xv, is a lesser-known poem, *Judith*, that retells the biblical story of a female heroine who matches Beowulf in traditional Germanic virtues: courage, boldness of spirit, and fame. The text of *Judith* is surrounded by mysteries. First, the poem itself is incomplete. It begins in midsentence, leaving scholars to speculate about how much of the text has been lost and what details the missing segment might have contained. A second cause for perplexity is the poem's inclusion in the *Beowulf* manuscript in the first place. Finally, readers puzzle over how differently this Judith is rendered from the Judith of the apocryphal source, and what this poem implies about a culture whose heroic literature tends to oppose women's role as "peace-weavers" to men's role as warriors.

The poem itself "begins" with the last word of a poetic line. The rest of it up to this word is simply missing, probably because the poem was originally separate from the *Beowulf* poem preceding it. The manuscript suffered considerable damage in a 1731 fire in the Cotton library. Scholars have tried to repair the damage by comparing this English version of Judith with its biblical source in the Apocrypha, a group of books in the Old Testament that were later considered noncanonical by the Protestant churches. Some believe that the missing part must have been three times as long as the surviving poem, while others think that the poem lacks only a few lines. The first view, based on comparison with the apocryphal account, is the more popular.

The Old English story of Judith begins at what is the climax in the story in the Apocrypha. The biblical version describes Holofernes's rise to power as king of the Assyrians, his conquest and exploitation of many lands, and finally his siege of the Israelites in the land of Bethulia. Just when the Israelites surrender all hope of being able to stave off Holofernes and the Assyrians, Judith, a lovely and pious widow, steps forward to prophesy the death of Holofernes at her own hand and the victory of the Israelites.

This is where the Old English text begins, four days after Judith has entered the Assyrian camp, with one of the finest scenes of drunken mead hall antics in Anglo-Saxon literature. After Holofernes has drunk his fill, he has Judith brought to his tent. He passes out before she arrives, and she seizes the opportunity to decapitate him. She then returns triumphant to the amazed Bethulians, rallying them against the Assyrians as she brandishes Holofernes's bloody head. The Israelites finally give battle to the Assyrians, who are routed decisively.

HERO OR SAINT?

Although the Old English poem follows the general plot of the biblical story of Judith, it is no mere translation. It transforms the figure of Judith from the attractive widow of the biblical version, who uses her beauty to seduce and overcome Holofernes, to someone more like Beowulf, a woman who battles a monster no less horrible than Grendel in order to save her people. The Old English Judith is an uncanny hybrid of Christian saint and Germanic hero, who demonstrates her courage and achieves that elusive reward so dear to the *Beowulf* poet—glory—through her assault on the forces of evil. At the same time, she embodies Christian virtues of humility and self-sacrifice, qualities that likewise define Beowulf in his victories over Grendel and Grendel's mother. Judith never boasts of her victories in the mead hall, nor is she awarded Assyrian booty to equal what Beowulf receives from Hrothgar, but she is clearly cut from the same cloth of the heroic Germanic tradition that produced Beowulf.

Judith as hero departs from the Beowulfian type in her resemblance to saints, whose life stories, or "legends," were popular reading in the Middle Ages. Like female saints, Judith renounces the cultural roles and expectations of women to take on a heathen tyrant. The virgin saint's frequently ensuing struggle with a political despot stages a conflict between Christianity and paganism, but it also figures a kind of political and social resistance on the saint's part. Saints' lives typically end in martyrdom, by which the saint not only wins in the debate between Christianity and paganism but often powerfully affects witnesses, who convert in great numbers. Judith clearly is not such a saint, but the Old English version of her story does lend her the kind of physical strength and virtue usually accorded female saints, and Holofernes plays the heathen hound. Like female saints, Judith possesses a certain amount of power, revealed in her prayers to God for help and in her speeches later to her countrymen. In addition, her strength is grounded in her "true belief," a faith that the poet converts into a decidedly Christian rather than Jewish one. She becomes the "Savior's servant," in the manner of other saints, rather than a pious Hebrew widow dedicated to the God of Israel. Lost in the translation of Judith from Old Testament heroine to Christian saint is some of her spunk, too: in the apocryphal book of Judith, she uses her beauty, fine clothing, and jewelry to seduce Holofernes. Because the first part of the poem is missing, however, it is difficult to say what the Old English Judith did to prepare herself to meet Holofernes, but the remaining text does not refer to her beauty or adornment. Clearly, in the end, the glory of the Old English Judith comes not from passive martyrdom but from her brave and violent slaying of her people's foe.

JUDITH AND GENDER

Aside from critical discussion regarding the poem's missing segment, scholars have more recently taken an interest in the poem because of the gender issues it raises. Women in Anglo-Saxon literature often play relatively marginal roles. Where they do appear, as in *Beowulf*, their gender roles are clearly restricted to "peace-weaving," an Anglo-Saxon descriptor for a good, aristocratic woman who mediated the hostilities of men either through words of wisdom and advice or through an arranged marriage as a pawn of larger political strategies. Wealhtheow, Hrothgar's wife in *Beowulf*, fits the role of peace-weaver in both senses of the word. There are, however, exceptions to this gender ideal in Old English literature, such as Elene and Juliana in poems of the same name, and there are also antitheses of this ideal, such as Modthrytho in *Beowulf*, who has any man who gazes upon her killed.

Judith exists outside these heroic and sacred frameworks for representing women in Anglo-Saxon literature. Feminist scholars of the past ten years have pointed to Judith's agency as a woman in the poem, particularly in her capacity as Beowulfian hero who decapitates the monster Holofernes. Others have seen in the poem an explicit critique of the masculine culture of the mead hall and warrior society glorified in *Beowulf*. In *Judith*, the feasts that celebrate the relationships of king to retainers and the homosocial world of heroic society degenerate into drunkenness and bellowing. Judith's intervention, according to this view, is more than a rescue mission for the Bethulians: it is the poet's critical reflection on epic society, including heroic masculinity. This reading of the poem provides one plausible answer to the puzzle of why *Judith* follows *Beowulf* in the manuscript: it serves as a critical reflection on that poem, even as it shares with it some of the same heroic and Christian coordinates.

[*See also* Beowulf; Medieval Saints' Lives; *and* Old English.]

EDITIONS AND TRANSLATIONS

Crossley-Holland, Kevin, trans. *The Anglo-Saxon World: An Anthology*. Oxford, 1994.

Dobbie, E. V. K., ed. *Beowulf and Judith*. Anglo-Saxon Poetic Records, IV. New York, 1953.

Griffith, Mark, ed. *Judith*. Exeter, U.K., 1998.

FURTHER READING

Belanoff, Patricia A. "*Judith*: Sacred and Secular Heroine." In *Heroic Poetry in the Anglo-Saxon Period: Studies in Honor of Jess B. Bessinger, Jr.*, edited by Helen Damico and John Leyerle, 247–264. Kalamazoo, MI, 1993. A good overview of the sacred and heroic elements of the poem.

Hermann, John P. *Allegories of War: Language and Violence in Old English Poetry*. Ann Arbor, MI, 1989. The chapter on *Judith* presents the poem as a critique of heroic masculinity.

Lochrie, Karma. "Gender, Sexual Violence, and the Politics of War in the Old English 'Judith.'" In *Class and Gender in Early English Literature: Intersections*, edited by Britton J. Harwood and Gillian R. Overing, 1–20. Bloomington, IN, 1994. A consideration of how class and gender are treated in the poem.

Magennis, Hugh. "Gender and Heroism in the Old English *Judith*." In *Writing Gender and Genre in Medieval Literature: Approaches to Old and Middle English Texts*, edited by Elaine Treharne, 5–18. Cambridge, U.K., 2002. Argues that Judith becomes a hero without becoming male.

JULIAN OF NORWICH

Sarah Beckwith

Julian of Norwich (1342–after 1416), named after the East Anglian church in whose anchorhold (enclosed cell) she lived, was the author of the astonishingly bold and original Middle English work *A Revelation of Love*. This prose meditation, sometimes also known as *A Book of Showings*, was based on a series of revelations Julian experienced in May 1373. Imagining that she was dying, she received the last rites, and as her priest held a crucifix in front of her, she had a sequence of visions of Christ's Passion. In the written form in which she communicated her visions, she incorporated into them abstruse, difficult, but deeply moving meditations on the nature of the human will, sin, God as mother, and the Trinity. The overwhelming emphasis of the visions is on the relation of the human soul to God as one founded, maintained, and redeemed in love; there is a serene and unprecedented sense of the impossibility of God's wrath and of the existence of a "godly wille" in the soul that never consents to sin, as well as an understanding that God wants to be known as loving and by means of love, and finally, a sense that although sin is, in Julian's words, "behovely" ("necessary", "beneficial"), "all shall be well."

Scholars have disputed how much Latin Julian knew, and it is unclear whether she was a nun or a laywoman, but she clearly was familiar with contemporary writings on affective spirituality—treatises written for those in the contemplative life, which often centered on meditations on the life and Passion of Christ. Her work distinguishes her as a daring theologian, a consummate rhetorician, and a spiritual advisor of tact, depth, and subtlety. Because she thought in the vernacular through words whose semantic range she tested and stretched to accommodate a sense of the whole of creation in relation to God, and in perfectly patterned sentences embodying strenuous Trinitarian concepts, she was also a brilliant writer. The sheer difficulty and daring of her ideas is nevertheless at home (a favorite word and concept) in her text. Though she was fully orthodox, her conceptual daring and ability to think theologically in the Middle English vernacular, at a time when writing and learning were a nearly exclu-sive Latinate clerical preserve, are even more surprising given both her femininity and the climate of danger surrounding vernacular theology in the late fourteenth and especially the early fifteenth century. The archbishop of Canterbury, Thomas Arundel (1353–1414), issued "Constitutions" (1407-9) restricting unauthorized translation and speculation about theology in the vernacular, but even before that, visionary writing had been vigilantly monitored and adjudicated by means of diagnostic techniques known as *discretio spirituum* ("the discretion of spirits"), by which spiritual advisers were advised to test the authenticity, orthodoxy, and God-derived nature of revelation. Women visionary writers, newly controversial through the writings and canonization (in 1391) of Birgitta of Sweden, were often mediated through male aman-uenses or confessors and were anxious to define themselves as the mere transparent vessels of the voice of God—even when their visions, like Birgitta's, were of political importance. The authority of these female mystics was thus, paradoxically, premised on the denial of their own voices. Julian, by contrast, was exegete and commentator on her own visions, and in this she was a profoundly revisionist writer, reenvisioning the nature of visionary experience and visionary writing, which for her were inseparable.

THE TEXTS

Julian's visions exist in two different versions. The first, known by scholars as the Short Text, was probably written shortly after her illness and visions of May 1373, and was intended for people vowed to the contemplative life, a life that in the late Middle Ages increasingly included lay people. This text, rediscovered in 1909, surviving in one manuscript—British Library MS Additional 37790, also known as the Amherst Manuscript—sounds like a speaking voice and appears to remain close to the experience of the visions. It seems that between the writing of the short and long texts, Julian may have entered an anchor-hold, perhaps inspired by her visions and wishing to meditate further upon them. Norwich appears to have had a community of anchoresses, women committed to the solitary contemplative life who entered permanently closed cells in a ceremony that was at once a funeral rite as they "died to the world" and a wedding ceremony as they married Christ—a way of life beautifully described in the early thirteenth century text, the *Ancrene Riwle* or *Guide for Anchoresses*. In her anchorhold, Julian was consulted by Margery Kempe, a lay visionary from Bishop's Lynn, Norfolk, whose spiritual memoirs were discovered in the twentieth century and published as *The Book of Margery Kempe*; Julian advised Margery about the veracity of the latter's visions.

The second version, the Long Text, appears to have been written between fifteen and twenty years after the Short Text. In it Julian meditated and reflected on the visions, greatly expanding especially those sections in the Short Text that describe her "Revelations" Fourteen to Sixteen. Here she developed the theology of God as mother and added a vision not present in the Short Text, whose understanding transformed and united her understanding of all the others: the Lord and Servant "example." None of the manuscripts of *A Book of Showings* dates from before the seventeenth century, and the versions we have are associated with the communities of Catholic women exiled during the Reformation from England to Cambrai and Paris. There Benedictine nuns under the direction of Father David Augustine Baker (spiritual director at Cambrai from 1624 to 1633) and Anne Clementine Cary (1615–1671), who founded the Paris convent, copied and preserved Julian's writings.

JULIAN'S PASSION

In the late Middle Ages, the Passion of Christ became the focus for intense forms of identification, imitation, and meditation. In meditations that followed the Hours of the Cross, or in narratives that encouraged participatory drama, the religious were urged to hold dear everything connected to the sacred body of the suffering Christ, and to imagine themselves at the foot of the Cross with Mary and John the Evangelist. These forms of imaging and imagination are plastic and visual as well as narrative and textual. Julian of Norwich's visions take their cue from such contemplation, and yet one of the striking distinctions of her descriptions is that they do not stop at an identification with the suffering of Christ. This is partly the effect of her startling everyday similes, which render the body of Christ at home in the ordinary things in the

world: the blood trickling down from under the crown of thorns is in its roundness like the scales of a herring, in its copiousness like the drops of rain falling from the eaves; the Church in its anguish and tribulation will be shaken like a cloth in the wind. This refusal to stop at identification with Christ comes from Julian's linking the Crucifixion with love rather than with abjection. Julian, in her text, never actually sees Christ die. Christ asks her where is the point of her grief and pain, so that neither the center, the actual moment, nor the meaning (the point and purpose) of grief is given substance, but the suffering is "comprehended" (a Julian pun, "understood and encompassed") in the triune nature of God (rather than the second person focus of much Passion meditation), and in the loving acts of creation, which Julian calls "keeping," or maintenance and redemption. In the later sections on God as mother, the Crucifixion is seen as a permanent, creative act of giving birth to redeemed souls through the very act of dying. In her use of another favorite verb, "beclosyng," Julian even envisages pregnancy as mutual between God and the soul: God "beclosyses" us in himself, and creation is from the beginning entwined with redemption. God has no contempt for what he has made, and in a startling moment Julian even describes defecation as beautiful and fitting—the body unlocking itself like a purse in the time of need. God has no disdain for even this simplest of offices: just as the body is clad in cloth, and the flesh in the skin, and the bones in the flesh and the heart in the trunk, so are we, soul and body, clad and enclosed in the goodness of God (Long Text, chapter 6). In the fifth Revelation, in which the fiend is overcome and in which she describes God as incapable of anger, Julian describes herself as laughing mightily and enjoying the shared laughter she thereby inspires in those around her. There is nothing in medieval Passion narratives akin to this delightful and eminently social moment.

WHAT IS SIN?

Julian's vision that "all manner of thing shall be well" and her conviction that God can never be angry sounds strange in relation to the conventional medieval teaching that sin is original to our depraved being and necessitates punishment from which we are relieved only by virtue of Christ's sacrifice. That sacrifice was repeated in every mass when priestly consecration made the body of Christ on the altar, thereby interceding with God on the behalf of sinful souls. Julian never talks about the sins of others—only her own. For her sin is the subject of confession, not accusation, as it so often became in Lollard writing, whose authors could be so obsessed with clerical sin that they forgot their own. Although Julian is reticent about the medieval penitential system—contrition, confession, and penance are mentioned but are essentially marginal—penance was a central sacrament of the Church, which could alone dispense the balm of forgiveness. Julian's sense of the discrepancy between her visions and the teachings of the Church cause her some anguish until they are resolved in the lengthy chapter 51 of the Long Text, in which she expounds an "example" about a Lord and his servant. This example conflates two scriptural texts, Genesis 3 and Romans 5, the texts through which Augustine had evolved his fearsome, massively influential account of God's wrathful and rightful punishment of sinners.

In Julian's recounting of the Lord and Servant parable, the servant rushes to fulfill the wishes of the Lord and, because he is too eager and too enthusiastic, clumsily stumbles into a ditch. In that ditch he can no longer sense the closeness and presence of God, which, though he cannot see it, is always there. He falls into despair. As Julian expounds her vision, it becomes clear that the servant is both Adam and Christ. When Adam falls into sin, Christ falls into incarnation, into human flesh. The absolute simultaneity of fall and redemption, expressed in the identity of Christ and Adam in the servant, and the conviction that the fall happens merely through a zealous desire to please and not through malice or wickedness, mean that, for Julian, sin is a desolate sense of God's absence. This deprival turns out to be blindness to what is always already there—the loving, all-pervading, enclosing love of the Creator for his creation. Sin is "behovely" ("necessary") because through it we attain a knowledge of who we are. And because our souls are made in the Trinitarian image of God, self-knowledge and the knowledge of God are bound together. God's love affords our self-knowledge as sinful, but that knowledge will not drive us to despair and desolation if we learn to know God through loving him. For Julian, God wants to be known by us, and that knowledge is experienced only through loving. The Lord and Servant parable give her an understanding of all the revelations; after this exposition she begins to see all the "shewings" as one coherent whole. All the Lord's "menyng" is contained therein.

Julian's use of the word "menyng" is dense and highly significant in the Long Text, and much of her theology is conveyed through semantic compression and skillful ver-

bal economy. "Menyng" carries the sense of "meaning" as well as "intermediary," and there appears to be an oblique critique here of the "menes" used to speak with God. We use many "menys" ("intermediaries, methods, means") for lack of understanding, she says in chapter 6 of the Long Text, but God does not need such means; the chief and principal "mene" is the "blissid kynde" that he takes from the Virgin Mary. "Kynde" is another beautifully complex word in Julian's writing (as it is in *Piers Plowman* and in Shakespeare's reanimation of it in *King Lear*), for "kynde" can mean "natural constitution," "order of creation," or "innate disposition" as well as the more familiar meaning of "benevolent, cherishing" as in modern "kind." What God means and the way he mediates it (through "kynde," through his kindness, through his innate disposition which he shares with us) is love: that is why Julian can sound the very grammar of love in her last words, in which love is God's agent, object and very purpose: God's "menes." Love, she says, was his "mening" in the *Showings*. "Who shewid it the [to you]? Love. What shewid He the? Love. Wherefore shewid it He? For love. Hold the therin, and thou shalt witten and knowen more in the same."

WHAT IS A SHEWING?

The notion of God as mother does not appear in the Short Text, and the Lord and Servant example is not mentioned in the summary of showings in chapter 1 of the Long Text. It is possible that both notions were developed in a second revision of the Long Text. Julian tells us with great frankness that it took her nearly twenty years to understand the nature of the Lord and Servant vision. The status of the Lord and Servant example raises fascinating questions about what a "shewing" was for Julian. Although the visions emanated initially from what she saw, seeing for her was always a form of understanding, and what she saw was not the same as what she was shown. Indeed, her vision was deeply temporal—subject to reversal and even denial (as in the temptation in which she dismisses her showings as "ravings"; chapter 66, Long Text)—and it never transcended the nature of human understanding. Her characteristic locutions ("as to my syte," "in my understonding") mean that her understanding was a participant in what the vision actually was. She was never "shown" something that existed independently of her understanding, and this may be the reason that she deferred discussing the Lord and Servant for a full twenty years. This is a sense of visionary writing radically different from that of many of her contemporaries—a vision that incorporated her fine intellect, an intellect that was profoundly interrogatory and yet never restless, and that included a process of prolonged, patient ratiocination and commentary as she became her own exegete. In the work she made out of this, doctrine is never separable from experience, and theology does not forget how it learns its own language.

[*See also* Margery Kempe; The Lollards; *and* Medieval Devotional Prose.]

EDITIONS AND TRANSLATIONS

Baker, Denise, ed. *The Showings of Julian of Norwich.* New York, 2005.

Colledge, Edmund, and James Walsh, eds. *A Book of Showings to the Anchoress Julian of Norwich.* 2 vols. Studies and Texts 35. Toronto, 1978. Based on the Paris manuscript in the Bibliotheque Nationale, the earliest extant version of the Long Text. This edition includes both the Short and the Long Text, discussion of the manuscripts, and a long essay on Julian's learning, which the editors take to be extensive.

Colledge, Edmund, and James Walsh, trans. *Julian of Norwich: Showings.* Classics of Western Spirituality. New York, 1978. Translates both Short and Long Texts and includes a long, informative introduction.

Crampton, Georgia Ronan, ed. *The Shewings of Julian of Norwich.* Kalamazoo, MI, 1993. An excellent edition based on ms. Sloane 2499, with glosses of the Middle English at the foot of the page, a useful bibliography, and helpful introduction.

Glasscoe, Marion, ed. *Julian of Norwich: A Revelation of Love.* Exeter, U.K., 1986. Based on ms. Sloane 2499, which the editor believes to be closer than others to Julian's Middle English text.

Spearing, Elizabeth, trans. *Revelations of Divine Love.* London and New York, 1998.

Wolters, Clifton, trans. *Julian of Norwich: Revelations of Divine Love.* Harmondsworth, U.K., 1966.

FURTHER READING

Aers, David, and Lynn Staley. *The Powers of the Holy: Religion, Politics and Gender in Late Medieval English Culture.* University Park, PA, 1996. A chapter by Aers demonstrates how Julian's representation of the crucified Christ refuses to hypostatize suffering and abjection, and a chapter by Staley explores the *Showings* against the backdrop of her time's crisis of authority.

Baker, Denise Nowakowski. *Julian of Norwich's Showings: From Vision to Book.* Princeton, 1994. Includes analysis of the Lord and Servant example as a revision of Augustinian theodicy and a theologically informed description of Julian's understanding of sin and soul.

Heimmel, Jennifer. *"God is Our Mother": Julian of Norwich and the Medieval Image of Christian Feminine Divinity.* Salzburg, 1982. Traces the genealogy and development of the idea of God as Mother in medieval and earlier sources and explores Julian's distinctive deployment of the image.

Jantzen, Grace. *Julian of Norwich: Mystic and Theologian.* Rev. ed. New York, 2000.

Nuth, Joan M. *Wisdom's Daughter: The Theology of Julian of Norwich.* New York, 1991. Explores the sapiential dimensions of Julian's theology.

Tanner, Norman. *The Church in Late Medieval Norwich, 1370–1532.* Toronto, 1984. Useful survey of Norwich's ecclesiastical institutions and personnel.

Watson, Nicholas. "The Composition of Julian of Norwich's *Revelation of Divine Love.*" *Speculum* 68 (1993): 637–683. Argues for a late date for the Long Text of the *Showings*, possibly as late as the 1410s.

Windeatt, B. A. "Julian of Norwich and Her Audience." *Review of English Studies* n.s. 28 (1977): 1–17. A study of what the differences between Short and Long Texts can tell us about Julian's audience.

JUNIUS MANUSCRIPT

Elaine Treharne

The Old English Junius Manuscript, formally cata-logued as Oxford, Bodleian Library, Junius 11, is one of the four major poetic volumes surviving from the Anglo-Saxon period. It is unique among these manuscripts because of its lavish sequence of line-drawn illustrations elucidating the text—a sequence that was, unfortunately, never finished. Junius 11 is part of the important collection of medieval manuscripts named after the donor, Francis Junius, an antiquarian scholar of the seventeenth century, who studied the biblical poems in the Junius codex and published the first edition of them. Because Old English poems were not given titles in their manuscripts, modern editors have been responsible for naming them.

CONTENTS, AUTHORSHIP, AND DATE

The Junius Manuscript includes four poems: the first three, *Genesis, Exodus*, and *Daniel*, are based on the Old Testament books of those names; the fourth, written in a slightly later script and now called *Christ and Satan*, is based on three major events—the Fall of the Angels, Christ's Crucifixion to the Last Judgment, and Christ's Temptation. At one time scholars thought that these four poems were by a single author, whom they identified with Cædmon, the divinely inspired poet of whom Bede wrote in his *Ecclesiastical History*. Because of this attribution, Junius 11 is sometimes known as the Cædmon Manuscript. However, all four poems seem to have been composed by different authors, probably at different times, and may have been collated into this manuscript because they share major themes of Christian salvation history.

There is a great deal of scholarly debate about the structure of the manuscript and its overall unity. Section numbers occur sporadically through the volume, up to page 209. At the end of *Christ and Satan* is a scribal *explicit* (closing words) that reads "Finit Liber. II. Amen" ("Here ends the second book. Amen"). Since *Christ and Satan* seems to have been thought of by the scribe as making a second book, many scholars think that the first three poems in the manuscript comprise an original Liber I, a first book, that lost its *explicit* because the last page or pages of the poem *Daniel* have been excised or lost through damage. This reading of the manuscript's physical makeup would therefore regard the volume as of two parts, with its Old and New Testament division effectively reflecting the Bible itself. Whether the later addition of *Christ and Satan* was part of the original design or this was simply regarded as an appropriate text to add on is another matter for scholarly debate. There is no doubt, however, that its themes extend those of the first three poems.

Junius 11 is typical of Anglo-Saxon books in that very little is known about the historical and cultural contexts of the manuscripts' production. Not only do we not know how Junius 11 was originally conceived or by whom, or when the texts themselves were composed, but we are also unsure of the manuscript's date of composition and its place of production. In some respects, these concerns are secondary to interpreting the poems—reading and analyzing what is there. In other important respects, however, the vacuum of information about the manuscript's conception and manufacture means that we cannot contextualize what we do know: we do not know by whom, for whom, where, why, or how the manuscript was put together. We cannot know the compiler's intentions for these four poems, or the audience's reception of them. In general, scholars agree that the first three poems in the manuscript were copied by one scribe in the later tenth century, and *Christ and Satan*, written by three scribes, was added early in the eleventh century. Possible places of origin are Christ Church, Canterbury, or Winchester, capital of Anglo-Saxon England, or, less plausibly, Malmesbury in Wiltshire. All three places were the sites of famous Benedictine monasteries in the tenth and eleventh centuries, so monks may have produced the Junius manuscript either for use within the monastery or for a lay patron. Because the manuscript is elaborately illustrated with line drawings that elucidate the text (though none survives for *Christ and Satan*) and can therefore be considered an expensive, deluxe volume, it is possible that a wealthy patron paid for it to be put together. It was never finished, though, as the sequence of incomplete illustrations testifies.

GENESIS

The composite Old English poem *Genesis*, on pages 1–134 of Junius 11, is the longest of the texts in the manuscript. As a complete work, divided into forty-one parts, it tells the history of the Fall of the Angels, the Fall of Man, Cain and Abel, God's covenants with Noah and Lot, and the extensive story of Abraham, ending with his obedience to God in his envisaged sacrifice of Isaac. The poem is 2,936 lines in total but is actually composed of two originally independent poems. *Genesis A*, which comprises lines 1–234 and 852–2936, is closely based on chapters 1–22 of the Old Testament book of Genesis. A major focus is on those whose loyalty and obedience to God results in their salvation (Abel, Noah, Lot, and Abraham) and those whose disobedience results in damnation (Lucifer, Cain, and the Sodomites, for example). *Genesis B*, interpolated as lines 235–851, is a complete poem translated into Old English from the Old Saxon poem *Genesis*, fragments of which survive in the Vatican Library, Rome. This poem deals with the fall of humanity after the temptation of Adam and Eve (with Adam being tempted first, and Eve portrayed in a relatively sympathetic manner), and it recapitulates the story of the Fall of the Angels, depicting Satan as an audacious warrior in the Germanic-heroic mold. Throughout the *Genesis* texts, these familiar Old Testament characters are brought to life in a lively and dynamic narrative that adapts and manipulates its biblical source to demonstrate the victory of those who practice fidelity and obedience to God.

EXODUS

Exodus is without doubt one of the finest and most complex poems in Old English, despite the occurrence of some gaps in the text as it survives. Its 590 lines on pages 143–171 of the manuscript detail, in a dense and difficult narration, the events of the Israelites' crossing of the Red Sea, adapted from chapters 12, 13, and 14 of the Old Testament book of Exodus. The poem focuses on Moses, linking him with his predecessors Noah and Abraham and demonstrating his leadership and heroism as he brings his people through the parted sea to salvation from their Egyptian captors. The emphasis on the movement of the faithful people toward their homeland is reminiscent of the spiritual journey of all Christians, and the waters of the Red Sea reflect the saving water of baptism. Rather like *Genesis B*, this is a poem that interweaves the heroic with the Christian message, and the vivid and terrifying depiction of the death of the pursuing Egyptians in the waves of the closing sea could not have failed to have an impact on an Anglo-Saxon audience.

DANIEL

On pages 173–212 of Junius 11 is the poem *Daniel*, based on chapters 1–5 of the Old Testament book of Daniel. Parts of the song of Azarius within *Daniel* are also included in *Azarius* in the manuscript Exeter Book of Old English poetry. *Daniel*'s 764 lines may or may not represent the entire original text, and scholars have not reached agreement on how much, if anything at all, of the poem is missing. This is an account of the salvation of the three Jewish boys Hannaniah, Azariah, and Mishael, who were placed within the fiery furnace by the Babylonian king, Nebuchadnezzar, and the subsequent role of the prophet Daniel in interpreting the king's dreams. The downfall of the king and his successor contrasts with the uplifting of the three boys, and the poem focuses on the themes of obedience, loyalty, and perseverance in contrast to pride, disobedience, and brutish behavior.

CHRIST AND SATAN

Christ and Satan, the last poem in Junius 11 on pages 213–229, was added at a slightly later date than the preceding three texts. It is regarded by scholars as either a composite poem created from three separate short works on the Fall of the Angels (lines 1–314), the Harrowing of Hell (lines 315–662), and the Temptation of Christ (lines 623–729), or as a single poem with three distinct parts. Each of these parts reflects on the Old Testament poems: the Fall of the Angels clearly highlights the theme of pride and disobedience and can be related to *Genesis*, although the story of Satan's downfall is itself apocryphal in origin; the Harrowing resonates with the themes of salvation and the rescue of the just, presaged by the three youths in the fiery furnace of *Daniel*; and the Temptation of Christ by Satan during his forty days in the desert is prefigured by the Israelites' forty years of wandering after their escape from Egypt. *Christ and Satan* might therefore be seen as the text that, in its encapsulation of salvation history from the exile of the fallen angels and of mankind from Paradise, brings us back to the heavenly homeland with Christ's defeat of evil and his redemption of humanity.

[*See also* Exeter Book *and* Old English.]

EDITIONS

Doane, A. N., ed. *Genesis A: A New Edition.* Madison, WI, 1978. The major scholarly edition of *Genesis*, lines 1–234 and 852–2936, with a full introduction to the poem and to criticism on it.

Doane, A. N., ed. *The Saxon Genesis: An Edition of the West Saxon Genesis B and the Old Saxon "Vatican Genesis."* Madison, WI, 1991. The major scholarly edition of both lines 235–851 of the Junius *Genesis* and its ultimate source, the Old Saxon version discovered in the nineteenth century in Rome. This edition analyzes all aspects of the works, including meter and linguistic and stylistic issues.

Farrell, R. T., ed. *Daniel and Azarius.* London, 1974. This scholarly edition of *Daniel* from Junius 11 also includes the analogous text, *Azarius*, from the Exeter Book.

Finnegan, Robert E., ed. *Christ and Satan: A Critical Edition.* Waterloo, ON, 1977. A significant scholarly edition that regards the three parts as distinct elements of a single unified work.

Irving, E. B., Jr., ed. *The Old English Exodus.* New Haven, CT, 1953; rev. ed, Hamden, CT, 1970. An erudite and lucid edition; the reprint includes numerous emendations and addenda.

Lucas, Peter, ed. *Exodus.* London, 1977. An excellent edition of the poem with a comprehensive introduction, elucidating the allegorical and typological aspects of the poem.

Muir, Bernard, ed. *A Digital Facsimile of Oxford, Bodleian Library, MS. Junius 11.* With Nick Kennedy. Bodleian Digital Texts, 1. Oxford, 2004. This CD includes a full-color digitized reproduction of the codex with numerous scholarly materials: introduction about the manuscript's date, physical makeup, and critical history, a comprehensive bibliography, translations and transcriptions, and analyses of the line drawings.

FURTHER READING

Karkov, Catherine E. *Text and Picture in Anglo-Saxon England: Narrative Strategies in the Junius 11 Manuscript.* Cambridge Studies in Anglo-Saxon England 31. Cambridge, U.K., 2001. An interesting full study of the extensive sequence of illustrations in Junius 11.

Liuzza, Roy M., ed. *The Poems of MS Junius 11: Basic Readings.* Basic Readings in Anglo-Saxon England 8. New York, 2002. An excellent collection of important studies on various aspects of Junius 11, including indispensable articles by Joyce Hill, J. R. Hall, and James W. Earl.

O'Brien O'Keeffe, Katherine. *Visible Song: Transitional Literacy in Old English Verse.* Cambridge Studies in Anglo-Saxon England 4. Cambridge, U.K., 1990. Examines in detail the visual format of the major poetic works in Old English, and proposes numerous conclusions about methods of reading and interpreting the texts.

PATRICK KAVANAGH

Patricia McManus

Patrick Kavanagh (1904–1967) is now recognized as one of the greatest of Ireland's post-independence poets, and his work is a staple of school and university curricula alike. A novelist, journalist, and literary critic as well as a poet, he has been immortalized in Dublin by a statue placed on the bank of the Grand Canal to the west of Baggot Street Bridge.

Kavanagh lived in Dublin for nearly twenty years, inhabiting a variety of bed-sitters, rented flats, and hostel beds, becoming a well-known face in the city's pubs as alcoholism began to destroy him in the late 1950s. His work, however, is most intimately associated with a different type of social space: the rural villages of County Monaghan, the region where he was born and lived for the first thirty-five years of his life.

As the writer from Monaghan, a poet who wrote of land and its care, Kavanagh gained a reputation as a "plowman poet" in the 1930s, the decade when his work first began to be published nationally. In the wake of the Irish "literary revival" that marked the early decades of the twentieth century, there was a taste for all things peasant in literary Ireland. In plays at the Abbey Theatre and in novels, poems, and prose, the countryman, the scholar and drover, the plowman mystic were popular tropes for an essential and earthy yet mystical Irishness.

For a young poet desperate for publication, there was a seductive ease about the role, and Kavanagh on his trips to Dublin in the 1930s and in his poems of the same decade did play the rural dreamer and charmer, the bogland enigma. But it was also a role forced on him, a background and context he was not allowed to forget. Literary activity in Ireland was then carried on by an elite of university-educated and Dublin-centered men. When Kavanagh and his work first appeared, both were frequently caricatured as crude, making up in vigor for what they lacked in polish (but lacking in polish nevertheless). Kavanagh's biographer Antoinette Quinn notes, for example, that Seán O'Faoláin, writing to Frank O'Connor in 1942, expressed his weariness with what he termed "turfsmoke" in Irish writing by targeting Kavanagh's

work. In the case of "what we please to call (optimistically) the New Ireland," he wrote, there should be a "literature of the city": "One wants civilisation. Kavanagh doesn't wash his poetry's ears" (p. 155).

O'Faoláin's is a tellingly simple insult. Kavanagh had been writing poetry for more than twenty years by the time O'Faoláin indicted its unwashed quality. In 1929 he had been published in the *Irish Statesman*, the influential weekly journal of arts and ideas edited by A. E. (George Russell, 1867–1935), then the grand old man of Irish literature. Over the next six years, Kavanagh built a strong literary reputation in Dublin, publishing poems in the prestigious quarterly review journal the *Dublin Magazine* and in the *Irish Times*, as well as in the popular English papers *John O'London's Weekly* and the *Spectator*. In September 1936, Macmillan published *Ploughman and Other Poems*, Kavanagh's first collection, a selection of thirty-one poems which was well reviewed in both the Irish and English press.

But Kavanagh was also a farmer. The poetry he wrote and published in the 1930s was written for the most part in the fragments of time he squeezed out of the daily round of milking, feeding, herding, sowing, tilling, and reaping that defined his life on the small family farm in the parish of Inniskeen, County Monaghan. In early twentieth century Ireland, farming was still a labor-intensive and seasonal business, dependent on manual labor and knowledge won from experience. Born in 1904 to James Kavanagh, a cobbler from the Inniskeen townland of Mucker, and Bridget Quinn, a laborer's daughter from Killaney, Kavanagh was the fourth child and first son in a family that eventually comprised ten children. Through long hours of labor and careful saving, Kavanagh's parents had accumulated enough money to buy a nine-acre farm in 1910. In rural Ireland at that time, land still equaled status; land rather than education was the route to security and the vehicle of social mobility. As the eldest son, Patrick Kavanagh would inherit land. He left Kednaminsha primary school just months before his fourteenth birthday to begin a double apprenticeship, learning the craft of shoemaking from his father and that of farming from the local farmers he was hired out to as seasonal labor. When Kavanagh's father died in 1929, Patrick took over his position as nominal head of the Kavanagh household, answerable to his mother Bridget for how he ran the farm but publicly visible as its owner and manager. By the time he turned thirty in 1934, he had been working the land for over fifteen years.

UNWASHED POETRY

Those years are described by Quinn in her biography of Kavanagh as forming "a saturation course in farming, folklore and masculinity, Innishkeen style" (p. 34). A life so closely devoted to the land, the care of land and the experiences of those who care for land, could not be separated from the poetry Kavanagh was writing simultaneously—and mostly daily—in the late 1920s and 1930s. His early pieces are often derivative, drawing their inspiration and diction from the canonical English poets collected in the school textbooks and anthologies that formed Kavanagh's first point of contact with poetry. In "To the Man after the Harrow" (1940), it is the figure of the seed sower who dominates the landscape of "April clay" and the movements of the horses pulling the harrow. The sower is a figure romanticized by the poet's address, the call to "forget" local cares and rivalries so as to see the biblical potency of the far-flying seeds and his destiny to enter the "mist where Genesis begins." Similarly, in "Ploughman" (1930), the plowman is given the otherworldly role of dreamer; a joyous "tranquillity" walks with him as he magically alters the landscape, painting "the meadow brown / With my plough." And in "Inniskeen Road: July Evening," one of the most beautiful of Kavanagh's early sonnets, the bicycles that go by in twos and threes carrying locals to the dance in Billy Brennan's barn amid "the half-talk code of mysteries," the "wink-and-elbow language of delight," are watched by a poet who is separate, exiled in the land of solitary contemplation where the poet is "king / Of banks and stones and every blooming thing."

When O'Faoláin used Kavanagh to illustrate the lack of urbanity in Irish poetry, it was poems like these he had in mind. However, O'Faoláin's insult is more complex than it at first appears. The established older writer is indeed scorning as crude and uncivilized the material and technique of Kavanagh's early work. But the direction in which O'Faoláin, together with Frank O'Connor, wanted Irish writing to move so as to be fit for the "New Ireland"

was precisely to a new realism, to a documentary aesthetic that could represent all the diverse threads of Free State Ireland.

In the *Bell*, founded in October 1940 with O'Faoláin as its editor and O'Connor as its poetry editor, a literary and cultural program for ridding Irish culture of the powerful remnants of romantic nationalism had been put forward. With the death of William Butler Yeats in 1939, both O'Faoláin and O'Connor, then two of the most influential voices in Irish literary circles, saw an opportunity finally to overcome the legacy of the Irish literary revival. The nationalist symbols upon which the revival had fed belonged to "the time when we growled in defeat and dreamed of the future. That future has arrived and, with its arrival, killed them," announced the *Bell*'s first editorial (cited in Smyth, p. 164). The task of Irish writers now was to write of what they knew, to make Irish writing fit for the contemporary reality of Irish life.

But reality, the raw material of local places and patterns of living, was precisely what Kavanagh was disciplining himself to produce in the early 1940s. Having made two aborted attempts to live in London in the late 1930s, he had finally moved to Dublin in 1939 to work at being a full-time writer. Even before he made the move, however, he had expressed dissatisfaction with both the artifice of his plowman-poet persona and the redundancy of the poetry it produced. The semiautobiographical novel he was writing throughout 1937, *The Green Fool* (1938), makes clear the distance between the reified world of the plowman poems and the reality of plowing a bad plot of land: it was only an ill-nourished imagination that could produce the "ploughman ecstasy" that turned a "kicking mare in a rusty, old plough tilling a rood of land for turnips" into the pleasant lilt of finding "a star-lovely art / In a dark sod." The experience of writing *The Green Fool* taught Kavanagh the value of precision, of detail, and of the richness of color and sound to be found in the real idioms and idiosyncrasies of local life.

Encouraged by O'Faoláin and O'Connor—both of whom acted as friends and mentors to Kavanagh as well as publicizing his work—Kavanagh in the early 1940s set about ridding his work of the abstract romantic symbolism he had wrongly come to identify as the language of poetry. In "Stony Grey Soil," a poem first published in the *Bell* in 1940, land is addressed as an enemy of all that is generous and pleasurable in life. The powerful images of the poem contain an anger and aggression new to Kavanagh's poetry. He castigates the narrow mold that farming life is forced into: the stony gray soil "took the gay child of my passion" and gave only a "clod-conceived":

You sang on steaming dunghills
A song of cowards' brood,
You perfumed my clothes with weasel itch,
You fed me on swinish food.

However, Kavanagh's sense of what constituted "realism" still differed from O'Faoláin's. O'Faoláin—and with him, the *Bell*—demanded an Irish culture modeled on the idea of the higher arts as a civilizing force. Irish writing should represent Irish life but should do so with forms and techniques taken from the canon of English literature. Kavanagh had neither the benefit nor the burden of a university education. He was an autodidact who had fed himself eclectically on whatever literature he could find in his own or in neighbors' houses. In his earlier work, this lack of a formal foundation for his writing led to an uncertainty and hesitancy about his own powers, an uncertainty often expressed in imitative and deferential verse. By 1940, however, Kavanagh possessed both a confidence in his ability as a writer and a grim certainty that the realities of rural life were matter not merely fit for poetry but necessary to Irish poetry. It is a mark of his brilliance as a poet that he survived the often ill-disguised condescension of those like O'Faoláin to produce a new Irish poetry.

ORIGINALITY IN NORMALITY

At first Kavanagh's confidence and dedication expressed themselves in an aesthetic of rage, an anger directed as much at those who would beautify the lives of the country poor (in the name of a romantic vision of Ireland as an idyllic non-English place) as against the life of "the peasant ploughman who is half a vegetable," "a sick horse nosing around the meadow for a clean place to die." Those are lines from Kavanagh's most celebrated long poem, *The Great Hunger* (1942), a savagely antipastoral rendering of the life of Patrick Maguire, a Monaghan plowman who did not get away.

The bachelor Maguire, obeying Church, mother, and custom, made "the field his bride" and endured consequently the shriveling of his life and being as his "great hunger" went unsatisfied. In the epic anger of *The Great Hunger*, Kavanagh fulfilled with brilliance the realist remit set out by the *Bell*. The poem documents the appalling scars wrought on individual and communities' lives by the rural realities of decline and depopulation, emigration, late marriage, and failure to marry. But Kavanagh

did so with a poetic voice saturated with the world it spoke of. No detached anonymity mediates the portrait of Maguire slowly stagnating. The poem's voice to Seamus Heaney sounded "as if the 'stony grey soil of Monaghan' suddenly became vocal": Kavanagh's achievement here is, according to Heaney, "to find an Irish note that is not dependent on backward looks towards Irish tradition, not an artful revival of poetic strategies from another tongue but a ritualistic drawing out of patterns of run and stress in the English language as it is spoken in Ireland" (p. 123). Kavanagh's long poems of the 1940s, *The Great Hunger* and *Lough Derg* (written 1942, published 1978), attempt to move outward from the personal to the social, and by using scenes of individual life to embody the textures and significances of a totality, these two pieces constitute an ambition to restore poetry to the public domain, to "reestablish the rights of poetry in the larger arena of twentieth-century historical experience" (Browne, p. 133).

The eighteen poems in Kavanagh's second collection, *A Soul for Sale*, also express his new realist and rural aesthetic. Published in London in 1947 to positive reviews, the collection includes poems that have become Irish classics: in addition to *The Great Hunger*, there are "Spraying the Potatoes," "A Christmas Childhood," "Stony Grey Soil," and "Advent." However, despite the positive reception given to *A Soul for Sale*, Kavanagh appeared in print in the late 1940s and 1950s mostly as a journalist and a columnist who specialized in rendering detailed and often polemically critical scenes of Irish country life. Poetry did not pay well, and for most of his time in Dublin, Kavanagh existed on the margins of poverty, continually seeking and failing to find the paid employment he thought would give him the security to write.

With the exception of *Tarry Flynn* (1948), a novel that traces the family- and parish-centered confines of its protagonist's daily life, Kavanagh's next major work did not appear until 1960, with the poems collected in *Come Dance with Kitty Stobling and Other Poems*. *Tarry Flynn* continued the anticlerical and antiromantic realism Kavanagh had first expressed so profoundly in *The Great Hunger*. But in the novel he also worked a detached and comic vein that lifts the text above a grim realism. The poems collected in *Come Dance with Kitty Stobling* are also notable for a lyrical energy and celebratory tone. Love poems addressed to a world of present-tense objects and places—canals and streets as well as country lanes and open fields—they are full of color and movement, a love of the irrational, and a frequent joyous recklessness.

The two canal sonnets open the collection on a note of rich reconciliation, and the thirty-two pieces that follow consolidate and elaborate a vibrant yet peaceful aesthetic. In "Is" and "To Hell with Commonsense," Kavanagh finds life to lie in an abandonment to the here and now, in surrender to love, and in the human capacity to be imaginatively transformed by love. *Come Dance with Kitty Stobling* secured Kavanagh's reception as the most significant Irish poet since Yeats. He had influential admirers among a younger generation of Irish poets, a generation that included John Hewitt and Seamus Heaney, and by his death in 1967 both his *Collected Poems* (1964) and *Collected Pruse* (1967; the self-mocking misspelling was his choice) had been published.

In refusing to wash his poetry's ears, then, Kavanagh had opened the way to and developed a post-independence poetry, a lyric realism capable of coping with the contradictions of twentieth-century Irish life. "It is only in normality that you can have originality" was one of Kavanagh's favorite sayings, and his gift to Irish literature was the restoration to it of that originality and that normality.

[*See also* Abbey Theatre *and* Brendan Behan.]

SELECTED WORKS

Ploughman and Other Poems (1936)
The Green Fool (1938)
The Great Hunger (1942)
A Soul for Sale (1947)
Tarry Flynn (1948)
Come Dance with Kitty Stobling and Other Poems (1960)
Collected Poems (1964)
Self-Portrait (1964)
Collected Pruse (1967)
The Complete Poems of Patrick Kavanagh (1972)

FURTHER READING

Brown, Terence. "The Counter-Revival: 1930–1965; Poetry." In *The Field Day Anthology of Irish Writing*, edited by Seamus Deane, vol. 3. Derry, 1991. This brief essay contains a sharp analysis of the situation of Irish poetry in the 1940s, 1950s, and 1960s; it locates Kavanagh's work in relation to his contemporaries and offers an insightful analysis of that work.

Heaney, Seamus. "From Monaghan to the Grand Canal: The Poetry of Patrick Kavanagh." In his *Preoccupations: Selected Prose, 1968–1978*. London, 1980. An excellent and provocative close reading of some of Kavanagh's longer poems, also offering a sense of how Heaney himself has been influenced by Kavanagh.

Kiberd, Declan. *Inventing Ireland: The Literature of the Modern Nation*. London, 1995. By now a classic, Kiberd's analysis of the making of the canon of modern Irish literature contains a brief but fascinating analysis of Kavanagh's place in that canon.

Quinn, Antoinette. *Patrick Kavanagh: A Biography*. Dublin, 2001. This meticulously researched biographical study offers invaluable readings of Kavanagh's work as well as documenting his life.

Smyth, Gerry. *Decolonisation and Criticism: The Construction of Irish Literature*. London, 1998. A strong description of post–World War II Irish literary and intellectual life, using as one of its case studies the journal Kavanagh and his brother produced in the 1950s.

Warner, Alan. *Clay Is the Word: Patrick Kavanagh, 1904–1967*. Dublin, 1973. This early study of Kavanagh's work is still one of the best brief studies available.

JOHN KEATS

James Chandler

The life of John Keats (1795–1821) has become the stuff of modern legend, although it is a tale told with a variety of inflections. It is the story, for example, of an orphaned young city dweller who lived and breathed poetry but perished of consumption before his twenty-sixth birthday. It is also the fable of the impoverished apothecary student in fashion-conscious Regency London who suffered and died for his aesthetic commitments. In its most dramatic form, and from as early as Percy Shelley's brilliant elegy, *Adonais* (1821), the life of Keats is the quasi-Christian narrative of a supremely sensitive artist who was crucified for his poetry. Keats's was a sensibility so exquisite, the legend has it, that he was killed by adverse criticism of an early volume of poetry (*Endymion*, 1818). Thus Lord Byron, no friend of Keats nor fan of his work, could quip, in *Don Juan*, canto 11 (1822–1823), "'Tis strange the mind, that very fiery particle, / Should let itself be snuffed out by an Article." Although the legend assumes various forms, it remains clear that reports of his premature death, and the late volume of poems that appeared not long before it, assured his role as the English romantic martyr to the creative imagination. Keats's achievement was not, in fact, much recognized in his own lifetime, but the *story* of Keats helped secure his place as avatar of what he himself once called "the poetry of earth."

Aggrandized as it would be, Keats's life was nonetheless on several scores a decidedly modest affair. And because he died young, it is centered in the years of growth. Keats was not what is called well-born. At the time of his birth near London Wall in Finsbury on 31 October 1795, his father, Thomas Keats, managed the livery stables that belonged to the family of his wife, née Frances Jennings. The eldest of the Keats children, John was followed by

John Keats
Portrait by Joseph Severn, 1819
NATIONAL PORTRAIT GALLERY, LONDON

two brothers, George and Tom, and a sister, Fanny; he remained close to all of them. The Thomas Keatses were not impoverished. There was even some talk of sending John to Harrow, Lord Byron's school. They settled instead on a small academy in Enfield, just north of London, where Keats matriculated in 1803, the shortest of seventy-odd students in the school. (He would never reach five feet one inch in stature.) The school was capably run by John Clarke, a member of London's Dissenting and reforming circles, and Keats was well educated there in a curriculum more modern than classical in its orientation. It was here, too, that Keats came to be befriended by John Clarke's son Cowden, eight years Keats's senior, who served as his tutor. Cowden Clarke would later introduce Keats into the literary circle of Leigh Hunt, where he soon became infatuated with poetry, and eventually with the idea of being a poet.

Much adversity, however, lay in his path. Thomas Keats died in a riding accident in 1804. John's mother remarried badly, and almost immediately, having waited no longer than did Hamlet's mother Gertrude. The effect of all this on Keats was to turn him pugnacious. In spite of his diminutive stature, he became something of a brawler, his reputation surviving in the school for some time after he left it. Six years after the death of his father, his mother died of consumption, the disease that would later claim his brother Tom and eventually Keats himself. He was again transformed by the death of a parent, this time from scrappy pugilist to scholarly introvert. Meanwhile, the orphaned children were placed in the care of their grandmother, who would herself be dead in three years. At this point, the Keats estate would be entrusted chiefly to one Richard Abbey, a source of frustration to Keats in his subsequent financial transactions.

EARLY POEMS

In 1811, Keats left Clarke's school and entered into a bound apprenticeship with Thomas Hammond, a local surgeon in Edmonton. While embarking on this career, Keats stayed in touch with the Clarkes, and especially with Cowden Clarke, with whom he discussed books and the theater on visits back to Enfield. The lonely tedium of the apprenticeship and the lively intellectual camaraderie with Clarke would prove to be a conjuncture crucial to Keats's future. Prominent among the writers Keats and Clarke discussed stood the Elizabethan poet Edmund Spenser. When Clarke read aloud Spenser's *Epithalamion* to him one day in 1813, Keats borrowed his first book from Clarke's library: Spenser's *The Faerie Queen*. After devouring this book, Keats returned with what Clarke later described as scintillating commentary on certain of its passages. The event can be taken to mark Keats's in-auguration into the world of poetry: he soon composed his "Imitation of Spenser," which still appears first in chronologically ordered collections of his poetry. And he later wrote a generous verse epistle to Clarke to thank him for his support.

Not least of Clarke's interventions was his introduction of Keats to Leigh Hunt, the editor of the *Examiner*, a fashionable London poet, and a notorious opponent of Tory policies. Hunt became his new support and the ex-clusive publisher of Keats's earliest poems. The first of Keats's letters that survive, fittingly, is a note of October 1816 to Cowden Clarke expressing his delight at the pros-pect of being introduced to Leigh Hunt, one that pre-dicted, accurately, that this meeting would be "an era in my existence." Hunt promoted Keats's work among the many literati he numbered his friends. He hosted Keats at his place in Hampstead, exposed him to his library, his informal salon, and his Italianate tastes in literature and art. Keats's early poetic manifesto, "Sleep and Poetry," was written in Hunt's study, and he invoked the room's books and objects in the course of the poem's aesthetic rumi-nations. Hunt not only helped to persuade his friend Charles Ollier to publish Keats's first volume of poems in 1817; he also published favorable commentary to help win them an audience. Without Hunt's cultivation, it is unlikely that Keats would have made the career decisions he did in these crucial years. For after Keats had had enough of the apprenticeship to Hammond, he elected to pursue his medical studies at Guy's Hospital in South-wark, where he matriculated with other surgeons' pupils in October 1815. By early 1817, however, flushed with his new appetites for the world that Hunt opened up to him,

Keats had decided to try to make a go of it as a writer—indeed as a poet.

Thus began Keats's internal struggle with the question of poetic success. William Wordsworth, who supplied the gold standard in contemporary poetry for Keats, had broached just this question in his own prose writings of 1815, this after the tepid reception of his epic poem, *The Excursion*, which Keats considered one of the three cul-tural wonders of the age. Wordsworth's central claim is that no great and original poet could also enjoy popular success in his own lifetime. Keats seems to have been both more vexed about this question than Wordsworth and more ambivalent. Keats knew that the best-selling poets of his time such as Byron, Thomas Campbell, Thomas Moore, and Walter Scott could all make a living from their poetry—not that all of them actually depended on it. He would later express resentment about the popular and financial success of such poets. At the same time, there was a part of Keats that aspired to reach beyond such vulgar considerations and that indeed anticipated the modern opposition of artist and society that would later find a more explicit articulation in the early Alfred, Lord Tennyson, in Charles Baudelaire, and in William Butler Yeats. These tensions would leave their mark on the poetry itself—even, or especially, on the best of it.

None of these "events" in Keats's life is of earth-shaking significance, of course, and one further aspect of the modesty of Keats's life is the limited extent of his travels. At the time Keats committed himself to a life in poetry, he had scarcely ventured beyond London and its environs. Even through 1819, his last and most productive year of writing, he had stepped foot off the island of Great Britain only for a short stay on the Isle of Wight and (during his ten-day walking tour of Scotland with Charles Brown in 1818) for a couple of days in Northern Ireland. The Scottish tour was in fact the only time he traveled beyond England until his move to Rome in 1820. He did occasionally seek a change from the London-Hampstead scene, however, sometimes for holiday, sometimes for work. He spent significant periods in Margate, Oxford, Devon, and Winchester at various times between 1816 and early 1820.

Although Keats embarked on no grand tour, these ex-cursions had their own importance for his evolving poetic career. For one thing, they prompted him to send letters back to friends and family in London, and thus to add to the remarkable body of correspondence that records his steep learning curve in these years. Keats used the familiar letter as a kind of laboratory for thinking and feeling his way through various problems of life and poetry. His were not primarily views worked out in public forms, such as the pamphlet, the essay, or the speech. Indeed, although Keats numbered a few writers of renown among his acquaintances, he explored his most deeply felt issues most freely with friends and relations whose names we now know precisely because they were his correspondents: Benjamin Bailey, John Hamilton Reynolds, Richard Woodhouse, Charles Brown, Joseph Severn, Fanny Brawne, and of course George, Tom, and Fanny Keats.

DEVELOPING IDEAS AND OPINIONS

It can truly be said that the familiar letter was the perfect vehicle for Keats's reflections on his life and work, though it may be equally true that the fact that he produced these reflections in epistolary contexts helped to shape his ideas in the first place. He was not, at all events, a systematic thinker. The doctrine with which his name is perhaps most famously associated is what he called "*Negative Capability*, that is when a man is capable of being in uncertainties, Mysteries, doubts, without any irritable reaching after fact & reason," as he wrote in a December 1817 letter to his brothers. The letters tend to keep faith with this non-principle. One of the other paradoxes of Keats's body of letters is that, while they chart a trajectory of steep intellectual growth, there is also a strange consistency about them from the first. Not that there is always an immediate translation of the letters into the poetry—admirers of the great poems of 1819 can be surprised to find that letters that seem to provide the most apposite commentaries on these texts were written much earlier.

Some of Keats's earliest ideas have to do with the critique of orthodox religion in favor of his own distinctive form of sentimental aesthetics. Benjamin Bailey, a divinity student at Cambridge, and later a parson, was a correspondent who early on brought out Keats's views on this head. In November 1817, Keats wrote to Bailey that he sought "a recourse somewhat human independent of the great consolations of religion." Later that same month, Keats returned to this theme with Bailey, announcing the extent of his skepticism: "I am certain of nothing but the holiness of the Heart's affections and the truth of imagination." In this same letter he also sounds a theme that would likewise be sustained over months and years, finding its poetic articulation in such mature works as "The Eve of St. Agnes," "Lamia," and the Great Odes. That theme: "What the imagination seizes as beauty must be truth." In this letter, too, he offers his famous speculation

on the afterlife, "that we shall enjoy ourselves here after by having what we called happiness on Earth repeated in a finer tone." All this was written for Bailey the divinity student. But on this very same day—his intuitions always seemed to come in bursts—Keats likewise wrote to John Hamilton Reynolds, a fellow poet, with a more technical observation about poetics that would also come to shape much that he later thought and wrote. Keats reports having just read through a volume of Shakespeare's poems with a new insight into what makes them so extraordinary: "I neer found so many beauties in the sonnets—they seem to be full of fine things said unintentionally—in the intensity of working out conceits."

In the conjunction of these two letters—one emphasizing the role of the "heart" in materialist poetry and the other emphasizing the technical aspects of Keats's Shakespearean literary ideal—we find the basic elements of what is perhaps his central aesthetic challenge in this period of his poetic apprenticeship. It was a challenge Keats carried on in his engagement with many authors, many of them his contemporaries, and some of these contemporaries members of his circle of acquaintance. With Percy Shelley, for example, Keats shared (as he did with Hunt) a skepticism about organized religion and a belief that poetry could play a liberating role in English society. But he thought Shelley's own poetry deficient in those virtues he praised in Shakespeare. Shelley needed, Keats told him in reference to one of his compositions, "to 'load every rift' of your subject with ore." With Wordsworth, Keats shared a view of the holiness of the imagination, a respect for the philosophic blank verse of John Milton, and a distrust of the general public. But, like many writers of his generation, Keats came to see Wordsworth as a renegade to his earlier political and religious views, a poet too dependent on "thought" as opposed to "sensation," and, in the end, an egotist. Keats's famous exclamation—"O for a life of sensation rather than of thoughts"—seems to be partly aimed at Wordsworth.

With the critic William Hazlitt, whose London lectures he attended in 1818 and 1819, Keats probably shared as much as it was possible for him to share with anyone who was not a poet. Keats had long maintained that the true poet has no identity per se but must always have the capacity to enter sympathetically into all other identities. He found this contention corroborated in Hazlitt's praise of Shakespeare's dramatic imagination. And likewise he probably had help from Hazlitt in framing his still-influential distinction between Shakespeare as the "camelion [sic] poet" and the antithetical posture of the Miltonic-Wordsworthian "egotistical sublime."

None of this reading and thinking was enough by itself to enable Keats to solve the great problems posed in his letters to Bailey and Reynolds in 1817. What he sought was a new spontaneity that could also be grounded in material life. This grounding in material life, in "sensations" scientifically understood, had to resist the Wordsworthian reflection—the kind of "habits of meditation" that turned feelings into thoughts (the representations of our past feelings). By contrast, Keats's broad sensations had to be established not in reflection but in the indirect intensity of poetic elaboration. The story of how Keats negotiated this problem is a complicated one, and probably unfinished. It seems worth noting, though, how many of the poems Keats wrote before 1819 are composed in highly conventional verse forms. Of the more than two hundred poems, fully sixty are sonnets (in both the Italian and English varieties). And most of the verse he composed for longer poems before 1819—"Sleep and Poetry," "I Stood Tip-Toe on a Little Hill," and of course the four-thousand-line *Endymion*—were written in heroic couplets, the iambic pentameter rhyming verse pairs favored by Augustan poets such as Alexander Pope. It is quite true that Keats attempted to vary syntax and rhythm in his instantiation of the couplet verse form (although a remarkably high proportion of his lines are in fact end-stopped). It is also true that within the sonnet form he attempted to follow Shakespeare's example in achieving intensity by indirection; one thinks of promising early exercises in sonnets in which he himself is registering the experience of intensity, such as "On First Looking into Chapman's Homer." Yet the task of intentionally producing unintentional effects, central though this task might be for Romantic poetics generally, is not a small challenge.

THE SPRING OF 1819

One of Keats's breakthrough poems in 1819, "The Eve of St. Agnes," interestingly marks his return to the very first verse form in which he was struck by indirect intensity as a reader, and in which he first composed as a poet: the rhymed, eight-line Spenserian stanza. Occasioned by a chilly January encounter with the medieval monumentality of Stansted Abbey, and written under the double emotional charge of the recent death of his brother Tom and the first flush of his love affair with his Hampstead neighbor Fanny Brawne, it combines the associationist logic of the loco-descriptive poem with the license of eroticized romance. Like *Romeo and Juliet*, whose plot elements and complex conceits it self-consciously borrows, it hovers between the sacred and the profane, the reverent and the ribald, troubadour poetry and gothic fiction: one scene of voyeurism actually seems to come straight from Matthew Lewis's gothic romance *The Monk* (1796). In the intensity of its sensuous language, the liberties it takes with religion and sex, the poem manages to be a kind of wonder without quite achieving a full aesthetic success. And of course it remains in the Spenserian verse form.

After "St Agnes," there was almost nothing for three months, one of Keats's longest ever poetic droughts. He was living with Charles Brown in the house at Wentworth Place in Hampstead (now a shrine to his memory). He was troubled by the turn of events with Fanny Brawne, anxious about his career, and concerned about his health. Since he was medically trained, he may well have recognized early symptoms of the tuberculosis that would soon cause his death. He was also worried about his brother George and George's young bride, Georgiana, who had gone off to the wilds of Illinois some months before and had experienced serious hardship there. He was adding entries to a long journal letter for them in these weeks, and in these entries he was vicariously exploring the world abroad. He was not, however, writing much else.

Then, in April, things began to converge for the better. The weather improved, for example, and Keats's health along with it. He even tried his hand at cricket on the nineteenth. That week Keats had a chance encounter with the great Samuel Taylor Coleridge on a walk along Hampstead Heath, with stimulating conversation about many topics, including nightingales, dreams, and the nature of poetic sensation. Keats undertook some experimental exercises, including a sonnet on the sonnet, which seems to have returned his attention to his poetic craft in new and interesting ways. The great experimental ballad "La Belle Dame Sans Merci" emerges on the twenty-first, a poem that would set the template for the nineteenth-century art poetry of Tennyson and the Pre-Raphaelites. And then there was a long entry in a letter (14 February–3 May 1819) to George and Georgiana in America in which Keats explored the idea of imagining the experience of a suffering world not as a vale of tears but as a "vale of soul-making." This was a mature and sober revisiting of the spiritual themes Keats had sounded in November 1817. Out of this confluence of conditions came an extraordinary five-month period of productivity, and more immediately, an astounding month of work (from the end

186

of April to the end of May), in which Keats produced, among other things, five of his six great odes.

Keats himself registered the sense of a new level of achievement in the very first of these poems, the "Ode to Psyche," which most immediately picked up on the theme of "soul-making." Transcribing it (as he had done with "La Belle Dame") in his journal letter to George and Georgiana, he explained that it was "the first and only one [of his poems] with which I have taken even moderate pains." It seems that taking pains with a poem was for Keats a mark of how to take pain into a poem. Certainly the encounter with pain—with ache, loss, and sorrow—would now be a constitutive part of "poetic intensity" and a key in the search for non-Christian forms of consolation. The "Ode to Psyche"—perhaps the closest Keats ever came to writing a poetic manifesto—celebrates its titular goddess as the crucial figure in the untraveled course of religious modernity, a deity conceived "too late for the fond-believing lyre" of the more ancient world order of the Greeks and earlier Romans. Keats's source was Apuleius's first-century story of the eventual apotheosis of the all-too-human woman who was punished for her failure to heed the prohibition against gazing on Cupid, the divine lover who visited her by night and left her to wonder about his identity by day. Keats saw in this myth of the human made divine a salutary alternative to the morbid story of Christ (almost perfectly contemporary with that of Psyche) that had displaced Psyche's influence for the subsequent history of the West. In the central conceit of the poem, Keats offers himself as priest and prophet of a neomodern cult of Psyche's devotees, avatar of an aesthetic rite composed of and by the experience of poetic sensations that derive from the poem's elaboration of just these conceits.

In the "Ode to Psyche," Keats's long-standing project to think and feel his way toward a solution to the great challenges he set himself in 1817 was now bearing major fruit. Part of the reason for his success, one might speculate, has to do with his new interest in formal experimentation beyond the limits of the largely conventional verse designs with which he had been working. While the ode was a genre that goes back to the time of Pindar, its verse form was not a settled question. In the spring of 1819, Keats put his now-intuitive command of the sonnet form in the service of new kinds of stanzaic structure for his odes, a structure made from transformed and transposed pieces of both the Italian and the English traditions. It is as if, in having to address these formidable formal challenges, Keats managed precisely the kind of indirect intensity that he had praised in Shakespeare.

Whatever the explanation, it is undeniable that Keats followed "Psyche" with a most impressive series of odes, a series that features a pairing of poems that are as much studied, and as much admired, as any poems in the English language: "Ode to a Nightingale" and "Ode on a Grecian Urn." Not surprisingly, these profoundly meditative lyrics feature more questions than answers. They reflect Keats's wariness about poetry that has "a palpable design on us." They are in this sense not didactic, but at the same time they are not without a sense of aesthetic design. Indeed, the two poems taken together make a pair of studies that address the human senses by way, respectively, of the ear and the eye.

In "Nightingale," the poem's speaker attends to the song of the unseen bird—heard one morning by Keats in his Hampstead garden—to the exclusion of all other sensory impressions. The discipline of the poem then extends to the conjuring, by imaginative surmise and poetic invention, of a world synesthetically composed around the absence of vision: "I cannot see what flowers are at my feet, / Nor what soft incense hangs upon the boughs, / But, in embalmed darkness, guess . . ." Conversely, the poet-speaker of the "Grecian Urn" focuses on an exquisite visual object that he initially locates in a world of utter silence. The task in this poem is to conjure up a synesthetic world around the absence of sound—to find a way to tell the tale of the urn, to sing its song, recite the "leaf-fring'd legend" that haunts about its shape. Both poems load every rift with ore, employing the poet's full array of resources to generate poetic sensation. Yet at the same time, and crucially, both seem to acknowledge the limits of this endeavor. Each imaginative reverie leads the poet-speaker to a moment or a place where some suppressed pain or anxiety is allowed to return the poet from his sensations, as it were, to his senses.

MORTAL THOUGHTS

It has been suggested that the odes and the other lyrics of the spring of 1819—"Bright Star," for example—signal a new phase in Keats's humanism. This shows in the development of his longer poems as well. Ever since he embarked on *Endymion* in early 1817, Keats had been haunted by the idea that to make his mark as a poet he had to succeed with the long form. The romantic and sentimental excesses of *Endymion* had given way, even before it was published, to the Miltonic abstract austerity of *Hyperion*, a poem about how the tyranny of Saturn and Old Night gave way to the enlightened regime of Apollo. Now, in the months after his great spring odes, Keats would reframe his still-unfulfilled plan for the epic by way of a complicated dream vision that would serve as its prelude: *The Fall of Hyperion*. Keats employed the meditative periods and rhythms of a highly enjambed blank-verse style to launch his most searching account to date of the responsibilities of the modern poet. The poet-speaker approaches the altar of the goddess Moneta in the midst of a postlapsarian garden, amid scraps of a feast of summer fruits, "the refuse of a meal / By angel tasted, or our mother Eve." As he tries to ascend the steps of the altar, he is confronted and interrogated by the goddess, who accuses him of belonging to the tribe of dreamers, not that of poets: "What benefit canst thou do, or all thy tribe, / To the great world?" It was a profound question that Keats now made central to his mission as a poet. He would not stay healthy long enough to find an answer to it, however, and the *Fall of Hyperion*, too, remained but a fragment.

Happily, while at work on the *Fall*, in September 1819, Keats did undertake a seasonal ode that would form a complement to the great odes of the spring. It would indeed come to be treasured with the best of them. Keats was living in Winchester at this period, while great events were astir in town. In mid-September he went to London to negotiate with the Dickensian trustee Richard Abbey, on behalf of his brother George, whose financial troubles in America were aggravated by a bad deal struck with the naturalist John James Audubon. Keats's path that day happened to take him along the route prepared for "Orator" Henry Hunt, who was returning to London to stand trial for his part in the great public demonstration in Manchester where workers and their families were killed and maimed the month before, the so-called Peterloo Massacre. Hunt would be cheered by a crowd estimated in the many tens of thousands, almost certainly already assembled by the time that Keats passed along the parade route earlier that day.

After returning to the quiet of Winchester, Keats spent the ensuing Saturday writing to the George Keatses about the history of England's progress toward liberty and the current state of religion and politics in the nation. On Sunday morning he awoke and took a walk past Winchester Cathedral and into the picturesque sallows of the River Itchen. When he returned that day he composed the poem that is probably his best effort to provide a balm for a world that needed consolation in the face of death.

It would be a redemptive poem that, as he put it in April, would not offend against our reason and humanity. Often called the most perfect poem in English, "To Autumn" goes as far as can be imagined toward realizing its impossibly high goals.

The thought of his own death would weigh more heavily on Keats's mind in the coming weeks and months. Back in Hampstead in October, he would briefly contemplate a career in journalism "on the liberal side of the question." This was in part a response to his increasing financial straits, which had worsened with the failure of the play he wrote with Charles Brown that summer to gain production support. By the end of the year he was showing new signs of deteriorating health. On February 3 he made an ill-advised trip to London without his greatcoat and suffered his first severe hemorrhage. The second hemorrhage came a few months later. Before the end of 1820 he had moved to Rome, where he was nursed in his final months by his friend Joseph Severn in a house overlooking the Spanish Steps—the house is now a small museum of his life and work. He died there 23 February 1821 and was buried in the Protestant cemetery at Rome three days later.

A body of work so impressive completed before the poet's twenty-sixth birthday—indeed, almost all of it before his twenty-fourth birthday—raises questions about what Keats might have done if he had lived. Such questions will go on being debated as long as Keats is read. The question of whether he would have done so much without a sense of the urgency about his remaining time is perhaps the more significant one. Given his family history, his medical knowledge, and his curious realism about such things, it seems a mistake to see the remarkable intensity his work of 1819 as unconditioned by a perception of impending doom. What is not a matter of debate is Keats's impressive legacy in English and English-language poetry—in Tennyson, Yeats, Elizabeth Barrett Browning, Thomas Hardy, William Carlos Williams, Wallace Stevens, and many other writers. He managed to find a place not only "among the English Poets," as he once confessed he hoped to do, but among the great lyricists of the modern world.

[*See also* George Gordon, Lord Byron; John Clare; Samuel Taylor Coleridge; William Hazlitt; Leigh Hunt; Romanticism; Percy Bysshe Shelley; Edmund Spenser; Alfred, Lord Tennyson; *and* William Wordsworth.]

MAJOR EDITIONS

The Letters of John Keats 1814–1821. 2 vols. Edited by Hyder E. Rollins. Cambridge, MA, 1958.

The Poems of John Keats. Edited by Jack Stillinger. Cambridge, MA, 1978.

FURTHER READING

Bate, Walter Jackson. *John Keats.* Cambridge, MA, 1963. This biography includes detailed commentary on the formal innovations Keats made within the English poetic tradition.

Butler, Marilyn. *Romantics, Rebels, and Reactionaries: English Literature and Its Background.* New York, 1981. Helpfully places Keats among the Romantic writers who constitute the "cult of the South" and directs attention to Romanticism's neoclassical directions.

Chandler, James K. *England in 1819: The Politics of Literary Culture and the Case of Romantic Historicism.* Chicago, 1998. Extended discussions of Keats's relation to Romantic conceptions of history and of the importance for Keats of his brother's move to America.

Gittings, Robert. *John Keats.* Boston, 1968. An incisive biography that, like Gittings's other work on Keats, is especially good in addressing Keats's "living year."

Levinson, Marjorie. *Keats's Life of Allegory: The Origins of a Style.* New York, 1988. A theoretically informed critical study that takes as its starting point Byron's disparaging remarks about Keats's poetry as dandified and onanistic.

McGann, Jerome J. *The Beauty of Inflections: Literary Investigations in Historical Method and Theory.* New York, 1985. Includes an important long essay on Keats and "historical method" that analytically traces the production and reception histories of some key poems.

Motion, Andrew. *Keats.* New York, 1998. A readable biography of Keats by a practicing poet with genuine enthusiasm for his subject.

Roe, Nicholas. *John Keats and the Culture of Dissent.* New York, 1997. Places Keats's thought and writing in the context of dissenting religious writers to clarify the poet's own political commitments.

Sperry, Stuart M. *Keats the Poet.* Princeton, NJ, 1973. Includes a revealing discussion of how Keats's apprenticeship as an apothecary shaped some of his most central notions about poetry and poetics.

Ward, Aileen. *John Keats: The Making of a Poet.* New York, 1963. Perhaps the most politically astute of the biographers of Keats.

Vendler, Helen. *The Odes of John Keats.* Cambridge, MA, 1983. An impressively sensitive reading of the Great Odes both as single poems and as a coherent constellation of work.

JAMES KELMAN

Willy Maley

James Kelman, the leading figure in the literary resurgence of the 1980s known as the "Glasgow renaissance," has put the Scottish city on the world map of literature by producing novels, short stories, essays, and plays in a language bristling with angry intelligence, creating a compelling voice utterly anchored in his hometown, yet richly resonant for readers worldwide.

Oppressed individuals, usually messed-up men, are his subject matter, handled in a language best described as "page rage." One character in a Kelman story asks another if he's still writing "wee stories with a working-class theme." Kelman writes big stories with a big theme: individuals up against authority. "Kelmanesque" has become a byword for a new "social surrealism," gritty renditions of post-industrial working-class life, particularly as experienced by lone—and lonesome—males who "lose the plot" and are prone to furious flights of fancy.

None of the terms applied to Kelman's back-to-the-wall style—"demotic," "dialect," "idiom," "slang," "swearing," or "vernacular"—do justice to his explosive prose and his refusal to draw a distinction between the language of narrative and the language of dialogue. The first Scottish writer to take the "God voice" and make it Glaswegian, by capturing the rhythms of speech he has made poetry of what had before been characterized as "inarticulate." With his ear to the ground—some would say the gutter—Kelman captures the tenderness of tough-talking dissidents, drifters, down-and-outs, and dudes. Kelman took Glaswegian, a low-prestige "accent" of English, and turned it into one of the most forceful and fluent literary languages of the twentieth century. Kelman has waged war on genre and popular fodder fiction as well as the privileged literary canon. In its place he offers serious engagement with real people and real issues, but it is a realism riddled with absurdist humor and surrealist politics.

Kelman's language extends beyond accent and expletives. From at least the time of his novel *The Busconductor Hines* (1984) he has been experimenting with new kinds of narrative voice. Kelman has been described as a late modernist but has also been seen as part of a wave of new literatures in English that would place him alongside writers like Chinua Achebe. Kelman's existential angst led one critic to call him a "Glasgow Hamlet." His native resistance prompted another to speak of "the rage of Caliban." Both are right. In his fundamental questioning of the nature of "being" and "representation," of speaking for oneself versus being spoken for, and in his rigorous examination of the motives and meanings of tortured individuals, Kelman resembles the dark prince, watching over the battlements, or tenements, of Glasgow. In his tireless campaigning for the human dignity of the oppressed, and relentless berating of those whose authority usurps his rightful place on this earth, he conjures up Caliban: "You taught me language, and my profit on't is, I know how to curse." Cursing in the language of the master, while showing a stronger grasp of human thoughts and actions than those in authority, sums up Kelman. Credited with opening doors to a succession of new Scottish authors, including Janice Galloway, Alison Kennedy, Alan Warner, and Irvine Welsh, he is both an experimental writer of tremendous patience and craft and a postcolonial polemicist who combines the streetwise delivery of a rapper with the absolute authority of an Old Testament prophet.

BEGINNINGS

Born in Glasgow on 9 June 1946, Kelman left school at fifteen and served two years of a six-year apprenticeship as a compositor. He says of this experience that "the way words look on the page has been important to me ever since." He left the printing trade to follow his family to the United States, an effort at emigration that proved successful only for his older brother. His father, a picture framer, worked for a time in a gallery in Pasadena, California, but the American experiment never worked out and the family, minus the older brother, returned to Scotland. In 1971 Kelman became part of the Glasgow group of writers mentored by Philip Hobsbaum that included

Alasdair Gray, Tom Leonard, and Liz Lochhead. He studied philosophy and English at Strathclyde University, developing an admiration for Noam Chomsky. Associated with the development of a distinctive Glasgow voice and vision, Kelman's intense, unsentimental imaginings of that city bear comparison with James Joyce's dour depictions in *Dubliners* (1916), and his work has also drawn comparisons with writers such as Samuel Beckett, Albert Camus, Anton Chekhov, Fyodor Dostoevsky, Nikolay Gogol, Franz Kafka, and Émile Zola. European realist, modernist, and existentialist traditions inspired Kelman, but so too did the American culture he experienced in his youth, including the Westerns of Louis L'Amour, the novels of Nelson Algren and Jack Kerouac, and the music of the blues. Kelman was first published in the United States, and he received his first major academic appointment there as a professor at the University of Texas, Austin (2000–2001). *You Have to Be Careful in the Land of the Free* (2004), his first all-American novel, is the fruit of a forty-year personal and thirty-year publishing connection with the United States.

Kelman's career as a short story writer started in 1973 with an American publication, *An Old Pub near the Angel*, by the Maine-based Puckerbrush Press, with payment in the form of two hundred copies. This was followed by *Three Glasgow Writers* (1976, with Alex Hamilton and Tom Leonard) and *Short Tales from the Nightshift* (1978). His breakthrough came with *Not Not while the Giro* (1983), a collection that established Kelman as a voice of distinction. *Lean Tales* (1985, with Alasdair Gray and Agnes Owens) consolidated that position, but it was the award-winning volume *Greyhound for Breakfast* (1987), winner of the Cheltenham Prize, that sealed Kelman's reputation. By then he had published his first novel, but he remained resolute in his commitment to the short form, publishing two major collections over the next ten years—*The Burn* (1991), winner of the Scottish Arts Council Book Award, and *The Good Times* (1998), a collection consisting entirely of monologues, which won both the *Scotland on Sunday*/Glenfiddich Spirit of Scotland Award and the Stakis Prize for Scottish Writer of the Year. The collection *Busted Scotch* (1997) was published in the United States on the back of the success of *How Late It Was, How Late* (1994), which won the Booker Prize for fiction, Britain's top literary award, as well as the Writers' Guild Award for best fiction. *Selected Stories* appeared in 2001. Kelman's work includes a number of very short stories in a form sometimes called flash fiction, micro-

fiction, or sudden fiction, ranging from a paragraph to a couple of pages.

NOVELS

Kelman has published six novels. Most can be described as a week in the life of a working-class man going through a crisis brought on by a clash with the authorities. His first, *The Busconductor Hines*, is the story of Rab Hines, a ticket collector on Glasgow's public transport system at a moment when conversion to driver-only buses is making the job a redundant occupation. Hines has aspirations to social mobility that would mean becoming a driver, but he also has "issues" that make the transition a problem. Kelman had himself worked as a bus conductor in Glasgow—while reading Camus—and the novel is shot through with the authenticity of a dying breed. Kelman's second novel, *A Chancer* (1985), is the story of a gambling man, or rather a betting boy, young Tammas, told in a pared, third-person style.

A Disaffection (1989), about a week in the life of a schoolteacher, won the James Tait Black Memorial Prize for fiction and was short-listed for the Booker Prize. Here, the main character is Patrick Doyle, a working-class teacher at odds with his profession. His period of upward mobility ends in unemployment but not before he has given his bosses and colleagues a piece of his mind. Doyle is typical of Kelman's antiheroes, alienated, frustrated, and denied—or denying—the possibility of social or communal action. A recurring feature of Kelman's fiction is individual characters coming up against the powers that be, their struggle always a solitary one.

How Late It Was, How Late (1994), the story of Sammy Samuels, eyeless in Glasgow after being blinded by a police assault, won the Booker Prize and has been compared to *Samson Agonistes* in its epic anger against authority. Kelman insisted that the book was about "welfare," but it was also about class warfare, the warfare waged by the authorities on the poor, the voiceless, and the unseen. Controversy surrounded the award. One of the Booker judges, Rabbi Julia Neuberger, questioned whether the novel counted as "literature." Some British members of Parliament wanted the book banned. Sections of the press spent time counting occurrences of the word "fuck" (four thousand). Kelman's acceptance speech was a powerful defense of the right to self-expression, as well as a blistering attack on censorship and elitism: "My culture and my language have a right to exist, and no one has the authority to dismiss that right."

Translated Accounts (2001) combines the invention of Kelman's creative prose with the machine-stitched precision of his critical essays. Only a writer schooled in Ludwig Wittgenstein and Chomsky and steeped in the politics of repression and resistance could have produced such an unsettling account of a totalitarian state and its victims. *Translated Accounts* is a challenging work, but one bearing the characteristic strengths of Kelman's craft: sparseness, stark description, and defiant dignity in desperate circumstances. It also demonstrates the way in which, for Kelman, self-expression and existence are intimately bound up: challenge one and you challenge the other. The novel appeared to mark a radical departure from the manic monologues of *Hines* and *How Late*; it comprises fifty-four pieces by a handful or more individuals under interrogation by officialdom. Their experiences of disappearance, murder, rape, and torture, recounted in a language stripped of emotion in an English as broken as the victims of the regime, make for a disturbing book, but no less so than the earlier tale of a man blinded by police brutality, though it lacks the dark humor of *How Late*.

You Have to Be Careful in the Land of the Free (2004) is the story of a Scottish immigrant, Jeremiah Brown, trying to get back to "Skallin" from "Uhmerka" (Rapid City, South Dakota, to be precise). The Kafkaesque America that Jeremiah inhabits is riddled with post–September 11 paranoia, a police state suspicious of aliens with strange accents like his. But Kelman's novelistic jeremiad suggests that paranoia, racism, and surveillance follow any grand act of "terror." Although he has changed gear and shifted ground in his novels, close followers of Kelman see a clear thread running from Rab Hines's clashes with authority on the buses through Sammy Samuels's blind battling with bureaucracy in *How Late* to Jerry Brown's railing against the state in *You Have to Be Careful in the Land of the Free* (2004). Sammy Samuels disappears "out of sight" at his story's end. Disappearances haunt the ghostly characters of *Translated Accounts*. Jerry, in *You Have to Be Careful*, says: "Everybody vanishes, that is what life is, unresolved business." Kelman's writing makes the unseen visible by getting up close and political with characters overlooked by mainstream fiction.

DRAMA AND ESSAYS

Kelman is less familiar to international audiences as a playwright, but his plays have been performed to capacity audiences, and he has written for radio, stage, and screen.

The historical prison drama *Hardie and Baird: The Last Days* (1991), the story of two nineteenth-century Scottish weavers condemned by the British state, is political theater with a strong philosophical basis, staging a discussion around activism and change.

Kelman's career as a critic and public speaker is central to his identity as a politically committed writer. For Kelman, "good art is about dissent." Kelman has been involved in a series of public campaigns, illustrative of his belief in the role of the artist as being one of commitment, intervention, opposition, and engagement. Two collections of his essays bear witness to his seriousness of mind. *Some Recent Attacks* (1992) deals with questions of literary censorship and elitism as well as with local political struggles. "And the Judges Said . . ." (2002) is a much more formidable collection of criticism with a thirty-thousand-word essay on Kafka at its heart.

Kelman's writing has been called "prison literature," in which the smallest act or gesture is viewed through the eyes of a man caught, condemned, and confined. It has also been seen as "protest literature," a literature of campaign, commitment, and complaint. Patrick Doyle, in *A Disaffection*, says of his students, "making them angry's a start." Kelman makes his readers livid. He also makes them laugh out loud.

[*See also* Postcolonial Literature.]

SELECTED WORKS

NOVELS

The Busconductor Hines (1984)
A Chancer (1985)
A Disaffection (1989)
How Late It Was, How Late (1994)
Translated Accounts (2001)
You Have to Be Careful in the Land of the Free (2004)

PLAYS

Hardie and Baird, and Other Plays (1991; includes *The Busker*, *In the Night*, and *Hardie and Baird*)
The Return (1991)
One, Two—Hey! (1994)

SHORT STORIES

An Old Pub near the Angel (1973)
Three Glasgow Writers (1976, with Alex Hamilton and Tom Leonard)
Short Tales from the Nightshift (1978)
Not Not while the Giro (1983)

Lean Tales (1985, with Alasdair Gray and Agnes Owens)
Greyhound for Breakfast (1987)
The Burn (1991)
Busted Scotch (1997)
Seven Stories (audio cassette, 1997)
The Good Times (1998)
Selected Stories (2001)
The Close Season (2002, with Ken Grant)

ESSAYS AND CRITICISM

Fighting for Survival: The Steel Industry in Scotland (1990)
Some Recent Attacks: Essays Cultural and Political (1992)
Tantalising Twinkles: Some Thoughts on a First Order Radical Thinker of European Standing (1997)
"And the Judges Said . . .": Essays (2002)

FURTHER READING

Baker, Simon. "'Wee Stories with a Working-Class Theme': The Reimagining of Urban Realism in the Fiction of James Kelman." In *Studies in Scottish Fiction: 1945 to Present*, edited by Susanne Hagemann, 235–250. New York and Frankfurt, 1996.

Bernstein, Stephen. "James Kelman." *Review of Contemporary Fiction* 20, no. 3 (2000): 42–80.

Bittenbender, J. Christopher. "Silence, Censorship, and the Voices of *Skaz* in the Fiction of James Kelman." *Bucknell Review* 43, no. 2 (Fall 1999): 150–165.

Böhnke, Dietmar. *Kelman Writes Back*. Cambridge, MA, 1999.

Chapman 57 (1989). Special issue of the journal devoted largely to Kelman.

Craig, Cairns. "Resisting Arrest: James Kelman." In *The Scottish Novel since the Seventies*, edited by Randall Stevenson and Gavin Wallace, 99–114. Edinburgh, 1993.

Jackson, Ellen-Raïssa, and Willy Maley, eds. *Kelman and Commitment*. Special issue of Edinburgh *Review* 108 (2001).

Kirk, John. "Figuring the Dispossessed: Images of the Urban Working Class in the Writing of James Kelman." *English* 48, no. 191 (1999): 44–63.

Maley, Willy. "Swearing Blind: Kelman and the Curse of the Working Classes." *Edinburgh Review* 95 (1996): 105–112

McGlynn, Mary. "'Middle-Class Wankers' and Working-Class Texts: The Critics and James Kelman." *Contemporary Literature* 43, no. 1 (2002): 50–84.

McLean, Duncan. "James Kelman Interviewed." *Edinburgh Review* 71 (1985): 64–80.

Milne, Drew. "The Fiction of James Kelman and Irvine Welsh: Accents, Speech and Writing." In *Contemporary British Fiction*, edited by Richard J. Lane, Rod Mengham, and Philip Tew, 158–173. Cambridge, U.K., 2003.

Milne, Drew. "James Kelman: Dialectics of Urbanity." In *Writing Region and Nation: Proceedings of the Fourth International Conference on the Literature of Region and Nation, Swansea 1992*. Swansea, Wales, 1994. Special issue of the *Swansea Review*; see pp. 393–407.

Pitchford, Nicola. "How Late It Was for England: James Kelman's Scottish Booker Prize." *Contemporary Literature* 41, no. 4 (2000): 150–165.

Zagratzki, Uwe. "'Blues Fell This Morning': James Kelman's Scottish Literature and Afro-American Music." *Scottish Literary Journal* 27, no. 1 (2000): 105–117.

MARGERY KEMPE

Sarah Salih

The *Book of Margery Kempe* is an oddity, and many of its readers have concluded that its author and protagonist was one, also. Probably written in 1436–1438, it narrates the life of Margery Kempe of Lynn, the daughter and wife of prosperous Norfolk merchants, mother of fourteen, who one night leapt from the marital bed crying out that it was "full merry in heaven" and thereafter enacted her love of God through a program of ascetic exercises, visions, and travel. Very little additional information supplements the *Book*'s representation of Margery Kempe, the historical figure. There is a single record of the admittance of a woman of that name to Lynn's Trinity Guild in 1438, and brief extracts from the *Book* were printed in 1501 and 1521, attributed to "Margery Kempe of Lynn," with the later edition adding the unreliable detail that she was "a devout anchoress" (female recluse).

The *Book*'s Proem describes how it came to be written. Although often urged to record her visions, Margery waited for more than twenty years until she felt she had a divine command to do so. Unable to write herself, she dictated the bulk of the book to a layman, perhaps her own son, who died before it could be completed; she then turned to a priest, who after several false starts transcribed, rewrote, and finished it. The relative claims to authorship of Margery and of the scribes, and the extent to which their contributions can be distinguished, have been much debated. The *Book* is often described as the first autobiography in English, but this categorization, although not inaccurate, obscures its mixture of genres. Readers of modern autobiography may be surprised or alienated by techniques such as the third-person narrative, which refers to Margery throughout as "the creature." The *Book* is in part an autohagiography or self-written saint's life, a rare and inherently unstable genre, with added elements of mystical treatise and devotional guide: Margery or her scribes, or all of them, may have intended it as a bid for her canonization as a saint after her death. Such a document would be characterized by two slightly contradictory imperatives: to prove that Margery conformed to accepted models of holy life, and to

establish the historical truth of any miraculous events or signs of divine favor that occurred in her vicinity. Hence the *Book* includes both the concrete details of Margery's life and a continuous interpretive commentary on it. For example, the *Book* proclaims that when a piece of masonry fell on her from the church vault as she prayed, her escape unscathed was miraculous; it records the weight of the offending object, three pounds of stone and six of wood. Although only a minority of modern critics read the *Book* as if it were wholly fictitious, it undoubtedly models its protagonist and her narrative on textual exemplars, freely omitting materials—such as Margery's household responsibilities or her relations with her children—that do not contribute to a picture of her spiritual development. The form of hagiography, however, fits imperfectly with the life story of a living person. The narrative covers Margery's life between the ages of twenty and sixty-five in a roughly chronological structure, but it differs from its hagiographic models by omitting her childhood and that staple element of saints' lives, a pious death scene.

Margery was born and lived in Bishop's Lynn, now King's Lynn, in Norfolk, then a prosperous port and the first place where new goods and ideas would arrive from northern Europe. The town's religious and commercial activities were interdependent: it displayed its wealth by building and furnishing grand churches and chapels, and its guilds were at once the town's government, its banks, and its religious fraternities. Margery's father, John Brunham, was among Lynn's richest and most influential merchants and served five terms as its mayor. Her husband, John Kempe, was also a member of Lynn's elite, but, as Margery reminded him, a less successful one. Margery evidently held property independently of her husband, for in the early years of their marriage she set up and ran first a brewery and then a mill, despite his opposition, and later was able to pay his debts in part exchange for his permitting her to make a vow of chastity. Even following her religious conversion, she retained mercantile habits of thought. Margery and many other figures in the

Book routinely measured spiritual experience in material terms, from the investment of "three or four pounds" in masses which she recommended to a widow to hurry her husband's soul through purgatory, to the more extravagant twenty pounds at which a cleric valued her gift of tears. In this milieu even Jesus spoke of heavenly merit as a commodity that could be invested and exchanged.

THE LIFE

The *Book*'s main narrative opens with Margery, married at twenty and soon pregnant, "as nature would have it," suffering so badly in childbirth that, fearing for her life, she sent for a priest so that she might confess a long-hidden sin. The priest's unsympathetic response left her unable to complete her confession, and fear of damnation drove her mad for approximately eight months. This madness opened up the supernatural realm: Margery saw devils threaten her with damnation, driving her to despair, to abuse her husband and family, and to harm herself so severely that she was restrained for her own safety. Her madness ended when, suddenly, Jesus appeared, "dressed in a mantle of purple silk, sitting on her bedside," and asked her, "Daughter, why have you forsaken me when I never forsook you?" She was instantly cured and able to take charge of her household keys. It is an arresting opening, introducing several themes—confession, marriage, demonic attacks, Margery's visionary abilities—that persist throughout the *Book*. It is at once a vividly persuasive and particularized narrative, and a morality tale that demonstrates the frailty of the human body and soul when unaided by divine mercy and the sacraments of the Church.

This tender encounter with Jesus in the privacy of the marital bedroom began a process of replacing familial relationships with spiritual ones. Margery considered herself to be the bride of Christ, a status often ascribed to nuns and holy women, and understood this to be a passionate relationship between individuals: Jesus told her, "Daughter, you greatly desire to see me, and you may boldly, when you are in your bed, take me to you as your wedded husband." He was almost continually available to her for advice, comfort, and affection. Commitment to this relationship required Margery to renegotiate the terms of her marriage to John Kempe. The next stage of her conversion was marked by a repulsion from sex with her husband, which she had previously enjoyed, and the conviction that it was displeasing to God. A low point of the marriage ensued, during which John refused Mar-

gery's request that they should desist from sex, and "used her as he had done before," as was his right under the church laws governing marriage. Several of their children must have been conceived in these conditions, and it was during this period that Jesus comforted Margery with the information that many, if not most, married women longed for widowhood. Eventually, perhaps when Margery was nearing the end of her childbearing years, John agreed to a vow of chastity. He asked in return that Margery should continue to share his bed, give up fasting on Fridays, and pay his debts before she set off on a pilgrimage to Jerusalem. After consulting Jesus, she accepted these terms. If medieval marriage customs treated women as commodities, transferred from father to husband, then Margery was a commodity who bought herself back with hard cash and a promise of decorous behavior.

Freedom from her marital obligations enabled Margery to continue developing a set of behaviors that constituted her mature spirituality. She followed a recognized model of visionary, affective, penitential spirituality, influenced by the lives and writings of Continental holy women, but she continually customized it in practice. Having begun immediately after her conversion an ascetic program of fasting, sleep deprivation, and wearing a hair shirt, she systematically moderated her bodily pieties once she had secured her chastity. She also concentrated on travel. She had already journeyed around England in search of shrines or spiritual counsel, and she now set out on the great pilgrimage to Jerusalem and Rome, a journey of approximately eighteen months which intensified and transformed her devotional life. Approaching Jerusalem, she was so excited that she nearly fell off her donkey; arriving at the holy sites, she experienced more vivid versions of her affective visions of the lives of Christ and the Virgin. Her devotional behavior already included weeping for the sins and sorrows of the world, but now the weeping took a more intense form: "She fell down, for she could not stand or kneel, but wallowed and writhed with her body, spreading her arms open, and cried with a loud voice as though her heart should burst asunder." Such involuntary outbreaks were to recur for many years afterwards, polarizing observers into those who accepted them on Margery's terms as exterior signs of devotion, and those who thought her mad, drunk, or demonically possessed. In Rome she underwent a formal mystical marriage to the Godhead, attended by the Virgin Mary and a congregation of saints: it is a curious scene, for Margery made it plain that her preference was for the humanity of Christ. Here also she began to dress in white,

195

gave away all her money (and some she had borrowed from other people) in order to experience real poverty, and practiced humility by serving a poor old woman. She used her travels to experiment with extreme or non-English devotional behaviors and then carried home with her those she found serviceable.

Margery's relations with the institutionalized Church were variable. The *Book* recounts that while traveling through the Midlands and northern England in 1417 she was twice questioned by the authorities on suspicion of adherence to the Lollard or Wycliffite heresy. Some readers have suspected that the never-specified youthful sin that Margery failed to confess consisted of heretical opinions, perhaps learned from William Sawtre, burned as a Lollard in 1401, who had been a priest in Lynn during her youth. However, if Margery had in fact ever held heretical views, the *Book* would certainly conceal such a lapse; on its evidence, her enthusiasm for pilgrimages, the visual arts, and the sacraments placed her firmly in the orthodox camp. Her traveling, white clothes, noisy devotion, and claim to a special but not officially recognized relationship with God were enough to arouse suspicion in a time of heightened anxiety about heretics. As the *Book* tells it, however, her interrogators accepted that her allegiance and beliefs were orthodox and so did not proceed against her, although many seemed keen to hurry her out of their jurisdiction. Indeed, Margery's religion had no inherent conflict with the Church. Although she might criticize or quarrel with individual priests, her devotional life was dependent on clerical support. She successfully applied to Thomas Arundel, the heretic-hunting archbishop of Canterbury, for permission to confess and receive the Eucharist weekly (something few laypersons did at the time). Anxious about the status of her visions, she continually consulted clerics for reassurance that she was not deceived by demonic illusions, and on several occasions she relied on clerics to defend her from the hostility of laypeople. Some priests even appreciated her screaming during sermons, taking the opportunity to extemporize on the spiritual value of such devotion.

CRITICAL RESPONSES

The history of the critical reception of *The Book of Margery Kempe* is instructive. Contemporary evidence indicates that it gained respect in limited and specialist mystical circles but did not circulate widely nor acquire the popular appeal necessary for a cult. The sole surviving manuscript belonged to the library of mystical writings collected by the contemplative Carthusian monks of Mount Grace, Yorkshire, where annotations indicate that it had intelligent and engaged readers. Another copy must have been used as the source of the printed extracts, which present a contained and normalized version of Margery, emphasizing interior mystical experience and excluding details of her external life. The *Book* itself was thus assumed to be a mystical treatise until it was rediscovered in 1934, when its idiosyncrasies caused surprise and some consternation among scholars of mysticism. There was a marked streak of misogyny in some early commentaries on the *Book* which held Margery to be a false or failed mystic, a woman too enmeshed with the world and the body to be capable of true spiritual insight. Since the 1980s, however, feminist critics have taken a more sympathetic view of Margery as a woman making the best of the cultural materials available to her. Contemporary opinions of the *Book* vary considerably, but its importance for the study of late medieval lay piety and of medieval women's writing has been securely established. It is now canonical: several editions are in print; it regularly features in undergraduate courses on medieval literature and history; and it has been the subject of a mass of scholarly articles and a handful of books. The *Book* has even made some appearances in the non-academic world: it was serialized in adapted form on BBC Radio 4 in 2000 and inspired at least one novel, Robert Gluck's postmodern, sexually explicit *Margery Kempe* (London, 1994). However, Margery is rarely taken seriously as a Christian exemplar; unlike her contemporary Julian of Norwich, she has no visible devotional cult, although the Church of England permits her a minor commemoration.

The Book of Margery Kempe presents modern readers with a disconcerting mixture of the accessible and the alien. It is easy to sensationalize or to mock Margery. She made the Virgin Mary a hot drink to comfort her at the Crucifixion! She had a vision of priests brandishing erections in Hell! In fact, such incidents are not unique or original to Margery: the detail of feeding the Virgin is derived from the orthodox devotional *Meditations on the Life of Christ*, and almost every East Anglian parish church held depictions of naked sinners writhing in Hell. The *Book* engages with the mainstream of medieval lay devotional practices in idiosyncratic ways, showing a spirituality in lively dialogue with the historical conditions that formed it. It offers modern readers a wealth of information on medieval marriage, travel, and urban life. Perhaps accidentally, it is also a significant milestone in

English life-writing, an unforgettable portrait of a complex individual struggling to find a place in a complex society.

[*See also* Julian of Norwich *and* Medieval Devotional Prose.]

EDITIONS

Staley, Lynn, ed. *The Book of Margery Kempe: A New Translation, Contexts, Criticism*. Norton Critical Edition. New York, 2001.

Windeatt, Barry, trans. *The Book of Margery Kempe*. Harmondsworth, U.K., 1985.

FURTHER READING

Aers, David. *Community, Gender, and Individual Identity: English Writing 1360–1430*. London, 1988. Includes a chapter on Margery and details her social context.

Arnold, John H., and Katherine J. Lewis, eds. *A Companion to the Book of Margery Kempe*. Woodbridge, U.K., 2004. An edited collection surveying a range of contextual and textual issues and summarizing scholarship to date.

Ashley, Kathleen. "Historicizing Margery: The Book of Margery Kempe as Social Text." *Journal of Medieval and Early Modern Studies* 28 (1998): 371–388. Subtle reading emphasizing the complexity of medieval East Anglian society.

Atkinson, Clarissa. *Mystic and Pilgrim: The Book and the World of Margery Kempe*. Ithaca, NY, 1983. A contextualizing introduction.

Beckwith, Sarah. "Problems of Authority in Late Medieval English Mysticism: Language, Agency, and Authority in the Book of Margery Kempe." *Exemplaria* 4 (1992): 171–199.

Beckwith, Sarah. "A Very Material Mysticism: The Medieval Mysticism of Margery Kempe." In *Medieval Literature: Criticism, Ideology, and History*, edited by David Aers, 34–47. Brighton, U.K., 1986. Densely argued and influential article on the problems of feminine mysticism.

Delany, Sheila. *Writing Woman: Women Writers and Women in Literature, Medieval to Modern*. New York, 1983. A chapter compares the treatment of the economics of sexuality in the *Book* and in Chaucer's *Wife of Bath's Prologue*.

Dinshaw, Carolyn. "Margery Kempe." In *The Cambridge Companion to Medieval Women's Writing*, edited by Carolyn Dinshaw and David Wallace, 222–239. Cambridge, U.K., 2003. Argues for Margery's offering a life possibility for the present.

Gibson, Gail McMurray. *Theater of Devotion: East Anglian Drama and Society in the Late Middle Ages*. Chicago, 1989. Survey of late medieval East Anglia's religious culture in its verbal and visual arts, including a chapter on the *Book*.

Goodman, Anthony. *Margery Kempe and Her World*. London, 2002. Focuses more on the world than on the *Book*, but full of invaluable historical information.

Lochrie, Karma. *Margery Kempe and Translations of the Flesh*. Philadelphia, 1991. Psychoanalytically informed feminist critique.

McEntire, Sandra J., ed. *Margery Kempe: A Book of Essays*. New York, 1992. Consolidates the first wave of feminist and historicizing scholarship on Kempe, though now looking somewhat uneven in quality.

Salih, Sarah. *Versions of Virginity in Late Medieval England*. Woodbridge, U.K., 2001. Includes a chapter arguing that the *Book* represents a performance of virginity.

Staley, Lynn. *Margery Kempe's Dissenting Fictions*. University Park, PA, 1994. Places the *Book* in the context of fifteenth-century social and religious tensions; argues for the character "Margery" being the fictive construct of the author, "Kempe."

Watt, Diane. *Secretaries of God: Women Prophets in Late Medieval and Early Modern England*. Woodbridge, U.K., 1997.

THOMAS KILLIGREW

Paul D. Cannan

Thomas Killigrew (1612–1683) provides an instructive foil to his more famous contemporary, William Davenant. Both were courtiers who, at a young age, wrote plays to please the court. Both were Royalists during the English Civil Wars, serving Queen Henrietta Maria and Charles II in exile. Both were granted royal patents to open theaters after the Restoration, Killigrew forming the King's Company and Davenant the Duke's Company. Both were buried in Westminster Abbey, Killigrew next to Ben Jonson and Davenant with an epitaph echoing Jonson's. Despite these parallels, however, Killigrew's literary and historical significance has been almost completely eclipsed by that of Davenant. Davenant was a more successful playwright both before the theaters were closed in 1642 and after they reopened in 1660; he had more experience as a theater manager, and, perhaps more important, he had a vision for the London stage that emphasized music and spectacle and was successful in implementing it. In contrast, Killigrew wrote only a handful of plays; many of them were never intended to be staged, and only one, *The Parson's Wedding* (premiere 5 October 1664) was successful. Finally, owing to poor management and bad luck, the King's Company was forced to merge with the Duke's Company in 1682. Nevertheless, Killigrew remains noteworthy as an influential figure in an important transitional moment in English literary and political history. His earliest plays, with their emphasis on idealistic love-and-honor conflicts, anticipate the Restoration rhymed heroic play. In addition, Killigrew's troupe's inheritance of the King's Company's pre-1642 repertory assured the dominance of Shakespeare, Jonson, and Francis Beaumont and John Fletcher on the early Restoration stage.

Thomas Killigrew
Portrait by William Sheppard, 1650
NATIONAL PORTRAIT GALLERY, LONDON

THE ILLITERATE COURTIER

Killigrew's family had been well connected to the court since the reign of Henry VIII. Accordingly, Thomas and his many siblings found employment in the Stuart court in a variety of capacities, some more illustrious than others. His sister Elizabeth, a maid of honor to Queen Henrietta Maria, later became the exiled Charles II's mistress. His brother William was knighted by James I, and both William and brother Henry received honors from Charles I and were successful playwrights. By comparison, Thomas's accomplishments seem wanting. His lack of education is sometimes exaggerated—even he referred to himself in the epilogue to *The Parson's Wedding* as "the illiterate Courtier"—but it is true that he had only a grammar school education. He learned from experience: the diarist Samuel Pepys repeated an anecdote about how the young Killigrew gained admittance to the Red Bull Theatre by playing the role of an extra. Killigrew began his court education as early as 1625, when he became Page of Honour to Charles I.

Killigrew's first three plays are the product of this court education: divertissements written to satisfy the tastes of Queen Henrietta Maria. *The Prisoners*, *The Princess*, and *Claricilla* were all written and staged between 1633 and 1637, and are so imitative of the French heroic romances popular with the queen that they are essentially indistinguishable. All three are pseudo-histories which tell the stories of embattled heroes who must, in order to win the hand of a virtuous woman, overcome obstacles presented by rivals, villains, and pirates. The fact that it was revived at least four times after 1660 suggests that *Claricilla* was the most successful of Killigrew's early efforts, probably because of the effective characterization of the villain Seleucus. *The Prisoners* was evidently never revived, and when Pepys saw *The Princess* on 29 November 1661, he and the packed house were greatly disappointed. Today these early plays are of interest mainly to scholars searching for antecedents to the Restoration rhymed heroic play.

Killigrew's most popular (and notorious) play, *The Parson's Wedding*, was written in 1640–1641 but, because of the revolutionary government's closing of the theaters, it probably was not performed until after the Restoration. It is the polar opposite of his previous work: in stark contrast to his dramas of idealistic love, *The Parson's Wedding* revels in the harsh sexual realities of Killigrew's London. It recounts the exploits of Tom Careless and Ned Wild, two young wits just back from France, and their hangers-on, Jolly and Captain Buff. The title derives from one plot line in the play in which Captain Buff exacts vengeance on the Parson by marrying him off to his old mistress, Wanton. Wanton makes the Parson's life difficult; and when the Parson is tricked into committing adultery, he pays a bribe to Captain Buff rather than go to jail. The main plot involves the coupling of Ned and Tom with, respectively, Mistress Pleasant and the Widow. The women are similarly tricked into a compromising situation where marrying the wits provides the only honorable resolution. Killigrew's motive for writing such a play is thought to have been a crisis in his life: his wife, Cecilia, died in 1638, a year and a half after they married; and he was living beyond his means and harassed by creditors. Accordingly, rather than writing to please the queen, Killigrew was evidently trying to make money in the public theater. The play's racy situations and vulgar dialogue clearly contributed to its success when it was finally staged in 1660. A revised version premiered in October 1664 at Killigrew's theater in Bridges Street, with an all-female cast, and this production was very successful. When *The Parson's Wedding* was revived in June 1672, it was again played with an all-female cast. Although Killigrew never wrote a play like this again, he clearly had a sense for the type of comedy that would eventually define the Restoration stage.

THE BANISHED CAVALIER

Given Killigrew's association with the court, it is not surprising to see him supporting the Royalist cause with the outbreak of civil war. In 1641 he acted as a courier and liaison officer. For these services, he was arrested by Parliament in September 1642 but probably not actually imprisoned. In 1643 he sought Parliament's protection against his creditors, and, as a result of a prisoner exchange, he was eventually returned to the Royalist army.

In all likelihood, Killigrew left England in 1644 with Queen Henrietta Maria. In exile he quickly entered the service of Prince Charles and the duke of York, acting as the latter's Groom of the Bedchamber. Sometime during this period, probably between 1645 and 1646, Killigrew wrote *The Pilgrim*, considered by modern scholars to be his most promising play. It may have been intended for a roving troupe of actors who performed for the exiled court, but it was never staged. Like all of Killigrew's previous efforts, *The Pilgrim* is derivative—the plot is borrowed from James Shirley's *The Politician* (premiere c. 1639) with hints of *Hamlet*—but it is also his most original and dramatically effective work. The play is a complexly plotted story of court intrigue, recounting the story of the evil Duchess Julia, who conspires with her lover Martino to put their illegitimate child Cosmo on the throne. Becoming privy to their plan to murder the rightful heir, Sforza, Cosmo disguises himself as a pilgrim in a search for the culprits and the truth. In the end, Cosmo unwittingly kills his father, Martino, and Julia unwittingly kills her disguised son. The play is not perfect—the plot is plodding, the action is interrupted with unnecessary exposition, and the comic business is superfluous—but it does exhibit solid characterization, some poetry, and real tragic effect. One wonders how talented a playwright Killigrew might have become if he had written more often and more consistently.

In 1649 Killigrew became ambassador to Venice and the northern states of Italy for the exiled court. While serving as ambassador, he wrote two of his three closet dramas (plays intended for private reading rather than stage production): *Cicilia and Clorinda*, composed in Turin and Florence between 1649 and 1650, and *Bellamira Her Dream*, composed in Venice between 1650 and 1652. These sprawling, two-part works, each essentially a ten-act play, represent a return to his earliest drama and its indebtedness to the French heroic romance. In fact, *Cicilia and Clorinda* is largely based on one episode in Madeleine de Scudéry's monumental epic *Artamene ou Le Grand Cyrus*. Of these two closet dramas, *Cicilia and Clorinda* is regarded as the stronger effort because, working within the rigid conventions of the genre, Killigrew still managed to produce flashes of effective characterization and dramatic action. He was dismissed from his post as ambassador in 1652 when the presence in Italy of two representatives from England—one from Cromwell and another from the exiled Charles II—proved too controversial. The years between 1652 and 1654 are generally regarded as the bleakest of Killigrew's exile; toward the end of this period, he wrote his last and now best-known closet drama, *Thomaso, or The Wanderer*. Like his others, *Thomaso* is a lengthy, two-part work, but in contrast to those romances it is a boisterous comedy drawing on a completely different literary lineage—the plays of Thomas Middleton, Ben Jonson, and Beaumont and Fletcher. The story of banished, impoverished, and depraved cavaliers running amuck in Madrid is also clearly based on personal experience, a connection that Killigrew and his contemporaries made explicit: while in Italy, Killigrew signed his correspondence "Thomaso," and Richard Flecknoe titled his satire on Killigrew *Life of Tomaso the Wanderer* (1667). Killigrew's *Thomaso* is best known today for inspiring Aphra Behn's play *The Rover, or The Banish't Cavaliers* (Part I, premiere March 1677; Part II, premiere January 1681). Behn's indebtedness to Killigrew was so obvious to her audience that she felt obliged to offer a disclaimer at the end of the printed text of *The Rover* (1677). Behn's protestations aside—she asserted, "the Plot and Bus'ness (not to boast on't) is my own: as for the Words and Characters, I leave the Reader to judge"—the plot, characters, and several of the speeches are clearly borrowed from Killigrew. Nevertheless, without the success of Behn's adaptation, Killigrew's closet drama and even the author himself would enjoy less literary and critical prestige today.

THE RESTORATION THEATER MANAGER

Killigrew had far more impact on the history of English drama as a theater manager than as a playwright. Because of his close association with the court, and Charles II in particular, Killigrew was able to secure a patent to open his own theater upon the Restoration. While a number of hopefuls scrambled to form troupes and stage plays in 1660, Killigrew and William Davenant (who had been granted a patent by Charles I to open a theater in 1639) quickly quashed all competition. The patent of 21 August 1660 issued to Killigrew and Davenant created a duopoly that defined the London theater world until the early nineteenth century.

Early on, Killigrew's company seems to have had the upper hand. In the autumn of 1660, Killigrew and Davenant formed a united company; but by 5 November, Killigrew's King's Company, boasting such experienced actors as Charles Hart and Michael Mohun, was performing separately in the Red Bull Theatre. In addition to hiring more experienced actors, Killigrew's company also evidently laid claim to the King's Company's pre-1642 repertory of plays, which included many of the most popular works of Shakespeare, Jonson, and Beaumont and Fletcher. By contrast, Davenant, whose troupe was made up of comparatively inexperienced actors, had to petition for the right to stage his own plays. Both companies were slow to produce new plays, but the King's Company had the distinction of staging the first entirely new English play on the Restoration stage—Sir William Killigrew's *Selindra* (premiere March 1662). Over the next few years, Killigrew produced plays by his relatives and dramatists closely connected to his theater, notably Sir Robert Howard, a shareholder in the King's Company. Howard's brother-in-law John Dryden also wrote for the King's Company, and in 1668 he signed a contract with Killigrew, becoming, in essence, the first professional playwright of the Restoration. Despite these advantages, the nature of theatrical competition on the London stage changed significantly in 1661, when Davenant opened his new theater in Lincoln's Inn Fields with its innovative wing-and-shutter stage. The theater's inaugural performance ran for almost two weeks and completely cleared out Killigrew's house. Killigrew was forced to respond by building his own changeable-scenery theater, which opened in Bridges Street on 7 May 1663. Like the two-patent monopoly, the wing-and-shutter theater defined the nature of the London stage until the nineteenth century.

While the King's Company enjoyed major successes in the 1660s and 1670s—with, for example, heroic tragedies by Dryden and comedies by William Wycherley—it also continually struggled to compete with the blooming talent and increasing innovations of the Duke's Company. Killigrew did not share Davenant's talent as a playwright and theatrical visionary. Nor did Killigrew possess Davenant's managerial skills: while Davenant seized control of his troupe early on, Killigrew was often forced to defer to his well-connected veteran actors. Killigrew's company also had a string of very bad luck. In early 1672, just when the Duke's Company's Dorset Garden Theatre began staging its multimedia operatic spectaculars, the Bridges Street theater burned to the ground. For several years, the King's Company was forced to stage plays at the Duke's Company's old theater in Lincoln's Inn Fields while a new playhouse was built. The Theatre Royal in Drury Lane opened on 26 March 1674, but even this new venue, which Dryden referred to apologetically as a "Plain Built House," could not compete with the Dorset Garden Theatre. Indeed, the King's Company could respond to the Dorset Garden spectaculars only by staging parodies of them (for example, Thomas Duffett's *Psyche Debauch'd* in August 1675, an answer to Thomas Shadwell's *Psyche* of February 1675). In addition, squabbling among Killigrew, the actors, and his son Charles put serious strain on the King's Company, often causing productions to be canceled and the theater to close. In early 1677, Thomas Killigrew, forced to honor a promise he had made to Charles, turned his interest in the King's Company over to his son. At the same time, Thomas transferred to Charles the office of the Master of the Revels, a post he had held since 1673. This change in leadership did little to stop the precipitous decline of the King's Company, however. In the summer of 1678, the King's Company's two star playwrights, Dryden and Nathaniel Lee, deserted to the Duke's Company. Moreover, the tumultuous political climate created by the Popish Plot and the Exclusion Crisis in the late 1670s and early 1680s hurt the London theater in general and the troubled King's Company in particular. In 1682 the King's Company was forced to merge with the Duke's Company; the United Company remained the sole acting troupe in London until 1695. Killigrew died on 19 March 1683 and was buried in Westminster Abbey next to Ben Jonson. Even in Killigrew's heyday the two playwrights were in entirely different leagues, but this fact perhaps gives us a sense of Killigrew's status and critical esteem among his contemporaries. In 1691, Gerard Langbaine, in his entry for Killigrew in *An Account of the English Dramatick Poets*, praised his service to the court and confidently asserted that *The Parson's Wedding* and *Thomaso* "will always be valu'd by the best Judges and Admirers of Dramatick Poetry." Today Killigrew has been eclipsed by Davenant and Behn, but he remains important as a promising (albeit not prolific) playwright who, as a theater manager, had a prominent role in one of the most significant transitional periods in the history of the London stage.

[*See also* Aphra Behn; Francis Beaumont; Censorship; Closet Drama; William Davenant; John Dryden; John Fletcher; *and* Restoration Drama.]

SELECTED WORKS

The Prisoners and Claracill: Two Tragæ-Comedies (1641)
Comedies, and Tragedies (1664)

FURTHER READING

Harbage, Alfred. *Thomas Killigrew: Cavalier Dramatist, 1612–83.* Philadelphia, 1930; reprinted New York, 1967. The only book-length study of Killigrew's life and works; dated but thoroughly researched and still useful as a starting point.

Hotson, Leslie. *The Commonwealth and Restoration Stage.* Cambridge, MA, 1928; reprinted New York, 1962. Still standard documentary history of the London stage in the mid-seventeenth century.

Hume, Robert D. "Securing a Repertory: Plays on the London Stage 1660–5." In *Poetry and Drama, 1570–1700: Essays in Honour of Harold F. Brooks*, edited by Antony Coleman and Antony Hammond. London, 1981. A clear, concise reconsideration of the complexities surrounding the reestablishment of the London theaters in the 1660s.

Pepys, Samuel. *The Diary of Samuel Pepys: A New and Complete Transcription.* Edited by Robert Latham and William Matthews. 11 vols. Berkeley, CA, 1970–1983. Pepys knew Killigrew and recorded several substantive conversations he had with him about actors, the King's Company's new playhouse in Bridges Street, and other theatrical gossip.

Vander Motten, J. P. *Sir William Killigrew (1606–1695): His Life and Dramatic Works.* Ghent, Belgium, 1980. A well-documented study of Thomas's famous brother.

RUDYARD KIPLING

Patrick Brantlinger

From the 1890s until India and Pakistan gained independence in 1947–1948, Joseph Rudyard Kipling (1865–1936) was the best-known and most influential author writing about the British Raj and indeed about other parts of the British Empire such as South Africa. Both a superb writer of fiction and poetry and an advocate of imperialism, he became known as the "unofficial laureate of the British Empire." He was also the first English writer to be awarded a Nobel Prize in literature, in 1907. Kipling was born in Bombay, India, in 1865, son of Alice Macdonald and John Lockwood Kipling. His father was an artist, designer, and teacher; two of his mother's sisters had married well-known artists, Pre-Raphaelite painter Edward Burne-Jones and Edward Poynter, who became president of the Royal Academy. A third sister married politician Alfred Baldwin; their son Stanley would become prime minister. The Kiplings were also friends with William Morris, the leader of the Arts and Crafts Movement.

The Kiplings traveled to India in 1865, after Lockwood had accepted the principalship of the School of Art in Bombay. A decade later they moved to Lahore, where Lockwood served as principal of the Mayo School of Industrial Arts and as curator of the City Museum (he and the "Wonder-House" Museum are depicted at the start of *Kim*). Rudyard spent the first five and a half years of his life in India, absorbing the exotic, colorful world around him through the indulgent tutelage of his ayah, or Indian nurse, and his Hindu "bearer," Meeta. In his posthumously published autobiography, *Something of Myself*, Kipling recalls nostalgically the trips to markets and temples with Meeta, the ayah, "and my sister in her perambulator":

Rudyard Kipling
Photograph by Elliott & Fry
NATIONAL PORTRAIT GALLERY, LONDON

In the afternoon heats before we took our sleep, [the ayah] or Meeta would tell us stories and Indian nursery songs all unforgotten, and we were sent into the dining-room after we had been dressed, with the caution "Speak English now to Papa and Mamma." So one spoke "English," haltingly translated out of the vernacular idiom that one thought and dreamed in.

When he was almost six and his sister Alice just three, their parents took them to England and boarded them in Southsea, near Portsmouth, in what Rudyard later called "the House of Desolation." It was typical for Anglo-Indian parents to send their children to England for both education and health reasons. The woman in charge of the Southsea establishment and her son treated Rudyard harshly; his memories of those years were of abuse and desperate unhappiness, which his parents did not discover until 1877. Once they did, they enrolled him in the United Services College, which trained young men mainly for military careers. Kipling would write about his experiences there in his school fiction, *Stalky & Co.* (1899), featuring three boys learning pluck, loyalty, honesty, and a sizable measure of cruelty—all qualities that he associated with imperial mastery.

When he returned to India at age sixteen, in 1882, he felt he was returning home, and "my English years fell away, nor ever, I think, came back in full strength." He took a position in Lahore as a reporter for the *Civil and Military Gazette*, in which, besides news items, he began to publish his first poems and short stories. In 1887 Kipling moved to Allahabad to become a reporter for the more important *Pioneer*, for which he visited and wrote about so-called native states, territories still nominally independent of British rule. These experiences influenced both his early fiction and his masterpiece, *Kim* (1901).

Many of his early poems appeared in *Departmental Ditties* in 1886; the stories were published as small volumes, marketed in Indian railway stations, starting with *Plain Tales from the Hills*, followed by *Soldiers Three*, *The Story of the Gadsbys*, *In Black and White*, *Wee Willie Winkie*, *The Phantom Rickshaw*, and *Under the Deodars*, all in 1888. When later published in Britain, the short stories in particular made Kipling one of the most popular authors of the 1890s and early 1900s.

As a teenage reporter at the Punjab Club in Lahore, Kipling listened to the shoptalk of "picked men at their definite work—Civilians, Army, Education, Canals, Forestry, Engineering, Irrigation, Railways, Doctors, and Lawyers." He admired these Anglo-Indians for their practicality and hard work in the service, as he saw it, both of ordinary Indians and of the Empire. He celebrated such men—and, although rarely, women—and their virtues in many of his short stories, including "The Bridge-Builders," "William the Conqueror," and the tales featuring his white subalterns or "soldiers three": Mulvaney the Irishman, Learoyd the Yorkshireman, and Ortheris the Cockney. In equal measure, Kipling detested those who, often from the safe distance of England, criticized the empire and advocated Indian "home rule" or independence. A number of his stories express his belief that Indians would never be able to govern themselves ("The Head of the District," for instance) or become fully rational members of modern civilization ("In the House of Suddhoo," "The Strange Ride of Morrowbie Jukes," and others).

Kipling saw himself as a realist in the mold of Robert Browning's Renaissance painter, Fra Lippo Lippi: irreverent, engaged in the pleasures as much as the pains of life, and insistent on painting the flesh as the only true way of painting the soul. Many of his poems collected in *Barrack-Room Ballads* (1892) and later volumes emulate Browning, taking the form of dramatic monologues; they often give voice to lower-class, Anglo-Indian soldiers ("Tommy," "Mandalay") and sometimes express admiration for Indians. "Though I've belted you and flayed you," declares the white subaltern narrator of "Gunga Din," "By the livin' Gawd that made you, / You're a better man than I am, Gunga Din!" Often, too, his poems like his stories offer direct ideological support for empire ("Recessional," "For All We Have and Are," "The White Man's Burden," "The Islanders"). As a poet, Kipling for the most part contented himself with Victorian models, eschewing the modernist experimentalism associated with Ezra Pound and T. S. Eliot. Yet he declared that,

when he started writing poetry, "There were few atrocities of form and metre that I did not perpetrate, and I enjoyed them all." Throughout his career, he did "perpetrate" many experiments with poetic and fictional form, and it seems fair to say, with G. K. Chesterton, that Kipling's mastery both of the short story and of the dramatic monologue expresses the modernist sense of "fleetingness and fragility; it means that existence is only an impression." On the other hand, T. S. Eliot wrote an appreciative introduction to a collection of Kipling's poetry arguing that Kipling was primarily a writer of ballads—a storyteller of a very traditional kind—but a great one. Certainly, Kipling was one of the greatest late-Victorian and Edwardian writers, but he remained too much the journalist—and, at least after 1900, too much a public figure engaged in politics—to treat literature as a higher calling, after the manner of such modernists as Eliot and Pound.

In fiction Kipling succeeds most often as a short-story writer practicing a version of realistic narration that Virginia Woolf, James Joyce, and other modernists rejected. Even in the 1890s, Kipling was viewed as "vulgar" by such "decadent" writers as Oscar Wilde. Assessing *Plain Tales from the Hills*, Wilde declared:

> One feels as if one were seated under a palm-tree reading life by superb flashes of vulgarity. The jaded, second-rate Anglo-Indians are in exquisite incongruity with their surroundings. . . . The mere lack of style in the story-teller gives an odd journalistic realism to what he tells us. From the point of view of literature Mr. Kipling is a genius who drops his aspirates.

Nevertheless, even in the early short stories Kipling at his best offers something more than "journalistic realism" and Anglo-Indian "vulgarity." Such short stories as "Without Benefit of Clergy," "Lispeth," "Muhammad Din," and "The Man Who Would Be King" capture some of the complexity and tragedy of the human condition—power, love, and misunderstandings across racial and cultural boundaries and the costs of European hubris and adventurism in Asia and other parts of the world. He was a champion of imperialism who could be sharply critical of what he saw as the wrong sorts of imperial domination.

With the one exception *Kim*, Kipling was less successful as a novelist than as a poet or a short-story writer. Henry James called Kipling's first novel, *The Light That Failed* (1890), "the most youthfully infirm of his productions." A self-pitying, partly autobiographical tale of botched love, art, war, and life, it nevertheless expresses Kipling's early views on all those topics. The earlier *Stalky & Co.* is not a novel but a series of school stories about a trio of boys, based on Kipling's friendships with George Beresford (M'Turk) and Lionel Dunsterville (Stalky; Kipling portrayed himself as Beetle). And *Captains Courageous* (1897) is, like countless other works of fiction in the second half of the nineteenth century, an adventure novel addressed to an adolescent, male readership. Rescued at sea, its boy protagonist, the spoiled son of an American millionaire, learns the virtues of hard work and manliness from the cod fishermen who take him on board their vessel.

With his American friend, Wolcott Balestier, Kipling coauthored *The Naulahka*, which is set in both India and the United States. In 1892 he married Wolcott's sister, Caroline Balestier, and settled for a time in Vermont (1892–1896), where he learned enough about the United States to see it as one of Britain's rivals for world dominion and as presenting still another model of imperialism—and as far as he was concerned, not an attractive model. In *Captains Courageous* and some of the stories in *The Day's Work* (1898), Kipling views American culture as materialistic and American motives for colonial expansion as mercenary rather than moral or idealistic. During the Spanish-American War, Kipling wrote "The White Man's Burden" as a sermon to the Americans about their responsibility to the "dark" races of the world; he clearly thought the British version of imperialism, as exemplified by the Raj in India, morally superior to the American version:

> Take up the White Man's burden—
> Send forth the best ye breed—
> Go bind your sons to exile
> To serve your captives' need;
> To wait in heavy harness
> On fluttered folk and wild—
> Your new-caught, sullen peoples,
> Half devil and half child.

In South Africa at the turn of the century, Kipling met and became friends with the empire builder Cecil Rhodes, whom he admired for many of the same reasons that he admired another, American friend, Theodore Roosevelt. Kipling and his family made South Africa their home for six months each year from 1900 to 1907, through most of the Boer War and the movement toward the Union of South Africa (1910). Rhodes built the Kiplings a house,

the "Woolsack," on his estate of Groote Schuur, and this became for them their "paradise" at the Cape of Good Hope. Kipling did not just relax in South Africa; he served as a war correspondent and saw some of the fighting at firsthand. Although some of his fiction and poetry deal with South African topics (the short stories "A Sahib's War" and "Mrs. Bathurst," for instance), Kipling hardly had the same relationship to that territory that he had to India. Perhaps his friendship with Rhodes and his patriotic support of the British during the Boer War prevented him from having much interest in or empathy for the colorful, diverse, and dynamic indigenous cultures of Africa—the very sort of ethnographic interest expressed by his friend H. Rider Haggard and that energizes much of Kipling's Indian fiction and poetry.

Kipling's stories and poems for children include some of his best, most inventive writing. His two *Jungle Book*s (1894 and 1895), featuring the adventures of the wolf-boy Mowgli and a cast of personified animal characters such as Kala Nag the Elephant, Kaa the Rock Python, and the Bandar-log, or Monkey People, have never been out of print and have been made into a number of films, including an animated version by Disney Studios in 1967. The books were also a model for the popular Tarzan of the Apes stories by the American writer Edgar Rice Burroughs. *Just So Stories for Little Children* (1902) consists mainly of animal fables, both prose tales and poems, such as "How the Rhinoceros Got His Skin" and "The Cat That Walked by Himself," and was illustrated by Kipling himself. In *Puck of Pook's Hill* (1906) and its sequel, *Rewards and Fairies* (1910), two children, Dan and Una, encounter Puck from Shakespeare's *A Midsummer Night's Dream*, who introduces them to a series of episodes from English history. *Captains Courageous* is a more realistic story for boy readers, and both *Stalky & Co.* and *Kim* are aimed at adolescent as much as adult readers.

The deaths of Kipling's daughter, Josephine, at age six in 1899, and his son, John, at the Battle of Loos in 1915 during World War I, deepened the note of tragedy in his later writing and contributed to his interest in supernatural possibilities in stories such as "Wired" and "They." Although he had explored such possibilities in earlier stories, including "The Phantom Rickshaw" and "The Mark of the Beast," the later works—especially "They"—strike a more personal note. Some of his later stories and poems also reveal more of the thematic depth and interest in formal experimentation associated with literary modernism. But he remains an author identified with the heyday of British imperialism around the turn of the century, one who could write about other races and cultures sympathetically and yet believed in the ultimate authority and destiny to rule of the "white race," and above all of the English. Virginia Woolf, who opposed the patriarchal and racist domination of European males of much of the rest of the world, declared: "Kipling makes up the whole British Empire to amuse the solitude of his nursery, [and] the result is curiously sterile and depressing."

Despite Woolf's condemnation, *The Jungle Books* and *Just So Stories* are likely always to have admiring readers of all ages. Although many of Kipling's more realistic stories—"Without Benefit of Clergy," "The Man Who Would Be King," and others—will also continue to be read and admired, his fiction for children perhaps expresses most fully and complexly his worldview, entailing a morality and politics at once authoritarian (or imperialist) and tolerant of all races and creatures (everyone deserves equal treatment under an eternally just Law). In *The Jungle Books*, the Law of the Jungle is inescapable, and yet capacious enough to embrace all species who adhere to it. But for both adult and younger readers, it is without doubt *Kim* that best expresses the ethnographically curious, tolerant, and even admiring side of Kipling—that is, Kipling at his best. Although Kipling called his masterpiece "nakedly picaresque and plotless," it is its openness to cultural difference and its lack of teleological structure—typical of the picaresque (the "Great Game" played on the "Road of Life")—that allow Kim, despite his role as a spy, and Kipling through him, despite his authoritarian politics, to be the "Friend of all the World." And Kim's companion on the Road, the Teshoo Lama, offers still another model of how to approach the world and everything in it—not a possessive, imperialist model but just the opposite: an unworldly way of appreciating the world and getting along with it.

The orphaned son of an Irish trooper and a housemaid, Kimball O'Hara—Kim—is a streetwise boy indistinguishable from the Indian street urchins he lives among in Lahore. Like Kipling, he delights in the sights, sounds, and scents of India. He soon proves his worth to Mahbub Ali, Hurree Babu, Lurgan, and other agents of the British Secret Service, under the supervision of Colonel Creighton, who teach him the fine arts of disguise and espionage. This diverse, colorful crew—but Kim especially—is able to foil the plans of the Russian agents to seize control of Afghanistan and, perhaps, all of India. Much of the novel finds Kim on the Grand Trunk Road with still another mentor, the gentle, childlike Lama who is seeking enlightenment. The worldly business of spying

and the unworldliness of the Lama's spiritual quest both find an open receptiveness in Kim, who enjoys these and all other aspects of the experience of India. "India was awake," writes Kipling, "and Kim was in the middle of it, more awake and more excited than anyone."

T. S. Eliot noted that the chief problem with assessing Kipling's total contribution to literature is his "versatility." Great writers, Eliot declared, ordinarily express some sort of powerful "inner compulsion" or unifying theme: "With no writer of equal eminence to Kipling is this inner compulsion, this unity in variety more difficult to discern." But it is not really difficult to discern a "unity" in Kipling's very diverse writings. That unity was supplied by his belief in the ultimate justice and virtue of the British Empire and of the English in their dealings with the rest of the world. For Kipling, it was the duty of the white servants of the empire or, as he understood it, of civilization, to try to bring law and progress to what he called, in "Recessional," "the lesser breeds without the Law." Because of the racial inferiority of those "lesser breeds," empire building was an unending, perhaps ultimately tragic endeavor. Hard work, honesty, and selfless devotion to duty were the qualities that redeemed imperialism and its servants in India and elsewhere, even if the ultimate goals of the full civilization and independence of India were—as Kipling seems always to have believed—impossibilities. For Kipling, as for his friend Haggard and many other turn-of-the-century European and American authors, imperialism did not mean primarily political domination or a system of economic exploitation but a moral ideal, even a surrogate religion.

[*See also* H. Rider Haggard *and* Orientalism.]

SELECTED WORKS

Departmental Ditties and Other Verses (1886)
Plain Tales from the Hills (1888)
Soldiers Three: A Collection of Stories Setting Forth Certain Passages in the Lives and Adventures of Privates Terence Mulvaney, Stanley Ortheris, and John Learoyd (1888)
The Story of the Gadsbys: A Tale Without a Plot (1888)
In Black and White (1888)
Under the Deodars (1888)
The Phantom Rickshaw and Other Tales (1888)
Wee Willie Winkie and Other Child Stories (1888)
The Light That Failed (1890)
Life's Handicap: Being Stories of Mine Own People (1891)
The Naulahka: A Story of West and East, coauthored by Wolcott Balestier (1892)

Barrack-Room Ballads and Other Verses (1892)

The Jungle Book (1894)

The Second Jungle Book (1895)

The Seven Seas (1896)

"Captains Courageous": A Story of the Grand Banks (1897)

The Day's Work (1898)

Stalky & Co. (1899)

Kim (1901)

Just So Stories for Little Children (1902)

Traffics and Discoveries (1904)

Puck of Pook's Hill (1906)

Collected Verse of Rudyard Kipling (1907)

Rewards and Fairies (1910)

A Diversity of Creatures (1917)

Debits and Credits (1926)

Limits and Renewals (1932)

Something of Myself for My Friends Known and Unknown (1937)

EDITIONS

Complete Works. The Sussex Edition. 35 vols. 1937–1939. Republished as the Burwash Edition. 28 vols. New York, 1941.

Pinney, Thomas, ed. *Kipling's India: Uncollected Sketches, 1884–88.* Basingstoke, U.K., 1986.

FURTHER READING

Birkenhead, Lord. *Rudyard Kipling.* London, 1978. "The long suppressed biography."

Carrington, C. E. *Rudyard Kipling: His Life and Work.* London, 1955. The authorized biography.

Eliot, T. S. Introduction to *A Choice of Kipling's Verse.* London, 1941. Astute criticism by a leading modernist poet.

Gilmour, David. *The Long Recessional: The Imperial Life of Rudyard Kipling.* New York, 2002. Detailed account of Kipling's role as a public, political figure.

Green, Roger Lancelyn, ed. *Kipling: The Critical Heritage.* New York, 1971. A useful collection of early critical responses to Kipling.

Keating, Peter. *Kipling the Poet.* London, 1994. Essential commentary on the poetry.

Mallett, Phillip. *Rudyard Kipling: A Literary Life.* Houndmills, U.K., 2003. Succinct, well-balanced study.

Page, Norman. *A Kipling Companion.* London, 1984. Useful summaries of many of the short stories and poems.

Rao, K. Bhaskara. *Rudyard Kipling's India.* Norman, OK, 1967. Offers a critical account from an Indian perspective.

Tompkins, J. M. S. *The Art of Rudyard Kipling.* London, 1959. From a formalist, appreciative perspective, explores Kipling's development as a writer.

ARTHUR KOESTLER

Frank Day

Few intellectuals participated more intensely in the midcentury turmoil of Europe than the Communist apostate Arthur Koestler (1905–1983), who was sentenced to death by the Nationalists during the Spanish Civil War and whose fictional exposé of the Moscow show trials became one of the most important books of the era. Many of his most dramatic experiences are chronicled in the several autobiographical works discussed below.

Koestler was born 5 September 1905 in Budapest, to Hungarian-Jewish parents. From 1922 to 1925 he studied science at the polytechnic in Vienna but left the university without a degree to serve the Revisionist Party in Palestine. In 1929 he moved to Paris, where he worked for Ullstein's, the German newspaper chain. When he moved again, to Berlin in 1930, he became science editor of *Vossische Zeitung* and foreign editor of *Zeitung am Mittag*. His success as a journalist earned him the honor of being the only newsman to accompany the *Graf Zeppelin* on its flight to the North Pole in 1931. Koestler quit Ullstein's in 1931 and spent several months touring the Soviet Union before settling down in Paris for three years and working for the Comintern. When the Spanish Civil War broke out in 1936, he went to Spain as a correspondent for the London *News Chronicle* but was soon arrested by the Nationalists, jailed in Seville, and sentenced to death before being released thanks to British intervention. He then recorded his experience in *Spanish Testament* (1937), later revised as *Dialogue with Death* (1942). In 1938 he resigned from the Communist Party in disillusionment with Stalinism and the Moscow show trials.

Koestler returned to Paris in 1939 but was again imprisoned, this time in a French internment camp for aliens, an ordeal he described in *Scum of the Earth* (1941). Released in January 1940, he made his way to England, where he spent two years in the British Pioneer Corps. *Darkness at Noon* was published in 1940, translated by his longtime companion Daphne Hardy, and its appearance in French in 1946 as *Le zéro et l'infini* caused an immediate uproar among Paris's leftist intellectuals. His essay in *The God That Failed* (1950) traces his gradual disillu-

sionment with Communism and is accompanied by similar confessions from Richard Wright, Ignazio Silone, Louis Fischer, Stephen Spender, and André Gide. Koestler's reputation as an apostate to Communism led to two lecture tours in America and an appointment for 1950–1951 as a Chubb Fellow at Yale. In 1950 he divorced Dorothy Asher, his first wife, and married Mamaine Paget, whom he took to Pennsylvania to live for two years before their separation and his return to England. His abandonment of political writing, announced in *The Trail of the Dinosaur and Other Essays* (1955), was followed by the unexpected publication of *The Sleepwalkers: A History of Man's Changing Vision of the Universe* (1959) and two later volumes on the psychology of creativity, *The Act of Creation* (1964) and *The Ghost in the Machine* (1967). Mamaine died in 1954, and in 1965 Koestler married his secretary, Cynthia Jefferies. Koestler must have felt that 1973 justified the efforts of a lifetime. Not only was he made a Companion of the Royal Society of Literature that year, but he was also accepted into the Amicale des Anciens Internés du Camp de Vernet d'Ariège, a brotherhood of his fellow concentration-camp inmates in 1939–1940. Thus were the novelist, the autobiographer, and the journalist honored along with the veteran of Europe's ideological struggles. He and Cynthia Jefferies settled in London, where he continued writing until, drained by Parkinson's disease and leukemia, he committed suicide with his wife on 3 March 1983.

FICTION AND DRAMA

In a postscript to the Danube edition of *The Gladiators* (1939) Koestler explains that it forms, along with *Darkness at Noon* and *Thieves in the Night* (1946), a trilogy "whose leitmotif is the central question of revolutionary ethics and of political ethics in general: the question whether, or to what extent, the end justifies the means." Of these three novels, only *Darkness at Noon*, one of the most important novels of the twentieth century, endures on university reading lists. It tells the story of a veteran

Bolshevik, Rubashov, who finds he can no longer connive with the Party in its hypocritical detours on the road to a Socialist Utopia. The end does not justify the means, Rubashov concludes, and the individual ego, the I, is not a mere "grammatical fiction" with its outline blurred by the sweep of the historical dialectic. Rubashov insists, as did Koestler in *The God That Failed*, that the individual cannot be brutalized in the name of history. Rubashov thus rejects the thesis of Koestler's first novel, *The Gladiators*, which was suggested by the Roman slave war of 73–71 BC and which approves the "law of detours," the need sometimes to sacrifice means to ends. The third novel of the group, *Thieves in the Night*, dramatizes life in a commune in Palestine and depicts the stresses of communal life and the effect on Palestine of international politics in 1937–1939. Its central character, a young English-born Jew named Joseph, joins a terrorist group at the novel's end, thus endorsing what George Orwell rejected as "catastrophic gradualism," or the theory defined in the banality that you cannot make an omelet without breaking eggs.

Koestler's other three novels achieved less distinction. *Arrival and Departure* (1943) explores the psychology of the revolutionary mentality as a congeries of grudges and neuroses, but the narrator concludes that ultimately revolutionary motives cannot be conclusively explained by psychoanalysis and psychobiography. *The Age of Longing* (1951) depicts Cold War angst in Paris and is enlivened only slightly by Koestler's satirical portrait of the Marxist existentialist philosopher Jean-Paul Sartre as Professor Pontieux, author of *Negation and Position*. The inspiration for *The Call-Girls* (1972) was the highbrow symposium in Alpbach, Switzerland, that Koestler attended in 1968. The characters are mere mouthpieces, but they dramatize the author's intense contempt for behaviorist psychology, and the story becomes a psychomachy between the soulless behaviorists and the advocates of humanity's existential freedom. Besides his six novels, Koestler wrote one uninspired play, *Twilight Bar*, in 1933, but it was not staged until 1946, in Paris as *Bar du Soleil*.

AUTOBIOGRAPHY, ISRAEL, AND SCIENCE HISTORY

Spanish Testament and *Scum of the Earth* were followed by two superb volumes of autobiography. *Arrow in the Blue* (1952), which covers the period 1905–1931, describes his youthful preoccupation with mathematics and attributes his attraction to the Promised Land and the Communist Party to his hunger for the Infinite. The appeal of Zionism and its Revisionist leader, Vladimir Jabotinsky, prompted him to abandon his engineering studies in Vienna and move to Palestine, but he soon returned to Europe and joined the Communist Party in 1931. *The Invisible Writing* recounts the story of the struggles between his Party cell and the Nazis in Berlin in 1932, summarizes his wanderings in Ukraine and central Asia (accompanied much of the time by Langston Hughes), and explains his resignation from his Party job after a spell in Paris as a propagandist for the Communist organizer Willy Muenzenberg. Koestler testifies to how his imprisonment in Seville by the Nationalists induced a mystical state in him, a belief in an occult dimension that holds a text for life written in invisible ink. After his release from prison he wandered around Europe before resigning from the Party in 1938, thus climaxing an extraordinary journey through midcentury ideologies.

An important element in Koestler's thinking was his attitude toward Jews and Jewishness, an attitude that many Jewish critics condemned. In *Promise and Fulfilment* (1949) he asserts that modern Jews should either migrate to Israel or assimilate into the culture in which they lived. His ambivalence toward Jews appears in the revulsion he expresses for Jews on one hand and his strong support for Jews' civil rights on the other. In *The Thirteenth Tribe* (1976) Koestler argues that the Jews of Eastern Europe are descendants of the Turkish people of the Khazar empire, which flourished between the Black Sea and the Caspian from the seventh century to the tenth. If the Ashkenazic Jews are not of Semitic racial stock, he reasons, then the term "anti-Semitism" loses all meaning. Reviewers were generally harsh in their judgments, seeing his thesis as another claim that Jews should either go to Israel or assimilate. Koestler's one masterpiece of science history, *The Sleepwalkers*, proposes that creativity is often a kind of sleepwalking in which reason is strongly influenced by some irrational element. An earlier, related study, *Insight and Outlook* (1949), and the long companion volume, *The Act of Creation* (1964), continue these concerns but leave no clear impression. His book on the Austrian biologist Paul Kammerer, *The Case of the Midwife Toad* (1971), provides a very readable account of that biologist's experiments and his probable faking of evidence demonstrating the inheritance of acquired characteristics, but his defense of parapsychology on the grounds that it is legitimized by the paradoxes of quantum physics fails to convince. At his death he left almost one million pounds for establishing a chair in parapsychology in Britain, an offer accepted by Edinburgh University.

SELECTED WORKS

AUTOBIOGRAPHY

Spanish Testament (1937)

Scum of the Earth (1941)

Dialogue with Death (1942)

The God That Failed (as one of six contributors), edited by Richard Crossman (1949)

Arrow in the Blue (1952)

The Invisible Writing (1954)

NOVELS

The Gladiators (1939)

Darkness at Noon (1940)

Arrival and Departure (1943)

Thieves in the Night (1946)

The Age of Longing (1951)

The Call-Girls: A Tragi-Comedy with Prologue and Epilogue (1972)

DRAMA

Twilight Bar (1945)

NONFICTION

The Yogi and the Commissar and Other Essays (1945)

Insight and Outlook: An Inquiry into the Common Foundations of Science, Art, and Social Ethics (1949)

Promise and Fulfilment: Palestine, 1917–1949 (1949)

The Trail of the Dinosaur and Other Essays (1955)

Reflections on Hanging (1956)

The Sleepwalkers: A History of Man's Changing Vision of the Universe (1959)

The Lotus and the Robot (1960)

The Act of Creation (1964)

The Ghost in the Machine (1967)

Drinkers of Infinity. Essays 1955-1967 (1968)

The Case of the Midwife Toad (1971)

The Roots of Coincidence: An Excursion into Parapsychology (1972)

The Heel of Achilles: Essays 1968–1973 (1974)

The Thirteenth Tribe: The Khazar Empire and Its Heritage (1976)

Janus: A Summing Up (1978)

Bricks to Babel: Selected Writings with Comments by the Author (1980)

FURTHER READING

Cesarani, David. *Arthur Koestler: The Homeless Mind.* London, 1998. This first full biography of Koestler pays close attention to his attitude toward Jews.

Day, Frank. *Arthur Koestler: A Guide to Research.* New York, 1987. Annotated bibliographies of both the primary and the secondary works.

Goodman, Celia, ed. *Living with Koestler: Mamaine Koestler's Letters 1945–1951.* New York, 1985. Celia Goodman is Mamaine Paget Koestler's twin sister, and Mamaine wrote these revealing letters to her when she was living with Koestler in Wales, France, and Pennsylvania.

Harris, Harold, ed. *Astride the Two Cultures: Arthur Koestler at 70.* London, 1975. A dozen essays evaluating many aspects of Koestler's work.

Merrill, Reed, and Thomas Frazier. *Arthur Koestler: An International Bibliography.* Ann Arbor, MI, 1979. Lists all publications by Koestler through July 1978.

HANIF KUREISHI

Scott Cohen

Hanif Kureishi (born 1954) has earned a place as one of the most important voices in contemporary literature for his vivid, if often unsettling, portraits of postcolonial Britain. A gifted storyteller and self-appointed—and hence far from uncontroversial—translator for the new multiethnic communities of Britain and of London in particular, Kureishi sheds light on some of the darker urban spaces of the former imperial metropolis. Although much of his work can be read as exercises in autobiography, failing to recognize its significance beyond its charismatic and provocative author risks diminishing its importance and the extent to which Kureishi's plays, screenplays, and novels have shaped contemporary perceptions of race, class, and sexuality. Several themes are prominent in his writing: the liberating aspects of sex; cross-generational debates over the futures of minority cultures in Britain as youths weigh assimilation against ethnic solidarity; the difficulties of traditional and modern family life as men and women clutch ancient tradition in the face of modernity; and racism as a force of personal brutality ratified by formal institutions. Kureishi utilizes personal encounters and private emotions in order to animate his parallel depictions of global institutions and concepts. Even in the most deeply intimate moment the wider social world is not far away, and even the most personal plight has social relevance.

Kureishi was born on 5 December 1954 in the southeastern London suburb of Bromley, Kent. His father, Kafiushan, came from a wealthy Muslim family that moved to Karachi, Pakistan, after the partition of India in 1948. His mother, Audrey, was the daughter of an English shop owner. Kureishi recalls being haunted by the question of origins: "I found it almost impossible to answer questions about where I came from." Subject to racism and class alienation, Kureishi focused on solitary and creative activities, and decided at the age of fourteen to become a writer. He studied philosophy at Lancaster University and then at King's College, London, where he earned a BA in 1977. During college, he was invited to work odd jobs at the Royal Court Theatre, where he was introduced to the life of intellectuals and the "fringe" theater—which he found both exhilarating and frustrating. It was there that his first short play, *Soaking the Heat* (1976), was produced in the Court's studio Theatre Upstairs.

PLAYS AND FILMS

Kureishi claims to have been initially attracted to the theater because drama promised to give life to particular narratives and experiences that the novel seemed unable to address. Similarly, the shared and performative nature of the theater resembled pop music, which Kureishi would always distinguish as the ideal form for the exchange of ideas. This formula clearly pervades his early plays, from the social realist portrait of a woman's obsession with an American pop icon in *The King and Me* (1980) to the racial and class conflict at the heart of *Birds of Passage* (1983). His early plays anticipate many of the themes—forbidden desire, generational rifts, racial segregation and fear, and class anxiety and anger—that he would develop with increasing sophistication.

In 1981, two of Kureishi's most important plays debuted in London. First produced at the Royal Shakespeare Company's Warehouse Theatre, *Outskirts* (1981) describes the divergent paths of two boyhood friends from white working-class families. The men are united by their secret, random, and senseless beating of an Indian man twelve years earlier. Del remains ashamed and horrified by his involvement, while Bob has deployed his past actions to bolster his standing in a local neofascist group. Turning to the other side of London's growing racial divide, *Borderline* (1981) is set in the South Asian immigrant community of Southall. Largely centered on the story of Amina, a British-born young woman who attempts to reconcile her Pakistani parents' conventional expectations with her own vaguely formed desires, *Borderline* is the story of the clash of cultures and generations within Britain.

During the 1980s, Kureishi's best-known work was written for the screen. In what amounts to an extended refutation of Thatcherism, Kureishi wrote three screenplays that would forever change perceptions of London. Written during a visit to Pakistan, *My Beautiful Laundrette* (1985) centers on a young second-generation Pakistani immigrant, Omar, and his love affair with a school friend and former National Front member, Johnny. In addition to highlighting the racial and class divisions in London, the script focuses on how cross- and intragenerational conflict is intensified by the immigrant experience. Part romantic fantasy and part gangster thriller, the film, directed by Stephen Frears, portrays a rough and decaying London with an atmosphere of eerie foreboding. The film at once foregrounds and transcends racial conflict, not only through its rendering of a homosexual romance between two young men from very different backgrounds but also in its assertion that the Asian immigrant community is determined to succeed despite guaranteed resentment and retaliation. *My Beautiful Laundrette* met with considerable critical as well as popular acclaim, winning numerous awards and earning a nomination for an Academy Award.

Sammy and Rosie Get Laid (1988) sharpens Kureishi's critique of Margaret Thatcher's policies, their effect on London's poor, and Thatcher's redeployment of imperialist tropes and nationalist thinking. Also directed by Stephen Frears, the film uses the open relationship between Sammy, an accountant of South Asian descent, and Rosie, a white social worker, as a window into the state of contemporary Britain. When Sammy's father, Rafi, arrives in the city he loved and left decades earlier, he finds his London and his son altered almost beyond recognition. Unable to understand fully the nature of his son's relationship with Rosie or why they choose to live in a South London neighborhood racked by urban problems, Rafi figures as the returning disciple of empire, haunted and forced into exile by his own actions abroad and bewildered by the riots that are tearing apart the city that for centuries stood as the pinnacle of civilization. A subplot involving a commune of squatters and their eviction offers a moving critique of Tory policies and mourns the enfeebled position of liberalism.

Delineating the city in muted, almost monochromatic, tones, *London Kills Me* (1991) follows the often brutal and haphazard lives of a motley crew of drug dealers and addicts adrift in London. Despite this grim-sounding summary, Kureishi's directorial debut is rife with tender, lighthearted, and farcical moments. *London Kills Me* is a study of appetite and the contradictory impulses that must inform the life of the addict, featuring characters who are at once completely content with their situation and desperately unhappy, trapped in a world of bloated excesses and indefinite cravings.

NOVELS AND SHORT STORIES

Densely packed with allusions to popular culture, Kureishi's first novel, *The Buddha of Suburbia* (1990) is a lively and rowdy portrait of a young man dedicated to experiencing the world through a variety of countercultural vehicles, including sex, drugs, rock and roll, and fringe theater. Drawing on the conventions of the picaresque and confessional novels as well as the Bildungsroman and the novel of manners, *The Buddha of Suburbia* is set in 1970s suburban London, where the first-person narrator, Karim Amir, confronts bourgeois morality and hypocrisy, racial intolerance, and adolescent boredom. The opening line— "I am an Englishman born and bred, almost"—signals the unstable ground on which his adventures are inaugurated; however, by the end of the novel, Karim and others find themselves slipping into lives grounded by stability and convention. Identity in the novel is fluid, as Karim's father deploys a hodgepodge of oriental tropes in order to serve as a suburban mystic and Karim explores sexual relationships with men and women, and Kureishi insists on the ambivalence of hybrid identities. Hailed as both vividly imaginative and autobiographical, the novel won the Whitbread First Novel Award.

Kureishi's second novel, *The Black Album* (1995), also tells a coming-of-age story and is equally concerned with identity formation. But here Kureishi examines the relation between authenticity and ethnicity. Shahid Hasan, a young British Asian university student, finds himself romantically involved with his white, hip cultural studies professor, Deedee Osgood. In this novel of extremes, Deedee, who gladly blends critical thinking, drug taking, and sex, stands as a relatively stable counterbalance to the influence of a militant Muslim student group with whom Shahid has found common cause. Drawn to the group by its apparent triumph over the self-loathing induced by racism, Shahid becomes disillusioned when the group publicly burns a book it finds offensive. While a number of readers of have suggested that Kureishi's fundamentalist characters in this novel and elsewhere are merely caricatures, Kureishi's treatment of extremism nevertheless predicts many of the social contradictions that have since contributed to the radicalization of second-generation British Asians.

The bulk of the stories collected in *Love in a Blue Time* (1997) and *Midnight All Day* (1999), as well as Kureishi's third novel *Intimacy* (1998), examine midlife crises in masculinity and the consequent—almost inevitable—decay of human relationships. This equation and Kureishi's unyielding embrace of the "violence" and "delight" of separation have not been popular with many critics. Even the generous reader is tested by these stories, which feature sexist and self-destructive characters in their darkest moments. Other readers have been disappointed by Kureishi's recent departure from the familiar terrain of politics and ethnicity. The complex dynamics of the modern family provide the backdrop for Kureishi's novel *Gabriel's Gift* (2001); his novel *The Body* (2004) returns to the subject of identity in a fantasy in which an aging writer has his brain transplanted into a younger body. At once a meditation on the connection between the human body and mind and a tale of excess, the novel offers a compelling study of frailty, agency, and regret.

[*See also* Orientalism; Postcolonial Literature; *and* Salman Rushdie.]

SELECTED WORKS

PLAYS AND SCREENPLAYS

Soaking the Heat (1976)

The King and Me (1980)

Borderline (1981)

Birds of Passage (1983)

Outskirts, The King and Me, Tomorrow-Today! (1983)

My Beautiful Laundrette (1985)

Sammy and Rosie Get Laid (1988)

London Kills Me (1991)

Outskirts and Other Plays (1992)

My Son the Fanatic (1997)

Sleep With Me (1999)

The Mother (2003)

When the Night Begins (2004)

FICTION

The Buddha of Suburbia (1990)

The Black Album (1995)

Love in a Blue Time (1997)

Intimacy (1998)

Midnight All Day (1999)

Gabriel's Gift: A Novel (2001)

The Body and Seven Stories (2002)

NONFICTION

London Kills Me: Three Screenplays and Four Essays (1992)

The Faber Book of Pop, coedited with Jon Savage (1995)

Dreaming and Scheming: Reflections on Writing and Politics (2002)

FURTHER READING

Kaleta, Kenneth C. *Hanif Kureishi: Postcolonial Storyteller.* Austin, TX, 1998. Savvy and intelligent reading of Kureishi's writing through published and unpublished materials.

MacCabe, Colin. "Hanif Kureishi on London." *Critical Quarterly* 41 (1999): 37–56. Illuminating interview addressing Kureishi's background and thoughts concerning postcolonial London.

Moore-Gilbert, Bart. *Hanif Kureishi.* Manchester, U.K., 2001. Theoretically informed overview of the author's life, works, and context.

Needham, Anuradha Dingwaney. *Using the Master's Tools: Resistance and the Literature of the African and South-Asian Diasporas.* London, 2000. Reads Kureishi alongside C. L. R. James, Salman Rushdie, and others to investigate the nature and defense of cultural heterogeneity.

Ranasinha, Ruvani. *Hanif Kureishi.* Devon, U.K., 2002. Helpful introductory overview, paying particular attention to the contemporary political and ethnic contexts.

CHARLES LAMB

Andrea Bradley and Mark Schoenfield

When Samuel Taylor Coleridge in "This Lime-Tree Bower My Prison" characterized Charles Lamb (1775–1834) as a captive of the "City," bearing patiently the "strange calamity" of his life, three times he named him "gentle-hearted Charles"; more characteristic of Lamb than this address is Lamb's response to it: "For God's sake (I never was more serious), don't make me ridiculous any more by terming me gentle-hearted in print, or do it in better verses." Lamb declared that "gentleness" is an "equivocal" compliment at best, "fit only to be a cordial to some green-sick sonneteer."

Lamb's combination of independence, irony, self-effacement, and wit illustrates the complex quality of his writing and his place in Romantic literature: both like and radically unlike his contemporaries, Lamb had to negotiate his Enlightenment sensibility of rationality and wit while confronting the despised myth of his own "gentle," ethereal quality. Lamb's success as a writer came relatively late in his career; only after he had explored poetry, drama, and children's literature did he hit upon Elia essay form he made famous under his pseudonym, Elia. These pseudo-biographical narratives have canonized both the "gentle-hearted Charles" and the "drunken dog" that he had suggested to Coleridge as a superior epigraph. The essays draw on rich but tumultuous experience: a difficult personal life tightly entwined with that of his sister, Mary, a long and steady career at the East India House, and a persistent engagement with the great artists and thinkers of his day.

EARLY YEARS

Born 10 February 1775 to John and Elizabeth (Field) Lamb, Charles was the youngest of three surviving children; his brother, John, was born in 1763 and his sister,

Charles Lamb
Chalk and pencil portrait
by Robert Hancock, 1798
NATIONAL PORTRAIT GALLERY, LONDON

Mary, in 1764. The family home was in London's Inner Temple legal district, where John Lamb served as clerk to Samuel Salt, a lawyer and later an important patron to Charles and his brother. Salt likely ensured their enrollment at Christ's Hospital, a school which Charles attended between October 1782 and November 1789. There Lamb befriended Coleridge and excelled in his studies, despite a stammer that impeded his attaining a university education. Lamb wrote feelingly of his years at Christ's, first under his own name in 1813 ("Recollections of Christ's Hospital"), and as the more critical Elia in 1820 ("Christ's Hospital Five and Thirty Years Ago").

Lamb started work at the South Sea House in September 1791, and the subsequent year he entered the employ of the East India House as a clerk in the accountant's office, a position he would hold for the next thirty-three years. The Lambs' benefactor, Samuel Salt, died in July 1792; despite a bequest to John Lamb, the family's financial circumstances became straitened, and their support fell largely to Charles's clerkship and Mary's needlework. The next year Charles moved the family into smaller lodgings in Holborn, inaugurating a lifelong pattern of changing addresses. The beginning of Charles's business career coincided with his first literary aspirations: inspired by his early friendships with Coleridge and Robert Southey, Lamb began contributing verses to their volumes as well as to several London papers.

Lamb's affection for Ann Simmons, his first known romance, was apparently discouraged by his maternal grandmother, who reminded him of his paternal legacy of hereditary insanity. Simmons died in 1792, and Lamb's romantic disappointment, combined with the pressures of family provision and the rigors of full-time employment from the age of fourteen, produced a brief nervous breakdown. As he reported to Coleridge in May 1796, Lamb voluntarily entered a mental institution in the winter of 1795: "I am got somewhat rational now, and don't bite any one. But mad I was—and many a vagary my imagination played with me, enough to make a volume if all told." Lamb's first extant letter reveals the depth of his attachment to Coleridge and links his mental illness to love, friendship, and literary potential. Speculating on the cause of his madness, Lamb wrote, "Coleridge, it may convince you of my regards for you when I tell you my head ran on you in my madness, as much almost as on another Person, who I am inclined to think was the more immediate cause of my temporary frenzy." That other person, Ann Simmons, reappears as the titular heroine of the novella *Rosamund Gray*, as "Anna" in the poetry, and as "Alice W—n" in the essays.

Charles seems never to have suffered another mental collapse, but the family legacy fell heavily and more frequently on his sister, Mary. In a sober letter to Coleridge, Lamb described the tragedy of 22 September 1796, "the day of horrors": "My poor dear dearest sister in a fit of insanity has been the death of her own mother. I was at hand only time enough to snatch the knife out of her grasp." Mary was taken to a madhouse in Islington, and the coroner's jury returned a verdict of lunacy. Charles then undertook her care, thus initiating the siblings' life together in a "double singleness," as he described it. In the same letter to Coleridge, Lamb declared his resolution to abandon his literary attempts as frivolity: "mention nothing of poetry. I have destroyed every vestige of past vanities of that kind. Do as you please, but if you publish, publish mine (I give free leave) without name or initial, and never send me a book." Despite this renunciation, Lamb soon took up his pen to compose verse, drama, and prose for periodicals and compilations.

In the years leading up to his Elia essays, Lamb divided his time between the East India House and the various lodgings in which he and Mary hosted a revolving crowd of family, friends, and acquaintances. In the posthumously published "Charles Lamb's Autobiography" (composed 1827), Lamb drily observed that his "true works may be found on the Shelves of Leadenhall Street, filling some hundred folios." Aside from these files of bookkeeping, Lamb also wrote proto-Elian essays for the *Morning Post*, the *Albion*, and the *Morning Chronicle*, and Leigh Hunt's periodicals, the *Reflector* and the *Examiner*. His other major works of the pre-Elian period (1796–1820) include a novella, *A Tale of Rosamund Gray* (1798); two dramas, *John Woodvil: A Tragedy*

(1802) and *Mr. H—: A Farce in Two Acts* (1806); and an anthology of Elizabethan poetry, *Specimens of English Dramatic Poets* (1808). Despite later accomplishment as a theatrical reviewer and a lifelong enthusiasm for performance, Lamb was not a successful dramatist.

The extra-Elian writing that did achieve success was Lamb's children's literature, produced in collaboration with his sister. Encouraged by William Godwin and Mary Wollstonecraft to contribute several volumes to their Juvenile Library, the Lambs wrote a famous compilation of Shakespeare redactions, *Tales from Shakespear* (1807), and other adaptations or story collections: *The King and Queen of Hearts* (1806) and *The Adventures of Ulysses* (1808), both by Charles, and *Mrs. Leicester's School* (1809), seven of whose ten stories were penned by Mary. Eschewing a morally didactic approach to children's literature, the Lambs encouraged imagination in their young readers and tried to whet their appetites for more sustaining adult literary fare.

Just as he rejected the heavy authorial hand in the composition of juvenile literature, Lamb resisted the imposition of the writer's will in his adult literary criticism. Although he later responded favorably to Wordsworth's *Excursion*, Lamb censured his friend's authorial intrusion in the *Lyrical Ballads*. In a letter from January 1801, Lamb wrote, "It appears to me a fault in the Beggar, that the instructions conveyed in it are too direct and like a lecture: they don't slide into the mind of the reader, while he is imagining no such matter. An intelligent reader finds a sort of insult in being told, I will teach you how to think upon this subject." Lamb's aesthetic criticism was fragmentary and frequently oral; while he claimed lack of interest in story, he gravitated toward the idiosyncratic: "Out-of-the-way humours and opinions—heads with some diverting twist in them—the oddities of authorship" delighted him.

Lamb's Shakespeare criticism is notable for its interest in psychological complexity and its determined preference for the plays as read rather than performed texts. "It may seem a paradox," he wrote in "On the Tragedies of Shakespeare," "but I cannot help being of opinion that the plays of Shakespeare are less calculated for performance on a stage, than those of almost any other dramatist whatever." Shakespeare's faculties of interior vastness and essential textuality Lamb also located in another great English artist, William Hogarth, whose name he coupled with Shakespeare's in "On the Genius and Character of Hogarth." The painter's faces "have not a mere momentary interest"; like Shakespeare's characters, "they are permanent abiding ideas. Not the sports of nature, but her necessary eternal classes. We feel that we cannot part with any of them, lest a link should be broken."

ELIA YEARS

Unusual among the canonical Romantics, Lamb did not find his finest form until relatively late in life. Introduced to John Scott, the editor of the *London Magazine*, through his good friend William Hazlitt, Lamb contributed his first essay to that magazine under the pseudonym of Elia in 1820. From August of that year to July 1825, Lamb regularly wrote his Elia pieces, the first collected edition of which appeared in 1823 as *Elia: Essays Which Have Appeared under That Signature in the London Magazine*. A later collected edition of the final Elia essays was published in 1833 as *The Last Essays of Elia: Being a Sequel to Essays Published under That Name*. The Elia persona flourished under Scott's editorship; Scott, however, was killed in February 1821 in a duel with J. H. Christie, the result of a literary dispute with J. G. Lockhart of *Black-wood's Magazine*. Lamb continued to produce Elia essays for the new editors, Taylor and Hessey, but his regret for the loss of the *London*'s charismatic leader dampened his enthusiasm; in February 1825, he wrote to Bernard Barton, "Our 2nd No. is all trash. . . . Why did poor Scott die! There was comfort in writing with such associates as were his little band of Scribblers, some gone away, some affronted away, and I am left as the solitary widow looking for water cresses." Lamb's first essay for the *London*, "The South-Sea House," establishes the parallels between writer and clerk that run throughout the Elia texts. The periodicals themselves were by now marked with a new professionalism bound up with personality and the vexed urban self-image at the core of the Elian canon.

Posturing as a man lacking refinement, the "drunken dog" and not the "green-sick sonneteer," Lamb presented his work as unformed and authentic, ragged and singular. The pseudonym, though, belies authenticity, as do Lamb's various explanations for its origin: "Elia" is an anagram for "a lie," but in a letter to John Taylor, his second editor at the *London*, Lamb explained that Elia was the name of a former fellow clerk at the South Sea House, an Italian who "added the function of an author to that of a scrivener, like myself." Lamb's assumption of another's name for his own pseudonym illustrates the complex interweavings of person and persona in the Elia essays. In "A Character of the Late Elia," Lamb defends the "egotism" of Elia's persona: "What he tells us, as of himself, was often true only (historically) of another." His method was to "imply and twine with his own identity the griefs and affections of another—making himself many, or reducing many unto himself."

Elia's lack of polish is both a self-criticism and a boast in Lamb's writing. Especially pointed in the identification of his vexed masculinity, Lamb displays a fascination with childhood, his resistance to age and "the age": "He did not conform to the march of time, but was dragged along in the procession," he writes of Elia in the "Preface" to *The Last Essays of Elia*. "His manners lagged behind his years. He was too much of the boy-man. The *toga virilis* never sate gracefully on his shoulders." Lamb calls these "weaknesses," but he claims that "such as they were, they are a key to explicate some of his writings." Both roughly unfinished and quaintly ethereal, the Elian essays are drawn to the incomplete and the incondite in life: memory, desire, dream, the past. Many of his best known essays—"Mackery End," "Dream-Children," "Blakesmoor," "New Year's Eve," "The Old Benchers of the Inner Temple"—proceed from a position of loss, incompletion, or regret. In "New Year's Eve," for example, the writer claims to know the past year only in the moment of its death: "Of all sound of all bells . . . most solemn and touching is the peal which rings out the Old Year. I never hear it without a gathering-up of my mind to a concentration of . . . all I have done or suffered, performed or neglected—in that regretted time. I begin to know its worth, as when a person dies." One can only love the past when it is past, Elia goes on: "I play over again *for love*, as the gamesters phrase it, games, for which I once paid so dear." For Elia and his creator, the experience of loss or incompletion becomes the condition for writing itself: remembrance produces words.

As he did with his own life, Lamb transformed the lives of those close to him into the stuff of essayistic fiction. In the Elia articles, his brother John becomes his cousin James and his sister Mary becomes his cousin Bridget. Bridget makes frequent appearances in the Elia essays, most prominently in "My Relations" and "Old China." In the latter, Lamb as Elia speaks through Bridget/Mary's voice to argue that one only experiences true pleasure when it comes seldom and at great cost: "'I wish the good old times would come again,'" Bridget sighs, "'when we were not quite so rich. I do not mean, that I want to be poor; but there was a middle state . . . in which I am sure we were a great deal happier. A purchase is but a purchase, now that you have money enough and to spare. . . . A thing was worth buying then, when we felt the money that we paid for it.'" So, too, in "The Superannuated Man" does Elia/Lamb lament the paradox of loss in the midst of good fortune. Newly pensioned off from his place of business, Elia marvels, "I was in the condition of a prisoner in the old Bastille, suddenly let loose after a forty years' confinement. I could scarce trust myself with myself. . . . Having all holidays, I am as though I had none."

Conversation, however, was something the Lambs never lacked. Their evenings were filled with guests: Wordsworth, Coleridge, Leigh Hunt, Hazlitt, Godwin, Benjamin Haydon, George Dyer, Henry Crabb Robinson, Thomas Noon Talfourd (Lamb's early biographer), and Sarah Burney, the sister-in-law of Frances Burney. Coleridge and Lamb often met at the Salutation and Cat, a Newgate Street tavern. Having met Wordsworth in 1797, Lamb responded to the poet's work with acuity, candor, and affection throughout their long correspondence. Lamb's association with Hazlitt, which began in 1802, proved significant in the establishment of the Elian vehicle; Lamb was best man at Hazlitt's wedding and was his funeral's sole mourner. The variety of Lamb's acquaintance is also shown in the wealth of his correspondence. From the news of his sister's matricide, to his wittily sensible criticism, to his proposal of marriage at forty-four to the young actress Fanny Kelly (she declined), Lamb's letters communicate the tenderness and rage, delight and anxiety of his life.

After his retirement from the East India House at fifty, Lamb enjoyed a solidly middle-class annual pension of £450. He continued to contribute essays to a number of magazines and albums, including William Hone's *Every-Day Book* and *Table Book*, the *New Monthly Magazine*, the *Spectator*, the *Athenaeum*, and the *Englishman's Magazine*. He also published a collection of poems, *Album Verses*, in 1830, and *The Last Essays of Elia* in 1833. He saw the marriage of Emma Isola, the child he and Mary had adopted in 1823 when Emma was twelve, to Edward Moxon, his own publisher. On 27 December 1834, Charles Lamb died of an infection caught after he fell during one of his long walks. He was buried in Edmonton Churchyard. On 20 May 1847, Mary Lamb died at the age of eighty-two; she did not suffer a single mental relapse after the death of her beloved brother.

[*See also* Samuel Taylor Coleridge; Romanticism; *and* William Wordsworth.]

EDITIONS

Bate, Jonathan, ed. *Elia and The Last Essays of Elia*. Originally published 1823 and 1833. Oxford, 1987.

Lucas, E. V., ed. *The Works of Charles and Mary Lamb*. 7 vols. London, 1903–1905.

Marrs, Edwin., ed. *The Letters of Charles and Mary Anne Lamb*. 3 vols. Ithaca, NY, 1975–1978.

FURTHER READING

Aaron, Jane. *A Double Singleness: Gender and the Writings of Charles and Mary Lamb*. Oxford, 1991. Crucial biography of both Charles and Mary from a psychologically informed feminist perspective.

Ackroyd, Peter. *The Lambs of London*. London, 2004. A novel that interweaves the lives of the Lambs with a famous Shakespeare hoax of the Romantic period.

Burton, Sarah. *A Double Life: A Biography of Charles and Mary Lamb*. London, 2003. A more popularizing look at the Lambs.

McFarland, Thomas. *Romantic Cruxes: The English Essayists and the Spirit of the Age*. Oxford, 1987. Locates Lamb within the essayist tradition of De Quincey and Hazlitt.

McKenna, William. *Charles Lamb and the Theatre*. Gerrards Cross, U.K., 1978. Charts Lamb's complex attitudes to theatrical culture and composition.

Monsman, Gerald. *Charles Lamb as the London Magazine's "Elia."* Lewiston, NY, 2003.

Monsman, Gerald. *Confessions of a Prosaic Dreamer: Charles Lamb's Art of Autobiography*. Durham, NC, 1984. Explores Lamb's life and his transformation of it into the Elia essays.

Parker, Mark. *Literary Magazines and British Periodicals*. Cambridge, U.K., 2000. An extensive look at the periodicals, demonstrating Lamb's significance in that social enterprise.

Randel, Fred. *The World of Elia: Charles Lamb's Essayistic Romanticism*. Port Washington, NY, 1975. Explores Lamb's anxieties and pleasures in his literary confrontation with time.

Ross, Ernest. *The Ordeal of Bridget Elia: A Chronicle of the Lambs*. Norman, OK, 1940.

LETITIA LANDON

Mary Ellis Gibson

In the 1820s and 1830s Letitia Elizabeth Landon (1802–1838) was among the best-known literary figures in Britain. Her fame was acknowledged in America and throughout the British Empire. In the minds of many, the poet and her poems were inseparable, and readers responded strongly to the image of the lovelorn poetess projected in her work. Although Landon's reputation declined after her death, in recent years she has again become the subject of significant critical attention.

Landon (known by her signature L. E. L., and nicknamed Letty) was a transitional figure between the decades of high Romanticism and the Victorian era. Her best work yokes contradictory qualities of sentimentalism and irony, autobiography and performative mask. The two decades following the Napoleonic wars saw economic dislocation in Britain, accelerating urbanization and imperial power, the rise of the literary marketplace, and the demise of an older patronage economy of art. Landon's work evolved in this vortex of change.

Born 14 August 1802, Landon was the eldest of three children; her sister, Elizabeth Jane, died at thirteen, and she had a brother, Whittington. Although they came from the gentry, by the time of Landon's birth her family had lost much of their money. Her father initially earned a respectable middle-class income with an army supply agency. His attempt to become a scientific gentleman farmer, however, resulted in the loss of his remaining fortune. At his death in 1824, Landon became the sole support of her family. Like her immediate predecessor, Felicia Hemans, by far the best-known British woman poet before her, Landon was obliged to publish much and often. Over the course of her short life, she provided most of her brother's support at university, promoted his career, and despite what was evidently a vexed relationship with

Letitia Landon
Portrait by Daniel Maclise, c. 1830–1835
NATIONAL PORTRAIT GALLERY, LONDON

her mother, worked to secure her remaining parent's old age.

THE POET AND THE PUBLIC

Landon came before the public at a very early age, and like Felicia Hemans, she was an immediate success, even a sensation. Jerome McGann and Daniel Riess point out that Landon made her debut in the "volatile cultural arena" of literary journalism. This scene was not only public but strongly gendered, and the difficulties encountered by a young and single woman were still more daunting than those faced by her male peers. The cult of respectability for women mingled uneasily with the tropes of Byronic Romanticism, and even Lord Byron's popularity by this time was beginning to collapse in scandal. As she entered this controversial world, Landon would in any case have been the subject of talk, but she provoked unfriendly speculation when she moved out of her grandmother's house and into her own rooms.

A woman in the literary marketplace, Landon led at once an intensely public and an intensely private life. On the one hand, Landon's texts present her as the biographical guarantor of the image of the "poetess," whose power is grounded in a public display of suffering and anguish and who perishes for her art. On the other hand, her poems, especially those published in the 1830s in the annuals and as headnotes to her novel, resonate oddly with this myth.

In the late twentieth century, when critics began to read Landon, they remarked on the implicit discontinuities in her myth of the poetess. Isobel Armstrong speaks of this discontinuity as characteristic of women's poetry in the period: she argues that "the doubleness of women's poetry" results from its "ostensible adoption of an affective mode, often simple, often pious, often conventional," which is also questioned and "used for unexpected purposes" (*Victorian Poetry*, p. 324). Another way of elaborating the doubleness of Landon's writing is to see, as Tricia Lootens does, her increasing willingness in both poetry and fiction eventually to abandon the persona of the poetess in favor of one confronting power and moral ambiguity. McGann and Reiss characterize Landon's poetry as "oblique, or held in reserve, or self-censored" (p. 23). Landon's reserve acquired a new biographical resonance with Cynthia Lawford's discovery that Landon had a fifteen-year affair with her editor, William Jerdan. Between 1822 and 1829 Landon gave birth to three of his children. During her lifetime Landon and her friends went to great lengths to dispel rumors about her sexual activity, including those pairing her with Jerdan and others. She also seems to have had an intense relationship or affair with Rosina Wheeler, later Lady Lytton, who when estranged from Bulwer Lytton also perpetrated rumors about the poet. The scandal surrounding Landon stood in marked contrast to the figure of the poetess in her work. The myth of the abandoned poetess in her early poems frequently relies on either historicization or the protestation of sexual innocence. The poet-heroines of *The Improvisatrice* and *The Golden Violet* may recount the stories of Sappho and others, but their own moral power is guaranteed by their innocence.

Given the social strictures of the time and the cultural tropes created by Landon herself, it is remarkable that she managed to maintain her reputation at all. She was defended both in life and after her death by numerous friends and biographers who, although unable to lay rumor to rest, nevertheless made her appear more an innocent victim than the agent of her own fate. Rumors about her sexual conduct led her, at least by her own account, to break an engagement with John Forster, later the biographer of Charles Dickens.

EARLY WORKS

Landon's first publisher, William Jerdan, brought her to the public in an ostensibly avuncular manner. Her neighbor in Brompton, a London suburb, Jerdan was by 1817 the editor of a new periodical, *The Literary Gazette*. Under his editorship the *Gazette* was widely read among the middle classes. Priced well below the more expensive quarterlies, such as *Blackwoods*, which began publication the same year, the *Gazette* was published weekly and included long excerpts as well as complete poems. It found many readers who could seldom afford the quarterlies or

even volumes of verse. The *Gazette*'s readership prefigured the audience for the gift-books and annuals that were soon to become a sensation. Landon's literary career was a function of her ability to gauge the needs of this new market. As one of Jerdan's most frequent contributors, she gradually took on significant responsibilities for writing critical essays and reviews as well as poems.

Landon's first poem, "Rome," appeared in the *Gazette* on 11 March 1820. Its first line, "Oh! how thou art changed, thou proud daughter of fame," announces a theme of late Romanticism—the meditation on ruins—that was to be adumbrated later in Thomas Babington Macaulay's *Lays of Ancient Rome*. It also strikes the theme of meditation on empire, which comes second only to love and poetic inspiration among Landon's frequent subjects. This first published poem was signed only with the initial "L." Soon Landon was signing her work "L. E. L.," and Jerdan brilliantly allowed speculation about the author's identity to increase demand for the *Gazette*. L. E. L. became the object of various poetic outpourings, and when Bernard Barton, a Quaker poet, offered his poem "To L. E. L." to the *Gazette* two years later, Jerdan appended a note indicating (not quite accurately): "We have pleasure in saying that the sweet poems under this signature are by a lady, yet in her teens! The admiration with which they have been so generally read, could not delight their fair author more than it has those who in the *Literary Gazette* cherished her infant genius."

So, turning twenty, Landon found herself a very youthful "fair author." She published several collections of poetry in the subsequent decade, beginning with *The Fate of Adelaide, A Swiss Romantic Tale; and Other Poems* (1821), and continuing with *The Improvisatrice and Other Poems* (1824), *The Troubadour* (1825), *The Golden Violet* (1827), and *The Venetian Bracelet* (1828).

In *The Improvisatrice* (the title bears the feminine form of the Italian word for a male poet who composes extempore), Landon illustrates "that species of inspiration common in Italy" experienced by a "young female with all the loveliness, vivid feeling, and genius of her own impassioned land" (from "Advertisement" in her *Poetical Works*). The title character's genius overflows in various songs, including Sappho's farewell and the song of a Hindu girl, but these effusions and other interpolated tales are framed by a story of crossed love. The heroine's beloved Lorenzo is betrothed to another and does the honorable thing by marrying her; his wife dies beautifully and even conveniently. On seeking his beloved poet after his wife's death, Lorenzo finds he has arrived too late. The *improvisatrice* has already entered a fatal decline. She remains only in a painting where she appears "All soul, all passion, and all fire; / A priestess of Apollo's, when / The morning beams fall on her lyre." As Glennis Stephenson points out, this is the first of many appearances of the poet as Pythia, Apollo's priestess at Delphi. The Pythian performance of the poet reappears in other poems, such as "Erinna" or "Corinne at the Cape of Misena," and establishes a powerful "link between women's poetry and performance" (*Letitia Landon*, p. 109). L. E. L. here, as in her later poetry, is keenly aware of the power of spectacle.

The spectacle of the poetess resides in a gap between L. E. L. the persona and Landon the professional writer, and perhaps in the further contradiction between Landon the writer and Letty the private subject. As her friends S. C. and Anna Maria Hall observed, "it was not in her nature to open her heart to any one; her large organ of 'secretiveness' was her bane; she knew it and deplored it." Whether Landon found the "organ of secretiveness" a bane or a blessing no one can say. It is true, nonetheless, that from the publication of her first volume she was never wholly captive to the sentiments in which she traded. As early as 1820 she wrote as much to her cousin, clearly aware of the ways that her youth and celebrity were both a blessing and curse:

> Are you pleased with me? Am I not happy? "An elegance of mind peculiarly graceful in a female;"—is not this the praise you would have wished me to obtain? . . . The poem is now entirely finished. I hope you will like [The Fate of] "Adelaide." I wished to pourtray a gentle soft character, and to paint in her the most delicate love. I fear her dying is a little romantic; yet, what was I to do, as her death must terminate it? Pray do you think, as you are the model of my, I hope, charming heroine, you could have contrived to descend to the grave "Pale martyr to love's wasting flame?"

POETRY AND FICTION IN THE 1830S

In the 1830s Landon's poetry and fiction began to contain the complexities of attitude reflected in this early letter to her cousin. She wrote three novels of high society, in the genre popularly called "silver fork novels": *Romance and Reality* (1831), *Francesca Carrara* (1834), and *Ethel Churchill* (1837). In addition, she published a collection of poems, *The Vow of the Peacock* (1835). A final collection, *The Zenana and Minor Poems* (1839), was edited posthumously by Landon's friend Emma Roberts. Landon published widely in annuals, popular precursors of the modern coffee-table book. The annuals boasted elaborate covers and engravings and were the first print commodities widely favored by the Victorian middle classes. The text of the annuals was generally written to illustrate engravings rather than the other way around. Landon's work for *Fisher's Drawing-Room Scrapbook* and her poetical illustrations for *The Easter Gift* (also published by Fisher, 1832) evince a gradual shift in the market toward more explicitly religious works. Whatever her own personal skepticism about conventional piety, which seems to have been considerable, Landon nevertheless accommodated Fisher's growing presence in the evangelical market.

From 1832 to 1839 Landon edited the *Drawing-Room Scrapbook*, writing virtually all its poetry herself. Among these poems are many written in response to engravings from the sketchbook of Captain Robert Elliott, who had been in the service of the British East India Company and was a friend of Landon's sometime housemate Emma Roberts. With considerable work in the *Asiatick Researches* and other learned journals and books, Landon created a series of poems remarkable for both furthering and revealing the contradictions in the British imperial project. Also published in *Fisher's* was a poem that rivals Samuel Taylor Coleridge's "Christabel" and John Keats's "La Belle Dame sans Mercy"; "The Fairy of the Fountains" re-creates the story of the femme fatale as a haunted family romance. While many poems in the annuals replicate themes of her earlier work, Landon's poems for *Fisher's* share with her fiction a certain ironic distancing from her subject. In *Fisher's* contrary sentiments are juxtaposed without comment, and footnotes and headnotes provide ironic framing.

THE MYTH OF L. E. L.

On 7 June 1838 Landon married George Maclean, governor of Cape Coast Castle, West Africa (now Ghana). Theirs had been a difficult relationship, with Maclean inclined to break off the connection upon hearing rumors about Landon's earlier life. In his turn, Maclean was rumored to have an African common-law wife. By whatever agreement, the couple were married and left London some weeks later on the day of Victoria's coronation. They arrived in Africa on 15 August. On 15 October Landon was found slumped against her bedroom door, on the point of death, clutching a vial of prussic (hydrocyanic) acid. There was no autopsy. After a somewhat perfunctory inquest, she was buried within the walls of the fort.

Landon's death gave rise to many rumors. Whatever her friends or detractors had earlier thought of her conduct, she was now portrayed as a victim of suicide or murder. Maclean, who had been under investigation for allowing slave-trading vessels to resupply at Cape Coast Castle, came under suspicion. L. E. L. had accomplished the fate of the poetess—dying in the most dramatic of circumstances.

Anne Ethel Wyly argues that Landon's death may have been from epileptic seizure, for which hydrocyanic acid and other drugs in Landon's possession were sometimes prescribed. No account of the bruises on Landon's hands and cheek, noted at the inquest, has been satisfactory. Whatever explanations occurred to her friends and to later biographers, Landon's death became international currency. From Canada to Calcutta, readers and writers lamented her demise. Although her poems defined the very Englishness of empire, in her death L. E. L. became an embodiment of imperial melancholia.

[*See also* Felicia Hemans *and* Romanticism.]

SELECTED WORKS

The Improvisatrice and Other Poems (1824)
The Troubadour (1825)
The Golden Violet (1827)
The Venetian Bracelet (1828)
Ethel Churchill (1837)
The Zenana and Minor Poems (1839)
Poetical Works (1841)

FURTHER READING

Armstrong, Isobel. *Victorian Poetry: Poetry, Poetics, Politics.* London, 1993. Places Landon in the context of Victorian gender politics and poetics.

Blanchard, Laman. *Life and Literary Remains of L. E. L.* 2 vols. London, 1841. The best Victorian biography of Landon, including some of her correspondence.

Hall, Anna Maria, and S. C. Hall. "Memories of Authors: Miss Landon." *Atlantic Monthly* 15 (1865): 330–340. Key reminiscence by Landon's close friends.

Lawford, Cynthia. "Diary." *London Review of Books*, 21 September 2000, 36–37. First revelations about Landon's private life.

Leighton, Angela. *Victorian Women Poets: Writing against the Heart.* New York, 1992. Groundbreaking study of Landon along with seven other nineteenth-century women poets.

Lootens, Tricia. "Receiving the Legend, Rethinking the Writer: Letitia Landon and the Poetess Tradition." In *Romanticism and Women Poets: Opening the Doors of Reception*, edited by Harriet Kramer Linkin and Stephen C. Behrendt. Lexington, KY, 1999.

McGann, Jerome, and Daniel Riess, eds. *Letitia Elizabeth Landon: Selected Writings.* Peterborough, Ont., 1997. The only modern critical edition of Landon, including extremely useful materials on her literary reputation and influence on other poets. Contains an important index to Landon's periodical publications.

Stephenson, Glennis. *Letitia Landon: The Woman behind L. E. L.* Manchester, U.K., 1995. The best modern bio-critical study of Landon.

Wyly, Anne Ethel. "Letitia Elizabeth Landon: Her Career, Her 'Mysterious' Death, and Her Poetry." MA thesis, Duke University, Durham, NC, 1942. Most detailed discussion to date of Landon's death and the legend surrounding it.

WALTER SAVAGE LANDOR

Rebecca Cole Heinowitz

The extensive writings of Walter Savage Landor (1775–1864) have become something of a terra incognita to the contemporary reader. Their enigmatic quality is due largely to Landor's general disinterest in literary fame, frequent anonymous or pseudonymous publications, and predilection for writing much of his major poetry in Latin. The sheer range and multiplicity of Landor's work also make it difficult to define. "Genius," wrote Landor, "shows its power by its multiformity." Beloved by eminent friends such as Robert Southey, Henry Crabb Robinson, Robert Browning, and Charles Dickens, Landor's personality seems to have mirrored his work in its dynamism, eccentricity, and strength. Indeed, the prose and poetry he produced during his extraordinarily long writing life remain testaments to one of the most acute aesthetic and political sensibilities of his generation.

EARLY LIFE

On 30 January 1775, Walter Savage Landor was born in Warwick, England, the first son of a well-to-do provincial doctor. In 1783 he entered Rugby School, where he acquired his passion for literature and remarkable talent for the classics. When he was only twelve years old, he composed a Latin poem of such caliber that the headmaster, Thomas James, chidingly accused him of plagiarism. As Landor's classical attainments flourished, so did his refractory pride. He refused to address the sons of the nobility as "Mister," as was the custom, and frequently challenged James's authority, both verbally and in satiric verses. Though he was kind to the other boys at Rugby, often extravagantly so, well liked, and among the top of his class, James had Landor removed at the age of sixteen for being "rebellious" and "incit[ing] others to rebellion."

Landor's political views, like his literary abilities, developed early. His father, like many Whigs, swung toward the Tory government after the French Revolution. Dr. Landor's turn had the effect of strengthening his son's support of the Whigs and ardent opposition to the war with revolutionary France. In November 1792 Landor matriculated at Trinity College, Oxford. The freshman quickly developed a reputation as a dangerous republican (in the original sense of the term) and was one of the first students to wear his hair without powder. In June 1794 he was suspended for two terms after firing a volley of small shot against the shutters of his neighbor's room during a party. He never returned to Oxford.

By 1795 Landor had moved to London, and his first volume of poetry had appeared. The collection illustrated the young poet's love of Latin literature, especially Lucretius, Catullus, Tibullus, and John Milton. It also reflected his revolutionary zeal and his violent opposition to the Tory government. Although only thirty-six of the one thousand copies printed were sold, reviews were generally positive. Nevertheless, Landor disowned the collection several years later on the grounds of its fashionably sentimental style: "I had imprudently sent into the world a volume, of which I was soon ashamed. . . . I was then in raptures with what I now despise."

Ever disinclined to take up a respectable profession, Landor spent much of the next two years writing and wandering through South Wales. In 1796 he encountered Clara Reeve's *Progress of Romance* (1785), in which he first read "The History of Charoba, Queen of Ægypt," which suggested the narrative for his first significant poem, *Gebir* (1798). In an addendum to the Latin version of the poem, published in 1803, Landor identified *Gebir* as a Hellenistic "heroic idyl." He argued, against common opinion, that the great Greek idylls were not simply pastoral poems treating the loves of shepherds and nymphs, but rather that their composition in heroic verse suggested lofty themes, albeit portrayed in miniature. But the influence of classical simplicity on *Gebir* is significant in another respect. Even before William Wordsworth's famous dicta in the *Lyrical Ballads* against elevated and ornate poetic diction, Landor wrote in his postscript to *Gebir*, "I have avoided high-sounding words. I have attempted to throw back the gross materials, and to bring the figures forward."

Gebir also offers a useful window onto the complexities and contradictions of Romantic-era radicalism. Behind the story of the king of Cadiz who must avenge the suffering of his ancestors by conquering Egypt, one sees Landor's admiration of Napoleon and contempt for English kings. Alongside his radical idealism, however, one also notes a decidedly colonialist tendency in the poem. Although Landor specifies that those who flee injustice in their native land are more righteous than those who colonize foreign lands on behalf of their mother country, his portrait of conquest ending in love has disturbing implications. The fact that Landor felt entitled to adapt Oriental source material (in this case, an Arabian history of ancient Egypt) for the purpose of addressing European politics has also led modern critics to question the limits of his radical egalitarianism. Similar criticisms have been directed at better-known Romantic writers such as Percy Bysshe Shelley, Thomas de Quincey, Samuel Taylor Coleridge, and Robert Southey. What is interesting about Landor's Orientalism is its early appearance and its subsequent influence on these authors. Southey, for example, commented, "My verse was greatly improved by [reading *Gebir*]" and dedicated his own Oriental epic, the *Curse of Kehama*, to Landor.

Despite *Gebir*'s success with Southey and his circle, critics received the poem unfavorably. Although Landor was pained by their judgment, he went on to publish *Poems from the Arabic and Persian* in 1800. This work followed the Romantic taste for Orientalism and literary impostures (or false translations). As did *Gebir*, *Poems from the Arabic and Persian* linked the lure of the Orient with a revolutionary agenda, commending Napoleon's appreciation of the eastern territories he had conquered. Similarly, *Poetry by the Author of Gebir* (printed in 1800, published in 1802) stands out for the "Story of Crysaor," an exoticist work that thinly veils Landor's opinions on contemporary European politics.

Landor's political allegiances were profoundly altered in the summer of 1802, when Napoleon crowned himself First Consul for life. Although he had renounced his faith in the French Revolution, Landor protested until the end of his life that his views remained coherent: "Let me never be called inconsistent if I praised the good and true, abhorring and detesting the vicious and the false." The following year he published a revised edition of *Gebir* in which his early praise for Napoleon was largely revoked. In 1806, with the failure and dissolution of the Ministry of All the Talents, headed by Charles Fox, Landor's renunciation of the Whigs and their sympathy for the French government was complete.

When Spain rose up against the Napoleonic invasion in 1808, Landor, with characteristic spontaneity and enthusiasm, learned Spanish and shipped off to Spain as a private soldier. His stay was cut short, however, by the Convention of Cintra, in which the victorious British made a number of overly generous concessions to the French, thereby failing to thwart Napoleon's imperial ambitions. Landor returned to England in October, enraged and ashamed for his country. Yet his service in Spain was not fruitless. The following year, while reading the classic medieval epic *El Cid* and closely following events on the Iberian Peninsula, he began work on his Spanish tragedy, *Count Julian*. It tells the tale of the legendary conqueror who, having heroically routed the Moors, then leads them back into Spain to avenge the rape of his daughter by the Spanish king. Although he completed the play in January 1811, Landor could not find a publisher until February 1812, when John Murray (Lord Byron's publisher) released it on Southey's recommendation.

As a result of his failure to find remunerative work, his economic ineptitude, and his generosity to friends, Landor was plagued throughout his life by financial strain. Even after the death of his father in 1805, which left him with an annual income of £1,100 a year and a significant amount of property, Landor struggled to make ends meet. In 1807 he purchased Llanthony Abbey in Monmouthsire, South Wales, without even having seen the property. But Landor had no knowledge of estate management; this naivete, combined with a vehemently litigious tendency when he felt himself wronged, quickly made him an enemy of both his tenants and the local authorities. In 1813 Landor left Llanthony, followed by an angry trail of creditors and lawsuits, and in 1815 he renounced all control of the property.

ITALY

In 1811 Landor married, and by the end of 1815, he and his wife Julia had relocated to Italy. The Landors' arrival there coincided with the opening of peace talks between France and Britain. Landor immediately scripted a pamphlet (under the pseudonym "Calvus") in which he maintained that any peace was untenable unless Napoleon were stripped of his power and France divested of all its imperial conquests. This was not to be the last of Landor's prose writings, as witnessed by an 1820 pamphlet advising Neapolitan revolutionaries on the principles of representative government; *Letters of a Conservative* (1836), a reformist pamphlet decrying the corruption of the Church of England; *High and Low Life in Italy* (1837–1838), a study of Italian society and manners; and numerous contributions to literary journals, ranging from letters on the Irish question to essays on the poets Theocritus and Petrarch. But Landor's most significant prose work was the *Imaginary Conversations of Literary Men and Statesmen* (1824–1853). Bringing together such varied topics as the Emperor Alexander, Mohammed, Wordsworth, Ovid, Italian politics, French literature under Louis XIV, Geoffrey Chaucer, Oliver Cromwell, the German dramatist August Kotzebue, and spelling and diction (about which he was passionate), the *Imaginary Conversations* were the perfect form for expressing the immense scope of Landor's concerns.

One of the factors that pushed Landor toward the conversational form was the discouragement his Latin writings met on the publication of *Idyllia Heroica Decem* (Ten Heroic Idylls) in Italy in 1820. In "De Cultu atque Usu Latini Sermonis" ("Concerning the Cultivation and Use of Latin Speech"), an essay that comprised a large part of this volume, Landor critiqued Latin poetry, both ancient and modern, extolled the poetry of Wordsworth and Southey, and rebuked the works and character of Byron. Southey included Landor's treatment of Byron in his damning *Vision of Judgment* later that year, and Landor quickly found himself embroiled in the poetry wars between Southey's circle and the so-called Satanic School, namely Byron and Leigh Hunt. What principally angered Landor, however, was the publisher's removal of those of his poems that criticized Italian statesmen. Indeed, during his early years in Italy, Landor developed a hefty police record (not unlike that he left behind in Wales). Though it was well received by those few who read it, no British publisher wanted to distribute the book, and Landor's friends dissuaded him from further publication in Latin.

The decisive event in the genesis of the *Imaginary Conversations* occurred when Landor received a letter in which Southey explained his new undertaking, *Colloquies on the Progress and Prospects of Society*, a dialogue between a modern man (Southey himself, under the guise of one "Montesinos") and Sir Thomas More. Because Landor envisioned the *Conversations* as personal essays in the form of dialogues, only a few stand out for dramatic power or careful characterization. While his characters often serve as mouthpieces for Landor himself, they also allow him to express opinions that would have compromised his publisher or with which he did not in fact agree. He also used historical characters as ciphers for himself, as when Sophocles complains of his mistreatment by petty diplomats and foreign secretaries, much as Landor often did.

The *Conversations* had difficulty finding a publisher because of the controversial opinions they expressed. Landor finally convinced the publisher of the prominent *London Magazine*, John Taylor, to accept the work, provided that he omit or qualify several of the more inflammatory conversations. Although his alliance with Southey still rendered him vulnerable to jibes in the pages of liberal periodicals, Landor's reputation visibly benefited from such negative exposure. By 1824, when the first two volumes of the *Conversations* were finally published, Landor's name was already familiar to the reading public and, for the first time, his writings began to reach a sizable audience. That the *Conversations* were so widely respected despite their tendentiousness reveals how misleading divisions such as Tory and Whig can be with regard to political and intellectual currents during the Romantic era. In 1828 the third volume of the *Conversations* was published, and in 1835 the fourth and fifth. Landor, however, would revise and add to the *Conversations* almost until the end of his life.

Although Southey was to remain a close friend of Landor's until the end of his days, the two men's political opinions diverged significantly after 1820. Landor supported Catholic emancipation and electoral reform, two issues that Southey vociferously opposed. Landor dedicated the first volume of the *Imaginary Conversations* to his brother-in-law, Colonel Edward Stopford, who had fought for South American independence under Simón Bolívar, and the third volume to Bolívar himself. He defended the Greek struggle for liberty and foresaw the downfall of England resulting from its colonial mismanagement and complicity with Austrian and Russian imperialism. Though he did not predict the immediate destruction of England, he could look forward with a certain detached enjoyment to the elegant ruins of "York Cathedral, a thousand years hence, when the Americans have conquered and devastated the Country."

In the 1820s Landor's relationship with the Satanic School also shifted. In 1823 Leigh Hunt (co-editor, with Lord Byron, of the controversial journal, *The Liberal*) moved to Florence, near where Landor was residing. In time Landor found himself the intimate friend of his erstwhile enemies, even reversing his early negative opinion of Shelley. As Landor's circle of literary friends and admirers expanded during the 1820s and early 1830s, however, his domestic life was disintegrating. In 1835, twenty-one years after he had moved to Italy, he left his wife, family, and his beloved Villa Gherardesca in Fiesole, and returned to England.

VICTORIAN ENGLAND

With his separation from Julia and return to England, a new chapter opened in Landor's life. The sixty-year-old Romantic poet now found himself in the company of men such as Browning, Dickens, John Forster, and Thomas Carlyle—soon to become among the most eminent Victorian writers. One can find an illuminating caricature of Landor during these years in the person of Lawrence Boythorn, the fierce, tender, eccentric character in Dickens's *Bleak House*. Landor's years in England were also the most prolific of his life, yielding such works as *Pericles and Aspasia* (1836), *The Pentameron and Pentalogia* (1837), *Andrea of Hungary* (1839), and *Giovanna of Naples* (1839). Drawing on his favorite pastime, dining, as a metaphor for literary attainment, Landor wrote, "I shall dine late, but the dining-room will be well-lighted, the guests few and select."

Pericles and Aspasia was immediately hailed as Landor's best composition to date. The work explores the literary and political history of fifth-century Athens via a series of letters, interspersed with poetry, dramatic blank verse, and prose fragments allegedly written by ancient Greeks. Equally well received, *The Pentameron and Pentalogia* consists of five "interviews" or imaginary conversations featuring Petrarch and Boccaccio, as well as five dramatic scenes between such figures as Orestes and Electra, Francis Bacon and the earl of Sussex, and the parents of Martin Luther. *Andrea of Hungary* and *Giovanna of Naples*, which John Forster called Landor's masterpieces, treat the marriage of Giovanna to Andrea of Hungary, the accusation that his mother plotted to murder the boy, and the queen's vindication. In addition to displaying a dramatic continuity that *Count Julian* lacks, *Andrea* and *Giovanna* reveal a new richness of characterization.

During the 1840s Landor undertook the enormous task of translating much of his Latin poetry, particularly the idylls, which appeared in 1847 as *The Hellenics*, dedicated to the new liberal pope, Pius IX. During these years he suffered increasingly from his separation from his children and, perhaps as a result of this sadness, threw himself with renewed vigor into political writing and charity work. Then, with the outbreak of revolutions across Europe in 1848, Landor's flagging faith in the future of human liberty was revitalized. He quickly drafted seven poems in praise of revolution that were published in February under the title *The Italics*, one week before the revolution in France and two months before that in Hungary. Nor did Landor's productivity wane in the following decade: during his mid-seventies he contributed more than one hundred prose works and almost an equal number of poems to English periodicals, in addition to his own published volumes.

Despite his undiminished productivity and the constant quality of his work, however, Landor's writings began to show a bittersweet acquiescence to old age. The title of the 1853 volume collecting his new Imaginary Conversations, satires, articles, dramatic scenes, and poems, tells much: *The Last Fruit off an Old Tree*. His next volume of poetry, appearing in 1858 with a dedication to the president of Hungary, followed in a similar vein: *Dry Sticks, Fagoted by Walter Savage Landor*. What is perhaps most remarkable about Landor's dotage is that although he came to consider himself a Tory, unlike Southey and Wordsworth, his radicalism did not fade with age. The outbreak of the Crimean War saw Landor vigorously criticizing the Russian tsar; regarding domestic politics, he wrote in favor of liberal causes, the Chartists, and workingmen's organizations.

The last years of his life brought illness and personal distresses from which Landor never fully recovered. Falsely accused of indecent conduct toward a young woman with whom he had developed a sentimental friendship, Landor struck back at his assailant in the local papers and was charged with libel. During that same time a failed assassination attempt aimed at the French emperor resulted in the death of almost a hundred members of a crowd near the emperor's carriage. This event attracted particularly negative attention to Landor because he was known to have advocated tyrannicide as a means of alleviating oppression and was said to have had friendly relations with the assassin, Felice Orsini. In 1858, fearing a guilty verdict if he stood trial in the libel case, Landor's family arranged for his flight back to Italy. His reappearance at Fiesole was met with familial indifference and even cruelty. Nevertheless, he continued to write, revise, and publish, dedicating much of his energy to various public vindications of his honor. With the help of the Brownings and Forster, he relocated to a small private cottage where, in September 1864, he died.

Shelley's love of *Gebir* and Wordsworth's praise for *Count Julian* were not unfounded, and much of Landor's poetry deserves to be revisited by the contemporary reader. Although inconsistent, Landor's verse often attains a beauty that ranks it among the greatest literature:

And the long moon-beam on the hard wet sand
Lay like a jaspar column half uprear'd

During his lifetime Landor's circle of admirers included such luminaries as Wordsworth, Charles Lamb, Thomas Beddoes, Leigh Hunt, William Hazlitt, the Brownings, Ralph Waldo Emerson, Dickens, Isaac D'Israeli, Alfred, Lord Tennyson, and Algernon Charles Swinburne, among hundreds of lesser-known intellectuals. Even those who disagreed with him attested to his astonishing powers of language, both in his prose style and in his ingenious conversation. Today Emerson's evaluation of Landor still holds true: "Year after year the scholar must still go back to Landor for a multitude of elegant sentences—for wisdom, wit, and indignation that are unforgettable."

[*See also* Orientalism; Romanticism; Robert Southey; *and* William Wordsworth.]

SELECTED WORKS

The Poems of Walter Savage Landor (1795)
Gebir (1798, published 1801)
Poems from the Arabic and Persian (1800)
Poetry by the Author of Gebir (1802)
Simonidea (1806)
Count Julian (1812)
Idyllia (1815)
Idyllia Heroica Decem (Ten Heroic Idylls, 1820)
Imaginary Conversations of Literary Men and Statesmen, vols. 1 and 2 (1824)
Imaginary Conversations, vol. 3 (1828)
Gebir, Count Julian, and Other Poems (1831)
Citation and Examination of William Shakespeare (1834)
Imaginary Conversations, vols. 4 and 5 (1835)
Pericles and Aspasia, 2 vols. (1836)
The Pentameron and Pentalogia (1837)
Andrea of Hungary (1839)
Giovanna of Naples (1839)
Fra Rupert (1841; the final part of the dramatic trilogy beginning with *Andrea of Hungary* and *Giovanna of Naples*)
The Works of Walter Savage Landor, 2 vols. (1846)
Hellenics (1847)
Italics (1848)
Imaginary Conversations of the Greeks and Romans (1853)
The Last Fruit off an Old Tree (1853)
Antony and Octavius (1856)
Scenes for the Study (1856)
Dry Sticks, Fagoted by Walter Savage Landor (1858)
Heroic Idyls (1863)

EDITIONS

de Sélincourt, E., ed. *Imaginary Conversations: A Selection*. Oxford, 1914.

Welby, T. Earle, and Stephen Wheeler, eds. *The Complete Works of Walter Savage Landor*. 16 vols. London, 1927–1936.

Wheeler, Stephen, ed. *Letters of Walter Savage Landor, Private and Public*. London, 1899. Good representation of Landor's witty, conversational style.

FURTHER READING

Colvin, Sidney. *Landor*. New York, 1881. Excellent although somewhat dated biography.

Elwin, Malcolm. *Savage Landor*. New York, 1941. Useful biography, including letters from Landor to his family.

Forster, John. *Walter Savage Landor: A Biography*. 2 vols. London, 1869. The first biography of Landor by one of his closest friends; a wellspring of information, including many personal accounts, though Forster often misquotes Landor's letters.

Super, Robert Henry. *Walter Savage Landor: A Biography*. New York, 1954. The definitive treatment of Landor's life and work.

AEMILIA LANYER

Susanne Woods

Aemilia Bassano Lanyer (1569–1645) published one volume of verse, *Salve Deus Rex Judaeorum* (Hail God, King of the Jews, 1611), notable for its variety, quality, and protofeminist stance. Lanyer may also have been the first woman writing in English both to claim divine calling as a poet and to seek patronage through a community of intellectual women whom she praised and sought to represent. Her book consists of eleven introductory dedications to highborn women, nine in verse and two in prose, followed by the long title poem (1,840 lines in rhyme royal stanzas, ababbcc), followed by the first country-house poem published in English, "The Description of Cookham" (210 lines of couplets). The title poem tells the story of Christ's Passion entirely from the point of view of women, including a witty "Defense of Eve" in the voice of Pilate's wife (lines 753–832). "Cookham" portrays an idyllic sojourn with Margaret Russell, countess of Cumberland, and her daughter Anne Clifford shortly before she became countess of Dorset, at the royal leasehold home of Margaret's brother. Margaret is Lanyer's principal dedicatee for the long poem as well as for "Cookham."

LIFE

Aemilia Bassano was born a member of the minor gentry in 1569 (the year of Edmund Spenser's first publication), the daughter of the court musician Baptista Bassano and his "reputed wife," Margaret Johnson. Aemilia's father, a native of Venice, was the youngest of several brothers brought to England by Henry VIII to enrich the music of the court. Her mother was an Englishwoman with ties to families associated with the Reformation wing of the English Church, notably the Vaughan family, which included Anne Vaughan Lock (Dering Prowse), who translated John Calvin and wrote a series of religious sonnets published in 1560. Baptista Bassano died when Aemilia was seven and Margaret Johnson when Aemilia was eighteen. At some time in her childhood Aemilia was educated in the household of Susan Bertie, the young dowager duchess of Kent, where she was exposed to standard Renaissance humanist texts and ideas. Probably after her mother's death, Aemilia became the mistress of the much older Lord Chamberlain, Henry Cary, Lord Hunsdon, Queen Elizabeth's cousin. Aemilia told the astrologer Simon Forman in 1597 that "the old Lord Chamberlain kept her long and she was maintained in great pomp," that he "loved her well," and that she "had been favored much of her majesty [Queen Elizabeth I]." When Aemilia became pregnant by the Lord Chamberlain in 1592, she was married in October to a musician cousin, Alfonso Lanyer. She gave birth in early 1593 to a son, whom she named Henry.

Lanyer lost direct access to the glamour and pomp of the Elizabethan court when she ended her relationship with the Lord Chamberlain, and her poetry shows her frustration with the class and gender distinctions that prevented her return. There were no avenues for a woman to rise independently in the social hierarchy. While her husband volunteered as a gentleman-soldier with the earl of Essex and developed contacts with important courtiers, including the earl of Southampton and Thomas Egerton (Lord Chancellor under James), Aemilia could only hope he would be knighted so she could rise to the rank of "lady." Although he was eventually awarded income from a hay- and grain-weighing patent, a typical reward for government service that Aemilia Lanyer fought to collect after her husband's death in 1613, Alfonso never was knighted.

A. L. Rowse fit into this era of Aemilia's life the conjecture that Lanyer was Shakespeare's "Dark Lady." and a few others, notably Roger Prior, have followed his lead. The majority of Lanyer scholars, however, consider this merely distracting speculation supported by circular reasoning, bits of information taken out of context, and wishful thinking (Lewalski, p. 213; Woods, chap. 1; Bevington in Grossman, pp. 10–24). Lanyer may possibly have encountered Shakespeare, whose acting company (as the Lord Chamberlain's Men) came under the protection of Lord Hunsdon and then his son after Lanyer was forced to leave the court, but it is hard to believe so ambitious a woman would have left the bed of one of the mightiest peers of the land for that of a player who had not yet achieved the rank of gentleman. The major poets of the period with whom Lanyer was more plausibly acquainted include Spenser, who was at the Elizabethan court for periods between 1589 and 1591, when Lanyer was enjoying the queen's favor, and Ben Jonson, who consorted with court musicians and numbered among his closest friends Alfonso Ferrabosco, who married Aemilia Lanyer's sister-in-law, Ellen Lanyer, in 1610.

Aemilia Lanyer's best hope for advancement lay in her friendships with Margaret, countess of Cumberland, and her daughter Anne Clifford. The countess of Cumberland, like the countesses of Pembroke and Bedford, was a well-known patron of the arts. Spenser dedicated verse to her. Samuel Daniel lived in her household and was tutor to Anne Clifford. At some time during the first decade of the seventeenth century, Lanyer resided with the countess and her daughter at the Crown manor at Cookham, where she apparently enjoyed patronage similar to Daniel's. Lanyer's book of poems is, among other things, an effort to bridge the gap in class by encouraging and justifying patronage support.

When Alfonso died in 1613, Lanyer was forced to support herself and her son, who eventually became a court musician, married, had two children, and then predeceased his mother. From 1617 to 1619 Lanyer ran a school for young women until a dispute with her landlord forced her out of the building she was using. She negotiated with Alfonso's relatives over the hay and grain patent, eventually getting a settlement on behalf of herself and her grandchildren. When she died in 1645 (the year John Milton's *Poems* appeared), she was buried in the churchyard of Saint James Clerkenwell, the parish in which her son and his family had settled in the 1620s.

SALVE DEUS REX JUDAEORUM

The story of Lanyer's life suggests an ambitious woman at odds with many of the class and gender assumptions of her time. Her one extant book shows that she was familiar with classical and vernacular literature, with perhaps the most influence from Spenser and the poetic narratives of Shakespeare, Daniel, and Michael Drayton. In the long *Salve Deus* poem she refers to Lucrece, Rosamund, and Matilda, stories told respectively by these three authors. In addition to the rhyme royal of *Salve Deus* and the heroic couplets of "Cookham," Lanyer proves adept with ballade stanzas and quatrains among the dedicatory poems and shows an ability to write elegant rhetorical prose.

The dedications are, in order: "To the Queenes most Excellent Majestie" (Queen Anne); "To the Lady *Elizabeths* Grace" (Anne's daughter, Princess Elizabeth); "To all virtuous Ladies in generall" (a general encomium as prelude to the rest of the specific dedications); "To the Ladie *Arabella*" (Arbella Stuart, King James's cousin); "To the Ladie *Susan*, Countesse Dowager of Kent, and Daughter to the Duchesse of Suffolke" (Susan Bertie, in whose household Lanyer had been educated); "The Authors Dreame to the Ladie *Marie*, the Countesse Dowager of *Pembrooke*" (Mary Sidney, preeminent woman poet and patron of her day and sister to the late Sir Philip Sidney); "To the Ladie *Lucie*, Countesse of Bedford" (reputed to be a fine writer herself, though nothing remains extant, and the most important woman patron after Mary Sidney); "To the Ladie *Margaret* Countesse Dowager of Cumberland" (a prose dedication); "To the Ladie *Katherine* Countesse of Suffolke" (who was reputedly interested in learning and gave receptions at Magdalene College, Cambridge, when her husband was chancellor of the university); "To the Ladie *Anne*, Countesse of Dorcet (Margaret's daughter, herself an important patron and eventually a major figure in the English North Country until her death in 1676); and immediately before the long poem itself, "To the Vertuous Reader" (a general prose dedication with some protofeminist themes). This last is worth particular note, especially Lanyer's condemnation of women who disparage other women. She accuses them of imitating the practice of "evill disposed men, who forgetting they were borne of women, nourished of women, and that if it were not by the means of women, they would be quite extinguished out of the world, and a finall ende of them all, doe like Vipers deface the wombes wherein they were bred, onely to give way and utterance to their want [lack] of discretion and goodnesse" (lines 19–24). The Ciceronian periodicity of the prose is remarkable for its art and persuasive logic.

Also of note are the dedications to Queen Anne and the countess of Pembroke. The dedication to the queen begins the book by both acknowledging and overcoming the disadvantages of gender, using many of the same gestures male poets used to acknowledge and bridge class differences between themselves and their patrons. Like Spenser approaching Queen Elizabeth in *The Faerie Queene*, Lanyer asks only that the grace of the great queen overcome her inadequacies and promises in return the grace of her own gift, the long poem she presents.

In "The Authors Dreame" to Pembroke, the "Author" (an audacious word for a woman in this period) envisions the countess centering classical figures of beauty, intellect, and power, including the Graces, Minerva, and Bellona, and reconciling the traditional dispute between nature and art. From Pembroke's example issues a new harmony that enables the author to offer boldly her own vision of Christ's Passion. In addition to showing clearly that women writers did have a tradition of their own, the poem is a delicate recasting of the classical figures who pervaded male Renaissance humanist discourse. The Muses, for example, provide the musical background for the speaker-dreamer's vision of first Minerva (who trumpets the countess's fame), then the countess, who effectively replaces them as inspiring motives and is later presented as a figure who can resolve the ancient conflict between nature and art.

The main poem of the volume, *Salve Deus*, highlights the suffering of Christ as an analogue to women's suffering, notably that of Lanyer's patron, the countess of Cumberland, who endured an unfaithful husband and, in her widowhood, a dispute with King James over the inheritance rights of her only child, Anne Clifford. The countess's suffering surrounds the central story as Lanyer begins the poem with dedicatory language to her along with reference to tales of faithful and misunderstood women from history, romance, and the Bible. The Passion story itself moves peripheral biblical characters to the center, emphasizing the wisdom of women as opposed to the malice of men, as in the warning of Pilate's wife, the tears of the daughters of Jerusalem, and the suffering of Mary, the mother of Jesus (line 1287). It ends with Christ's Resurrection and the triumphant marriage between Christ and the Church, the latter fully embodied in the countess of Cumberland, whose devotion is portrayed as greater than that of a series of classical and biblical women (notably the queen of Sheba) and even greater than famous martyrs.

The whole poem, with its effort to redefine beauty, to gaze on the male body, and to affirm a woman poet's divine calling, is a powerful and original construction of verse narrative. The poem's best-known section, however, is "*Eves* Apologie," in which Pilate's wife condemns those who would execute Christ and uses the perfidy of men to refute the old claims of women's guilt in Eve's fall. The section's conclusion seems almost modern in both sentiment and language:

Then let us have our Libertie againe,
And challendge to your selves no Sov'raigntie;
You came not in the world without our paine,
Make that a barre against your crueltie;
Your fault being greater, why should you disdaine
Our being your equals, free from tyranny?
 If one weake woman simply did offend,
   This sinne of yours hath no excuse, nor end.

(ll. 825–832)

"The Description of Cookham," the poem that concludes the volume, is 210 lines of often elegant pentameter couplets, describing what Barbara Lewalski has called "a valediction by author and residents to an Edenic pastoral life and place" (p. 234). Though it is the first of the formal genre known as the "country-house poem" printed in English, the traditional "first," Ben Jonson's "To Penshurst," printed in 1616, may have been written around the same time and makes an effective pair with Lanyer's poem. "Cookham" presents a woman's vision of "an Edenic pastoral life," in which neither men nor class distinctions mar conversation and song under a lovely oak tree with a wonderful view of the countryside. But all must end, as "occasions" (line 147) call the countess and her daughter away. The speaker is left reflecting on the class distinctions that leave her behind:

Unconstant Fortune, thou art most to blame
Who casts us downe into so lowe a frame:
Where our great friends we cannot dayly see,
So great a difference is there in degree.

(ll. 103–106)

Lanyer's work illustrates three major concerns of the Jacobean period: poetic authority, "wit," and religion. The swaddling of dedications to highborn patrons and the topic of Christ's Passion finesse the general issue of whether women have a right to speak publicly. Lanyer's claim that she was born to praise the countess of Cumberland (*Salve Deus*, lines 1457–1464) and that she had a divine calling to "performe this Worke" ("To the doubtfull Reader") make her claim for authority more direct. Lanyer's wit fits the classic Johnsonian dictum of "discordia concors" and provides a lively balance to the more famous wit of John Donne. Her principal technique is to use logic to turn traditional biases around. So she notes in her poem to Queen Anne, for example, that women are not expected to have the learning or artfulness of men and are therefore not expected to write, yet women are generally conceded to be closer to nature:

And since all Arts at first from Nature came,
That goodly Creature, Mother of Perfection,
Whom *Joves* almighty hand at first did frame,
Taking both her and hers in his protection:
  Why should not She now grace my barren Muse,
  And in a Woman all defects excuse.

(ll. 151–156)

She flips the usual connotations upside down. Instead of women's closeness to nature making them less sophisticated artists, it makes them more authentic ones. Similarly in the "*Eves* Apologie" section of the *Salve Deus,* Lanyer alters both Eve's guilt and man's boast of knowledge: "Yet Men will boast of Knowledge, which he tooke / From *Eves* faire hand, as from a learned Booke" (lines 807–808).

As a religious poet Lanyer challenges patriarchal assumptions about Christianity and offers a rich description of the central event of Christian belief. In *Salve Deus* her crucified Christ is the beautiful object of female gaze, a risen bridegroom worthy of the rapturous language of the Song of Songs:

This is that Bridegroom that appears so faire,
So sweet, so lovely in his Spouses sight,
That unto Snowe we may his face compare,
His cheekes like skarlet, and his eyes so bright
As purest Doves that in the rivers are,
Washed with milke, to give the more delight;
  His head is likened to the finest gold,
  His curled lockes so beauteous to behold.

(ll. 1305–1312)

Although unquestionably Protestant in background and theology, Lanyer's "sensuous baroque passage[s]" (Lewalski, p. 234) are more reminiscent of Robert Southwell or even Richard Crashaw than they are of, say, Fulke Greville's plain-style Calvinist sonnets. Lanyer's topic places her, with Southwell, Greville, and Donne, at the beginning of the great period of English religious poetry. At the same time her unique perspective makes her a particularly valuable contrast to the major religious poets, including Donne, George Herbert, and Milton. Her narrative subtlety, boldness, and wit combine to make her an important figure in English poetry of the early seventeenth century.

[*See also* Ben Jonson; William Shakespeare: The Poems; Mary Sidney, Countess of Pembroke; *and* Isabella Whitney.]

EDITIONS

Salve Devs Rex Ivdaeorum. Containing, 1. The Passion of Christ. 2. Eues Apologie in defence of Women. 3. The Teares of the Daughters of Ierusalem. 4. The Salutation and Sorrow of the Virgine Marie. London, 1611. STC 15277 and 15277.5 The former has four-line, the latter five-line publisher's imprint; nine extant copies, not all complete.

Rowse, A. L., ed. *The Poems of Shakespeare's Dark Lady: "Salve Deus Rex Judaeorum" by Emilia Lanier.* London, 1978. Introduction argues Rowse's case that Lanyer was Shakespeare's "Dark Lady."

Woods, Susanne, ed. *The Poems of Aemilia Lanyer: "Salve Deus Rex Judaeorum."* New York, 1993. Based on the Huntington Library copy.

Woods, Susanne, Betty S. Travitsky, and Patrick Cullen, eds. *Salve Devs Rex Judaeorum* in *The Early Modern Englishwoman, 1500–1700: A Facsimile Library of Essential Works.* Vol. 10, *The Poets, I: Isabella Whitney, Anne Dowriche, Aemilia Lanyer, Rachel Speght, and Diana Primrose.* Burlington, VT, 2002.

FURTHER READING

Benson, Pamela Joseph. "To Play the Man: Aemilia Lanyer and the Acquisition of Patronage." In *Opening the Borders: Inclusivity in Early Modern Studies; Essays in Honor of James V. Mirollo,* edited by Peter C. Herman, 243–264. Newark, NJ, 1999.

Bowen, Barbara. "Aemilia Lanyer and the Invention of White Womanhood." In *Maids and Mistresses, Cousins and Queens,* edited by Susan Frye and Karen Robertson, 274–2303. New York, 1999.

DiPasquale, Theresa M. "Woman's Desire for Man in Lanyer's *Salve Deus Rex Judaeorum.*" *Journal of English and Germanic Philology* 99 (2000): 356–378.

Grossman, Marshall, ed. *Aemilia Lanyer: Gender, Genre, and the Canon.* Lexington, KY, 1998. Essential collection, including David Bevington's rejection of Rowse's "Dark Lady" argument (pp. 10–28) and foundational essays by Leeds Barroll, Barbara Lewalski, Kari Boyd McBride, Susanne Woods, Janel Mueller, Marshall Grossman, Naomi Miller, Michael Holmes, and Achsah Guibbory.

Herz, Judith Scherer. "Aemilia Lanyer and the Pathos of Literary History." In *Representing Women in Renaissance England,* edited by Claude J. Summers and Ted-Larry Pebworth, 121–135. Columbia, MO, 1997.

Keohane, Catherine. "'That Blindest Weakenesse Be Not Over-Bold': Aemilia Lanyer's Radical Unfolding of the Passion." *ELH* 64 (1997): 359–389.

Lamb, Mary Ellen. "Patronage and Class in Aemilia Lanyer's *Salve Deus Rex Judaeorum.*" In *Women, Writing, and the Reproduction of Culture in Tudor and Stuart Britain*, edited by Mary E. Burke, Jane Donawerth, Linda L. Dove, and Karen Nelson, 38–57. Syracuse, NY, 2000.

Lasocki, David, with Roger Prior. *The Bassanos: Venetian Musicians and Instrument Makers in England, 1531–1665.* Aldershot, U.K., 1995. Useful research on Lanyer's extended Bassano family. Prior contributes an unconvincing rehash of Rowse's "Dark Lady" theory and makes a circumstantial but more interesting case that the Bassano family had Jewish origins.

Lewalski, Barbara Kiefer. *Writing Women in Jacobean England.* Cambridge, MA, 1993. The whole work contextualizes Lanyer, the specific subject of chap. 8, "Imagining Female Community: Aemilia Lanyer's Poems," pp. 213–241.

Loughlin, Marie H. "'Fast ti'd unto them in a golden Chaine': Typology, Apocalypse, and Women's Genealogy in Aemilia Lanyer's *Salve Deus Rex Judaeorum.*" *Renaissance Quarterly* 53 (2000): 133–179.

McBride, Kari Boyd. "Aemilia Lanyer (1569–1645): Bibliography." 24 May 2005. http://jamaica.u.arizona.edu/ic/mcbride/lanyer/lanbib.htm. Regularly updated.

Nelson, Karen. "Annotated Bibliography: Texts and Criticism of Aemilia Bassano Lanyer." In *Aemilia Lanyer: Gender, Genre, and the Canon*, edited by Marshall Grossman, 234–254. Lexington, KY, 1998. Mostly complete up to 1998.

Ng, Su Fang. "Aemilia Lanyer and the Politics of Praise." *ELH* 67 (2000): 433–451.

Powell, Brenda J. "'Witnesse thy wife (o Pilate) speakes for all': Aemilia Lanyer's Strategic Self-Positioning." *Christianity and Literature* 46 (1996): 5–23.

Rogers, John. "The Passion of a Female Literary Tradition: Aemelia Lanyer's *Salve Deus Rex Judaeorum.*" *Huntington Library Quarterly* 63 (2000): 435–446.

Schleiner, Louise. "Discourse Analysis and Literary Study: Aemilia Lanyer's 'Epistle' as Sample Text." *Mosaic* 30 (1997): 15–37.

Seelig, Sharon Cadman. "'To All Vertuous Ladies in Generall': Aemilia Lanyer's Community of Strong Women." In *Literary Circles and Cultural Communities in Renaissance England*, edited by Claude J. Summers and Ted-Larry Pebworth, 44–58. Columbia, MO, 2000.

Shea, Colleen. "Literary Authority as Cultural Criticism in Aemilia Lanyer's 'The Authors Dreame.'" *English Literary Renaissance* 32 (2002): 386–407.

Trill, Suzanne. "Reflected Desire: The Erotics of the Gaze in Aemilia Lanyer's *Salve Deus Rex Judaeorum.*" In *Women and Culture at the Courts of the Stuart Queens*, edited by Clare McManus, 167–192. Basingstokew, U.K., 2003.

Woods, Susanne. *Lanyer: A Renaissance Woman Poet.* New York, 1999. Biography based on primary sources followed by chapters situating Lanyer in relation to her contemporaries (Spenser, Shakespeare, Jonson, and religious poets including Donne).

PHILIP LARKIN

James Booth

It seems at first sight easy to determine the place of Philip Larkin (1922–1985) in literary history. Reaching maturity in the middle years of the twentieth century, he rejects the avant-garde modernism of Ezra Pound and T. S. Eliot. His poetry avoids elaborate mythic structures and obscure allusions. His subject matter, in poems such as "Church Going," "Afternoons," and "The Whitsun Weddings," is everyday urban or domestic life: an empty church, young mothers in a park, working-class weddings glimpsed from a train. He exclaimed "I love the commonplace" and frequently cited the homespun doctrine that the poet should touch the reader's heart by showing his own. His highly quotable poetry distills familiar emotions: from the cynical "They fuck you up, your mum and dad," to the sentimental "What will survive of us is love."

But there is another, contradictory, Larkin: a poet of the inexpressible, who yearns for transcendence and who rejects the ties of marriage and commitment in order to devote himself to his art. In this Larkin's hands the commonplace stereotypes of advertising become, in "Essential Beauty" and "Sunny Prestatyn," for instance, archetypes of unattainable perfection. His poetry of the commonplace modulates at a touch into extravagant rhetoric in the Romantic Decadent tradition, as in "Money":

> I listen to money singing. It's like looking down
> From long french windows at a provincial town,
> The slums, the canal, the churches ornate and mad
> In the evening sun. It is intensely sad.

The closing lines of "Absences," "Here," and "High Windows" are the work of a poet of metaphorical abstraction who has, in his own way, learned as much from the French symbolists as did Eliot.

From 1944, when he was twenty-two, until 1980, when he was fifty-eight, Larkin wrote virtually all his poetic drafts with a 2B pencil in a series of eight workbooks, dating each poem as it reached completion. An intensely deliberate writer, he claimed that in his early novels he would avoid reusing a word he had employed on page 15 on page 115. His poetic oeuvre shows a unique economy and coherence, each poem possessing its own form and its own genre or mixture of genres. He almost never writes the same kind of poem twice. He published only four major collections during his lifetime, at intervals of roughly a decade: *The North Ship* in 1945, *The Less Deceived* in 1955, *The Whitsun Weddings* in 1964, and *High Windows* in 1974. In each of the three mature volumes great care is devoted to the contrasts and modulations between poems. Consequently, some readers objected when in the *Collected Poems* of 1988 Larkin's editor, Anthony Thwaite, reordered the poems into chronological sequence and added more than sixty unpublished works. The 1988 volume, however, does enable the reader to trace the development of the poetry through false starts and periods of blockage that are obscured by the calculated harmonies of the volumes published in Larkin's lifetime.

THE NORTH SHIP AND THE FICTION

Throughout the 1940s Larkin was determined to be a novelist. For his first extended fiction, written following his graduation from Oxford in the summer of 1943, he adopted the assumed persona of a lesbian writer of girls' school stories, "Brunette Coleman." For Larkin, whose poor eyesight had secured his exemption from military service, and who claimed to be "uninterested" in the war, "Brunette" seems to have provided an imaginative defense against the patriotic masculinity of the time. "Brunette's" *Trouble at Willow Gables*, which Larkin carefully typed up and sent to an agent, never saw publication until a posthumous edition appeared in 2002, and her sequence of poems, *Sugar and Spice*, also remained unpublished during the poet's lifetime. "Brunette's" poetry is of interest, however, in the way it anticipates Larkin's mature poetry, particularly in its use of stereotype and cliché to comic-elegiac effect. The grown-up schoolgirl laments: "Now the ponies all are dead." She has learned that, sadly, even "Games mistresses turn grey."

The "serious" poetry that Larkin wrote in the early 1940s is less original than his "lesbian" work. He imitates first John Keats, then W. H. Auden, then William Butler Yeats. His first collection, *The North Ship*, published in 1945 by the Fortune Press, shows the influence of Auden, as in "Is it for now or for always":

> Shine out, my sudden angel,
> Break fear with breast and brow,
> I take you now and for always,
> For always is always now.

But the predominant voice is that of Yeats: "Love, we must part now: do not let it be / Calamitous and bitter." The mature Larkin mocked the "Celtic fever" of this volume and related, with some simplification, how he was "cured" in the mid-1940s by the example of the plain but moving poetry of Thomas Hardy.

In 1943 Larkin became librarian in the Midland town of Wellington in Shropshire, a job that involved attention to the heating boiler as well as the books. Here he completed two novels in which his female self-identification assumed a more realistic form. In *Jill*, published by the Fortune Press in 1946, John Kemp, a timid northern scholarship boy at Oxford, implausibly invents a schoolgirl sister, Jill, in order to impress his middle-class roommate, Chris Warner. Kemp's fantasy takes on a strange poetic intensity when he starts sending real letters to this presexual dream of innocence, excited by the idea of their circulation, forever undelivered, through the postal system. At this point a real, ordinary "Gillian" appears, whom Kemp pursues and finally kisses. She breaks down in tears, upon which he is roughed up by Warner and his friends and suffers a nervous breakdown.

Larkin's second completed novel, *A Girl in Winter* (1947), published by Faber and Faber, shows the same clash between poetic dream and hard reality, but viewed through a female consciousness. Katherine Lind, a refugee whose nationality is never specified, escapes from her snowbound loneliness in a dreary Midland town by resurrecting memories of a prewar summer spent with an English family, during which she had developed a crush on Robin, the son of the household. Like Kemp, Katherine is a version of the Pygmalion-like artist, creating an unreal perfection with which she then falls in love. And, like Kemp's, her dream is shattered by reality and sex. Robin reappears, now a drunken and importunate soldier, probably bound for death. She yields to his demands and at the end of the novel drifts numbly to sleep through an inner realm of blizzards and icebergs.

In 1946 Larkin had escaped the backwater of Wellington and taken the post of sub-librarian at the University College of Leicester. In the months that followed, Faber rejected his proposed second collection of poems, *In the Grip of Light*, as did five other publishers. Around the time of these rejections, in early 1948, his father fell ill and died. Soon thereafter, Larkin became engaged to be married to his Wellington girlfriend, Ruth Bowman, and began sharing a house, claustrophobically, with his bereaved mother. Not surprisingly, perhaps, Larkin stopped writing poetry altogether for nearly a year.

Instead, he attempted to mature beyond what he called the "diffused poetry" of his two completed novels, in two more works of fiction, this time with thoroughly prosaic protagonists: a car manufacturer and an assistant lecturer in a provincial university college. The latter character was based on Monica Jones, a young lecturer at Leicester, who ultimately became Larkin's lifelong partner. Larkin also helped his Oxford friend Kingsley Amis with his comic university novel *Lucky Jim*, which had its origin in Amis's first impressions of Larkin in the senior common room at Leicester. The immediate success of Amis's novel when it was published in 1954 made Larkin intensely jealous. He always regretted that he himself had failed in what he felt to be the more demanding genre of fiction. In falling back on poetry, he found his true voice, but also, in his own eyes, he confirmed his selfish failure to engage with reality. As he said in an interview: "If you tell a novelist 'Life's not like that,' he has to do something about it. The poet simply replies, 'No, but I am.'"

THE LESS DECEIVED

In 1950 Larkin broke off his engagement to Ruth Bowman and escaped life with his mother by taking the post of sub-librarian at Queen's University in Belfast. His next attempt to make his mark, *XX Poems*, printed in 1951 at his own expense in an edition of a hundred copies, went unnoticed, and it was not until 1955 that he finally secured the publication of the first of his three great mature collections, *The Less Deceived*, with the Marvell Press in Hull, which had recently been founded by the working-class poetry lovers George and Jean Hartley.

The Less Deceived established Larkin's reputation. His name was at once associated with "the Movement," a group including Kingsley Amis, Robert Conquest, Donald Davie, and Thom Gunn, whose work was in revolt against both modernism and the extravagant rhetoric of Dylan Thomas. The "Movement" style possessed a prose-like coherence; its tone was skeptical, robust, ironic; and its themes were those of a postwar, welfare-state England. The speaker of Larkin's "Church Going" seemed to many readers to typify "the Movement": taking off his cycle-clips "in awkward reverence" as he enters the empty church, and referring dismissively to "some brass and stuff / Up at the holy end." The poem seems intended as a skeptical response to the wartime Anglo-Catholic piety of Eliot's "Little Gidding."

Distinctive to Larkin, however, is the shifting interplay between the poem's dramatized "I" and the implied author. There is an element of self-parody in the elevated closing section of the poem. "A serious house on serious earth it is," the speaker intones, with a "poetic" inversion of word order. In the church's "blent air," he continues, "all our compulsions meet, / Are recognised, and robed as destinies." The words are vacuous, and the poet seems to be mocking himself. Though Larkin conceded that he was culturally an "Anglican agnostic," he emphatically denied that "Church Going" was a religious poem. Equally, however, it is not an antireligious satire. To be a satirist, Larkin said, requires that the poet believes that he knows better than other people. Larkin is not didactic in this way. "Church Going" is an emotional drama of failed transcendence, not a philosophical or ideological statement.

Other poems in *The Less Deceived* adopt the robust, demotic register that Larkin made peculiarly his own:

Why should I let the toad *work*
  Squat on my life?
Can't I use my wit as a pitchfork
  And drive the brute off?

(Toads)

He admits that he is not courageous enough to shout "Stuff your pension!" since his own "toad" squats within him and will never allow him to blarney his way to getting "The fame and the girl and the money / All at one sitting." Both the poem's defiance of convention and its resignation to convention are similarly imaged in terms of colorful stereotypes.

At the opposite end of the spectrum of *The Less Deceived* is "Deceptions," from which the volume derives its title. In this dramatization of the suffering of a sixteen-year-old Victorian rape victim, Larkin no longer attempts to appropriate the female voice. Instead, a male speaker offers useless consolation across slums and years. Though miserably impelled to apologize on behalf of her rapist, he is uncomfortably aware of his impertinence. "For you

would hardly care / That you were less deceived, out on that bed, / Than he was." Some critics read this poem as an apology for rape; but this is to miss the scathing self-accusation in the speaker's excuses. In biographical terms the poem can be read as dramatizing the guilts of Larkin's recently ended engagement.

"If, My Darling," however, reflects a new and different relationship with the witty and acerbic Monica Jones. Here the tragic collision between male and female worlds is recast as comedy. The poet imagines his beloved jumping, like Lewis Carroll's Alice, with floating skirt, into his head and being aghast to find not a tidy feminine parlor of undisturbed embers and small-printed books for the sabbath, but a sordid masculine attic: "A Grecian statue kicked in the privates, money, / A swill-tub of finer feelings." The raucous performativeness of the poet's aggression makes the poem ambiguous. He is still, after all, trying to see things from the woman's point of view.

A different, delicately artificial complex of tones is heard in "Lines on a Young Lady's Photograph Album," inspired by Winifred Arnott, a twenty-year-old library assistant in Belfast. Unlike Ruth Bowman and Monica Jones, Winifred Arnott, being engaged to someone else, did not threaten him with commitment. The poem inventively unites the genres of seduction poem, address to the muse, and reflective elegy, as the poet's pornographic leering over the photo album shifts into an idealistic yearning for the unattainable. The photographs keep the girl's "Unvariably lovely" image immune from aging and contract his heart by being "out of date."

THE WHITSUN WEDDINGS

By coincidence Larkin found himself a neighbor of the publishers of his 1955 volume *The Less Deceived* when, in that same year, he was appointed librarian at the University of Hull. Larkin lived in Hull for the remaining three decades of his life, and here he wrote the poems of *The Whitsun Weddings* and *High Windows*, both published by Faber. However, he did not see himself as a local poet. He liked Hull, he insisted, simply because it was so far away from everywhere else. Though he is sometimes seen as a quintessentially English poet, Larkin lacks ideological nationalism. In "The Importance of Elsewhere," he presents his recent return from Ireland not as a welcome return home but as a loss of precious freedom. In England "no elsewhere underwrites my existence." Without the "excuse" of "difference" he cannot so easily refuse to conform.

Larkin's early years in Hull were the happiest of his life. As the university's librarian, he had the satisfaction of overseeing a huge building program and a steady expansion in both books and staff. Like Wallace Stevens, Larkin had a "real job," although he hated the implications of the label "librarian-poet" and at first made the Hartleys promise not to distribute *The Less Deceived* in local bookshops.

Larkin had dedicated *The Less Deceived* to Monica Jones. By the early 1960s, however—although he visited her regularly in Leicester, and he holidayed with her each year—he had also become emotionally involved with a member of his library staff, Maeve Brennan. Monica Jones shared his Oxford background; Maeve Brennan, by contrast, was a local "Hull girl." She was also a strict Catholic who resisted the poet's sexual advances for nearly two decades after they first met. Nevertheless, Larkin told her that she had taught him more about his emotions than anyone else, and he considered *The Whitsun Weddings* to be "her book."

Maeve Brennan, more intensely than Winifred Arnott, was Larkin's muse of everyday reality: innocent and ordinary, but at the same time satisfyingly out of reach. His one love poem addressed to her, "Broadcast," makes the very distance between the lovers into a precious part of their relationship. She had attended a concert in the City Hall, to which the poet listened at home on the radio. The poem focuses on the poet's inner vision of the beloved, "beautiful and devout" in the darkened hall, a glove unnoticed on the floor beside her, while he, in his darkened flat, strains desperately to pick out her hands, "tiny in all that air, applauding."

In *The Whitsun Weddings*, Larkin's "less-deceived" style thaws into something warmer and more generous. "Love Songs in Age," "Faith Healing," "The Large Cool Store," and "Ambulances" all follow the same basic structure: a casual social realist observation generates a surprisingly elaborate meditation, leading to a rhetorical climax of poignant emotion. In "The Whitsun Weddings," the same absurd but touching wedding ritual is reenacted at each station on the journey to London: the mothers loud and fat, an uncle shouting smut, frowning children, and the girls, "unreally" marked off in their "lemons, mauves, and olive-ochres." The picturesque working-class images serve to dissolve the poet's middle-class reserve, and by the closing stanza the "I" of the opening has become "we." However, though he celebrates this communal spring ritual, the poet himself remains disengaged, behind the window of his traveling room. The newlyweds

share this "frail / Travelling coincidence" with him, but none of them, he reflects, will think of the others, nor of "how their lives would all contain this hour." Such reflections are only for the poet, for whom a railway carriage is also an ivory tower.

The opening poem in *The Whitsun Weddings*, "Here," enacts a more intensely intimate withdrawal from social involvement. Its title is not the topographical proper noun, "Hull," but an existential adverb. Passing through the city, with its cut-price crowd, busy buying red kitchenware and iced lollies, the poem (there is no "I" or "we") withdraws into a landscape of "Loneliness," "silence," and "heat." The original title in the workbook draft was "Withdrawing Room," an archaic form of "drawing room." Larkin's work constantly presents a stereotypical or archetypical room as a measure of existence: attic, tower, garret, cave, cell, bedsit, waiting room. In "Here" the "unfenced existence" of a limitless land, sea-, and skyscape becomes the most elusive of his living rooms.

During 1963 and 1964 Larkin, having just turned forty, worked for ten months on a long tragicomic poem, "The Dance," which he hoped would form the centerpiece of *The Whitsun Weddings*. In it the speaker half-willingly socializes with the "sad set" of his beloved's friends. He is excited by the invitation in her eyes as they dance, but finds himself unable to supply the question to her "tremendous answer." Can the poet at last go beyond unreal dreams and commit himself to a real woman? In real life Larkin could neither marry nor resolve the triangle of his relationships. The poem remained a fragment, and the impersonal, collective epithalamium of "The Whitsun Weddings" became, instead, the centerpiece of the collection. The trauma of this failure left him unable to write poetry for six months, and it also put a definitive end to the debate over marriage that had occupied his poetry for much of the previous two decades.

HIGH WINDOWS AND AFTER

In the poems collected in *High Windows*, aging becomes the dominant theme. The tone is increasingly mannered and extreme, and the symbolist element comes to the fore. The title poem of the volume opens with a stereotype of the utmost self-parodic crudity. The poet sees "a couple of kids" and guesses that "he's fucking her" and she is using contraception. This, he concludes, is the paradise that "Everyone old has dreamed of all their lives." But he is aware that such envy of the young is not unprecedented. His own youthful freedom from religious inhibitions, he guesses, would have inspired just such envy from the previous, spiritually haunted generation.

Then, with an abrupt poetic leap, the poet abandons these sterile envies in a vision of high windows: "the deep blue air, that shows / Nothing, and is nowhere, and is endless." His self-irony has not, however, been dispelled. It is apparent that his euphoria has been achieved by a verbal trick. Placed at the end of the poem "endless" implies a sublime permanence; "endless nothing" would not be so rhetorically satisfying. In the workbook Larkin derisively acknowledges his trick in a penciled comment at the end of the poem: "and fucking piss." For readers with a postmodern disregard for traditional textual boundaries, this barely articulate anger at the failure of transcendence is as much a part of the poem as is the published text.

In 1975 Larkin engineered a belated affair with Betty Mackereth, who had been his secretary since 1957. The relationship produced some of his best love poems. "We met at the end of the party," unpublished during his lifetime, conjures evocative symbols out of the flattest realism. An aging lover describes how his beloved, at the end of the party of life, when "most of the drinks were dead," cheerfully offers him "this that's left" in a dirty glass. She is content with "what survives," cheerfully insisting that "There's autumn too." But the poet is lost in his memories of June, when the party guests were still arriving. Now he is no longer there to greet them. This beloved plays the role of an unconventional muse, unattainable and awesome not because of her beauty, nor her innocent ordinariness, but simply because of her vitality.

Larkin's father had died of cancer at the age of sixty-three and he himself was convinced that he would die at the same age, as he did. He was always aware of the ticking of his inner biological clock, and as he aged, his poetry aged with him. Metaphors falter or reveal their inadequacy; eloquence is the more eloquent for sounding hollow. In "The Building," the sheer tower-block of a hospital is described with a grand gesture: "Higher than the handsomest hotel." But the *h* alliteration sighs exhaustedly, and at the end of the stanza the register sinks into prosiness and comic zeugma as both "creepers" and "a frightening smell" "hang" in the hospital entrance.

In "The Old Fools," the mixture of horror and humor is even more shocking, as the poet jeers at the inhabitants of a nursing home: "Do they somehow suppose / It's more grown-up when your mouth hangs open and drools, / And you keep on pissing yourself . . . ?" Again, as in "High Windows" the poem modulates into a yearning for tran-

scendence, but here instead of a symbolist leap upward and outward, we are taken inward:

> Perhaps being old is having lighted rooms
> Inside your head . . .
> . . . .
> . . . chairs and a fire burning,
> The blown bush at the window, or the sun's
> Faint friendliness on the wall some lonely
> Rain-ceased midsummer evening.

This versifies the cynical description of dementia: "the lights are on but there's nobody at home." It also offers the most moving of all Larkin's images of escape. In a chilling metaphorical twist the same words that convey the reduced humiliation of senility also convey a consolatory transcendence.

The self-elegy "Aubade," published in the *Times Literary Supplement* in 1977, puts a final, deliberate full stop at the end of Larkin's writing career. The traditional aubade genre, in which lovers part at dawn, is brutally transformed into an "in a funk about death" poem, as the poet lies in bed contemplating "the total emptiness for ever, / The sure extinction that we travel to / And shall be lost in always." The mood is the plainest indicative, and the imagery is flatly prosaic: "It stands plain as a wardrobe, what we know." Not only does this poem anticipate the poet's death; its exhaustion of metaphorical vitality also enacts, as he put it, "the death-throes of a talent." The poetry in extremis of Larkin's late elegies provokes contradictory responses. Some readers find it disconcerting. Others are inspirited by its refusal of consolations, whether of religion, philosophy, or even of poetry itself. As Larkin said in an interview: "A good poem about failure is a success."

Larkin is preeminently a poet. However, the essays and reviews that he collected in *Required Writing* (1983) contain some of the most memorably opinionated literary criticism of his time. In his essay "A Neglected Responsibility," he attempted to warn his fellow librarians against the loss of modern British literary manuscripts to wealthy libraries in the United States. He gained a separate reputation as jazz reviewer for the *Daily Telegraph* newspaper. When he collected his reviews in *All What Jazz* (1970), he added an introduction in which (with a hint of self-caricature) he launched a provocative attack on the "mad lads" of modernism for their irresponsible exploitation of technique and disregard of their audience.

The posthumous revelations about Larkin's private life in the *Selected Letters* (1992) and the biography by Andrew Motion (1993) allowed hostile critics to cast him as a sexist and racist. He inherited a taste for iconoclastic political opinions from his father, who had admired the efficiency of the Nazi state. Some readers countered that the objectionable opinions of Larkin the man were irrelevant to the poetry. Others contended that the offending passages were addressed only to particular right-wing friends and should not be taken seriously. After all, he had excellent relations with Monica Jones's Indian colleague, R. K. Biswas, gave encouragement to the young Indian poet Vikram Seth, and was passionate about black American jazz music. The coherence of his work is to be found on a deeper, simpler level than that of cultural politics. His is essentially a lyric sensibility. He is an existential vagrant of no fixed ideological abode, who never lost the vulnerable openness to experience which he expressed in an early letter: "The ultimate joy is to be alive, in the flesh. Shake that thing."

[*See also* Kingsley Amis *and* Thom Gunn.]

SELECTED WORKS

The North Ship (1945)
Jill (1946)
A Girl in Winter (1947)
The Less Deceived (1955)
The Whitsun Weddings (1964)
All that Jazz: A Record Diary 1961–68 (1970)
High Windows (1974)
Required Writing: Miscellaneous Pieces 1955–1982 (1983)
Collected Poems (1988)
Selected Letters of Philip Larkin, 1940–1985 (1992)
Further Requirements: Interviews, Broadcasts, Statements and Book Reviews (2001)
Trouble at Willow Gables and Other Fictions (2002)
Collected Poems (2003; this new edition excludes the poems first published in 1988)
Early Poems and Juvenilia (2005)

FURTHER READING

Booth, James, ed. *New Larkins for Old: Critical Essays.* Basingstoke, U.K., 2000. Includes insightful essays by Barbara Everett, John Carey, Raphaël Ingelbien, John Osborne, and Penelope Pelizzon.

Booth, James. *Philip Larkin: The Poet's Plight.* Basingstoke, U.K., 2005. A wide-ranging study of Larkin's mature poetry.

Morrison, Blake. *The Movement: English Poetry and Fiction of the 1950s.* London, 1986. An absorbing historical account of "the Movement."

Motion, Andrew. *Philip Larkin: A Writer's Life.* London, 1993. Motion was authorized by Larkin to write his life, and this remains the standard biography, although it has been attacked by some as too negative.

Regan, Stephen, ed. *Philip Larkin: Contemporary Critical Essays.* Basingstoke, U.K., 1997. Contains important essays by Seamus Heaney, Barbara Everett, Janice Rossen, Tom Paulin, and Alan Bennett.

Swarbrick, Andrew, *Out of Reach: The Poetry of Philip Larkin.* Basingstoke, U.K., 1995. A sensitive study, focusing on the transcendental and symbolist elements in Larkin's work.

D. H. LAWRENCE

David Seelow

When most people hear the name David Herbert, or D. H., Lawrence (1885–1930), they think of *Lady Chatterley's Lover*, and *Lady Chatterley's Lover* prompts one to think of sex. The number of those who have read *LCL* or seen a popular movie version will always be fewer than those who have simply heard of the novel. A celebrated court case catapulted the novel into infamy; the scandal replicated the novel's immediate reception in England, Paris, and other locales in 1928. Lawrence had already suffered through censorship battles with his novel *The Rainbow*. He printed *Lady Chatterley's Lover* through Giuseppe Orioli's private press in Florence, Italy, but that attempt to circumvent a moralistic public met with contradictory responses. The small printing sold well, and circulated Lawrence's name among the general public, but also deprived Lawrence of income and resulted in a barrage of pirated editions; the novel acquired a worldwide reputation, but failed to bring the author any royalties. As early as 1930, the manager of the Dunster House Bookshop in Cambridge, Massachusetts, was convicted for selling *LCL*. The novel had been deemed obscene. Lawrence refused to accommodate censors, but his legal and moral battles only exacerbated his failing health. After Lawrence's death in 1930, expurgated editions of *LCL* appeared on bookshelves, but the genuine novel had to await the American Grove Press publication of 1959.

In England, the unexpurgated *Lady Chatterley's Lover* was the first novel brought to court under the new 1959 Obscene Publications Act. This watershed trial, *Regina v. Penguin Books, Ltd.*, established the use of expert witnesses in authenticating a book's literary merit and also established the convention of requiring a jury to consider

D. H. Lawrence
Photograph by Ernesto Guardia, 1920s
NATIONAL PORTRAIT GALLERY, LONDON

the text as a whole, not simply its objectionable segments (those sections and words that "clean" versions eliminated), when determining whether or not the work should be ruled obscene. Penguin's success at the trial made possible the wide publication of an inexpensive paperback version of Lawrence's final novel. Their legal victory also signaled a change in social morals in the direction of the emancipation movements that mushroomed during the subsequent decade. Lawrence's work challenged both the moral and social values of the early twentieth century, and just past the century's midpoint the novel contributed, in effect, to a major social transformation concerning sexuality, morality, and social status.

Yet ironically, scarcely had the 1960s liberation movements heralded Lawrence's genius than segments of the same movements consigned Lawrence's works to the historical wastebasket. Kate Millet's blistering attack on Lawrence in *Sexual Politics* (1970) pushed the boulder that launched an avalanche of political correctness down on the once-revered writer. Millet did not object to the sex in Lawrence's fiction; she objected to the type of sex it seemed to valorize. For instance, when the narrative of *LCL* demotes Connie's clitoral orgasm in favor of her mutual climax with Mellors, Millet cries foul. Gary Adelman has further shown how, from at least the 1980s onward, Lawrence has been marginalized within the academic world. Lawrence no longer commands the same degree of serious scholarship that his modernist peers enjoy. Understanding the roller coaster Lawrence lived—a roller coaster that his ghost continues to inhabit—requires a closer look at his final novel and the texts surrounding its publication.

THE LADY'S MAN

Lawrence revised his fiction wholesale. Rather than tinker with a word (à la Flaubert), he restarted from scratch. He wrote *Paul Morel* into his first major novel, *Sons and Lovers* (1913), and he rewrote *LCL's* predecessor "Quetzalcoatl" as *The Plumed Serpent* (1926). Lawrence wrote *LCL* three times, beginning with *The First Lady Chatterley*, then *John Thomas and Lady Jane*, until he reached the satisfactory third version. Rewriting the novel says much about Lawrence's final message to the world. First, all versions of the novel stress the affair between Lady Chatterley and a gamekeeper (named Parker at first, then renamed Mellors). The story's real challenge consists precisely in the affair's social transgression, not in its moral impropriety. After all, the main character is Lady Chatterley, not Mrs. Chatterley. Indeed, at the book's obscenity trial, the prosecuting attorney famously asked the jury, "Would you allow your maidservant to read this book?" The attorney bluntly implies that only the educated should read "dangerous" literature. Additionally, only a privileged and educated jury could pretend to have servants in the first place, and the novel's protagonist is a not only a servant, but a servant who serves a very privileged lady in a way her impotent husband cannot. Lawrence subverts social hierarchies, thus signifying social transgression through the couple's sexual transgression. Affairs hardly made news in England's artistic circles; many of Lawrence's intellectual friends such as Richard Aldington, Katherine Mansfield, and Bertrand Russell had rather steamy and public liaisons—but they did not mess with the lower class.

So Connie Chatterley is a lady, but the novel is entitled *Lady Chatterley's Lover*. Mellors has the story's focus. The gamekeeper persona appealed to Lawrence ever since his very first novel. The attraction stems from Lawrence's long admiration for the working class, whether coal miners like his father or the peasants he admired in the Tuscany countryside. Lawrence grew up as part of a working-class family in Eastwood, Nottingham. He valued the men's connection with the earth, their physicality and spontaneity. In fact, at the same time he was composing *LCL*, Lawrence wrote a number of poems he called *Pansies* (also subject to censorship), a variation on Pascal's *Pensées*. Yet, as Lawrence stressed in the volume's preface, his thoughts emerged out of the soil, and referenced the body below the navel—not the rarefied region of the brain that Pascal addressed. For Lawrence, the beauty of life, whether a blossoming flower or a revelatory thought, remained inextricably part of the manure that fertilized its

glorious exhibition. Consequently, Lawrence's protagonist Mellors reflects a strong, physical connection with the landscape he traverses.

This man of the land is then set in opposition to the exploiter of land. Lawrence railed against industrialization from his earliest writings to his last. He admired the miners, but hated the industrialists who stripped the landscape of its resources and decimated nature's beauty for personal wealth. Lawrence represented this industrialist type most powerfully in the character of Gerald Crich (*Women in Love*, chapter 5), and Clifford Chatterley must be understood as the last incarnation of it. Clifford Chatterley's success as a businessman symbolizes Lawrence's growing despair at mankind's fate.

On the other hand, the evolving relationship between Connie and Mellors also signifies Lawrence's fleeting hope for humanity's renewal. The revised version of the novel downplays the gamekeeper's social role and increases his personal connection to Connie. Lawrence rejected the idea of leadership he had described in a series of novels during the 1920s—*Aaron's Rod* (1922), *Kangaroo* (1923), and *The Plumed Serpent* (1926)—in favor of marriage as the symbol for social transformation. The unequal relationship between leader and follower is replaced by the equal and interdependent relationship between a man and a woman. This change partly reflects Lawrence's prescient understanding of the Fascist forces emerging in both Italy and Germany and the need for an alternative to social movements and their mob mentality.

At one point Lawrence thought of calling his novel *Tenderness*. He explains his shift in direction in the posthumously published essay "Apropos of Lady Chatterley's Lover" (1930), contrasting modern, nervous sex with "sex as blood-contact." For Lawrence, the English had lost their capacity to have passionate sex; the new England that Lawrence advocates would celebrate the "phallus as a bridge to the future." He valorizes the phallus as a ritualistic symbol that restores reverence for natural cycles. Lawrence's use of phallic symbolism can be best understood by briefly reviewing two texts that significantly contribute to Lawrence's overall vision for *LCL*, the travel essays *Etruscan Places* (1927, published posthumously in 1932) and the novella *The Escaped Cock* (1929).

LORD I WAS BORN A TRAVELING MAN

Lawrence made a whirlwind visit to see tombs in the Etruscan landscape with his close friend Earl Brewster in April 1927. He had recently completed the second version of *Lady Chatterley's Lover* (the version called *John Thomas and Lady Jane*), and he wanted very much to visit Etruria, an area northwest of Rome. Unlike his Buddhist friend, Lawrence sought his inspiration from the outer landscapes of the West, that is, from southern Europe, the southwestern United States, and Mexico. He locates the essence of Etruscan civilization in its use of two dominant archetypal symbols: the arx and the phallus, which represent the female and the male sex organs.

What really impresses Lawrence about the Etruscans is their symbolism, which he contrasts with the more directly anthropomorphic gods of the Greco-Roman world. For Lawrence, Etruscan symbols, like those he discovered in Mexico and among Native American tribes in the United States, signify an animate, holistic world of elemental forces that link life and death. He continually contrasts the Etruscan worldview with that of the Roman Empire, which exterminated the Etruscan civilization in, according to Lawrence, the Romans' relentless pursuit of conquest and wealth. Traces of Etruscan civilization remain only in the tombs and artifacts collected in a few Italian museums.

As Lawrence visits the tombs, he also makes a variety of stunning observations on the Italian landscape and its significance. He notes, for instance, the physiognomy of local peasants and reads in their faces innocence "not deadened by morals." The peasants are a final link to a pre-Roman world that the Great War has virtually extinguished. The twin forces of destruction—war and industrialism—appear again and again on the periphery of Lawrence's description of his journey. Consequently, the peasants will soon become the exploited workers of a developing Italy, and, more ominously, will provide the fodder for the growing Fascist movement.

Museums also reflect a certain death. Lawrence's visit to a museum in Perugia sparked his interest in the Etruscans, but he lashes out at the institutional nature of museums. From Lawrence's perspective, museums tear away a culture's artifacts from their natural environment and reposition or exhibit them in a foreign context, geographically separate from their origin. In a sense, museums create displaced cultures. As Lawrence makes these observations on the changing Italian landscape, he pays homage to the natural world that industrialism continues to eat away. The prose of his travel books often approaches the exquisite lyricism of Lawrence's best nature poems. Lawrence evokes nature as a continuing process that "long after the words of Jesus and Buddha are gone into oblivion the nightingale will still sing because it is

neither preaching nor teaching nor commanding nor urging. It is just singing. And in the beginning was not the word, but a chirrup." This ongoing natural process is precisely how he sees the Etruscan tombs and their depiction of death as "the natural continuance of the fullness of life."

Lawrence's journey to the Etruscan past culminated a lifelong thirst for travel and a parallel love for the Italian countryside and Mediterranean world that dates back to around 1912. Lawrence met Frieda Weekley, the wife of one of his former professors, and they quickly began a torrid affair that led to Frieda and Lawrence eloping on 3 May 1912 for Germany and Italy; thus, Lawrence's wanderlust precisely coincides with his passionate love for Frieda. A year after Lawrence embarked on his affair and later marriage to Frieda (13 July 1913), England entered war against Germany. Lawrence vociferously opposed the war and failed, for health reasons, to qualify for service and his citizenship prohibited him from traveling abroad. Meanwhile, marriage to a German whose cousin was a notorious German fighter pilot exposed Lawrence to spying, harassment, and general hostility. Lawrence lived out the war as an internal exile in Cornwall. Consequently, Lawrence's thirst for travel combined his love for Frieda, a disgust at England, and his emerging utopian dreams.

A famous letter of 15 January 1915 to Willie Hopkin (a Congregationalist and prominent Eastwood intellectual who introduced Lawrence to local literary figures) announced Lawrence's desire to found a utopian community called Rananim, which would consist of a small group of like-minded people living in a quasi-monastic society in some tropical location. The letter to Hopkin speaks of a desire to "sail away from the world," hence anticipating the final sailing into oblivion evoked in his poem "The Ship of Death." Lawrence searched for this utopia across many frontiers, including Germany, Austria, Switzerland, France, Italy, Sardinia, Capri, Sicily, Australia, Ceylon, Mexico, Tahiti, and New Mexico. He appeared quite comfortable on the ranch outside Taos, New Mexico, and most happy near the Mediterranean, especially in Italy. Lawrence indicates his sympathy for the sun in the symbolic conclusion to *Twilight in Italy* (1916), with its trek from the cold despair of Switzerland to the warmth of a Mediterranean sun.

As Paul Fussell remarks in "The Places of D. H. Lawrence," Lawrence's travel books are preeminently about "moving and freedom and the delight of feeling your feet in contact with the road," and this desire to keep moving propels the great novella *The Escaped Cock* (later published as, and commonly known as, *The Man Who Died*). Lawrence arrived at the idea for the story on the same travels with Earl Brewster that inspired *Etruscan Places*. In *The Escaped Cock*, Lawrence retells the story of Jesus, who is referred to in the tale as simply "the man who died." Lawrence twists the gospel by imagining Jesus rejecting his Christ role and deciding to live life in the flesh. Lawrence's Jesus has his feet planted firmly on the ground. Like Lawrence, the Jesus figure wanders the countryside until he finds healing in the touch of a priestess of Isis. Lawrence thus superimposes the Egyptian myth of Osiris and Isis onto the gospel story. The narrative represents the resurrection of "the man who died" as the emergence of the man's erection: "he felt the stir of something coming: a dawn, a new sun." The pun on "son" reinforces the narrative inversion of the Christian resurrection story. The sun, in Lawrence, always signifies sexuality in its old, pagan guise. Consequently, the narrative inverts Jesus's rebirth into eternal life by describing a rebirth into a fully lived temporal life. Lawrence does not reject Jesus's spirituality; on the contrary, he underscores the historically diluted Christian belief in the resurrection of the body. For Lawrence, the spirit participates in the flesh. What the novella rejects is Jesus's Christ role—the dying of the self so that others may live. Lawrence reverses the traditional Christian message: his Jesus refuses death so the self may live.

Lawrence grew increasingly preoccupied with Jesus's story as his own death appeared more imminent. In addition to *The Escaped Cock*, he produced a striking essay, "The Risen Lord," poems such as "Resurrection" and "The Risen Lord," the posthumously published essay *Apocalypse*, and a painting titled *Resurrection*. The painting portrays a dying Jesus who bears a distinct resemblance to Lawrence. In all cases Lawrence turns the Christian obsession with death into his own affirmation of life.

A FISH OUT OF WATER,
OR LAWRENCE'S COUNTERPOETICS

Only Thomas Hardy surpassed D. H. Lawrence as a master of both the modern novel and the modern lyric. Nonetheless, Lawrence, unlike Hardy, scarcely merits a mention in poetry anthologies, and even less in critical commentary. Gary Adelman describes the curious gulf between other poets' appreciation of Lawrence's poetry and critics' condemnation in his chapter "Political Correctness, Working Poets, and Lawrence's Poetry" (*Reclaiming D. H. Lawrence*, pp. 105–153). Proceeding under

the assumption that practicing poets know a good poem when they read or hear one, Adelman suggests that Lawrence's verse may be best approached through an understanding of how he is so frequently misread. Similarly, I. A. Richards's classic text *Practical Criticism* (1929) offers D. H. Lawrence's lyric "The Piano" as a case study. Richards used a group of twelve poems with his poetry students to demonstrate the difference between poor reading and good reading, or misunderstanding and understanding, a lyric. Of the twelve poems Richards used, his students ranked Lawrence's lyric eleventh. Students objected to the poem's gross sentimentality, poor word choice, unrealistic descriptions, and run-over lines. Richards shrewdly points out that poor readers bring a certain preconceived expectation to the poem, and when that expectation is not met, they simply dismiss the poem.

Lawrence rarely meets a conventional reader's expectations, and the "The Piano" is no exception. The brief three-stanza lyric evokes the poet's memory of a childhood scene: listening to his mother sing religious hymns on a wintry Sunday evening. The cozy room contrasts with the cold outside, and the mother's smile signifies the scene's simple joy at family togetherness. The poet's mind drifts to such memories as he listens to a lady sing at a grand piano; he knows that modern norms prohibit the adult male's weeping over such childish sentiments as remembering his mother sing a hymn. Nonetheless, Lawrence describes the sentiment head-on, while still recognizing that the past is past. As Richards explains, the risk of sentiment succeeds when the scene works "into a close and living relation with some other scene concretely and tastefully realized, which may act as a standard of reality and awaken the dream-infected object of the sentiment into actuality" (p. 254).

Despite Richards's critical acumen, his own book and its preconceptions have, paradoxically, prevented a genuine appreciation of Lawrence's poetry. Practical criticism's methodology argues for the importance of understanding the author's intention, and also privileges a very tightly constructed poetic object, or the "well wrought urn." Lawrence's best poetry remains open and, generally, antithetical to New Criticism. Amit Chaudhuri has recently discussed how practical criticism's attention to a particular form and the need to explicate a text's deeper meanings has entirely misread Lawrence's verse. Unfortunately, Chaudhuri's method simply deconstructs Lawrence's poetry into a group of random lines or a free play of difference. Contrary to the deconstructive position, Lawrence articulates a very clear poetics, which he espouses in the preface to the American edition of *New Poems* (1918).

Lawrence wrote the preface after the publication of the book *Look! We Have Come Through!* (1917), which records, through a series of beautifully rendered imagist poems, Lawrence's journey with Frieda. The preface exhibits Lawrence's profound debt to Walt Whitman. Lawrence titles his essay "The Poetry of the Present," a poetry that he contrasts with the gemlike, perfectly crafted verse of John Keats and Percy Bysshe Shelley. Lawrence praises a poetry that captures the instant and then lets that instant go. This antiteleological poetry necessarily embraces free verse. Lawrence explores the underpinnings of the poetry of the present in his famous essay on Walt Whitman.

Few essays capture Lawrence's prophetic message better than this meditation on Whitman that closes *Studies in Classic American Literature* (1923; the same publication year as *Birds, Beasts, and Flowers*). Lawrence describes Whitman as the American Moses, "pioneering into the wilderness of unopened life." Whitman becomes the first writer to break the "mental allegiance" and bring the soul back down into contact with the body. Whitman's primacy of the body—the fleshliness of man's connection to women, to other men, and to nature—represents a "doctrine of life." When Lawrence claims that Whitman rejects a morality of salvation in favor of "a morality of actual living," he proclaims his own doctrine of life. Whitman exemplifies Lawrence's religion of blood consciousness, but this rather mystical formulation needs to be understood as a very basic metaphor for a celebration of the body. Lawrence uses Whitman to praise the physical self and to provide a poetics for Lawrence's collected work.

Robert Langbaum beautifully captures the essence of Lawrence's strand of modern poetics in his essay "Romanticism as a Modern Tradition." This tradition valorizes the "doctrine of experience that the imaginative apprehension gained through immediate experience is primary and certain, whereas the analytic reflection that follows is secondary and problematical." Lawrence's devotion to experience, and his mastery of free verse as exemplification of experience, can be rivaled only by his poetic mentor, Whitman.

Although Whitman inspired Lawrence's verse, Lawrence could never accept Whitman's democratic perspective. He rejected Whitman's easy incorporation of the common man, since Lawrence resisted any submergence of the individual into a larger unit. For Lawrence, Whitman's catalogues incorporate all of America into Whitman's own ever-expanding ego, with no differentiation among diverse groups of people. Lawrence struggled throughout his life to unify a passionate belief in radical individualism with a counterdesire to realize a utopian community of like-minded people. Lawrence's dialect poems, such as "The Collier's Wife," portray with naturalistic detail his divided attitude about midland mining families, and complement such early short stories as "Odour of Chrysanthemums," "A Sick Collier," and "Strike Pay." "The Collier's Wife" tells a story similar to that of "Odour of Chrysanthemums," without the tragic ending. Lawrence beautifully realizes the familial pain of a wife tormented by her husband's drinking, coarseness, and flashes of violence. Nonetheless, the poem renders an equally deep sympathy for men forced to work the earth in dehumanizing conditions in order to provide for their struggling families. Lawrence's late didactic poems "How Beastly the Bourgeoisie Is" and "Wages" likewise condemn modern man's enslavement to the soul-crushing industrial machine of capitalism.

Lawrence's rejection of capitalism results in an ambiguity similar to the psychological division he feels about the working masses. The poem "Hibiscus and Salvia Flowers" exhibits this internal division at its deepest level. Written in Taormina, Sicily, the poem appears in *Birds, Beasts, and Flowers* (1923), one of the most accomplished books of verse in modern literature. "Hibiscus and Salvia Flowers" forms part of the book's flower sequence, and tells the story of Italian socialists/anarchists through the flowers' symbolism; the salvia, for instance, is a metaphor for rage. The Italian socialists assume the flowers as symbols for their fight to cleanse the world of capitalist domination, and while Lawrence admires the flowers' fiery beauty, he despises their appropriation by what he considers a violent lower-class mob. His disdain for the Italians' socialist tendency, however, must be measured against his desire to wipe the world clean of its money-driven corruption.

Lawrence complicates the poem's message by linking the socialists with the ancient Jews and the Passover story. Consequently, the poem's imagery superimposes the socialist revolt against the bourgeoisie with the Jews' escape from Egyptian bondage. Yet for all this, Lawrence's sympathy with the attack on a corrupt civilization concludes with disgust at the socialists' presumptuous embrace of the hibiscus. Beauty, in Lawrence's eyes, resides in individuality, which the socialist equalizing agitation would destroy. The socialists would bring the beautiful hibiscus into the same plane as the cabbage, a symbol for Lawrence of the industrial wasteland.

Lawrence's philosophy of individualism and the mystical connection between separate entities appears most strongly in the volume's beast sequence. The whimsical "Man and Bat" tells the story of the speaker trying to rid his room of a swooping bat that is trying to evade the daylight shining through his window. The frustrated speaker concedes that the bat is doing what it must naturally do, and he safely releases the little furry lump to the open sky at twilight. In "Snake," the speaker encounters a kingly snake and recognizes the importance of letting nature be nature. Lawrence does not identify with the snake in order to incorporate or humanize it, but rather he creates, as Marjorie Perloff observes, "a new space . . . in which the mind and its objects are present in a single realm of proximity" ("Lawrence's Lyric Theatre").

The poet's proximity to nature's majestic otherness finds superb expression in the tortoise poems (originally published independently in 1921). "Baby Tortoise" describes the tortoise's slow birth with an exactitude rarely present even in the best of William Wordsworth. Lawrence glorifies the stubborn little creature, even comparing it to Ulysses. Nature's adventures parallel, but can never be reduced to, the most heroic of man's quests.

Lawrence alludes to the Osiris myth in "Tortoise Shout," and this allusion recurs in the book's fruit sequence. "Pomegranate" describes the primeval fruit that predates Eve's apple as the sign of sexuality. In "Medlars and Sorb-Apples," Lawrence relishes in the sensuality of autumn, and in "Peach," fruits—symbols of the vagina— signify nature's resistance to man's technology, which makes unnatural, perfectly shaped objects. For Lawrence, nature is a process of transformation that precludes any possibility of closure, and hence mastery, by man and his drive for a fixed order. The peach's perfection resides precisely in its imperfection—a fitting trope for Lawrence's own immense poetic oeuvre.

TRUST THE TALE, NOT THE TELLER

In the academic world, Lawrence's short stories have fared much better than his poetry. After all, Lawrence is thought to rank along with Anton Chekhov, Guy de Maupassant, and Ernest Hemingway as a master of the genre. "Odour of Chrysanthemums" (1909) and "The Rocking-Horse Winner" (1926) remain Lawrence's most anthologized stories. Written at the beginning and the end of

his career, these two stories display Lawrence's range as storyteller. The early story uses a traditional, realistic narrative style, with naturalistic detail reminiscent of Émile Zola, to portray a struggling mining family. The reader's initial sympathy for the wife who suffers from her husband's alcoholism, anger, and violence slowly expands into a complex identification with the abusive husband. Despite the wife Lizzie's unhappiness at her husband's distant, abusive behavior, she also fears what would happen to her if her husband did not return. The narrative's divided sympathy discloses itself through the appearance of the husband's mother. The dialogue between wife and mother-in-law reveals the wife's complicity in the husband's pain: "You've had a sight of trouble with him Elizabeth, you have indeed. But he was a jolly enough lad wi' me, he was, I can assure you."

Tragically, the husband dies smothered by coal. Yet the story focuses on the women's reactions to the man's death rather than on the death itself. Ironically, as the mother weeps, Lizzie attends to preparing the body for burial. During her practical activity, Lizzie experiences an epiphany that illuminates her essential estrangement from the man she married. Lizzie carries the unborn child of a man she never really knew, and never tried to love. She contemplates her own complicity in her husband's death, and the story ends, as Kingsley Widmer notes, with her absolute aloneness. The wife's estrangement places her in the no-man's-land typical of the early twentieth century. She has been unhappy living with her husband, but his death signifies an uncertainty more frightening than the stability his presence allowed.

At the other end of Lawrence's fictional spectrum, "The Rocking-Horse Winner," composed for Cynthia Asquith's *The Ghost Book*, takes the form of a fable. The story's protagonist, the child Paul, habitually retreats to his room where he secretly rides his hobbyhorse until he enters a trancelike state. When Paul reaches this state, both mystical and sexual, he can miraculously predict the winner of upcoming horse races. Paul's secret habit, a metaphor for masturbation, takes place in a strangely animated house that whispers, "more money." Paul's lower middle-class family wants more money in order to climb the social ladder. Paul learns that his magic power allows him to make his mother more money, and he escalates the riding until the story's tragic climax.

Early in the story, Paul overhears his uncle talk about "filthy lucre," which Paul misunderstands as "filthy lucker." The uncle's proverbial phrase sees money as a corrupting influence on people. However, the filthy money that Paul hears as "filthy lucker" brings his mother more money. His mother had previously explained to Paul that luck helps one obtain money, and money is what the mother, Hester, wants. Since Paul wants his mother's attention, he wants to provide her with money, and the luck exhibited by his winning predictions helps quiet the house's whispers and temporarily satisfies his mother. In keeping with the tale's fablelike narration, the "luck" turns out to be tragically unlucky. Paul's ultimate prediction as his mother enters his room leads to an £80,000 winning bet, but Paul falls into a trance at this climactic moment and ends up dying three days later. Paul's final words resonate with irony: "Mother, did I tell you? I am lucky?"

The fable's simple moral that money corrupts hides both psychological and social dimensions. The story's oedipal configuration suggests that Paul wants to give his mother a baby, that is, what she truly desires most. Thus, money acts as a metaphor for the baby. Yet Hester, not the peripheral father, represents the punishing parent, a castrating mother who refuses any baby and denies oedipal gratification even on the sublimated level of possessing money. In effect, Hester exchanges her son for the £80,000. Society dictates that the male must provide resources for the family, and Paul admirably tries to provide what his father cannot, but, being so young, he necessarily fails. Hester uses up this resource, and Paul, over-identifying with the aggressive mother, loses himself. From the psychoanalytic perspective, Paul's transgression (riding the horse being a metaphor for masturbation, then later displaced as a symbol of desired copulation with his mother) requires his punishment or death.

Psychoanalytic readings of this richly symbolic fable also benefit from a more materialist reading. In the end, the mother ends up in literal filth, and her son has been disposed of as a waste product. Hester symbolically digs Paul's grave. The middle-class family requires more money to maintain or improve its status, and the class system of an increasingly industrialized England demands that this insatiable appetite be fed at all costs, including that of a child's life. In practical terms Paul works as child laborer. If Lawrence's "Odour of Chrysanthemums" paints a dark portrait of the working-class family, then "The Rocking-Horse Winner" paints an even darker portrait of the expanding English middle class.

In between these two stories of 1909 and 1926, Lawrence composed volumes of classic short stories. "The Horse Dealer's Daughter" portrays a rather twisted pastoral love story. A virginal country girl, Mabel, has de-

voted her life to domestic chores. Her mother died when Mabel was fourteen. The family had some prosperity from the father's horse dealing, but that money has all gone by the wayside, and as the story begins the family's business has evaporated, leaving family members bankrupt. Following the father's death, everyone has made individual plans that do not include their siblings. The three brothers expect Mabel to move in with her sister, but Mabel emphatically does not make any such plans. Her mother's death has left her a lonely and displaced person, and she devotes her time to caring for her mother's gravesite.

The horse dealer's family has firmly entrenched patriarchal values. Mabel is an invisible figure among the brothers, "they had talked at her and around her for so many years." Consequently, Mabel's choice not to live with her sister leaves her in a precarious state. She cannot support herself, but she does not want to be supported by anyone else, either. Trimming her mother's gravesite, and later walking into the water, wipes the past clean but does not prepare her for a world that still disapproves of the independent woman. Mabel seems both to relish the liberation from her patriarchal family, and to fear the unknown world that "liberation" might bring.

One day, in a trancelike state, Mabel wanders into a nearby lake in an apparent suicide attempt. Fortunately, Jack, the country doctor, happens to spot Mabel in the lake. He walks into the water and brings her back from the brink of death. Jack takes the still unconscious Mabel back to her house where he undresses her, wraps her in blankets, and places her near a fire. When Mabel awakens she asks, rather oddly, if Jack loves her. Although Jack is a close friend of Mabel's brother, he has never shown any interest in Mabel. In fact, earlier in the story Jack stops to visit with the brothers but does not even acknowledge Mabel's presence. Yet now Jack kisses her, and he even decides that they will marry—despite Mabel's proclamation that she is horrible. What can a reader make of such odd happenings in the English countryside?

For one thing, Jack dismisses Mabel only when she resides with her brothers. When Jack observes her isolated from the family, her face "mesmerizes him." In addition, Lawrence originally called the story "The Miracle," which implies Mabel's rescue has some religious significance. In terms typical of Lawrence, Mabel appears to be reborn into the flesh. Her exposure to Jack's male gaze has lit a fire that Mabel can only quench by marriage. Reading the story as a resurrection of Mabel's body or the emergence of her blood consciousness, however, leaves the story half read. Her marriage may symbolize a happy conclusion for a previously dead life—a life that denied sexuality—but what does marriage hold for the good doctor? Jack proposes marriage to Mabel entirely out of an obsolete social obligation that concludes the story on an ominous note. Mabel's eldest brother Joe is about to marry as a response to the family's breakup, and the narrator's characterization of that impending marriage presages Jack's prospective marriage to Mabel: "He would marry and go into harness. His life was over, he would be a subject animal now." Mabel shows no interest in her marriage. In fact, she appears ready to succumb to tradition, just as Jack succumbed to tradition, but for a different reason. Mabel, like Lizzie in "Odour of Chrysanthemums," finds herself in an impossible state: trapped between a family that denied her presence and a future that will just as surely relegate her to secondary status. Thus, Lawrence's story denies any rescue fantasy and presents a complex critique of family structure that feminist attacks on his work completely miss.

"Tickets Please" dramatizes the inverse of "The Horse Dealer's Daughter." In this story, women are no longer domestic servants to the patriarchal family, but instead are employed servants of the war economy. As men fight on the front, women and infirm men perform those jobs previously occupied by the nation's primarily male workforce. The story shows women conducting local trams, and Annie, the protagonist, enjoys her newfound freedom. The social role reversal extends, in the story's sadistic twist, to male-female relationships.

The tram inspector, John Thomas, has his way with the many available young women riding and working the trams: with few men available in town, the burly, handsome young inspector seduces an endless line of single women. He meets the girls during the day, sleeps with them at night, and discards them in the morning, off in search of a new conquest (the name John Thomas coincidently foreshadows Mellors's affectionate nickname in *Lady Chatterley's Lover*). The newly independent Annie enjoys John Thomas's company, but does not appreciate being treated as a toy. John Thomas dismisses her, and Annie plots revenge. Late one night, Annie rallies the group of scorned girls and sets a trap for the inspector. As John Thomas enters the waiting room full of ex-lovers, he is ambushed by the girls, who seem to be transformed into a group of vicious maenads turning on their Dionysian tram inspector. John Thomas is turned face against the wall and then slapped, scratched, hit by a belt buckle, and generally humiliated by the girls. A maddened Annie,

in the sexually superior position on top of the inspector, demands that John Thomas choose one of the girls as his bride. The maenads' violence subsides when the tortured man proclaims his choice of Annie. Annie refuses to touch John Thomas, but as the narrative describes her, Annie now seems a broken woman. John Thomas, face averted, takes his torn coat and cap and leaves the lionesses' den.

Annie's Pyrrhic victory is an example of Lawrence's irony. She has chosen her mate, but it is a mate she does not really want. John Thomas has only a superficial and ironic relationship to Lawrence's dark, pagan gods. He pursues sex without intimacy and ends up the prey of his victims. Equally humiliated, Annie has turned into an aggressive force that strips her of intimacy and renders her the hunter she had despised in John Thomas. Her anger appears fueled by the social constrictions of the time. Annie's freedom to work and sleep with men represents only a temporary release from women's submissive place within the family structure. John Thomas still controls the women's response. Before Annie's rallying cry, the girls appeared content to have some sex and then move on with their lives. Annie, the most independent girl, realizes the temporary or illusory sense of freedom the war had made possible, and she erupts at the awareness that when the war ends things will return to the way they were. After all, John Thomas holds the power to make a choice, and marriage to a dominant man would be precisely the future that produces Annie's rage.

This mock-heroic story takes place in the inferno of the British midlands. The tram ride, an obvious symbol of copulation, shuffles from the ninth circle of the colliery to the perhaps upper circle of town. Lawrence draws analogies between the hell of industrial England and the hell of international war. These two horrors of the early twentieth century frame Lawrence's embattled vision of a new intimacy that his novels strive to imagine.

SMASHING WALLS, CROSSING BOUNDARIES

History has been unkind to Lawrence's reputation as a novelist, but his reputation as a whole rests on his novels. His reputation suffered first from the great moderns and their pretense to scientific objectivity, which saw Lawrence as a rather hortatory loose canon; his reputation suffered next (or simultaneously) from the moral puritanism that continues to strangle creativity even in those countries with long-standing democratic traditions; and most recently, Lawrence's reputation suffers from the vagaries of a political correctness that emanates from the ivory tower. Undoubtedly, Lawrence would embrace his outsider position. He had at best a begrudging admiration for James Joyce's *Ulysses* (fate frequently linked Joyce and Lawrence over censorship issues) and he scorned the famous Bloomsbury group, whose most accomplished writer, Virginia Woolf, thought equally little of Lawrence. Certainly, no honest reader would venture to claim Lawrence a better novelist than Joyce or Woolf; many have, in fact, ventured the opposite claim. T. S. Eliot and his followers blasted Lawrence for his disregard of tradition, his lack of impersonality, and his general trashing of hierarchies, generic and otherwise. F. R. Leavis remained a lone wolf defending Lawrence against the snobby uppercrust literati who had no respect for a miner's son.

Graham Martin has outlined the general debate over Lawrence's modernism, situating Lawrence between the H. G. Wells and Henry James poles of early-twentieth-century literary production. James considered Wells, a friend of Lawrence, to be a journalist, and a journalist could not polish the shoes James walked in. For his part, Wells thought little of a finely crafted story like James's, seeing it as empty of ideas. Although Lawrence was perceived by Eliot and others as lacking form, nothing could be further from the evidence the novels proffer. Indeed, to compare Lawrence to Woolf or Joyce is to succumb to the proverbial apples and oranges fallacy. Modernism has many rooms, and different styles occupy different sections of a sprawling single-story ranch. Lawrence's novels contain both a cornucopia of frequently contradictory ideas as well as technical innovations from which contemporary fiction continues to benefit.

Admittedly, his first two novels are minor league. *The White Peacock's* (1911) chief virtue resides in its portrayal of the gamekeeper Annable, a prefiguration of the more completely drawn Mellors of *Lady Chatterley's Lover*. The novel also exhibits some underlying homoerotic tension and the dynamics of male friendship that resurface in *Women in Love* and the novels of the 1920s. *The Trespasser* (1912) shows a development in narrative technique, but nothing to suggest the masterpieces on the horizon.

With *Sons and Lovers* (1913) Lawrence made his breakthrough. A classic Bildungsroman, the story dramatizes Paul Morel's emergence from a constricted family environment dominated by an overpowering mother. In additional to the novel's oedipal dynamics, Lawrence describes the decimation of the English countryside with devastating accuracy. In Lawrence's novel, the landscape metamorphoses into an object for man's manipulation rather than his admiration. Man no longer participates in the natural world, but tears up the hills in search of coal to fuel his appetite for technology and town building. The novel concludes with Paul's emergence from the dark looking toward the town lights. This open-ended conclusion represents the novel's ambiguity; Paul pulls free from the net of family suffocation, but awaits the iron net of urban civilization that Lawrence's next two novels describe in detail.

Lawrence followed *Sons and Lovers* with a major work in progress called *The Sisters*, which bifurcated into two complementary masterpieces, *The Rainbow* (1915) and *Women in Love* (1916, published in 1920). The first novel is a hymn to Eros and the second a threnody about the war. *The Rainbow* extends the Victorian novel's Augustan sweep and brings to a close the realist novel. Lawrence narrates the saga of the Brangwen family over three generations. The intergenerational family story parallels England's change from a rural society to a heavily industrial-based one. Lawrence gives the novel's events historical specificity, including the beginning of the Midland Counties Railway in 1840. The narrative symbolizes the difference between premodern and modern England through a comparison between Marsh Farm and Wigginston colliery. Lawrence marks this movement from farm to industry in a linear fashion; however, the story's apocalyptic imagery brings a mythic dimension and satiric edge to the novel. Lawrence would clearly be one of Freud's "discontents," and the novel's indictment of industrial civilization surfaces at numerous points.

Contrary to the Victorian novel's organic movement, *The Rainbow*'s chronological development clashes with the narrative's radical oscillation between Eros and Thanatos (life and death). The narrative dramatizes conflicting drives through the rhythms of relationships: Tom and Lydia in the first generation, Will and Anna in the second, and Ursula and Anton in the third. On one hand, the marital relationship strives for a mythic evocation of the unconscious, and on the other hand, couples become locked into a personal love that constricts development and signifies the mechanical state of modernity that Lawrence despised. Nonetheless, Lawrence could only signify the mythic power of an archetypal love that transgresses the limits of consciousness, and speaks the body's primal drives or the "living unconscious," through a highly self-conscious narrative style. Similarly, the novel's unromantic depiction of a cannibalistic sexual desire, or of sex as a form of Nietzschean will to power, devours the sex scenes, which are unfolding against a natural backdrop.

The Rainbow also offers a radical critique of British imperialism, and, implicitly, a critique of England's role in World War I. Surprisingly, Lawrence speaks through the female character Ursula, the most completely drawn character in his entire oeuvre, against the military-minded Anton Skrebensky. Anton stands willing, against Ursula's beliefs and wishes, to serve the British army in India. Additionally, Ursula and Anton's relationship evolves and then devolves against the background of the Boer War. Ursula's attack on imperialism parallels Lawrence's own antinationalist stance during World War I. Censors objected to *The Rainbow's* rather muted depiction of sexuality, but they objected even more strenuously, under the cover of morality, to the novel's unpopular politics.

The story does conclude with a rainbow, the biblical sign of hope, but Ursula, member of the third generation, refuses marriage. Moreover, the rainbow signifies the transitory after-image of a storm, and this tenuous bridge disappears in the endless, opaque fog of *Women in Love.* Lawrence returns to the archetypal conflict between forces of life and death when *Lady Chatterley's Lover* recomposes and combines *The Rainbow* and *Women in Love.* Ultimately, Lawrence's final message in his fiction is at best ambiguous. He imagines a new world based on tenderness, on the loving connection of a male and female—together but separate, as Birkin proposes in *Women in Love.* But this utopian image is not actualized; Lady Chatterley does not marry Mellors, and the couple ends apart. Meanwhile, in real life, writing, publishing, and defending his last masterpiece drained what little energy Lawrence had left, and on a symbolic, but also on a nearly literal, level, *Lady Chatterley's Lover* killed him.

Nonetheless, Lawrence narrated sex, brought sex into the open, and let sex speak the joys of the body, making possible the discourse that so consumes our contemporary landscape. He also left a vast amount of work that crosses all genres, from novels and poetry to short stories and travel writing. Even his letters (published in seven massive volumes) represent an epic masterpiece of autobiography. Ultimately, life dealt David Herbert Lawrence an invalid's system, but he lived a triathlon athlete's life. Should any of us achieve a small portion of what D. H. Lawrence accomplished in his brief forty-four years, we, too, can say we have lived a full life.

[*See also* Censorship; T. S. Eliot; Sigmund Freud; F. R. Leavis; Modernism; *and* Virginia Woolf.]

SELECTED WORKS

The White Peacock (1911)
The Trespasser (1912)
Sons and Lovers (1913)
The Prussian Officer and Other Stories (1914)
The Widowing of Mrs. Holyroyd (1914)
The Rainbow (1915)
Twilight in Italy (1916)
Look! We Have Come Through! (1917)
New Poems (1918)
The Lost Girl (1920)
Women in Love (1920)
Psychoanalysis and the Unconscious (1921)
Sea and Sardinia (1921)
Aaron's Rod (1922)
England, My England and Other Stories (1922)
Fantasia of the Unconscious (1922)
Birds, Beasts, and Flowers (1923)
Kangaroo (1923)
The Ladybird, the Fox, the Captain's Doll (1923)
Studies in Classic American Literature (1923)
Reflections on the Death of a Porcupine (1925)
St. Mawr (1925)
David (1926)
The Plumed Serpent (1926)
Collected Poems (1928)
Lady Chatterley's Lover (1928)
The Woman Who Rode Away and Other Stories (1928)
The Escaped Cock (The Man Who Died) (1929)
Pansies (1929)
Pornography and Obscenity (1929)
Apropos of Lady Chatterley's Lover (1930)
Love Among the Haystacks and Other Pieces (1930)
The Virgin and the Gipsy (1930)
Apocalypse (1931)
Etruscan Places (1932)
Last Poems (1932)
Phoenix (1936)
The First Lady Chatterley (1944)
The Collected Letters (1962)
The Complete Poems (1964)
The Complete Plays (1965)
Mr. Noon (1984)

EDITIONS

The standard scholarly edition of D. H. Lawrence's work is being published by Cambridge University Press under the general editorship of James T. Boulton and Warren Roberts. A less expensive edition of the scholarly publications is available through Penguin's Twentieth-Century Classics series. Major works discussed or referred to in the article are indicated with the Cambridge editor and date of publication by Cambridge. Books not yet published by Cambridge, including *The Complete Poems*, edited by Vivian de Sola Pinto and Warren Roberts, are available through Penguin. *The Escaped Cock*, edited by Gerald M. Lacey, is published by Black Sparrow Press.

FURTHER READING

Adelman, Gary. *Reclaiming D. H. Lawrence: Contemporary Writers Speak Out.* Lewisburg, PA, 2002. Describes the large gap between the academic treatment of Lawrence and Lawrence's treatment by creative writers; an important book for understanding the problems with political correctness in the academic world.

Chaudhuri, Amit. *D. H. Lawrence and "Difference": Postcoloniality and the Poetry of the Present.* Oxford, 2003. Applies postmodern theory to Lawrence's poetry.

Donaldson, George, and Mara Kalnins, eds. *D. H. Lawrence in Italy and England.* London, 1999. Includes three important essays: "Lawrence and Cambridge," by James T. Boulton; "Play and Carnival in *Sea and Sardinia*," by Mara Kalnins; and "Lawrence and Modernism," by Graham Martin.

Ellis, David. *D. H. Lawrence: The Dying Game, 1922–1930.* Cambridge, U.K., 1998.

Fernihough, Anne, ed. *The Cambridge Companion to D. H. Lawrence.* Cambridge, U.K., 2001. Collects a wide range of solid essays on all aspects of Lawrence's work, including his usually neglected drama.

Fernihough, Anne. *D. H. Lawrence: Aesthetics and Ideology.* Oxford, 1993. Offers stimulating readings of Lawrence's thinking from a philosophical perspective that engages Lawrence's ideology in some creative ways.

Friedman, Alan W. "D. H. Lawrence: Pleasure and Death." *Studies in the Novel* 32, no. 2 (Summer 2000): 207–228. Traces the dialectic of life drives and death drives across Lawrence's major fiction.

Fussell, Paul. "The Places of D. H. Lawrence." In *Abroad: British Literary Traveling between the Wars*, 141–164. New York, 1980. Fussell's chapter on Lawrence's travel books is far and away the best essay on the design and significance of Lawrence's travel writing and its relationship both to his nomadic life and to his response to England's political climate.

Gilbert, Sandra. *Acts of Attention: The Poems of D. H. Lawrence.* Carbondale, IL, 1990. The best general introduction to Lawrence's poetry; includes many excellent readings of individual poems.

Hayles, N. Katherine. "Evasion: The Field of the Unconscious in D. H. Lawrence." In *The Cosmic Web: Scientific Field Models and Literary Strategies in the Twentieth Century*, 85–110. Ithaca, NY, 1984. Offers an original and convincing account of Lawrence's theory of the unconscious and its relation to narrative and characterization.

Ingersoll, Earl G. *D. H. Lawrence, Desire, and Narrative.* Gainsville, FL, 2001. Examines Lawrence's narrative in light of Lacanian theory.

Kermode, Frank. *D. H. Lawrence.* London, 1973. Kermode's book is a brief but highly insightful introduction to Lawrence.

Kinkead-Weekes, Mark. *D. H. Lawrence: Triumph to Exile, 1912–1922.* Cambridge, U.K., 1996.

Langbaum, Robert. *The Poetry of Experience: The Dramatic Monologue in Modern Literary Tradition.* New York, 1957. Langbaum's classic text, though primarily addressing nineteenth-century verse, provides a theoretical foundation for understanding Lawrence's poetry as belonging to a countertradition rejected by T. S. Eliot and the high modernists.

Leavis, F. R. *D. H. Lawrence: Novelist.* London, 1955. The most important defender of Lawrence's work, Leavis discusses Lawrence's fiction in relation to the tradition of the novel.

Millet, Kate. *Sexual Politics.* New York, 1970. The classic feminist attack on D. H. Lawrence and Henry Miller, Millet's book severely damaged Lawrence's academic reputation, but spurred Norman Mailer's powerful defense of both Lawrence and Miller in *The Prisoner of Sex* (1971).

Millett, Robert W. *The Vultures and the Phoenix: A Study of the Mandrake Press Edition of the Paintings of D. H. Lawrence.* Philadelphia, 1983. Includes excellent reproductions of Lawrence's paintings along with an indepth discussion of them, their exhibition, and their dissemination through the Mandrake edition.

Oates, Joyce Carol. *The Hostile Sun: The Poetry of D. H. Lawrence.* Los Angeles, 1973. Focuses on Lawrence's sun imagery and its relation to his overall philosophy.

Perloff, Marjorie. "Lawrence's Lyric Theatre: *Birds, Beasts, and Flowers*." In *Poetic License: Essays on Modernist and Postmodernist Lyric.* Chicago, 1990. Perloff provides the best single essay on Lawrence's poetry, reading the lyrics of Lawrence's best volume of verse as an integrated text that exhibits Lawrence's persona performing diverse roles.

Rexroth, Kenneth. "Poetry, Regeneration, and D. H. Lawrence." Reprinted in *World Outside the Window: Selected Essays of Kenneth Rexroth*. New York, 1987. An accomplished poet, Rexroth in his 1947 essay discusses the entire range of Lawrence's work in a lively style and favorably compares Lawrence to Thomas Hardy.

Richards, I. A. *Practical Criticism: A Study of Literary Judgment*. New York, 1929. Richards uses "The Piano" as part of his experiment in poetry reading with a group of students.

Seelow, David. *Radical Modernism and Sexuality: Freud/Reich/D. H. Lawrence and Beyond*. New York, 2005. Reexamines Lawrence's work from a postmodernist perspective and provides detailed readings of *Women in Love, Lady Chatterley's Lover, The Fox, The Man Who Died*, and a variety of Lawrence's short stories.

Siegel, Carol. *Lawrence Among the Women: Wavering Boundaries in Women's Literary Traditions*. Charlottesville, VA, 1991. Siegel's book is an excellent alternative to the feminist attacks on Lawrence.

Squires, Michael, and Lynn K. Talbot. *Living at the Edge: A Biography of D. H. Lawrence and Frieda von Richthofen*. Madison, WI, 2002. A husband-and-wife team writes about Lawrence and Frieda in an engaging style with a fine sense of scholarship and a refreshing dual perspective on one of literature's most famous marriages.

Widmer, Kingsley. *The Art of Perversity: D. H. Lawrence's Shorter Fiction*. Seattle, WA, 1962. Although an early book, Widmer's reading of Lawrence's short stories remains convincing and provocative.

Worthen, John. *D. H. Lawrence: The Early Years, 1885–1912*. Cambridge, U.K., 1991.

T. E. LAWRENCE

Waïl S. Hassan

Few celebrated figures have combined the range of talents and interests of T. E. Lawrence (1888–1935), who by the age of thirty achieved the status of legendary national hero and cult figure. His fame rests on his role as a British liaison officer to the leaders of the Arab Revolt against Ottoman rule during the last two years of World War I, and on his *Seven Pillars of Wisdom: A Triumph*, a detailed memoir of that campaign.

Born in Wales on 15 August 1888, Thomas Edward Lawrence was the second of five illegitimate sons of an Anglo-Irish baronet, Thomas Chapman, and Sarah Lawrence (or Sarah Junner), the Scottish governess to Chapman's four daughters from his marriage to Edith Chapman. Chapman changed his name to Lawrence after leaving his first family in 1884. After living in various locations, including two years in France, the couple and their children eventually settled in Oxford in 1896, where Ned (Thomas Edward) attended the City of Oxford High School for Boys and eventually won a scholarship to study history at Jesus College. By then he had already developed a passion for medieval heraldry, chivalry, and architecture, collecting brass rubbings and pottery fragments in Oxford and surrounding villages, and cycling around France to visit medieval castles. During that period he also subjected himself to rigorous physical and mental discipline of an often eccentric nature: fasting for days at a time, trekking across country in midwinter, riding his bicycle uphill and walking it downhill, cycling nonstop until falling exhausted by the roadside, reading the newspapers upside down. To research his bachelor's thesis on medieval architecture, Lawrence took a walking tour of Syria and Palestine, eventually writing a thesis for which he was awarded first-class honors upon graduation in 1910, and which was published in 1936 as *Crusader Cas-*

T. E. Lawrence
Pencil portrait by Augustus Edwin John,
c. 1929
NATIONAL PORTRAIT GALLERY, LONDON

tles. At Oxford he came under the influence of the Orientalist, archaeologist, and intelligence officer D. G. Hogarth, who later took Lawrence with him for excavation work in the Middle East and helped him get appointed in the British intelligence bureau in Cairo at the outbreak of the war. Lawrence later wrote, "He is the man to whom I owe everything I have had since I was seventeen."

In 1916, Hussein ibn Ali, Sharif of Mecca, launched the Arab Revolt against the Turks. The Allies saw the advantage of supporting the Revolt so as to weaken the Ottomans and distract them on the eastern front. In an intelligence memo in January 1916, Lawrence described the Arab Revolt as "beneficial to us, because it marches with our immediate aims, the break up of the Islamic 'bloc' and the defeat and disruption of the Ottoman Empire, and because *the states* [Sharif Hussein] *would set up to succeed the Turks would be . . . harmless to ourselves . . .* The Arabs are even less stable than the Turks. *If properly handled they would remain in a state of political mosaic, a tissue of small jealous principalities incapable of cohesion*" (emphasis in original). Lawrence was sent to the Hizaj (western Arabia) on a fact-finding mission and began serving as a liaison between the British military command in Cairo and Faisal, the leader of the Arab forces and one of Hussein's sons. Lawrence participated in the military campaign and became increasingly guilt-ridden as he realized that the British did not intend to honor their promise, made in the McMahon-Hussein correspondence of 1915–1916, to grant Arab independence after the war: the Sykes-Picot agreement signed with the French in 1916 envisioned the partition of Ottoman territories between Britain and France. Nevertheless, Lawrence convinced Faisal that it would still be in the Arabs' best interest to go on fighting the Ottomans. After the success of the Revolt and the

Arab capture of Damascus in 1918, Lawrence lobbied for Arab independence at the Versailles peace conference in 1919 and the Cairo conference in 1921. Those efforts failed both in maintaining the territorial integrity of the Arab land, which he had promised to the leaders of the Revolt, and in limiting French influence in what later became Syria and Lebanon. Meanwhile, the British placed Palestine, which they had promised to the Zionists in the Balfour Declaration of 1917, under mandate, and divided the remaining territory into the kingdoms of Iraq and Transjordan, assigning them to Faisal and his brother Abdallah, respectively. Those arrangements precipitated the subsequent instability of the Middle East.

Lawrence began writing *Seven Pillars* after the war but lost the manuscript in 1919. With a seven-year fellowship at All Souls College, Oxford, he produced two more drafts, one of which he destroyed in 1922, and in the same year eight proof copies were printed of the other (the "Oxford" text), which he revised and abridged continuously until its publication to subscribers in 1926–1927; it was not reissued for general circulation until 1935. A further abridgment was published in 1927 as *Revolt in the Desert* to defray the costs of publication.

Lawrence attained the rank of colonel by the end of the war. He was then assigned to the Colonial Office as Middle East adviser under Winston Churchill, but disappointed with the outcome of postwar diplomacy and tired of "the shallow grave of public duty," as he called it, he resigned in 1922 and enlisted as a private in the Royal Air Force under the assumed name of John Hume Ross. His experience as a new recruit furnished the material for *The Mint*, an autobiographical account of his life in the ranks. Eventually published in 1936, *The Mint* embarrassed the RAF with its depiction of the violation of the recruits' dignity. Lawrence's identity was quickly discovered by the press, and he was discharged from the RAF. With the help of friends, he enlisted in the Royal Tank Corps in 1923 under the name T. E. Shaw, a name he assumed legally in 1927. Intercession of friends allowed him to return to the RAF, serving in India in 1926–1929. Back in England, he translated Homer's *Odyssey* and worked on improving high-speed motorboats until his retirement from the RAF in February 1935. He died in a motorcycle accident on 19 May of that year.

LEGEND AND CONTROVERSY

Several of Lawrence's more than forty biographers have speculated about the psychological effect of his discovering his illegitimacy at an early age: it has been seen variously as a deep wound that caused his aloofness, sense of isolation, and distaste for intimacy; as a spur for him to prove himself worthy by his accomplishments of the aristocratic distinction he could never claim; or as the root cause of his masochistic self-discipline and contempt for corporeality. Biographers have also speculated about the lasting effects of his brief capture, torture, and rape by Turks in Deraa, Syria, an episode graphically, and contradictorily, described in the two surviving texts of *Seven Pillars* and in a letter to Charlotte Shaw. Controversy also surrounds his ambiguous sexuality, the regular secret flagellations he arranged for himself in his later years with a young Scotsman called John Bruce, and whether his intense passion for speedboats and motorcycles evidenced an unconscious death wish.

The legend of Lawrence may have been initiated by one man, but it quickly grew at the hands of a few biographers, friends, devotees, and to some extent Lawrence himself. In 1919 the American journalist Lowell Thomas, who had met Lawrence briefly, gave a series of sensational lectures, complete with a film and slide presentation, titled "With Allenby in Palestine and Lawrence in Arabia," at London's Covent Garden theater, then Albert Hall, and later at Madison Square Garden in New York. The crusades, the romance of the desert, and the *Thousand and One Nights* heavily colored Thomas's depiction of Lawrence, who quickly became the sole focus of the lectures as an uncrowned English king of the Arabs, uniting and marching them to victory over their Turkish oppressors. England was ready for such a glamorous, larger-than-life hero who could salve the national trauma over the horrors of war on the western front. In *With Lawrence in Arabia* (1924), Thomas paradoxically depicted Lawrence as an "Arabian knight," the Arab Revolt as "war in the Land of the Arabian Nights" and as "the most romantic campaign in modern history," Faisal as "the George Washington of Arabia," and Sir Edmund Allenby as "Britain's modern Cœur de Lion." Two of Lawrence's friends, Robert Graves and Liddell Hart, followed suit with adulatory, if more sober, biographies in 1927 and 1934, respectively. By then the legend of Lawrence was firmly established, confirmed by Lawrence's own exaggerated self-portrait in *Seven Pillars* as a prophetic leader of the Revolt who meant to remake the Arabs into "a new nation, to restore a lost influence, to give twenty million of Semites the foundation on which to build an inspired dream palace of their national thoughts." Throughout the 1920s and 1930s, Lawrence's numerous friends and admirers (including George Bernard and Charlotte Shaw, E. M. Forster, Winston Churchill, W. H. Auden, and other high-profile figures) also contributed to his fame, albeit sometimes with a touch of irony, as did other biographers, dramatists, poets, and novelists who modeled their heroes on him.

It was perhaps inevitable, especially after World War II, that the legend of Lawrence would invite debunking. The most notable among the detractors was Richard Aldington, whose 1955 biography focused attention for the first time on Lawrence's illegitimacy and his capture at Deraa. Aldington concluded that Lawrence was driven by the desire to overcome guilt and shame to use his considerable talents to excel in various pursuits, and that he consistently relied on lying, deceit, and self-dramatization to embellish his image. Other disillusioned post–World War II writers, including Terence Rattigan, Anthony West, Alan Bennett, and James Aldridge, satirized nationalistic and militaristic heroism in the figure of Lawrence. Philip Knightly and Colin Simpson's biography (1969) uncovered Lawrence's secret flagellations, heightening the interest in his sadomasochism, a theme already explored in Robert Bolt's commercially successful film *Lawrence of Arabia* (1962), which otherwise depicted Lawrence as a romantic, visionary hero. Matthew Eden's thriller *The Murder of Lawrence of Arabia* (1979) takes its cue from Desmond Stewart's speculation about Lawrence's death in a 1977 biography and imagines him returning to the Middle East in the 1930s to lead another rebellion against the Mandate authorities in Palestine. Such a plot clearly reflects longstanding speculation about Lawrence's role in the shaping of the modern Middle East. Two noteworthy Arab scholars have challenged Lawrence's account of his activities in *Seven Pillars* and British views of both Lawrence and the postwar settlement: George Antonius (1938), who knew Lawrence, gives a detailed history of the Arab national movement from the nineteenth century through the 1930s, and Suleiman Mousa wrote a biography of Lawrence (1966). After the declassification in 1968 of wartime documents, academic study of Lawrence has intensified, with dozens of new biographies, the formation and regular symposia of the T. E. Lawrence Society, which sponsors the *Journal of the T. E. Lawrence Society*, and the Castle Hill Press publication of the 1922 "Oxford" edition of *Seven Pillars* and, beginning in 2000, volumes of Lawrence's massive correspondence.

THE WRITER

Lawrence wanted to be remembered more as a man of letters than as a man of action, although characteristically he never devoted himself completely to writing or to any of his diverse interests. His works include his graduation thesis, a coauthored manual on Sinai written for the British Intelligence Bureau in Cairo and another for the RAF, two commissioned translations, and scattered poems and articles collected after his death. He was also an avid correspondent, leaving behind more than six thousand letters to some of the most prominent literary and political figures of his day. His claim to fame as a writer, however, rests on the tremendous popularity of *Revolt in the Desert*, an abridgment published in advance of, and immediately superseded by, *Seven Pillars*, which has sold more than a million copies and was the basis for an international blockbuster movie. *The Mint*, though well received, has been much less popular for interesting reasons having to do with the stark contrast between the scope, style, narrative voice, and ambition of the two books. While *Seven Pillars* has been described as a modern epic, *The Mint* has been compared to prison diaries. Taken together, the two books represent phases of Lawrence's career and psychic development: his grand ambition and romantic idealism confronted with imperialist manipulation and double-dealing, and his subsequent profound guilt and self-mortification.

Seven Pillars is for the most part a fast-paced, action-packed war memoir written in a style that fluctuates between literary affectation and self-effacing economy. Edward Said in *Orientalism* (1978) and David Spurr in *The Rhetoric of Empire* (1993) have analyzed Lawrence's use of colonial discourse and nineteenth-century racial theory—for example, in the initial chapters on the nature of "Semites," in his use throughout of rhetorical strategies like the idealization, naturalization, and eroticization of the Arabs, and in the static vision of an inert Orient prodded into action by the European imperialist (or prophet, in Lawrence's romantic self-image). In that sense, Lawrence was very much a product of his time and culture. The sporadic spells of introspection in the book, however, register some of the personal complexity that continues to fascinate his biographers, and result partly from Lawrence's own complicated motives and partly from the contradictions between Orientalist discourse and his experiential knowledge of Arabs. Those tensions are heightened halfway through the military campaign when rumors spread about the Sykes-Picot agreement and British intentions to betray the Arab aspirations for independence. Lawrence is then forced not only to acknowledge the duplicity of his role but also to continue to play it while trying to salvage his own idealism. In this context, the episode at Deraa functions, structurally, as the climax of Lawrence's psychological drama: the breaking of his will under torture and the loss of his "bodily integrity," as he described it elsewhere, parallel his sense of loss of ethical integrity. The frenzied and fruitless diplomacy after the war, his rejection of high office in favor of the obscurity and "mental suicide" of life in the RAF, his signing away of all sales profits from *Revolt in the Desert* to charity, the flagellations of his later years, and possibly also his suicidal behavior all seem to fit into a pattern of atonement.

The searing description of intense daily humiliation and the stylistic austerity of *The Mint* reflect this dramatic shift from prophetic leader to penitent, masochistic recluse. *The Mint* is in one sense the second act of the psychic drama staged in *Seven Pillars*, and in another sense is its dialectical counterpart, deflating the myth of "Lawrence of Arabia" that *Seven Pillars* with its epic aspirations participates in creating. The remarkable disparity in the popularity of the two narratives is a testimony to the endurance of national myths.

[*See also* Robert Graves *and* Orientalism.]

SELECTED WORKS

The Wilderness of Zin, with C. Leonard Woolley (1915)

The Forest Giant (1924; translation of Adrien le Corbeau's novel *Le gigantesque*)

Revolt in the Desert (1927)

The Odyssey of Homer, translated by T. E. Shaw (1932)

The 200 Class Royal Air Force Seaplane Tender, Provisional Issue of Notes (1932)

Seven Pillars of Wisdom (1935)

Crusader Castles (1936)

The Mint (1936)

EDITIONS

Garnett, David, ed. *The Letters of T. E. Lawrence*. London, 1938.

Graves, Robert, and Liddell Hart, eds. *T. E. Lawrence to His Biographers Robert Graves and Liddell Hart*. 2 vols. London, 1962.

Lawrence, M. R., ed. *The Home Letters of T. E. Lawrence and His Brothers*. Oxford, 1954.

Weintraub, Stanley, and Rodelle Weintraub, eds. *Evolution of a Revolt: Early Postwar Writings of T. E. Lawrence*. University Park, PA, 1968.

Wilson, Jeremy, ed. *Minorities*. London, 1971.

Wilson, Jeremy, and Nicole Wilson, eds. *T. E. Lawrence, Correspondence with Bernard and Charlotte Shaw 1922–1926*. Volume 1 of T. E. Lawrence, *Letters*, Jeremy Wilson, series editor. Fordingbridge, U.K., 2000.

FURTHER READING

Aldington, Richard. *Lawrence of Arabia: A Biographical Enquiry*. London, 1955. A well-researched though singlemindedly damning investigation into Lawrence's motives.

Allen, M. D. *The Medievalism of Lawrence of Arabia*. University Park, PA, 1991. Focuses on Lawrence's interest in medieval history and romance and how it influenced his writing.

Antonius, George. *The Arab Awakening: The Story of the Arab National Movement*. Beirut, 1938. A detailed historical account of Arab nationalism from the mid-nineteenth century that is indispensable to understanding Lawrence's role in modern Arab history.

Crawford, Fred D. *Richard Aldington and Lawrence of Arabia: A Cautionary Tale*. Carbondale, IL, 1998. An exhaustive study of the controversy over Aldington's biography of Lawrence.

Knightley, Philip, and Colin Simpson. *The Secret Lives of Lawrence of Arabia*. London, 1969. A biography emphasizing Lawrence's psychology.

Lawrence, A. W., ed. *T. E. Lawrence by His Friends*. London, 1937. Homage by some ninety family members, friends, and acquaintances on the occasion of his death.

Mousa, Suleiman. *T. E. Lawrence: An Arab View*. Translated by Albert Butros. London, 1966. A biography and an assessment of the Lawrence legend from an Arab perspective.

Tabachnick, Stephen E., ed. *The T. E. Lawrence Puzzle*. Athens, GA, 1984. Thirteen scholars discuss various aspects of Lawrence's career.

Weintraub, Stanley, and Rodelle Weintraub. *Lawrence of Arabia: The Literary Impulse*. Baton Rouge, LA, 1975. Helpful companion to and background information about his writings.

Wilson, Jeremy. *Lawrence of Arabia: The Authorised Biography of T. E. Lawrence*. London, 1989. The most detailed biography to date, relying on declassified documents.

LAȜAMON

Andrew Galloway

The first Arthurian poem in Middle English, and the best long poem in Middle English until the masterpieces of the later fourteenth century, is the *Brut*, written around 1215 by Laȝamon or Lawemon, whose name is usually modernized as Layamon (or Lawman, or Loweman). Unlike the episodic structure of Chaucer's *Canterbury Tales*, Gower's *Confessio Amantis*, or Langland's *Piers Plowman*, however, its narrative is a single continuous history, more than sixteen thousand lines long, with an especially elaborate and poetically rich presentation of the deeds of King Arthur. Its source is primarily a single work, the Anglo-Norman *Brut* by the courtly poet Wace (died before 1183), who presented a relatively direct translation of Geoffrey of Monmouth's Latin *History of the Kings of Britain* (c. 1138), in which the stories of Arthur first appeared in full scope. Laȝamon made clear in his prologue that he lived at King's Areley in Worcestershire; he mentioned his own name and his father's name, and his identity as a "preost." But his precise dates are obscure, as are many other aspects of his literary affinities, original audience, and impetus for writing, including patronage, and these are left tantalizingly available for varying interpretations.

The prologue mentions that Wace presented his French poem to Eleanor of Aquitaine, whom Laȝamon described in the past tense as Henry II's wife (after her marriage to Louis VII of France was annulled, nominally on the grounds of consanguinity). Since Eleanor outlived Henry, the past tense means that Henry's death in 1189 provides the earliest possible date for Laȝamon's poem. The latest possible date is the period of the two medieval copies of the work, catalogued as British Library, MS Cotton Caligula A. IX and Cotton Otho C. XIII; both are datable by paleography (the historical study of handwriting) to the last quarter of the thirteenth century, although the Caligula copy employs a style and diction suggesting a much earlier period—as early as the late twelfth century—while the Otho copy uses diction more contemporary with its copying. E. G. Stanley influentially argues that the poet was consciously archaizing his language, just

as he presented a metrical form that superficially resembles the Anglo-Saxon alliterative long line, although in its multiple-stress structure and frequent use of internal rhyme it by no means truly resembles an Old English poetic meter; this possibility of lexical and perhaps poetic archaizing has allowed the poem's dating to range between the late twelfth and mid-thirteenth centuries.

Scholars now generally agree that *Brut* was probably a product of King John's reign (1199–1216) or a few years after; Rosamund Allen, who thinks the poem dates from 1216, notes that Laȝamon's unique statement that King Arthur came from Brittany to claim the crown on Uther's death (lines 9898 and 9935) indicates some allusion to Prince Arthur of Brittany. Arthur of Brittany, the son of King Richard's and John's long-dead brother Geoffrey, was a likely heir to the English throne when Richard died in 1199, but Arthur was edged out by Richard and then probably murdered in 1203, at age sixteen, by John, who thus removed the alternate claimant to the English throne. Ralph Coggeshall, a chronicler writing in the 1220s, declared that the connection between Arthur of Brittany and the ancient King Arthur had earlier been widespread among the Bretons, and this suggests further confirmation of the general period of John's reign for the poem's composition or the recent memories on which it relied.

Laȝamon's poem is best considered a historical epic, although throughout it relates past, present, and future in complex and perhaps deliberately interwoven ways. Laȝamon, for instance, follows Wace in noting that after King Arthur's death, "the Britons await him" (13279–13282), but Laȝamon adds suggestively, "Bute while wes an witeze Mærlin ihate; / he bodede mid worde his quiðes weoren soðe, / þat an Arður sculde zete cum Anglen to fulste" (14295–14297: "But once upon a time there was a wise man named Merlin; / he made his predictions with words, and his sayings were true, / that *an Arthur* would yet come as a help to the English"). The open-ended quality of this observation does not make the poem any easier to date, but it suggests its open connections to early thirteenth century political sentiment and history.

An interwoven view of history is also clear in La-ʒamon's deft and vivid prologue, itself a small literary masterpiece, which follows in general claims and form the often elaborate prologues in Latin historical works of the period. Unlike most Latin histories, however, this original prologue presents intriguingly misleading claims about his range of sources, although it offers a compelling view of the poet as compiler, setting three very different books together, beholding them devoutly, then "pressing them into one," as if making a kind of consecration of a eucharistic host (which embodies the nation's times and cultures, and becomes his own poem). He names as his sources three "books" in the three chief languages of England, English, Latin, and French; and all are from very different moments of English history. That in "Englisca" is Bede, a Latin history, albeit one translated into English in the ninth century, which Laʒamon shows no signs of having used, and which perhaps thus simply represents the Anglo-Saxon period. The book he claims to have used "on Latin" is an impossible collaboration or compilation by "Seint Albin" (difficult to identify with any firmly historical figure, and but perhaps simply a historical symbol, the first English martyr, Saint Alban) and also by the "feire Austin" (Augustine) who brought Christianity to England, together suggesting writers of the pagan Saxon period. The last source, by Wace, "a Frenchis clerc," is merely listed as the third book that Laʒamon traveled to collect in order to be able "of Engle ða æðelæn tellen, / wat heo ihoten weoren & wonene heo comen" ("to tell about the noble English, / what they were called, and from where they came"), and this one seems mentioned chiefly to point to the world of Anglo-Norman England, the post-conquest, French-speaking political community that destroyed the world of the Anglo-Saxons whose language and poetic forms contributed so much to Laʒamon's own poetry.

The details that Laʒamon added about Eleanor herself receiving Wace's book perhaps imply the high social circles in which his own work ought to be welcome, if only the royal court were still interested in English rather than French verse writing; yet his poem epically describes (like all of the Arthurian materials that so captivated post-conquest English culture) the destructive efforts of the ancestors of the English whose language and poetic form he invokes. The golden world of the Britons, including their chief glory—a King Arthur who in Laʒamon is nearly a poet-king—is callously brought down by the pagan ancestors of the Anglo-Saxons, whom the Normans in turn conquered. Laʒamon's poem has thus been

called essentially paradoxical or "ambivalent," in imitating an Anglo-Saxon literary tradition only to describe the least unflattering aspects of the culture creating that tradition. But twelfth- and thirteenth-century English historical writing is shot through with such critical and self-critical assessments of English culture, as described by an intelligentsia that was often conscious of its culturally hybrid identity (the great twelfth-century Anglo-Latin historian William of Malmesbury, for example, emphasized that since his mother was Anglo-Saxon and his father Norman, he could present the Norman Conquest evenhandedly).

Even Laʒamon's portrayal of his great hero, Arthur, is deeply ambivalent. Arthur is imagined as a visionary poet-king, able to produce soaring similes, prone to extraordinary prophetic dreams (like that which presents Mordred like a giant rat gnawing on the posts of his royal house; lines 13964–14021), and willing to let his worst enemies go free simply so that they can travel back home to "tellen tidende of Arðure kinge" ("tell tales about King Arthur"; line 10425). Laʒamon added repeatedly to his source, Wace, indications that Arthur's men are too fearful to offer him wiser counsel against such rash actions (for example, lines 14022, 10428–10429). In Laʒamon, Arthur's ability to transcend his moment in song, story, and prophetic dream seems as much part of his tragedy as of his grandeur.

Laʒamon's poem participated in a complex intellectual and literary world that may be broadened to include Latin epic as well as French courtly poetry, and some sort of contact with Anglo-Saxon literary traditions. His work thus poses a fascinating and useful problem for medieval literary history. In meter, it moves between the rhyme used by French and Latin verse (including half-line rhymes of leonine Latin verse) and the alliteration used by Old English (and some later Welsh) writings, but with a persistent avoidance of the simple four-stress structure that fundamentally informs Old English meter. Cable suggests that this evasion is deliberate; if so, the poem's chosen relation to the traditional "Englishness" in meter is all the more elusive. In language, the poem (in the Caligula copy) uses many formulae and type-scenes, but it does so with deft pertinence: a particularly exquisite formula is the poet's mention of a moment of silence after a moving statement or episode has occurred, as when King Leir—in the first English presentation of that story—returns finally after his downfall to his daughter Cordoille to make his lament: "þe quene Cordoille seæt longhe swþe [very] stille" (lines 1760). But the phrase is clearly formulaic (see also 8512, 9922). In poetics, Laȝamon's use of Virgilian similes rises to a crescendo with the section on Arthur's reign (lines 10040, 10048, 10061, 10402, 10603, 10702); his use of character portrayal, dialogue, and irony all fundamentally reimagine his French source to a degree comparable with Chaucer's remaking of Boccaccio's *Teseida* into the *Knight's Tale* but sustained over a far longer span, with a continued variety of interest for those who can become familiar with its odd language and peculiar and distinctive literary greatness.

[*See also* Arthurian Literature; Geoffrey of Monmouth; *and* Middle English.]

EDITIONS AND TRANSLATIONS

Laȝamon: Brut. Edited by G. L. Brook and R. F. Leslie. 2 vols. Early English Text Society 250, 277. London, 1963, 1978.

Lawman: Brut. Translated with commentary by Rosamund Allen. New York, 1992.

Layamon's Arthur. Edited and translated by W. R. J. Barron and S. C. Weinberg. Exeter, U.K., 2001. The Arthurian section only, with facing-page translation.

Wace. *Roman de Brut: A History of the English.* Edited and translated by Judith Weiss. Exeter, U.K., 1999.

FURTHER READING

Allen, Rosamund, Lucy Perry, and Jane Roberts, eds. *Laȝamon: Contexts, Language, and Interpretation.* London, 2002. A substantial collection of critical essays, including studies of his meter, context, social vision, genre, and editorial history.

Galloway, A. "Laȝamon's Gift." *Publications of the Modern Language Association* 121 (2006). A recent discussion of the poem's complex position in literary and cultural history, focusing on how it looks back to traditional ideas of lordly gift exchange but reshapes those to correspond to new cultural issues and new possibilities for literary power.

Le Saux, Françoise H. M. *Laȝamon's Brut: The Poem and Its Sources.* Cambridge, U.K., 1989. A scrupulous examination of the range of possible sources for the poem, and the poet's ways of using them.

Le Saux, Françoise H. M., ed. *The Text and Tradition of Laȝamon's Brut.* Arthurian Studies 33. Cambridge, U.K., 1994. A valuable collection of critical essays.

Stanley, Eric G. "Laȝamon's Antiquarian Sentiments." *Medium Ævum* 38 (1969): 23–37. A classic essay arguing for Layamon's calculated archaizing effort.

F. R. LEAVIS

William E. Cain

The literary critic F. R. Leavis (1895–1978) is difficult to describe and assess fairly. He wrote a number of seminal books; he edited *Scrutiny* (1932–1953), one of the premier journals of the twentieth century; he re-shaped the English literary canon in both poetry and prose; and he prompted countless readers and students to share his passion for critical analysis and evaluation. Leavis's strength is his dedication to principles and ideals, which during his peak years of the 1930s and 1940s he embodied in brilliant interpretive work. His limitation is a rigidity of mind that ultimately led to an absence of intellectual curiosity and an inability or unwillingness to reflect on the nature and implications of his judgments. Leavis thus provokes extreme frustration in readers even as he manages to win from many of them high appreciation and respect.

F. R. Leavis
Charcoal by Robert Sargent Austin, 1934
NATIONAL PORTRAIT GALLERY, LONDON

must have been a harrowing experience for Leavis (it lasted twenty-one months), but he kept his feelings about "the blood deluge" (as he termed it) mostly to himself, except to remark, decades later, that throughout the war years he carried in his knapsack the World's Classics edition of John Milton's poetry.

After the war Leavis returned to Cambridge and completed a dissertation titled "The Relationship of Journalism to Literature: Studied in the Rise and Earlier Development of the Press in England." Key inspirations for him in the 1920s were I. A. Richards, whose lectures on the analysis of poetry were elaborated in *Principles of Literary Criticism* (1924) and *Practical Criticism* (1929), and T. S. Eliot, whose haunting verse and keen critical prose (for example, *The Sacred Wood*, 1920) were provocative and who in 1926 at Trinity College, Cambridge, presented eight lectures on metaphysical poetry.

Impatient with the Victorian spirit of belles lettres and with gentlemanly reflection on the classics, devoted to modern poetry and literary criticism, and responsive to such scandalous authors as James Joyce and D. H. Lawrence, Leavis was an oppositional critic-teacher within the university. He became in 1927 a probationary lecturer on poetry and "modern problems in criticism," and in 1932 he was named the Director of Studies in English for Downing College. But Leavis's position at Cambridge was precarious and it took many years for him to reach the standing in the university he deserved. In 1929 he married Queenie Dorothy Roth (1906–1981), an undergraduate at Girton College and one of his pupils; always her husband's fiercely loyal supporter, she would achieve renown in her own right for *Fiction and the Reading Public* (1932), an investigation of mass culture and of reading habits since the eighteenth century, and for her cogent essays on

LIFE AND CAREER

Frank Raymond Leavis was born in Cambridge, England, on 14 July 1895. His parents were Harry Leavis (1862–1921), a piano dealer and proprietor of a music shop, and Kate Sarah Moore (1874–1929). He attended local elementary school, and then Cambridge and County School and Perse Grammar School, where he studied Greek under William Henry Denham Rouse (a founding editor of the Loeb Classical Library); he was an excellent student and participated in sports and in the theater (among his roles was the lead in *Macbeth*).

From Perse, Leavis proceeded to Emmanuel College, Cambridge, but World War I intervened, and in 1916 he left the university to join the Friends' Ambulance Unit (a Quaker medical service), which by train transported the dying and the dead from the battlefields to the rear. This

Jane Austen, the Brontës, and other English and American novelists.

LEAVIS'S CRITICISM

Leavis's first major book, *New Bearings in English Poetry: A Study of the Contemporary Situation*, examining Gerard Manley Hopkins, William Butler Yeats, Eliot, and Ezra Pound, was published in 1932 (2d ed. 1950). In the same year, two of his associates, Lionel Charles Knights and Donald Culver, launched a journal they named *Scrutiny*, and with the third issue Leavis became a senior editor. At once literary and much more, *Scrutiny* offered essays and reviews on education, politics, philosophy, music, and other subjects. Contributors in the beginning were diverse and included Richards, William Empson, Goldsworthy Lowes Dickinson, Michael Oakeshott, Herbert Butterfield, and W. H. Auden.

Leavis's own essays and reviews usually appeared first in the pages of *Scrutiny*, and he then organized and developed them for publication in critical books, including *Revaluation: Tradition and Development in English Poetry* (1936), *The Great Tradition: George Eliot, Henry James, Joseph Conrad* (1948), and *D. H. Lawrence: Novelist* (1955), and in collections, notably *The Common Pursuit* (1952). In 1954 Leavis was at last invited to join the English faculty board at Cambridge. And in 1959 he was given an appointment as university reader (which is one level below that of professor)—in part, it is said, because the authorities knew he would soon retire, which he did three years later. Leavis lectured in Great Britain and the United States, and held visiting appointments at the universities of York (1965), Wales (1969), and Bristol (1970). He died on 14 April 1978.

During his final decades, Leavis's critical writing became narrow and repetitive, marked by incessant celebration of Lawrence and Dickens and rejection of nearly everyone else. In *New Bearings in English Poetry* and *Revaluation*, Leavis had shown himself to be a superb practitioner of and advocate for "close reading" of literary texts. He furthermore had emphasized that critics and teachers should be engaged with the contemporary literary scene, and, especially in *Education and the University: A Sketch for an "English School"* (1943, 2d ed. 1948), had outlined an approach to cultural criticism that was keyed to close reading yet that reached beyond it into politics, history, economics, and the media. But by the late 1940s and early 1950s Leavis was becoming mired in waging the same polemical battles year after year and increasingly he shunned contemporary literature. He neither practiced nor fostered the cultural analysis and critique, growing out of close reading, that he had called for in *Education and the University*.

In *Two Cultures?: The Significance of C. P. Snow* (1962), *Lectures in America* (1969), *English Literature in Our Time and the University* (1969), and *Nor Shall My Sword: Discourses on Pluralism, Compassion, and Social Hope* (1972), Leavis devoted nearly all of his energy to polemical warfare—the "higher pamphleteering," he called it. His dogged determination was impressive up to a point, but no longer was he changing minds, as he had done in his stimulating books on poetry and in his essays and reviews for *Scrutiny*.

Leavis's best books of his later period are *Dickens the Novelist* (coauthored with Q. D. Leavis, 1970) and *The Living Principle: "English" as a Discipline of Thought* (1975). But both reprinted or adapted much material written a good deal earlier, and both are padded with lengthy quotations, laments about the decline of cultural standards, and jibes at T. S. Eliot, the Bloomsbury group, the BBC, the *Times Literary Supplement*, and other symptoms of cultural corruption. Leavis insisted he had been maligned and mistreated for decades. "They say I have persecution mania," he said: "Comes of being persecuted, you know." He was caught in the grip of an idealized esteem for (and identification with) D. H. Lawrence, whom he celebrated again in *Thought, Words, and Creativity: Art and Thought in Lawrence* (1976).

Leavis deployed Lawrence and Dickens to indict modern civilization as a spectacle of deterioration and decay. This wasteland sense of things is there in Leavis's work from the beginning: it simply grew more vivid and unrelenting. Industrialism, technology, the mass media, and the ever-encroaching horrors of "Americanization" (cheap entertainment, collapse of critical standards, mediocrity rampant in schools and universities) had crushed the harmonious culture and community that England had once enjoyed. "What we have lost," Leavis professed as early as 1933 in *Culture and Environment: The Training of Critical Awareness*,

is the organic community with the living culture it embodied. Folk songs, folk dances, Cotswold cottages, and handicraft products are signs and expressions of something more: an art of life, a way of living, ordered and patterned, involving social arts, codes of intercourse, and a responsive adjustment, growing out of immemorial experience, to the natural environment and the rhythm of the year. (pp. 1–2)

"The machine" has utterly destroyed "the old ways of life, the old forms, and by reason of the continual rapid change it involves, prevented the growth of new" (p. 3). And the result is the ravaging of soul and spirit: "life impoverishment—the human emptiness" (*Nor Shall My Sword*, p. 60). But Leavis made his case in such stark terms that he ended up dramatizing the futility of the remedy he proposed:

> We can't restore the general day-to-day creativity that has vanished; we shall have no successor to Dickens. But we *have* Dickens, and we have the English literature that (a profoundly significant truth) Dickens himself had, and more— for there is the later development that includes Lawrence. There *is* English literature—so very much more than an aggregation or succession of individual works and authors. It reveals for the contemplation it challenges—in its organic interrelatedness reveals incomparably—the nature of a cultural continuity, being such a continuity itself. (*Nor Shall My Sword*, p. 185)

This is a powerful critique of modernity, but it is so sweeping and absolute that no response or alternative to it feels even remotely plausible. All that Leavis seems able to invoke is a handful of novels that keep alive for us the memory of a world we have irretrievably lost.

WHY LEAVIS MATTERS

Combative and contentious, Leavis is a militant figure whose precursors in the nineteenth century are Thomas Carlyle, John Ruskin, Matthew Arnold, and William Morris. His roots as a dissenter indeed extend further back, into the seventeenth century. Q. D. Leavis once observed at a social gathering that in the English Civil War her husband would have been "one of Cromwell's generals." He heard her across the room and replied, "No, my dear, I would have been Cromwell." His research supervisor in the 1920s, Arthur Quiller-Couch, noted Leavis's "self-sufficiency," and a friend, the critic Marius Bewley, said trenchantly about this same trait of personality that Leavis would "never learn, and there is something irritating about a person who won't."

Too often it seems that Leavis does not want others to learn, either. His evaluations can be coarse, as when he says that a student "will have no use at all for Hazlitt or Lamb" (*Education and the University*, p. 133), and when he scorns "the ruck of Gaskells and Trollopes and Merediths" (*The Great Tradition*, p. 15). There are many things that Leavis knew little or nothing about—even as he dis-

missed them as worthless. Popular culture was a blank to him and he was baffled by anyone who showed an interest in any dimension of it; he was shocked, for example, when he was told that the philosopher Ludwig Wittgenstein, whom Leavis knew at Cambridge, attended the movies twice a week.

Nowhere does Leavis consider Karl Marx, Friedrich Nietzsche, or Sigmund Freud. He paid no attention to Thomas Mann, Franz Kafka, and other major figures of European modernism. There is nothing in his sizable output on the literature of the British Empire. Nor has Leavis an understanding of and feeling for American literature, though he tried—unconvincingly—to graft Nathaniel Hawthorne, Herman Melville, and Mark Twain to the "great tradition" of the English novel.

Yet Leavis was a great critic. He defined "tradition" in English poetry (the "line of wit" extending from John Donne and Ben Jonson to T. S. Eliot) and in fiction (Jane Austen, Dickens, George Eliot, Henry James, Joseph Conrad, and Lawrence); he edited a journal that for two decades published pioneering work on literature, criticism, and higher education; in *Mass Civilization and Minority Culture* (1930), *Culture and Environment*, and *Education and the University*, he laid the foundations for the field of cultural studies, making connections between literary interpretation and other disciplines, foreign languages and literatures, and topics in history, politics, and the media; and he insisted, forcefully, on the centrality of English in the modern university and the value of literary criticism as an activity and commitment.

Leavis was passionately drawn to the organization of language in complex, challenging poems and novels. This, for him, constituted the center of literary studies, and his analyses and judgments of specific works, above all in his books and essays of the 1930s to the early 1950s, remain valuable and instructive. Here is Leavis in action in an essay comparing Shakespeare's *Antony and Cleopatra* and John Dryden's *All for Love*, in which he focuses on Enobarbus's description of Cleopatra: "The barge she sat in, like a burnish'd throne, / Burn'd on the water. . . .":

> The assonantal sequence, "barge"—"burnish'd"— "burn'd"—is alien in spirit to Dryden's handling of the medium (it reminds us of Hopkins who, though he has a technical deliberateness of his own, is, in his use of English, essentially Shakespearean). The effect is to give the metaphor burn'd a sensuous realization that it wouldn't otherwise have had; the force of "burn" is reflected back through "burnish'd" (felt now as "burning" too) upon "barge", so that

the barge takes fire, as it were, before our eyes: we are much more than merely told that the barge "burn'd." (The Living Principle, pp. 146–147)

For Leavis, the best English poets and novelists possess in common an intimate feeling for the resources of English. Through their handling of the medium, they create for readers an experience of profound moral exploration and testing:

In coming to terms with great literature we discover what at bottom we really believe. What for—what ultimately for? What do men live by?—the questions work and tell at what I can only call a religious depth of thought and feeling. (*Nor Shall My Sword*, p. 56)

Leavis maintains that for critics, teachers, and students of literature, certain questions are fundamental and must be asked and answered: What are we reading and why? Even more: What do we believe in, and why? Leavis thus matters because of the intense moral and intellectual demands he makes on us. He is not ironic; he does not apologize; he is direct and forthright. This is a critic who expects us to be as serious about life and literature as he is.

[*See also* Literary Theory.]

SELECTED WORKS

Mass Civilization and Minority Culture (1930)

D. H. Lawrence (1930)

New Bearings in English Poetry: A Study of the Contemporary Situation (1932, 2d ed. 1950)

How to Teach Reading: A Primer for Ezra Pound (1932)

For Continuity (1933)

Culture and Environment: The Training of Critical Awareness (1933), with Denys Thompson

Revaluation: Tradition and Development in English Poetry (1936)

Education and the University: A Sketch for an "English School" (1943, 2d ed. 1948)

The Great Tradition: George Eliot, Henry James, Joseph Conrad (1948)

The Common Pursuit (1952)

D. H. Lawrence: Novelist (1955)

Two Cultures?: The Significance of C. P. Snow (1962)

Anna Karenina and Other Essays (1967)

English Literature in Our Time and the University (1969)

Lectures in America (1969), with Q. D. Leavis

Dickens the Novelist (1970), with Q. D. Leavis

Nor Shall My Sword: Discourses on Pluralism, Compassion, and Social Hope (1972)

Letters in Criticism (1974), edited by John Tasker

The Living Principle: "English" as a Discipline of Thought (1975)

Thought, Words, and Creativity: Art and Thought in Lawrence (1976)

EDITIONS

Singh, G., ed. *The Critic as Anti-Philosopher: Essays and Papers.* London, 1983.

Singh, G., ed. *Valuation in Criticism and Other Essays.* Cambridge, U.K., 1986.

FURTHER READING

Bell, Michael. *F. R. Leavis.* New York, 1988. Considers Leavis's "critical rhetoric" and literary judgments.

Bilan, R. P. *The Literary Criticism of F. R. Leavis.* New York, 1979. Expert overview.

Boyers, Robert. *F. R. Leavis: Judgment and the Discipline of Thought.* Columbia, MO, 1978. Brief but stimulating.

F. R. Leavis: Reminiscences and Revaluations. Special issue of *The Cambridge Quarterly* 25, no. 4 (1996).

Kinch, M. B., William Baker, and John Kimber. *F. R. Leavis and Q. D. Leavis: An Annotated Bibliography.* New York, 1989. An essential resource.

MacKillop, Ian. *F. R. Leavis: A Life in Criticism.* London, 1995. A solid biography.

MacKillop, Ian, and Richard Storer, eds. *F. R. Leavis: Essays and Documents.* Sheffield, U.K., 1995. Biographical and interpretive essays on Leavis as teacher and critic.

Mulhern, Francis. *The Moment of "Scrutiny."* London, 1979. Focuses on the journal *Scrutiny* and its historical and cultural significance.

Samson, Anne. *F. R. Leavis.* New York, 1992. Examines Leavis in the context of modern literary theory and cultural criticism.

Thompson, Denys, ed. *The Leavises: Recollections and Impressions.* New York, 1984. Firsthand accounts and essays.

JOHN LE CARRÉ

Kevin J. H. Dettmar

David John Moore Cornwell was born in 1931 into family circumstances almost guaranteed, in retrospect, to make a person obsessed with double-dealing and intrigue. His father, Ronnie, muddled along through a series of low-rent scams and schemes; his mother, Olive, left the family when Cornwell was just four years old, on the occasion of her husband's being imprisoned for fraud. Ronnie, however, continued to entertain exalted social aspirations for his two sons, and David was sent to an exclusive boarding school at the tender age of five.

Though he was successful academically, Cornwell hated the elitism and hypocrisy of the schools—both Sherborne School, the model for James Hilton's *Goodbye, Mr. Chips* (1934), and then England's most prestigious school for boys, Eton. Cornwell left school at age sixteen to spend time living in Switzerland with relatives, where he studied German language and literature at the University of Bern; he then secured a position as an intelligence officer posted in Vienna. Having completed his National Service duty, Cornwell returned to England and resumed university studies at Oxford; he took an honors degree in German and seems to have contemplated a career in academics, but the young family he had started with Ann Sharp forced him to secure a more immediate and dependable income. This he did first as a teacher at Eton; but when the school proved as odious to him as a teacher as it had as a student, Cornwell joined the British Foreign Office, working in the embassy in Bonn, Germany. It was in this position, bored with the work and writing fiction on his commute to and from the office, that Cornwell transformed himself into a professional author.

APPRENTICE WORK
AND INTERNATIONAL FAME

David Cornwell went "under cover" and published his first book, *Call for the Dead*, in 1961; as the Cold War approached its nadir, Cornwell became John Le Carré ("the square" or "the unremarkable"—his nom de plume was necessitated by his work with the Foreign Office), and

set out on a course to become the undisputed master of postwar spy fiction. *Call for the Dead* is really a novella rather than a fully developed novel; it also has one foot in the world of detective fiction and the other in the world of espionage where Le Carré would make his name. A second book, the novella *A Murder of Quality* (1962), is accomplished but even more entirely a piece of detective fiction. Both were reviewed favorably on their release; neither, it seems fair to say, would have secured Le Carré's reputation, nor did they suggest a firm foundation for the writing career Le Carré has subsequently built. One element of these first two works, however, would endure: the character George Smiley, Le Carré's unprepossessing, understated spy.

Le Carré's first full-length novel changed his life, and it changed the genre of which he quickly became the unquestioned master. *The Spy Who Came In from the Cold* (1963) was a huge success; Le Carré had looked forward to the day when he might make a modest living off his writing, and give up his dreary job at the Foreign Service. *The Spy Who Came In from the Cold*, which has sold more than 40 million copies to date worldwide (making it the best-selling spy novel of all time), did that and much more. With it, Le Carré invented the serious, thought-provoking Cold War spy novel. Ian Fleming, creator of the James Bond franchise, had been there earlier and more flashily; but as the reality of the Cold War sank in, the almost camp figure of 007 seemed further and further removed from the real experience of British citizens, and less and less useful as they sought a way to understand the shrinking British Empire's diminished place in a vastly changed world theater. James Bond was all flash and style—all surface, it sometimes seemed, and no substance; George Smiley, on the other hand, was a slovenly, intellectual spy, and one who recognized and wrestled with the complicated moral and ethical dilemmas that his work brought him. In a visible symbol of just how much the world of espionage had changed in the previous quarter-century, *The Spy Who Came In from the Cold* opens and closes at that newest of Cold War monuments, the Berlin Wall; indeed the novel's spy protagonist, Alec Leamus, is killed on that wall because he will not betray the woman he loves.

Le Carré followed up on the success of *The Spy Who Came In from the Cold* with *The Looking-Glass War* (1965) and *A Small Town in Germany* (1968). Both examine the politics of the Cold War, and how those large political structures insinuate themselves into the moral decisions of individual citizens. To what extremes will the defenders of democracy go in order to protect their way of life? And if the citizens of the "free world" stoop to the tactics of the oppressive regimes behind the "iron curtain," have they in fact forfeited their freedom and moral superiority in the process? These two novels, however, wear their political and ethical dilemmas somewhat on their sleeves, and are long and slow into the bargain; neither enjoyed the critical or popular success of Le Carré's breakout novel.

A DEPARTURE, AND A RETURN

Given the disappointing reception of *The Looking-Glass War* and *A Small Town in Germany*, and concerned that he was quickly being pigeonholed as a writer exclusively of spy stories, Le Carré's next step looks, in retrospect, not so surprising as it must have seemed at the time: the frankly embarrassing romance *The Naive and Sentimental Lover* (1971), whose titular adjectives are only too honest. Based on a love triangle in which Le Carré had been involved, the material is insufficiently distanced to be anything but sentimental; one reviewer—hardly the novel's harshest—called it "an unhappy venture into the metaphysics of love." In an irony that Le Carré himself would come to recognize, his spy novels of the 1960s were in part precisely about "the metaphysics of love"; but approached through the world of espionage, the topic had a kind of immediacy and context that prevented it from becoming maudlin. All of Le Carré's novels have, as one of their concerns, the complex and contradictory nature of love; the one novel in which this is made the explicit focus, however, fails to hit the mark.

Reviewers and readers urged Le Carré to go back "under cover." He heeded their advice, and the result is a powerful, loosely connected trilogy of novels that comprised Le Carré's output for the 1970s: *Tinker, Tailor, Soldier, Spy* (1974), *The Honourable Schoolboy* (1977), and *Smiley's People* (1980); the three were published together in 1982 as *The Quest for Karla*. The moral landscape in which George Smiley (brought out of retirement) now

operates is, if anything, more ambiguous and troubling than in the novels of the 1960s. Loyalty within "the Circus" (the intelligence-gathering agency that Smiley is charged with pulling back into shape) seems to be a thing of the past; the quintessential "us versus them" Cold War mentality will no longer suffice, since on many important occasions the lives of the agents are put in danger by domestic threats, not foreign ones—by "moles" burrowed within the British espionage community. The relations of British spies to one another, the antagonism between the British and Soviet intelligence communities, even the relationship of a spy to his or her lover: all are relationships of power, exploitation, deceit. Most disturbingly, the closer Smiley comes to his goal of eliminating his Soviet opposite Karla, the more he realizes that Karla is also his doppelgänger. The novels of this trilogy, especially the first and third, are among Le Carré's most successful; they are also among his bleakest. When he had finished *Smiley's People*, Le Carré vowed that he was done with George Smiley. He was wrong.

TOWARD A POST–COLD WAR ESPIONAGE

As the thaw in Soviet relations with the West so welcomed in diplomatic circles set in, Le Carré recognized that it meant a fundamental shift in the role of East-West espionage. Or at least it ought to: one thing that Le Carré's novels of the 1980s suggest is that despite the official rhetoric of *glasnost* ("openness"), in some ways the spy game went on just as before. Nevertheless, in his first novel after the trilogy, Le Carré changed the venue to the Middle East; *The Little Drummer Girl* (1983) both demonstrates real insight into the conflict between the Israelis and Palestinians—the result of Le Carré's careful research—and also suggests, if quietly, that there is something hauntingly similar in all such national and international struggles. His next novel, *The Perfect Spy* (1986), written a decade after the death of his difficult father, uses a thinly veiled autobiographical frame to investigate the dynamics of the father-son relationship. *The Russia House* (1989) explores the inability, or unwillingness, of British diplomatic and intelligence services to work in accordance with the ideals of *perestroika* ("restructuring").

Despite his earlier vow, in 1991 Le Carré did bring his best-known character, George Smiley, back, in the loosely constructed *The Secret Pilgrim*; the collection works something like a retrospective of Smiley's career, contrasting his experience and wisdom with that of a new generation of spies who are facing a very different political reality from the one in which Smiley came of age. In the 1990s and beyond, with the official destruction of the Berlin Wall (central to Le Carré's first great success) and the splintering of the former Soviet Union, Le Carré's cold warriors find themselves with no Cold War left to fight; his novels since *The Night Manager* (1993) have sometimes had little to do with the world of espionage upon which he made his reputation, and they have been published to mixed reviews.

But whatever the decades to come might bring, John Le Carré has succeeded in endowing the spy novel with a degree of intelligence, moral questioning, and self-examination it had found previously only in the work of Graham Greene; and it brought these gifts into a Cold War world that politicians were altogether unwilling to deal with in anything other than crisp black and white. John Le Carré restored to the Cold War and post–Cold War landscape its proper shades of gray.

[*See also* Ian Fleming *and* Graham Greene.]

SELECTED WORKS

Call for the Dead (1961)
A Murder of Quality (1962)
The Spy Who Came In from the Cold (1963)
The Looking-Glass War (1965)
A Small Town in Germany (1968)
The Naive and Sentimental Lover (1971)
Tinker, Tailor, Soldier, Spy (1974)
The Honourable Schoolboy (1977)
Smiley's People (1980)
The Little Drummer Girl (1983)
A Perfect Spy (1986)
The Russia House (1989)
The Secret Pilgrim (1991)
The Night Manager (1993)
Our Game (1995)
The Tailor of Panama (1996)
Single and Single (1999)
The Constant Gardener (2000)
Absolute Friends (2004)

FURTHER READING

Aronoff, Myron Joel. *The Spy Novels of John Le Carré: Balancing Ethics and Politics.* New York, 1998.

Bloom, Harold, ed. *John Le Carré.* New York, 1987.

Bruccoli, Matthew J., and Judith S. Baughman, eds. *Conversations with John Le Carré.* Jackson, MS, 2004.

Cobbs, John L. *Understanding John Le Carré.* Columbia, SC, 1998.

Hoffman, Tod. *Le Carré's Landscape.* Montreal, 2001.

Monaghan, David. *Smiley's Circus: A Guide to the Secret World of John Le Carré.* London, 1986.

NATHANIEL LEE

Timothy Decker

The plays of Nathaniel Lee (c. 1647–1692) articulate conflicts central to Restoration England: conflicts between passion and reason, authority and rebellion, society and the individual. Lee managed to preserve the tension of these conflicts and thereby capture the anxieties of his age, while also reintroducing to English tragedy the psychological depth and moral complexity of Jacobean and Caroline drama. Most prolific from 1674 to 1684, Lee primarily wrote heroic dramas. Known for their extravagant verse, violent subject matter, larger-than-life protagonists, and lavish stage productions, these dramas provided Lee with the opportunity to entertain audiences while exploring the tensions and passions that became his trademark.

Lee probably nurtured his sense of intellectual conflict in the large library owned by his father, an Anglican minister who turned Presbyterian and supported Oliver Cromwell's Commonwealth government, but then supported Charles II's return to the throne in 1660. The library contained a wide variety of religious writings, ranging from orthodox Anglican doctrine to Puritan tracts. Lee's education was continued at the Charterhouse and then at Trinity College, Cambridge (BA 1668–1669, possibly a Fellow in 1669–1670). After leaving Cambridge, he briefly worked as an actor. Most notably, he played Duncan in Sir William Davenant's version of *Macbeth* (1673). However, stage fright drove him from performance to playwriting.

Lee's plays exemplify the new direction that drama was taking by the early 1670s. The previous decade had been dominated by the plays of Roger Boyle, earl of Orrery, which show heroic characters struggling with the conflict between love and honor—and always choosing honor. These plays, by showing heroes rejecting chaotic passions in favor of duty, reenacted the Restoration's return to tradition, reason, and royalty after the chaos of the civil wars. Lee's plays, however, present dubious heroes; instead of describing their virtue, Lee depicts their error, confusion, and emotional turmoil, and he includes powerful heroines in addition to the standard warriors of heroic drama.

The shift toward complexity and emotion shows that dramatists were registering doubts about whether Charles II, whose appetites for mistresses and lavish entertainment conflicted with his role as an upholder of tradition and stability, had indeed expelled the turmoil of the civil wars and interregnum. Lee's emphasis on passion also indicates the general direction English drama would take: away from stoical warriors and toward the affective dramas of the 1690s and early eighteenth century.

EARLY WORKS

Lee's first play, *The Tragedy of Nero, Emperour of Rome*, was produced at Drury Lane in May 1674 and met with moderate success. Nero's excesses allowed Lee to reveal his penchant for violence and bombast (the play begins with the emperor ordering the execution of his mother, Agrippina). The play also includes Lee's first experiment with psychological contrasts, a technique he learned from John Dryden. Nero's vehemence is offset by the passive escapism of Britannicus, the rightful heir to the throne, who, following the murders of his sister, Octavia, and his wife, Cyara, goes mad. He is afterward poisoned by Nero. Britannicus's death leaves the audience yearning for a hero who would be a compromise between the emperor's passion and Britannicus's irresolution. The play concludes with the villain dying—perhaps by poisoning as well, although this remains unclear—while thunder sounds to indicate a providential design. Lee nevertheless launched his playwriting career by presenting a world in which heroism is scarce. Only divine intervention can restore reason and stability, while humankind remains unable to defend itself against the uncontrollable appetites of a Nero.

With a run at Drury Lane that lasted a week or more, Lee's second play, *Sophonisba* (1675), became his first smash hit. Complicating his use of character contrasts, Lee structured *Sophonisba* around Hannibal's passion for his Roman mistress, Rosalinda, and the infatuation of Massinissa, the King of Nubia and an ally of Rome, with

Sophonisba, his Carthaginian mistress. Both women play large roles and contribute to the bombast as much as the men. Hannibal debates whether to continue the war after he visits an oracle, where priestesses produce a vision of Rosalinda dying from a wound. The prophecy comes true: Rosalinda disguises herself as a soldier in order to aid Hannibal and is killed, renewing Hannibal's uncertainty over whether to continue fighting. Meanwhile, Massinissa rescues Sophonisba from a Numidian usurper, but he is consequently ordered by Scipio to surrender his mistress to the Roman camp because she is an enemy. Massinissa drinks poison with his mistress when Scipio insists on executing her. Hannibal and Massinissa therefore experience parallel tragedies: their role as warriors ultimately destroys the women they love. Yet their ways of handling this are vastly different. Hannibal will continue fighting Rome until he can place Rosalinda's statue on the Capitol. His counterpart, however, surrenders to his passion and his sorrow, committing suicide with his beloved. Although Scipio, grieving over the Nubian king's fate, returns to Rome "with Drooping Eagles," the play opposes such resignation to the renewed vigor of Hannibal only moments before and invites the audience to question which is preferable. *Sophonisba* therefore concludes with two potential heroes whose opposite reactions to the love-and-honor conflict cancel each other out, suggesting that there is no easy answer to the dilemmas the characters face.

LATER WORKS

Over the nine years following *Sophonisba,* Lee wrote nine more plays and collaborated with Dryden on two others. The two most significant of his later works are *The Rival Queens* and *Lucius Junius Brutus.* The first became Lee's most popular play. Following a wildly successful first run in March 1677, *The Rival Queens* was performed every year throughout the Restoration and remained a stock offering through the mid-nineteenth century. Lee was again influenced by Dryden, this time in switching from rhyme to blank verse. Taking place after Alexander's entrance into conquered Babylon, the play contrasts the fiery Roxana, Alexander's mistress during the war, to the devoted Statira, Alexander's wife. Lee, however, complicates the contrast. Statira, for instance, chooses to hear Alexander's apology for the affair only because she has been angered by the cruel delight Roxana takes in having stolen him. At one point, Roxana describes how Statira will suffer from dreaming about Alexander and his new

mistress in bed together. Statira's angry reaction to her rival's cruelty is the true motive behind Statira's decision to return to Alexander—during a fierce exchange in which Lee briefly reverts to rhymed couplets to sharpen the women's lines, Statira tells Roxana, "thou hast wak'd a rage, / Whose boiling now no temper can asswage" (3.1.248–249). Lee therefore invites the audience to consider whether the play truly offers a heroine, just as *Sophonisba* invites the audience to question whether Hannibal or Massinissa is a true hero. The play's conclusion creates similar ambiguities. Statira is poisoned by Roxana while awaiting Alexander in a bower. The scene certainly shows Roxana as the play's villain, yet she escapes punishment when Alexander forgives her. She takes the opportunity to curse Alexander, for although he shows her mercy, he exiles her from Babylon. Alexander's decision could be seen as diabolically appropriate: Roxana's desire for him is so intense that death may be preferable to banishment. Yet Roxana remains on stage long after Statira has quietly disappeared, suggesting that her fury can outlast the tamer personality of her rival. True heroes are as scarce as true heroines. The play has opened with Alexander's followers discussing his harsh treatment of the Babylonians and pointing out his weakness for luxury (Statira is later murdered while Alexander is at a banquet). One such follower, the old soldier Clytus, constantly warns others about Alexander's uncontrollable passions. When he forcefully voices his displeasure to Alexander himself, the conqueror runs Clytus through. Yet Clytus is drunk at the time, casting doubt on his own self-control. The play concludes with Alexander dying after his followers poison him because they fear his rages.

Lucius Junius Brutus has generated more critical attention than Lee's other plays because of the debate over whether the eponymous character is a republican hero or a self-serving villain. The play had a strong first performance, but it was immediately banned because the theme of rebellion was too risky for the time (December 1680, at the height of the Exclusion Crisis, during which James II was banned from accession to the throne because he was a Roman Catholic). The play begins with the seditious Brutus feigning madness to avoid capture by the tyrannical Roman king, Tarquin. When Tarquin's son rapes Lucrece, the daughter of a prominent family, Brutus uses the crime to incite a rebellion. Brutus's son Titus, however, loves Tarquin's daughter, Teraminta, a relationship that Brutus forbids. Titus, like Britannicus, remains passive throughout the play; his love for Teraminta allows his pro-Tarquin brother, Tiberius, to draw Titus into a conspiracy against Brutus. After discovering the plot, Brutus orders the execution of both sons. He justifies the harsh sentence by envisioning himself as a mere instrument of fate. His destiny is to become the liberator of Rome, and he argues that he must coldly serve that destiny. Before the Roman Senate, Brutus focuses on the political expediency of an execution, which will "stop the mouth of loud Sedition" (5.2.42). His reaction to the rape of Lucrece is likewise calculating. Although Brutus can imagine her "ruffled, wet, and dropping tears," he thinks of her pain only in terms of how she can aid the rebellion: "So Lucrece comes to Rome, and summons all her blood" (1.1.97–102). While many of Lee's characters are marred by excessive passion or excessive passivity, Brutus's flaw is his excessive reliance on reason. The true enemy for Lee seems to be any kind of excess. Recent critics note the play's cynical attitude toward language, which becomes merely another instrument with which Brutus can achieve his desires. A distrust of language became a popular theme during the Restoration and is often central to comedies by authors such as Aphra Behn and William Wycherley. Brutus may be the defender of Roman republicanism, and Lee does not envision the overthrow of Tarquin as unfortunate. Yet the Machiavellian way in which the goal was accomplished invites audiences to question the consequences of political efficiency.

Lee's only comedy, *The Princess of Cleve* (c. 1682), has also occasioned significant critical commentary. Lee borrowed most of the plot from Madame de Lafayette's famous short novel, *La Princesse de Clèves* (Paris 1678; translation, London 1679). Its hero, the rake Nemours, is usually considered a satiric portrait of the libertine John Wilmot, earl of Rochester, who supported Lee early in the playwright's career but then abandoned him. More likely, Lee was commenting on the excesses of libertinism in general. By doing so, *The Princess* served as Lee's revenge on his audience of court wits for the banning of Lee's *The Massacre of Paris* (c. 1679), a dramatization of the mass murder of French Huguenots by Catholics on Saint Bartholomew's Day 1572, which, like *Brutus*, was too political for the volatile times. In the comedy, the French queen, Catherine de Medici (who never appears on stage), uses Tournon, Nemours's procuress, to distract the rake from Marguerite and thereby convince the Princess to abandon him. The queen wants her to marry the Dauphin (heir to the French throne), creating an alliance of Protestant and Catholic forces. Tournon introduces Nemours to several available women, including the dissatisfied wives of two foolish would-be rakes, Saint André and Poltrot. These two characters allow Lee successfully to execute several standard scenes from Restoration comedy. Saint André and Poltrot are tested by their wives, Celia and Elianor, who appear in disguise and best the men at repartee. Later, Tournon arranges for Poltrot to sleep with Celia while her husband, Saint-André, sleepwalks, but Nemours takes Poltrot's place. Meanwhile, another character, the Vidame, sleeps with Poltrot's wife. A related plot involves the passion of the Princess of Cleve for Nemours. Her husband dies of heartbreak after the princess confesses her love for Nemours. Nemours's wooing of the Princess and her relationship with her husband create the high plot (spoken in blank verse) of this split-plot comedy, with the adventures of Saint-André and Poltrot serving as the low plot (spoken in colloquial prose). Nemours occupies a prominent role in both parts because he is a master of deception; lacking any essence, he simply speaks whatever language is appropriate for the task at hand.

The play ends on a bitter note. The Princess swears to retire from society to mourn her husband (Statira from *The Rival Queens* had made a similar commitment, only to abandon it after hearing Alexander's pleas). She also leaves open the possibility of returning to Nemours by confessing that she will always love him, and Nemours believes that she will eventually reciprocate his affection, swearing that he will "bed her eighteen months three weeks hence at half an hour past two in the morning" (5.3.256–257). His prediction belies his promise to mend his ways after marrying a reconciled Marguerite. Nemours concludes the play with a couplet asserting that "death-bed sorrow rarely shows the man," an allusion to Rochester's famed last-minute repentance and a rejection of any hope for redemption from the depravity that Lee exposes (5.3.306). Nemours combines the consuming passions of Nero and Alexander with the dehumanizing logic of Brutus. The result is a monster of lust incapable of the genuine love felt by Lee's more sympathetic heroes, and it is telling that Lee saved his most sinister characterization for an analysis of the world in which he actually lived.

Lee's final play, *Constantine the Great; A Tragedy* (1683), provides an audience with some hope for redemption from the pervasive evil of human affairs. The play depicts the Roman emperor's near-collapse into madness, a descent provoked by his treacherous advisor, Arius. The villain's schemes include inciting the Romans to rebellion, encouraging an assassination of the emperor, and marrying Constantine's betrothed, Fausta, to the emperor's son, Crispus. At the conclusion, Arius's plots are revealed and Constantine regains his sanity and his control over Rome. Yet he attributes the revelation to "the hand of Heav'n" (5.2.328), not to any abilities of his own. As in Lee's first play, in which Nero dies to the thundering of heaven, human beings remain too weak and confused to resolve their own problems.

REPUTATION

Lee's playwriting career ended abruptly when he suffered a mental collapse and was confined to Bedlam (Bethlem Royal Hospital) on 11 November 1684. He was released in the spring of 1688, but for the remaining four years of his life he produced only occasional verse. Lee was respected as a dramatist in his day, but the bombastic quality of his verse, in combination with his mental collapse, prevented his reputation from moving beyond the stigma of "Mad Nat Lee." He was slighted by Rochester, Joseph Addison, and John Dennis as an incoherent writer lacking restraint. Even when his contemporaries praised him, they felt obligated to mention his illness. Gerard Langbaine, in *An Account of the English Dramatic Poets* (1691), complimented Lee as a successful poet and playwright, but wishes that "his Madness had not exceeded that Divine Fury which Ovid mentions." Although Lee criticized extremes in his plays, the extremes of his verse and his life prevented his contemporaries from appreciating this. He died in the spring of 1692, following a drinking bout.

[*See also* John Dryden *and* Restoration Drama.]

SELECTED WORKS

The Tragedy of Nero, Emperour of Rome (1674)
Sophonisba, or Hannibal's Overthrow (1675)
Gloriana, or The Court of Augustus Caesar (1676)
The Rival Queens, or The Death of Alexander the Great (1678)

Mithridates, King of Pontus: A Tragedy (1678)
Oedipus: A Tragedy (c.1679; written in collaboration with John Dryden)
The Massacre of Paris (c.1679)
Caesar Borgia; Son of Pope Alexander the Sixth (c.1679; written with John Dryden)
Theodosius: or, The Force of Love, A Tragedy (1680)
Lucius Junius Brutus; Father of his Country (1680)
The Princess of Cleve (c.1682)
Constantine the Great; A Tragedy (1683)

EDITION

Stroup, Thomas B., and Arthur Cooke, eds. *The Works of Nathaniel Lee.* New Brunswick, NJ, 1954.

FURTHER READING

Armistead, J. M. *Nathaniel Lee.* Boston, 1979. Analyzes all plays except the Dryden collaborations, emphasizing Lee's use of character contrasts and emphasis on psychology.
Cannan, Paul D. "New Directions in Serious Drama on the London Stage, 1675–1678." *Philological Quarterly* 73 (1994): 219–242.
Ham, Roswell Gray. *Lee and Otway: Biography from a Baroque Age.* New York, 1932; repr. 1969. Summarizes the evidence on Lee's education, career in London, personality, illness, and treatment at Bethlem Hospital.
Kewes, Paulina. "Otway, Lee, and the Restoration History Play." In *A Companion to Restoration Drama*, edited by Susan J. Owen, 355–377. Oxford, 2001.
Rothstein, Eric. *Restoration Tragedy: Form and the Process of Change.* Madison, WI 1967. Recounts the development of Restoration tragedy from 1660 through the end of the century; shows how Lee contributed to this development in the 1670s.

J. S. LE FANU

Nicholas Daly

Joseph Thomas Sheridan Le Fanu (1814–1873) occupies an important transitional position in literary history between the gothic novelists of the Romantic era (e.g., Ann Radcliffe, Matthew Lewis, and Mary Wollstonecraft Shelley) and the writers of late Victorian supernatural fiction (e.g., Robert Louis Stevenson, H. Rider Haggard, and Bram Stoker). For many, he is the exemplary practitioner of the Victorian ghost story. Beginning in the 1980s, some have also placed him within a specifically Anglo-Irish gothic tradition, noting that many of the best-known writers of nineteenth-century supernatural fiction came from the minority Protestant population of Ireland.

EARLY LIFE AND CAREER

Le Fanu was born on 28 August 1814 (some sources give 24 August), at 45 Lower Dominick Street in Dublin. The Le Fanus were of Huguenot stock, descendants of Protestants driven from France by Catholic persecution, and they were firmly part of the professional middle class. Le Fanu's father, Thomas, was a Church of Ireland clergyman; and his mother, Emma, née Dobbin, was also from a clerical background. The Le Fanus were also proud of their connection to the distinguished Anglo-Irish literary family, the Sheridans; Le Fanu was related to Frances Sheridan, the eighteenth-century novelist, and to her son, the playwright Richard Brinsley Sheridan. Le Fanu spent his early years in Dublin, where his father was a chaplain at the military school in Phoenix Park, but in 1826 the family moved to Abington, County Limerick, when Thomas Le Fanu became dean of Emly. At the time this was far from being a move to rural tranquility, since Catholic tenants were bitterly opposed to paying taxes, or tithes, to support the official Protestant Church, and a campaign of nonpayment and sporadic violence was underway. The Le Fanu family found themselves living in a state of veritable siege, never leaving the house without arms. Moreover, the family finances became increasingly precarious as a result of the tithe war. (Money would continue to be a problem for most of Le Fanu's life, and

it would at times cause him to produce literary work that was beneath his abilities.) Le Fanu's biographer, W. J. McCormack, sees the early experience of isolation and violence as formative for the later fiction, but the young writer was also consciously imbibing useful material from other sources. Among these were the books in the library at Abington, which included Ann Radcliffe's *Mysteries of Udolpho* and the anti-Enlightenment horror novel *The Mummy*; it was also in Limerick that Le Fanu had his first encounters with the Irish fairy lore that he would later employ in his own literary tales of the supernatural.

Le Fanu's career as a writer did not begin until the late 1830s. By then he had earned his degree from Trinity College, Dublin, and was training as a barrister at the King's Inns. In January 1838 he published his first piece, "The Ghost and the Bonesetter," in the *Dublin University Magazine*, a periodical unofficially associated with Trinity College; its other contributors included its editor, Isaac Butt (later a campaigner for Home Rule for Ireland) and the Irish novelist William Carleton (1794–1869). In 1838 Le Fanu also visited London, where he attended the literary salon of Samuel Carter and Anna Maria Hall; whether or not this glimpse of the professional literary life persuaded him to persevere in his writing, more stories followed.

Le Fanu's first story is more farcically grotesque than horrific, but its use of framed narration—the story purports to be from the edited papers of a Catholic priest, the late Reverend Francis Purcell, parish priest of Drumcoolagh—situates it very much in the gothic tradition, and the stories that follow it in the "Purcell Papers" series announce many of Le Fanu's favorite themes: the Faustian pact, aristocratic decadence and decay, betrayal by one's own family, and the powerlessness of the individual before implacable supernatural agents or retributive figures from the past. Some of the stories are set among the vanished eighteenth-century Catholic gentry, a device that may have allowed Le Fanu to express in gothic form his fears for the political perils of his own class, though the same sense of paralysis and vulnerability is hard to miss even in the other tales. The house, like the Gothic castle, provides little safety in these stories. In "Passage in the Secret History of an Irish Countess" the bedroom becomes a literal death trap, and the young narrator sees her cousin brutally murdered as she sleeps beside her. In "Schalken the Painter" a girl is pledged by her greedy father to a sinister but wealthy old man. One night she returns in an agitated and half-starved state to tell her father and his apprentice that "the dead and the living can never be one," and she begs them not to leave her alone for even a moment. When they do, the door immediately locks behind them; they hammer on it in vain, and when they open it she has vanished, seemingly carried off to her marriage to a dead man. Another of the most successful stories, "A Chapter in the History of Tyrone Family," is thought to have provided the plot of Charlotte Bronte's *Jane Eyre* (1847).

On 18 December 1843, in St. Peter's Church in Dublin, Le Fanu married Susanna Bennett, the daughter of a prosperous family who lived on Merrion Square. He had acquired a stake in two newspapers, the *Statesman* and the *Warder*, both staunchly conservative, and he turned his hand to writing editorials in the Tory cause. The first of these papers folded in 1846 and was anything but remunerative for Le Fanu, but he maintained his involvement in the *Warder* until 1870. He seems to have had little success as a barrister, but he had some income from his post as tipstaff to the Court of Common Pleas, effectively a legal sinecure.

EARLY NOVELS

Le Fanu's first novels appeared in the 1840s, and in them he forsook the supernatural for historical romance. His first novel, set in early eighteenth century Ireland, was *The Cock and Anchor* (1845), and a second historical novel, *Torlogh O'Brien* appeared in 1847, though critics have suggested that the order of publication may reverse the order of their composition. These narratives recall the work of Sir Walter Scott in their attempts to come to terms with the nation's political past, and they figure the possibility of religious and political reconciliation in love matches between Catholic heroes and Protestant heroines (though only in *Torlogh O'Brien* is such an imaginary resolution fully entertained). A selection of Le Fanu's short fiction from the *Dublin University Magazine* appeared in 1851 as *Ghost Stories and Tales of Mystery*. However, some of the stories are markedly different from the versions that appeared in the magazine. The Irish tale "Richard Mar-

ston," for example, reappears as "The Evil Guest," a story with an English setting. Here we see the beginning of Le Fanu's career-long practice of rewriting or recycling earlier work. At times, his return to earlier work seems compulsive, extending to the almost cabbalistic repetition of certain character names and verbal patterns.

TRAGEDY AND REBIRTH

After the story "An Account of Some Strange Disturbances in Aungier Street" appeared in the *Dublin University Magazine* in December 1853, there was an extended hiatus in Le Fanu's output. It was during this period, on 26 April 1858, that Susanna Le Fanu died suddenly at the age of thirty-four, and Le Fanu was left with four children (two girls and two boys) and a precarious financial position. Yet though he acquired a reputation as the "Invisible Prince" of Dublin society, this seems to exaggerate the extent of his reclusiveness. What is true is that Le Fanu was extremely troubled by religious doubts after his wife's death, and he possibly suffered from depression.

Then, in 1861, Le Fanu acquired the periodical in which he had published much of his early writing, the *Dublin University Magazine*, and this seems to have spurred him to fresh creative work. As a major contributor of serial novels to his own magazine he could, of course, save money as editor, though one consequence of this thrift was that he churned out a novel a year until 1869, and not always his best work. *The House by the Churchyard*, his first novel since the 1840s, appeared in the magazine from October 1861 to February 1863 under the pseudonym Charles de Cresseron. Le Fanu dispensed with this pseudonym for the novels that followed: *Wylder's Hand* (1863–1864), *Uncle Silas* (1864), *Guy Deverell* (1865), *All in the Dark* (1866), *The Tenants of Malory* (1867), *Haunted Lives* (1868), and *The Wyvern Mystery* (1869). *The House by the Churchyard*, the only one of these novels with an Irish setting, is a historical novel centering on a murder mystery, but its loose structure allowed Le Fanu to devote a good deal of space to conjuring up a vanished social world. Like many other Victorian writers, he extracted additional profit from the serial by republishing it as a three-volume novel.

THE LATER NOVELS

At this point a London publisher, Richard Bentley, offered Le Fanu a contract for another novel on the condition that it would be "the story of an English subject and in modern times." All of Le Fanu's subsequent novels followed this formula, and they sometimes possess a curiously palimpsestic quality, since he often reworked his Irish short fiction for these "English" novels. The use of modern English settings also meant that critics tended to perceive him as a "sensation novelist," part of the wave of contemporary crime fiction that followed the massive success of Wilkie Collins's *The Woman in White* (1860). Le Fanu himself protested at this categorization, and in his preface to *Uncle Silas* he represents himself as following in the footsteps of Sir Walter Scott and the "legitimate school of tragic English romance." This is not entirely accurate, however, for although Le Fanu's work does differ from that of his contemporaries in its dependence on atmosphere rather than suspense, he did not share Scott's vision of historical modernization.

Uncle Silas is generally regarded as Le Fanu's best novel, although *The House by the Churchyard* and *Wylder's Hand* also have their admirers. Serialized in 1864 as *Maud Ruthyn*, and later *Maud Ruthyn and Uncle Silas*, it is a first-person narrative of Maud, a young heiress who is sent to live with her uncle Silas, a once romantic figure now reduced to obscurity and genteel poverty by his own profligacy, and living under the shadow of the mysterious death of one of his guests many years before. To vindicate his brother's name, Maud's father not only entrusts her to Silas's care but also bequeaths everything to him in the event of her death. As Le Fanu acknowledges in the preface, the novel is in fact an extended reworking of his earlier "Passage in the Secret History of an Irish Countess," but the heroine is now English, and the setting is more or less contemporary England. It is also, in effect, an updated gothic novel, in which the formulaic castle in the Apennines has been replaced by a neglected and ramshackle English country house and the swarthy foreign villain is now an elderly but rapacious relative. For the most part, the brisk suspense and rapidly alternating locations of the sensation novel are eschewed in favor of creating a pervasive sense of claustrophobic menace in a single, brilliantly realized domestic setting.

Le Fanu's later novels generally suggest that he was writing too much too quickly, and that the three-volume novel was perhaps not the ideal mode for his particular narrative gifts. That he fully recognized this himself is attested to by a letter of 1866 in which he confessed that "it seems so up-hill a march, so destitute a progress, so mere a treadmill . . . if I could dispense with the little money a novel brings me in, I should never write another."

In marked contrast to his novels, Le Fanu's short fiction continued to be of excellent quality, and in 1872 he published some of his very best work in the collection *In a Glass Darkly* (1872). The best-known of these is the vampire story "Carmilla," in which, as in *Uncle Silas*, the events are relayed by a convincingly realized female narrator. It is often cited as a source for Bram Stoker's far more famous *Dracula* (1897), which it resembles in using vampirism to figure sexuality. More than in Stoker's novel, however, one is never quite sure where one's sympathies should lie—whether the monster is Carmilla or the patriarchal group that hunts her. One of the most successful stories in the collection, "The Room at the Dragon Volant," is not a supernatural tale but an adventure story that describes the progressive ensnaring of a cocksure hero in a murderous plot in France just after Napoleon's first defeat. Its description of the hero's drug-induced paralysis and burial alive are as effective as any of Le Fanu's more ghostly tales.

Le Fanu maintained his literary connections with London, and shortly before the appearance of *In a Glass Darkly* he published a number of stories in Charles Dickens's magazine *All the Year Round*. These are literary treatments of Irish folk stories, possibly ones that he heard in his youth in Limerick or that he encountered through his acquaintance with the folklorist and *Dublin University Magazine* contributor, Patrick Kennedy. Perhaps the best is "The Child that Went with the Fairies," which in many ways recalls his "Schalken the Painter" of some thirty years earlier, another instance of the continuity of Le Fanu's literary themes and situations.

Le Fanu died on 7 February 1873. His final novel, *Willing to Die* (1873), was published posthumously. Of all his prolific output as a novelist, it is *Uncle Silas* that has ensured his place in literary history. His reputation as a writer of short fiction is considerable, and it was already partly established by the end of the nineteenth century, helped by Alfred Graves's 1880 collection of Le Fanu's early fiction, published as *The Purcell Papers*. In the twentieth century, the masterly ghost-story writer Montague Rhodes James recognized Le Fanu's particular genius and edited a collection of his short fiction, *Madame Crowl's Ghost and Other Tales of Mystery* (1923). Other writers have been equally admiring. Although his work has never been as widely read—or as widely adapted—as that of Bram Stoker, in the best of his fiction he is a far more conscious literary artist. In addition, Le Fanu's career casts an interesting sidelight on Dublin as a literary marketplace in the nineteenth century, especially in his balancing of the demands of Irish and metropolitan readerships. If his displacement of Irish material to English settings is sometimes simply unconvincing, in *Uncle Silas* it produced one of the most haunting Victorian novels, one that has a peculiar and nightmarish self-contained reality missing from his Irish novels.

[*See also* Detective Fiction; The Gothic; Sensation Novel; *and* Bram Stoker]

SELECTED WORKS

The Cock and Anchor (1845)

The Fortunes of Colonel Torlogh O'Brien (1847)

Ghost Stories and Tales of Mystery (1851)

The House by the Churchyard (1863)

Wylder's Hand (1864)

Uncle Silas (1864)

Guy Deverell (1865)

All in the Dark (1866)

The Tenants of Malory (1867)

Haunted Lives (1868)

The Wyvern Mystery (1869)

Checkmate (1871)

The Rose and the Key (1871)

Chronicles of Golden Friars (1871)

In a Glass Darkly (1872)

Willing to Die (1873)

The Purcell Papers (1880)

The Poems of Joseph Sheridan Le Fanu (1896)

FURTHER READING

Browne, Nelson. *Sheridan Le Fanu.* London, 1951. A brief introduction to Le Fanu's work.

Coughlan, Patricia. "Doubles, Shadows, Sedan-Chairs and the Past: The 'Ghost Stories' of J. S. Le Fanu." In *Critical Approaches to Anglo-Irish Literature,* edited by Michael Allen and Angela Wilcox, 17–39. Gerrards Cross, U.K., 1989.

Heller, Tamar. "The Vampire in the House: Hysteria, Female Sexuality, and Female Knowledge in Le Fanu's 'Carmilla.' " In *The New Nineteenth Century: Feminist Readings of Underread Victorian Fiction,* edited by Barbara Harman and Susan Meyer, 75–95. New York, 1996.

Howes, Marjorie. "Misalliance and Anglo-Irish Tradition in Le Fanu's Uncle Silas." *Nineteenth- Century Literature* 47, no. 2 (1992): 164–186.

McCormack, W. J. *Sheridan Le Fanu and Victorian Ireland.* Oxford, 1980. An insightful biography that also contains some of the best critical readings of Le Fanu's work, especially *Uncle Silas.*

McCormack, W. J. *Dissolute Characters: Irish Literary History through Balzac, Sheridan Le Fanu, Yeats and Bowen.* Manchester, U.K., 1993.

Sage, Victor. *Le Fanu's Gothic: The Rhetoric of Darkness.* New York, 2003. A detailed critical analysis that focuses on the narrative structure of the fiction.

CHARLOTTE LENNOX

Eve Tavor Bannet

Charlotte Lennox (1720–1804) was a transatlantic writer by biography, by influence, and as the author of two important British-American novels. She lived in colonial America during the late 1730s and early 1740s, the young daughter of a British (probably Scottish) military officer, much as the "American" novelist Susanna Rowson (1762–1824) did. She wrote about her experiences in colonial Albany, Schenectady, and New York in her first novel, *The Life of Harriot Stuart, Written by Herself* (1750), which is often read as a fictionalized biography, and again in her last novel, *Euphemia* (1790). Lennox has therefore been described in some quarters as either the "first American novelist" or the "first novelist of colonial America" (Séjourné). However, she spent the bulk of her professional life in London, where she mixed with such luminaries as Samuel Johnson, Samuel Richardson, Henry and Sarah Fielding, David Garrick, and Johnson's friend Hester Thrale (who disliked her). Dr. Johnson is said to have crowned Lennox with a laurel wreath after reading her best-known novel, *The Female Quixote* (1752); and she was painted as one of the "Nine Living Muses of Great Britain" in a famous Ladies Pocket Book engraving of 1778. Feminist scholars have therefore regarded her as a British woman writer. As these different attributions indicate, Lennox does not fit seamlessly into either British or American national literatures. But national literatures were creations of a later date.

During most of Lennox's active writing career, the American mainland and island colonies were still cultural provinces of England (much like Scotland and Ireland), and Lennox was one of the numerous Scottish, Irish, and American provincials eking out a precarious living as writers in London, which dominated Britain and the em-

Charlotte Lennox
Stipple engraving
by Francesco Bartolozzi,
after Sir Joshua Reynolds, 1793
NATIONAL PORTRAIT GALLERY, LONDON

pire as the major center of patronage and of the printing and bookselling trades. Like many other eighteenth-century women writers, she was driven to take up her pen by a shiftless husband and a failed marriage, which left her with two children and in acute financial distress. Consequently—again, like other authors who wrote for bread—she produced poems and plays as well as novels, and she did translations from the French and adaptations as well as original work. In addition to five novels she certainly wrote, and four that have been attributed to her, she also published *Poems on Several Occasions* (1747), a "dramatic pastoral" called *Philander* (1758), a periodical, *The Lady's Museum* (1760–1761), and a critical comparison of Shakespeare plays with the narratives on which they were based, *Shakespeare Illustrated* (1753–1754). Most critical attention to date has focused on Lennox's novels, particularly *The Female Quixote*, which was hugely popular on both sides of the Atlantic and had literary progeny into the early Republic, most notably in Tabitha Gilman Tenney's novel *Female Quixotism* (1801).

THE FEMALE QUIXOTE

Like Cervantes's *Don Quixote*, Lennox's Arabella "supposed Romances were real Pictures of Life" and drew from them "all her Notions and Expectations." Unlike the Spanish Don, her view of the world was formed by bad translations of the woman-centered, seventeenth-century French romances of Mlle. de Scudery and La Calprenede. Besides absorbing the assumptions built into their hyperbolic, complemental language and courtship rules, Arabella derived from these romances the idea that love—understood as faithful service of an adored mistress by chivalrous knights who obeyed her every wish—was "the ruling principle of the world," as well as the belief that a lady normally agreed to marry only after a lover had won her heart by proving his devotion for many years through a long series of extraordinary adventures and distresses. The novel's satire derives from the confrontation of such expectations with ordinary life in an upper-class English country house, where Arabella is presented with the husband that her guardian has chosen for her, for the economic, dynastic, and self-interested reasons usual in England at this time. Lennox punctuated her comic scenes with serious discourses about the epistemological power of a variety of closely allied eighteenth-century narrative genres: "imagined or fictitious histories," such as romance; the newer and more probabilistic "familiar histories," now called novels; and the "true histories," now called history. In the process, she demonstrated that men's fears about the power of fictions to shape women's expectations of men and of life were justified, while at the same time reassuring men (perhaps tongue in cheek) that, in the end, a few rapid magisterial words from a doctor (then and since identified with Dr. Johnson) would convince a young woman that the narratives she had always read "as Copies of Life and Models of Conduct" were "empty Fictions," and thus effect an instantaneous cure. The novel ends quite abruptly with Arabella's cure and marriage to the husband that her guardian has designated.

The abruptness of the ending has been attributed to the novelist Samuel Richardson's insistence, in two letters of 1751 and 1752, that Lennox complete her story and "finish [her] Heroine's cure" in two volumes rather than in the three she had originally planned (Isles, "The Lennox Collection"). However, later women writers, such as Jane Austen and Charlotte Brontë, used similarly perfunctory conventional endings to underline the artifice—and undermine the credibility—of the expected "happy end" that, through a marriage, reintegrates the heroine into patriarchal society (Barreca, *Untamed and Unabashed*). Like Lennox's contemporary Lady Mary Wortley Montagu, many modern critics have found unconvincing Arabella's too rapid transformation from a powerful, spirited, and adventurous heroine to a defeated, obedient, and dutiful wife. They point out that Lennox's satire works both ways: "reality" may subvert romantic ideals, but the feminine ideals inscribed in romance also reveal the conduct and beliefs of Arabella's guardian, noble suitors, and possible female alter egos in English society to be nothing more than the artifices, courtship customs, and epistemological fictions of a later date.

In *The Progress of Romance* (1785), Clara Reeve dismissed Lennox's satire on romance as superfluous, stating that, by the time Lennox wrote *The Female Quixote*, "the taste for those Romances was extinct, and the Books exploded." This was a self-interested argument by someone who had capitalized on the vogue for gothic romance by writing one herself (*The Old English Baron*, 1778). It ignored the relationship of Lennox's treatment of French romances to contemporary arguments in Britain about what many viewed as excessive French influence on English manners, and it also overlooked the very different ways in which the novel's satiric confrontations played in geographic terms. For instance, in England during the 1740s, Eliza Haywood's *Female Spectator* (1744–1746) was pointing out that—if she wished her daughter to enjoy gentlemanly gallantries and to be addressed with "elegance and delicacy"—"Mrs. Oldfashioned" must take the girl to France, because men in England treated courtship, sex, and marriage "but as a thing necessary to be done, either for the sake of propagating their families, or for clearing their estates from mortgage, or for the payment of younger children's fortunes" (vol. II, p. 68). However, in colonial Albany during the same years, as the memoirist Anne McVicar Grant (1755–1838) and Lennox's novel *Harriot Stuart* both confirm, the language, gallantries and "seductive courtesies" of the "fine gentlemen" in highflown seventeenth-century comedies and romances were identified with English gentility; they were copied by anglicizing provincials and shaped the expectations of more than one provincial girl, including Harriot herself. In England, *The Female Quixote* remained among the most popular of the many "infernal," "political," and other quixotes that proliferated everywhere in literature to "turn authority into jest"; as such, it formed part of the Enlightenment project. However, in America at the turn of the nineteenth century, in a curious reprise of Harriot Stuart's problem, the novel was recast by Tabitha Gilman Tenney (1762–1837), in *Female Quixotism*, as a critique of the deluding influence of English literature on the expectations of her heroine, Dorcasina, "a middling kind of person, like the greater part of her country women," and as a comment on the less attractive social and marital choices available there.

VARIATIONS ON A THEME

Three of Lennox's other four novels took up *The Female Quixote*'s implicit theme: the difficulties faced by an outsider to English society who either misunderstands its codes and values or acts by different moral and social principles. The heroine of *Henrietta* (1758) is an orphaned colonel's daughter who has the beauty, virtue, and gentle birth—but not the fortune or manners—to make a place for herself in upper-class English society. As the novelist Fanny Burney would later do in *Evelina* (1778), Lennox used the "ignorance of forms and inexperience in the manners of the world" of a "young woman of obscure birth but conspicuous beauty" upon her "entrance into the world" as "instructions into life" for her readers. But Burney's young orphan is safely protected by the patronage of Lady Howard, the guardianship of the Reverend Mr. Villiers, the chivalry of a suitor, and the championship of a long-lost brother, and she lives the comfortable life of a lady despite her lack of fortune. Lennox's young orphan has, perhaps more realistically, to face up to all the disadvantage of her state of "beggarly gentility" without protectors—and to struggle to preserve her virtue, reputation, native honesty, and religious integrity—despite repeated betrayals by brother, guardian, noble relations, noble ladies, wealthy upstarts, and female friends. Evelina learns the social forms expected of a lady; but Henrietta learns that a woman will not be the beneficiary of favor or patronage for long if she is unwilling either to flatter or to compromise her principles; that the lady without fortune who will not trade her virtue for money by becoming a rich man's mistress must go into service as a maid; and that she who "enters upon the world with high notions of disinterestedness, friendship, sincerity and candor" will learn the hard way that most persons will "abuse our confidence and the good opinion we have of them." Evelina's satire is reassuringly directed against outsiders—foreigners like Mme. Mirval, the vulgar nouveau riche, and "masculine" women. Henrietta, however, turns to satire as a means of dealing with the pain of losing caste, in defiant rejection of her repeated humiliations at the hands of "lovers" who do not think her rich enough to marry and of ladies who wish to "gratify [their] pride" by having "the daughter of a gentleman subjected to [their] caprice, and dependent on [their] bounty." *Henrietta* is thus a far more disturbing novel than *Evelina* and has, from the first, been far less popular as a result. Lennox eliminated the novel's biting critique of English society when she later based her play *The Sister* on book V of *Henrietta*, in which the heroine's brother reappears and arranges for Henrietta to marry the wealthy son of a noble lord. By reducing the story to a mere matter of recognitions and intrigues, she no doubt hoped that her play would please enough to run to a third-night benefit for the author and bring in much-needed funds.

Lennox's first novel, *Harriot Stuart*, is a less accomplished performance than either *The Female Quixote* or *Henrietta*, though it prefigures them by measuring genteel English life against the idealistic values in familiar literary genres, by its naive heroine's difficulty in distinguishing fictions from the practiced deceptions of polished English life, and by its account of the distresses Harriot faces in England as she strives to reenter the ranks of birth, fortune, and privilege. The interest and importance of this novel lie in its account of English colonization in Albany and New York, and in its historically accurate representations of many actual people and situations, albeit under borrowed names. Lennox passes comment on these by developing analogies between the greed and violence lurking under the polite and gallant words of the English officers who court Harriot while repeatedly trying to capture or rape her and the colonists' conduct in the land. In *Harriot Stuart*, every relation of courtship, family, government, and trade among the English is infected with the violence and rapaciousness of a trading people individually and nationally on the make, who use their polite manners and genteel ceremonies as instruments in their competition with the French and the Dutch for domination of the Indians, the fur trade, and the resources of the new world. When Harriot's unwilling body is captured by Englishmen posing as Indians, Lennox also turns the familiar captivity narrative back upon itself by showing that it is a projection of the colonist's own worst traits upon the colonized other.

Euphemia (1790) foregrounds a secondary element in *Harriot Stuart*'s portrayal of colonial life: the conduct, fate, and fortunes of those liminally aristocratic families who went out to America to serve in administrative offices and military postings, and whose migrations linked the mother country to the frontiers of empire. Looking back well after the Revolution on the same years, people, and events during the 1740s that she had explored in *Harriot Stuart*, *Euphemia* is a more compassionate rewrite of *Harriot Stuart*, which lays bare both the financial and social insecurities of English colonial functionaries and the mistakes in English conduct toward the other nations they attempted to rule. While mixing the epistolary novel with the travelogue, and describing the lives and customs of the Indians and the Dutch, *Euphemia* explores the insecurities of the English families at the fort in Albany who, though seeking to make or mend their fortunes in America like the merest adventurer, pretended to a gentility and status they lacked in the mother country, and who used polite English manners to construct themselves as the first families in the place. While distinguishing them from those British soldiers who planted themselves in the colony and wished to remain, she shows how the defensive superiorities and xenophobic racism of this would-be English elite alienated the Indians and the Dutch, and she models a different, more accepting, and more multicultural form of international exchange.

SOPHIA

Sophia (1762), which was serialized in Lennox's periodical *The Lady's Museum* before it was sold independently as a novel, stands somewhat apart from these other works, but in a way that, finally, seems to reinforce them. The most conventional of Lennox's novels, *Sophia* is a version of the standard "two sisters" plot, which prefigures Jane Austen's *Sense and Sensibility* (1811). Lennox shows how a virtuous, educated, and sensible young lady with small fortune, who is able to stand firm against the bad advice of a foolish and socially ambitious mother and resist the seduction of wealthy suitors, ultimately triumphs over her more beautiful, coquettish, socially successful, and sexually permissive sister. While Harriot is banned from good society and forced to emigrate to America, Sophia achieves the ambition of all the daughters in Lennox's novels: she is confirmed in her proper rank, despite her poverty, by her marriage to a wealthy English peer.

Sophia affirmed the values of conservative, matriarchal women writers in the bluestocking circle by condemning the coquette and showing a proper lady obtaining her proper reward. Since Lennox had lost her earlier patrons with Lord Bute's rise to power at George III's accession in 1760, *Sophia* and the tracts on education in *The Lady's Museum* may have been her bid to join the ranks of bluestocking writers such as Sarah Scott, Sarah Fielding, Catherine Talbot, and Elizabeth Carter—all impoverished learned ladies who promoted matriarchal values and benefited from the society, patronage, and financial support of wealthy members of fashionable society. But Lennox was never quite considered a lady in these circles; her nails were too dirty, her temper too passionate, and her manners too brash. No patronage was forthcoming from these sources, and Lennox wrote comparatively little thereafter. With the exception of what is unquestionably a major novel, *Euphemia* (1790), her important writing was published between 1750 and 1762.

During her last years, Lennox subsisted in England on the charity of Eva Garrick, on small gifts of money from fellow Grub Street writers like Samuel Johnson and Henry Fielding, and on the philanthropy of the Royal Literary Fund, which was supported by printers, painters, and professionals. Perhaps people such as this understood better what it meant to depend on the caprices of fine ladies, to struggle to exist in England in "beggarly gentility," and why, in 1793, it was necessary to give Lennox the money to send her son back to America. The wheel may be said to have come full circle.

[*See also* Frances Burney; Epistolary Novel; *and* The Novel.]

SELECTED WORKS

NOVELS

The Life of Harriot Stuart, Written by Herself (1751)
The Female Quixote (1752)
Henrietta (1758)
Sophia (1762)
Euphemia (1790)

PLAYS

The Sister (1769)
Old City Manners (1775)
The Heiress (1786)

TRANSLATIONS

Memoirs of Mme de Maintenon (1757)
Pierre Brumoy's Greek Theater (1760)
Memoirs of Maximillian de Bethune, the Duke of Sully (1778)

FURTHER READING

Bannet, Eve Tavor. "The Theater of Politeness in Charlotte Lennox's British-American Novels." *Novel: A Forum on Fiction* (Fall 1999): 73–92.

Barreca, Regina. *Untamed and Unabashed: Essays on Women and Humor in British Literature.* Detroit, MI, 1994.

Griffin, Dustin. *Literary Patronage in England, 1650–1800.* Cambridge, U.K., 1996.

Isles, Duncan. "The Lennox Collection." *Harvard Library Bulletin* 18.4 (1970): 317–344; 19.1 (1971): 36–60; 19.2 (1971): 165–186; 19.4 (1971): 416–435.

Langbauer, Laurie. *Women and Romance: The Consolations of Gender in the English Novel.* Ithaca, NY, 1990.

Motooka, Wendy. *The Age of Reasons: Quixotism, Sentimentalism, and Political Economy in the Eighteenth Century.* London, 1998.

Paulson, Ronald. *Don Quixote in England.* Baltimore, 1998.

Séjourné, Philippe. *The Mystery of Charlotte Lennox: First Novelist of Colonial America.* Aix-en-Provence, France, 1967.

Small, Miriam R. *Charlotte Ramsay Lennox: An Eighteenth Century Lady of Letters* (1935). Hamden, CT, 1969.

Spacks, Patricia Myer. "Sisters." In *Fetter'd or Free: British Women Novelists, 1670–1815,* edited by Mary Ann Schofield and Cecilia Macheschi. Athens, OH, 1992.

DORIS LESSING

Debrah Raschke

Any biographical summation of Doris Lessing (born 1919) must contend with her less than amicable views on critics and biographers. In *Under my Skin* (1994), the first volume of her autobiography, she scorns any attempted biographies of her as concoctions and admits to having secrets she will never tell. The facts, then, are easiest. Lessing was born of British parents in Kermanshah, Persia (now Iran). When she was five, she moved with her parents and her younger brother to Rhodesia (now Zimbabwe), the backdrop of her early fiction. She moved to London in 1949. She likes cats.

In addition to her twenty-four novels, Lessing has written in a plethora of genres: short fiction, metafiction, poetry, drama, autobiography, memoir, fabular (a subgenre of speculative fiction), and opera. Her early foray into realism that characterized *The Grass Is Singing* (1950), *The Children of Violence* (1952–1969), and many of her short stories was followed, to the dismay of some of her enthusiasts, by a plunge into the mythic in *Briefing for a Descent into Hell* (1971), *Memoirs of a Survivor* (1974), *The Fifth Child* (1988), and *Ben in the World* (2000), and into the realm of science fiction in the series *Canopus in Argos: Archives* (1979–1983). Between these periods came *The Golden Notebook* (1962), a durably popular work hailed as a groundbreaking encapsulation of an era. Much of her latest fiction attempts to break taboos on aging.

Lessing's life story mirrors the complexity of her writing. From 1927 to 1931, she was educated in a Catholic convent just outside Salisbury, where, as she notes in the 1994 volume of her autobiography, she heard "horrific sermons" on "hellfire" and the "undying worm." After a short stint at home, she spent a year in Girls' High, a government school in Salisbury. That ended her formal education. She married twice and divorced twice, leaving

Doris Lessing
Photograph by Roger Mayne, 1959
© ROGER MAYNE/NATIONAL PORTRAIT
GALLERY, LONDON

the two children from her first marriage with her first husband and taking the one child from her second marriage with her to London. Engaged tenuously in Marxist politics, Lessing flirted with the Communist Party while still in Rhodesia, joined officially in 1951 when she moved to London, and then quit in 1956, disillusioned with what she deemed its propensity for dogmatic and tyrannical thought—a subject of *The Good Terrorist*, *A Ripple in the Storm*, and the Red notebook in *The Golden Notebook*. She went through a Catholic phase as young girl but soon declared herself an atheist; much later she became interested in Sufism, an interest that continued throughout her life.

Marxist, materialist, mystic, feminist, social critic, experimentalist, and visionary: Lessing earned all these epithets—and rebuffed them all. Her "habitual gesture" toward critics, in Virginia Tiger's words, has been to swat them "as though they are irritating black flies." Like Proteus, who, when firmly grasped, revealed an underlying consistency, Lessing's wing has taken many different forms but has remained constant in one thing: the voice of the social critic-seer who attempts to change materiality by changing vision. What entraps and liberates has changed markedly through her career, as has her understanding of method, but the attempt to implode those cultural narratives that imprison is constant. Whether in the mode of realism or fantasy, Lessing has observed the shifting Zeitgeist with a keen eye, enjoining the world to change or face disaster.

BEGINNINGS

Lessing's early work set in colonial Rhodesia unmasks the brutal ideology inherent to white settlement culture. The short story collection *This Was the Old Chief's Country* enacts what Edward Said later identified in *Orientalism* as the orientalizing and the subsequent diminishment of the Other. Black Africa, wild and primitive, set apart from the white settlements, is eroticized and forbidden, something to be conquered and tamed. *The Grass Is Singing* probes the baseness of this ideology through Dick Turner and his frigid and disconnected wife, Mary, whose physical and mental abuse of her black servants mirrors the abuses of apartheid. When Moses, Mary's last servant, whom she eroticizes and belittles, murders her, he revolts against her constant dehumanization to which he has been subjected. The ending is the beginning, suggesting the self-perpetuation of an ideology yet unbroken. This unmasking continues in *Martha Quest*, the first of the five-volume series *Children of Violence* (1959–1962), where Martha learns that the destructiveness of racism is not limited to black/white tensions but instead is a product of a whole way of thinking. *Martha Quest*, as Roberta Rubenstein notes, situates its protagonist in the throes of the same racist and conventional ideology of which Mary Turner was a product. Her departure from the farm, which initiates this volume, is a metaphor of flight from the conventional racist and parochial thinking of white settler ideology. Thus, *Children of Violence*, best known as a female Bildungsroman, depicts Martha as gradually extricating herself from of all kinds of conventional thinking and institutions. In *A Proper Marriage*, second in the series, the now married Martha finds her "proper" marriage to be another cultural prison in which women are doomed to the "cycle of procreation." The novel ends with her abandoning this role for what initially seems like a panacea in Communist activism. *A Ripple from the Storm* (1958), third in the series, written after Khrushchev's censure of Stalin and the Soviet invasion of Hungary, depicts Martha as initially enamored with her new political life. However, when she discovers that her devout Communist husband wants a conventional marriage and when her political group collapses, she becomes disillusioned.

Landlocked continues Martha's disaffection with leftist politics, mirroring Lessing's own and also reflecting a shift in Lessing's style: a break from realism that parallels her increasing interest in Sufism. Shadia Fahim examines Lessing's work as reflecting the Sufi principle of balance, and Müge Galin relates it to the Sufi process of attuning oneself to higher harmonies. In Sufi thought, old patterns must be eradicated in order for a new way of seeing to transpire; as Gayle Greene observes, for Lessing that includes the revision of literary form. In the beginning of *Landlocked*, Martha has a recurring dream in which the half-dozen rooms of a house must be kept separate; here Lessing's interest in Carl Jung contributes the notion that the structure of a house reflects the individual's psyche. Aptly, Martha's consciousness is divided. When Martha meets the Jewish immigrant and gardener Thomas Stern, who adds a "new room" to her life, the division in the house ends. Boundaries dissolve and a center deeply rooted in nature prevails. The relationship for Martha becomes the "most real thing that happened to her." Set against the Cold War, the volatile 1960s, and the threat of nuclear annihilation, *The Four-Gated City* (1969), the fifth and final novel of the series, offers, amid its ruins, similar glimpses of connectedness: the imagined mythic four-gated city that never emerges in the novel, the Scottish island where the telepathic people escape disaster, and individual scenes of natural fullness. The only novel of *Children of Violence* set in London, *The Four-Gated City*, although it ends with multiple cities in ruin, accentuates Lessing's vision shifting under the influence of Sufism into a belief in an expanding and evolving consciousness that extends beyond the material and visible world.

EXPANDING FORAYS

The possibility of multivalent visions as a conduit for understanding becomes a recurrent theme in Lessing's fiction, as well as in her autobiography, *Under My Skin*. Using the metaphor of rooms in a house, Lessing writes of memories being played out behind a wall: the known rooms shared by many, which she calls "communal dreams," and the empty rooms, which unveil undiscovered rooms, undiscovered floors, or "even other houses." These empty rooms offer the possibility of layered landscapes "never known in life." As Roberta Rubenstein reflects, the structure of the house thus takes on a kind of living presence, melding exterior and interior structures with the body and with the psyche.

This motif is perhaps most evident in Lessing's apocalyptic and semiautobiographical novel *Memoirs of a Survivor*, which poses the question of how one survives the wasteland. Three parallel vistas emerge in this novel: the looming chaos outside (nomadic gangs, new diseases, mysterious deaths, failing communal services); the scene depicting the narrator's flat that she shares with the adolescent girl Emily and her cat-dog (both inexplicably left on her doorstep); and the rooms the narrator visits behind the wall of her flat—the personal rooms, which are unyielding and confining, and the impersonal ones, which are chaotic but offer the possibility of freedom. On a literal level the novel seems to offer only three alternatives: join the apocalypse outside, remain in the tenuous sanctuary inside, or succumb to a surreal wandering akin to madness. The novel ends with the principal characters all disappearing behind the walls of the flat. The inner and outer narratives break down, which some critics regard as failure; however, this narrative collapse juxtaposed with visible alternatives is the point. Lessing suggests that survival in an increasingly problematic world entails thinking outside traditional structures, including narrative structures. Insularity of dwelling or of the mind fosters denial, encourages aggressivity, and breeds demise. Identified in *The Prisons We Choose to Live Inside* (1987) as "You are damned, We are Saved" narratives, this way of thinking, Lessing implies, is deeply internalized. It does not matter if the narrative is religious or political, liberal or conservative, as Lessing suggests in *The Small Personal Voice* and elsewhere; it is the embedded structure of the narrative that needs to change.

Lessing's foray into science fiction in *Canopus in Argos: Archives* uses an alien universe to startle the reader into seeing the familiar world anew. Set after the nuclear annihilation of World War III, *Re: Colonised Plant 5, Shikasta* (1979), the first of the series, features a Canopean emissary whose role, as Katherine Fishburn notes, stages a rethinking of the origins and structures of both sacred and public history. Through the marriage of the ethereal Al·Ith and the highly physical Ben Ata, the fabular *The Marriages Between Zones Three, Four, and Five* (1980), the second of the series, explores difference, particularly sexual difference, as necessary for change and growth. *The Sirian Experiments* (1981) reveals the narrator Ambien II moving beyond her Sirian imperial identity, collectively marked by suspicion, envy, exploitation, colonialization, and misuse of technology. In *The Making of the Representative for Planet 8* (1982), the inhabitants of Planet 8, doomed by an encroaching ice age, must learn to see beneath the solidity that defines their landscape and subsequently their view of the world to uncover an underlying fluidity and oneness that defines the universe. Although Shikasta is the only site identified as earth, the nationalistic zones of *Marriages*, the technologically sophisticated Sirian Empire, the complacent Planet 8, Shammat (the power hungry empire that opposes Canopus), and the rhetorically slippery Volyen empire of *Sentimental Agents* (last of the series) are all manifestations of our world as well. Lessing keeps changing the landscape to complicate the lesson and to demonstrate that the problems themselves are not unchanging.

Throughout *Canopus* and at the end of *The Four-Gated City*, which leaves Britain in apocalyptic ruins, failure to break out of intractable thinking invites disaster. This dynamic is played out again in the implosion that occurs in *The Fifth Child* (1988), which poses as domestic fiction. The focal couple, Harriet and David Lovatt, fall in love at first sight and soon go on to create what seems like the perfect marriage. They purchase a huge, rambling Victorian house, where holidays go on forever and where they bear four lovely children, with the hope of bearing four more. All is well until the arrival of the fifth child, Ben, who is perceived as distinctly foreign, as a monster. The houseguests stop coming, and the other four children begin to suffer not only from neglect but also from fear for their lives. In desperation, Harriet and David institutionalize Ben. Harriet, however, relents after later visiting the hospital and finding a nineteenth-century house of horrors, with Ben drugged and naked in a straitjacket. Harriet brings Ben home, but his return permanently fractures the family: David leaves the household, and three of the children take refuge in boarding school. It is surprising not that this domestic idyll fails, but that it is staged in an era long past that of the "angel in the house," the ideal of Victorian womanhood.

The disjunction suggests there is more to this tale than failed domesticity. As previously in her fiction, Lessing extends beyond the limits of the diegetic narrative (the recounting of narrative events). Domestic practices thus become inseparable from colonial ones, and the Lovatt house itself, with its great room depicted as a "the heart of the kingdom," becomes metonymic for colonial politics. Interweaving the turn-of-the-century fascination with eugenics and paradigms of colonial control, *The Fifth Child* suggests that the domestic scene is a breeding ground for colonial domination. Inherent in this fantasy of empire is the separation of the dominant race from those who are conquered—a fantasy that was replicated in the architectural structures of the English housing constructed in the colonies. This division was not just a physical means of separating the white settlements from the Africans, but also an extension of the cultural imaginary (the fantasies particular to a culture) that permeated Britain during the late nineteenth century. In *The Fifth Child*, this division is enacted by the eugenic fantasy that permeates the text. All is lost: Harriet's family, her house, and her marriage. No one benefits.

The Golden Notebook (1962) moved many readers in the 1960s, as the women's movement was gaining momentum. It depicts difficult issues not previously verbalized, speaking to and transforming individual women and capturing the spirit of the times. Lessing, however, admonished those who focused on its feminist concerns. Stylistically ambitious, *The Golden Notebook* contains four sections of the narrative *Free Women*, each of which is followed by a notebook: the Black notebook, business transactions regarding Anna's successful novel; the Red notebook, delineating her affiliation with the Communist Party; the Yellow notebook, exploring her fictional projection Ella, who struggles with sexual relationships and writing; and the Blue notebook, Anna's journal. These four sections are followed by the Golden notebook, written by Anna and her lover, and a final section of *Free Women*, which provides a tritely conventional ending. It is finally disclosed that *Free Women*, which draws from the notebooks, is a novel written by Anna. Thus, the reader is reading Anna's novel from the beginning, but does not know it. Controversial and provocative, the novel brings together themes that haunted Lessing, but in a way that shows Lessing's dissatisfaction with the novel's conventional form. There are many Annas in this novel, and each notebook, though focused on a particular subject, intersects with the others, reinforcing Lessing's continual censure of compartmentalization and her belief that disintegration may sometimes be necessary before reintegration can occur. The novel, however, eludes any attempt to analyze it as a unified whole. In the fiction of her later years, Lessing continues to unsettle conventional paradigms, particularly those concerning women and aging. In an interview with Bill Gray (2003), Lessing quoted the phrase, "Lucky the culture where the old can talk to the young and the young can talk to the old." Lessing begins this dialogue with aging in earnest in *The Summer before the Dark* (1973), where forty-five-year-old Kate Brown gradually comes to terms with her changing physicality. Lessing broaches the subject again in *The Diaries of Jane Somers* (1984), first published as a literary hoax under the pseudonym of Jane Somers and under the combined titles of *The Diary of a Good Neighbor* and *If the Old Could . . .* (1983–1984). When magnetic Janna Somers meets ailing Maudie Fowler, the contact generates for Janna a "changed conception of self." *Love, Again* (1995), featuring sixty-five-year-old Sarah Durham falling tumultuously in love with a younger man, presents a conundrum. Ruth Saxton sees Sarah, tormented by a nostalgic loss for her younger body, as internalizing the culture's ageist dictums, while Phyllis Perrakis sees Sarah as working through this nostalgia and relinquishing entrapping definitions of love. In *The Sweetest Dream* (also

a novel about the 1960s), Lessing enables Francis Lennox, in her sixties, to fall in love with a younger man and to enjoy the physical fruits of that relationship.

Lessing's ability to change her literary landscapes over fifty years of writing, to adjust the scene as the world's problems in our world take on different valences reflects her ability to chronicle changing times and her stature as a writer and a visionary. *Grandmothers* (2003) seems to present four separate novellas. The first, "Grandmothers," breaks the taboos of aging by featuring two attractive grandmothers who years earlier had affairs with each other's teenage sons. "The Reason for It," a fabular, gives us a once plentiful society whose democratic processes, initially their strength, become their ruination when they succumb to the charms of a "stupid" leader. Warning against disarming charm is a theme that haunts all these novellas, as Lessing continues to stir readers to think beyond the fiction before them.

[*See also* Postcolonial Literature *and* Science Fiction.]

SELECTED WORKS

NOVELS

The Grass Is Singing (1950)

Martha Quest, vol. 1 of *Children of Violence* (1952)

A Proper Marriage, vol. 2 of *Children of Violence* (1954)

Retreat to Innocence (1956)

A Ripple from the Storm, vol. 3 of *Children of Violence* (1958)

The Golden Notebook (1962), reissued with preface (1972)

Landlocked, vol. 4 of *Children of Violence* (1965)

The Four-Gated City, vol. 5 of *Children of Violence* (1969)

Briefing for a Descent into Hell (1971)

The Summer before the Dark (1973)

The Memoirs of a Survivor (1974)

Re: Colonised Planet 5: Shikasta, vol. 1 of *Canopus of Argos: Archives* (1979)

The Marriages Between Zones Three, Four, and Five, vol. 2 of *Canopus* (1980)

The Sirian Experiments, vol. 3 of *Canopus* (1981)

The Making of the Representative for Planet 8, vol. 4 of *Canopus* (1982)

Documents Relating to the Sentimental Agents in the Volyen Empire, vol. 5 of *Canopus* (1983)

The Diaries of Jane Somers (1984)

The Good Terrorist (1985)

The Fifth Child (1988)

Love, Again (1995)

Mara and Dann (1999)

Ben in the World (2000)
The Sweetest Dream (2001)
The Grandmothers: Four Short Novels (2003)

SHORT STORY COLLECTIONS

Five: Short Novels (1953)
Habit of Loving (1957)
A Man and Two Women (1963)
African Stories (1964)
Nine African Stories (1968)
Doris Lessing's Collected African Stories, 2 vols. (1973)
Collected Stories, 2 vols. (1978)
The Real Thing: Stories and Sketches (1987)

DRAMA, OPERA, AND POETRY

Each His Own Wilderness (1959)
Play with a Tiger: A Play in Three Acts (1962)
The Making of the Representative for Planet 8: An Opera in Three Acts, with Philip Glass (1988)
The Marriages Between Zones Three, Four, and Five, with Philip Glass (1997)
Fourteen Poems (1959)

AUTOBIOGRAPHY

Under My Skin: Volume One of My Autobiography, to 1949 (1994)
Walking in the Shade: Volume Two of My Autobiography 1949–1962 (1997)

NON-FICTION

Going Home (1957)
The Habit of Loving (1957)
In Pursuit of the English: A Documentary (1960)
Particularly Cats (1967)
A Small Personal Voice: Essays, Reviews, Interviews (1974)
Prisons We Choose to Live Inside (1987)
The Wind Blows Away Our Words (1987)
Particularly Cats and Rufus the Survivor (1991)
African Laughter: Four Visits to Zimbabwe (1992)
The Old Age of El Magnifico (2000)

FURTHER READING

Fahim, Shadia S. *Doris Lessing: Sufi Equilibrium and the Form of the Novel*. New York, 1994. Attempts to reconcile Lessing's early realistic fiction with her later mystical works through the Sufi principle of equilibrium.

Fishburn, Katherine. *The Unexpected Universe of Doris Lessing: A Study in Narrative Technique*. Westport, CT, and London, 1985. Examines how Lessing's experimentation with form in her mythic novel and science fiction encourages reevaluation of the premises of our world.

Galin, Müge. *Between East and West: Sufism in the Novels of Doris Lessing*. Albany, NY, 1997. Examines the influence of Idries Shah on Lessing, and how the Sufi vision materializes in selected works.

Greene, Gayle. *Doris Lessing: The Poetics of Change*. Ann Arbor, MI, 1994. Examines Lessing's relationship to feminism and realism and the impact of *The Golden Notebook*.

Perrakis, Phyllis, ed. *Spiritual Exploration in the Works of Doris Lessing*. Westport, CT, and London, 1999. An essential edited essay collection that explores the multivalent spirituality in Lessing's works.

Pickering, Jean. *Understanding Doris Lessing*. New York, 1990. A good introduction to Lessing's work through *The Fifth Child*; includes plot summaries.

Rubenstein, Roberta. *The Novelistic Vision of Doris Lessing: Breaking the Forms of Consciousness*. Urbana, IL, 1979. A groundbreaking study with invaluable attention to Lessing's use of form.

Sage, Lorna. *Doris Lessing*. New York, 1983. Focuses on the significance of Lessing's experience in colonial Rhodesia.

Saxton, Ruth, and Jean Tobin, eds. *Woolf and Lessing: Breaking the Mold*. New York, 1994. Insightful collection emphasizing the two authors' treatments of female subjectivity, class or insider status, creativity, the female body, and mother-daughter relationships.

Schlueter, Paul. *The Novels of Doris Lessing*. Carbondale, IL, 1973. A key early examination of Lessing's work through *Briefing for a Descent into Hell*; emphasis on themes of social justice and ways to discover freedom.

Seligman, Dee. *Doris Lessing: An Annotated Bibliography of Criticism*. Westport, CT, 1981. Although dated, in addition to its annotated bibliography of criticism, cites Lessing's lesser-known writings.

Sprague, Claire. *Rereading Doris Lessing: Narrative Patterns of Doubling and Repetition*. Chapel Hill, NC, 1987. Examines hidden patterns, doubling, and numerology in selected works.

Sprague, Claire, and Virginia Tiger, eds. *Critical Essays on Doris Lessing*. Boston, 1986. Important essay collection that provides an overview of the critical positions on Lessing.

C. S. LEWIS

Wesley A. Kort

Clive Staples Lewis (1898–1963) retains, more than forty years after his death, a high visibility in English-speaking cultures as a literary and religious author. All of his major works are in print, several likely available at any local bookseller, while books and articles about him appear with noticeable regularity. Conferences on his work are held annually, and several organizations disseminate his ideas and writings.

While Lewis retains a high level of visibility, his stature as a literary/cultural scholar and critic, as a literary artist, and as an advocate of Christianity is a matter of contention. Indeed, responsible and intelligent people hold sharply differing opinions of him. Admirers, especially in the United States, have canonized him or placed him, with the likes of Sigmund Freud,

C. S. Lewis
Photograph by Walter Stoneman, 1955
NATIONAL PORTRAIT GALLERY, LONDON

among the most influential and imposing intellects of the twentieth century. But others dismiss him as a dilettante or an imposter. The high visibility and uncertainty of his stature may well arise from his many-faceted career. He was, by profession, a historian of medieval and Renaissance English literature, but, as one who came on the literary scene at just the time that English literature established itself as a major field of study at Oxford and Cambridge, he took seriously the moral role of literature for the national culture. This allowed him to relate historical literary studies to Christian moral and religious beliefs that, he believed, had been marginalized and even discredited in contemporary English culture generally and in its academic culture particularly. In the early 1940s his name became a household word because of his contribution to the attempt, principally prosecuted by the BBC, to articulate a national character, a character that Lewis believed required religious and specifically Christian content. These broadcasts, which began in 1941 and

continued until 1944 (published in 1952 as *Mere Christianity*), coincided with, among other things, the serialization and publication of his widely popular epistolary novel, *The Screwtape Letters* (1941 and 1942), and the second novel of his space trilogy, *Perelandra* (1943).

Lewis produced a line of poetic and fictional work that ran from his early adulthood ("Death in Battle," 1919) to his later years (*Till We Have Faces*, 1956). This output continues to attract readers not only because it is layered by moral and religious interests but also because it is diverse, inventive, and accessible. He seems to have been undaunted by the differing efforts required by, among other genres, science fiction, autobiography, children's stories, and lyric and narrative poetry, and by retrieving and refashioning classical myth.

Lewis read philosophy and classics as a student at Oxford, and this enabled him to include in his output works on moral philosophy and on such perennial problems in the philosophy of religion as miracles and evil. In addition, the accuracy and value of his critique of modernity arose from his firsthand knowledge of the principal assumptions of modern epistemology and ontology. This critique was also driven by his deep concern for the health of English culture, and it accounts for the attention he gave to the educational ethos of English schools (*The Abolition of Man*, 1944, and *Surprised by Joy*, 1955). Finally, Lewis, while he did not think of himself as a theologian, clarified and advocated what he took to be the basic principles of Christianity; Lewis felt that those principles provide a more adequate account of one's place in the world and one's relations to and within it than do its secular rivals. His purpose in this was to call English Christians back to their religious identity and to make Christianity credible and workable in and for everyday, contemporary life.

Lewis may have high visibility but unclear stature not only because of his many-faceted career but also because he did not fully identify himself with any established intellectual or vocational styles, assumptions, or movements. He combined highbrow and popular culture. He was professional and amateur, scholar and imaginative writer, Christian advocate and man of the world, historian and explorer of space and the future, a pedant and a provocateur, a political conservative and a person with radical views of power and its abuses. While his circles of friendships are well known, his friends held various convictions. He took exception to many of his literary contemporaries who viewed the world wars as having revealed the true condition of humanity, as having torn away the illusions and facades of the Victorian and Edwardian periods. He also did not share his contemporaries' general disparagement of the Romantics. And while in many respects he was similar in his literary and cultural interests to F. R. Leavis and company, he thought they were overly self-conscious and self-important, and his own view of culture was more inclusive, more like what Raymond Williams called a "whole way of living." Finally, as an advocate of Christianity, he was not a spokesperson for the Church. While a participant, he was also critical of it and did not posit church affiliation as essential to a Christian identity. In his theological writings and debates he advanced his own views, which were often elusive because of their mediating or combinatory position relative to clear theological alternatives or contraries.

The many ambiguities and complexities in Lewis, his elusiveness and sense of difference with his surroundings, may owe something to his being born in Belfast but giving his life to the English literary, academic, and cultural scene. He had few and eventually no sense of ties to Ireland, but he also seems not to have felt himself fully included within the English academic or literary ethos.

While there is much in Lewis that keeps him from being easily pinned down, it is possible to infer from his work some constant and controlling characteristics and preoccupations. The first is his relation to the great divide that defines modernity, namely the separation between attention to the massively external and physical, especially the city, and attention to the intensely internal and spiritual. Lewis stands, in relation to this divide, on the personal, spiritual side. He took little interest in urban life and puzzled over the attachment of Charles Williams to London, which he himself largely avoided. As a young man he explored various spiritualist options, and, in his construction of Christianity, personal devotions, especially private prayer, are paramount. His elaboration of Christian morality is largely in personal rather than in social, economic, or political terms. And while he thought that his contemporaries who were interested in spiritualism and magic were toying with matters they did not understand, he did not dismiss those interests as vacuous.

A second characteristic is that Lewis was consistently anti-Cartesian. That is, he denied the gap that modernity had made axiomatic between subjects and objects, body and mind, nature and culture, or fact and value. He wanted to restore continuity between such contraries. He was, in fact, a relationalist, if that word can be used, in all possible respects. This is why he saw morality as not alien to human nature but as consistent with it. One of the theses that motivated his space trilogy, especially *Out of the Silent Planet* (1938), was that space was not, as H. G. Wells presented it, alien and hostile to human feelings but supportive of and exhilarating for them. Personal identity was established, he thought, by one's human and non-human relationships, such as those he describes in *The Four Loves* (1960). This stress on relationship does not mean that he condemned the scientific method. But he thought of the separation of fact from value as tactical, abstract, and appropriate only in some and not in all circumstances and certainly not as a general description or one's position in and relation to the world.

A third characteristic of Lewis's work is its idealist tendencies. These tendencies were not only in opposition to materialist insights but also complementary to and corrective for them. Lewis resisted materialism not as a form of analysis but as an adequate account of the world and the place of persons in it. He thought that materialism could not take morality, spirituality, and thought adequately into account. Materialism, like scientific analysis, is reductive, and, while he accepted reduction as a legitimate form of analysis, he also thought that science needed to be housed within a culture that moved not in a downward and reductive direction but in an upward and expansive one. He revealed a typically idealist interest, as well, in his concern for the whole, not only the whole of the universe and the whole of humanity but also the whole of English culture. Finally, his idealism appears in the way he returned to Christianity by means of idealist philosophy (*Surprised by Joy*) and in the way he looked behind Christian diversity to shared essentials (*Mere Christianity*).

A final characteristic of Lewis's work is that, in spite of his professional identity as a literary and cultural historian, his imagination and intellect were primarily spatial. The language of place and space is prominent in his narratives. This is clear in the space trilogy. In *Out of the Silent Planet*, the reader is transported to Malachandra (Mars) and encounters, through the experience of Elwin Ransom, not only an alternative world but another society. In *Perelandra* (1943) Ransom is carried to Venus, a newly created world, in which he resists and finally overcomes the force of Western modernity represented by the physicist Weston, who arrives on Perelandra to embark on a project of domination. *That Hideous Strength* (1945) projects an English academic future that is under the sway of a power both politically massive and scientifically and technologically advanced. Spatiality is also prominent in such theological fictions as *The Great Divorce* (1945) and *The Screwtape Letters*, and a central matter for the novel that some take to be his greatest achievement, *Till We Have Faces* (1956), is the standing and quality of Psyche's new home.

THE CHRONICLES OF NARNIA

The spatial quality of his imagination is fully realized in his best-known set of fictions, *The Chronicles of Narnia*. These seven narratives take the reader, often in the company of children from this world, into another world—one that, when initially entered in *The Lion, the Witch, and the Wardrobe* (1950), suffers from the results of a witch's curse, a constant winter with no Christmas. Starting with the delivery of Narnia from this curse, the whole life span of Narnia is narrated, from its creation in *The Magician's Nephew* (1955) to its ending in *The Last Battle* (1956). *The Chronicles of Narnia* presents an alternative world, one that resembles many of the conflicts and deficiencies of the cultural world of modern England and one in which events occur that are Narnian counterparts to those affirmed in and by a Christian account of the world. Not only is there a creation story and an apocalyptic ending, but there is also, in the first of the chronicles, a Narnian counterpart to the doctrine of redemption wrought by the suffering and death of Aslan, the lion. Aslan, indeed, provides—within all the complexities, vagaries, and dynamics of the Narnian world and its history—a constant presence. By him Narnia is created, redeemed from the witch's curse, and brought to its eschatological destruction and fulfillment. In the *Chronicles*, as in all of his fiction, Lewis deploys an alternative world

to view more clearly, by means of differences and similarities, the moral and spiritual condition of modern English culture. At the same time the *Chronicles* prepare young readers for the kinds of situations, characters, and events they will encounter when, it is hoped, they read the Christian narrative, consider its theological explications, and apply its principles to their own experience.

It could be argued that the characteristics of Lewis and his work, both those that make him complex and elusive and those that give his work consistency and continuity, are characteristics more appropriate to a postmodern than to a modern cultural context. An orientation more spatial than temporal, a disregard for the coherence or consistency of professional and personal identity, a high view of rhetoric and of literature as a form of advocacy, an autobiographical impulse, an active cultural theory and critique, and a persistent attention to the relation of culture to moral and spiritual beliefs and behaviors—all these things seem to make him more a part of the present academic, literary, and religious scene than of that which pertained in the first half of the twentieth century. Perhaps his continuing prominence and the sharply differing evaluations of him arise from his similarity to the current and controversial cultural context.

[*See also* The Inklings *and* J. R. R. Tolkien.]

SELECTED WORKS

THE CHRONICLES OF NARNIA

The Lion, the Witch, and the Wardrobe (1950)
Prince Caspian (1951)
The Voyage of the Dawn Treader (1952)
The Silver Chair (1953)
The Horse and His Boy (1954)
The Magician's Nephew (1955)
The Last Battle (1956)

OTHER FICTION

Out of the Silent Planet (1938)
The Screwtape Letters (1941 and 1942)
Perelandra (1943)
The Great Divorce (1945)
That Hideous Strength (1945)
Till We Have Faces: A Myth Retold (1956)

NONFICTION

The Allegory of Love: A Study in Medieval Tradition (1936)
The Problem of Pain (1940)

A Preface to Paradise Lost (1942)

The Abolition of Man (1944)

Miracles: A Preliminary Study (1947)

The Weight of Glory and Other Addresses (1949)

Mere Christianity (1952; based on radio talks of 1941–1944)

English Literature in the Sixteenth Century Excluding Drama (1954)

Surprised by Joy: The Shape of My Early Life (1955)

Reflections on the Psalms (1958)

The Four Loves (1960)

Studies in Words (1960)

An Experiment in Criticism (1961)

The Discarded Image: An Introduction to Medieval and Renaissance Literature (1964)

FURTHER READING

Ford, Paul F. *A Companion to Narnia.* San Francisco, CA, 1994.

Hooper, Walter. *C. S. Lewis: A Companion and Guide.* New York, 1996.

Kort, Wesley A. *C. S. Lewis Then and Now.* New York, 2001.

Meyers, Doris T. *C. S. Lewis in Context.* Kent, OH, 1994.

Purtill, Richard. *C. S. Lewis' Case for the Christian Faith.* San Francisco, CA, 2004.

Sayer, George. *Jack: A Life of C. S. Lewis.* San Francisco, CA, 1984.

Schakel, Peter J. *Imagination and the Arts in C. S. Lewis: Journeying to Narnia and Other Worlds.* Columbia, MO, 2002

Wilson, A. N. *C. S. Lewis: A Biography.* New York, 1990.

WYNDHAM LEWIS

Sharon Stockton

Canadian-born Percy Wyndham Lewis (1882–1957) is remembered as an aggressively vocal mouthpiece for that aspect of British revolutionary modernism that led to an attraction to fascism. Although in one sense true, the accusation is also to some extent unfair. Even as early as 1934, as Vincent Sherry has pointed out, Lewis was already doubting the profascist rhetoric of his own earlier assertions. By the time he wrote *Rude Assignment* (1950), Lewis had long since thoroughly recanted, expressing not only horror at the atrocities of fascism in practice but self-condemnation in his honest appraisal of his own earlier mistaken logic: "As a portraitist I feel I should have detected the awful symptoms, even if I was wanting in the visionary power to see this little figure, only a few years later, popping into his gas ovens." It is ironic that Lewis would near the end of his life castigate himself for not *seeing* Hitler truly—vision being the one characteristic of human ability that grounded his fierce dream of a radically new and unified aesthetic. Thus, although one must take Lewis in the context of his early celebrations of Hitler, one must also remember the positive and powerful influence he had on early-twentieth-century art and literature. Or, perhaps more accurately, a study of Lewis's enemy stance offers an indispensable window into an often conveniently ignored aspect of high modernism. Along with T. S. Eliot and Ezra Pound, Lewis was central to the foundation of an English-speaking avant-garde.

Born on a yacht off Amherst, Nova Scotia, in 1882, the son of a British mother and an American father, Lewis was sent to school in England in 1888 and thought of himself as English for most of his life. His young adulthood in England was marked by a series of fiery confrontations: he was dismissed from the Rugby School, the Slade School of Art, the Camden Town Group (1911), and the Omega workshops (1913). Aptly, he joined the Rebel Art Centre in 1914. Soon after, he decisively entered the public sphere as spokesperson for Vorticism, the English response to Futurism and Cubism.

LEWIS AS EDITOR

The rhetoric that led Lewis to his explicit support of fascism was grounded in the first place in his "enemy" stance—a self-conscious performance that staged Lewis himself as a marginalized and persecuted member of a small group desperately clinging to traditional value in the face of what he tended to define as the encroaching flood of modernist corruption. The "enemy" stance was a dramatic public presentation that no doubt coincided with his own personal proclivity for causing trouble. The professional, public version of this enemy stance he first developed and deployed in the establishment of *Blast* (1914–1915)—a literary and artistic journal as well as Vorticist manifesto in support of a new, aesthetically energized machine in the face of old, nineteenth-century sentimentality. "Vorticism" was itself a term coined by Ezra Pound to suggest the power and energy of a cyclone, or vortex, to devastate the existing landscape; in theory, Vorticist art was intended to speak to the new, industrial man, violent and single-minded in his mechanized goals. Vorticism was a specifically British movement; some have termed it "Cubo-Futurism." In his editorial position at *Blast*, Lewis relished the role of outsider, "enemy" of the established order, a stance he articulated in shrill, self-righteous condemnation of a variety of species of modernist decay, including materialism, philistinism, chaos, and especially democracy—which last he perceived to threaten all that is or could be worthwhile in Western culture. The extravagance of this rhetoric is most positively interpreted as an example of the general cultural fear of the growing democratization that accompanied World War I.

In spite of the editorial excesses of *Blast*, the enemy rhetoric of the journal is also (perhaps ironically) recalled as having fiercely defended experimental aesthetic practice. It brought together artists of poetry, fiction, and the visual in an explicit effort to rewrite the parameters of the humanities. It is a mark of the historical importance of this journal that T. S. Eliot's "Preludes" was first published here, in 1915. Thus, although short-lived, *Blast* was nonetheless crucial in amalgamating the disparate individuals who would later become the central players of modernism. It is for the publication of *Blast* that Lewis will always be remembered within studies of literary history.

The Enemy, a later short-running magazine of which three issues were published between 1927 and 1929, had less aesthetic merit to legitimate the editorial enemy stance. In this journal, Lewis defined himself not only as enemy but outlaw, one who has consciously moved outside the social order in order to provide and provoke with hostile criticism those still languishing mindlessly on the inside. The objects of attack in this later magazine are even more diffuse and abstract than those in *Blast*. The heightened tone of the enemy rhetoric in this journal—often described as hysterical—makes the 1931 publication of *Hitler* seem almost inevitable.

LEWIS AS ARTIST

Today Wyndham Lewis is more often positively remembered as a visual artist than as a writer, his painted works seeming to have more staying power than his written. His creation of the school of Vorticist painting combined the power and structure of Cubism with the humanism of Futurism—and established for Britain its only avant-garde movement, making an original contribution to European modernism. Lewis's paintings are noted for their marked geometrical lines, sharp angles, and bold planes—all of which fuse a sense of mechanized power with temporal stability. In his art—as in his philosophy—he was vocally resistant to what he considered the irresponsible flux of the "time-philosophers" such as Henri Bergson. Lewis fiercely resisted the notion that humans perceive the world as a flashing series of disconnected and meaningless fragments; he believed that we see pictures—full, enduring, and complete. He would continue throughout his artistic and written career to give ontological priority to the visual spectacle and the seer; such derivations as theory, idea, and time would always be set down as secondary and parasitic.

The Vorticist movement broke up in 1915, partly as a result of World War I. Soon after the group's only exhibition, Lewis was posted to the western front, and he served as an official war artist from 1917 to 1919. It was during this time that he painted some of his most enduring works, including most notably *A Battery Shelled*, from sketches made on Vimy Ridge. In addition, throughout his career, he painted a number of semiabstract portraits, including those of Edith Sitwell (1935), Ezra Pound (1938), and T. S. Eliot (1938 and 1939), all recognizably Lewis's work because of their aggressive lines and static structure. Long after World War I and the beginnings of modernism, he was still struggling visually with urban, mechanistic forms of representation, including *The Surrender of Barcelona* (1936), a well-known painting that evidences a nostalgia for the adversarial and mechanistic possibilities of early modernism, a nostalgia that would dominate Lewis's artistic work until the end of his visual career (which occurred when he went completely blind in 1951 as a result of a brain tumor). His paintings can be found in several museums, including the Tate Gallery in London and the Museum of Modern Art in New York City.

LEWIS AS WRITER

With the publication of his first novel, *Tarr*, in 1918, Lewis turned most of his energies toward writing. This first novel works to incorporate the violent, mechanistic characteristics of Lewis's visual art into written form, and it thus sets the pace for all of his following fictional works. *Tarr* has often been criticized for its violence and its misogyny; it has nonetheless impressed many with its distillation of a certain—perhaps ultimately sad—strand within modernist thought, one that tried to incorporate the machine into humanity as a way to protect humanity from the machine. The novels that follow *Tarr* are similar in tone: as is the case in his painting, Lewis seemed not able to move beyond his initial, violent stance, in spite of the increasingly visible cost to himself and to the modern humanity he hoped to portray (or create). *The Apes of God* (1930), a biting satire of the cultural politics of London's 1920s art world, highlighted Lewis's conflicts with his contemporaries, including most notably (and disastrously for Lewis) the Sitwell family. *The Human Age*, a trilogy composed of *The Childermass* (1928), *Monstre Gai* (1955), and *Malign Fiesta* (1955)—a fourth volume, *The Trial of Man*, was left uncompleted at the time of Lewis's death—never became popular. *Revenge for Love* (1937) is generally thought to be his best novel, poignantly set in pre–civil war Spain—as is, in fact, his most famous painting, *The Surrender of Barcelona* (1936). His semiautobiographical novel *Self Condemned* (1954) shares the honest, if abrasive, strength of Lewis's other prose works.

Lewis's nonfiction prose works tend to be stronger and more believable than his fiction. His major theoretical and cultural statements are found most articulately stated in *The Art of Being Ruled* (1926). The essay collection *Time and Western Man* (1927) is crucial to any study of modernist thought for its attacks on the "time philosophy" of Henri Bergson and for its fresh, if polemical, critique of James Joyce. Lewis's unfortunate 1931 publication of *Hitler* waxed embarrassingly poetic about the role the German leader would and could offer the new modern world. Lewis's formal retraction, *The Hitler Cult* (1939), given its historical moment, struck its audience as too little too late. He was never forgiven: not by the London art scene, not by the critical English-speaking public at large—not then, and not now. Nonetheless, there is no denying that *Men Without Art* (1934) is a superb book of literary criticism, being one of the first to recognize, for example, William Faulkner. *Men Without Art* also provides a substantial study of Ernest Hemingway. Lewis is also remembered for an autobiographical account of his wartime experiences, *Blasting and Bombardiering* (1937), and his later autobiographical statement, *Rude Assignment* (1950). He is less known for *The Writer and the Absolute* (1952). Percy Wyndham Lewis continued to write, in blindness, until his death in 1957.

[*See also* T. S. Eliot *and* Modernism.]

SELECTED WORKS

Blast, as editor (1914–1915)

Tarr (1918)

The Art of Being Ruled (1926)

Time and Western Man (1927)

The Childermass (1928)

The Apes of God (1930)

Hitler (1931)

Men Without Art (1934)

Blasting and Bombardiering (1937)

Revenge for Love (1937)

The Hitler Cult (1939)

Rude Assignment (1950)

The Writer and the Absolute (1952)

Self Condemned (1954)

Malign Fiesta (1955)

Monstre Gai (1955)

FURTHER READING

Edwards, Paul. *Wyndham Lewis, Painter and Writer.* New Haven, CT, and London, 2000. Paul Edwards is the foremost scholar of Wyndham Lewis. In addition, this text draws Lewis's painting and writing together: an unusual—although much welcomed—approach.

Jameson, Fredric. *Fables of Aggression: Wyndham Lewis, the Modernist as Fascist.* Berkeley, CA, 1979. Marxist approach; invaluable for understanding the political critique of Lewis.

Meyers, Jeffrey. *Wyndham Lewis: A Revaluation.* London, 1980. First significant and most important attempt to redeem Lewis of his association with German fascism.

O'Keeffe, Paul. *Some Sort of Genius: A Life of Wyndham Lewis.* London, 2000. The only significant biography of Lewis.

Sherry, Vincent. *Ezra Pound, Wyndham Lewis, and Radical Modernism.* New York, 1993. Effectively places Lewis within a general cultural, philosophic, and aesthetic context.

GEORGE LILLO

Susan Staves

George Lillo (1693–1739) was a versatile and innovative playwright most famous for creating a new bourgeois domestic drama in *The London Merchant* (1731), *The Fatal Curiosity* (1736), and *Arden of Feversham* (1759). In *The London Merchant*, Lillo took the radical step of writing tragedy in prose rather than in verse; of all Lillo's plays, *The London Merchant* has attracted the most attention from critics. However, Lillo's eight surviving plays include a comic ballad opera, *Silvia; or, The Country Burial* (1730); romances; and one of the more successful eighteenth-century adaptations of a Shakespearian romance, *Marina* (1738), adapted from *Pericles, Prince of Tyre*.

The son of a Dutch jeweler, Lillo had an unusual class background for an eighteenth-century playwright. Unlike many contemporary writers of tragedy who came from gentry families and were educated at the universities or in law, Lillo was a goldsmith and jeweler. He was thus not a gentleman but a "tradesman," albeit one engaged in an elite trade. He pursed his trade in London until, at thirty-seven, he offered *Sylvia* to be performed at Lincoln's Inn Fields. Nevertheless it is known that he was an unusually serious student of drama, including ancient Greek and Roman drama and Elizabethan drama.

Lillo's class position prompted him to develop a penetrating critique of gentry ideology, including its assumptions about work. He was vividly aware of the social condescension the upper classes directed at people who worked for their livings. In *Arden of Feversham* he allows a character to make sardonic remarks at the expense of his own trade of goldsmith, which had come to include taking in deposits of customers' valuables and lending money at interest. When Bradshaw moralizes to two discharged soldiers that in time of peace they ought to apply themselves "to some honest creditable business," Black Will, retorts: "Yes, as you have done. I'm told you keep a goldsmith's shop . . . and like a mechanical rogue, live by cheating. I have more honour." Black Will goes further to invoke the traditional moral animus against taking interest as usury, calling Bradshaw a "*cent. per cent*. Rascal."

While Lillo does give voice to merchants' arguments for their respectability and social value, far from simply offering a counterideology simplistically celebrating the values of the middle classes, he raises sharp questions about what work is honest and what constitutes value.

THE LONDON MERCHANT

In *The London Merchant*, Lillo intentionally broke with key conventions of classical and neoclassical tragedy, conventions that naturalized assumptions of upper-class ideologies. Instead of presenting as tragic hero a king or other upper-class person, characters the older conventions assumed possessed the most significant human experience, Lillo offered an eighteen-year-old merchant's apprentice. Instead of drawing his subject from classical mythology or the histories of rulers, Lillo used a story from a popular ballad, "George Barnwell." Instead of writing in verse, he wrote in prose.

The London Merchant is often thought of as the first significant bourgeois drama. In the neoclassical literary environment of the 1730s, Lillo's use of formal elements of comedy—a low protagonist and prose—in a tragedy was potentially ridiculous, cousin to an intentionally funny mock-epic or burlesque like Henry Fielding's *Tragedy of Tragedies; or, The Life and Death of Tom Thumb the Great* (1731), in which Tom is eaten by a cow. Lillo's admirerers, therefore, especially relished the story of a fashionable gentleman who came to the premiere of *The London Merchant* with copies of the ballad intending to make "ludicrous comparisons between the ancient ditty and modern play," but was converted to rapt attention and tears.

Barnwell, hitherto a diligent servant of his master, the merchant Thorowgood, in a single meeting is seduced by Millwood, a woman whose trade is exchanging sexual favors for money. She quickly persuades him to steal from his master to supply her with money she insists she desperately needs. Not satisfied, Millwood next persuades him to attempt to steal money from his uncle

288

and to kill his uncle to cover up the crime. Barnwell is astonished at the speed of his fall from virtue into criminality, often viewing his own actions as a stunned spectator. Masked, he stalks his kindly uncle, alternately drawing and withdrawing his pistol. As the uncle discovers this masked man and draws his sword, Barnwell has already thrown down his pistol. Yet Barnwell stabs him. Instead of robbing his uncle, however, Barnwell reveals himself to his dying benefactor, seeking and obtaining forgiveness. Millwood, who has never cared for Barnwell but only sought to exploit him, is outraged and reproaches the bloody Barnwell—in words often quoted by the play's detractors, who have sometimes agreed with her—as a "whining, preposterous, canting Villain." In the fifth act a repentant Barnwell and a defiant Millwood both stand before a crowd of spectators and a gallows, waiting to be hanged.

Although there are moments of ineptness and stilted language in *The London Merchant*, this profoundly original play has mythopoeic power. Lillo grapples with a fundamental problem of emerging capitalism: how to create a person who has enormous desire for wealth, desire sufficient to compel him to work hard and to take risks, yet at the same time is a controlled person who can delay gratification, not spending resources while he amasses capital. A successful capitalist man cannot simply be content with a quiet life such as Barnwell leads before the play begins. Tellingly Lillo often revised his sources to make the characters of his striving protagonists more virtuous, to add language about the horrors of economic dependence, or to reduce the stigmatization of those who seek to better their economic circumstances and become financially independent.

While the stage action unsurprisingly shows Millwood offering Barnwell physical contact with her attractive body to arouse his desires, Millwood's servant is surprised that her mistress arranges an elaborate supper at her house, with music and—presumably—expensive plate on display. Barnwell seems to succumb not only to the feast of the senses Millwood provides but to the display of opulence that arouses his hitherto quiescent desires for adventure and wealth. As he goes off to bed with Millwood, Barnwell does not speak of the delights of the female body but likens himself to a merchant beginning a risky "adventure" in hope of future profit:

> Reluctant thus, the Merchant quits his Ease,
> And trusts to Rocks, and Sands, and stormy Seas;
> In Hopes some unknown golden Coast to find.

Even as the play fears the connection between appetite and criminality, it calls for some sympathy for George's capacity for desire and his appetite for risk.

Critics have argued over whether *The London Merchant* is tragic or is too didactic or too sentimental to be tragic. Barnwell, like sentimental heroes, is a man of feeling, said by his friends to be Millwood's victim. His tearful final repentance and hope of salvation have made some consider Lillo guilty of a sentimentalism that detracts from the moral seriousness of Barnwell's crimes by separating feeling from action and valuing feeling over action. Yet the action of the play calls into question its commands that people make reason govern desire. Thorowgood's famous speech about how humanity can improve itself by studying "the Method of Merchandise" as "a Science, to see how it is founded on Reason, and the Nature of Things" comes after reason has proven ineffectual in preventing his disciple's fall. His humane forgiveness of Barnwell's first error—like forgiveness in many of Lillo's plays—demonstrates his humanity—and perhaps his sentimentality—yet instead of averting catastrophe, forgiveness contributes to it. Lillo here does not ultimately embrace the Enlightenment optimism that is the ground of sentimental drama. His plots express a more Calvinist sense that humankind is stained with irremediable evil. Millwood, who throughout the play voices a trenchant critique of the corruption of her society and its injustices toward women, at the gallows not only refuses to embrace the possibility of redemption but cries out, "I was doom'd before the World began to endless Pains."

FATAL CURIOSITY

In *Fatal Curiosity*, a second domestic tragedy, one in verse, Lillo creates characters with more realized psychological depth than Barnwell or Thorowgood. He powerfully explores the extent to which individual identity in capitalist society is grounded in the possession of wealth. The play is set in Penryn, a town on the Cornwall coast where the local inhabitants profit from plundering the frequent shipwrecks. Here, as in other Lillo plays, the sea is both a highway to riches and a site of storms and wrecks, a powerful image both visually and in the verse. As the eponymous heroine in *Marina*, who is born in a storm at sea in which her mother dies, puts it:

> This world, to me, is like a lasting storm,
> That swallows, piece by piece, the merchant's wealth,
> And in the end, himself.

Fatal Curiosity begins as Young Wilmot returns from seven years in the Indies, is shipwrecked on the coast, but is able to preserve his life and a casket filled with jewels, "wealth / Enough to glut even avarice itself." Because his once prosperous parents have fallen into poverty, he went off seeking to restore the family fortunes and suffered enslavement. While he is absent, Old Wilmot and his wife Agnes become destitute. A compelling character, Old Wilmot was once high-minded, generous, and well regarded. Now he is suicidal, convinced that his son is dead, and in despair about his loss of wealth and of the social regard he now discovers was a consequence of that wealth. Both Old Wilmot and Agnes are obsessed with the aging body—a body no longer capable of generating hope by a capacity for reproduction—introducing an unusual subject for serious drama. Once Old Wilmot found that stoic philosophy made sense, but now, under conditions of material deprivation, he tells Agnes to sell his copy of Seneca to buy bread.

Old Wilmot's anger explodes in a plot that has a ballad-like inevitability, although Lillo derived it from what was supposed to be a story of real seventeenth-century crime. The plot presents two kinds of fatal curiosity. First, instead of simply presenting himself to his parents, Young Wilmot has a complicated modern desire to make his reunion with them a psychological spectacle. Very much a man of sensibility, he is fascinated by the operations of the mind, acutely aware that ideas can generate emotional states, and wants to indulge himself in what he recognizes is a kind of "wanton" pleasure. Using deception, he tries to stage a scene in which his friends, his faithful fiancée Charlot, and his parents will all be present as he gradually discloses his identity. He expects that, as his parents are astonished by "floods of transport," all, regarding one another, will experience permutations and combinations of sympathetic emotions as pleasure flows "in torrents" and "more extatick grows." A servant warns Young Wilmot that he grows "luxurious in mental pleasures" and that his "boundless curiosity" is a weakness. Certainly it contributes to the catastrophe, yet, like Barnwell's desires, "boundless curiosity" was a useful quality for the capitalist adventurer.

Instead of experiencing "floods of transport," Young Wilmot's parents murder him. Visited by a man she thinks is a young stranger, a friend of Charlot's, and asked to safeguard his casket, Agnes, in a second act of fatal curiosity, opens the casket. She is overwhelmed by the sudden possibility of escaping from "the galling scorn" attendant upon poverty to reclaim the sense of dignified selfhood she had when the Wilmots had money. Charlot observes that poverty and grief have not humbled Agnes but rather increased her pride, creating a vicious cycle in which "pride increasing" aggravates grief and anger. Agnes convinces Old Wilmot to stab their guest. When Charlot and the others arrive, they witness not torrents of pleasure but the dying groans of Young Wilmot. This powerful play, translated into German, had an important influence on the fatalistic *Schicksalstragödie* ("fate tragedy") of the late eighteenth century.

ROMANCE

Tragedy was not a congenial form for Enlightenment writers, despite its continued literary prestige. Enlightenment ideologies emphasized human beings' potential for good and were often less interested in metaphysics than in more worldly issues of politics and social organization. Theorists argued that classical tragedy, as a pagan literature, was not a suitable model for modern Christian writers, who ought rather to seize opportunities for originality afforded by the challenge of inventing a Christian poetry. The more congenial form for serious drama in the Enlightenment was, therefore, romance. Three of Lillo's plays are romances: *The Christian Hero* (1734–1735), *Marina* (1738), and *Elmerick; or, Justice Triumphant* (1739–1740).

The best of these, *Elmerick*, is a historical and political romance that addresses issues of guilt, law, and punishment central to Lillo's plays. Andrew II, a virtuous patriot king, rules over Hungary. Since Jerusalem has fallen to Saladin in 1187, he decides to lead a crusade to recapture the city for Christianity and appoints his subject Elmerick to rule as regent. As Andrew departs for Jerusalem, he gives Elmerick the sword of justice and abjures him to punish all acts of "bold injustice," no matter how highly placed the wrong doers. As elsewhere in Lillo and in the political philosophy of the patriot opposition with which he sympathized, the sound administration of justice is understood to be important to creating a society of virtuous individuals, and individual virtue, in turn, is understood as an essential ground of freedom and protection against tyranny.

Elmerick's commitment to the vigorous and impartial administration of justice is promptly tested. Queen Matilda and her brother Conrade conspire to effect Conrade's rape of Elmerick's wife, Ismena. Elmerick's conduct, once he discovers the crime, is remarkable, apparently combining a modern enlightened humanity with commitment to the enforcement of justice. Yet his efforts to combine humane kindness with justice leave the spectator with questions about their compatibility. That the virtuous Ismena could be raped, of course, moves the play away from romance and toward tragedy, even though the overall plot remains that of romance. Showing a trust in his wife's truthfulness and honor surprising in a plot of the early eighteenth century, a weeping Elmerick unquestioningly believes that Ismena was raped rather than guilty of adultery and attempts to console her by declaring, "thou art innocent, / Thy mind unstain'd." This possibility that a raped woman might be innocent was later a center of the debate over Samuel Richardson's novel *Clarissa* (1747–1748). Elmerick is determined to mete out just punishment to Matilda and Conrade, despite their high rank. Speedily, having heard Matilda's confession of guilt, he summons the executioners. In a lurid scene, as the queen declaims that a mere subject has no right to judge her, Elmerick gives his order. The executioners pull the queen into a recess in the back scene, where they strangle her.

Debate ensues among the Lords of the Assembly whether Elmerick's "dreadful act" of "Unprecedented Justice" merits "reproach or praise." Recognizing that Lillo was addressing contemporary political issues, including whether a subject had a right to judge a monarch, one early commentator worried that the apparently exemplary regent acts "contrary to the strict notions of justice" (Genest, *Account of the English Stage*, vol. 3, p. 608), when he condemns Matilda without a trial. Yet Lillo's setting his action so far back in time disorients easy judgment about this and similar questions, making the spectator uncertain about the applicability of modern standards to Elmerick's acts. The play, while clearly celebrating Elmerick's actions as heroic, thus forces the audience to question the essential elements of justice.

RECEPTION AND INFLUENCE

While *Marina* had reasonable success as a Shakespearian adaptation, Lillo's other romances attracted little attention after their first performances and publications. *The London Merchant* survived as a repertory play well into the nineteenth century. William Hazlitt, the great Romantic drama critic, intriguingly reproduced the critical schizophrenia about the merits of *The London Merchant*, in one essay savagely ridiculing it as "a piece of wretched cant" that insulted the virtues of human nature and in another naming Lillo along with Thomas Southerne and Edward Moore as the only dramatists who escaped the frigidity and insipidity of eighteenth-century tragedy. *The Fatal Curiosity* was less famous than *The London Merchant*, but late eighteenth-century adaptations and revivals, particularly a revival of 1797 in which the great actress Sarah Siddons played Agnes, rekindled English interest. Most important, Lillo's domestic tragedy had a significant influence on French drama and dramatic theory, especially on Denis Diderot, and hence on the development of a European theory and practice of bourgeois serious drama.

[*See also* Romantic Drama.]

SELECTED WORKS

Sylvia; or, The Country Burial (performed and published 1730)

The London Merchant; or, The History of George Barnwell (performed and published 1731)

The Christian Hero: A Tragedy (performed 1734–1735; published 1735)

Fatal Curiosity: A True Tragedy of Three Acts (performed 1736; published 1737)

Marina: A Play of Three Acts (performed and published 1738)

Elmrick; or, Justice Triumphant: A Tragedy (performed 1739–1740; published posthumously 1740)

Arden of Feversham: An Historical Tragedy (performed 1756; published 1762)

EDITION

Steffensen, James L., and Richard Noble, eds. *The Dramatic Works of George Lillo*. Oxford, 1993. The best edition, with a lengthy critical introduction, excellent explanatory notes, and a careful discussion of Lillo's use of his sources.

FURTHER READING

Borkat, Roberta F. S. "The Evil of Goodness: Sentimental Morality in *The London Merchant*." *Studies in Philology* 76 (1979): 288–312. An example of the attack on *The London Merchant* as sentimental and immoral.

Burgess, C. F. "Lillo sans Barnwell." *Modern Philology* (1968): 5–29. A strong-minded critical essay with judgments on all the plays and an argument against the exclusive emphasis on *The London Merchant*.

Carlson, Julia A., ed. "Domestic/Tragedy." *South Atlantic Quarterly* 98.3 (1999): 331–624. A special issue of the journal on domestic tragedy in both England and Germany that includes a provocative introduction by Carlson and an article by Lisa A. Freeman historicizing middle-class ideology (pp. 539–561) in relation to *The London Merchant.*

Genest, John. *Some Account of the English Stage from the Restoration in 1660 to 1830.* 10 vols. London, 1832; reprinted New York, 1964.

Grace, Domicick M. "*Fatal Curiosity* and Fatal Colonialism." *English Studies in Canada* 28 (2002): 385–411. A good example of postcolonial critical approaches to Lillo.

Massai, Sonia. "From *Pericles* to *Marina*: 'While Women Are to Be Had for Money, Love, or Importunity'." *Shakespeare Survey* 51 (1998): 67–77. Considers Lillo's adaptation of *Pericles.* Overdoes Lillo's sympathy with the realistic values of the brothel but rightly argues that the play presents a dialectical confrontation between traditional and modern ideologies and models of theater.

Price, Lawrence Marsden. "George Barnwell Abroad." *Comparative Literature* 2 (1950): 126–156. An important account of the French and German reception. Points out French adaptations that transform *The London Merchant* into a truly sentimental play. For the German reception, the serious student should also consult the Carlson volume and subsequent German articles.

DAVID LINDSAY

Greg Walker

Sir David Lindsay of the Mount (c. 1486–1555), the most gifted Scottish poet and dramatist of the sixteenth century, came from a wealthy family with lands in Cupar in Fife and Lothian. He was a lifelong courtier, and his first definite appearance in the documentary records fittingly notes his role in a play performed before King James IV and his wife Queen Margaret at Holyrood Abbey in October 1511. Thereafter, he was appointed to the household of the king's son, the future James V, and would spend the rest of his life offering poetic counsel to James and to successive minority regimes, chronicling their successes and, more frequently, lamenting their failures.

James IV died in 1513, following the disastrous Scottish defeat at the Battle of Flodden, but Lindsay continued to serve the new boy-king James V. His formal appointment was as an usher, but he seems to have taken on other unofficial duties too, including acting as companion, tutor, and entertainer to the young sovereign. For in his earliest extant poem, *The Dreme*, written at some point between 1526 and 1528 and dedicated to James, he recalled how:

> Quhen thow wes young, I bure ye in myne arme,
> Full tenderlie tyll thow begouth to gang,
> And in thy bed oft happit the[e] full warme
> With lute in hand, syne, swetlie to the[e] sang;
> Sumtyme in dansing feiralie I flang;
> And sumtyme playand fairsis on the flure;
> And sumtyme on myne office takkand cure . . .
>
> (ll. 8–14)

> So, sen thy birth I have continewalye
> Bene occupyit, and aye to thy plesoure;
> And sumtyme, seware, Coppare, and Carvoure
>
> Thy purs maister and secreit Thesaurare,
> Thy Yshare, aye sen thy natyvitie,
> And of thy chalmer cheiffe Cubiculare,
> Quhilk to this houre hes keipit my lawtie.
>
> (ll. 19–25)

Factional squabbles were endemic to sixteenth-century Scottish politics, and Lindsay lost his place at court for a time during the ascendancy of Archibald Douglas, sixth earl of Angus. In *The Complaynt* he would describe this short-lived loss of office as an abject humiliation, in which he was "tramplit doun in to the douste" (255). But when Angus himself fell and the young king took up the reins of power in person, Lindsay returned to court and took on new and more substantial roles as a diplomat, in which guise he made a number of trips to France, and herald. He became first Snowden Herald, and then, in 1540, Lyon King of Arms, the principal herald of Scotland, one of whose duties was to sit before the throne in Parliament and act as interlocutor between the king and the three estates of lords, senior clergy, and commoners.

WORKS

Both Lindsay's close relationship with James V and his experiences in Parliament color his writings, most of which were primarily satirical and addressed the social and political ills besetting Scotland. Although not a fully fledged radical, Lindsay was nonetheless also reformist in his religious views, fiercely critical of what he saw as the economic and moral abuses of bishops and parish priests alike. Characteristically, he voiced his criticisms in texts for a royal audience, sharp, witty counsels and passionate appeals for justice aimed at a king who was himself intent on a measure of reform.

The Dreme, for all its affectionate reminiscences of the poet's loyalty and love for the king, ends with an acerbic petition voiced by John the Commonweal that James redress the injustices rife in Scotland. In *The Testament of the Papyngo* (1530), a work designed for oral delivery in the royal household, he reworked the death of the king's pet bird into an allegorical commentary on the avarice of the regular clergy, who, in the guise of predatory birds, strip bare the overambitious courtly papyngo (parrot) who has fallen from the top of the tree. In *The Tragedie of The Cardinall*, a rumination on the murder of Scotland's premier ecclesiast Cardinal David Beaton, the anti-clericalism was more direct. Lindsay had Beaton's ghost confess that he had planned to destroy all religious reformers along with his personal enemies and critics:

> Sum with the fyre, sum with the sword and knyfe;
> In speciale mony gentle men of Fyfe,
> And [I] purposit tyll put to gret torment
> All favouraris of the auld and new Testament.
>
> (ll. 213–216)

And, in a short early version of the play that was to become his greatest work, *Ane Satyre of the Thrie Estaitis*, performed before James V at Linlithgow in 1540, he presented the petition of the Poor Man against the clerical and lay oppressors who had driven him and his family from their home to beg for bread. Significantly, the play (of which only a brief prose description survives) ended with a reference outward from the parliament of the play to the real king in the audience, calling on him to take on the task of social and ecclesiastical reform that his theatrical surrogate could only gesture toward.

On the death of James V in 1542 Lindsay faced a personal and political crisis. Without an adult king to write for, his role as a counselor was in danger of becoming redundant. It was this dilemma, and the plight of benighted, leaderless Scotland, that he reflected on in the preliminary epistle to his last and most substantial poem, *The Monarche: Ane Dialog Betuix Experience and ane Courteour* (c. 1552):

> We have no kyng the[e] to present, allace!
> Quhilk to this countre bene ane cairful cace;
> And als our Quene, of Scotland Heretour,
> Sche dwellth i France: I pray God saif hir grace.
> It war to[o] lang for the[e] to run that race,
> And far langer or that young teder flour
> Bryng home tyll [us] ane kyng and governour,
> Allace, tharfor, we may with sorrow syng,
> Quhilk moste so lang remane without ane kyng.
>
> (ll. 10–18)

His solution was to turn outward from the court toward the Scottish nation as whole, dedicating the poem "To faithfull, prudent, pastouris spirituall, / To nobyll erlis, and Lordis temporall" (37–38), and in the hope that it might also be read by "unlernit knawis" who knew no Latin (547), the colliers, carters, and cooks of Scotland. Lindsay went on to reflect the uncertainties of minority rule and the religious ferment of the Early Reformation in both *The Monarche* and the reworked drama that was to be his principal achievement, *Ane Satyre of the Thrie Estaitis*. In *The Monarche* he denounced "the gret idolatrye, / And manifest abominatioun" of the traditional Catholic religious processions in Edinburgh with a rigor of which John Knox himself would have been proud:

> Aschame ye nocht, ye seculare prestis and freris,
> Tyll so gret superstitioun to consent?
> Ydolateris ye have ben mony yeris,
> Expresse agane the Lordis Commandiment.
>
> (ll. 2509–2512)

The Thrie Estaitis he greatly expanded from the short interlude of 1540, turning it into a sweeping, panoramic play, comprising two huge acts, divided by a carnivalesque comic interlude and preceded by a set of broadly comic banns. In the first half a king, Rex Humanitas, falls prey to a group of courtier vices: Placebo ("I will please"), Solace, and Wantonness, who lead him into sin before he is redeemed by Divine Correctioun. In the second half a parliament is summoned to redress the grievances of the poor and reform the Church. The play was performed in Lindsay's hometown of Cupar in Fife in 1552 and again on Calton Hill in Edinburgh in 1554. Based in part on the *moralité* and *sottie* (fools plays) he would have witnessed in France, it both voices Lindsay's own disillusionment with successive failed regimes and reprises the complaints of the downtrodden commons of Scotland, represented here by two distinct figures, the humble John of the Commoun Weill, resurrected from *The Dreme*, and the more aggressively radical Pauper. The misfortunes of the former at the hands of greedy, self-interested lords and churchmen are powerfully described:

> With singular profeit he hes bene sa supprysit,
> That he is baith cauld, naikit, and disgysit.
>
> (ll. 3767–3768)

The play reaches a climax in the apocalyptic vision of reform brought about by the descent from heaven of the winged Divine Correctioun (seemingly a figure of the Archangel Michael), who purges the corrupt clergy and hangs a number of personified vices (Falset [Falsehood], Dissait, and Common Thift) symbolic of the forces that have oppressed the commonwealth. The last word, however, is left to the phallic fool, Folly, whose parodic sermon on the theme "infinite are the number of fools" returns the play to the present day with the suggestion that so long as there are fools in positions of power, the realm will never be amenable to true reform.

In his last years Lindsay wrote a chivalric romance based on the life of a friend and neighbor, *The Historie of*

Squyer Meldrum, and completed the political and moralized world history, *The Monarche*. In the latter he combined an encyclopedic copiousness of historical and thematic sweep with his characteristically uncompromising focus on the practical need for reform here and now and in Scotland:

> I traist to se gude reformatione
> from tyme we gett ane faithfull prudent king
> Quhilk knawis the trueth and his vocatione.
> All Publicanis, I traist, he wyll doun thring,
> And wyll nocht suffer in this realme to ring;
> Corrupit Scrybis, nor fals Pharisiens
> Agane the treuth quhilk planely doith maling.
> Tyll that kyng cum we mon tak paciens.
>
> (ll. 2605–2612)

REPUTATION

Lindsay's religious views, although never unequivocally Lutheran, were nonetheless sufficiently reformist and anticlerical to commend him to subsequent generations of Scottish Protestants, ensuring his status as the most popular and widely read Scottish Renaissance poet into the modern era. He stood alongside the "Scottish Chaucerians," Dunbar, Douglas, and Hennryson, as the central figures in the efflorescence of Scottish verse in the later fifteenth and early sixteenth centuries. But in the later twentieth century it was his political radicalism, and especially his championing of the oppressed poor, most evident in *The Thrie Estaitis*, that guaranteed him appreciative audiences in Scotland and beyond. The play, probably the most accomplished dramatic work produced in Britain before *The Spanish Tragedy*, was revived by Tyrone Guthrie for the Edinburgh Festival of 1948 and has been performed many times since, although not as frequently outside Scotland as it deserves, owing in part to the untranslatable nature of its resonant Middle Scots vocabulary.

[*See also* Gawin Douglas; William Dunbar; *and* Robert Henryson.]

SELECTED WORKS

The Dreme (written 1526–1528)

The Complaynt (1530)

The Testament and Complaynt of the Papyngo (1530)

The Complaint and Publict Confessioun of the Kingis Auld Hound, Callit Bagsche (?1530–1542)

The Historie of Squyer Meldrum (1550)

Ane Satyre of the Thrie Estaitis (first version 1540, full version 1552 and 1554)

The Monarche: Ane Dialog Betuix Experience and ane Courteour (1554)

EDITION

Hamer, Douglas, ed. *The Works of Sir David Lindsay, 1490–1555*. 4 vols. Edinburgh, 1931–1936. The definitive edition of Lindsay's works.

FURTHER READING

Edington, Carol. *Court and Culture in Renaissance Scotland: Sir David Lindsay of the Mount*. Amherst, MA, 1994. The best modern study of the intersection between Lindsay's writing and his political career.

Jack, R. D. S., ed. *The History of Scottish Literature: Origins to 1660*. Aberdeen, U.K., 1988. Places Lindsay in the wider context of late medieval and Renaissance Scottish literature.

Kantrowitz, Joanne Spencer. *Dramatic Allegory: Lindsay's "Ane Satyre of the Thrie Estaitis."* Lincoln, NE, 1975. A sustained analysis of *The Thrie Estaitis*.

McGavin, J. J. "The Dramatic Prosody of Sir David Lindsay." In *Of Lion and Unicorn*, edited by R. D. S. Jack and K. McGinley, 39–66. Edinburgh, 1993. An excellent analysis of the versification in *Ane Satyre*.

Mill, Anna Jean. *Medieval Plays in Scotland*. Edinburgh, 1927. A seminal study of early Scottish drama.

Riddy, Felicity. "Squyer Meldrum and the Romance of Chivalry." *Yearbook of English Studies* 4 (1974): 26–36. An excellent reading of one of Lindsay's "lighter" poems.

Walker, Greg. *The Politics of Performance in Early Renaissance Drama*. New York, 1998. Contains a long chapter on *The Thrie Estaitis*.

Williamson, J. E. H. " 'Althocht I beir nocht lyke ane baird' ": David Lyndsay's *Complaynt*." *The Scottish Literary Journal* 9 (1982): 5–20. Analyzes one of Lindsay's longer political poems.

Williamson, J. E. H. "Shady Publishing in Sixteenth-Century Scotland: The Case of Sir David Lindsay's Poems." *Bibliographical Society of Australia and New Zealand Bulletin* 16 (1992): 97–106. An excellent overview of Lindsay's cultural roles and the publishing history of his verse.

LITERARY JOURNALS

Mark S. Morrisson

To gauge the range and cultural significance of literature published in the twentieth century, we must not ignore literary journals, where many works we now know in book form first appeared. Such journals circulated literary production, shaped its public reception, and created public identities for its authors and even for entire literary movements, bringing poems, short stories, novels, and other literary forms into explicit contact with the other cultural and political dimensions of a society.

EDWARDIAN PERIODICALS:
THE ADVENT OF THE MASS-MARKET PRESS

The emergence of a truly modern mass-market press in the late nineteenth and early twentieth centuries and the proliferation of "little magazines" helped set the course of literary journals for the next century. During the Edwardian period several important periodical genres published or reviewed literature. General reviews often featured literary discussions, and some even published a few poems and short stories, but they included this literary material among discussions of many other cultural and social phenomena—politics, the arts, commerce, and technological advances, for example. A few quarterlies that had been important to the earlier nineteenth century, such as the venerable *Edinburgh Review* (1802–1929), still survived. But the later Victorian period had seen the rise of other types of general reviews that were less expensive than the quarterlies but also aimed primarily at a middle-class, university-educated readership. Such reviews, particularly the monthlies, remained prominent in the Edwardian era. Beginning with the *Fortnightly Review* in 1865, the monthlies reviewed and published a wide range of primary literary work and popularized the signed article, breaking with earlier reviews' tradition of anonymity. An issue usually ran to around 150 to 200 pages, cost two shillings sixpence per issue (as opposed to six shillings, equal to the cost of a new novel, for a quarterly), and included such prominent names as the *Contemporary Review*, *Nineteenth Century*, *National*, *Blackwood's*, and *Westminster Review*. Weekly reviews, often more explicitly partisan in their politics, also flourished. These cost between threepence and sixpence per issue, and they included the *Athenæum*, *Academy*, *Spectator*, and *Saturday Review*. Monthly magazines with a more literary focus, such as the *Cornhill* (1860–1975) at one shilling, thrived as well, publishing mainstream fiction serials, short stories, some poetry, and articles on literature. And one literary journal was born that still occupies a prominent position today: the *Times Literary Supplement* (*TLS*). The *TLS* was created in 1902 and quickly became a key voice in the British literary world, maintaining a circulation of between twenty thousand and forty-five thousand for the rest of the century. A typical middle-class family at the turn of the century might subscribe to more than one of these popular reviews.

But technological developments such as the Linotype machine, the rotary press, cheap paper, and inexpensive illustrations (eventually including photographs), as well as newly sophisticated advertising practices, led to a vast expansion of the periodical press in the 1890s that eventually began to undermine the established reviews. At the century's turn, new illustrated mass-market periodicals were beginning to reshape the literary marketplace. The lavishly illustrated *Strand*, founded in 1891 by George Newnes, cost only sixpence per issue (half the cost of the *Cornhill*, and one-fifth the cost of the monthly reviews). It quickly hit a circulation of more than half a million readers. By the beginning of 1914 the *Strand* was at the height of its popularity, selling 110 pages of advertising per issue and adding color advertisements. The magazine featured work such as Arthur Conan Doyle's *Sherlock Holmes* stories, humorous tales by W. W. Jacobs, and science fiction by H. G. Wells, and it targeted a broad middle-class audience.

Mass-market periodicals reached beyond the middle class as well. Newnes's *Tit-Bits* (1881) and Harmsworth's penny weekly *Answers* (1888), and even the new mass-market daily and evening newspapers, aimed at both middle- and working-class readers and included serial fiction and short stories. Although much of this literary material was forgettable, such notable modernist authors as James Joyce, Joseph Conrad, and Virginia Woolf submitted work to *Tit-Bits*, though they were rejected. Over time, the demand for ever-larger circulation as the reading public expanded and advertisers became more influential led to the waning of the general reviews, but they were not simply replaced by cheap tabloids. The twentieth century saw the rise of more specialized magazines, of journals of academic literary criticism, and, above all, of socalled little magazines.

MODERNIST LITTLE MAGAZINES

In Britain, little magazines came into their own in the early twentieth century. There were little magazines in the Victorian period, of course, such as the Pre-Raphaelite publication *The Germ* (1850) and the Decadents' infamous *Yellow Book* (1894–1897). In France, symbolist little magazines abounded in the 1880s and early 1890s. But as Alvin Sullivan notes, "The moderns of the twenties and thirties published more of their work in periodicals and anthologies than did any of their predecessors except for the nineteenth-century writers of serial fiction." Modernism was largely born in little magazines.

Little magazines are typically low-budget periodicals, often supported out of the pockets of their editors or a few patrons—or, later in the twentieth century, by Arts Council grants—rather than by large publishing houses. They usually enjoy great freedom to choose their content. Unlike explicitly commercial ventures, they need not seek maximum profit from advertising and subscription revenues. The term "little magazine" refers to their limited circulation; subscribers usually number in the hundreds, and generally have been fewer than five thousand. Most early-twentieth-century little magazines railed against the formulaic, sentimental fiction that flooded the market, but many still sought much higher circulation than they achieved, and a few did have notable commercial success. Some adopted, to varying degrees, advances in advertising, using everything from brand-name strategies and advertising typography to street sellers and publicity stunts. Others accepted a limited audience, a market niche often consisting of authors, scholars, and devotees of a particular brand of literature.

The little magazines served several purposes. They fostered dialogue between literature and the other arts and areas of social and cultural revolt. Dora Marsden's *Freewoman* (1911–1912) and its successors *The New Freewoman* (1913) and *The Egoist* (1914–1919), for instance,

and A. R. Orage's *New Age* (1907–1922) placed modernist literature alongside political stances such as egoism, anarchism, syndicalism, and guild socialism, as well as social debates about feminism, women's suffrage, and sexual orientation.

These magazines also helped to create or consolidate group identity. Wyndham Lewis's avant-garde magazine *Blast* (1914–1915) self-consciously created an identity, Vorticism, for a group of painters, sculptors, and writers. *The Egoist* became something of a house organ for Imagist poetry in Britain. Publication in some other little magazines, such as Harold Monro's *Poetry and Drama* (1913–1914) or the *English Review* during Ford Madox Ford's editorship (1908–1910), marked one's writing as generally modern, if not connected to a specific movement.

Little magazines established a bridge between experimental authors and the mainstream publishing world. As Peter Keating has demonstrated, nineteenth-century shifts toward single-volume novels, paperbacks, and royalty systems for authors helped to expand fiction publishing. These shifts, however, also made it more difficult for new or experimental novelists to sustain themselves on the money from a first novel long enough to write a second. Such authors were virtually forced to make journal publication supplement the small income they derived from book publication, especially until they had built enough of a reputation to negotiate better deals with publishers. Little magazines also helped authors find an initial audience for their work. Hoffman, Allen, and Ulrich have shown that the accumulated exposure of publication in several little magazines might get an author into better-paying commercial magazines, and eventually a book contract.

Writers quickly began to realize that little magazines could be part of a larger field of literary publication, not merely an alternative to it. As Lawrence Rainey has explained, T. S. Eliot was savvy enough about publishing to bring out *The Waste Land* first in his own London little magazine, *The Criterion*, and, almost simultaneously, in a culturally prestigious (and larger circulation) American little magazine, *The Dial*, and then in book form. Rainey notes that modernist authors even came to adopt a tripartite publication strategy: publication in a little magazine, then in an expensive limited edition, and finally in a mainstream publisher's edition. The little magazines thus acted as venues for nonmainstream literature but also contributed to its eventual commercial publication.

Modernist authors used the literary reviews and little magazines to lambaste the mainstream press for advancing mediocre literature and poor critical judgment—and to promote their literary agenda. In the summer of 1914, Ezra Pound used *Blast* and *The Egoist* to promote the short-lived Vorticist movement and to excoriate the literary establishment. Having caught the public's attention with the provocative polemics in *Blast*, he subsequently published an article in the *Fortnightly Review* explaining Vorticism in much more restrained terms for a broader middle-class audience. Modernists likewise ridiculed the judgments of the *Times Literary Supplement* (Pound dragged some of its most facile critiques through the wringer in the pages of *The Egoist*), yet several modernist authors, including William Butler Yeats, Virginia Woolf, and Richard Aldington, published anonymous reviews or letters in the *TLS* to advance their aesthetic theories in the literary marketplace. T. S. Eliot published a number of influential essays as lead reviews in the *TLS*, and Bruce Richmond, its editor, helped support Eliot's *Criterion* when it lost its patron in 1925.

LITERARY JOURNALS AFTER 1939

These developments took place largely between 1900 and 1939, but the trends continued across the century. The highly capitalized mass-market press continued to flourish; the *TLS* was recognized as part of the literary establishment. Although radio and, increasingly, television began to make inroads into readers' leisure time, literary magazines proliferated. Little magazines largely ceased publishing serial novels by 1939, but they remained important venues for poetry, short stories, and critical writing. Regional little magazines (some supported by regional arts councils) took off in the post–World War II years, with publications in Wales, Scotland, and Northern Ireland focusing on issues of national and cultural identity. Some even published in Celtic languages. Moreover, the move toward scholarly literary criticism that had begun to grow in journals such as *The Criterion* came to fruition in F. R. Leavis's Cambridge-based *Scrutiny* (1932–1953), which combined practical criticism with critiques of the metropolitan literary world.

Little magazines continued to publish work by new authors or by those whose work was too far out of the commercial mainstream to find a large audience, and they have been especially important to poets. Görtschacher estimates that perhaps as many as 80 percent of British authors in the second half of the century got their start in little magazines. Moreover, as in the modernist era, the postwar little magazines often helped to consolidate group identities for writers and promote literary movements. The year 1939 saw the demise of many key magazines (*Criterion*, *London Mercury*, *Twentieth Century Verse*, and *New Verse*, for instance), and other major periodicals, such as the *Cornhill*, suspended publication during the war. Some magazines, however, circumvented paper rationing and the ban on new magazines enacted in 1940 by disguising themselves as anthologies. Two such magazines—Meary Tambimuttu's *Poetry (London)* and Henry Treece's *Kingdom Come*, both founded in 1939— became identified with the "New Apocalypse" movement and broader New Romanticism of the 1940s, publishing such writers as Dylan Thomas, J. F. Hendry, G. S. Fraser, and Norman MacCaig. The 1950s saw the rise of a backlash against modernism and against New Romanticism that became known as The Movement. Philip Larkin, Kingsley Amis, D. J. Enright, and Donald Davie were its spokesmen, and it too came to be associated with specific little magazines: *Departure*, *The Isis*, *Trio*, and *New Poems*.

The prevailing pattern of new movement followed by reaction against it, and the birth of new magazines to promote the new direction and attack the old, was reenacted in the years that followed. Many little magazines that sprang up in the 1960s and 1970s espoused experimental work along modernist lines, looking to Basil Bunting or Hugh MacDiarmid, for instance, rather than to the Movement and Larkin for inspiration. Others looked abroad to find new currents of experimental poetry. These magazines fostered a transatlantic aesthetic that admired the experimentation of the Beats, New York poets, and Black Mountain artists in America as well as other veins of what would eventually be called postmodernism in poetry. Cambridge and London, in particular, became centers of the Poetry Revival. The Cambridge poets (including J. H. Prynne, Tim Longville, John Riley, Andrew Crozier, Peter Riley, Veronica Forrest-Thomson, and Anthony Barnett) were published by such little magazines as the *Grosseteste Review*, *English Intelligencer*, *Perfect Bound*, and *Ochre Magazine*. These venues were crucial to the group's developing poetics and identity. Similarly, the London scene that emerged around Bob Cobbing, Eric Mottram, Allen Fisher, Ken Edwards, Maggie O'Sullivan, Barry MacSweeney, Bill Griffiths, Denise Riley, and others relied on little magazines such as *Alembic*, *Reality Studios*, and *Spanner*. The Poetry Revival was perhaps at its height when, quite surprisingly, Eric Mottram was elected in 1971 to the editorship of the *Poetry Review*, the magazine of the conservative Poetry Society. Mottram used the magazine to foster international experimental poetry and to promote the Cambridge and London poets of the Revival, although he was forced out in 1977 in a feud with the Arts Council.

END OF THE CENTURY AND BEYOND

Two literary journals of the last quarter of the twentieth century—*London Review of Books* and *Granta*—illustrate the continuing audience for and even commercial success of the general literary review and little magazine genres. During a 1979 lockout at the *Times* during which the *TLS* was not published for several months, the *London Review of Books* came into existence, taking advantage of the *TLS*'s absence. The fortnightly *LRB* was partially inspired by the *New York Review of Books*, which had instituted signed reviews, longer articles, and freestanding articles not connected to published books. Emerging during the Thatcher years, the *LRB* has been a consistent voice in British intellectual life, launching critiques primarily from the left. Its founder, Karl Miller, had been trained by Leavis at Cambridge, served as the literary editor of the *New Statesman* and the *Spectator*, and then edited *The Listener*. (He was also the Lord Northcliffe Professor of Modern English Literature at University College, London.) But the *LRB* has not resembled those journals, nor anything Northcliffe himself would have launched, and its editors like to compare it to the general reviews of the nineteenth century, with their emphasis on lengthy essays. It has a circulation of almost forty-three thousand, and is read in about eighty countries by a highly educated and fairly affluent audience.

The case of *Granta* shows that a little magazine can occasionally become commercially successful. *Granta* began in 1889 as a student magazine at Cambridge. It published work by writers such as A. A. Milne (who was an editor) and Rupert Brooke as well as by men who became members of Parliament and government figures. But in 1979 Bill Buford transformed the magazine into a showcase for new fiction and nonfiction. *Granta*'s editors see its "championing of forms such as the travel account, the memoir, and reportage" as doing "much to expand the idea of what 'literature' could be or do" (Jack). While *Granta* seeks to discover and support new and innovative writing—notable contributors have included Martin Amis, Julian Barnes, Gabriel García Márquez, Hanif Kureishi, Ariel Dorfman, and John Berger—it has extended its reach and scope well beyond what is often achievable by little magazines. Its quarterly issues pack in some 250 to 300 pages of literature, and it averages almost 70,000

copies sold, with more than 56,000 of those sales to subscribers. Its special issues can sell as many as 90,000 copies. And like *The Egoist* in the early twentieth century, which created the Egoist Press to publish books and pamphlets by authors featured in the magazine, *Granta* expanded to create Granta Books in 1989. Indeed, *Granta* could serve as a model for how a literary magazine can realize its aspirations to publish writing by nonestablished authors, but to do so in an influential and commercially viable way.

Some scholars and critics have bemoaned the demise of the Victorian reviews with their high-quality, comprehensive essays in the first half of the twentieth century. They lament the increasing power and presence of advertising in journals, and they believe that expanded reading audiences have diluted and cheapened the content of periodicals. The literary historian Denys Thompson thus complains of the "disintegration of the reading public" in Britain. Yet there is much evidence that Britain's literary journals remain healthy and even vigorous. Even after the demise of the modernist little magazines of the earlier twentieth century, the proliferation of small-budget and low-circulation little magazines has responded to diverse literary imperatives and (in the aggregate) has allowed literary movements and scenes to flourish. Hundreds of little magazines have been published in the postwar era—more than four hundred of them in the 1965–1975 decade alone (Görtschacher). Most do not survive long, but new little magazines still arise to provide platforms for new literature and to meet a dizzying array of aesthetic, regional, and ethnic needs. Historians of postwar poetry find it hard to avoid discussing the little magazine affiliations of authors. Although some establishment literary figures in Britain have lamented that not much occurred in poetry in the 1960s and 1970s, other critics, more attuned to experimental and international trends in poetry, look at the 1960s and 1970s through the lens of little magazines and small presses and find instead the British Poetry Revival.

The history of the British Poetry Revival also highlights the importance of technology for literary journals. Just as advances in manufacturing allowed both mass-market illustrated magazines and little magazines to bloom in the early twentieth century, technology helped to drive literary production in the latter part of the century. The Poetry Revival was enabled by duplicating machines and cheap production technologies for both little magazines and small-press books. During this period, some "plastic bag mags" eschewed binding altogether: they were simply loose copied sheets in a plastic bag. Desktop publishing has allowed relatively high production values for even the most underfunded little magazines. At century's end, electronic publication may well augment the ability of print-based little magazines to publish largely unknown or nonmainstream authors—and to connect British literature even more strongly to global literary movements. Such an easy destruction of national boundaries may well transform British literature in ways that can hardly be imagined at the beginning of the twenty-first century.

[*See also* Serialization.]

FURTHER READING

Görtschacher, Wolfgang. *Little Magazine Profiles: The Little Magazines in Great Britain 1939–1993*. Salzburg, Austria, 1993. An excellent history of the little magazine after 1939, including interviews with editors, critics, and poets, and reflections on the magazines' audiences, contributors, and media.

Hoffman, Frederick J., Charles Allen, and Carolyn F. Ulrich. *The Little Magazine: A History and a Bibliography*. Princeton, NJ, 1946. Seminal work on the little magazine form, with brief accounts of hundreds of titles.

Jack, Ian. "Motley Notes: A River, a Magazine, and Many Apologies." *Granta* 87 (Autumn 2004): 9–18. A good brief history of *Granta* and reflections on its significance by its editor.

Keating, Peter. *The Haunted Study: A Social History of the English Novel 1875–1914*. London, 1989. Crucial account of the transformation of the institutions of the periodical press and book publishing and of the publication practices of fiction writers.

May, Derwent. *Critical Times: The History of the Times Literary Supplement*. London, 2001. A thorough history of the *TLS* and exploration of its influence and its contributors.

Morrisson, Mark S. *The Public Face of Modernism: Little Magazines, Audiences, and Reception 1905–1920*. Madison, WI, 2001. An exploration of modernist little magazines' relationships to consumer culture via a study of the audience, promotional practices, and public ambitions of early little magazines during the expansion of the mass-market press.

Rainey, Lawrence. *Institutions of Modernism: Literary Elites and Public Culture*. New Haven, CT, 1998. An ambitious and thought-provoking study of the publication practices of modernists in the face of the expanding commodity culture of the early twentieth century.

Sullivan, Alvin, ed. *British Literary Magazines*. 4 vols. Westport, CT, 1983–1986. Very useful account of British literary magazines from 1698 to 1984. See especially vol. 3, *The Victorian and Edwardian Age, 1937–1913*, and vol. 4, *The Modern Age, 1914–1984*.

Treglown, Jeremy. "Literary History and the *Lit. Supp.*" *Yearbook of English Studies* 16 (Literary Periodicals Special Number) (1986): 132–149. Treglown was editor of the *TLS*. This special issue contains many useful essays on literary periodicals over the past two centuries.

LITERARY THEORY

Dolora Chapelle Wojciehowski

The modern word "theory" derives from the Greek *theoria*, a "looking at," "witnessing," or "observing," "contemplation" or "speculation," as well as "a sight" or "spectacle." In contemporary usage "theory" refers to a conceptual system, often with its own special terminology, that names and explains complicated phenomena that cannot be understood through observation alone. Theory is often opposed to "practice"; theory is the abstract reasoning or hypotheses guiding actions, decisions, ethical choices, or political strategies.

Within literary studies, theory might be loosely defined as the field of inquiry devoted to problems of signification and interpretation. Literary theorists analyze the language, structure, or function of the text, often in relation to the culture in which that text circulates. Theorists may also assess the aesthetic, social, political, ethical, or economic value of a text for particular groups. There are always multiple perspectives on what texts are and what they mean; hence it is important to recognize that there is not just one literary theory but many theories that overlap, complement, or contradict one another.

Literary theory has a long and venerable history, for in one form or another it has existed for more than two thousand years. However, within the field of literary studies today, the word "theory" commonly refers to several schools of interpretation—deconstruction, feminism, or postcolonial theory, for example—that arose or achieved new prominence during the 1960s and 1970s or thereafter, partly in response to the profound social and cultural upheavals of that era. Many of these theories first developed with disciplines other than literary studies and are often contrasted with the literary criticism prevalent in the Anglo-American academy earlier in the twentieth century.

Interdisciplinary and often politically engaged, contemporary theory has revolutionized the teaching, reading, and writing of literature, as well as the production and interpretation of popular culture. Theory has had a profound impact on other disciplines as well, including philosophy, history, anthropology, communications, and legal studies; indeed, it has helped to redraw or to break down the boundaries that previously separated various disciplines within the humanities and social sciences.

STRUCTURALISM

In order to begin to understand the complex cultural phenomenon called theory, together with its intriguing history, it is necessary to analyze the conditions that brought it into being. In its late-twentieth-century incarnation, theory developed as a reaction to, and as an extension of, earlier intellectual trends, philosophical currents, and interpretive traditions—among them, structuralism.

Structural anthropology. The French anthropologist Claude Lévi-Strauss (1908–) launched the structuralist movement in anthropology with the publication of *Les Structures élémentaires de la parenté* (1949; English trans., *The Elementary Structures of Kinship*, 1962). In that study, Lévi-Strauss applied key concepts of the Swiss linguist Ferdinand de Saussure (1857–1913), founder of modern semiology (the study of signs), to his field research conducted among tribal peoples in Brazil.

Saussure had developed a revolutionary theory of language by examining the relations between its component parts, its signs (words). He contended that signs "mean" because they are similar to, or different from, every other sign in the system, not because they have an intrinsic connection to their "referents"—the external objects they seem to name. When Lévi-Strauss applied this differential notion to his own field, anthropology, he focused on the connections between the phenomena he observed (the system) rather than on the phenomena themselves (its signs). This structuralist paradigm enabled him to recognize the hidden structures of tribal kinship networks, social rituals, and mythology.

Psychoanalysis. During the 1930s and for several decades thereafter, a young French psychiatrist, Jacques Lacan (1901–1981), conducted in Paris a different kind of field research. Initially a specialist in the form of mental illness known as paranoid psychosis, Lacan pursued his study of the deep structures of the human psyche. Lacan ushered in the structuralist era in psychoanalysis by applying the theories of Saussure and Lévi-Strauss to signature concepts of Sigmund Freud (1856–1939), the father of psychoanalysis.

In essays such as "L'instance de la lettre dans l'inconscient ou la raison depuis Freud" (1957; English trans., "The Agency of the Letter in the Unconscious, or Reason Since Freud," 1977), Lacan expanded Freud's theory of the unconscious mind by describing its differential linguistic organization. He also explored the systematic imprecision of metaphor and metonymy, the two modes of representation used by the unconscious to represent its own obscure desires. There and throughout his writings, Lacan highlighted misrecognition as a structural feature of the human mind—an enormously influential concept for later theory.

Cultural criticism. Roland Barthes (1915–1980), a leading French literary critic and a younger contemporary of Lévi-Strauss and Lacan, was also a leader of the structuralist movement. In 1957, also in Paris, Barthes published *Mythologies* (English trans., *Mythologies*, 1972), a set of essays on topics as diverse as French wine-drinking habits, soap powders and detergents, Einstein's brain, and plastic. This breakthrough study, like those of Lévi-Strauss and Lacan, applied Saussure's semiology to yet another context—popular culture. Instead of taking detergent or plastic more or less at face value, Barthes read the "myths" underpinning those products, revealing deep structures that before had remained hidden or only dimly perceived.

The impact of structuralism. During the 1950s and 1960s, structuralism spread to other fields, including political science, history, philosophy, and literary studies. Other noted structuralists include the Marxist political theorist Louis Althusser (1918–1990), the literary critics Gérard Genette (1930–) and Tzvetan Todorov (1939–), the polymath cultural critic Michel Serres (1930–), and the intellectual historian Michel Foucault (1926–1984). Because of its linguistic roots, structuralism also had affinities with Russian formalism, an influential theoretical movement of the early twentieth century combining linguistic and literary analysis, and its successor movement, the Prague School of linguistics. The Russian literary theorist Mikhail Bakhtin (1895–1975) is also sometimes classified as a structuralist. Bakhtin's pathbreaking theory of dialogue in the novel added a social and political dimension to Saussure's theory of language as a differential system. Bakhtin's highly original theories of the self, always in dialogic relation to others, remain highly influential within literary studies.

In its many applications, structuralism directed attention to the impersonal structures governing human thought, behavior, and culture. Certain branches of structuralism also challenged the concepts of the conscious control, will, desire, or freedom of individuals, concepts that had been central to two twentieth-century philosophical schools, phenomenology and existentialism. These philosophical challenges to humanist notions of individual autonomy would become even more pronounced in the era of poststructuralist theory.

POSTSTRUCTURALISM AND DECONSTRUCTION

As its prefix suggests, poststructuralism came after structuralism, both chronologically and conceptually. The differences between these two movements are subtle, yet significant. Any explanation of those differences is complicated by the fact that many structuralists (for example, Lacan, Barthes, and Foucault) were also considered poststructuralists in their later phases. One key difference is the relative optimism of the former school, confident in its power to explain in a manner both systematic and scientific the concealed structures of thought, culture, and social organization. Poststructuralism, by contrast, presented a more radical and thoroughgoing critique of our ability to find coherence in such structures, and also in our own explanations and analyses thereof. For that reason, poststructuralism is often considered "antifoundationalist," because it questions claims to objective knowledge. Instability, indeterminacy, and undecidability are all central motifs of the later theory, especially deconstruction.

How did this theoretical sea change come about, and why? The political and cultural radicalism of the late 1960s contributed in no small part to this skeptical and paradoxically Utopian turn in the world of theory.

The Tel Quel ***group.*** One important forum for theory was the literary and philosophical journal *Tel Quel*, published in Paris between 1960 and 1982. Edited by the novelist Philippe Sollers (1936–), *Tel Quel* (French for "as such") promoted experimental creative writing and innovative theories that often engaged the psychoanalytic concepts of Freud and Lacan, while critiquing or modifying certain premises of structuralism. Contributors to the avant-garde journal included semiologist and psychoanalyst Julia Kristeva (1941–), feminist philosopher Luce Irigaray (1932–), literary theorist René Girard (1923–), and philosopher Jacques Derrida (1930–2004), as well as Barthes, Todorov, Genette, and Foucault, and numerous other intellectuals and artists of note. Their critiques, conversations and debates gradually helped give rise to a new body of theory later referred to as poststructuralism.

Derrida and deconstruction.

Among the most influential members of the *Tel Quel* group was the Algerian-born philosopher Jacques Derrida, principal founder of the theoretical school called deconstruction. Derrida's form of poststructuralism was based on a set of interpretive approaches that focus on the linguistic complexities within philosophical, literary, or indeed *any* texts. The radical nature of Derrida's thought comes into relief when viewed against the backdrop of the Western philosophical tradition. Throughout the ages, philosophers have sought to understand the nature of truth or reality based on a transcendental origin. This fundamental impulse of philosophy, which Derrida called logocentrism (from the Greek *logos*, "word" or "reason"), he critiqued in analyses of key philosophers of that tradition (Plato, Jean-Jacques Rousseau, Edmund Husserl, and Martin Heidegger, to name a few). Derrida explored the subtle contradictions within their theoretical systems, and even, at the same time, within his own. Following in the skeptical tradition of German philosopher Friedrich Nietzsche (1844–1900), Derrida held that human conceptual systems remain trapped in linguistic and conceptual structures from which they cannot escape; within those structures, meaning is never transparent, fully present, or attainable. Language, knowledge, and experience, he argued, must be understood without the transcendental grounding of truth, presence, or logos. The famous Derridean statement in *De la grammatologie* (1967; *Of Grammatology*, 1976) that "there is nothing outside the text" is not a denial of reality but a rethinking of reality outside of traditional metaphysical norms.

Derrida also demonstrated the degree to which Western thought is organized according to pairs of concepts (for example, presence–absence, mind–body, nature–culture, reason–madness, male–female, and white–black). These binary terms do not occupy separate yet equal positions within the philosophical tradition; rather, each pairing is structured hierarchically, with one term typically taking precedence over the other. Derrida provided a technique for "deconstructing" these binary pairs. In doing so, he questioned the ways that people usually think about the world, building political and moral systems out of those separate-but-unequal binary oppositions. Extraordinarily versatile, witty, and perplexing to many, Derrida's work has had an enormous impact on literary studies, philosophy, and theory itself.

Michel Foucault.

Like Derrida, Michel Foucault was one of the principal theorists associated with the emergence of poststructuralism. Originally trained as a philosopher of psychology, Foucault later described himself as a specialist in the history of systems of thought. More historically oriented than many theorists of his day, Foucault studied various structures of social control, discipline, and repression, analyzing the evolution of those structures over time. Foucault conducted archival research on a broad and intriguing array of topics, including the history of insanity, the development of the modern penal system, and the history of sexuality.

Throughout his works Foucault emphasized the large and impersonal social forces that regulate people's lives and dictate bodily conduct. Subjects (a word for deindividualized selves) are, in Foucault's analysis, inevitably tangled in a network of powerful forces—some subtle, others quite blatant or brutal—that determine not only public and private behaviors but also identity itself. Foucault's metaphor for this mode of control and containment is "panopticism," a term coined by the British philosopher Jeremy Bentham (1748–1832) to describe his model for a circular prison (from the Greek *pan-* [all] and *optikos* [from *optos*, visible]). In his landmark study *Surveiller et punir: La naissance de la prison* (1975; English trans., *Discipline and Punish: The Birth of the Prison*, 1978), Foucault argued that modern men and women cannot escape the implied prison of constant surveillance within society, even if, he argues, more extreme forms of coercion and punishment have declined in popularity over the last few centuries.

Foucault's determinist theory of power relations was frequently criticized for its apparent denial of human agency (the capacity to take conscious action or to create change), although the philosopher was simultaneously preoccupied with transgression and other modes of resistance. Foucault's legacy has been profound and wide-ranging across the humanities and social sciences, influencing other branches of poststructuralist thought, such as cultural studies, new historicism, queer theory, and postcolonial theory.

PSYCHOANALYTIC THEORY

The idea that hidden structures play a powerful role in determining individual or collective identity has a long history within the psychoanalytic tradition, as it does within structuralism and poststructuralism, which are in many ways coextensive with the Freudian tradition. The dialogue between psychoanalytic, literary, and social theorists is complex, extensive, and resistant to summary, although certain themes and trends may be highlighted.

Literary criticism and psychoanalysis.

Throughout the twentieth century and into the current one, psychoanalytically inclined literary scholars (or literary-minded psychoanalysts) applied various components of Freudian theory to the study of literature. Early psychoanalytic critics tended to read literature as a mirror of the author's psychic life. For example, the British psychiatrist Ernest Jones (1879–1958) argued in *Hamlet and Oedipus* (1949) that Shakespeare's famous play revealed its author's unresolved Oedipus complex. Freud had contended that children experience erotic desire for the opposite-sex parent and jealousy for the same-sex parent; he named this conflictual family dynamic, which he considered universal, after the Greek playwright Sophocles' character Oedipus, a man who killed his father and married his mother before realizing his relationship to both. Jones's reading assumed a direct correspondence between the ambivalent character Hamlet and Shakespeare himself. However, Jones's critics argued that the relation between art and artist is more complicated, nuanced, and difficult to trace.

Nevertheless, psychobiographical interpretations of writers and their works have a long and influential history. The literary critic Harold Bloom (1930–) applied Freud's Oedipal model of psychic development to another context: the writer's creative development and the relation between literary works. In *The Anxiety of Influence: A Theory of Poetry* (1973), Bloom argued that writers are necessarily in the position of "sons" who must compete with and overcome their "fathers"—that is, earlier authors serving as their literary models—in order to write effectively. In this and other works, Bloom stressed the writer's unconscious, as well as conscious entrainment with his literary forebears. Bloom locates the Oedipal struggle in the rhetoric of a literary work, thus combining psychoanalytic theory and rhetorical reading.

Psychoanalysis and poststructuralism.

By the late 1970s, most psychoanalytic theory in Europe and America had taken a poststructuralist turn. Countering American ego psychology, as well as other earlier traditions emphasizing the potential unity and coherence of the psyche, later theorists, many of them Lacanian, describe a "decentered self." These theorists emphasize misrecognition, irrationality, and fragmentation as key features of human psychic life.

Julia Kristeva, the Bulgarian-born semiologist and psychoanalyst, ranks among the most noted of these theorists. In *Pouvoirs de l'horreur* (1980; *The Powers of Horror*, 1982), Kristeva presented her provocative theory of "abjection." In a decentering analysis focusing on the real and imagined powers of the maternal body, Kristeva explored the child's necessary yet traumatic separation from its mother (the process of abjection) as it develops a sense of its own body image, discreet from its mother's. However, Kristeva argued that these imagined boundaries of the body and of identity itself are unstable, potentially subject to collapse. Kristeva's work, strongly influenced by that of Jacques Lacan, continues to define the more psychoanalytically oriented branches of poststructuralism. Her analyses of the female body and maternity have also had a major impact on feminist and gender theory.

The philosopher Gilles Deleuze (1925–1995) and the psychoanalyst Félix Guattari (1930–1992) also represent an important strand of poststructuralist theory. In their coauthored book *Anti-Oedipe* (1972; English trans., *Anti-Oedipus*, 1977) the two men contended that psychoanalysis, in tandem with capitalism, limits, represses, and controls the expression of desire within modern culture. In their elaborate retheorizing of desire itself, Deleuze and Guattari rejected the validity of Freud's model of the Oedipus complex, offering an alternative model of the mind as a factory of "desiring machines." With this mechanical metaphor, they sought to depersonalize and, as it were, de-transgress desire, thereby subverting the Freudian familial paradigm of sexuality and desire.

Trauma theory, a more recent development fusing psychoanalysis and poststructuralism, explores the psychic repercussions of physical or emotional trauma—for example, among Holocaust survivors, Vietnam veterans, and victims of assault, abuse, or torture. Trauma is understood as an event that is not fully experienced as it occurs; it returns later in repetitive behavioral symptoms, disturbing dreams, or other unwanted aftershocks of a traumatizing event. Trauma theorists such as Cathy Caruth, Shoshana Felman, and Dori Laub have analyzed the dimension of trauma within narrative (novels, films, personal histories, and other forms). Trauma, they argue, is an elusive and often repetitive element of such narratives, manifesting as enigmatic linguistic or figural symptoms. Trauma theory has provided an important lens for interpreting not only individual but also collective history, and comments on the fundamentally traumatic nature of modernity itself.

MARXISMS

If the figure of Freud looms large within contemporary theory, so too does that of the nineteenth-century political philosopher Karl Marx (1818–1883). Marx and his fellow theorist Friedrich Engels (1820–1895) developed a "materialist" interpretation of history (so named for its emphasis on the material conditions of existence). They argued that culture is a direct manifestation of the particular economic system that determines it; in their terms, culture is a "superstructure" founded on the "base" of a given political economy (for example, feudalism or capitalism). They also held that cultural expressions such as literature, philosophy, and religion are freighted with "ideology," the largely concealed and collectively held justifications for the distribution of wealth within a political system. They contended that persons seeking to create a more equitable society, less stratified by social and economic class divisions, should understand and interpret ideology at work (or play).

The Frankfurt School.

The relation of culture, politics, and ideology was a vexing and often urgent question throughout the twentieth century—a question theorized by Marxists in a variety of ways. Among the most influential theorists to elaborate on Marx's paradigm, as well as Freud's, were the philosophers Theodor Adorno (1903–1969), Max Horkheimer (1895–1973), Herbert Marcuse (1898–1979), and other associates of the Institut für Sozialforschung (Institute for Social Research) established at the University of Frankfurt in 1923. The literary critic Walter Benjamin (1892–1940) is also regarded as an affiliate of this group.

The Nazis shut down the Frankfurt School in 1933, and many of its members emigrated to the United States before returning to Germany in the 1950s. During the postwar period, Adorno and Horkheimer critiqued the Western "culture industry" as a capitalist tool for social control—a case made in their book *The Dialectic of Enlightenment* (1947; English trans. 1972). In *The Authoritarian Personality* (1950), Adorno and other members of the school explored the social and psychological causes of authoritarian behavior, prejudice, and group aggression. Marcuse's seminal work *One-Dimensional Man* (1964) examined the "false needs" and imaginary choices provided by capitalism and communism alike. Although their work was tinged with pessimism regarding the supposed advances of modernity, Frankfurt School theorists nevertheless held out some hope for rationality as a means of combating authoritarianism in its many forms.

Marxism and structuralism.

During the 1960s, the French philosopher Louis Althusser (1918–1990) brought structuralism to bear on the classical Marxist concept of ideology. Althusser challenged the prevailing notion of ideology as "false consciousness," a potentially removable veil of illusion, arguing that ideology is truly inescapable. Social organizations like churches, schools, and trade unions shape identity and behavior profoundly by transmitting ideologies. Hence, despite appearances to the contrary, individuals do not freely choose their own belief systems. In a paradoxical way, those systems choose *them* through the process that Althusser calls "interpellation" (from the French *interpeller*, "to hail" and "to interrogate"). Althusser's determinist view of ideology was consonant with strong forms of structuralism, as well as certain de-individuating strands of poststructuralist thought.

Cultural materialism and cultural studies.

Two influential British Marxists, the literary critics Raymond Williams (1921–1988) and Terry Eagleton (1943–), analyzed the specific role of literature and other writing in the creation of ideology. They argued that literary texts are neither apolitical aesthetic artifacts removed from the world nor straightforward reflections of an economic system (for example, industrial capitalism), as some earlier Marxists had held. Writers do not write in a vacuum, as Williams argued in *Culture and Society* (1958); they are profoundly influenced by the material realities and class conflicts of their time. By supporting or challenging those material conditions, their representations of the world can have a significant impact. Writers may also represent social conflicts within their culture without fully understanding those conflicts or their role in them. Cultural materialism seeks to reveal the dialectical relation between writer and culture, and between culture and society.

Postmodernism.

The American literary theorist Fredric Jameson, the French sociologist Jean Baudrillard, the poststructuralist philosopher Jean-François Lyotard, and the Lacanian-Marxist critic Slavov Zizek (1949–), among others, have turned their gaze on our own historical moment, the "postmodern." A period marked by accelerated economic, scientific, and technological changes after World War II, postmodernity is viewed by many theorists as an era of vacuous consumerism. For Lyotard (1924–1998), the "postmodern condition" is one of skepticism or incredulity toward the "grand narratives" of the past—for instance, democracy, Marxism, or science. These "metanarratives" were themselves illusions, he argued, and liberation from them a step forward. Although we may be passing out of the postmodern moment, the brave new world of multinational capitalism and globalization continues to inspire new lines of critical inquiry.

POSTCOLONIAL THEORY

The phenomenon of globalization has motivated postcolonial theorists, whose concerns often align with those of Marxists, to examine the ideologies of race and ethnicity, as well as class, defining colonized societies of the past and present. While globalization may seem like a recent occurrence, its origins may be traced back at least as far as the early modern age, when Vasco da Gama sailed to Africa and the Indies, and Columbus to the "new" world in the Western Hemisphere. By the sixteenth century, Portugal, Spain, the Netherlands, England, and other European nations had established colonies around the world, which in most cases greatly enriched the colonizing countries while enslaving or impoverishing native populations and decimating local cultures. Fundamental to the colonizing process was the slave trade, the dehumanizing practice of forced labor, based largely in Africa, which drove the economies and shaped the values of the early modern age, and the legacy of which continues to impact the world today.

Decolonization. The late 1940s to the 1960s was an era of accelerated decolonization, marking a new phase in the history of globalization. At that time, numerous colonies sought and achieved independence from European rule and formed new nations, including India and Pakistan (1947), Vietnam (1954), Iraq (1958), Congo (1960), Algeria (1962), and dozens of others. During those decades the poet Aimé Césaire (1913–) and the psychoanalyst and philosopher Frantz Fanon (1925–1961), both born in the French colony of Martinique; the Tunisian writer

Albert Memmi (1920–); and the Nigerian novelist Chinua Achebe (1930–) published works theorizing the colonial situation in revolutionary ways. Fanon's influential study *Peau noire, masques blanchs* (1952; English trans. *Black Skin, White Masks*, 1967) examined the psychopathology of colonialism and the damaging effects of racism. In *Les Damnés de la terre* (1961; English trans., *The Wretched of the Earth*, 1963), Fanon analyzed the place of violence in anticolonial struggles, and the strategic difficulties faced by new African nations.

Decolonizing the mind. As Fanon and others had argued, colonialism is as much a state of mind as an economic and political condition. Later theorists continued to analyze the ideological underpinnings of colonialism, transmitted through literature, art, and other forms of culture. In 1978 the Palestinian-born literary critic Edward Said (1935–2003) published *Orientalism*, a pathbreaking book exploring the negative stereotypes, fantasies, and pseudo-knowledges that Europeans have projected onto the Eastern world (Said focuses on the Near East in this work, which he identifies as the site of Europe's oldest colonies). In the European colonial mind, Said argued, the East functions as a kind of imaginary "Other," alternately strange, exotic, duplicitous, and altogether different from the West. Said also explained how supposedly neutral fields of study—for example, philology (the study of languages)—are permeated with these same "Orientalist" stereotypes. Occidental "knowledge" about the East, he argued, is problematic, because it manifests persistent yet sometimes subtle prejudice toward Arabo-Islamic peoples.

European colonizers also imposed their languages, literature, and cultural on those they colonized. The effect of such impositions, the Kenyan author and critic Ngugi Wa Thiong'o (1938–) argued, is to alienate colonized peoples from their own traditions and history. In *Decolonizing the Mind: The Politics of Language in African Literature* (1986), Ngugi called for an Afrocentric approach to education in his own country and throughout Africa, one aimed at recovering the suppressed oral and written cultures of that continent. The importance of cultural resistance has also been analyzed by theorists such as Gayatri Spivak (1942–), Barbara Harlow (1948–), and Abdul JanMohamed (1945–).

Subaltern studies. In notebooks written during his imprisonment in the late 1920s and early 1930s, the Italian Marxist Antonio Gramsci (1891–1937) analyzed the complex relations of the ruling classes and the dominated. Gramsci used the term "subaltern" to describe those classes (primarily workers) excluded from roles of significant power within a given political regime. Postcolonial theorists have applied the term more generally to persons or groups deemed inferior because of race or ethnicity, gender or sexuality, and/or religious or political beliefs, as well as class. In her influential essay "Can the Subaltern Speak?" (1988), the Bengali-born feminist Gayatri Spivak reflects on the situation of the most disenfranchised laborers of the world, especially women, and the co-opting of their voices and interests by many other groups, including Western theorists. The "speaking-for" problem— the question of who speaks for whom, and why—remains a key topic of debate in subaltern studies, as well as other branches of postcolonial theory.

Globalization and diaspora. As the economies and cultures of the world become increasingly interconnected, the sociologist Paul Gilroy (1956–) and the cultural theorists Stuart Hall (1932–) and Homi Bhabha (1949–) have argued that we live not only in a postcolonial world but also a post- or transnational one. "Diaspora," the movement or dispersal of peoples resulting from slavery, colonialism, or ethnic conflict, is a useful concept for describing contemporary migrations of people around the globe, and the fluidity of national and cultural identities resulting from these movements. Deconstructing the binary category of colonizer–colonized and others like it, Homi Bhahba posits in his book *The Location of Culture* (1994) an in-between form of identity resisting classification: "hybridity." To embrace hybridity is not simply to relabel oneself or others but to think of the world in fundamentally different terms, resisting the separatism and exclusions of outmoded notions of nationality, race, and other markers of "essential" identity.

Analyzing the conjunctions of race, ethnicity, and class in the context of British national history, as well a larger, transatlantic and transnational one, Paul Gilroy underscores the complexity of black identity, shaped by the diasporic forces of slavery and colonialism. In seminal works such as "*There Ain't no Black in the Union Jack*": *The Cultural Politics of Race and Nation* (1987) and *The Black Atlantic: Modernity and Double Consciousness* (1993), Gilroy provides a nuanced theory of hybrid identities in the postcolonial world, while also exploring the persistence of racialized and racist categories of thought across the spectrum of contemporary politicals and culture. Postcolonial theory clarifies the origin and history

of these categories, as well as useful strategies for challenging them.

THEORIES OF RACE AND ETHNICITY

During the 1950s and 1960s, the era of decolonization, a parallel struggle unfolded in the United States, as the Civil Rights movement sought to end the oppression of African Americans. Similar movements for equal rights and cultural recognition were led by Native Americans, Chicanos, Asian Americans, and other ethnic minorities in the United States. The landmark Supreme Court decision *Brown v. Board of Education* (1954) reversed the "separate but equal" policy previously used to defend segregation, although the actual end of that practice lay well in the future. Sit-ins, demonstrations, and other forms of direct action during these decades helped accomplish what the courts could or would not—the beginning of a national transformation of consciousness. Theory, too, played a part in that transformation.

African American literary theory. In the 1960s and 1970s, the Black Arts Movement, sponsored in part by publisher and poet LeRoi Jones (Amiri Baraka [1934–]) and allied with the Black Power movement, inspired a new generation of poets and playwrights to explore African American culture in its own terms.

By the 1970s, universities had begun to institute courses and programs in African American literature, history, and culture. New forms of theory exploring the uniqueness of black literature, language, and culture in America would emerge at the same time.

In *Blues, Ideology, and Afro-American Literature: A Vernacular Theory* (1984), the activist literary critic Houston Baker (1943–) analyzed as a site of resistance the "vernacular" speech of black Americans. A "non-standard" language often marginalized or ignored, the vernacular defines musical forms such as the blues, as well as other expressions of popular culture. The literary theorist, editor, and public intellectual Henry Louis Gates Jr. (1950–) synthesized deconstruction theory, African folklore, and African American cultural traditions in works such as *The Signifying Monkey: A Theory of African-American Literary Criticism* (1988). There Gates examines the vernacular practice of "signifyin(g)," a form of word-play in African American literature, music, and daily life involving humor, insults, irony, and improvisation—a practice that he traces back to African oral and textual traditions.

The novelist and critic Alice Walker (1944–) explored the literary and cultural traditions of African American women, focusing on the works of Zora Neal Hurston (1891–1960), an influential writer and theorist of the Harlem Renaissance. Walker's book *In Search of Our Mothers' Gardens: Womanist Prose* (1983) studied female creativity, a neglected issue within African American cultural theory of the time—an issue further theorized by feminists such as Barbara Christian, Barbara Smith, Hortense Spillers, Hazel Carby, and bell hooks (Gloria Watkins).

The place of African Americans within the white American literary imagination has also inspired important lines of theoretical inquiry. In *Playing in the Dark: Whiteness and the Literary Imagination* (1992), the novelist and Nobel-laureate Toni Morrison (1931–) analyzes the "Africanist" presence in the literature of white Americans—that is, the racialized fears and desires refracted through the lens of a literary tradition colored by slavery and its legacy. The representational honesty of writers, however partial or unwitting, enables critical readers a means of confronting that legacy.

Theory's borders. Closely related to African American and postcolonial studies, border theory explores the literature and cultural experiences of Chicanos and Chicanas in historical and economic contexts. The border between the United States and Mexico is not only a territorial boundary but also an economic, cultural, and psychological one; hence, its crossings are freighted with meaning. Border theory, inspired by writer and folklorist Américo Paredes, and developed by Gloria Anzaldúa, Ruth Behar, Ramon Saldívar, Héctor Calderón, José David Saldívar, José Limon, Guillermo Gomez-Peña, and others, focuses on the complex exchanges between the United States, Mexico, Latin America, and the Caribbean across these real and imagined borders. Works such as the multilingual *Borderlands/La Frontera* (1987) by Gloria Anzaldúa (1942–2004) foreground "boundary" issues such as immigration and diaspora; the intersections of racism, sexism, and homophobia; and cultural hybridization and creativity.

The boundaries of ethnic and cultural identity are also key themes within Native American studies. Writers and theorists such as N. Scott Momaday, Paula Gunn Allen, Leslie Marmon Silko, Louise Erdrich, Arnold Krupat, and Gerald Vizenor have examined the history and traditions of native peoples in America and Canada, often marginalized within the dominant culture.

In the field of Asian American studies, theorists note that Asian Americans are a broad and heterogeneous group whose experiences cannot be reduced to a hyphenated identity. Asian American writers such as Maxine Hong Kingston, Amy Tan, Frank Chin, Bapsi Sidhwa, Lois-Ann Yamanaka, and Bharati Mukherjee, as well as theorists Lisa Lowe, Shirley Leok-lin Lim, Yen Le Espiritu, E. San Juan, and Ronald Takaki have analyzed the complex problems of ethnic assimilation, identification, and discrimination, as well as the ambiguous distinction of "model minority," within U.S. culture.

Critical race studies. In the past three decades, the concept of race—largely neglected within earlier theories—became the focus of Critical Race Theory, originally a branch of legal studies, and later also a movement within the humanities. The legal scholars Derek Bell, Richard Delgado, Alan Freeman, Patricia Williams, Kimberle Crenshaw, Angela Harris, and David Theo Goldberg; the philosopher Kwame Anthony Appiah; the cultural historian Cornell West; and many others have analyzed concepts of race, their history, and their problematic application within the American legal system, the academy, and the culture at large. They argue that race and racism, although seemingly "deconstructed" by a society that aims to be "color-blind" in its administration of justice, remain entrenched and often unconscious forces.

FEMINISM AND QUEER THEORY

In 1949 the philosopher and novelist Simone de Beauvoir (1908–1986) published her landmark book, *Le deuxième sexe* (English trans., *The Second Sex*, 1984), arguing that "One is not born, but rather becomes, a woman." De Beauvoir held that women might achieve their liberation only by understanding their status and roles as second-class citizens within patriarchal (male-dominated) societies.

By the late 1960s, the women's movement in the United States and England was well underway. Thousands of American women participated in consciousness-raising groups, analyzing the multiple causes of women's oppression. Popular works such as *The Feminine Mystique* (1963) by Betty Friedan (1921–), *Sexual Politics* (1970) by Kate Millett (1934–), and *The Female Eunuch* (1970) by Germaine Greer (1939–) and the edited collections *Sisterhood Is Powerful* (1970) and *Women in a Sexist Society: Studies in Power and Powerlessness* (1971) helped galvanize mass resistance to gender inequality. In England, seminal works such as *Women: Resistance and Revolution* (1972), by Juliet Mitchell (1940–), and *Women's Consciousness, Man's World* (1973), by Sheila Rowbotham (1943–), helped advance the women's movement.

Feminist theory in England and America. Feminists in literary studies noted the cultural neglect or suppression of women writers—a situation they sought to remedy by publishing forgotten or little-known writings by women authors, and by theorizing the nature of women's writing and creativity. In *A Literature of Their Own* (1977) Elaine Showalter (1941–) studied generations of British women writers, identifying a distinctive female tradition and literary aesthetic. Sandra Gilbert (1936–) and Susan Gubar (1944–) analyzed the psychological difficulties faced by nineteenth-century women writers in Britain as they combated the misogynistic fantasies and stereotypes projected upon them (*The Madwoman in the Attic: The Woman Writer and the Nineteenth-Century Literary Imagination*, 1979).

Yet by the 1980s, the monolithic category of "woman"—initially a powerful organizing concept in feminism—soon began to give way to a plurality of definitions and accompanying theories that explored differences between women. In her essay "Compulsory Heterosexuality and Lesbian Existence" (1980), poet and essayist Adrienne Rich (1929–) questioned the feminist rhetoric of sisterhood by pointing out the homophobia of certain sectors of the women's movement. Similarly, feminists of color analyzed the exclusions implicit in white, middle-class feminist theory. In *Ain't I a Woman?* (1981), bell hooks (1953–) argued that the mainstream feminist movement was reinforcing rather than challenging the racial and class prejudices of the culture. *This Bridge Called My Back: Writings by Radical Women of Color* (1981), an influential anthology of essays, poetry, and short fiction edited by Gloria Anzaldúa and Cherríe Moraga (1952–), also drew attention to the blind spots of feminist theory regarding racism, homophobia, misogyny, and classism.

French feminism. At the same time, the ideas of French feminists began to reshape the Anglo-American feminist conversation—especially those of Julia Kristeva, Luce Irigaray, and Hélène Cixous. In different ways, each member of this trio, deeply influenced by Lacanian psychoanalysis and deconstruction, had emphasized the role of language, the body (male and female), and the unconscious in the construction of patriarchy.

In her influential essay "Rire de la Méduse" (1975; English trans. "Laugh of the Medusa," 1976), Cixous (1937–) posited the notion of *écriture féminine* ("feminine writing"), a nonlinear, associative style of writing that "writes the body" through its foregrounding of sexuality and erotic desire. By its very nature *écriture féminine* challenges "phallocentric" (masculinist) thought structures—including those of psychoanalysis itself. Liberating on several levels, *écriture féminine* is a style of writing available to women *and* to men. Such writing, Cixous argued, taps into the basic bisexuality of all humans with its fearless imaginings of the body.

Gender and queer theory. In the 1980s, psychoanalytic feminists such as Jane Gallop, Jacqueline Rose, Mary Jacobus, and Toril Moi introduced Lacanian and French feminist theory to enthusiastic new audiences in the United States and Britain. Because of its emphasis on sexual difference, French feminism helped give rise to a new branch of feminist theory focusing on the "sex-gender distinction"—"sex" connoting biological differences of males and females and "gender" the socially constructed ones. In *Gender Trouble* (1990) and *Bodies that Matter* (1993), the American philosopher Judith Butler (1956–) further theorized the sex–gender distinction. Gender identity, she argued, depends on a culturally dictated set of roles that one performs continually, rather like an actor following a script. Normative gender roles are frequently constricting or destructive, while deviance from such roles often results in punishment or disapproval. Despite its socially determinist overtones, Butler's theory allows for individual and collective resistance. For example, the performance of certain "queer" roles, such as wearing drag, destabilizes the existing categories and gender identities attached to them.

In the 1980s and 1990s, gay and lesbian activists had adopted the "derogatory" term "queer" as a means of confronting and resisting homophobia in the culture, also using the term as a rallying cry. Queer theory seeks to dispel heterosexist prejudice by analyzing its structures in new ways. Employing a set of deconstructive interpretive moves inspired by Derrida, theorists such as Butler, Monique Wittig, Eve Kosofsky Sedgwick, Paul Morrison, and Michael Moon have analyzed the "queer" elements implicit in normative heterosexual culture. They also explore the contingent nature of sexuality, its historical variability, and its inexhaustible representations in literature, film, the visual arts, and popular culture. Queer theory, together with feminism, has had a tremendous impact on the humanities and social sciences.

THEORY AND THE TRANSFORMATION OF LITERARY STUDIES

By the late 1970s and 1980s, theory had become a topic of intense interest in colleges and universities in the United States and Britain. Theorists of various schools debated their positions in classrooms, conferences, books, and journals. These debates were not merely academic, since they had important consequences for how literature, languages, and writing would be taught to the next generation.

The Anglo-American formalist tradition. The term "formalism" designates any method of critical interpretation that focuses on the form rather than the content or context of a literary work. New Criticism, the formalist method that held sway in the American academy from the 1930s until the 1970s, was predicated on the view that poems, novels, and other literary texts are self-contained aesthetic artifacts. New Critics held that a genuine understanding and appreciation of a text's literariness could be achieved only through an objective analysis of its formal construction, rhetoric, and internal cohesion, rather than from the study of the author's biography or intention, or the social or historical context of the work.

Leading exponents of the New Criticism in the United States included the literary critics Cleanth Brooks, John Crowe Ransom, R. P. Blackmur, W. K. Wimsatt, and Monroe Beardsley. In England, the Cambridge literary scholar F. R. Leavis, his wife and coauthor Q. D. Leavis, and the literary theorists I. A. Richards and William Empson developed similar methods of formalist criticism, influential for decades. Two midcentury formalists, whose innovative works cannot be easily categorized, also exerted considerable influence on Anglo-American literary studies: the American rhetorician and aesthetic theorist Kenneth Burke and the Canadian critic Northrop Frye, author of the influential study of literary genre *Anatomy of Criticism* (1957). Insisting on the systematic and objective approach to literature and the aesthetic, the formalists contributed to the rise of English literature as a serious field of study. Their techniques of interpretation are still taught today as the practice of "close reading," the careful analysis of literary texts and their rhetorical devices.

The Deconstructive Turn. By the 1970s and 1980s, literary scholars at Yale University, including Paul de Man, J. Hillis Miller, Geoffrey Hartman, Barbara Johnson, and Shoshana Felman, had introduced Derrida and his works to an American audience. Deconstruction, primarily a philosophical movement until that point, became a literary critical one in the United States, as deconstruction fused with earlier formalisms to create a new approach to close reading. Instead of focusing on the unity and cohesion of literary works, the mark of New Criticism, deconstructionists looked at the difference between the presumed "meaning" of a literary text and the rhetorical structures that convey them. This technique of rhetorical reading, foregrounding "undecidability," was pioneered by Paul de Man (1919–1983), generally considered the founder of deconstruction in America.

Deconstruction opened up a new range of interpretive possibilities as exciting to some as they were unsettling to others, depending on their tolerance for ambiguity. Deconstruction, though highly controversial, had a profound impact on literary studies in the United States. Derrida's decentering critiques of binaries hierarchies had many useful applications within feminist and queer studies, postcolonial theory, and other discourses challenging the status quo. Deconstruction, together with other forms of poststructuralist theory, would also open up an intense debate regarding the canon of English and American literature.

The culture wars. From the early twentieth century until roughly the 1970s, the curricula of most literature departments were organized around the teaching and transmission of the literary canon, the generally agreed-upon roster of great books in English, beginning with *Beowulf* and culminating in modernist works such as T. S. Eliot's poem "The Wasteland." This consensus would change with the gradual percolation of theory through the Anglo-American academy.

By the 1980s, the sociologist Pierre Bourdieu, the literary and legal theorists Barbara Herrnstein Smith and Stanley Fish, the philosopher Richard Rorty, and other theorists of axiology (the study of value) had offered influential relativist accounts of ethical and aesthetic judgments. Reader-response critics such as Jane Tompkins, Wolfgang Iser, Stephen Mailloux, and Janice Radway emphasized the role of the reader in the interpretive process, contesting the New Critical credo that meanings are contained and fixed within a literary text; rather, they argued, interpretive communities of readers generate meanings.

The net effect of these and related theoretical debates was a collective rethinking of the traditional literary canon, which had previously been consolidated and defended with claims of its timeless and self-evident excellence.

Soon a nationwide debate on the canon, often acrimonious, was underway both inside and outside the academy. While traditionalists defended the older canon and argued for its preservation, progressives argued for an expanded and more inclusive multicultural canon and for the restructuring of English department curricula. As literary historians brought to light important works by women and minority writers of the past, the canon of British and American literature began to expand. Partly as a result of increasing globalization, the works of Anglophone (English-speaking) writers from Africa, South Asia, the Caribbean, and Australia, and of a new generation of American and British writers more diverse than at any previous point in U.S. history, also achieved greater prominence within the literary canon. Significantly reconfigured in the past several decades, the canon continues to evolve rapidly.

The rise of cultural studies. While many scholars have contested or defended the literary canon, others have sought to dissolve the distinction between high and low culture implied by the concept of "literature," and to focus instead on the study of everyday culture. A theoretical school originating in Britain, cultural studies was developed in the 1970s and 1980s by Raymond Williams, Stuart Hall, Dick Hebdige, and others. It theorizes the ways in which people create and consume culture, especially within Western capitalist societies. Film, television, rock music, advertisements, or any other forms of expression serve as objects of analysis and ideological exploration for cultural studies theorists, along with the subcultures that may crystallize around certain popular phenomena. As a critical discourse, cultural studies has revolutionized literary studies by reconfiguring and expanding the field.

New historicism. Closely allied with cultural studies is the interpretive school known as New Historicism, a form of historically and socially oriented theory that arose in the 1980s and 1990s within the field of early modern literary studies. Pioneered by Stephen Greenblatt, Louis Montrose, and Leah Marcus and many others in the United States, New Historicism showed strong affinities with the cultural materialism of the British critics Catherine Belsey, Alan Sinfield, Peter Stallybrass, and Jonathan Dollimore. New Historicism transformed the study of

Shakespeare and the English Renaissance—and of other historical periods as well—by situating plays, poems, and prose of a given era in novel cultural, social, and economic contexts. New Historicist interpretations illuminate the hidden fantasies, beliefs, desires, fears, and power relations particular to a given time and place and refracted through cultural artifacts. Counteracting the aestheticism of earlier Anglo-American literary criticism, as well as the ahistorical textual analyses of deconstruction, New Historicism became a critical norm within English departments by the mid-1980s and continues to be practiced today. Like cultural studies, New Historicism has been a major force in the transformation of literary studies in the United States and Britain.

The future of theory. As the dust settles after the major upheavals in the United States and British academies resulting from the theoretical debates of the past several decades, some would say that theory is now dead, its various missions more or less accomplished. Although it may be true that some theoretical debates have played themselves out, and that the field has entered a phase of consolidation rather than rapid transformation, there is always room for more theory. New theories are likely to emerge in response to scientific and medical discoveries, technological developments, to political, social, and environmental quandaries, and, finally, to art—new and old, and defined in new and artful ways. Fortunately for the next generation of theorists, all the questions have not been asked, nor will they ever be.

With special thanks to Cathy Caruth, Eric Chapelle, Jeffrey Kahan, Sidney Monas, and Helena Woodard.

[*See also* The Author; Black British Literature; The Canon; Sigmund Freud; Genre; F. R. Leavis; Literature; Karl Marx; Narrative; Orientalism; Reading; *and* Raymond Williams.]

FURTHER READING

GENERAL REFERENCE

Culler, Jonathan. *Literary Theory: A Very Short Introduction.* Oxford, 1997. An excellent pocket guide to the basics, focusing on topics rather than schools of theory.

Groden, Michael, Martin Kreiswirth, and Imre Szeman, eds. *The Johns Hopkins Guide to Literary Theory and Criticism.* 2nd ed. Baltimore, 2005. The most comprehensive encyclopedia of theory to date.

Knellwolf, Christa, and Christopher Norris, eds. *The Cambridge History of Literary Criticism.* Vol. 9, *Twentieth-Century Historical, Philosophical and Psychological Perspectives.* Cambridge, U.K. 2001. This important collection of essays provides deep background on recent theory, including several schools not covered by this essay.

Macey, David. *The Penguin Dictionary of Critical Theory.* London, 2000. A succinct and highly useful reference work defining key concepts, figures, and schools of contemporary theory.

Murfin, Ross, and Supryia M. Ray. *The Bedford Glossary of Critical and Literary Terms.* 2nd ed. Boston, 2003. A valuable reference work for students of literature, this detailed glossary explains fundamental concepts of literary criticism and literary theory.

ESSAY COLLECTIONS AND SECONDARY WORKS ON SCHOOLS OF LITERARY THEORY

Ashcroft, Bill, Gareth Griffiths, and Helen Tiffin. *The Empire Writes Back: Theory and Practice in Post-Colonial Literatures.* 2nd ed. London, 2002. An introduction to the major debates on postcolonial writing and theory.

Best, Stephen, and Douglas Kellner. *The Postmodern Turn.* New York, 1997. An excellent overview of the postmodern debate and its ramifications in many fields.

Brannigan, John. *New Historicism and Cultural Materialism.* New York, 1998. A useful study describing the rise of historicist literary study in England and America.

Calderón, Héctor and José David Saldívar. *Criticism in the Borderlands: Studies in Chicano Literature, Culture, and Ideology.* Durham, NC, 1991. An important collection of essays on Chicano literary theory.

Culler, Jonathan. *Structuralist Poetics: Structuralism, Linguistics, and the Study of Literature.* Ithaca, NY, 1975. Classic introduction to structuralism and its impact on literary studies.

Descombes, Vincent. *Modern French Philosophy.* Translated by L. Scott-Fox and J. M. Harding. 1973; Cambridge, U.K., 1980. An advanced introduction to the works of Foucault, Derrida, and other poststructuralists in relation to the key figures in continental philosophy.

Eagleton, Terry, ed. *Marxist Literary Theory: A Reader.* Oxford, 1996. An extensive collection featuring works of key Marxist theorists.

Ellmann, Maud. *Psychoanalytic Literary Criticism.* Harlow, U.K., 1994. A helpful collection of influential statements linking psychoanalysis and literature.

Greenblatt, Stephen, and Giles Gunn. *Redrawing the Boundaries: The Transformation of English and American Literary Studies.* New York, 1992. Insightful and informative essays tracing the impact of theory on many subdisciplines within literary studies.

Lim, Shirley Geok-lin, and Amy Ling. *Reading the Literatures of Asian America.* Philadelphia, 1992. An influential, topically organized collection of Asian American literary criticism and theory.

Marks, Elaine, and Isabelle de Courtivron, eds. *New French Feminisms: An Anthology.* New York, 1980. An important introduction to French feminist writers in their own words.

Mongia, Padmini, ed. *Contemporary Postcolonial Theory: A Reader.* New York, 1996. An anthology of the major theorists in the field of postcolonial studies, with a useful bibliography appended.

Morland, Iain, and Annabelle Wilcox, eds. *Queer Theory.* New York, 2005. A recent anthology of theoretical writings providing an excellent overview of the field.

Napier, Winston, ed. *African American Literary Theory: A Reader.* New York, 2000. A highly useful collection of writings representing the major movements and trends of African American theory.

Norris, Christopher. *Deconstruction: Theory and Practice.* 3rd ed. London, 2002. Acclaimed guide to deconstruction with a useful updated bibliography of the field.

Patai, Daphne, and Wilfrido Corral, eds. *Theory's Empire: An Anthology of Dissent.* New York, 2005. These new "counter-theory" essays identify the parameters of recent theoretical debates and challenge their perceived limitations.

Sturrock, John, and Jean-Michel Rabaté. *Structuralism.* 2nd ed. Oxford, 2003. A concise introduction to structuralism presented in a reader-friendly fashion.

Tompkins, Jane P. *Reader-Response Criticism: From Formalism to Post-Structuralism.* Baltimore, 1980. Well-regarded collection presenting a broad range of theorists analyzing the role of the reader.

Turner, Graeme. *British Cultural Studies: An Introduction.* 3rd ed. London, 2003. Popular introduction to the field of cultural studies in relation to other theoretical discourses.

Vizenor, Gerald. *Narrative Chance: Postmodern Discourse*

on Native American Indian Literatures. Reprint, Norman, OK, 1993. The essays in this influential collection analyze Native American literature through the lens of postmodernism.

Warhol, Robin, and Diane Price Herndl. *Feminisms: An Anthology of Literary Theory and Criticism.* 2nd ed. New Brunswick, NJ, 1997. A comprehensive and well-organized anthology of feminist criticism and theory.

Wright, Elizabeth. *Psychoanalytic Criticism: A Reappraisal.* 2nd ed. London, 1998. Advanced introduction to the principal schools of psychoanalysis and their applications for literature and art.

LITERATURE

Trevor Ross

"Literature" is the collective noun for the category of verbal art that includes poems, plays, novels, and short stories. Though this use of the word is a relatively recent application, the kinds of works it denotes are among the oldest and most widely produced forms of creative expression. Philosophers and literary critics have long tried to describe the essential characteristics of these works and to distinguish them from those of other genres of oral and written communication. That they have never agreed on a workable definition for literature and that the word is one of many terms that have been used to identify these works may indicate that the category is protean and its boundaries porous. Yet people generally know what is meant by literature and can freely cite examples of it. The idea of literature is, at the least, conventionally intelligible. It is equally possible that literary writings satisfy human desires that run far deeper than prevailing conventions of thought.

The origins of literature are prehistoric. It was developed, it appears, to address a number of basic cognitive and psychological needs, which may well have become ingrained through evolution (Hernadi 2001; Turner). Other forms of communication have served similar purposes, but literature remains the one most recognized as specially designed to address these needs. A work that meets these needs gives pleasure, and the nature of this pleasure is largely the same whether the work is serious in tone, suspense inducing, wildly imaginative, semantically rich, rhetorically inspiring, or harshly satiric. Since this pleasure springs from so deep a source and is available from so great a variety of works, neither its nature nor literature's may finally be amenable to abstract definition. Not all literary works succeed at pleasing, and in fact by "literature" is often meant a canon of esteemed writings, as is implied by "British literature" in the title of this encyclopedia. But even failed examples of literature share with other literary works certain features and conventions intended to fulfill the form's essential purposes.

These features fall into two groups, those involving the expressive use of words and those involving their use in representation. These groups intersect at some points, and it is possible to see their features as forming a broad spectrum of literary effects, with verbal figures at one end and fictional modes at the other. But there is no simple relation between these features and their possible effects. Several features perform more than one purpose or produce more than one effect. Metaphors, for example, can have both affective uses as forms of wordplay and cognitive uses as creative ways of depicting experience. Most literary works aim to satisfy more than one need by containing examples of both types of features, and authors are daily altering these features in novel uses and variations. This may explain why theories of literature have tended to emphasize one or the other group of features as literature's defining properties, since it has so far not proven easy to identify what all of these features have in common.

LITERATURE AS A VERBAL ART

The features of the first type rely on the inventive use of language's physical or signifying dimensions. Sound patterning is essential to verse, if not literature in general. Poets have occasionally utilized aural elements, such as the onomatopoeic mimicry of natural sounds, as a rudimentary form of representation to reinforce their meaning, but these elements are principally used for sensory purposes and hence operate at a level mostly below rational cognition. Iambic meter, for instance, is widely prevalent in English poetic and dramatic verse because it approximates the sound of the human heartbeat. The regularity of metrical expression makes it easy to remember, and for much of history and especially in oral cultures, poetry has been championed as an aid to communal memory. Since it also stimulates the ear through resonant patterns of rhythm and cadence, poetry partakes of many of the same somatic and harmonizing functions of music and dance. Other sound patterns in poetry, such as rhyme and stanza structure, perform similar functions while equally appealing to the understanding. Rhyme, for one, can be used to suggest balance and closure, which are deeply satisfying to the mind. From time to time literary writers have also experimented with another basic mode of sensory processing, pictorial recognition, to supplement a text's meaning with aspects of its visual design. Shaped or concrete poetry, as well as such self-reflexive exercises in book layout as Laurence Sterne's in *Tristram Shandy*, engage higher rational processes than do simple emblems, but part of their agreeable effect involves the sudden recognition of congruity between visual and verbal elements.

The ability to compare unlike things is one of the mind's default modes for organizing experience, and its primary mechanism for developing this ability is metaphor. Literature, according to some theories, represents a peculiarly refined and inventive use of metaphor and other figures to extend the range of signification. Russian formalist critics believed that literature's essential quality, its "literariness," lay in how it deviated from everyday speech in order to defamiliarize readers with ordinary ways of perceiving and describing the world. New Critical and deconstructive theorists have similarly emphasized how literary writings, unlike other discourses, compress or complicate meaning so as either to suggest underlying unities of thought or to reveal language's instabilities and referential limits. Whether or not such a thing as literary language could ever be firmly distinguished from ordinary speech, it is historically the case that poets and prose stylists have long been celebrated for enriching the language of their community, enlarging its vocabulary and enlivening sense with apt phrases and devices. Tropes, symbols, and rhetorical figures are a necessary if not sufficient ingredient in most poetic genres and perform at least an important secondary role in dramatic dialogue, prose satires, modernist fiction, and oratorical speech. Like sound patterns, they are almost always deployed in conjunction with other elements, though some, like irony, can be sustained over an entire work.

Poetic sounds and figures have sometimes been assigned additional moral and psychological functions over and above their formal and semantic values. Critics in Latin antiquity and early modern Europe, two cultures deeply informed by rhetorical norms, not only equated poetry chiefly with the arrangement and figurative use of words but laid great store by its power to persuade, instruct, and ultimately give shape to social life. For them it was an article of faith that eloquent, sublime, or impassioned speech could bring about in its auditors emotional and intellectual responses so intense as to over-power the mind. Philosophers since Plato have likewise worried over these effects in a way that implied that they too believed that what set literature apart from other utterances was its affective force. To some degree this belief survives in a modified version within aesthetic accounts of how creative works refine the sensibility by attuning the senses to the intellect, the passions to the understanding. In accordance with their modern liberal faith in the freedom of the mind, however, aesthetic theorists diverge from earlier rhetoricians in insisting that the affectivity of literary art cannot be used to subdue reason since it is severely impaired when utilized for instrumental purposes like persuasion.

LITERATURE AS A REPRESENTATIONAL ART

Features of the second type involve the use of words to describe, order, or reimagine experience. Not so conventionalized as techniques of verbal form, these features serve four essential cognitive functions: mimesis, story making, fiction, and identification. Theories of mimesis, beginning with Aristotle's, emphasize literature's truth content and ability to present compelling verbal imitations of life as we know it. These theories diverge in how they describe the nature of literary knowledge, as either consisting of close accounts of particular perceptions or partaking of general truths and insights, though this knowledge remains difficult to define, seeing as literary works vary tremendously in how they convey it. Some genres, such as georgic description, realist fiction, autobiography, and the literature of travel, rely heavily on factual accuracy to arrive at plausible renderings of reality, while other nonfictional modes, like verse epistles, odes, and the essay, offer more abstract reflections. Most literary works refer in some measure to details and circumstances of the actual world, and all literary works can be interpreted for their moral and thematic relevance to life. In this way literary writing is unlike most other discourses, save perhaps for myth and parable, in that its meaning has wide applicability to multiple situations in life even if it is not usually expressed as constative statements of general truth. Yet precisely because it is mediated through verbal representations of particular aspects or episodes of life, literary knowledge has been dismissed by some, notably Plato, as trivial and superficial.

Story making is the mind's default mode for making sense of events. With effort it is possible to interpret the flow of experience in other ways, but story making is vital to survival since it allows the mind to develop memory by relating actions to their causes and to predict the their probable consequences. While it can take many forms, it is familiarly identified with narrative or the relating of connected events by one or more storytellers. Narrative is the defining attribute of several literary genres, from epic and fabliau to the short story and popular fiction, but it is also widely deployed as a method of ordering information in nonliterary discourses, including jokes, anecdotes, histories, films, and serial television. Dramatic genres are conventionally opposed to narrative forms because their stories are enacted rather than narrated. But plays present plotted sequences of actions performed by characters in given settings, which is why it is more precise to say that much literature, including drama, is composed of stories if not necessarily storytelling. Plots, or the cognitive patterning of events in time, are structurally indispensable in comedies and comic novels, among other genres, but stories are by definition absent from the lyric. That stories are not part of this ancient category of poetry may explain why few theories of literature posit story making as its primary function.

More common are theories that equate literature with fiction or, more broadly, world making. Story making is not possible without fiction, since the mind must envisage different possible outcomes for an action before it can determine its most probable consequence. But fiction, the cognitive invention of experiences beyond the known and familiar, has functions in addition to its role in stories. Dreams, fantasies, or rational speculation on hypothetical scenarios can be at once the source and manifestation of human desire and so impel and influence behavior. In contrast to communal fictions, such as myths and legends, literary writings work to articulate private or particularized fictions in a way that renders them intelligible and compelling to multiple readers. Most longer literary works present detailed virtual worlds, while many non-fictional genres, such as love poems, are at least fictive in encouraging readers to imagine a lyric speaker talking within a given situation. Some critics suggest that figurative language is itself a kind of world making, although it is hard to see what is gained by broadening the concept of fiction in this way (Miller). Fiction, unlike metaphor, is not in itself a means of understanding experience, so it does not satisfy all of the basic needs that literary works are expected to supply. This is likely why most theorists note the prevalence of fiction in literary discourse but stop short of proposing it as literature's defining essence. For similar reasons moralists have long distrusted fiction, which they see as an indulgence of the mind that en-courages impressionable readers to escape and even obliterate the mundane world for no constructive purpose. In response, literature's defenders like Sir Philip Sidney have claimed that, as literature does not purport to state factual truth, its use of fiction cannot deceive; yet the claim does not so much answer the moralists' qualms as obscure literature's relation to truth. Though fiction has important cognitive uses in helping readers transcend habitual thinking, a literary work's significance is usually believed to derive from what it says about the world and how it says it.

Identification overlaps with fiction in that it has to do with how literature engages readers in imaginatively perceiving life from the point of view of another. Individuals learn to become social beings by opening themselves to otherness through impersonation and vicarious experience. Literature is only one of a number of discourses whose purpose it is to inspire this hermeneutic process, but several literary genres extend special opportunities for identifying with others. Acting in drama is the most immersive form of role-playing, yet drama also depends for some of its effect on the experience of impersonation in the sense that audiences are invited to examine the dynamics of both actors performing and characters engaging in public self-presentation. Sympathetic identification with fictional characters is not only a common response readers have to literary works but one they are quite conscious of and keen to share and discuss with other readers. Identification is not restricted to fiction and can be shaped by techniques other than characterization or the depiction of virtual lives. Tone, point of view, and the use of authorial personae are all methods for positioning readers so as to encourage them to entertain and side with particular attitudes toward a work's subject. Readers may also be positioned in a different way by the peculiarly intimate yet indirect quality of soliloquy, interior monologue, and lyric utterance—poetry is "overheard," in John Stuart Mill's dictum—which inspire them at once to share and contemplate the private feelings of another. Identification is thus integral to how a great deal of literature works and a major source of its appeal, but it is neither its primary nor distinguishing feature.

LITERATURE AS A CONVENTIONAL CATEGORY

Given the difficulty of identifying a feature or function common to all literary works, authors and critics have long tried to suggest what literature is by opposing it to

316

what it is not. It is easy enough to say that, unlike other representational arts, literature uses only words and, unlike abstract arts like music, it relies largely on signification. Ordering the arts in this way does not assist in understanding the nature of literary composition. More influential have been those comparisons, like Horace's notion of *ut pictura poesis* (as is painting, so is poetry), that reveal parallels in what the sister arts aim to achieve.

Literature is commonly assumed to differ from other ways of communicating in either kind or degree of creativeness. Traditionally it has been contrasted with history and philosophy in terms of what knowledge each provides and how it provides that knowledge. Nowadays literature is popularly opposed to informative or analytical discourses, such as science and journalism, while its world-making functions appear to set it apart from the problem-solving tenor of legal, political, economic, and other discourses within the public sphere. Aesthetic theories stress literature's incompatibility with utilitarian speech, such as propaganda, and some treat literature as a normative category comprising works that can be shown to possess beauty, thematic richness, or other artistic quality. More informally critics have long discriminated between literature, as representing an evaluative standard, and anything they feel falls below that standard, from entire genres of popular fiction and escapist entertainment to works they merely consider distasteful, incomprehensible, or inadequate. Finally, literary criticism has sometimes been claimed as a branch of literature, and certainly some examples of criticism demonstrate sufficient formal traits to qualify as literary, but criticism is generally regarded as ancillary to creative writing.

All these are conventional discriminations whose force depends as much on belief as demonstrable evidence. Recognizing this, some critics have proposed that literature is no more than a cluster of genres linked by a family of discursive features, a cluster that expands or contracts in accordance with changing ideas of literature's value (Fowler). Other critics, notably cultural materialists and sociologists of literature, have gone further and argued that literature is merely what a culture or influential people within it have deemed as such (Bennett). Literature in this view is equivalent to the canon, to a set of works that have been preserved for either their artistic or historical interest, or to everything that is taught in literature departments and criticized by literary critics. These institutional definitions of literature are meant to contest claims for its autonomy and exclusiveness, but they do not necessarily explain why certain works are designated literature and not others. For any definition to give a sense of what literature is, it must identify the criteria of eligibility that people follow in deciding which writings are literary.

FROM POETRY TO LITERATURE

The word "literature" was first applied to the category of creative writings at the end of the eighteenth century. Originally, the word denoted the ability to form letters or, more usually, the quality of being learned in diverse subjects (Marino). By the eighteenth century this older meaning had begun to compete with a newer sense of literature as a body of printed matter related by form or subject matter. This sense survives in modern usage, as when one speaks of pamphlet literature or the literature on biomedical ethics. In some contexts the term can still be used to refer to a range of rhetorically sophisticated works that are not necessarily imaginative in content. This is especially the case with writings from earlier periods, in that it is possible to think of the King James Bible, Dorothy Osborne's letters, or Edmund Burke's *Reflections on the Revolution in France* as works of British literature and as material for literary study. Before the nineteenth century this range of writings could be designated as polite learning or belles lettres, but the oldest and most commonly used word for it was "poetry." Poetry had originally referred to the making of verses, which is why Aristotle had reservations about using it as a label for works of tragedy or epic, which he believed were primarily representational genres. After him, critics thought nothing of applying the label to plays, prose romances, didactic verse, or anything they regarded as fine writing.

This shift in terminology from "poetry" to "literature" perhaps signaled a narrowing of the category, henceforth to include principally imaginative writings. It may have also, as some believe, reflected a change in how literary writing was valued. "Literature" displaced "poetry," it is said, as a consequence of the activity becoming in some way autonomous. Gradually emancipated from the oversight of state and church, literature emerged as a distinct cultural field with its own rules for its production and reception (Bourdieu); once free speech was guaranteed by law, literature became the space where one could say anything without being obligated to refer to the world and ideas of what already existed (Derrida); while other discourses were developed to regulate knowledge, literature was left to itself to turn inward and become pure in the search for an intransitive language (Foucault); and severed from social hierarchies of speech, literature was no longer an instrument for imposing the will of the rulers upon the ruled but was transformed into something that anyone could write, in any form or style, and could use to interpret and remake the world (Rancière). All of these accounts locate the cause of literature's emergence in the rise of modernity and so imply that literature as we know it was effectively invented only at the turn of the nineteenth century.

It may be worth asking, however, why "literature" was chosen as the name for this invention. It was hardly a new word, after all, and its meaning was already well established. Arguably it was chosen to replace "poetry" as the term for imaginative writings because it more aptly connoted how people thought of the value and purpose of the writings. Whereas poetry had to do with making, with the craft of versifying and the creation of fictions, literature had long pertained to reading, either the condition of being well read or the books that were available to read. Whatever else may have happened to the category of verbal art at the end of the eighteenth century, the shift from "poetry" to "literature" implied a change in emphasis in how the category was defined, a change from writing to reading, production to consumption. The change was the upshot of several related developments, including a growth in readership at all ranks, the rise of the book trade and the subsequent commodification of books, the increasing pedagogical use of English writings as both models for composition and material for study and interpretation, and the ascendancy of the doctrines of taste and aesthetics that located literature's value in its beneficial effects upon the judgment and sensibility of the reader (Ross). Unlike poetry, literature was not something people did, it was something that could change them.

The distinction shapes thinking to this day. Courses of instruction in how to write poems, plays, or stories are designated programs in "creative writing" rather than "imaginative writing." Conversely, the poems, plays, and stories taught in literature classes are referred to as works of the imagination. The distinction has stayed in place in spite of the fact that literature has come to share most of its functions and features with the newer arts of radio, film, television, and computer games. For many this diffusion of imaginative expression across new media and technologies augurs the end of literature (Kernan), or at the least confirms that it makes little sense to treat liter-

ature as a category separate from other cultural works and practices. Yet it seems safe to say that, so long as reading is considered essential to self-formation, we will be reading literature.

[*See also* The Author; The Canon; Literary Theory; *and* Reading.]

FURTHER READING

Bennett, Tony. *Outside Literature.* London and New York, 1990.

Bourdieu, Pierre. *The Field of Cultural Production: Essays on Art and Literature.* Edited by Randal Johnson. New York, 1993. A collection of Bourdieu's important early position papers setting out his sociology of culture.

Derrida, Jacques. *Acts of Literature.* Edited by Derek Attridge. New York and London, 1992. A collection of the philosopher's writings on literary texts and the concept of literature.

Foucault, Michel. *The Order of Things: An Archaeology of Human Sciences.* London, 1970. Comments briefly but suggestively on the relation of literature to the discourses of knowledge.

Fowler, Alastair. *Kinds of Literature: An Introduction to the Theory of Genres and Modes.* Cambridge, MA, 1982. Important study of genre and its implications for understanding literature.

Hernadi, Paul. "Literature and Evolution." *SubStance* 94/95 (2001): 55–71.

Hernadi, Paul, ed. *What Is Literature?* Bloomington, IN, and London, 1978. A collection of essays on the problem of defining literature.

Kernan, Alvin. *The Death of Literature.* New Haven, CT, 1990. Typical of many laments from the culture wars about how the literature has been devalued in an age of electronic media.

Marino, Adrian. *The Biography of "the Idea of Literature" from Antiquity to the Baroque.* Translated by Virgil Stanciu and Charles M. Carlton. Albany, NY, 1996. Exhaustive survey of early notions of literature.

Miller, J. Hillis. *On Literature.* London and New York, 2002.

Rancière, Jacques. "The Politics of Literature." *SubStance* 33 (2004): 10–24. Important summary account linking the concept of literature to the rise of modern democratic politics.

Ross, Trevor. "The Emergence of Literature: Making and Reading the Canon in the Eighteenth Century." *ELH* 63 (1996): 397–422.

Terry, Richard. *Poetry and the Making of the English Literary Past, 1660–1781*. Oxford, 2001. A lively corrective to claims that date the invention of literature to the eighteenth century.

Turner, Mark. *The Literary Mind*. New York and Oxford, 1996. A provocative essay on how stories shape thought.

ANNE VAUGHAN LOCK

Susan M. Felch

The date is September 1545, the place the court of the bishop of London. A young schoolteacher, Master Cob, is again being examined for his radical religious views. Two years earlier he had been arrested for translating an illegal Lutheran commentary on the Gospels. A year later he was back in court, rescued on this occasion by the queen, Katherine Parr, who sent a personal emissary to plead on his behalf. Now in his third appearance, it is no light thing to stand accused in "matters of religion," for September 1545 lies almost midway between the arrest of the queen's friend, Anne Askew, in March 1545 and her death at the stake on 16 July 1546. In the middle of this high drama, court intrigue, and religious dispute stands an eleven-year-old girl, Anne Vaughan. This trial of her tutor, Master Cob, is the earliest documented glimpse we have of a woman who would become an important reformer in her own right.

Anne Vaughan (later Anne Vaughan Lock Dering Prowse) was born about 1534 in London to parents who served in the court of Henry VIII and died sometime before 1607. Her father, a cloth merchant, was a diplomat, and her mother was a silkwoman who supplied clothes for Henry's succession of queens. Anne received a rigorous education at home along with her younger brother and sister; she could read and write in English, French, and Latin, and probably in Greek and Italian as well. She was also deeply embroiled in the emerging Protestant Reformation from an early age. Her father defended William Tyndale, the man who first translated the Bible into modern English and was burned at the stake for his pains; her tutor got himself arrested; and Anne herself hosted the fiery Scottish preacher John Knox (c. 1513–1572) when he came to London to preach for Edward VI. By that time she was married to Henry Lock (also spelled Lok or Locke; died 1571), the son of another London cloth merchant whose family had smuggled banned Protestant books into England in the 1530s.

Anne Lock's friendship with Knox, some thirty years her senior, would prove decisive both for her life and for her writing. In the summer of 1553 outspoken Protestants in London found themselves faced with a difficult situation. King Edward died suddenly, and his sister Mary Tudor, who was devoted to the memory of her mother Katherine of Aragon and to her mother's Roman Catholicism, came to the throne. Knox, along with many others, fled to the Continent, and he soon began a correspondence with Lock, urging her to leave London and come to Geneva in Switzerland. Although her letters to him have been lost, fourteen of his letters to her survive; in them he warmly praises their friendship, responds to her questions, and asks for her advice and help.

With pressures mounting on Protestants, Lock left London in 1557 and traveled to Geneva with her two small children. Her husband apparently remained behind to look after the extended family's financial interests. Four days after she arrived in Geneva, her infant daughter Anne died. Yet despite this tragedy, Lock remained in Geneva with the colony of English exiles, participating in their social and religious life, and listening to the weekly sermons of the French reformer John Calvin. When she returned to London in 1559, after the accession of Elizabeth I, she published her first book.

LOCK'S FIRST BOOK

The main body of Lock's first book (1560) is a translation of four sermons preached by Calvin in November 1557 on the song of Hezekiah as found in Isaiah 38. These sermons address the subject of suffering, a topic about which Lock at age twenty-three knew a great deal. They also feature the biblical King Hezekiah, who was praised as a model Reformation hero for destroying a brass serpent that had degenerated from an emblem of healing to an object of superstitious adoration. The translation itself shows considerable skill; Lock worked from the manuscript transcriptions of Calvin's sermons, and her English version appeared before the French edition. But more impressive than the translation are the two original pieces that frame the book.

Lock presented her book as a New Year's gift to Katherine Willoughby Brandon Bertie, the dowager duchess of Suffolk (1520–1580), herself an exile during Mary Tudor's reign and one of the most prominent women in England. The preface is a masterpiece of elegant and persuasive rhetoric. Lock interweaves references to suffering and Hezekiah, the two themes of Calvin's sermons, with compliments to the duchess and covert advice to the new queen, Elizabeth. Taking as her central image the contrasting effects of good and bad medicine, Lock urges her readers to accept the good medicine of God's word, the Bible, as it is mixed into a powerful drug by the apothecary John Calvin and then delivered to his patients in an "English box" prepared by Lock herself. Along the way, Lock demonstrates her knowledge of contemporary medical practice, using technical terms for prescribed remedies and distinguishing between university-educated male physicians and nonbaccalaureate practitioners like herself. She crafts her language, using the rhetorical tools Master Cob had drilled into her, as she spins out long, balanced sentences or paints vivid word pictures. With theological and literary acuity, she extends the central image of good and bad medicine into a story of three oils: the oil of the scorpion (a contemporary wonder drug) that morphs into the brass serpent Hezekiah destroyed; the oil that lights the lamps of the wise (Protestant) virgins as they await the coming of their Lord (based on a parable first told in Matthew 25:1–13); and the oil the Good Samaritan uses to heal the wounded man (Luke 10:25–37), now identified as King Hezekiah on his deathbed. The parentheses of the previous sentence hint at the intricate and layered construction of Lock's writing.

Her rhetorical skill is again demonstrated in the closing section, a sequence of twenty-one sonnets on Psalm 51 that are preceded by five introductory, narrative sonnets and accompanied by an original prose translation of the psalm in the margins. Although other English writers, most notably Thomas Wyatt and Henry Howard, earl of Surrey, had begun to write sonnets a generation earlier, Lock was the first to construct a coherent sequence, and one that draws not only on the genre of sonnets with which we are still familiar, but also on the genre of biblical paraphrase or commentary popular in her own day. She called her sequence "A Meditation of a Penitent Sinner: Written in [the] Manner of a Paraphrase upon the 51st Psalm of David," and her poems combine the intensity of sonnet love and despair with the disciplined reflection that paraphrase demands.

The five introductory sonnets form a narrative frame for the anguished cries of repentance that are repeated in the psalm sonnets. In the first sonnet the speaker is par-alyzed as she sees her own stained life and the threatening sword of judgment. This double vision—one eye looking inward and one upward—characterizes the entire sequence, but it is a vision that is blurred, almost obscured, by a boiling cauldron of tears. In the second sonnet Lock moves to the prostrate body of a narrator who is unhorsed in an uneven jousting match. The third poem changes the scene to a courtroom where a personified Despair prosecutes the narrator, using her own admission of guilt to argue that she be banished from God. In the fourth poem an external Despair becomes unnecessary as the narrator's conscience performs the roles of prosecutor, judge, and executioner. She is dragged, insentient, into the very throat of Hell yet finds, in the fifth sonnet, just enough breath to murmur, "Mercy, mercy," at which point she is ready to articulate the prayer of repentance that is Psalm 51.

The "she" of the sonnets, however, is not merely a private individual but a representative of King David, that powerful but guilty monarch who first penned the psalm. Like Wyatt before her, who had crafted his poetic version of Psalm 51 in 1536 while imprisoned in the Tower of London, Lock was speaking to a nation faced with choices: Would England and her new ruler confess the sins committed under Mary Tudor's reign and return to God, or would they squander this opportunity? The concluding poems of the sequence anticipate the blessings that will come to the entire nation if its ruler and citizens repent and begin to rebuild the walls of Jerusalem, a figure that stands both for the Church and for England itself.

LOCK'S LATIN POEM

Lock's religious intensity did not abate in the years that followed her return from Geneva. After the death of her first husband, she married Edward Dering (c. 1540–1576), an elegant scholar turned preacher, who angered Elizabeth I when he warned her not to become like "an untamed and unruly heifer." That sermon, and the consequent loss of preaching privileges for Dering, led directly to Lock's single extant Latin poem. In 1572, the same year that Lock and Dering were married, the Cooke sisters undertook to rehabilitate his reputation with the queen. These sisters were writers as well as prominent, well-educated women with impeccable connections. Daughters of Anthony Cooke (1504–1576), who had tutored Edward VI, they were married to some of the most powerful men in England: Mildred (1526–1589) to William Cecil, Lord Burghley, one of Queen Elizabeth's chief counselors; Anne (1527/28–1610), the mother of Francis Bacon, to Nicholas Bacon, Lord Keeper of the Great Seal; Elizabeth (1528–1609) to Thomas Hoby, translator of Baldassare Castiglione's *The Courtier*, and later to John, Lord Russell, heir of the second earl of Bedford; and Katherine (c. 1530–1583) to Henry Killigrew, a diplomat in Queen Elizabeth's court. They were also friends with Anne Lock and Edward Dering. Together, this circle of reformers produced a beautifully illustrated manuscript of an Italian encyclopedia, the *Giardino cosmografico coltivato* (The cultivated garden of the world), prefaced by poems they had written in a variety of languages. Ostensibly dedicated to Robert Dudley, earl of Leicester, it was in fact addressed to the queen and was intended to convince her that her loyal opposition was indeed loyal—and learned.

Lock's contribution to the volume is a Latin quatrain that puns on the author's name: she praises Bartholo Sylva for providing as much delight to his readers as they might experience on a walk through a shady grove of trees.

Edward Dering died just four years after he married Anne Lock (1576), but she continued to exercise a potent influence on the political and religious world. In 1576 James Sanford, an unmemorable but prolific translator, dedicated a slightly revised volume to Christopher Hatton (1540–1591), captain of the royal guard. The revision, in fact, was merely a pretext for the preface, a sustained panegyric to Queen Elizabeth that praised her wisdom, polity, and learning but also offered reproof by setting before her the example of women who were not only wise and learned, but godly: "England hath had and hath at this day," said Sanford, "noble Gentlewomen famous for their learning, as the right honorable my Lady Burghley [Mildred Cooke Cecil], my Lady Russell [Elizabeth Cooke Hoby Russell], my Lady Bacon [Anne Cooke Bacon], Mistress Dering [Anne Lock], with others." Sanford's preface confirmed what the rest of London already knew—that the Cooke sisters and their circle, especially Anne Lock Dering, were women who mattered.

LOCK'S SECOND BOOK

By 1583 Anne Lock had married Richard Prowse of Exeter (died 1607) and moved with him to Devonshire. But she had hardly retired. John Field, preacher, printer, and pamphleteer, dedicated a book to her in 1583 noting that she was "no young scholar" in the school of Christ. That same year she was instrumental in bringing Christopher

Goodman, a friend since the Genevan exile, to preach at St. Peter's Church in Exeter. In 1590 she published her second book. Like the first, it was composed in three sections: an introductory preface, this time addressed to Anne Russell Dudley, the countess of Warwick and sister-in-law of Elizabeth Cooke Russell; the translation of a French devotional text on suffering by Jean Taffin; and an original poem urging England, once again, to repent.

Lock's religious community desperately needed her new book. The leadership had been decimated through death, imprisonment, and exile after a bitter struggle with the archbishop of Canterbury, John Whitgift, which culminated in an exchange of polemical pamphlets known as the Marprelate Controversy (1588–1589). In this context, Lock chose to translate Jean Taffin's *Of the Markes of the Children of God*, recently written for a persecuted church in Holland. *Of the Markes* proved to be both a comfort to the struggling English Puritans, among whom Lock counted herself, and a rebuke to the established Church. In her preface Lock reminded the countess not to hide her gifts under a bushel, but rather to use her political influence "to give light unto many." Lock herself acknowledged that although "great things by reason of my sex, I may not do . . . that which I may, I ought to do," and concluded that "I have according to my duty, brought my poor basket of stones to the strengthening of the walls of that Jerusalem, whereof (by grace) we are all both Citizens and members," thus recalling the conclusion of her own poems on Psalm 51 written some thirty years earlier.

LOCK'S INFLUENCE

That "poor basket of stones" was, in fact, enough to build a lasting edifice. Anne Lock remained a potent force in England throughout her own lifetime (she died before 1607) and into the seventeenth century. Her name as translator on her second book is printed as large as that of the author; as a mother of the church, her presence and authority—her imprimatur, as it were—were essential to the beleaguered members of her community, who republished her book seven times in the next forty-five years.

Her literary presence was also felt by her son, Henry Lok, who seemed unable to escape the sonnet form: he wrote hundreds of sonnets, and his versification of the book of Ecclesiastes imitates his mother's work on Psalm 51, combining doubled seven-line stanzas and paraphrase with a marginal prose translation. More important,

Lock's influence can be traced in the works of Mary Sidney Herbert, the countess of Pembroke, and Aemelia Lanyer, and her figure of Despair uncannily predicts the threatening Despaire who almost overwhelms the Redcrosse Knight in Edmund Spenser's *The Faerie Queene* (Book 1, Canto 9).

Lock maintained the friendships she had formed while an exile in Geneva and through them exercised considerable influence in Scotland. Christopher Goodman brought Lock's sonnets to Holy Trinity, the parish church in St. Andrews, and had Andrew Kemp create a polyphonic four-part setting for them. Thomas Wode included this musical rendition in the *St. Andrews Psalter* (University of Edinburgh, MSS La.III.483.1–3). Margaret Cunningham, a Scottish gentlewoman entrapped in a difficult marriage, took Lock's second book as her model. In 1607, she crafted a poem that appealed to her erring husband to repent and justified her remonstrances with these words: "It is little or nothing that I can do which I hope ye will consider in respect of my weak sex, but I pray God that every one of us according to that measure of grace the Lord hath given us may bring our poor basket of stones to the strengthening of the walls of Jerusalem whereof (by grace) we are all both citizens and members" (National Library of Scotland, MS 906).

Even after her death, Anne Lock was unable to escape the drama, intrigue, and disputes that had marked her life. But that, perhaps, is fit tribute for a writer who offered both good medicine and a basket of stones to her readers.

[*See also* Aemelia Lanyer; Mary Sidney, Countess of Pembroke; The Sonnet in the Renaissance; Henry Howard, Earl of Surrey; *and* Thomas Wyatt.]

SELECTED WORKS

Sermons of John Calvin, upon the songe that Ezechias made after he had bene sicke, and afflicted by the hand of God, conteyned in the 38. Chapiter of Esay (1560; Short Title Catalogue #4450)

"Ut iuvat umbriferum" [As a shadowy grove] in *Giardino cosmografico coltivato* [The cultivated garden of the world] (1574; Cambridge University Library, MS li.5.37)

Of the Markes of the Children of God, and of Their Comforts in Afflictions (1590; Short Title Catalogue #23652)

EDITION

Felch, Susan M., ed. *The Collected Works of Anne Vaughan Lock.* Tempe, AZ, 1999. The definitive edition of Lock's writings, with an extensive introduction to her life and works.

FURTHER READING

Baxter, Jamie Reid. "Thomas Wode, Christopher Goodman and the Curious Death of Scottish Music." *Scotlands* (1997): 1–20. Describes the content and context of the *St. Andrews Psalter.*

Collinson, Patrick. "The Role of Women in the English Reformation Illustrated by the Life and Friendships of Anne Locke." In *Godly People: Essays on English Protestantism and Puritanism,* edited by Patrick Collinson, 273–287. London, 1983. The seminal article on Anne Lock's life, with some attention to her writings.

Hannay, Margaret P. "'Unlock my lipps': The *Miserere mei Deus* of Anne Vaughan Lok and Mary Sidney Herbert, Countess of Pembroke." In *Privileging Gender in Early Modern England,* edited by Jean R. Brink, 19–36. Kirksville, MO, 1993. An important article dealing with Lock's influence on later writers.

Schleiner, Louise. *Tudor and Stuart Women Writers.* Bloomington, IN, 1994. The chapter on the Cooke sisters' circle includes a discussion of Anne Lock and her Latin poem.

Spiller, Michael R. G. "A Literary 'First': The Sonnet Sequence of Anne Locke (1560)." *Renaissance Studies* 11 (1997): 41–55. A literary consideration of the Psalm 51 poems, focusing on sonnet conventions.

White, Micheline. "Renaissance Englishwomen and Religious Translations: The Case of Anne Lock's *Of the Markes of the Children of God.*" *English Literary Renaissance* 29 (1999): 375–400. A contextual look at Anne Lock's 1590 book.

Woods, Susanne. *Lanyer: A Renaissance Woman Poet.* New York and Oxford, 1999. Includes substantive materials on the connections between Lock and Lanyer.

JOHN LOCKE

Zachary Sng

The multitude of topics that John Locke (1632–1704) wrote on in his lifetime might astonish the modern reader. The divisions between spheres of knowledge that we take for granted today were, however, largely irrelevant for the seventeenth-century man of letters. Together with such contemporaries as Robert Boyle, John Evelyn, and Isaac Newton, Locke participated in informal meetings and learned discussions dedicated to the investigation of matters as diverse as epistemology, monetary theory, physics, and forestry. These meetings resulted in the formation in 1662 of the Royal Society for Improving Natural Knowledge, which brought together thinkers committed to knowledge gained through experience and observation rather than theoretical speculation. Locke was elected a member in 1668, and his writings reflect a strong dedication to the principles and aims of the society.

Born to Puritan parents, Locke received an excellent education at Westminster School and at Christ Church, Oxford. As a student, he was exposed to the traditional brand of academic philosophy that he would later reject as hopelessly removed from human experience. Turning away from philosophy, Locke devoted much of his time at Oxford to the study of medicine and the natural sciences. In 1667 he accepted an invitation to move into the London household of Anthony Ashley Cooper, Lord Ashley, later the earl of Shaftesbury. There he became Cooper's secretary, family physician, and tutor, and a trusted advisor on political and commercial matters. As a member of the Shaftesbury household, Locke wrote a number of papers on trade and monetary policy, responding to the pressures of an impending currency crisis. Although his patron's fall from power in 1673 brought this phase of Locke's career to an end, it did not terminate his interest in state affairs. Locke eventually left England and spent a long period abroad in France and Holland, but

John Locke
Bronze medal by Jean Dassier, 1704
NATIONAL PORTRAIT GALLERY, LONDON

he returned in 1689 after the Glorious Revolution. He resumed his activities as a commentator on monetary and political matters and was soon appointed to the Board of Trade and Plantations as well as the Bank of England.

Upon his return to London, Locke began publishing a number of works that he had written and revised while abroad. *The Letter Concerning Toleration, Two Treatises of Government,* and the *Essay Concerning Human Understanding* all appeared within a year of his return, and they established Locke's reputation in England, France, and Germany. He also continued his activities with the Royal Society, and he turned his attention to new areas of inquiry such as pedagogy and religion, publishing *Some Thoughts Concerning Education* in 1693 and *The Reasonableness of Christianity* in 1695. The financial troubles of the new government prompted Locke to revisit his early work on money, and he published a number of economic papers in the 1690s in response to renewed debates. After a long struggle with illness, Locke died on 28 October 1704.

ESSAY CONCERNING HUMAN UNDERSTANDING

The aim of the *Essay,* Locke's best-known work, is to investigate the nature and limits of human knowledge. True to the spirit of the Royal Society, it claims to do so not by laying down axioms or universal truths from which to proceed, but rather by a disinterested observation of how knowledge is formed in the individual mind. Largely directed against the philosophy of René Descartes, its first book challenges the assumption that fundamental truths slumber within the soul, awaiting discovery by intellectual activity. Instead, Locke argues that ideas must enter the mind through some process, the description of which must be the starting point of the *Essay.*

The task of understanding "understanding" itself can therefore only begin with book II proper, after the ground has been cleared and prepared. Locke appeals to the reader's observation and experience, asking that we suppose the mind to resemble "white paper, void of all characters, without any ideas," and he proposes that everything with which it becomes supplied has to come from one or both of the two fountains of knowledge: sensation and reflection. The first provides the mind with impressions about external objects, and the second allows the mind to perceive its own operations. Together, they make up what Locke calls "experience." Locke further divides ideas into simple and complex ones. Simple ideas are the basic elements of experience: they are provided in discrete form through one or more senses, through reflection, or through a combination of both. Examples are heat and cold for simple ideas of sensation, thinking and willing for ideas of reflection, and pleasure and pain for simple ideas originating in both sensation and reflection. Simple ideas are perceived and not created by the mind, but the mind can combine them arbitrarily, thus producing complex ideas. In addition to combination, the mind is also capable of other operations on ideas, such as comparison and abstraction.

After this account of the origin and types of ideas, Locke plans to move on to describe how the understanding forms knowledge from ideas. He interrupts himself at this point, however, with a lengthy discourse on language that takes up the entirety of book III. This detour is, he claims, necessary because there is a close connection between ideas and words that has to be explicated. Locke's comments turn out, however, to be much more than an aside; he ends up delivering a historically important discourse on language and meaning. One major claim in this section is the challenge to an assumed relationship between words and things. Locke argues that words stand, instead, for ideas—first and foremost, ideas in the mind of the speaker, and then corresponding ideas that must be excited in the minds of the listeners. In addition, he rejects any natural connection between words and the ideas they stand for, and proposes instead that this connection is made by voluntary imposition—that is, by common agreement within a community of speakers. These and related claims are usually referred to as Locke's version of the "arbitrariness thesis" with regard to language. In taking this position, Locke disagreed with many seventeenth-century theorists of language who supported the notion of a divinely inspired and motivated original language.

Only after this outline of a theory of language is Locke able to move on to book IV, which is devoted to knowledge. This, Locke claims, is nothing but the perception of the connections between our ideas: that is, it is the perception of relationships such as agreement, disagreement, connection, and identity between particular ideas. The main innovation in this section is Locke's strict separation between the kinds of knowledge that involve a claim about "real existence," and those that do not. Knowledge about the identity or necessary connections obtaining between ideas is, for example, not knowledge about real existence. Even propositions concerning the supposed "essence" of things are removed from the question of their real existence, because they implicate only that peculiar mediating abstraction that Locke calls the "nominal essence" of things (basically, the set of properties that leads us to classify a thing in a certain way), as opposed to their "real essence."

TREATISES OF GOVERNMENT

The aims of Locke's *Two Treatises of Government* are twofold: first, to refute the doctrine of absolute monarchy, and second, to propose in positive terms an alternative theory of power. Locke's main opponent here was Robert Filmer, who had argued in *Patriarcha, or The Natural Power of Kings* (1680) for a divine basis for the authority of monarchs, passed down from Adam himself. In his *First Treatise*, Locke mounts a comprehensive critique of Filmer through a reading of numerous biblical passages. His own theory of government, expressed in the *Second Treatise*, is grounded in an argument for the natural rights of individuals and a social contract theory of political power.

Locke's starting point is the individual with natural rights to life, liberty, health, and property. Prior to the introduction of government, in a "natural state," all individuals have equal rights to these, and a natural law obtains. This law is revealed upon the application of reason, and it leads individuals to respect each other's rights as much as they value their own. Locke argues that the choice to violate this law is what results in slavery or war, thus taking issue with Thomas Hobbes, who equated the natural state with the state of war. In order to enforce this law of nature, and to mete out just punishment for its violation, civil government is introduced. This account of the origin of government carries important implications: because civil government is instituted to safeguard the natural rights of individuals, its power depends solely on the explicit consent of those governed. Any government that fails in its charge to protect the individuals it governs is thus illegitimate, and rebellion against it is, in turn, legitimate.

ECONOMIC AND RELIGIOUS WRITINGS

Locke's economic writings were produced in response to a series of crises during the period; as such, they do not provide a systematic theory of money or wealth. Nonetheless, Locke's pamphlets contain some early insights into the nature of money. He observes, for example, that there is a close connection between the value of money and the amount of it in circulation—in addition to being a unit of exchange, money is thus also a commodity whose price is determined by supply and demand. Although this idea is not fully worked out in Locke's writings, it has been read as one of the first articulations of the so-called quantity theory of money. Also original, although never consistently developed and thus frequently misunderstood, is Locke's insistence on the intrinsic value of coinage. For him, this refers not to some fixed value of the precious metal contained in coins, but rather to the value that common consent has placed on a particular denomination of coin. His commitment to this intrinsic value motivates him to reject intervention on the part of the state through the devaluation of coinage or a reduction of interest rates. For Locke, these measures would be tantamount to state-sponsored fraud, for they would cause coinage to have a different value from its intrinsic one.

Locke's main contribution to the history of religious thought came in the form of his arguments for religious toleration in three *Letters*. Although he did not challenge the antipapist trend of treating Roman Catholics as subjects of a foreign political power and therefore dangerous to British society, Locke's general stance was that matters of faith are to be individually decided and lie outside the purview of civil government. Religious persecution on the part of the state is therefore an illegitimate use of power. In essence, the view expressed in the *Letters* is compatible with Locke's view of government as laid out in the *Two Treatises*, the logical conclusion of which should be a separation of state and church.

LOCKE AND LITERATURE

The eighteenth century produced a number of important positive responses to Locke's views on the mind, on language, and on politics, alongside some very negative re-

actions, most notably from Samuel Taylor Coleridge and William Hazlitt. In general, however, modern scholars acknowledge Locke's importance for the development of British thought in the centuries that followed. Some historians of philosophy even refer to him as the "father of British empiricism," referring to the tradition of using experience as the ground of philosophy, as exemplified by thinkers such as George Berkeley or David Hume. Recent scholarship, however, has challenged this narrative by uncovering Locke's debt to earlier French sources such as Pierre Gassendi and Nicolas de Malebranche, and by pointing out the rationalist elements of the *Essay*.

In the field of literary studies, discussions of Locke's influence have been dominated by investigations into his importance for two developments in the eighteenth century: the rise of the novel, and the emergence of the Romantic aesthetic. The studies on Locke and the novel focus on his epistemology as part of a general philosophical climate that privileged individual experience over universal truths and eventually produced a skeptical stance by suspending the guarantee of knowledge (whether moral, psychological, or religious). The scholarship on Locke and Romanticism is more diverse. One major strand takes Locke's articulation of the complex relationship between mind and world as the inauguration of a philosophical problem to which Romanticism responded. In the vocabulary of M. H. Abrams's classic study, the question is whether the mind's role is like that of a mirror that passively reproduces, or like that of a lamp that actively functions as the source of illumination. Modern scholarship has moved away from the strong claim of a historical break between these two positions to favor a more nuanced account of the complexities present in both Locke's and the British Romantics' thoughts on the matter. Another important line of inquiry addresses the influence of Lockean theories of language on Romanticism. By freeing language from the constraints of the word-thing relationship, and insisting on the arbitrary character of the word-idea relationship that replaces it, Locke's theory of language could be read as the harbinger of the celebration of the creative, positing power of language that we associate with Romanticism. Percy Bysshe Shelley's remarks on the imagination in "A Defence of Poetry," for example, give it priority in the production of language and ideas that is thinkable only once the restraints of the word-thing correspondence have been loosened.

The collection and republication of Locke's economic writings in 1991 have also attracted the attention of literary scholars. By grounding coinage in a concept of intrinsic value as determined by common consent, these writings invite comparison with similarly central appeals to original, collective agreement in Locke's theories of language and of government. A corollary of Locke's position is a heightened anxiety about policing and safeguarding the integrity of these agreements; indeed, warnings about the consequences of corrupted integrity occur frequently in Locke's political, philosophical, and economic writings. Scholars have begun investigating the extent and implications of these correspondences, but this area of research is still in its early stage.

Another emerging area of interest is Locke's own rhetoric. Eloquence and the use of figural language were suspect for him because they open the door to misunderstandings and, even worse, to deliberate manipulation and abuse. Locke thus made several explicit condemnations of rhetoric in his texts. Paradoxically, however, his own writing depends heavily on rhetorical devices. For instance, a rich series of metaphors is employed for the mind in the *Essay*; examples include white paper, dark room, candle, mirror, and ship. Earlier commentators found it sufficient to abstract from these individual images the general idea of a tabula rasa ("blank slate," and a phrase that occurs nowhere in the *Essay*), but some modern critics, such as Paul de Man, raise questions about what epistemological consequences these images and the sheer fact of their proliferation might have for Locke's project in general. Such work, along with important studies of Locke's narrative technique in the *Essay*, suggests that it would be inadequate to take his statements about plain language and common sense at face value.

[*See* Joseph Addison; Thomas Hobbes; Romanticism; *and* Laurence Sterne.]

SELECTED WORKS

Letter on Toleration (1689)
Second Letter on Toleration (1690)
Two Treatises of Government (1690)
Essay Concerning Human Understanding (1690)
Some Considerations of the Consequences of Lowering of Interest, and Raising the Value of Money (1691)

Third Letter on Toleration (1692)
Some Thoughts Concerning Education (1693)
The Reasonableness of Christianity (1695)

EDITION

Kelly, Patrick Hyde, ed. *Locke on Money*. 2 vols. Oxford, 1991. An invaluable collection of Locke's writings on money. The introduction is especially informative on the historical context of Locke's economic thought.

FURTHER READING

Aarsleff, Hans. *From Locke to Saussure: Essays on the Study of Language and Intellectual History*. Minneapolis, MN, 1982. The introduction and the chapters on Locke provide a good introduction to his place in the history of European theories of language.

Abrams, M. H. *The Mirror and the Lamp: Romantic Theory and the Critical Tradition*. Oxford, 1953. The classic study on the relationship between British Romanticism and eighteenth-century philosophy.

Caffentzis, Constantine G. *Clipped Coins, Abused Words, and Civil Government: John Locke's Philosophy of Money*. New York, 1989. A brief study that attempts to establish connections among Locke's economics, philosophy, and theory of language.

Caruth, Cathy. *Empirical Truths and Critical Fictions: Locke, Wordsworth, Kant, Freud*. Baltimore, 1991. An insightful study of Locke's narrative technique in the *Essay*.

de Man, Paul. "The Epistemology of Metaphor." *Critical Inquiry* 5 (1978): 13–30. A brief but insightful reading of some key metaphors from the *Essay*.

Shapin, Steven. *A Social History of Truth: Civility and Science in Seventeenth-Century England*. Chicago, 1994. Discusses Locke in the context of the Royal Society's commitment to reliable testimony and decorous discourse in order to safeguard truth.

Walker, William. *Locke, Literary Criticism, and Philosophy*. Cambridge, U.K., 1994. A useful study of Locke's importance for the modern literary critic.

DAVID LODGE

Gavin Keulks

Few writers have so deftly worn the dual masks of creative writer and literary theorist as has David Lodge (born 1935). From the publication of his first novel, *The Picturegoers*, in 1960 to his 2002 collection of essays, *Consciousness and the Novel*, Lodge has published a dozen novels, nearly as many critical monographs, a handful of plays, and scores of scholarly essays, reviews, and reflections. These numbers assume eye-raising proportions when the circumstances behind their productivity are revealed: besides his duties as a writer and a scholar, Lodge has also worked full-time as a university professor, husband, and father of five children. When his first child was diagnosed with Down's syndrome, Lodge realized it would be financially impossible to walk away from academe; it was not until he was offered early retirement (and a pension) in 1987 that he could pursue writing full-time, becoming increasingly productive rather than slouching into retirement.

Throughout the many demands placed on his time and his patience, Lodge has consistently achieved remarkable levels of professional acuity and achievement. Irrespective of the work he will produce in the future, he has already solidified his reputation as one of the most lucid, intelligent, and entertaining writer-scholars of his generation.

THEORY AND BEYOND: LITERARY CRITICISM

Although Lodge has largely abandoned scholarship for creative writing since retiring from the University of Birmingham, his contributions to the field of literary criticism remain equally (if not more) impressive than his creative work. One might even argue, as others have, that Lodge is a major scholar and a minor novelist, provided that one perceives such classifications to be complimentary, not critical.

Few scholars since the 1960s have matched Lodge's ability to synthesize complex theories into intelligible, comprehensible patterns. His major books—*Language of Fiction* (1966); *The Novelist at the* Crossroads (1971); *The Modes of Modern Writing* (1977); *Working with Structur-*

alism (1981); and *After Bakhtin* (1990)—successfully elucidate the increasingly specialized academic debates that flourished during the late twentieth century. Many of these controversies were remarkably austere, and numerous critics crashed upon their rocks. Yet Lodge was able to complement his analysis with the patience, clarity, and concern for his audience that too often disappeared from more combative theorists. *The Language of Fiction*, for instance, argues persuasively for prose fiction to be as carefully studied as poetic diction. *The Novelist at the Crossroads* clarifies the highly contested evolution from modernism to postmodernism, yet Lodge's book is distinguished from similar texts on the subject through its historical grounding, its critical acumen, and its well-balanced prose. As numerous essays in these collections (and elsewhere) make clear, Lodge never concurred that the efficacy of "classical realism" had diminished in the postmodern age, yet his scholarly voice remains one of mediation, not provocation; of communication, not obfuscation.

The Modes of Modern Writing, *Working with Structuralism*, and *After Bakhtin* extend his earlier ideas into new terrain. In the late 1960s, especially 1968, the field of literary criticism segmented into diverse subjects, many of which seemed foreign to traditional literary analysis. This so-called linguistic turn differed dramatically from earlier analytical systems—such as Moral Formalism or New Criticism—that had been dominant from the 1930s to the 1950s. Whereas Lodge's earlier scholarly works could still invoke the orderings of those earlier movements—even if only as nostalgia—such invocations proved increasingly difficult after the rise of poststructuralism.

Impressively, Lodge's mind—and prose—proved to be equally as capable of clarifying post-Saussurean linguistics as they had previously managed to do with realism, modernism, and postmodernism. *The Modes of Modern Writing* arguably continues where *The Novelist at the Crossroads* left off—at the intersection between realism and postmodernism. It enlists Roman Jakobson's distinction between metaphor and metonymy to clarify the nuances of contemporary theories of mimesis. *Working with Structuralism* and *After Bakhtin* can also be perceived as symbolic "updatings," extending and refining the ideas of *The Language of Fiction*. Whereas that earlier text had preceded some of the more controversial theories, these latter works strive to reconcile structuralism and poststructuralism, textuality and postmodernism.

Near the turn of the century, Lodge would also articulate one of the best sustained objections to the High Theory of earlier decades. His later works of criticism—*The Art of Fiction* (1992), *The Practice of Writing* (1996), and *Consciousness and the Novel* (2002)—are thoughtful meditations on creativity, writing, and the role of the artist within society. They return to classical scholarly roots and are decidedly antitheoretical. In these books, Lodge seeks a more universal audience, and as a consequence his analyses are less sophisticated—although arguably longer-lasting—than his earlier publications. In many ways, they reflect the culmination of his dual careers as a writer and scholar, the product of six decades devoted to literature.

Successively, these nonfiction works established Lodge as one of the leading scholars of his generation—a position he never relinquished, even in the midst of the controversial theoretical upheavals that often ensnared lesser critics.

CHANGING PACES: FICTION

Throughout his career, David Lodge has perfectly balanced creative and academic work, often alternating between novels and scholarship. Many of his novels elucidate theoretical issues, striving to provoke creative solutions to critical quandaries. He was not always successful—reviewers sometimes found his experiments with narrative perspective or multiple endings intrusive—but many of his novels won major awards (e.g., *Changing Places* [1975], *How Far Can You Go?* [1980]), and two were short-listed for the coveted Booker Prize (*Small World* [1984] and *Nice Work* [1988]). The latter also won the Sunday Express Book of the Year Award for its year. In general, Lodge's novels reflect the tradition and tenets of literary realism, even though he occasionally vacations from that mode by dabbling with postmodern reflexivity, intertextuality, and pastiche. *The British Museum is Falling Down* (1965), for instance, is a tour de force of stylistic mimicry, an homage to many of the author's artistic influences—and his academic syllabi. It followed a series of coming-of-age, semi-autobiographical novels—*The Pic-*

turegoers (1960), *Ginger, You're Barmy* (1962), and *Out of the Shelter* (1970)—which satirized Lodge's discomfort with military action, surveying his own experiences in the army (*Ginger, You're Barmy*) and surviving Nazi blitzkriegs as a child in London (*Out of the Shelter*).

Among his many talents as a novelist, Lodge excels in creating precise and lively dialogue, well-defined characters, complex parallels and doubles, and wonderfully comic situations. Often these trademarks buttress commonplace themes, especially the opposition between Catholicism and sexuality, restraint and desire. A lifelong Catholic, Lodge strives in his fiction to reconcile the contingencies of human longing with the Vatican's reluctance to moderate doctrine.

The British Museum is Falling Down, for instance, leverages absurdist frustration against the Church's refusal to lift a contraception ban during the liberal 1960s. *How Far Can You Go?* resumes this critique twelve years after Pope Paul VI reaffirmed Church policy. Both novels lambaste the institutional irresponsibility of endorsing the rhythm method—comically labeled "Vatican Roulette" in *The British Museum*—which Lodge blames for marital discord, medical complications, and, ultimately, divorce. Later in his career Lodge returned to this theme of contrapuntal disappointment, both sexual and spiritual, with *Paradise News* (1991).

Readers generally agree that Lodge is most successful when writing within his hallmark subjects: Catholicism and academia. Lodge is far more than a Catholic author, however, and attempts to assimilate his work under the rubric of academic comedies of manners similarly underestimate his achievements. Like two of his satiric mentors—Kingsley Amis and Evelyn Waugh—Lodge is capable of traversing comic registers that range from the serious to the absurd. Such an expansive range affords him the liberty to experiment with narrative form in ways that Amis and Waugh never preferred. *How Far Can You Go?*, for instance, employs a series of self-reflexive narrative asides; *Small World* and *Nice Work* occasionally morph into heavily intertextual novels of ideas; and sections of *Therapy* (1995) manipulate credibility by celebrating their own artificiality. *Changing Places* is even more exhibitionist: throughout the novel Lodge adopts wildly divergent literary styles, ranging from Joycean minutiae—newspaper clippings, advertisements, and so on—to epistolary prose and the controversial final chapter, which is presented as a film script and proffers numerous conclusions to the reader.

For many readers, *Changing Places* remains Lodge's most memorable and important novel. Others opt for *Small World*, its sequel. In the first book, Lodge creates two of his most famous characters—Morris Zapp and Philip Swallow, two academics from different sides of the Atlantic who swap countries, universities, and, ultimately, wives. Its delicate equilibrium between academic discourse and comic morality is perfectly achieved until the final chapter, which Lodge extends only sufficiently to suggest possibilities for closure before ending abruptly, parodying the postmodern indeterminacy that was gaining favor at that time.

Small World resurrects Zapp and Swallow's characters. Although not as groundbreaking, the sequel is arguably more complex, tracing its parodic heroes from conference to abstruse conference in quest of romance, infidelity, narcissism, and the UNESCO Chair of Literary Criticism. Whereas Lodge satirized some of his own experiences teaching abroad in *Changing Places* (State University of Euphoria is a thinly veiled University of California, Berkeley), he playfully mocked academic superciliousness in *Small World*, especially the Modern Language Association annual convention and contemporary trends in scholarly discourse. These novels remain highly valued within academic circles for their aesthetic and cathartic pleasures; they are also responsible for generating scholarly interest in Lodge's fiction. *Changing Places* was the first of Lodge's novels to gain widespread coverage in the United States (he was always more popular in England), whereas *Small World* was widely successful.

Nice Work, *Paradise News*, and *Therapy* continue Lodge's examination of academia, faith, and the dualities of the modern world. An updated "Condition of England" novel, *Nice Work* narrates the opposing stories of Robyn Penrose and Vic Wilcox, headstrong doppelgängers who negotiate the hypocritical boundaries of each other's profession. Penrose is a Marxist-feminist professor at Rummidge University, the same school as Philip Swallow and a surrogate for Lodge's own University of Birmingham. Swallow and Zapp even make playful cameo appearances in the novel, traipsing between conferences (Zapp) or mellowing into middle age and midlevel management (Swallow, who is now a dean). Completing the opposition between town and gown, Wilcox labors as an engineering manager.

Paradise News and *Therapy* are less successful than Lodge's earlier novels, but they definitely reveal a new emphasis on human relationships—irrespective of the orthodox, often restrictive, worlds of academia and Church.

The first portrays a transformative journey to Hawaii that assimilates literary tropes of confession, renewal, and salvation. In the end, however, the novel can only suggest secular and agnostic redemption. As Dennis Jackson explains, the "spiritual salvation it offers lies in making deep personal connections with loved ones: family, friends, and lovers." *Therapy* extends such meditations while adding a philosophical component—the theological philosophy of Søren Kierkegaard.

Since the early 1990s, Lodge has devoted more of his energy to writing for the screen and stage. During this time he has adapted a number of his novels (and those of other people) for serialization on British television, and he has composed two full-length plays: *The Writing Game: A Comedy* (1990) and *Home Truths* (1998). In many ways this artistic swerve is structurally intriguing: like many of his novels, which often invoke their origins in their endings, Lodge seems to be returning to an earlier stage. In the mid-1960s he had collaborated on two dramatic productions in Birmingham.

His first creative works of the twenty-first century—*Thinks [. . .]* (2001) and *Author, Author* (2004)—are inventive, well-written, and enlivening, yet seem somewhat derivative of earlier work. The earlier book alternates stream-of-consciousness narration with diary entries to portray the indelicacies of love and study at the fictitious University of Gloucester. The latter novel—certainly the more ambitious of the two—is a "docunovel" on Henry James's life, which one reviewer called "singularly undramatic."

Whatever the future may hold for Lodge's creative and critical reputations, few people would contest that he was a central figure in scholarly debates for more than four decades. That is more than most people ever achieve. During this period Lodge also established himself as a highly successful comic novelist, thereby cementing his status as one of the most productive, ambitious, and clever writer-scholars of his time.

[*See also* Malcolm Bradbury.]

SELECTED WORKS

NOVELS

About Catholic Authors (1957)
The Picturegoers (1960)
Ginger, You're Barmy (1962)
The British Museum is Falling Down (1965)
Out of the Shelter (1970)
Changing Places: A Tale of Two Campuses (1975)

How Far Can You Go? (1980; republished as *Souls and Bodies*, 1982)

Small World: An Academic Romance (1984)

Nice Work (1988)

Paradise News (1991)

Therapy (1995)

Home Truths: A Novella (1999)

Thinks [. . .] (2001)

Author, Author (2004)

DRAMA

Between These Four Walls, with Malcolm Bradbury and James Duckett (1963)

Slap in the Middle, with James Duckett and David Turner (1965)

The Writing Game: A Comedy (1990)

Home Truths (1998)

NONFICTION

Language of Fiction: Essays in Criticism and Verbal Analysis of the English Novel (1966)

Graham Greene (1966)

"Emma": A Casebook (1968)

The Novelist at the Crossroads and Other Essays on Fiction and Criticism (1971)

Evelyn Waugh (1971)

Twentieth-Century Literary Criticism: A Reader (1972)

The Modes of Modern Writing: Metaphor, Metonymy and the Typology of Modern (1977)

Working with Structuralism: Essays and Reviews on Nineteenth- and Twentieth-Century (1981)

Write On: Occasional Essays '65–'85 (1986)

Modern Criticism and Theory: A Reader (1988)

After Bakhtin: Essays on Fiction and Criticism (1990)

The Art of Fiction: Illustrated from Classical and Modern Texts (1993)

The Practice of Writing: Essays, Lectures, Reviews, and a Diary (1996)

Consciousness and the Novel: Connected Essays (2002)

FURTHER READING

Amman, Daniel. *David Lodge and the Art-and-Reality Novel.* Heidelberg, Germany, 1991.

Arizti, Barbara. *Textuality as Striptease: The Discourses of Intimacy in David Lodge's Changing Places and Small World.* Frankfurt, Germany, and New York, 2002.

Martin, Bruce K. *David Lodge.* New York, 1999.

Morace, Robert A. *The Dialogic Novels of Malcolm Bradbury and David Lodge.* Carbondale, IL, 1989.

Moseley, Merritt. *David Lodge: How Far Can You Go?* San Bernardino, CA, 1991.

Schürer, Norbert. *David Lodge: An Annotated Primary and Secondary Bibliography.* Frankfurt, Germany, and New York, 1995.

THE LOLLARDS

Fiona Somerset

The Lollards, also known as Wycliffites, were religious reformers, then considered heretics by the Roman Catholic Church, who were active in England from the 1370s, when their ideas were inspired by the views of John Wyclif (c. 1330–1384). Many scholars think that Lollard writings continued to be read by persons interested in the heresy up until the Reformation in England in the 1530s, when some texts indeed gained renewed attention as proof that sixteenth-century reforming ideas were not mere novelties from abroad but had a long history within England. Certainly there are records of Lollards being tried for heresy up through the 1520s. Other scholars have been more inclined to dismiss Lollardy's influence and importance.

PRIMARY SOURCES

We know of the Lollards from four main kinds of written sources, each of which has limitations as well as strengths. The first category is chronicles by historical writers active in the late fourteenth and fifteenth centuries. These writers were typically biased quite strongly against the Lollards and may have been misinformed as well, but they show us what people were thinking about Lollards, and how Lollards were being criticized. Second, we have legal records of attempts to suppress Lollards, as well as of the prosecutions and trials of individuals and groups. Legal records can show us who was involved in quelling Lollardy and how they went about it, as well as what social groups participated in Lollardy. They can sometimes show us what books Lollards owned and what they read, since books circulated within a certain group are often listed. They can even give us some insight into what beliefs Lollards held, since suspects testified about their beliefs, usually in the form of a brief list but sometimes at great length; the longer written testimonies are often considered among Lollard writings (see below). But as always, laws may tell us more about what their makers hoped to achieve than about what really happened, and legal proceedings may often reflect what prosecutors expected to find more than what Lollards really thought—especially since suspects were usually questioned about their beliefs according to a set list of possible heresies. What is more, the Lollards who were prosecuted may not accurately represent the movement as a whole, since persons with power and influence were less likely to find themselves in trouble unless they annoyed someone more influential still.

Our third group of sources is the writings of the Lollards' opponents, typically attempting to refute Lollard ideas. Opponents of Lollardy sometimes discussed its thought in great detail, and they give us insight into why educated writers were worried about Lollardy; but the opponents might also misunderstand or even distort Lollard ideas, whether or not they meant to.

Finally, we have the extensive translations into English and writings in both Latin and English of the Lollards themselves, together with the evidence about how these works were written and read that can be derived from the manuscripts in which they are preserved. These writings are our best window on how Lollards themselves expressed their ideas. But they may tell us more about the views of the elite of the movement who could write, and how these Lollards wanted to try to spread their beliefs, than they do about what more ordinary Lollards believed. And manuscripts containing Lollard writings and translations were owned by persons who were not Lollards as well as by those who were.

THE EVIDENCE OF LOLLARD WRITINGS

Thus, although writings by the Lollards themselves will be the main emphasis when we consider the movement as a literary phenomenon, we should remember that Lollard writings give us only part of the history of Lollardy. In some ways, what they can tell us is frustratingly vague and imprecise. Most Lollard writings are anonymous, and most manuscripts whose contents are predominantly Lollard bear no marks of ownership. It is not hard to see why when we recall that Wyclif's writings were condemned as heretical at the Blackfriars Council in 1382, a year that also brought edicts against his followers; that the 1401 statute *De heretico comburendo* ("On the burning of heretics") made it more likely that heretics in England would be handed over to the secular arm and burned; and that Arundel's *Constitutions* of 1407–1409 attempted to restrict vernacular translation and the ownership of vernacular biblical materials. Most Lollard writings are also undated; some refer to specific events in a way that allows us to fix their date with relative precision, but for others we cannot state more than the approximate dates of their manuscripts. Some writings, indeed, are preserved only in post-Reformation printed copies. Although their printers claim they are medieval, and these claims seem to be supported by the content, we may never know for sure.

LOLLARDS AND THE BIBLE

Nonetheless, there is a great deal that Lollard writings can show us. We know that the Lollards were the first to translate the full text of the Bible into Middle English, over the course of several years in the last two decades of the fourteenth century. The Lollards' translation from the Latin Vulgate (the Latin version of the Bible in common use in the later Middle Ages) is the first version of the whole Bible in language that can still be fairly easily understood today, and it remained in use until the time of Tyndale's partial translation (1520s) and perhaps beyond. The Wycliffite Bible was the product of extended collaborative effort and went through at least one revision, from an early version closely based on the Latin but difficult to read in English into a more idiomatic version more friendly to readers unversed in Latin. It is unlikely that Wyclif himself was involved in the project (though popular writings claiming his authorship are still easy to find, and a very few scholars are still devoted to proving it). About 250 manuscripts of part or all of this Bible are extant, ranging from sumptuous copies owned by royalty to excerpts copied into workaday manuscript compilations.

The Lollards were plainly very interested in the Bible, so it is unsurprising that their extant manuscripts also include a great deal of ancillary material: indexes, summaries of biblical books, prologues to biblical books (both composed by Lollards and translated from previous sources), line-by-line commentaries on particular books that draw on a wide variety of pre-Lollard sources, adaptations of previous vernacular translations and com-

mentaries, and extended commentaries in the form of freestanding treatises. There are also Lollard defenses of biblical translation, both in freestanding tracts and within writings on broader topics. Most of this material (with the exception of some of the defenses of translation) has not received the attention it deserves, and little of it has ever been printed. Those who have looked to the Lollards as a historical precursor of their own beliefs do not examine these biblical materials because they think they know how Lollards read the Bible (and usually they think, wrongly, that the Lollards were resolutely attentive only to its literal historical meaning). Those who do want to read Lollard writings are usually more fascinated with the polemical and the more literary works. This gap in interest is unfortunate, because it is in their work with the Bible that we can most clearly see the Lollards' extensive engagement with previous sources and with the culture around them. The Lollards' polemical writings tend to foreground their rejection of their contemporaries' and predecessors' beliefs, but this provides anything but a full picture of Lollards as readers and writers.

TRACTS, SERMONS, AND PASTORAL AND INSTRUCTIONAL WRITINGS

The polemical writings are, however, very useful in coming to understand what Lollards believed and how they felt their beliefs differed from those of their contemporaries. Most often examined, and probably most useful as a starting point, is a brief, assertive list of beliefs such as the *Twelve Conclusions*. Posted on the doors of Westminster Hall while Parliament was in session in 1395, the *Conclusions* advocates the reformation of the English Church through reduction of its possessions. It urges the abolition of the Church hierarchy and of priestly celibacy, religious orders, and vows of continence for women. It criticizes the Church's use of some sacraments (the Eucharist, confession), as well as of various rituals (exorcism, consecration) and other practices (prayers for the dead, pilgrimage, offerings to images, crusades, employment of goldsmiths and other luxury craftsmen). As in any piece of Lollard polemic, some of these items are specific to the occasion (for example, the mention of goldsmiths) while others are frequent complaints (Church possessions, hierarchy, priesthood, religious orders, the Eucharist and confession, pilgrimage, images, crusades). Perhaps even more useful as an introduction to Lollard beliefs are works that seem to have been written not as defiant responses to outside criticism, but for a more receptive audience seeking a comprehensive discussion; this category includes the *Testimony of William Thorpe* (a fictionalized account of William Thorpe's confrontation with Archbishop Arundel while imprisoned before any official trial for heresy in 1407) and the *Lanterne of Light* (a pastoral handbook laying out the Lollard faith for interested readers, c. 1409–1414). Many other short Lollard writings on a specific issue or a range of issues are extant in manuscript, and a good number have been published, though mostly in nineteenth-century editions without the kind of commentary that can aid novice readers (they also reveal an earlier tendency to ascribe these works to Wyclif himself). Longer works especially worthy of attention include the *English Wycliffite Sermons*, five sets of sermons apparently composed by a coordinated team of writers in the late 1380s to 1390s, and a sermon and tract on the Eucharist by the same author written between 1409 and 1414 and recently published in *The Works of a Lollard Preacher*. Polemical reference works include the *Rosarium*, an alphabetical list of controversial topics, and the *Lollard Chronicle of the Papacy*.

LOLLARDS AND POETRY

Readily accessible to modern readers with some background in Middle English literature are *Piers the Plowman's Creed* and *The Plowman's Tale*. *Piers the Plowman's Creed* was probably written shortly after 1393, since it refers to the trial of the Wycliffite Walter Brut in that year. It is a response to William Langland's *Piers Plowman* and is written in the same alliterative long lines, but with a sharper, less meditative, and more satirical edge. The narrator is awake rather than dreaming, and he searches in vain among the four orders of friars for an honest man who will teach him his creed, only to learn it in the end from a poor plowman. *The Plowman's Tale* is extant only in printed texts from the 1530s on, and it probably did not acquire the narrative frame that turns it into a spurious contribution to Geoffrey Chaucer's *Canterbury Tales* until the mid-sixteenth century, when editors of Chaucer were eager to give him a Protestant pedigree. Most of the rest of the poem, however, is probably medieval, and though written in a very different idiom from *Piers the Plowman's Creed* (stanzaic rhyme rather than alliterative long lines), it too criticizes the Church in verse, and there is even a probable reference to *Piers the Plowman's Creed* (lines 1065–1069). Another, more literary Lollard work written partly in verse is the *Upland Series* (c. 1380–1410),

including *Jack Upland*'s seemingly naive questions, in prose, about the behavior of the friars, *Friar Daw*'s verse answers, and the further replies, again in verse, in *Upland's Rejoinder*. The debate among these texts is in many places so allusive that the university controversies it references make no sense without excellent notes (no current edition is adequate in this respect), but the invective in the exchange is entertaining. This text too was printed in the sixteenth century, as Lollards began to take on their new role as the perceived precursors to the English Reformation—a role that continues to influence their reputation up to the present day.

[*See also* The English Bible; Middle English; *and* Piers Plowman.]

EDITIONS

Arnold, Thomas, ed. *Select English Works of John Wyclif.* Vol. 3. Oxford, 1871.

Barr, Helen, ed. *The Piers Plowman Tradition.* London, 1993.

Cigman, Gloria, ed. *Lollard Sermons.* London, 1989.

Embree, Dan, ed. *The Chronicles of Rome: An Edition of the Middle English "Chronicle of Popes and Emperors" and "The Lollard Chronicle."* Woodbridge, U.K., 1999.

Gradon, P., and Anne Hudson, eds. *English Wycliffite Sermons.* 5 vols. Oxford, 1983–1996.

Heyworth, P. L., ed. *Jack Upland, Friar Daw's Reply, and Upland's Rejoinder.* Oxford, 1968.

Hudson, Anne, ed. *Selections from English Wycliffite Writings.* Cambridge, U.K., 1978.

Hudson, Anne, ed. *Two Wycliffite Texts: The Sermon of William Taylor 1406. The Testimony of William Thorpe 1407.* Early English Text Society 301. Oxford, 1993.

Hudson, Anne, ed. *The Works of a Lollard Preacher.* Early English Text Society 317. Oxford, 2001.

Matthew, F. D., ed. *The English Works of Wyclif Hitherto Unprinted.* Early English Text Society, o.s. 74. London, 1880; 2d rev. ed., 1902.

McCarl, Mary Rhinelander, ed. *The Plowman's Tale: The c. 1532 and 1606 Editions of a Spurious Canterbury Tale.* New York and London, 1997.

FURTHER READING

Aston, Margaret. *Lollards and Reformers: Images and Literacy in Late Medieval Religion.* London, 1984. Essays on Lollard beliefs in relation to later Reformation beliefs.

Ghosh, Kantik. *The Wycliffite Heresy: Authority and the*

Interpretation of Texts. Cambridge, U.K., 2002. Chapters on the controversy over biblical translation and on the English Wycliffite Sermons.

Hudson, Anne. *Lollards and Their Books*. London, 1985. Essays on Lollard writings and on aspects of Lollard book production.

Hudson, Anne. *The Premature Reformation: Wycliffite Texts and Lollard History*. Oxford, 1988. A comprehensive survey of the Lollard movement focused on the writings of Lollards and of their opponents, drawing on all the types of sources enumerated in this entry.

Somerset, Fiona. *Clerical Discourse and Lay Audience in Late Medieval England*. Cambridge, U.K., 1998. Chapters on the *Upland Series*, the *Twelve Conclusions*, and *The Testimony of William Thorpe*.

Somerset, Fiona. "Wycliffite Prose." In *A Companion to Middle English Prose*, edited by A. S. G. Edwards, 195–214. Woodbridge, U.K., 2004. A survey of Lollard prose writings in English.

Somerset, Fiona, Jill C. Havens, and Derrick G. Pitard, eds. *Lollards and Their Influence in Late Medieval England*. Woodbridge, U.K., 2003. In addition to recent essays, includes Pitard's comprehensive bibliography of published work on Lollardy.

MALCOLM LOWRY

Kevin J. H. Dettmar

The short and turbulent life of the novelist Malcolm Lowry (1909–1957) competes with that of his sometime drinking partner, the poet Dylan Thomas, as one of the most disturbingly compelling of the twentieth century. It is difficult to talk about Lowry's career without quickly devolving into Romantic clichés about the tortured artist—though in Lowry's case, the artist was quite clearly tortured by his own demons rather than, in Rimbaud's formulation, made to suffer for the sins of a decadent society. For a short time, Lowry turned that turbulence to aesthetic ends; his one great novel, *Under the Volcano* (1947), represents perhaps the last great flowering of the modernist novel in English, before the sea change of postmodernism. But Lowry's self-destructive bent robbed us of any further, fully realized creative work.

A TORTURED UPBRINGING BY DESIGN

Clarence Malcolm Lowry was born into extremely privileged circumstances, if saddled with what he considered to be an unfortunate given name; he despised it, and never used it. Lowry was born on 28 July 1909, in New Brighton, near Liverpool, the fourth of four brothers. His father was a successful businessman possessed of a sizable fortune; Malcolm was sent to exclusive boarding schools, with the expectation that he would matriculate at Cambridge in due course, and eventually enter the family business, along with his brothers. Lowry, however, rebelled in the most odious way he could: he left school at seventeen and chose to earn his own living, becoming a deckhand on a ship bound for Yokohama. He returned five months later cured of this particular Romantic notion, but now had broken more or less definitively with his father and his family, and had stored up a body of experience that he would draw upon in his earliest writing.

Lowry's writing life had begun in modest fashion during his school days; he published some poetry and short fiction for his school's magazine. More ominously, Lowry set down the pattern of heavy drinking that was to circumscribe both his life and his art. While he wrote further

poetry—one volume of it was published after his death—it soon became clear that fiction was Lowry's métier. After two aimless years, in which he wrote some and continued to drink heavily, Lowry belatedly entered Cambridge University in 1929, where his two passions—writing and drinking—continued apace. He was an indifferent student, but when his time at Cambridge was finished, he had completed work on his first novel. Lowry's time at sea had suggested material for a half dozen early stories; these were then reshaped, along with new writing, into the somewhat uneven *Ultramarine* (1933).

Ultramarine, published the year after Lowry's graduation, bears the impress, even in its title, of the American poet Conrad Aiken's 1927 experimental novel *Blue Voyage*; and Aiken's novel, like so many of those produced by young writers during this period, itself evidences everywhere the not always salutary influence of James Joyce's *Ulysses* (1922). While *Ultramarine* is impressive as the work of a precociously talented writer, and contains passages of real psychological power, these strengths are for many readers overbalanced by passages of "purple," overwrought prose; indeed Aiken, with whom Lowry developed a friendship, jokingly suggested that the novel ought to have been titled "Purple Passage." Although ostensibly dealing with a voyage, that voyage is, as so often in modernist literature, both what Virginia Woolf called a "voyage out" and, almost indistinguishably, a voyage inward: the dual structure of Joseph Conrad's *Heart of Darkness* (1902), for instance. It is also, according to another common modernist pattern, a thinly autobiographical Bildungsroman, or novel of development; the novel's protagonist, Dana Hilliot, makes a voyage to the Far East, but his overly sensitive nature puts him at odds with his fellow crew members.

The novel's interest today, however, has little to do with either the plot or the scenic description one might reasonably expect of such a narrative; for the landscapes that finally interest Lowry, again like Conrad, are the psychological ones. After the publication of *Under the Volcano*, Lowry himself declared *Ultramarine* "not worth reading," and contemporary critical reception was mixed: while some reviewers admired both the stylistic experimentation and the psychological profundity of the novel, others found the balance in Lowry's collage tipping toward incoherence. In retrospect, it is perhaps Lowry's experiments with stream of consciousness that represent *Ultramarine*'s primary contribution to experimental modernist fiction.

STORMY WEATHER

In April 1933, after a stay of a few months in London, Lowry resumed the itinerant life that would become his characteristic mode. He began by visiting Spain with Aiken; while there, he met an American woman, Jan Gabrial, and married her in January 1934 after a whirlwind courtship. There were difficulties from the start, and the marriage seems never to have enjoyed any real stability; Lowry writes about it, in fictional guise, in the story "In Le Havre." Gabrial seems to have decided quickly to cut her losses, abandoning Lowry in Paris and returning alone to New York. Lowry later followed Gabrial to New York, and the marriage was patched up for a time; before long, however, Lowry's drinking landed him in the psychiatric ward of New York's infamous Bellevue Hospital. As with most of the powerful incidents in his life, this harrowing experience became the impetus and raw material for a piece of writing, the unpublished short novel "The Last Address," later substantially rewritten as "Swinging the Maelstrom"; an amalgam of the two, *Lunar Caustic*, was published after Lowry's death. *Lunar Caustic* is thought by many to be the most nearly successful of Lowry's opus posthumous; the novel's protagonist Bill Plantagenet comes to consciousness interned at Bellevue, with no recollection of the events that led to his incarceration, or even of his own identity and personal history. The novel re-creates in haunting detail the experiences of Lowry's own hospitalization.

Attempting a new start, in 1936 Lowry and Gabrial moved to Cuernavaca, Mexico, the landscape that he would make his own in *Under the Volcano*. The move was not sufficient to salvage the marriage; Lowry continued to drink excessively, Gabrial to carry on affairs with other men: by the following year, the relationship had broken apart for good. This time it was Gabrial who wrote the fictional chronicle; her short story "Not with a Bang" anatomizes the last days and months of their unhappy marriage. During this period Lowry was at work on another psychological novel, "In Ballast to the White Sea,"

which he worked on by turns until the end of the 1930s, by which point it filled a thousand manuscript pages. Aiken admired it inordinately, but it was judged unpublishable, and the manuscript languished. It was later lost in a fire.

On his own again, Lowry traveled the Mexican countryside looking for the country's best mescal (to be found in Oaxaca), and made a close friend in the Mexican socialist Juan Fernando Márquez; the two became (predictably) drinking buddies, and Lowry again landed in prison for disorderly behavior. He returned to the United States in 1938, settling, though only temporarily, in Los Angeles.

UNDER THE VOLCANO

Miraculously, given the chaos of his day-to-day life, Lowry had by this time started work on his masterpiece, *Under the Volcano*. He submitted the manuscript to publishers in 1939, and it was rejected; while in Los Angeles, he met Margerie Bonner, an actress, and the two, despite the mayhem that Lowry created all around him, remained together until Lowry's death. The couple were married in December 1940, after Lowry's American visa expired and they had moved across the border to Vancouver. The couple sustained this vagabond existence, living by turns in and around Vancouver, then Ontario, and later returning to Mexico. Living just outside Vancouver in a squatter's cabin, Lowry brought *Under the Volcano* into final form; evicted by a fire, he finished the novel in the last days of 1944.

Under the Volcano is truly a novel like no other; at its most fevered and anxious, it resembles the hallucinatory atmosphere of the "Circe" chapter of Joyce's *Ulysses*. Like that famous fictional episode, *Under the Volcano* imitates, in part, a kind of alcoholic stupor; with an alcoholic as its protagonist, and alcohol seemingly providing its modus operandi or stylistic conceit, reading the book proves a challenging and deeply disturbing experience. The story concerns the bleak last days of Geoffrey Firmin, British consul to Mexico; with the exception of a prefatory first chapter, the entire action unfolds on a single tragic day, 2 November 1938, by the end of which Firmin is dead. The autobiographical layer is undeniable: the Mexican mise-en-scène, the alcoholic husband, the unfaithful wife, the marital strife, and the generally bleak atmosphere of mutually assured destruction. The 1984 John Huston film captures this aspect of the novel quite well, with Lowry's hallucinatory effects translating especially well to the big screen; another unrelated film, Mike Figgis's *Leaving Las Vegas* (1995), inadvertently captures Lowry's sense of sodden doom quite vividly.

Lowry's masterpiece might be characterized as a piece of late modernism: by 1947 the modernist moment had largely passed into literary history, with Joyce's *Finnegan's Wake* (1939), for instance, pointing the way toward the future just as his *Ulysses* had marked the finest flowering of the modernist past. *Under the Volcano*, however, uses resolutely modernist means for a thoroughly modernist end: the vivid psychological evocation of what one must, inevitably, call a "tortured soul." Lowry himself described the novel as "concerned with the guilt of man, with his remorse, with his ceaseless struggling towards the light under the weight of the past, and with his doom." One might be forgiven for mistaking these words as coming from the contemporaneous American novelist William Faulkner; though Faulkner and Lowry exerted no direct influence on one another, Faulkner's fiction provides the most useful analogue to Lowry's fiction, a similarity underremarked to date in the criticism. Lowry also shares with Joyce, Faulkner, and many other great modernist writers a fascination with myth and symbol, and a belief in the ability of mythic resonances to (as T. S. Eliot wrote about Joyce's use of myth in *Ulysses*) give "a shape and a significance to the immense panorama of futility and anarchy which is contemporary history." Geoffrey Firmin takes his place as one of the very last in a long line of modernist protagonists searching desperately for order in a world that seems to offer none; and like many others, his search is in the end fruitless, as he is killed by a fascist sympathizer, the victim of partisan political violence.

The occasional naysayer notwithstanding, *Under the Volcano* was received to critical acclaim; the book also sold well, spending months on the best-seller lists. Having completed the book, Lowry and his wife returned to Mexico, a land foreign to her but, now, the imaginative landscape of his greatest artistic triumph. Lowry hoped for a reunion with his friend Márquez, only to discover that he had been shot years before; the sojourn ended when the couple was ingloriously deported on an immigration violation. It was not the triumphant return with which Lowry had hoped to regale Margerie. Hard on the heels of this experience, Lowry began to write a novel in tribute to his dead friend; *Dark as the Grave Wherein My Friend Is Laid* remained unfinished at Lowry's death, but was published in 1968, to rather tepid reviews. Critical consensus sees the book as marred by its overreliance on autobiography, and its dearth of novelistic structure and tension.

"SUCCESS IS LIKE SOME HORRIBLE DISASTER"

Lowry never quite recovered from the success of *Under the Volcano*; having written his magnum opus he seems also to have written himself out, and the last decade and more of his life found him casting about for subjects for new fiction, with little apparent success. The Lowrys traveled nearly constantly, visiting Europe, the Caribbean, the American South, and New York; ultimately they returned to Canada in 1949. For a time, Lowry gave up fiction, or the novel at least, and embarked on a screenplay for F. Scott Fitzgerald's own tale of alcoholic ruin and conflicted relationships, *Tender Is the Night*. The screenplay was never produced, though it was subsequently published; nevertheless, Lowry was pleased with the results, and it seems to have buoyed him for a time. Over the next few years, Lowry complemented work on his final novel, *October Ferry to Gabriola*, with a series of accomplished short stories, which were collected in the volume *Hear Us O Lord from Heaven Thy Dwelling Place*.

INGLORIOUS AND UNTIMELY END

October Ferry never got further along than a first draft; Random House, the premier publisher of literary fiction in the United States at the time, terminated its contract with Lowry for the book, pessimistic about its chances for successful publication. This vote of no confidence rattled Lowry profoundly; he traveled a great deal, drank a great deal, and wrote but little after 1954. In 1956 Lowry and his wife rented a cottage on the south coast of England; on 27 June 1957, after a fight with his wife, Lowry took his own life with an overdose of sleeping pills.

Many writers whose names live on enjoy a reputation based on the strength of just one book; Djuna Barnes has entered the canon based on little more. *Under the Volcano* ensures that Lowry will continue to be read and studied, with admiration and with a kind of morbid fascination, if not with pleasure—for one does not take a draft as strong as this one with pleasure. Given the power of that one novel, we can but regret that he did not live to create another.

[*See also* James Joyce; Modernism; *and* Dylan Thomas.]

SELECTED WORKS

Ultramarine (1933; rev. ed., 1962)
Under the Volcano (1947)

Hear Us O Lord from Heaven Thy Dwelling Place
  (1961)
Selected Poems of Malcolm Lowry (edited by Earle Birney;
  1962)
Lunar Caustic (edited by Earle Birney and Margerie Lowry;
  1963)
Dark as the Grave Wherein My Friend Is Laid (1968)
October Ferry to Gabriola (1970)

FURTHER READING

Bowker, Gordon. *Pursued by Furies: A Life of Malcolm Lowry.* New York, 1997. The most comprehensive biography.

Costa, Richard Hauer. *Malcolm Lowry.* Boston, 1972. Best general introduction to Lowry's life and work.

Cross, Richard K. *Malcolm Lowry: A Preface to his Fiction.* Chicago, 1980. Intelligent critical overview of Lowry's small oeuvre.

Day, Douglas. *Malcolm Lowry: A Biography.* New York, 1973. The standard scholarly biography; winner of the National Book Award.

Gabrial, Jan. *Inside the Volcano: My Life with Malcolm Lowry.* New York, 2000. The most recent biography, by Lowry's ex-wife and the fictional Yvonne from *Under the Volcano.*

Vice, Sue, ed. *Malcolm Lowry: Eighty Years On.* London, 1989. Widely varying appraisals of the lasting importance of Lowry's work.

Walker, Ronald G. *Infernal Paradise: Mexico and the Modern English Novel.* Berkeley, CA, 1974. Includes two chapters on Lowry: one biographical, with a consideration of *Dark as the Grave Wherein My Friend Is Laid,* and one focusing on *Under the Volcano.*

JOHN LYDGATE

John M. Bowers

John Lydgate (c. 1371–c. 1449) wrote close to 140,000 lines of verse, thus ranking as one of the most prolific poets in English literary history. This accomplishment is remarkable on several scores. First, he was a monk in the great Benedictine abbey of Bury Saint Edmunds, and members of monastic orders did not typically concern themselves with vernacular writing, least of all poetry on the secular themes of love and war. Lydgate's monastery was in Suffolk moreover, far from the center of literary activity in London. Furthermore, he defined his entire career as a self-conscious continuation of the Chaucer tradition at a time when copies of works such as the *Canterbury Tales* were rare and expensive. He would remain the principal mediator of Chaucerian style and subject matter to successors into the sixteenth century. Finally, Lydgate wrote for money—really the first paid English poet on record—having secured a host of high-profile commissions to become the uncrowned poet laureate of England during the entire first half of the fifteenth century.

Born around 1371, Lydgate was ordained a priest in 1397 and continued his studies at Oxford during the first decade of the fifteenth century. While at university, he first attracted the attention of the Prince of Wales, the future Henry V. Even at this early date, Lydgate's poetry was recognized for its potential usefulness in consolidating national unity and creating English cultural identity. Lydgate spent much of his early career outside the cloister. He enjoyed long periods in London, presumably at his abbot's luxurious townhouse at Buries Markes. In 1426 he traveled as far as Paris, where he saw the famous paintings and texts that inspired his *Danse Macabre*, which was subsequently inscribed in the cloister of St. Paul's Cathedral in London. He received a royal annuity in 1439 and seems to have spent most of the last decade of his life back in his monastic community. Written in old age, his *Testament of Dan John Lydgate* is a rather touching pseudo-autobiography framing the narrative of his life in traditional penitential terms.

Lydgate wrote in almost every conceivable medieval genre spanning about 160 items—classical epic, courtly love vision, saint's life, political allegory, religious hymn, memento mori, moral satire, Aesopic fable, amorous ballade, verse prayer, debate, genealogical romance, devotional hymn—while inventing at least one new genre, the literary mumming, which became a direct ancestor of the Renaissance masque. He expanded the English vocabulary by coining many new words, especially through the importation of scientific terms. He carried forward Chaucer's major metrical forms of rhyme royal, octosyllabic couplets and iambic pentameter couplets, modified with his own distinctive "headless" or "broken-backed" lines (lacking a syllable), which were closely imitated by successors such as Benedict Burgh and Steven Hawes. Since he wrote on commission for particular patrons, there are peculiar items in his oeuvre, such as *The Treatise for Laundresses*. To judge by the number of surviving manuscripts, *The Dietary*, on health-giving nutrition, was his most popular work.

Lydgate's commitments as Lancastrian propagandist, however, were a consistent preoccupation throughout most of his career. Shortly after Henry V's coronation in 1413, Lydgate wrote *A Defence of Holy Church* as a testimonial to the new king's commitment to orthodoxy. Later, his *Title and Pedigree of Henry VI* (1427) publicized the young king's legitimate claim to the throne of France. Royal governance remained unstable after the deposition of Richard II; more than three decades later, Lydgate's *Of the Sudden Fall of Princes in Our Days* defended this usurpation by claiming that King Richard willingly resigned the Crown to Henry IV. Though more secure on the throne than his father had been, Henry V needed to quell Sir John Oldcastle's Lollard uprising in 1413 and the Southampton plot just prior to the French campaign that was crowned with resounding victory at Agincourt in 1415. In terms of the long-standing mutual support between the monarchy and the monasteries, Lydgate's commitment to the stability of Lancastrian rule made perfect sense. All of his political texts stand strangely at odds with themselves, however, forever haunted by the pessimistic counter-awareness that political ambitions were foredoomed by the flawed terms of their own undertaking.

Although he probably never knew Geoffrey Chaucer personally, Lydgate did know the poet's son, to whom he addressed the charming lyric *On the Departing of Thomas Chaucer*. The younger Chaucer was a mainstay of the new Lancastrian dynasty and their number-one man in Parliament. Since he was presumably the caretaker of his father's literary papers, Thomas was able to give the monk early access to the manuscripts of the major poems that served as the basis for Lydgate's subsequent career, perhaps in Chaucer's own draft versions housed in the precinct of Westminster Abbey where the poet died; Thomas Chaucer continued to lease his father's tenement residence there until his own death in 1434. Lydgate's *Complaint of the Black Knight* is a reworking of *The Book of the Duchess*, and his *Temple of Glass* revisits the thematic concerns of *The House of Fame*. Thought to have been composed early his career, these imitations remain among the best of Lydgate's writings. Courtly poetry, like courtly love, was a game that operated according to rules even a monk could learn and elaborate. As a member of a religious order sworn to celibacy, he brought real sympathy to the plight of a lover committed to an impossible passion, an unattainable lady, and long service in the cause of unrequited longing.

Thomas Chaucer apparently shared Henry V's sense that Lydgate could be useful in helping to dignify or even legitimate the royal house of Lancaster. The monk-poet continued his relationship with the Chaucer family through the poet's granddaughter, Alice, for whom he wrote a pious commentary, *The Virtues of the Mass*. For her second husband, he produced his monumental translation of *The Pilgrimage of the Life of Man* (1428). Alice Chaucer owned a manuscript of Lydgate's *Pilgrimage* which she donated to the almshouse in her home village of Ewelme, Oxfordshire. The best manuscript of *The Siege of Thebes* bears the heraldic arms of her third husband, William de la Pole, duke of Suffolk.

Introducing the highly ornamental "aureate" (meaning "gilded") style of diction, Lydgate continued Chaucer's classicizing practices as an early form of Renaissance humanism, writing the 30,000-line *Troy Book* (1412–1420) for Henry V as an expansion of the historical narrative surrounding *Troilus and Criseyde*. His encyclopedic habits of mind make him a prime resource for understanding late medieval intellectual culture. He next wrote *The Siege of Thebes* (1420–1422) as a supplement to the tragic history recounted in the *Knight's Tale*. The celebratory allusions to the 1420 Treaty of Troyes link the classical work to the topicality of Henry V's military successes

in France. Lydgate's project of continuing the Chaucerian tradition often became an overambitious effort at surpassing his master, however, in an almost Oedipal drama of a son trying to outdo his literary father figure. Aptly enough, the Lydgate work in which the Oedipal competition is most obvious, *Siege of Thebes*, was adapted from the French *Roman de Edipus*. But where Chaucer had produced elegant conciseness, subtle psychological insight, and outrageous comedic wit, Lydgate provided instead material bulk, simplified morality, and showy stylistic complexity sometimes descending into grandiloquence and obscurity. Yet much as Lydgate has been disparaged as the "driveling monk of Bury," it is hard to gauge how Chaucer's posthumous reputation might have fared if his imitator had not worked steadily at elevating the older poet's status as the founding author of the English literary tradition.

The Prologue to the *Siege of Thebes* represents Lydgate's most obvious effort at supplementing what he perceived as Chaucer's major shortcoming: his failure to complete the *Canterbury Tales* by not dramatizing the homeward journey. The chivalric epic's first lines were clearly meant to recall the famous opening of Chaucer's General Prologue; the passage also demonstrates how Lydgate's ambitions at Chaucerian imitation often faltered from trying too hard (Edwards, p. 29, ll.1–26):

Whan brighte Phebus passed was the Ram
Myd of Aprille and into Bole cam
And Satourn old with his frosty face
In Virgyne taken had his place,
Malencolik and slowgh of mocioun,
And was also in th'oposicioun
Of Lucina the mone moyst and pale
That many shour fro hevene made avale,
Whan Aurora was in the morowe red,
And Jubiter in the Crabbes hed
Hath take his paleys and his mansioun,
The lusty tyme and joly fressh sesoun
Whan that Flora the noble myghty quene
The soyl hath clad in newe tendre grene
With her floures craftyly ymeynt,
Braunch and bough with red and whit depeynt,
Fletinge the bawme on hillis and on valys,
The tyme in soth whan Canterbury talys
Complet and told at many sondry stage
Of estatis in the pilgrimage,
Everich man like to his degré,
Some of desport, some of moralité,
Some of knyghthode, love and gentillesse,
And some also of parfit holynesse,

And some also in soth of ribaudye
To make laughter in the companye . . .

The sentence continues rambling onward for thirty-eight more lines before reaching its end.

In this Prologue, Lydgate depicted the pilgrims under the direction of the Host leaving Canterbury on the road back to London. Spotting Lydgate himself among the departing pilgrims, the Host invites him to join the fellowship and to tell the next tale (which becomes the only tale) for the return trip. As a pilgrim, Lydgate provides a self-portrait calculated scrupulously to correct every defect of monastic conduct that Chaucer had originally invested in his Monk. At just this time, Henry V had launched an investigation into the laxity of discipline at Benedictine foundations, and Lydgate clearly wanted to publicize his own innocence. His larger intention was to vindicate his status as a voice of moral authority and a credible adviser to princes.

As a storyteller in *The Siege of Thebes*, Lydgate aimed at correcting Chaucer's Knight by providing a comprehensive history of Theban political history prior to the intervention of Duke Theseus. His story became a gigantic prequel to the *Knight's Tale*, a concatenation of tragic episodes leading to the total destruction of a kingdom. His ambition to imitate Chaucer's high style, however, missed the concentrated pathos of the story of Palamon and Arcite, just as his efforts at rivaling his master's low style in the Prologue achieved something coarser and more vulgar than Chaucer ever wrote, even in his most risqué passages. In any head-to-head competition between the two poets, Lydgate invariably takes second prize.

When the energetic Henry V died unexpectedly in 1422, Lydgate was quick to find new footing. He immediately wrote one of the first political pamphlets in English, the prose *Serpent of Division*, warning against the evils of civil discord during this period of uncertainty. He then associated himself with the earl of Warwick, traveled overseas with the duke of Bedford, and generally shifted his allegiance to Humphrey, duke of Gloucester, as the new patriarch of the Lancastrian dynasty during the long minority of Henry VI. Duke Humphrey was an enthusiast for books, as witnessed by the Oxford library that bears his name, and Lydgate produced a number of poems for him, notably the immense 36,000-line *Fall of Princes* during the 1430s. Based on a French version of Boccaccio's *De casibus illustrium virorum* (Examples of Famous Men), this mega-composition marked Lydgate as a professional man of letters, not just a court poet, employed for the advancement of historiography, classical learning, and piety.

The Fall of Princes constituted a major addition to the growing syllabus of English vernacular literature and stimulated a native posterity in works such as *The Mirror of Magistrates*. As a vast expansion of Chaucer's *Monk's Tale*, this work did much to establish tragedy as a genre in the English tradition for later writers in the Tudor period, including Shakespeare. Its advocacy of the "great man" view of history remains potent even today. As in all of his versions of political history, however, Lydgate instinctively reverted to an old-fashioned monastic view that secular careers were tragically flawed because of the inescapable mutability of earthly things, so that royal ambitions inevitably ended in personal disappointment and national disaster. Greed, arrogance, treason, slander, vengeance, family betrayal, female perfidy, and the arbitrary malignancy of Dame Fortune directed the course of political events inexorably toward catastrophic ends. His poetry abounds in dire warnings but contains few optimistic examples for the would-be perfect prince. When Shakespeare's Richard II says pathetically that he will "sit upon the ground and tell sad stories of the death of kings," it is as if he has already spent too much time reading *The Fall of Princes*.

Lydgate's output of religious poetry was enough to establish a whole separate career. Composed as a vast compendium of Marian lore and symbolism, his *Life of Our Lady* was produced for Henry V just before the king's death and survives in more than forty copies, several of them high-quality illuminated manuscripts—evidence that his religious works found an elite audience beyond the cloister. Other pious pieces were produced for aristocratic ladies such as the countess of Warwick and Queen Katherine, widow of Henry V. Religious works such as the *Exposition of the Paternoster* developed the florid rhetoric and Latinate vocabulary most characteristic of the "aureation" which inspirited later imitators such as William Dunbar.

When not obliged to perform as a storyteller, Lydgate was able to exploit his rhetorical strengths in splendid passages of invocation, interpretation, prayer, prophecy, and pious exclamation. Two hagiographic works celebrating the founders of England's two great Benedictine houses achieve almost epically monumental size. *The Life of St. Edmund and St. Fremund* was produced for his home monastery of Bury St. Edmunds, while his *Life of St. Albon and St. Amphabell* was commissioned by John

Whethamstede, abbot of St. Albans. The Abbot's Register records a payment to Lydgate of £3.6s.8d., the first English record of an actual payment to a writer for his literary services.

Lydgate's poetry provided ready merchandise for William Caxton's printing presses. By the end of the fifteenth century, therefore, he was secure as a member of the triumvirate of English authors—Chaucer, Gower, and Lydgate—which remained canonical into the Renaissance. In addition to his obvious coup of career promotion, Lydgate made a decisive contribution to the more innovative and far-reaching project of creating the *idea* of a national literary tradition. He nominated Chaucer as the "first finder" of a poetic language for all of Britain, not just England, and then he successfully inserted himself as the heir apparent in this literary lineage. Lydgate thus bolstered the concept of the English tradition as a genealogy passed along from father to son. This orderly succession from one author to the next was an artificial, cobbled-together enterprise, like the succession of Lancastrian kings from Henry IV to Henry VI but more enduring. Lydgate's systematic consolidation of Chaucer's achievement established a high-style poetic standard for English literature that would remain the norm for centuries.

[*See also* William Caxton; Geoffrey Chaucer; *and* Medieval Devotional Prose.]

EDITIONS

Bergen, Henry, ed. *The Fall of Princes.* Early English Text Society, extra series 121–124, 1924–1927.

Bergen, Henry, ed. *Troy Book.* Early English Text Society, extra series 97, 103, 106, 126, 1906–1935.

Edwards, Robert R., ed. *The Siege of Thebes.* Kalamazoo, MI, 2001.

Furnivall, Frederick J., and K. B. Locock, eds. *Pilgrimage of the Life of Man.* Early English Text Society, extra series 77, 83, 92, 1899–1904.

MacCracken, Henry Noble, ed. *Minor Poems: (1) Religious Poems, (2) Secular Poems.* Early English Text Society, extra series 107, 1911, and original series 192, 1934.

FURTHER READING

Bowers, John M. "Controversy and Criticism: Lydgate's *Thebes* and the Prologue to *Beryn*." *Chaucer Yearbook* 5 (1998): 91–115.

Gibson, Gail McMurray. "Bury St. Edmunds, Lydgate, and the *N Town Cycle*." *Speculum* 56 (1981): 56–90.

Kline, Daniel T. "Father Chaucer and the *Siege of Thebes*: Literary Paternity, Aggressive Deference, and the Prologue to Lydgate's Oedipal *Canterbury Tales*." *Chaucer Review* 34 (1999): 217–235.

Patterson, Lee. "Making Identities in Fifteenth-Century England: Henry V and John Lydgate." In *New Historical Literary Studies,* edited by Jeffrey N. Cox and Larry J. Reynolds, 69–107. Princeton, NJ, 1993.

Pearsall, Derek. *John Lydgate.* Charlottesville, VA, 1970.

Pearsall, Derek. *John Lydgate (1371–1559): A Bio-Bibliography.* University of Victoria English Literary Studies, no. 71. Victoria, B.C., 1997.

Schirmer, Walter F. *John Lydgate: A Study in the Culture of the XVth Century.* Translated by Ann E. Keep. London and Berkeley, 1961.

Strohm, Paul. "Hoccleve, Lydgate and the Lancastrian Court." In *The Cambridge History of Medieval Literature,* edited by David Wallace, 640–661. Cambridge, U.K., 1999.

JOHN LYLY

Mike Pincombe

John Lyly (1554–1606) was the most celebrated English writer of the 1580s. His first novel, *Euphues: The Anatomy of Wit*, published in December 1578, won him instant fame as the inventor of the witty ornamental style subsequently called "euphuism." He was then just twenty-four years old. Within five years he became the unofficial purveyor of drama to the royal court, and he wrote at least five plays—probably more—for performance before Elizabeth I. But his involvement in political controversy led to the inhibition of his company of juvenile actors, Paul's Boys, around 1590; thereafter he left London for several years and was never able to relaunch his career either as a writer or as a courtier. He died in London, probably of plague, and was buried in the churchyard of St. Bartholomew the Less in Smithfield on 30 November 1606.

THE GENTLEMAN OF LETTERS

Lyly is the earliest but in some ways the least typical member of a group of Elizabethan writers often termed the "university wits." The others usually cited are George Peele, Thomas Lodge, Robert Greene, Christopher Marlowe, and Thomas Nashe. All these men were educated at either Oxford or Cambridge (or both universities) before making their way to London to seek their fortune by the exercise of their "wit," or what we might now call "literary talent." Lyly stands out because, unlike the others, he had a humble but relatively well-established place in the social order. The others had to struggle to make ends meet—literally "living off their wits." But Lyly enjoyed the steady patronage of one of the more cultivated young noblemen of the period, Edward de Vere, earl of Oxford; and, as the impresario of Paul's Boys, he had a source of income from their performances not only at court but also in their metropolitan playhouses, first at the Blackfriars and later in St. Paul's Cathedral itself. Lyly owed this social security less to his wits, though they were very considerable, than to his family connections. A gentleman born and bred, with friends in very high places,

he was a relative of one of the three most powerful men in England—William Cecil, Lord Burghley, the queen's most trusted minister throughout the first forty years of her reign. Indeed, Burghley was in this respect probably more important to Lyly than his own family, despite its scholarly and academic credentials. Lyly's grandfather, William Lily, was the first master of St. Paul's Cathedral School, and he was the coauthor of the Latin grammar ("Lily's Grammar") studied by his grandson and every other Elizabethan schoolboy. Lyly's uncle, George Lily, was a scholar of international renown, who spent most of his adult life in Italy; nearer to home, Lyly's London family was firmly based in schoolteaching (he had an aunt called Scholastica). Lyly himself tried to set up as an Oxford don in 1573, but he failed and came to London to seek his fortune instead.

Lyly thus belongs to that numerous group of Tudor writers whom we could call "gentlemen of letters." He defined himself not only by the education in classical literature he had received at school and university, but also by his status as a gentleman rather than a mere commoner, and as a member of the establishment, albeit a minor one, rather than an upstart. This was the social basis of the more "courtly" inflection of Elizabethan humanism, with its twin emphases on learning and courtesy. The key to Lyly's success as a writer and a courtier ultimately lay in the easy grace with which he managed to combine these two elements of *litterae humaniores*, a gift first revealed in the learned but urbane style he developed as England's first best-selling novelist.

STYLIST AND NOVELIST

Unlike most modern novels, *Euphues* (1578) and *Euphues and His England* (1580) do not place much emphasis on plot or character, though these elements are not entirely overlooked. In the first, Euphues and his friend Philautus fall out over a young woman called Lucilla; the sequel takes the pair to England, where Philautus falls fruitlessly in love with Camilla and once again quarrels with Euphues, but he eventually drops his pursuit and is reconciled to his friend once more. The narrative action is thus slight, and Lyly seems to have chosen it because it offered him the opportunity to display his own rhetorical and discursive abilities. Both books abound in witty conversation, formal orations, letters, and essays on various topics ranging from education to exile, from the topography of England to a eulogy of its queen. Much of this material, as Lyly's early critics were quick to note, was borrowed, often without acknowledgment, from classical and modern authors ranging from the classical Greek biographer Plutarch to the modern Dutch scholar Erasmus, from the classical Roman poet Ovid to the modern English historian William Harrison. This method of composition was not uncommon among the Elizabethans, but what makes Lyly unusual is his extraordinary ability to transform these quite various materials into the highly ornate style that soon came to be known as "euphuism." Modern critics have tended to emphasize its use of devices such as alliteration and antithesis to produce an ordered but specious form of argumentation that reflects its speakers' willfulness or self-delusion; but Lyly's contemporaries were more interested in his ornamental use of proverbs and maxims, and especially his far-fetched similes and other comparisons drawn from what is often called "unnatural natural history," such as the "tree in Tylos, whose nuts have shells like fire, and being cracked, the kernel is but water" (*Galatea*).

It is hard to overestimate the immense popularity of the two parts of *Euphues*: no fewer than thirteen editions of both books were published in Lyly's lifetime. *Euphues* set the style for a whole generation, as is witnessed not only by the number of imitations but also by the degree of criticism it excited. Yet Lyly did not follow up this success by writing more installments of the story, probably because there was no more gain to be had from it. All the financial profits went to the publisher, and, as a gentleman, Lyly could hardly be seen to write for money. Moreover, a more acceptable means of furthering his career by his literary talents soon presented itself: court drama.

DRAMATIST AND IMPRESARIO

By the time Lyly completed *Euphues and His England* in early 1580, he was in the service, probably as a personal secretary, of the earl of Oxford. There were family connections here, since Oxford was Burghley's ward; but no doubt the poetical young earl—he has sometimes been claimed as the author of Shakespeare's plays—relished the literary reputation of his new gentleman-servant. Then, in 1583, through a complicated series of events, Oxford came to be the patron of a company that combined the members of the two main children's troupes: Paul's Boys and the Children of the Chapel Royal. Both companies had been playing semiprofessionally for several years, with the claim that such public performances were rehearsals for eventual performance at court. It was under these auspices that Lyly, referred to in the court accounts as "my Lord of Oxenford's man," produced his earliest plays: *Campaspe* and *Sappho and Phao*, both of which were performed first at the Blackfriars in London, and then at court on New Year's Day and on Shrove Tuesday, 1584, respectively. This particular enterprise soon collapsed, but Lyly recouped his fortunes and within a year or two he and Paul's Boys were producing regular performances at a theater somewhere in the precincts of St. Paul's Cathedral. Nor had he lost his connection with the court: *Galatea* was performed before the queen on New Year's Day 1588, *Endymion* on Shrove Tuesday the same year, and *Midas* on Twelfth Night 1590.

However, by virtue of his pamphlet *Pap with an Hatchet* (1589), Lyly had also become embroiled in the Marprelate Controversy, a particularly vitriolic phase in the prolonged struggle throughout the Elizabethan period between the established Church and radical reformers. The involvement of Paul's Boys in anti-Marprelate plays led, it seems, to the closure of their theater at Paul's, and with it Lyly's main source of livelihood, which apparently forced him to retire to his wife's estates in Yorkshire for the early 1590s. This interruption makes it hard to trace his later career and to place the three other plays from his hand: *Mother Bombie* (printed 1594), *The Woman in the Moon* (printed 1597), and *Love's Metamorphosis* (printed 1601). These are difficult to date, but the first and last were probably written before the closure of Paul's, while *The Woman in the Moon* may have been composed around 1594. This play and *Love's Metamorphosis* may have been presented at court, though the Terentian comedy *Mother Bombie* probably was not, as it makes no such claim and turns away from the kind of drama that had established Lyly as a unique voice in the late Elizabethan theater: the mythological play.

Figures and fables from ancient Greek and Roman mythology were by no means unheard of in Tudor drama before Lyly, but they tended to be found not so much in the main theatrical tradition of the interlude and its variants as in entertainments devised especially for certain festive occasions, such as the shows written for performance before the queen as she toured the provinces on her summer progresses. Here, it may said, mythological material was almost obligatory, and Lyly was keenly aware of recent specimens of this kind of drama presented to Elizabeth at Kenilworth Castle, Warwickshire, in 1575 and at Norwich in 1578. What Lyly did was to pour this material into the mold of the interlude (and although we tend to follow Lyly's contemporaries' habit of calling his plays "comedies," he was always careful to avoid this or any other neo-or pseudo-classical generic designation). These shows were generally outdoor productions, performed in field and forest, and this supplied Lyly with the other key element in his new kind of drama: the pastoral world of nymphs and shepherds. Thus was born the central pentad of Lylian drama: *Sappho and Phao*, *Galatea*, *Midas*, *The Woman in the Moon*, and *Love's Metamorphosis* all mingle mythological and pastoral elements in varying proportions.

Moreover, they are all concerned with the main theme of the Elizabethans' favorite storybook: Ovid's epic mythological poem *Metamorphoses*. Venus uses her magic to make Phao irresistibly beautiful to Sappho; Neptune turns himself into a shepherd and Galatea and Phyllida are disguised as boys; Midas is given an ass's ears; Pandora becomes the Woman in the Moon only after having been temperamentally transformed by the other six planets in turn; and the title of *Love's Metamorphosis* speaks for itself. It is this ingredient, metamorphosis, that binds Lyly's most famous play, *Endymion*, into this central corpus, for although *Endymion* is shaped out of the materials of chivalric romance, the play also features the metamorphosis of its main character from a young man to an old man and then back to a young man in a sequence of miraculous alterations.

It should by now be clear that the dramaturgy Lyly favored was one that emphasized the magical properties of theater, and his prologues and epilogues are full of allusions to conjurors, labyrinths, novelty boxes, dreams, shadows, fairies, and so on. This is especially true of those spoken at the court, where Lyly sometimes cedes a formative—or transformative—role to the royal spectator. In the court prologue to *Campaspe*, for example, which deals with a brief amour of Alexander the Great, he says: "Whatsoever we present we wish it may be thought the dancing of Agrippa his shadows, who in the moment they were seen were of any shape one would conceive." This is a reference to the famous crystal ball of the German magus Heinrich Cornelius Agrippa, mentioned, among others, by Christopher Marlowe in *Doctor Faustus*; but

Lyly uses it here to subordinate his own imaginative processes to the queen's fancies, thus turning the place where his play was being performed—in this case, the royal palace of Whitehall—into a metamorphic theater in its own right, with Elizabeth I as the divine entity at the center of its magic. Indeed, Lyly often incorporated into his plays characters who bear a striking symbolic resemblance to the queen, and at one level his drama may be seen as a complex and occult courtship of Elizabeth's favor. For example, when Endymion is rejuvenated by a kiss from the virgin lady Cynthia, critics have detected a discreet request on Lyly's part that Elizabeth should reward his own loyal service with some form of remuneration. Sadly, nothing came of Lyly's many petitions to the queen, who declined to wave her magic wand for him in the form of a pension or a small monopoly such as were given to several other writers in the period. He aimed at the office of the Master of Revels, the impresario of the court theater with a lucrative sideline in the licensing of plays in London; but this went to a lesser man with better connections.

REPUTATION AND INFLUENCE

Lyly was disappointed in his career as a courtier, but as a poet his place on Parnassus is far more elevated than that of his rival for the mastership, the minor verse-maker Sir George Buc. Euphuism shaped fashionable prose in England for a decade and more, and several writers used the name of Lyly's hero to sell their own productions, such as Robert Greene's *Euphues His Censure to Philautus* (1587), which has nothing to do with these two characters at all. His influence as a dramatist is equally pervasive, but on the whole less obvious. Perhaps his main contribution was the witty and charming comic heroine, such as Campaspe and Sappho, the forerunner of many of Shakespeare's best-loved female characters. If one play were to be singled out as especially important and enduring, it must be *Galatea*. This play is particularly attractive to modern critics because of its complex games with gender and sexuality: two girls dressed as two boys fall in love with each other. But the play is also eminently actable, and it has been staged at least four times in recent years, in England at Oxford (1979) and Stratford-upon-Avon (1994), in Armidale, Australia (1995), and in Lyon, France (1998). Perhaps *Galatea*, of all his works, is the best way for the modern reader to begin an exploration of Lyly's distinctive literary and dramatic world.

[*See also* Elizabeth I; Christopher Marlowe; Patronage; *and* William Shakespeare: The Comedies.]

SELECTED WORKS

Euphues: The Anatomy of Wit (1578)

Euphues and His England (1580)

Campaspe (1584)

Sappho and Phao (1584)

Pap with an Hatchet (1589)

Endymion (1591)

Galatea (1592)

Midas (1592)

Mother Bombie (1594)

The Woman in the Moon (1597)

Love's Metamorphosis (1601)

EDITIONS

The best edition is the one currently in preparation by Manchester University Press, edited by G. K. Hunter, David Bevington, and Leah Scragg. By 2005 the following volumes had been published: *Campaspe* and *Sappho and Phao* (Hunter and Bevington, eds., 1996); *Galatea* and *Midas* (Hunter and Bevington, eds., 2000); *Endymion* (Bevington, ed., 2002); and *Euphues* and *Euphues and His England* (Scragg, ed., 2003).

Bond, R. Warwick, ed. *The Complete Works of John Lyly.* 3 vols. Oxford, 1902. The standard old-spelling edition of Lyly's works.

FURTHER READING

Alwes, Derek. " 'I Would Faine Serve': John Lyly's Career at Court." *Comparative Drama* 34 (2000/2001): 399–421.

Bennett, Josephine Waters. "Oxford and *Endymion.*" *PMLA* 57 (1942): 354–369. The only really convincing "topical" reading of a play by Lyly.

Donovan, Kevin J. "Recent Studies in John Lyly (1969–1990)." *English Literary Renaissance* 22 (1992): 435–450.

Houppert, Joseph W. *John Lyly.* Boston, 1975. Short introduction in the Twayne's English Authors Series.

Hunter, G. K. *John Lyly: The Humanist as Courtier.* London, 1962. Still the most complete study of Lyly's life and works.

McCabe, Richard. "Wit, Eloquence, and Wisdom in *Euphues: The Anatomy of Wit.*" *Studies in Philology* 81 (1984): 299–324. The best account of the relation between *Euphues* and "humanism."

Pincombe, Mike. *The Plays of John Lyly: Eros and Eliza.* Manchester, 1996. Deals with all eight plays in the courtly (and anticourtly) context.

Saccio, Peter. *The Court Comedies of John Lyly: A Study in Allegorical Dramaturgy.* Princeton, 1969. Mainly focused on *Campaspe* and *Galatea.*

Scragg, Leah. *The Metamorphoses of Galatea: A Study in Creative Adaptation.* Washington, DC, 1982. Detailed account of the influence of this play on later drama.

THE MABINOGION

Bettina Arnold

The *Pedair Cainc y Mabinogi* (*Four Branches of the Mabinogi*) is a collection of eleven medieval Welsh tales committed to writing between the twelfth and fourteenth centuries. They are full of magic, supernatural personages, and other characteristic elements of Celtic myth and legend. The two surviving complete manuscripts are in the *Llyfr Gwyn Rhydderch* (White Book of Rhydderch), written in the early fourteenth century, and in the *Llyfr Coch Hergest* (Red Book of Hergest), from the late fourteenth century. Two fragments of the second and third Branches are found in Peniarth 6, a manuscript from the early thirteenth century. The correct Welsh term for the Four Branches is *mabinogi*, but the scribal error *mabinogion*, found uniquely at the end of book I, was used by Lady Charlotte Guest as a title for the first English translation (1838–1849), which includes all eleven tales, and this has since become the accepted form. The etymological source of the title is probably *mab* ("tale of youth," or "of a youth"), but a reference to the Romano-British deity Maponus ("divine youth" or "great son") may be intended as well. The *Mabinogion* is one of the best-known collections of Celtic literature of the British Isles, but there is little consensus regarding the origins of the tales or their relationship to one another.

The *Red Book of Hergest*, named after its former home in Hergest, Herefordshire, consists of 362 red leather-bound folios containing most of the extant Welsh prose and verse from before 1400. One of the copyists, Hywel Fychan fab Hywel Goch of Buellt, worked for Hopcyn ap Tomas ab Einion (c. 1330 to 1403 or later) of Ynysforgan, Swansea, who may have commissioned the work, which remained in Hergest from 1465 until the early seventeenth century. The manuscript was donated to Oxford University in 1701 by the Reverend Thomas Wilkins and is now at the Bodleian Library, Oxford (MS Jesus College 111). The White Book of Rhydderch, in the collections of the National Library of Wales, is bound in two volumes known as Peniarth MS 4 and Peniarth MS 5. By about 1634 the manuscript was in the hands of the famous Flintshire antiquary and copyist John Jones of Gellilyfdy.

In 1658 the manuscript, which had been divided into two volumes, became part of the library of Robert Vaughan at Hengwrt in Merionethshire, which was transferred to Peniarth by W. W. E. Wynne in 1859. In 1904 it was bought by Sir John Williams, who presented it to the National Library as one of its founding collections. Lady Guest's *Mabinogion*, first published in Llandovery in 1838–1849, brought the tales out of obscurity and was the definitive translation for almost a century. Subsequent scholarship has focused on dating the transcription of the tales, the relationship between the two manuscript versions and other fragmentary versions, the authorship of the tales, and their impact on later literature.

THE TALES

The eleven tales of the *Mabinogion* are *The Four Branches of the Mabinogi* (*Pwyll, Branwen, Manawydan,* and *Math*), *Culhwch ac Olwen* (*Culhwch and Olwen*), *Breuddwyd Rhonabwy* (*The Dream of Rhonabwy*), *Breuddwyd Macsen Wledig* (*The Dream of Macsen Wledig*), *Cyfranc Lludd a Llefelys* (*Lludd and Llefely*), *Peredur Son of Efrawg, Owein or the Lady of the Fountain,* and *Gereint Son of Erbin*. Some scholars do not include the romances *Peredur, Owein,* and *Gereint* in the *Mabinogion* because of the obvious influence in them of the later Continental Arthurian tradition. There is also disagreement as to when the tales were redacted (rendered from oral to written texts) and when they were actually composed. Patrick Ford dates the *White Book of Rhydderch* between 1300 and 1325, and the *Red Book of Hergest* between 1375 and 1425, while Proinsias Mac Cana argues that the manuscripts were composed no earlier than the eleventh century. Rachel Bromwich and D. Simon Evans date the *White Book* about 1350 and the *Red Book* between 1382 and 1410, while Gwyn Williams suggests that the tales were compiled in their present form sometime in the late eleventh or early twelfth century. Caerwyn Williams agrees with Sir Ifor Williams that the Four Branches may have been the work of a native of Dyfed in southern Wales around

1060, when all three provinces were under a single ruler, Gruffudd ap Llywelyn ap Seisyll. There is also disagreement about the identity and social status of the authors: some scholars assume the redactors were members of the intelligentsia; some believe that a single author was responsible for all the tales, or at least the Four Branches; and some, such as Andrew Breeze, suggest that the author of the Four Branches may have been female.

The First Branch deals with the youthful exploits of *Pwyll* (literally "wisdom, reason"), the ruler of Dyfed, a peninsula of southwestern Wales, in the Otherworld, his marriage to Rhiannon, and the birth of their son, Pryderi. The Second Branch, entitled *Branwen, Daughter of Llyr*, actually deals with several of the children of Llyr, the Welsh sea god, including Bendigeidfran—also known as Bran ("crow/raven"), the Blessed—his brother Manawydan, their sister Branwen, and two half-brothers, the evil Evnisien and the gentle Nisien. Branwen is married off to Matholwch, the king of Ireland, who is insulted by Evnisien, resulting in a war between the children of Llyr and the Irish. Branwen dies, and Bendigeidfran is killed; his severed head is ultimately buried in London. The Third Branch, *Manawydan, Son of Llyr*, features some of the same characters found in the First and Second branches, notably Rhiannon, now widowed, and Pryderi. Magic plays an important role here, but the wanderings of Manawydan and Cigfa also provide useful and evocative descriptions of the lives of Celtic craft workers and the patronage system that supported them. In the Fourth Branch, *Math, Son of Mathonwy*, revenge and the relatively powerless state of elite women are important elements. The tale features two magicians, Math and Gwydion, as well as Gwydion's sister Arianrhod ("silver wheel") and her unwanted son, Lleu Llaw Gyffes ("fair one of the steady hand").

In *Culhwch ac Olwen*, an Arthurian narrative probably redacted sometime in the eleventh century, Culhwch, the hero, born in a pigsty, falls in love with Olwen, daughter of the giant Ysbaddaden and journeys to Arthur's court to ask for help in winning her. *The Dream of Rhonabwy*, also considered an Arthurian narrative, may be one of the last surviving texts in the Middle Welsh tradition. It is found in its entirety only in the *Red Book of Hergest*, but it is set in the reign of Madog ap Meredudd, prince of Powys, who died in 1159. The tale consists mainly of a dream sequence in which Arthur's champions and those of his enemies are named and described in detail more reminiscent of a laundry list than a narrative. *The Dream of Macsen (Maxen) Wledig* has been interpreted as related to the *ailing* tradition in Irish poetry, which features dreams with an underlying political subtext. Maxen, emperor of Rome, dreams of a maiden named Elen and falls in love with her. He sets out to find her and must then fight to reclaim his kingdom, which has been usurped during his absence. Both Maxen and Elen have been equated with historical personages, the former with the Spanish-born Maximus (or Magnus), Roman emperor from 383 to 388, and the latter with Elen Luyddog of Segontium (Carnarvon), wife of the historical Magnus. *Lludd and Llefelys* tells how Lludd, son of Beli Mawr, ruler of Britain, and his brother Llefelys, ruler of France, rid Britain of three plagues: the Coraniaid, a sly and malicious alien people; a horrific scream heard in every household in Britain at midnight on Beltaine (May Eve), frightening people half to death; and the disappearance of all the provisions in the king's court each night.

Peredur, Son of Efrawg, one of the Tair Rhamant ("Three Romances") in the *Mabinogion*, was redacted sometime in the thirteenth century. It has obvious connections to the story of Percival, and manuscripts are found in both the *White Book* and the *Red Book*. *Peredur, Owein or the Lady of the Fountain*, and *Gereint Son of Erbin* have been linked to works of Chrétien de Troyes (fl. 1160–1182) that deal with identical or clearly related protagonists.

DOCUMENTS OF A CULTURE

Modern readers' tendency to treat the *Mabinogion* as a work of literature rather than a transcription of a living oral tradition obscures the existence of older themes embedded within the text that predate the introduction of writing and Christianity. Many of these themes are also attested in the archaeological record of Iron Age Celtic Europe as well as Celtic Britain. The Otherworld is depicted as a mirror of the world of the living, in which life continues according to the status of the individual; burials of both Continental and, where preserved, Island Celts bear out the existence of such a belief in the Celtic world. Feasting and drinking are important in the creation and maintenance of sociopolitical relations in the stories, and there is archaeological evidence for the mead, ale, and wine mentioned there. Alcohol serves as a social lubricant and a form of elite currency used to bind followers to their lord in the texts, as is also reflected in the cauldrons, drinking horns, flagons, cups, dippers, and beakers that have been found in elite Iron Age Celtic graves. Alcohol as a psychoactive agent links this world to the Otherworld in several texts, especially those dealing with the inauguration of rulers.

Reciprocity and the generous ruler are represented in the tales and in the archaeological record, while the warband, or *teulu*, and the cult of the warrior play significant roles in the texts. Sovereignty is personified as a female figure in several tales, but the contest between *Pwyll* and *Gwawl* in the Second Branch is probably the best example. Rhiannon confers the kingdom upon her husband with her person, but the wedding feast is hers to command, and by withholding it from Gwawl she manages to delay the nuptials long enough for Pwyll, whom she has chosen to be her consort, to outwit his rival.

The material culture associated with elite status in the archaeological record is surprisingly consistent with the texts. Feasting equipment (drinking horns, cauldrons, cups of gold or silver) is a good example, as is hunting equipment. Bows and arrows are found exclusively in elite male graves on the Continent. The link between hunting and the Otherworld is present in both the Continental archaeological record and the *Mabinogion*, exemplified by the meeting of Pwyll and Arawn over the body of a slain stag. Torcs (neck rings of bronze, silver, or gold) and metal weapons, especially swords and spears, are found in elite burials in both contexts, and metalworking as an activity imbued with high status and magical associations is archaeologically attested and represented in the literature. Animal imagery in elite culture is reflected in some of the names and symbols in the literature, especially boars, bulls, hounds, birds of prey or corvids, and waterfowl. Shape-shifting and animal-human hybrid forms, as seen in *Math ab Mathonwy*, are clearly represented in Iron Age iconography.

We also learn about the social structure of these ancient people through the stories' references to fosterage and matrilineal succession (note the importance of mother's brothers and sister's sons; Culhwuch and Arthur are each other's mothers' sisters' sons). Their belief system is reflected in number symbolism in material culture as well as text (triplism; multiples of three; three and seven as auspicious and powerful numbers) and in the Celtic "cult of the head."

The close correlations between those elements of the archaeological record related to elite culture and ritual practices and the insular texts, especially from Wales and Ireland, should be taken into consideration in attempts to interpret this material, allowing analyses that move beyond relatively sterile debates over style, dates, or authorship. Interpretations that include an anthropological perspective put the *Mabinogion* back into the context of the living society that created these richly imagined and densely layered tales.

[*See also* Arthurian Literature.]

EDITIONS AND TRANSLATIONS

Bromwich, Rachel, and D. Simon Evans. *Culhwuch and Olwen: An Edition and Study of the Oldest Arthurian Tale.* Cardiff, U.K., 1992. Detailed and definitive study of one of the most important tales, with extensive discussion of themes and phrasing.

Ford, Patrick K., trans. *The Mabinogi and Other Medieval Welsh Tales.* Berkeley, CA, 1977.

Gantz, Jeffrey, trans. *The Mabinogion.* Harmondsworth, U.K., 1976.

Jones, Gwyn, and Thomas Jones. *The Mabinogion.* London, 1949; rev. ed., 1993.

FURTHER READING

Arnold, Bettina. "'Drinking the Feast': Alcohol and the Legitimation of Power in Celtic Europe." *Cambridge Archaeological Journal* 9 (1999): 71–93. Anthropological interpretation of Celtic alcohol consumption as a sociopolitical activity.

Breeze, Andrew. *Medieval Welsh Literature.* Dublin, Ireland, 1997. A controversial but intriguing interpretation suggesting that the *Four Branches of the Mabinogi* were written by Princess Gwenllian (c. 1098–1136) of Gwynedd and Dyfed.

Mac Cana, Proinsias. *The Mabinogi.* Cardiff, U.K., 1977; 2d ed., 1992. Seminal interpretation and analysis of the text.

Roberts, Brynley F. *Studies on Middle Welsh Literature.* New York, 1992. Includes an extensive section on the *Mabinogion*.

Williams, Gwyn. *An Introduction to Welsh Literature.* Cardiff, U.K., 1992. Outlines the development of Welsh literature from the sixth century to the twentieth.

Williams, J. E. Caerwyn. *The Poets of the Welsh Princes.* Rev. ed. Cardiff, U.K., 1994. Detailed discussion of the writers of poetry and prose in Medieval Wales and their social context.

THOMAS BABINGTON MACAULAY

Jennifer Ruth

A historian and a poet, a colorful essayist and a riveting orator, an administrator in English India and a leading Whig reformer in Britain, Thomas Babington Macaulay (1800–1859) was a much-discussed, admired, and, sometimes, resented figure in Victorian England. He continues to provoke conversation today as scholars debate the legacy of two documents: his *History of England from the Accession of James II*, a narrative sprawling over five volumes, though spanning only seventeen years, and his "Minute on Indian Education," a statement calling for the study of English in Indian Education. While there is no doubt that both texts greatly influenced Macaulay's contemporaries, whether that influence proved beneficial or detrimental remains an open question.

THE MACAULAY FAMILY

Macaulay was the first of nine children born to Zachary and Selena Macaulay. A member of the Clapham sect (a group of humanitarian-minded Evangelicals), Zachary Macaulay worked tirelessly for the abolition of slavery. Zachary expected great things of his son, and Macaulay showed signs of promise from an early age, reading at age three and writing what he called a "universal history" at eight. Macaulay's novel reading, though, annoyed Zachary, who wanted Macaulay to occupy himself with more solemn studies. However, Macaulay's passion for literature led to what made arguably his biggest impact on history: the "Minute on Indian Education," which helped spawn English literature as a modern discipline (see below). What warmth and applause he did not receive from his father, he got in abundance from his mother and siblings. Later, after Macaulay left Trinity College, Cambridge, and began his double career as essayist and member of Parliament, these family members provided an audience upon whom he could test his essays and speeches before they were unleashed on *Edinburgh Review* readers or on the House of Commons. Throughout his adult life, he supported his family financially and remained devoted to them, never marrying or forming significant new attachments but looking to them—particularly his sisters Hannah and Margaret—to fulfill his emotional needs.

ESSAYIST

While Macaulay had published a few pieces in *Knight's Quarterly Magazine*, a small mouthpiece for himself and a few friends from Cambridge, his literary life began in earnest when he published "Milton" in the leading Whig journal *Edinburgh Review* in August 1825. "Like Byron, [Macaulay] awoke one morning and found himself famous," his grandnephew George Trevelyan later wrote of the effect of that essay. With "Milton," "Johnson," and other essays in the *Edinburgh Review*, Macaulay quickly developed a distinctive, rhetorical style. His essays abound in paradox, evocative concrete detail, and eviscerating sarcasm. A famous example of the sarcasm is his comment on James Mill's *Essays on Government*. "We have here," Macaulay wrote, "an elaborate treatise on Government, from which, but for one or two passing allusions, it would not appear that the author was aware that any governments actually existed among men." He was indefatigably entertaining, though his humor was often at another's expense. About one poor writer's work, Macaulay wrote, "Compared with the labour of reading through these volumes, all other labour, the labour of thieves on the treadmill, of children in factories, of negroes in sugar plantations, is an agreeable recreation." He could sustain his readers' attention through even the longest article, and his were regularly seventy thousand to eighty thousand words. In 1843, when he collected these writings together and published them in three volumes, nobody was surprised when they sold as well as if they were penny dreadfuls.

The essays did not succeed on wit alone. Called "a book in breeches" by Sydney Smith, one of the founders of the *Edinburgh Review*, Macaulay was a voracious reader of history and literature, and he peppered his writings with historical references and literary allusions. He could even marshal statistics when necessary. In Macaulay's review of Robert Southey's *Colloquies on Society*, for example, that poet's disdain for the Victorian present and his nostalgia for the paternalistic past look obtusely indulgent next to Macaulay's string of statistics testifying to the masses' increased longevity and improved diet. Such stinging critiques of the works of eminent men made him a few enemies, and posterity has not always agreed with the judgments he pronounced on his contemporaries. He disliked, for example, the writings of Charles Dickens, Thomas Carlyle, and, most typically, the Romantics. He dismissed all things abstract or mystical, preferring the practical and pragmatic ("An acre in Middlesex is preferable to a principality in Utopia," he quipped). His biggest failings, though, were his complacence about the virtues of the middle class and his readiness to believe that England had magically transformed into a meritocracy after the Reform Act of 1832. "Men of real merit will, if they persevere, at last reach the station to which they are entitled," he wrote confidently. For these and other reasons, Lytton Strachey called him a "philistine," and yet one cannot help but nurse a quiet conviction that time has proved Macaulay right more often than it has proved him wrong. He did not need to wait for Sigmund Freud, to take one example, to scoff at the utilitarians' notion that men always act in their own self-interest.

WHIG STATESMAN

Nowhere was Macaulay more right than in his outspoken support of the 1832 Reform Act enfranchising much of the middle class. On 2 March 1831, only one year after gaining a seat representing Calne in Parliament, Macaulay urged the House of Commons to pass the act. In doing so, he secured his place at the forefront of the Whig Party, that reasonable party which neither called for revolution, like the Radicals sometimes seemed to do, nor reclined on their privileges, like the Tories. "I do, in my conscience, believe that, unless the plan proposed, or some similar plan, be speedily adopted, great and terrible calamities will befall us," Macaulay declared of the Reform Act; "entertaining this opinion, I think myself bound to state it, not as a threat, but as a reason. I support this bill because it will improve our institutions; but I support it also because it tends to preserve them." Macaulay steered an enormously effective course between alarmism and reason as he strove to convince his peers of the necessity of reform. While he warned Parliament that the middle class would revolt if the act were not passed, he also stressed

the middle class's investment in averting revolution. Precisely because this class owned property, it had a stake in preserving stability, he argued. But it was not simply to appease the middle class that Macaulay felt reform was required, it was also because Macaulay believed in the superior capabilities of the middle class and viewed this class's interests as largely synonymous with the nation's own.

Macaulay left Parliament to accept a position in India but returned to it in 1839, representing Edinburgh. In 1847, he lost the election for Edinburgh but was invited to run again in 1852 and won handily this time. He continued to represent Edinburgh until 1856, when he resigned because of deteriorating health. Macaulay championed a number of progressive causes during this long career. In particular, he was a consistent and insistent champion of religious liberty, arguing for the secularization of the state and the abolition of any institutionalized biases against non-Anglicans. Undoubtedly, though, the passing of the Reform Act was the defining event of his political career. After the House voted in favor of it, he wrote to a friend: "If I should live fifty years the impression of it will be as fresh and sharp in my mind as if it had just taken place. It was like seeing Caesar stabbed in the Senate House, or seeing Oliver taking the mace from the table, a sight to be seen only once and never to be forgotten." The act was both the occasion for his most dramatic and impressive Parliamentary speech, and the standard by which he judged history. In Macaulay's view, as would become clear when he wrote his *History of England*, history was a series of events leading slowly but surely up to the Reform Act.

HISTORIAN

Despite his career in Parliament, and during breaks from it, Macaulay continued to write. His book of poetry *Lays of Ancient Rome* came out in 1842 and sold very well. The work for which he had the highest hopes, however, was his *History of England from the Accession of James II*, begun after his defeat in the 1847 general election. Originally, Macaulay planned to start with the Glorious Revolution in 1688 and continue up to the Reform Act in 1832, but by his death he had only reached 1702. Despite the small amount of time covered, the history was both a popular and a critical success, showcased in bookstores throughout Britain and propped on the desks of all budding historians. The first two volumes appeared in 1848, the second two in 1855, and the last posthumously in 1861. The sales of the *History of England* rivaled even those enjoyed by the works of Charles Dickens and Sir Walter Scott, and it was translated into German, Polish, Danish, Swedish, Italian, French, Dutch, Spanish, Hungarian, Russian, Bohemian, and Persian. Perhaps the greatest testimony to the *History*'s success, though, is that largely due to it, Macaulay was made Baron Macaulay of Rothley in 1857, the first person ever to be given a peerage in honor of literary achievement.

The most famous chapter of the *History of England* is a model of social history that is one of the first examples of the genre. In an 1828 essay, Macaulay first explained his idea of what he termed "domestic history." He wrote:

> The circumstances which have most influence on the happiness of mankind, the changes of manners and morals, the transition of communities from poverty to wealth, from knowledge to ignorance, from ferocity to humanity—these are, for the most part, noiseless revolutions. Their progress is rarely indicated by what historians are pleased to call important events. . . . He who would understand these things rightly must not confine his observations to palaces and solemn days. He must see ordinary men as they appear in their ordinary business and in their ordinary pleasures. He must mingle in the crowds of the exchange and the coffee-house. He must obtain admittance to the convivial table and the domestic hearth.

Twenty years later, in chapter 3 of the *History of England*, Macaulay offered an example of this mode of history in his detailed snapshot of England in 1685. He begins the chapter by speculating about the size of the population in that year, then describes the largely still-rural landscape, before moving to the social and political climate. He moves seamlessly between concrete specificity and insightful generalization. "In Covent Garden a filthy and noisy market was held close to the dwellings of the great," we learn on one page; "fruit women screamed, carters fought, cabbage stalks, and rotten apples accumulated in heaps at the thresholds of the Countess of Berkshire and the Bishop of Durham." "In the seventeenth century," we read on the next page, "the pulpit was to a large portion of the population what the periodical now is." The style he cultivated in his essays pays off in his history, as he brings history closer by playing on his reader's emotions. A gruesome image likely to make the reader queasy, for example, is followed by a line likely to raise a smile: "Multitudes assembled to see gladiators hack each other to pieces with deadly weapons, and shouted with delight when one of the combatants lost a finger or an eye. The

prisons were hells on earth, seminaries of every crime and of every disease. At the assizes the lean and yellow culprits brought with them from their cells to the dock an atmosphere of stench and pestilence which sometimes avenged them signally on bench, bar, and jury."

In the twentieth and twenty-first centuries, critics have continued to applaud the dynamic social history exemplified by chapter 3, but they have grown impatient with the *History of England*'s simplistic narrative of inevitable progress. Two world wars have made it hard to believe that civilization is, as Macaulay claimed, always moving "rapidly forward." Critics also argue that the history as a whole is told from the specific perspective of the middle class. They charge that, in his eagerness to view all of history as leading ineluctably toward the Reform Act of 1832, Macaulay anachronistically implies that Britain owes even the Glorious Revolution to the strivings of that class.

ADMINISTRATOR IN ENGLISH INDIA

Not long after Macaulay first entered Parliament, he was offered a position on the Supreme Council of the East India Company. He did not want to go to India, but he knew that if he did, he could save enough money in five years to buy himself and his family economic independence for decades. He lived in India from 1834 to 1838, returning home one year early after receiving an inheritance from an uncle. While in India, Macaulay developed virtually from scratch the entire Indian Penal Code. As passionate about English literature as ever, he also dramatically swayed the 1835 debate over whether the British should encourage the "natives" to study English literature rather than, as had been the policy, Sanskrit, Arabic, or Persian.

Ironically, English literature as a discipline of study first began in India before carrying over to England. Whether Macaulay's "Minute on Indian Education" directly or indirectly influenced this development is debated, but certainly this writing is the most forceful articulation of the British policy of instructing Indians in English literature. As such, the "Minute" has been criticized in recent decades as testifying to Britain's use of literature as a kind of ideological weapon among its colonies. Most notably, Gauri Viswanathan (1989) has argued that the institutionalization of English studies in India "created a blueprint for social control in the guise of a humanistic program of enlightenment" (p. 10). Macaulay intended English literature to refine the sensibilities of the Indian elite who would, in turn, transmit the new culture they were imbibing to those below them. "We must at present," Macaulay declared, "do our best to form a class who may be interpreters between us and the millions whom we govern; a class of persons, Indian in blood and colour, but English in taste, in opinions, in morals, and in intellect." Used first to justify literary study in the colonial periphery, Macaulay's understanding of English literature as a civilizing, humanizing force became the rationale for literary study at the empire's center as well.

[*See also* Orientalism.]

SELECTED WORKS

Lays of Ancient Rome (1842)

Critical and Historical Essays Contributed to the Edinburgh Review, 3 vols. (1843)

History of England from the Accession of James II (1849–1861)

Speeches, Parliamentary, and Miscellaneous, 2 vols. (1854)

The Indian Education Minutes, edited by Henry Woodrow (1862)

EDITIONS

Pinney, Thomas, ed. *The Letters of Macaulay.* 3 vols. Cambridge, U.K., 1974–1976.

Trevor-Roper, Hugh R., ed. *The History of England.* Harmondsworth, U.K., 1979.

FURTHER READING

Beatty, Richmond Croon. *Lord Macaulay: Victorian Liberal.* Norman, OK, 1938. Good biography, also containing discussion of the liberal tradition and thoughtful analyses of Macaulay's writings and speeches.

Clive, John. *Macaulay: The Shaping of the Historian.* New York, 1973. Biography with three useful chapters on Macaulay's Indian period.

Ghosh, Peter R. "Macaulay and the Heritage of the Enlightenment." *English Historical Review* 112 (April 1997): 358–395. Excellent, in-depth discussion of the *History of England.*

Hamburger, John. *Macaulay and the Whig Tradition.* Chicago, 1976.

Trevelyan, George Otto. *The Life and Letters of Lord Macaulay.* 2 vols. 1875. Repr. New York, 1901.

Viswanathan, Gauri. *Masks of Conquest: Literary Study and British Rule in India.* New York, 1989. Analysis of the implications of English study in India.

Wahrman, Dror. *Imagining the Middle Class: The Political Representation of Class in Britain, c. 1780–1840.* New York, 1995. A study of the way the term "middle class" was used by various political groups from the French Revolution to the Reform Act. Useful for contextualizing Macaulay's invocations of the "middle class."

HUGH MacDIARMID

Nancy K. Gish

Born in the Scottish Border town of Langholm, Christopher Murray Grieve (1892–1978) chose "Hugh MacDiarmid" as his pen name in 1922. In ancient Gothic, he said, "Hugh" meant "divine wisdom," and "MacDiarmid" identified him with the Gaelic. He made that name an emblem of Scottish nationalism and a distinct modernism, parallel to but separate from the modernism developed in England. As the key figure in the cultural and literary movement called the Scottish Renaissance, he fused his nationalism with poetry as a way of renewing what he considered an intellectually exhausted and linguistically limited tradition. His personal and public life were thus in a sense inseparable: the poet's goal was to discover a new and expanded Scottish consciousness, which the political persona worked to establish. Though he left school at eighteen already planning to write, the catalyst for his emergence as a Scottish nationalist and a major modernist poet was World War I.

MacDiarmid enlisted in 1915 and served throughout the war at hospitals in Salonika and Marseilles. Travel, experience with soldiers from all over the world, and the horror of war led to a sharp break with the past. But the impact of the Great War on MacDiarmid's language and poetry, and thus on Scottish modernism, differed significantly from the impact on writers in England. MacDiarmid said he encountered, at Salonika, camaraderie shared among soldiers of all nations, except those of England. They used a mixture of languages he called "polyglottery," the medium of expression used to communicate across nationalities. He returned to Scotland determined to redefine "Scottishness" in opposition to English dominance in Britain, and to find an alternative poetry, inexpressible in English. Between the Wars, he promoted the Scottish Renaissance as an editor, publisher, and critic: he edited a three-volume anthology of Scottish poets, *Northern Numbers* (1920–1922), he edited and published a series of Scottish literary and cultural journals—the *Scottish Chapbook* (1922–1923), the *Scottish Nation* (1923), and the *Northern Review* (1924)—and he wrote nearly all of his poetry, which was to be published in book after book

into the 1970s. While his prose advocacy sustained a continuing argument for Scottish renewal, his poetry was to demonstrate cultural difference and a Scottish modern literature.

The initial result of this intense activity was the appearance, in 1922, of a prose monologue and several poems in Scots by "Hugh M'Diarmid." The Scottish Renaissance thus began the same year that *The Waste Land* and *Ulysses* were published and with comparable radical experimentation. Like T. S. Eliot and Ezra Pound, MacDiarmid needed a new language for the complexity of the postwar experience, but unlike them he had an existing lexicon. As Pound and Eliot turned to Latin and French, MacDiarmid began writing in what he called "Synthetic Scots," using words—rare, archaic, unknown—from any period of Scottish history or region of Scotland, words with sounds lost to Modern English. Although he later wrote in equally unfamiliar English, his poetic experimentation remained focused on words. While his vast output showed great thematic and technical variety, it retained a focus on Scotland, the expansion of human consciousness, and the discovery, in words, of the unknown. In *Sangschaw* (1925) and *Penny Wheep* (1926), he created lyrics in Braid Scots (Broad Scots), forms he expanded into long poetic sequences in *A Drunk Man Looks at the Thistle* (1926) and *To Circumjack Cencrastus* (1930). During the 1930s, he shifted increasingly to philosophical "poems of fact" in "Synthetic English," a pastiche of languages and vocabulary from science and technology. Like "Synthetic Scots," it focused on the creative possibilities of individual words but aimed at larger, more international ideas and experiences. These late experimental developments are most fully worked out in *Stony Limits, and Other Poems* (1934) and *In Memoriam James Joyce* (1955). Though the early lyrics established his reputation in Scotland, and political activity made him a prominent figure, international recognition came late: in the 1950s and 1960s he traveled widely, and through the 1970s he received many honors.

MacDiarmid's most important work shares key characteristics. He demonstrated that great poetry could be written from alternative British cultures and languages; he developed original forms of linguistic experimentalism; and he developed open, inclusive, multilingual poetic styles. He sought to create new, distinctively Scottish ways of feeling and experiencing the world, and to connect these with other forms of experimental work not only in English but in Russian and in European languages. To do this, he tapped into the vast storehouse of the Scots Vernacular and, later, into Gaelic, world languages, and every available source in dictionaries.

EARLY SCOTS LYRICS

Prior to his World War I experience, Christopher Grieve had opposed the use of the Scots Vernacular as sentimental, rural, and limited. As "Hugh MacDiarmid," he transformed the language by creating "Synthetic Scots." Though no one spoke exactly this kind of Scots, the rhythms, sounds, and most of the vocabulary were familiar. The combination of aural familiarity with archaic, rare, or unfamiliar words allowed a range of expression not available in either English or any single Scottish dialect; in his early lyrics this new "polyglottery" produced startling images and striking juxtapositions. For MacDiarmid, art was the extension of consciousness into the unknown, and the Scottish Vernacular provided access to that consciousness. Scots words, he claimed, provided an inexhaustible source of unique perception and insights, and many of the early poems derive key words and images directly from John Jamieson's *Etymological Dictionary of the Scottish Language* (1808). The result can be uncanny and moving, as in the opening line of his first Scots poem, "The Watergaw": "Aye weet forenicht i' the yow-trummle" (One wet early evening in the cold weather in July after the sheep shearing [literally "ewe-tremble"]). There is no way to say this in English without sounding clumsy, and there is no exact equivalent for the image. Similarly, in "The Eemis Stane" ("The Unsteady Stone"), the opening line is carried by the Scots words: "I' the how-dumb-deid o' the cauld hairst nicht" (In the silent dead center of the cold harvest night) and by the Germanic sound of "nicht," which does not exist in Modern English. For MacDiarmid, such lapsed words could evoke lapsed feelings and experiences that were distinctively Scottish, and, at the same time, could allow for a new, modern vision of a changed world. While this work shares the difficulty and estrangement of other modernisms, it remains based in Scotland and does not focus on urban life or a mechanized world. Rather, it characteristically takes a stance outside earth altogether, observing from a cosmic perspective. The "watergaw" is that "antrin (rare) thing," an indistinct rainbow, revealing a sense of the meaning of death. The eemis stane "wags" in the heavens—part earth, part gravestone—and is inexplicably linked with memory and history. MacDiarmid claimed that using a Scots word was like hitting a chord rather than a note because the words carried many meanings, some of them contradictory. By juxtaposing these multiple meanings, he wrote lyrics that repeatedly startle with their strange and sometimes eerie possibilities of perception. Although the early lyrics create the distinctive effects MacDiarmid saw as new and essential to the creation of a Scottish modernism, he wanted to explore broader themes and experiences. He turned to long poetic sequences that combine many poetic styles and forms.

His masterpiece, and the most important modern Scottish poem, is *A Drunk Man Looks at the Thistle*, which aims to achieve a kind of "whole" by plunging into all human experience—drunkenness, sexuality, hysteria, and social collapse, as well as love, desire, and the possibility for a renewal of Scotland and all humanity. Influenced by Dostoevsky, among others, MacDiarmid explored antitheses of human experience. He consciously eschewed all external structures, including the template of myth, seeking instead a kind of inclusiveness through the reiteration of key central symbols: thistle (the national symbol of Scotland), moon, man and woman, body and soul, transcendence and despair. All are illumined by "spirit" or spirits: drunkenness is a form of vision, and "whisky" comes from a Gaelic word meaning "water of life." In *A Drunk Man*, MacDiarmid moved beyond sudden, extraordinary lyric moments to claim a Scottish history, culture, and philosophical vision in which the narrator, freed by whisky from all conventional categories, "looks at" the state of Scotland and the contradictory, chaotic, tragic, and comic condition of humanity. It retains the use of rare Scots words but places them in the larger context of what he called "the puzzle o' man's soul." *To Circumjack Cencrastus* (1930) aimed at a complementary vision of synthesis but was less successful. It served less to resolve poetic antitheses than to reveal the need for a new medium.

NEW FORMS OF POETRY

In the early 1930s, MacDiarmid's first marriage broke up, he was unable to sustain regular employment, and he met and married his second wife, Valda Trevlyn. In 1932 they moved to Whalsay, a tiny island in the Shetlands—stark, bare, and often solitary. He began to write poems in English as well as Scots and to try new experiments with language, including a series of poems evoking the water and light of his childhood home and "Synthetic English" poems combining words from science and technology as well as many languages. The "Synthetic English" poems focus on "fact" and the natural world. Perhaps the finest achievement in this new medium is "On a Raised Beach," which opens and closes with passages of scientific and rare English as well as old Norn words, so dense as to be almost unreadable and yet intensely compelling. Like the early lyrics, it opens with a rhythm and sound that evokes deep feeling even before it is understood: "All is lithogenesis—or lochia, / Carpolite fruit of the forbidden tree, / Stones blacker than any in the Caaba, / Cream-colored, caen-stone, chatoyant pieces," (All is the process of the production of rock—or the watery discharge after birth, / Fossil fruit of the forbidden tree, / Stones blacker than the sacred black stone in the shrine of Mecca, / Cream-colored, lightish-yellow building stone, stone with undulating or floating lustre). When the poem moves to a kind of materialist and scientific meditation on creation and human existence, the stones retain immediacy and the sensuality of touch and color. Throughout the 1930s MacDiarmid wrote increasingly massive "poems of fact," using Whitmanesque lists and Joycean linguistic multiplicity. He planned an enormous, interrelated set of poems called *Mature Art*, of which only a small part was published, most importantly *In Memoriam James Joyce* (1955). In this last, very long poem, he celebrated world languages and denied the centrality of English.

ACHIEVEMENT AND INFLUENCE

It is difficult to define a single pattern in the life's work of a poet who sought constant movement into new consciousness, yet the first Braid Scots lyrics and the late, voluminous and open-ended "English" compositions have comparable aesthetic purposes. Having exhausted one form, MacDiarmid tried another and another. What changed was the nature of experimentation with words and the degree to which he could achieve his purpose. As the vision of language and its role in culture expanded, the proportion of success may have lessened, but in poems like "On a Raised Beach" or *Dìreadh I, II, and III* (1974), the results are as arresting and original.

Throughout his life, as an essayist, critic, journalist, and political figure, MacDiarmid promoted ideas he demonstrated in his poetry. While he has remained outside the mainstream of critical discussion despite the innovation and brilliance of much of his poetry, his achievements include the creation of modernist poetry that influenced Irish as well as Scottish poets to recover cultural visions other than those of England; techniques that evolved increasingly into large, open, multilingual and international poetry; and an original experimentalism that is unlike either mainstream or avant-garde poetry of England or America and that helped make possible the continuing creation of new and individual ways of Scottish writing. His poetry remains the major achievement of the Scottish Renaissance he largely created and promoted, and his commitment to an alternative culture continues to influence new kinds of work.

[*See also* Edwin Muir.]

SELECTED WORKS

Annals of the Five Senses (1923)
Sangschaw (1925)
Penny Wheep (1926)
A Drunk Man Looks at the Thistle (1926)
Contemporary Scottish Studies: First Series (1926)
To Circumjack Cencrastus, or The Curly Snake (1930)
First Hymn to Lenin, and Other Poems (1931)
Scots Unbound, and Other Poems (1932)
Scottish Scene, or The Intelligent Man's Guide to Albyn (with Lewis Grassic Gibbon; 1934)
Stony Limits, and Other Poems (1934)
At the Sign of the Thistle: a Collection of Essays (1934)
Second Hymn to Lenin, and Other Poems (1935)
Lucky Poet: A Self-Study in Literature and Political Ideas, Being the Autobiography of Hugh MacDiarmid (Christopher Murray Grieve) (1943)
In Memoriam James Joyce: From A Vision of World Language (1955)
Complete Poems, 1920–1976, 2 vols. (1978)
The Raucle Tongue: Hitherto Uncollected Prose, 3 vols. (1996–1998)

FURTHER READING

Bold, Alan. *MacDiarmid: Christopher Murray Grieve, A Critical Biography*. Amherst, MA, 1988. The only full-length biography. Critical commentary on all the major works. An essential source for the life and Scottish context.

Buthlay, Kenneth. *Hugh MacDiarmid*. Edinburgh, 1982. An introduction to and seminal reading of MacDiarmid's work. Revised and updated from the original text published in 1964.

Carruthers, Gerard, David Goldie, and Alastair Renfrew, eds. *Beyond Scotland: New Contexts for Twentieth-Century Scottish Literature.* Amsterdam and New York, 2004. An edited collection of essays rethinking twentieth-century Scottish literature. Includes essays on MacDiarmid as well as new perspectives on his place in Scottish modernism.

Gish, Nancy K. *Hugh MacDiarmid: The Man and His Work.* London, 1984. A study of the poetry drawing on extensive interviews with the poet and Scottish writers as well as criticism. Includes biographical first chapter.

Gish, Nancy K. *Hugh MacDiarmid: Man and Poet.* Orono, ME, and Edinburgh, 1992. An edited collection of essays on the poet's life, works, and contexts. Includes interviews with family and other poets, and an extensive bibliography.

Kerrigan, Catherine. *Whaur Extremes Meet: The Poetry of Hugh MacDiarmid 1920–1934.* Edinburgh, 1983. Defines MacDiarmid as a Romantic poet linked to both the traditional Scottish ballad tradition and modern discoveries in science and art. Covers only work published through 1934.

McCarey, Peter. *Hugh MacDiarmid and the Russians.* Edinburgh, 1987. Examines the work in relation to modern Russian philosophy and poetry, connections that distinguish MacDiarmid from most modernists writing in English.

Riach, Alan. *The Poetry of Hugh MacDiarmid.* Glasgow, 1999. An introduction for first-time readers, placing MacDiarmid in the contexts of Scottish cultural tradition and modern Scottish literature.

Whyte, Christopher. *Modern Scottish Poetry.* Edinburgh, 2004. A poet's reconsideration of modern Scottish poetry in relation to Scottish national identity. Includes discussion of MacDiarmid's early poetry as a response to a crisis in language and of *In Memoriam James Joyce* as a move to postmodernism.

HENRY MACKENZIE

George E. Haggerty

Henry Mackenzie (1745–1831), the son of a prominent physician, was born in Edinburgh, where he spent much of his life working in government service. His three novels were all written before his mid-thirties. He is important to literary history because of these novels—*The Man of Feeling* (1771), *The Man of the World* (1773), and *Julia de Roubigné* (1777)—and because of his contribution to the periodicals *The Mirror* (1779–1780) and *The Lounger* (1785–1787), both of which he edited. He also wrote a number of plays, none of which had much success on the Edinburgh stage.

THE MAN OF FEELING

Mackenzie's first novel is one of the set pieces of the Age of Sensibility, and it has justifiably been celebrated as one of the key texts of the age. A bizarre novel in many ways, it tells the story of Harley, a sensitive, self-effacing hero who can never bring himself to express the love he feels for the elusive Miss Walton. His passivity comes to seem self-defeating, and his desires are fulfilled only at the moment of his death, at which time Miss Walton recognizes his love and tells him that she loves him in return. If Harley is attempting to reach beyond the privacy of his own feeling, his effort simply fails. Issues of gender and class are so vividly depicted in this novel that it is almost an allegory of the capitalist crisis of middle-class experience. Here the alienated bourgeois subject wanders in search of engagement with the world, hoping that it will somehow liberate him from himself. He feeds on others, consumes them as it were, as a way of giving substance to his own responses. He is passive and self-involved, for all his professed interest in others, and his action is a kind of unwitting aggression that emotionally commodifies whomever he encounters. Out of this self of pseudosuffering subjectivity emerges the "Man of Feeling," who sighs, sheds a tear or two, and dispenses "goodness" in a patronizing, victimizing, and ultimately self-victimizing way. To witness the experience of the man of feeling, however, is like watching someone make his way through a hall of mirrors: everything he thinks he sees, everything he tries to react to, everything that causes him to feel— all are merely reflections of himself. If readers do not immediately recognize the position of the man of feeling as narcissistic, it is perhaps because the mirrors in question do an awfully good job of distorting the subject.

As the physical dynamic of feeling, as it was understood during the later eighteenth century, sensibility makes physical response the source of the self. Feeling, or sensation, is, in other words, the foundation of selfhood ("I feel, therefore I am"), and the act of feeling itself becomes tantamount to self-knowledge. The "organs of sense," as they are described in Chambers's *Cyclopedia*, have a crucial function in the activity of self-definition. The problem inevitably arises, however, that the body—separate from, and potentially a brute exposure of, the lie of the language of sentimental response—undermines the process of ideological mystification that the man of feeling would represent. Mackenzie is aware of this dilemma, but the plot of the novel suggests that he sees no solution. Although language is essential to any attempt to give feeling form, it always threatens to appropriate that feeling for the purposes of ideological reconstruction. Hysteria, hypochondria, melancholy, and other eighteenth-century illnesses are symptomatic of this dysfunction, and of the resulting confusion of discourse and desire. While the language of sensibility offers the terms for physical response, it also diagnoses physicality itself as a kind of illness. Writers of sensibility are aware of this tension, but they are not always successful in avoiding it. Their characters rarely do. If Mackenzie and other writers of the Age of Sensibility are opposed to the mind-body duality that paralyzed the previous age in a ritual of self-negation, they repeatedly express their concern in terms of the difficulty of using language to represent private experience. Another way to look at this crisis, however, is to say that they must find their bodies in language in order to be able to feel, that they must discover their sexual selves in the language of sensibility in order to know pleasure. Discourse precedes desire in a way that the literature of the later eighteenth century repeatedly laments. The crisis of the thinking, feeling bourgeois male was already in place before the turn of the nineteenth century.

This crisis of representation is present in Mackenzie's first novel. Harley looks for some way to represent his feelings, but even narrative fails him. The novel, constructed "from a bundle of little episodes," as the "editor" tells us, seems to collapse before the attempts to represent intense feeling in language. This breakdown means that Harley is distracted from the world, at odds with himself, and in some ways destined to succumb to this disjunction. "There is a helplessness in the character of extreme humanity," the editor says, that makes him "unfit for the world." Harley is unfit for the world because of the depth of his feeling; in other words, the intensity with which he experiences the world makes it impossible for him to remain alive. For Mackenzie this is a comment on the state of the world, but this attitude resonates in other ways throughout the later eighteenth century. The man of feeling often seems at odds with a pernicious world, and he pursues instead a world that exists only in his own imagination. This is true for Gray's poet in "Elegy Written in a Country Churchyard," Sterne's Yorick in *A Sentimental Journey*, and even Goldsmith's vicar in *The Vicar of Wakefield*. What Mackenzie manages to do in *The Man of Feeling*, however, is to theorize this position for the age. Mackenzie's poor, sensitive, debilitated hero comes to represent the very concept of the man of feeling. As such, he suggests just how problematic such a position must inevitably be.

Mackenzie was fully aware of these problems, and they are present in different ways in all his writings. How internal feelings could be represented in the world, and how their representation could remain true to the feeling behind them—this was Mackenzie's obsession. John Mullan argues that "With the publication of Mackenzie's *Man of Feeling* in 1771, the sentimental novel has evolved into a terminal formula precisely because, with all its talk of virtue, it cannot reflect at all on the problems of conduct, the practices of any existing society" (*Sentiment and Sociability*, p. 119). This argument is anticipated in the conservative self-analysis of Mackenzie himself: his own fear that sentimentalism places nature before law suggests its power to undo so-

cial classification and revolutionize society. The implications of the code of sentimentalism are potentially far more radical than modern critics have suggested. Like other "men of feeling," Mackenzie, in this novel, postulates a world in which feelings are paramount and which gives absolute value to personal emotion. By implication, political relations are structured to reflect communal value, and personal identity remains unfixed by class or even gender restrictions. Feeling liberates individuals into a communism of sympathy and a nonhierarchical system of relations based on benevolence and goodwill. But Mackenzie draws back from his radical project because he learns that to give way to feeling is to open an abyss of narcissistic self-appreciation that threatens to undermine the integrity of society itself. He fears that dissolution even more than he desires emotional liberation. Mackenzie is caught, then, between a radical reformulation of male subjectivity as the locus of feeling and a desire not to threaten hierarchical social arrangements, or even to lose the power of male prerogative in an age of social flux. Mackenzie sees how high the stakes of narcissistic identification really are, and his character Harley dies because of an inherent anxiety about where this might lead.

THE MAN OF THE WORLD

The novel *The Man of the World* tells a more coherent but somehow less engaging story of the ways in which a wicked individual can take advantage of simple, sensitive souls who see only good in the world. The well-meaning hero, Richard Annesly, who has resisted his father's expectations by dedicating himself to the Church rather than to business, finds unhappiness in retirement. His wife dies in childbirth, and he finds himself left with two children, Billy and Harriet, and a tiny income with which to support them. The neighboring squire, Sir Thomas Sindall, seems to take an interest in the children, but his real interest is nefarious: he plots to seduce the girl. In order to do so, he ensnares the boy in a series of transgressions, including armed robbery, that result in Billy's being transported to America for fourteen years. In the meantime, Sir Thomas manages to abduct the girl, drug her, and rape her. Later, when she finds herself with child, she seeks out Sir Thomas, but he rejects her. She dies in childbirth as a result of this treatment, and her baby is lost and presumably drowned.

In the second part of the novel, Sir Thomas has reproduced this situation in his own house; his ward, Lucy, and his cousin, Bolton, are like the young Anneslys, except that it quickly becomes obvious that they are in love. Sir Thomas has designs on the girl, and again he tries to send the boy away. As Bolton passes through London to fulfill his commission, a series of encounters leaves him rich, and he decides to return to seek the hand of Lucy. On the way he meets a young man who turns out to be Billy, returning from America, and they proceed together. On arriving, they hear the screams of a young girl—Lucy, who is being attacked by Sir Thomas. They rescue her, wounding Sir Thomas, and at this moment the nurse enters and declares that Lucy is the daughter of Harriet and Sir Thomas. He acknowledges her and dies repentant, and Lucy and Bolton are allowed to marry. As in other novels of the period, it takes two generations to resolve this tale. The final marriage is meant to mitigate some of the more excessive details of the narrative.

What this novel has to do with *The Man of Feeling* may not at first be obvious. But even here, the ease with which a wicked man can repeatedly use the trust of these simple, sensitive souls to exert his power over them reminds us of some of the concerns of the earlier novel. A personal crisis of social dimensions animates the tale; rape and victimization are the result of a world in which there are no values except financial values, and these characters seem trapped in repeating history until they are ready to fight and claim what they feel they deserve. This novel is a kind of morality tale, and it shows how good characters can suffer. But their suffering is also their salvation, because it is a measure of the intensity of their feeling, and therefore of the depth of their souls.

JULIA DE ROUBIGNÉ

Mackenzie's last novel, *Julia de Roubigné,* tells the story of a young girl who is forced through circumstance to marry a man she does not love. Although her heart belongs to her childhood friend Savillon, Julia finds herself indebted to a local gentleman who has been kind to her continually indebted father and who has pressed his suit in a gentle if insistent way. She has in the meantime heard that Savillon, who has been in Martinique on his uncle's plantation, has married a woman in the colony. When her mother, on her deathbed, pleads with Julia to accept the hand of the wealthy Montauban, her resistance breaks down and she does marry him.

Unique among Mackenzie's heroes, Savillon is able to find satisfaction in the world even as he nurses his heightened sensibility. From Martinique, he writes to a friend:

> Yet I am happier here than I could venture to expect. Had I been left to my own choice, I should probably have sat down in solitude, to think of the past, and enjoy my reflections; but I have been forced to do better. There is an active duty, which rewards every man in the performance; and my uncle has so contrived matters, that I have had very little time unemployed. He has been liberal of instruction, and, I hope, has found me willing to be instructed. Our business, indeed, is not very intricate; but in the simplest occupations, there are a thousand little circumstances, which experience alone can teach us. In certain departments, however, I have tried projects of my own: some of them have failed in the end, but all gave me pleasure in the pursuit. In one I have been successful beyond expectation; and in that one I was the most deeply interested, because it touched the cause of humanity. (Letter XXVII)

This unexpected enthusiasm for business is explained in the next letters, when it becomes clear that Savillon's experiment has to do with the management of slaves, and that in fact his plan involves raising a slave, Yambu, who had been a prince in Africa, to a position of authority over the slaves so that they are, in effect, working for him and not for the white masters. This experiment is a success, and Savillon feels justified in putting his faith in human nature. It is interesting, and perhaps inevitable, that the man of feeling in the later eighteenth century would turn his attention to slavery. But it is especially significant that it is in relation to slavery that a hero of sensibility is able to get out of himself and be moved by his ability to change circumstances in the world. Later Savillon even says, "I begin to suspect that the sensibility, of which young minds are proud, from which they look down with contempt on the unfeeling multitude of ordinary men, is less a blessing than an inconvenience" (Letter XXX).

The conclusion of the novel is tragic. When Savillon returns and finds that Julia is married, he begs her to meet with him. Julia reluctantly agrees, but Montauban finds out about the meeting and imagines that they have already had illicit sexual relations. In his jealousy, he decides to poison the pair. Julia alone is poisoned, however, and as she dies, Montauban discovers that she has not been unfaithful. Distraught at her death, he kills himself. Only Savillon survives. In this case, the man of feeling is the sole survival in a world of misdirected affection.

Julia de Roubigné is Mackenzie's masterpiece, and it deserves greater critical recognition.

[*See also* The Novel *and* Sensibility.]

SELECTED WORKS

The Man of Feeling (1771)
The Man of the World (1773)
Julia de Roubigné (1777)

FURTHER READING

Barker, Gerard A. *Henry Mackenzie.* Boston, 1975.

Haggerty, George E. *Men in Love: Masculinity and Sexuality in the Eighteenth Century.* New York, 1999.

Mullan, John. *Sentiment and Sociability: Language and Feeling in the Eighteenth Century.* Oxford, 1988.

LOUIS MacNEICE

John Goodby

During his lifetime and for more than a decade after his death, the poetry of Louis MacNeice (1907–1963) was read almost wholly in terms of the 1930s "Auden Generation." Given his witty discursiveness, attention to contemporary social surfaces, conversational tone, and leftist politics, it was undoubtedly correct to set MacNeice beside Cecil Day Lewis, Stephen Spender, and W. H. Auden himself. Since the 1970s, however, it has become increasingly clear that the differences between his work and that of his contemporaries is at least as important as the similarities. MacNeice, it can now be seen, while a "Left" poet, was consistently skeptical of his contemporaries' faith in Marxism and the Soviet Union, and the importance to his writing of his Northern Irish provenance was overlooked in the process of fitting him into an English literary myth. Most important, the "1930s poet" label had distracted critics from attending sufficiently to the powerful and original poetry MacNeice wrote in the final years of his life.

Frederick Louis MacNeice was born on 12 September 1907 in Belfast, the third child of Lily and John Frederick MacNeice. His father, a rector in the Church of Ireland, was a liberal and ecumenical churchman who rose to become bishop of Down and Dromore. Lily MacNeice died when her son was five years old, a devastating loss that overshadowed his early years and is alluded to in several poems, most nightmarishly in "Autobiography": "The dark was talking to the dead; / The lamp was dark beside my bed. / Come back early or never come." The very title of the poem, however, consciously frames the notion of "autobiography" as a way of "explaining" a writer's work, and it cautions against crudely psychological interpretations. MacNeice's childhood was spent at the Northern Irish seaside town of Carrickfergus, although both parents

Louis MacNeice
Portrait by Nancy Culliford Sharp, 1938
© ESTATE OF NANCY SHARP/NATIONAL
PORTRAIT GALLERY, LONDON

had family ties to the west of Ireland. His upbringing and background established a set of oppositions (northern versus southern; Irish versus English; hard versus soft; colorful versus drab; disciplined versus dissipated; cold versus warm; paternal versus maternal) that inform much of his writing. From 1917 on he was educated in English public schools, entering Merton College, Oxford, in 1926, where he took a degree in classics, met Auden, and edited *Oxford Poetry 1929* with Spender. On graduating in 1929, MacNeice became an assistant lecturer in classics at the University of Birmingham, and in the same year he published his first collection, *Blind Fireworks*, which established him as a promising younger poet.

THE LYRICISM OF SURFACES

MacNeice's earliest lyrics toy with modernist and Romantic models, and they show traces of the mild dandyism and emotional detachment that he had acquired as an aesthete at Marlborough, partly under the influence of his closest friend there, Anthony Blunt. The poems reflect modernism's use of myth, and some explore the physical textures of sounds and silences, dwelling on the materiality of language through onomatopoeia, refrain, rhyme, assonance, and alliteration. Like others of his generation, however, MacNeice had already rejected the linguistic autonomy and formal experimentalism prized by T. S. Eliot and Ezra Pound. His poems of the early 1930s display instead a mastery of rhyme and stanza forms, as well as an urbane, liberal, and modern sensitivity keenly aware of the fragility of its aspirations and pretensions. To the rising tide of economic depression and fascism in Europe, MacNeice's response was a pragmatic, skeptical socialism rather than the communism of many of his friends: "To a Communist" (1933), indeed, warns against basing sweeping generalizations upon contingent historical circumstances. His own poems tend to switch between empirical close-up and the long view, asserting the importance of the moment. This is a philosophical, even a political, position as much as a form of carpe diem: both speakers in "An Eclogue for Christmas" (1933), for example, agree that "We shall go down like paleolithic man / Before some new Ice Age or Genghis Khan," but set against it the desire that "all these ephemeral things / Be somehow permanent, like the swallow's tangent wings."

The apprehension of the tension between surface and void finds less apocalyptic expression in "Birmingham," from his second collection, *Poems* (1935), with its mimetic relish of city life: "Smoke from the train-gulf hid by awnings blunders upward, the brakes of cars / Pipe as the policeman pivoting round raises his flat hand." This opening verse ends by observing that "beyond this centre the slumward vista thins like a diagram: / There, unvisited, are Vulcan's forges who doesn't give a tinker's damn," and the poem proceeds to elaborate on the contrast between an incipient society of the spectacle, defined by consumer commodities—"Cubical scent-bottles artificial legs arctic foxes and electric mops"—and the backbreaking work of those upon whom such superabundance and display rests. But for all the irony at the expense of the middle classes, ignorant of the source of their comfort and busy "climbing tentatively upward on jerry-built beauty and sweated labour," MacNeice does not denigrate the modern city as Eliot had, nor does he indulge in revolutionary self-flagellation over his own complicity in its injustices. Rather, the instinct to find beauty in the quotidian is set beside social awareness in a nonjudgmental way. Indeed, it is suggested that popular culture, toward which MacNeice had an ambivalent attitude, may mediate between these worlds: "Next week it is likely in the heart's funfair we shall pull / Strong enough on the handle to get back our money; or at any rate it is possible." The acceptance of the simultaneity of opposed states poises his best work between deathly certainty and dissolving flux, and is memorably expressed in "Snow," which brings together "Spawning snow and pink roses" separated by a window from the winter weather outside, perceived as

Soundlessly collateral and incompatible:
World is suddener than we fancy it.

World is crazier and more of it than we think,
Incorrigibly plural.

Such pluralism leads to an awareness of "The drunkenness of things being various," and the recognition that the world is "more spiteful and gay than one supposes" with "more than glass between the snow and the huge roses." Even at his most discursive, then, MacNeice is never convinced that language is merely a means to an end; that is, a transparent (like the glass of the window) and neutral vehicle for sense.

IMPURE POETRY AND WORLD WAR II

In the later 1930s, with the breakup of his first marriage, MacNeice began to travel abroad, registering the premonitions of world war. He visited Spain in 1936 on the eve of the civil war, and again in 1938 just as the final nationalist onslaught began, and the experience found its way into several poems. More famously, he spent several months with Auden in Iceland in 1936, returning to co-author *Letters from Iceland* (1937), a largely successful mixture of travelogue, journalism, letters, satire, parody, fantasy, and poetry. MacNeice attempted a similar formula in *I Crossed the Minch* (1938), an account of a visit to the Hebrides with Nancy Coldstream, while *Zoo* (1938) is also travelogue of sorts. It is possible to see in these works a striving for a more heterogeneous and impure form of utterance than the lyric; or, rather, an attempt to separate out the dramatic potential of the various elements that make up a lyric. This is clear in MacNeice's first extended statement on poetry, *Modern Poetry* (1938), which defends the engaged, "impure" quality of 1930s writing against critics such as Virginia Woolf, and it is manifest in his third collection, *The Earth Compels* (1938).

The Earth Compels reveals the variety of MacNeice's lyric talent—in the semisurreal satire of "Bagpipe Music," for example, or "The Sunlight on the Garden," which infuses a deceptively slight poem with the full plangent weight of the English lyric tradition. The culmination of MacNeice's fascination with "impure poetry," however, and his single greatest work, is *Autumn Journal* (1939). This is a long poem in twenty-four sections, taking the form of a survey of MacNeice's life set against the background of the British and French betrayal of Czechoslovakia to the Nazis in the Munich Agreement. As gas masks are issued and antiaircraft gun emplacements dug in London, MacNeice sums up the debates and dilemmas of the 1930s with unexampled brilliance, in a verse diary that leaps backward and forward in time, reflecting with melancholy flamboyance on Spain, Birmingham, London, marital breakdown, and his own amusedly ironic but angst-ridden and unstable self. Section XVI memorably wrestles with MacNeice's divided Irish allegiances in stereotypes that (though often unfair) hint at the source of his self-division, preferring Ireland to England, but only able to live in the latter:

> Why do we like being Irish? Partly because
>   It gives us a hold on the sentimental English
> As members of a world that never was . . .
> And partly because Ireland is small enough
>   To be still thought of with family feeling . . .
> Why should I want to go back
>   To you, Ireland, my Ireland? . . .
> I hate your grandiose airs,
>   Your sob-stuff, your laugh and your swagger,
> Your assumption that everyone else cares
>   Who is king of your castle

The poem as a whole captures the seedy but not wholly regretful end-of-decade, prewar mood more generously and complexly than does Auden's "September 1, 1939," with its dismissal of the "low, dishonest decade." This is partly because *Autumn Journal* is tentatively oriented toward the future, as well as to some kind of participation in the violent events about to unfold. "Aristotle was right," MacNeice claims in section XVII, "to think of man-in-action / As the essential and really existent man . . . I cannot lie in this bath for ever, clouding / The cooling water in rose-geranium soap." This is not to say that MacNeice was unambiguously attached to Britain: he spent several months of 1939 and much of 1940 in the United States, wondering whether to spend the war there. He left partly because of a failed love affair and partly because of a "vulgar curiosity" to witness the war, thinking that "if I stayed another year out of England I should have to stay out for good, having missed so much history, lost touch."

In 1936 MacNeice had written a well-received version of Aeschylus' *Agamemnon*; now, in 1941, he joined the BBC and found an outlet for his dramatic talents in its features department. He wrote dozens of radio dramas and features, as well as more overtly propagandistic material; his best work in this medium is *The Dark Tower* (1947). He was also responsible for the first, and still one of the best, short critical studies of W. B. Yeats, published in 1941. Yet although he was productive, and made a generally happy second marriage to the singer Hedli Anderson in 1942, MacNeice was severely tested by the war. He also lost several close friends, suffered the death of his father, was overworked, and was angered by the Republic of Ireland's neutrality. Despite several outstanding poems written during the period (including "Prayer before Birth," "The Trolls," and "The Strand"), the proportion of flaccid over good verse rose in *Plant and Phantom* (1941), *Springboard* (1944), and *Holes in the Sky* (1948).

POSTWAR AND PARABLE

The nadir of MacNeice's postwar poetry was *Autumn Sequel* (1954), a wooden and largely misconceived attempt to revisit the success of *Autumn Journal*. As he put it in "Day of Renewal" (1951), "This middle stretch / Of life is bad for poets." Yet it was during the late 1940s and 1950s that, out of touch with new literary trends, he was accumulating the experiences that would feed a new kind of poetry. These included a visit to India for the BBC in 1947 to cover the celebrations of independence (in which he encountered the horror of communal bloodletting), the directorship of the British Council in Athens in 1950–1951, and other trips, including one to South Africa in 1959. "House on a Cliff" (1955) and "Death of an Old Lady" (1956) are poems whose somber subjects are belied by the buoyancy of their treatment of loss and the return of lyric compression, revealing an adjustment to the darker climates of Cold War and middle age. It was this creative realignment that yielded the poems collected in *Visitations* (1957), *Solstices* (1961), and *The Burning Perch* (1963). In these, MacNeice broke from realism, renewing his interest in riddle, refrain, nursery, and nonsense rhyme. In addition, the seeming inconsequentiality of many of the subjects nags the reader without being fully resolvable, as in "Nature Notes," four short pieces that repeat the words "incorrigible" and "childhood." The feeling is summed up in the final lines of "Indoor Sports": "It is time / We left these puzzles and started to be ourselves / And started to live, is it not?" MacNeice also developed his affinities with parabolic and allegorical authors, such as Samuel Beckett, William Golding, John Bunyan, and Edmund Spenser, further exploring these in his 1963 Clark Lectures. The late poems reflect a growing interest in the questions and structures of belief derived from his Anglican and Ulster background, though offering no consolation in the normal sense of the word. In "The Taxis," "Soap Suds," and "The Truisms," for example, the uncertain identities of the earlier poems is intensified—"How can you prove your minds are single?" one asks—as the speakers attempt to wrest some kind of agency from near-impossible predicaments. Real and parabolic worlds are blurred, as in "Charon," in which the bus initially "mov[ing] through London" with its "pigeons" and "rumours of wars" gradually acquires a more mythic quality as it reaches a bridgeless Thames. Here the passengers are obliged to board a boat with a ferryman

> . . . just as Virgil
> And Dante had seen him. He looked at us coldly
> And his eyes were dead and his hands on the oar
> Were black with obols and varicose veins
> Marbled his calves and he said to us coldly:
> If you want to die you will have to pay for it.

Amid the grimness and darkness (which the collapse of his second marriage and heavy drinking undoubtedly intensified) there is an indefatigable quality, as in "The Wiper," which insists that, despite the loss of memory and purpose, "yet we hold the road," or the dogged insistence elsewhere that "Round the corner is—sooner or later—the sea." It was a severe blow to British poetry that MacNeice did not live to develop this powerful, pared-down style; as it was, he caught a chill while visiting a cave to record sound effects for his final radio play, *Persons from Porlock*, and died of pneumonia on 3 September 1963.

REPUTATION

Perceptions of MacNeice began to change with the 1960s poetry revival in Northern Ireland and his championing by Michael Longley, Derek Mahon, Paul Muldoon, and other Northern Irish poets. This revaluation has proceeded alongside critical and theoretical complications of the exclusivity of earlier definitions of what an "English" or an "Irish" poet might be (albeit this has arguably now gone too far in diminishing MacNeice's English and cosmopolitan aspects). Similarly, where MacNeice's status as an Irish writer was previously questioned by critics from the Irish Republic, essentialist definitions have now largely been replaced by more pluralistic notions of Irishness. Indeed, MacNeice's interest in relativity and flux, his constant attempts to deconstruct binaries, his concern with the self and with tradition as potential self-betrayal make him an exemplary Irish writer, particularly in the Anglo-Irish line that includes Beckett, Elizabeth Bowen, and Francis Stuart.

[*See also* W. H. Auden; Paul Muldoon; *and* Stephen Spender.]

SELECTED WORKS

Blind Fireworks (1929)
Poems (1935)
The Agammemnon of Aeschylus (1936)
Letters from Iceland (with W. H. Auden; 1937)
The Earth Compels (1938)
I Crossed the Minch (1938)
Modern Poetry: A Personal Essay (1938)
Autumn Journal (1939)
Plant and Phantom (1941)
The Poetry of W. B. Yeats (1941)
Springboard (1944)
The Dark Tower and Other Radio Scripts (1947)
Ten Burnt Offerings (1952)
Autumn Sequel: A Rhetorical Poem in XXVI Cantos (1954)
Solstices (1961)
The Burning Perch (1963)
The Strings are False: An Unfinished Autobiography (1965)
Varieties of Parable (1965)

EDITIONS

Dodds, E. R., ed. *Collected Poems of Louis MacNeice*. 2d corrected ed. London, 1979.

Heuser, Alan, ed. *Selected Literary Criticism of Louis MacNeice*. Oxford, 1987.

Heuser, Alan, ed. *Selected Prose of Louis MacNeice*. Oxford, 1990.

FURTHER READING

Brown, Terence. *Louis MacNeice: Sceptical Vision*. Dublin, 1975.

Longley, Edna. *Louis MacNeice: A Critical Study*. London, 1986; repr. London, 1996.

Stallworthy, Jon. *Louis MacNeice*. London, 1995.

THE MACRO PLAYS

John C. Coldewey

The designation "Macro plays" refers collectively to the three medieval plays preserved in the Macro manuscript, arguably the most important textual witness to the morality play tradition in England. Of the five English morality plays surviving anywhere (*The Pride of Life, The Castle of Perseverance, Wisdom, Mankind,* and *Everyman*), three are found in this composite manuscript, now housed at the Folger Shakespeare Library in Washington, DC (Folger MS V.a.354). The manuscript takes its name from one of its earliest owners, the Reverend Cox Macro (1683–1767), a native of Bury St. Edmunds in Suffolk and a collector of manuscripts. The plays appearing in it are *The Castle of Perseverance, Wisdom,* and *Mankind.* These are widely considered to be, respectively, the most theatrically elaborate, the most ostentatiously pious, and the most obscene of all morality plays, so that together they bear witness to a remarkable range of theatrical experience. Of equal theatrical interest in the Macro manuscript is the frequently reproduced drawing of a medieval theater in the round, a fifteenth-century stage plan for the *Castle of Perseverance.* Further links between the Macro manuscript, its plays, and Bury St. Edmunds have been explored in recent years, and it now seems likely that the town acted as a center for late medieval dramatic activity, much of it sponsored by the monastery for which the town was named.

THE MACRO PLAYS AND EAST ANGLIAN THEATRICAL TRADITIONS

Each of the Macro plays presents a unique specimen requiring individual attention, but some general observations are first in order regarding the Macro manuscript itself as well as some of the features shared by the play texts. To begin with, the plays all date from the fifteenth century and are associated with East Anglia, that part of England extending east of London and north from the Thames to the Wash, traditionally including the counties of Norfolk, Suffolk, and Essex, and eastern parts of Hertfordshire and Cambridgeshire. During the fifteenth and sixteenth centuries this area developed its own traditions of theater distinct from those found in large cities further north, owing in large part to geographic circumstance and population settlement patterns. Unlike the North or West Midlands, where substantial towns had grown to dominate an entire region, East Anglia's mainly flat or slightly rolling countryside supported a dense network of small towns and villages that prospered in the fifteenth century because of the wool trade. Performance traditions evolved here quite unlike those in major centers such as York or Chester, where town councils and guilds supported the production of large cycle plays. In East Anglia, by contrast, towns and villages and parishes were close enough to share plays and costumes, and traveling between nearby communities to see or to take part in local productions was common. The result was a different kind of play, not part of a cycle but portable, and composed with a shrewd eye toward doubling roles, controlling scenic shifts, and pleasing an audience. The staging was mainly place-and-scaffold (held in one central site such as the town market square) rather than processional or on pageant wagons. Unlike cycle plays, these had to be commercially viable. Almost by definition, then, the plays produced in East Anglia were highly theatrical, spectacular, entertaining, written to be self-sustaining, and performed for money. Numbered among the non-cycle East Anglian plays are most of the English moralities, those entertaining allegories that evolved into the Moral Interludes of the humanists, which often featured the ever-popular Vice figures in later Elizabethan fare. Chief among the moralities are the Macro plays.

PROVENANCE, DATE, AND LANGUAGE

All three of the Macro plays are linked to East Anglia by manuscript provenance and dialect. Originally three separate manuscripts, the plays were bound together sometime before 1819 and have been rebound twice since then. *The Castle of Perseverance,* the oldest of the plays, was probably composed between 1400 and 1425, although the manuscript dates from sometime around 1440. The language of the play and the scribal habits of its copyist point strongly toward the dialect of Norfolk. *Wisdom* seems to have been composed between 1460 and 1470 and exists in two manuscripts: the Macro version and an incomplete version in another manuscript collection at the Bodleian Library (Bodley MS Digby 133), from which the Macro *Wisdom* seems to have been copied sometime in the late fifteenth century (judging from the watermarks on its paper, almost certainly after 1471). As in the copy of *The Castle of Perseverance*, the language and scribal habits of the copyist of *Wisdom* tie the play to East Anglia; more than that, an inscription at the end of the play by its earliest owner, one "Hyngham monachus" (Monk Hyngham) ties the play directly to the abbey of St. Edmund in Bury St. Edmunds. Monk Hyngham's handwriting matches that of Thomas Hyngham, a Bury monk known to have owned a number of manuscripts, who was resident at the abbey at the time *Wisdom* was copied; he may well have been its scribe. Hyngham wrote the same inscription at the end of *Mankind*, the third of the Macro plays, which he may also have copied. Like *Wisdom* it dates from the mid-1460s, and both its dialect and the scribal habits of its copyist show strong East Anglian features; beyond that, the play refers to a great number of towns in Norfolk and Cambridgeshire, and Bury St. Edmunds is explicitly mentioned in the text.

THEATRICALITY: PAGEANTRY AND STAGECRAFT

The general outlines of plot and action in each of the three Macro plays are discussed in the entry "Morality Plays" in the *Encyclopedia of British Literature*, but it was their theatricality and spectacle that made these plays memorable to their original audiences, still delightful and instructive to watch today. Some of those features deserve mention here, since they nearly jump off the Macro manuscript folios.

***Formality and* Wisdom.** Of the three, *Wisdom* is the most spectacular in terms of costume and display. The play opens with the sweeping entrance of the character Wisdom dressed as Christ the King, and the manuscript describes his costume in glowing detail: he enters "in a rich purple cloth of gold robe with a mantle of the same material lined with ermine, about his neck a royal hood furred with ermine, upon his head a wig with bangs, a beard of curled Cypress gold, wearing a rich imperial crown set with precious stones and pearls, in his left hand

a gold orb set with precious stones and pearls, in his right hand a royal scepter." (Quotations are from Riggio's modernized text.) Wisdom will be contesting with Lucifer for the soul of the character Anima, whose contrasting simplicity is conveyed by her costume as well: she enters "as a maiden, in a white cloth of gold handsomely bordered with miniver, a mantle of black over it, a wig like that of Wisdom, with a rich coronet laced at the back, from which hang long tassels with two knots or buttons of gold." When Lucifer makes his appearance, he enters "wearing a devil's suit on the outside, dressed underneath as a proud gallant," and soon enough he disposes of the devil's suit to pursue his temptations as a gallant. The characters Mind, Will, and Understanding each have six allegorically liveried servants of their own as a retinue; Mind's are specified as having "red beards and lions rampant on their crests, and each with a warder in his hand" and the others are equally colorful. Each group of six masquers conducts a formal dance, and the three retinues of six servants are counterpointed by six whores who perform a masked dance to a hornpipe, perhaps with the defiled Anima. At one point toward the end, Anima emerges "in the most horrible costume, fouler than a fiend," and we can tell even without her pitiful dialogue that she has gone wrong. In this morality play she will, of course, come to Wisdom again, and be dressed once more in finery. But it is clear that here allegorically fitting clothes make the character, and allegorical character drives the action to its salvific, satisfying ending.

Other kinds of pageantry and music play their parts in *Wisdom*, too. Besides the hornpipe for the whores, stage directions specify that minstrels play trumpets and bagpipes, and Anima sings "in the most mournful manner, drawing out the notes as is sung in Passion week." Taken all together, with its costumes and music the play exhibits a kind of processional rhythm, like a sequence of *tableaux vivants*. Tellingly, of the thirty-eight characters who appear in *Wisdom*, only seven have speaking parts, and despite a number of frantic moments in the action—for example, when small boys dressed as devils rush out from and back under the skirts of Anima—the play seems as choreographed as a modern ballet. The theatrical qualities of *Wisdom*, then, have a formal quality; this is in keeping with the main source of the play, Henry Suso's static and mystical *Orologium Sapientiae* (*The Clock of Wisdom*), which is quoted extensively at the beginning and end of the play. Other sources of wisdom literature inform the play as well, but the main point to be noticed is that *Wisdom*'s allegorical theatricality suits it thematically, making a spectacular, formal show of serious meditation. All of a piece, the play's pleasures are rooted as much in its performance as in its language.

Learned lewdness in Mankind.

The theatricality of *Mankind* offers a series of sharp contrasts to that of *Wisdom*. If *Wisdom*'s action seems formal and choreographed, *Mankind*'s takes informality to the edge of obscenity. Like *Wisdom*, *Mankind* opens with a static and impressive figure, Mercy, who speaks soberly in moral tones, introducing himself and urging spiritual improvement for all, including the audience: "ye soverens that sytt and ye brothern that stonde ryght uppe." Within this play, however, the effect could not be more different from *Wisdom*. Instead of eliciting the devoted response of a soulful acolyte like Anima, Mercy rouses the taunting figure of Mischief, a lowlife farm worker who mocks not only what Mercy says but also how he says it. Mischief is soon joined by his country cronies New Gyse, Nowadays, and Nought, and Mercy's "talkyng delectable" receives wild parody. Once the mocking characters leave together, singing, Mercy's speech does actually seem to take on a pompous and preachy tone. Thus, when the main character, Mankind, enters with spade in hand, the battle lines have already been drawn. The war for his soul is on; in this play, however, it will be conducted mainly with language. In contrast to *Wisdom* with its formal pairings and elaborate masque-like staging, the action of this play follows a simple line: Mankind receives instruction from Mercy; he is tempted by the band of lowlife figures and resists; he is tempted again by the Devil Titivillus and he succumbs; following further indignities and nearing despair, he repents and is saved. As the early part of the play suggests, however, the real battle is guided by the dialogue, which ranges from learned Latin to an obscene pun on "holy" ("hole-lick") and lurches in quick succession through the dialogue between Mankind and his tempters and Mercy. Fast-paced like the fast talkers facing Mankind, the play moves swiftly and riotously toward its happy conclusion, pausing only for the players to take up a collection from the audience in anticipation of Titivillus, the devil with a big head and a net for snaring souls. It might be noted that as they perform the collection, or quête, Nowadays, New Gyse, and Nought explicitly call on people from nine different places in Norfolk and Cambridgeshire. These local habitations and names have been taken to refer to towns where *Mankind* may actually have been played, or whence audiences might have come to see

such plays performed. Whatever its immediate application, collecting from named audience members—present or not—lends local flavor and an informal intimacy to the performance.

In *Mankind*, then, spectacle takes on quite a different character than in *Wisdom*. To be sure, some costuming and props are necessary, but nothing more elaborate than gallant costumes and a devil's suit for Titivillus. As part of his ordeal, Mankind's tunic is cut short during the course of the play, no doubt too short for modesty, but there is no need for anything in this play resembling Wisdom's ermine-lined regalia or any of the other ostentatious livery that helps determine meaning in *Wisdom*. More important is the emphasis on the slippery inner allegorical battles fought between Mankind and the frustrations of his own World, between Mankind and the temptations of the Flesh—his own cupidity—and between Mankind and his own demons. This inner battle, *Mankind* suggests, starts with words—the mockery of piety, the soft whisper in the ear, the noisy distraction from the eternal possibilities of Mercy—and where the battle might lead from named places in East Anglia might be disastrous indeed.

Stage as soul in The Castle of Perseverance.

Wisdom seems to trade on allegorical displays of costume and formal action, while *Mankind* foregrounds an allegory of inner character and sin with loaded dialogue. In the most widely known and longest (3,649 lines) of the Macro plays, *The Castle of Perseverance*, stage machinery itself provides an elaborate allegory of the embattled human psyche and a site for redemption. As the remarkable stage plan reveals, the same forces that appear in *Mankind* show up here, bent on taking over the soul of the main character, Humanum Genus (also called Mankinde): the World, the Flesh, and the Devil. In this play they occupy colossal structures, towering scaffolds perched on the edge of an enormous circular playing space 125 feet (38 meters) across. To the south is the stage of Flesh and his minion sins Gluttony, Sloth, and Lechery; to the west is the stage of the World, who oversees his servant Covetousness, and to the north is the stage of the Devil, Belial, with his own sins of Pride, Wrath, and Envy, poised for action. At the center of the playing place lies the Castle of Perseverance itself, at least two stories high, where Mankinde is born and where he dies. To the east, standing against the predatory forces at the other points of the compass, is the scaffold of God. The elaborate course of action in the play requires a constant balancing act that echoes the inner turmoil of a soul going through life: the Good Angel opposing the Bad Angel, or the seven deadly sins being opposed by the seven cardinal virtues. Battle sequences involving attacks on the castle are spectacular and at the same time comic in their failure; as the play proceeds, they help to highlight the abstract qualities of vices and virtues and they demonstrate that the fortified soul can withstand such assaults. Still, vice figures like Backbiter roam the playing space freely, misleading Mankinde; and even though he learns to repent, Mankinde falls prey to Covetousness at the end, just before being struck by Death's spear. His last cry for mercy is answered in the play by a surprising posthumous debate in the playing space among the four daughters of God (Mercy, Truth, Righteousness, and Peace) over the fate of his soul. In the end he is saved and welcomed into heaven, and the audience is enjoined to learn from his example.

As in *Wisdom* and *Mankind*, the meaning of *The Castle of Perseverance* is embedded in its staging. The scale of its playing space illustrates the importance of its themes, while its elaborate action mimics the inner conflicts of real moral turmoil. It may be impossible not to laugh at characters like the devil Belial, who, the stage plan warns, must have "gunpowder burning in pipes in his hands and in his ears and in his arse," but he is nonetheless a figure of malice, capable in fact of deploying the very spiritual sin of Pride that causes such derisive laughter. As in *Wisdom*, the allegory of costumes and props informs the larger sense of the play; as in *Mankind*, the danger to the human soul remains constant, despite the foolishness or incompetence of the agent. Taken together, these three Macro plays demonstrate different ways that theatricality and pageantry can mix to add personal and moral significance to their sometimes unwieldy allegorical freight.

[*See also* Everyman; Morality Plays; *and* Mystery Plays.]

EDITIONS

Bevington, David, ed. *The Macro Plays: A Facsimile Edition with Facing Transcription.* New York, 1972. Facsimile edition and transcription of the plays.

Bevington, David, ed. *Medieval Drama.* Boston, 1975. The most comprehensive textbook edition of medieval plays, including *Mankind* and *The Castle of Perseverance.*

Coldewey, John, ed. *Early English Drama: An Anthology.* New York, 1993. Edition of many non-cycle plays, including *Mankind* and *Wisdom.*

Eccles, Mark, ed. *The Macro Plays.* Early English Text Society 262. London, 1969. Definitive edition of the Macro plays.

Knittle, Frank, and G. Fattic, eds. *A Critical Edition of the Medieval Play* Mankind. New York; 1996. Useful edition of one play.

Riggio, Milla Cozart, ed. *The Play of Wisdom: Its Texts and Contexts.* AMS Studies in the Middle Ages 14. New York, 1990. An elaborate edition of *Wisdom* with facing-page text in modernized English.

FURTHER READING

Coldewey, John C. "The Non-cycle Plays and the East Anglian Tradition." In *The Cambridge Companion to Medieval English Theatre,* edited by Richard Beadle, 189–210. Cambridge, U.K., 1994. Introduction to dramatic traditions in medieval East Anglia; includes references to the Macro plays; with bibliography.

Cox, John D. *The Devil and the Sacred in English Drama, 1350–1642.* Cambridge, U.K., 2000. Stresses the formal and moral dimensions of holy power in medieval plays, including some the Macro plays.

Davidson, Clifford. *Visualizing the Moral Life: Medieval Iconography and the Macro Morality Plays.* AMS Studies in the Middle Ages 16. New York, 1989. Dovetails literary and iconographic imagery in the Macro plays.

Gibson, Gail McMurray. "Bury St. Edmunds, Lydgate, and the N-Town Cycle." *Speculum* 56 (1981): 56–90. Seminal work locating Bury St. Edmunds as a major site of interest for medieval theater studies.

Gibson, Gail McMurray. *The Theater of Devotion: East Anglian Drama and Society in the Late Middle Ages.* Chicago, 1989. In-depth exploration of devotional theater and culture in East Anglia.

Griffiths, Jeremy. "Thomas Hyngham, Monk of Bury and the Macro Plays Manuscript." *English Manuscript Studies* 5 (1995): 214–219. Identifies the handwriting in the Macro manuscript with that of Thomas Hyngham.

Kelley, Michael R. *Flamboyant Drama: A Study of the Castle of Perseverance, Mankind, and Wisdom.* Carbondale, IL, 1979. Examines the "controlling aesthetic" of the Macro plays, treating costumes, realism, stage plan, music, and props.

King, Pamela M. "Morality Plays." In *The Cambridge Companion to Medieval English Theatre,* edited by

Richard Beadle, 240–264. Cambridge, U.K., 1994. Useful introduction to morality plays, including the Macro plays; with bibliography.

Potter, Robert. *The English Morality Play: Origins, History, and Influence of a Dramatic Tradition.* London, 1975. Standard work of criticism on the morality plays, including the Macro plays.

Riggio, Milla Cozart, ed. *The Wisdom Symposium.* AMS Studies in the Middle Ages 11. New York, 1986. A collection of incisive essays on *Wisdom.*

Southern, Richard. *The Medieval Theatre in the Round: A Study of the Staging of the Castle of Perseverance and Related Matters.* 2d ed. London, 1975. Classic study of the play's performance possibilities.

THOMAS MALORY

Stephen H. A. Shepherd

An anonymous sixteenth-century transcription records the words inscribed on a now-lost tombstone in Greyfriars churchyard, near Newgate Prison in London:

Dominus Thomas Malleré valens miles obiit 14 Mar 1470 de parochia Monkenkyrby in comitatu Warwici.

("Sir Thomas Malory, a valiant knight of the parish of Monks Kirby in Warwickshire, died 14 March 1471" [date adjusted to modern reckoning])

Malory is thought to have been born around 1416. If no other record of his life existed, "valiant" might seem a formulaic obsequy appropriate to any knight in the late fifteenth century. Because of what he wrote, however, and where he wrote, and what contemporary authorities wrote about him, the word might seem to his readers to resonate with proud, personalized defiance.

What Malory wrote was a prose romance, *The Hoole Book of Kyng Arthur and of His Noble Knyghtes of The Rounde Table*; it is otherwise known by the Norman French title *Le Morte Darthur*. It is a 370,000-word compendium of Arthurian legend, derived mostly through earnest translation and adaptation of French prose sources, but also making striking use of a variety of English poems. Alone–and we know of no other works certain to be by him—this work made Malory one of the most influential medieval writers in English, and the most influential of those who appeared in the century after Chaucer. On rare occasions within the *Morte Darthur*, Malory extemporized with emotive comments about himself or about life and thought in his own times; these are among the most significant of all statements about Malory and is discussed in more detail below.

By his own admission, early in the *Morte Arthur*, Malory was writing in prison: "this was drawyn by a knyght presoner, Sir Thomas Malleorré" (Shepherd, p. 112; all quotations are from this edition). In the year in which he claims to have finished the work (between 4 March 1469 and 3 March 1470), he is recorded as witnessing a deathbed declaration of an inmate at Newgate Prison; and Ma-lory's burial nearby, a year later, suggests that he did not leave prison before he himself died. It was an ending in kind, insofar as Malory had been constrained for a variety of charges, more or less continuously, for over a decade. In an age when even the royal infrastructure—Lancastrian or Yorkist, whoever had the upper hand in the latest round of wars—depended upon a creative application of official documentation to sustain its approval and power, the documents that allege Malory's crimes cannot be trusted for neutrality. Yet they could be said to represent the earliest body of Malory "criticism," and there is enough to suggest that Malory's extemporaneous comments in the *Morte Darthur* have a dialectical relationship to the "narrative" sketched by the allegations. This body of allegation, and other contemporary records, are discussed below.

MALORY ON MALORY

There is some uncertainty about the order in which Malory wrote the tales that comprise the *Morte Darthur*, but the following account assumes that Malory himself determined the order in which the tales are preserved in their two medieval witnesses, the "Winchester Malory" manuscript and William Caxton's 1485 printed edition. In an early aside Malory speaks with the authority of one experienced in battle, aware of the danger, and worthiness, of a competitive psychology in the field:

Oftetymes thorow envy grete hardynesse is shewed, that hath bene the deth of many kyd [reputable] knyghtes—for thoughe they speke fayre [equitably] many one unto other, yet whan they be in batayle eyther wolde beste be praysed. (p. 137)

Here is an age-old paradox typical of literary heroism, but Malory implicitly links it to his own nonliterary experience. In the process, he steps away from an "equitable" recapitulation of his source (the *Alliterative Morte Arthure*) into a moment of personal validation—a version of the phenomenon he describes.

As he begins his "books" of Trystram de Lyones, Malory reflects on Trystram's renown as an author on the arts of hunting. This turns into a reflection on the distinctive language of those of gentle birth:

> All jantyllmen that beryth olde armys [come from old gentry families] ought of ryght to honoure Sir Trystrams for the goodly tearmys that jantylmen have and use and shall do unto the Day of Dome, that thereby in a maner all men of worshyp may discover [distinguish] a jantylman frome a yoman [servant] and a yoman frome a vylayne [churl]. (p. 231)

The distinguishing vocabulary of Malory and his class is also that of the hero about whom he writes. "Olde armys" in this context applies not just to long-established family coats of arms but also to a species of verbal heraldry whose genesis lies in Arthurian antiquity; again, writing functions for Malory as a means of self-validation, but it also takes on the potential of auto-iconography, where Malory as Trystram-Malory implies that he is what he writes. A further implication is that of an anxiety about being distinguishable from lesser men when external signs of status are absent; and in another aside in the same tale, Malory considers the case of unlikely triumphs in combat:

> Here men may undirstonde, that bene [are] men of worshyp [honor], that man was never fourmed that all tymes myght attayne, but somtyme he was put to the worse by malefortune; and at som tyme the wayker [weaker] knyght put the byggar knyght to a rebuke. (p. 293)

The story of Trystram—one full of misidentification and "malefortune," the inhumane agent of improper reversals—constitutes the largest single body of related matter in the *Morte Darthur*; and yet it is not a traditional component of the cycles of tales that lead up to the death of Arthur and that comprise the main sources for the rest of Malory's work. Perhaps, as a prisoner with time on his hands, Malory worked with any source book he could get, borrowed from friends or associates. The personal note of identification with iniquitous disenfranchisement seems to continue, however, as he considers Trystram imprisoned by Sir Darras:

> So Sir Trystram endured there grete payne, for syknes had undirtake hym—and that ys the grettist payne a presoner may have, for all the whyle a presonere may have hys helth of body, he may endure undir the mercy of God and in hope of good delyveraunce.
>
> But whan syknes towchith [touches] a presoners body, than may a presonere say all welth ys hym berauffte [he is

bereft of all wealth], and than hath he cause to wayle and wepe. (p. 327)

Malory wrote that he finished the *Morte Darthur* in the ninth year of the reign of Edward IV, which ran from 4 March 1469 to 3 March 1470 by our modern calendrical reckoning (p. 698). If the Greyfriars epitaph is accurate, this means he died no more than two years later. Perhaps at the time he was writing of Trystram, Malory already knew his own health was gravely compromised, although inevitable familiarity with the most common cause of death in medieval prisons would be enough. Whatever the case, the identification between text and history of the oppressed Trystram and Malory persists.

Later, in the closing tales of the *Morte Darthur*, Malory's extemporary comments retain their personal implication, but they do so by comparative reference to the excesses of fifteenth-century political and cultural opportunism. When a great fire is prepared with which to burn Queen Guinevere for adultery—should a trial of champions (fought, for summary efficiency, in the same place) prove her guilt—Malory reflects on the corruptions of justice prevalent in his own day:

> Such custom was used in tho [those] dayes, for favoure, love, nother affinité [alliances with noble families] there sholde be none other but ryghtuous jugemente, as well upon a Kynge as uppon a knyght, and as well upon a quene as uppon another poure lady. (p. 595)

If Malory's legal record provides reliable evidence for anything, it is that favor, love, and affinity were his constant antagonists, just as they were the main instruments of a litigious sovereignty and counter-sovereignty throughout the Wars of the Roses, and in this instance Guinevere is, like Trystram, Malory's fellow prisoner. In this portion of the *Morte Darthur* she is more than once charged with adultery by traitorous schemers (however accurate their charges may be), and so she is also a fellow criminal, also excessively incriminated by opportunists rather than judicial integrity. Indeed, for Malory, the adultery is admirable for being unadulterated:

> So faryth the love nowadayes, sone [soon] hote, sone colde: thys ys no stabylyté. But the olde love was nat so; for men and women coude love togydirs seven yerys, and no lycoures [lecherous] lustis was betwyxte them—and than was love trouthe and faythefulnes.
>
> And so in lyke wyse was used such love in Kynge Arthurs dayes. Wherefore I lykken love nowadayes unto sommer and wynter: for, lyke as the tone ys colde and the othir ys hote,

so faryth love nowadayes. And therefore all ye that be lovers, calle unto youre remembraunce the monethe of May, lyke as ded [did] Quene Gwenyver, for whom I make here a lytyll mencion, that whyle she lyved she was a trew lover, and therefor she had a good ende. (p. 625)

The last phrase suggests an acute awareness on Malory's part of the relation between stable endings—of lives, and of texts—on the one hand, and public stability and personal vindication on the other. Throughout the year in which Malory was finishing the *Morte Darthur* and perhaps contemplating his failing health, England was enduring one of the most intense periods of instability of the long Wars of the Roses. Richard, earl of Warwick ("the Kingmaker") was orchestrating uprisings against Edward IV, the man for whom he had been instrumental in winning the throne; his aim was to restore his old enemy, Henry VI, as a puppet king. It can hardly be in doubt that Malory had this turmoil in mind when, in the last and best known of his major direct addresses, he strove against dissolution. Contemplating the disloyalty of Arthur's subjects as they turn to support the would-be usurper Mordred, Malory addresses "ye, all Englysshemen," accusing them (and himself, it seems) of a bad habit of fickleness: "thys is a greate defaughte of us Englysshemen, for there may no thynge us please no terme" (p. 680). "The moste kynge and nobelyst knyght of the worlde" is brought down by the same species of instability that captivated Malory intellectually, emotionally, and legally—and which, as Malory seems to have understood for himself, was destined to make a life lived virtually coterminous with a life written.

MALORY'S ERA ON MALORY

Official records show that Malory was born between 1415 and 1417 into an old gentry family of Warwickshire, in the south central Midlands of England. His father, John, died around 1433, and had been at various times a sheriff, a member of Parliament, and justice of the peace for Warwickshire, all positions of considerable local power and influence. Thomas was knighted around 1441 (the circumstances are unknown); he was member of Parliament for Warwickshire from January 1445 to April 1446, and had married Elizabeth Walsh by 5 February 1448; they had a son, Robert, born around 1447 or 1448. Between October 1462 and January 1463, Thomas Malory participated in the military expedition of Edward IV and the Kingmaker against Lancastrian strongholds in northern England; he may also have been with the Yorkists at the battle of Towton in 1461, after which Edward IV was crowned. These are the major known details in the non-criminal record of Malory's life; they trace a life typical of a fifteenth-century man of his background.

To some extent, so do the criminal records, insofar as Malory lived in a perilous time, when knights worked in the service of more powerful lords whose legal power and contingent administration of coercive force were potentially absolute over the territories and honors they controlled, and highly effective at satisfying their ambitions to acquire the territories and honors of others. One lord's legality could be another's violation, and a loyal servant to one lord could be a dangerous criminal to another. The first known accusation of criminal activity against Malory came in 1443, when he was said, with an accomplice, to have insulted, wounded, and imprisoned one Thomas Smythe of Spratton, Northamptonshire, while also stealing the man's goods to the value of £40 (an exorbitant amount, equivalent to the annual income expected of a knight). Such charges among the gentry were formulaic, and they were often fabricated with the aim of achieving some form of settlement; in this case, there is no evidence of a trial. Two things are to be adduced, however, as signals of what is arguably a pattern in Malory's record: he convinced others into complicity or affront, and he was no stranger to bodily violation.

On 23 August 1451, Malory was charged at Nuneaton, Warwickshire, with several serious crimes. The charges were made in the presence of a powerful Lancastrian, Humphrey Stafford, duke of Buckingham, suggesting that Malory was no mere jurisdictional irritant. The charges included the attempted ambush-murder of the duke, with the aid of twenty-six other men, on 4 January 1450; the rape of Joan Smith, at Coventry, first on 23 May and again on 5 August 1450; the extortion of money from two monks of Monks Kirby, Warwickshire, 31 May 1450; the theft of seven cows, two calves, 335 sheep, and a cart worth £22 at Cosford, Warwickshire, on 4 June 1451; the theft of six does and infliction of £500 worth of damage in the duke of Buckingham's deer park at Cauldon, Warwickshire, 20 July 1451; escaping imprisonment at the house of Sheriff Sir William Montford at Coleshill, Warwickshire (where Malory allegedly swam the moat at night), 27 July 1451; robbery, with ten accomplices, of £46 in money and £40 worth of ornaments from Combe Abbey, 28 July 1451; and further robbery at Combe Abbey, with one hundred accomplices, of £40 in money and five rings, a small psalter, two silver bells, three rosaries, and two bows and three sheaves of arrows.

The variety (perhaps artificially enriched) of charges suggests Buckingham's insistence that Malory be constrained one way or another; and indeed records show him held at various prisons, without trial, at least as early as the beginning of 1452, and until July 1460. It is unlikely that the charges were entirely fabricated. Aware of this, most commentary on Malory has until recently danced about the perceived problem of a "writer of genius" being a rapist; but historically contextualizing studies such as those by Field and Batt have begun to replace embarrassment with sanguine insight. For instance, that Malory is charged with raping Joan Smith twice is likely to represent a legal understanding of adultery as a form of sexual violation (an understanding that privileges the husband, who would make the charge): by his own defiant standard, Malory may in retrospect have considered himself, or Joan, "a trew lover," as he did Guinevere.

By 14 July 1468, Malory was back in prison (again without record of trial), and he appears to have stayed there until his death. This time his imprisonment seems to have been for pro-Lancastrian activities, though this has not been proved. A viable explanation, however, would be that he was in the "affinité" of Warwick the Kingmaker and had little choice in undertaking his reversal—whence, perhaps, his lament over the "great defaughte of us Englysshemen." Such a lament might indicate a criminal threat, however, to anyone whose power was secured through revolt. This and the other charges construct an implied "reading" of Malory as dangerously effective at both corporeal and discursive persuasion. His discursive power is monumentally confirmed by the entirety of the *Morte Darthur*, and by such passages as those quoted above that demonstrate a compelling solipsistic affect, and even an ability to compel through deft command of paradox. In prison, Malory's corporeal power was by definition contained; but one might sense in his vast Arthuriad a projection of his physical agency, for in any paper edition it has a mass resistant to movement, and, if moved, has a momentum that must be checked.

[*See also* Arthurian Literature *and* Middle English Romance.]

EDITION

Shepherd, Stephen H. A., ed. *Le Morte Darthur*. New York and London, 2004. Includes landmark essay by Catherine Batt on Malory and rape.

FURTHER READING

Field, P. J. C. *The Life and Times of Sir Thomas Malory*. Cambridge, U.K., 1993. The most detailed and informative study of Malory's life; convincingly rules out other proposed candidates for author of *Le Morte Darthur*.

Field, P. J. C. "The Malory Life-Records." In *A Companion to Malory*, edited by Elizabeth Archibald and A. S. G. Edwards, 115–130. Cambridge, U.K., 1996.

Hicks, Michael. *Richard III and His Rivals: Magnates and Their Motives in the Wars of the Roses*. London, 1991.

Kim, Hyonjin. *The Knight without the Sword: A Social Landscape of Malorian Chivalry*. Cambridge, U.K., 2000.

Meale, Carol M. "Manuscripts, Readers, and Patrons in Fifteenth-Century England: Sir Thomas Malory and Arthurian Romance." *Arthurian Literature* 4 (1985): 93–126.

Riddy, Felicity. *Sir Thomas Malory*. Leiden, The Netherlands, 1987.

Sutton, Anne F. "Malory in Newgate: A New Document." *The Library*, seventh series, 1 (2000): 243–262.

THE TRAVELS OF SIR JOHN MANDEVILLE

John M. Bowers

For more than two centuries, Sir John Mandeville was the most famous world traveler who probably never existed. The popularity of *Mandeville's Travels* is attested by some three hundred surviving manuscripts dated from the 1360s on. Available in French, English, and Latin—as well as Czech, Italian, Danish, Spanish, and other languages—this classic of travel literature surpassed other contenders for popularity, including Marco Polo's *Divisament dou Monde* (1299). Early cartographers incorporated its geographical information into their mapmaking. When his crew sighted land in 1492, Christopher Columbus had been reading *Mandeville's Travels* as a practical guidebook for information about Asia. During the fifteenth and sixteenth centuries, seventy-two printed editions indicate its continuing influence in its original version, which also spawned various adaptations, such as the one that Samuel Taylor Coleridge was reading when he was inspired to write "Kubla Khan."

Near the beginning of the text, the knight-narrator states that he was born in England in the town of St. Albans. Near the end, another biographical insertion restates the chronology of the journey:

> And I, John Mandeville, knight, left my country and crossed the sea in the year of Our Lord Jesus Christ 1322; I have traveled through many lands, countries and isles, and have been on many honorable journeys, and many honorable deeds of arms with worthy men, although I am unworthy; I am now come to rest, a man worn out by age and travel and the feebleness of my body, and certain other causes which force me to rest. I have compiled this book and written it, as it came into my mind, in the year of Our Lord Jesus Christ 1356, that is to say in the thirty-fourth year after I left this land and took my way to those parts.

No reader seems to have questioned the authenticity of this claim during the first two hundred years of the work's circulation, even when sixteenth-century explorers began bringing back contradictory reports.

The genealogical relations among the different versions indicate that *Mandeville's Travels* was first composed in French around 1357. The lost French-language original was adapted as the "Continental Version" by 1371. An Anglo-French text was widespread by 1390, and some scholars have argued that this "Insular Version" was the original work, composed in England. This version was translated into Latin by 1390 and finally rendered into English before 1400. This English translation is called the "Defective Version" because its archetype had lost a number of pages describing the wonders of Egypt. Four other English variations followed, including the "Metrical Version." The work's initial availability in French meant that it quickly achieved an international readership; its subsequent translation into Latin gave it a respectability bestowed by the language of scholarship and science.

The work can be read as a medieval *summa* or compendium drawn, sometimes verbatim, from sources available in northern France. These included such reliable, up-to-date travelogues as the Franciscan friar Odoric of Pordenone's story of his missionary expedition from India to Cathay (1330) and the Dominican friar William of Boldensele's account of his travels in Egypt and the Holy Land (1336). Unlike other medieval writers, the author of the *Travels* concealed his sources rather than advertising them to boost his credibility, which rests instead on claims of personally visiting these distant lands. Too much tacit reliance on these sources often counts heavily against the narrator's credibility, however. When he claims residence with the Great Khan at Manzi (lifted from Odoric's account), he cannot be trusted, because the kingdom of Manzi fell in 1278. Consequently, skeptical critics have accused the author of traveling no farther than the nearest monastic library. Even his name seems derived from the satirical French romance *Le Roman de Mandevie* (1340).

The text's mosaiclike assemblage of prior accounts undercuts claims for a real English traveler. Specifically, the text relies heavily on the Benedictine monk Jean le Long's 1351 French translation of a collection of previous travel narratives. Le Long himself has been suggested as a plausible candidate for authorship. With its own local adaptation of the work surviving in seven manuscripts, the town of Liège made steady claims for the man himself; a grave epitaph in a local church, no longer surviving, once recorded that the Englishman Mandeville "who traveled over the whole world" had ended his days in the town. Two of Liège's residents have indeed been proposed as possible authors—the physician Jean de Bourgogne and the chronicler Jean d'Outremeuse—but these speculations are based on evidence insufficient to win wide support. The case for Continental composition is bolstered somewhat by the writer's failure to use the two source-texts regarded as most authoritative in England, Bartholomaeus Anglicus's *De proprietatibus rerum* (c. 1245) and Ranulf Higden's *Polychronicon* (c. 1347).

On the other hand, the great Benedictine monastery of St. Albans was a center for disseminating copies of the work, and its famous chronicler Thomas Walsingham claimed Mandeville as a notable person associated with his abbey. In 1357 the French-born Queen Isabelle was served by a John Mandeville, park-keeper of Enfield twelve miles from St. Albans and liegeman of the book-loving Humphrey Bohun, earl of Hereford. The Tudor antiquarian John Leland recalled hearing as a child that the author of the *Travels* lived at "Hainvilla" (Enfield). Queen Isabelle entertained King Jean II and other French noblemen taken prisoner at Poitiers in 1356, a year before the putative dating of the *Travels*, so there was suddenly a ready-made audience for French-language literature in England at exactly this date. Aristocratic captives confined in England would have found much to appreciate in the stories of a freelance knight exploring remote corners of the world. Overall, Mandeville's fantastic reports found a European audience at a time when Ottoman expansion and Timur's revival of the Mongol Empire made the prospect of actual contact with the East increasingly unrealistic.

Local knowledge, such as his reference to barnacle geese, lends some credibility to the writer's Englishness, as does his reference to the letters yogh (ȝ) and thorn (þ) that "we have in our language in England." If merely ruses, these references point to the writer's savvy efforts at encouraging credibility. Why would a French-speaking writer concoct the fiction of an English knight traveling to Cathay? The text itself mentions the longstanding reputation of Englishmen for restlessness and their obsession with visiting foreign lands, so the persona of an English traveler would confirm this ethnic stereotype of men addicted to visiting far-flung parts of the world.

The work's international success owed much to the authority of a shrewd, often skeptical eyewitness. He claims personally to have drunk from the Fountain of Youth: "I, John Mandeville, saw this well and drank of it three times, and so did all my companions. Ever since that time I have felt the better and healthier." He had entered the service of the sultan of Egypt and spent sixteen months in the household of the Great Khan. Yet he is cautious about accepting unverified lore, such as the report that Noah's Ark could be visited on the summit of Mount Ararat. Like Herodotus, he is prone to repeat hearsay but usually careful to note that he has not personally seen the marvel being described. This status as a trustworthy witness made everything else believable. His account strongly implies that he himself had seen gold-digging ants and the marks on the earth where crocodiles dragged their large bodies. He reports what he learned at first hand about the Buddhist doctrine of reincarnation and weird Tibetan funeral rites. He personally crossed the Vale Perilous in the company of two Lombard friars. Many of these details smack of firsthand knowledge, such as the names of the most recent Egyptian sultans and the number of steps at the Church of the Nativity in Bethlehem, details not found in his sources. In one interesting example, he reports that the Great Khan's palace walls were covered with the sweet-smelling red skins of panthers—probably red pandas—a detail missing in Odoric.

Since the work assimilates the genres of chronicle, romance, bestiary, and hagiography, the manuscripts indicate that *Mandeville's Travels* appealed to different classes of readers who brought different interests to the work. Some of the earliest copies were owned by royals such as Charles V of France, Juan I of Aragon, Duke Thomas of Gloucester in England, Valentina Visconti in Milan, and her son Charles of Orléans. A group of English manuscripts interpolate an elaborate dedication to Edward III (d. 1377) as evidence of this intention to appeal to high-status readers by associating the work with the stylishness of the royal court. Aristocratic audiences would have identified with the chivalric values of the knightly narrator who served the sultan of Egypt, his courage and sense of adventure in the wilds of Asia, and his account of fabulous races drawn from the literary tradition of the Alexander Romances. When Chaucer incorporated material from this work in his *Squire's Tale*, he reflected aristocratic fascination with the exotic lore of Genghis Khan and the marvels of the Mongol Empire. One Czech manuscript, the Textless Mandeville, jettisons the narrative altogether to provide instead a series of high-quality illuminations showing the spectacles described in the *Travels*.

The work also found its way into monastic libraries from England to Germany. In English manuscript anthologies, for example, it appears five times with William Langland's religious allegory *Piers Plowman*, and an anonymous English contemporary of Langland incorporated its information on the Dead Sea into his sermonlike poem *Cleanness*. Here Mandeville's readers would have found religious history, accounts of Christian martyrs and relics, and a reliable itinerary for pilgrimage to the Holy Land, actually used as a road map by the owner of one manuscript. The Christian world is literally mapped according to the relics and miracles that imbue these place names with sacred meaning. Some manuscripts abridge the second half of the work after the descriptions of the Holy Land, evidence that the audience's interest was in the biblical rather than the fabulous. The menace of Islamic nations, counterbalanced by their personal piety and lack of ecclesiastical corruption, formed a steady concern of both aristocratic and religious audiences. Transforming human curiosity into a virtue, the work reinforces a religious geography, centered physically and spiritually on Jerusalem, which stresses the unity of the world while allowing and containing its diversity. Some English versions of the *Travels* interpolate a section telling how Mandeville stops in Rome to get papal approval—"our holy father the Pope has ratified and confirmed my book in all points"—a supplement clearly designed to sanction contents that were often unflattering to Christian practices while lauding the virtues of non-Christians.

The geography of the *Travels* corresponds to the fourteenth-century map of the world with its "T in O" configuration of the three continents: Asia, Europe, and Africa. Jerusalem stands at the center of the T, with the East materializing as the domain of despotism, strangeness, and monstrosity. Recent postcolonial studies have located in Mandeville's accounts a medieval version of the Orientalism discussed in Edward Said's seminal work as the geographical category of human otherness. As a Christian and an Englishman, however, the narrator embodies a remarkable degree of cultural relativism that values outlandish peoples without any impulse to convert them, conquer them, trade with them, or plunder their riches. He is the model of the perfect Baedeker-toting tourist. Of course, this open-minded tolerance may have been the privilege of a library-bound writer who never actually dwelled among the alien races he describes.

A superior storyteller who surpassed the narrative skill of authentic eyewitnesses, the author of *Mandeville's Travels* offered the fabulous descriptions that established Amazons, Cannibals, Pygmies, the Juggernaut, and the Fountain of Youth as permanent fixtures in the European imagination. When Shakespeare's Othello boasts about his encounters with "the Cannibals that each other eat, / And Anthropophagi, and men whose heads / Do grow beneath their shoulders" (act 1, scene 3, lines 143–145), he shows himself inhabiting the same twilight world of real-life adventure and fantastic exaggeration. The fourteenth-century work stands as the progenitor of a whole genre of philosophic travel literature that includes Thomas More's *Utopia*, Shakespeare's *Tempest*, and Samuel Johnson's *Rasselas*, reaching forward into science fiction classics such as television's *Star Trek*. Indeed, the first scholarly edition (1725) of the British Library's Cotton manuscript coincided with the publication of Jonathan Swift's *Gulliver's Travels*. Fantasy literature and films can hardly avoid this legacy. When J. R. R. Tolkien described Frodo's dangerous trek across the Dead Marsh in *Lord of the Rings*, he was clearly recalling Mandeville's near-fatal crossing through the Vale Perilous.

The debate over whether an actual Englishman named Sir John Mandeville really traveled as far as the court of the Great Khan in Cathay—or whether the account was completely fabricated out of prior travel books—will remain difficult to resolve. In a modern instance of a Englishman's adventures among Arabs, *The Seven Pillars of Wisdom* contains so many distortions and outright errors that some critics have suggested the book is best read as a novel, and yet we know that T. E. Lawrence actually visited the places he described and knew the main players personally. It is appealing to take a middle position in allowing that the narrator of *Mandeville's Travels* made an actual pilgrimage to Jerusalem and then fabricated the rest. Or maybe he did make the trip to Cathay and then consulted travel books when he came home in order to verify information such as place names. Benjamin Disraeli confessed similar lapses of memory: "Like all great travelers, I have seen more than I remember, and I remember more than I have seen."

Sometimes, however, a popular text's factual basis becomes less important than its imaginative reach. During the eighteenth century, when its reliability as a travel narrative had been discounted, *The Tatler* could still praise Mandeville for the "copiousness of his invention and greatness of his genius," and Dr. Johnson's Preface to his *Dictionary* of 1755 valued the work's "force of thought and beauty of expression." Sir John Mandeville's account of his journey, after all, made circumnavigation of the globe into a physical possibility for later explorers such as Columbus and Martin Frobisher, who had a copy of the *Travels* with him as he lay off Baffin Bay in 1576. Ponce de Leon explored Florida when actually searching for Mandeville's Fountain of Youth, and Sir Walter Ralegh quoted Mandeville by name in his *Discovery of Guiana.* It would be no exaggeration to claim that *Mandeville's Travels* firmly established travel literature as a prominent genre for the entire later British tradition.

[*See also* Orientalism *and* Travel Writing.]

EDITIONS

Moseley, C. W. R. D., trans. *The Travels of Sir John Mandeville.* Harmondsworth, U.K., 1983. Translation of the Insular Version, supplemented with major interpolations from other versions.

Seymour, M. C., ed. *The Defective Version of Mandeville's Travels.* Early English Text Society, original series 319. London, 2002. Based on Oxford, Queen's College MS 383.

Seymour, M. C., ed. *Mandeville's Travels.* Oxford, 1967. Middle English edition of the Cotton manuscript.

FURTHER READING

Greenblatt, Stephen. "From the Dome of the Rock to the Rim of the World." In his *Marvelous Possessions: The Wonder of the New World,* 26–51. Chicago, 1991. Traces the origins of Columbus's notions of the East.

Hanna, Ralph III. "Mandeville." In *Middle English Prose,* edited by A. S. G. Edwards, 121–132. New Brunswick, NJ, 1984.

Higgins, Iain Macleod. *Writing East: The "Travels" of Sir John Mandeville.* Philadelphia, 1997. Insightful readings of the major versions.

Said, Edward W. *Orientalism.* New York, 1978. Foundational text for postcolonial studies.

Seymour, M. C. *Sir John Mandeville.* Authors of the Middle Ages, 1. Aldershot, U.K., and Brookfield, VT, 1993. Reviews authorship evidence and catalogues the many manuscripts.

Tzanaki, Rosemary. *Mandeville's Medieval Audiences: A Study on the Reception of the "Book" of Sir John Mandeville (1371–1550).* Aldershot, U.K., and Burlington, VT, 2003.

Zacher, Christian K. *Curiosity and Pilgrimage: The Literature of Discovery in Fourteenth-Century England.* Baltimore, 1976.

DELARIVIER MANLEY

Ellen Pollak

Delarivier Manley (c. 1667/71–1724) was one of the three most popular women writers of the Restoration and first half of the eighteenth century. In an enduring phrase, the eighteenth-century poet John Sterling included her along with Aphra Behn and Eliza Haywood in "the fair Triumvirate of Wit" and attributed to her a "greater Name" than that of her predecessor Behn (dedicatory verse to Haywood's *Secret Histories, Novels, and Poems*, 1725). Manley's political scandal narrative *Secret Memoirs and Manners of Several Persons of Quality of Both Sexes, from the New Atalantis, an Island in the Mediterranean* (1709), better known as the *New Atalantis*, was the most sensational and influential best seller published during the reign of Queen Anne (1702–1714). A thinly veiled political allegory that targeted prominent Whigs by weaving a blend of fact and fashionable gossip into steamy accounts of the sexual and political intrigues of the rich and famous, the *New Atalantis* inspired so much popular interest that, as Fidelis Morgan has commented, it "was read not only in literary circles but by practically everybody who could read" (p. 144). So powerful an intervention was the *New Atalantis* in the political controversies of its day that Manley is credited with helping to bring down the Whig ministry, which lost its power over Parliament and its consequent influence over the queen to the opposing Tory party in 1710. The work does seem to have been received as a political threat by Whig leaders, as its author, publishers, and printers were held briefly on charges of seditious libel just days after its second volume appeared in October 1709.

Although Manley's work has only recently begun to receive the serious critical attention it deserves, her notoriety as a scandalmonger survived into the twentieth century, in part through the influence of Sir Winston Churchill, whose ancestor the duke of Marlborough was the primary target of her satire. In his biography of Marlborough, Churchill, lamenting that Manley could not "be swept . . . back into the cesspool from which she should never have crawled," characterized her writings as "the lying inventions of a prurient and filthy-minded under-

world, . . . paid for by party interest and political malice" (*Marlborough; His Life and Times*, vol. 1 [1933], pp. 130–132), a view of Manley's devotion to smut and aggression echoed a decade later in Bridget MacCarthy's declaration that Manley "collected filth with the relentless energy of a dredger, and aimed it with the deadly precision of a machine-gun" (p. 216).

Since the mid-1980s, however, feminist scholarship on early women writers and more broadly cultural approaches to literary texts have brought Manley's importance in eighteenth-century literary and political circles into better focus. A friend and collaborator of such literary notables as Jonathan Swift and Richard Steele, and of the Tory statesmen Robert Harley and Henry St. John Bolingbroke, Manley experimented with allegory and narrative voice to turn cultural stereotypes of women as gossips into a compelling form of cultural critique. Amatory prose became in her hands an instrument of political agency worthy of the new interactions of print, politics, and sexuality that had come to characterize modern public life in England at the turn of the eighteenth century. The author of some twenty works altogether, including at least four plays, a few poems, and three extremely popular works of scandal fiction (her signature métier), Manley served for a time as editor of the Tory journal the *Examiner* and was a key player in the pamphlet wars waged between the two reigning political parties, the Whigs and the Tories, during the last years of Queen Anne's reign. Her unique blend of fact and fiction in the form of political allegory based on themes of seduction and the quest for power played an important role in the early development of British prose fiction.

LIFE AND EARLY CAREER AS A PLAYWRIGHT

What little we know about Manley's life comes from her own pen in two semifictionalized autobiographical narratives that rework the same events: the inset story of Delia in the second volume of the *New Atalantis*; and *The Adventures of Rivella*, in which Manley presents the story of her life through the words of a male admirer—a project she undertook anonymously in 1714 to preempt publication of a scurrilous biography of her by the hack writer Charles Gildon. These two narratives offer contrasting characterizations of Manley (as Delia, she is an innocent victim; as Rivella, a shrewd and seductive woman of the world), but the events they record are consistent and largely borne out by historical research.

Manley was probably born between 1667 and 1671 in the Channel Islands, where her father, Sir Roger Manley, a Tory scholar and translator who had been knighted for his support of Charles I during the English Civil Wars, served as lieutenant-governor of the Isle of Jersey. Her mother seems to have died when she was very young and certainly before the family (including Sir Roger, Delarivier, and her four siblings) moved to Landguard Fort in Suffolk in 1680. After Sir Roger's death in 1787, she was left in the care of her older cousin John Manley, who deceived her into a bigamous marriage and took her to London, where she bore him a son in 1691. After Manley's discovery of her cousin's treachery and his subsequent abandonment of her in London with an illegitimate child, she became a friend and retainer of Charles II's former mistress, the duchess of Cleveland (Lady Castlemaine), with whom she lived for several months, until the fickle duchess (later to be portrayed in the *New Atalantis* as Madame de L'Inconstant) traded her for a new favorite. At the duchess's residence Manley first became acquainted with the gossip and scandal surrounding such "Persons of Quality" as John Churchill (the duke of Marlborough) and his wife, Sarah, who later would figure so centrally as the butts of her political satire. Here she may also have been introduced to the world of the London theater, where her writing career began with a poem in praise of Catherine Trotter on the occasion of the Drury Lane Theatre's production of Trotter's play *Agnes de Castro* in 1695. Manley's own first play, *The Lost Lover*, a comedy performed on the same stage the following year, was a flop.

Manley's second play, a tragedy entitled *The Royal Mischief*, was performed later that same year by a rival acting company at Lincoln's Inn Fields. The ruthless ambition and sensuality of its lusty heroine, a Persian queen, Homais, launched her reputation for frank and potentially provocative eroticism. Manley claims in her preface to the play to have confined herself solely to a "feminine" eros, but the name Homais (French for "manly") hints that other motives may underlie her heroine's predatory sexuality while at the same time signaling, through a veiled onomastic pun, her own developing penchant for political narrative that masquerades as purely amatory fiction. Be that as it may, *The Royal Mischief* clearly exemplifies Manley's skill at satirically exploiting sensational themes and effects to arouse public interest (at one point in the play, after a man is shot alive from a cannon, "his carcass shattering in a thousand pieces," his grief-stricken wife gathers the "smoking relics of her lord / . . . bestowing burning kisses/And embraces on every fatal piece").

At about the same time that Manley made her debut as a London playwright, an unauthorized work entitled *Letters Written by Mrs Manley* (1696) appeared in print, containing correspondence to a friend identified only as J.H. (possibly James Hargreaves) during a trip she had taken to the west country in 1694, probably to recover from the debacle of her failed "marriage" and her dismissal by Lady Castlemaine. This work was almost immediately withdrawn on Manley's request, reappearing only after her death as *A Stagecoach Journey to Exeter* in 1725. During this same period Manley was also ridiculed, along with her fellow playwrights Trotter and Mary Pix, in *The Female Wits*, an anonymous play performed by the acting company she had recently walked out on at Drury Lane and in which she is portrayed in the character of Marsilia, a vain poetess. In 1700 she contributed two poems to *The Nine Muses*, an anthology (which she may also have organized) of elegiac poems by women writers on the death of the poet John Dryden.

PRINT, POLITICS, AND SCANDAL: MANLEY AS TORY SATIRIST

Manley first ventured into the arena of political satire with the anonymous 1705 publication of *The Secret History of Queen Zarah and the Zarazians*, a sustained satirical account of the marriage and rise to power of Queen Anne's childhood friend and confidante Sarah Churchill (née Jennings). Anne had named Sarah Keeper of the Privy Purse, Mistress of the Robes, and Groom of the Stole when she took the throne in 1702, and as a reward for John Churchill's victorious military leadership against France in the War of the Spanish Succession (sometimes called Queen Anne's War) she gave the Churchills a huge estate and the money to begin building a palace there in 1705 (Blenheim Palace, named for Churchill's decisive victory at Blenheim in 1704). In *Queen Zarah* Manley portrays Sarah as the avaricious and power-hungry Zarah, who, by exploiting the fame of her unprincipled husband, Hippolito, seeks nothing less than total domination of

Albania (Queen Anne) and, ultimately, usurpation of the monarchy. Through an extended political allegory, she levels a scathing attack on the integrity of the Churchills, portraying them as callously prepared to exploit Anne (and, through her, the nation) to satisfy their own insatiable desires for wealth and personal advancement. *Queen Zarah* was so instantly successful that Manley wrote and published a second part in the same year, and subsequent editions appeared in 1707, 1709, 1711, 1712, with French translations in 1708 and 1711.

Manley's most famous attack on Anne's Whig ministry, the *New Atalantis*, followed in 1709. Broader in focus and more complex in plot than *Queen Zarah*, this narrative uses elaborate framing devices to tell a series of titillating amatory tales containing a much larger cast of characters. To disguise and distance her satiric representations, Manley presents her narrative as a double translation (from Italian into French into English) and sets it on an unknown island in the Mediterranean. A panorama of anecdotes of public and private life is related by the voluble female figure of Intelligence to Virtue and the latter's daughter, Astrea (Justice), who having formerly abandoned Earth in despair has returned to survey the progress of humanity. Making her visitors invisible, Intelligence takes them on a tour of the goings-on of the island, which to contemporary readers was easily recognizable as England. Modeled on the seventeenth-century French gossip novels of Madame d'Aulnoy, which had recently been printed in England for the first time, Manley's best seller recirculated damaging rumors about influential statesmen and aristocrats, as well as some less prominent contemporaries and even a few Tories (such as her unscrupulous cousin John Manley). John Churchill figures here as an inveterate opportunist under the aliases Count Fortunatus and the Marquis de Caria. Like her frame narrative, Manley's use of fabricated names and recycled gossip served as an elaborate defense against prosecution; and, indeed, when she was arrested for libel she managed to extricate herself from the authorities by insisting on the purely fictive character of her work. Her brush with the law seems to have added to her fame, and the *New Atalantis* went into at least seven editions by 1736. Several of these were accompanied by elaborate keys to the identities of its characters. A French translation came out in 1713.

To Manley, the model of ministerial government that emerged under Queen Anne represented a crisis in political authority that dated back to the Glorious Revolution of 1688, in which a Whig victory had limited the

prerogatives of the monarchy and given Parliament unaccustomed political influence. The Crown, now answerable to Parliament, was also subject to being swayed by the interests of whichever of the two influential parties of the day—the Whigs and the Tories—was in political ascendancy. As a Tory, Manley favored a strong monarchy and feared the incipient intrusion into government of party politics, which through the interventions of print and the literary marketplace was increasingly coming to play a role in the formation of public opinion. It was clear to her that the dispersion of sovereign power among a cadre of ministers and partisan journalists produced dangerous openings for political manipulation through strategies of false representation. The *New Atalantis* repeatedly crosses narratives of sex and politics, and of private and public life (including an allegory of Manley's own story of seduction by her cousin John), to make the point that monarchs, like lovers, are vulnerable to breaches of trust and constancy by those who court their favor. The irony, of course, is that no one was more thoroughly a product of, or more vigorous a participant in, this emerging modern political culture than Delarivier Manley herself; indeed, no one more effectively deployed the power of print to sway public opinion and produce political effects. Encouraged by Sarah Churchill's visible loss of influence over Anne, whose new favorite, Abigail Masham, was a Tory, Manley includes in the second volume of the *New Atalantis* a wishful prefiguration of the Whigs' fall and the Tories' rise to power in terms that correspond eerily to events that would in fact unfold almost a year later. In the interim she also published a two-volume sequel to the *Atalantis*, *Memoirs of Europe* (1710), largely an anticipatory celebration of Tory success dedicated to Abigail Masham. This, the last of her scandal chronicles, was the first to which she openly admitted authorship. *Memoirs* was advertised as "done into English by the author of *New Atalantis*" and carried Manley's initials on its preface, thus officially announcing what by then, like the scandalous stories Manley loved to retell in her fiction, was already an open secret.

After *Memoirs* Manley turned from scandal fiction to political journalism, succeeding Jonathan Swift in 1711 as editor of the recently established Tory journal *The Examiner*, to which she contributed numbers 7 and 46–52. Between 1711 and 1714 (the year of Queen Anne's death) she also wrote several important pamphlets for the Tory cause, in addition to her autobiographical *Adventures of Rivella*.

In 1717 the last of Manley's extant plays, *Lucius, the First Christian King of Britain*, was produced, under the patronage of Richard Steele, to whom the play is dedicated. This was Manley's first return to the stage since 1707, when her protofeminist and politically inflammatory play *Almyna* (an anagram of Manley) played, perhaps fortunately, to an audience too small to instigate any trouble. Manley had known Steele since the late 1690s, and *The Lady's Pacquet of Letters* (1707; reissued in 1711 as part of *Court Intrigues*) was based in part on their correspondence, but the two had become estranged in 1702 when Steele refused to lend Manley money in a time of need—an incident that earned him the name Monsieur L'Ingrat in the *Atalantis*. Steele's support of Manley late in her life seems to have been motivated by his wish for reconciliation. On the other hand, despite a payment of fifty pounds sent by Robert Harley in 1714 for her service to the Tory cause (plagued by illness and dwindling resources, she had petitioned him for one hundred pounds), Manley never received the financial reward or protection she felt she deserved from the Tory ministry for her work. In 1720 she published her last known work, *The Power of Love*, a set of novellas based on William Painter's *Palace of Pleasure*. Manley died 11 July 1724 in London, at the home of John Barber, the chief Tory printer, who had produced a number of her works. It has been assumed that because Manley lived with Barber for approximately the last ten years of her life she must have been his mistress, but this is sheer speculation. She was buried in the church of St. Benet Paul's Wharf.

At a time when women could not officially hold political office, Delarivier Manley's fiction not only established an arena for the exercise of women's political agency in the public sphere but tackled a number of delicate and difficult topics, including seduction, incest, adultery, and lesbian separatism, from a protofeminist point of view. Along with her predecessor Aphra Behn and her successor Eliza Haywood, she was one of the most important writers of British fiction to explore the important interconnections between sex and politics as domains of power before the Richardsonian novel domesticated the discourse of sexuality and, some would argue, obscured its politics.

[*See also* Aphra Behn; Eliza Haywood; Satire; *and* Jonathan Swift.]

SELECTED WORKS

Letters Written by Mrs Manley (1696); reissued as *A Stagecoach Journey to Exeter* (1725)

The Lost Lover; or, The Jealous Husband (1696)

The Royal Mischief (1696)

The Nine Muses (1700)

The Secret History of Queen Zarah and the Zarazians (1705)

Almyna: or, The Arabian Vow (1707)

The Lady's Pacquet of Letters in Memoirs of the Court of England (1707); reissued as *Court Intrigues in a Collection of Original Letters from the Island of the New Atalantis* (1711)

An Heroick Essay upon the Unequal'd Victory Obtain'd by Major-General Webb over the Count de la Motte at Wynendale (1709)

Secret Memoirs and Manners of Several Persons of Quality of both Sexes, from the New Atalantis, an Island in the Mediterranean, Written Originally in Italian (1709)

Memoirs of Europe towards the Close of the Eighth Century, Written by Eginardus, Secretary and Favourite to Charlemagne, and Done into English by the Translator of the New Atalantis (1710)

The Duke of Marlborough's Vindication: In Answer to a Pamphlet, Lately Published, Called Bouchain; or A Dialogue between the Medley and the Examiner (1711)

The Examiner, no. 7 (14 September 1710) and nos. 46–52 (14 June–26 July 1711)

A Learned Comment on Doctor Hare's Sermon (1711)

A True Narrative of What Pass'd at the Examination of the Marquis de Guiscard at the Cock-Pit the 8th of March 1710/11: His Stabbing Mr. Harley and Other Precedent and Subsequent Facts Relating to the Life of the Said Guiscard (1711)

The Honour and Prerogative of the Queen's Majesty Vindicated and Defended against the Unexampled Insolence of the Author of the Guardian (1713)

The Adventures of Rivella; or, The History of the Author of the Atalantis (1714)

Lucius, the First Christian King of Britain (1717)

The Power of Love in Seven Novels: 1) The Fair Hypocrite, 2) The Physician's Strategem, 3) The Wife's Resentment, 4 and 5) The Husband's Resentment, 6) The Happy Fugitives, and 7) The Perjured Beauty (1720)

FURTHER READING

Anderson, Paul Bunyan. "Delariviere Manley's Prose Fiction." *Philological Quarterly* 13, no. 2 (1934): 168–188. This and the following article are valuable early efforts to rehabilitate Manley's reputation as an important literary figure.

Anderson, Paul Bunyan. "Mistress Delarivière Manley's Biography." *Modern Philology* 33 (1935–1936): 261–278.

Ballaster, Ros. *Seductive Forms: Women's Amatory Fiction from 1684 to 1740*. Oxford, 1992. Contains a substantial chapter on Manley and is groundbreaking in its serious critical engagement with women's amatory fiction and the role of such narratives in the development of the British novel.

Fabricant, Carole. "The Shared Worlds of Manley and Swift." In *Pope, Swift, and Women Writers*, edited by Donald C. Mell, 154–178. Newark, DE, 1996. Argues that the work and careers of Manley and Swift as satirists and political propagandists can be mutually illuminating.

Gallagher, Catherine. *Nobody's Story: The Vanishing Acts of Women Writers in the Marketplace, 1670–1820*. Berkeley, CA, 1994. Includes an important chapter on Manley's use of allegory as a rhetorical strategy in light of the discursive interactions among fiction, femininity, and politics in the early literary marketplace.

Herman, Ruth, *The Business of a Woman: The Political Writings of Delarivier Manley*. Newark, DE, 2003. The first full-length study of Manley as a political propagandist.

MacCarthy, Bridget. *Women Writers: Their Contribution to the English Novel 1621–1744*. Cork, Ireland, 1944.

McDowell, Paula. *The Women of Grub Street: Press, Politics, and Gender in the London Literary Marketplace, 1678–1730*. Oxford, 1998. A third of this book is devoted to a discussion of Manley as a political writer.

Morgan, Fidelis. *A Women of No Character: An Autobiography of Mrs Manley*. London, 1986. A biographical account of Manley's life based on Manley's own autobiographical narratives and supplemented by historical research.

Needham, Gwendolyn B. "Mary de la Rivière Manley, Tory Defender." *Huntington Library Quarterly* 12 (1948–1949): 253–288. An important early contribution to scholarship on Manley that seeks to record the "extraordinary achievement of this pioneer female journalist."

Pollak, Ellen. *Incest and the English Novel, 1684–1814*. Baltimore, 2003. Includes a chapter on incest and the dangers of representation in *The New Atalantis*.

Richetti, John J. *Popular Fiction before Richardson: Narrative Patterns, 1700–1739*. Oxford, 1969. An important early contribution to the study of eighteenth-century popular writing, with discussion of the plots of Manley, among others. Now dated in its assessment of women writers, but it has been reprinted with a new introduction in the wake of feminist scholarship.

Todd, Janet. *The Sign of Angellica: Women, Writing and Fiction, 1660–1800*. New York, 1989. One of the first important literary histories of women writers in the eighteenth century; includes a short chapter on Manley's life and work.

KATHERINE MANSFIELD

Kevin Bell

Even those stories by Katherine Mansfield (1888–1923) that are generally denigrated or dismissed by the relatively small number of critics who have undertaken serious consideration of her work possess a unique plenitude of Imagistic effects—whose essence might be said to be time itself. There are few better examples of this quality than the following passage from Raoul Duquette, the dissipated narrator of one of her most respected efforts, "Je ne Parle pas Français" (1920):

> I don't believe in the human soul. I never have. I believe that people are like portmanteaux—packed with certain things, started going, thrown about, tossed away, dumped down, lost and found, half emptied suddenly, or squeezed fatter than ever, until finally the Ultimate Porter swings them on to the Ultimate Train and away they rattle. . . .

Not but what these portmanteaux can be very fascinating. Oh, but very! I see myself standing in front of them, don't you know, like a Customs official.

"Have you anything to declare? Any wines, spirits, cigars, perfumes, silks?"

And the moment of hesitation as to whether I am going to be fooled just before I chalk that squiggle, and then the other moment of hesitation just after, as to whether I have been, are perhaps the two most thrilling instants in life.

THE ESSENCE OF MANSFIELD

The moment of hesitation, we discover only after the fact, is often the central element in the reading and interpretation of Mansfield's work—it is the moment in which the details of the presented image's texture separate us not only from the continuity of facts and meanings in the

Katherine Mansfield
Photograph by Adelphi Studios Ltd., 1913
NATIONAL PORTRAIT GALLERY, LONDON

story but also from the unspoken demand that we connect them in the first place and organize them into something identifiably "whole." Raoul's moments of hesitation are suspended frames in which the *intensity* of what seems *all* of life's possibility is made to surface. What is "thrilling" about such instants has nothing to do with the content of "what" the voyeuristic Raoul may discover or "what" he may miss, but is rather the split-second invention of the very *promise* that something distinctly new and singular is going to happen. In its distance from whatever concrete answer is promised, the indeterminacy of the promise itself, creates the sensation—and exhilaration—of uncertainty's *duration*. Promise is the step onto the edge of new discovery and what Mansfield's writing forces is the sense that to stand on that edge is to step outside of time itself, as anticipation and possibility begin to swell. Even as early as 1908, in one of her first and most evocative stories, "The Tiredness of Rosabel," Mansfield's work is already seriously investigating the ways in which a Jamesian narrative scrutiny of mental work and imagery might complicate and even undo the notion of real time in short fiction.

In the way that time is so frequently condensed and intensified in Katherine Mansfield, the notion of individual identity is by turns fragmented or multiplied. Again, the cited passage is exemplary, because immediately the status of subjectivity or selfhood is converted into objecthood; the thinking "subject" of decision and feeling is made into a passive recipient or observer of life's experience, instead of its agent. The "outside" world, in all its speeds, colors, and energies, is shown to create and to contour human life instead of being molded by an organizing point of human view. When Raoul finds it necessary to leave himself in order to enjoy the sight of himself interrogating the "portmanteaux," we see that Raoul cannot "be himself" unless it is by *not* being himself; he cannot take full pleasure from the encounter unless he is removed from the field of direct participation and made able to witness the encounter as theater.

For at least a few years before she died from tuberculosis in 1923, at the age of thirty-four, Mansfield's concentrated imaging and exacting detail of emotion had been recognized and celebrated by artists and critics such as D. H. Lawrence, T. S. Eliot, and Virginia and Leonard Woolf, whose Hogarth Press published 1918's "Prelude." This would be the first of her later great pieces such as "The Man without a Temperament" (1920), "The Stranger" (1920), and "At the Bay" (1922).

While they are sometimes technical marvels of temporal suspension, Mansfield's stories are also often oblique, digressive studies of personal isolation, disillusionment, and impatience or boredom with cultural convention. The earlier stories in particular, composed during Mansfield's initial taste of continental bohemianism in her early twenties, nearly always reflect a certain indebtedness of sensibility to the nineteenth-century Russian author and playwright Anton Chekhov. Most Mansfield scholars have at some point observed the centrality of Chekhov to Mansfield's development. In 1921, Malcolm Cowley was one of the first to celebrate this critical relation astutely, suggesting that, like Chekhov, Mansfield had "come to a point where she writes most of her stories around a situation instead of around a plot. Sometimes she goes farther. She has written one story around two themes instead of around a situation; she approaches here to the construction of music."

AN EPHEMERAL LIFE,
AN ENDURING OEUVRE

Mansfield was born Kathleen Beauchamp on 14 October 1888, in Wellington, New Zealand, the third daughter of Harold Beauchamp and Annie Burnell Beauchamp. At nineteen, in 1908, having returned to New Zealand after completing Queen's College in London, she quickly turned around and went back to London, determined to live and work as an artist. She traveled and wrote across Europe, where she suffered a miscarriage that may have initiated the interminable series of physical ailments that would circumscribe the remainder of her life so heavily. Her first book of stories, *In a German Pension*, was published in 1911 under the name Katherine Mansfield. That

year she also met the British critic and writer John Middleton Murry, whom she would marry in 1918. In such stories as "The Man without a Temperament," "Marriage à la Mode" (1921), "Bliss" (1918), and "The Stranger," some of the insecurities, disappointments, and occasional joys of the marriage are thematized. In Mansfield's posthumously published *Journal* (1954) and in several volumes of letters, all edited by Murry, these themes are given historical body. The volumes are themselves controversial, in that they are frequently said to be the basis of a certain Mansfield "cult of personality"—oriented around her seemingly ephemeral character and early death, and managed, a great many critics charge, by an exploitative Murry himself.

The first Mansfield volume, *In a German Pension*, is generally regarded by her critics as the ugly stepchild in her oeuvre, relying as it does on the grotesquely flattened and exaggerated characterizations of its figures, whose names ("Herr Rat," "the Vegetable Lady") playfully correspond in some way to their weaknesses of personality such as gluttony, hypocrisy, or narcissism. Generated from several lonely months in a Bavarian boardinghouse where she stayed during her pregnancy and after her miscarriage, the direct, even hard-edged, language and driving rhythm of the thirteen stories stir the swift-moving procession of their images into something like a dingy dream, unpleasantly punctuated by precisely worded insults, condescensions, and scenes of disgust. But if this is true, it is also the case that the rendering of those images is a writing that gestures toward liberation from the dark immediacy of their worlds; a liberation in which the free play of thinking, of desire, and of language can imagine itself in frivolity or wildness—thus making real for each of these three dimensions the strange, unsettling, and thoroughly unrepresentable powers they *each* contain at every moment. The titular "Modern Soul" of the sixth sketch, Sonia Godowska, is a failing actor who thinks herself a genius because she identifies with the freedom expressed in the works of other people—and is failing, she thinks, because she is duty-bound elsewhere:

"Now I must put Mamma to bed," whispered Fraulein Sonia. "But afterwards I must take a walk. It is imperative that I free my spirit in the open air for a moment. Would you come with me, as far as the railway station and back?"

[. . .]Thus the modern soul and I found ourselves under the stars.

"What a night!" she said. "Do you know that poem of Sappho about her hands in the stars . . . I am furiously

Sapphic. And this is so remarkable—not only am I Sapphic, I find in all the works of all the greatest writers, especially in their unedited letters, some touch, some sign of myself . . . like a thousand reflections of my own hands in a dark mirror."

"But what a bother," said I.

"I do not know what you mean by 'bother'; is it rather the curse of my genius . . ." She paused suddenly, staring at me. "Do you know my tragedy?" she asked.

I shook my head.

"My tragedy is my mother. Living with her I live with the coffin of my unborn aspirations . . . I long to do wild, passionate things. And Mamma says, 'Please pour out my mixture first.' Once I remember I flew into a rage and threw a washstand jug out of the window. Do you know what she said? 'Sonia, it is not so much throwing things out of windows, if only you would—' "

"Choose something smaller?" said I.

"No . . . 'Tell me about it beforehand.' Humiliating!"

Once again the question of time eclipses that of action's content; the point is not in what is thrown out the window, but in the moment "beforehand," the moment in which the mindless act of throwing is required to explain itself—an injunction that effectively kills the act, since the throwing is an expression of "wild, passionate" impulse, not subject to the preemptive ordering of self-accounting. Sonia's wish is to momentarily surrender to breakdowns of the mastery and control that structure her life and to thereby, presumably, enter the domain of "pure" experience represented for her by the "unedited" letters of great writers. That she discerns this wildness less in the fictional or poetic works of those writers than in their personal letters and histories suggests the kind of imaginative impoverishment on her part that not only diminishes her reading but also seems to account for the limitations of her own career. What surfaces quickly is the profound force of alienation that marks so much of Mansfield's writing, so dense in this case as to divide Sonia not only from her mother and, indeed, from her own possibilities (of genius, no less), but from any sense of personal responsibility for that failure or any sense of personal agency that might reverse it.

In the final five years of her life, Mansfield produced her most inventive and most perfectly realized works, beginning with "Prelude" and followed by "Bliss," "Je ne Parle pas Français," "The Daughters of the Late Colonel" (1921), "The Garden Party" (1922), and "The Fly" (1923). By 1978, when the critical journal *Modern Fiction Studies* devoted an entire issue to discussion of her work, she had become an icon of both experimental high modernism and feminist literary practice, whose early departure from the modernist scene has since produced a demand for an energy and unpredictability of style now largely defined by its very nonfulfillment. "But though I can do this better than she could, where is she, who could do what I can't," wondered Virginia Woolf upon the death of her onetime friend and rival. "I was jealous of her writing," Woolf would write—"the only writing I have ever been jealous of."

[*See also* The Bloomsbury Group; Modernism; *and* Virginia Woolf.]

SELECTED WORKS

In a German Pension (1911)
Bliss and Other Stories (1920)
The Garden-Party and Other Stories (1922)
The Dove's Nest and Other Stories (1923)

EDITION

Murry, John Middleton, ed. *The Journal of Katherine Mansfield*. London, 1954.

FURTHER READING

Brown, Sally. "Hundreds of Selves: The British Library's Katherine Mansfield Letters." *British Library Journal* 14, no. 2 (1988): 154–164.

Cather, Willa. "Katherine Mansfield." In her *Not Under Forty*, 139–166. London, 1936. A perceptive and artful, if uneven appreciation.

Cowley, Malcolm. Review of "Bliss." *Dial* 71, no. 3 (September 1921): 365.

Daly, Saralyn R. *Katherine Mansfield*. New York, 1965; rev. ed., 1994. An important and original study, marred by a dogmatic and often flatteningly reductive brand of feminism.

Dunbar, Pamela. *Radical Mansfield: Double Discourse in Katherine Mansfield's Short Stories*. New York, 1997. A sharp critical analysis of language in Mansfield and of modernist aesthetic signatures, the close readings included in this text are at once theoretically sophisticated and crisply written.

Modern Fiction Studies 24, no. 3 (Autumn 1978). Katherine Mansfield special issue.

Moran, Patricia. *Word of Mouth: Body Language in Katherine Mansfield and Virginia Woolf*. Charlottesville, VA,

1996. An inventive and overdue comparison of major works from each writer; manages not to sink into historiography.

Nathan, Rhoda B., ed. *Critical Essays on Katherine Mansfield.* New York, 1993.

Pilditch, Jan, ed. *The Critical Response to Katherine Mansfield.* Westport, CT, 1996. A valuably representative collection of critical writings on Mansfield, from the publication of *In a German Pension* in 1911 until 1988.

Stead, C. K. "Katherine Mansfield and the Art of Fiction." *New Review* 4, no. 43 (September 1977): 27–36. Magisterially balanced and perceptive essay, integrating sophisticated readings and biographical information.

MARIE DE FRANCE

Matilda Tomaryn Bruckner

Coined in the sixteenth century, the name "Marie de France" offers an enticing puzzle rather than a clear reference to a specific historical person. It shapes the contours of a portrait of the artist that emerges from a number of twelfth-century works signed "Marie," a rare woman who wrote in a world dominated by men and male writers, and a trailblazer whose geographical designation suggests a dialogue across French-speaking milieus of the Anglo-Norman domain on either side of the English Channel. "Marie ai nun, si sui de France" ("My name is Marie and I am from France"), she declared in the epilogue to her *Fables*. All three works commonly attributed to the same Marie locate her at the intersection of multiple cultures, languages, and traditions—clerical and lay, written and oral, popular and learned, Latin and vernacular (English, French, and Breton). Shared concerns connect the *Lais* (or *Lays*), the *Fables*, and *L'Espurgatoire de saint Patrice* (*The Purgatory of Saint Patrick*) across their generic differences; they range from secular tales of adventure to moralizing animal fables and journeys into the Other World. The links cluster around themes of translation and transmission that are vital to Marie's call to remember, whether it be remembrance of the story matter she passed along to new publics or of the author "who does not forget herself" when she signed her name in the prologue to the first lay of her collection and thus took her place in the chain of transmitters. The same gesture closes the *Espurgatoire*: "I, Marie, have placed in memory the book of Purgatory in French so that it may be understood by lay people."

Marie was probably born on the Continent and wrote for French-speaking aristocratic circles in England, most likely the court of Henry II and Eleanor of Aquitaine. Possible identifications of her are based on the literary patrons she designated (a "noble king" for the *Lais*, "count William" for the *Fables*) and the approximate dating of her works—most reasonably between 1160 and 1190, although some push the *Espurgatoire* to 1208–1215. A fourth work by an author called Marie, *La vie seinte Audree* (The Life of Saint Audrey), based on a Latin vita, has also been proposed for inclusion in Marie de France's corpus. Its early thirteenth century date, recently determined, brings it into the possible period of her activity. Suggestions for the historical Marie have included the abbess of Reading, where the only manuscript containing all twelve lays with the General Prologue probably originated, the abbess of Shaftesbury (Henry II's half-sister), and daughters of King Stephen or the count of Meulan. No single candidate has prevailed, and our knowledge of Marie centers by necessity on the character of her works, which show that she was well educated, capable of translating from English and Latin, and familiar with written and oral literary traditions from the classics (especially Ovid and the Greco-Latin tradition of Aesopic fables) to contemporary Latin and vernacular works, including Geoffrey of Monmouth's *History of the Britons* (1135), the Old French translation of the *Aeneid* (c. 1155–1160), and some versions of the Tristan story. Although she was clearly operating in the same orbit as other great writers of the twelfth-century renaissance, it has been impossible to determine her relationship to the romances of Chrétien de Troyes (fl. 1165–1191) and Thomas of England (fl. mid- or late twelfth century). Some have even questioned her identity as a woman or as the author of all twelve lays presented in the manuscript catalogued as Harley 978. Nevertheless, the popularity of "dame Marie" among counts, barons, kings, and especially ladies was attested by Denis Piramus in his *Life of Saint Edmund the King* (c. 1170), when he complained about the lack of truthfulness in her rhymed lays, which were read aloud and much praised at court. The questions of gender and genre are important in for modern readers of her work.

THE *LAIS*

When she assembled a group of the traditional narratives called *lais* ("lays" in English) and put them into writing, Marie showed herself to be an artist as bold as she was subtle. In the General Prologue, she explained her decision to translate short tales "you've heard" told by Breton storytellers to commemorate an adventure. Ever conscious of rivalries at court—and the envy good work could elicit—Marie wanted to do something new rather than translate from Latin as others had done. In doing so, she appears to have launched the genre of written, narrative lays in verse. At the same time, she gave her own collection a weight and resonance that brought it into competition with romance, whose story matter it shares, while developing a distinctive character across the continuities and discontinuities of twelve juxtaposed lays: *Guigemar, Equitan, Le Fresne* (*The Ash*), *Bisclavret* (*Werewolf*), *Lanval, Deus Amanz* (*Two Lovers*), *Yonec, Laüstic* (*Nightingale*), *Milun, Chaitivel* (*The Wretched One*), *Chievrefoil* (*Honeysuckle*), and *Eliduc*. The success of Marie's enterprise can be measured not only by a critical bibliography begun in the sixteenth century and multiplied exponentially since the end of the nineteenth. The enthusiasm of modern readers and writers inspired by her work continues the chain of transmission and has yielded further fruits (as she anticipated in her prologue to *Guigemar*) in translations and rewritings like John Fowles's retelling of *Eliduc* in *The Ebony Tower* and Ursula LeGuin's "The Wife's Story," a recasting of *Bisclavret* from a radically different point of view.

The length of the lays varies considerably (from 118 to 1,184 verses), but most of them recount a single anecdote. All are framed by short prologues and epilogues that include the identifying titles; as a group, these highlight the important role of female characters in the lays. Specific actions and situations individualize heroes and heroines, uniformly noble and courteous. Many adventures occur when the marvelous intervenes in normal experience (magic animals and rings, shape shifters, passages that cross into another world, etc.); others remain realistic in time and setting but also involve contrasting planes of existence. What unifies the collection is their thematic focus on adventure and love, as well as their tendency to form constantly reforming subsets as similar situations are replayed with different characters and circumstances: the adulterous love triangles of *Laüstic* and *Chievrefoil*, couples threatened then reunited in *Guigemar* and *Le Fresne*, cross-generational love stories in *Yonec* and *Milun*, and so on. The interaction made possible by the arrangement of the collection explores the varieties of human experience, the happy endings as well as the unsatisfactory, sad, or tragic ones, for which no single doctrine of love accounts—although Marie seems to prefer well-matched couples, regardless of marital status.

The most problematic passage in the General Prologue describes Marie's view of the Latin literary tradition, whose rhetorical lessons she had clearly mastered. It gives insight into her own art as a writer transforming oral tales into written verses that require all our skills of interpretation to unpack. Citing Priscian as her authority, she speaks of the obscurities that ancient poets placed in their writings for later generations to discover (or invent) as they become more capable of "glossing the letter" and revealing the "surplus of meaning" contained (or inspired). Scholars have disagreed in reading these verses, assigning the "surplus de sen" to the original writers or their later interpreters: Marie's syntax involves us in the very activity she describes and thus prepares us to read tales whose stylistic economy and apparent simplicity belie their complexities. Their artful ambiguities invite countless interpretations and disagreements among readers, even in deciding whether a given ending is a happy one.

A ONE-ACT *TRISTAN*

A brief look at *Chievrefoil* reveals the richness hidden in Marie's art. In the shortest lay of her collection, Marie concentrated the story of Tristan and Iseut into one episode and a single powerful image. Her lays frequently contain an emblem that encapsulates the adventure—for example, a knot in *Guigemar*, or the swan who carries messages in *Milun*. The emblem chosen here reveals Marie's characteristic wrapping of metaphor and metonymy to encapsulate the truth of the adventures recounted. As Tristan tells the queen, they can live only as long as they remain intertwined like the honeysuckle and the hazel tree. The metaphors for Tristan and Iseut in the plant world twist around each other metonymically: honeysuckle and hazel are not simply parts standing for the whole; they are two parts of the same whole, complementary parts of a single self, which live and die together. In Tristan's words, "Fair beloved, so it is with us: neither you without me nor me without you."

To bring about their reunion during his exile, Tristan sends this message to the queen using a piece of hazel wood left on a forest path. Much critical discourse on *Chievrefoil* focuses on what Tristan wrote on the wood. Twenty-four verses spell out the message conveyed, but it remains unclear whether Tristan carves all these words in the wood, implies them by the mere presence of his name inscribed, or has already sent them to the queen. The problem in glossing Tristan's words relates to their excess:

there seem to be too many to fit reasonably on a branch that the queen can read as she passes by on horseback. This debate exactly parallels the other commonplace of criticism focused on Marie's writing activity and the "surplus de sen." Paradoxically, the common thread of extra words, surplus meaning, connects character and author.

Presented as a composer of lays in *Chievrefoil*'s epilogue, Tristan has frequently been recognized as a figure for Marie herself. We might even speak of twins, the artist as twin who duplicates and doubles (compare the literal twins thematized in *Le Fresne*). Marie implicitly twinned her artistic activities with Tristan's: he composes one lay; Marie, so as not to forget herself, repeated the gesture twelve times. Her arrangement of lays in a collection is the excessive production that allows us to read a surplus between economic lines, held in memory by writing. Marie's is the art of brevity, not the excess of amplification typical of her rival, romance; but the paradox of her writing is to achieve excess through ellipsis, within each lay and across the set of twelve.

THE *FABLES*

In the Middle Ages, animal fables were not simply tales for children, as they have become in modern times. The twenty-three extant manuscripts of Marie's *Fables* reflect their popularity among vernacular readers, who gained access to Greek and Roman traditions through her translation, the first of several "Isopets," or French collections of Aesopic fables. In her prologue, Marie claims to have translated from King Alfred's English version, although no trace of this work has been found. About half of her 102 fables derive from a fourth-century Latin fable collection entitled *Romulus Nilantii*; the remaining fables reflect the classical tradition and folkloric sources. Marie may also have had access through oral translation to the Eastern fable tradition represented by Arabic collections. All her transpositions into French remind us how flexible the concept of translation was in medieval usage: the translator exercised considerable leverage in moving the earlier work into a new cultural milieu, shaping it for a new audience. Where exact comparisons are possible, Marie's lively narrative style and the particular twists given to her moral lessons stand out clearly to give her collection an underlying unity across the quickly moving scenes of weak and strong animals fighting for their existence, or the equally energetic stories where animals compete with peasants for their livelihood.

The structure of each fable expresses the genre's pedagogical imperative and suggests comparisons between

Marie's fables and the "mirror of princes" tradition. Short narratives (8 to 124 verses) lead to moral lessons that explain how we should apply the fables' actions when lords exploit those who serve them, vassals lack loyalty, judges are bribed, or accusations are false. The explicit character of the meaning assigned in the moral separates the fables from the lays (except for the hybrid *Equitan*) and brings them close to another short narrative type, the fabliaux (comic, often ribald tales), which enjoyed a similar popularity in the twelfth and thirteenth centuries. The amorality that typically hides behind the lessons in fabliaux (as in the stories of Renard the Fox) contrasts significantly with the desire to instruct and improve that guides the application of the moral in Marie's fables. If her political stance is basically conservative and aristocratic, Marie nevertheless shows concern that justice be available to all classes. Social hierarchy should be maintained for the sake of harmony; all people should accept their places and responsibilities.

Indirectly, the combination of fables works to raise questions about how much nature and nurture allow us to control our actions. Consider the first fable, in which a rooster spurns the gem he finds on a dung heap. He acts "according to his nature," and the moral may surprise us by warning about those who "similarly" despise the better and prefer the worse. Apparently we should be capable of better. But the last fable's dialogue between a hen and a woman leads to the opposite conclusion. The hen rejects an improvement in her manner of feeding: "Likewise people cannot change their nature or their custom." A tension appears between nature as fixed and the desire to correct. In this light, the repeated appearances of the fox are instructive. He usually plays the role of the tricky deceiver (when matched with cat or rooster, dove or female bear), but he may also find himself in the position of sympathetic victim, as in "The Fox and the Eagle." Unlike medieval bestiaries, Marie's fables offer a range of possible behaviors open to each animal, depending on circumstances. A kind of situational ethics thus emerges from the interplay between narratives and morals across the collection.

L'ESPURGATOIRE

A single surviving manuscript contains Marie's translation of Henry of Saltrey's Latin account of Saint Patrick's Purgatory (c. 1179–1186), the first in a series of medieval visionary poems that culminates in Dante's *Divine Comedy*. It offers another opportunity to see how Marie dealt with her sources: a good Latinist, she produced a faithful translation but did not hesitate to recast her material for a lay and aristocratic, rather than monastic, audience. Through her we hear layers of voices, as she speaks within a long tradition of otherworldly journeys. Her more than two thousand verses contain a variety of materials (romanesque, hagiographic, and homiletic) but give primary attention to chivalric adventure, as the knight Owein descends into the pit that gives entrance into Purgatory for those brave enough to endure its torments. Armed with the name of Jesus Christ, Owein overcomes the devils' tortures and temptations, reaches the Earthly Paradise, and returns to be confirmed in his role as now purified knight. The work of devils is not limited to Purgatory: a series of anecdotes follow as reinforcement through experience for our belief in an incredible tale. They remind us how much Marie delighted in combining stories with multiple levels of reality, making different worlds available to her vernacular public, and keeping memory (and interpretation) alive in writing.

[*See also* Arthurian Literature *and* Breton Lays.]

WORKS

Les Lais (*The Lays*; between 1160 and 1189)

Les Fables (*The Fables*; between 1167 and 1189)

L'Espurgatoire de saint Patrice (*The Purgatory of Saint Patrick*; c. 1190 or between 1208 and 1215)

EDITIONS AND TRANSLATIONS

Burgess, Glyn S., and Keith Busby, trans. *The Lais of Marie de France*. 2d ed. New York, 1986, 1999.

Curley, Michael J., trans. *Saint Patrick's Purgatory: A Poem by Marie de France*. Binghamton, NY, 1993. Karl Warnke's edition of the Old French text is reproduced on facing pages.

Ewert, Alfred, ed. *Marie de France: Lais*. Oxford, 1944; reprinted with introduction and bibliography by G. S. Burgess, Bristol, U.K., 1995.

Spiegel, Harriet, ed. and trans. *Fables: Marie de France*. Toronto, 1987.

FURTHER READING

Bloch, H. Howard. *The Anonymous Marie de France*. Chicago and London, 2003. Argues for the continuity of authorship in all three works attributed to Marie, using an arsenal of modern critical approaches to demonstrate the sophistication of Marie's writing.

Bruckner, Matilda Tomaryn. "Textual Identity and Marie de France's *Lais*." In her *Shaping Romance: Interpretation, Truth, and Closure in Twelfth-Century French Fictions*, 157–206. Philadelphia, 1993. Analyzes how the *Lais* work as a collection, with special attention to the first and last lays, as well as the subtleties of Marie's narrating style.

Burgess, Glyn S. *Marie de France: An Analytical Bibliography*. London, 1977. Supplement No. 1, 1985; Supplement No. 2, 1997. Comprehensive, well organized, and extensively annotated.

Maréchal, Chantal A., ed. *In Quest of Marie de France: A Twelfth-Century Poet*. Lewiston, NY, and Lampeter, U.K., 1992. A wide variety of articles and approaches to Marie's *Fables* and *Lais*.

McCash, June Hall. "*La vie seinte Audree*: A Fourth Text by Marie de France?" *Speculum* 77 (2002): 744–777. Argues convincingly for reopening the attribution question.

CHRISTOPHER MARLOWE

Patrick Cheney

Christopher Marlowe (1564–1593) was the first author in English to write both poems and plays of an artistically superior order. He is perhaps best known as a founding father of English drama, especially tragedy, along with Thomas Kyd and William Shakespeare. When Marlowe died at the age of twenty-nine, he had written seven plays: *Dido, Queen of Carthage*; *Tamburlaine the Great, Parts One and Two*; *The Jew of Malta*; *Edward II*; *The Massacre at Paris*; and *Doctor Faustus*. Marlowe also left behind four extraordinary poems, and these would qualify him for a similar historic role in the development of English poetry: *Ovid's Elegies*, "The Passionate Shepherd to His Love," *Lucan's First Book*, and *Hero and Leander*. What is historic is the presence of masterpieces in both lyric poetry ("The Passionate Shepherd") and stage tragedy (*Faustus*). Remarkably, Marlowe was an inventor of both the English history play (*Edward II*) and of Ovidian narrative verse in English (*Hero and Leander*).

By combining plays with poems in an early phase of modern English literature, Marlowe pioneered the compound template of English authorship itself, which his two greatest heirs, Shakespeare and Ben Jonson, bequeathed even more momentously to the ensuing centuries: to John Milton and John Dryden, Lord Byron and Percy Bysshe Shelley, and William Butler Yeats and T. S. Eliot.

LIFE AND WORKS

Marlowe was christened 26 February 1564, twenty days after his birth, in Canterbury. He was the eldest son of John Marlowe (c. 1536–1605), a shoemaker, and Katherine Arthur Marlowe (died 1605), who would bear five surviving daughters and one other surviving son. In 1579 Marlowe won a scholarship at the King's School, Canterbury, indicating that he had been attending grammar school, learning Latin, and studying Virgil, Ovid, and Seneca. In 1580 he won a Matthew Parker Scholarship (named after the archbishop of Canterbury), which allowed him to enter Corpus Christi College, Cambridge.

There he continued to develop his mastery of Latin literature and studied rhetoric, the art of persuasion. Yet Archbishop Parker had set aside the three-year scholarship for boys "who were likely to proceed in arts and afterward make Divinity their study" (Riggs, in Cheney, ed., 2004, p. 27). Marlowe's education led to an unsettling collision between English Protestantism, with its doctrine of God's grace as the conductor of salvation, and classical philosophy, with its emphasis on human choice as the shaping force of destiny. This dissonance provided a crucible for Marlowe's creation of poems and plays.

The chronology of Marlowe's works is notoriously uncertain. Scholars believe that while at Cambridge he produced his first poem, *Ovid's Elegies* (a translation of Ovid's *Amores*), and his first play, *Dido* (a critique of Virgil's imperial epic, the *Aeneid*). In 1584 he completed his BA degree, and in 1585 he began the MA. Yet on 29 June 1587, Queen Elizabeth I's Privy Council (or main governing body) wrote a letter asking the university to grant Marlowe his MA despite a rumor that he had "gone beyond the seas to Reames" (the English Catholic seminary in France), for he "had done her Majestie good service . . . in matters touching the benefitt of his countrie" (Kuriyama, pp. 202–203). From this letter and other evidence, scholars believe that Marlowe was working as a government agent.

Later in 1587 Marlowe was in London, where he wrote (or had brought with him) the plays that would mark the new Elizabethan drama: the two-part *Tamburlaine*, his only work published in his lifetime, although anonymously. During the next six years, in arguably the most meteoric career of early modern English literature, he would compose the remainder of his poems and plays. Scholars tend to date the composition of "The Passionate Shepherd" in 1587–1588, alongside the *Tamburlaine* plays, which echo the poem's famed sentiment, "Come live with me, and be my love." *The Jew of Malta* followed soon after, and then either *Edward II* or *The Massacre at Paris*. *Doctor Faustus* is a special case, because it was printed in two different editions, the "A-text" of 1604 and the "B-text" of 1616; scholars now believe the earlier text is closer to Marlowe's authority, but they are divided over whether he wrote the great tragedy in 1588–1589 or 1592–1593. When the theaters closed owing to plague in 1592–1593, and Marlowe was seeking a patron in Thomas Walsingham (1563/68–1630), he likely wrote *Lucan's First Book* (a partial translation of the Roman poet Lucan's counter-imperial epic, the *Pharsalia*) and *Hero and Leander*. Two other works are assigned to him, both dating to these years: a short Latin epitaph on Sir Roger Manwood, a Canterbury judge who died on 14 December 1592; and a Latin prose dedicatory epistle prefacing Thomas Watson's *Amintae Gaudia* (1592), addressed to Mary Sidney Herbert.

These details suggest that Marlowe was intensely busy during the last years of his life. He was also traveling—and not merely to France. Kyd reports that he was "perswad[ing] . . . with men of quallitie to goe unto the k[ing] of Scotts" (MacLure p. 36), suggesting his criticism of Elizabeth and support for James VI of Scotland, who would become king of England in 1603. A letter written 26 January 1592 in the Netherlands by Sir Robert Sidney (1563–1626) to William Cecil, Lord Burghley (1520–1598), announces Marlowe's arrest for counterfeiting. Yet no evidence exists that he was ever prosecuted—testifying perhaps to his intelligence work.

In fact, Marlowe had repeated run-ins with the law, especially during the last sixteen months of his life. In 1589 he was arrested with Thomas Watson for killing William Bradley in Hog Lane, London; both men went to Newgate Prison before being released. In 1592 Marlowe was bound to keep the peace by the constable and subconstable of Holywell Street, Shoreditch. Later in 1592 Marlowe fought with William Corkine of Canterbury, although Corkine's subsequent suit was settled out of court.

This violent activity was preparation for the most famous event of Marlowe's brief life: his death. Through painstaking research, scholars have pieced together the following account. On 5 May 1593, an anonymous libel attacking Protestant immigrants was posted on the wall of the Dutch Church in London, signed "per Tamberlaine" and containing allusions to Marlowe's plays. On 11 May, the Privy Council ordered the Lord Mayor to arrest persons suspected in connection with the libel. On 12 May, Marlowe's former roommate, Kyd, was arrested, imprisoned, and tortured. During the search of Kyd's room, the investigators found a heretical document that Kyd claimed was Marlowe's. Perhaps between 12 May and 27 May, an unnamed spy wrote "Remembrances of words &

matter against Richard Cholmeley," which reported that Marlowe had been lecturing on atheism. On 18 May, the Privy Council issued a warrant for Marlowe's arrest. On 20 May, he appeared before the Privy Council and was instructed to "give his daily attendance," but he was released on his own recognizance. On or around 27 May, Richard Baines delivered a deposition against Marlowe, including charges of atheism and sodomy; the young man reportedly said, "all they that love not Tobacco & Boies were fooles" (Kuriyama, p. 221). Three days later, on 30 May, Marlowe was killed by Ingram Frizer in Deptford in the house of Eleanor Bull, in a quarrel over who would pay the "reckoning," or bill, for the day's expenses. The witnesses to the event were Robert Poley and Nicholas Skeres, well-known espionage figures. Subsequently Frizer was freed on the grounds of self-defense, and Marlowe was buried in an unmarked grave at St. Nicholas' Church, Deptford. Shortly afterward, Kyd wrote two documents to Sir John Puckering, the Lord Keeper, accusing Marlowe of atheism.

HETERODOX AUTHOR: RELIGION, POLITICS, SEXUALITY

The archival evidence portrays Marlowe as a heterodox intellectual in religion, politics, sexuality, and literature. Accused not merely of atheism but of being unpatriotic and advocating sodomy, he wrote poems and plays in the new Elizabethan literary milieu. The paradox at the heart of his career is that such a gifted poet and playwright could be implicated in so much violence and scandal. The poet who would pen some of the greatest lines ever on the loss of female virginity—"Jewels being lost are found again, this never; 'Tis lost but once, and once lost, lost for ever" (*Hero and Leander* 1.85–86)—evidently "report[ed] St John to be our saviour Christes Alexis . . . that is[,] that Christ did love him with an extraordinary love" (Kyd, in MacLure).

Not surprisingly, Marlowe's contemporaries were divided over his character. If Kyd could call him "intemperate & of a cruel hart" (MacLure, p. 33), fellow poet-playwright George Peele could speak of "Marley, the Muses darling for thy verse" (MacLure, p. 39). The Puritan Thomas Beard reduced Marlowe to a "barking dogge" whom "the Lord" hooked by "the nosthrils" (MacLure, p. 42), yet the poet Michael Drayton imagined Marlowe "bath[ing] . . . in the Thespian springs" and having "in him those brave translunary things, / That the first Poets had" (MacLure, p. 47). In *As You Like It*

(3.5.79–80, 3.3.15), Shakespeare eulogized Marlowe as "the dead shepherd"; he quoted *Hero and Leander*'s "Who ever loved, that loved not at first sight" (1.176); and he echoed *The Jew of Malta*—"Infinite riches in a little room" (1.1.37)—when referring to Marlowe's death as "a great reckoning in a little room." In 1633 Thomas Heywood looked back on Marlowe as "the best of Poets in that age" (MacLure, p. 49), but during the English Civil War (1642–1660), when the theaters closed, Marlowe's plays virtually disappeared. A revival occurred during the Romantic era, when Marlowe emerged as a free-thinking rebel fighting against orthodoxy. During the twentieth century, his works were thoroughly edited and his life and death studiously researched. Most notably, scholars began to suspect that the original coroner's report was spurious. The two most important conspiracy theories agree that Marlowe was politically assassinated. The first (Nicholl) argues that Marlowe got caught in a crossfire between two rival factions, that of Robert Devereux, earl of Essex, and that of Sir Walter Ralegh. The second argues that Queen Elizabeth herself ordered Marlowe's murder (Riggs 2004).

The fact that such a brilliant poet and dramatist died young amid swirling controversy has given rise to the industry of Marlowe scholarship, to regular productions of his plays (and occasionally films, such as the 1967 *Faustus* starring Richard Burton and Elizabeth Taylor), and to recent novelizations of his life (e.g., Anthony Burgess's 1993 *A Dead Man in Deptford*).

At the beginning of the twenty-first century, Marlowe's stature as a major canonical author of English poems and plays rests secure. So does his reputation as a heterodox thinker in religion, sexuality, and politics. The main problem has become to relate these three forms of heterodoxy to their corresponding literary representations in his works.

INTERPRETING CHRISTOPHER MARLOWE

While Marlowe is usually thought of as a dramatist, a more accurate view begins with his simultaneous production of poems and plays, and then witnesses how his representations of religion, sexuality, and politics unfold from this literary foundation. Such a model recognizes that the combination of poems and plays is fundamentally a sixteenth-century phenomenon, becoming a durable legacy of the "Renaissance" (Cheney, *Poet-Playwright*, pp. 17–48). English precursors of the poet-playwright include John Skelton, George Gascoigne, and Watson, while precursors on the Continent include

Lope de Vega (1562–1635) in Spain; Torquato Tasso (1544–1595) in Italy; and Marguerite de Navarre (1492–1549) in France. No doubt the simultaneous emergence of a print culture and a theater culture undergirded the authorship of the new English and European poet-playwright. Although print had been invented in the fifteenth century, it became a budding institution in England only late in the sixteenth. Similarly, the first viable commercial theaters were built in the 1570s.

Yet an authoritative classical precedent existed in Ovid. This widely imitated Roman author composed elegiac poetry (represented by the *Amores*) and narrative verse (his *Metamorphoses*). But he also wrote a tragedy, *Medea*, extant in two lines. Jonson's *The Poetaster* (1601) put this "Ovid" on the stage. The *Amores, Metamorphoses*, and *Medea* belong to the genres of amorous poetry, myth narrative, and tragedy, and together they counter the famous Virgilian model of pastoral, georgic, and epic. In the *Amores*, Ovid tells a story about his attempt to write epic and tragedy, his initial failure and turn to love elegy, and his final turn to tragedy.

Others had written poems and plays, but by translating the *Amores*, Marlowe made the Ovidian *cursus* (or career) available to Renaissance culture, and his works followed this career path. *Ovid's Elegies* and "The Passionate Shepherd" form a phase of amorous poetry; the plays, of tragedy; and the minor epics, *Lucan's First Book* and *Hero and Leander*, of epic. Although Marlowe's Ovidian *cursus* remained truncated, he produced a canon right on the cusp of a literary career—probably in opposition to England's Virgil, Edmund Spenser.

Marlowe's heterodox representations of religion, sexuality, and politics map onto this model. In addition to a literary career, he also had a new theology, a bold sexuality, and a dangerous politics. His atheism, homoeroticism, and subversion have been the subjects of much recent scholarship. The religious thinker who emerged in *Faustus* was a gifted scholar who found Christian grace dissatisfying. Yet Marlowe's attack on Christianity simultaneously engaged him in a titanic wrestling match with the angel of grace itself. Similarly, the sexual figure who appears in *Edward II* is a homoerotic lover who defies heterosexual norms. Yet Marlowe also penned some intriguing portraits of women, from Dido and Zenocrate in the plays to Corinna and Hero in the poems. Finally, the political thinker who emerged in *Tamburlaine* was a dissident who opposed monarchy yet was obsessed with "republican" (antimonarchical) thinking to the 1590s. Scholars are even beginning to see Marlowe's translation of Lucan, "the central poet of the republican imagination" (Norbrook, p. 24), as grounds for placing Marlowe at the forefront of the literary republican movement, which reached political fruition in the English Civil War of the 1640s (Cheney in *Cambridge Companion*, p. 15).

HISTORICAL ACHIEVEMENT

Marlowe's corpus of poems and plays was indeed a historic enterprise in early modern English literature. He is notable for his development of the "mighty [blank verse] line" (Jonson's phrase), which quickly became the gold standard for the new stage, represented in *Tamburlaine* and leading to Shakespeare and Jonson; and for epic poetry, represented in *Lucan's First Book* and leading to Milton. Marlowe was also the most important inventor of the English couplet (*Ovid's Elegies* and *Hero and Leander*), anticipating Alexander Pope. In fact, *Ovid's Elegies* was the first translation of the *Amores* into any European vernacular, while *Lucan's First Book* was the first translation of the *Pharsalia* into English. The poet Algernon Charles Swinburne called "The Passionate Shepherd" "one of the most faultless lyrics . . . in the whole range of descriptive and fanciful poetry." When these achievements in poetry are placed alongside those in drama, with *Faustus* long held to be a world masterpiece, Marlowe can be seen to have made a singular contribution to the formation of an English canon. Finally, the distinction of Christopher Marlowe may be that he was the first dissident intellectual in regard to religion, sexuality, and politics to become a major canonical author of poems and plays in English.

[*See also* Thomas Heywood; Ben Jonson; *and* William Shakespeare.]

SELECTED WORKS

Ovid's Elegies (composed 1584–1585?; published mid-to-late 1590s?)

Dido, Queen of Carthage (composed 1584–1585?; published 1594)

Tamburlaine the Great, Part One and Part Two (composed 1587–1588; published 1590)

"The Passionate Shepherd to His Love" (composed 1587–1588?; published 1599)

The Jew of Malta (composed 1588–1589?; published 1633)

Edward II (composed 1591?; published 1594)

The Massacre at Paris (composed 1591?; published early seventeenth century?)

Doctor Faustus (composed 1588–1589, 1592–1593?; published 1604, 1616)

Lucan's First Book (composed 1592–1593?; published 1600)

Hero and Leander (composed 1592–1593?; published 1598)

Latin Epitaph on Sir Roger Manwood (composed 1592–1593; exists in manuscript)

Latin Dedicatory Epistle to Mary Sidney Herbert (composed 1592; published 1592)

EDITIONS

Gill, Roma, general ed. *The Complete Works of Christopher Marlowe*. 5 vols. Oxford, 1987–1998. Vol. 1, Translations, edited by Roma Gill; vol. 2, *Doctor Faustus*, edited by Roma Gill; vol. 3, *Edward II*, edited by Richard Rowland; vol. 4, *The Jew of Malta*, edited by Roma Gill; vol. 5, *Tamburlaine the Great, Parts 1 and 2* and *The Massacre at Paris with the Death of the Duke of Guise*, edited by David Fuller and Edward J. Esche. The most recent old-spelling edition, with some authoritative editing and commentary, however unevenly completed.

FURTHER READING

Bartels, Emily C. *Spectacles of Strangeness: Imperialism, Alienation, and Marlowe*. Philadelphia, 1993. An engaging look into outsiders in the imperial dynamic of Marlowe's plays.

Bloom, Harold, ed. *Christopher Marlowe*. New York, 1986. A useful collection of previously published essays from distinguished critics.

Cartelli, Thomas. *Marlowe, Shakespeare, and the Economy of Theatrical Experience*. Philadelphia, 1991. The most important study relating Marlowe to Shakespeare.

Cheney, Patrick. *Marlowe's Counterfeit Profession: Ovid, Spenser, Counter-Nationhood*. Toronto, 1997. The first full study of Marlowe's literary career.

Cheney, Patrick. "Recent Studies in Marlowe (1987–1998)." *English Literary Renaissance* 31 (2001): 288–328. An annotated essay on recent criticism.

Cheney, Patrick. *Shakespeare, National Poet-Playwright*. Cambridge, U.K., 2004. Relates Shakespeare to Marlowe and Spenser in the writing of English nationhood.

Cheney, Patrick, ed. *The Cambridge Companion to Christopher Marlowe*. Cambridge, U.K., 2004. New essays on Marlowe's life, texts, style, politics, religion, sexuality, classicism, and afterlife in theater, film, and fiction. Each essay contains a recommended reading list.

Dabbs, Thomas. *Reforming Marlowe: The Nineteenth-Century Canonization of a Dramatist*. London, 1991. A helpful study for understanding the modern making of Christopher Marlowe.

Eliot, T. S. "Christopher Marlowe." In his *Elizabethan Dramatists*. London, 1963. A seminal essay and point of origin for modern Marlowe criticism.

Ellis-Fermor, Una. *Christopher Marlowe*. 1927; repr. Hamden, CT, 1967. The first modern book-length study of great merit.

Friedenreich, Kenneth, Roma Gill, and Constance B. Kuriyama, eds. *A Poet and a Filthy Play-Maker: New Essays on Christopher Marlowe*. New York, 1988. A valuable collection of previously unpublished essays.

Greenblatt, Stephen. "Marlowe and the Will to Absolute Play." In his *Renaissance Self-Fashioning: From More to Shakespeare*. Chicago, 1980. The most important essay on Marlowe in the late twentieth century.

Healy, Thomas. *Christopher Marlowe*. Plymouth, UK, 1994. An accessible introduction to Marlowe's life and works.

Honan, Park. *Christopher Marlowe: Poet & Spy*. Oxford, 2005.

Hopkins, Lisa. *Christopher Marlowe: A Literary Life*. Basingstoke, U.K., 2000. A useful biography emphasizing Marlowe's literary career.

Hopkins, Lisa. *A Christopher Marlowe Chronology*. Basingstoke, U.K., 2005. An invaluable resource tool, with detailed information and dates for all events surrounding the life and death of Marlowe.

Kuriyama, Constance Brown. *Christopher Marlowe: A Renaissance Life*. Ithaca, NY, 2002. An authoritative recent biography rejecting conspiracy theories of Marlowe's death, with an indispensable printing of important archival documents.

Leech, Clifford. *Christopher Marlowe: Poet for the Stage*. Edited by Anne Lancashire. New York, 1986. A full study of Marlowe's life and works by an eminent scholar.

Levin, Harry. *The Overreacher: A Study of Christopher Marlowe*. Cambridge, MA, 1954. A groundbreaking study, with its influential model of the Marlovian "overreacher."

MacLure, Millar, ed. *Marlowe: The Critical Heritage 1588–1896*. London, 1979. A useful assembly of commentary on Marlowe over three centuries.

Nicholl, Charles. *The Reckoning: The Murder of Christopher Marlowe*. New York, 1992. Perhaps the most influential recent study of Marlowe's death by political assassination.

Norbrook, David. *Writing the English Republic: Poetry, Rhetoric, and Politics, 1627–1660*. Cambridge, U.K., 1999. A magisterial study of the English republican imagination in the seventeenth century.

Riggs, David. *The World of Christopher Marlowe*. London, 2004. A full biography with excellent commentary.

Steane, J. B. *Marlowe: A Critical Study*. Cambridge, U.K., 1964. The first full study of Marlowe's life and works to give balanced credit to his poems.

Thomas, Vivien, and William Tydeman, eds. *Christopher Marlowe: The Plays and Their Sources*. London, 1994. An indispensable resource tool.

White, Paul Whitfield, ed. *Marlowe, History, and Sexuality: New Critical Essays on Christopher Marlowe*. New York, 1998. An important collection of previously unpublished essays.

Wilson, Richard, ed. *Christopher Marlowe*. London, 1999. A useful collection of important criticism from the 1980s and 1990s.

JOHN MARSTON

Ceri Sullivan

John Marston (c. 1575–1634) was baptized at Warding-ton, Oxfordshire. His father, John, was a lawyer at the Middle Temple and his mother, Maria Guarsi, was the daughter of an Italian surgeon. He graduated from Brasenose College, Oxford, in 1594 and joined his father at the Temple. However, his relationship with the latter, who had hoped his son would enter law rather than, as he said in his will, take "delight in plays and vain studies and fooleries," was strained. So were his relations with other authorities. His satires, with a preface by "Kin-sayder" ("kinsing" meant castrating—marring—the "stones" of a dog, so Marston's biting satires aim to ruin his rivals' powers), were publicly burned by the order of Archbishop Whitgift of Canterbury and Bishop Bancroft of London in 1599. His cowriters of *Eastward Ho!*, Ben Jonson and George Chapman, were imprisoned for criti-cizing Scots courtiers in 1605. The years following his marriage in 1605 to Mary, the daughter of William Wilkes, a chaplain to James I, show a change of direction. He moved out of the Middle Temple in November 1606. Although in 1608 he was briefly held in Newgate (perhaps in connection with a play, now lost, satirizing James's mining policies), by 1609 he was ordained. He was rector of Christ Church, Hampshire, between 1616 and 1631. Tellingly, Marston insisted that his name be removed from a collected edition of his plays in 1633, and his tombstone read *oblivioni sacrum* ("sacred to forgetful-ness").

THE WRITING

The Scourge of Villany (1598), a collection of verse satires, is fashionably melancholic, attacking those who intend to repent tomorrow (satire four), tricks of self-promotion (five), contemporary poets (six, eight, and nine), extrav-agant dress and legal delay (seven), and gallants (ten)—no original topics here. *The Metamorphosis of Pygmalion's Image* (1598), an erotic epyllion (a short narrative poem, similar to an epic in theme, tone, or style) that dwells on the delights of the sculptor in his creation, follows the louche tone of Christopher Marlowe's *Hero and Leander* (1598) and Shakespeare's *Venus and Adonis* (1593), al-though with less of their light irony and pastiche. The satires published with *Pygmalion* attacked Joseph Hall's satires in *Virgidemiarum, or Toothless Satires* (1597) as obscure and pedantic, focused on little faults rather than great sins. Their main result was to bring Marston to attention as an antagonistic figure rather than a champion of a particular principle. He took this stance further in the second of his two attacks, this time on Ben Jonson. The "war of the theatres" between 1599 and 1601 took the form of an escalating series of parodies and critiques of the other author in, on Jonson's side, *Every Man Out of His Humour* (1599) and *Poetaster* (1601) and, on Mar-ston's side, *Histriomastix* (c. 1599, speculatively attributed to Marston), *Jack Drum's Entertainment* (1600), and *What You Will* (c. 1600–1601). Marston charged Jonson with dull pedantry, malice, hypocrisy, and arrogance—and was, Jonson boasted to William Drummond, beaten and disarmed by Jonson, and then lampooned in *Poetaster*.

Antonio and Mellida (1599; for Paul's boys) starts with an induction that shows the boy actors commenting on how they should play their roles, uncertain about how to handle the play's sudden moves from farce to tragedy to romance. The play is a romantic comedy, surprisingly based on a man rather than a woman cross-dressing. Mel-lida's father, the duke of Venice, Piero, has defeated An-drugio, duke of Genoa. The latter's son, Antonio, arrives at the Venetian court as an Amazon, and persuades Mel-lida to flee with him. Piero recaptures her but is per-suaded both by Andrugio's courage in challenging him and by the feigned death of Antonio to let the two marry. In the succeeding play, *Antonio's Revenge* (1599; for Paul's Boys), however, Piero recovers his despotic verve, mur-ders Andrugio, and plots the same fate for Antonio, slur-ring his daughter's honor to prevent a match. Mellida dies in misery, and—shades of *Hamlet*—is revenged by her lover and the ghost of his father in a masque in which the duke eats a fricassee of his own son before his own tongue is ripped out. Finding even their own actions untenable the disillusioned servants of justice retire to a monastery.

Eastward Ho! (for Children of the Revels at the Black-friars) was cowritten in response to Thomas Dekker and John Webster's *Westward Ho!*, and takes its satirical strand from the customary features of the city comedy displayed by the latter: the wastrel apprentice, Quicksilver; the upwardly mobile merchant's daughter, Gertrude; the needy knight, Sir Petronel Flash. But the merchant, Touchstone, has a second apprentice, Golding, who by thrift and hard work gains both Touchstone's daughter Mildred and the post of deputy alderman. The unusual double helix of citizen and city comedy has caused a rabbit/duck perception of the play. It has been alternately held to be a genial ethical critique of cupidity in the world of trade and a satire on gentry fantasies of an obedient and serviceable city. *The Dutch Courtesan* (1605; for the Children of the Revels at the Blackfriars), however, reserves good nature for its subplot. Its central device is the attempt by a courtesan, Franceschina, to revenge herself on a former lover, Freevill, by persuading her new lover, Malheureux, to kill him. A pretense of this is made, but when Freevill disappears, Malheureux is arrested and sentenced. Only at the last moment does Freevill reappear, having both cured his friend of his desire for Franceschina and forced Malheureux to admit that neither rigid codes nor satire had protected him from the effects of ill-aimed desire.

Two tragedies mark out different areas: a "tragi comoedia" (according to the Stationers' Register) and a monument of self-control. *The Malcontent* (1604; for Children of the Revels at the Blackfriars and the King's Men at the Globe) directs the machinations of the disguised banished duke of Genoa, Altofronto, against the lover, Mendoza, of Aurelia, the wife of the current duke, Pietro. Tiring of Aurelia, Mendoza turns to Altofronto's wife, Maria, which in its turn brings Altofronto into a revenge partnership with Pietro. Altofronto's disguise as the malcontent, Malevole, makes him the collaborator of choice for other court malcontents, as he works his way back to the top. Maria's sexual and political fidelity is contrasted with the uncontrolled lusts of the duke's wife, Aurelia; the new order of virtue begins when Maria and Altofronto are reunited. As with the comedies there is an induction (this time by John Webster) that features an audience member chatting with the actors about his expectations for the play as they prepare to go onstage; Henry Condell and Richard Burbage express some anxiety about whether this is a "bitter play," either as a satire or as a moral tale. In fact, Altofronto's position allows a satirist's swift, acute, ad hoc commentary on the action even while encouraging all in "that to which they are most affected"—the commentator is part of what he comments on. By contrast, *Sophonisba* (1606; for the Children of the Revels at the Blackfriars), relating the suicide of its newly wed heroine to avoid captivity, opposes the violent and sudden switches in her fortunes to her own stoic reception of them. The wedding of the Carthaginian noble, Sophonisba, and the prince of Libya, Massinissa, is interrupted by a military threat from Rome. The groom answers his new country's call and leaves the bride with his promise to protect her from Roman enslavement. Sophonisba has her own battles to win, warding off an attempt by his rival, Syphax, to take Massinissa's place in her bed by substituting first a male slave then a witch. When Massinissa returns with a new allegiance to Scipio and is ordered to send Sophonisba to him, she poisons herself to protect her husband's honor. In the scholar George Hunter's words, the characters "move through the chaos of history with measured calm . . . *pathos* is rewritten as *admiratio*."

CRITICAL HISTORY

The improbability of the plots and the artificial nature of the character's motivations are obvious. This was accentuated by both the metadramatic inductions and the age of the actors (from around twelve to eighteen). Just as disordered as Marston's plots are his characters' speeches: each character searches desperately for neologisms, breaks off suddenly, moves into Italian, reverts to wild gesture, repeats words senselessly, and falls to exclamation or grunt (Algernon Charles Swinburne said reading this "crabbed and convulsive" style was like struggling "through a cactus hedge"). This characteristic was ridiculed in the figure of Crispinus in *Poetaster*, who is given a pill to vomit up the hard words he had swallowed (prorumped, furibund, oblatrant . . . "who would have thought there should ha' beene such a deale of filth in a poet?"), and in the Parnassus plays in the character of Furor Poeticus, with his "great battering-ram of terms" and his indecency. The following generation felt disinclined to find the appropriate aesthetic to deal with Marston's dramatic structure or language. His plays were not revived with the opening of the theaters after the English Civil War, nor did they appeal to eighteenth-century taste. Charles Lamb's *Specimens of English Dramatic Poets* (1808) and William Hazlitt's *Lectures on the Dramatic Literature of the Age of Elizabeth* (1820) were more sympathetic: they picked out Marston's "turbulent greatness" and his "impatient scorn and bitter indignation against the vices and follies of men"; he is, according to Hazlitt, a freethinker and skeptic, whose uneven register shows the playwright's shifts in interest not in power. Like other city comedians and revenge tragedians, Marston was rescued for reading by Swinburne in 1908 as an essentially moral writer, who displayed "in a spirit of healthy disgust . . . the vicious exuberance or eccentricity of affectation or of self-indulgence." This line continued alongside a second criticizing Marston's ability and engagement, following T. S. Eliot's sharp comment that the plays "give the effect of work done by a man who was so exasperated by having to write in a form which he despised that he deliberately wrote worse than he could have written, in order to relieve his feelings."

Current commentary on Marston takes two routes. One reads his plays as fantastic compensations for the experience of being rejected for substantial employment. As one of London's turn-of-the-century, overeducated, underemployed, young Turks, Marston separates himself from the corruption of popular applause and looks to the long-withheld approval of monarch, repeatedly displaying phallic traits of aggression and exhibitionism—although, as Mark T. Burnett (2002) points out, his characters' masculinity is often fragile, choked off, or split apart. The second line follows Eliot's perception of Marston's innovative indiscipline but bends it back as a positive comment on the play's ironic, parodic, and meta-dramatic qualities. Now, Marston's understanding of the discontinuities of existence—an extreme skepticism, which postmodern readers can appreciate—is held to reveal itself in the plays' language and structure. The contributors to T. F. Wharton's collection of essays (2000) take this into exciting areas: censorship and the free speech of the satirist, the "revenge musical" that playfully "unglues" genre and the market paradigms behind it, textual and linguistic interplay, homosocial and auto-erotic impulses, an anti-Horatian impulse to delight not instruct, an anarchic attitude toward Calvinist providentialism, and male hysteria as a symptomatic work of art.

[See also George Chapman and Ben Jonson.]

SELECTED WORKS

The Metamorphosis of Pygmalion's Image: And Certain Satires (1598)

The Scourge of Villany (1598)
Antonio and Mellida (c. 1599–1600)
Antonio's Revenge (c. 1599–1601)
The Malcontent (c. 1603, revised 1604)
The Dutch Courtesan (c. 1604–1605)
Eastward Ho! (1605) with George Chapman and Ben Jonson
Sophonisba (c. 1605–1606)

FURTHER READING

Burnett, Mark T. "Staging the Malcontent in Early Modern England." In *A Companion to Renaissance Drama*, edited by Arthur F. Kinney. Oxford, 2002.

Eliot, T. S. *Elizabethan Essays*. London, 1934.

Finkelpearl, Philip. *John Marston of the Middle Temple: An Elizabethan Dramatist in His Social Setting*. Cambridge, MA, 1969. Considers the politics, ethics, and tastes of this tight, critical community of clever young men.

Geckle, George. *John Marston's Drama: Themes, Images, Sources*. Rutherford, NJ, 1980. Sensible and scholarly introduction to the plays.

Hazlitt, William. *Lectures on the Dramatic Literature of the Age of Elizabeth*. London, 1820.

Hunter, G. K. *English Drama, 1586–1642: The Age of Shakespeare*. Oxford, 1997. Skeptical, assured, concise, and sometimes impish judgments, more on Marston's technical abilities than his worldviews.

Lamb, Charles. *Specimens of English Dramatic Poets, Who Lived about the Time of Shakespeare: With Notes*. London, 1808.

Pascoe, David. "Marston's Childishness." *Medieval and Renaissance Drama in England* 9 (1997): 92–111.

Swinburne, Algernon Charles. *The Age of Shakespeare*. London, 1908.

Wharton, T. F. *The Critical Fall and Rise of John Marston*. Columbia, SC, 1994. Reception history to the present.

Wharton, T. F., ed. *The Drama of John Marston: Critical Re-Visions*. Cambridge, U.K., 2000. Essential reading.

Whigham, Frank. *Seizures of the Will in Early Modern English Drama*. Cambridge, U.K., 1996. Context for Burnett's line.

HARRIET MARTINEAU

Deirdre David

Harriet Martineau (1802–1876) was one of most prolific and versatile writers of the Victorian period. From an article for a Dissenting (Unitarian) monthly periodical about female religious writers that appeared in 1821 to the posthumous publication of her three-volume *Autobiography* in 1877, Martineau examined such things as English politics, American slavery, Eastern harems, the Woman Question, military reform, and how to endure lengthy confinement to the sickroom. Her career is characterized by devotion to the professional business of writing, by a democratic willingness to popularize for the general public abstract political and philosophical ideas, and by an admirable physical fortitude that defied disability (she was deaf from the age of sixteen and confined to bed for five years, from age thirty-seven to forty-two, with a uterine tumor). She also experienced the difficulties of working as a successful woman intellectual in a male-dominated literary marketplace, a dilemma she solved by casting herself always in an ancillary role. By insisting that her work was mere "auxiliary usefulness," she diffused the threat that her assertiveness and professional success posed to the cultural establishment. In her *Autobiography* she characterized herself as gifted with an "earnestness and intellectual clearness within a certain range" and as limited by "small" imaginative powers and an inability to "discover" or "invent" new ideas. In summing up her career, she declared that she had never written for amusement, money, or fame; rather, "things were pressing to be said; and there was more or less evidence that I was the person to say them."

In a remarkable variety of texts—religious tract, essay, newspaper leader, travel narrative, novel, political tale, children's story, and translation—Martineau displayed her skill in popularizing influential political ideas of the

Harriet Martineau
Chalk portrait by George Richmond, 1849
NATIONAL PORTRAIT GALLERY, LONDON

moment, whether they concerned the benevolent workings of capitalism, the superiority of English imperialism, or the progressivist nature of competitive individualism. When she was firmly established as arguably the most prominent popular writer of the age, in 1852 she joined the staff of the *Daily News* and over the next sixteen years she wrote some sixteen hundred articles for the newspaper. Martineau's cheerfully chosen work, from the early 1820s to the end of her life, was to record and to legitimate the values of the English middle class, even if these values were often at odds with her views on the position of women in society. A major challenge in her career was to reconcile the prevailing middle-class relegation of women to the home and hearth with her popularization in the public sphere of the values of this social class. To a large degree, she met this challenge through consistent articulation of the need for both women and men to acquiesce in evolving laws of social progress: she cast her work, with its accompanying contradictions, as part of this acquiescence. Her fervent articulation of the need to educate women so that they might willingly assent to abstract laws not of their own construction must, therefore, be seen as but one expression of her overall political position. Even while Martineau was strongly committed to social causes that were important to women's lives, such as birth control and the Contagious Diseases Acts of 1871, she implicitly advocated woman's educated acceptance of patriarchal governance.

Every day of her writing life—that is, when she was not engaged in the travel that invariably became the subject of yet another article or book—Martineau was at her desk from seven-thirty in the morning until two in the afternoon. First, last, and always a writer, regardless of what she was writing about, she was dedicated to the development of crisp, clear, and accessible prose and scornful of the sterile eloquence she attributed to her contemporary Thomas De Quincey, whose memoir *Confessions of an English Opium Eater* appeared in 1821: De Quincey, in her view, recklessly spent his intellect in a sterile flow of language—"Marvellous analytical faculty he had, but it all oozed out in barren words." For George Eliot, Martineau was the most fertile and fluent of writers: Eliot announced Martineau to be a "*trump*—the only English woman that possesses thoroughly the art of writing," and Eliot's praise expressed the appreciation of many of Martineau's fellow writers for her ability to adapt her style to the writing moment without any compromise of clarity or commitment.

"AUXILIARY USEFULNESS" AND THE WOMAN QUESTION

The daughter of a Norwich bombazine (a type of fabric) manufacturer and his religiously strict wife, Martineau was encouraged in her intellectual precocity by her Unitarian parents; although her formal education was limited to attendance at a local school from the age of eleven to thirteen and one year at the age of sixteen at a school run by an aunt and uncle, she was educated by her brothers in Latin and arithmetic and by her sister in French, and was allowed to read all the newspapers in the house and to study Shakespeare on her own. She never married and apart from a brief engagement seems to have had no romantic attachments; rather, she was happily married to her career—as she put it, "My work and I have been fitted to each other."

The work began with articles on women's education for the Dissenting periodical, *Monthly Repository*, and gathered financial importance with the death of her father in 1826 and subsequent fall in the family income. With the encouragement of her mother, Martineau, at thirty, moved to London, where she began working regularly for the Reverend William Fox, the editor of the *Repository* and publisher of religious tracts. With her characteristic efficiency and speed, she began producing a series of religious books on devotional exercises for children and the family. Cannily, though, she quickly suspected that she might earn more money through the popularization of the "new science" of political economy that was derived principally from Adam Smith's *An Inquiry into the Nature and Causes of the Wealth of Nations* (1776) and James Mill's *Elements of Political Economy* (1821). She persuaded Fox's brother, Charles Fox, to publish the first of a series

of tales illustrating particular principles of the "new science" that were currently obscure to her intended readership, literate artisans and tradesmen who found themselves quickly featured as characters in the subsequent stories. The first tale was so astonishingly successful that readers clamored for the next with the fervor customarily reserved for the latest monthly installment of a novel. Martineau was on her way to professional and financial success, her expository talents almost immediately solicited by the government to produce a pamphlet explaining the need for increased house taxes.

As a whole, the twenty-four *Illustrations of Political Economy* that Martineau produced from 1832 to 1834 propounded a social theory that amalgamated the principles of Jeremy Bentham's Utilitarianism, which advocated social actions based upon the greatest happiness for all; Adam Smith's laissez-faire doctrine; Thomas Malthus's *Essay on the Principle of Population* (1798), and David Ricardo's arguments for free trade. As expressed in Martineau's homespun narratives, political economy is a social theory grounded in a firm belief in the benevolent workings of capitalism and of competitive individualism. The *Illustrations* argue that capital must be preserved in times of recession, that the enclosure of lands by wealthy farmers is in the best interest of all because it brings laborers to depressed agricultural communities, that workers should save money instead of supporting strikes, that a regular supply of cheap food will be guaranteed by free trade in wheat, and that colonization is essential for the expansion of British markets. Complex social problems are translated into happy fables. It was in this work that Martineau discovered an alignment of the textual form of the *Illustrations* and her cultural identity as working woman intellectual in a male-dominated culture: she became the intelligent, well-paid, professional popularizer of difficult economic principles developed not by herself or by any other woman, but by male philosophers and economists. She filled an established textual form (the chatty tale) with received political ideas. This was, indeed, "auxiliary usefulness," which is not to say she ignored the Woman Question, a sustained subject of heated debate in Victorian culture, either in the *Illustrations* or in any of the writing to follow.

In her Malthusian tale "Weal and Woe in Garveloch" (1832), for instance, Martineau advocated birth control as a means of improving the impoverished lives of rural women, for which she was roundly scolded for dealing with matters unsuitable for treatment by a female author. Her travel in America from 1834 to 1836, which she undertook in common with many other Victorian writers eager to inspect the former colony and turn their impressions into lucrative travel narratives, provided many opportunities to attack "The Political Non-Existence of Women" (the title of a chapter in *Society in America* [1837], a work seen today by many critics as evidence of Martineau's important status as a pioneer sociologist). Never one to waste time, as she crossed the Atlantic she set up her portable writing desk and began a book about how to become an informed and informative traveler that also articulates her feminist opinions; in *How to Observe Manners and Morals* (1838) she declares that women have risen from a state of slavery (unfortunately exemplified by the subservience of the "Indian squaw") to the present condition in which they are "less than half-educated, precluded from earning a subsistence, except in a very few ill-paid employments, and prohibited from giving or withholding their assent to laws, which they are yet bound by penalties to obey." Women must be decently educated, freed by adequately compensated employment from humiliating dependence on their families, and accorded fair participation in determining the laws that govern their lives. Above all else, Martineau wanted women to become rational agents in control of their emotions and their intellect.

Martineau not only thundered against the denial of equal opportunities for women to become educated and support themselves (in other words, to become much like herself), she also urged them to perfect their domestic skills, an imperative sometimes seen by her biographers as a contradiction in her sexual politics. However, Martineau's feminism must be situated within the context of her distinction between the abstract evolution of immutable laws of social progress and the material construction of laws governing daily life. One would misread this distinction if one saw, for example, her call to women to perfect their baking, preserving, starching, and ironing as a directive for them to remain sequestered in the domestic sphere; rather, Martineau believed that the women in rural and artisan families to whom she addressed these remarks in *Household Education* (1849) would advance beyond the kitchen by achieving excellence in everything they did. Martineau herself took as much pride in her complicated needlework as she did in her skillful writing.

SLAVERY, HISTORY, AND REFORM

From her first published attack on slavery in the *Monthly Repository* to the end of her life, Martineau was fiercely opposed to the ownership of slaves. In "Demerara" (1832), the fourth of the tales demonstrating the theories of political economy, she argues that slaves lose money for their owners. Purchasing a man is a very poor bargain: "Where the labourer is held as capital, the capitalist not only pays a much higher price for an equal quantity of labour, but also for waste, negligence, and theft, on the part of the labourer." In *Society in America* she mounts a moving and persuasive attack on the entire American system, punctuating arguments anchored in the economic inefficiency of owning a laborer rather than purchasing his labor power, with shocking accounts of violence, including the sexual abuse of slave children. If one considers Martineau's consistent deployment of the metaphor of family for social organization, then a significant connection begins to emerge between her calls for women to become rational wives or economically independent workers, for the lower classes to become independent through acquisition of education, and for slaves to become proprietors of their own labor. All must liberate themselves from the social parent (or, in the case of slaves, be freed) in order to achieve active, rational, and adult participation in the public sphere of politics and government. Her *History of England* (1864), a popularizing run through events from the beginning of the nineteenth century to the Crimean War (1854–1856), supports this view through many pages devoted to the participation of the artisan class in saving England from the revolutions that swept the Continent in the middle of the century.

Because artisans and tradesmen properly aligned their interests with those of their employers in the solid middle class and realized that unionization could only imperil rather than advance their welfare, they absorbed the potentially destructive revolutionary energies that were expressed in the rick-burning, machine-breaking, and agitation for parliamentary reform that dominated the early 1830s. Martineau believed that this social group prevented violence on 10 April 1848, the day of the last great meeting of Chartists in London (so named for the 1838 "People's Charter" that demanded parliamentary reform of the inequities remaining after the Reform Act of 1832): peace was kept "by the citizens themselves . . . From that day it was a settled matter, that England was safe from revolution." In writing her *History*, Martineau's principal aim was to celebrate the achievements of English society, whether to be found in the establishment of Mechanics Institutes for working-class education or in the growth of the railways that permitted better distribution of agricultural products and thus improved everyone's diet.

The attacks on slavery, the celebrations of the spirit of sensible reform in place of destructive revolution, and the enthusiasm for technological change found affirmation in the despotic and backward conditions of Middle Eastern life that Martineau elaborated in *Eastern Life, Present and Past*, published in 1848 after she returned from an eight-month journey with Liverpool friends that began in Cairo, proceeded up the Nile, and covered three months in the Sinai. *Eastern Life* offers a diverting travel narrative, many helpful hints for women travelers, and a postulation of the superiority of Christianity over the religions that preceded it and of the superiority of European civilization over the Egyptian. It is a work that constructs dominant mid-nineteenth-century ideologies of Oriental backwardness and European advance through Martineau's belief in the evolution of an ever-improving social order. Nowhere is this dichotomy better illustrated than in her descriptions of the harem: incarcerated women loll around in an abhorrent condition of sloth and inertia. Privileged they may have been in terms of Orientalist guardianship, but for Martineau these women were sad and repellent creatures.

WRITING ABOUT THE SELF

Martineau was never reluctant to introduce her own experiences into her writing: directly, she recounted her sociological observations of America and the East, described in detail her five years of illness, and capaciously presented the triumphs and pains of her life in the posthumously published *Autobiography*; indirectly, she wrote about her waning religious belief in the controversial *Letters on the Laws of Man's Nature and Development* (1851) and also about her cure from illness through mesmerism (so she believed) in *Letters on Mesmerism* (1844). As her own best model for the discipline of disruptive passion by rational intellect that she urged upon her readers, she placed herself on the path of self-governance from early childhood. The *Autobiography* chronicles a direction of naked desire for recognition from her family (particularly her brother James) into dedication to the writing life that received accolades from numerous politicians, Victorian social critics, American abolitionists, and thousands of grateful readers. That she transformed her five years confined to bed into a lengthy essay about how to endure such an experience exemplifies Martineau's heroic self-reliance. (The nonmalignant tumor diagnosed in 1839 shifted position through the enforced rest and permitted her reentry into public life in 1844.)

Only twice in her long and productive writing life did Martineau venture into the novel form, with *Deerbrook* (1839), a rural chronicle of mismatched love, and *The Hour and the Man* (1840), a romanticized tribute to the life of the slave leader Toussaint-Louverture, who led the Haitian revolution in the 1790s. She endows her major characters in these novels with the traits whose development she urged upon her readers in much of her nonfictional writing. Whether in the case of a lame and sensitive governess in *Deerbrook* or of the leader modeled upon Rousseau's Noble Savage in *The Hour and the Man*, self-reliance and love of learning permits the survival of loneliness and unrequited love in the first and the heroic defiance of oppression in the second. Martineau abhorred self-pity and celebrated intellectual ambition, and although the tension between her assertive feminism and the conventional ideas about women's roles ascribed to by the social class she aimed to serve—that composed of merchants, tradesmen, and artisans—sometimes created contradictions in the vast body of her work, she presented no conflicted front to the world. When she returned from the Middle East she visited the illustrious Victorian sage Thomas Carlyle, who wrote immediately to his friend the poet Robert Browning, "Miss Martineau has been to Jerusalem and is back; called here yesterday, brown as a berry; full of life, loquacity, dogmatism, and various 'gospels of the east wind.'" This loquacious, vital, and sometimes dogmatic woman intellectual, here full of life and bronzed from trekking across the desert in her sensible boots, may have believed she performed only "auxiliary usefulness," but she was a splendidly heroic and tough-minded thinker, dedicated to her dying day to the life of writing. Her achievements place her at the vortex of Victorian culture and society.

[*See also* Orientalism.]

SELECTED WORKS

Illustrations of Political Economy (1832–1834)
Society in America (1837)
How to Observe Manners and Morals (1838)
Retrospect of Western Travel (1838)
Deerbrook (1839)
The Hour and the Man (1840)
Letters on Mesmerism (1844)
Life in the Sick-Room (1844)
Eastern Life, Present and Past (1848)
Household Education (1849)
Letters on the Laws of Man's Nature and Development (1851)

British Rule in India: A Historical Sketch (1857)

The History of England from the Commencement of the Nineteenth Century to the Crimean War (1864)

Autobiography (1877)

FURTHER READING

David, Deirdre. *Intellectual Women and Victorian Patriarchy: Harriet Martineau, Elizabeth Barrett Browning, and George Eliot.* Ithaca, NY, 1987. A study of three important Victorian women intellectuals.

Logan, Deborah Anna. *The Hour and the Woman: Harriet Martineau's "Somewhat Remarkable" Life.* DeKalb, IL, 2002. Comprehensive coverage of the life and especially useful for analysis of the journalism.

Logan, Deborah Anna, ed. *Writings on Slavery and the American Civil War: Harriet Martineau.* DeKalb, IL, 2002. Carefully annotated collection of the important writings about America and slavery.

Peterson, Linda H. *Victorian Autobiography: The Tradition of Self-Interpretation.* New Haven, CT, 1986. Important discussion of Martineau as autobiographer.

Roberts, Caroline. *The Woman and the Hour: Harriet Martineau and Victorian Ideologies.* Toronto, 2002. Astute analysis of Martineau's place in Victorian intellectual history.

Webb, R. K. *Harriet Martineau: A Radical Victorian.* New York, 1960. An important pioneering work in Martineau scholarship.

Wheatley, Vera. *The Life and Work of Harriet Martineau.* London, 1957. Straightforward and factual biography.

Yates, Gayle Graham. *Harriet Martineau on Women.* New Brunswick, NJ, 1985. Useful selections for an introduction to further reading.

MARTIN MARPRELATE

Jesse M. Lander

"Martin Marprelate" was the pseudonym adopted by the anonymous writer or writers of a series of pamphlets written in 1588 and 1589 that attacked the established English Church. These tracts caused a furor by rejecting the rule of bishops in language that was richly colloquial and deeply abusive. The scandal caused by Marprelate was extensive; the pamphlets offered offense not only to the church hierarchy, which was subject to a scathing critique, but also to the godly advocates of presbyterianism, who felt that the cause of presbyterianism—a church government composed of elders, deacons, doctors, and ministers—was deeply hurt by Marprelate's rollicking and irreverent attack. Marprelate's attacks also caused concern because they were so clearly aimed at a broad lay readership—Elizabethan ecclesiastical controversy had been largely an insider's affair, conducted chiefly among men who had been educated at either Cambridge or Oxford. Marprelate decisively broke out of the circle of orthodoxy not only by insisting on a radical change to the current institutional structure of the English Church but also by taking his appeal directly to the people in a demotic language that was not calibrated to convey the subtleties of theological dispute. Unable to immediately locate and shut down the clandestine press that was producing the pamphlets, the English government took the unprecedented step of commissioning responses not only from divines but also from playwrights and pamphleteers who answered Martin's scurrilous manner with their own version of emphatic abuse. For a brief moment, Marprelate was lampooned on the London stage where he was subjected to ritual abuse and purgation; at the same time, the London presses produced a flurry of anti-Martinist tracts. As a consequence, the name "Marprelate" resonated broadly throughout the literary culture of early modern England. A source of enormous scandal in the late sixteenth century, Marprelate had a significant afterlife in English literature, influencing figures as diverse as Thomas Nashe, John Milton, Andrew Marvell, and Jonathan Swift.

Although the Marprelate pamphlets were immediately recognized as a radical departure from the existing conventions of religious controversy, they were not without precedent. The pamphlets drew on an established tradition of Protestant satire that used invective in pursuit of reform. Indeed, Martin's great namesake, Martin Luther, had deployed a vigorous—even scatological—language of abuse, and in some respects Marprelate's tracts were a return to this earlier robust language of unmasking. At the same time, the Marprelate pamphlets are a genuine departure. What makes them innovative is their volatile combination of oral and print elements. Marprelate manages to deploy in print a series of highly oral techniques: anecdote, direct address, imagined dialogue, colloquialisms, and dialect language. Despite the extemporaneous style of his discourse, his use of print is deeply sophisticated and carefully executed. Throughout, the pamphlets reveal a steady awareness of their own status as printed documents as well as a critical interest in the books printed in defense of the establishment.

The seven pamphlets attributed to Marprelate exhibit a consistent sensibility but take a variety of forms. The first, commonly referred to as *The Epistle*, appeared in 1588 and offers itself as an introduction to a forthcoming book that will epitomize the ponderous work of John Bridges, the dean of Salisbury, whose *Defence of the Government Established in the Church of England* (1587) ran to 1,401 prolix pages. The promised *Epitome* followed soon within the same year and continued the attack on Bridges. Not only was Bridges pilloried for his diffuse and rambling style—in the *Epistle*, Marprelate asserts, "I cannot very often at one breath come to a full point," and in the *Epitome* he worries, "I was never so affraid in my life that I should not come to end till I had bene windlesse"—he was also ridiculed for his extravagant use of paper: "You may see when men have a gift in writing howe easie it is for them to daube paper." The complete work is "very briefely comprehended in a portable booke if your horse be not to weake of and hundred threescore and twelve sheets of good Demie paper." Shortly after the appearance of the *Epitome*, Thomas Cooper, the bishop of Winchester, entered the fray with *An Admonition to the*

People of England (1589). As his title indicates, Cooper was aware that Marprelate was taking his cause to the people and was horrified that "at this present time, we shoulde see in mens handes and bosomes, commonly slanderous pamphlets fresh from the press against the best of the Church of Englande." He summarizes the dire consequences of such behavior: "But if this outragious spirit of boldenesse be not stopped speedily, I feare he wil prove himselfe to bee, not onely *Marprelate*, but *Mar-prince, Mar-state, Mar-lawe, Mar-magistrate,* and all together, until he bring it to an Anabaptisticall equalitie and communitie."

Marprelate turned to attack this new adversary with evident relish, first in *Certaine Mineral and Metaphisicall Schoolpoints* (1589), a broadsheet that listed erroneous theses to be defended by various members of the clergy (a large number of which were culled from Cooper's book), and then in *Hay Any Worke for Cooper* (1589), a more substantial work. In response to *Hay Any Worke for Cooper,* a number of anti-Martinist tracts were published that attempted to imitate the irreverent scoffing of their target; meanwhile, the Martinist press issued *Theses Martinianae,* usually referred to as *Martin Junior,* and *The Iust Censure and Reproofe of Martin Iunior,* or *Martin Senior.* These two pamphlets signal a shift in approach: *Martin Junior* purports to be the work of Martin's son, who casts himself in the role of literary executor by printing a manuscript of his father's; *Martin Senior* continues the conceit by posing as an older brother who chastises Martin Junior for exposing their father's imperfect papers to public view. Soon after, on 14 August 1589, John Hodgskin, Valentine Symmes, and Arthur Thomlin were caught in Manchester printing "More Worke for Cooper," which would have made for a total of eight Marprelate tracts had it been completed. In early September, Henry Sharpe, a bookbinder who was involved in the manufacture and distribution of the pamphlets, was also arrested. The examination of these individuals allowed the authorities to reconstruct the printing history of the pamphlets, and it was soon revealed that the Martinist press had been sheltered by several members of the Puritan gentry. However, no conclusive proof regarding the actual authorship of the pamphlets emerged. Nor did this calamity silence Marprelate; the last of the tracts, the *Protestatyon,* appeared in late September. In it, Marprelate claimed that the capture of the press at Manchester would not silence him and urged his readers to "Resone not frome the successe of thinges untoe the goodness of the cause." Despite such professions, this final tract does not maintain the boisterousness of the earlier pamphlets, and the writer increasingly dwells on the possibility of martyrdom as opposed to the hope for further reform.

METHOD

The standard method used in the pursuit of Protestant ecclesiastical controversy was scriptural citation combined with syllogistic reasoning. While Marprelate did not abandon this fundamental commitment, his attachment to logical demonstration was consistently playful. When Marprelate refers to a "lustie syllogisme of my owne making," he manages to invest the scholastic mode with physical life. A similar effect is achieved when he writes, "I wil presently proue both maior and minor of this sillogisme. And hold my cloake there somebody that I may go roundly to worke." Syllogistic disputation is elsewhere figured as a duel or wrestling match: "but first you & I must go out alone into the plain fields and there we wil try it out even by plaine syllogisms."

Despite these joking invocations, Marprelate never denies the efficacy of the syllogism; not only does he expose the logical fallacies of the bishops, but he also makes use of the syllogism to mount his own argument. Unlike the usual form of religious polemic, which entailed copious quotations from the adversary's text, Marprelate is relentlessly opportunistic in seeking out contradictions and weak points in his opponent's work. Rather than painstakingly follow the movement of an opponent's argument, Marprelate jumps from one point to the next without providing any obvious structure. The haphazard organization of his text contributes to the sense that one is reading an extemporaneous performance, and this sense is increased by Marprelate's frequent use of damning anecdotes that reveal the bad behavior of assorted members of the hierarchy.

This aspect of Marprelate's method is informed by several earlier practices. The attack on particular individuals reveals the influence of the common practice of "libeling" or "ballading." Sometimes sung, sometimes circulated in manuscript, and only rarely printed, these libels were a common part of Elizabethan life. At the same time, a more clearly historiographical practice had been established by John Foxe, who collected such anecdotes for his *Actes and Monuments* (1583), a practice that was later taken up by Puritan writers eager to amass an archive of ecclesiastical misdeeds. Finally, the ridiculous anecdote as a literary form owes a debt to both the jest book and the collection of merry tales.

STYLE

From the moment of his first appearance, Marprelate was recognized for his innovative prose style. As Marprelate acknowledges in the opening of *Theses Martinianae*: "The Bishops and their traine, though they stumble at the cause, yet especially, mislike my maner of writing. Those whom foolishly men call Puritanes, like of the matter I haue handled, but the form they cannot brooke." Literary historians of the twentieth century were more positive: J. Dover Wilson hails Marprelate as "the great prose satirist of the Elizabethan period." The most obtrusive aspect of Marprelate's style is its restless energy, an animation that rejects the normal cadences of written discourse in favor of the lively rhythms of direct address punctuated by asides, exclamations, and interjections.

Even the space of the printed page is used to depict a public scene of oral dispute. In the *Epistle*, an interruption from the audience initially appears within parentheses: "Therefore no Lord B. (nowe I pray thee good Martin speake out if ever thou diddest speake out that hir Maiestie and the counsell may heare thee) is to be tolerated in any christian commonwealth." This intrusive endorsement angers Marprelate, who comments in the margin: "What malapert knaves are these that cannot be content to stand by and here but they must teach a gentleman how to speake." The typographic conventions of margin and parentheses are here used to imagine a dynamic and fluid situation in which Marprelate, the gentleman, holds forth to an enthusiastic and unruly audience. On the next page, it is the bystanders who now appear in the margin. Marprelate has constructed a syllogism to establish that bishops are "petty popes," but in the conclusion he adds that they are "proud prelates intolerable withstanders of reformation enemies of the gospell and most covetous wretched priests." The marginal note complains, "M. Marprelate you put more then the question in the conclusion of your syllogisme." This provokes another outburst from Marprelate: "This is a pretie matter that standers by must be so busie in other mens games: why sawceboxes must you be pratling? you are as mannerly as bishops in medling with that you have nothing to doe as they do in taking upon them civill offices." However, Marprelate pronounces himself glad to see that the bystanders have learned to stay on the margin rather than interrupt the central text.

Print conventions are used alongside oral modes in order to create an engaging sense of immediacy. Having digressed to describe the railing of John Whitgift, the bishop of London, Marprelate returns to the subject of John Bridges: "But now alas, alas brother Bridges, I had forgotten you all this while, my brother London and I were so busie that we scarce thought of you." Such conversational markers are accompanied by a novel attempt to render a range of ejaculations and interjections into print. Laughter is represented by "Ha ha ha" and "py, hy, hy, hy"; sniggering appears as "Tse tse tse." At one point the huntsman's call, "soho," used to draw attention to a started hare, appears at the beginning of a sentence addressing Bridges. The novelty of Marprelate's use of exclamations was recognized by one of his adversaries, who complained that Martin spoke only in "whoopes and haloes." Elsewhere the accents of spoken English appear, as "ide a kept him" for "I would have kept him." Similarly, the dialect of the West Country turns up regularly. In addition, Marprelate has a penchant for colloquial phrases, as when he urges an opponent to "stand to thy tackling," and proverbs, such as "enough is as good as a feast."

Marprelate upended the decorum of religious controversy by insisting on the homely language of daily conversation, but he also invented words to express his outrage. A facility for punning and wordplay resulted in a series of scurrilous epithets. The archbishop of Canterbury becomes "His Cantiburinesse"; Convocation, "Confocation"; vicars, "fickers"; Divinity, "Divillitie"; civilians, "seevillaines." In addition, Marprelate offered coinages such as "hublication" (publication), "madmonition" (admonition), "bepistle" (assail with letters), and "bumfeg" (thrash). The same interest in the sound of words is visible in Marprelate's fondness for alliteration, as in "braue bounsing priest" and "pettie popes." *Pappe with an Hatchet* (1589), one of the anti-Martinist tracts, alludes to Marprelate's "holie day English," suggesting that it represents a carnivalesque abandonment of the usual linguistic order. In particular, the writer points to Marprelate's tendency to coin words and "inkhornize" (itself a neologism). One of the more thoughtful contemporary commentators, Francis Bacon, objected to having matters of religion "handled in the style of the stage," but conceded that "bitter and earnest writing may not hastily be condemned." In *Hay Any Worke*, Marprelate offered his own defense:

> I sawe the cause of Christs government and of the Bishops Antichristian dealing to be hidden. The most part of men could not be gotten to read any thing written in the defence of the on and against the other. I bethought me therefore of a way whereby men might be drawne to do both perceiving

the humors of men in these times (especialy of those that are in any place) to be given to mirth. I tooke that course. I might lawfully do it. I for jesting is lawful by circumstances even in the greatest matters.

CONSEQUENCES

The Marprelate pamphlets failed to achieve their ostensible purpose. If anything, the tracts brought the presbyterian cause into further disrepute. According to Josias Nichols, writing at the end of Elizabeth's reign, the appearance of Marprelate "did greatlie astonish vs, & verie much darken the righteousnesse of our cause." Although the immediate goal was not met, the pamphlets and the many responses they provoked had a galvanic effect on the Elizabethan reading public. The Marprelate episode was an early instance of consequential public debate in print, and it would continue to resonate in years to come. When the presbyterian cause recovered, Marprelate was not forgotten: *Hay Any Worke* was reprinted under the title *Reformation No Enemie* in 1641 and again, using the original title, in 1642. In addition, beginning in 1645, Richard Overton, representing the political agitators known as the Levellers, published a series of radical tracts using the pseudonym "Mar-priest." As Marprelate was recovered, so too his old opponents reappeared: in 1642 John Taylor published *Tom Nash His Ghost*, which claimed on its title page to have been "Written by Thomas Nash his Ghost . . . a little revived since the 30. Year of the late Qu. Elizabeths Reigne, when Martin Mar-Prelate was mad as any of his Tub-men are now." Although Taylor's short pamphlet reveals no direct familiarity with Marprelate, a name that had long since become a general term of abuse, his linking of Nashe with Marprelate is significant, for in terms of literary style Marprelate's most obvious influence was on Thomas Nashe. Nashe's precise role in the Marprelate controversy remains unclear (several of the anonymous anti-Martinist tracts have been attributed to him), but scholars have long recognized a significant stylistic debt to Marprelate. Although Nashe's own exuberant prose has no imitators, Marprelate's distinctive method begins a vein of religious satire that runs directly to Milton, Marvell, and Swift. More generally, Marprelate's influence can be traced in the pamphlet writings of the 1640s, texts that influenced the plain prose of the Dissenting tradition represented by John Bunyan and Daniel Defoe.

[*See also* Censorship *and* Thomas Nashe.]

WORKS

Oh Read Ouer D. John Bridges, for It Is a Worthy Worke; or, An Epitome of the Fyrste Booke, of That Right Worshipfull Volume, Written against the Puritanes [*Epistle*] (1588)

Oh Read Ouer D. John Bridges, for It Is Worthy Work [*Epitome*] (1588)

Certaine Minerall and Metaphisicall Schoolpoints To Be Defended by the Reuerende Byshopps (1589)

Hay Any Worke for Cooper; or, A Brief Pistle Directed to the Reuerende Byshopps (1589)

Theses Martinianae: That Is Certain Demonstratiue Conclusions [Martin Junior] (1589)

The Iust Censure and Reproofe of Martin Iunior [Martin Senior] (1589)

The Protestatyon of Martin Marprelat (1589)

EDITION

Pierce, William, ed. *The Marprelate Tracts, 1588, 1589*. London, 1911. The only modern edition of the Marprelate tracts.

FURTHER READING

Anselment, Raymond A. *"Betwixt Jest and Earnest": Marprelate, Milton, Marvell, Swift, and the Decorum of Religious Ridicule*. Toronto, 1979. The only major literary study that treats Marprelate at length; gives him a place at the heart of the English satirical tradition.

Black, Joseph. "The Rhetoric of Reaction: The Martin Marprelate Tracts (1588–89), Anti-Martinism, and the Uses of Print in Early Modern England." *Sixteenth Century Journal* 28 (1997): 707–725. Suggests that the Marprelate controversy helped foster a world of print debate in early modern England.

Carlson, Leland H. *Martin Marprelate, Gentleman: Master Job Throckmorton Laid Open in His Colors*. San Marino, CA, 1981. An indispensable resource; the only recent full-length study devoted to Marprelate.

Hill, Christopher. "Radical Prose in Seventeenth-Century England: From Marprelate to the Levellers." *Essays in Criticism* 32 (1982): 95–118. Argues that Marprelate was an important influence on the Leveller writers and that they, in turn, spread the "prose of everyday speech" beyond the stage and pulpit preparing the way for John Bunyan, Daniel Defoe, and Jonathan Swift.

Lander, Jesse M. "Martin Marprelate and the Fugitive Text." *Reformation* 7 (2002): 135–185. Analyzes Marprelate's argumentative strategies, especially his sophisticated use of print conventions.

Poole, Kristen. "Saints Alive! Falstaff, Martin Marprelate, and the Staging of Puritanism." *Shakespeare Quarterly* 46 (1995): 47–75. Argues that Falstaff is a parody of the grotesque Puritan, a stereotype that emerges from the Marprelate controversy.

Summergill, Travis L. "The Influence of the Marprelate Controversy upon the Style of Thomas Nashe." *Studies in Philology* 48 (1951): 145–160. Claims that an early engagement with Marprelate was central to the development of Nashe's mature style.

ANDREW MARVELL

Nigel Smith

Andrew Marvell (1621–1678) was born on 31 March 1621, in the rectory at Winestead in the East Riding of Yorkshire, the fourth child and elder son of the Reverend Andrew Marvell (c. 1584–1641) and his first wife, Anne Pease (died 1638). Marvell was educated in the grammar school at Kingston upon Hull, and at Trinity College, Cambridge. Dabbling with Roman Catholicism was not the cause of his being deprived of his Cambridge scholarship in 1641; more probably, he did not meet the residence requirement. By this time or soon afterward, Marvell was apparently living in London, probably enjoying the distractions it provided for young gentlemen, and in pursuit of preferment from the great. His father's death had indirectly resulted in limited access to funds, and Marvell spent the middle of the civil war decade traveling abroad in Holland, France, Spain, and Italy. He had published Latin and Greek verse while an undergraduate, but it is usually supposed that his flourishing as a lyric poet began in these years abroad. It has also been conjectured that Marvell met George Villiers, the young duke of Buckingham, and his brother, Lord Francis Villiers, in this period, probably at Rome.

Back in London by late 1647, Marvell was soon confronted with some difficult choices. His father had been a moderate Church of England divine, someone who would have looked to a follower of Archbishop William Laud (1573–1645) like a nonseparating Puritan, but the poet's connections and sentiments suggest Royalism. There are two Royalist elegies and a verse letter to the Cavalier poet Richard Lovelace from these years. Nonetheless, the rise of the republic meant that many young men in search of preferment now had to readjust their affiliations. Marvell was part of a group of younger men of letters, among them John Hall and Marchamont Ned-

Andrew Marvell
Anonymous portrait, c. 1655–1660
NATIONAL PORTRAIT GALLERY, LONDON

ham, who were finding a new poetry and aesthetic ethos for a new age. Marvell's "An Horatian Ode upon Cromwell's Return from Ireland" belongs to this period and is a prime (even the best) example of the literary production of these "Commonwealth Cavaliers."

Substantial preferment did not arrive, however, and Marvell settled for a tutorship in the Yorkshire household of the recently retired chief commander of the New Model Army, Thomas Fairfax. Marvell taught Fairfax's daughter Mary languages, having been found by the family to be sufficiently godly. Here began another period—known as the Nun Appleton period, in reference to the former nunnery that was part of Fairfax's domain—of intense but different creativity, from which the "mower" poems and "Upon Appleton House" emerged. In this period or just before it Marvell met John Milton, who was anxious to secure the younger man's services for the Commonwealth. "The Character of Holland" was written in early 1653 with that aim in mind, but despite the recognition in inner circles that he was worthy of being a secretary of state, Marvell became a household tutor again, this time at Eton in the house of John Oxenbridge, teaching William Dutton, a ward of Oliver Cromwell. This began another rich period of creativity for Marvell, including "Bermudas," "A Letter to Dr. Ingelo," and "The First Anniversary of the Government of the Lord Protector." Marvell was involved in the production of diplomatic poetry for Cromwell, and with Dutton he traveled to Paris and Saumur in 1656. The final reward came on 2 September 1657, with an appointment as a senior protectorate civil servant. One year later Cromwell died; Marvell penned an important elegy for him (although it did not appear in print) and progressed in January 1659 to being Hull's member of Parliament, where he voted with the government against the opposition republicans. The collapse of the protectorate in the spring meant that Marvell lost his seat in May, although he remained in Whitehall as Latin secretary. It is reported that he spoke at the "Rota," the club organized by James Harrington to debate constitutions prior to the restoration of the monarchy.

With that restoration Marvell regained his parliamentary seat, but he was now effectively an "out," and he spent the remaining eighteen years of his life playing a key role in the foundation of what would become the first Whig Party, as well as being assiduous with respect to his constituency. He was rebuked in December 1660 for complaining about Milton's harsh treatment and was notorious for allegedly trading blows with an archenemy, Sir Thomas Clifford, in the House of Commons. Marvell spent two periods abroad: one in Holland (1662–1663), and one as secretary on an embassy to Russia, Sweden, and Denmark (1663–1665). Both times he served Charles Howard, the Roman Catholic earl of Carlisle, who had formerly compromised with Cromwell and who remained a protector of Dissenters in the 1660s. All of Carlisle's diplomatic aims were frustrated, and Marvell's choice of Latin phrasing at one point offended the tsar.

In the late 1660s Marvell played an important role in the emergence of critical opposition to the regime of Edward Hyde, first earl of Clarendon, notably in the context of English embarrassment during the Second Dutch War (1664–1667). While working hard in Parliament, in the debating chamber and on committees, especially with respect to investigating the causes of administrative miscarriage during the Dutch Wars, Marvell was also involved in the surreptitious production of salacious and defamatory poetic satires of Clarendon: a substantial number of the group of poems known as the "Advice to a Painter" poems. Marvell did not personally benefit from the fall of Clarendon (and at one point he spoke against precipitate treatment of the disgraced earl), but he remained an "opposition" MP. His counsel was respected by various anticourt aristocrats, including Thomas Wharton; Arthur Annesley, first earl of Anglesey; and Anthony Ashley Cooper, first earl of Shaftesbury. In their turn, they provided access to libraries, protection, and support, especially when Marvell began his defense of religious toleration in a series of sensational prose pamphlets, nearly all of them published anonymously; *The Rehearsal Transpros'd* and *Mr. Smirke* are the best known. As the new decade began, Marvell was alarmed by the rise of royal power and the problems it presented for religious toleration. In 1671, with an indefinite proroguing or sus-

pension of Parliament threatened, Marvell considered the possibility of a post in Ireland.

In March 1672, Charles II joined the French king, Louis XIV, in a third war against the Dutch. Marvell is thought to have acted as a secret agent in Holland during this time. In a clever and libelous mock speech composed in February 1675, Marvell attacked Charles's policy and his personal behavior as well. Whether Marvell wrote a related series of verse satires—"The Statue in Stocks-Market" (after October 1674), "The Statue at Charing Cross" (July 1675), and "A Dialogue between the Two Horses" (late 1675)—is a subject of critical dispute. Before the parliamentary session ended, Marvell was given responsibilities for revoking the right of Catholics to sit in Parliament and for investigating recusancy (the return from Anglicanism to Catholicism) in Yorkshire.

The concern with religious liberty continued, and Marvell's republican/Whig associations strengthened toward the end of his life as Charles II appeared to be listing again toward a French-style absolutist government— hence the poems on Scotland and in defense of the tortured Scottish Covenanter James Mitchell. On 16 August 1678, after returning from a visit to Hull, Marvell died of a fever complicated by inappropriate medical treatment and was buried in the church of St. Giles in the Field.

Marvell died intestate, and a dispute arose after his death between John Farrington and Mary Palmer/Marvell concerning his alleged assets (the size of which has never been accurately established), and in connection with this, the matter of whether he was ever married. In September 1680, Mary Palmer, known to be Marvell's housekeeper, claimed to be his widow and by the following March had been granted administration jointly with her lawyer, one of his creditors. She also signed the preface to the 1681 *Miscellaneous Poems*. While we cannot at present prove that Marvell was married, we cannot prove that he was not. The question then turns on the nature of the marriage and the kind of household he kept. How this information reflects on Marvell's sexuality and his views on sexuality is a topic that has often been engaged in interpretations of his poetry.

THE POETRY

Marvell is best known today for his poetry, which was hardly known at all during his lifetime, and then mostly to a small circle of intimates. Most of it was first published in collected form two years and five months after his death.

The lyrics are various in form: pastoral dialogues and monologues, religious lyrics, garden poems, erotic love poems. They are notable for their ability to hold contraries in balance (rather than forcing their collision) and to suspend expected coordinates of time and place. Some of them bear a close relationship with the emblem-book tradition or with painting, especially portraiture. They make the excitingly original emerge from the greatest clichés of the age, as in "To His Coy Mistress." Marvell's ability to extract poised ambiguity through syntactic contraction, or punning (especially on Latinate senses of English words), has been widely admired. So is the "liberty" that has been seen as dramatized in the texture of the verse: a combination of the highly disciplined (regular couplet rhymes, highly formed, regular stanzas) and the relatively liberal—frequent deviation from regular stress patterns, but never enough to endanger the metrical shape of the whole. The verse has been praised for its notable evenness of rhythm with very regular end-stopping and a marked caesura, so that rhyme becomes a significant part of the meaning of the poem. "Thick-rhyming" creates a sense of deep pleasure and profound passivity, extending even to bliss, as exemplified in many passages from "Upon Appleton House."

That the sequential arrangement of the poems in the 1681 volume might be significant has been the subject of critical discussion. There are five poems known to be written before 1650 that were not included in 1681: two panegyrics, one in Latin, one in Greek, written while Marvell was an undergraduate; two apparently Royalist elegies; and a dedicatory verse epistle addressed to the Cavalier poet Richard Lovelace. The elegy on Lord Hastings and the Lovelace poem are considered to be among the best examples of their kind and have been seen as key to Marvell's understanding of poetry's function and the relationship between poetry and the civil crisis of his time. Marvell's mastery of the new genre of the country house poem is attested by the inclusion of "Upon Appleton House" in the 1681 volume, in addition to other poems either from the Nun Appleton period or associated with Fairfax, such as the "mower" poems or "Upon the Hill and Grove at Bilbrough." The 1681 volume also originally contained the three great poems on Oliver Cromwell, including *An Horatian Ode*, often regarded as the most distinguished political poem in the English language. These poems were canceled from most copies of 1681: only two uncanceled copies are known to survive today. Only one of these poems, *The First Anniversary*, was published in printed form before 1681. A further collection of occasional poems, including the Latin verse letter to Dr. Ingelo and the insightful and combative prefatory poem to Milton's *Paradise Lost*, completes the volume.

Contrary to a once common view, Marvell remained active as a lyricist during the Restoration, but most of the poetry he wrote at this time appears to be satires of the government, notably Clarendon and his administration in the late 1660s. This includes the elaborate "The Last Instructions to a Painter" but also the second and third "Advices to a Painter," long and possibly collectively composed satires to which Marvell's authorship is now fairly confidently attached. Further poems on issues of court and royal corruption and toleration circulated in the decade before Marvell's death. Many have been attributed to Marvell, but only some can be accepted with certainty. Of this group, the excellent and politically original "The Loyal Scot," built out of one passage in "The Last Instructions," stands out, as does the hitherto overlooked Latin poem "Scaevola Scoto-Brittannus." We will never know with precision how much of Marvell's poetry has been lost, but we do know that in September 1677 he wrote an epitaph on a friend, the republican theorist James Harrington, but suppressed it because, claimed Aubrey, it would have given offense.

PROSE

Marvell was most famous in his own time and long afterward for *The Rehearsal Transpros'd*, published in the autumn of 1672. Its target was Samuel Parker, later bishop of Oxford, whom Marvell had first met in Milton's house in 1662–1663. Parker conformed and by 1670 was upholding the power of the civil authority over religious externals in *A Discourse of Ecclesiastical Polity*. It was, however, the attack on toleration of nonconformity that Parker prefaced to John Bramhall's *Vindication of Himself and the Episcopal Clergy from the Charge of Popery* in September 1672 that provoked Marvell to respond. The title of his anonymously published reply, and the name of the chief character Mr. Bayes, which he uses to mock his opponent, derive from the duke of Buckingham's satirical play *The Rehearsal*, where the protagonist, a caricature of John Dryden, defines his practice of turning prose into verse as "transversing."

Marvell's tract is an extended piece of needling jest, but at its heart Marvell produces a distinct view on the sources of religious intolerance in his country. The real schismatics, in Marvell's view, are the Arminians of Charles I's reign: the high churchers with whom Parker now allies himself. While the intolerance of the Anglican bishops is exposed, Marvell also quotes extensively from his now deceased acquaintance John Hales, another "Arminian" but one who argued that "schism" was nothing more than a mechanism of control adopted by malevolent parties within a given church.

Marvell made sly insinuations concerning Parker's love habits; in return, the five printed replies and a scurrilous verse lampoon accused Marvell of sodomy and impotence, and alleged that he had been surgically castrated. A second issue was allowed to pass by the censor with slight changes, after the king read it and opined that "Parker has done him wrong, and this man has done him Right." The collapse of the indulgence policy a year later aided Parker in his long *Reproof*, to which Marvell replied with the second part of *The Rehearsal Transpros'd* (1673), this time issued under his own name and quoting on its title page a threat made against his life if he should publish any further "Lie or Libel" against his opponent. Marvell was assumed to be the victor, and a generation later Jonathan Swift, hailing him as an innovative genius, remarked that "we still read *Marvel's* Answer to *Parker* with Pleasure," whereas Parker had been forgotten.

During the fifteen-month prorogation that began in late 1675, Marvell defended the views of Herbert Croft, bishop of Hereford, who had advocated accommodation with nonconformists. Marvell mocked Croft's critic, Francis Turner, in *Mr. Smirke; or, The Divine in Mode* (May 1676), published under the pseudonym Andreas Rivetus junior (Andre Rivet was a famous French Calvinist, but the borrowed identity makes an anagram of *res nuda veritas* ("naked truth"). Marvell appended to this *A Short Historical Essay, Concerning General Councils*, discussing disputes between rival Christian sects in the third century and attributing these conflicts to the bishops. Marvell escaped government prosecution again, though his publisher was briefly imprisoned.

Marvell's hope for the rehabilitation of Charles II finally failed, resulting in his anonymously published *An Account of the Growth of Popery and Arbitrary Government* (1677), which traces an alleged conspiracy "to change the Lawfull Government of *England* into an Absolute Tyranny, and to convert the established Protestant Religion into down-right Popery." The alarmed government posted a sizable reward for identifying the author and printer. Marvell's last published work, the anonymously issued *Remarks upon a Late Disingenuous Discourse*, takes up a debate between conforming and nonconformist thinkers on God's influence in the world.

POSTHUMOUS REPUTATION

Marvell's poetry had circulated almost entirely in manuscript until 1681, and where we can tell from echoes in the verse of other poets, or in terms of direct evidence of response (such as from Queen Christina), that it was highly respected. Anthony à Wood attests that the volume was "cried up as excellent" by those of the author's own persuasion, the Whigs. Unsurprisingly, it contained none of the political pieces attributed to Marvell after the revolution of 1688. But with regard to the satires in poetry as well as in prose, Marvell was not without admirers. Aubrey, who became acquainted personally with Marvell in the 1670s, called him "an excellent poet in Latin or English: for Latin verses there was no man would come into competition with him."

Marvell was honored in death by a grant of £50 from the city of Hull for funeral expenses and a gravestone, and by elegies written by John Ayloffe and other admirers. In 1726, Thomas Cooke, who viewed Marvell as a "sincere and daring Patriot," reprinted his lyrics and satires in *The Works of Andrew Marvell Esq.*, supported by a biographical note and some private letters. The formerly expurgated Cromwell poems eventually resurfaced in a folio collected works published fifty years later by Edward Thompson. Increasing recognition of Marvell's poetry through the nineteenth century culminated in a *Complete Works* (1872) edited by Alexander Grosart.

The twentieth-century critical appreciation of Marvell was signaled by T. S. Eliot's essay for a volume issued to commemorate Marvell's tercentenary in 1921. H. M. Margoliouth edited the *Poems and Letters* (1927), and the French critic Pierre Legouis produced a major biographical and critical study in 1928. In following decades, Marvell's work has been perhaps the most extensively analyzed of all seventeenth-century lyric verse. The recent annotated editions of his poetry and his prose confirm his status as a major canonical author, while recent historical interpretation points up his significance as a key player and observer in mid- and late-seventeenth-century political life.

[*See also* Cavalier Poetry *and* Satire.]

EDITIONS

Donno, Elizabeth Story, ed. *The Complete Poems*. New York, 1972. Reprinted in 2005, with revised reading list and an introduction by Jonathan Bate.

Dzelzainis, Martin, and Annabel Patterson, eds. *The Prose Works*. 2 vols. New Haven, CT, 2003.

Margoliouth, H. M., ed. *The Poems and Letters of Andrew Marvell.* 3d ed. rev. by Pierre Legouis with the collaboration of E. E. Duncan-Jones. Oxford, 1971.

Smith, Nigel, ed. *The Poems of Andrew Marvell.* London, 2003.

FURTHER READING

Chernaik, Warren. *The Poet's Time: Politics and Religion in the Work of Andrew Marvell.* New York, 1983.

Chernaik, Warren, and Martin Dzelzainis, eds. *Marvell and Liberty.* New York, 1999.

Colie, Rosalie L. *"My Ecchoing Song": Andrew Marvell's Poetry of Criticism.* Princeton, NJ, 1970.

Collins, Dan S. *Andrew Marvell: A Reference Guide.* Boston, 1981.

Friedman, D. M. *Marvell's Pastoral Art.* London, 1970.

Healy, Thomas, ed. *Andrew Marvell.* New York, 1998.

Hunt, John Dixon. *Andrew Marvell: His Life and Writings.* London, 1978.

Kelliher, Hilton. "Andrew Marvell." In *Oxford Dictionary of National Biography.* Oxford, 2004.

Kelliher, Hilton. *Andrew Marvell: Poet and Politician, 1621–78: An Exhibition to Commemorate the Tercentenary of His Death.* London, 1978.

Legouis, Pierre. *Andrew Marvell: Poet, Puritan, Patriot.* Oxford, 1965. Abridged version of the 1928 French edition.

Leishman, James Blair. *The Art of Marvell's Poetry.* London, 1966. 2d ed., New York, 1968.

Murray, Nicholas. *World Enough and Time: The Life of Andrew Marvell.* London, 1999.

Norbrook, David. *Writing the English Republic: Poetry, Rhetoric, and Politics, 1627–1660.* New York, 1999.

Parker, G. F. "Marvell on Milton: Why the Poem Rhymes Not." *Cambridge Quarterly* 20.3 (1991): 183–209.

Patterson, Annabel. *Marvell: The Writer in Public Life.* New York, 2000.

Ray, Robert H. *An Andrew Marvell Companion.* New York, 1998.

Rees, Christine. *The Judgment of Marvell.* New York, 1989.

Wallace, John M. *Destiny His Choice: The Loyalism of Andrew Marvell.* London, 1968.

Zwicker, Steven N. *Lines of Authority: Politics and English Literary Culture, 1649–1689.* Ithaca, NY, 1993.

KARL MARX

Timothy Bewes

Karl Heinrich Marx (1818–1883) was born in Trier, Germany, the son of a bourgeois Jewish lawyer who converted to Lutheranism after the passing of anti-Jewish laws in 1816. As a young man he studied law and philosophy in Bonn and Berlin during a period of further political reaction under Frederick William IV. German philosophy was then under the stultifying influence of conservative, "orthodox" Hegelianism. Marx arrived in London in 1849, a refugee from the political fallout of the failed revolutions in Europe the year before, which he and his coauthor Friedrich Engels had helped to foment with the publication of the *Communist Manifesto* (1848). There he lived out his "sleepless night of exile," as he put it in a letter to Engels, until his death in 1883, producing works that would shake and polarize the worlds of philosophy, politics, and literature through the following century.

Marx's permanent displacement in London, from the age of thirty-one, says a great deal about England at this time, although precisely what it says depends on one's point of view. For the British historian of ideas Isaiah Berlin (1909–1997), the hospitality extended to Marx, Engels, and other European radicals speaks of "the isolation of England intellectually and socially from the main currents of Continental life," as much as its fabled "tolerance." Culturally and geographically, England felt insulated from the events that shook the Continent, enabling it to regard its guests with patronizing indifference. One of Marx's recent biographers, Francis Wheen, observes that England "has never known whether to feel pride or shame at its connection with the father of proletarian revolution." As Marx seems to have intuited, the English were enamored with the idea of their own tolerance, to which Marx and Engels explicitly appealed in a joint letter to the *Spectator* protesting their constant surveillance by police spies: England, they wrote in 1850, was in danger of losing its reputation as "the safest asylum for refugees of all parties and all countries."

London was a growing metropolis. By 1800 it was the first urban center with a million people, and when Marx arrived the population was over two and a half million, more than a third of whom were migrants. The extremes of poverty and wealth existed side by side, a situation Charles Dickens vividly depicted in *Bleak House* (1853). Marx and his family lived closer to the former than the latter extreme—at times far too close for comfort: two children died during the first two years they spent in London, and a third in 1855. Yet what more suitable backdrop could there be for the work of a thinker inclined to celebrate the bourgeoisie for having "rescued a considerable part of the population from the idiocy of rural life," who welcomed the industrial era for dismantling "all feudal, patriarchal, idyllic relations," and who imagined capitalism itself as a force that would hasten the elevation of the proletarian struggle from the national level to the international?

HISTORICAL MATERIALISM

For a passage from Marx's works that can sum up the impact of his thought on literary studies, it would be difficult to improve on the following, from *The German Ideology*, written two years before the *Manifesto* (1846):

> In direct contrast to German philosophy which descends from heaven to earth, here we ascend from earth to heaven. That is to say, we do not set out from what men say, imagine, conceive, nor from men as narrated, thought of, imagined, conceived, in order to arrive at men in the flesh. We set out from real, active men, and on the basis of their real life-process we demonstrate the development of the ideological reflexes and echoes of this life-process.

For the first time, material interests were being put forward as the motor of human history. Everything in the realm of human consciousness (art, religion, philosophy, literature, subjectivity, science, law) would be regarded not as the necessarily imperfect attempts of free and gifted individuals to describe or otherwise make sense of the world, but as the precise opposite: the complete expression of class positions in the economic and social structure that are in themselves specific and incomplete.

The German Ideology is a dense, 650-page work much taken up with bellicose attacks on numerous, now mostly forgotten contemporaries. Like much of Marx's writing, the book was considered unpublishable during his lifetime, and it did not appear in print until 1932. For all its verbosity and polemical lopsidedness, it contains the first, most lucid account of "historical materialism," the methodology underpinning the body of political and philosophical thought that has come to be called Marxism. The sentences quoted are from the opening section, where Marx and Engels outlined their main objections to the prevailing currents in German philosophical idealism. Their principal targets were a group of leftist thinkers calling themselves the "Young Hegelians." The various philosophical projects of the Young Hegelian thinkers—who included Max Stirner, Bruno Bauer, and Ludwig Feuerbach—were all attempts to replace the supposed mysticism of Hegel's concept of "spirit" (*Geist*), the animating principle of his philosophy of history, with human rationality. The error they had in common, according to Marx and Engels, was to seek to change reality by changing the consciousness of men and women; their thought was founded on a powerful belief in the force of revolutionary ideas—in particular, the critique of religious and superstitious conceptions, the traces of which they detected everywhere. Yet their approach, according to Marx and Engels, amounted to nothing more than a demand "to interpret reality in another way, i.e. to recognize it by means of another interpretation." The Young Hegelians thereby preserved the separation between reality and our perception of it by their faith in the integrity of the critical consciousness. Hegel's idealism survived their critique of it, since human intellect remained independent of material interests. For Marx and Engels, the Young Hegelians' philosophy was still a thoroughly contemplative discipline, abstracted from reality and therefore covertly invested in maintaining the world as it is.

Historical materialism, by contrast, aimed to be not a contemplative but a practical theory. Marx concludes his "Theses on Feuerbach" (1845)—a work contemporary with *The German Ideology* that restates many of its central points in aphoristic form—with the famous statement, "The philosophers have only *interpreted* the world, in various ways; the point is to *change* it." Marx and Engels drew attention to the "relations of production" which determine all output, and thus all purely contemplative activity. Human fantasies of intellectual autonomy are the first thing to be eliminated in Marx and Engels's approach.

What Marx and Engels propose is not simply an inversion of priorities, but a fundamental shift in the understanding of humanity's relationship to the world—away from history as the disembodied evolution of consciousness, and toward what might be called an embodied, or material, history. For Marx and Engels, "Man" (a word they frequently put in quotation marks) does not simply confront his world as something to be cultivated, or that oppresses him; rather, man does not exist in separation from the material conditions of his existence, the need for shelter and food, the actuality of his oppression, and the system of wealth and privilege that enables reflection. "Man," in short, produces himself simultaneously with what he produces through labor. Thus everything in the realm of imagination—including everything that purports to transcend his conditions of existence—arises from, and must be referred primarily to, those conditions. Art and literature, even at their most "elevated," express not the "above and beyond" of the material world, but precisely the relations of production. In a feudal or capitalist society these are inevitably relations of exploitation.

This is the essence of historical materialism, and its most important political implication is a rejection of the idea of "civil society," the liberal conception of the state that emerged from Hegel's *Philosophy of Right* (1821). In "civil society" the state consists of a series of contracts entered into between necessarily free individuals and the sovereign power, in which each of these two parties has duties that it owes to the other, as well as corresponding rights. Should the state fail in its duties to the citizen, the citizen has the right to depose the state. Likewise, should the citizen fail to observe his duties to society, the state has the right to imprison or otherwise exclude him from it. "Civil society," for Marx, is an idealist representation of society predicated on a fantasy of independence and autonomy that appeared historically alongside the bourgeoisie as a class, and it should be regarded as that class's ideological expression, perfectly in tune with its material interests. For Marx and Engels, rather, "the history of all hitherto existing society is the history of class struggles." German Idealism, they write in a celebrated image, relates to the materialist dialectic ("the study of the actual world") in the same way as masturbation to "sexual love."

CONSCIOUSNESS AND IDEOLOGY

This is far from saying that consciousness is a realm of illusion. In another graphic analogy in *The German Ide-*

ology, the Young Hegelians' critique of religion is compared to a man who fights against the danger of drowning by insisting that gravity is an illusion: if only men and women were able to knock this superstition out of their heads, they would be insured against any danger from water. For Marx and Engels, there is no such realm of conscious "illusion" that is separable from the world of materiality; that is, there is no false consciousness as such, just as there is no "Man" as such. It is ironic, then, that a crude notion of "false consciousness" has frequently been attached to the name of Marx himself; in fact, the existence of such a notion among his contemporaries infuriated the young Marx.

Other misperceptions also help to give Marx's thought a bad name. "Religion is the opium of the people," a phrase from another early work, Marx's Introduction to *A Critique of Hegel's Philosophy of Right* (1843), is often interpreted as a demand for the elimination of religion as a stage—the first step, even—in the process of establishing a communist society. Yet if the passage is read in context, it is clear that Marx does not mean that religion is simply a tool for the oppression of working people, but that religion is "the fantastic realization of the human essence" in a society that does not allow the essence "any true reality." The struggle against religion as such is a distraction as long as it fails to understand itself as part of a struggle against a world of which religion is the "spiritual aroma." Put simply, religious belief is for Marx not an illusion to be uprooted and expunged, but the symptom of a falsity that extends through every aspect of capitalist society, including all "critique" of it, and that will disappear only when exploitation and inequality disappear.

A passage in *The Eighteenth Brumaire of Louis Bonaparte* (1852), Marx's polemical dissection of the failed French revolution of 1848–1851, which elevated the nephew of Napoleon I to the presidency, reiterates this sense of the material (or structural) basis of ideology. For Marx, the strategic failure to grasp this point was one of the factors behind the collapse of the Second Republic. To ignore the material basis of ideology—to replace a Marxist concept of ideology with a liberal one—is to remove any obstacle to the idea that the interests of the proletariat can be represented just as easily by the bourgeoisie as by the proletariat itself. The bourgeoisie may believe itself to be acting in the general interest; yet the very idea of the "general interest" is an idealist abstraction, a means of betraying the proletariat. For Marx, this is exactly what happened with Louis Bonaparte. A "gro-

tesque mediocrity," "a nothing," was able to turn himself into a hero by presenting himself as the legitimate representative of the peasantry. The results were catastrophic (at least for the proletarian revolution). In Marx's account, a bourgeois monarchy—the deposed Louis-Philippe—was simply replaced by a bourgeois republic, the only difference being that "whereas a limited section of the bourgeoisie ruled in the name of the king, the whole of the bourgeoisie will now rule in the name of the people." Among the lessons of 1851—when Bonaparte, the elected president, abolished the Constituent National Assembly in a coup d'état and established a dictatorship with himself as emperor—is that no alliance is possible between the peasantry or the urban proletariat and the bourgeoisie, for reasons that are embodied in the very principle of historical materialism. "As in private life one differentiates between what a man thinks and says of himself and what he really is and does," writes Marx in the *Eighteenth Brumaire*,

> so in historical struggles one must distinguish still more the phrases and fancies of parties from their real organism and their real interests. . . . Thus the Tories in England long imagined that they were enthusiastic about monarchy, the church and the beauties of the old English Constitution, until the day of danger wrung from them the confession that they are enthusiastic only about *ground rent*.

This passage introduces a quandary that has long generated debate within the Marxist tradition. Differences of opinion on this question within the Communist League—the London group of German émigré intellectuals at whose request Marx wrote the *Communist Manifesto*—caused it to split around this time, and it appears that Marx largely engineered the rupture. In a speech to the League in September 1850, Marx described the issue as a clash between the "universal" approach put forward in the *Manifesto*—which demonstrated that revolution was impossible if instigated "prematurely," before objective conditions enabled the proletariat to assume its history-defining role—and the view that the "will" of the party, rather than "real relationships," could be the motivating force of revolution. The word "proletariat," claimed Marx, could not be used in the same "empty" (that is, idealist, representative) way that democrats use the word "people," as it had been, by implication, in France. Any alliance with the bourgeoisie, however "pragmatic," represented a departure from the materialism of the *Manifesto*. The empirical basis of the party is not the imposition of democratic ideas and theoretical principles upon a receptive subaltern class, but the opposite: "actual relations springing from an existing class struggle."

The point is not that individuals are incapable of ideas, or that consciousness is a mystical concept per se; rather, consciousness has a material existence from which it is inseparable. False consciousness, as the Hungarian philosopher and critic Georg Lukács (1922) maintained, is "neither arbitrary, subjective nor psychological," but rather objective: "it is the class situation itself." This historical-materialist principle underpins the incongruity of Marxism with any idea of representative democracy, but also with any idea of party dictatorship. The Soviet regime of 1929–1953 under Stalin, for example, had far more in common with the state terrorism practiced by Louis Bonaparte than with the future proletarian revolution envisaged by Marx and Engels.

THE *COMMUNIST MANIFESTO*

The *Communist Manifesto* is the most widely read of Marx's works, and it expounds for the first time the thesis of the historical inevitability of proletarian revolution. Commissioned by the Communist League, completely rewritten by Marx after an initial attempt by Engels, and published in London on the brink of the 1848 French revolution, the *Communist Manifesto* sets out a program for the complete transformation of society. The systematic quality of its argumentation, the tenacity with which it strives for a "scientific" explanation of the logic of historical change, and its fascination with the transformative power of capital are the qualities that make this work so compelling and so constantly surprising. It is fair to say that the real revolutionary hero of the *Communist Manifesto* is the bourgeoisie, and it is a peculiarity of the text, although one completely consistent with the methodology rehearsed in *The German Ideology*, that its most lyrical passages are those that deal with its antagonist. Marx was undeniably captivated by the revolutionary energy of capitalism. The following passage is perhaps the best known in all of Marx's writing:

> Constant revolutionizing of production, uninterrupted disturbance of all social conditions, everlasting uncertainty and agitation distinguish the bourgeois epoch from all earlier ones. All fixed, fast-frozen relations, with their train of ancient and venerable prejudices and opinions, are swept away, all new-formed ones become antiquated before they can ossify. All that is solid melts into air, all that is holy is profaned, and man is at last compelled to face with sober senses, his real conditions of life, and his relations with his kind.

For Marx and Engels, the effects of the bourgeois epoch not only had a positive dimension, but also established the precondition for the development of communism. It was precisely the bourgeois expansion of the market that made the internationalization of the proletariat imaginable. Further foreseen benefits include the eradication of racism ("the barbarians' intensely obstinate hatred of foreigners"), the eclipse of nationalist provincialism, and the dissolution of people's "religious and political illusions." In the lines that follow, Marx appears to predict the phenomenon of globalization: "The need of a constantly expanding market for its products chases the bourgeoisie over the whole surface of the globe. . . . The bourgeoisie has through its exploitation of the world-market given a cosmopolitan character to production and consumption in every country."

It was these sentences that prompted the resurgence of interest in Marx around the time of the 150th anniversary of the publication of the *Manifesto*. In an October 1997 edition of the *New Yorker*, John Cassidy declared Marx to be "the next big thinker," publishing a lengthy article arguing that Marx's importance is less that of a theorist of communism than as a "student of capitalism." To oppose Marx the thinker of capitalism to the socialist revolutionary, however, is to do exactly what Marx's project is intent on showing us cannot be done. Historical materialism is not an "ethical" (and therefore subjective) political theory about how to temper the "extremes" of capitalism, but an analysis of history from the point of view of objective relations between historical processes and between social and economic classes. For Marx, the two moments of capitalism and communism are historically inseparable. Communism is inconceivable without capitalism, though it is also more than just a historical stage that succeeds capitalism. Communism, rather, is a completely new dispensation in which even the opposition between capitalism and communism has to be rethought. Not only is capitalism swept away by the proletarian revolution, but the very conditions for the existence of class antagonisms, and classes in general, disappear as well. "Communism" write Marx and Engels in *The German Ideology*, "is for us not a state of affairs which is to be established, an ideal to which reality [will] have to adjust itself. We call communism the real movement which abolishes the present state of things. The conditions of this movement result from the premises now in existence."

THE WRITING OF *CAPITAL*

We should expect that a thinker so alert to the unreliability of habitual appearances would be acutely interested in and influenced by literature. Even before Marx, Defoe's *Robinson Crusoe* (1719) had provided political economists with a model for bourgeois individualism, the fantasy of "man on his island" that Marx deflates in the opening chapter of *Capital*. Marx consumed Victorian novels, but his taste extended to Aeschylus, Dante, Fielding, Gogol, Pushkin, and Walter Scott. He admired Honoré de Balzac's depictions of bourgeois society; he named the French encyclopedist Denis Diderot as his "favourite prose writer" in a questionnaire filled in for two of his daughters in 1865; and his writing includes hundreds of citations of Dickens, Shakespeare, and Goethe, as well as innumerable references to classical literature. In his later works, Marx's own literary style becomes progressively more distinctive. The mature Marx is an intensely figurative writer; his metaphors have a dramatic, corporeal quality, reminiscent of earlier English writers such as Jonathan Swift and Laurence Sterne.

Capital (1867) is Marx's largest and most influential work, yet he left it unfinished; only the first of its three volumes was published during his lifetime. More than any other of his works, its literary merits are as pronounced as its theoretical and analytical ones. Francis Wheen remarks on the "picaresque" quality of Marx's account of the transnational movement of capital, and he characterizes the whole work as "a Victorian melodrama or a vast gothic novel"—this is a world of heroes "enslaved and consumed by the monster they created," he writes. "A spectre is haunting Europe" are the words with which Marx and Engels introduce the imminence of the proletarian revolution in the *Communist Manifesto*. In *Capital*, however, the supernatural domain is found on the other side of the equation; we read of the "vampire-like" character of capital, which, as dead labor, lives "only by sucking living labor, and lives the more, the more labor it sucks." Its need of a ready source of surplus labor is described as a "werewolf-like hunger." Surplus-value, Marx's term for the "congealed" labor time amassed by the capitalist from the hours worked by the laborer over and above those necessary for his or her subsistence, "has all the charms of something created out of nothing." And for Marx, the commodity—the opening chapter on which could be taken as a showpiece for the three-volume work as a whole—has a positively "phantasmatic" quality. Marx is describing the transformation from "use value" to "exchange value" in the object produced by the capitalist mode of production, a distinction inherited from the British political economist David Ricardo. Marx writes:

> The form of wood . . . is altered if a table is made out of it. Nevertheless the table continues to be wood, an ordinary sensuous thing. But as soon as it emerges as a commodity, it changes into a thing which transcends sensuousness. It not only stands with its feet on the ground, but, in relation to all other commodities, it stands on its head, and evolves out of its wooden brain grotesque ideas, far more wonderful than if it were to begin dancing of its own free will.

No other thinker has written so powerfully, and with such originality, about the material actuality of the exchange economy: the relations of producer, consumer, and worker to almost everything he or she encounters. The subject of *Capital* is the economic organization of society in its totality—the logic of the processes of production, distribution, and exchange; the impact of commodification on every aspect of human existence; and the world-shattering consequences of the development and expansion of the capitalist mode of production in the future. Political economy, Marx argues, is concerned not with abstract, disembodied laws but with people, their situations, and their activities. And *Capital*, for the most part, is not a philosophically abstract book; much of it—particularly the middle chapters "The Working Day," "Large-Scale Industry," and "Wages"—is based on data from government Blue Books, reports by British factory inspectors, and the 1861 census, all dealing with real working conditions at that time.

England was the crucible in which industrialization, the capitalist mode of production, and the discipline of political economy had their origin. In 1850 Marx described it as the "demiurge of the bourgeois cosmos"—"the original process always occurs in England," he declared. Thus, for all the hardship he suffered there, Marx could not have chosen a better position from which to observe and anatomize the logic of capitalism. This is particularly so if we take into account his alliance with Engels, who had written *The Condition of the English Working Classes* (1845) when he was working at his father's textile factory in Manchester. Throughout the writing of *Capital*, Engels was back in Manchester managing the family firm and providing further material for Marx's researches, as well as regular funds. The year 1851—when Marx embarked upon the intensive economic studies in the British Museum that would lead to the production of *Capital*—was the year of the great Industrial Exhibition in London, and the beginning of a period of industrial prosperity in Britain that would ensure, according to Marx, that the revolution would not happen anytime soon, thereby justifying his own lengthy absence from more direct revolutionary activity.

Marx's statement in an afterword to the second edition of 1873 helps us to understand his debt to Hegel: "With [Hegel the dialectic] is standing on its head. It must be inverted, in order to discover the rational kernel within the mystical shell." Capitalism, for Marx, is mystifying in the extreme—and never more so than in those moments when it appears to demystify. The "fetishism of commodities" is a metaphor lifted, says Marx, from the "misty realm of religion"; however, it applies not to moments of subjective or spiritual intoxication, but to everyday activities and practices. Once objects are produced to be exchanged with other objects, rather than for immediate use, the fabric of social relations in which they are embedded, and their ability to express those relations, is obscured. The commodity "transcends sensuousness" because, like the transcendent specters of religious belief, a creation of human beings here appears infused with a life of its own; the mundane relations of exploitation and oppression it expresses are forgotten.

The commodity is not an object misperceived by a subject, but a category in which consciousness itself is ensnared and implicated. In commodity fetishism, subject and object are completely reconstrued; the term "misrecognition," used by the French structuralist-Marxist Louis Althusser to explain the paradox in which the self is simultaneously addressed by and constituted through ideology, applies also to commodity fetishism, the most concrete instance of ideology discussed in Marx's writings.

Not only is Marx's prose distinctly "literary" therefore, it is also motivated by the desire to transmit the sensuous dimension of human life, to infuse words and sentences with sensation. This quality, perhaps, is what has led some readers to characterize his imagery as "grotesque." Yet, at least as much as it is a rhetorical device, this attention to physical description is a commentary on the impoverishing effects of capital on our "human" senses—a symptom of the totality of capitalist exploitation. When Engels, looking over the proofs of the first volume of *Capital,* noticed certain passages where Marx's troublesome carbuncles (a purulent skin condition) had "left their mark," Marx expressed the hope that the bourgeoisie would come to regret every one of his carbuncles. This is a story much loved by Marx's biographers, but its significance may be more than anecdotal. The writing of *Capital,* it suggests, aspired to a form in which the conditions of its production would be sensuously present in the very body of the prose.

MARX'S LITERARY LEGACY

A passage in the posthumously discovered *Economic and Philosophical Manuscripts,* a collection of notes written in Paris in 1844—just weeks before the encounter that would inaugurate the long collaboration with Engels—is where Marx first connects the erosion of sensation with the bourgeois form of production. The young Marx believed that private property alienates men and women from their humanity by diverting all their "natural" human senses toward acquisition. Thus, what seem to be the most visceral and unnegotiable elements of humanity do not survive the appearance of private property unchanged. Marx is talking not only about the five physical senses but also what he calls the "spiritual" senses—such as will, contemplation, and love—which he groups together as the "human sense." Seeing, hearing, smelling, tasting, loving, and so on, are replaced, with the appearance of private property, by *having.* "The supersession of private property" by communism," he writes in the fragment entitled "Private Property and Communism," represents "the complete emancipation of all human senses and attributes . . . precisely because these senses and attributes have become human, subjectively as well as objectively."

Marx acknowledges the historical role of the bourgeoisie in opening up the distinctively "human" sense, elevating man above crude animal "necessity" to a level at which the senses begin to be cultivated in themselves—this is when humanity as such takes form. Private property thereby "objectifies" the essence, alerting us to the fact of its absence by giving us a distinct aesthetic sense. Its gratification by, say, the creation and appreciation of works of art and literature is a provisional but necessary compensation. The society that is "fully developed"—communism—will produce man "in all the richness of his being, the *rich* man who is *profoundly and abundantly endowed with all the senses,* as its constant reality." The implication is that art and literature, at least in their bourgeois form, will wither away, along with the state. The eye will become a human eye, says Marx, since "its object has become a social, *human* object, made by man for man"—no longer subordinated to the ethos of acquisition. The senses, freed from their "egoistic" nature, will at this stage "become *theoreticians* in their immediate praxis"—meaning that subject and object will coexist in sensuous, mutual immediacy.

Perhaps the greatest lessons that Marx's work holds for the study of literature are to be found here—not in the debates over the attributes of a properly "realist" artwork, which were brought to an abrupt, unresolved end by Modernist experimentation, nor in the prescriptive High Modernism of Frankfurt School ideology-critique, but in the proposition that, in capitalist society, art and literature can work to break down the alienation of the individual from society by inserting him or her into a relationship of material, sensuous continuity with it. A Marxist approach to literature does not necessarily attempt to "awaken" men and women to the "truth" of their oppression; in fact, such a project may not even be Marxist at all. With the indefinite suspension of the conditions that could ensure proletarian revolution, literature can perform a real revolutionary, or prerevolutionary, function: transporting men and women out of their oppression by turning the sense organs into agents of material transformation; abolishing the ego, even if only momentarily, and reminding us, in an accessible and immediate form, of the human impoverishment of the world we ordinarily inhabit.

[*See also* Realism *and* Utopianism.]

SELECTED WORKS

The Holy Family, or Critique of Critical Criticism (with Friedrich Engels, 1845)
Manifesto of the Communist Party (with Engels, 1848)
The Class Struggles in France (1850)
The Eighteenth Brumaire of Louis Bonaparte (1852)
Capital: A Critique of Political Economy (vol. 1, 1867; vol. 2, 1885; vol. 3, 1894)
The German Ideology (with Engels, 1846; published 1932)
Economic and Philosophical Manuscripts (1844; published 1936)
Grundrisse: Foundations of the Critique of Political Economy (c. 1857; published 1939)

EDITIONS

Arthur, C. J., ed. *The German Ideology* [with Friedrich Engels]. London, 1974. A student edition, judiciously abridged and highly readable, which has become the standard English edition. Also includes *Theses on Feuerbach* and the "Introduction to a Critique of Political Economy" (1857).

Bender, Frederic L., ed. *The Communist Manifesto: A Norton Critical Edition.* New York, 1988. This comprehensive, rigorously annotated edition attributes the au-

thorship of the *Manifesto* solely to Marx, but later prefaces by Marx and Engels, and a number of contextualizing sources and interpretive essays, are provided. The translation is the classic English version by Engels's favorite translator, Samuel Moore, with his creative additions to the German text meticulously signposted.

The Communist Manifesto [with Friedrich Engels] New York, 1998. Published by Monthly Review Press, this is one of several editions marking the 150th anniversary of its original publication. Includes a useful introductory essay by Ellen Meiksins Wood.

Fowkes, Ben, trans. *Capital: A Critique of Political Economy*, vol. 1. Harmondsworth, U.K., 1976. This excellent modern translation corrects many errors and approximations in the 1887 version by Samuel Moore and Edward Aveling. Vols. 2 and 3, posthumously edited by Engels, are translated for Penguin (1978, 1981) by David Fernbach. A fourth volume, assembled from Marx's notebooks by Karl Kautsky, was published in English in 1969 with the title *Theories of Surplus Value.*

Livingstone, Rodney, and Gregor Benton, trans. *Early Writings.* Harmondsworth, U.K., 1975. An indispensable volume, containing the Introduction to *A Contribution to the Critique of Hegel's Philosophy of Right*, the 1844 *Economic and Philosophical* [or "Paris"] *Manuscripts*, "On the Jewish Question," and the *Theses on Feuerbach.*

FURTHER READING

Louis Althusser. "Ideology and Ideological State Apparatuses." In his *Lenin and Philosophy and Other Essays.* London, 1971. Widely anthologized essay in which the case is forcefully argued for the material basis of ideology.

Anderson, Perry. *Considerations on Western Marxism.* London, 1976. A synthetic essay on the aftermath and influence of the body of work produced by Marx and Engels, focusing on the later "Western Marxism" of twentieth-century European thinkers; the introductory analysis of the evolution and supersession of the preceding "classical tradition" is comprehensive and incisive.

Berlin, Isaiah. *Karl Marx: His Life and Environment.* London, 1939; repr. 1995. An erudite, extremely readable, "balanced" biography from a thinker whose sympathies lie finally not with "savage and menacing" revolutionary socialism but with the "tolerance" of liberalism; Berlin's understanding of the European intellectual milieu in the mid-nineteenth century is nuanced and vivid.

Berman, Marshall. *All That Is Solid Melts into Air: The Experience of Modernity.* New York, 1982. Berman's modernist and humanist reading of Marx is unorthodox, but narrative force and excitement make this an important addition to recent literature on Marx and Marxism.

Cassidy, John. "The Return of Karl Marx." *New Yorker* 73, no. 32 (20–27 October 1997): 248–259. The article that signaled the latest revival of fashionable interest in Marx.

Lukács, Georg. *History and Class Consciousness: Studies in Marxist Dialectics.* Translated by Rodney Livingstone. London, 1971. Originally published in 1922, the founding text of "Western Marxism" contains complex but fascinating essays on historical materialism as method, class consciousness, reification, and an equally fascinating preface from 1969 in which Lukács all but disavows the entire work on the basis of its idealism.

McLellan, David. *Karl Marx: His Life and Thought.* London, 1973. The most thorough, reliable and scholarly biography available.

Wheen, Francis. *Karl Marx.* London, 1999. A recent and sympathetic biography situated in the context of Marx's 1990s "rediscovery" as a theorist of capitalism; largely succeeds in giving us "Marx the man," and elegantly distills much existing scholarship, but also turns up some fresh material.

JOHN MASEFIELD

Philip W. Errington

John Edward Masefield (1878–1967) was one of the most prolific, versatile, successful, and popular writers of the twentieth century. Yet as a poet, novelist, historian, playwright, and writer for children, Masefield outlived his contemporary reputation and mismanaged the literary marketplace. John Betjeman anticipated that Masefield's two poems "Sea-Fever" and "Cargoes" would be "remembered as long as the language lasts," but Masefield's canon is more eclectic and variable than his current reputation allows.

Masefield claimed that as a child he "lived in Paradise." He was born in Ledbury on 1 June 1878, and the Herefordshire countryside had a profound influence. Masefield wrote that "at a very early age," while in the garden, "I became aware, for the first time, that I had an imagination, and that I could tell this faculty to imagine all manner of strange things." It is easy to identify a quasi-Wordsworthian communion with nature. This was not to last. Masefield was orphaned, and his guardians hoped that training for the merchant marine would crush youthful aspirations to become a writer. He was therefore educated between 1891 and 1894 aboard the school ship *Conway*, moored on the Mersey River in Liverpool. As an apprentice, Masefield sailed round Cape Horn in 1894, but he was classified a Distressed British Sailor upon arrival in Chile. After his convalescence in England, he secured a new position aboard a ship docked in New York. Masefield crossed the Atlantic but failed to report for duty. He later wrote, "I was going to be a writer, come what might." Early biographical details resonate through Masefield's work. Herefordshire gave the writer a love of England and the English countryside. Sea experiences opened to him the folklore of the sea, a working knowledge of ships, and the beauty and wonder of seascapes. He also displays a reaction to the violence, disease, and coarseness of naval life. "Sea-Fever"—a poem of yearning for the sea—suggests disease in its title and comes from a collection of verse in which the sea causes much suffering and death.

Masefield's sympathy for the underdog dates from his time of homeless vagrancy in America. Many Masefield "heroes" are antiheroes: the ending of "The Wanderer" is "Life's battle is a conquest for the strong; / The meaning shows in the defeated thing." Eventually, the youthful Masefield secured work in a bar and then a carpet mill, and he spent his spare time and money on books. He first read Geoffrey Chaucer in 1896 and enjoyed a poetic revelation. John Keats and Percy Bysshe Shelley followed. With increased desire to become a writer, Masefield returned to England in 1897. After encouragement from William Butler Yeats, his first published poem appeared in the *Outlook* in 1899, and his first volume, *Salt-Water Ballads*, was published in 1902.

Masefield's career can be viewed in four periods. During 1899–1911 the writer sought an individual voice and style. He married in 1903, and his first child was born in 1904. With a family to support, the writer experimented with different genres and produced many volumes in addition to articles and book reviews for newspapers. *Salt-Water Ballads* (considered by the author as "something new said newly") was followed by the more lyrical *Ballads* (1903), which includes the poem "Cargoes." Short stories, naval histories, and editions of selections from Restoration writers failed to bring much success. Consequently, Masefield approached the Literary Agency of London in 1906 and was represented by them until early in the First World War. His publisher and agent helped shape Masefield's output. The novel *Captain Margaret* (1908) was the first result and was considered by A. E. Housman to be "quite readable, and containing a number of interesting details; but bad." Masefield's play *The Tragedy of Nan* (produced in 1908) enjoyed greater success, with J. M. Synge reporting Yeats's view that it was "a wonderful play—the best English play since the Elizabethans." Works for children, including *Martin Hyde* (1910) and *Jim Davis* (1911), were largely written to order, as was a critical work on Shakespeare. Modest critical success, however, failed to yield financial stability. In 1911 Masefield found his own inspiration and burst upon the literary scene with a new and shocking voice.

The long narrative poem *The Everlasting Mercy* (1911) tells of the spiritual enlightenment of a drunken poacher.

Lord Alfred Douglas branded it "nine tenths sheer filth," yet J. M. Barrie described it as "incomparably the finest literature." The first printing (in the *English Review*) replaced numerous examples of the word "bloody" with blank spaces. Robert Graves later claimed Masefield's innovation in this poem emboldened Bernard Shaw to make the word the dramatic climax of *Pygmalion*. The period 1911–1922 reveals Masefield's success with long narrative poetry and widespread critical acclaim. *The Widow in the Bye Street* (1912) is a rural tragedy set in Ledbury in which lust provokes a murder and a hanging. *Dauber* (1913) draws on Masefield's sea experiences and tells of an aspiring artist receiving contempt from his fellow sailors. The character of Dauber eventually falls to his death after an act of heroism. *Reynard the Fox* (1919) describes a foxhunt from the perspective of both the hunter and the hunted. Noted by Muriel Spark as "a classic of its kind" and "a great poem," the work can be classified as war poetry (Masefield later wrote of the fox being "a symbol of the free soul of humanity, then just escaped from extinction").

Masefield's other work is frequently overshadowed by his poetry. In a historical work such as *Gallipoli* (1916), the precision of the poet produces a powerful and crafted prose. Edward Marsh called it "supreme," while Neville Lytton described the book as "a masterpiece." Widespread success led to an invitation from Sir Douglas Haig to chronicle the battle of the Somme, although government bureaucracy eventually forced Masefield to abandon the plan.

In the period 1922–1930 Masefield returned to novels and drama. *Sard Harker* (1924), a fast-paced adventure telling of a sailor's quest after a dream vision and a last-minute escape from torture and sacrifice at the hands of a demonic mystic, was Masefield's first novel for over a decade and was originally written as a play. Living outside Oxford, Masefield organized amateur theatrical productions and recitations. A private theater in his garden (the Music Room) provided a forum in which poets could develop work with freedom from the censorship of the Lord Chamberlain. *The Trial of Jesus* was one such challenge to censorship and was first produced privately in 1925. The work depicted Christ on stage and became known by the author as "my forbidden play." Masefield also experimented with drama in the community (the "bad" quarto of *Hamlet* was staged in 1927), and verse recitals led to an annual competition (the Oxford Recitations) and later an annual festival (the Oxford Summer Diversions). Written at the invitation of the dean of Canterbury, *The Coming of Christ* (1928) was first performed in Canterbury Cathedral and became the first play staged in an English cathedral since medieval times. The innovation, with music by Gustav Holst and designs by Charles Ricketts, included the representation of Christ on stage (leading the Lord Chamberlain to note the performance was "carried out" on the responsibility of the dean of Canterbury). Success led to a Canterbury drama festival and T. S. Eliot's *Murder in the Cathedral*—Eliot being approached only after Masefield had rejected an invitation to write on the murder of Thomas à Becket. With the death of Masefield's close neighbor, Robert Bridges, the position of poet laureate fell vacant, and in 1930 Masefield was appointed.

The fourteenth laureate since John Dryden, Masefield commenced his official career noting that he would only provide verse when he felt moved to do so. He ended his career churning out dutiful verses for any royal or significant occasion. This stance—in addition to an incorrect anecdote that verses were sent for publication in the *Times* accompanied by a stamped addressed envelope in case of rejection—has had an adverse effect on Masefield's reputation.

Between 1930 and 1967 Masefield increasingly shunned attention. *The Bird of Dawning* (1933) is a novel of the China Tea Race and was described by a contemporary reviewer as "the finest sea-yarn ever penned," while the children's fantasy *The Box of Delights* (1935) is a classic of the fantasy genre. Yet Masefield was beginning to lose touch with his public. He was unenthusiastic about the interest of film companies (adaptations proposed for Douglas Fairbanks, Richard Burton, and Katharine Hepburn failed to develop), he actively discouraged broadcasting, and he largely dismissed paperback publishers. The elderly writer increasingly became a recluse.

In 1957 Masefield cheerfully noted that of 300 million English-reading people in the world, three read him, and four wrote criticisms of him. Yet the author was also capable of surprising his dwindling public. Publication on a long-playing record of *The Story of Ossian* in 1959 was the first time a work was released in a sound recording prior to book publication. The *Grammophone* hailed it as "the most important record ever issued in the history of the grammophone," but despite the apparent modernity of the project, Masefield was merely advocating the art of spoken poetry. For the author this dated back to Yeats's Monday evenings and his own experiments in the 1930s. The author, who had witnessed the coming of the railways at the edge of his childhood garden and was first read by the late Victorians, was now in the nuclear age and commemorated the assassination of John F. Kennedy in verse. Masefield died on 12 May 1967, and his ashes were interred in Poets' Corner, Westminster Abbey. Robert Graves, in a memorial address, stated that in Masefield "the fierce flame of poetry had truly burned."

Masefield always considered himself a "writer," not a poet, novelist, or playwright. Narrative, not modernist doctrine or any specific literary movement, was Masefield's interest, and narrative poetry in the twentieth century was his innovation. Increasingly, the writer's style became unfashionable. He is not an intellectual or modernist poet. His works are frequently expansive in scope and form; his language, allusions, and poetic form are simple; and his readers are welcomed into accessible works. Focus occasionally becomes indulgent, and moreover his canon is highly variable in quality. Here is a writer, however, who is engaging, eloquent, and honest. Reading Masefield can be a highly rewarding and entertaining experience. He can be witty, emotionally charged, and shocking. He can also spin a good yarn.

[*See also* Poet Laureate.]

SELECTED WORKS

POETRY

Salt-Water Ballads (1902)

Ballads (1903)

The Everlasting Mercy (1911)

The Widow in the Bye Street (1912)

The Daffodil Fields (1913)

Dauber (1913)

Reynard the Fox (1919)

Enslaved and Other Poems (1920)

Right Royal (1920)

King Cole (1921)

Collected Poems (1923; revised 1932, 1938; reprinted as Poems, 1946)

Midsummer Night and Other Tales in Verse (1928)

South and East (1929)

Minnie Maylow's Story and Other Tales and Scenes (1931)

A Tale of Troy (1932)

A Letter from Pontus and Other Verse (1936)

The Country Scene (1937)

Tribute to Ballet (1938)

A Generation Risen (1942)

On the Hill (1949)

The Bluebells and Other Verse (1961)

Old Raiger and Other Verse (1964)

In Glad Thanksgiving (1967)

Sea Fever: Selected Poems of John Masefield, edited by Philip W. Errington (2005)

SHORT STORY COLLECTIONS

A Mainsail Haul (1905)

A Tarpaulin Muster (1907)

HISTORICAL

Sea Life in Nelson's Time (1905)

On the Spanish Main (1906)

Gallipoli (1916)

The Old Front Line (1917)

The Nine Days Wonder (1941)

The Twenty-Five Days (1972)

NOVELS

Captain Margaret (1908)

Lost Endeavour (1910)

Sard Harker (1924)

Odtaa (1926)

The Hawbucks (1929)

The Bird of Dawning (1933)

Eggs and Baker (1936)

The Square Peg (1937)

Dead Ned (1938)

Live and Kicking Ned (1939)

PLAYS

The Tragedy of Nan and Other Plays (1909)

The Tragedy of Pompey the Great (1910)

Philip the King and Other Poems (1914)

The Faithful (1915)

Good Friday (1916)

Melloney Holtspur (1922)

The Trial of Jesus (1925)

Tristan and Isolt (1927)

The Coming of Christ (1928)

WORKS FOR CHILDREN

Jim Davis (1911)

The Midnight Folk (1927)

The Box of Delights (1935)

LITERARY CRITICISM

William Shakespeare (1911; revised 1954)

John M. Synge: A Few Personal Recollections (1915)

Shakespeare and Spiritual Life (1924)
Chaucer (1931)
Some Memories of W. B. Yeats (1940)
A "Macbeth" Production (1945)
Thanks before Going (1946)

AUTOBIOGRAPHICAL

In the Mill (1941)
New Chum (1944)
So Long to Learn (1952)
Grace before Ploughing (1966)

FURTHER READING

Babington-Smith, Constance. *John Masefield: A Life.* Oxford, 1978. A full-length biography.

Drew, Fraser. *John Masefield's England: A Study of the National Themes in His Work.* Rutherford, NJ, 1973.

Errington, Philip W. *John Masefield, the "Great Auk" of English Literature: A Bibliography.* London, 2004. Extensive use of publishers' archives.

Spark, Muriel. *John Masefield.* London, 1953; revised 1992.

Sternlicht, Sanford. *John Masefield.* Boston, 1977.

MASQUE

Stephen Orgel

Disguisings and masked entertainments had always been a feature of the Christmas season throughout Europe, adapting elements of the Roman Saturnalia—the world turned upside down, masters and servants changing places—to the Christian festival, with its central element of epiphany, or revelation. In Jacobean and Caroline England the court masque developed into a literary and poetic genre of real consistency and distinction through the work of a small number of dramatic poets, chiefly Ben Jonson, and perhaps more significantly through the instigation and lavish support of a small number of aristocratic and institutional patrons. But it is important to emphasize that the Stuart court masque, which is for us a chapter in the history of British drama, was in its own time only the most extravagant version of a type of entertainment that existed at all levels of society, and whose form was infinitely various—novelty was itself a virtue in such festivities, and the norms were always changing.

The masque differs from drama in its direct involvement of patrons and audience within the mimetic act, generally as masked participants, and almost always in the concluding dance, called the "revels," in which masquers took partners from among the spectators, and which came to be a defining feature of the form. Masques are in many respects a better index to the complex nature of Renaissance society than drama is. Understanding this social and celebratory genre requires us to take into account not only plot, character, language, and the constraints and economics of the theatrical medium, but also the demands of patronage, the nature of artistic collaboration, the often arcane but nevertheless ubiquitous forms of early modern symbolism, and most important, the presence of an active and specific audience. Moreover, dealing with these celebratory works only through the surviving speeches and descriptions (almost invariably the only evidence available to us) constantly reminds us of how much in this quintessentially Renaissance form—as in many artistic forms of the period—is lost to us: spectacle, music, choreography, complex imagery; most of all, the participation of identifiable patrons and performers who also constitute what is being celebrated. Indeed, the masque was, in a sense, what much of Renaissance art was all about. Quintessentially collaborative in conception and execution, it was more of a game than a show, more an expression of aristocratic identity and privilege than of poetic and dramatic mastery, with the masks providing a degree of freedom, even if only notional, from the constraints of place, office, and self.

FORMAL DEVELOPMENT

It is thanks principally to Ben Jonson that the Stuart masque, uniquely in the history of the genre, exhibits some genuine formal development. Queen Anne had commissioned Samuel Daniel to write the first of her Christmas shows, *The Vision of the Twelve Goddesses*, in 1604. This was a conservative but exemplary work, a majestic procession of idealized roles for the queen and her ladies to enact. In turning to Ben Jonson the next year, she revolutionized the form—the reconception of the masque was clearly as much her work as her poet's, and Jonson says that he "apted" his invention to her commands. The queen proposed a masque in which she and her ladies could appear in blackface—the choice of subject has been considered transgressive or perverse. It is true that one spectator later objected that as African nymphs, the ladies were ugly, and that their delicate costumes were "too light and Curtizan-like"; but other reports describe the performance as rich and exotic, which was surely the queen's intention. Jonson produced, in *The Masque of Blackness* (1605), a work rich in learning, symbolism, and serious poetry, a highly literate and intellectually challenging setting for the songs, dances, and visual splendor that made up most of the evening's entertainment. The striking costumes and ingenious scenery—the body of the work, as the text was its soul—were by Inigo Jones, Jonson's collaborator on these spectacles for the next two decades. For the masque, Jones invented a stage unlike anything the English had seen before, employing perspective settings and complex machinery, and arranging the masquing hall according to the principles of optics, with the royal seat at the apex of the perspective—the king, the best spectator, had the best seat, and indeed, optically only the king's place was perfect. This was the first of a series of court productions through which, over the next three decades, Inigo Jones revolutionized the mechanics and visual properties of the English stage. Though the union of poet and architect ultimately dissolved in a bitter quarrel over the relative importance of their respective roles, the Stuart masque was truly the creation of a uniquely responsive collaboration.

The form as Jonson conceived it was built around antitheses: *The Masque of Blackness* was to be followed and completed by *The Masque of Beauty* (1608), in which the black nymphs become white, bleached by the radiance of the king's presence at the center of both the audience and the spectacle. From this initial progression Jonson developed a bipartite structure, antimasque (which he calls "a foil, or false masque"), and main masque. The antimasque was generally grotesque or comic and, since it included dialogue, was always performed by professional performers—the courtly masquers would not take speaking parts, since this would reduce them to the level of actors; but dancing was the prerogative of every lady and gentleman, and their carefully rehearsed choreographic performances were the high point of the entertainment. Jonson's first fully realized antimasque was in *The Masque of Queens* (1609), in which a coven of witches is banished and superseded by Queen Anne and her ladies in the character of twelve heroic queens of history—Queen Anne, of course, plays a version of herself, Bel-Anna, queen of the Ocean. Thereafter Jonson gradually developed the antimasque into a little comic or satiric prologue, not so much an antithesis to the courtly spectacle as a preparation for it, announcing the conceit of the masque, and epitomizing the world of complexity and disorder that the idealizations of the courtly fiction are to transform and transcend. Notable works in this mode are *Oberon* (1611), written for James's elder son Henry, Prince of Wales, to dance in; *Pleasure Reconciled to Virtue* (1618), in which James's favorite, George Villiers, the marquess (later duke) of Buckingham, did a spectacular impromptu dance; and *The Gipsies Metamorphosed* (1621), commissioned by Buckingham for a visit of the royal family to his country estate. In this, Buckingham and his family played a troupe of gypsies who told the fortunes of the royal party and the other aristocratic guests—a rare instance of the courtly masquers taking speaking roles. The king liked the work so well that it was performed before him three times.

THE MASQUE UNDER CHARLES I

After James's death in 1625 Jonson fell from favor. Under Charles I, masques for the court became more spectacular, more philosophical, and more overtly political, specifically concerned with celebrating and justifying policies that were increasingly unpopular. Unlike James, his son and daughter-in-law took active roles in their masques, and the form focused with a new intensity on the king and queen, and on the idealization of the monarchy. The texts, conceived by more courtly imaginations than Jonson's—Aurelian Townshend, William Davenant, Thomas Carew—adapted recent French and Italian entertainments and invoked the rich symbolism of contemporary Neoplatonism, in which the French-born queen Henrietta Maria had a particular interest. The productions, too, were far more elaborate scenically than any Jones had designed with Jonson. Predictably, the royal penchant for masquing was regularly cited by critics of the regime as a prime instance of its profligacy and immorality, and the impending civil war marked the end of masquing as a feature of English court life; the last court masque, Davenant's *Salmacida Spolia*, performed in 1640, presented the king as an embattled hero, patient and suffering—an incipient martyr. John Milton sneered at the Whitehall theatricals; nevertheless, his *Masque Presented at Ludlow Castle* ("Comus"), performed at a provincial court in 1634, and revised and included in his collected poems in 1645, is evidence enough of the continuing vitality of the form even to the Puritan moral imagination, and Andrew Marvell was employed to compose songs for a masque celebrating the marriage of Oliver Cromwell's daughter as late as 1657.

[*See also* Inigo Jones; Ben Jonson; *and* John Milton.]

EDITIONS

Orgel, Stephen, ed. *The Complete Masks.* New Haven, CT, 1969.

Herford, C. H., and Percy Simpson, eds. *Works.* 11 vols. Oxford, 1925–1952.

FURTHER READING

Bevington, David, and Peter Holbrook, eds. *The Politics of the Stuart Court Masque.* Cambridge, U.K., 1998.

Fletcher, Angus. *The Transcendental Masque: An Essay on Milton's Comus.* Ithaca, NY, 1971.

Johnson, Anthony W. *Ben Jonson: Poetry and Architecture.* Oxford, 1994.

Kogan, Stephen. *The Hieroglyphic King: Wisdom and Idolatry in the Seventeenth-Century Masque.* London and Toronto, 1986.

Lindley, David, ed. *The Court Masque.* Manchester, U.K., 1984.

Orgel, Stephen. *The Illusion of Power: Political Theater in the English Renaissance.* Berkeley, CA, 1975.

Orgel, Stephen. *The Jonsonian Masque.* Cambridge, MA, 1965.

Orgel, Stephen, and Roy Strong. *Inigo Jones: The Theatre of the Stuart Court.* London and Berkeley, CA, 1973.

Strong, Roy. *Splendor at Court: Renaissance Spectacle and the Theater of Power.* Boston, 1973.

W. SOMERSET MAUGHAM

Philip Holden

William Somerset Maugham (1874–1965) occupies a paradoxical position in twentieth-century British literature. In a literary career that spanned seven decades, Maugham wrote his first novel, *Liza of Lambeth*, before the end of the nineteenth century and published his most popular fictional work, *The Razor's Edge*, fifty years later, during the World War II. The range of Maugham's oeuvre is equally expansive: he wrote highly successful novels, short stories, plays, and volumes of travel writing and criticism. If we look at the works more closely, further variety emerges. In the genre of short fiction alone, Maugham was both the originator of the espionage story and a caustic chronicler of colonial society so effective that British Malaya between the wars is often thought of as "Maugham country." Yet although he was an important influence on writers as diverse as George Orwell, Ian Fleming, and V. S. Naipaul, Maugham's critical stock has remained low. Maugham, not altogether convincingly, maintained throughout his life and expressed in the autobiographical *The Summing Up* that he had no "illusions about my literary position," preferring to please an ever-expanding reading public rather than solicit critical acclaim. If he outlived contemporaries such as James Joyce, Virginia Woolf, or D. H. Lawrence, he could not match them in terms of stylistic innovation or thematic complexity. Nevertheless, Maugham remains popular with a transnational reading public. With the rise of critical approaches such as postcolonial and queer studies which stress the social position of literary works above an evaluation of their intrinsic literary merits, the writer's stock may well rise again. Scholars will perhaps be able to follow generations of casual readers and answer Joseph Epstein's anxious question "Is it all right to read Somerset Maugham?" in the affirmative.

Somerset Maugham
Photograph by John Gay, 1949
NATIONAL PORTRAIT GALLERY, LONDON

EARLY WRITING

Maugham's early novels exhibit considerable variety as the author explores the possibilities afforded by a variety of genres. The most enduring are *Liza of Lambeth*, an account of South London slum life influenced by popular late nineteenth century "new realist" writers such as Arthur Morrison, and *Mrs. Craddock*, a sympathetic description of the travails of an intelligent and impulsive woman caught in the stifling embrace of English provincial society. *Mrs. Craddock* introduces four elements that would be central to most of Maugham's fictional works. First, in Maugham's own words, "fact and fiction are . . . intermingled": the small Kentish town of Blackstable is in reality Whitstable, the town in which Maugham spent his later childhood under the care of his uncle after his mother's death. The clear parallels between Maugham's own life and the fictional worlds he created have formed the focus of much critical attention. Maugham's greatest fictional achievement, indeed, may have been the creation of his own public persona as an urbane writer and man of letters; scholars have found it difficult to look away from the spectacle of Maugham's self-created "author function" and instead to focus on the works themselves. Second, *Mrs. Craddock* introduces a central dynamic of passion and enslavement that would feature in much of Maugham's writing. Bertha Leys, the protagonist, wishes to "abase herself before" her oafish lover, Edward Craddock, consumed by the "despotic possession" of her passions that prevent rational action. Third, Maugham is keen to expose the hypocrisy of Edwardian social pretensions, especially those involving class relations: this would become a major object of attention in his plays and short stories. Finally, in its descriptions of Edward, the novel embodies a coded homoeroticism that is present in most of Maugham's writing. Maugham was a medical student in London during the trials of play-wright Oscar Wilde in 1895 and his conviction for "gross indecency"; Maugham's own homosexuality remained closeted throughout his lifetime—even to the extent of his hiding it from his first biographer, Richard Cordell—but it is an important subterranean element in his fiction.

Maugham achieved popular success and financial independence with the performance of his play *Lady Frederick* in 1907, and he devoted much of the next decade to writing theatrically conventional but socially acerbic dramas. His novel *Of Human Bondage* (1915) marks a second turning point in his career. First drafted almost fifteen years before its publication, *Of Human Bondage* returns to the concerns of Maugham's earlier fiction. It is, on Maugham's own admission, an "autobiographical novel," drawing on material from his early life to construct a Bildungsroman in which we follow the growth of its protagonist, Philip Carey. Yet the confident tone of the Victorian Bildungsroman is challenged: Philip is involved in a consuming and humiliating passion for his boyish lover, Mildred Rogers. The ending of the novel, in which Philip makes a decision to marry the homely Sally Altheny, provides narrative closure but does so unconvincingly, given the depth of Philip's earlier humiliation at Mildred's hands.

LATER FICTION

Of Human Bondage would be the last time that Maugham drew extensively on material from his childhood. Other experiences had overtaken him: the short stories in *Ashenden*, for instance, were inspired by his work for the British intelligence services in Switzerland during the early part of World War I. Yet Maugham's most important subject matter was to be found further afield. On 14 November 1916, he and his companion Gerald Haxton arrived in Honolulu on the steamer S.S. *Great Northern*. This was the first of a series of journeys he made beyond Europe and North America over the two decades that followed. Maugham would travel to Australia, China, Southeast Asia, and India, and he would make Asia the setting for his best-known and most ambitious writing.

Maugham's short stories, novels, and travel writing set in Asia and Polynesia gain their strength from a central contradiction: they succeed because of, not despite, their writer's scanty firsthand knowledge of the countries he visited. Preceding and succeeding British writers of fiction with an Asian setting, such as Rudyard Kipling, Hugh Clifford, Joseph Conrad, Leonard Woolf, and George Or-

well, had a diversity of experiences in Asia, but they all shared a period of prolonged residence in the regions that they chose to write about. Maugham's fictions show his status as a visitor. They are set in the world of colonial European elites and have few complex Asian characters, frequently repeating rather than challenging Orientalist binarisms between a primordial, sensuous East and a modern, rational West. The classic Maugham short story replicates this binarism on the level of narrative structure. The writer makes extensive use of nested narratives, in which the rational structure of a discussion between two British men at a club or restaurant contains the wildness of a narrative of transgression. One man tells his story to the other, often a writer or a doctor with a barely concealed similarity to Maugham himself: after the story is told, we return to the scene of narration, and order is restored.

Maugham's Asian stories and novels, however, use their underlying binarisms to launch a devastating critique of the hypocrisies of European elites in colonial society. Britain's colonies had already played a key role in Maugham's early work: *Smith* and several of his other plays, for instance, expose the rigidity of Edwardian and Georgian England through the return of a less socially punctilious but more fundamentally human character from a transformative sojourn in the colonies; early novels like *The Explorer* draw their inspiration from the British Empire as a scene of imagined frontier romance. From *The Moon and Sixpence* onward, Maugham's fictions contrast the putative natural world of Asia and Polynesia to the artificiality of the morally hypocritical colonial societies that govern it. As an outsider with no stake in the colonial order, Maugham could write stories that cut close to the bone. Many of his stories were based on a conscious intermingling of fiction and fact: "The Letter," for instance, in which a lawyer and a planter conspire to conceal the planter's wife's cold-blooded murder of her lover, was cleverly adapted from a 1911 court case in Kuala Lumpur. Such thin fictionalization did not go unchallenged; under threat of legal action, Maugham had to change the names of the protagonists of *The Painted Veil* and move its setting from Hong Kong to the imaginary colony of Tching-Yen.

DOUBLENESS, LONELINESS, AND MODERNITY

From the perspective of the twenty-first century, it would be anachronistic to call Maugham in any way anticolonialist. In many aspects—for instance, in its enactment of conflicts regarding social respectability through the sexualized bodies of European women—Maugham's exotic fiction simply reiterates colonial discourse in a different key. Yet the best of the Malayan stories, collected in *The Casuarina Tree* and *Ah King*, as well as the often overlooked novel set in the Dutch East Indies, *The Narrow Corner*, have something more than this to offer. In a preface to a collection of travel writing, Maugham describes himself as someone who continually lived "two modes of life," who experienced the world through "two liberties, two points of view," living always with doubleness. The superficial reference here is to Maugham's birth, childhood, and later residence in France and his adolescence and literary success in England. However, as Jeffrey Meyers points out, the duality of Maugham's life and works runs much deeper than this. Maugham's closeted homosexuality and production of a public persona introduce a dynamic of surfaces and concealed depth into his fiction: his narrators are strangers, fascinated by the truths they uncover but fundamentally estranged from them.

In his essay "El Greco," one of his few published comments on homosexuality, Maugham noted homosexual men's attachment to "decoration" and focus on the superficial, their "small power of invention but . . . wonderful gift for delightful embroidery." The homosexual, Maugham asserted, "stands on the bank, aloof and ironical, and watches the river of life flow on." Seen retrospectively and shorn of the societal homophobia to which they respond, Maugham's comments seem prescient of the insights of theorists of gender and sexuality such as Judith Butler, that dissident sexualities may result in the performance of conventional sexual roles in a manner which is slightly "off key" and thus reveals their constructed nature. Maugham's distant, ironic narrators and focalizers are alternately amused, appalled, or fascinated by the stories of heterosexual passion and unmanly or unwomanly behavior that they observe or are told, but they never completely identify with them. This central dynamic of investment and distance might be extended outward to a view of Maugham as a quintessentially modern writer, detached from community, negotiating continually in his texts between the intratextual stories of fiction and the extratextual narrated reality of everyday life. Novels such as *The Narrow Corner* are indeed densely intertextual, populated by characters from the world of Maugham's earlier fiction. In his last novel on Asia, *The Razor's Edge*, Maugham goes further in his play on the doubleness of life and art, introducing a narrator who is named W. Somerset Maugham.

In the final three decades of his life, Maugham continued to produce novels, criticism, and a series of autobiographical works that concealed as much as they told. "In my twenties," Maugham wrote in a summary of his career in *The Summing Up*, "the critics said I was brutal, in my thirties they said I was flippant, in my forties they said I was cynical, in my fifties they said I was competent, and now in my sixties they say I am superficial." In comparison with his peers in the twentieth century, critical and literary historical assessments are likely to stress competency and superficiality. One might see Maugham's vast and varied oeuvre as filler, mortar in the cracks between his greater contemporaries. Yet Maugham's consciously middlebrow fiction might be as interesting as more avant-garde writing in terms of the social formations in which it is embedded. In its elegant but always slightly uncomfortable conformity with generic and discursive conventions, Maugham's best work hints at the brutality and cynicism of the ordinary, the calculated cruelties of the everyday in modern life.

[*See also* The Bildungsroman *and* Orientalism.]

SELECTED WORKS

NOVELS

Liza of Lambeth (1897)
The Making of a Saint (1898)
The Hero (1901)
Mrs. Craddock (1902)
The Merry-Go-Round (1904)
The Bishop's Apron: A Study in the Origins of a Great Family (1906)
The Explorer (1908)
The Magician (1908)
Of Human Bondage (1915)
The Moon and Sixpence (1919)
The Painted Veil (1925)
Cakes and Ale: or the Skeleton in the Cupboard (1930)
The Narrow Corner (1932)
Theatre (1937)
Christmas Holiday (1939)
Up at the Villa (1941)
The Hour Before the Dawn (1942)
The Razor's Edge (1944)
Then and Now (1946)
Catalina (1948)

SHORT STORY COLLECTIONS

The Trembling of a Leaf (1921)
The Casuarina Tree (1926)
Ashenden: or The British Agent (1928)
Six Stories Written in the First Person Singular (1931)
The Book-Bag (1932)
Ah King (1933)
East and West: the Collected Stories (1934)
Cosmopolitans: Very Short Stories (1936)
The Mixture as Before (1940)
Creatures of Circumstance (1947)
Quartet (1948)
Trio (1950)
Encore (1952)
The World Over (1952)
The Complete Short Stories of W. Somerset Maugham (1953)
Seventeen Lost Stories (1969)

PLAYS

A Man of Honour (1903)
Lady Frederick (1912)
Jack Straw (1912)
Mrs. Dot (1912)
Penelope (1912)
The Explorer (1912)
The Tenth Man (1913)
Landed Gentry (1913)
Smith (1913)
The Land of Promise (1913)
The Unknown (1920)
The Circle (1921)
Caesar's Wife (1922)
East of Suez (1922)
Our Betters (1923)
Home and Beauty (1923)
The Unattainable (1923)
Loaves and Fishes (1924)
The Constant Wife (1927)
The Letter (1927)
The Sacred Flame (1928)
The Bread-Winner (1930)
For Services Rendered (1932)
Sheppey (1933)
Collected Plays (1931–1934)
The Noble Spaniard (1953)

TRAVEL WRITING

Orientations (1899)
The Land of the Blessed Virgin: Sketches and Impressions of Andalusia (1905)
On a Chinese Screen (1922)
The Gentleman in the Parlour: A Record of a Journey from Rangoon to Haiphong (1930)
Don Fernando: or Variations on Some Spanish Themes (1935)
My South Sea Island (1936)

CRITICISM, MEMOIRS, AND MISCELLANEOUS

The Summing Up (1938)
France at War (1940)
Books and You (1940)
Strictly Personal (1941)
Great Novelists and Their Novels (1948)
A Writer's Notebook (1949)
The Writer's Point of View (1951)
The Vagrant Mood (1952)
Points of View (1958)
Purely for My Pleasure (1962)
Selected Prefaces and Introductions (1963)
A Traveller in Romance: Uncollected Writings (1984)

FURTHER READING

Bassett, Troy James. "W. Somerset Maugham: An Annotated Bibliography of Criticism, 1969–1997." *English Literature in Transition (1880–1920)* 41 (1998): 132–184. Lists critical articles in several European languages, in addition to listing and supplementing earlier bibliographical resources.

Calder, Robert. *Willie: The Life of W. Somerset Maugham.* London, 1989. The most sympathetic biographical account, written in part in response to Morgan; draws on extensive interviews with Maugham's companion Alan Searle.

Curtis, Anthony, and John Whitehead, eds. *W. Somerset Maugham: The Critical Heritage.* London, 1987. Useful collection, largely of contemporary reviews of Maugham's works.

Holden, Philip. *Orienting Masculinity, Orienting Nation: W. Somerset Maugham's Exotic Fiction.* Westport, CT, 1996. Explores Maugham's fiction set in Asia and the South Pacific through the lens of colonial discourse analysis and queer theory.

Innes, Christopher. "Somerset Maugham: Popular Comedy Versus Social Criticism." In *Modern British Drama: The Twentieth Century,* 253–261. Cambridge, U.K., 2002. Critically astute overview of Maugham's plays in the context of twentieth-century British comic drama.

Meyers, Jeffrey. *Somerset Maugham: A Life.* New York,

2004. Competent scholarly biography with extensive commentary on the literary works; Meyers had access to several new sources and corrects errors in Morgan's account.

Morgan, Ted. *Maugham.* New York, 1980. The only scholarly biography to receive assistance from Maugham's literary executor, Spencer Curtis Brown; paints a harsh but not unconvincing portrait of "a man whose defects were glaring, but . . . should not be used to diminish his accomplishments" (p. xxi).

IAN MCEWAN

Megan M. Quigley

Since Ian McEwan's first collection of stories, *First Love, Last Rites*, won the Somerset Maugham Award in 1976, he has been a major voice in contemporary British fiction. He is often called the best British writer of his generation, which includes Martin Amis, Julian Barnes, Angela Carter, Salman Rushdie, and Kazuo Ishiguro. McEwan has written novels, screenplays, children's stories, and a libretto for an oratorio on the topic of nuclear annihilation. His subject matter is as varied as his choice of genre, alternating between sadomasochism (which earned him early in his career the title Ian MacAbre) and feminism, between historical fiction and contemporary psychological intrigue. Nonetheless, there is something distinctive about reading a work by McEwan. His writing has been called "the art of unease," an apt term for the discomfort and disquiet his works invoke. In *The Child in Time*, McEwan's protagonist realizes his marriage ended because "there had been a malevolent intervention." McEwan's works exquisitely portray "malevolent interventions"—child snatchings, hot-air balloon disasters, and car crashes. His characters' efforts to make sense of such incidents and to regain or to maintain some kind of security in the incidents' aftermath often motivate his plots. The novels' occasional failures to coalesce into more than distinct set pieces may say less about McEwan's skill in plotting than about his reluctance to give coherence to a world that he says "distresses me and makes me anxious."

THE MYTH OF THE TWO McEWANS

McEwan made his name as a writer of dark short stories in which disturbing subject matter (incest, murder, violence) is rendered in stark, unemotional prose. For example, in "Homemade," an adolescent boy rapes his ten-year-old sister and is proud of losing his virginity, while "Dead as They Come" describes a man's erotic obsession with a store mannequin. McEwan's later works widen their scope, taking on political topics (government propaganda, patriarchy, terrorism) and a greater cast of char-

acters and historical time periods. What Kiernan Ryan has skeptically called the "received wisdom" about McEwan's career is that he began as a "writer obsessed with the perverse, the grotesque, the macabre," but grew out of this adolescent style of writing "to a more mature engagement with the wider world of history and society" (p. 2). This easy division fails to account for important continuities in McEwan's work, overstating the sensationalism of the earlier stories while underestimating the eroticism and perverse power games still at large in the later works.

Ian Russell McEwan was born on 21 June 1948 in Aldershot, Hampshire, though he spent much of his childhood abroad, in Singapore and in Libya, where his father, a Scottish sergeant major in the British Army, was stationed. McEwan has said that he was mentally an only child, since his step-siblings were a decade older than he, and his early stories and his first novel, *The Cement Garden* (1978), seem fascinated by potential sibling relationships. *The Cement Garden* has been described as a modern *Lord of the Flies*, wherein four siblings, recently bereft of both parents, first bury their mother's body in cement in the basement, and then unsuccessfully attempt to reconstruct a "normal" family life. Another element of McEwan's childhood that reverberates thematically throughout his works was his experience of being gathered for safety into armed military camps when Britain and France invaded Egypt over the Suez Canal in 1956. He has remarked that his childhood realization that political changes intimately affect individuals' experiences underscores the political engagement in his works. In his work for television his political bent is particularly self-evident. *The Imitation Game* (1981), for example, renounces the patriarchal limitations on women during World War II and their continuation in today's society, and in *The Ploughman's Lunch* (1985) the antihero is writing a revisionary work on the Suez Crisis. After being educated at Woolverstone School in Suffolk and the University of Sussex, McEwan earned his MA at the University of East Anglia, under the auspices of two famous literary figures,

Malcolm Bradbury and Angus Wilson. Stories from his thesis became his acclaimed first collection *First Love, Last Rites*. By 1983, having published another collection of stories and two novels, he was named one of the Twenty Best Young British Novelists by *Granta*.

McEwan himself, though, was feeling the need for a change in his writing. He told John Haffenden in an interview, "I had begun to feel rather trapped by the kinds of things I had been writing. I had been labeled as the chronicler of comically exaggerated psychopathic states of mind or of adolescent anxiety, snot and pimples" (p. 173). The difference between *The Comfort of Strangers* (1981) and *The Child in Time* (1987) seems to be a thematic watermark in McEwan's oeuvre. *The Comfort of Strangers*, reminiscent of Thomas Mann's *Death in Venice*, examines a young couple's boredom while on holiday until they meet two strangers. The strangest characteristic of this horrifying tale may be the young couple's apparent complicity in their doom, the similarity between their erotic rejuvenation and the fatal "comfort" provided by their psychopathic new friends. *The Child in Time*, published after McEwan's writing for television and—importantly, he has said—after he had become a father, turns away from this earlier gothicism. It begins rather than ends with an awful event, in this case the kidnapping of a man's three-year-old daughter, and certainly returns to earlier themes, in particular the desire to regress to childhood. However, the regression of the aspiring statesman in *The Child in Time*, as he carefully builds his tree house and begins to live like a boy, is somehow beautiful, whereas the treatment of a similar theme in an earlier collection, the monologue "Conversation with a Cupboard Man," provokes disgust and alarm. *The Child in Time*, moreover, works toward a positive resolution, an affirmation of life and love. A mixture of tones and genres (sometimes realism, sometimes magical realism), *The Child in Time* varies between a polemic against the Thatcher government and a love letter. It received much critical acclaim, and won the Whitbread Novel Award in 1987. McEwan's other works of this middle period include *The Innocent* (1990), a spy thriller set in Cold War Berlin that was compared to the achievements of John LeCarré and Graham Greene, and *Black Dogs* (1992), wherein a young man tries to stitch together his family's memoirs.

The controversy over the BBC's censorship of McEwan's "Solid Geometry" in 1979 demonstrates how the myth of the two McEwans has more to do with the audience's expectations than with the actual written material. "Solid Geometry," a screenplay adapted from a story in his first collection of the same name, depicts the end of a marriage between a man obsessed with his edition of his great-grandfather's journals and his new-age wife. Four days before its recording the BBC halted the production. In the play, the husband, ironically, must submit to his wife's belief in nonrational ideas—ideas such as "Dimensionality is a function of consciousness"—in order to make her disappear. In life, with further irony, McEwan himself needed to accept the irrationality of the censors when the play, which is more interested in the relationship between science and faith than in perversity, was censored for its "grotesque and bizarre sexual elements." Though the only real grotesquerie is the presence of a "pickled penis" on Albert's desk, trepidation over another Ian MacAbre work led to the play's censorship.

FROM *ENDURING LOVE* TO *SATURDAY*

McEwan's admiration for Nabokov's remark that readers must first "learn to fondle the details" certainly applies to the appreciator of McEwan's own clear prose. Undoubtedly one of the most powerful images in his works is that of the man clinging to the hot-air balloon at the beginning of *Enduring Love*:

> He had been on the rope so long that I began to think he might stay there until the balloon drifted down or the boy came to his senses and found the valve that released the gas, or until some beam, or god, or some other impossible cartoon thing, came and gathered him up. Even as I had that hope, we saw him slip down right to the end of the rope. And still he hung there. For two seconds, three, four. And then he let go. Even then, there was a fraction of time when he barely fell, and I still thought there was a chance that a freak physical law, a furious thermal, some phenomenon no more astonishing than the one we were witnessing, would intervene and bear him up. We watched him drop. You could see the acceleration. No forgiveness, no special dispensation for flesh, or bravery, or kindness. Only ruthless gravity. And from somewhere, perhaps from him, perhaps from some indifferent crow, a thin squawk cut through the stilled air. He fell as he had hung, a stiff little black stick. I've never seen such a terrible thing as that falling man.

McEwan combines suspense writing, "two seconds, three, four," with liturgical references, "no special dispensation for flesh," with literary resonances (we are back to Icarus in W. H. Auden's "Musée des Beaux Arts" or to the "indifferent" drop in W. B. Yeats's "Leda and the Swan"), all delivered in the consistent first-person narration of his protagonist. The reader learns much about the science writer Joe Rose from the language he chooses, just as the religious obsessions of Jed Perry, Joe's stalker, are foreshadowed. A central conflict in McEwan's book—theology versus science—is crystallized in a single passage, just as the apparently minor shift between "I" and "we" becomes entirely significant as Jed's feeling of unity leads to his obsessive "enduring love."

Amsterdam, Atonement, and *Saturday*, McEwan's three most recent novels (which stand out in his canon for their one word titles), demonstrate his ability to assimilate vast quantities of knowledge for the benefit of his fiction. *Amsterdam*, which tells the story of three men who reconnect at their former lover's funeral, is a cutting social satire, sending up the sixties generation who seem to have resigned their former rebelliousness for creature comforts. In this short book, McEwan demonstrates his copious knowledge of music and journalism in order to describe the occupations and preoccupations of his characters. Although McEwan won the prestigious Booker Prize for *Amsterdam* in 1998, many critics believe the prize was really overdue and perhaps awarded to the wrong book in his oeuvre. *Atonement*, in contrast, earned rave reviews, and was also a popular best seller on both sides of the Atlantic. McEwan's research at the Imperial War Museum bears fruit in the careful descriptions of Briony Tallis's experience as a nurse trainee at a London hospital during World War II and of Robbie Turner's bewilderment during the British Army's retreat from Dunkirk. *Atonement* asks why Briony, a young girl who would be writer, pinpoints an innocent neighbor as the criminal who has assaulted her cousin, and why she clings to her story even in the face of doubt. The sexual nature of the crime, as well as the erotic encounter Briony accidentally interrupts between her sister and her sister's lover, returns McEwan's readers to the anxious adolescent sexuality of his early stories. Briony's desire to atone, however, and the novel's self-conscious questioning of a literary work's effectiveness as a remedy for a grievous sin are new to *Atonement*. McEwan writes, "Did she really think she could hide behind some borrowed notions of modern writing, and drown her guilt in a stream—three streams!—of consciousness?"

Saturday has been hailed as the best post-9/11 work of fiction, and it is also McEwan's most obviously autobiographical work yet. A book set over the course of one twenty-four-hour period, it shares characteristics with earlier masterpieces of that genre including *Ulysses* and *Mrs. Dalloway*, and it is also McEwan's first effort at writing entirely in the present tense, a quality that explains *Saturday*'s occasional resemblance to John Updike's *Rabbit* novels. Henry Perowne, the protagonist, is a brain surgeon—a profession that lends well to the novel's absorption in the mental health of individuals in current society. Perowne dislikes literature but he shares McEwan's love of wine, squash, and his wife; "What a stroke of luck, that the woman he loves is also his wife," Perowne muses. *Saturday* strives to capture and present current society as it is, in all its ambiguities and anxieties, while also depicting what a man is willing to do when his family falls under threat. Although it received mostly glowing reviews, the display of scientific knowledge and terminology has led some critics to despair, whereas others have feared that its political agenda overwhelms the plot. McEwan himself is not unaware of such a concern, both in *Saturday* and as he goes forward in his career: "I am aware of the danger that in trying to write more politically," he has stated, "I could take up moral positions that might preempt or exclude that rather mysterious and unreflective element that is so important in fiction." However, the reading public and critics concur—no matter whether they prefer the early, brutal stories, or the later, longer novels of ideas—that McEwan has mastered the "mysterious and unreflective element" which creates great fiction.

[*See also* Martin Amis; Angela Carter; *and* Reading.]

SELECTED WORKS

First Love, Last Rites (1975)
In Between the Sheets, and Other Stories (1978)
The Cement Garden (1978)
The Comfort of Strangers (1981)
The Imitation Game: Three Plays for Television (1981)
Or Shall We Die? Words for an Oratorio Set to Music by Michael Berkeley (1983)
The Ploughman's Lunch (1985)
The Child in Time (1987)
The Innocent (1990)
Black Dogs (1992)
The Daydreamer (illustrated by Anthony Browne; 1994)
Enduring Love (1997)
Amsterdam (1998)
Atonement (2001)
Saturday (2005)

FURTHER READING

Byrnes, Christina. "Ian McEwan—Pornographer or Prophet?" *Contemporary Review* 266 (June 1995): 320–

323. Assessment of McEwan up through *The Day-dreamer*, weighing contradictory reactions to his works.

Finney, Brian. "Briony's Stand Against Oblivion: The Making of Fiction in Ian McEwan's *Atonement*." *Journal of Modern Literature* 27, no. 3 (Winter 2004): 68–82. Powerful reading of *Atonement*.

Haffenden, John. *Novelists in Interview*. London, 1985. An excellent early interview with McEwan, particularly good on the early works and the changes of his career.

"Ian McEwan with Martin Amis." *Writers Talk: Ideas of Our Time*. ICA Video, 1989. Humorous and insightful video of an interview between the two authors.

Malcolm, David. *Understanding Ian McEwan*. Columbia, SC, 2002. Comprehensive overview of McEwan's works up through *Amsterdam*.

Ryan, Kiernan. *Ian McEwan*. Writers and Their Work Series. Plymouth, U.K., 1994. Influential study of McEwan's works up through *Black Dogs*, particularly interested in continuities in McEwan's career and his relationship to feminism.

Slay, Jack L., Jr. *Ian McEwan*. English Author Series. New York, 1996. Good introduction, especially for a contextualization of McEwan among his generation of British writers.

Tait, Theo. "*A Rational Diagnosis*." 11 February 2005. Moderate review of *Saturday* but useful analysis of McEwan's craft through 2005.

JOHN McGAHERN

Eamon Maher

John McGahern was born in Dublin in 1934, one of the seven children of his father, a sergeant in the newly formed police force, and his mother, a teacher. He spent most of his youth in the western counties of Leitrim and Roscommon, and after finishing school he traveled to Dublin for training to become a teacher. In spite of a relatively modest output of six novels, three collections of short stories, and one play, McGahern's oeuvre illuminates the evolution of Irish society during the second half of the twentieth century. His works chart the emotional lives of individuals who struggle to find a worthwhile role in society, and who have been marked by oppressive and sometimes abusive childhoods. The Ireland he captures is a far cry from the economic boom and cultural sea change brought about by the phenomenon known as the "Celtic Tiger." Perhaps this explains his popularity in Ireland and abroad: his work is the swan song of a traditional rural Ireland that is on the verge of extinction.

AN UNEVEN START

With the publication of *The Barracks* in 1963, McGahern broke out spectacularly on the Irish literary scene. The novel earned him the prestigious AE Memorial Award and a Macauley Fellowship. It relates the final months in the life of Elizabeth, a middle-aged woman forced to come to terms with the news that she has terminal cancer. She had returned to Ireland exhausted from her work as a nurse in London during the Blitz and met her future husband, Reegan. Elizabeth tends to the needs of her husband and stepchildren while always remaining something of an outsider. Reegan is one of the many disillusioned veterans of the Irish War of Independence against British hegemony that one encounters in McGahern's writings. His life after the struggle never achieves the same intensity, and he is frustrated at having to take orders from superiors like Quirke, who is younger than he is, and for whom he feels nothing but disdain.

The most striking aspect of this novel is how a young novelist manages to get inside the mind of his heroine.

On the threshold of death, the most ordinary scenes assume a beauty and an intensity that they never possessed before the onset of Elizabeth's illness. She uses her memory and her deep spirituality to help her to die with dignity. Her husband is unable to offer her any real support, as he has difficulty facing up to the prospect of losing a second wife and is obsessed by his conflict with Quirke.

In his second novel, *The Dark* (1965), McGahern presents an adolescent male who is haunted by a promise he made to his mother that he would one day say a mass for her. This vocation to the priesthood is never realized, however, as the young man feels unworthy in the face of God because of his problems with masturbation and the sexual abuse inflicted on him by his widowed father. To describe taboo issues such as these, and even to hint at clerical sexual abuse, as McGahern does in *The Dark*, was to place oneself at a remove from the dominant ideology of 1960s Ireland. The Catholic Church was quite suspicious of writers in general, but it was certainly not going to tolerate such a stark portrayal of the hidden Ireland as that contained in this novel. The book was promptly banned by the Censorship of Publications Board, and the archbishop of Dublin, John Charles McQuaid, insisted that McGahern be removed from his position as a schoolteacher in Clontarf, Dublin. Sickened by the affair, the writer chose to leave Ireland for a few years.

McGahern's second novel, therefore, is better known for the controversy associated with it than for its literary qualities. In addition, its stark realism and gloomy atmosphere, the presence of a domineering and abusive father, and the terrible feelings of guilt and sinfulness that take hold of the main character combine to create a picture of a repressed and repressive society.

EXPERIMENTS WITH STYLE

The Leavetaking was first published in 1974, and McGahern took the unusual step of rewriting parts of it and publishing the revised text in 1984. In his preface to the second edition, he speaks of having been "too close to the

'Idea,' " as a result of which "the work lacked that distance, that inner formality or calm, that all writing, no matter what it is attempting, must possess." The book is divided into two parts, the first of which deals with the death of the narrator's mother and his guilt at not having fulfilled his promise to her that he would become a priest. There are obvious autobiographical overtones in the relationship between the narrator and his mother, a schoolteacher. As in McGahern's real life, the children stay with their mother in their country cottage while the father works as a policeman in the town of Cootehall, some distance away. One evening the father arrives from Cootehall and impregnates his wife, despite warnings against her conceiving again after she underwent a mastectomy. When she dies shortly after giving birth, the young man feels anger at his father. He also resents the fact that he did not spend every moment he could have with his mother as she was dying, but he was fearful that if he stayed any longer, he would not have the strength to leave at all.

All these events are played out in the mind of the narrator, who is spending his last day as a schoolteacher before his dismissal by the parish priest for his irregular marriage to an American divorcée in a registry office in London. (McGahern was similarly married to a Finnish theater director and translator during the year he spent in London before the publication of *The Dark*, which contributed to his own dismissal.) The book is notable for the way in which it is narrated (it alternatively uses "I," "You," and "He" narrators) as well as for the fact that it portrays a couple who have the possibility of enjoying a healthy sexual relationship and a happy life together.

The Pornographer (1979) explores the changing face of Ireland, with its dance halls, sexual promiscuity, and hard drinking. The traditional religious practices and strong family bonds of the early novels set in the country give way to the blind search for pleasure and new experiences in Dublin and London. The nameless pornographer gets involved with a thirty-eight-year-old bank clerk, Josephine, who does not want him to use condoms and ends up getting pregnant. The pornographer decides that she should give up the child for adoption (the abortion option is ruled out by Josephine, who travels to London to give birth), and he resolves not to have anything to do with their child once it is born. His heartlessness on this front is in stark contrast to the kindness he displays toward his aunt, who is dying in a hospital. He falls in love with a nurse he meets during one of his visits and, at the end of the novel, decides that he will go back to the farm that was bequeathed to him by his dead parents and live there with the nurse, if she will agree to marry him.

SHORT STORIES

McGahern is rightly hailed as a master of the short story genre. He published three collections: *Nightlines* (1970), *Getting Through* (1978), and *High Ground* (1985). In 1992 he brought all three collections together in slightly amended form in *The Collected Stories*. He has described the short story as a "small explosion," a genre that demands that the reader fill in the blanks and that the writer get straight into the action. The themes and settings are similar to what one encounters in the novels: strained relationships and misunderstandings between sons and their fathers, a futile search for sexual and emotional harmony between men and women, and the daily grind of working the land and making ends meet. Among the best stories are "The Country Funeral," "Gold Watch," "Wheels," "Old-fashioned," and "Peaches."

CHRONICLING THE LAST MOMENTS OF TRADITIONAL RURAL IRELAND

Amongst Women (1990) is the book that gave McGahern international recognition as a novelist of genuine capacity. Short-listed for the Booker Prize, it won many literary awards in Ireland and was made into a highly successful television drama. A tightly constructed and beautifully written novel, it portrays the fortunes of the Moran family and their farm near the west coast of Ireland. It is clear that the eleven-year gap between this work and McGahern's previous novel was spent honing the prose and capturing the personality of the book's enigmatic main character, Michael Moran. Yet another veteran of the War of Independence, this patriarch rules his family with the same military efficiency that he displayed as leader of a guerrilla unit. Aloof and self-absorbed, he is capable of both charm and violence. At the end of the novel, Moran bemoans the departure of all his children, who go to work in London and Dublin. He is left alone with his second wife, Rose, and sees with poignancy the beauty of the landscape which had escaped him all the years he was struggling to bring it under his control: "To die was never to look on all this again. . . . He had never realised when in the midst of confident life what an amazing glory he was part of." While the farm, called Great Meadow, seems like a monument to the unchanging rituals of rural life, it can be seen that transformations are near at hand. None of the Moran children stay on the land, and the emergence of the automobile and a more relaxed attitude to sexuality seem to threaten the equilibrium and sobriety espoused by their father's generation.

That They May Face the Rising Sun (2002) relates a year in the life of a community around a lake, in a setting that is close to McGahern's own abode in County Leitrim. Not a traditional novel in that it has no real plot or character development, it is more an elegiac evocation of a way of life about to disappear. It is significant that no inhabitant of the lakeside community is less than middle-aged, and there is a real sense that they are the last of their kind. Hence the comment of the local handyman, Patrick Ryan, is significant: "After us, there'll be nothing but the water hen and the swan."

The various incidents that occur are related mainly from the point of view of a returned emigrant and former seminarian, Ruttledge, who comes back from London with his wife, Kate, to try his hand at farming. There are many similarities between him and McGahern, who continues to farm in Leitrim. There is a wonderful array of characters: Ruttledge's uncle, a local businessman familiarly known as "The Shah"; a committed womanizer, John Quinn; the loveable Jamesie and his wife, Mary; and the hired hand Bill Evans. There is a wistful tone in the descriptions of the landscape, and one gets the impression that McGahern is telling over the plants and animals before the full impact of modernity changes everything.

With this novel McGahern broke new ground, for there is a sense that he is now celebrating an Ireland that had formerly been the object of critical appraisal and a source of pain. The book was warmly received by the critics and outsold *Amongst Women* in the United States within months of its publication (under the title *By the Lake*).

[*See also* Seamus Heaney *and* Paul Muldoon.]

SELECTED WORKS

NOVELS

The Barracks (1963)
The Dark (1965)
The Leavetaking (1974; revised version 1984)
The Pornographer (1979)
Amongst Women (1990)
That They May Face the Rising Sun (2002; American ed., By the Lake)

SHORT STORY COLLECTIONS

Nightlines (1970)
Getting Through (1978)
High Ground (1985)
The Collected Stories (1992)

DRAMA

The Power of Darkness (1991)

FURTHER READING

Irish University Review 35.1 (Spring/Summer 2005). Special ssue on John McGahern.

Maher, Eamon. *John McGahern: From the Local to the Universal.* Dublin, 2003.

Sampson, Denis. *Outstaring Nature's Eye: The Fiction of John McGahern.* Washington, DC, 1993.

Sampson, Denis, ed. *Canadian Journal of Irish Studies* 17.1 (July 1991). Special issue on John McGahern.

Whyte, James. *History, Myth, and Ritual in the Fiction of John McGahern: Strategies of Transcendence.* Lewiston, NY, 2002.

MEDIEVAL ANGLO-LATIN LITERATURE

David Townsend

Most literature produced in England up to the fourteenth century was written not in the native tongue of its authors but in an acquired language of high culture associated with a distant metropolitan center whose hold on the European imagination long survived that city's collapse as an imperial capital. That is to say, this literature was written in Latin, the classical language of Rome. The circumstances in which Anglo-Latin literature was produced thus necessarily emphasize complex negotiations of center and periphery, of the literary work and its supplementary context, of the individual's subjectivity split by the exigencies of language, of self and other. Such a characterization troubles certain idealized assumptions about the cultural unity of the Latin Middle Ages that were enshrined in much twentieth-century medievalist scholarship. At the same time, the similarity of such cultural tensions to those addressed by postcolonial interpretation, or for that matter by psychoanalytic or "queer" interpretation, may surprise students more familiar with later eras. That surprise may expose a blind spot in these later fields of study. Anglo-Latin literature matters, then, at least in part because its existence forces us to rewrite the grand narrative of English literature—or, more specifically, to reconsider the representation of its earliest cultural dynamics.

FROM THE CONVERSION
TO THE SACK OF LINDISFARNE (793)

Shortly after their arrival in the year 669, Archbishop Theodore and his assistant Hadrian founded an influential school at Canterbury. The seventh-century English also had access to Latin letters through Irish scholars active in Northumbria. These two sources of erudition flowed into the beginnings of an Anglo-Latin tradition. From its outset, Latin literature in England involved a linguistic estrangement that distinguished it from contemporary Continental practice. The radical difference of England's Germanic vernacular from the acquired language of high culture must have emphasized to native speakers the gap between the two spheres of their linguistic experience, in a way that the relative proximity of Latin to the emerging Romance vernaculars would not for the earliest English writers' Frankish contemporaries.

Anglo-Latin begins with Aldhelm, bishop of Sherborne (c. 630–709). Aldhelm's prose works—that is, his letters and the prose *De virginitate* (On virginity)—display notoriously extended sentence structure and exuberant vocabulary, though the complexities are usually more a matter of lexical accretion than of elaborate syntax. (He often reads like an unfortunately clever teenager making too free with a thesaurus.) His verse works include a collection of one hundred riddles, which originally formed an appendix to a treatise on metrics, and a verse version of *De virginitate*. The riddles circulated separately in medieval manuscripts, often with extensive glosses that attest their importance for centuries as a teaching text. Several bear significantly as analogues on the study of the vernacular Exeter Book riddles. The double prose and verse *De virginitate* together constitute the first instance in England of the *opus geminatum*—twin prose and verse versions of the same work, explicitly announced by the author as two halves of a single whole.

The first sustained flowering of Anglo-Latin literature encompassed the eighth century (extended to the death of Alcuin of York in 804). Its center of gravity lay not in the southern kingdoms under Canterbury's more direct influence, but in Northumbria, where the Irish presence was more strongly felt. The opening decades of the century produced a wealth of hagiography (texts having to do with the veneration of saints), including an anonymous life of Pope Gregory the Great written at Whitby (between 680 and 704), an anonymous life of Saint Cuthbert (between 699 and 705), Felix of Croyland's life of the hermit Saint Guthlac (between 713 and 749), and Stephan of Ripon's life of the litigious romanizing bishop Wilfrid (between 710 and 720). Various texts connected to English missionary figures active on the Continent also survive. The preeminent author of the early eighth century was Bede (673–735); in addition to his masterpiece, the *Historia ecclesiastica gentis Anglorum* (Ecclesiastical history of the English people), he wrote verse and prose versions of the life of Cuthbert, as well as many "nonliterary" works such as biblical commentaries and treatises on grammar, metrics, and the computation of time.

It is useful here to look at a key passage from Bede's *Historia* and a parallel version of the same story from the Whitby life of Gregory. According to Uppinder Mehan and David Townsend, together they illustrate something of the dynamics by which the literary supremacy of Latin introduced the alienation of the split subject into the earliest recorded stages of English cultural self-consciousness. The two passages record variants of an anecdote wherein the future pope, en route through the Roman Forum, encounters several English boys whose exotic appearance—notably their pale skin and blonde hair—attracts him and fires his subsequent dedication to the conversion of their race. In both versions, the authoritative gaze of the Roman ecclesiastic not only observes the national identity of these youths from afar, but in some real sense confers that identity upon them. Being told that their people are called the Angles, he twists the name into significance through a Latin pun: "Not Angles," he replies, "but angels." He thus elides the fragmentation of the warring minor kingdoms of the English into a unified national identity. He imposes that identity from without and privileges observation of the nation's life from the vantage point of a metropolitan center (and in its linguistic terms) over the subjective experience of the English themselves. The ideal reader implied by the rhetoric of Bede's text is not so much a member of the English people as an inhabitant of a generalized Latin Christendom for whom English proper names, here and elsewhere, require glossing. Bede's text, in other words, invites English readers to regard themselves from a vantage point outside English national identity. At the same time, Bede's Latin style is noteworthy among eighth-century texts for its purity and classicizing sophistication. Bede's English boys are slaves put up for sale in the Forum, and Gregory discusses their identity with his retinue in the third person. In the Whitby version of the story, by contrast, the English are young men, they are asked directly about their identity, and they answer for themselves. The Whitby text, moreover, deploys a notoriously ungrammatical Latin and an eccentric formal structure far removed from the normative conventions of the saint's life as a genre. In addition to recording Gregory's Latin puns on English proper names, it introduces English puns on Latin words that privilege the vernacular as the repository of deeper meaning. The two versions' respective narrative

agendas suggest the extent to which agency, identity, and control of the norms of the metropolitan language were contested in early-eighth-century Northumbria. Bede and the Whitby anonymous both appropriated the norms of Latinity, but they did so according to dramatically contrasting strategies. Each in his (or her?) own way staked out the relation of metropolitan perspective and metropolitan language to the lived experience of specifically English cultural conditions.

Alcuin of York (c. 735–804) dominates the later eighth century. Most of his works date from his tenure on the Continent as arbiter of intellectual life at the court of Charlemagne. Like Bede's, much of Alcuin's output is by modern categories nonliterary, including pedagogical treatises on language and numerous biblical commentaries. A large body of surviving verse includes pastoral poetry, short occasional pieces addressed to favorite pupils, a long poem on the saints and treasures of the church of York, and a verse version of the life of Saint Willibrord, an Anglo-Saxon missionary to the Frisians approximately half a century before Alcuin wrote his text between 785 and 797. This latter poem, together with a prose version of the same saint's life, is another example of the *opus geminatum*. Other prose saints' lives and a substantial corpus of letters round out his oeuvre.

The vogue for the *opus geminatum* also instantiates the decentered position of the early English reader. Aldhelm, Bede, and Alcuin all offered jejune explanations for their choice of the form. Aldhelm suggested that the prose and verse halves of his work constituted its walls and roof, respectively. Both Bede and Alcuin justified the creation of an *opus geminatum* as an appeal both to the simplicity of the mass of the faithful (in the prose) and the sophistication of the learned (in the poetry). Alcuin suggested that his prose was appropriate for public recitation and his verse for private reading. The halves of each work differ from one another to varying degrees. The first twenty chapters of Aldhelm's arcane prose have scant parallel in his relatively straightforward verse, while a quarter of the verse text bears minimal correspondence to the prose. The halves of Bede's diptych differ in substance, but not quite so dramatically. The correspondence of Alcuin's prose to his verse is more consistent, but the verse is so compressed in its allusion to events more fully narrated in the prose that the reader must often already know the story in order to follow along. This allusiveness illustrates dramatically a central issue with these texts: that beneath their explicit protestations of unity, they palpably expose the impossibility of the text's full presence to itself, or to its reader. The reader's experience of the text necessarily remains always partial, always in need of a supplement drawn from elsewhere—in this case, from the other half of the work itself. That the supplement (or at least part of it) is brought within the frame of the work itself exposes the self-sufficient unity of the reading experience as chimerical.

THE NINTH AND TENTH CENTURIES

Viking depredations that began with the sack of Lindisfarne in 793 brought Anglo-Latin letters to a nearly complete standstill in the ninth century. The most notable exceptions are a poem by Æthelwulf on the abbots of Wearmouth and Jarrow, dating from the first decades of the century, and Asser's biography (893) of Alfred the Great of Wessex. The latter text, of paramount historical importance, is a strange and engaging pastiche of disparate materials, stitched together from a Latin translation of the *Anglo-Saxon Chronicle* and narrative sections that bear comparison to Einhard's *Life of Charlemagne* and the tradition of secular biography descending from the Roman writer Suetonius. (Over the past century and a half, its authenticity has been repeatedly challenged, and each time vociferously defended.)

The resurgence of Anglo-Latin in the tenth century is closely associated with the revival of Benedictine monasticism, a movement connected with several great reformers of the English Church, but from a literary point of view its most important association is with Æthelwold, bishop of Winchester from 963 to 984, whose school formed many writers of his generation. Most tenth-century Anglo-Latin demonstrates a love of implausibly recondite expression, drawing some of its inspiration from a revived interest in the works of Aldhelm but far outstripping his stylistic excesses. The touchstone works of this period include Frithegod's wickedly difficult verse *Breviloquium* on the life of Wilfrid, from the middle of the century; Lantfred of Winchester's account of the translation and miracles of Saint Swithun, from after 971; works of Wulfstan the Cantor, including a prose life of Æthelwold and a verse recasting of Lantfred's work; and engagingly bizarre lives of Saint Oswald of York and Saint Ecgwin, both now attributed to Byrhtferth of Ramsey. The Latin works of Ælfric of Eynsham (c. 950–c. 1010), better known for his vernacular homilies, represent a stylistically more sober strain of tenth-century Anglo-Latin.

LATIN LITERATURE IN LATE ANGLO-SAXON ENGLAND

The eleventh-century English produced relatively few Latin works, but there survives the *Encomium Emmae reginae* (In praise of Queen Emma, written between 1040 and 1042), a laudatory biography of Emma, queen in turn of Æthelred II and Cnut, which also gives an important account of the Danish conquest of England. In the generation after the Norman Conquest there followed a great wave of prose hagiography. Many of these texts record the biographies of pre–Norman Conquest English saints for the first time; others offer revised accounts of saints commemorated by earlier *vitae*. Goscelin, a peripatetic Flemish monk who eventually settled at Canterbury in the 1080s, was the preeminent hagiographer of his generation in England, though two other Canterbury monks, Osbern and the somewhat younger Eadmer, rivaled him in prestige.

The interplay between an eleventh-century vernacular text and its Latin source, the latter not itself produced in England, illustrates particularly well the interpenetration of Latin and English literary culture, as discussed by David Townsend. Indeed, one cannot do justice to the cultural work performed by this text without attending to that interpenetration as itself lying within the work's own frame of reference. The earliest known version of the romance of Apollonius of Tyre in any European vernacular is a fragmentary Old English translation extant in one manuscript of the second quarter of the eleventh century—the only surviving example of romance in Old English. The level of translation is generally accurate and unobtrusively idiomatic. Yet the translation's very success, in its transparency, veils the meaning of the process by which the late Greco-Roman fantasy world of the Latin text was transposed into categories intelligible to the Old English audience. At both representational and linguistic levels, the text stages an implicit dialectic between what must have been familiar and what must have been rich and strange to an English reader around 1025 or 1050. The reader's negotiation of that dialectic depended on his or her awareness of an intertextual relay between the Latin source text and the vernacular adaptation, an oscillation between the presence and absence of full meaning within the English text.

If this dynamic is similar to that sketched earlier in regard to the *opera geminata* of the eighth century, perhaps both examples point to the essentially interlinguistic nature of English medieval culture—to what Robert Stanton has called the "culture of translation" in Anglo-Saxon

England. English literary culture, from its precocious beginnings some centuries before the rise of most other European literary vernaculars, depended fundamentally on the articulation of linguistic difference. Anglo-Latin literature is one of the most palpable manifestations of the constitutive Other of English-language literature, from its beginnings through the Norman period to at least the fourteenth century. With the suppression of English as a literary language from the decades after 1066 until well into the thirteenth century, the concept of a distinct Anglo-Latin literature became attenuated, and the dynamics of the dialectic between the two languages and their literatures so central to the Anglo-Saxon period more diffuse.

ANGLO-LATIN LITERATURE
AFTER THE NORMAN CONQUEST

With the conquest, and particularly during the reign of Henry II, Continental ties came close to overwhelming what was uniquely English about Latin literature written in England, and uniquely important about its dialectic with literature in the vernacular, but some writers remained quintessentially insular by virtue of subject matter or of biography, or both. They include some of the period's best-known and most readable authors: Geoffrey of Monmouth, whose *Historia regum Britanniae* (*History of the Kings of Britain*, 1137) was the fountainhead of the Arthurian tradition; Walter Map (c. 1135–1209/10), whose quirky commonplace book of ironic narrative, *De nugis curialium* (Courtiers' trifles), defies easy categorization; Nigel of Canterbury (c. 1130–c. 1200), author of the satirical epic *Speculum stultorum* (The Mirror of Fools); Gerald of Wales (1146–1243), an invaluable source for Welsh and Irish culture, and for the rise of proto-colonial discourse, in the twelfth century; Peter of Blois (c. 1135–1212), whose letters document the mores of Henry II's court, but whose surviving poetry is not sufficiently extensive to warrant fully his contemporary characterization as one of the foremost poets of his age; the classicizing epic poet Joseph of Exeter (fl. c. 1180–1194), nephew of an archbishop of Canterbury; and the polymath churchmen John of Salisbury (c. 1115–1180) and Alexander Neckam (1157–1217). Two decades before these luminaries, English historiography had risen to illustrious stylistic heights in the works of William of Malmesbury (c. 1090–1143).

Joseph of Exeter's masterwork, the *Iliad of Dares Phrygius*, is an apposite though by no means unique illustration of the sophistication of Anglo-Latin literature in the twelfth century. Written around 1185, it retells the story of the Trojan War versifying a Latin prose source of little distinction but considerable medieval popularity, which purported to give an eyewitness account from the perspective of a Trojan survivor. Joseph freely adapted his source, pulling out all rhetorical stops in order to present his material as a convincing simulacrum of Silver Latin epic style. (The poem, which enjoyed a modest popularity, was later known to Chaucer and figures as an important context of *Troilus and Criseyde*.) Joseph's work, however, offers far more than a mere exercise in antiquarian stylistics. Among its genuinely innovative aspects is its involved and often self-reflexive meditation on the representation of the body within the generic conventions of epic. Such issues are mediated through tensions between flesh and speech. They are perhaps most striking in those passages where, as discussed by Sylvia Parsons, Joseph uses the bodies of his female characters as screens on which to project metaphorically the unifying thematic imagery of his poem. (Joseph also wrote an epic on the Crusades, the *Antiocheis*, of which a mere twenty-five lines survive.)

Anglo-Latin writers of the thirteenth century do not perhaps rival the scope and wit of their twelfth-century predecessors, but they include figures of paramount importance in the literary culture of their age, whose work speaks well enough to modern critical sensibilities to warrant ongoing study for other than purely historical reasons. The academic strain of thirteenth-century culture produced such writers of literary treatises as Geoffrey of Vinsauf, whose *Poetria Nova* (The new art of poetry, c. 1200–1202) was its generation's most influential manual of verse composition, and John of Garland (c. 1195–after 1252), who complemented his *Parisiana Poetria* with a range of mythological and religious poetry. The considerable international prestige of the itinerant professional poet Henry of Avranches (c. 1200–c. 1262) rested largely on a series of highly readable and often rhetorically ingenious versified saints' lives, written mostly for English patrons. The Franciscan satirical and devotional poet Walter of Wimborne (active from the 1220s through the 1260s) and the religious lyricists John of Hoveden (died c. 1275) and John Pecham (archbishop of Canterbury from 1279 to 1292) represent the more thoroughly clerical side of the period's culture.

With the fourteenth century, the rising prestige of English as a literary language overtook the intellectual energy and variety of Anglo-Latin literature, but John

Gower "hedged his bets on literary immortality," as A. G. Rigg puts it, by writing in Latin as well as in English and French. His major work of Latin verse is the *Vox Clamantis*, a poem of more than five thousand elegiac couplets, while the Latin verses of the *Confessio Amantis* stand as a reminder that English literary culture in the age of Chaucer remained self-consciously polyglot, and that such linguistic pluralism often generated a deep skepticism of claims of absolute authority. Siân Echard has discussed the complex and self-undermining ways that Gower layers registers of authority within his work: the dialogic tensions he sets up between Latin and English portions of the *Confessio*, unresolved as they often are, invest his work with an epistemological uncertainty often imputed to Chaucer, but sometimes not recognized as more widely endemic to the literary circumstances of his generation precisely by virtue of the troubling ongoing presence of Latinity as a supplement to vernacular culture.

[*See also* Ælfric; Alfred; Arthurian Literature; Bede; Geoffrey of Monmouth; John Gower; Medieval Devotional Prose; Medieval History and Chronicle; *and* Medieval Saints' Lives.]

FURTHER READING

Bolton, Whitney French. *A History of Anglo-Latin Literature, 597–1066.* Vol. 1, 597–740. Princeton, 1967. An older account that provides an overview but must be used with caution on a number of points of factual detail. (No subsequent volumes were published.)

Echard, Siân. "With Carmen's Help: Latin Authorities in the *Confessio Amantis*." *Studies in Philology* 95 (1998): 1–40. Discusses the destabilization of authority through the gaps between the Latin and English portions of Gower's text.

Lapidge, Michael. *Anglo-Latin Literature, 600–899; and Anglo-Latin Literature, 900–1066.* London, 1993, 1996. Collected papers by an eminent authority on pre-conquest Anglo-Latin.

Mantello, F. A. C., and A. G. Rigg. *Medieval Latin: An Introduction and Bibliographical Guide.* Washington, DC, 1996. An omnibus volume that includes much information on Anglo-Latin authors.

McGowan, Joseph P. "An Introduction to the Corpus of Anglo-Latin Literature" and "Anglo-Latin Prose." In *A Companion to Anglo-Saxon Literature*, edited by Phillip Pulsiano and Elaine Treharne, 11–49, 296–323. Oxford, 2001. Two articles that together provide a recent survey of the pre-conquest material.

Mehan, Uppinder, and David Townsend. "'Nation' and the Gaze of the Other in Eighth-Century Northumbria." *Comparative Literature* 53 (2001): 1–26. On the usefulness (and pitfalls) of postcolonial categories for analysis of early Anglo-Latin literary culture.

Parsons, Sylvia. "The Representation of the Body in Twelfth-Century Latin Epic." Ph.D. diss., University of Toronto, 2004. A reading of Joseph of Exeter's *Ylias* and Walter of Châtillon's *Alexandreis* through and against current theories of body, gender, and violence.

Rigg, A. G. *A History of Anglo-Latin Literature, 1066–1422.* Cambridge, U.K., 1992. The definitive survey of Latin literature in England after the Norman Conquest.

Stanton, Robert. *The Culture of Translation in Anglo-Saxon England.* Cambridge, U.K., 2002. An argument for the gap between Latin and English as a pervasive dynamic of Anglo-Saxon literary culture.

Townsend, David. "The Naked Truth of the King's Affection in the Old English *Apollonius of Tyre*." *Journal of Medieval and Early Modern Studies* 34 (2004): 173–196. A case study of how English–Latin interlinguistic dynamics articulated late Anglo-Saxon self-understanding.

MEDIEVAL DEVOTIONAL PROSE

Nicholas Watson

"Devotional prose" is a modern term for a loose category of writings in Middle English, Anglo-Norman French, and Latin that were designed for edification and the stimulation of individual religious feeling. These writings are associated with the affective (emotion-centered) spirituality that grew up with the reform movements of the twelfth century, which emphasized desire, fear, and love, not formal obligation, as the most significant ties binding God and the soul. Although some prose texts from Anglo-Saxon England might also be reckoned "devotional," this link with the affective means that, for readers today, the history of English devotional prose starts with Anselm's *Orationes sive meditationes* (*Prayers and Meditations*) in 1100. It then expands into several genres: *meditations* on Christ's passion or other topics, aimed at arousing affective states in the reader; *remedies*, aimed at sustaining readers through times of difficulty; *mirrors*, exemplary texts, aimed at inculcating proper habits of living, sometimes by describing the life of Christ; informal *rules*, aimed at integrating the affective relationship to God with religious living in general; and *ladders*, in which this integration is presented as an ascent from one level of selfhood to another.

Devotional reading was an important part of the monastic routine throughout the medieval period and was also practiced in lay households across a widening social spectrum; vernacular devotional reading was especially associated with women. Although these traditions of devotional writing were interrupted at the Reformation (Saint Thomas More's *Dialogue of Comfort against Tribulation* is a late "remedy"), they survived within Catholicism and, in altered forms, in Protestantism: John Bunyan's *Pilgrim's Progress* is straightforwardly a "mirror," and Thomas Traherne's *Centuries of Meditation* a meditation. Beyond this, the earnestness with which even modern readers approach serious fiction and self-help books suggests strong continuities between present-day assumptions about leisurely reading and those of our predecessors.

DEFINITIONS

Like many apparently objective labels in common use, the phrase "devotional prose" encodes certain questionable assumptions. To call a work "devotional" is to imply that it is not several other things. It is not *visionary*: it is neither the record of profound personal experience nor liable to theological speculation on the relationship between the soul and God. It is not *scholastic*: it does not build complex intellectual arguments nor use specialized academic vocabularies. It is not mainly *didactic* or *pragmatic*: it is more concerned with the development of the inner self than with codified rules of behavior or credal formulas. It is not *official*: it does not form part of an individual's liturgical responsibilities, nor of a collective act of worship such as communal prayer or preaching. It is not *reformist* or *polemical*: it does not aim at effecting large-scale change in the church or in secular society, and it does not devote much attention to castigating the sins and errors of others.

Such exclusions can be helpful both because they are partly true and because they draw attention to the quality that comes closest to unifying the works described as "devotional" into a field of inquiry: their association with the voluntary and with the use of leisure, the periods of time that fall outside preset social and religious responsibilities. Yet these exclusions can also encourage preemptive decisions, both about what counts as "devotional prose" and about how works so categorized are read. The relationships between inner self and outer form of living, individual and collective religiosities, personal devotion and reformism were all matters for vigorous argument in late medieval prose texts—not surprisingly, since there is a lot at stake in how these relationships are imagined. How far does the outward appearance of religiosity—the status of nun, monk, hermit, or lay person with no special training—matter? When is it right to practice an individual devotion to God and withdraw from communal celebrations of worship? Is a proper attitude toward God and a sense of one's sinfulness compatible with the criticism of others and an activist attitude to church reform for those who are not preachers or clerics, or must the devout soul be pacifist, allowing God to work as he wills? To insist on too fixed a definition of the devotional is to take sides in these arguments, making the most unworldly texts seem the most representative and sealing off devotional writings from the controversies that swirled around them. Like its companion activities, prayer and meditation, contemplative reading took place in the privacy of cloister or chamber, and, like most reading, it involved a mental act of detachment from the present. But it was not thereby disengaged from the world, and many devotional texts have fierce ideological agendas. Indeed, the cumulative effect of devotional writing and reading was profound and extended well beyond the end of the Middle Ages.

MEDITATION

Reading, prayer, and meditation are enjoined on monks and nuns in the sixth-century Benedictine Rule, the foundational work of Western monasticism, as private activities meant to offer relief from the demands of community worship imposed by the liturgy. Partly because reading was seen as a form of manual labor—a physical act involving the mouth and, through gesture, the whole body—the Rule sees it as a constructive use of leisure and defense against idleness. The *Orationes sive meditationes* of Saint Anselm (1033–1109), monk, philosopher, and archbishop of Canterbury, represent a momentous intensification of this way of thinking about reading. This deeply considered set of addresses to God and the saints fuses reading, meditation, and prayer into a single activity, demanding of its users a vivid awareness of the crisis state in which the human soul is situated, trapped between desire for the good and an awestruck awareness of its own inadequacy; indeed, it is hard to identify such reading with leisure in any modern sense of that term. According to Anselm's prologue, reading his book provides means "to excite the mind to the love or the fear of God or to an investigation (*discussionem*) of the same" through "intent and profound meditation." Although solitary, this is an essentially interactive process, in which the reader, temporarily deprived of the comforts of community and of ritual offered by the liturgy, sits or kneels in the presence of the saints, the Virgin Mary, and God, weeping, praising, desiring. "Now, little man (*homuncio*), leave just a while your earthly business, hide just a season from the tumults of your thoughts . . . make just a little space for God, and rest just a little in him. Enter into the chamber (*cubiculum*) of your mind and shut out everything but

God." Inside that chamber, an emotionally complex series of relationships with God can play itself out undisturbed: "Alas, from what a height have I fallen, into what a depth have I plunged!" cries the meditator at the reproofs of the justly punishing father; "Console me, console me . . . for I am yours," she calls at the embraces of the merciful mother and desiring lover; "Truly, Lord, you live in light inaccessible, truly there is nothing that can penetrate it to see you there—truly I do not see this light for it is too dazzling, yet whatever I do see I see by it," she marvels at the majesty of the universal creator and the redeemer.

If there is a refuge from God or the self in these remarkable meditations, it is to be found in the beauty of their language and the supreme control with which they offer the reader an imagined habitation with Anselm himself, the first soliloquizer of the meditations, as he lays out the needs and aspirations of the soul with a fierceness worthy of one of the West's foremost logicians. Anselm had studied Augustine's autobiographical works, especially the *Confessions*, and his narrative voice has all the sinuous self-reflexiveness and lyricism of his predecessor's. Offered up to his readers for their appropriation, Anselm's voice in soliloquy became a training ground for the imagining of countless individual selfhoods as his meditations were disseminated, used, and imitated over several hundred years. In one popular form of late medieval meditation, termed Passion meditation, the self confronts the death of Christ, finding there fear, compassion, and an agonized comfort in the redeeming power of Christ's suffering. In another, erotic meditation, the self chooses Christ over earthly lovers and bathes in sensuous appreciation of "the wooing of our Lord." In a third, *contemptus mundi* ("contempt for the world") meditation, the self sees itself pitifully deranged and disordered by the effects of human sin on the divine creation. Meditative reading remained a basic practice inside and outside the monastery throughout the Middle Ages and beyond, as devout individuals chose and developed scripts for personal dramas through which they performed their increasingly confident sense of their private inner selves, stripped of social and domestic obligation, as more "real" than any other aspect of their being: an image of the self many still share and all have to contend with.

REMEDY

A specialized form of meditation in which the narrator addresses the reader rather than voicing her words is the remedy, a genre that explains the benefits of suffering (the

Twelve Profits of Tribulation, as a thirteenth-century work of that title calls them) and offers "comforts" to those in need. If meditation shapes selves, remedy aims to keep them in balance, both during general crises and especially when the psychological demands of the quest for perfection become overwhelming and inner or demonic voices threaten to draw the self into lassitude or despair. An adventurous work of the 1380s names what is happening at these moments in its title: *The Chastising of God's Children*. The *Chastising* is an invaluable resource for our knowledge of topics such as the English attitudes toward visions; another remedy, the *Book of the Craft of Dying* (c. 1420) offers fascinating insights into the spiritual comforts available to the dying. But the most psychologically intricate remedy is *De remediis* (c. 1350; Englished as the *Remedy against the Trouble of Temptations* by an English friar turned Italian hermit, William Flete). This work shows to an impressive degree both the responsiveness of the remedy to the specificities of individual spiritual experience and the flexibility of its theological tools. Sensitivity toward the idea of divine justice and conviction of one's sinfulness were problems for devout people in the Middle Ages, despite the optimism of most vernacular salvation theologies. Flete encouraged readers appalled at their own inclinations towards evil to divide their perception of themselves into "two wylles," one good and begotten by grace, the other evil, and then to identify their truer selves with the godly will, not repenting so much as disassociating themselves from their evil impulses: "Though ye through suche wycked thoughtes and sterynges by vyolence and sharpnes be enclyned to sensualyte [evil], yet ye do it not ne [nor] consent therto; but it is the sensualyte that dooth it in you." This solution to the chaos of conflicting impulses that can rise to the surface of the most ordered life (a solution closely studied by Julian of Norwich) is as sophisticated as any modern system of therapy. If meditation tends to nurture a private sense of self, remedy notices that selves are in practice permeable to invasion from within and without; but it also proposes a view of the self (one inconceivable in many Protestant theological traditions) as at bottom inherently good.

MIRROR

The remedy is thus especially helpful in responding to the actual daily experience of devout people. But is there not something inherently escapist about some kinds of devotional reading, as there is said to be about romantic modern fiction? A derivate of Anselmian meditation, Nicholas Love's sentimental *Mirror of the Life of Christ*, written around 1410 and read for three hundred years after its publication, brings this question home because escape is so exactly what it insists on for its lay readers: "symple soules . . . that kan not thenke bot [are only capable of conceiving of] bodyes or bodily thinges." Love wrote at a time when religious reading available to laypeople was increasingly challenging and critical of the Church (the free-thinking dialogue *Dives and Pauper* and the radical apocalypse *The Lantern of Light* date from almost the same year), and when the religious authorities had decided that one root of the problem was the vernacular Bible, notably the Wycliffite Bible. Published in conjunction with a major piece of legislation, Archbishop Arundel's *Constitutions*, which attempted (for the first time in English history) to impose official restrictions on lay access to the Bible, the *Mirror* is a substitute Bible from which everything controversial has been removed. A devotional biography based partly on the Gospels and partly on "devoute ymaginacions" (episodes and speeches embellished in the manner of a novel), the *Mirror* offers readers a costume-drama version of Christ's life: a narrative full of charm, feeling, and genteel behavior that hopes to stand in for a more thorough intellectual and political engagement with religion. As Mary cuddles the newborn Jesus, "swetly clippyng and kissyng" him and washing his face with milk from her "fulle pap, as she was taght of [taught by] the Holi Gost," ox and ass kneel down and warm the baby with their breath while Joseph looks on, adoring. This kind of image was much in demand (the link, via Victorian piety, with the Christmas card is genuine), and its hyperrealism was not necessarily conservative in its effects, for all the scorn the *Mirror* has been subjected to in recent years; one of the work's most attentive readers was the mystic Margery Kempe, and her discovery of the radical possibilities of the work's literalism deserves attentive respect. But the view of the laity's spiritual needs that the *Mirror* projects is at odds with those in contemporary texts. A medieval literary "mirror" offered two things to readers: encyclopedic knowledge of a subject, and ways of seeing the self ethically in that subject. A lesser-known mirror of Christ's life, contemporary with Love's, is the *Speculum devotorum* (*Mirror for the Devout*), written in English by a monk for a nun. It shows how these two impulses can work in practice, for here affect takes second place to a scrupulous formal structure, a careful account of sources, and a willingness to leave problems of interpretation to the ethical intelligence of the reader. By contrast, although Love's *Mirror* is more mirror than meditation—the self-reflexive engagement in Christ's life fostered by meditation is lacking here—the reflections this mirror casts back both of its subject and of its reader are unambitiously generalized.

RULE

The *Mirror*'s social agenda was to promulgate a model that Love's older contemporary, Walter Hilton, termed "mixed" life, in which laypeople were assumed to be in sophisticated charge of their secular affairs but were expected to be less masterful or inquiring in their devotions. This model sought to diffuse demands for lay involvement in church government by a careful separation of outer ("active") and inner ("contemplative") selves; that separation at once sealed the secular off from complex engagement with religion and, paradoxically, gave religious justification to a mode of living in which religion had mostly an overseeing presence. Although this "mixed life" understanding of lay religiosity was influential in the fifteenth and early sixteenth centuries, most devotional prose texts from the thirteenth century on promulgated a different model, in which inner and outer selves are understood to be so intricately interrelated that private and social, political and devotional, can never be clearly divided. This led to the rise of informal "rules" (sometimes called "forms," as in Richard Rolle's *Form of Living*, 1348–1349), handbooks of religious living based partly on formal monastic rules such as the Benedictine Rule, and partly on the extensive tradition of Latin writings on interiority by such thinkers as Bernard of Clairvaux, Hugh and Richard of Saint Victor, and Bonaventure.

Two early thirteenth-century works are foundational: Archbishop Edmund of Canterbury's *Mirour de Seinte Eglyse* (*Mirror of Holy Church*) or *Speculum religiosorum* (*Mirror for Religious*), probably first written in Latin around 1215, and the anonymous *Ancrene Wisse* (*Advice for Anchoresses*), perhaps written a few years later in a West Midland dialect of English. Both works circulated in all three of England's literary languages into the sixteenth century and provided generic models and material for many imitations. Although both offer advice on daily behavior, the *Mirour* to all "religious" and *Ancrene Wisse* primarily to female hermits or anchoresses, neither calls itself a rule; indeed, both could also be described as "anti-rules," for both are as suspicious of the formalism that can result from the rule's focus on the outer self, not the inner, as they are of a singleminded emphasis on interi-

ority. The term Edmund uses to describe his readers, "genz de religiun" ("religious people"), is a case in point, for "religion" in thirteenth-century French and English is a word poised between denoting an institutional identity (that of monk, friar, canon, or nun) and a spiritual one (in the sense of "devout"). The word thus suggests that the same demands—to live "honorably, meekly, and lovingly," as Edmund put it—are to be made of all members of the Church, whatever their status. Honorable, meek, and loving living involves keeping clearly in mind the perfection that is the goal of human life, the sinful nature of the self, the being of Christ, the articles of the faith, the scriptures, the beauty of creation, and the needs of others: on awaking each day, the reader prays first for those in prison or those who have died in the night, before proceeding to meditation on Christ's life. The intensity of meditation, the more distanced reflectiveness of the mirror, are here put to work in service of a religiosity that is designed to be adaptable for any kind of living and to infuse any activity with spiritual purpose.

Ancrene Wisse's initial sense of audience seems more specific. However, anchoresses—women who lived lives of prayer, meditation, and reading in cells attached to churches—bridged the divide between professional religious and the laity in much the same way as the word "religion" did, and *Ancrene Wisse* is aware from the start of the broad audience the work gained in practice. The work's sense of the relation between inner and outer, tenor and vehicle, is so fluid that the anchoritic cell it describes constantly shimmers between representing a physical cell (with curtained windows and a door always shut) and the selves that live within that cell (with their carefully guarded senses and celibate bodies). The "outer rule" (parts I and VIII of the work) describes the austere regime to which anchoresses dedicated themselves, their vigils, constant prayers, vegetarian diet, and rough clothing. In the "inner rule" (parts II–VII), the rigors to which anchoresses are subjected are metaphorical. Here the anchoritic life is a pilgrimage, a race, a bout of upstream rowing, a frantic digging for buried treasure, a pelican feeding its young with its heart's blood, a bitter journey through the desert, a crucifixion, a death; Christ's own anchoritic cells, the humiliating enclosures his divine being condescended to enter, were the womb and the tomb. Under this rhetorical regime, the anchoresses themselves become representatives of devout Christian being in general, and their lives models for the spiritual attitudes of those who live in the world. In adaptations such as the *Simple Tretis* (c. 1400)—influenced by the topos of the "cloister of the soul" elaborated in *The Abbey of the Holy Ghost* (c. 1350), where the soul is not a cell but an entire monastery—the anchoresses have become "inner hermits," allegorical residents of the soul who continue their devotions even while the lay reader is occupied in everyday business. The hermit is a powerful identity to offer readers, figuring passionate independence from institutional attachments, immediate intimacy with God, and a prophetic awareness of how spiritual reality haunts the earthly. If Edmund's *Mirour* gives readers a daily regime in which inner and outer, active and contemplative, are in dynamic balance, *Ancrene Wisse* provides ways of framing this balance, not as a compromise between the active and the contemplative but as one of the most arduous forms the Christian's pursuit of perfection can take.

LADDER

Rules are multigeneric works; not only the *Mirour* and *Ancrene Wisse* but also their closest late medieval imitators (for example, two "rules" for the laity, *The Holy Book Gratia Dei* and *Book to a Mother* from 1375–1400) incorporate all of the five genres discussed here. The same is only sometimes true of "ladders," those works that construct life as an ascent "as by a laddir of dyverse runges" from earth to heaven (the compilation *Pore Caityf*, echoing *A Ladder of Foure Ronges*, 1375–1400). Here, different theologies of ascent demand different attitudes to its "rungs," the parts of the spiritual life that are progressively left behind. In Hilton's *Scale of Perfection* (c. 1380–1395), the most influential work of late Middle English prose into the seventeenth century (when its admirers included the Benedictine mystic Augustine Baker), the chaos that sin has introduced into the soul has displaced the image of God and replaced it with an image of sin itself. A pagan idol stands in blasphemous mockery in the heart of the temple of the soul. To restore the divine image for brief periods, the devout person may read, meditate, pray, confess, and do penance for sin. But to attack sin in any thorough way, she must look into her own corruption and take the shock of the dismay this induces, learning to dwell within that dismay as it enables divine grace to enter the soul and rekindle the sparks of created goodness that still linger there. This intense labor does slowly lead the soul up a ladder whose rungs include the image of life as a pilgrimage to Jerusalem, recitation of the holy name of "Jesus," and, in the second book of the *Scale*, contemplation of heaven and, ultimately, God in Trinity. But the way to this end lies

through such turmoil—Hilton's attitude to sin is as horrified as Anselm's, although he also has the delicacy in his treatment of the sinner that one would expect from a student of Flete—that all the resources of meditation, mirror, and remedy, all the forms imposed by a rule, are needed to keep the self in comfort, steadying it as it returns, fragile to the last, back to the height from which it fell.

The extraordinary *Cloud of Unknowing* (1380s), in contrast, eschews as far as it can all literary genres and any relation to the reader except that of assistant in the act of imageless contemplation that lies at its heart. In this act, the contemplative—who, as a precondition for even reading the work, has already ascended from the active life to the state of lonely desire that is solitary life—sits in silence, pressing down into a cloud of forgetting everything earthly, including religious language itself. The intensity of Anselmian meditation has no place here, as the soul waits in a "cloude of unknowyng" that is the distance between Earth and the incomprehensible God. Unique among Middle English writers, the anonymous author of the *Cloud* drew on a distinct, originally Greek tradition of "negative theology" stemming from the fifth- or sixth-century Neoplatonic theologian "Dionysius the Areopagite," who held that God is so far beyond understanding that any human means of knowing, including revealed theology, hides more than it reveals. They come closest to God, then, who rest in the most fully realized knowledge of their ignorance of him. For the *Cloud* author, imbued with the assumptions of late medieval affectivity, this is a most energetic rest; the soul waits for the "sodeyn steryng" of love to spring to God "as sparcle fro the cole" ("as a spark from a coal"). The prose of the *Cloud* is energetic too, but not with the energy of evocation, whether of God or the self, found in other texts discussed here. All its intensity goes into the construction and deconstruction, in lyrical prose, of the metaphors on which the work relies in order to lead its reader beyond metaphor. Language comes under as corrosive a suspicion as the contemplative must bring to bear on wandering thoughts; the word "up" in the phrase "lift up your herte" is as dangerous as sexual temptation, for God is not "up." Only "God" and "love" survive unchallenged, as monosyllables on which the contemplative rides into the silence. The *Cloud*'s antirhetorical devotion produces a negative image of the tradition that began with Anselm's crafted and astute wordiness. Here the self is still seated in the cell of the soul, but now as a singularity; all drama, posture, and complexity of being are gone, and the contemplator is as cut off from worldly concerns as Nicholas Love could possibly have desired. Affectivity has come to have all the austere solipsism of Descartes's "Cogito ergo sum" ("I think, therefore I am").

RECEPTION

Except for a few works read in translation by modern Christian believers or studied in university courses, medieval devotional prose tended until recently to be regarded as a significant but isolated phenomenon, likely to interest only specialists. Things have changed somewhat in the last few years, and parts of this large body of work are beginning to find their place in medieval literary history and in studies of pre-Reformation vernacular theology. This body of works, however, deserved to reach more deeply into literary studies. For in its representations of complex selfhoods, in its ministrations to individual psychologies, and in its ability to imagine processes of transformation from one level of being to another, medieval devotional prose offers an archive of psychologically sophisticated material with few parallels in premodern literature—material whose assumptions may feel alien in some ways, but in others are profoundly familiar. The gap between general intellectual assumptions about the Middle Ages and the historical record is always baffling, and never more so than in relation to the history of the self. A fuller knowledge of this extraordinary body of writing would help to narrow that gap.

[*See also* John Bunyan; Julian of Norwich; Margery Kempe; Thomas More; Richard Rolle; *and* Thomas Traherne.]

EDITIONS AND TRANSLATIONS

Anselm. *The Prayers and Meditations of St. Anselm with the Proslogion.* Translated by Benedicta Ward. Harmondsworth, U.K., 1973. Excellent annotated translation.

Colledge, Edmund, ed. and trans. *The Mediaeval Mystics of England.* New York, 1962. Excellent translations and discussions of devotional prose works including Edmund's *Mirour de Seinte Eglyse* and Flete's *De remediis.*

Edmund of Canterbury. *Mirour de Seinte Eglyse.* Edited by A. D. Wilshere. London, 1982.

Gallacher, Patrick G., ed. *The Cloud of Unknowing.* Kalamazoo, MI, 1997.

Hazenfratz, Robert, ed. *Ancrene Wisse.* Kalamazoo, MI, 2000. Readable edition of this centrally important Middle English religious prose work.

Hilton, Walter. *The Scale of Perfection.* Edited by Thomas H. Bestul. Kalamazoo, MI, 2000. First modern edition of Hilton's masterpiece.

Hilton, Walter. *The Scale of Perfection.* Translated by John P. H. Clark and Rosemary Doward. New York, 1991. Scholarly translation with a full account of Hilton's career.

Horstmann, Carl, ed. *Yorkshire Writers: Richard Rolle of Hampole, an English Father of the Church.* 2 vols. London, 1895–1896. Extensive set of transcriptions of Middle English devotional prose works, still indispensable although annoyingly difficult to use.

Savage, Anne, and Nicholas Watson, trans. *Anchoritic Spirituality: "Ancrene Wisse" and Associated Works.* New York, 1991. Annotated translations of works in the "*Ancrene Wisse* Group."

Spearing, A., trans. *The Cloud of Unknowing and Other Works.* Harmondsworth, U.K., 2001. Translation of all the works by the anonymous *Cloud* author.

FURTHER READING

Dean, Ruth J., with Maureen B. M. Boulton. *Manual of Anglo-Norman Literature.* London, 1999. Annotated bibliography of surviving works of Anglo-Norman literature.

Georgianna, Linda. *The Solitary Self: Individuality in the "Ancrene Wisse".* Cambridge, MA, 1981.

Glasscoe, Marion and Jones, E. A., eds. *The Medieval Mystical Tradition in England.* 7 vols. Exeter, U.K., 1980, 1982, and Cambridge, U.K., 1984, 1987, 1991, 1999, 2004. Ongoing series of conference papers representing much of the best work being done in the field.

Hartung, Albert E., ed. *A Manual of the Writings in Middle English, 1050–1500.* 10 vols. New Haven, 1967–1998. Relevant here are "Works of Religious and Philosophical Instruction" by Robert R. Raymo (in vol. 7), and "English Mystical Writings" by Valerie M. Lagorio and Michael G. Sargent (in vol. 9).

Southern, Richard W. *St. Anselm: Portrait in a Landscape.* Cambridge, U.K., 1990. Detailed study of the religious and intellectual milieu of the author of *Orationes sive meditationes.*

Wallace, David, ed. *The Cambridge History of Medieval English Literature.* Cambridge, 1999. Several relevant chapters and extensive bibliography.

Watson, Nicholas. "Censorship and Cultural Change:

Vernacular Theology, the Oxford Translation Debate, and Arundel's *Constitutions* of 1409." *Speculum* 70 (1995): 822–865. Account of the embattled political and cultural situation of late Middle English religious writing.

Wogan-Browne, Jocelyn, et al., eds. *The Idea of the Vernacular: An Anthology of Middle English Literary Theory, 1280–1520.* University Park, PA, 1999. Includes selections from many devotional prose works, with accompanying discussions and full bibliography.

MEDIEVAL HISTORY AND CHRONICLE

Andrew Galloway

The visions and literary forms of history from late antiquity and early Christianity provided a general basis for chronicles and history writing in the British Isles throughout the medieval period, yet these traditions were continually and almost immediately adapted into unique historical styles, narrative forms and trajectories, and perspectives, bespeaking the particular circumstances and, above all, the cultural interactions that made medieval British history writing a major literary and cultural phenomenon.

FROM LATIN BEGINNINGS
TO ANGLO-SAXON HISTORY

The earliest historians in the British Isles whose works have survived tended to write histories of the Church and its martyrs and saints, following models like Eusebius (fourth century), or histories of a people, following models like Orosius (also fourth century); often they charted their histories with an eye on biblical models, especially the Old Testament's patterns of the trials and punishments of God's chosen people, or the New Testament's glimpses of the advance of the early Church. Christianity had arrived in the British Isles in many quarters by the second century, but with the gradual departure of the Roman legions after the sack of Rome in 410 and the collapse of the Roman Empire, only scattered pockets of Christianity persisted among the remaining Britons, and the successive invasions of Germanic non-Christian and nonliterate peoples (who merged into the Anglo-Saxons) pressed the earlier Christian British to the edges of the islands. Thus, it is no surprise that the British (that is, Celtic) Christian historian known as Gildas (probably sixth century), in *On the Fall of Britain*, compared the pagan Saxon assaults to the attacks "of the Assyrian of old upon Judea," by which "the Lord in his wonted way might try in this nation, the modern Israel, whether it loves him or not." Yet the "Assyrian" Anglo-Saxons themselves, once numbers of them had generally adopted Christianity and thus Roman literacy (with some runic modifications)—both of which then helped to establish their cultural dominance over what would become the nation of England and to press the Celtic natives to the margins—produced the greatest historian of the early Middle Ages, and among the greatest of all time: the Northumbrian monk Bede.

Bede's Latin *History of the English Church* (c. 731) charts, more optimistically than Gildas, a process of the advance of Roman Christianity into the lives and politics of the English people. It also established many of the standards of later English historical writing. One need only compare his emphasis on an exacting and realistic presentation with the very popular ninth-century Irish historical fantasia *The Voyage of St. Brendan*, or even the more sober ninth-century Latin prose history by the Welsh Nennius, to feel the distinctively "English" mode of historical writing: empirical, scenically realistic and dramatic, concerned with the legitimacy of its sources, and insistently universal in its claims of seeking "truth"—which Bede carefully defined as what pious witnesses have declared.

Bede's vision everywhere announces a gentle cultural imperialism. An epitome of this is his famous story of the shy swineherd Cædmon, an illiterate servant who, departing because of stage fright from a raucous evening of secular and possibly pagan poetry-telling, enjoys the private arrival of an angel in a manger, who serves as midwife to a new kind of English poetry. The angel is like Gabriel to Cædmon's Mary, since by his new annunciation Cædmon suddenly produces a Christian hymn in the body of Old English poetic formulas (even adapting the pagan epithet "Frea almihtig" for God); henceforth, Cædmon voluminously produces Christian Old English poetry transformed out of Latin Christian writing, "like some clean animal chewing the cud" (IV.24), further emphasizing a gently maternal mode for this triumphant appropriation of living English culture by the English Church. The prospect of authoritative, vernacular English history begins here, since Cædmon's hymn describes the creation of the world. Indeed, two of the earliest copies of Bede's *History*, the earliest from no later than 737, include an

Old Northumbrian (English) version above Bede's Latin translation of Cædmon's first hymn. As those rare early glosses in English show, Bede stirred the possibility of authoritative English vernacular history writing more than two centuries before anything of that kind has come down to us.

ANGLO-SAXON AND BRITISH HISTORY

With King Alfred's and his heirs' ambitious program for English cultural dominance in the ninth century (partly on the model of Charlemagne's gathering of Latin intellectuals and poets to his Holy Roman Empire in the eighth century), a wide range of historical writing suddenly appeared in English. Bede's *History* was translated into Old English in the ninth century, automatically constituting a major achievement in West Saxon history writing. The translated Bede in turn contributed a preface to most versions of the Anglo-Saxon Chronicle, the first sustained contemporary English vernacular history, which appears to have started in the ninth century, too. Earlier English annals almost certainly existed, evidently in the kingdom of Mercia in central England; and in Ireland, contemporaneous annals in Old Irish may also well have existed from roughly this date, although we know these only by the annals of prose and poetry compiled by the eleventh-century abbot of Clonmacnois, Tigernach hua Braein, and from other, later sources. Those annals are less stylistically unified than the Anglo-Saxon Chronicle because they include many poems describing the events (especially in the "third fragment" in Old Irish); but they suggest that the inclusion of occasional poems in the Anglo-Saxon Chronicle is not as pioneering as it appears. The Irish materials reflect a long interaction between monastic annalists and generations of Irish Cædmons, or perhaps in some cases Irish versions of Cædmon's more secular companions, since many of the impressively detailed Irish chronicle poems do not mention Christianity.

The Anglo-Saxon Chronicle, however, achieved a dominance and circulation that none of these other works enjoyed. It doubtless derived its reverence for the annalistic form from its origins in Easter tables, required to calculate Easter by the Roman Christian method; yet this material basis should not obscure the broader English commitment to the broad cultural and literate utility of dating anno Domini. Dating a history by the years of the Lord, rather than of individual kings or popes or fifteen-year indiction cycles, was also Bede's innovation, introduced to coordinate punctiliously the lives and reigns of

kings and the missions of saints and bishops drawn from a wide array of sources. The lost originals for the Irish annals evidently did not date anno Domini, just as the annual dates in the later, magnificent Welsh annals, the *Brut Y Tywysogyon* (Brut of the princes), were clearly inserted at a later stage. The Anglo-Saxon Chronicle, in contrast, adheres so rigorously to dating anno Domini that even years without entries have their place, and many of the poems in the Chronicle conform to the annalistic style. The entry for 937, for instance, opens with a line that folds neatly into the other annalistic openings, beginning, as often in the Chronicle, with an initial "here" (such and such happened or so and so died), as if designating a spot in time fixed by God's eternal view and the English monastic calendar: "Her Æthelstan cyning . . ." ("Here King Athelstan . . ."). But what follows under the year 937 is the "Battle of Brunanburh," a work written out as prose except for metrical punctuation, but a fully metrical historical poem brilliantly celebrating victors and denouncing enemies. King Athelstan's victory with a coalition of West Saxon and Mercian warriors over the "five young kings" with their armies of Irish, Scots, and Strathclyde Britons proclaims an almost "national" expression of Anglo-Saxon triumph over a combined force of Celtic and Norse peoples, in a spirit that prose alone could not convey, and it must have been recited in courtly as well as monastic settings. In the poem, time itself pauses to allow this glorious battle's slaughter to be complete, persisting "from when the sun, the glorious star, rose up in the morrow tide, glided over the lands—God's bright candle, the eternal Lord's—until that noble creation sank to rest." While this poem's taunting rhetoric and formulaic phrasing declare the importance of English secular history at a moment of triumphant unity and victory, the original monastic readers and copyists of the entry might also contemplate the parallels to the biblical history of the chosen people, such as the five kings whom Joshua defeated at Gabaon. For did not the sun stand still there also, "in the midst of heaven, and hastened not to go down the space of one day" (Jos. 10:13)?

HISTORICAL FORMS
AFTER THE NORMAN CONQUEST

The Anglo-Saxon Chronicle continued to be kept in at least two monastic houses after the Norman Conquest of 1066, but its language and its historical focus became generally more local, though also more scenic, politically elaborate, and piquant. With the Conquest and the installation of Anglo-Norman aristocrats as heads of the Church and of the secular government (two entities that for the first time became legally and administratively distinct), Latin historians once again dominated English history. Almost all offspring or half-offspring of the victorious Normans, these writers usually adopted a more pessimistic view of earlier English history than had prevailed in Anglo-Saxon culture itself. England, in their view, was a repeating record of conquests, by the Anglo-Saxons over the Celts and Britons, by the Danes over the Anglo-Saxons, and of course by the Normans over the Anglo-Saxons; that conquest was made less traumatic, more inevitably part of fortune's lessons, in view of the earlier conquests. Henry of Huntington structured his Latin history (1129–1154), filled with laments for fortune, around the "five plagues" (the prior conquests) of England. Relying, haltingly, on the Anglo-Saxon Chronicle as his source, Henry noted with the patronizing appreciation of an aesthete or antiquarian that the style of his source changes at the entry we call the "Battle of Brunanburh" into "a kind of song, using strange words and figures of speech," which he himself imitated (with some translation errors) in Latin "so that from the solemnity [*gravitas*] of the words we may learn of the solemnity of the deeds and thoughts of that people" (V.18). A permanent chasm divided his world from "that" one, and English history everywhere began to seem full of such chasms.

Indeed, this melancholic and nostalgic view of the intellectual class of England's conquerors led to another kind of model for national history: the matter of Troy, connecting the founding of Rome (as known from the works of Virgil and Livy) to the first peopling of the British Isles by drawing on the tradition of the travels and settlement of Brutus, from Nennius and perhaps other lost Welsh sources. Thus, Geoffrey of Monmouth's Latin *History of the British Kings* (c. 1136) offered to a mostly sympathetic and certainly a very wide readership a claim that, since Geoffrey had found a "certain very ancient" British book that a Welsh friend of his could translate, he could now for the first time make available the sequence of much earlier British cultural flowering and conquest, and Arthur's pinnacle of civilization, before that in turn was destroyed by the barbaric Saxons whom his own Anglo-Norman people would conquer. In later English kings' hands, Arthuriana was often fancifully or menacingly self-affirming of their political power and English claims to empire; but in the hands of those seriously situating it in English history, it was always intrinsically melancholic and nostalgic. It was also fraught with ethical complexity. The founder and first king of that British people, Brutus, was an ambiguous figure who fled Italy as an accidental matricide and patricide.

LATE MEDIEVAL CULTURAL INTERACTIONS AND VERNACULAR HISTORY

The connections between England and Troy that the Brutus story involved, especially as translated from Geoffrey of Monmouth's Latin into French by the courtly historian Wace (d. 1183), helped to foster other versions of ancient works, as in two twelfth-century French poems, the massive and influential *Roman de Troie* and the *Roman d'Eneas*, which in turn fed into a broad historical model of "Troy material" that rapidly became a more fertile basis for historical writing than Orosius or even the Bible. The "matter of Troy" also readily led, in later medieval English historical writing in English, French, and sometimes Latin, to what we would define as historical fiction. Middle English romances are often prefaced or pointed in ways that suggest connections to such "real" English history; examples are seen in *Sir Gawain and the Green Knight*, *Athelston*, the somewhat more popular *Arthour and Merlin*, and the still more widely rooted *Havelok the Dane*, versions of which actually appear in chronicles such as Gaimar's and the prose *Brut*. Some cases, like Layamon's *Brut* (c. 1220), are difficult to place in either category.

Post-Conquest historical writing also shows a new inclination for testing sources, however: it cites documents and compares evidence to a far greater degree than do any earlier medieval writings. This is especially clear in the Latin monastic tradition that by this time was inundated with administrative documents and collections of books, from monastic writers like Matthew Paris in the mid-thirteenth century to Ranulph Higden in the mid-fourteenth, whose Latin universal history not only identifies his sources but also notes his own sometimes resistant or critical commentary on those sources. His kind of independent response to the Latin monastic tradition was widespread through the end of the Middle Ages, as we can see from the many copies of his works and of his many continuators; the form was followed even by English poets like Chaucer and Gower, both of whom similarly adopted the posture of a compiler commenting on his sources. Higden's first English translator, John Trevisa (c. 1386), singlehandedly created a massive and original English work—almost inevitably original, since individual commentary is solicited by Higden's example. Thus, whereas Higden noted his objections and additions to the sources and signed those comments with his initial, Trevisa noted his responses to Higden's comments and signs those with his own name. Where Higden throughout presented his doubts about the veracity of King Arthur (in opposition to Geoffrey of Monmouth), Trevisa vigorously denounced the monk's logical bases for attacking that authority and that king's historical plausibility, while leaving Higden's and his own sources' disparate views all present before the reader: "Ranulphus his resouns [arguments], that he meveth ayenst Gaufridus and Arthur, schulde non clerke moove that can knowe an argument." Yet, Trevisa added, "it may wel be that Arthur is ofte over-preysed, and so beeth meny othere" (V.337–339).

As England rose to increasing dominance over its Celtic neighbors, historical debate offered a cultural means to negotiate those conflicts, and Higden's work offered an obvious vehicle for this through the end of the Middle Ages. The major Latin Scottish chroniclers, John of Fordun (writing c. 1370) and Walter Bower (c. 1440), directly critiqued Higden's accounts of Britain's origins but, like Trevisa, they relied closely on Higden's work to do so. Much later medieval vernacular history writing, however, engaged in such cultural and political interaction, conflict, and debate from another tradition, based on the "matter of Troy" or the Arthurian tradition, using the Brutus story to frame political and sometimes social history in terms of each king's reign.

Wace's late twelfth-century translation of Geoffrey of Monmouth had set the terms for this tradition, but it was only fully followed—in hundreds of copies, and in several varieties—by later vernacular histories based on the Brut, first in French by the early fourteenth century, translated into Middle English by the fifteenth, and translated and copied at roughly the same time in Welsh from a Latin original. These vernacular, usually prose Bruts do not usually engage in elaborate displays of authenticating their materials (as the tradition branching from Higden does), but their contemporary political detail is much more notable, and they include intense political arguments and sentiments, as important as facts for defining cultural history. Brut writers in Wales and Scotland sometimes included views of ancient "liberty" from the Celtic cultures of the British Isles, a notable aspect of history's power in those regions. Thus, the Welsh Brut Y Tywysogyon, whose unified narrative ends with most of Wales' independence after its chief principalities were made subject to Edward I in the late thirteenth century (although

this core survives only in later copies), begins a long narrative under the year 1197 (1198 in modern reckoning, owing to later calendar reform): "In that year Gwenwynwyn gathered a mighty host to seek to win for the Welsh their original rights and to restore their bounds to their rightful owners, which they had lost through the multitude of their sins" (Peniarth manuscript version). In the late fourteenth century John Barbour modeled his long Scots verse history of Robert the Bruce's struggle to claim independent Scottish sovereignty early in that century on the basic princely focus of the Brut, similarly pausing to expound on how "Fredome is a noble thing . . . He levys at es [lives at ease] that frely levys" (lines 225 ff.). The theme of the British calling for lost liberty appears as early as, and probably in some sense derives from, Geoffrey of Monmouth's account of Brutus's speeches when Brutus's men are captured by the Greeks; but this lineage does not explain its persistence in such politically charged historical writings—even in the Scottish Declaration of Arbroath (1320), an open letter to Pope John XXII complaining of English attacks on the Scots as a further assault on a long-suffering people. The theme appears less often in English Brut histories, but it features in Robert Mannyng's comments, in his 1338 verse translations of Wace's Brut and a more contemporary French verse Brut by Pierre Langtoft, that William the Conqueror "sette vs in seruage" ("put us into slavery," 2.1244).

Historical writing thrives on cultural interactions and conflict; and Edward I's age of conquest over England's Celtic neighbors, from which all of the last examples directly or indirectly derive, produced some of the most vivid and paradoxical vernacular historical writing of the Middle Ages. Robert Mannyng's (fl. 1288–1338) poetic Middle English Chronicle of England is a remarkable instance. Written in Lincolnshire in the shadow of Scotland (and even mentioning Mannyng's attendance at a feast at Cambridge given by the brother of King Robert Bruce of Scotland), it raises unusually acute questions about its political, religious, and literary features and perspectives. Mannyng initially stressed the necessity to write simply and clearly for "lewed men," and especially to avoid "tailrhyme"; but for his second part, Mannyng used a virulently anti-Scottish source, Pierre Langtoft's Brut, which includes amid its French verse many tail-rhyme poems, in English, against the Scots. Such ephemeral English diatribe is preserved not only in Langtoft's French verse but also in the short political poems found in the French and English prose Bruts, where the Scots' versified taunts back to the English are uniquely preserved, and in the still more viciously anti-Scottish short historical poems by another Northern English poet of this period, Laurence Minot. Topical, partisan praise or abuse is one of the raw elements of any contemporary historical literature; the "Battle of Brunanburh" is merely an elegant early instance. But Mannyng took up such heated historical writing only to complicate its point. Where his source "Pers" (Langtoft) presented a brief diatribe in tail-rhyme against the perfidious Scots at a meeting at Berwick where John Baliol offered fealty to Edward I, in which Langtoft says that Merlin's prophecy announced that all Britain should be "al on" (under English rule), Mannyng added in his own tail-rhyme, "it is no so: [the British nations] er o sundere . . . Ye haf wele herd / the Brus Robert / was Scottis kyng / wele tuenti yere / in gode powere / mayntend that thing" (2.6841–6846). Smuggled into his version of this anti-Scottish tail-rhyme poem is the view that the Scots have a time-tested right to their own country after all.

Tracing the short polemical history poem up through Mannyng's use of it suggests that his political and literary postures were deeply complex, and this is borne out by considering his treatment of Edward I, who reigned during Mannyng's lifetime. Mannyng is often critical of the English king who most realized the goal of an English empire in the British Islands; "His folie was the more," as Mannyng says, significantly altering his source Langtoft, as often when he comments on Edward. Mannyng criticizes Edward for having "ouerhipped" ("leapt over") his barons by not sharing his wealth or his power, and this arrogant presumption, Mannyng makes plain (in another visible shift from Langtoft), led to England's many losses in this period. Mannyng uses the same word when he chides Langtoft because he "ouerhippis" ("skips over") parts of his source, Geoffrey of Monmouth. The arrogance of mistreating history is tantamount to the arrogance of imperial tyranny. Yet Mannyng closes with praise for Edward as the "floure of cristendam," at the climax of a final list of great men who have fallen—starting with Adam, bringing Mannyng's poem back to the biblical history, and thus to the universal human sin, with which his narrative began.

Mannyng's is far from the last major English medieval history, but it serves to show some subtle possibilities for originality in a period when English historical writing continued to depend on French and Latin sources. In part, Mannyng's originality emerges in his adaptations of ephemeral and natively English political diatribes, and more broadly in his pervasive awareness of the literary forms of history. He rigorously follows his principles of textual fidelity to the truth as found in earlier writings: for instance, since "noither Gildas, no Bede, no Henry of Hyntynton, / no William of Malmesbiri, ne Pers of Bridlynton / writes not in ther bokes" about Havelok the Dane, he refused to recount this material. Yet he spends a long passage describing the local Lincolnshire beliefs and even physical relics supporting the Havelok story, and in this as throughout his work he shows a sense that fiction-making too has its place in history, and that historical writing is itself a form of narrative and literary creation. His sense of this alone confirms his central place in the vast body of writings merely indicated here, among the most complex and significant in British culture.

[*See also* King Alfred; Arthurian Literature; Bede; Cædmon; Geoffrey of Monmouth; Laȝamon; Medieval Anglo-Latin Literature; Middle English; Old English; *and* Thomas Usk.]

EDITIONS

Early Middle Ages to the Norman Conquest

"The Battle of Brunanburh." In *Eight Old English Poems*, edited with commentary and glossary by John C. Pope. 3d ed. revised by R. D. Fulk. New York, 2001.

Bede. *Ecclesiastical History of the English People*. Edited and translated by Betram Colgrave and R. A. B. Mynors. Oxford, 1969; reprint 1991.

Dumville, David, and Simon Keynes, eds. *The Anglo-Saxon Chronicle: A Collaborative Edition*. Cambridge, U.K., 1983–. English translation by M. J. Swanson, *The Anglo-Saxon Chronicle*. New York, 1998.

Gildas. *De excidio Britanniae*. Edited and translated by M. Winterbottom. Chichester, U.K., 1978.

Nennius. *Historia Brittonum cum additamentis Nenni*. Edited by Theodor Mommsen. Berlin, 1898. English translation by A. W. Wade-Evans, *Nennius's History of the Britons*. London, 1938.

Selmer, Carl, ed. *Navigatio Sancti Brendani* [Voyage of St. Brendan]. Dublin, 1989. English translation by J. F. Webb and D. H. Farmer in *The Age of Bede*, 233–267. London, 1965; reprint 1998.

Stokes, Whitley, ed. *The Annals of Tigernach*. 2 vols. Felinfach, Wales, 1993. Facsimile reprint of the edition and translation published in *Revue Celtique* 16 (1895), 17 (1896), and 18 (1897).

Twelfth Century

Geoffrey of Monmouth. *Historia Regum Britannie*. Vol. I. Bern Burgerbibliothek MS. 568. Edited by Neil Wright.

Cambridge, U.K., 1985. English translation by Lewis Thorpe, *The History of the Kings of Britain*. London, 1966.

Henry, Archdeacon of Huntingdon. *Historia Anglorum* [History of the English people]. Edited and translated by Diana Greenway. Oxford, 1996.

William of Malmesbury. *Gesta Regum Anglorum* [Deeds of the kings of the English]. Edited and translated by R. A. B. Mynors. Oxford, 1998.

William of Newburgh. *The History of English Affairs*. Book 1. Edited and translated by P. G. Walsh and M. J. Kennedy. Warminster, U.K., 1988.

LATER MIDDLE AGES

Barbour, John. *The Bruce*. Edited by A. A. M. Duncan. Edinburgh, 1999. Includes a translation of the Declaration of Arbroath.

Brie, Friedrich W. D., ed. *The Brut, or the Chronicles of England*. 2 vols. Early English Text Society Original Series 131, 136. London, 1906, 1908.

Hector, L. C., and Barbara F. Harvey, eds. and trans. *The Westminster Chronicle, 1381–1394*. Oxford, 1982.

Higden, Ranulph, and John Trevisa. Polychronicon Ranulphi Higden Monachi Cestrensis, *Together with the English Translations of John Trevisa and of an Unknown Writer of the Fifteenth Century*. 9 vols. Edited by Churchill Babington and J. R. Lumby. Rolls Series. London, 1865–1886.

Jones, Thomas, ed. and trans. *Brut Y Twysogyon* [The chronicle of the princes]. 2 vols. Peniarth MS. 20 Version. Board of Celtic Studies no. 6 and 11. Cardiff, U.K., 1941, 1952.

Knighton, Henry. *Knighton's Chronicle, 1337–1396*. Edited and translated by G. H. Martin. Oxford, 1995.

Mannyng of Brunne, Robert. *The Chronicle*. Edited by Idelle Sullens. Binghamton, NY, 1996.

Minot, Laurence. *The Poems of Laurence Minot*. Edited by Richard H. Osberg. Kalamazoo, MI, 1996.

Usk, Adam. *The Chronicle of Adam Usk, 1377–1421*. Edited and translated by C. Given-Wilson. Oxford, 1997.

FURTHER READING

Galloway, Andrew. "Writing History in England." In *The Cambridge History of Medieval English Literature*, edited by David Wallace, 255–283. Cambridge, U.K., 1999, 2002. A selected survey of chroniclers and the development of historical writing in England from 1066 to 1535.

Gransden, Antonia. *Historical Writing in England i: c. 550–c. 1307*. Ithaca, NY, 1974. *Historical Writing in England ii: c. 1307 to the Early Sixteenth Century*. Ithaca, NY, 1982. The standard survey of the known facts about historical writing and historical writers in medieval England, with brief commentary on the contents, structures, and historical reliability of the works.

Jones, Charles W. *Saints' Lives and Chronicles in Early England*. Ithaca, NY, 1947. A pioneering study of the origins of the English annalistic chronicle form and its relation to other kinds of early medieval narrative forms.

Partner, Nancy. *Serious Entertainments: The Writing of History in Twelfth-Century England*. Chicago, 1977. A sensitive appreciation of the literary style and outlook of four twelfth-century Anglo-Latin historians.

Pearsall, Derek. *Arthurian Romance: A Short Introduction*. Oxford, 2003. A thorough survey of the literary tradition spawned by the *Brut* materials.

MEDIEVALISM

Allen J. Frantzen

Medievalism can be defined as the reception of the art, artifacts, literature, history, and ideas regarded as characteristic of medieval cultures. It appears throughout the arts, from attempts to re-create authentic performances of medieval drama to the production of films loosely based on *Beowulf*. Whether academic or popular, re-creative or creative, medievalism assumes clear boundaries for a period known as "the Middle Ages." The phrase "Middle Age" was first used in 1605 by William Camden, an English historian interested in geography. He offered his readers "a taste of some of middle age," a period "ouercast with darke clouds, or rather thicke fogges of ignorance." The plural, "Middle Ages," appeared in 1616 in the work of Sir Henry Spelman, a church historian, to designate a period between the decline of classical learning in Late Antiquity and its revival in the Renaissance. This "middle" was supposedly dark and undeveloped, simultaneously barbaric and excessively pious. This stereotype persists today in all its marvelous contradictions.

MEDIEVAL AND MEDIEVALISM

Most readers today associate medievalism with the Pre-Raphaelite movement, launched in England in 1848 by the poet and painter Dante Gabriel Rossetti and the painters and designers John Millais, William Morris, and Edward Burne-Jones. Working in a variety of media, the Pre-Raphaelites aimed for pictorial realism. They sought to return art to the social usefulness it was thought to have had in the time of the Italian artist and architect Raphael (died 1520). Believing that art should serve the cause of truth as well as beauty, the Pre-Raphaelites adhered to a medieval aesthetic, which they defined as the expression of simple faith in clean lines. They also produced texts, including handsome editions of Chaucer's *Canterbury Tales* and translations of manuals of chivalry. Authors and artists in this movement contrasted the individual qualities of medieval works of art to the mass-produced art of Victorian England and to what the Pre-Raphaelites saw as the debased taste of an industrialized society.

BEFORE THE VICTORIANS

Medievalism did not begin in the nineteenth century, however. At a point still close to the Middle Ages, Edmund Spenser drew on England's medieval history and on Chaucer's poetry in *The Faerie Queene* (published 1590–1596). Well before Spenser's time, and standing closer still to medieval beliefs and taste, is the work of the English historian John Bale (1495–1563). Bale, a priest who left the Roman Catholic Church to join the English Reformation, fashioned an entire literary history out of the English Middle Ages. He was familiar with a wide range of medieval English and Latin texts and in 1548 published a catalog of hundreds of British authors and their works, arguably the first national history of writing in England. Bale also collected manuscripts written in Old English (or Anglo-Saxon) that had been discarded when Henry VIII seized the English monasteries; books in Old English could not be read by most educated people and were often sold as scrap. Bale could not read Old English either, but he understood that these manuscripts were vital links in England's ancient history.

Bale's creative work shows another side to his medievalism. He wrote plays that adapted both themes and techniques from the great "mystery" or "cycle" dramas of the late Middle Ages and used medieval devices (such as personification allegory) to satirize the medieval Church. Like his historical works, Bale's plays were polemical. (*A Comedy Concernynge thre lawes, of Nature, Moses, & Christ, corrupted by the sodomytes, Pharysees and Papystes*, published in 1538, seems to be the only drama from sixteenth-century England in which Sodomy is a character.) Like those who would follow him in reconstructing the Middle Ages, Bale reshaped medieval materials to suit a specific vision of history and culture.

Real or imagined similarities between early English history and his own time were the basis of Bale's medievalism. His contemporaries concentrated instead on the differences between England's past and their present. Their reception of the poetry of Geoffrey Chaucer (d. 1399) is the exception that proves the rule. Chaucer's work was continuously available in manuscript or printed form after his death. His poetry was seen as having the timeless value of a classic, while the works of his contemporaries (not to mention that of earlier authors) were dismissed as "rude" and barbaric, in part because their work was written in dialects more difficult to read than Chaucer's own. One of Chaucer's biggest proponents was John Dryden, who translated five of the *Canterbury Tales* in 1700. Like Camden, Dryden praised Chaucer as the English Homer and was eager to promote an early English author to the literary pantheon. Of Chaucer's ability to create distinctive characters, Dryden wrote, "'Tis sufficient to say according to the Proverb, that here is God's Plenty."

Admiration for Chaucer kept much of the rest of medieval English literature in the dark until the publication of Thomas Warton's *History of English Poetry* in 1774. Warton embraced English literature from the eleventh century through the sixteenth; his study, despite its flaws, is still considered important for its range and breadth. Warton was also a poet, just as the historian Bale was also a dramatist, and his poetry captures the flavor of a second, more popular kind of medievalism. Warton wrote that he wanted to "muse on the magnificence of yore" and "with Gothic manners Gothic arts explore." ("Gothic" in his day meant "medieval" and was not related to the Germanic tribe of the Goths.) The "Gothic Revival" in literature was already under way, launched by Horace Walpole's *The Castle of Otranto: A Gothic Story* in 1764. Not all "Gothic" work was set in the Middle Ages, although Ann Radcliffe's best-selling *The Mysteries of Udolpho* (1794) was. Mary Shelley's more influential *Frankenstein* (1817) and many other gothic novels emphasized the macabre and the sinister but had later settings.

Warton's work also helped to make medieval poetry available to amateur scholars known as "antiqueries," who were unattached to institutions and supported their own work (unlike Warton, who was a professor at Oxford). The "antiqueries" included Sir Walter Scott (1771–1832), who drew on the Middle Ages as inspiration for novels and poetry that, many have argued, inspired the cult of chivalry in nineteenth-century England. His novel *Ivanhoe* (1819) concerns the war between Normans and Saxons, and *The Talisman* (1825) is about Christian-Muslim conflict. Scott also produced a scholarly edition of a medieval romance, *Sir Tristrem*. By midcentury, spurred by Warton's and Scott's work, private clubs were formed to sponsor editions of medieval texts. David Matthews has pointed out that these clubs were not always, as one might expect, elite groups of wealthy readers. Stimulated by the recovery of medieval texts, artists and others developed a taste for medieval ceremonies, clothing, and architecture. Country houses were renovated to look like medieval castles, and genuinely ancient architecture was sometimes destroyed in the process.

MEDIEVALISM TODAY

Medievalism today has lost the cultural particularity of the Middle Ages. Readers now think of a vast, undifferentiated Middle Ages, peopled alternately by barbarians doing battle or aristocrats dancing in gardens. Readers a century ago saw the Middle Ages differently and understood them as a period of origins for contemporary religious and social practices. In England, France, and Germany, to take only the most prominent examples, medievalism was propelled by the development of strong nationalist traditions.

"Medievalism" now means, to some, the scholarly study of the Middle Ages and its theoretical and methodological bases; in this sense, "medievalists" seek the fullest and most subtle understanding of medieval people and their culture. To others, however, "medievalism" is a name for the interpretation and imitation of medieval culture by artists and thinkers whose work reinterprets the conventions of the Middle Ages for the modern world. It is customary to regard these as distinct activities, one scholarly (for example, editing Arthurian romances) and the other popular (for example, making a film based on the adventures of King Arthur). But as earlier examples show, popular medievalism can demonstrate deep respect for the particularity of medieval cultures; conversely, scholars sometimes adapt medieval evidence to their political and social agenda.

It is often argued that the idealization of medieval culture ended with World War I, which exposed the vulnerability of chivalric combat and individual heroism to mechanized warfare. Archaic standards of combat were pitifully inadequate to the techniques of modern war, but medieval themes, especially the Passion and death of Christ, were powerful tools both in wartime propaganda and in postwar memorials. Rather than putting an end to heroic associations, the war can be said to have revived them and, through countless memorials, to have preserved them for generations. In the popular British lexicon, the phrase "getting medieval" has referred to undisciplined violence. At the same time, recruiting videos for the United States Marine Corps feature knights in shining armor. Modern medievalism, however different from the medievalism of the past, preserves the conflicts and contradictions of medieval culture.

[*See also* John Bale; The Gothic; Pre-Raphaelites; Dante Gabriel Rossetti; *and* Walter Scott.]

FURTHER READING

Bloch, Howard, and Stephen G. Nichols, eds. *Medievalism and the Modernist Temper.* Baltimore, 1996. Theoretical studies of medievalism and medieval scholarship, focused on French sources.

Camden, William. "Poems." In his *Remaines Concerning Britain*, 336–344. 2 vols. London, 1605; repr. London, 1870.

Dinshaw, Carolyn. *Getting Medieval: Sexualities and Communities, Pre and Postmodern.* Durham, NC, 1999. Uses gender and queer theory to discuss modern understandings of medieval social and sexual behavior.

Dryden, John. Preface. In his *Fables, Ancient and Modern.* Repr., Menston, U.K., 1973.

Fairfield, Leslie P. *John Bale: Mythmaker for the English Reformation.* West Lafayette, IN, 1976. The best history of Bale's career.

Frantzen, Allen J., ed. *Desire for Origins: New Language, Old English, and Teaching the Tradition.* New Brunswick, NJ, 1990. Traces the development of Anglo-Saxon studies from the Renaissance to the modern era.

Girouard, Mark. *The Return to Camelot: Chivalry and the English Gentleman.* New Haven, CT, 1981. A brilliant, richly illustrated history of chivalry in the nineteenth century up to World War I.

Matthews, David. *The Making of Middle English, 1765–1910.* Minneapolis, MN, 1999. A rich and insightful discussion of the origins of scholarship in Middle English language and literature.

Patterson, Lee. *Negotiating the Past: The Historical Understanding of Medieval Literature.* Madison, WI, 1987. Sets medievalism in a philosophical and theoretical context, with special emphasis on Chaucer.

Simmons, Clare A. *Reversing the Conquest: History and Myth in Nineteenth-Century British Literature.* New Brunswick, NJ, 1990. An excellent analysis of how the Norman Conquest was used to influence national identity in the nineteenth century.

Simons, John, ed. *From Medieval to Medievalism.* New York, 1992. Essays relating medieval studies to modern criticism and the shaping of ideas of the Middle Ages.

Utz, Richard, and Tom Shippey, eds. *Medievalism in the Modern World: Essays in Honour of Leslie J. Workman.* Turnhout, Belgium, 1998. See especially the interview with Workman, pp. 439–440.

Warton, Thomas. *The History of English Poetry, from the Close of the Eleventh to the Commencement of the Eighteenth Century.* London, 1774–1806; repr. New York, 1968.

Warton, Thomas. "Verses on Sir Joshua Reynolds' Painted Window at New College, Oxford, 1782." In his *Poetical Works.* 5th ed. Oxford, 1802; repr. 1969.

MEDIEVAL SAINTS' LIVES

Karen A. Winstead

Saints' lives are by far the largest part of the vast body of literature known as hagiography, or "writings about the holy." Figures from the New Testament and Apocrypha, such as John the Baptist, Mary Magdalene, Paul, and the Apostles, were the earliest Christian saints and among the most enduringly popular. Their stories established concepts of holiness and literary motifs that would be used by hagiographers for centuries to come—for example, imitation of Christ as a guide to life, miracle-working, penitence, and asceticism as marks of sanctity, confrontation with a pagan tyrant as a climactic plot episode, and martyrdom as the supreme act of devotion.

In late antiquity (the period between the fall of the Roman Empire and the Middle Ages), two important hagiographical genres took shape: the martyr legend and the life of the confessor. (The term "legend" in this context comes from a Latin word meaning "something to be read" and does not have its present-day connotation of untruth.) Martyr legends celebrate the heroism of Christians who died during the Roman persecutions of the second, third, and early fourth centuries, while the first lives of confessors (non-martyrs) mostly honor "desert fathers" who demonstrated their heroism through extreme asceticism. The division of saints into martyrs and confessors persisted throughout the Middle Ages. Martyr legends typically focus on the protagonist's trial before a pagan official, courageous endurance of horrible torments, and excruciating death. Though lives of confessors came to vary considerably depending on whether the saint was male or female, hermit or king, abbess or wife, they typically recount portents attending the saint's birth, a devout childhood, an adult life marked by miracles, an exemplary death, and further, posthumous miracles.

Saints' lives rarely reflect modern ideas of biography. Not only are they full of miracles, but the lives of many different saints are improbably similar. Indeed, medieval hagiographers were, by modern standards, shameless plagiarists, borrowing plots, passages, and sometimes whole lives from legends of other saints. Many of the most popular saints were largely or wholly invented, their first "bi-ographies" composed centuries after they supposedly lived. The dashing George, who fought a dragon to save a damsel in distress, is a famous example. Hundreds of legends were written about virgin martyrs—women who died for refusing to surrender either their faith or their bodies to lecherous pagans—legends that are as formulaic and sometimes as graphic as paperback romances. Even the legends of historical saints like Francis of Assisi, who are well documented in reliable sources, often contain fabulous elements. As the lives of saints were continually rewritten, authors felt free to embellish and otherwise modify the texts they had inherited to suit either their own agendas or the tastes and interests of their audiences. However, medieval hagiographers who took what we might consider egregious liberties with historical fact did not think they were writing fiction; rather, their chief concern was to convey moral, not historical, truth. They wrote to celebrate Christian heroism and to inspire awe and devotion.

Saints' lives formed an important part of medieval popular culture, and they were enjoyed by all sectors of society. Depending on their audience, they might be somber accounts of piety or sensational adventure stories. Saints' lives were also literary vehicles for exploring social issues such as sexuality, gender roles, family relations, politics, and national identity. Though historians and literary critics long disparaged saints' lives for lacking artistry and historical accuracy, recent scholars of medieval culture have mined them for the insights they offer into the values and attitudes of medieval authors and their audiences.

EARLY BRITISH LIVES

The earliest British hagiographers wrote in Latin during the late seventh and early eighth centuries, inaugurating a rich literature of native saints. The first surviving text in this genre is an anonymous prose life of Saint Cuthbert, a seventh-century monk who became bishop of Lindisfarne. Other early Anglo-Latin lives include a life of Bishop Wilfrid (died 709) by Stephen of Ripon; Felix's life of the hermit Guthlac, a sort of Anglo-Saxon desert father who abandoned a successful military career to battle the demons haunting the fens of Mercia; and a life of Gregory the Great, the pope who, in 597, dispatched missionaries to convert the Anglo-Saxons.

It is appropriate that Cuthbert be the earliest known subject of English hagiography, for he would become one of Britain's best-known saints, and his cult spread to many parts of Continental Europe. Cuthbert's fame owed much to the efforts of the English historian, hagiographer, and biblical exegete Bede (673–735), who produced two lives of Cuthbert, one in verse and one in prose, each significantly elaborating and refining the story recounted in the anonymous life. One of the most important hagiographers of the Anglo-Saxon period, Bede also wrote the first "narrative" martyrology, providing short biographies to flesh out the standard list of saints' names and feast days, and lives of English saints pervade his widely circulated *Ecclesiastical History of the English People*.

Saints' lives were also well represented in Old English literature. In the ninth or tenth century, Cynewulf composed three saints' lives in verse. *Elene* recounts the discovery of the Cross by Helen, mother of Emperor Constantine; *Juliana* is the earliest surviving virgin martyr legend in a Western European vernacular tongue; and *The Fates of the Apostles* briefly describes the heroic deaths of each of Christ's disciples. Three other, anonymous Old English saints' poems probably date from about Cynewulf's time. *Andreas* recounts the Apostle Andrew's mission to convert the Mermedonian cannibals and rescue his comrade Matthew from their clutches. The other two deal with Guthlac, one focusing on his life as a hermit and the other on his death. As these summaries suggest, Old English poets tended to recount heroic episodes rather than full biographies. Though based on Latin sources, their poems are distinctively Anglo-Saxon, suffused with elements of native epic and elegy. The saints are Christian versions of Beowulf, thanes devoted to their leader, Christ, willing to endure loneliness and exile for his sake and eager to wage war against the demons and nonbelievers who are his enemies.

Anglo-Saxon England also produced an impressive body of vernacular hagiography in prose. An Old English martyrology, written in the ninth century in the narrative tradition established by Bede, is the first vernacular prose martyrology in all Europe and perhaps the earliest example of Old English narrative prose. Prose saints' lives flourished from the tenth century on, thanks in part to King Alfred's campaign to provide vernacular religious instruction to the laity. By far the most influential and prolific Old English hagiographer was Ælfric, tenth-century Abbot of Eynsham, whose anthology of saints' lives and two homily collections include lives of more than sixty saints, from Roman martyrs to native confessors like Cuthbert. Ælfric's lives, written in a distinctive rhythmic and alliterative style, constitute about two-thirds of the extant hagiography in Old English prose.

THE POST-CONQUEST TRADITION TO 1400

Although a few were written in Old English following the Norman Conquest of 1066, there was a lull in the production of vernacular saints' lives until the late 1000s and early 1100s, when the first surviving lives in Anglo-Norman French were written. However, the century following the Conquest produced a rich corpus of Latin hagiography, much of it on Anglo-Saxon saints. Some of these native saints had never been commemorated until they came to the attention of Norman hagiographers or hagiographers sponsored by Norman patrons.

Among the earliest lives in Anglo-Norman French is one of Saint Alexis, who abandoned his bride on their wedding night to embrace a life of exile and asceticism, which is widely considered the finest vernacular rendition of the popular Alexis legend. It is preserved in the *St. Albans Psalter*, a manuscript probably created for the twelfth-century recluse Christina of Markyate, who may have had Alexis in mind when she forsook her own spouse to devote herself to God. During the mid-twelfth century, two lives were written by Wace, the canon of Bayeux best known for originating King Arthur's Round Table in his verse chronicle, the *Roman de Brut*. One is a life of Margaret of Antioch, the virgin martyr who emerged unscathed from a dragon's belly to become patron saint of childbirth; the other is a life of Nicholas of Myra, the wonder-working bishop whose feats included the resurrection of three students who had been minced and pickled by a thieving innkeeper. Fascination with the spectacular deeds of early saints continued throughout the Anglo-Norman period. At the beginning of the fourteenth century, the most prolific Anglo-Norman hagiographer, Nicholas Bozon, wrote lives of six virgin martyrs, as well as of Martha, Mary Magdalene, and two desert fathers; his only life of a later saint is that of Elizabeth of Hungary.

Lives of saints native to the British Isles also proliferated in Anglo-French hagiography. During the late twelfth century, the monk Benedeit recounted the fantastic sea voyage of the Irish monk Brendan. Benedeit also composed a life of Archbishop Thomas Becket, who became the subject of a tremendous cult and vast hagiography almost immediately after his 1170 assassination in Canterbury Cathedral. Other noteworthy examples include Denis Piramus's late-twelfth-century life of Edmund, a king of East Anglia slain by the Danes, and Matthew Paris's mid-thirteenth-century lives of Alban, Edward the Confessor, Thomas Becket, and Edmund of Abingdon. Piramus and Paris exemplify a trend toward longer saints' lives with an interest in character and historical detail.

Women played an important role in the development and preservation of the Anglo-Norman hagiographical tradition as we know it. Christina of Markyate's probable association with the life of Alexis has already been noted, and many other lives likewise were either written for women or survive in manuscripts owned by women. Moreover, at least three Anglo-Norman lives of the twelfth and thirteenth centuries were written by women: a life of Katherine of Alexandria by Clemence, a nun of Barking Abbey; a life of Edward the Confessor, also by a nun of Barking (possibly Clemence); and a life of Etheldreda by a woman identified only as "Marie." The importance of women as readers, patrons, and authors may account for the rich representation of female holiness in Anglo-Norman saints' lives, encompassing virgin martyrs, penitents, abbesses, nuns, and holy laywomen, both legendary and historical.

Although women would not exert a similarly pervasive influence on Middle English hagiography until the fifteenth century, the first Middle English saints' lives were of virgin martyrs—Katherine, Margaret, and Juliana—and were probably written for nuns or female recluses. These lives, in alliterative, rhythmic prose, form part of a set of devotional texts known as the "Katherine Group" that appears intended to strengthen the professed virgin's devotion to celibacy and to her heavenly bridegroom, Christ.

Middle English saints' lives of the late thirteenth and fourteenth centuries tend to be short, action-centered, and morally simple. Most were composed within, or added to, anthologies of saints' lives called "legendaries." Legendaries, at first written in Latin, became widespread during the thirteenth century as reference works for priests charged with educating the laity. Later, vernacular legendaries were read by both the clergy and laypeople. The largest and most widely circulated in Middle English is the so-called *South English Legendary*, which originated during the late thirteenth century and was extensively revised and supplemented during the following two centuries. More than sixty manuscripts of it survive, containing lives in verse of more than ninety saints. Most are

martyrs and confessors of the early Church, but a substantial minority are British—kings, bishops, and nuns of the Anglo-Saxon past, along with Thomas Becket, whose exceptionally detailed life is, at 2,500 lines, the longest narrative in the collection and indeed one of the longest Middle English lives composed before 1400.

The most popular subjects of freestanding saints' lives—that is, lives not composed as part of a legendary—appear to have been virgin martyrs, especially Katherine and Margaret. A predilection for virgin saints seems natural among celibate priests and nuns, yet the only two Middle English saints' lives known to have been written by laypeople are also virgin martyr legends. Before 1390, Geoffrey Chaucer composed a rhetorically polished but otherwise very conventional life of Saint Cecilia, which he later incorporated into the *Canterbury Tales* as the "Second Nun's Tale." Around 1400, Chaucer's contemporary William Paris produced a life of Saint Christine. With its strong-willed, combative heroine, Paris's narrative epitomizes the fast-paced, conflict-oriented martyr legend popular at the time; it also features a rare biographical epilogue in which Paris, a political prisoner on the Isle of Man, reflects on his fate.

THE HAGIOGRAPHICAL TRADITION AFTER 1400

The fifteenth century brought extraordinary innovation in Middle English hagiography; indeed, it might well be called English hagiography's Golden Age. Perhaps because English had supplanted French as the language of culture, Middle English saints' lives became far more complex in their plots and themes, their rhetoric became more ornate, and they began to evince the interest in history and psychology that is found in Latin and French lives from the twelfth century forward. For the first time, moreover, and reflecting broader trends in English literature, much of this hagiography is in prose.

John Lydgate, a prolific author of history, romance, and hagiography, inaugurated a more sophisticated and self-consciously "literary" hagiography during the first half of the fifteenth century. His six-thousand-line *Life of Our Lady* is a novel hybrid of saint's life and meditative tract that uses episodes from the Virgin Mary's early life as occasions for extended spiritual reflection and doctrinal instruction. His verse *Lives of Saints Edmund and Fremund* and *Lives of Saints Alban and Amphibalus* are suffused with historical detail and evoke issues and complexities that had not been explicit concerns in the past. Alban agonizes over his conversion, while Edmund struggles to reconcile his conceptions of Christian and kingly duty. Around 1445 John Capgrave produced a rhyme-royal *Life of Saint Katherine* that brought the complex, literary hagiography of Lydgate to a wider audience. Capgrave's *Katherine*, told through an obtrusive, Chaucerian narrator, recounts her life as simultaneously a religious triumph and a political failure. A young female scholar who longs to escape the demands put on her as a woman and a ruler, Katherine is one of the most nuanced heroines of Middle English literature.

Hagiographical epics in the Lydgate tradition continued to be written into the early sixteenth century, and the same epic impulse informs the Mary Magdalene play found in the Digby manuscript, which was written about 1500. The Magdalene play is one of only two surviving Middle English saints' plays (the other, on Paul, is also in the Digby manuscript) and is one of the most complex and spectacular works of medieval English drama.

The fifteenth century saw a broader spectrum of female holiness represented in Middle English hagiography, perhaps because women were becoming important readers and patrons. Lives of holy wives began to appear; among the most popular was Mary's mother, Anne. Lives of Continental holy women from the recent past—Catherine of Siena, Bridget of Sweden, Marie d'Oignies, Christina "the Astonishing" of Saint-Trond, and Elizabeth of Hungary—were translated into English for the first time. Notable among authors who wrote explicitly for women is Osbern Bokenham, who composed verse lives of female saints for East Anglian gentlewomen. Female readers, though, were not interested only in lives of women: Symon Wynter composed a prose life of Jerome for Margaret, duchess of Clarence, and Capgrave's life of Augustine was commissioned by an unnamed gentlewoman.

One of the first books printed in English was William Caxton's *Golden Legend*, a prose translation of Jacobus de Voragine's popular thirteenth-century Latin legendary supplemented with lives of English saints. First published in 1483, Caxton's legendary went through nine printings by 1517. More than any other work, it defined the saint's-life genre for early modern readers.

[*See also* Ælfric; King Alfred; Bede; Osbern Bokenham; John Capgrave; William Caxton; Geoffrey Chaucer; Cynewulf; Digby Plays; *and* John Lydgate.]

EDITIONS AND TRANSLATIONS

Bradley, S. A. J, ed. *Anglo-Saxon Poetry*. London, 1982. Includes translations of *Andreas, Elene, The Fates of the Apostles*, and both Guthlac poems.

Head, Thomas, ed. *Medieval Hagiography: An Anthology*. New York, 2000. Wide selection of major texts in translation; British works include Bede's *Martyrology* and lives of Alexis, Margaret of Antioch, and Marie d'Oignies.

Webb, J. F., and D. H. Farmer, eds. *The Age of Bede*. New York, 1983. Translation of early Anglo-Latin lives, including Bede's prose life of Cuthbert.

Winstead, Karen A., trans. *Chaste Passions: Medieval English Virgin Martyr Legends*. Ithaca, NY, 2000. Translations of Middle English texts from the Katherine Group, *South English Legendary*, and works of Chaucer, Paris, Lydgate, and Bokenham.

Wogan-Browne, Jocelyn, and Glyn Burgess, trans. *Virgin Lives and Holy Deaths: Two Exemplary Biographies for Anglo-Norman Women*. London, 1996. Translations of Clemence of Barking's life of Katherine and an anonymous life of Lawrence.

FURTHER READING

Ashley, Kathleen M., and Pamela Sheingorn, eds. *Interpreting Cultural Symbols: Saint Anne in Late Medieval Society*. Athens, GA, 1990. Seminal introduction discusses cultural approaches to hagiography.

Bynum, Caroline Walker. *Holy Feast and Holy Fast: The Religious Significance of Food to Medieval Women*. Berkeley, CA, 1987. Influential study of late medieval women saints, focusing on Continental Europe.

Coletti, Theresa. *Mary Magdalene and the Drama of Saints: Theater, Gender, and Religion in Late Medieval England*. Philadelphia, 2004. The social and cultural contexts of the Digby Mary Magdalene play.

Lapidge, Michael. "The Saintly Life in Anglo-Saxon England." In *The Cambridge Companion to Old English Literature*, edited by Malcolm Godden and Michael Lapidge, 243–263. Cambridge, U.K., 1991.

Rollason, David W. *Saints and Relics in Anglo-Saxon England*. Oxford, 1989.

Thompson, Anne B. *Everyday Saints and the Art of Narrative in the South English Legendary*. Burlington, VT, 2003. An accessible introduction to the major legendary.

Winstead, Karen A. *Virgin Martyrs: Legends of Sainthood in Late Medieval England*. Ithaca, NY, 1997.

Wogan-Browne, Jocelyn. *Saints' Lives and Women's Literary Culture c. 1150–1300: Virginity and Its Authorizations*. Oxford, 2001. An important study of the Anglo-Norman hagiographical tradition.

MELODRAMA

Emily Allen

When melodrama burst onto the London stage at the beginning of the nineteenth century, it not only revolutionized theatrical aesthetics and practice, it also marked the rise of a cultural form that would have a profound and lasting impact on modern life. Melodrama is both a theatrical genre and a way of imagining the world that infiltrated other artistic forms (particularly the novel and film) and came to influence many aspects of British life, from public politics to private family dynamics. With characteristic vigor, melodrama found its way into courtrooms and newsrooms, parlors and parliament, onto television and cinema screens, and across the Atlantic and around the globe. Although often diminished and overlooked as a "popular" form, melodrama cannot be underestimated as a flexible and pervasive cultural force.

THE RISE OF MELODRAMA

Given how revolutionary the history of melodrama has been, it makes perfect sense that melodrama was born of revolution; namely the French Revolution of 1789. Prior to the revolution, licensed French theaters produced only "traditional" plays: tragedy or high comedy. Unlicensed theaters were allowed by law to play only wordless drama, and they developed a drama of visual spectacle and action that was considered inappropriate for elite theater audiences, although tremendously popular with the lower classes. One result of the revolution was the deregulation of French theaters, which allowed the populist drama of the streets and unlicensed theaters free theatrical reign on the nation's stages.

Mélo-drame (literally, "music-drama" or "song-drama," from the Greek) came of age in the 1790s, and its highly theatrical, physical, and sensational aesthetic drew strongly on the tradition of wordless spectacle. Although Jean-Jacques Rousseau was the first to use the term *mélodrame*, referring to his play *Pygmalion* (1770), in which dramatic monologue alternates with pantomime and musical accompaniment, the true "father" of the genre is considered to be Guilbert de Pixérécourt, who wrote the most successful melodramas of the late 1790s and famously claimed to write for those who could not read. Pixérécourt's exceptionally popular *Victor, ou l'enfant de la forêt* (Victor, or the Child of the Forest, 1798) was followed by *Coelina, ou l'enfant de mystère* (Coelina, or the Child of Mystery, 1800), which crossed the channel in 1802 as A Tale of Mystery, adapted for the London stage by Thomas Holcroft.

While Holcroft's *A Tale of Mystery* is frequently cited as the first British melodrama (another candidate is Thomas Dibdin's 1804 *Valentine and Orson*), it would be too simple to claim that British melodrama was taken directly from France, for the genre had a complicated and in many ways parallel development in Britain, where theatrical licensing laws similarly produced a two-tiered system of "legitimate" and "illegitimate" theater. Early French melodrama also borrowed heavily from the British gothic novel, which further muddies lines of intersection and influence.

Following the 1737 Licensing Act, which gave the monopoly on spoken drama to London's two "patent theaters," Drury Lane and Covent Garden (and, later, the Haymarket), nonpatent theaters developed a flourishing culture of spectacular entertainment, which mixed song, dance, pantomime, animal acts, pyrotechnics, and many kinds of elaborate and thrilling visual extravaganza. British melodrama is descended from, and often overlaps with, these earlier spectacular forms, which include traditional pantomime (or "panto"), *pose plastique* (live models in static attitudes), and *tableau vivant* (or "living pictures," costumed actors grouped in still poses, as in a painting).

The melodramatic aesthetic is highly visual and gestural, relying on the expressions of the body. Melodramatic acting was characterized by physical, facial, and vocal exaggeration, and it likewise sought to produce thrills and chills of emotion in the bodies of its large (and largely working-class) audience. As in France, melodrama in Britain was initially considered a "low" and "illegitimate" genre, tied to the sensation-hungry urban working class.

468

Because of its class ties, and because of its connection to revolutionary France, melodrama was at first considered a dangerous and radical form, although its politics turned out to be highly flexible as it developed during the nineteenth century.

Also highly flexible was the melodramatic "formula," which was capable of almost infinite variety when it came to producing types of the form: gothic, Oriental, urban, Irish, nautical, military, domestic, historical, imperial, crime, temperance, and even equestrian, canine, and feline melodramas proliferated on British stages, as melodrama spread out from industrial centers to captivate rural and eventually colonial audiences.

Within this amazing variety, certain structures remained fairly constant, however. At its core, melodrama provided a morally legible confrontation between good and evil, resulting in the sometimes violent and necessarily spectacular overthrow of the villain and the restoration of moral order. Along with the villain, who often stole the show in a scenery-chewing, moustache-twirling turn of sheer dastardliness, stock melodramatic characters included the upright and handsome hero (often more upstanding than clever) and the long-suffering and virtuous heroine, whose efforts to resist the evil machinations of the villain generally lend the melodramatic plot its suspense, pathos, and center of moral gravity. Comic and pathetic characters—children, aged parents, and the like—rounded out the melodramatic cast, but the basic confrontation usually took place between the villain (often representing an authority figure of some type, such as a landlord or factory owner) and the hero and heroine (often representing the weak and downtrodden, which is to say, in melodrama, the morally pure).

In a standard melodramatic plot, the play initially establishes the virtue of the hero and/or heroine (along with the base intentions of the villain), dispatches the hero in such a way as to leave the heroine vulnerable to the villain's wiles, produces a crisis in which the forces of evil look certain to triumph over those of good, and finishes with a spectacular turn in which good and evil receive their just deserts. And, of course, everyone sings or, alternatively, speaks their lines to musical accompaniment or punctuation, which helped set the emotional tone of productions and cue an audience response.

Given the thousands upon thousands of melodramas produced in Britain during the nineteenth century, it is not surprising that the melodramatic "formula" given above had many variations, some of which troubled the clear moral distinctions of the traditional plot. In Douglas

Jerrold's famous nautical melodrama *Black-Ey'd Susan* (1829), for example, the sailor-hero, William, is torn between his national duty to the navy and his domestic duty to his wife, Susan. Everything works out at the last moment, when William is disclosed as having been discharged from the navy before he struck a superior officer for making unwanted sexual advances on Susan, but the moral and political choices staged by the play are difficult ones.

Rather than viewing melodrama as an escapist and emotionally manipulative form that delivered simplistic moral lessons to the masses, as it was often characterized by its detractors, we can see it as a heightened dramatic form that staged historically specific conflicts, allowing its audience to negotiate the most pressing ideological contradictions of the day (for example, the conflict between state authority and domestic duty). Understanding melodrama as ideological work helps to explain not only its vast popularity and tremendous longevity, but also its peculiar political flexibility.

While melodramas dealt with the most important and sensitive political issues of the day (national and imperial identity, gender roles, class formations, racial relations, socioeconomic changes), they did so in both strikingly radical and conservative ways—sometimes within the same play. If the "happy ending" of melodrama appears to force moral and ideological closure, the plays themselves can question the status quo in thrilling and disturbing ways. In C. H. Hazelwood's 1863 melodramatic adaptation of Mary Elizabeth Braddon's sensation novel, *Lady Audley's Secret*, for example, the female lead is the villain, and her final (and shockingly abrupt) mad scene raises as many questions about female identity and agency as it lays to rest:

> Aye—aye! [Laughs wildly.] Mad, mad, that is the word. I feel it here—here! [Places her hands on her temples.] Do not touch me—do not come near me—let me claim your silence—your pity—and let the grave, the cold grave, close over Lady Audley and her Secret. [Falls—dies—Music—tableau of sympathy—George Talboys kneels over her.]

In the decade following the 1857 Matrimonial Causes Act, which first gave women the right to divorce, and when women's roles were being vigorously contested, the sympathetic madness of a bigamous woman—one who has attempted to murder her first husband by tossing him down a well—was hot stuff indeed.

Melodrama's heady stew of sensational plotting, emotional and visual excess, gestural largesse, and political sensitivity (not to mention its murders, floods, fires, avalanches, shipwrecks, and many, many explosions) made it the most popular and influential theatrical form of the nineteenth century. As it swiftly came to dominate the stages of "illegitimate" theaters after the turn of the nineteenth century, it swept the capital and the country, borrowing its plots from wherever it chose (French melodramas and novels, British novels, "legitimate" drama, true crime stories and court proceedings, naval battles, etc.). Nothing was sacred: even Shakespeare, the high priest of the legitimate spoken drama, was given the melodramatic treatment, with plays radically shortened, leavened with music, and often given the requisite happy ending (Hamlet sings—and lives!). With packed houses attending melodramatic fare, the patent theaters could not compete, and Drury Lane and Covent Garden almost immediately got into the melodramatic act themselves.

By the time the 1843 Theatre Regulation Act legally abolished the difference between legitimate and illegitimate productions, that difference had largely ceased to exist, and by midcentury much "melodrama" had simply become "drama," losing some of its music but none of its emotion or flair. By midcentury, too, melodrama's audience had come to include the theater-going middle classes as well as its working-class core audience.

The standard critical trajectory for melodrama sees the form becoming increasingly conservative over the course of the century, as it moves from such radical or working-class plays as Jerrold's *The Rent Day* (1832) and John Walker's *The Factory Lad* (1832), both of which premiered just before the passage of the 1832 Reform Bill that expanded voting rights, through the more bourgeois domestic melodrama of midcentury, such as T. W. Robertson's "cup and saucer" drama *Caste* (1867) and T. A. Palmer's 1874 theatrical adaptation of Ellen Wood's novel *East Lynne*, to the patriotic and jingoistic fantasies of late-nineteenth-century imperial melodrama. Recent critical thinking, however, allows for a more complicated narrative, in which the politics of melodrama were always quite mixed. Both the audience and the cultural function of melodrama changed during its long nineteenth-century run, but in ways that were at once historically specific and ideologically complex.

MELODRAMA OFFSTAGE

The curtain fell on British stage melodrama sometime shortly after the turn of the twentieth century, when more realistic theatrical forms had largely taken its spot in the

cultural limelight. But like the traditional stage pantomime to which it was related, melodrama proved to be something of a changeling, capable of great feats of transformation as it moved from one cultural and artistic register to the next. By the time melodrama bowed its way off the stage, it had long since found other homes no less hospitable and influential.

MELODRAMA AND THE NOVEL

One such home was in the pages of the nineteenth-century novel, which shared with melodrama an intense and sometimes vexed relationship of mutual influence. Stage melodramas frequently borrowed plots from best-selling novels (there were, for example, thousands of melodramatic productions launched by the novels of Sir Walter Scott and Charles Dickens), and the novel returned this regard by incorporating into itself melodramatic plotting and character. While obviously less visual and musical than staged drama, the novel was similarly given to sentiment and sensation, and as a popular and commercial form it naturally played to the public—a public it shared, and for which it competed, with the popular stage. Because of this competition, and because the novel was itself an "illegitimate" form seeking cultural legitimacy, nineteenth-century novels often downplayed their connection to melodrama, claiming instead a greater realism and gravity. In spite of such claims, however, the novel clearly bears the melodramatic mark, particularly in the sensational cliffhangers of serialized fiction (analogous to the "sensation scene" of theater) and in the domestic novel's highly emotional vision of familial morality. Popular novel genres tied most closely to melodrama include the gothic novel, the Newgate novel (crime fiction named after the prison), the penny dreadful (suspense fiction named after its price), and the sensation novel (so-called for its wild popularity, sensational plotting, and presumed effect on its reader).

MELODRAMA ON SCREEN

Another important locus of nineteenth-century melodrama is film, which took many of its early scripts, and much of its early aesthetic, from the stage. Silent film, in particular, owes a heavy debt to stage melodrama, and its gestural economy obviously draws on the melodramatic tradition. Two prominent examples of silent cinematic melodrama are D. W. Griffith's *Broken Blossoms* (1919) and *Orphans of the Storm* (1921), the latter film set during the French Revolution at the "birth" of melodrama. Contemporary film criticism has come to use the term "melo-drama" to describe films of heightened visual style and intense emotional effects, such as Hollywood's "women's films" of the 1930s and 1940s, which focus on the point of view of the suffering heroine, as in King Vidor's 1937 remake of Henry King's 1925 tearjerker, *Stella Dallas,* or Michael Curtiz's 1945 *Mildred Pierce.* Hollywood's "family melodrama" of the 1940s and 1950s has also received much critical attention; high-water marks of the genre include films by Vincente Minnelli, Nicholas Ray, and particularly Douglas Sirk, whose films include *All that Heaven Allows* (1955), *Written on the Wind* (1956), and *Imitation of Life* (1959). Melodrama has also made the move to serialized television, such as day- and nighttime "soap operas," in which the genre's emotional excess is on full display. As with theater and the novel, melodramatic film and television have often been dismissed as superficial, escapist, manipulative, and crassly commercial, but recent critics have come to recognize these popular forms as spaces of ideological conflict and negotiation that bear close examination.

OTHER MELODRAMATIC DISCOURSES

Nineteenth-century melodrama also had, and continues to have, a considerable influence on nonartistic forms of representation. In public life, for example, melodrama both gave the masses a way to understand and express their opposition to authority (as they famously did during the 1809 "O.P. Wars," or "Old Price Riots," when melodramatic crowds protested official changes at the national theater, Covent Garden) and gave national authority a way to express itself to the masses (as it did, for example, in the lavish pageants of state that characterized the Victorian period). In journalism, melodrama helped produce a sensational style that marked many Victorian publications (such as *Illustrated Police News* and *The Divorce Court Reporter*) and is still with us today. Criminal trials likewise took a page from melodrama's book. Perhaps melodrama's most important contribution to modern life, however, is that it has given us a rubric through which to understand our moral and emotional lives. The aesthetic and thematic patterns of melodrama still limn our daily existence and remain culturally resonant long after the descent of melodrama's final curtain.

[*See also* Detective Fiction; The Gothic; Popular Romance; *and* Sensation Novel.]

FURTHER READING

Booth, Michael R. *English Melodrama.* London, 1965. The first important and still standard text on the topic, this is an excellent and readable introduction for any student of English stage melodrama.

Bratton, Jacky, Jim Cook, and Christine Gledhill, eds. *Melodrama: Stage, Picture, Screen.* London, 1994. A significant and wide-ranging collection of essays that brings together critical discussions of melodrama in its many visual forms (theatrical, cinematic, pictorial). Includes essays by Peter Brooks, Martin Meisel, Laura Mulvey, and others.

Brooks, Peter. *The Melodramatic Imagination: Balzac, Henry James, Melodrama, and the Mode of Excess.* New Haven, CT, 1976. A landmark book that initiated much critical work on the topic. Brooks argues that the "melodramatic mode" has become the "central fact of the modern sensibility" that takes over the moral function of the sacred in a post-sacred era.

Hadley, Elaine. *Melodramatic Tactics: Theatricalized Dissent in the English Marketplace, 1800–1850.* Stanford, CA, 1995. An important reconsideration of the politics of nineteenth-century melodrama. Hadley argues that the melodramatic mode provided a public and theatricalized paradigm for resistance to the hierarchies of market capitalism.

Hays, Michael, and Anastasia Nikolopoulou, eds. *Melodrama: The Cultural Emergence of a Genre.* New York, 1996. A helpful collection of essays on the cultural function of nineteenth-century stage melodrama. Includes essays by Michael Booth, Jeffrey N. Cox, Thomas Postlewait, and others.

Landy, Marcia, ed. *Imitations of Life: A Reader on Film and Television Melodrama.* Detroit, MI, 1991. A useful introduction for students of cinematic or televisual melodrama. Includes essays by Mary Anne Doane, Thomas Elsaesser, Tania Modleski, Linda Williams, and others.

Meisel, Martin. *Realizations: Narrative, Pictorial, and Theatrical Arts in Nineteenth-Century England.* Princeton, NJ, 1983. The most influential study of the connections among drama, painting, and fiction, with strongest emphasis on the theatricality of the pictorial image.

Moody, Jane. *Illegitimate Theatre in London, 1770–1840.* Cambridge, U.K., 2000. A full-scale account of London's "illegitimate" theaters and theatrical forms, which provides a lively history of early melodrama and its adjacent (and overlapping) genres.

GEORGE MEREDITH

Daniel Hack

By the time of his death, the novelist and poet George Meredith (1828–1909) had achieved quasi-official status as one of the greatest writers of his time: president of the Society of Authors and recipient of the Order of Merit, he had been showered with testimonials from heads of state and men of letters alike on his eightieth birthday. In view of his difficult childhood and the trouble he had in becoming established as an author, Meredith's ascent to such eminence was a remarkable achievement. Also remarkable, however, was the rapid and sustained decline of his posthumous reputation: by 1928 Virginia Woolf could declare that "the general conclusion would seem to be [that] he has not worn well," and today he is far less often read, taught, and studied than almost any other authors with whom he was ranked during his long career, such as George Eliot, Thomas Hardy, and Henry James. Yet if for many readers the frustrations presented by Meredith's notoriously mannered prose style outweigh its rewards, he remains a significant, at times compelling writer whose restless testing of the formal limits of the Victorian novel—and indeed, his very willingness to frustrate his readers—helped pave the way for the more radical experiments of modernism.

George Meredith
Photograph by Alvin Langdon Coburn, 1904

FINDING HIS WAY

Meredith was born 12 February 1828 in Portsmouth, the only child of Augustus Meredith, a naval outfitter and tailor, and Jane Meredith (née Macnamara). His childhood was marked by loss and dislocation: his mother died when he was five years old, and his father, who had inherited his own father's prominent tailoring establishment, declared bankruptcy in 1838 and moved away, first to London and later to South Africa, leaving George a ward in chancery (that is, under the supervision of the courts). Supported by a small legacy from his mother's family, Meredith briefly attended a boarding school in England and spent two formative years at a progressive Moravian school in Neuwied, Germany. At the age of twenty-one, he married Mary Ellen Nicolls, the widowed daughter of the writer Thomas Love Peacock, but the ensuing decade proved no less turbulent than his youth: the couple had little success in their attempt to support themselves by writing, and their marriage broke up in 1857, when Mary left Meredith and their young son to elope with the painter Henry Wallis, who had used Meredith the previous year as the model for his widely reproduced painting *The Death of Chatterton*. Mary died in 1861, and three years later Meredith married Marie Vulliamy, with whom he had two children. Domestically, the second half of Meredith's life was as stable as the first half was unsettled; his second marriage was a happy one, and the family's finances slowly improved. In 1867 the Merediths moved to Flint Cottage, near Box Hill, Surrey, and lived there the rest of their lives, Marie dying in 1885 and Meredith himself in 1909.

Although a famous talker, Meredith rarely discussed his family background and early experiences; he could be evasive about even such basic facts as his place of birth. However, recognizable versions of individuals and situations from his private life—along with the sense of shame that no doubt contributed to his reticence—recur in his writings, especially those from the period in the late 1850s and early 1860s when he solidified his career. That career began slowly. Meredith contributed poems and articles to a number of periodicals in the early 1850s and, at his own expense, published a volume of poetry that received some good reviews but did not sell. Turning to prose fiction,

Meredith wrote *The Shaving of Shagpat* (1856), a collection of linked stories subtitled "An Arabian Entertainment" and modeled on the *Arabian Nights*. This work also met with limited commercial success but received some very positive reviews, with Marian Evans (the future George Eliot) praising it as a work of "poetical genius." This book also marked the beginning of Meredith's association with Chapman and Hall, a firm that would publish many of his novels and for which he worked for over three decades as a reader of manuscripts. In this capacity, Meredith helped launch the careers of George Gissing and Thomas Hardy, although he rejected Hardy's first novel, the now lost *The Poor Man and the Lady*.

Meredith followed *The Shaving of Shagpat* with another pastiche, *Farina: A Legend of Cologne* (1857), which received mixed reviews and has attracted little later attention. Next, however, he produced the first of the works that make him a significant figure in the history of the English novel: *The Ordeal of Richard Feverel* (1859), a determinedly unconventional Bildungsroman which introduces Meredith's career-long interests in generational conflict, egoism, and the perils of romantic idealism. Subtitled "A History of Father and Son," the novel tells the often comic but ultimately tragic story of Richard Feverel's formation by and fitful rebellion against the authoritarian, quasi-scientific "System" of moral and sexual education devised by his father—like Meredith, a man left to raise his son alone after losing his wife to another man. Although the novel is sufficiently explicit in its handling of sexuality that Mudie's, the leading circulating library, canceled its order, its unconventionality lies less in its candor than in its formal properties. Most striking are the allusive, baroque style and generic and tonal variability, even instability: refusing to settle into any one voice or genre, the novel mixes discourses, aligns itself at various times with New Comedy, chivalric romance, and the novel of education, and shifts with dizzying speed between "levity, fierce thought, high-spirited humour, garish drama, lyricism and integrity of insight," as the critic Gillian Beer puts it. Its experimental spirit, self-reflexiveness, ostentatious wit, and occasional, seemingly willful obscurity are typical of the dozen novels Meredith would write over the next three and a half decades.

Richard Feverel firmly established Meredith as one of the first British novelists to achieve a prestige not matched by popularity. Moreover, this prestige was based largely on the very qualities that were seen to preclude popularity, such as a highly figurative style and an emphasis on the analysis of character at the expense of plot. Much more strongly than most of his Victorian predecessors, then, Meredith experienced the relationship between his authorial strengths and interests and the demands of the marketplace as one of tension, or even opposition. However, even as he anticipated the modernist model whereby commercial failure became a sign of artistic integrity, Meredith did not fully inhabit this model, especially in the first two decades of his career; instead, he sought a wider readership and was willing to make certain compromises to attain it. The novels written in the decade or so following *Richard Feverel* therefore move uneasily between continued experimentation and attempts at more straightforward narrative interest. These works include *Evan Harrington* (1860), a study of snobbery and social mobility that draws heavily on Meredith's own family history; *Emilia in England* (1864; later retitled *Sandra Belloni*), a treatment of sentimentalism featuring analytical interventions by both narrator and "Philosopher"; *Rhoda Fleming* (1865), a work that, in its plot if not its narration, reflects the contemporary vogue for "bigamy novels"; a sequel to *Sandra Belloni* titled *Vittoria* (1867), a novel of the failed Italian revolution of 1848–1849 which, unlike most of Meredith's novels, is crowded with incident; and *The Adventures of Harry Richmond* (1871), by Meredith's standards a relatively conventional Bildungsroman that, like the more audacious *Richard Feverel*, centers on a father-son relationship. These novels did not provide the increased popularity Meredith hoped for, nor were they all equally well received. On the whole, though, they did enhance his reputation, even though none is now ranked among his strongest.

Meredith's most significant publication of the 1860s was not his fiction but a volume of poetry, *Modern Love and Poems of the English Roadside* (1862). Although he wrote and published poetry throughout his career, it is above all upon this book's title poem that his enduring reputation as a poet rests. A sequence of fifty sixteen-line "sonnets" (as Meredith called them), "Modern Love" begins in the third person but is spoken mainly in the first person by a husband who has discovered his wife's infidelity. The poem combines lyric and narrative forms to create a searing, ultimately tragic portrayal of a disintegrating marriage. In its irony, syntactic and symbolic intricacies, psychological insight, and sexual frankness, "Modern Love" powerfully distills central strategies and preoccupations of Meredith's fiction, and it stands as one of the major long poems of the period.

THE MIDDLE YEARS

By the 1870s Meredith seems to have come to terms with his limited popularity, and he went on to produce much of his best work. *Beauchamp's Career* (1876) recounts the intertwined political and romantic fortunes of an idealistic but callow young man, Nevil Beauchamp, who breaks with his aristocratic family to make an unsuccessful bid for Parliament as a Radical. The novel, which displays Meredith's typical tonal instability and narrative indirection, ends abruptly with Beauchamp's death by drowning while saving a young working-class boy. While Meredith defended this ending as inevitable, many readers have found it gratuitous; one may suspect that its necessity for Meredith lay precisely in its thwarting of conventional readerly expectations. With its nuanced depiction of Cecilia Halkett, a Tory heiress who attempts to withstand the pressures of family and caste and grapple with the alien political convictions and romantic fickleness of the man she loves, *Beauchamp's Career* also demonstrates Meredith's increasingly acute and sympathetic (if also ironic) attention to the interiority of his leading female characters. This emphasis is especially prominent in his next novel, *The Egoist* (1879).

Considered by many Meredith's masterpiece, *The Egoist* tells the story of a young woman's desperate, ultimately successful attempt to free herself from her precipitous engagement to a monstrously self-centered baronet. Subtitled "A Comedy in Narrative," the novel puts into play ideas articulated in Meredith's 1877 lecture "On the Idea of Comedy and the Uses of the Comic Spirit" (commonly known as the "Essay on Comedy") and recalled in the first chapter of the novel. These ideas include comedy's corrective, civilizing nature and, more surprisingly, the notion that comedy, as exemplified by the plays of the seventeenth-century French dramatist Molière, not only focuses on the battle of the sexes but also shows that when men and women "draw together in social life their minds grow liker," as the "Essay" puts it. Yet whereas the "Essay" tends to make deviations from social norms the target of "the Comic Spirit," in *The Egoist* and elsewhere Meredith frequently criticized social conventions themselves, in particular those defining and delimiting women's roles. In *The Egoist*, for example, the monstrousness of Sir Willoughby Patterne's egotism marks less a departure from the norms of patriarchal English society than its epitome, as his very name suggests. At the same time, the novel's tone of comic detachment and its farcelike plot clash provocatively with the felt urgency of the characters' predicaments. As is so often true of Meredith (and so rarely true of earlier Victorian novelists), readers are left unsure of just how much or how little is meant to be at stake in what they have read.

More so than *The Egoist*, Meredith's next two novels develop another significant aspect of *Beauchamp's Career*: the increasingly overt use of the referential practices of the roman à clef, or fiction based on factual events and persons. *Beauchamp's Career* borrows freely but tacitly from the naval and political experiences and family background of Meredith's friend Frederick Maxse (and *The Egoist* includes an easily recognizable depiction of the man of letters Leslie Stephen); *The Tragic Comedians* (1880) is more explicitly based on fact, here a love affair of the German politician Ferdinand Lasalle—the work is subtitled "A Study in a Well-Known Story"; and *Diana of the Crossways* (1885), one of Meredith's finest works, openly recalls the sexual and political scandals involving the author Caroline Norton, a confidante of politicians who was involved in a well-publicized divorce case. In Meredith's hands, the ostentatiously referential nature of prominent characters—that is, their basis in real people—does not so much compensate for as mimic on another plane the ambiguously antireferential playfulness of his highly wrought language. The use of this technique in *Diana of the Crossways* also had unexpected commercial consequences: interest in the historical material helped make that novel by far Meredith's greatest popular success. Its strong sales prompted the publication of a uniform edition of his novels, many of which had gone out of print. Popularity and prestige came together here, as the appearance of this edition led to critical appreciations that further enhanced Meredith's reputation.

LATE CAREER AND LEGACY

Meredith wrote three more novels after *Diana of the Crossways*: *One of our Conquerors* (1891), *Lord Ormont and His Aminta* (1894), and *The Amazing Marriage* (1895). These works continue to feature his trademark stylistic hybridity and extravagance, while further sharpening his criticism of marriage as an institution. In this last phase of his career Meredith also devoted renewed attention to his poetry, which ranges both topically and formally but returns most often to the question of humanity's relationship to nature. Meredith's poems were often valued at the time less for their formal qualities than for their progressive politics and Vitalist philosophy, but this didactic strain has not worn well. It is almost entirely on his fiction, along with "Modern Love," that Meredith's influence and reputation rest today.

In his lifetime Meredith was often embraced by critics and younger writers for his breaks with Victorian literary and social orthodoxies and for his refusal to accommodate his style to the mass market. His formal experimentation, lyricism, focus on interiority, and relatively frank treatment of sexuality all left their mark on such leading modernist writers as James Joyce, D. H. Lawrence, and Virginia Woolf. Paradoxically, however, the further innovations of these writers helped locate Meredith more firmly in the nineteenth century than he had seemed at the time, and in retrospect his preoccupations and narrative practices may appear more late Victorian than modern. There is no shame in that, of course, although Meredith himself and many of his early admirers might disagree; at the same time, the gap between what these admirers promised and what Meredith's works deliver surely contributed to the rapid decline of his posthumous reputation.

Meredith remains important both for his transitional role in the development of the English novel and for the distinctive challenges and insights afforded by his work. It is virtually tautological to say that the techniques Meredith uses to break readers' habits can be off-putting. At his best, however, as in *Richard Feverel*, *The Egoist*, and "Modern Love," Meredith generates a complex and even unique reading experience that centers on the very play of engagement and detachment. Such play constitutes a major concern of his work as well as its signature effect. The persistent inventiveness with which he manipulated and explored this fundamental dynamic of absorption and reflection lies at the heart of his achievement and helps give it enduring value.

[*See also* Thomas Hardy; Modernism; *and* The Novel.]

SELECTED WORKS

Poems (1851)
The Shaving of Shagpat (1855)
Farina (1857)
The Ordeal of Richard Feverel (1859)
Evan Harrington (1860)
Modern Love, and Poems of the English Roadside (1862)
Rhoda Fleming (1865)
Vittoria (1866)
The Adventures of Harry Richmond (1871)
Beauchamp's Career (1876)
The Egoist (1879)
The Tragic Comedians (1880)
Poems and Lyrics of the Joy of the Earth (1883)
Diana of the Crossways: One of our Conquerors (1885)
Ballads and Poems of Tragic Life (1887)
A Reading of Earth (1888)
One of Our Conquerors (1891)
Poems (1892)
Lord Ormont and His Aminta (1894)
The Amazing Marriage (1895)
Odes in Contribution to the Song of French History (1898)
A Reading of Life (1901)
Last Poems (1909)
Celt and Saxon (1910)

FURTHER READING

Beer, Gillian. *Meredith: A Change of Masks, a Study of the Novels.* London, 1970. Analyzes the ways in which Meredith's formal innovations serve his novels' thematic concerns and shape the reading experience.

Fletcher, Ian, ed. *Meredith Now: Some Critical Essays.* New York, 1971. Excellent collection of essays spanning Meredith's entire career.

Jones, Mervyn. *The Amazing Victorian: A Life of George Meredith.* London, 1999. Sympathetic account of Meredith's life and beliefs.

Muendel, Renate. *George Meredith.* Boston, 1986. Good introductory survey of the full range of Meredith's writings.

Roberts, Neil. *Meredith and the Novel.* New York, 1997. Readings of Meredith's novels through the lens of Mikhail Bakhtin's theory of dialogism.

Stevenson, Lionel. *The Ordeal of George Meredith: A Biography.* New York, 1953. Remains the standard biography.

Williams, Ioan, ed. *Meredith: The Critical Heritage.* New York, 1971. A generous collection of contemporary reviews of Meredith's works.

METAPHYSICAL POETS

Ceri Sullivan

The aggregation "metaphysical" was formed unevenly by later readers over four centuries and has no coherent definition. John Donne was the first to be recognized by his contemporaries in the 1630s as writing in a startling new style about the self's failures in secular and divine love. George Herbert, Donne's relation and friend, also wrote on the heart's response to God, but in the plain style. A generation later Andrew Marvell speculated ingeniously on philosophical, religious, and erotic matters in the mode of Donne. Meanwhile, Henry Vaughan's and Richard Crashaw's sacred poems took up Herbert's concerns, in the transcendent and Catholic registers, respectively. Two subgroups were added in the twentieth century: the discovery of Thomas Traherne's manuscripts led to his recognition as a poet of sublimity analogous to Vaughan, and new interest in baroque poetics brought forward the work of Robert Southwell and William Alabaster's Jesuit lyrics.

THE THEMES AND STYLE

Thomas Carew's "Elegy upon the death of . . . Dr. John Donne" (1633) is one of the first and most acute literary commentaries on the metaphysical style. Donne, muses Carew, recovered a "language of both words and sense," moving away from the amplified style of the Elizabethans toward a deliberately terse style that paid close attention to strict logic rather than emotional affect. He threw away "the lazy seeds of servile imitation" (thus renouncing the principal poetic technique of the schoolroom, where the classical authors were read, copied, and varied), and in doing so demonstrated a vigorous mind operating independently of received tenets, both of form and of concept. He has "opened us a mine / of rich and pregnant fancy; drawn a line / Of masculine expression" on the substantial topics of divinity; used his "imperious wit" to awe "our stubborn language"—"soft melting phrases" would have been too weak for his "giant fancy." In short, Donne "committed holy rapes upon the will." This, then, is a poetry of force and point, aimed at arguing a reader—or

the self—into submissive agreement. It is skeptical about habitual positions, attempting to draw out first principles from the situation in which the poem's speaker finds himself. It focuses on the self not because interiority per se is interesting (contrary to current opinion) but because the self is the primary and most trustworthy material to consider in working toward truth.

Although the "group" of metaphysical poets is not homogeneous in style and content, two features Carew identifies are common to all: a deep concern with exploring the self's relationship with God, and an unorthodox (even desperate) desire to find the appropriate means to express this. Both arise from the problem that it is impossible for the human to understand the divine. This is not just the problem of speaking about God, about which Donne himself says, "who ever dare / Seek new expressions, do . . . thrust into strait corners of poor wit / Thee, who are cornerless and infinite" ("Upon the Translation of the Psalms"). Thus, Herbert cries, "but who hath praise enough? nay, who hath any?" and begs for "a root, that gives expressions" ("Providence"), and Crashaw apostrophizes "mighty nothing" and sardonically praises the Pharisees' reply to Christ, since "while they speak nothing, they speak all" (epigrams on Matthew 27 and 22). It is primarily the problem of whether one can know God. Thus, in his sermons Donne repeatedly warns that "if you limit God with any definition, hee growes larger by that definition; for even by that definition you discerne presently that he is something else then that definition comprehends." How then to say anything about or to God? The Italian Jesuit Emanuele Tesauro put marvel, created by metaphor, at the center of the devotional aesthetic. Wit, *ingegno*, acknowledges that its representations of the links between the divine and the human are provisional fictions, both startling and false (*Il cannocchiale Aristotelico* [Aristotle's Lens], 1654). In the metaphysical poem this marvel is sometimes evident in single phrases or images, "conceits," that are self-consciously and deliberately inadequate or extraordinary. As Traherne put it, the worshiper "can never Exceed, nor be too High. All Hyperboles are but little Pigmies, and diminutiv Expressions, in Comparison of the Truth." On occasion the chains between the creator and created are long and careful arguments composed of definitions, partitions, similarities and differences, antecedents and consequences, contradictions and corollaries. In such poems the prepositions are the most telling words, demanding that their readers display intelligence and tenacity similar to the poet's in following the argument (getting to the end of a metaphysical poem still understanding its flow is a moment for self-congratulation).

Not all poets tortured their verse to reach the truth. Herbert's arguments with a sulky or bumptious self are made with the cooperation of a loving God who supplies many of the missing links. This God speaks directly to Herbert, alternately chiding and encouraging, often in the domestic register. Vaughan and Traherne, while acknowledging their debt to Herbert, respond with delight to God's sustaining presence in their affairs and the natural world, which is therefore a world of light. All three poets tend to use the plain style, avoiding conceits and overt dialectic, but are—like Donne, Marvell, Alabaster, Southwell, and Crashaw—still astounded by the paradox of divine love for God's faulty creatures.

Unsurprisingly, the burning triumphs and aching losses of secular passion provided many analogies for sacred love; more extraordinary was the return compliment, where the religious register was used for the erotic. Donne and Marvell subject their mistresses to the same narrow-eyed scrutiny, harangue them with the same intensity, laud them with the same passion, play with their positions as wittily as they do their own consciences. The effect is to make the mistress a discursive area rather than a separate person. When they turn from love to address current social and political events, this skeptical, ironic, disengaged, and intelligent stance is maintained.

CRITICAL HISTORY

An early response to such complexity was voiced in John Dryden's snide comment about Donne's "songs and sonnets" that the latter "affects the metaphysics . . . and perplexes the minds of the fair sex with nice speculations of philosophy, when he should engage their hearts and entertain them with the softnesses of love." Samuel Johnson, asserting that faith should keep quiet about what it cannot utter, was scandalized: "what they wanted . . . of the sublime they endeavoured to supply by hyperbole." Although Johnson fair-mindedly praised the analytical intelligence

that lay behind the "heterogeneous ideas . . . yoked by violence together," he argued that the poems overlooked the topic at hand in a self-congratulatory play of wit. With the exception of Herbert (whose verses were largely read as devotional models), in the next two centuries the metaphysical poets were little regarded. Their dialectical focus on the self was not in accord with a public-spirited aesthetic that valued clear debate on facts that could be empirically verified. Not until the early twentieth century was there a reassessment of their worth, with H. J. C. Grierson's new edition of metaphysical verse and a series of essays and reviews by T. S. Eliot that lauded the style as one that fused thought and feeling. Eliot praised the way its complex and original explorations into the self capture the fragmented and complex experience of life, clearly regarding the work as akin to modernist verse's concern with the uneasy and alienated status of the individual in urban society after World War I (understandably, he did not include Vaughan's poetry, and Traherne's work had yet to be recovered).

Since, evidently, the term "metaphysical" has been remade by readers to their own tastes, early-twenty-first-century debates about this poetry will sound familiar. They take four directions. The first views the work as a Protestant poetry that arises from the scriptural and the interior godly word or, alternatively, is influenced by Catholic meditation techniques that visualize biblical scenes and insert the meditator within them. This discussion is enriched by revisionist history on the Caroline Church in particular. The second considers how far this poetry is baroque in intention and form; while in secular terms it would be politically suspect as an attempt to amaze or even lose the spectator rather than appeal to his or her mature judgment, the subordination of speaker and reader in the divine poems is regarded as the inevitable and proper response to dialogue with an infinitely superior interlocutor. The third debates how far a writing of physicality is also one of a new interiority—a new self-consciousness—perceiving conscience as apart from the all-seeing eye of God. The fourth considers the poets individually to give sympathetic treatment to their damaged careers, broken faiths, failed politics, or split families. This group sometimes offers psychoanalytic and sociological explanations for their strained expression of self, or genders the poems' speakers as female, anxiously confined to a passive mode, awaiting the response of a lover or God.

[*See also* Thomas Carew; Richard Crashaw; John Donne; T. S. Eliot; George Herbert; Andrew Marvell; Robert Southwell; Thomas Traherne; *and* Henry Vaughan.]

EDITIONS

Alabaster, William. *The Sonnets.* Edited by G. M. Story and Helen Gardner. London, 1959.

Crashaw, Richard. *The Poems, English, Latin, and Greek.* Edited by L. C. Martin. Oxford, 1957.

Donne, John. *The Complete English Poems.* Edited by A. J. Smith. Harmondsworth, U.K., 1976.

Herbert, George. *The English Poems.* Edited by C. A. Patrides. London, 1975.

Traherne, Thomas. *Selected Poems and Prose.* Edited by Alan Bradford. London, 1991.

Vaughan, Henry. *The Complete Poems.* Edited by A. Rudrum. New Haven, CT, 1981.

FURTHER READING

Carey, John. *John Donne, Life, Mind, and Art.* London, 1981.

Colie, Rosalie. *Paradoxica epidemica. The Renaissance Tradition of Paradox.* Princeton, NJ, 1966.

Corns, Thomas N. *Cambridge Companion to English Poetry: Donne to Marvell.* Cambridge, U.K., 1993.

Dryden, John. *A Discourse Concerning the Original and Progress of Satire.* London, 1693.

Eliot, T. S. "The Metaphysical Poets." In *Selected Essays.* London, 1932.

Estrin, Barbara. *Laura: Uncovering Gender and Genre in Wyatt, Donne, and Marvell.* Durham, NC, 1994.

Fish, Stanley. *Self-Consuming Artifacts: The Experience of Seventeenth-Century Literature.* Berkeley, CA, 1972.

Guibbory, Achsah. *Ceremony and Community from Herbert to Milton: Literature, Religion, and Cultural Conflict in Seventeenth-Century England.* Cambridge, U.K., 1998.

Hammond, Gerald. *Fleeting Things: English Poets and Poems, 1616–1660.* Cambridge, MA, 1990.

Harman, Barbara. *Costly Monuments. Representations of the Self in George Herbert's Poetry.* Cambridge, MA, 1982.

Healy, Thomas F. *Richard Crashaw.* Leiden, Netherlands, 1986.

Johnson, Samuel. "Life of Cowley." In *Lives of the English Poets.* London, 1779.

Lewalski, Barbara. *Protestant Poetics and the Seventeenth-Century Religious Lyric.* Princeton, NJ, 1979.

Martz, Louis L. *The Poetry of Meditation: A Study in English Religious Literature of the Seventeenth Century.* New Haven, CT, 1962.

Praz, Mario. *The Flaming Heart: Essays on Crashaw, Machiavelli, and Other Studies in the Relations between Italian and English Literature from Chaucer to T. S. Eliot.* Garden City, NY, 1958.

Reid, David. *The Metaphysical Poets.* New York, 2000.

Sawday, Jonathan. *The Body Emblazoned: Dissection and the Human Body in Renaissance Culture.* London, 1995.

Schoenfeldt, Michael. *Prayer and Power: George Herbert and Renaissance Courtship.* Chicago, 1991.

Shuger, Deborah. *The Renaissance Bible: Scholarship, Sacrifice, and Subjectivity.* Berkeley, CA, 1994.

Slights, Camille Wells. *The Casuistical Tradition in Shakespeare, Donne, Herbert, and Milton.* Princeton, NJ, 1981.

Smith, A. J. *Metaphysical Wit.* Cambridge, U.K., 1991.

Strier, Richard. *Love Known: Theology and Experience in George Herbert's Poetry.* Chicago, 1983.

MIDDLE ENGLISH

Seth Lerer

"Middle English" is the term used to describe the spoken and written vernacular in England between the period of the Norman Conquest (1066) and the early sixteenth century. It differed from its predecessor, Old English, in three key areas: its loss of the Germanic inflectional system and grammatical gender; its absorption of a large French and Latin vocabulary; and its system of pronunciation. Throughout the Middle English period, England was a trilingual culture. Law, government, and social life were conducted largely in French. Church administration, scholarship, and intellectual activity were conducted mainly in Latin. Nonetheless, Middle English was a vehicle for literary, religious, and intellectual inquiry almost from the start. Lyric and narrative poetry, historical prose, and biblical drama all developed as major literary genres in it. Writers such as Geoffrey Chaucer, John Gower, William Langland, Julian of Norwich, and Margery Kempe developed notions of authorial identity and vernacular social consciousness. For all these writers, language was not simply a vehicle of expression but a theme, as they addressed relationships between word and thing, intention and expression, past and present. The study of the Middle English language is thus inseparable from the study of medieval English literature, social life, and spiritual experience.

THE DEVELOPMENT OF MIDDLE ENGLISH

English was changing even before the Norman Conquest, and in parts of England relatively untouched by French influence we may witness Middle English emerging out of its Old English matrix. The *Peterborough Chronicle*, from East Anglia, illustrates how Anglo-Saxon traditions of historiography continued even after the conquest. Each entry in the *Chronicle* begins with a statement of what happened in that year. The entry for 1083, for example, uses the opening formula in precisely grammatical Old English: "On þissum geare" ("in this year"). The *-um* and *-e* endings signal the dative masculine singular forms of the adjective and noun, following the preposition. As the case endings began to lose their prominence in the spoken language, they became harder to reproduce in the written. The entry for 1117 opens, "On þison geare." Here, the adjectival ending has leveled to an indiscriminate back vowel, *o*, plus an indiscriminate nasal, *n*. Perhaps this spelling represents a scribe's attempt to preserve what he thought was a grammatical ending. The entry for 1135 opens, "On þis geare." Here we see a total loss of the adjectival ending, together with what may be thought of as a fossilized dative final *-e* in the noun. Concord (case agreement) in grammatical gender has obviously gone by this time. The last entry in the *Peterborough Chronicle*, 1154, opens, "On þis gaer." Endings have completely dropped away, but the preposition *on* still has its Old English sense of "in" or "at this point," not the more modern sense (emerging in Middle English) of spatial location.

These examples reveal some of the ways in which the English language was grammatically changing apart from any direct influence of French. In other parts of England, French grammar and syntax were beginning to have an effect, however, and by the early fourteenth century, English idioms (even if they were made up completely of Old English phrases) were shaping themselves to French word order. For example, the expression "to hold dear" is modeled directly on French *tenir chier*; "to put to death" comes directly from the French *metre a mort*. Even though the words are English, the idioms are French. So, too, verbs such as *do, give, have, make,* and *take* came to be used in their French equivalent senses: thus emerged the English idioms "do battle," "give offense," "have mercy," "make peace," "take pains," and so on.

Another important change lay in word stress. Old English, like all other Germanic languages, had fixed stress on the root syllable of a word: regardless of what prefixes or suffixes were added, or what the grammatical category of the derived word was, the stress remained fixed on the root. The Romance languages had variable word stress, sometimes on the root syllable and at other times on a prefix or suffix. Changes in this regard facilitated the En-

479

glish adoption of Continental verse forms. From the Old English alliterative line (where the number of stressed syllables alone mattered), verse moved to a quantitative line (where the number of alternating stressed and unstressed syllables mattered), in which rhyme was the organizing principle. Look at the opening lines of the *The Owl and the Nightingale*, probably composed in the late twelfth century and preserved in two manuscripts of the mid-thirteenth:

> Ich war in one summere dale,
> In one suïe diȝele hale.

The lines are in iambic tetrameter and they rhyme, but every word is an Old English word, and several of them preserve inflectional endings. The Romance features of Middle English were emerging, then, even when no loan words were being used.

The Middle English vocabulary differed markedly from that of Old English not simply in its voracity for French and Latin terms, but also in the ways in which it formed word compounds and established different registers for usage. Like its fellow Germanic languages, Old English tended to rely on compounds based on native words rather than borrowing terms from other languages. Noun compounding, in particular, became one of the defining features of the Old English poetic lexicon (witness, for example, such terms as *swan-rad* "swan road," or *hwæl-rad* "whale road," for the sea), but it was also a feature of everyday speech (our Modern English word "nostril," for example, comes from an Old English compound, *nase-þyrel*, a "puncture in the nose"). The Romance languages did not form compounds in this way, and Middle English relied on loan words from Latin and French to enhance its vocabulary. The Normans brought new words for learning, commerce, administration, the church, technology, cooking, and other cultural domains. Such words are easily recognized. They are often polysyllabic; often words for the institutions of the conquest (church, law, government, etc.); words for things imported with the Normans (castles, courts, prisons, etc.); and words distinguished by certain sounds and spellings. Old English and new French words survived in common use, often distinguishing shades of meaning or connotation. An obvious example is the Modern English set of words for food. The Anglo-Saxon raised the food, while the Norman Frenchman ate it. Our animals remain Old English: sow, cow, calf, sheep, deer. Our meats are French: pork, beef, veal, mutton, venison.

By the middle of the thirteenth century, French vocabulary had permeated a good deal of Middle English literary writing, even if the French language itself remained largely impenetrable to British speakers. An English nobleman, Walter of Bibbesworth, wrote a treatise at this time explaining the differences between the two languages—a handbook for the native aspirant wishing to make it in a gallicized society. The fact that Walter had to explain the concept of grammatical gender (the difference between French *le* and *la*) indicates that this feature of the English language had functionally disappeared. Walter also called attention to the variations and technical language that French had in contrast to English. He offered the example of the handsome knight whose hair is red (*rous*), whose horse is red (*sor*), whose shield is red (*goules*), and whose lance is red (*rouge*). Walter's treatise is an education in culture, as it recognizes that the study of linguistic change remains a social enterprise.

MIDDLE ENGLISH LANGUAGE AND LITERARY EXPRESSION

Nowhere is this fact clearer than in medieval English poetry. In the famous opening lines of Geoffrey Chaucer's *Canterbury Tales*, words of French and Latin origin stand side by side with words from the Old English lexicon. The pilgrims are on their way to Canterbury, we are told, "The hooly blissful martir for to seke." All the words but one in this line are Old English: only *martir* comes from French, a word that signals not just a religious category but a distinctive social one for Saint Thomas's condition. The little birds that "slepen al the nyght with open eye" (all Old English words) have not "hearts" but "corages"—a French term that had, by Chaucer's time, begun to shift in sense from simply meaning the bodily organ (heart) to the moral quality of heartiness (our Modern English word "courage"). Thus, twenty-odd lines later, when the poem's narrator notes how he set out on his pilgrimage "with full devout courage," he links religious conviction with the idioms of Francophone desire: devout courage, now not simply a good heart but something approaching moral virtue.

Middle English literature is rife with such awareness of the social and the moral registers of language variation. The play known as *Mankind*, probably written in the mid-fifteenth century but certainly reflecting dramatic idioms of earlier decades, shows us the rowdy characters Newguise, Nowadays, and Nought taunting the effete Mercy (notice, again, the difference between the English names of the fools and the French name of the moral character). Early in the play, Mercy announces:

"Mercy" is my name by denominacion.
I conseive ye have but a lityll favour in my
   communicacion.

Newguise responds tauntingly:

Ey, ey, yowr body iss full of englisch Laten!
I am aferde it will brest.

(Bevington, ll. 122–125)

Mercy's polysyllabic, Latinate vocabulary and his periphrastic syntax easily become the butt of popular humor.

If medieval English audiences were cognizant of differences in language, they were also acutely sensitive to differences in dialect. The major Middle English regional dialects—the Midlands, the South, Kent, and the North—were distinguished by features of pronunciation, by grammatical and morphological characteristics, and by certain lexical elements. Chaucer could humorously recreate the dialect of his northern clerks in the "Reeve's Tale." "See how the hoppur wagges til and fra," says one; "I is as ill a millere as are ye," chimes in the other. Here, the southern long *o* [o:] becomes the northern long *a* [a:]: thus, *from* becomes *fra*, and, later on, *bones* becomes *banes* (in the curse "for Goddes banes"). Southern grammar, "I am," comes out as northern "I is." A northern, Scandinavian vocabulary (words such as *ill*, *ugly*, *muggy*) appears here too, as does, later on, the characteristic use of the northern *k* sound for the southern *ch* spellings (when one of the clerks later in the poem uses the word *slyk* for southern *such*).

But the North could also mock the South. In the well-known *Second Shepherd's Play* from the Wakefield Cycle, the sheep-stealing Mak shows up, affecting the linguistic airs of a messenger of the king. He speaks in southern dialect and with words redolent of gallicism:

Fie on you! Goith hence
Out of my presence!
I must have reverence,
Why, who be ich?

The shepherds of the play find this speech "quaint," and one jousts back:

Now take outt that Sothren tothe,
And sett in a torde!

(Bevington, ll. 204–216)

The dialect tables are turned here, as the Northerners make fun of the pretentiousness of the Londoners. As John of Trevisa put it in his translation of Ranulph Higden's *Polychronicon* (1385), the language of the North seems "so sharp, slyttyng and frotyng, and unschape, þat we Southeron men may that langage unneþe understondey." If the southern men can barely grasp the gratings of the North, the Northerners bristle at the mock mellifluousness of Mak's southern tooth.

THE END OF MIDDLE ENGLISH

By the late fifteenth century, the language of Chaucer was becoming increasingly opaque. The Great Vowel Shift (the systematic raising and fronting of the Middle English long, stressed monopthongs, so that, for example, the vowel of *that* changed from an "ah" sound to its present-day one) had begun, rendering the sound of spoken English markedly different from what it was in Chaucer's time. Chancery (the official organ of documentary production in the English court) had begun to regularize spelling, and English gradually came to be spelled according to fixed standards rather than according to pronunciation. And the vocabulary still burgeoned with words borrowed not just from French and Latin but also from the languages of commerce, intellectual and artistic exchange, and science (Dutch, Italian, and Greek). In his 1490 preface to his printed translation of the *Eneydos*, William Caxton reflected on these changes: "And certainly our langage now vsed varyeth ferr from that whiche was vsed and spoken whan I was borne." Regional dialect variation still made the speech of London incomprehensible to rustics of the provinces. Caxton told a devastatingly funny story about some London merchants shipwrecked on the Kentish shore who try to get some food from a Kentish farmwoman: "And the good wyf answered. That she coude speke no frenshe. And the marchaunt was angry. For he also coude speke no frenshe." We Englishmen, he wrote, "ben borne vnder the domynacyon of the mone." Language is a sublunary and thus changeable thing, and though poets of the late fifteenth and early sixteenth centuries continued to compose in Chaucer's forms and idioms, their words and sounds were no longer the Middle English of their master. It would be left to nineteenth-century philologists and editors to recover this language and firmly place its study in the literature departments of the modern university.

[*See also* Geoffrey Chaucer; John Gower; Julian of Norwich; Margery Kempe; Medieval Devotional Prose; Medieval History and Chronicle; Medieval Saints' Lives; *and* Old English.]

FURTHER READING

Baugh, A. C., and Thomas Cable. *A History of the English Language.* 5th ed. Englewood Cliffs, NJ, 2002. The standard textbook on the history of the language, best on vocabulary changes and loan words in the Middle English period.

Bennett, J. A. W., and G. V. Smithers. *Early Middle English Verse and Prose.* 2d ed. Oxford, 1968. A standard anthology of literary texts from the late twelfth century through the early fourteenth, together with a full philological introduction to the language and detailed linguistic annotations for each selection.

Benson, Larry D., ed. *The Riverside Chaucer.* 3d ed. Boston, 1987. The standard edition of Chaucer's works, containing an excellent introduction on Chaucer's language.

Bevington, David., ed. *Medieval Drama.* Boston, 1975. The standard student's anthology of pre-Shakespearean English drama, with excellent annotations to the cycle and morality plays, in particular.

Burrow, J. A., and Thorlac Turville-Petre, eds. *A Book of Middle English.* 3d ed. Oxford, 2004. An excellent student anthology of major texts, with a precise linguistic and historical introduction.

Cannon, Christopher. *The Making of Chaucer's English.* Cambridge, U.K., 1999. A seminal scholarly study of how Chaucer used the resources of his vernacular to position himself as a linguistic innovator in English literary history.

Clanchy, M. T. *From Memory to Written Record, England 1066–1307.* Cambridge, MA, 1979. A groundbreaking study of literacy and social change in medieval England, with important information on early Middle English documents, Walter of Bibbesworth, and the trilingual nature of Britain in the period.

Fisher, John Hurt. "Chancery English and the Emergence of Standard Written English." *Speculum* 52 (1977): 870–899. An important scholarly study of how written English emerged in the late fourteenth and fifteenth centuries.

Matthews, David. *The Making of Middle English, 1765–1910.* Minneapolis, MN, 1999. A provocative account of the history of Middle English studies, concentrating on the rise of nineteenth-century philology and textual criticism, and with a compelling polemic for the sustained study of the subject in the modern university.

Mossé, Fernand. *A Handbook of Middle English.* Translated by James A. Walker. Baltimore, 1968. The standard grammar of the language, together with an anthology of representative texts, philologically annotated. Best on the details of Middle English dialects.

Wogan-Brown, Jocelyn, et al. *The Idea of the Vernacular: An Anthology of Middle English Literary Theory, 1280–1520.* University Park, PA, 1999. An important collection of texts and essays illustrating the richness of Middle English vernacular thought in the period.

MIDDLE ENGLISH ROMANCE

Stephen H. A. Shepherd

The joys and the challenge of engaging with the many texts in the broad genre of romances written in Middle English lies partly in developing a sense of how to "see" them without predilection. This is not to say that full sight of what they "really are" or "really were" can truly be recovered today, but it points out that, perhaps more than any other body of Middle English texts, the romances are imagined by readers' desire and fantasy well before they are read. How could "romances" be anything other than tales of idealized allure and adventure? As products of the Middle Ages, how could they not promise chivalric and courtly victories over oppression? That more than a few authors of the Middle English romances effectively asked the same questions of their own medium, or even worked as if such questions were irrelevant, should be caution enough to encourage "seeing" these works rather than "foreseeing" them, to remain open to the many and varied intelligences that, over so much time, they have enabled, conjoined, and preserved.

CLASSIFICATION

It is impossible to arrive at a critical definition that keeps in sharp focus all of the hundred and more Middle English texts conventionally called "romances." French and Hale call them "the first large body of English fiction," an exciting intimation of historic triumph for the vernacular imagination, and an intimation of their importance to such authors as Sidney, Spenser, Shakespeare, Milton, Johnson, Keats, Scott, Wordsworth, Tennyson, Twain, Tolkien, and many more—but it is also a great generalization. Erich Auerbach's paradigm of a lone knight riding forth to destined adventure and undergoing a process of spiritual realization conceives an attractively specific template against which to measure any given text, especially Old French courtly romances, but with the Middle English romances its primary effect is to reveal that little more than one-tenth of those texts conform to that model.

Taxonomic approaches have proved durable, if necessarily uncritical. In the late twelfth century, Jean Bodel's *Les saisnes* identified three "matters" that concerned imaginative martial texts, and the categories have stuck: the Matter of Britain concerns tales mostly of King Arthur; the Matter of France concerns tales mostly of Charlemagne in his battles with non-Christians; and the Matter of Rome deals principally with classical legends such as those of Alexander the Great and Troy. Other categories have been added, such as the Matter of England, the Breton Lays, Eustace-Constance-Florence-Griselda Legends, and Ancestral Romances; each group has a convenient topical referent, but such categorization risks, if not indeed enacts, a faux-critical isolationism, or even evaluative stratification. For instance, implicit in much criticism is the idea that Arthur has to be "greater" than Alexander, who is in turn greater than Charlemagne (or vice versa); and it is thought unlikely that greater matters condescend to the influence of lesser.

Distinctions based on metrical form are also common. Distinctive forms are the tail-rhyme, alliterative long line, alliterative stanza (often with rhyme and "bob and wheel" pendant stanzas), and four-stress couplet, each sometimes treated as representative of a certain "school" of poetic tradition. In some instances, as with the alliterative poems, a good case can be made for the existence of such tradition, where the mechanical exigencies of the form effect a richness of verbal association and thematic interweaving. At the same time, isolationism and stratification of the kinds noted above can easily creep into the analysis of representatives from these groups.

Even when a text is internally labeled a "romance," just what the word meant in the late Middle Ages is not always clear. Reflection on its etymology can nevertheless be enlightening. At its most literal and universal, "romance" indicates a text written in or translated from a Romance language. For English vernacular writers of the Middle Ages this meant, primarily, Anglo-Norman French and the kinds of French works popularly read and translated. These included the formative chivalric and courtly works of Chrétien de Troyes and Marie de France, but also heroic works (*chansons de geste*), regional founding and dynastic legends, and satiric allegories such as the *Romance of the Rose*, suggesting a spectrum of adventive and adventurous meanings that the Modern English word "romance" still retains. At the same time, the fact that the word in its earliest English senses had much to do with translation, with the abstraction and assimilation of verbal distance and cultural boundaries, suggests an originary way of "seeing" these texts. It is a way modeled by the most influential of all critics of Middle English romance, Geoffrey Chaucer (who died in 1400).

CHAUCER

Chaucer's contribution can be read for evaluative convenience or for contextual complexity. In the mid-1990s, a prominent Chaucerian was overheard to say, "The romances have not attracted the best minds." It is a judgment easily arrived at from a reading of some of Chaucer's own treatments of romance in the *Canterbury Tales*. Most notably, Chaucer elected to give his "elvyssh" avatar, Chaucer the Pilgrim, the *Tale of Sir Thopas*, a poem in tail-rhyme that outrageously ranks itself high among other well-known English romances: *King Horn, Bevis of Hampton, Guy of Warwick*, and *Lybeaus Desconus*. The tale, one the teller learned "longe agoon," is replete with formulaic tag lines and conventional motifs (a knight errant, his love of an elfin queen, his proposed fight with a giant who obstructs them). Another avatar, the Host, soon interrupts, with justifiable accusations of "drasty rymyng," "dogerel," and wasting of time; and Chaucer the Pilgrim is compelled to stop and resubmit, this time telling the moral *Tale of Melibee*, in prose. Burlesque and satire can have elements of affirmation and flattery, but here the impression of Chaucer's authoritative condescension and pejoration is hard to resist. And the categorical imperatives of the dressing-down—choice of verse form, a high percentage of formulas, nostalgic affectation, lack of ideological direction, "elvyssh" trifles—persist in modern generalizations about the romances (one might add to this the Parson's dismissal of what he sees as the provincial linguistic features of alliterative poetry: "I am a Southren man; / I kan nat geeste 'rum, ram, ruf,' by lettre").

English romance also takes a beating in varying ways at the hands of the Wife of Bath, the Man of Law, the Clerk, and the Franklin, all of whom seem to have subjective agendas that justify a heady reworking and transformation of received English romance plots, motifs, and motives. One could say that silk purses are the result. For instance, the *Wife of Bath's Tale* retrofits an Arthurian romance of the "Loathly Lady" type—one likely to have been familiar to Chaucer's readership—to create a tale that in its modifications to the type vicariously satisfies the Wife's declared will to female matrimonial power. Perhaps more impressively, the retrofitting also enacts female writerly power for a woman who in her long prologue claims women are read ("glosed") like books but are forbidden the writing of such books: "Who peynted the leon," she asks, "tel me who?"—calling to mind the truism that only the victors get to write history. In the process the Wife alludes to, paraphrases, and outright reinvents passages from the great *auctorités* of her time, in a fashion worthy of the clerical training her fifth husband would have received at Oxford. What, then, of non-Chaucerian romance in light of such extraordinary transmutation? The sows' ears by easy implication are positivistic, atavistic, and unresearched, and they obscure the authorial subject.

If read for contextual complexity, however, the same evidence reveals the insights of a great mind moving upon the attractions and challenges of received difficulty. Perhaps more frequently than in any other form he adopts, Chaucer understood romance as a medium for experimentation. What is significant about *Sir Thopas* is not the rejection of the pilgrim-Chaucer's "drasty" English romance, but the author-Chaucer's recognition of a medium well suited to the expression of strange excellence: this has to be one of the best deliberately rotten poems ever written, and certainly the earliest of the best. It is hard to think of another medieval literary genre or mode—saint's life, sermon, exemplum, debate, chronicle, epistle, tragedy, folk tale, even fabliau—so available to apostate "translation" and redactive disturbance.

King Horn, Bevis of Hampton, Guy of Warwick, and *Lybeaus Desconus*, the romances that *Thopas* identifies as its peers, are also translations and adaptations, and all have heroes who, in their own ways, survive by translating themselves through geographic, social, intellectual, and physiognomic boundaries. So does the loathly-lady-made-beautiful of the *Wife of Bath's Tale*, and, to a lesser extent, the knight-rapist who under her discursive tutelage learns to be marriageable. The "Loathly Lady" poems have an ancient and diverse heritage, traceable to an early legend personifying the sovereignty of Ireland whence the core issue, through Welsh, Breton, and French intermediaries, was translated into one about the balance of power in marriage. The Wife thus transforms a tale about transformation which itself has a continuously transformative genealogy—a genealogy characteristic of the multicultural matrix that the English language had become by the time Chaucer claimed it for his own innovations. That the Wife's transformations radicalize conventions of authorship further contributes to an impression of Chaucer's view of romance not as predictable and derivative, rehearsed for an unimaginative readership, but as an author's medium already known to be for and about the challenges of translation in more than just its linguistic form.

BESIDES CHAUCER

Though mindful of the risks of classification noted above, the discussion that follows distinguishes between metrical (verse) and prose romances. The earliest Middle English metrical romance, *King Horn*, dates from the first quarter of the thirteenth century, but examples in Middle English prose did not appear much before 1400 (even though examples in French prose appeared in the twelfth century), and arguments can be made for their signaling new contextual responses. Space does not permit discussion of more than a handful of inviting texts—even full-length studies of the entire notional corpus are hampered by a need to move along—but the aim of this discussion is to advocate a heuristic like that evinced by Chaucer, one sensitive to a literature of transformation.

METRICAL ROMANCES

Sir Gawain and the Green Knight (written c. 1375–1400) is the most commonly read and most intensely studied of the metrical romances. Whoever wrote it knew Celtic and Arthurian tradition well and knew how to play with a well-read audience's anticipation of tradition transformed. Of its 2,530 alliterative lines, fewer than fifty are assigned to conventional knightly adventure—in this case, travel into strange lands attended by a series of struggles against beasts and monsters (lines 691–739). The rest is arguably devoted to a piecemeal disassembly of fourteenth-century chivalric infrastructure—literature, symbology, and ethical imperatives—to the point where Gawain, a traditional paragon, seems to emerge aware of, and yet no longer able to conform to, the fictions that constitute his only existence. The "green" magic of Bertilak and Morgan le Fey, a mix of earthy Celtic preternaturalism and the kind of empirical cunning bred among the most gracious practitioners of fine courtesy, is the undoing of Gawain's idealized being.

To commemorate the cowardice, covetousness, and perfidy that Gawain knows this magic has revealed in him, he sports a green sash. The response of Arthur's court is first to laugh, perhaps nervously, and then for the other knights to agree also to wear a green sash, for Gawain's "sake." For this "the renoun of the Rounde Table" is "acorded," or resolved, and Gawain is thereafter honored "in the best boke of romaunce." What is honored, however, may be a courtly cover-up—a mere change of clothes—rather than a genuine recognition of the need for redemptive change. The coy vocabulary here, for a poem so attentive to detail and known for its lexical depth, cannot be accidental. One could wonder if the posited "best boke of romaunce" can be anything but an ironic decoy—unless, that is, the phrase refers to this poem itself, where "romance at its best" shows how romance idealism, once translated into the empirical, cannot be wholly translated back.

A century earlier, *Havelok*, an impassioned investigation of the relationship between personal character and the health of nations, emerged from the deft integration of a remarkably diverse body of Insular (British and Irish) source material. The author was likely a local government official, writing in the environs of the city of Lincoln. The poem is informed by a detailed knowledge of administrative rank and legal procedure, as well as of thirteenth-century English regnal history, especially as it pertains to the key event in *Havelok*, usurpation. In addition to knowing the fields, streets, bridges, and buildings of Lincoln, the poet also knew local legends of the Lincolnshire hero Havelok, and he is likely to have known courtly Anglo-French historical poems such as the *Lai d'Haveloc* (c. 1190–1220) and Gaimar's *l'estoire des Engleis* (c. 1135–1140). Much of the poem's diversity across classes, cultures, and localities is organized by a rigorous management of narrative parallelism, tracing the cooperative triumph of two young royal heirs over their ruthless and corrupting usurper-regents. Even the names of the regents appear to be chosen to emphasize the parallelism. Godrich, earl of Cornwall, is the regent of England, and Godard the regent of Denmark: once "God" is removed from their Christian names, the evil that ramifies is "rich-ard," possibly a reference to Richard, Earl of Cornwall, younger brother of Henry III (1207–1272). Richard was notorious for his inconstancy in supporting the king against threats of rebellion.

For this poet, inconstancy of character is the greatest threat to the sovereignty of a nation and the equitable protection of its citizens; and yet it is potentially also the greatest resource. Thus the two regents figure in some ways as admirable leaders and strategists, but quickly they become felonious schemers, eventually drained by avarice of any charitable impulse that they once might have had. But two erstwhile loyal servants of Godard, the cruel fisherman Grim and the brigand nobleman Ubbe, both manifest charitable reformation when exposed not just to supernatural signs of Havelok's nascent royalty, but also to his ability to commune with them, even though one of them is of high birth and one low. Because of these reformations, Havelok is allowed first simply to survive exile as an orphan (Grim raises him in England), and second to regain his throne and the throne of his wife, Goldeborw of England, with unyielding military support (Ubbe rallies the troops). Havelock's "communal" ability is emblematized in great detail throughout with lists of the kinds of fish and other food harvested, hauled, and consumed by him, the roads and rivers he traveled, the locations where he worked as a porter, the kinds of local games in which he competed, the ranks of officialdom with which he successfully negotiated, and the legal loopholes and word games used in attempts to constrain him—all of which derives from the author's own "communal" transformation of the diverse sources remarked above. As does the *Wife of Bath's Tale*, the poem enacts what it recommends.

Sir Orfeo (c. 1300–1330) is another study in transformation. It relocates the classical legend of Orpheus and Eurydice amid Celtic mythology, where the underworld of abduction is an atemporal, nightless simulacrum of this world, and where the poem identifies itself, and not just its hero, with the restorative power of music. The poem also eschews the brooding allegorizing characteristic of important medieval treatments of the legend such as *Ovide moralisée* and *The Consolation of Philosophy* (where, for instance, Boethius warns against the perils of looking back on infernal things—that is, returning to old sins). *Sir Orfeo* even gives its version of the legend a happy ending in which the king-harpist's wife, Heurodis, is fully restored to him and never lost again. This is nothing less than a challenge to an implied standard of medieval readership; one will only get alternatives to what one "wants" here. Critics who perhaps want to see no more than an archetypal fairy tale—it is the earliest known English example—have found one disappointment with the poem: it should end sooner, so that the climax comes with Orfeo's recovery of long-lost love, not with the subsequent emphasis on the recovery of his kingdom. Other critics are disappointed by how its introduction is marred by ignorance of the tale's classical heritage: Thrace is identified with Winchester, Juno is male, and Pluto is Orfeo's ancestor rather than his opponent.

As for the latter disappointment, all three surviving manuscripts of the poem, each with a good degree of independent authority, attest to most of these "errors"; and one might think about what the modern critical response to them would be if Chaucer were the author. The Wife of Bath's "Prologue" is a compendium of deliberate error, compelling her audience to consider an alternative perspective on authorship, and, as remarked above, her *Tale* (which, like the *Franklin's Tale*, shows signs of Chaucer's acquaintance with *Sir Orfeo*) embodies an audacious alteration of a traditional story. To an astute reader likely to know the traditional form of the legend, the early signals in *Sir Orfeo* of an imminent translation of form would have been obvious. As for the first disappointment to critics, Orfeo's restoration is in fact framed with emphatic symmetry: Orfeo loses his wife, who is abducted by the King of Fairies (who also appears to have stolen her sanity); Orfeo then resigns his kingdom, and retreats for more than ten years to a directionless life in the woods (a self-abductive madness); at the exact midpoint of the poem, he spots his wife in a party of fairies; he finds out where they go, recovers his wife, and then recovers his kingdom. This will not be just a poem about love; it is also about physical and psychological desolation, where utter restoration is mandated—and for this world, not the next. Music is the principal modality of this temporal resurrection, and the poem reminds us of its own origin at the harps of Breton minstrels, suggesting that it is itself an instrument of the restorative magic it celebrates. Seth Lerer has effused over the self-promotional positivism of the poem, but Derek Pearsall is right to say this reads the poem too much like "a memorandum to an Arts Funding Council." What is extraordinary about *Sir Orfeo* is its insistence on the possibility of transfigurative solutions to the most profound forms of human loss outside of death.

Many other such witnesses to a translative understanding of romance exist in the Middle English corpus; the three discussed above suggest the depth of innovation to be found but only begin to disclose its variety. The briefer discussions that follow expand on the latter quality.

Using the Saracen-fighting context of the Matter of France, romances, *Rauf Coilȝear* (Scottish, c. 1475–1500) also draws on alliterative "Gawain-testing" romances like

Sir Gawain and the Green Knight, The Turke and Gawen, and *Golagros and Gawain*. The unlikely combination generates another just as unlikely: an amusing travesty of the source materials, in which a collier defeats a Saracen and gives Emperor Charlemagne Green-Knight-like lessons in courtesy, combined with an implicitly grave satire on the politics of subjugation in late-fifteenth-century Scotland. *Sir Launfal* (c. 1385), ostensibly a traditional Arthurian romance depicting the moral growth of a knight nurtured by a supernatural love, is significantly refashioned in response to a dialectic on prodigality brought about by a burgeoning post-plague mercantile class. *Sir Perceval of Galles* (c. 1300–1340) is the work of an author familiar with standard Continental accounts of Perceval's role in the quest for the Holy Grail, but who, of all things, eliminates the Grail quest from Perceval's story. Perceval himself is translated into a hero realized, not unlike Havelok, more through native character and familial loyalty than through an institutionalized and privileged mission. Also, the poem is written in a demanding sixteen-line tail-rhyme stanza, and each stanza is linked to adjacent stanzas by repeated keywords or whole lines, as if to confirm an understanding of this specimen of English romance as a medium of indigenous sophistication.

The *Alliterative Morte Arthure* (c. 1350–1400), one of the most influential poems for subsequent writers of romance, reconceives standard British legendary representations of Arthurian endeavor in terms of national heroism and personal tragedy. Over the course of the poem, the Arthur of legend who defends Britain against chaos becomes a would-be world emperor who wages an obsessive war on Rome and the papacy, only to leave his own nation exposed to the irreparable destruction of his incestuously conceived son, Mordred. Arthur dies and is buried; the legend of his living retreat to the Isle of Avalon is abandoned—a move consistent with the poet's explicit interest in the fatalistic allegory of the Wheel of Fortune.

One of that poem's romance heirs is *The Awntyrs off Arthure at the Terne Wathelyne* (c. 1400–1430), which reassembles the former's account of Arthur's destruction as moralizing prophecies delivered to Guinevere and Gawain by the wailing ghost of Guinevere's mother, decayed and hellishly mutilated in accordance with the fashionable memento mori ("remember that you must die") iconography of the period. The salvation of Arthurian civilization, as well as the ghost, is tied up with the prophecies, which at their core advocate just treatment of the dispossessed. History confirms that the Arthurian prophecies went unheeded, and the poem refuses to confirm that measures taken in aid of the ghost—the singing of trental masses, as suggested by devotional legends of Pope Gregory—were successful. Amid all this comes Sir Galeron, a Scottish knight contesting Arthur's appropriation of his lands. He and Gawain fight to settle the dispute, but it is a bloody standoff, ended only by more wailing of women. Admiring pity compels Arthur to restore Galeron's lands and make him a member of the Round Table—an institution destined, of course, for destruction because of its excessive territorial ambition. The Galeron episode is modeled on a Saracen-Christian duel in the Charlemagne romance of *Otuel*, but where the Saracen challenger in that work is saved for eternity through religious conversion, the Celtic challenger of the *Awntyrs* regains lost land and is transplanted into a temporal institution of dubious reliability. The coruscating interaction of such a wide variety of adapted source materials makes this one of the most rigorously innovative poems in the corpus.

"Rigorous" can hardly be an appropriate characterization of the intertextual antics of the *Weddyng of Sir Gawen and Dame Ragnell*, a late Middle English romance written in the last quarter of the fifteenth century, though the resulting literary travesty (in its formal sense) is surely deliberate. Like the *Wife of Bath's Tale*, the *Weddyng* adapts a version of the "Loathly Lady" story, but it also adapts in turn elements of Chaucer's adaptation. The author had also been reading Malory's *Morte Darthur* and at least one of the Gawain-testing romances, possibly the *Awntyrs*. The result is a loathly lady more intelligent (and telling better jokes) than any of the men around her, a Gawain who has traded courtesy for glib gullibility, and an Arthur devoted to petty evasions; and the travesty is fully realized when the author, unable to conclude his poem efficiently, claims (like Malory) to be writing from prison. For all its irreverence, it is significant that the poem's novelty is sourced in romances known for their own provocative transformations.

PROSE ROMANCES

Of the more than two dozen surviving romances in prose, *King Arthur* (c. 1400–1425) is the earliest; *Arthur of Lyttell Brytane* (c. 1500–1520), by John Bourchier, Lord Berners, is often held to be the latest to retain a distinctively medieval character; and most of the others were written between about 1450 and 1500. The most famous and influential of these, Sir Thomas Malory's *Morte Darthur*, was completed in 1469–1470. Although many have metrical counterparts, and new metrical romances continued to be written alongside them, their virtually coincident emergence with the period of dynastic strife known as the Wars of the Roses suggests more than just a countermetrical vogue—and more, perhaps, than a style-conscious echo of a French interest in prose romance that had developed a century and more earlier. Before and during the wars, the conflict between the houses of Lancaster and York was in large measure discursive, comprising competing narratives of legitimacy, many of them in English prose, and all of them arguably studies of, or exercises within, the interstices between reality and verisimilitude. Claims were drawn up from "authorized" selective royal genealogies, from widely circulated (often forged) legal records of contested territorial and honorial rights, and from chronicle accounts of the claimants' chivalric and spiritual credentials. For prospective adaptors of romance with an interest in topicality, the transition to prose could well generate immediate mimetic dividends.

This seems to have been the case for Malory, about whose compositional processes we know the most. Malory's style is, for instance, noted for its simple coordination: sentences often begin with "And," "Then," or "So," appearing to affect the consecutive integrity of English prose chronicles of the period. Further, the great bulk of his sources, the French Arthurian cyclic romances, are themselves in prose; but even when he had a metrical source—most notably the English *Alliterative Morte Arthure* and the *Stanzaic Morte Arthur*—he translated into prose. The result in the case of the alliterative source is a conversion not to a natural speech pattern but to a stylized prose, alliterative yet arrythmic, as much a gesture of assimilative innovation as an effort to conform to the prose model of the French sources. Where Malory translated English metrics, he also introduced some of the English sources' most trenchant changes to the received tradition of Arthur's greatest successes and his greatest failures. The *Alliterative Morte Arthur* was the source of an early series of episodes in Malory's work concerning Arthur's victories in Europe, including his defeat of the Roman emperor Lucius; however, the former's distinctive tragic ending is deferred for hundreds of pages, and then taken up by recourse in large part to the distinctive tragic account given in the *Stanzaic Morte Arthur*. Thus, English metrical innovation was abstracted into prose innovation; and, in the final part of Malory's

work, the new topicality of Malory's choices achieved its author's most direct confirmation:

> Lo, ye, all Englysshemen, se ye nat what a myschyff here was? For he that was the moste kynge and nobelyst knyght of the worlde, and moste loved the felyshyp of noble knyghtes—and by hym they all were upholdyn [sustained]—and yet myght nat thes Englyshemen holde them contente with hym. Lo, thus was the olde custom and usayges of thys londe; and men say that we of thys londe have nat yet loste that custom. Alas, thys ys a greate defaughte [failing] of us Englysshemen, for there may no thynge us please no terme. (Shepherd edition, p. 680)

At the time Malory wrote this, apparently imprisoned for his partisan activities, the throne was changing hands through military coercion for the second time in ten years; some of those who had orchestrated the first change were now seeking to undo it. Henry VI would be restored, and Edward IV driven into exile; and yet, less than a year later, Edward would be king again, and Henry dead, probably murdered at Edward's command.

In an important study of the prose romances, Helen Cooper finds that, more than in most metrical romances, "treachery and murder within the body politic or the kin group, the slaying of father by son, the failure to pass on good rule in a strong and righteous order of succession, and sometimes also incest, are repeated and urgent themes in these works" (pp. 141–142). Besides Malory, Cooper remarks a "bias towards disaster" (p. 146) in eight works, all of them translation-adaptations: the *Prose Life of Alexander* (c. 1400–1450), the *Siege of Troy* (c. 1425–1450), the *Siege of Thebes* (c. 1450), *Turpines Story* (c. 1460–1461), *Melusine* (c. 1500), Henry Watson's *Valentine and Orson* (c. 1502), and William Caxton's *The Four Sons of Aymon* (c. 1489) and *Charles the Great* (1485). In these and other prose romances, there is also a persistent interest in the attractions and menaces of the heathen East, an interest likely to have been fueled by a revival of crusading ideology brought on by the Turkish capture of Constantinople in 1453, and of Belgrade in 1456. The Wars of the Roses may have compounded that interest, for in both instances catastrophic threats to a "righteous order of succession" were thought to be at issue.

Outside the *Morte Darthur*, and to some extent Caxton's translations, relatively little research has been published about the prose texts. Many are not even available in modern editions. Studies like Cooper's are thus to be encouraged, not least because they begin with historical and cultural contextualizing and invite more scrutiny at the level of the translative and adaptive strategies of individual texts.

CODICOLOGY

Manuscripts are sometimes referred to as "witnesses" when editors use their texts as evidence for the authority of particular readings. But broader meanings also obtain: manuscripts can bear witness not just to the work of authors but also to the interests of their contemporary readers, as well as the interests of those who copied, commissioned, and owned them. There are many potential records, then, of how the romances were "seen" in their own time. Publication of photographic facsimilies and book-length studies of important romances and collections of romances—such as the Auchinleck Manuscript, the Lincoln- and London-Thornton Manuscripts, the Winchester Manuscript, the Vernon Manuscript, and the manuscript containing *Sir Gawain and the Green Knight*—has facilitated research on these manuscripts and hinted at the complex critical insights available in the study of yet others.

The Winchester Manuscript, discovered in 1934, and the only manuscript of Malory's *Morte Darthur* to survive from before Caxton's 1485 printed edition, shows signs of having been in Caxton's printing shop for some years, yet many of its readings were rejected by Caxton, suggesting that he possessed what he considered another, more authoritative version. Textual divisions and many readings in Winchester, however, appear more likely to be authorial than those of Caxton's edition; so critical appreciation of the text must be sophisticated enough to acknowledge "sight" of the text as available only through refraction. The manuscript of another prose romance, *Turpines Story*, contains several English historical works and a few propagandistic texts in Latin advocating the claim of the Lancastrian, Henry VI, to the throne. The family that commissioned the manuscript (and possibly the writing of *Turpines Story* itself) was known for its active, sometimes violent support of the Lancastrian claim; one member was even imprisoned for his involvement in the same plot against Edward IV that appears to have precipitated Malory's imprisonment. *Turpines Story* then becomes more than the categorical term "romance" can accommodate, if the term is understood only in the sense of literary taxonomy rather than of literary production.

One romance-in-manuscript, *Sir Fermubras* (c. 1380), survives as a holograph, a text written in its author's handwriting, as is evident by many marginal and interlinear revisions in the same hand. Some of the revisions show that the writer was meticulously translating, retranslating, and adapting a French source. The manuscript's binding, made up of recycled ecclesiastical documents, shows portions of a rough draft of the poem in the same hand: compared to the corresponding "fair" copy, they reveal more of the author's drive to translate, retranslate, and modify the source. This author-translator-reviser (and bookbinder) has not been identified, but the ecclesiastical documents and the disciplined nature of the hand suggest a professional scribe working in a monastic scriptorium. It would be surprising if the production of this romance, a story of Christian war against unbelievers, did not hold spiritual significance for that person, but many of the revisions also show a determined enthusiasm to elaborate themes of mortal adventure, exotic detail, the testing of character, and the display of fatalistic humor—all commonly recognized as features of romance. But it could be argued that what really makes this a romance is its record of the adventive process that reinscribed such themes.

[*See also* Arthurian Literature; Breton Lays; William Caxton; Geoffrey Chaucer; Sir Gawain and the Green Knight; Genre; Laȝamon; Thomas Malory; Marie de France; *and* Popular Romance.]

FACSIMILE EDITIONS

The Auchinleck Manuscript. Introduced by Derek Pearsall and I. C. Cunningham. London, 1977.

Malory, Thomas. *The Winchester Malory: A Facsimile.* Introduced by N. R. Ker. Early English Text Society, s.s. 4. London, 1976.

Pearl, Cleanness, Patience, and Sir Gawain [and the Green Knight]: facsimile of BM MS. Cotton Nero A.x. Edited by I. Gollancz. Early English Text Society. London, 1923.

The [Lincoln] Thornton Manuscript. Introduced by D. S. Brewer and A. E. B. Owen. London, 1977.

The Vernon Manuscript. Edited by A. I. Doyle. Cambridge, 1987.

EDITIONS AND TRANSLATIONS

Benson, L. D., et al., eds. *The Riverside Chaucer.* Boston, 1987.

Fellows, Jennifer, ed. *Of Love and Chivalry: An Anthology of Middle English Romance.* London, 1993.

French, Walter Hoyt, and Charles Brockway Hale, eds. *Middle English Metrical Romances*. New York, 1964.

Hamel, Mary, ed. *Morte Arthure*. New York, 1984. An edition of the *Alliterature Morte Arthur*.

Herrtage, S. J., ed. *Sir Ferumbras*. Early English Text Society, e.s. 34. London, 1879.

Lupack, Alan, ed. *Three Middle English Charlemagne Romances*. Kalamazoo, MI, 1990.

Mills, Maldwyn, ed. *Six Middle English Romances*. London, 1992.

Mills, Maldwyn, ed. *Ywain and Gawain, Sir Percyvell of Gales, The Anturs of Arther*. London, 1992.

Shepherd, Stephen H. A., ed. *Middle English Romances*. New York and London, 1995.

Shepherd, Stephen H. A., ed. Thomas Malory: *Le Morte Darthur*. New York and London, 2004.

Shepherd, Stephen H. A., ed. *Turpines Story*. Early English Text Society, o.s. 322. Oxford, 2004.

Tolkien, J. R. R., and E. V. Gordon, eds. *Sir Gawain and the Green Knight*. 2d ed. Revised by Norman Davis. Oxford, 1967.

FURTHER READING

Barron, W. R. J. *English Medieval Romance*. London, 1987. Still the most thoughtful and comprehensive book-length study.

Beer, Gillian. *The Romance: The Critical Idiom*. London, 1970. Helpful guide to the history of the genre/mode.

Cooper, Helen. "Counter-Romance: Civil Strife and Father Killing in the Prose Romances." In *The Long Fifteenth Century: Essays for Douglas Gray*, edited by Helen Cooper and Sally Mapstone, 141–162. Oxford, 1997.

Cooper, Helen. *The English Romance in Time: Transforming Motifs from Geoffrey of Monmouth to the Death of Shakespeare*. Oxford, 2004.

Crane, Susan. *Insular Romance*. Berkeley, 1986.

Edwards, A. S. G., ed. *Middle English Prose: A Critical Guide to Major Authors and Genres*. New Brunswick, NJ, 1984.

Ellis, Roger, ed. *The Medieval Translator: The Theory and Practice of Translation in the Middle Ages*. Cambridge, U.K., 1989. Related subsequent volumes also published under this title.

Hanks, Thomas D., Jr., and Jessica G. Brogdon, eds. *The Social and Literary Contexts of Malory's "Morte Darthur."* Cambridge, U.K., 2000. See especially Karen Cherewatuk's "Sir Thomas Malory's 'Grete Booke,'" pp. 42–67.

Hardman, Phillipa, ed. *The Matter of Identity in Medieval Romance*. Woodbridge, U.K., 2002.

Heng, Geraldine. *Empire of Magic: Medieval Romance and the Politics of Cultural Fantasy*. New York, 2003.

Menuge, Noel James. *Medieval English Wardship in Romance and Law*. Woodbridge, U.K., 2002.

Mills, Maldwyn, Jennifer Fellows, and Carol Meale, eds. *Romance in Medieval England*. Cambridge, U.K., 1991.

Pearsall, Derek. "Madness in *Sir Orfeo*." In *Romance Reading on the Book: Essays on Medieval Narrative Presented to Maldwyn Mills*, edited by J. Fellows et. al., 51–63. Cardiff, 1996. There are many other useful essays in this volume.

Pearsall, Derek. "Middle English Romance and Its Audiences." In *Historical and Editorial Studies in Medieval and Early Modern English for Johan Gerritsen*, edited by Mary Jo Arn and Hanneke Wirtjes, 37–47. Groningen, 1985.

Rice, Joanne A. *Middle English Romance: An Annotated Bibliography, 1955–1985*. New York, 1987.

Severs, J. Burke, ed. *A Manual of the Writings in Middle English. Fascicle 1: Romances 1050–1500*. New Haven, CT, 1967. The standard catalogue of those texts commonly held to be romances, with brief plot summaries and (largely outdated) critical commentary.

Thompson, John J. *Robert Thornton and the London Thornton Manuscript*. Cambridge, U.K., 1987.

Weiss, Judith, Jennifer Fellows, and Morgan Dickson, eds. *Medieval Insular Romance: Translation and Innovation*. Cambridge, U.K., 2000.

THOMAS MIDDLETON

Neil Rhodes

Thomas Middleton (1580–1627) is the only English Renaissance dramatist besides Shakespeare who was equally successful as a writer of both comedies and tragedies. But he differs from Shakespeare in that all his writing is inflected by satire and by a sharp sense of the social and economic fabric of the city in which he lived, the volatile, dangerous metropolis of London. Even when his plays are set elsewhere, as the tragedies are, they are shaped by his unrelenting awareness of the many faces of manipulation and desire present in early-seventeenth-century London life.

Thomas Middleton
Engraving (1795) after an
anonymous portrait
NATIONAL PORTRAIT GALLERY, LONDON

PROSE SATIRE
AND CITY COMEDY

Middleton's career path was determined when he came down from Oxford in 1600 without taking a degree and began writing satirical plays and prose pamphlets in the style of Thomas Nashe. (He had already written some verse satires under the title of *Microcynicon: Six Snarling Tales* while at Oxford.) Nashe, who had recently died, would then have been the most fashionable model for a student anxious to make an impression in the London literary world. *The Black Book* (1604) is designed as a sequel to Nashe's *Pierce Penniless* and features Lucifer himself, disguised as a constable of the watch, who has arrived in London in response to Pierce's supplication in order to spy out some of the more vicious aspects of contemporary urban life. His first stop is a brothel in Pickt-hatch, a resort much in evidence in Middleton's city comedies. In sketching these scenes of vice and squalor, Middleton borrows from Nashe's vivid, grotesque style, but his sympathies are less conservative than Nashe's. This is clear from *The Ant and the Nightingale* (1604), another prose satire, but one that is a good deal sharper in its social criticism. A memorable scene involves a poor plowman who visits his young master at a house in the Strand and marvels at his wasteful finery: "it drunk up the price of all my ploughland in very pearl, which stuck as thick upon those hangers as the white measles upon hog's flesh."

In these early years, Middleton tried his hand at various popular literary forms, such as the mock almanac, the jest book, and the plague pamphlet, but he had also begun writing for the stage. In February 1601, at the age of twenty, he was reported to be "in London daylie accompaninge the players." His first play was probably *The Phoenix* (1603–1604), which uses the disguised ruler motif, as Shakespeare did in *Measure for Measure,* and it may well predate Shakespeare's play. But the young Prince Phoenix is also cast somewhat in the Lucifer role of *The Black Book,* as well as other satirical personae, surveying and exposing contemporary vice. The influence of prose satire on Middleton's drama is still evident in *Your Five Gallants* (1607). The play combines types from the prose "character," a series of clever tricks, brothel scenes, and plenty of opportunity for fashionable swearing, but it is also moralistic, for its Jonsonian agent of correction, Fitzgrave, deals out exemplary punishments to the gallants.

Many of Middleton's comedies were written to be acted by children. They were performed by Paul's Boys, based at the cathedral choir school. It is a remarkable feature of the children's companies that when they reopened in 1599, after being closed for a decade, they competed with the public theaters by offering a repertoire slanted heavily toward satire. Early modern English culture was not sentimental about children, and the spectacle of prepubescent boys pretending to be gentlemen-gallants or female prostitutes was clearly reckoned to be entertaining. Two of Middleton's successes for Paul's Boys were *Michaelmas Term* (1604) and *A Mad World, My Masters* (1605). The first of these plays is a dark story of a city usurer's attempt to cheat an easygoing young country gentleman out of his inheritance. As Quomodo, the usurer, puts it: "They're busy 'bout our wives, we 'bout their lands" (2.2.112). This Middletonian paradigm is acted out within the menacing entanglements of the law (the play's title refers to the autumn law term), from which young Easy eventually extricates himself and returns to rural safety. Operating at the edge of what might be called comedy today, the play has touches in it of both *Volpone* and *Bleak House*. *A Mad World, My Masters* is a lighter, more anarchic spectacle of elaborate deceptions and bewildering disguises involving two young rakes, Follywit and Penitent Brothel. In a variation on Quomodo's formula, this scheming pair divide their ambitions between money and sex respectively. The division is accentuated at the end of the play when Penitent lives up to his name and is suddenly jolted into piety, while the fortune-hunting Follywit ludicrously finds himself married off to his grandfather's former mistress.

Middleton had collaborated with Thomas Dekker in the first part of *The Honest Whore* (1604), which was revived at the Globe Theatre in 1998, but the best-known product of that partnership is *The Roaring Girl* (1611), in which Middleton may have had the major hand. Half fact and half fiction, the play tells the story of Mary Firth, a transvestite thief known as Moll Cutpurse, who provided Middleton with a highly original vehicle for satirical comment. Criminal and vagabond, Middleton's Moll is nonetheless sexually unassailable and has a moralistic role to play in the exposure of male hypocrisy. Both these plays were performed by adult companies, and what is probably Middleton's greatest comedy, *A Chaste Maid in Cheapside* (1613), was also performed by an adult company, Lady Elizabeth's Men. It is possible that writing for the wider audience of the public stage enabled Middleton to put his familiar themes into a wider perspective. In *A Chaste Maid*, satire moves towards saturnalia—albeit of a tainted, urban variety—and the double focus of sex and money is assimilated into the business of fertility itself and the matter of wanted and unwanted children. The situation is summed up by Touchwood Senior, who laments that "Some only can get riches and no children, / We only can get children and no riches" (2.1.11–12). In a further variation on earlier patterns, Middleton changes the trickster figure into a lazy, amoral, middle-aged husband—Allwit, the willing cuckold—who effectively prostitutes his wife to the lecherous Sir Walter Whorehound. Despite the play's pervasive cynicism, the centerpiece scene of Mrs. Allwit's lying-in and the news of the barren Lady Kix's pregnancy help to open up the play to issues of life and death. So does the apparent drowning of Moll Yellowhammer (the "chaste maid" herself) and the sudden remorse of Sir Walter after what he imagines to be a fatal injury, reminding us that Middleton is a moralist as well as a satirist. Though covering much of the same ground as the earlier city comedies, *A Chaste Maid* mines it more deeply and richly.

A Chaste Maid brought to an end Middleton's run of city comedies. Two years later he was given responsibility for the City of London pageants and he also branched out into the tragicomic drama made fashionable by John Fletcher. His tragicomedies include *A Fair Quarrel* (1617), written with William Rowley, and *The Witch* (c. 1616), which combines sexual and political intrigue with occultism. Middleton took his witchcraft material from Reginald Scot, attacked by King James in his *Daemonologie*, and he also used this to produce an adaptation of *Macbeth* at around the same time. This points to a rather different strand of Middleton's dramatic career.

TRAGEDY

Middleton made his first excursion into tragedy in distinguished company. In 1605–1606 he collaborated with Shakespeare on *Timon of Athens*, long regarded as one of Shakespeare's oddest plays. Middleton's share seems to have been substantial, representing most of the first half of the play and some later passages. What this means, very roughly, is that Middleton had more to do with the social scenes, presenting Timon in his days of prosperity and largesse, and Shakespeare with the antisocial scenes that show Timon in tragic isolation. A strangely bisected plot of this kind is obviously suited to collaboration, but the Middleton-Shakespeare partnership also helps to account for other aspects of the play, such as its mixture of tragedy and satire, and of religion and economics, which is unlike anything else in the Shakespearean canon.

The partnership with Shakespeare probably enabled Middleton to get his first solo attempt at tragedy performed by the King's Men at the Globe. *The Revenger's Tragedy* (1606), previously regarded as a play by Cyril Tourneur, is a mixture of morality play and sensational revenge drama. It opens in memorable fashion with Vindice, the revenger, brooding over the skull of his murdered fiancée and commenting on the ducal family responsible for her death as they pass silently over the stage. The terms "dysfunctional" and "decadent" are inadequate to describe this particular household, which amuses itself with incest, murder, and "stirring meats." Middleton's treatment creates something of a hybrid, combining morality play admonition with a more contemporary Jacobean relish for the aesthetics of slaughter. This is apparent in Act Three, when Vindice observes that "You deceive men, but cannot deceive worms" and his brother, Hippolito, replies by applauding "The quaintness of thy malice" (3.5.98,108). It is the second vein that dominates in the revenge itself, as the duke is killed when he kisses the poisoned skull of Vindice's fiancée and the rest of the family is dispatched during a postprandial masque. A screen version of the play was made in 2003, set in a post-apocalyptic Liverpool of the near future.

Middleton's other tragedies were written much later and are rather different. *Women Beware Women* (1621) translates the social and economic interests of the comedies into a different dramatic form. It centers on Leantio, a young clerk of limited means who marries Bianca, a material girl with aspirations. When the Duke of Florence takes a fancy to the young wife, she is procured for him by Livia, an aristocratic lady who arranges the liaison for him over a game of chess with Leantio's mother. This is the scene that provided T. S. Eliot with the title for the second section of *The Waste Land*. The Duke tries to mollify Leantio with career advancement, and Livia decides to take him as her lover, but he remains obsessed with Bianca. In the final scene, which celebrates the marriage of the Duke and Bianca, we are treated to another of Middleton's murderous masques: characters are killed by poisoned incense, poisoned arrows, and flaming gold, in a glittering series of tableaux. But despite the gothic excesses of the conclusion, this is a tragedy that turns on the issue of social class, as middle-class values (Leantio, Bianca) confront aristocratic ones (the Duke, Livia).

The Leantio-Bianca situation is a strikingly modern formula. So too is the plot of *The Changeling* (1622), Middleton's greatest play (also coauthored with Rowley), which has been reproduced in many a film noir. This is a powerful drama of murder and sexual obsession, focused on a single relationship, without the sensational, multiple deaths of Middleton's other tragedies. Its principal characters are Beatrice-Joanna, the spoiled only child of a rich nobleman, and De Flores, born a gentleman but now a servant in the household. De Flores's obsession with Beatrice-Joanna is matched by her apparent disgust for him (he suffers from a facial disfigurement),

but when she wants to get rid of an unwelcome suitor she decides to employ him as her hit man. The job is done, but to her horror the reward that De Flores claims is not money, but her body. The partners in crime become sexual partners, a relationship created by their complicity in "the deed." The words "act" and "deed" fuse murderous and sexual meanings. As De Flores tells her:

> Fly not to your birth, but settle you
> In what the act has made you. You're no more now;
> You must forget your parentage to me.
> You're the deed's creature; by that name you lost
> Your first condition, and I challenge you,
> As peace and innocency has turned you out,
> And made you one with me.
>
> (3.4.137–143)

Sharing the dark secret, the two snap together like magnets. The step they take into crime is irreversible and their deaths inevitable. While the "changeling" of the play's title ostensibly refers to the feigned idiot, Antonio, who appears in the subplot (written by Rowley), it comes to stand for Beatrice-Joanna herself. At the point of death she fulfills De Flores's prediction by telling her father:

> Oh come not near me, sir. I shall defile you.
> I am that of your blood was taken from you
> For your better health.

In *The Changeling*, social class is again an issue, but here it is assimilated into a profound psychological tragedy of desire and damnation.

POLITICS AND RELIGION

It seems fitting that Middleton's last play should be called *A Game at Chess* (1624), since calculation and intrigue structure so much of his work in both comedy and tragedy. The chesslike moves of Quomodo, planning his financial entrapment of Easy in *Michaelmas Term*, or the actual game of chess in *Women Beware Women*, which prefigures a sexual seduction, both point to a certain kind of dramatic intelligence—one, in fact, where the term "plot" may be understood in its fullest sense. This final drama, however, though technically a tragedy, is really in a genre of its own, and it is concerned with neither sex nor money. The play is a political allegory about Anglo-Spanish relations, with England represented by the white pieces and Spain by the black in a game of chess. Its immediate context is the anti-Spanish feeling aroused by the prospect of a marriage between Prince Charles and the Spanish Infanta, but it is also a dramatic enactment of the conflict between Protestantism and Catholicism, where the forces of the righteous (Protestantism) are ultimately successful. What is perhaps the most remarkable aspect of the work, though, is the fact of its appearance at all. Performed at the Globe to packed houses, it was allowed to run for nine days before being suppressed, and nobody was imprisoned. It would seem that Middleton had some powerful political support.

If it is appropriate that Middleton should have ended his career with a play based on the cerebral maneuvers of chess, it is appropriate too that these should have had a religious context. An acute social commentator, Middleton has also been seen as a writer with Puritan sympathies and Calvinist beliefs. There is certainly no doubt that his dark and acerbic dramas, both comic and tragic, are driven by a strong moral sense of human depravity.

[*See also* Thomas Dekker; T. S. Eliot; King James VI and I; Thomas Nashe; Revenge Tragedy; *and* William Shakespeare.]

EDITIONS

Dutton, Richard, ed. *Women Beware Women and Other Plays.* Oxford, 1999. The best selection, with an excellent introduction.

Jowett, John, ed. *Timon of Athens.* Oxford, 2004. Makes the case for Middleton's coauthorship and is the best edition of the play to date.

Taylor, G., ed. *The Collected Works of Thomas Middleton.* 2 vols. Oxford. Forthcoming. A new annotated edition of the entire corpus, with a freshly established canon, supplementary essays, and a textual companion.

FURTHER READING

Chakravorty, Swapan. *Society and Politics in the Plays of Thomas Middleton.* Oxford, 1996. The best recent overview of Middleton's drama, both scholarly and critically perceptive.

Eliot, T. S. "Thomas Middleton." In *Selected Essays.* 3rd ed. London, 1951. Brief, aphoristic account of Middleton's genius.

Heinemann, Margot. *Puritanism and Theatre: Thomas Middleton and Opposition Drama under the Early Stuarts.* Cambridge, U.K., 1980. Argues for connections between Middleton's work and the radical Puritan movements of the period.

Holdsworth, Roger V., ed. *Three Jacobean Revenge Tragedies.* Basingstoke, U.K., 1990. Essays on the staging of the tragedies (Holdsworth) and on Middleton's Calvinism (J. Stachniewski).

Howard-Hill, T. H., ed. *Middleton's "Vulgar Pasquin": Essays on "A Game at Chess."* Newark, DE, 1995. Scholarly research on the fascinating political riddles surrounding this remarkable theatrical event.

Hunter, G. K. *English Drama 1586–1642: The Age of Shakespeare.* Oxford, 1997. An outstanding guide to understanding Middleton's place in the drama of his time. Critically succinct and deeply knowledgeable.

Jowett, John. "Thomas Middleton." In *A Companion to Renaissance Drama,* edited by Arthur F. Kinney. Oxford, 2002. Excellent, thematically organized survey of Middleton's writing career by one of the associate editors of the Oxford editions of both Middleton and Shakespeare.

Linwand, Theodore B. *The City Staged: Jacobean Comedy, 1603–1613.* Madison, WI, 1986. Good on the urban contexts of Middleton's comedies.

Ricks, Christopher. "The Moral and Poetic Structure of *The Changeling.*" *Essays in Criticism* 10 (1960): 290–306. Classic critical exposition of Middleton's greatest tragedy.

Rowe, G. E. *Thomas Middleton and the New Comedy Tradition.* Lincoln, NE, 1979. Useful study of comic form and Middleton's relationship to his antecedents in the genre.

JOHN STUART MILL

Amanda Anderson

John Stuart Mill's early life is extraordinarily well known, not only because he famously served as an experiment in utilitarian education for his father, James Mill, but also because his response to this experience formed an integral part of his own writing and thinking, as revealed most dramatically in his *Autobiography*. The experiment, prompted by his father's belief that the mind was a blank slate and capable of extensive formation, especially in the earliest years, consisted of an ambitious program of study begun at the age of three. By the age of twelve, Mill was accomplished in Greek, Latin, mathematics, history, and politics, and at this point he embarked on a study of logic, followed by classical economics. The mental crisis that he recalled undergoing at the age of twenty-one, in which he suddenly realized that his ideas of social reform and his practices of intellectual reasoning held no real meaning for him, moved Mill, through the catalyst of literature and the emotional response it inspired, to attempt to balance the forces of reason with the forces of poetry and feeling. The moderating view that Mill settled on could be said to characterize many of his writings, where he routinely tried to counteract what he saw as extreme pendulum swings in one conceptual direction or the other. This is a primary feature of his thinking, and also why he is such a useful figure in intellectual history: his work internalizes the more sharply defining political, philosophical, and social debates of the century. But there is another way in which this canonical moment in literary history—the reflection in writing on the mental crisis—crystallizes something vitally central to the work and significance of John Stuart Mill. For Mill, the conceptual was intimately bound up with the experiential, philosophy with practice. Just as Mill's father sought to enact his philosophy by having his son actually embody

John Stuart Mill
Photograph by John and
Charles Watkins, 1865
NATIONAL PORTRAIT GALLERY, LONDON

it, Mill himself, even as he departed significantly from the belief system of James Mill, was always grappling with the ways in which ideas might be successfully realized through practice and self-cultivation. It is no accident that this subject of an educational experiment gone awry defended liberalism on the ground that it ideally promotes a diversity of freely chosen "experiments in living." (The problem in his own case was the fact that the experiment was chosen for him, imposed on him, and focused only on a narrow range of human faculties.) Given Mill's interest in experience as a crucial testing ground for ideas, therefore, there is no more misleading view of Mill than that which sets him apart as a dry, forbidding polymath. Whatever view one may hold of the prose (some find it linear and uninspired, but Isaiah Berlin accords it "moral and intellectual charm"), the work is unified by an ongoing commitment to making vivid the connections between philosophy and life.

LIFE AND WORK

John Stuart Mill (1806–1873) was born in London, the eldest son of James Mill, who was a prominent member of a utilitarian group called the Philosophic Radicals and also the author of the influential *History of India* and chief examiner of the East India Company, a trading company that eventually managed British holdings in India. In early adulthood, prompted by the direction of his father, Mill began an active public career as a proponent of utilitarian reform and a writer for the periodical press, the central nineteenth-century arena for the advancement and canvassing of new ideas. Over many years, Mill contributed to some of the most important newspapers and journals of the time, including *Tait's Magazine*, the *Monthly Repository*, and the *Edinburgh Review*. He also edited the

London Review from its founding in 1836 until 1840 (by which time a merger had made it the *Westminster and London Review*). Mill's continuing career as a writer of great breadth and depth was accompanied, amazingly, by a steady job as a commercial administrator. In 1823, when he was only seventeen years old, his father secured him a position in the East India Company, where he rose in the ranks and eventually assumed the chief administrative position formerly held by his father. Mill continued in this post throughout his life, stepping down only after the British government took over the Company's function after the so-called India Mutiny of 1857.

In 1830, four years after Mill's mental crisis, he met Harriet Taylor, the other strong moral and intellectual influence on his life. When he met her, she was married though living apart from her husband. She and Mill entered into a very close platonic relationship that eventuated in marriage in 1851, two years after the death of her husband. Mill always acknowledged a great debt to her intellectual participation in his various projects, which extended across the fields of philosophy, politics and social reform, economics, social issues, religion, and literature During a trip to Europe in 1858, Harriet died at Avignon and was buried there. For the remainder of his life, Mill passed half the year at Avignon so that he could be near her grave.

Mill's first major publication was his *System of Logic* (1843), which argues for the primacy of induction over deduction and which secured Mill's reputation as a philosopher. Although only the sixth and last book of this massive work, which focuses on the "moral sciences," has had any influence on literary studies, it is worth noting, as a context for comprehending the breadth of Mill's intellectual output and significance, that the *Logic* dominated its field for the rest of the century. *The Principles of Political Economy* (1848), Mill's next major publication, was equally influential within its own field, where it defined the liberal orthodoxy in economics. It was not until some years later, however, that the works that would determine Mill's lasting significance for philosophy and literature were published. These are *On Liberty* (1859), *Utilitarianism* (1861), *The Subjection of Women* (1869), and the *Autobiography* (published posthumously, with additions by Harriet's daughter Helen, in 1873). In the field of literature, the most widely anthologized texts have been the *Autobiography*, *On Liberty*, and *The Subjection of Women*. *On Liberty* and *Utilitarianism*, meanwhile, continue to make regular appearances in course syllabi in political philosophy and ethics. Interestingly, Mill's writ-

ings on literature proper have been less influential, though his fundamental claim about the importance of poetry and the life of the emotions, which finds voice in the *Autobiography* and in his writing on the genre of poetry and on writers such as Tennyson and Wordsworth, has helped to secure Mill's place in the literary curriculum. Reading Mill allows students of literature not only to grasp the broader intellectual contours of the nineteenth century, but also to experience a thoroughly lucid and deeply personalized rejection of the dominance of science and rational analysis, coupled with an eloquent plea for the importance of literature, precisely at a time when scientific imperatives were dominating the emergence of formal disciplines.

In 1865 Mill's consistent interest in the application of theory to practice was given new testing ground when he was elected as a Liberal member of Parliament for Westminster. He took part in debates over the passage of the 1867 Reform Bill and spoke out strongly in favor of Irish land reform, women's suffrage, and the importance of an active foreign policy in the cause of freedom. He was defeated in the election of 1868, partly because of his support of unpopular progressive causes, and he retired from active public life to devote time to writing. In May 1873, during a trip to France with Helen Taylor, Mill became ill and died. He was buried beside his wife in Avignon. Other noteworthy books by Mill include *Considerations on Representative Government* (1851), *Examination of Sir William Hamilton's Philosophy* (1861), and *Three Essays on Religion* (posthumous, 1874).

THE CENTRALITY OF CHARACTER

Mill humanized the life of the mind by showing the psychological and emotional costs of a narrowly rational attitude, of a science that cannot grasp the complexities of human life. One way he accomplished this humanizing effect was repeatedly to highlight the consequences that various methods of thinking, learning, and acting have on individual character, a concept that for Mill included both psychological and ethical dimensions. In his attention to character, Mill was interested in showing the deleterious effects of routinized behaviors and the beneficial ramifications of cultivated habits of self-control and self-development. His concept of character is close in spirit to the German concept of *Bildung*, which comprehends education and self-cultivation. For Mill, the educational experiment conducted by his father distorted his character, in part because of its limited conception of intellectual achievement and individual well-being, whereas the mental crisis he underwent changed it completely, prompting him to reject his developed habits of analysis and pursue an ongoing, multifaceted project of self-cultivation. Character was both the vehicle and object of this ongoing project. Its invocation allowed Mill to invest the life of the mind with both psychological depth and near-literary resonance: to focus on character is to insist on a tight and consequential relation between method and ethos, stance and virtue, thought and feeling.

As Janice Carlisle has usefully shown, the category of character emerges everywhere in Mill's thought—in his accounts of intellectual history, in his critique of utilitarianism, in his theory of liberalism, and in his attempt to elaborate a science of the human. In his famous essays on Jeremy Bentham and Samuel Taylor Coleridge, works of intellectual history that compare the opposing beliefs of the age in which he lived, intellectual temperament and disposition play a key explanatory role in the drama between rationalism and romanticism. Strikingly, in the essay on the rationalistic Bentham, Mill begins by stating that ideas determine history, but he goes on to say that character determines ideas, or at least the shape that ideas take. Character is thus fundamental to the ultimate actualization, and therefore significance, of ideas. Jeremy Bentham's thought was limited, and his truth could only be incomplete and partial, because he lacked the capacity for sympathy and imagination, and he "failed in deriving light from other minds."

Character and virtue are also the central concepts in *Utilitarianism*, Mill's defense and revision of Bentham's philosophy. Mill believed in and wanted to preserve the principle underlying utilitarianism, the claim that human beings are motivated above all to pursue happiness—to increase their pleasure and decrease their pain. But he felt that Bentham's narrow formulation of self-interest failed to give this principle its proper scope, and thereby prompted justifiable criticisms that utilitarianism held a reductive and ultimately dishonorable view of human nature. Mill faults Bentham for discounting the fact that honor, integrity, and the cultivation of character can (and should) be key elements motivating the pursuit of happiness. For Mill, the only Benthamite concept that comes even close to such motives is "love of reputation," yet this concept is itself limited in its subordination of honor to an outward-directed concern with the opinion of others. Beyond this fundamental critique of Benthamism, Mill also asserts that "the cultivation of an ideal nobleness of will and conduct" should prevail over any other standard of happiness with which it comes into conflict. Indeed, if it does prevail, Mill asserts, then a higher standard of happiness will necessarily be advanced. Further, Mill stresses that in utilitarianism the individual agent is called upon to consider not his or her own happiness alone, but the happiness of all. Individuals are thus enjoined to cultivate impartiality, as well as to nurture their own sense of honor rather than simply appease immediate desires.

The characterological ideal of impartiality underpins not only Mill's sympathetic critique of utilitarianism but also the theory of liberalism he advances in *On Liberty*. Readers of this text often stress Mill's careful elaboration of the classic no-harm principle of liberalism, which holds that one is free to pursue whatever ends one wishes to pursue as long as one causes no harm to others along the way. Also influential has been Mill's stress, in the spirit of Alexis de Tocqueville, on the possible tyranny of the majority over the minority in a democracy. But this text is also vitally important to an understanding of Mill's ongoing investment in individual character, as well as those political forms and cultivated practices that will most conduce to its strength and flourishing. The ideal of impartiality advanced in this text is central to this larger project, and it has bearing on the domain of truth as well as the domain of morality. *On Liberty* construes the search for truth (here limited to the nonscientific realm of ideology and belief) as a process utterly dependent on one's capacity to comprehend and consider opposing points of view, thereby achieving distance from one's own initial perspective and interests. The ideal is at once epistemological and ethical, in keeping with Mill's persistent commitment to imagining a living philosophy. Epistemological ends are served when truth claims are forced to justify and moderate themselves in the face of opposing arguments. But ethical aims are served as well, for in order for individuals to develop ideas and convictions as their own, Mill argues, they must engage in the practice he advocates. The characterological dimensions of what we might thus call vital impartiality gives ethical and psychological depth to what might otherwise appear as a potentially value-neutral liberalism, or a dry version of disinterestedness. Indeed, when advancing the ideal of public debate, Mill insists that ideas only remain alive when they constitute a form of "living belief"; doctrines that no longer inspire the active and articulate devotion of their adherents devolve into dead dogma, contributing to a situation that vitiates the intellectual and moral condition of society.

Mill's interest in elaborating the human dimensions of modern thought and science, and in reconciling the forces of reason and emotion, led him as early as the writing of the *Logic* to propose and begin to lay the foundations for a new discipline of ethology, which he construed as the science of character (the term is now used for the study of human and animal behavior). Mill's interest in this project was linked to his dissatisfactions with other emergent social sciences. He faulted Bentham and the political economist David Ricardo for elaborating what he called "geometrical" methods, which mistakenly understood social phenomena as issuing from a single cause (human self-interest, narrowly construed). Mill insisted that a multiplicity of causes determined individual action and social life. Indeed, for Mill, social life involved a complex field of effects and causes, as well as a reaction of effects upon causes. Because of this complexity, he believed that social science could never be anything more than a science of tendencies.

In the *Logic*, Mill aspired to lay the foundation for a science of character that would be sensitive to the complexity of social determinations. Yet while much of his appeals to character in his other works sought to give ideas a human face, the treatment in the last book of the *Logic* is, above all, a theory about agency, an attempt to solve the problem of free will and determinism—an issue that vexed Mill throughout his life. In essence, he put forth in this work an elaborate argument to the effect that while circumstances can be said to determine character, our own desire to change our character is itself one of the circumstances that can determine the formation and development of character. This conclusion was in keeping with his claims about the complex and reciprocal relation between causes and effects, and it was also in keeping with his tendency to privilege the formative power of self-cultivation.

Mill is both representative and distinctive in his insistence on a close and vital relation between intellectual practices and the development of character. He is distinctive because he gives such focused attention to this notion across so many works and bodies of thought. But the tendency was at the heart of much nineteenth-century European thought, for which character functioned in large measure as the site where new and seemingly impersonal intellectual methods might be given meaningful enactment, and where they might take form as embodied virtue. Indeed, in demonstrable ways, the postures of distancing that characterized scientific objectivity, omniscient realism, and aesthetic disinterestedness were understood by nineteenth-century thinkers as integrally linked to the moral fate of the practitioner. Scientific writers sought to project an ideal of "moralized objectivity," to borrow the term used by the historian of science Lorraine Daston, while writers such as Matthew Arnold and Mill integrated ideals of exemplary character into their discussions of disinterestedness and impartiality. There were also negative examples of character-damaging theoretical postures: Charles Dickens was haunted by the idea that the cultivation of a "systems-view" or third-person perspective on the social world—one that analyzed relations of hierarchy and power—was both necessary to the project of realism and potentially harmful to individuals, whose critical practices might become habits of suspicion that would undermine the bonds of affection that unite families and communities.

Across these disparate views lies a commitment to the notion that intellectual and aesthetic postures are also lived practices, and as such they allow and even invite the same kinds of ethical assessments that people bring to their personal, social, and political lives more generally. Recent scholarly trends have tended to treat earlier ideals of critical detachment as illusory, elitist, and dangerous, invested in unattainable perspectives and disregarding the existence and the experience of differently situated, and differently enfranchised, social groups. Such assumptions fail to capture the keenly reflective and vexed relation that many Victorian thinkers had toward the personal side of impersonal practices. Placing Mill within this broader intellectual and cultural context allows us to see how central he was to the defining intellectual challenges of his time. His works reveal the manifold ways in which an ideal of character emerged to provide ballast in a world that was losing the ethical moorings of traditional belief.

MILL AND MODERNITY

John Stuart Mill was one of the early theorists of modernity. But unlike Victorian critics of modernization such as Thomas Carlyle and Matthew Arnold, who decried the deleterious effects of machinery and industrialization, Mill was interested in modernity as a progressive mode of thought that had the potential to improve social practices and institutions. This view informed Mill's writings on human science, on politics, and on religion. As always, however, Mill was alive to the claims of both the traditionalists and the progressives. Indeed, in his appeal to the importance of sentiment, art, and tradition, he participated in the argument against the dominance of modern science and rationality. But he was fundamentally a progressive thinker, on the side of modernity even as he attempted to correct for its excesses. Mill was a moderate insofar as he tried to elaborate a synthesis of opposing principles and tendencies, but he was a great proponent of the modern insofar as he believed that certain forms of progress, including the emergence of reconciling syntheses, were inexorable. As a progressive, he believed that societies evolved so as to replace relations of force with a higher moral law; he believed that conceptual excesses were moderated over time; and he thought that individuals and societies could come to affirm, and even reinvest with a certain sacredness, liberal principles of democratic freedom and enlightened utilitarian practices of reflection. In his writings on religion he takes a similar approach: there he argues that we might direct our religious feelings away from the traditional notion of "supernatural being" and toward more properly human and worldly objects. Mill believed that religious sentiments might animate utilitarian commitments, and he furthermore suggested that the personal allegiance to Christ, so central and important a part of Christian practice, should be replaced with an attachment to examples of human excellence and virtue.

Mill's great interest as a theorist of modernity derives from those elements of his thinking that reflect the challenges involved in trying to replace cherished customs and traditions—or even ingrained habits of thinking and feeling—with more modern (liberal, secular, and scientific) attitudes and aspirations. Mill was so profoundly aware of the force of ingrained habit and sentiment that he sought to elaborate how the critique of custom might become customary, and how the scrutiny of habit might become habitual. In order for such transformations to take hold, however, it is necessary to recruit the forces of education and otherwise to promote ongoing practices of self-cultivation. These practices, in their most noble forms, endow with the force of custom those liberal and utilitarian principles first brought to light through a rigorous examination of embedded custom. Another way of putting this is to say that Mill strove to give modern practices the force of tradition (and in doing so he managed to disarm traditionalists by appropriating some of their key notions, such as habit and custom).

It would be wrong to draw the conclusion that Mill's interest in habit was fundamentally strategic, however. In his political and social thinking, Mill was genuinely concerned with the value of habit and sentiment as binding forces for societies and states. Certain passages in *On Liberty* have led critics to emphasize Mill's concern about the negative impact of mass society on political vitality. But Mill was also deeply concerned with the attenuation of traditional forms of affiliation and the loss of whole ways of life, even as he promoted the liberal principles of individual autonomy and freedom. In the essay on Coleridge, a thinker he admired for his awareness of the importance of tradition, Mill asserts the hope that it will become a modern custom to feel loyalty and attachment to democratic principles, however counterintuitive that may seem to his readers. He in fact saw democracy as the form of political attachment most likely to prevail in modern times. But he also implied at various points that attachment to freedom and principle does not constitute a sufficiently binding element for modern politics, and in doing so he appealed to an idea of national cohesion that extends beyond the mere formal commitments of the liberal attitude. Mill might thus be seen as an early proponent (but also an internal critic) of what today is described as civic, as opposed to ethnic, nationalism.

Mill's importance as a theorist of modernity derives from his ability to apply a kind of experiential, even existential, test to the forms and principles associated with modern political institutions and modern intellectual practice. He consistently attempted to forge connections between everyday life and practice on the one hand, and the most advanced or abstract forms of thought on the other. His attentiveness to the power of habit and ingrained sentiment allowed him not only to suggest ways in which new habits might be cultivated, but also to diagnose with insight and force the ways in which systems of power embed themselves in the most intimate practices of daily life. This is especially apparent in *The Subjection of Women*, in which he argues that the central difficulty facing those who wish to address the subordination of women is the fact that such subordination is woven into the most intimate habits and feelings. Because of the deep emotional bonds between women and their oppressors, because both women and men are invested in keeping their relations intact, and because forms of subordination are accompanied by rich rewards of affection and pleasure, Mill felt it was very hard for a critic of the prevailing societal arrangements even to get a hearing.

For Mill, the relative impotence of rational argument in the face of such entrenched sentiments and ways of being is indicative of a general cultural overinvestment in custom and feeling that impedes the progress of modernity by allowing the law of physical force to continue to determine relations that should be regulated by moral law. The state of servitude in marriage, underwritten as it was by legal sanction, was a profound contradiction of the guiding principles of the modern world—equality, justice, and freedom. Moreover, for Mill, any arguments that based their defense of women's subordination on a claim about woman's nature were fundamentally flawed, insofar as it was simply impossible, under the system then current, to know women's true nature, so distorted had it become by artificial social forces. As was the case with his own education and upbringing, then, enforced habits and the coercive force of intimacy issues for women resulted in a fatal stunting of those powers of self-development and conditions of freedom and reciprocity that would insure the full flowering of individual capacities. It is surely no accident that Mill repeatedly asserted a parallel between vulnerability of women to their household oppressors and the vulnerability of children to their parents.

THE LIMITS OF MILL'S VISION

Although Mill was a great champion of liberal ideals, and sharply critical of various forms of oppression, his work also displays certain forms of elitism. His deep belief in the power of ideas and the possibilities held out by the life of the mind give his work a certain intellectualist bias. Mill tended to believe that progress was ultimately in the hands of a few rare thinkers who would advance the causes of modernity and principles of liberalism. He also tended to fear that premature extension of the voting franchise would allow the mediocrity of the majority to dominate over the enlightened and the educated. The principles of self-development and individual flourishing that undergirded his liberalism took precedence over the principle of universal suffrage, so that Mill thought the former might be in danger if one gave extended democratic rights and freedoms to an uncultivated society. In *Considerations on Representative Government*, Mill went so far as to discuss measures that might guard against such a danger, including proportional voting to ensure proper representation of various groups, weighted or plural votes for the educated, and an educational requirement for voters.

Ultimately, Mill wished to see the whole populace benefit from education and the forms of self-cultivation that it would engender. His desire to guarantee the authority and power of the educated minority was in the service of what he saw as a future good, the achievement of an enlightened democratic society in which every member had

been trained to lead the examined life. Nonetheless, he compromised his own liberal ideals in attempting to guard against what he saw as the ignorance of the working classes and the uneducated. Despite his democratic impulses, Mill's highest value was enlightened self-cultivation, and his political principles of freedom and autonomy could not be allowed to stand apart from, let alone override, this powerful compass guiding his political and ethical thought.

Mill's differential assessment of various social groups, particularly his tendency to measure their capacity for enlightened self-governance, extended outside of the realm of domestic politics and into the international arena. Although he was a great critic of slavery, Mill often reflected dominant cultural biases against other races and cultures, particularly the cultures of the East, which he tended to associate with a stagnant traditionalism. His belief in modernity as a progressive force involved a framing Eurocentric opposition between civilization and barbarism, and he thought that intervention in the affairs of other nations was justified if they were underdeveloped with respect to liberty and "civilization." This accounts for a series of tensions in his writings. On the one hand, Mill was a prominent figure in the Governor Eyre controversy, which erupted when Eyre, the British governor of Jamaica, brutally put down the 1865 Morant Bay Rebellion. Mill pressed for justice in the form of a murder charge against Eyre and argued strenuously and eloquently against what seemed to him the authoritarian views of his opponents, who were led by Thomas Carlyle and included many other prominent Victorian writers (Charles Dickens, John Ruskin, Alfred Tennyson). In this debate, Mill stood out as a strong voice on the side of progressive principles. Yet Mill also believed that the use of force against China during the Opium Wars was warranted, and he strongly supported the East India Company after the "India Mutiny" of 1857. Mill reflected a prevalent Victorian view when he argued that so-called barbarous states have no rights as nations, and that civilized nations are justified in interfering in their affairs so as to bring them closer to the point of becoming developed nations with civilized laws and practices. Mill thus held other nations to the standard of liberal democracy, rather than simply extending the principle of tolerance to them. To the extent that this became a justification for colonization and willful intervention, this form of liberalism certainly compromised its own moral foundations. But Mill was nonetheless directly confronting some of the issues that would be at the center of the development of international law in the twentieth century. His life and work provide not only an astonishingly vivid intellectual history of his time, but also, in many respects, an illuminating preview of social and political debates that were on the horizon.

[*See also* Thomas Carlyle; Samuel Taylor Coleridge; *and* Modernism]

SELECTED WORKS

"Bentham" (1838)

"Coleridge" (1840)

A System of Logic (1843)

Principles of Political Economy (1848)

On Liberty (1859)

Considerations on Representative Government (1861)

An Examination of Sir William Hamilton's Philosophy (1865)

Utilitarianism (1861)

The Subjection of Women (1869)

Autobiography (1873, posthumous)

Three Essays on Religion (1874, posthumous)

FURTHER READING

Bain, Alexander. *John Stuart Mill: A Criticism.* London, 1882. A biography and criticism, by one of Mill's disciples.

Berlin, Isaiah. "*John Stuart Mill and the Ends of Life.*" London, 1959. A reading of Mill's political thought which argues for the primacy of the concepts of freedom and individual variety.

Carlisle, Janice. *John Stuart Mill and the Writing of Character.* Athens, GA, 1991. An illuminating and wide-ranging analysis of the concept of character in Mill's thought, with special attention to his interest in ethology and the way his own character was revealed in his writings.

Donnor, Wendy. *The Liberal Self: John Stuart Mill's Moral and Political Philosophy.* Ithaca, NY, 1991. A discussion of Mill's utilitarianism and liberalism, with special emphasis on the doctrine of self-development.

Packe, Michael St. John. *The Life of John Stuart Mill.* London, 1954. A useful biography.

Ryan, Alan. *J. S. Mill.* London, 1974. An excellent introduction to Mill's philosophy, organized by extensive discussion of the major works.

Ryan, Alan. *The Philosophy of John Mill.* London, 1970. Argues for a general unity to Mill's thought, particularly with respect to the reach of his ambition to develop a science of society.

Semmel, Bernard. *John Stuart Mill and the Pursuit of Virtue.* New Haven, CT, 1984. A discussion of the importance of virtue within Mill's liberalism and across his political thought more generally.

Skorupski, John, ed. *The Cambridge Companion to Mill.* Cambridge, U.K., 1998. A set of strong essays on different aspects of Mill's work, with an indispensable bibliography.

A. A. MILNE

Richard C. Davis

Alan Alexander Milne (1882–1956), the author of one of the happiest books of childhood, enjoyed a happy childhood himself. Born on 18 January 1882, the precocious Milne grew up in Henley House School, the school that his father, John Vine Milne, ran on the outskirts of London and that had H. G. Wells on its teaching staff. Milne's father was an enlightened educator, and the child-centered world he fostered—both in his school and in his home—nurtured a respectful bond between father and son. Much has been speculated about A. A. Milne's complicated relationship with his own son, Christopher, who complained that his "father's heart remained buttoned up all through his life." Whatever the truth may be, the golden relationship between narrator/father and son depicted in *Winnie-the-Pooh* seems an accurate reflection of A. A. Milne's memories of his own father.

Milne attended Westminster School in 1893. His father chose Westminster, which Milne attended as a Queen's Scholar, for its sound educational reputation, even though it emphasized mathematics more than literary studies. Nevertheless, Milne nurtured his aptitude for words outside the formal constraints of the classroom, and during his years at Westminster, he developed a passion for reading, for light verse, and, later, for *Granta*, the Cambridge undergraduate magazine. When Milne went up to Trinity College, Cambridge, in 1900—again on scholarship—he immediately started to write for *Granta*, becoming its editor less than two years later. These were formative years for Milne, both as an individual and as a writer, and he established a lifelong pattern of shunning anything that seemed to take itself too seriously or that required him to engage in activity that was not fun at the moment.

While much of Milne's early academic promise had been in mathematics, by the time he left Cambridge he knew he wanted to write for a living. With a small nest egg provided by his father upon graduation, Milne returned to London determined to work as a freelance journalist. In 1903 he published a poem in *Punch*, and by 1905 he had managed to place thirty pieces of prose and light verse in that widely read magazine, as well as in other serials. By February 1906, while still only twenty-four years old, Milne was invited to fill the post of assistant editor of *Punch*, an offer he accepted jubilantly. Soon after, the initials "A.A.M." were immediately recognized by *Punch*'s readers, for Milne continued to make weekly contributions to the magazine. Ironically, those familiar initials would have been different had Milne's father not—as an afterthought—changed the name he had given his son at birth—Alexander Sydney Milne—to the more familiar Alan Alexander Milne. In 1913 he married Dorothy de Sélincourt. When Milne, a pacifist, capitulated to patriotic pressure in 1914 and volunteered in support of the war effort, he went on half-pay as *Punch*'s assistant editor. By that time, three separate collections of his writings from *Punch* had appeared in book form. His popularity as a satirist, essayist, and author of light verse in the years before the war was remarkable.

But Milne began to feel the pressure that weekly deadlines and the constant need for new material imposed. *Punch*, which had first offered him an avenue to a writerly life, now restricted that life, and he began to look to plays as a more agreeable source of income. To his good fortune, Milne's regiment was posted to the Isle of Wight, where, as a signals officer, he could continue to live with his wife and to write. But then, in the middle of 1916, he was shipped out to France and the horrors of warfare. By November of that year, he was invalided home with "trench fever," hospitalized for a few weeks, and then returned to his regiment on the Isle of Wight. Early in 1917, a comedic play he had written (*Wurzel-Flummery*) became Milne's first dramatic work to be professionally produced. It was followed by *The Lucky One*, *The Boy Comes Home*, *Belinda*, *Mr Pim Passes By*, *The Truth about Blayds*, *The Dover Road*, and many others. While he had initially been reluctant to cut ties completely with *Punch*, both out of a sense of loyalty to the magazine that had established his career and out of his own doubt that he could succeed solely as a playwright, by 1922 Milne earned more from his plays in one week than most people earned in a year. *Mr. Pim Passes By* was by far his most popular play, and like all Milne's work, it remained light in tone, was clever, and exhibited an easy, engaging style. It opened in London in 1920, running to 246 performances; in February of the next year, it opened to similar success in New York. So the man who had once been celebrated as Britain's most popular magazine humorist was now one of London's most successful playwrights. In addition, Milne published a detective novel, *The Red House Mystery*, in 1922, again to wide acclaim.

A WRITER FOR CHILDREN

With the birth of his only son in 1920, both Milne's life and his writing began to alter in ways he had never anticipated. While his publishers waited for another novel, Milne turned his hand to verse for children. Beginning in January 1924, *Punch* ran the first of twenty-five poems by Milne for and about children, and late in the same year most of these poems reappeared in the book *When We Were Very Young*, illustrated by E. H. Shepard. It was celebrated as the greatest children's book since *Alice's Adventures in Wonderland*, and sales were staggering. By March 1926 Milne had nearly completed the stories that would make up *Winnie-the-Pooh*, which was published in October. The now famous book built on some of the ideas and characters that appeared in *When We Were Very Young*, but it concentrated on a boy bearing the same name as Milne's son—Christopher Robin—and on his collection of animal friends, based on the stuffed animals resident in the Milne household. The publisher's confidence in the book was so great that the first English printing of *Winnie-the-Pooh* was seven times that of *When We Were Very Young*. No one was disappointed. The initial print run of Milne's *Now We Are Six*, published the next year, was greater still. Like *When We Were Very Young*, *Now We Are Six* was a collection of verse, but *The House at Pooh Corner*, published in 1928, returned to the same successful format of *Winnie-the-Pooh*. During the 1920s he also wrote *Toad of Toad Hall*, a dramatic adaptation of Kenneth Graham's *The Wind in the Willows*.

MILNE'S RECEPTION AND CONTRIBUTION

It is impossible to develop consensus about Milne's writing. His popular success in so many genres undoubtedly lies at the root of his frequent dismissal by literary critics.

All Milne's children's books—and *Winnie-the-Pooh* in particular—have been rejected for their smugness, for the sexist and imperialist values they embrace, and for their lack of social responsibility. But Milne's fascination with the sounds, rhythms, and uses of language, rather than its role as a cultural signifier, lies at the core of these books. He engages language in a way that at once reflects the immense confusion encountered by any young person learning to become literate, while at the same time amusing and engaging the adult reader who serves an essential role as intermediary between the text and the emerging reader. One critic claimed that children only like Milne's books in order to ingratiate themselves to adults, but the remark was made by someone who clearly underestimates the difficulty of simultaneously engaging the minds of younger children and those of adults who would like to encourage their literacy. Both reader and listener can derive pleasure again and again from Milne's children's books.

In all his writing, Milne uses language as a tool to entertain, not to instruct, probe, or philosophize. He is a writer of intelligence, not an intellectual writer. In much the same way that children's literature has moved away from didacticism and toward delight, Milne's writing shuns the overly serious and contents itself with being playful. Such an approach contributed to his immense popularity, but also to his easy dismissal by much of the academy. Nonetheless, the approach instills a formative appreciation of language in emerging readers. Milne, however, was never pleased that his reputation would rest on his work as a children's author.

He was content to leave the world pretty much as he found it, desiring only to enjoy it to the fullest extent that language would allow. His satirical work for *Punch* is more intent on laughing at the world than changing it. His plays lack the psychological and moral depth of classical drama. And what is best about his children's books is lost in their reconfiguration into animated cartoons and a commercial spin-off industry. But as an accomplished writer of light verse, an engaging prose stylist, and an intelligent mediator between adult reader and a child's developing consciousness, A. A. Milne has few equals.

[*See also* Children's Literature.]

SELECTED WORKS

WRITINGS FROM *PUNCH*

The Day's Play (1910)
The Holiday Round (1912)

PLAYS

First Plays (Wurzel-Flummery, The Lucky One, The Boy Comes Home, Belinda, The Red Feathers; 1919)
Second Plays (Make-Believe, Mr. Pim Passes By, The Camberley Triangle, The Romantic Age, The Stepmother; 1921)

WRITING FOR CHILDREN

When We Were Very Young (1924)
Winnie-the-Pooh (1926)
Now We Are Six (1927)
The House at Pooh Corner (1928)
Toad of Toad Hall (1929)

FICTION

The Red House Mystery (1922)

FURTHER READING

Crews, Frederick. *The Pooh Perplex: A Freshman Casebook.* New York, 1963. A fictional collection of scholarly essays on *Winnie-the-Pooh* and *The House at Pooh Corner* that parodies the excesses of critical writing.

Crews, Frederick. *Postmodern Pooh.* New York, 2001. Another satiric stab at more current critical writing.

Haring-Smith, Tori. *A. A. Milne: A Critical Bibliography.* New York, 1982. A comprehensive and briefly annotated bibliography of Milne's writing, as well as several pages of secondary criticism, now much dated.

Thwaite, Ann. *A. A. Milne: The Man Behind Winnie-the-Pooh.* New York, 1990. (Also published in London in 1990 under the title *A.A. Milne: His Life.*) An excellent definitive biography of Milne that addresses much of what has been written about his children's books.

JOHN MILTON

Thomas Festa

No author in the history of British literature has, during his own lifetime and after, proved more divisive and influential than John Milton (1608–1674). He was born on 9 December 1608 in Bread Street, Cheapside, London, the first son of John and Sara Milton. His early biographers, John Aubrey and Cyriac Skinner, tell us that, around the "beginning of Queen Elizabeth's reign," the poet's grandfather, a Roman Catholic, "disinherited" the poet's father after finding "a Bible in English in his chamber" (Darbishire, *The Early Lives of Milton,* 1932, pp. 1, 18); a Protestant, Milton's father left the family home in Oxfordshire and became a prosperous scrivener in London. After studying at Saint Paul's School, London, Milton attended Christ's College, Cambridge, where he earned his BA (1629) and MA (1632). Unwilling to conform to the Church of England, he considered himself to have been excluded or, as he says in *The Reason of Church Government* (1642), "Church-outed by the Prelates" (see Wolfe et al., *CPW*, vol. 1, p. 823). About the time he left university, Milton decided to become a poet rather than a minister.

Twenty-first-century readers will most likely encounter Milton first as an epic poet and later as a pamphleteer. While alive, however, he was best known as the author of controversial prose works dedicated to tearing down the church hierarchy, legalizing divorce, asserting authors' rights to publish under minimal censorship, and justifying regicide. Abroad, Milton became famous for his *Pro Populo Anglicano Defensio* (1651; A defence of the English people), which defended the fledgling republic against attack from a scholar employed by the future King Charles II, then living in exile in Paris. In 1650 the Council of State appointed Milton as secretary of foreign tongues, or translator of the regime's official correspondence into Latin, the language of diplomacy. He continued to work

John Milton
Engraving by William Faithorne, 1670
NATIONAL PORTRAIT GALLERY, LONDON

for the government during the Cromwellian Protectorate, though his duties were in all likelihood curtailed by the onset, in 1652, of blindness. At the Restoration, after hiding out while his books were burnt by the hangman, Milton was imprisoned in the Tower of London, then set free and allowed to live in relative quietude until his death in 1674.

The bare facts of Milton's life have always been adduced as an aid to understanding his poetical works. Yet Milton's role in the political life of his time deserves to be considered in its own right. For students of literature, this is true not only because the works respond so acutely to political exigencies, but also because Milton frequently meditates on the course of his life in his writings. The impression this tendency leaves can be somewhat misleading, since the author is unfolding the myth of a self that he is inventing as he goes along.

HIMSELF A TRUE POEM

Abstract statements about the nature of truth or the proper course of its pursuit often look like sentimental platitudes or, worse, propaganda covering over political self-interest. Against such forms of coercion and manipulation, Milton depicts a perpetual search for the first principles from which truth may achieve luminous if fleeting clarity, as in *Areopagitica* (1644):

And perhaps this is the doom which *Adam* fell into of knowing good and evil, that is to say of knowing good by evil. As therefore the state of man now is; what wisdom can there be to choose, what continence to forbear without the knowledge of evil? He that can apprehend and consider vice with all her baits and seeming pleasures, and yet abstain, and yet distinguish, and yet prefer that which is truly better, he is the true warfaring Christian. I cannot praise a fugitive and cloister'd vertue, unexercis'd & unbreath'd, that never sallies out and sees her adversary, but slinks out of the race. . . . (*CPW*, 2:514–515)

Milton encourages us to embrace the contingent, paradoxical status of knowledge in a world that has lost its innocence. We need to engage with the world and not just retreat into monkish contemplation of it. The "state of man" is now such that humanity must see and know evil and learn to abstain, for "that which purifies us is trial, and trial is by what is contrary." The wayfaring or "warfaring Christian" requires confrontation with evil to define what is good.

The ethical imperative to intervene in contemporary politics overrode, for the majority of his adult life, Milton's desire to become the nation's epic poet. In the *The Reason of Church Government*, Milton says he left behind the "calm and pleasing solitariness" of his studies in order "to imbark in a troubl'd sea of noises and hoarse disputes." Having descended from the heights of poetic thought to "the cool element of prose," he put off his "inward prompting" toward "something so written to aftertimes, as they should not willingly let it die." Poetic ability is "the inspired gift of God, rarely bestow'd" and carries with it duties that

> are of a power beside the office of a pulpit, to imbreed and cherish in a great people the seeds of vertu, and public civility, to allay the perturbations of the mind, and set the affections in right tune, to celebrate in glorious and lofty Hymns the throne and equipage of Gods Almightiness. (*CPW*, 1:808–817)

Milton merges the humanist's duty to plant the "seeds of vertu" with the prophet's obligation to speak truth to a corrupted, apostate tradition.

Milton argues for a society open to the dictates of individual conscience and not dependent on set forms of public worship as mandated by the church under Archbishop William Laud. Although for a time Milton sided with the Presbyterians against the bishops, he soon parted ways with all forms of church government that went beyond the locality. Even as he supports the Presbyterians, Milton insists that godly discipline begins with the self. In *An Apology against a Pamphlet* (1642), Milton admits that reading the love poetry of Ovid, of Dante, of Petrarch allured him. This was no evidence of perversion, he says, but rather served to establish in his mind a moral identity between poets and their subjects:

> he who would not be frustrate of his hope to write well hereafter in laudable things, ought himself to bee a true

Poem, that is, a composition, and pattern of the best and honourablest things. . . . (*CPW*, 1:890)

Milton committed some of his most fervent personal outbursts to the defense of this ethical imperative to write and to teach as a poet, a right and duty granted him as a result of the purity of his conduct; like Ben Jonson he deduced "the impossibility of any man's being the good Poet, without first being a good man."

FAITH, HOPE, AND "CHASTITY": *COMUS*

In *Comus* (1634), a devilish sorcerer tempts a young woman of marriageable age, Lady Alice Egerton, the fifteen year-old daughter of John Egerton, the earl of Bridgewater. The masque was commissioned for a viceregal ceremony at Ludlow Castle belatedly celebrating Bridgewater's installation as lord president of Wales back in 1631. The event promised to be both official, as is indicated by the audience, and intimate, as is suggested by the performers: in addition to Lady Alice, her brothers, aged nine and eleven, played in the masque alongside their music tutor, the court musician and composer Henry Lawes. As Milton said in his Latin oration *Prolusion 7* (1631), one family endowed with knowledge and wisdom may be sufficient to make a whole state virtuous. Milton designed the masque with precisely this idea in mind for the Egertons.

The children journey toward their father's castle through a mythic "wild Wood," which, in the absence of conventional social pressures, forces upon them an encounter with instinctual drives—a test of virtue that serves to reestablish the legitimacy of cultural identity. Not only faith in God is on trial, but also faith in community. The children "Are coming to attend their father's state, / And new-entrusted sceptre" (35–36). Progress toward the reunification of the family implies an allegory for cohesion on a larger scale in Wales.

Having lost her two brothers, the Lady is approached by Comus, who disguises himself as a local shepherd in order to offer her his supposed hospitality. The unsuspecting Lady graciously trusts

> thy honest-offered courtesy,
> Which oft is sooner found in lowly sheds
> With smoky rafters, than in tap'stry halls
> And courts of princes, where it first was named,
> And yet is most pretended
>
> (321–325)

Ironically, the audience knows what the idealistic Lady cannot, and yet the occasion affords her this opportunity to display her gentility. She begins to articulate a utopian vision of community. But of course she is wrong in her estimation of Comus's rustic "courtesy."

Later, however, after she has been taken into the enchanter's palace and affixed to a "marble venomed seat / Smeared with gums of glutinous heat" (915–916), she must measure the strength of her belief against Comus's power over her body. Milton casts Comus's challenge in verse that calls attention to the conventional topics of amorous poetry:

> List Lady be not coy, and be not cozened
> With that same vaunted name virginity;
> Beauty is Nature's coin, must not be hoarded,
> But must be current, and the good thereof
> Consists in mutual and partaken bliss,
> Unsavoury in the enjoyment of itself.
> If you let slip time, like a neglected rose
> It withers on the stalk with languished head.
> Beauty is Nature's brag, and must be shown
> In courts, at feasts, and high solemnities
> Where most may wonder at the workmanship.
>
> (736–746)

This is wonderfully inappropriate, since by its logic conspicuous expenditure of wealth (the occasion of the masque itself) justifies libertine sexuality. Advancing a worldly argument that challenges the Lady's naive abstemiousness, Comus charms with the lure of apparently reasonable pleasure. From *Comus* through *Paradise Lost*, Milton often gives the best lines to his villains.

The Lady is not, perhaps, as defenseless as she looks. And this is just Milton's point: she looks utterly vulnerable, yet, by virtue of her inner capacity to resist the incursion of lust, may unleash godly powers to counteract Comus's "magic structures." She wants society to be governed by temperance:

> If every just man that now pines with want
> Had but a moderate and beseeming share
> Of that which lewdly-pampered Luxury
> Now heaps upon some few with vast excess,
> Nature's full blessings would be well-dispensed
> In unsuperfluous even proportion.
>
> (767–772)

Against "the sun-clad power of chastity," Comus offers only "swinish gluttony." The magician has no mind for "the sage and serious doctrine of virginity" (a phrase Milton later applied to Edmund Spenser, "our sage and serious Poet"). The Lady's intellectual position remains unchanged, even though her physical situation makes her susceptible to abuse and, Comus suggests, rape.

Alone in the forest, the Lady had set forth a doctrine reliant on "Conscience" and involving an astonishing revision of Saint Paul's triad of faith, hope, and charity:

> O welcome pure-eyed Faith, white-handed Hope,
> Thou hovering angel girt with golden wings,
> And thou unblemished form of Chastity.
>
> (212–214)

Here she withholds "charity," the greatest of all virtues according to Saint Paul, though elsewhere she plots to redistribute "Nature's full blessing" (773).

The Lady's brothers, fortified by "haemony," a magical herb given them by the attendant Spirit who leads them to their sister's rescue, charge into the enchanter's cave in a moment of mock-heroic bombast and, despite a warning, let Comus escape into the woods. The Lady's rescuers cannot free her from the chair, so the attendant Spirit invokes Sabrina, the virginal genius of the Severn River, whose "office" is "To help ensnared chastity." The lord president's "three fair branches" return home, and the family dances to celebrate their reunion.

SHIPWRECK IS EVERYWHERE: "LYCIDAS"

If *Comus* critiques moral injustices perpetrated by the intemperate, then "Lycidas" (1637) concentrates this critical energy in an apocalyptic dirge. First published in 1638 as the last poem in a collection of elegies by fellow Cambridge poets for Edward King, a younger scholar and poet destined for the clergy, "Lycidas" was included in Milton's 1645 collection with a headnote that recast the funeral elegy as a prophecy of the bishops' decline: "In this monody the author bewails a learned friend, unfortunately drowned in his passage from Chester on the Irish Seas, 1637. And by occasion foretells the ruin of our corrupted clergy then in their height." "The pilot of the Galilean lake"—Saint Peter—inveighs against "the grim wolf with privy paw," Milton's figure for the appetitive clergy, who stuff themselves instead of feeding the "hungry sheep" of their flock. The model for all bishops and the rock on which Jesus founded the church, Peter assails the "Blind mouths! that scarce themselves know how to hold / A sheep-hook" (119).

In "Lycidas" the pastoral failure of the ministry coincides with the trumping of classical pastoral. Biblical authority supplants the parade of pagan deities and sylvan machinery from the poem's first allusion on: "Yet once more I shake not the earth only, but also heaven. And this word, Yet once more, signifieth the removing of those things that are shaken, as of things that are made, that those things which cannot be shaken may remain" (Hebrews 12:26–27). While mourning the death of a young man, "Lycidas" also laments the passing of pagan tradition, of its arguably facile consolations, and furnishes the poet with an occasion to meditate on mortality:

> But O the heavy change, now thou art gone,
> Now thou art gone, and never must return!
> Thee shepherd, thee the woods, and desert caves,
> With wild thyme and the gadding vine o'ergrown,
> And all their echoes mourn.
>
> (37–41)

Tonally, such lines assert the scope and power of Milton's ambivalence and nostalgia as he questions his affective reality. The irregular meter and rhyme articulate the mourner's jagged pain, just as mourning troubles life's regular rhythms, and the closure of rhyme comes unexpectedly as death can. The passage ends in an echo chamber of grief in which the direct object ("Thee shepherd"), having replaced the subject through inverted syntax, has disappeared from its conventional position following the verb. The very sentence structure requires the reader to remember Lycidas.

In the end, it is the speaker of the poem—the persona of the "uncouth swain"—who is relinquished. The final dissolution of the frame suggests that the shocking death has brought a new consciousness into being. Lycidas will now act as "the genius of the shore," a Protestant bulwark against the threat of Spanish Catholicism, but the fate of the "swain" at the poem's end is harder to decide: "Tomorrow to fresh woods, and pastures new." The voice separates from the poem's speaker, just as the ruin of the clergy has torn the church asunder. For true unity we must, as Milton says in *Of Reformation* (1641), await the "the universal and milde *Monarchy*"of "the Eternal and shortly-expected King" who shall "put an end to all Earthly *Tyrannies*" (*CPW*, 1:616).

THE COMMONWEALTH OF LEARNING: *AREOPAGITICA*

Milton's attack on the episcopacy in his pamphlets of 1640–1642 centered on the idea that "all Christians ought to know that the title of clergy St. Peter gave to all God's people," as he put it in *The Reason of Church Government* (*CPW*, 1:838). With the Presbyterians now dominating Parliament and the Westminster Assembly, their lock on power in the capital resembled, to the radical sectarians,

the bloc against which Parliament had rebelled. Milton charged the Presbyterians with hypocritical dissimulation in a sonnet "On the New Forcers of Conscience under the Long Parliament" (1646): "New *Presbyter* is but Old *Priest* writ large."

Milton's break with the Presbyterians was not occasioned by conscience alone. The Westminster Assembly disapproved of his *Doctrine and Discipline of Divorce* (1643), to which Milton added a preface for the second edition (1644) reflecting the analogy between government of household and country: "He who marries intends as little to conspire his own ruin as he that swears allegiance; and as a whole people is in proportion to an ill government, so is one man to an ill marriage" (*CPW*, 2:229). To swear an oath of allegiance to Parliament is to wed oneself to the fate of the revolution, for a nation that divorces its king to settle with Parliament has by analogy shown the need for the personal liberty to dissolve marriage on the basis of intellectual incompatibility.

Having been called before judges appointed by the House of Lords to justify his writings on divorce, Milton responded by writing one of his greatest prose works, *Areopagitica* (1644). Cast as an oration delivered before Parliament, it defends the "vigorously productive" quality of books against a licensing order mandating that Presbyterian divines censor all books prior to publication. Milton defends the value of unrestrained publication and of "books promiscuously read," except for those by Catholic authors: "I mean not tolerated Popery, and open superstition, which as it extirpates all religions and civil supremacies, so itself should be extirpate" (*CPW*, 2:565). Milton remained intractably anti-Catholic; his final pamphlet *Of True Religion* (1673) still resisted tolerating Catholics. His argument for toleration of religious difference was more restricted than those of contemporaries such as Roger Williams and William Walwyn, and was closer in this respect to that of John Locke.

Despite this common, irrational bias of his age, Milton's ethical defense of "the trial of vertue, and the exercise of truth" leads him to equate books with the divine gift of rationality: "he who destroys a good Book, kills reason itself, the Image of God, as it were in the eye" (*CPW*, 2:492). The spirit contained in books is godly, and the preservation of books is rightfully the duty of all who wish to reform society. Milton praises the industry of the people of London, "a City of refuge, the mansion house of liberty":

> the shop of warre hath not there more anvils and hammers
>   in defence of beleaguer'd Truth, then there be pens and heads

there, sitting by their studious lamps, musing, searching, re-volving new notions and ideas wherewith to present, as with their homage and their fealty the approaching Reformation: others as fast reading, trying all things, assenting to the force of reason and convincement. (*CPW*, 2:554)

Such passages communicate the great hope with which Milton lent his pen to the parliamentary cause.

Milton's faith in the people, such as it was, did not last; it reached its apex in *The Tenure of Kings and Magistrates* (1649), which locates the power of governance in the consent of the people. Long after such hope had died, Milton continued to dream of a godly republic, though the contrast between the confident earlier prose works and the later political vision is stark. After the failure of the revolutionary experiment and the scandal of the last years of the protectorate, *The Ready and Easy Way to Establish a Free Commonwealth* (1660), published at great personal risk on the eve of the Restoration, when the way was neither ready nor easy, resorted to advocacy of rule by a perpetual senate. By then Milton had begun to compose his epic on the Fall; the rational plans of the political advocate had given way to the furious zeal of the prophet.

THE "PARADISE WITHIN": *PARADISE LOST*

From the invocation of the muse, *Paradise Lost* (1667, 1674) questions the conventions of epic poetry and the identity of the poet. When, where, and how is the poetic voice situated in relation to the events depicted in the work? Where does this voice's authority come from, and how does the poem relate to scripture, which it in effect rewrites? The voice speaks to us directly, not merely in the proems to books 1, 3, 7, and 9, but often from within the body of the poem. This puritanical narrator comments on the action, renders verdicts about the moral outcome of the plot, but in the process makes such moralizing problematic, holds it up for scrutiny. The framing narrative bears a close resemblance in its particulars to the story of Milton's own life after the Restoration, including his blindness and his party's defeat, but it invites a mythic perspective by comparing the poet to "Blind Thamyris and blind Maeonides, / And Tiresias and Phineus prophets old" (3.35–36). As in "Lycidas," the frame becomes a means of interrogating the medium. Within the poem, several other narrators also shape the story: Adam, Eve, Satan, and God all tell tales, as do the "divine instructor" and "divine historian" deputized by God to relate much of the action. Raphael recounts the War in Heaven and Creation (books 5–7), and Michael explains

the historical consequences of the Fall by foretelling biblical history (books 11–12).

Milton summons his "heavenly muse," declares his prophetic ambition, and states his intention:

> what in me is dark
> Illumine, what is low raise and support;
> That to the height of this great argument
> I may assert eternal providence,
> And justify the ways of God to men.
>
> (1.22–26)

The "great argument" will be shown to inhere in the Gospel's promise that Christ will redeem fallen humanity. According to the conventional practice of typological interpretation—the adjustment of thought "From shadowy types to truth," as Michael tells Adam (12.303)—figures or events in the Hebrew Bible are read as signs that anticipate corresponding ones in the New Testament. The poem moves from "Man's first disobedience" to the victory of "one greater man" over sin and death. As the Son of God says to the serpent in book 10:

> Between thee and the woman I will put
> Enmity, and between thine and her seed;
> Her seed shall bruise thy head, thou bruise his heel.
>
> (10.179–181)

The narrator then confirms the sense of this biblical passage (Genesis 3:15), called the *protevangelium* by the Reformers:

> So spake this oracle, then verified
> When Jesus son of Mary second Eve
> Saw Satan fall like lightning down from heaven
> Prince of the air
>
> (10.182–185)

Mary is the "second Eve," just as Jesus is the "second Adam."

But it will take the reader some time to get from the opening of the poem to the Son's oracular utterance of the "great argument," and Adam, too, will have to learn through Michael's gradual instruction how to interpret this piece of scripture. Logically the poem starts in the midst of things seeking the cause "Of man's first disobedience": Satan, "The infernal serpent" (1.34), is an ambitious rebel, and his own language, as much as that of the narrator, contributes to our sense that he is a familiar literary type: "To reign is worth ambition though in hell: / Better to reign in hell, than serve in heaven" (1.262–263) echoes and distorts Achilles' lines to Odysseus in the underworld in the *Odyssey* (11.489–491). Tragically heroic from the start, Milton's Satan evokes the heroes of ancient martial epic and draws on the ethos of Greek and Roman literature that valorizes courage, steadfastness, and cunning: "The mind is its own place, and in itself / Can make a heaven of hell, a hell of heaven" (1.254–255). Resemblance between the pagan heroes and gods and the devils—such as we see in the catalog of devils in book 1—was a commonplace of Christian writers from at least the time of Origen. But Milton uses techniques of allusion and appropriation to create a massive texture of literary contest and revision. In an appropriation from the *Iliad* (1.591–595), Milton rewrites and ultimately challenges the veracity of traditional epic. The narrator says of Mammon, architect of Pandaemonium:

> Nor was his name unheard or unadored
> In ancient Greece; an in Ausonian land
> Men called him Mulciber; and how he fell
> From heaven, they fabled, thrown by angry Jove
> Sheer o'er the crystal battlements: from morn
> To noon he fell, from noon to dewy eve,
> A summer's day; and with the setting sun
> Dropped from the zenith like a falling star,
> On Lemnos the Aegaean isle: thus they relate,
> Erring: for he with this rebellious rout
> Fell long before
>
> (1.738–748)

Drawing out the comparison with Vulcan or "Mulciber," Milton lends the fallen angel the grandeur of the Homeric original only to dismiss the myth as untrue, or inexact, and revise it from within a Christian frame of reference. Milton grants his own poem priority over the Homeric source, since the subsequent poem attains precedence by virtue of a superior religious truth. One of the most celebrated effects of Miltonic verse appears in the break between the lines—"thus they relate, / Erring"—which boldly relegates the authority of the tradition out of which the poetic effect has been created, thereby illustrating the seductive allurement of the fictional, the mythic, the pagan. Only with a rigorous exactitude of knowledge and devotion can human beings maintain obedience to God. After the Fall, this realization comes belatedly and at a heavy cost to the imagination.

Milton also revises the story of origins from within the poem. In book 5, Raphael begins his mini-epic with an action that must come first chronologically, the anointing of the Son. God the Father suddenly announces:

> This day I have begot whom I declare
> My only Son, and on this holy hill

> Him have anointed, whom ye now behold
> At my right hand; your head I him appoint:
> And by myself have sworn to him shall bow
> All knees in heaven, and shall confess him Lord:
> Under his great vicegerent reign abide
> United as one individual soul
> For ever happy: him who disobeys
> Me disobeys, breaks union, and that day
> Cast out from God and blessed vision, falls
> Into utter darkness, deep engulfed, his place
> Ordained without redemption, without end.
>
> (5.603–615)

In one line—"For ever happy: him who disobeys"—Raphael shows the idea of rebellion to have been the Father's, as if God were providing a motive for civil war in heaven. And in that same line, as Neil Forsyth has argued, the Father's proclamation constructs "the whole duality of history" around a caesura, for "at the very moment the Son is said to be begotten in order to make everyone happy forever, God's word also calls Satan into being" (*The Satanic Epic*, p. 174). This pattern, whereby "first disobedience" is suggested in the very effort to prevent it, permeates the epic, as when Raphael, having been sent down to warn Adam of the threat posed by the fallen angels, explains that human "bodies may at last turn all to spirit, / Improved by tract of time," and

> may at choice
> Here or in heavenly paradises dwell;
> If ye be found obedient
>
> (5.499–501)

To which Adam replies: "What meant that caution joined, *If ye be found / Obedient?*" (5.513–514). The air of inadvertency clings to every effort at prevention. Human beings were created, as the Father says, "Sufficient to have stood, though free to fall" (3.99). Paradoxically, Adam and Eve must "know to know no more" (4.775). The Father proclaims the Son to have been "begotten," which seems to indicate that the Son has been procreated, though many critics have wanted to explain away this implication and make the word mean only "elevated in office." The elevation of the Son changes the political order of the universe by creating a "vicegerent."

By means of repeated keywords, such as "begot," which reappears in Satan's claim to be "self-begot," the epic builds up a complex self-referential series of analogies that elaborate its larger structure. Tracing keywords and identifying analogous contexts, as when Satan appropriates God's language, we question the legitimacy of these uses of rhetoric and witness the devil's manipulation of public discourse. Thus, Milton shows us the inward corruption that Satan turns to outward division through manipulations of speech.

It is precisely this talent for exploiting inward division that Satan wields as he seduces Eve into disobedience. Tempting Eve "our credulous mother," Satan plays on her sense of injustice at her subjugation to Adam. Disguised or "imbruted" in the serpent, Satan impresses her with his ability to speak, though she remains "yet sinless" as she accompanies him to the Tree. Milton is careful to point out that Eve did not sin until "she plucked, she eat" (9.781). The problem of her degree of culpability is further compounded when we recall that, in Satan's encounter with Uriel, the apostate angel is able to dupe the guardian of paradise, "the sharpest sighted Spirit of all in heaven," and remain "unperceived": "For neither man nor angel can discern / Hypocrisy" (3.682). Of course, Eve could have remained obedient, despite Satan's ploy. Eve wishes for knowledge of good and evil to render her "more equal" to Adam, "for inferior who is free?" (9.823–825). Fearing that he will let her die alone and that "Adam wedded to another Eve, / Shall live with her enjoying," she resolves to tempt him (9.828–829). Unlike Eve, Adam falls "undeceived," "Submitting to what seemed remediless" (9.919). The pathos of Adam's choice registers in the discrepancy between his emotional certainty and his intellectual ambiguity, in the mortal "resolution":

> Some cursed fraud
> Of enemy hath beguiled thee, yet unknown
> And me with thee hath ruined, for with thee
> Certain my resolution is to die;
> How can I live without thee . . . ?
>
> (9.904–908)

Although Adam is wrong doctrinally, he is by any other ethical standard acting humanely, which is at least part of what makes the passage so overwhelmingly tragic. It echoes Christ's offer of sacrifice, though as a blasphemous parody that engenders all future tragedy for humankind. Adam and Eve will have to learn to live without paradise. Michael suggests that faith, humility, charity, and above all acknowledged belief in the "redeemer ever blest" will guide fallen Adam through the new world he must enter:

> then wilt thou not be loath
> To leave this paradise, but shalt possess
> A paradise within thee, happier far.
>
> (12.585–587)

The world all before "Our lingering parents," Michael ushers them out onto "the subjected plain,"

> where to choose
> Their place of rest, and providence their guide:
> They hand in hand with wandering steps and slow,
> Through Eden took their solitary way.
>
> (12.646–649)

They have come to embody the contrariety and inward division that characterizes all consciousness after the Fall; they wander off "hand in hand" and yet "solitary."

"AS IN THE LAND OF DARKNESS YET IN LIGHT": *SAMSON AGONISTES*

No one knows precisely when Milton wrote his closet drama, but it was first published in 1671 in the volume titled *Paradise Regained . . . To Which Is Added Samson Agonistes*. The brief epic and the biblical tragedy thus form companion pieces, perhaps analogous in this way to the early poems "L'Allegro" and "Il Penseroso," though the magnitude, complexity, and gravity of the last poems invite deeper comparison. Their appearance together implies something of Milton's design for the volume: the two works would be read against each other, with the interplay between Old Testament type and New Testament fulfillment revealing a fuller structure of thought than either work, however accomplished in its own right, could address on its own.

Samson Agonistes has caused great critical controversy in recent years because it depicts violence that some have seen as unsanctioned by the divine guidance that the hero claims for his suicidal actions. Samson, "Eyeless in Gaza at the mill with slaves" (41), mulls over the fact of his present imprisonment. He knows what was prophesied before his birth: that he would deliver the Israelites from their bondage under the "Philistian yoke" (42). He must not blame God for his plight:

> Whom have I to complain of but myself?
> Who this high gift of strength committed to me,
> In what part lodged, how easily bereft me,
> Under the seal of silence could not keep,
> But weakly to a woman must reveal it.
>
> (46–50)

Samson has to keep reminding himself throughout the play that he "must not quarrel with the will / Of highest dispensation," which begs the question of his righteousness (60–61). Prone to fall, he acts on what he calls his "rousing motions" (1382)—though the legitimacy of Samson's claim remains a critical question.

Milton modified the biblical account when he placed the Philistine celebration in a "spacious theatre" (1605) rather than a "house" (Judges 16:27). This implies a critique of the Restoration culture in which Milton, as a dissenting voice, would have considered himself as a man chosen by God to tear down the idolatrous Philistine society persecuting the godly. Milton, like Samson, found himself "Blind among enemies" (67). The play "never was intended" for performance, as he says in his preface; the tragedy's iconoclastic conclusion implicitly critiques the revival of comedy on the Restoration stage. As long as Samson "preserved these locks unshorn, / The pledge of my unviolated vow" (1143–1144) he would enjoy special status as a Nazarite, etymologically one "separate to God." The fates of the sectarians and regicides after the Restoration and under the Clarendon Code are mirrored in the tale of the dissident hero forced to display his strength as an entertaining and vengeful spectacle.

This identification is, however, complicated by the dramatic context, which incorporates the commentary of several characters, including Samson's father Manoa and the Chorus of Danites, who recount Samson's former martial victories but now see him differently, "The glory late of Israel, now the grief" (179). Disclosing the secret superhuman strength symbolized by his long hair to Dalila, "a deceitful woman" and a Philistine, Samson has become the consummate fallen man, an idolater. The Chorus reports the suspicion of the Hebrew people:

> men wonder
> Why thou shouldst wed Philistian women rather
> Than of thine own tribe fairer, or as fair,
> At least of thine own nation
>
> (215–218)

Samson says confidently "That what I motioned was of God" (222), but we may doubt. His track record is hardly convincing, and his intemperate affection seems a pale and selfish thing next to the rending emotion that leads Adam to choose death in book 9 of *Paradise Lost*.

A strongly misogynistic interpretation of Dalila characterizes the play, whether in the Chorus's claim that

> God's universal law
> Gave to the man despotic power
> Over his female in due awe
>
> (1053–1055)

or in Samson's rather simpleminded reiteration that she betrayed him for gold rather than for her nation. Dalila contributes to the antifeminist strain but also recognizes the failure as Samson's: "Ere I to thee, thou to thyself wast cruel" (784), she says, and he concedes, "of what now I suffer / She was not the prime cause, but I myself" (234–235). He allowed himself to be "Softened with pleasure and voluptuous life / At length to lay my head and hallowed pledge / Of all my strength in the lascivious lap" (534–536). There can be no doubt of his regret, but he seeks to regenerate, not merely to grieve, for if "nature within me seems / In all her functions weary of herself" (595–596), then the way has, in one sense, been cleared for the visitation of grace on the fallen hero. Samson has a "sense of heaven's desertion" (632).

The Chorus alleviates his guilt: "Where the heart joins not, outward acts defile not" (1368). But Samson defies even this logic, since he mingles certainty about God's will with confusion about its significance:

> If there be aught of presage in the mind
> This day will be remarkable in my life
> By some great act, or of my days the last.
>
> (1387–1389)

At the play's conclusion, we know for certain only of his violent death offstage, though in his father's mind, "Samson hath quit himself / Like Samson . . ." (1709–1710). Bringing down the roof of the Philistine theater, Samson bears witness to his God, just as the hidden God "unexpectedly returns" to bear glorious witness "to his faithful champion" (1750–1751). Milton placed the tragedy at the end of the 1671 volume; the hero had come in the wake of the Restoration to represent the ambivalent condition of subjected yet inwardly resisting dissenters like the poet.

"EDEN RAISED IN THE WASTE WILDERNESS": *PARADISE REGAINED*

Thomas Ellwood, Milton's friend and student, tells a story about the circumstances leading to the composition of Milton's brief epic. After perusing *Paradise Lost*, probably around 1665, Ellwood returned the manuscript and said, "Thou hast said much here of *Paradise lost*; but what hast thou to say of *Paradise found*? He made me no answer, but sate some time in a Muse" The anecdote, if true, reveals the generosity that Milton extended to the young Quaker: "he shewed me his Second Poem, called *Paradise Regained*; and in a pleasant tone said to me, *This is owing to you; for you put it into my head by the question you put to me at* Chalfont; *which before I had not thought of*" (Carey, *Complete Shorter Poems*, p. 417).

Milton's Jesus triumphs over Satan's flamboyant escapism by countering fiction with plainspoken truth, answering hermeneutic subtlety with directness and clarity, with "deeds / Above heroic" (1.14–15). Interpretation of scripture—especially those parts of the Hebrew Bible, such as the messianic Psalms, that became the foundational texts for Christianity—forms the poem's chief "action." What does it mean to be the Son of God? At what point in his life did Jesus become aware that he was the Christ foretold in Hebrew prophecy? The transitional moment is Jesus's baptism in "the flood Jordan," which is told from opposing perspectives. Jesus arrives "as then obscure / Unmarked, unknown," but John the Baptist recognizes him:

> on him baptized
> Heaven opened, and in likeness of a dove
> The Spirit descended, while the Father's voice
> From heaven pronounced him his beloved Son.
>
> (1.29–32)

The event itself is uncontested, but Satan, "roving still / About the world," hears the Father's voice and claims to have seen "on his head / A perfect dove descend, whate'er it meant" (1.83–84). Although even in his doubt Satan confirms the identity of the Son, the "great dictator" (1.113) futilely tests Jesus, "Temptation and all guile on him to try" (1.123). Meanwhile God the Father explains to Gabriel, in terms deeply resonant of the plight of Job, the logic of exposing Jesus to the devil's assault:

> To show him worthy of his birth divine
> And high prediction, henceforth I expose
> To Satan. . . .
>
> (1.141–143)

In this way, Jesus will "lay down the rudiments / Of his great warfare" (1.157–158), which paradoxically consist in teaching the way of peace and charity: "By winning words to conquer willing hearts / And make persuasion do the work of fear" (1.222–223). Jesus is led by "some strong motion" (1.290) into the desert, and, regardless of whether we think Samson's "rousing motions" come from God, there can be no doubt that the impulse Jesus obeys is divine.

Disguised, like Edmund Spenser's Archimago in *The Faerie Queene*, as "an aged man in rural weeds" (1.314), Satan tries to convince Jesus to turn stones into bread, charitably feeding others as well as sating his own hunger. After quoting from the books of Exodus and 1 Kings, the Son responds tersely: "Why dost thou then suggest to me

distrust, / Knowing who I am, as I know who thou art?" (1.355–356). The devil is "undisguised" from this point on. The "action" of the poem is Satan's doing, whereas the meaning of the poem is Christ's suffering. Yet Satan, in his "grey dissimulation" (1.498), can feign piety as well as outrageous self-aggrandizement. While Jesus descends into himself, Satan becomes more extravagantly performative, as if stage managing a masque "to unfold some active scene" (2.239). The devils set up a banquet that recalls chivalric romance literature: "Alas how simple, to these cates compared, / Was that crude apple that diverted Eve!" (2.348–349).

Satan has misconstrued his genre to accommodate his vision of politics; the literary tradition on which he draws is shamelessly monarchical. Jesus, echoing *Prolusion 7*, internalizes power: "he who reigns within himself, and rules / Passions, desires, and fears, is more a king" than one who wears "a crown, / Golden in show" (2.466–467, 458–459). Satan offers Jesus control over the world's great empires, but Jesus requites the temptation by defining "true glory and renown" again through the example of Job: "God, / Looking on the earth, with approbation marks / The just man" (3.60–62). Satan clearly imagines Jesus's Davidic kingship literally, but Jesus thwarts the attempt to define power as military prowess, "argument / Of human weakness rather than of strength" (3.401–402).

For most readers of *Paradise Regained*, Jesus's rejection of pagan learning has proved the greatest obstacle to appreciation. The temptation of Athens is certainly more effective in luring scholars than "the undoubted Son of God" (1.11). Milton shows that Jesus, aware of what pagan knowledge has made possible, nonetheless subordinates it: "Greece from us these arts derived" (4.338). The Son's lyricism gives pause:

> Think not but that I know these things, or think
> I know them not; not therefore am I short
> Of knowing what I ought: he who receives
> Light from above, from the fountain of light,
> No other doctrine needs, though granted true.
>
> (4.286–290)

Jesus shows his mastery of what he dismisses, just as, in privileging Hebrew poetry and philosophy, he evokes the lesser greatness of Hellenic culture, "By light of nature not in all quite lost" (4.352). The rhyme of "not" and "ought" is, appropriately, internal. Books inspire idle curiosity in one who does not bring "A spirit and judgement equal or superior" to what he reads, "Deep-versed in books and shallow in himself" (4.324–327). Readers who are not properly attuned to the value of the books they take up are no more enriched than "children gathering pebbles on the shore" (4.330).

In the concluding temptation, Satan flies Jesus over Jerusalem, sets him down "on the highest pinnacle" of "the glorious Temple," and goads him, "show thy progeny; if not to stand, / Cast thyself down; safely if Son of God" (4.554–555). Satan then quotes Psalm 91:11–12, as he does in the Gospel of Luke, and Jesus counters with a quotation of Deuteronomy 6:16, "Also it is written, / Tempt not the Lord thy God, he said and stood" (4.560–561). If the climax seems less than spectacular, we must recall that the "show" has been Satan's, while the lucid interpretation of scripture has revealed the Son's true nature. The Son of God has "regained lost Paradise" and founded a "fairer Paradise" by "vanquishing / Temptation," just as Michael promised Adam he would find "Paradise within thee, happier far," Jesus restores us and regains the blissful seat (4.607–613). Henceforth, the "Queller of Satan" shall enter his "glorious work" and "begin to save mankind." In *Paradise Regained*, Milton represents "strenuous liberty" in a positive depiction of a radically new kind of heroism.

"AFTERTIMES": MILTON AND THE COUNTERTRADITION

Throughout Milton's works, a suspicion of narratives that pose as monolithic, coherent truth stands out. Milton made his standard for such evaluation ethical, so that it is not surprising to find both challenges and endorsements of his version of "strenuous liberty" in reflections on his personality. In contrast to the "negative capability" John Keats found in Shakespeare, Milton is inextricably bound to his greatest works, shadowing and even at times overshadowing them. Thus for Samuel Johnson, Milton was quintessentially "the surly republican" who "hated all whom he was required to obey." To such a critic, understanding the poetry becomes inseparable from grasping the obtrusive personality. As E. M. W. Tillyard quipped, "we feel that Milton, had he been stranded in his own Paradise, would very soon have eaten the apple on his own responsibility and immediately justified the act in a polemical pamphlet" (Milton, p. 239).

Milton's resistance to certain oppressive traditions of political and religious thought has won him greater sympathy of late, particularly amongst those eager to reclaim the field of literary history from its often conservative traditionalism. Even if the contention raised in William

Blake's *The Marriage of Heaven and Hell*, that Milton was "of the Devils party without knowing it," does not hold true for most who read past the early books of the epic, Milton's religious heterodoxy is now seen as a key to his importance in history. Milton's ongoing interest in such heresies as Socinianism and Mortalism contributed profoundly to his sense of the nature of selfhood. Milton may have belonged to a sect of one, but his commitments to political rights, to intellectual freedom, and to social reform animate his great poems. The unabashed scrutiny to which Milton subjected the founding myths and seminal texts of Christianity attests to his uniquely ethical and deeply personal engagement with his society. Milton's iconoclasm and learning, his dissidence and rigor, make him a figure of resistance within a tradition that for many he has, ironically, come to define.

[*See also* Censorship; Closet Drama; Masque; *and* The Sonnet in the Renaissance.]

SELECTED WORKS

POETRY

Lycidas (1638)
Comus (1634, first performance), a masque
Poems of Mr. John Milton (1646)
Paradise Lost, A Poem in Ten Books (1667)
Paradise Regain'd (1671)
Samson Agonistes (1671), a closet drama
Poems Upon Several Occasions (1673)
Paradise Lost, A Poem in Twelve Books (1674)

PROSE

Prolusion 7 (1631)
Of Reformation in England (1641)
The Reason of Church-Government Urg'd against Prelaty (1642)
An Apology against a Pamphlet (1642)
The Doctrine and Discipline of Divorce (1643)
Of Education (1644)
Areopagitica (1644)
Tetrachordon (1645)
The Tenure of Kings and Magistrates (1649)
Eikonoklastes (1649)
Pro Populo Anglicano Defensio (1651)
De Doctrina Christiana (?1655–1660s)
The Ready and Easy Way to Establish a Free Commonwealth (1660)
The History of Britain (1670)

EDITIONS

Carey, John, ed. *Complete Shorter Poems.* 2d ed. London, 1997. Poems cited here derive from this edition.

Dzelzainis, Martin, ed. *John Milton: Political Writings.* Cambridge, U.K., 1991.

Fowler, Alastair, ed. *Paradise Lost.* 2d ed. London, 1998.

Hughes, Merritt Y., ed. *Complete Poems and Major Prose.* New York, 1957.

Patterson, Frank Allen, et al., eds. *The Works of John Milton.* 18 vols. New York, 1931–1938.

Wolfe, Don M., et al., eds. *Complete Prose Works of John Milton.* 8 vols. New Haven, CT, 1953–1982. Prose cited here derives from this edition.

FURTHER READING

Barker, Arthur E. *Milton and the Puritan Dilemma, 1641–1660.* Toronto, 1942. Still the best book on Milton's prose.

Brown, Cedric C. *John Milton's Aristocratic Entertainments.* Cambridge, U.K., 1985. The most reliable source of information on *Comus.*

Corns, Thomas N., ed. *A Companion to Milton.* Oxford, 2001. An excellent place to start, with in-depth introductions written in an accessible style by leading scholars.

Darbishire, Helen, ed. *The Early Lives of Milton.* London, 1932. Reprinted London and New York, 1965. An essential collection of early biographies by Aubrey, Skinner, Wood, Phillips, Toland, and Richardson.

Empson, William. *Milton's God.* London, 1961. A witty reading of *Paradise Lost* that challenges complacent Christian interpretations.

Fish, Stanley. *How Milton Works.* Cambridge, MA, 2001. Strong and controversial readings of most of the works providing much that can be argued with, but little that can be ignored.

Forsyth, Neil. *The Satanic Epic.* Princeton, NJ, 2003. An unorthodox and learned treatment of *Paradise Lost* in the context of religious source materials.

Grose, Christopher. *Milton and the Sense of Tradition.* New Haven, CT, 1988. A rewarding interpretation of *Paradise Regained* and *Samson Agonistes.*

Hill, Christopher. *Milton and the English Revolution.* London and New York, 1977. A groundbreaking contextual study of Milton among the radicals of his day.

Knoppers, Laura Lunger. *Historicizing Milton: Spectacle, Power, and Poetry in Restoration England.* Athens, GA, 1994. A study of the major poems in their political and historical context.

Loewenstein, David. *Representing Revolution in Milton and His Contemporaries: Religion, Politics, and Polemics in Radical Puritanism.* Cambridge, U.K., 2001. A lucid historicist account focusing on relations between Milton and the radical sectarians that refines earlier studies by Hill and Barker.

Norbrook, David. *Writing the English Republic: Poetry, Rhetoric and Politics, 1627–1660.* Cambridge, U.K., 1999. A major revaluation of the period's literature in relation to republican politics, with useful chapters on Milton.

Parker, William R. *Milton: A Biography.* 2d ed. 2 vols. Edited by Gordon Campbell. Oxford, 1996. The standard modern biography, with a helpfully detailed index.

Radzinowicz, Mary Ann. *Milton's Epics and the Book of Psalms.* Princeton, NJ, 1989. An approachable study of Milton's use of scripture in his poetry.

Rogers, John. *The Matter of Revolution: Science, Poetry, and Politics in the Age of Milton.* Ithaca, NY, 1996. A stimulating reading of Milton's epic (and works by Winstanley, Marvell, and Cavendish) in the context of the period's revolutionary materialism.

Smith, Nigel. *Literature and Revolution in England, 1640–1660.* New Haven, CT, 1994. A vital survey of the literary and historical contexts for Milton's works.

Tayler, Edward W. *Milton's Poetry: Its Development in Time.* Pittsburgh, 1979. A helpful introduction to the period's intellectual history through close readings of the poems.

Tillyard, E. M. W. *Milton.* London, 1930. Revised ed., London, 1966. A solid and influential account of the life and works.

Turner, James Grantham. *One Flesh: Paradisal Marriage and Sexual Relations in the Age of Milton.* Oxford, 1987. An attractively subtle yet lucid account of one of the most vexing and contradictory aspects of Milton's works.

Von Maltzahn, Nicholas. *Milton's "History of Britian": Republican Historiography in the English Revolution.* Oxford, 1991. An excellent introduction to Milton's politics by way of one of his most neglected works.

Wittreich, Joseph A. *The Romantics on Milton: Formal Essays and Critical Asides.* Cleveland, OH, 1970. A collection of allusions by Wordsworth, Coleridge, Blake, Byron, Shelley, Keats, Lamb, Hazlitt et al.

A MIRROR FOR MAGISTRATES

Andrew Hadfield

A Mirror for Magistrates has the unenviable reputation of being a dull work that simply transposes much English history into verse and is worth reading only because Shakespeare used it as a source for his history plays. This is, however, an unfair perception of what was one of the best-selling works in sixteenth-century England, a book that began as a central element of a grand, radical literary experiment and went through a bewildering array of changes over its long publishing history. Although it is by no means the most sophisticated English literary work produced in the later sixteenth century, *A Mirror* is a complex and intelligent work, not a piece of hack writing; its authors sought to make a familiar genre, the "mirror for princes," relevant for a wider class of governors, England's magistrates.

ORIGIN

An attempt to publish the first edition of *A Mirror* was made in 1555 by the printer John Wayland, who wanted a supplementary work to accompany his new edition of John Lydgate's popular poem *The Fall of Princes*, a series of narrative tragedies on foolish or badly behaved rulers who brought about their own downfall. Wayland planned to collaborate with William Baldwin, one of the most prominent men of letters at the court of Edward VI, in writing a continuation of Lydgate's work, "concernynge the chefe Prynces of thys Iland, penned by the best clearkes in such kind matters that be thys day lyving." It is clear that by 1555 the work had already been done by a group of writers whom Baldwin had assembled for the task. Baldwin later claimed that he had managed to secure the services of seven, although only his own name and that of George Ferrers (c. 1500–1579), like Baldwin a well-known Protestant, are mentioned in the edition of 1559. The work had evidently been compiled over the previous few years, using material from several English histories: Edward Hall's history of the Wars of the Roses, *Union of the Noble and Illustre Famelies of Lancastre and York* (1542), Robert Fabyan's *The Concordance of Histories* (1516), and Thomas More's *History of Richard III* (printed in 1543). *A Mirror* was clearly part of the radical experimental political literature being encouraged at the court of Edward VI to help establish a more widespread and thoroughgoing Reformation in England. Unfortunately, Edward's premature death in 1553 had ruined the authors' plans, and the project had been put on hold until Wayland's overture to Baldwin. The first edition, however, was rapidly suppressed in 1555 on the orders of Mary's chancellor, Stephen Gardiner, and only a fragment of one copy is known to have survived.

FIRST EDITIONS

The first extant version (printed in 1559) appeared soon after Elizabeth I became queen (1558), having first been properly licensed in the Stationers' Register. This version of nineteen tragedies of eminent men from the reign of Richard II to Edward IV is evidently not the whole contents of the suppressed 1555 edition. The tragedies include those of Owen Glendower, the Welsh rebel against Henry IV who is vociferously condemned as a rebel against the king and God; Edward IV, an intemperate and self-indulgent king whose refusal to limit his appetites led to his downfall; and the rather more innocent Henry VI, who found the burden of government too much for him. The verse tragedies are connected by prose links in which the assembled authors discuss the significance of each tragedy and the lessons that might be learned from them by aspiring magistrates (invariably, what to avoid rather than what to copy). A new edition of *A Mirror* appeared in 1563, adding eight more narratives, including the tragedy of Jane Shore, mistress of Edward IV; it was written by Thomas Churchyard (c. 1520–1604), a prolific hack writer, and is probably his best work. More significantly, the edition also contains two poems by Thomas Sackville, earl of Dorset (1536–1608), coauthor of *Gorboduc* (1561): the often anthologized "Induction," and the tragedy of the duke of Buckingham.

REVISIONS AND LATER EDITIONS AND VERSIONS

The next revised edition of *A Mirror* appeared in 1571, and then a new edition containing a third part, with some material dating back to the first suppressed edition, was published in 1578. A further edition of 1587 added new material to the first part. All these versions of the text preserve the book's original design, outlining the successes, failures, and vicissitudes of fortune experienced by dead governors as a means of instructing living ones. However, *A Mirror* also inspired other versified narrations of English history, a sign of its influence and central importance as a literary text, as well as of the contradictory ways in which it was read. In 1574 the minor poet John Higgins (fl. 1570–1602) published *The First Part of the Mirror for Magistrates*, in which he used material from earlier British chronicles, especially Geoffrey of Monmouth's *History of the Kings of Britain*. Higgins included sixteen legends of early Britain in order to celebrate British achievements in repelling invaders and to tell exciting stories from times past, clearly a far cry from the original aims of the writers of *A Mirror*. He had Humber, the king of the defeated Huns, who drowns in the river where he left his name, tell the reader:

> If thou be forrayne bide within thy soyle:
> That God hath given to thee and thine to holde,
> If thou oppression meane beware the foyle:
> Beare not thy selfe, of thee or thine to bolde:
> Or of the feates thy elders did of olde,
> For God is just, injustice will not thrive:
> He plagues the prowe, preserves the good alive.

Such sentiments bear little relation to the "official" version of *A Mirror*.

Higgins's work was followed by a similar version by another minor writer, Thomas Blenerhasset (c. 1550–c. 1625), entitled *The Second Part of the Mirror for Magistrates*, which contains twelve tragedies on British history from Caesar's invasion to the Norman Conquest. A combined edition of 1587 collects the work of Higgins (but not Blenerhasset) and the tradition following Baldwin, as well as adding a series of new tragedies, such as those of James IV of Scotland and Cardinal Wolsey. The final version of *A Mirror* was edited by Richard Niccols in 1610. This combines all the material for the first time, omits the prose links, changes the order of some of the tragedies, and includes a new work by a substantial literary figure: Michael Drayton's poem on Thomas Cromwell,

the principal architect of Henry VIII's administrative reforms, who was executed in 1540.

LITERARY SIGNIFICANCE

The principal poetic form employed by all contributors to *A Mirror* is the complaint, one of the most fashionable literary genres of the second half of the sixteenth century, a vogue that *A Mirror* helped to create. The ghosts of the historical figures in *A Mirror* lament their fate—whether deserved or not—and point their audience, the writers of the tragedies, toward the moral that they draw from the tale. The opening tragedy of the 1559 edition describes "The fall of Robert Tresilian chiefe Justice of Englande, and his other felowes, for misconstruying the lawes, and expounding them to serve the Princes affections." Tresilian served Richard II, who was deposed by Henry Bolingbroke, the future Henry IV. The title shows not only that the purpose of *A Mirror* is to further better government, but also that the authors have a clear conception that both the monarch and his or her advisers need to live under the rule of law. Anyone who knew the relevant history would have seen that the tragedy warns readers what can happen if they abuse the laws and fail to serve their monarch properly. Good government might have saved Richard II from his excesses and so prevented his deposition and the subsequent series of civil wars. Tresilian's ghost explains how he and his fellow corrupt magistrates abused the laws to exploit ordinary men and women:

> So wurking lawe lyke waxe, the subjecte was not sure
> Of lyfe, lande, nor goods, but at the princes wyll:
> Which caused his kingdome the shorter tyme to dure,
> For clayming power absolute both to save and spyll,
> The prince therby presumed his people for to pyll
>   [exploit];
> And set his lustes for lawe, and will had reasons place,
> No more but hang and drawe, there was no better grace.

This abuse of the laws leads to the misery of both governed and governors. A more balanced and reasonable relationship between the two would lead to a more stable and happy country. Tresilian urges future magistrates to tread "the paths of equitie" and avoid his fate: "Let them that cum hereafter both that and this compare, / And wayling well the ende, they wyll I trust beware."

Other tragedies point to similar political morals. John Tiptoft, earl of Worcester (1427–1470), constable of England during the reign of Edward IV, was noted for his ruthless implementation of the law and was beheaded when Henry VI was briefly restored to the throne. He ends his tragedy with a warning that high office carries its penalties as well as its rewards:

> Warne all men, wisely to beware,
> What offices they enterprise to beare:
> The hyest alway most maligned are,
> Of peoples grudge, and princes hate in fear.
> For princes faultes his faultors all men teare.
> Which to avoyde, let none such office take,
> Save he that can for right his prince forsake.

Again, the moral is pointed to the need for the magistrate to pursue the right path rather than the expedient one, and to stand up to his king or queen if necessary, which belies *A Mirror's* reputation as a conservative text that simply supports the status quo. The authors do condemn rebels such as Jack Cade, who led an uprising against Henry VI in 1450. Cade admits his faults after he is mortally wounded: "Full litel knowe we wretches what we do. / Whan we presume our princes to resist. / We war with God, against his glory to, / That placeth in his office whom he list." But Cade is not a magistrate, and so he has no right to resist the will of the governing class. It is their duty to see that the law is implemented properly and fairly, and they have the right to oppose the excessive demands of monarchs, hence the proclaimed importance of the work.

The contrast between such tragedies and those that appear in subsequent editions shows how much the character of *A Mirror* altered over time. Thomas Churchyard's tragedy of Cardinal Wolsey opens with lines that suggest that we are about to read an adventure story rather than a historical political parable:

> Shall I looke on, when states step on the stage,
> And play theyr parts, before the peoples face?
> Some men live now, scarce four score yeares of age,
> Who in times past, did know the Cardinalls grace.
> A gameson worlde, when Byshops run at bace,
> Yea, get a fall, in striving for the gole,
> And body loase, and hazarde seely sole.

The tragedy continues as a rags-to-riches story, and Wolsey urges aspiring young readers to copy his example by rising early and studying until late. The conclusion that Wolsey's ghost draws seems almost willful in its refusal to draw the sort of moral that had characterized *A Mirror* as conceived by Baldwin:

> [T]he best is wee are gone,
> And worst of all, when wee our tales have tolde,
> Our open plagues, will warning bee to none,
> Men are by hap, and courage made so bolde:
> They thinke all is, theyr owne, they have in holde.
> Well, let them say, and thinke what they please,
> This weltring world, both flowes and ebs like seas.

The history of *A Mirror* shows how flexible—even unstable—literary forms can be, and how complex their history often is.

[*See also* John Lydgate *and* William Shakespeare: The History Plays.]

EDITIONS

Campbell, Lily B., ed. *A Mirror for Magistrates.* Cambridge, U.K., 1938.

Campbell, Lily B., ed. *Parts Added to 'The Mirror for Magistrates.'* Cambridge, U.K., 1946.

FURTHER READING

Campbell, Lily B. *Tudor Conceptions of History and Providence in "A Mirror for Magistrates."* Berkeley, CA, 1936.

Gresham, Stephen. "William Baldwin: Literary Voice of the Reign of Edward VI." *Huntington Library Quarterly* 44 (1980–1981): 101–116.

Hadfield, Andrew. *Literature, Politics and National Identity: Reformation to Renaissance* Cambridge, U.K., 1994. See chapter 3.

Lucas, Scott. "The Consolation of Tragedy: *A Mirror for Magistrates* and the Fall of the 'Good Duke' of Somerset." *Studies in Philology* 100 (2003): 44–70.